T0190110

Lecture Notes in Artificial Intelligence   13040

Subseries of Lecture Notes in Computer Science

More information about this subseries at http://www.springer.com/series/1244

Pietro Baroni · Christoph Benzmüller ·
Yì N. Wáng (Eds.)

Logic and Argumentation

4th International Conference, CLAR 2021
Hangzhou, China, October 20–22, 2021
Proceedings

 Springer

Editors
Pietro Baroni 🆔
Department of Information Engineering
University of Brescia
Brescia, Italy

Yì N. Wáng 🆔
Department of Philosophy (Zhuhai)
Sun Yat-sen University
Zhuhai, China

Christoph Benzmüller 🆔
Department of Mathematics
and Computer Science
Freie Universität Berlin
Berlin, Germany

ISSN 0302-9743 ISSN 1611-3349 (electronic)
Lecture Notes in Artificial Intelligence
ISBN 978-3-030-89390-3 ISBN 978-3-030-89391-0 (eBook)
https://doi.org/10.1007/978-3-030-89391-0

LNCS Sublibrary: SL7 – Artificial Intelligence

This Springer imprint is published by the registered company Springer Nature Switzerland AG
The registered company address is: Gewerbestrasse 11, 6330 Cham, Switzerland

Preface

This volume collects the papers accepted for presentation at the 4th International Conference on Logic and Argumentation (CLAR 2021).

The CLAR series started as a regional workshop hosted by Zhejiang University in 2016 and evolved through the years to become a successful international event attracting high quality contributions worldwide. It aims at bringing together researchers from various disciplines such as logic, formal argumentation, artificial intelligence, philosophy, computer science, linguistics, and law.

The success of the initiative is witnessed by the substantial increase of submissions over time: there were 11 at CLAR 2016, 16 at CLAR 2018, and 31 at CLAR 2020, while CLAR 2021 received 58 submissions.

After a careful reviewing process, 20 submissions were accepted as regular papers and 10 as short papers. The Program Committee of CLAR 2021 consisted of 65 top researchers from 19 countries. Submissions were – except for some special cases – reviewed by three Program Committee members, and attention and discussion were devoted to controversial judgments and peculiar situations.

The topics of accepted papers nicely cover the focus of the CLAR series, including formal models of argumentation, a variety of logic formalisms, nonmonotonic reasoning, dispute and dialogue systems, formal treatment of preference and support, and applications in areas like vaccine information and processing of legal texts.

We are indebted to the following invited speakers for accepting our invitation and for witnessing, with their talks and contributed papers, the rich diversity and vitality of the research areas covered by the conference:

- Annette Frank (Heidelberg University, Germany): On the Need of Knowledge for Computational Argument Analysis and Generation
- Giovanni Sartor (University of Bologna and European University Institute of Florence, Italy): Burdens of Persuasion and Standards of Proof in Structured Argumentation
- Ken Satoh (National Institute of Informatics, Japan): Implementation of Choice of Jurisdiction and Law in Private International Law by PROLEG Meta-interpreter
- Guillermo R Simari (Universidad Nacional del Sur and Institute for Computer Science and Engineering, Argentina): Focusing the Argumentative Process: Neighborhood-based Semantics in Abstract Argumentation
- Minghui Xiong (Zhejiang University and Sun Yat-sen University, China): Resolving the Cohenian Paradox in Judicial Probability Theory

The success of a conference depends on the contributions of many people.

First of all we thank all the authors for contributing to the conference with their hard work and commitment.

We are also very grateful to the members of the Program Committee and the additional reviewers for their invaluable efforts in providing high-quality reviews, which are crucial for the quality and success of the event.

In addition, we thank Springer for their generous support in publishing this conference proceedings and their sponsorship of a best paper award, and EasyChair for their invaluable technical infrastructure that helped us organize the review and publication process.

Last but not least, we are very grateful to Zhejiang University and Zhejiang University City College for their financial support and local organization efforts. In particular, we thank the main organizing team consisting of Beishui Liao, Quansheng Yu, Huimin Dong, Shengyu Dai, Zhihong Geng, Teng Ying, and Chonghui Li for their excellent support.

September 2021

Pietro Baroni
Christoph Benzmüller
Yì Nicholas Wáng

Organization

Program Committee Chairs

Pietro Baroni   University of Brescia, Italy
Christoph Benzmüller   Freie Universität Berlin, Germany
Yì Nicholas Wáng   Sun Yat-sen University, China

Program Committee

Thomas Agotnes	University of Bergen, Norway, and Southwest University, China
Natasha Alechina	Utrecht University, The Netherlands
Ofer Arieli	Academic College of Tel-Aviv, Israel
Pietro Baroni	University of Brescia, Italy
Christoph Benzmüller	Freie Universität Berlin, Germany
Antonis Bikakis	University College London, UK
Stefano Bistarelli	University of Perugia, Italy
Thomas Bolander	Technical University of Denmark, Denmark
Martin Caminada	Cardiff University, UK
Ilaria Canavotto	University of Amsterdam, The Netherlands
Walter Carnielli	University of Campinas, Brazil
Federico Cerutti	University of Brescia, Italy
Andrea Cohen	Universidad Nacional del Sur, Argentina
Marcos Cramer	Technische Universität Dresden, Germany
Mehdi Dastani	Utrecht University, The Netherlands
Jérémie Dauphin	University of Luxembourg, Luxembourg
Valeria de Paiva	Topos Institute, USA, and University of Birmingham, UK
Jérôme Delobelle	Université de Paris, France
Dragan Doder	Utrecht University, The Netherlands
Huimin Dong	Sun Yat-sen University, China
Bettina Fazzinga	ICAR-CNR, University of Calabria, Italy
Raul Fervari	Universidad Nacional de Córdoba, Argentina
Rustam Galimullin	University of Bergen, Norway
Sujata Ghosh	Indian Statistical Institute, India
Massimiliano Giacomin	University of Brescia, Italy
Sebastian Gottifredi	Universidad Nacional del Sur, Argentina
Guido Governatori	CSIRO, Australia
Andreas Herzig	University of Toulouse, France
Jesse Heyninck	Technische Universität Dortmund, Germany
Fengkui Ju	Beijing Normal University, China

Additional Reviewers

Alfano, Gianvincenzo
Alviano, Mario
Antonelli, Melissa
Botnan, Magnus Bakke
Budan, Paola
Cassano, Valentin
Chikobava, Margarita
Fuenmayor, David
Karmakar, Samr

König, Matthias
Maffezioli, Paolo
Morveli Espinoza, Mariela
Pavlovic, Edi
Rapberger, Anna
Santini, Francesco
Skiba, Kenneth
Trucco, Francisco

On the Need of Knowledge for Computational Argument Analysis and Generation (Abstract of Invited Talk)

Anette Frank

Department of Computational Linguistics, Heidelberg University, Germany
frank@cl.uni-heidelberg.de

Argumentation is deeply grounded in human society and communication. While formal argumentation has been studied for decades in philosophy and logic, only recently, computational argumentation has been established as a research field in the Natural Language Processing (NLP) community. Argumentation is a natural object of study for NLP, since arguments are framed in natural language – be it in discourse or dialogue. At the same time, analysing or even generating arguments computationally is a challenging goal. Humans frame arguments to deliberate issues that require careful reflection and deep analysis from various views and angles. The debated issues typically involve conflicting interests that need to be weighted in terms of their impacts and consequences.

In my talk I will highlight recent work on *knowledge-driven computational argument analysis* conducted in the ExpLAIN project. We perform argument analysis by integrating symbolic background knowledge with neural language processing models and show how leveraging such knowledge enhances performance and interpretability of results. We started from an empirical analysis of implicit knowledge in argumentative texts, and developed methods to integrate such knowledge in argument analysis tasks. Our work is the first to show how to combine structured and latent knowledge from pre-trained language models to perform reconstruction of implicit knowledge for argument analysis.

I will conclude by discussing avenues for moving from analysis to generative argumentation tasks, and the importance of knowledge for achieving these aims.

Contents

Short Papers and Extended Abstracts

Invited Papers

Resolving the Cohenian Paradox in Judicial Probability Theory

Wenjing Du[1], Zihan Niu[2], and Minghui Xiong[3]([⊠]) [iD]

[1] Wenbo College, East China University of Political Science and Law,
Shanghai, China
2178@ecupl.edu.cn
[2] Institute of Logic and Cognition, Sun Yat-sen University, Guangzhou, China
niuzh@mail.sysu.edu.cn
[3] Guanghua Law School, Zhejiang University, Hangzhou, China
xiongminghui@zju.edu.cn

Abstract. The Cohenian paradox is one of the main themes of judicial probability theory and one of the core topics discussed by the new evidence scholarship. To resolve this paradox, evidence scholars nowadays have proposed various solutions, including legal probabilism, Bayesian decision theory, and relative plausibility theory. These three solutions can be classified into two approaches, i.e., the probabilism and the explanationism. Among them, the former includes legal probabilism and Bayesian decision theory, and the latter includes the relative plausibility theory. However, the two approaches have recently begun to converge and become more understandable to each other. For example, Welch (2020) has recently defended and improved the relative plausibility theory by substantially improving it with the help of Bayesian decision theory. In this paper, by contrast, we attempt to defend the probabilistic approach - legal probabilism and Bayesian decision theory on the basis of relative plausibility theory.

Keywords: Cohenian paradox · Judicial probability theory · New evidence scholarship · Legal probabilism

1 Introduction

In 1968, John Kaplan [14] published a seminal paper Decision Theory and the Fact-finding Process, in which he discussed how some of the basic tools of decision theory could be applied to the fact-finding process in trials. It opens a precedent for the study of theories about judicial probability. Since then there has been rich literature that explains virtually all aspects of judicial proof, such as relevance and probative value of evidence at the micro level, as well as the standard of proof and the process of evidential reasoning or fact-finding, as probabilistic, from the basic nature of relevancy through the processing of information to the final decision about the facts [3] And then, Jonathan Cohen [4, p. 51] systematically discusses the theories about judicial probability. However, he

© Springer Nature Switzerland AG 2021
P. Baroni et al. (Eds.): CLAR 2021, LNAI 13040, pp. 3–19, 2021.
https://doi.org/10.1007/978-3-030-89391-0_1

criticizes the application of probabilistic methods in judicial proofs and raises the three critical questions: (a) But what is the nature of this juridical concept of probability, so often and so confidently employed? (b) Is it a mathematical probability? (c) Does it conform to the mathematical calculus of probabilities that Pascal originated? In part II of his monograph, he lists six difficulties for a Pascalian account of judicial probability, i.e., the difficulty about conjunction, inference upon inference, negation, proof beyond reasonable doubt, a criterion, and corroboration and convergence. For the sake of discussion, these difficulties are collectively referred to as the proof paradox [18] or the Cohenian paradox(es), which is one of the core issues in the contemporary new evidence scholarship.

In view of the Cohenian paradox, evidence scholars have proposed different solutions such as legal probabilism, Bayesian decision theory and relative plausibility theory [23]. Legal probabilism, whose origin can be traced back to the early days of probability theory, for example, Niklaus Bernoulli's dissertation De Usu Artis Conjectandi in Iure in 1709, is a research program that relies on probability theory to analyze, model and improve the evaluation of evidence and the process of decision-making in trial proceedings [22]. Allen and Pardo [3] and Pardo [16] have extended the Cohenian paradox, demonstrating the incompatibility of Bayesian reasoning with trials, and have proposed an analytical alternative - the relative plausibility theory - to improve the probabilistic paradigm. They argue that judicial proof is explanatory and have proposed relative plausibility theory based on the inference to the best explanation. During this controversy, many scholars have criticized probabilistic methods too radically, leading to the illusion that the probabilistic model of judicial proof is either inadequate or has little effect. As an analysis tool, probabilistic methods play a crucial role in the analysis of cases and the process of fact-finding. Probabilistic methods are consistent and normative and can avoid paradoxical conclusions and unfair verdicts.

In this paper we will respond to the Cohenian paradox and its related variants such as Blue Bus and Prisoner [18]. And then we will provide a possible resolution. Although the Cohenian paradox contains many difficulties, it is not intended or able to discuss all of them in this paper, and we will confine our discussion to the following three, i.e., the difficulty or problem of probability selection, calculation or computation, and conjunction. And these difficulties or problems are sometimes called paradoxes of proof [16, 18].

2   The Selection Problem: Subjective vs Objective Probability

The selection problem, also known as the probability selection problem or the difficulty of selection, refers to the situation in which it is difficult to choose between subjective probability and objective probability when probability theory is used for judicial proof. Judicial proof is a clear and evident declaration or demonstration of a matter which was doubtful before, conveyed in a judicial manner by sound arguments and other legal methods. The conviction or persuasion of the idea of a judge or jury, by way of the presentation of evidence, of the fact of a truth alleged: as, to prove, is to decide or persuade that a thing does or does not exist. Proof is the perfection of evidence, for without evidence there is no proof; although, there may be proof which does now not amount to proof: for example, a man is found murdered at a spot where some other had been seen on foot but a short time before, this truth would be evidence to show that the latter was the murderer, but, standing alone, would be very far from proof of it.

As the core of judicial proof, the standard of proof, in essence, can be loosely defined as the quantum of evidence that must be presented in a Court before a fact can be said to exist or not exist. As the type of cases before a Court can be classified into criminal or civil, so can the standard of proof. There is a clear understanding that the Courts follow according to which the standard of proof to be followed in a criminal case is that of "beyond reasonable doubt" whereas the standard of proof changes, even lowers to the "balance of probabilities" in cases of civil proceedings. Inferences may be deductive or inductive, but the inference in judicial proof process primarily involves inductive, in the board, non-demonstrative sense [17]. The standard of proof, even the criminal standard, are recognized as inherently "probabilistic", so he used probability theory to understand the role played the ordinary civil and criminal standards of proof the law's pursuit of factual accuracy [11]. A simple way of understanding standards of proof is in terms of degrees of probability [18], but Jonathon Cohen [4] and new evidence scholars with relative plausibility theory, such as Ronald Allen and Michael Pardo [17], have strongly opposed this approach. Generally speaking, there are two main standards for proof of fact in courts: the plaintiff in a civil case must prove on the balance of probability, including the preponderance of the evidence, and clear convincing evidence, and the prosecutor in a criminal case must prove his conclusion at a level of probability that puts it beyond reasonable doubt. In particular, to prevail in a civil case a claimant needs only prove his liability to a degree above 0.5. For the prosecution to succeed in a criminal case, it needs to prove guilt to a considerably higher degree of 0.95. In addition, there is a three-standard saying, i.e., preponderance = 0.5; clear and convincing = 0.6; beyond a reasonable doubt = 0.9.

Probability is a branch of mathematics regarding numerical descriptions of how probably an event is to occur, or how probable it is that a proposition is true. When it comes to practical application, there are two primary competing views of probability explanations. The one is that objectivists assign numbers to describe some objective or physical state of affairs. The most popular version of objective probability is frequentist probability. The other is that subjectivists assign numbers per subjective probability, that is, as a degree of belief. The most famous version of subjective probability is Bayesian probability. In the theory of judicial probability, two kinds of probability explanation exist simultaneously. However, Allen and Pardo [1] oppose the application of probabilistic approach to judicial proof and criticize both objective and subjective probability at the same time. According to them, the objective probability needs to be calculated by relative frequency or known statistical distribution data, and these data are difficult to obtain in reality. Even if the data is obtained, it may face the difficulty of selecting the "reference class". In addition, the problems in court trials tend to focus on what happened at a particular moment, and the final problem rarely appears in the relative frequency of a particular type of event. The only class that can accurately capture the "objective" value is the event itself, whose probability is either 1 or 0 [2]. Regarding subjective probabilities, they criticize that those prior probabilities and the likelihood values used to update the prior probabilities can be any number and are not affected by the quality or probative value of the evidence used to prove facts in the trial. Subjective probability is too subjective. It provides a way to maintain a consistent belief structure, but it is not necessarily related to the accuracy of the advancing results [3].

We don't share Allen and Pardo's views on this. If they were right, the whole theory of probability would be useless. Apparently, this is not true. The indisputable fact is that the probabilistic approach, which has been useful in almost all areas of scientific research, is normative, mathematical, and systematic. For example, statistical testing, confidence intervals, regression, and so on are widely used in social sciences. In addition, it permeates many aspects of philosophy. In epistemology, philosophy of mind, and cognitive science, we see that subjective probability functions can model the state of a particular point of view and learning can be modeled by updating these functions. Probability theory is the core of decision theory and game theory. It also has an impact on ethics and political philosophy. It occupies an important position in major metaphysical works such as causality and natural laws. Probability appears many times in the confirmation analysis, scientific explanation, and philosophy of specific scientific theories, such as quantum mechanics, statistical mechanics, and genetics, and can even occupy a central position in logic, philosophy of language, and philosophy of religion [10]. Therefore, we believe that the application of probabilistic methods in the judicial proof process is also natural and reasonable.

In judicial proof, the probability is normally defined as the degree of personal belief in a certain proposition, which is a probabilistic explanation provided by Bayesian theory that is both subjective and rational. Different analysts can hold different initial beliefs about a certain fact. When a Bayesian formula is used, these can be changed rationally based on new evidence. The subjective assignment leads to the cognitive consensus of the belief held by the analyst. Bayesian theory is a kind of cognitive proof theory, which claims that the condition for asserting a proposition being proved is if and only if the probability of trusting the proposition is high to a reasonable degree. As new evidence is continuously obtained, the cognitive proof will change. This probability will also occur in the corresponding change, which can be calculated and predicted according to the Bayesian formula. The Bayesian theory also provides a robust and unified framework for mixing objective statistical data and subjective factual evaluation. Even if the probability evaluation of a specific case has a frequency data basis, it also contains a subjective component based on personal knowledge. The "objective" probability judgment is the judgment on whether the consistency of intersubjectivity is achieved. For example, probabilistic evaluation based on knowledge of relevant statistical data is more "objective" than probabilistic evaluation without the support of relevant statistical data because rational people will think that if relevant statistical data is known, then personal beliefs should take the data knowledge into account. Statistical syllogism is the basis of probabilistic reasoning and has strong objectivity, but it also contains subjective factors. Its reasoning structure is as follows [21, pp. 21–22]:

1. The relative frequency of the property Q in the population R is γ;
2. a_i is an individual in the population R $(i = 1, 2, ..., n)$;
3. a_i has, for me, the same probability of possessing property Q as any other individual in the population R;
4. The probability, for me, that a_i has the property Q is γ.

The first two conditions examine statistical data information, which is objective, while the third condition expresses the state of the responder's knowledge and is subjective. The third condition can also be changed to a more subjective description. For the reasoner, a_i is the same as any other individual in the population R, and the possibility of having the property Q is the same.

It can be seen that Bayesian theory provides a unified framework for objective probability and subjective probability, which has both objective statistical data basis and subjective rationality. Or Allen [1] said, there are two versions of Bayesianism, an objective and subjective version. Allen and Pardo's critique seems to interpret the probability in the judicial proof as to either objective or subjective [3]. The probability can only choose one of them and cannot be integrated. This understanding is inappropriate. In a specific case, probability can be a fusion of objective frequency and subjective belief degree. The prior probability of some evidence or facts is reasonable for assignment with objective probability, while others are reasonable for evaluation with subjective probability. Here we are very glad to share the latest solution of Hunt & Mostyn [13]. They have given a solution to where the probability values come from. If the relevant data can be found and the appropriate reference class can be determined, the frequency should be calculated and assigned with objective probability. If no reasonable data can be found, there are three methods: The first is to adjust the content to be proved, appropriately enlarge or reduce the reference class, and then use objective probability assignment. The second is to make fuzzy objective probability assignments in terms of probability range and size comparison. The third is to assign values with subjective probability.

The difficulty of obtaining data is indeed a problem faced by the probabilistic approach. However, with the development of society, advances in science and technology, and the improvement of databases, this difficulty will be alleviated to some extent. It should be noted that the digital problem exists in the judicial field and exists in other social sciences. In other words, this is a common phenomenon of social science problems, but not a problem of probabilistic methods. The probability of an event itself is either 1 or 0, which refers to the "binary" legal principle; that is, if the judge initially believes that the probability of an event is greater than 0.5, then the probability of the event being valid will becomes 1, and if the judge initially believes that the probability of an event is less than

0.5, the probability of the event being true will become 0 [2,3]. Actually, this probabilistic method does not conflict with the binary legal principle. The binary principle is reasonable to be applied to the final probability of the event under consideration. In the calculation stage of probabilistic reasoning, the probability value can be continuous and should not be a binary value. Otherwise, it violates the relevant probability principle and lead to an absurdity or injustice factual verdict.

Allen and Pardo [3] criticize subjective probability as being too subjective and biased. However, judicial proof is a social science issue which is subjective. In judicial proofs, the objective facts of a case always occur before the facts are justified. The objective facts of many cases are difficult to restore to their original appearance due to the irreversibility of time. Therefore, the facts found by the fact-finder are legal, not necessarily objective. In a sense, a legal trial is not concerned for the "real truth of the matte", but for the making out of a legally proper case [19, p. 43]. Most of legal facts themselves are subjective. The relative plausibility theory developed by Allen and Pardo [3] as an alternative to probabilistic methods also completely relies on the subjective evaluation of the fact-finder. In addition, the subjective probability is not arbitrarily assigned. It needs to be constrained by evidence, legal principles, and related probability principles, such as the principle of probability multiplication, complementarity axioms, and Bayesian formulas. Untested and unconstrained subjective probability assignment does not have any significance. In fact, whether the fact-finder evaluates the subjective probability or changes or revises the subjective probability, it should be constrained by evidence and related principles. For example, suppose the fact-finder is evaluating the prior probability of the cause of death of a certain deceased, and combining the case and background knowledge, proposes three causes of death: suicide (H_1), homicide (H_2), and accidental death (H_3). According to the principle of probability, the probabilities of these three cases should be taken as numbers between 0 and 1, and the sum of these probabilities must be equal to 1. When new evidence is obtained, the probability should be updated according to the Bayesian formula to calculate the posterior probability. According to the rule of evidence exclusion, if a certain piece of evidence needs to be excluded, even if the fact-finder knows the existence of the evidence, his probability evaluation should not be changed at will.

3   The Calculation Problem: A Franklinian Solution

The calculation problem, also known as the calculation difficulty, which should be called the difficulty of computation in the sense of computer science or artificial intelligence, is directly related to the selection of reference classes, so it can also be called the difficulty of reference class selection or the reference class problem, which refers to deciding what data class to be used as the reference basis when calculating the probability of a single event. Allen and Pardo [2,3] as well as Colyvan, Reganm, and Ferson [5], have suggested the reference-class problem plays a role in the Cohenian paradox. When evaluating the probability of a single event, we usually first assign the event to a reference class based on a certain feature (attribute) and then calculate the frequency of this feature in the reference class. This frequency is considered as the probability of the event occurring. However, each event usually has many features, so it can belong to many reference classes or even an infinite number of reference classes. In different reference classes, the frequency of occurrence of a single feature is likely to be different, thus the probability of occurrence of the event is also different. The uncertainty and ambiguity of this probability lead to the so-called reference class problem, that is, how to choose the appropriate reference class to evaluate the probability of an event?

Probabilistic reasoning has the difficulty of reference class selection and severely criticized [2,3]. They use it as a basis to oppose the use of probabilistic methods in judicial proofs. In their paper *The Problematic Value of the Mathematical Model of Evidence*, they cite six cases to show that there are reference class problems in evaluating the probative value of evidence using probabilistic methods, and then come up with the relative plausibility theory, an explanationist approach, as a solution to these problems. One of these cases is called the "blue bus hypothetical" problem. Suppose a witness saw a bus strike a car but could not recall the color of the bus. Assume further that there are only two bus companies: The Blue Company and the Red Company. Which company is more likely liable for this accident? The most prevalent view in the legal literature of the probative value of the witness's report is that the ratio of Blue Company buses would determine it to Red Company buses in a reference class. Suppose the reference class is the street where the accident occurred, and suppose the Blue Company owns 75% of the buses in the street while the Red Company owns the remaining 25%. In that case, the Blue Company is more likely liable for this accident. But if the reference class is the town where the accident took place and suppose the Red Company owns 75% (and Blue the other 25%) of the buses in the town. Now the rate reverses, the Red Company is more likely liable. Furthermore, this would do so again if Blue owned 75% in the county and if Red owned 75% in the state, and so on. Similar reference classes can be divided endlessly, but we don't know which reference class is right. This example brings a lot of enlightenment to Allen and Pardo. First of all, the probative value of evidence is not the likelihood ratios of a given reference class. It corresponds to a variety of different reference classes. Evidence has an infinite number of likelihood ratios. Choosing any one of them, we must provide an explanation or reason, and a reasonable reason will always be found. Second, for the same reason, the value of evidence is not the information gain (the difference between the posterior probability and the prior probability) in the context of a given case. Finally, various statistical data or likelihood ratios from many reference classes are shreds of evidence, even more, complex evidence, and they need to be understood and explained [2]. Therefore, they believe that the likelihood cannot describe the probative value of the evidence very well, and the probability is difficult to obtain in reality. Even if it is obtained, it faces the difficulty of selecting the reference class.

The difficulty of reference class which exists in the field of judicial proof, is a universal problem because in any time of determining the probability of an individual thing or event with a certain feature, it may involve to select a reference class. Philosophers have elaborated on the universality and arduousness of the reference class problem, but they have not proposed solutions. Artificial intelligence experts who study common-sense reasoning also have encountered the reference class problem, and they also have found this problem to be tricky. Some scholars even believe that the difficulty of reference class selection is inherently unsolvable, and there is no principled method for determining reasonable reference classes [6].

This article will show that the reference class problem is not only solvable, but also has many solutions. From ancient times, the survival of human beings and even the survival of animals need to constantly evaluate risks based on frequency. People usually consciously or unconsciously determine the relevant reference classes based on their own experience and knowledge to evaluate the magnitude of the risk. In fact, we are solving the reference class problem every day in our life. For example, when you go out, referring to past weather conditions, you need to determine whether it will rain or not today and whether there is a risk of being caught in the rain. When riding an elevator, it is necessary to assess the risk of being trapped by the elevator based on the frequency of previous elevator failures. When traveling to a certain scenic spot, you need to assess your own risk of accidents according to the frequency of accidents in the scenic spot during the past, and so on. To stay alive, one must evaluate a good proportion of risk well, which is impossible if one cannot distinguish the few relevant reference classes from the many irrelevant ones. We solve relevant reference-class problems. Surely it is possible to say how. James Franklin [8] gives the following solution to the reference class problem: (a) A reference class should be defined by its features, so the problem reduces to explaining the relevance of features; (b) For statistical evidence, relevance is co-variation, for instance, a feature A is relevant to a prediction B if A and B co-vary or are correlated), and (c) The ideal reference class for an outcome B is the class defined by the intersection of all the feature relevant to B.

Applying Franklin's solution, we should pay attention to the following four points. First, we must distinguish between a set or class – the actual members - and the features defining it. For example, to evaluate the probability that the market price of a house (denoted as A) is greater than 3 million yuan (denoted as B), we need to find the "similar" houses that have been sold based on the features of house A (denoted as F). The collection of these similar houses is the reference class to be found. The features of determining similar houses may be the residential district (F_1) where the house is located, the area size (F_2), the apartment type (F_3), the floor (F_4), the house age (F_5), and so on. Secondly, we must find the correlation between the features F and the prediction or outcome B. The relevance of the four features of the residential area, area size, house type, and floor to the house price is co-variable. Once again, once the relevant features of A and a prediction B are identified and determined, the relevant reference class C is quite clear. The reference class C is composed of members similar to A that meet all relevant features. Finally, for the reference class selected according to Franklin's solution, a problem may arise: too few members meet all relevant features so that the reference class is too small to make a relevant frequency estimate. Under normal circumstances, a relevant reference class should contain enough members to make reliable estimates and predictions of the outcomes. Suppose the reference class is too small or even contains only one element of the original members. In that case, it will not support any reliable estimates because members rarely appear in such classes. One solution is to select several features from all relevant features to define multiple reference classes and then weigh the rationality of each reference class and select a class from them. For example, to predict the probability that the sales volume of book A exceeds 10,000 copies, the relevant features are the same author, the same topic, and the same publisher. If you want to meet these three features simultaneously, then the reference class will appear too small. We can define a reference class C_1 based on the features of "the same author," and then define another reference class C_2 based on "the same topic" and then tradeoff the outcome of these two reference classes to make a choice.

Discussing the judicial statistical evidence, the Charles Shonubi case is often much-discussed [2,17,18].[1] Regarding the dispute, in this case, scholars have mainly focused on the issue of reference class selection. The basic facts of this case are as follows: On December 10, 1991, Charles Shonubi, swallowed 103 balloons in the previous two days. The balloons contained a total of 427.4 g of heroin. He was arrested after arriving at John F. Kennedy Airport from Nigeria. The jury convicted him of drug smuggling. During the trial, the government also confirmed that Shonubi, a Nigerian citizen and a resident of the United States, smuggled drugs from Nigeria to the United States eight times from September 1, 1990 to December 10, 1991. At the time of the sentencing, Judge Jack Weinstein had to determine the amount of heroin that Shonubi had smuggled in the past seven times based on superior evidence. This amount constituted drug smuggling. Shonubi's sentence was based on the total amount of smuggling heroin eight times, not the amount of smuggling when he was arrested. During the trial, a government expert provided an important body of evidence concerning "the number of heroin seized from 177 Nigerian heroin abusers at Kennedy Airport during Shonubi's eight trips." Based on this data, Judge Weinstein concluded that Shonubi had smuggled 1,000 to 3,000 g of heroin during his eight trips and sentenced him accordingly. However, Shonubi appealed this sentence and the Second Circuit Court of Appeals vacated the sentence because the total quantity of drugs smuggled by Shonubi had not been established by a preponderance of evidence. This was partly because there was no "specific evidence" that Shonubi smuggled the quantity of drugs on which the sentencing was based. For this reason, the case was sent back to Judge Weinstein in the District Court for resentencing [5].[2]

---

[1] United States v. Shonubi, 895 F. Supp. 460 (E.D.N.Y. 1995).

[2] United States v. Shonubi, 103 F.3d 1085 (2d Cir. 1997).

Allen and Pardo [2] agree that the Shonubi case dealt with the problem of reference class selection, and do not reject the use of probabilistic reasoning. In the Shonubi case, they point out that the problem is that there is no detailed argumentation about the reasonable foundation of the selected reference class. For example, why can the amount of heroin seized from 177 Nigerian heroin users be used to predict the number of heroin smuggled by Shonubi? What is the basis for the selection of these 177 smugglers? What is its reasonable foundation? All need further justification. It should not be taken for granted that such reference classes are reasonable just because the data of these reference classes are easily available. The Shonubi case provides a vivid example of the importance of selecting reference classes and the necessity of demonstrating its reasonableness.

We agree with Allen and Pardo's point of view that in the use of probabilistic methods in judicial proof, the choice of reference classes and the reasonableness of the reference class needs to be justified. In fact, The Franklin's solution is the basis to ensure that the selected reference class is reasonable. In the Shonubi case, if "from Nigeria, it is a drug mule, at JFK Airport, within this period," these four features are considered to be related to the number of smuggled drugs. If there is no evidence that any of features available evidence are relevant, the reference class of these 177 smugglers is reasonable.

4   The Conjunction Problem: A Probabilistic Justification

Mathematicians have long developed what might be termed as conventional probability theory, in which probabilities theory obey certain basic principles, such as that the probability of proposition $A \cap B$, given a body of information O, equals the probability of A, give O, times the probability of B, given A and O. This is the multiplication principle in (conventional) probability theory. And most people understand the basic idea of probability with respect to proposition reflecting events that might recur in essentially identical form: thus, "The probability that any given flip of a fair coin will land heads up is 1 in 2". However, Friedman [9] questions this by saying what bearing does this have on litigation. In Cohen's view, neither the complementary principle for negation nor the multiplication principle for conjunction applies to the central core of any forensic proof in the Anglo-American legal systems [4, p. 2].

The difficulty of conjunction, also known as evidence aggregation problem, is first proposed by Jonathan Cohen [4, ch.5]. In most civil cases, the plaintiff's contention consists of several component elements [4, p. 58]. The multiplication principle for the mathematical probability of a conjunction entails that, if the contention as a whole is to be established on the balance of mathematical probability, there must either be very few separate components in the case or most of them must established at a very high level of probability. Since this constraint on the complexity of civil cases is unknown to the law, the mathematical analysis is in grave difficulties here.

Specifically speaking, when the facts claimed by the plaintiff include two or more individual elements, each element must be justified to make the litigation successful. In a traffic accident compensation case, for example, the car driver is suing an insurance company because it refuses to compensate him after an accident. The circumstances of the accident (denoted as A) and the terms of the insurance contract (denoted as B) may both be disputed. If he succeeds in the lawsuit, both of these elements must be justified on the basis of the plaintiff's benefit. On the contrary, as long as one elements of them has not been successfully justified, his claims will not be fully supported. Assuming that the "preponderance principle of evidence" of the civil proof standard can be interpreted as the probability requirement of asserting facts greater than 0.5, then should this requirement be applied to each element separately? Or is it applicable to their conjunction, that is, the entire case? We believe that there are three possible solutions for this problem. The first solution is that the principle of probability balance is only applicable to an individual element; that is, only the probability of each element is required to be greater than 0.5 without considering the probability of their conjunction. The second solution is that the principle of probability balance is only applicable to the entire case; that is, it only requires that the probability of all the elements is greater than 0.5, and there is no need to examine the probability of each element. The third solution is that the probability value of each element is required to be examined, and the combined probability of all elements is required to be greater than 0.5. The probabilistic method adopts the third solution. The probability of each element is examined. However, there is no requirement for its value to be greater than 0.5. Then the relevant probability formula is used to calculate the probability of conjunction, and its value is required to be greater than 0.5. Based on Cohen's analysis [4, p. 59], assuming that C is the conjunction of elements A and B, that is, $C = A \cap B$, according to the evidence provided, the fact-finder believes that A and B are two independent elements, each of which is determined with a probability of 0.7, then, according to the multiplication principle of probability, $P(C) = P(A) \times P(B) = 0.7 \times 0.7 = 0.49$. In other words, their joint outcome can be determined with a sufficiently high probability since 0.7 is greater than 0.49. Thus, although the probability of each element satisfies the proof standard of the principle of probability balance, the probability of the whole case does not. The point to require for a balance of mathematical probability seems a necessary consequence of construing the standard in civil cases, but it seems to be a rule that is unknown to judges and not respected by trier of fact.

Pardo and Allen [17] also mention the conjunction problem, the conjunction paradox called by them, and question the applicability of Bayesian probability theory in judicial proof. Most Bayesian theorists have reconstructed the probability of the standard of persuasion for the claimants' claim to mean that, under a preponderance of standard of 0.5 for a claim with two element, A and B, the probability of $A \times B$ exceeds 0.5, and for a three-element claim $A \times B \times C$ must exceed 0.5, and so on. This would mean that as the number of elements increases, the probability needed for each element would increase as well. In other words, for two elements, the average probability for each element must be approximately 0.707; for three elements, 0.794; for four elements, 0.841; and so on. From their point of view, it leads to some paradoxical conclusion such as the following: the plaintiff in a two-element claim wins when proving each element to 0.6 despite their conjunction probability is 0.36, and loses when proving one element to 0.9 and the other to 0.5 and having the conjunction probability of 0.45. That is why Cohen regards this finding as paradoxical, and telling against the application of probabilistic reasoning to a civil suit [7].

To avoid the difficulty of conjunction, Cohen points out that the rule of civil suits requires the plaintiff to prove each element of his case on the balance of probability [4, p. 58]. Cohen adopts the first solution. The car driver in the above case wins, even though the total probability (conjunctive probability) of the entire case is less than 0.5. While opposing probabilistic methods to judicial proofs, as mentioned earlier, Allen and Pardo [3] propose the theory of relative plausibility as an alternative. In the relative plausibility theory, they adopt the second solution, in which the fact-finder infers the best explanation of all the evidence as a whole. According to the applicable proof standards, the comparison between the competing explanations is also carried out at the overall level to determine the best explanation of the case. Once the best explanation is determined, we should compare the explanation with the various formal elements required by the substantive law to see if they are included in the explanation. If included, the explanation will be accepted, and the corresponding claim will win. Otherwise, the explanation will be rejected, and the corresponding claim will lose. The relative plausibility theory also avoids the emergence of the conjunction problems.

We consider that the third solution seems to be intuitive and natural. The first solution simply involves examining all of the elements one by one, using a local perspective, whereas our instinct is to evaluate the case as a whole. The second solution, which looks at the whole case, takes a holistic view, but ignores the individual examination of each element, making it easy to alter or even distort evidence. Simon's critique of this solution is that the holistic process itself has the potential to distort verdicts. Holism does not appear from nowhere. Rather, it is constructed via a cognitive process that entails a transformation of the fact-finder's mental representation of the evidence and drives the evidence towards a more extreme view of the cases [20]. For this cognitive process, we believe that it should be an analytic process from part to whole. The third answer is exactly in line with this idea, examining each element in part first, and then evaluating the whole, while probabilistic method is an inference method based on this cognition. In Pardo and Allen's example mentioned earlier, the probability of both elements in the first case is 0.6; In the second case, the probability of one element is 0.9 and the probability of the other is 0.5. According to the third solution, our interpretation is that the plaintiff will lose in both cases and will not lead to a paradoxical conclusion because the probability of their conjunction is less than 0.5, i.e., 0.36 for one and 0.45 for the other. They conclude that the plaintiff will win in the former case and lose in the latter case because he uses the first solution, which requires only a probability greater than 0.5 for each element. However, in both cases, according to the third solution, the plaintiff will lose and will not produce a paradoxical conclusion because the probabilities of their conjunction are both less than 0.5; that is, one is 0.36, and the other is 0.45.

In probability theory, according to the multiplication principle of probability, if $C = A \cap B$, and A and B are not independent of each other, then $P(C) = P(A) \times P(B|A) = P(B) \times P(A|B)$. If A and B are independent each other, then $P(C) = P(A) \times P(B)$. No matter which principle is applied, it is unlikely that the probability of C is greater than the probability of either A or B, and usually much less than the probability of either because a positive number greater than 0 times something less than 1 is definitely less than itself. It is correct for Allen and Pardo to understand that for the probability of conjunctions to be greater than 0.5, the probability values of the elements must be higher. The more elements the conjunction has, the higher its probability value is required, and correspondingly, the more difficult it is to prove. While Cohen's intuition seems to be that it is already very demanding to require the plaintiff to be satisfied by the court that the probability of each element is greater than 0.5. Thus, it would be unfair to further establish that the probability of conjunctions in the whole case is greater than 0.5.

Although Cohen [4] and Pardo and Allen [17] have exactly recognized this point, their mistakes are to apply this probability theory to judicial proof too simplistically. If the terms in the judicial proof are explained more comprehensively and formalized under the framework of probability theory, the conjunction problem will disappear. In fact, Dawid [7] has shown that Cohen's paradox and its related variants would have evaporated if the conjunction probability had been properly analyzed within the Pascal framework, in which he uses prior probability and posterior probability to demonstrate the reliability of the witness. He maintains that the combination of several independent pieces of evidence provides more support for the case than any of its individual evidence. Unlike Pardo and Allen's point of view, Dawid believes that if a case is divided into more and more individual elements, the increase in the number of elements will not greatly impact the overall effect. If there is any impact, it will give the claimant an advantage, even though he must determine each element with a high probability. Dawid [7] concludes that this probabilistic analysis, correctly performed, is in complete accord with logic and common-sense. However, in the field of evidence law, there are some scholars who discuss the difficulties of conjunction in the theory of judicial probability, and even question the applicability of this method. Therefore, we think it is necessary to make some responses to their criticisms.

To apply this probabilistic approach to judicial proof, the reasoner must first distinguish between the concept of evidence and proposition. A proposition is an assertion, a hypothesis, a fact to be proved, or an essential fact specified by substantive law. Evidence is a material used to establish the facts of a case. It's the evidence that we're evaluating, not the proposition. The supportive degree of the evidence to the proposition is also called the probative value of evidence. For the evidence E and the proposition H, the reasoner should distinguish the prior probability $P(H)$ and the *posterior* probability $P(H|E)$ of the proposition H and the likelihood of the evidence $P(E|H)$. The likelihood is used to measure the reliability of evidence, and the likelihood *ratio* $P(E|H)/P(E|not\ H)$ is used to measure the probative value of evidence. In the process of probabilistic reasoning, one must first evaluate the *prior* probability of the proposition and the likelihood of the evidence and then use probability theory to calculate the *posterior* probability of the proposition. The *posterior* probability is not only related to the likelihood but also the *prior* probability. Only *prior* probabilities and likelihoods can be assigned to probability numbers through relevant data or subjective experience. The *posterior* probabilities can only be calculated through the Bayes formula and cannot be directly assigned. When conducting probabilistic reasoning, people usually make three mistakes. One is to ignore the *prior* probability, the other is to confuse the likelihood and the *posterior* probability, and the *posterior* probability is directly assigned. The third is to use the *posterior* probability to evaluate the probative value of evidence. In fact, the probative value of evidence should be measured using the likelihood *ratio* model.

In the context of probability, the conjunction problem can be described as when two pieces of evidence a and b are considered at the same time, the *posterior* probability of proposition C will be less than the *posterior* probability of C when considering a single piece of evidence, that is, $P(C|a \cap b) < P(C|a), P(C|a \cap b) < P(C|b)$. The reason why the conjunction problem is counter-intuitive lies in the wrong calculation process; that is, if the evidence a and b are independent of each other, then $P(C|a \cap b) = P(C|a) \times P(C|b)$. The correct calculation should use the Bayesian formula to evaluate the evidence. Taroni *et al.* [21] give an example. Assuming that the *prior* probability of proposition C equals 0.5, namely $P(C) = 0.5$, the *posterior* probability $P(C|a) = P(C|b) = 0.7$. When evidence a and b are independent of each other, the Bayesian formula is used to calculate the likelihood *ratio* of evidence a and b, and the two likelihood *ratio* are equal to 2.33. However, the likelihood *ratio* of combined evidence $a \cap b$ is equal to 5.44, greater than their respective likelihood *ratio*. In addition, the *posterior* probability $P(C|a \cap b) = 0.84$, which is also greater than their respective *posterior* probabilities. This example shows that as long as probabilistic reasoning is used correctly, the probative value of conjunctive evidence can be greater than that of its individual branch evidence. The *posterior* probability given the conjunctive evidence can also be greater than the *posterior* probability given its branch evidence. The conjunction problem doesn't exist at all.

Going back to the traffic accident compensation case mentioned in the previous section, we think there is a lot of ambiguity in Cohen's statement. What is the evidence? Is 0.7 a *prior* probability, a *posteriori* probability or likelihood? The meaning of this number is unclear. Based on intuition Cohen uses the probability multiplication principle roughly, which leads to the so-called conjunction problem. There are at least four problems with Cohen's proof. First, his reasoning process does not clearly show the corresponding evidence, and without evidence, it is impossible to carry out formal evidential reasoning, and thus cannot guarantee the soundness of his argumentation. Second, according to Cohen's description, 0.7 should be a *posterior* probability, but due to the lack of relevant evidence, 0.7 is written as a *prior* probability, that is, $P(A) = P(B) = 0.7$. It can be seen that his use of symbols seems somewhat confusing. Third, Cohen does not explain how the *posterior* probability of 0.7 was calculated, nor does he explain the related *prior* probability and likelihood, making the mistake of directly assigning the *posterior* probability. Fourth, the probative power of evidence should be evaluated by likelihood rather than a *posteriori* probability. If the *posterior* probability is really to be used to evaluate it, then, according to the Bayesian probability, the *ratio* of the *posterior* probability to the *prior* probability needs to be evaluated, and if this *ratio* is greater than 1, then the likelihood rate is greater than 1. Therefore, in our opinion, it seems that Cohen should not compare the *posterior* probability 0.49 of conjunction C with the *posterior* probability of element A or B, but it is meaningful to compare it with the *prior* probability of C.

Assume that a and b evidence is the evidence of proposition A and B, respectively, and the reliability of evidence is 70%, namely, $P(a|A) = P(b|B) = 0.7$. When evidence a and b are independent of each other, proposition A and B are independent of each other. Apparently Cohen's final calculation is the *posterior* probability is $P(a \cap b|A \cap B)$. It is interesting to note that by the probability calculus, Dawid [7] find that to make the *posteriori* probability $P(a|A) = P(b|B) = 0.7$, the *prior* probability must be equal to 0.5, i.e. $P(A) = P(B) = 0.5$, so the *prior* probability of the conjunction is: $P(A \cap B) = P(A) \times P(B) = 0.25$, and $P(a \cap b|A \cap B) = P(a|A) \times P(b|B) = 0.49$. Here we reconstruct Cohen's reasoning by means of *prior* probability and a *posteriori* probability. This is obviously not result in a paradoxical conclusion because $P(a \cap b|A \cap B)/P(A \cap B) = 0.49/0.25 = 1.96 > 1$. It can be seen that the probability of the conjunctive evidence $a \cap b$ still provides positive support for the conjunctive proposition $A \cap B$, and does not reduce its probability. In addition, Dawid [7] also finds the law that the posterior probability of conjunction varies with its prior probability, as shown in the following table:

Table 1. Dawid on prior probability vs posterior probability

Priori probability $P(A \cap B)$	0.05	0.1	0.2	0.25	0.3	0.4	0.5
Posterior probability $P(a \cap b|A \cap B)$	0.16	0.27	0.43	0.49	0.55	0.64	0.72

As we can see from Table 1: (1) The *posterior* probability is always greater than its corresponding *prior* probability, and its *ratio* is greater than 1. Conjunctive evidence $a \cap b$ still provides positive support for the conjunctive proposition $A \cap B$; (2) As long as the *prior* probability is not below 0.3, the *posterior* probability will be greater than 0.5, satisfying the balance principle of the probability for the standard of proof. Therefore, in the case of 70% reliable evidence, as long as the *prior* probability $P(A \cap B)$ is greater than 0.3, Cohen's so-called conjunction problem ceases to exist.

5 Conclusion

As for the debate on the nature of judicial certification, we believe that it is impossible to reach a consensus and there is no ultimate winner. The relative plausible approach, i.e. interpretivism, based on the inference to the best interpretation is vague and not perfect in the normative aspect. The probabilistic approach, i.e., the probabilism, based on probabilistic reasoning requires too many probability values. These values are sometimes difficult to obtain, and there is no accepted method of probability assignment. Both of the two approaches are not incompatible but each has its pros and cons. Because of this, we may have to change the perspective of thinking that they are not absolutely opposed to each other, but can be considered the complementarity of their common application to judicial proof. In some cases, the best explanation in support of a decision may involve an explicit probabilistic reasoning process. Lipton [15, pp. 119–120], for example, has provided a brief exploration of the prospects for a compatibilist view of the relationship between the probabilism and the explanationism. In his view, it is compatible with the view that explanatory consideration helps us to perform what is in effect a Bayesian calculation and Bayesianism poses no particular threat to the relative plausibility theory. Specifically speaking, Bayes' theorem provides a constraint on the rational distribution of degrees of belief, but this is compatible with the view that explanatory considerations play a crucial role in the evolution of those beliefs and indeed a crucial role in the mechanism by which we attempt, with considerable but not complete success, to meet that constraint. That is why the Bayesian and the explanationist should be friends. According to Horwich [12], our full beliefs of degree would comply with the laws of deductive logic, and similarly, our degrees of belief should conform to the probability calculus. The elementary probabilistic models of degrees of belief often contains just the right balance of accuracy and simplicity to enable us to command a clear view of the issues and see where we were going wrong. The probabilistic method is an important analytical tool for judicial proof, but it is not a decisive tool. When the fact-finding process is reasonable for probability analysis, the advantages of quantitative analysis should be used rationally. To sum up, in our view, the probabilistic approach of judicial proof is not only self-consistent and normative, but also does not lead to paradoxical conclusions and unfair decisions. For the most part, the Cohenian paradoxes proposed by other schools of new evidence scholars are nothing more than misconceptions of probability.

Acknowledgments. This work was supported by the National Office and Social Science, P. R. China, for the project "Logical Model of Criminal Evidential Reasoning" (19BZX138).

References

1. Allen, R.J.: The nature of juridical proof: probability as a tool in plausible reasoning. Int. J. Evid. Proof **21**(1–2), 133–142 (2017). https://doi.org/10.1177/1365712716674794
2. Allen, R.J., Pardo, M.S.: The problematic value of mathematical models of evidence. J. Legal Stud. **36**(1), 107–140 (2007)
3. Allen, R.J., Pardo, M.S.: Relative plausibility and its critics. Int. J. Evid. Proof **23**(1–2), 5–59 (2019). https://doi.org/10.1177/1365712718813781
4. Cohen, L.J.: The Probable and the Provable. Clarendon Press, Oxford (1977)
5. Colyvan, M., Regan, H.M., Ferson, S.: Is it a crime to belong to a reference class. J. Polit. Philos. **9**(2), 168–181 (2001). https://doi.org/10.1111/1467-9760.00123
6. Colyvan, M., Regan, H.M.: Legal decisions and the reference class problem. Int. J. Evid. Proof **11**(4), 274–286 (2007). https://doi.org/10.1350/ijep.2007.11.4.274
7. Dawid, A.P.: The difficulty about conjunction. J. R. Stat. Soc. Ser. D (Stat.) **36**(2/3), 91–97 (1987)
8. Franklin, J.: The objective Bayesian conceptualisation of proof and reference class problems. Sydney Law Rev. **33**(3), 545–561 (2011)
9. Friedman, R.D.: Answering the Bayesioskeptical challenge. Int. J. Evid. Proof **3**(4), 276–291 (1997)
10. Hájek, A.: Explanations of probability. The Stanford Encyclopedia of Philosophy. Substantive revision 2019. Stanford Encyclopedia of Philosophy (2019). https://plato.stanford.edu/archives/fall2019/entries/probability-interpret/
11. Hamer, D.: Probabilistic standards of proof, their complements and the errors that are expected to flow from them. Univ. New Engl. Law J. **1**(1), 71–107 (2004)
12. Horwich, P.: Wittgensteinian bayesianism. Midwest Stud. Philos. **18**(1), 62–77 (1993)
13. Hunt, I., Mostyn, J.: Probability reasoning in judicial fact-finding. Int. J. Evid. Proof **24**(1), 75–94 (2020). https://doi.org/10.1177/1365712719875753
14. Kaplan, J.: Decision theory and the fact-finding process. Stanford Law Rev. **20**(6), 1065–1092 (1968)
15. Lipton, P.: Inference to the Best Explanation, 2nd edn. Routledge, Abingdon (2003)
16. Pardo, M.S.: The paradoxes of legal proof: a critical guide. Boston Univ. Law Rev. **99**(1), 233–290 (2019)
17. Pardo, M.S., Allen, R.J.: Juridical proof and the best explanation. Law Philos. **27**(3), 223–268 (2008). https://doi.org/10.1007/s10982-007-9016-4
18. Redmayne, M.: Exploring the proof paradoxes. Legal Theory **14**(4), 281–309 (2008). https://doi.org/10.1017/S1352325208080117
19. Rescher, N.: Dialectics: A Controversy-Oriented Approach to the Theory of Knowledge. State University of New York Press (1977)
20. Simon, D.: Thin empirics. Int. J. Evid. Proof **23**(1–2), 82–89 (2019). https://doi.org/10.1177/1365712718815350
21. Taroni, F., Aitken, C., Garbolino, P., Biedermann, A.: Bayesian Networks and Probabilistic Inference in Forensic Science. Wiley, New York (2006)
22. Urbaniak, R., Di Bello, M.: Legal Probabilism. Stanford Encyclopedia of Philosophy. First publshied 8 June 2021 (2021). https://plato.stanford.edu/archives/sum2021/entries/legal-probabilism/
23. Welch, J.R.: Rebooting the new evidence scholarship. Int. J. Evid. Proof **24**(4), 351–373 (2020). https://doi.org/10.1177/1365712720943329

Focusing the Argumentative Process: Neighborhood-Based Semantics in Abstract Argumentation

Melisa G. Escañuela Gonzalez[1], Maximiliano C. D. Budán[1,3],
Diego I. Martínez[2,3], Maria Laura Cobo[2,3], and Guillermo R. Simari[2,3(✉)]

[1] Depto. de Matemática, Universidad Nacional de Santiago del Estero (UNSE),
Santiago del Estero, Argentina
meliesca@unse.edu.ar, mcdb@cs.uns.edu.ar
[2] Depto. de Cs. e Ing. de la Comp., Universidad Nacional del Sur (DCIC UNS),
Bahía Blanca, Argentina
{dcm,mlc,grs}@cs.uns.edu.ar
[3] Institute for Computer Science and Engineering (ICIC UNS–CONICET),
Bahía Blanca, Argentina

Abstract. The introduction of abstract argumentation has allowed the study of many exciting characteristics of the argumentation process. Nevertheless, while helpful in many aspects, abstraction diminishes the knowledge representation capabilities available to describe naturally occurring features of argumentative dialogues. One of these elements is the consideration of the topics involved in a discussion. In studying dialogical processes, participants recognize that some topics are closely related to the original issue, while others are more distant to the central subject or simply refer to unrelated matters. Consequently, it is reasonable to study different argumentation semantics that consider the focus of a discussion to evaluate acceptability. In this work, we will introduce the necessary representational elements required to reflect the focus of a discussion, and we will propose an extension of the semantics for *multi-topic abstract argumentation frameworks* acknowledging that every argument has its own *zone of relevance* in the argumentation framework, leading to a concept of a neighborhood of legitimate defenses. Furthermore, other semantic elaborations are defined and discussed around this structure.

1 Introduction

Abstraction is a pathway to study argumentation without acknowledging the underlying logical structure, and thus the subject of study is centered on semantics. Thus, arguments are treated as abstract entities linked through interrelations between them, like support, attack, and weakening, among others [1,4,11,17]. In this conceptual direction, Dung in [11] introduced *Abstract Argumentation Frameworks* (*AFs*) with the top level of abstraction where arguments are atomic, and a binary attack relation is defined, leaving out of consideration most details with the goal of studying argument interaction and the

P. Baroni et al. (Eds.): CLAR 2021, LNAI 13040, pp. 20–39, 2021.
https://doi.org/10.1007/978-3-030-89391-0_2

possible outcomes of the argumentation process. Thus, recognizing the limits of the bare-bones, abstract framework introduced by Dung in his foundational work, researchers have advanced several extensions that augment the representational capabilities of the basic framework attaching additional features such as preference, support relations, probability, and values [1,4,6,7,16,17].

Recognizing this situation, in this work, we are interested in introducing the notion that corresponds to the *topics* associated with an argument. The fact that arguments could be linked to different topics and that these topics might or might not be closely related to each other introduces a topological aspect over the set of topics. Ignoring this intrinsic characteristic of dialogue may lead to "going off on a tangent" in the argumentation process; in other words, the topic an argument addresses may allow other arguments to be used or rejected in a particular dialogue.

In Budán *et al.* [5], a framework and its corresponding semantics in which arguments are associated with abstract labels denoting that a piece of reasoning may refer to different *topics* in the context of argumentation was introduced. For instance, an argument may refer to a *virus pandemia*, to the *quarantine*, and to the *welfare state*, while another argument may refer to *virus pandemia* and *music online streaming*. Although both arguments are related to one issue, the second argument may not be as helpful while discussing health topics as the first argument. Thus, based on the semantic network of topics, a nearness or "proximity" relation between arguments can be established, leading to a new notion of admissibility semantics where only sufficiently closely related arguments can be involved in the argument defense. In this direction, an argument is considered close enough to defend another argument if the distance between these is lower than a particular threshold τ, and any potential defender such that its topic is beyond τ will not be enabled as such. This is the basis of a proximity-semantics, but the original framework has a characteristic that can be improved towards a more realistic model. As defined, the threshold is the same for all the arguments leading to some unfair situations.

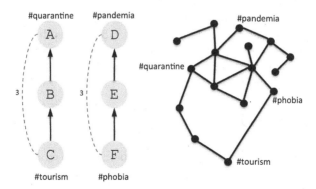

Fig. 1. Same-distance defenders under irregular network

Consider the framework of Fig. 1, where only the relevant hashtags are mentioned, and, for simplicity, there is only one hashtag per argument. Consider the distance between arguments as the length of the shortest path between their single hashtags. Here, the distance between A and C and between D and F is 3. If the threshold of proximity for the framework is 3, both A and D are defended by C and F, respectively. However, there seem to be more closely related topics in the upper zone of the graph, where health issues are addressed, than around #tourism. Since the semantic network of hashtags is not necessarily uniform, a universal threshold may not be adequate in all cases. Here an individual threshold for A may drop arguments about tourism, while a different threshold for D may enable all the arguments as defenders as long as they are both related to health issues. Thus, an improvement of this model should consider variations of distance for every piece of reasoning since the semantic network of topics, as abstract as it is, maybe dense or sparse in different regions or even related to different areas of interest.

In this work, we refine the proximity semantics by defining the proper defense scope for every argument, which may vary in range among the sets of arguments. Since the referred topics determine the associated distance in the network, an individual threshold is required, and therefore different sets of topics lead to different sets of potential defenders. Hence, in a sense, all the arguments "*close*" enough to a given argument A constitute a *neighborhood* for A. Given that the notion of closeness may differ for every argument, the attribute of being a neighbor is not universal: argument B may be a neighbor of A, but not the other way around. This idea leads to restricted forms of acceptability of arguments, where only defenders in the neighborhood are allowed. While in [5] a single, universal degree of proximity is applied to the whole framework yielding an admissible extension, here this attribute is defined for every individual argument. In Fig. 1 argument C is required to be in the neighborhood of A in order to provide a defense for A. Argument D may have a different neighborhood, and if F is not in it, then D has no close defense or, in other words, the defense provided by F is not relevant for D. The previous discussion leads naturally to a novel admissible semantics that we will address in this work.

This paper is organized as follows. In Sect. 2, the multi-topic abstract argumentation frameworks are reviewed, while in Sect. 3, we introduce a set of semantic notions that consider the "neighbourhoods" associated with the arguments in the argumentation process. Finally, Sect. 4 is devoted to the related work, concluding remarks, and further discussion.

2   Background

An *argumentation framework* is defined as a pair composed of a set of atomic arguments and a binary relation representing an attack relationship between them. To determine which arguments are able to survive the conflict, a well-defined systematic method is needed; such formal methods to identify conflict outcomes for an argumentation framework are referred to as *argumentation semantics.* All the well-known conceptual ideas introduced in [11] are assumed as given, and in this work, we will limit our focus on refining that framework by considering different metrics over a *topics network* affecting the argumentation discussion.

2.1 Hashtagged Argumentation Framework

We will present new forms of proximity-based semantics using hashtagged argumentation frameworks [5] as a starting point because it provides the elements for the consideration of a notion of distance. A hashtagged framework extends the representation capability of abstract frameworks by adding the *topics* addressed or referred to by the arguments. As it is usual in abstract frameworks, no reference to the underlying construction of the argument is made; however, Budán *et al.* in [5] gives relevance to *what* an argument refers to, not as a linguistic construction depending on its structure but as a whole. Topics are also treated abstractly through labels called *hashtags*, denoted with the prefix #; that is, a hashtag identifies subjects to which the argument refers, implicitly or explicitly. Since every argument is issued in the context of at least one subject or topic, arguments are always associated with at least one hashtag.

Definition 1 (Hashtagged Argument). *Given an argumentation framework* $\Phi = \langle \text{Args}, \text{Attacks} \rangle$, *let* $\mathcal{H}$ *be a finite non-empty set of hashtags. A* hashtagged argument structure, *or, when no confusion might arise, just a* hashtagged argument, *is a pair* $\langle A, \mathcal{H}_A \rangle$, *where* $A \in \text{Args}$ *and* $\mathcal{H}_A \subseteq \mathcal{H}$, $|\mathcal{H}_A| > 0$. *Then, given* $\langle A, \mathcal{H}_A \rangle$, *it is said that* A *is tagged with* $\mathcal{H}_A$. *When possible, hashtagged arguments will be succinctly denoted with the letters* A, B, ..., *possibly with subscripts or superscripts.*

Michel Foucault keenly pointed out that *"the frontiers of a book are never clear-cut (...) it is a node within a network"* in [12]; similarly, hashtags as topics attached to arguments usually are not isolated, and they might be related to others, leading to a semantic network of concepts. The resulting semantic network can be represented through a graph structure as follows.

Definition 2 (Hashtag Graph). *Let* $\mathcal{H}$ *be a finite set of hashtags, a hashtag graph is a graph* $\mathcal{G} = [\mathcal{H}, E]$, *where* $\mathcal{H}$ *is the set of vertices (hashtags) and* E *is a subset of* $\mathcal{H} \times \mathcal{H}$ *that represents a set of edges between the vertices (hashtags's relationship) in* $\mathcal{H}$. *When convenient, the graph* $\mathcal{G}$ *will be referred to as a hashcloud.*

In particular, the well-known concept of a path in a graph is relevant for the following definitions. A path is a finite or infinite sequence of edges that connects a sequence of vertices, assuming that they are all distinct from one another. Thus, using paths, we can represent connections between topics and, consequently, connections between arguments. Another essential component is the notion of distance in a graph, which is closely related to paths (see [3,10,13] for a comprehensive analysis). With these elements, not only the connections but also the distance between arguments can be analyzed.

Definition 3 (Distance Between Hasthatgs). *Let* $\mathscr{G} = [\mathcal{H}, E]$ *be a hashtag graph. The (geodesic) distance* $\mathsf{d}_{\mathscr{G}} : \mathcal{H} \times \mathcal{H} \to \mathbb{N}^0 \cup \{\infty\}$ *between two vertices* $\alpha, \beta \in \mathcal{H}$*, denoted* $\mathsf{d}_{\mathscr{G}}(\alpha, \beta)$*, is the number of edges in a shortest path connecting them; additionally, if there is no path between* α *and* β *we say that* $\mathsf{d}_{\mathscr{G}}(\alpha, \beta) = \infty$*, where* ∞*, conventionally, represents the greatest possible distance. For all* $\alpha, \beta, \gamma \in \mathcal{H}$*,* $\mathsf{d}_{\mathscr{G}}(\cdot, \cdot)$ *satisfies the following conditions:*

1) $\mathsf{d}_{\mathscr{G}}(\alpha, \beta) = 0$ *iff* $\alpha = \beta$ *(identity of indiscernibles),*
2) $\mathsf{d}_{\mathscr{G}}(\alpha, \beta) = \mathsf{d}_{\mathscr{G}}(\beta, \alpha)$ *(symmetry), and*
3) $\mathsf{d}_{\mathscr{G}}(\alpha, \gamma) \leq \mathsf{d}_{\mathscr{G}}(\alpha, \beta) + \mathsf{d}_{\mathscr{G}}(\beta, \gamma)$ *(subadditivity or triangle inequality).*

From the three items above, we obtain the non-negativity *or* separation *property* $\mathsf{d}_{\mathscr{G}}(\alpha, \beta) \geq 0$*.*

The hashtags network is independent of the argumentation graph, as it merely captures concepts and their semantic relations. From a knowledge representation point of view, the topological structure $\mathscr{G}$ implies that the closer the hashtags (vertices) are in the graph, the closer are the topics they stand for in the represented domain. Thus, given a pair of hashtagged arguments, a notion of proximity between these arguments can be induced by the *distance* existing between the referred topics in the hashtagged graph $\mathscr{G}$ [5].

Definition 4 (Distance between Hashtagged Arguments). *Given a hashtagged framework* $\Omega = \langle \Phi, \mathscr{G}_\Omega, \mathsf{d}_\Omega \rangle$*, where* $\Phi = \langle \mathtt{Args}, \mathtt{Attacks} \rangle$ *and* $\mathscr{G}_\Omega = [\mathcal{H}, E]$*, a distance function on* $\mathtt{Args}$ *is defined as* $\mathsf{d}_\Omega : \mathtt{Args} \times \mathtt{Args} \to \mathbb{N}^0 \cup \{\infty\}$*, where for all* $\mathbb{A}, \mathbb{B}, \mathbb{C} \in \mathtt{Args}$*, the following conditions should be satisfied:*

1) $\mathsf{d}_\Omega(\mathbb{A}, \mathbb{B}) = 0$ *iff* $\mathbb{A} = \mathbb{B}$ *(identity of indiscernibles),*
2) $\mathsf{d}_\Omega(\mathbb{A}, \mathbb{B}) = \mathsf{d}_\Omega(\mathbb{B}, \mathbb{A})$ *(symmetry), and*
3) $\mathsf{d}_\Omega(\mathbb{A}, \mathbb{C}) \leq \mathsf{d}_\Omega(\mathbb{A}, \mathbb{B}) + \mathsf{d}_\Omega(\mathbb{B}, \mathbb{C})$*.*
As before, the following can be obtained from the previous three.
4) $\mathsf{d}_\Omega(\mathbb{A}, \mathbb{B}) \geq 0$ *(non-negativity or separation).*

This formalization of the hashtags as a graph that represents both the topics and their abstract connections, highlighting the distance between the argument, will permit the examination of interesting semantic issues emerging from the abstract notion of *closeness*. The following definition provides a formal framework for hashtagged argumentation.

Definition 5 (Hashtagged Argumentation Framework). *A hashtagged argumentation framework* Ω *is represented as a 3-tuple* $\langle \Phi, \mathscr{G}_\Omega, \mathsf{d}_\Omega \rangle$*, where* $\Phi = \langle \mathtt{Args}, \mathtt{Attacks} \rangle$ *is an abstract argumentation framework in which* $\mathtt{Args}$ *is a set of hashtagged arguments and* $\mathtt{Attacks}$ *is a subset of* $\mathtt{Args} \times \mathtt{Args}$ *representing an attack relation defined on* $\mathtt{Args}$*,* $\mathscr{G}_\Omega = [\mathcal{H}, E]$ *is a hashtag graph, and* $\mathsf{d}_\Omega(\cdot, \cdot)$ *is a distance function defined over* Ω*. The graph* $\mathscr{G}_\Omega$ *will be called the* hashcloud *of* Ω*, and it will be denoted* $\mathscr{G}_\Omega$*.*

Given this formalization, an admissibility semantics is defined in [5], that uses the distance as a measure of relevance for defenses in the argumentation process.

2.2   Proximity-Based Semantics

The idea of argumentation-based reasoning is that an affirmation is believable if it can be defended successfully against attacking arguments. Hence, using hashtags is a pathway to further model proximity-based evaluations of argument extensions to further refine the abstract argumentation semantics. In particular, proximity semantics, as defined in [5] is applying the intuition that, for any argument, a closer defender is preferred over a distant one. Therefore, acceptability for hashtagged arguments considering a threshold τ of proximity is introduced. Under this interpretation of proximal defense, a potential defender that is beyond the threshold will not be considered as such.

Definition 6 (Basic Proximity-based semantics). *Let $\Omega = \langle \Phi, \mathscr{G}_\Omega, \mathsf{d}_\Omega \rangle$ be a hashtagged framework, $\mathsf{d}_\Omega(\cdot, \cdot)$ be a distance function defined in Ω, $\mathsf{S} \subseteq \mathtt{Args}$, and $\tau \in \mathbb{N}^0$ be a threshold. Then:*

- *A set S is said to be conflict free if there are no hashtagged arguments $\mathbb{A}, \mathbb{B} \in \mathsf{S}$ such that $\mathbb{B}$ attacks $\mathbb{A}$ (mirroring a similar definition in abstract frameworks).*
- *A hashtagged argument $\mathbb{A} \in \mathtt{Args}$ is τ-acceptable with respect to S when for every argument $\mathbb{B} \in \mathtt{Args}$ that attacks $\mathbb{A}$ there is a hashtagged argument $\mathbb{C} \in \mathsf{S}$ such that $\mathbb{C}$ attacks $\mathbb{B}$ and $\mathsf{d}_\Omega(\mathbb{A}, \mathbb{C}) \leq \tau$.*
- *S is said to be τ-admissible if every hashtagged argument in S is τ-acceptable with respect to S.*
- *An τ-admissible set S is an τ-complete extension iff S contains each argument that is τ-acceptable with respect to S.*
- *A set S is the τ-grounded extension of Ω iff S is a $\subseteq$-minimal τ-complete extension.*
- *A set S is an τ-preferred extension of Ω iff S is a $\subseteq$-maximal τ-complete extension.*

Next, we present a example showing how the concepts introduced above play a role in the argumentation formalism.

Example 1. Consider the hashtagged argumentation framework $\Omega = \langle \Phi, \mathscr{G}_\Omega, \mathsf{d}_\Omega \rangle$, graphically represented in Fig. 2, where:

$$\mathcal{H} = \{\#\alpha_1, \#\alpha_2, \ldots, \#\alpha_{25}\}.$$

$$
\begin{aligned}
E = \{ &(\#\alpha_1, \#\alpha_2), (\#\alpha_1, \#\alpha_8), (\#\alpha_1, \#\alpha_5), (\#\alpha_1, \#\alpha_{13}), (\#\alpha_2, \#\alpha_4), (\#\alpha_2, \#\alpha_5), \\
&(\#\alpha_2, \#\alpha_{24}), (\#\alpha_3, \#\alpha_6), (\#\alpha_4, \#\alpha_5), (\#\alpha_4, \#\alpha_8), (\#\alpha_4, \#\alpha_{16}), (\#\alpha_4, \#\alpha_{17}), \\
&(\#\alpha_5, \#\alpha_8), (\#\alpha_6, \#\alpha_7), (\#\alpha_6, \#\alpha_{20}), (\#\alpha_7, \#\alpha_{21}), (\#\alpha_7, \#\alpha_{10}), (\#\alpha_8, \#\alpha_{12}), \\
&(\#\alpha_8, \#\alpha_{11}), (\#\alpha_{11}, \#\alpha_{15}), (\#\alpha_{12}, \#\alpha_{13}), (\#\alpha_{15}, \#\alpha_{18}), (\#\alpha_{16}, \#\alpha_{23}), \\
&(\#\alpha_{21}, \#\alpha_{25}), (\#\alpha_{21}, \#\alpha_{22}), (\#\alpha_{22}, \#\alpha_{25}), (\#\alpha_{23}, \#\alpha_{24}),
\end{aligned}
$$

$\mathtt{Args} = \{\mathbb{A}, \mathbb{B}, \mathbb{C}, \mathbb{D}, \mathbb{E}, \mathbb{F}, \mathbb{G}, \mathbb{H}, \mathbb{I}, \mathbb{J}\}$.
$\mathtt{Attacks} = \{(\mathbb{A}, \mathbb{B}), (\mathbb{B}, \mathbb{H}), (\mathbb{C}, \mathbb{D}), (\mathbb{D}, \mathbb{F}), (\mathbb{E}, \mathbb{J}), (\mathbb{F}, \mathbb{E}), (\mathbb{H}, \mathbb{J}), (\mathbb{I}, \mathbb{A})\}$

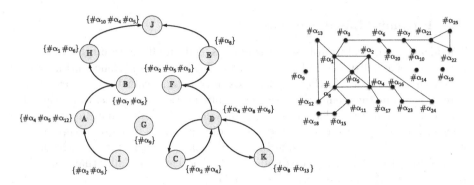

Fig. 2. Hashtagged argumentation framework and hashcloud for Ω

Then, consider the following non-intersection distance

$$
d_\Omega(\mathbb{A}, \mathbb{B}) = \begin{cases} max(d_\mathscr{G}(\alpha, \beta)) & \text{where } \alpha \in \mathscr{H}_\mathbb{A} \backslash \mathscr{H}_\mathbb{B} \text{ and } \beta \in \mathscr{H}_\mathbb{B} \backslash \mathscr{H}_\mathbb{A}, \\ 0 & \text{when } \mathscr{H}_\mathbb{A} = \mathscr{H}_\mathbb{B}, \\ \infty & \text{if for all } \alpha \in \mathscr{H}_\mathbb{A} \text{ and } \beta \in \mathscr{H}_\mathbb{B}, \\ & \text{there is no path between them.} \end{cases}
$$

Table 1 shows the distances between arguments, where "–" means that the distance is ∞. Consider a threshold $\tau = 4$, we obtain the following extensions:

Table 1. Distances between the hashtagged arguments in Ω

	$\mathbb{A}$	$\mathbb{B}$	$\mathbb{C}$	$\mathbb{D}$	$\mathbb{E}$	$\mathbb{F}$	$\mathbb{G}$	$\mathbb{H}$	$\mathbb{I}$	$\mathbb{J}$	$\mathbb{K}$
$\mathbb{A}$	0	5	2	–	1	2	–	3	2	5	1
$\mathbb{B}$	5	0	5	–	4	4	–	3	4	5	4
$\mathbb{C}$	2	5	0	–	2	3	–	4	1	5	3
$\mathbb{D}$	–	–	–	0	–	–	–	–	–	v	–
$\mathbb{E}$	1	4	2	–	0	2	–	2	2	5	2
$\mathbb{F}$	2	4	3	–	2	0	–	3	–	5	2
$\mathbb{G}$	–	–	–	–	–	–	0	–	–	–	–
$\mathbb{H}$	3	3	4	–	2	3	–	0	3	4	3
$\mathbb{I}$	2	4	1	–	2	–	–	3	0	5	2
$\mathbb{J}$	5	5	5	–	5	5	–	4	5	0	5
$\mathbb{K}$	1	4	3	–	2	2	–	3	2	5	0

The set $\mathsf{S}_1 = \{\mathbb{I}, \mathbb{B}, \mathbb{G}\}$ is τ-*complete* extension since it contains all the arguments that are defended by S_1. Furthermore, S_1 is a minimal set satisfying the previous conditions, and therefore it is the τ-*grounded* extension of Ω. That is, on the one hand, $\mathbb{G}$ and $\mathbb{I}$ have no attacker, while $\mathbb{I}$ is a proper defender of $\mathbb{B}$ (The reason is that $d_{\Omega}(\mathbb{I}, \mathbb{B}) = 4 \leq 4$). On the other hand, the even attack cycle between the arguments $\mathbb{D}$ and $\mathbb{C}$, and $\mathbb{K}$ and $\mathbb{D}$, limit the acceptance of other arguments in the discussion, under a skeptical position. The set $S_2 = \{\mathbb{I}, \mathbb{B}, \mathbb{C}, \mathbb{K}, \mathbb{F}, \mathbb{G}\}$ and $S_3 = \{\mathbb{I}, \mathbb{B}, \mathbb{D}, \mathbb{G}\}$ are τ-*admissible* and τ-*complete* extension since they contains all the arguments that are defended by S_2 and S_3, respectively. In addition, S_2 and S_3 are the maximal sets verifying the previous conditions, and therefore they are both τ-*preferred* extensions of Ω. Same analysis performed by the τ-*grounded* extension can be made for the preferred extension.

Note that in [5] the threshold is a unique property of the whole argumentation framework affecting all the possible extensions. This choice means that the same distance used to enable defenses is applied to every argument, leading to an extension that is induced by a given single threshold. As stated in the introduction, a more refined approach may consider individual thresholds for each argument; thus, the range of defenses available for a given argument becomes a local property of this argument. We will address this generalization in the following sections.

3   Argument Neighborhoods: A Topological View

As we mentioned before, as a piece of reasoning, every argument addresses certain specific topics, and every topic is naturally associated with many others in varying degrees of "closeness". Consequently, there is an underlying perception of *distance* between arguments when considering their topics. In a mathematical sense, a *topological space* may be intuitively described as a set of points along with a set of *neighborhoods* for each point. Any metric space will also be a topological space because, given a set, any properly specified distance function defined on it induces a topology on that set. The pair $(\text{Args}, d_{\Omega})$ associated with a Hashtagged Framework Ω can be regarded as a *metric space* in the topology sense, where a distance may be defined.

Intuitively speaking, a *neighborhood of a point* p is a set of points containing p and the points that can be reached within a given distance from p. A point p may have several neighborhoods of different sizes by considering different radius (distances). In Topology, a *ball* is the space bounded by a sphere. It may be a closed ball (including the boundary points that constitute the sphere) or an open ball (excluding them). Thus, a neighborhood associated with a point $x \in S$ with radius ε_x is the closed ball defined as

$$B(x; \varepsilon_x) = \{y \in S : distance(x, y) \leq \varepsilon_x\}.$$

It is important to remark that now the property of being a "neighbor" is local to each point since the threshold distance is not necessarily the same for every point. Illustrating this observation, Fig. 3 depicts three different situations.

In the first case, points a, b, and c do not have neighbors in common. In the second case, the neighbors of a are also neighbors of b, but no neighbor of c is a neighbor of a or b. In the third case, a has b as a neighbor, but not the other

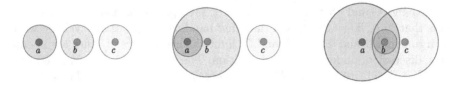

Fig. 3. Examples for balls and neighborhoods centering on a specific point

way around, since b does not include a in its neighborhood. Similarly, the point c has a b as neighbor but neither a nor c are neighbors of b. These concepts are suitable to be applied to argumentation frameworks by associating arguments with a neighborhood as follows.

Notation: We have switched the general notation for a threshold as τ to distinguish a local threshold ε subscripted with a particular argument making the change in perspective more apparent.

Definition 7 (Argument Neighborhood). *Let $\Omega = \langle \Phi, \mathscr{G}_\Omega, \mathsf{d}_\Omega \rangle$ be a hash-tagged framework, $\mathsf{d}_\Omega(\cdot, \cdot)$ be a distance function on the set* Args, *and* (Args, d_Ω) *be the metric space associated with the tagged framework Ω. Then, the neighborhood of an argument $\mathbb{A} \in$ Args with radius $\varepsilon_{\mathbb{A}}$ under the metric (Args, d_Ω) is defined as the set*

$$\mathfrak{N}_{\mathbb{A}}^{\varepsilon_{\mathbb{A}}} = \{\mathbb{X} \in \mathtt{Args} : \mathsf{d}_\Omega(\mathbb{A}, \mathbb{X}) \leq \varepsilon_{\mathbb{A}}, \text{ where } \varepsilon_{\mathbb{A}} \in \mathbb{N}^0\}.$$

The set of neighborhoods associated with arguments in Ω will be referred as $\mathfrak{N}_\Omega$.

A neighborhood is defined by a threshold that is based on a *distance* defined between arguments. Since several notions of distance could be introduced, we will focus on those influenced by the topics referred to by the arguments. A particularly interesting possibility is to consider the thresholds determined by the hashcloud created by the hashtags attached to every argument. Various alternatives can be advanced to define the neighborhood for an argument; for instance, their radius, centrality degree, topics classification, to mention just a few. Here, our primary purpose is only to allow defenses for an argument that are *close enough* to the topics represented by the set of hashtags associated with this argument. Since these hashtags may be closely related or widely dispersed, we need a measure of argument semantic coverage that will provide a reference about its size –always from the semantic point of view. Considering the observation just made, the radius and diameter appear appropriate since they are themselves a measure of size.

Definition 8 (Hashtag Metric Concepts). *Let $\Omega = \langle \Phi, \mathscr{G}_\Omega, \mathsf{d}_\Omega \rangle$ be a hash-tagged framework, where $\Phi = \langle$ Args, Attacks$\rangle$, $\mathscr{G}_\Omega = [\mathcal{H}, E]$ is a hashtag graph, and let $\mathsf{d}_\mathscr{G}(\cdot, \cdot)$ be a distance defined on $\mathscr{G}_\Omega$ and let $\mathfrak{I} \subseteq \mathcal{H}$ a finite, non-empty, subset of hashtags. Then:*

- *The* eccentricity *of a hashtag* $\alpha \in \mathcal{I}$ *is the maximum distance to any other hashtag in* $\mathcal{I}$, *i.e.,* $eccentricity(\alpha) = \max_{\beta \in \mathcal{I}} d_{\mathcal{G}}(\alpha, \beta)$. *If* $\alpha \in \mathcal{I}$ *is not connected to any other hashtag in* $\mathcal{I}$ *its eccentricity is associated with the constant* ∞, *which, conventionally, represents the greatest possible distance, i.e.,* $eccentricity(\alpha) = \infty$.
- *The* radius *of* $\mathcal{I}$ *is the minimum eccentricity among all hashtags in* $\mathcal{I}$, *i.e.,* $radius(\mathcal{I}) = \min_{\alpha \in \mathcal{I}} eccentricity(\alpha)$.
- *The* diameter *of* $\mathcal{I}$ *is the maximum eccentricity among all hashtags in* $\mathcal{I}$, *i.e.,* $diameter(\mathcal{I}) = \max_{\alpha \in \mathcal{I}} eccentricity(\alpha)$.

Note that if $\mathcal{I}$ contains a single element then the eccentricity, the radius, and the diameter will be zero. These graph-based topological concepts can be naturally extended to hashtagged arguments as follows.

Definition 9 (Hashtagged Argument Metric Concepts). *Given a hashtagged framework* $\Omega = \langle \Phi, \mathcal{G}_\Omega, d_\Omega \rangle$, *an argument* $\mathbb{A} = \langle A, \mathcal{H}_\mathbb{A} \rangle \in \text{Args}$, *the* radius *and* diameter *of* $\mathbb{A}$ *is the radius and diameter of* $\mathcal{H}_\mathbb{A}$, *respectively.*

The definition above provides a helpful characterization of the *influence of an argument* in the framework. It is important to remark that this influence is evaluated according to the topics and not to the underlying linguistic structure, which is not relevant here given our abstract approach. In Fig. 4, the radius and diameter of every argument are shown, and the directly induced neighborhoods are listed. In some cases, such as $\mathbb{A}$, there is a difference between the neighborhood induced by the radius and the one induced by the diameter; in others, such as $\mathbb{B}$ and $\mathbb{K}$, both neighborhoods coincide. The radius and the diameter are two criteria for establishing areas of semantic closeness, being the latter naturally wider than the former.

Definition 10 (Metric associated with the neighborhoods in Ω). *Let* $\Omega = \langle \Phi, \mathcal{G}_\Omega, d_\Omega \rangle$ *be a hashtagged framework,* $d_\Omega(\cdot, \cdot)$ *be a distance function over the set* Args, (Args, d_Ω) *be the metric space associated with the tagged framework* Ω, *and* $\mathfrak{N}_\Omega^{\varepsilon_\Omega} = \{\mathfrak{N}_\mathbb{X}^{\varepsilon_\mathbb{X}} : \mathbb{X} \in \text{Args}\}$ *be the set of neighborhoods associated with the arguments of* Ω. *Then:*

- *A neighborhood* $\mathfrak{N}_\mathbb{A}^{\varepsilon_\mathbb{A}} \in \mathfrak{N}_\Omega$ *is the* Greatest Neighborhood *iff there is no* $\mathfrak{N}_\mathbb{B}^{\varepsilon_\mathbb{B}} \in \mathfrak{N}_\Omega$ *such that* $\varepsilon_\mathbb{B} > \varepsilon_\mathbb{A}$. *We will use* $\mathcal{T}_\Omega^g$ *to denote the greatest radius associated with the greatest neighborhood of* $\mathfrak{N}_\Omega$.
- *A neighborhood* $\mathfrak{N}_\mathbb{A}^{\varepsilon_\mathbb{A}} \in \mathfrak{N}_\Omega$ *is the* Smallest Neighborhood *iff there is no* $\mathfrak{N}_\mathbb{B}^{\varepsilon_\mathbb{B}} \in \mathfrak{N}_\Omega$ *such that* $\varepsilon_\mathbb{B} \leq \varepsilon_\mathbb{A}$. *We will use* $\mathcal{T}_\Omega^s$ *to denote the smallest radius associated with the smallest neighborhood of* $\mathfrak{N}_\Omega$.

These two kinds of neighborhoods are also important to establish a connection between classical abstract frameworks semantics and the previous proximity-based extensions. In the following section, we analyze the proximity-based semantics [5] in this new context of individual thresholds.

Argument	Diameter	Neighborhoods for diameter dimension	Radius	Neighborhoods for radius dimension
A	2	C E F I	1	E
B	4	E F H I	4	E F H I
C	1	∅	1	∅
D	∞	A B C E F G H I J	1	∅
E	0	∅	0	∅
F	2	E	1	E
G	0	∅	0	∅
H	2	E	2	E
I	1	C	1	C
J	6	A B C E F H I	1	∅
K	2	A E F I	2	A E F I

Fig. 4. Arguments' neighborhoods

4   Neighborhood-Bounded Admissibility

Since each argument $\mathbb{X}$ has now a defense range $\varepsilon_{\mathbb{X}}$ related to its neighborhoods, it is necessary to provide a notion of *admissibility* that considers this range. A set of arguments is said to be admissible if every argument is acceptable with respect to that set by using defenses inside its own neighborhood.

Definition 11 (Conflict-freeness, Acceptability, and Admissibility). *Let* $\Omega = \langle \Phi, \mathcal{G}_{\Omega}, \mathsf{d}_{\Omega} \rangle$ *be a hashtagged framework,* $\mathsf{d}_{\Omega}(\cdot, \cdot)$ *be a distance function on the set* Args, *and* $(\text{Args}, \mathsf{d}_{\Omega})$ *be the metric space associated with the tagged framework* Ω. *Then:*

- *A set* S ⊆ Args *is said to be conflict free if there is no hashtagged arguments* $\mathbb{A}, \mathbb{B} \in$ S *such that* $\mathbb{B}$ *attacks* $\mathbb{A}$ *(usual notion in abstract frameworks).*
- *A hashtagged argument* $\mathbb{A} \in$ Args *is* η-acceptable *with respect to* S *if for every argument* $\mathbb{B} \in$ Args, *if* $\mathbb{B}$ *attacks* $\mathbb{A}$ *then there is a hashtagged argument* $\mathbb{C} \in$ S *such that* $\mathbb{C} \in \mathfrak{N}_{\mathbb{A}}^{\varepsilon_{\mathbb{A}}}$ *and* $\mathbb{C}$ *attacks* $\mathbb{B}$.
- S *is said to be* η-admissible *if every hashtagged argument in* S *is* η-acceptable *with respect to* S.

Under this notion of distance-bounded defense, an argument that may be a defender according to classical acceptability may not be a defender here; however, the quality of a set of being (classically) admissible is preserved, because, as it will be proved later, attacks are not restricted by distance, only defenses. Admissibility semantics is focused on the characterization of sets of arguments that provide mutual defenses within the set. By restricting defenses within to a particular neighborhood, we are *reshaping* the original notion of admissible sets (and also changing the notion of a focused, rational position) while respecting argument conflicts in the whole scenario.

Proposition 1. *Given* $\Omega = \langle \Phi, \mathscr{G}_\Omega, \mathsf{d}_\Omega \rangle$, *where* $\mathsf{d}_\Omega(\cdot, \cdot)$ *is a distance function on the set* Args, *and let* (Args, d_Ω) *be the metric space associated with the tagged framework* Ω. *Then: i) If* $\mathbb{A} \in$ Args *is* η-*acceptable w.r.t. a set* S *then it is acceptable w.r.t.* S; *and ii) If a set* S *is* η-*admissible then it is admissible.*

<u>Proff</u>: This demonstration follows directly from the definitions, and it will be done in two parts:

i) If $\mathbb{A} \in$ Args is η-*acceptable w.r.t.* a set S then it is acceptable *w.r.t.* S. Suppose that $\mathbb{A} \in$ Args is η-*acceptable w.r.t.* a set S but $\mathbb{A} \in$ Args is not *acceptable w.r.t.* a set S. Then, there exists a hashtagged argument $\mathbb{B} \in$ Args such that $\mathbb{B}$ attacks $\mathbb{A}$ and there not exists a hashtagged argument $\mathbb{C} \in$ Args such that $\mathbb{C}$ attacks $\mathbb{B}$. However, $\mathbb{A}$ is η-*acceptable w.r.t.* S and then for every attacker hashtagged argument $\mathbb{B} \in$ Args there exists a defender $\mathbb{C} \in$ S. Contradiction.

ii) If a set S is η-*admissible* then it is admissible. Suppose that S is η-*admissible* but it is not an admissible set. Then, there exists an hashtagged argument $\mathbb{A} \in$ Args such that $\mathbb{A}$ is not η-*acceptable w.r.t.* S. However, S is η-*admissible*. Thus, every hashtagged argument in S is η-*acceptablew.r.t.* S. Furthermore, by consequence of i) if a hashtagged argument $\mathbb{A} \in$ Args is η-*acceptable w.r.t.* a set S then it is acceptable *w.r.t.* S. Contradiction. □

The converses of the statements in Proposition 1 do not hold. For instance, an argument $\mathbb{A}$ may be acceptable with respect to the set $\{\mathbb{B}\}$, but not η-acceptable if $\mathbb{B} \notin \mathfrak{N}_\mathbb{A}^{\varepsilon_\mathbb{A}}$. Therefore, an admissible set may not be η-admissible. Furthermore, as we mentioned, these semantic notions are a refined version of the semantics proposed in Sect. 2.2. Thus, the following proposition hold.

Proposition 2. *Given* $\Omega = \langle \Phi, \mathscr{G}_\Omega, \mathsf{d}_\Omega \rangle$, *where* $\mathsf{d}_\Omega(\cdot, \cdot)$ *is a distance function on the set* Args, *and let* (Args, d_Ω) *be the metric space associated with the tagged framework* Ω, *and* $\mathfrak{T}_\Omega^s$ *and* $\mathfrak{T}_\Omega^g$ *be the radius associated with the smallest and greatest neighborhoods of* $\mathfrak{N}_\Omega$, *respectively; let* S $\subseteq$ Args. *Then: i) If* $\mathbb{A} \in$ Args *is* ε-*acceptable w.r.t.* S *with* $\varepsilon = \mathfrak{T}_\Omega^s$, *then it is* η-*acceptable w.r.t.* S; *ii) If* $\mathbb{A} \in$ Args *is* η-*acceptable w.r.t.* S *then it is* ε-*acceptable w.r.t.* S *with* $\varepsilon = \mathfrak{T}_\Omega^g$; *iii) If* S *is* ε-*admissible with* $\varepsilon = \mathfrak{T}_\Omega^s$, *then it is* η-*admissible; and iv) If* S *is* η-*admissible then it is* ε-*admissible with* $\varepsilon = \mathfrak{T}_\Omega^g$.

<u>Proff</u>: This demonstration will be done in fourth parts:

i) If $\mathbb{A} \in$ Args is ε-acceptable *w.r.t.* a set S with $\varepsilon = \mathfrak{T}_\Omega^s$, then it is η-acceptable *w.r.t.* S. Suppose that $\mathbb{A}$ is ε-acceptable *w.r.t.* a set S but $\mathbb{A}$ is not η-*acceptable w.r.t.* S. Then, there exists a hashtagged argument $\mathbb{B} \in$ Args such that $\mathbb{B}$ attacks $\mathbb{A}$ but there is no hashtagged argument $\mathbb{C} \in$ Args such that $\mathbb{C}$ attacks $\mathbb{B}$ verifying that $\mathbb{C} \in \mathfrak{N}_\mathbb{A}^{\varepsilon_\mathbb{A}}$. However, $\mathbb{A}$ is ε-*acceptable w.r.t.* S with $\varepsilon = \mathfrak{T}_\Omega^s$. Thus, the threshold applied to obtain the acceptable set of arguments is equal to the radius associated with the lowest neighborhood of $\mathfrak{N}_\Omega$. Then, for every attacked hashtagged argument $\mathbb{A} \in$ S there exists a defender $\mathbb{C} \in$ S such that $\mathbb{C} \in \mathfrak{N}_\mathbb{A}^{\varepsilon_\mathbb{A}}$. Contradiction.

ii) If $\mathbb{A} \in$ Args is η-acceptable *w.r.t.* a set S, then it is ε-acceptable *w.r.t.* S with $\varepsilon = \mathcal{T}_\Omega^g$. Suppose that $\mathbb{A}$ is η-acceptable *w.r.t.* a set S but $\mathbb{A}$ is not ε-*acceptable w.r.t.* a set S. Then, there exists a hashtagged argument $\mathbb{B} \in$ Args such that $\mathbb{B}$ attacks $\mathbb{A}$ and there is no hashtagged argument $\mathbb{C} \in$ Args such that $\mathbb{C}$ attacks $\mathbb{B}$ verifying that $\mathbb{C}$ is a defender of $\mathbb{A}$. That is, $d(\mathbb{C}, \mathbb{A}) > \varepsilon$. However, $\mathbb{A}$ is η-*acceptable w.r.t.* S. Thus, for every attacker hashtagged argument $\mathbb{B} \in$ S there exists a defender $\mathbb{C} \in$ S such that $\mathbb{C} \in \mathfrak{N}_\mathbb{A}^{\varepsilon_\mathbb{A}}$ where the radius of $\mathfrak{N}_\mathbb{A}^{\varepsilon_\mathbb{A}}$ is lower or equal than ε. Contradiction.

iii) If a set S is ε-*admissible* with $\varepsilon = \mathcal{T}_\Omega^g$, then it is η-admissible. Suppose that S is ε-*admissible* but it is not an η-admissible set. Then, there exists an hashtagged argument $\mathbb{A} \in$ Args such that $\mathbb{A}$ is not η-*acceptable w.r.t.* S. However, S is ε-*admissible*; then, every hashtagged argument in S is ε-*acceptable w.r.t.* S. Furthermore, as a consequence of i), if a hashtagged argument $\mathbb{A} \in$ Args is ε-*acceptable w.r.t.* a set S then it is η-acceptable *w.r.t.* S. Contradiction.

iv) If a set S is η-admissible then it is ε-admissible with $\varepsilon = \mathcal{T}_\Omega^g$. Suppose that S is η-*admissible* but it is not an ε-admissible set. Then, there exists a hashtagged argument $\mathbb{A} \in$ Args such that $\mathbb{A}$ is not ε-*acceptable w.r.t.* S. However, S is η-*admissible*; thus, every hashtagged argument in S is η-*acceptable w.r.t.* S. Furthermore, by consequence of i) if a hashtagged argument $\mathbb{A} \in$ Args is η-*acceptable w.r.t.* a set S then it is ε-acceptable *w.r.t.* S. Contradiction. □

As usual in abstract argumentation, Definition 11 leads to different notions providing a new proximity-based interpretation of classical admissibility. In this version, we propose an analysis more refined considering the admitted interaction field associated with the hashtagged arguments. This new notion allows the analysis of the argumentation process from a new point of view, where the scope associated with the hashtagged arguments is taken into account.

Definition 12. *Given* $\Omega = \langle \Phi, \mathscr{G}_\Omega, d_\Omega \rangle$, *where* $d_\Omega(\cdot, \cdot)$ *is a distance function over the set* Args, *and let* (Args, d_Ω) *be the metric space associated with the tagged framework* Ω; *let* S $\subseteq$ Args. *Then:*

- *An* η-admissible *set* S *is an* η-complete extension *iff* S *contains each argument that is* η-acceptable *with respect to* S.
- *Set* S *is the* η-grounded extension *of* Ω *iff* S *is an* $\subseteq$-*minimal* η-complete extension.
- *Set* S *is an* η-preferred extension *of* Ω *iff* S *is an* $\subseteq$-*maximal* η-complete extension.

Next, we present an example to make clear these novel acceptability concepts.

Example 2. Continuing with the hashtagged argumentation framework presented in Example 1, and based on the neighborhoods associated with each argument under the diameter dimension presented in Fig. 5, we have that: $\mathbb{I}$ is a defender of $\mathbb{B}$ since $\mathbb{I}$ is a neighbor of $\mathbb{B}$ (the distance between $\mathbb{I}$ and $\mathbb{B}$ is 4, where

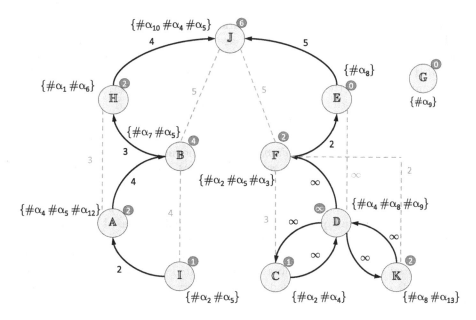

Fig. 5. Balls and neighborhoods

$\mathbb{B}$ has a neighborhood range of 4). Furthermore, $\mathbb{B}$ is a defender of $\mathbb{J}$ since the distance between $\mathbb{J}$ and $\mathbb{B}$ is 5 and $\mathbb{J}$ has a neighborhood range of 6. Thus, $\mathbb{B}$ is a neighbor of $\mathbb{J}$. On the other hand, $\mathbb{C}$ is not a defender of $\mathbb{F}$ since the distance between $\mathbb{C}$ and $\mathbb{F}$ is 3, while $\mathbb{F}$ has a neighborhood range of 2. However, $\mathbb{K}$ is a defender of $\mathbb{F}$ since $\mathbb{K}$ is a neighbor of $\mathbb{F}$ (the distance between $\mathbb{K}$ and $\mathbb{F}$ is 2, where $\mathbb{F}$ has a neighborhood range of 2). Thus, analyzing the acceptability notions presented in Definition 11, the sets $S_1 = \{\mathbb{I}, \mathbb{B}, \mathbb{C}, \mathbb{K}, \mathbb{F}, \mathbb{J}, \mathbb{G}\}$, $S_2 = \{\mathbb{I}, \mathbb{B}, \mathbb{K}, \mathbb{F}, \mathbb{J}, \mathbb{G}\}$, $S_3 = \{\mathbb{I}, \mathbb{B}, \mathbb{C}, \mathbb{G}\}$, and $S_4 = \{\mathbb{I}, \mathbb{B}, \mathbb{D}, \mathbb{G}\}$, and $S_5 = \{\mathbb{I}, \mathbb{B}, \mathbb{G}\}$ are the maximal η-admissible extensions. Furthermore, S_5 is the η-*grounded extension* while S_5 is the η-*preferred extension*, under the conditions established in Definition 12.

Note that admissibility discards argument defenders who do not belong to the neighborhood associated with the attacked argument in this proximity semantic version. If the argument has associated topics covering a particular thematic field, it will be defended by those arguments that are related to the same field. On the other hand, an opinion cannot be defended by formulations or assertions out of its spectrum of discussion.

As expected, if the smallest neighborhood is big enough, Dung's admissibility and η-admissibility coincide. Thus, the following connection will exist between the classical and the proximity-acceptable sets of arguments.

Proposition 3. *Given* $\Omega = \langle \Phi, \mathscr{G}_\Omega, \mathrm{d}_\Omega \rangle$, *where* $\mathrm{d}_\Omega(\cdot, \cdot)$ *is a distance function on the set* Args, *and let* $(\text{Args}, \mathrm{d}_\Omega)$ *be the metric space associated with the tagged framework* Ω. *If the smallest neighborhood* $\mathfrak{T}_\Omega^s \geq diameter(\mathcal{H})$ *then it holds that every* η-$\{admissible, complete, grounded, preferred\}$ *extension is an* $\{admissible, complete, grounded, preferred\}$ *extension respectively.*

Proff: For the acceptability-based semantics, it is sufficient to prove that the hashtagged defenders arguments in Ω are also present as defenders in the underlying abstract argumentation framework, for the η-admissible, complete, grounded, preferred extension. Suppose that an argument A is defended by an argument C from the attacks of B in the underlying abstract argumentation framework, but the counterpart hashtagged argument $\mathbb{A}$ is not defended in Ω by the hashtagged version of $\mathbb{C}$. This means that, by Definition 11, $d_\Omega(\mathbb{A}, \mathbb{C}) \in \mathfrak{N}_\mathbb{A}^{\varepsilon_\mathbb{A}}$ (†). However, the radius associated with the smallest neighborhood $\mathfrak{T}_\Omega^s \geq diameter(\mathcal{H})$ where $diameter(\mathcal{H})$ is the maximum eccentricity of the hashtags in $\mathcal{H}$. Nevertheless, the relation (†) is not possible since $diameter(\mathcal{H})$ is the maximum of the distances to all other hashtags in $\mathcal{H}$. Contradiction.   □

In abstract argumentation, a grounded extension is the skeptical position of acceptance, and it is unique. In our definition of proximity-based semantics, the notion of defense is bounded to a threshold associated with each hashtagged argument through their corresponding neighborhood. Thus, the skeptical position is related to the set of neighborhoods associated with the metric space, and different sets of neighborhoods lead to different η-grounded extensions; however, as in classical frameworks, the extension always exists.

Proposition 4. *Given $\Omega = \langle \Phi, \mathcal{G}_\Omega, d_\Omega \rangle$, where $d_\Omega(\cdot, \cdot)$ is a distance function on the set Args, and let (Args, d_Ω) be the metric space associated with the tagged framework Ω. Then, there always exists an unique η-grounded extension.*

Proff: In abstract argumentation the grounded extension is unique. Suppose there were two different sets S y S' that are both η-grounded extensions, and suppose $\mathbb{A} \in$ S, but $\mathbb{A} \notin$ S'. This means that $\mathbb{A}$ is not defended in S'. Since it is defended in S, then it must be because at least one defender $\mathbb{C}$ is not taken into account in S' due to a specific distance over the argumentation framework, and a particular position over the neighborhoods. But this cannot be so since S' is also η-grounded extension, *i.e.*, the neighborhoods defined in the framework are the same.   □

As we said before, hashtagged argumentation frameworks are an extension of abstract frameworks in the sense that we are considering additional elements; thus, if hashtags information is discarded, a classical abstract framework remains. The new proximity-based and the classical abstract semantics are related as the following theorem establishes by showing a link between this redefined proximity-based semantics and its corresponding abstract semantics counterpart, observing that the former is a refinement of the latter.

Theorem 1. *Given $\Omega = \langle \Phi, \mathcal{G}_\Omega, d_\Omega \rangle$, where $d_\Omega(\cdot, \cdot)$ is a distance function on the set Args, and let (Args, d_Ω) be the metric space associated with the tagged framework Ω. Then: i) If S_Ω is η-complete extension in Ω, then there exist a complete extension S_Φ in Φ satisfying that $S_\Omega \subseteq S_\Phi$; ii) If S_Ω is η-grounded extension in Ω, then there exist a grounded extension S_Φ in Φ satisfying that $S_\Omega \subseteq S_\Phi$; and, iii) If S_Ω is η-preferred extension in Ω, then there exist a preferred extension S_Φ in Φ satisfying that $S_\Omega \subseteq S_\Phi$.*

Proff: We separate the proof in three points:

i) If S_Ω is η-complete extension in Ω, then there exist a complete extension S_Φ in Φ satisfying that $S_\Omega \subseteq S_\Phi$. Suppose that S_Ω is η-complete extension in Ω, but there is no complete extension S_Φ in Φ satisfying that $S_\Omega \subseteq S_\Phi$. Thus, there exists an η-complete extension S_Ω in Ω and a complete extension S_Φ in Φ satisfying that $S_\Omega \supset S_\Phi$. Then, there exists the hashtagged argument $\mathbb{A}$ which is η-acceptable $w.r.t.$ the η-admissible extension S_Ω but the underlying argument (no hashtags) A is not acceptable $w.r.t.S$. Thus, $\mathbb{A}$ is defended by S_Ω but it is not defended by S in the underlying abstract argumentation framework. However, by Proposition 1, if $\mathbb{A} \in$ Args is η-*acceptable w.r.t.* a set S then it is acceptable $w.r.t.S$, and if a set S is η-*admissible* then S is admissible. Contradiction.

ii) If S_Ω is η-grounded extension in Ω, then there exist a grounded extension S_Φ in Φ satisfying that $S_\Omega \subseteq S_\Phi$. Trivially, since because of i) if S_Ω is η-complete extension in Ω, there exist a complete extension S_Φ in Φ satisfying that $S_\Omega \subseteq S_\Phi$. Thus, the proof of this point is a special case where S_Ω is the minimal η-complete extension in Ω and S_Φ is the minimal complete extension in Φ.

iii) If S_Ω is η-preferred extension in Ω, then there exist a preferred extension S_Φ in Φ satisfying that $S_\Omega \subseteq S_\Phi$. Trivially, since because of i) if S_Ω is η-complete extension in Ω, there exist a complete extension S_Φ in Φ satisfying that $S_\Omega \subseteq S_\Phi$. Thus, the proof of this point is a special case where S_Ω is a maximal η-complete extension in Ω and S_Φ is a maximal complete extension in Φ where the inclusion condition is satisfied. $\square$

Thus, the rationale of classic argumentation semantics is preserved. The addition of the concept neighborhood improves the argumentation model by introducing a new view on valid defenses for an individual argument; this idea is compelling because it leads to a new family of semantics, possibly parameterized with various metrics. Note that the notion of the neighborhood can be defined by considering different metrics associated with the hashcloud. Thus, different conceptualizations of the notion of neighborhood clearly influence the general outcome of the argumentation scenario. The relation of proximity between arguments is now relevant for the argumentation process.

Finally, considering the intuitions presented before, the following result establishes a connection between the proximity-based semantics, the proximity-based semantics based on the definition of neighborhood, and classical argumentation semantics.

Theorem 2. *Given* $\Omega = \langle \Phi, \mathscr{G}_\Omega, d_\Omega \rangle$, *where* $d_\Omega(\cdot, \cdot)$ *is a distance function on the set* Args, *let* (Args, d_Ω) *be the metric space associated with the tagged framework* Ω, *and* $\Phi = \langle \text{Args}, \text{Attacks} \rangle$ *be the underlying abstract argumentation framework. Then:*

i) *If* $\varepsilon = \mathcal{T}_\Omega^s$ *is the threshold associated with the smallest neighborhood of* Ω, S_Ω^η *is* η-complete (η-grounded, and η-preferred) extension respectively and S_Ω^ε *is*

ε-complete (ε-grounded, and ε-preferred) extension respectively, then it holds that $\mathbf{S}_\Omega^\varepsilon \subseteq \mathbf{S}_\Omega^\eta$.

ii) If $\varepsilon = \mathcal{T}_\Omega^g$ is the threshold associated with the greatest neighborhood of Ω, $\mathbf{S}_\Omega^\eta$ is η-complete (η-grounded, and η-preferred) extension respectively and $\mathbf{S}_\Omega^\varepsilon$ is ε-complete (ε-grounded, and ε-preferred) extension respectively, then it holds that $\mathbf{S}_\Omega^\eta \subseteq \mathbf{S}_\Omega^\varepsilon$.

Proff: We separate the proof in two parts, each one further divided in three items:

i) a) If $\varepsilon = \mathcal{T}_\Omega^s$ is the threshold associated with the smallest neighborhood of Ω, $\mathbf{S}_\Omega^\eta$ is η-complete extension and $\mathbf{S}_\Omega^\varepsilon$ is ε-complete extension, then it holds that $\mathbf{S}_\Omega^\varepsilon \subseteq \mathbf{S}_\Omega^\eta$. Suppose that $\mathbf{S}_\Omega^\varepsilon \supset \mathbf{S}_\Omega^\eta$. Then, there exists an hashtagged argument $\mathbb{A}$ which is τ-acceptable *w.r.t.* the τ-*admissible* extension $\mathbf{S}_\Omega^\varepsilon$ but $\mathbb{A}$ is not η-acceptable *w.r.t.* $\mathbf{S}_\Omega^\eta$. Thus, $\mathbb{A}$ is defended by $\mathbf{S}_\Omega^\varepsilon$ but it is not defended by $\mathbf{S}_\Omega^\eta$. However, by Proposition 2, if $\mathbb{A} \in \mathtt{Args}$ is ε-acceptable *w.r.t.* a set $\mathbf{S}_\Omega^\varepsilon$ with $\varepsilon = \mathcal{T}_\Omega^s$, then it is η-acceptable, and if a set $\mathbf{S}_\Omega^\varepsilon$ is τ-*admissible* then it is η-admissible. Contradiction.

b) If $\varepsilon = \mathcal{T}_\Omega^s$ is the threshold associated with the smallest neighborhood of Ω, $\mathbf{S}_\Omega^\eta$ is η-grounded extension and $\mathbf{S}_\Omega^\varepsilon$ is ε-grounded extension, then it holds that $\mathbf{S}_\Omega^\varepsilon \subseteq \mathbf{S}_\Omega^\eta$. Trivially, since by a) if $\mathbf{S}_\Omega^\eta$ is η-complete extension and $\mathbf{S}_\Omega^\varepsilon$ is ε-complete extension, then it holds that $\mathbf{S}_\Omega^\varepsilon \subseteq \mathbf{S}_\Omega^\eta$. Thus, the proof of this point is a special case where $\mathbf{S}_\Omega^\varepsilon$ is the minimal τ-complete extension in Ω and $\mathbf{S}_\Omega^\eta$ is the minimal η -complete extension in Ω.

c) If $\varepsilon = \mathcal{T}_\Omega^s$ is the threshold associated with the smallest neighborhood of Ω, $\mathbf{S}_\Omega^\eta$ is η-grounded extension and $\mathbf{S}_\Omega^\varepsilon$ is ε-grounded extension, then it holds that $\mathbf{S}_\Omega^\varepsilon \subseteq \mathbf{S}_\Omega^\eta$. Trivially, since by a) if $\mathbf{S}_\Omega^\eta$ is η-preferred extension and $\mathbf{S}_\Omega^\varepsilon$ is ε-preferred extension, then it holds that $\mathbf{S}_\Omega^\varepsilon \subseteq \mathbf{S}_\Omega^\eta$. Thus, the proof of this point is a special case where $\mathbf{S}_\Omega^\varepsilon$ is the maximal τ-complete extension in Ω and $\mathbf{S}_\Omega^\eta$ is the maximal η -complete extension in Ω.

ii) a) Let $\varepsilon = \mathcal{T}_\Omega^g$ be the threshold associated with the greatest neighborhood of Ω, $\mathbf{S}_\Omega^\eta$ is η-complete extension and $\mathbf{S}_\Omega^\varepsilon$ is ε-complete extension, then it holds $\mathbf{S}_\Omega^\eta \subseteq \mathbf{S}_\Omega^\varepsilon$. Suppose that $\mathbf{S}_\Omega^\eta \supset \mathbf{S}_\Omega^\varepsilon$. Then, there exists a hashtagged argument $\mathbb{A}$ which is η-acceptable *w.r.t.* the η-admissible extension $\mathbf{S}_\Omega^\eta$ but $\mathbb{A}$ is not τ-acceptable *w.r.t.* $\mathbf{S}_\Omega^\tau$. Thus, $\mathbb{A}$ is defended by $\mathbf{S}_\Omega^\eta$ but it is not defended by $\mathbf{S}_\Omega^\varepsilon$. However, by Proposition 2, if $\mathbb{A} \in \mathtt{Args}$ is η-acceptable *w.r.t.* a set $\mathbf{S}_\Omega^\eta$, then it is ε-acceptable, and if a set $\mathbf{S}_\Omega^\eta$ is η-*admissible* then it is ε-admissible. Contradiction.

b) If $\varepsilon = \mathcal{T}_\Omega^g$ is the threshold associated with the smallest neighborhood of Ω, $\mathbf{S}_\Omega^\eta$ is η-grounded extension and $\mathbf{S}_\Omega^\varepsilon$ is ε-grounded extension, then it holds that $\mathbf{S}_\Omega^\eta \subseteq \mathbf{S}_\Omega^\tau$. Trivially, since by a) if $\mathbf{S}_\Omega^\eta$ is η-complete extension and $\mathbf{S}_\Omega^\varepsilon$ is ε-complete extension, then it holds that $\mathbf{S}_\Omega^\eta \subseteq \mathbf{S}_\Omega^\tau$. Thus, the proof of this point is a special case where $\mathbf{S}_\Omega^\eta$ is the minimal η-complete extension in Ω and $\mathbf{S}_\Omega^\varepsilon$ is the minimal ε -complete extension in Ω.

c) If $\varepsilon = \mathcal{T}_\Omega^g$ is the threshold associated with the smallest neighborhood of Ω, $\mathbf{S}_\Omega^\eta$ is η-grounded extension and $\mathbf{S}_\Omega^\varepsilon$ is ε-grounded extension, then it holds that $S_\Omega^\eta \subseteq S_\Omega^\varepsilon$. Trivially, since by a) if S_Ω^η is η-preferred extension and S_Ω^ε is ε-preferred extension, then it holds that $S_\Omega^\varepsilon \subseteq S_\Omega^\eta$. Thus, the proof of this point is a special case where S_Ω^η is the maximal η-complete extension in Ω and S_Ω^ε is the maximal ε-complete extension in Ω.   □

As we postulated in the original proximity-based semantic, under this new interpretation of "defense", where we consider an admitted defense field associated with each argument, a potential defender argument maybe not be considered as such; however, the classical notion of admissibility is preserved. Note that, in this work, we have only analyzed the defense relation in the context of the neighborhood associated with an argument. However, this concept can be extended to the notion of attack, which we will discuss in future work. The reason for this decision is to stay within the spectrum of solutions originally proposed in abstract frameworks, intending to refine them. Considering the distance in the case of the attack relation and dismissing some of these attacks introduces a change in the argumentative process, obtaining other solutions that may be entirely different from the original ones. Another issue to avoid is: How can we improve the set of acceptable arguments considering the hashtags cloud representing the map of issues concerning a specific domain? In this sense, we can use the *centrality* and *peripheral* relations over this set of accepted arguments to prefer the more relevant arguments over the less relevant ones.

5   Related Work and Conclusions

In the context of classical abstract argumentation frameworks, there have been several proposals where other elements are added to the theoretical, abstract representational structure extending the possibility of representing more characteristics of the application domain. There exist approaches that provide mechanisms for discriminating attacks, making some of those attacks irrelevant and ignored under specific semantics. In particular, understanding how an attack comes into play has been the focus of a few works.

In [14], A. Hunter addresses the idea that attacks might have attached to them some uncertainty about whether these attacks hold, *i.e.*, some attacks might be believed, some might be disbelieved, and some might be unknown. The source of the uncertainty might be found in doubts that an attack holds or because of perceived imprecision in the way arguments are expressed. The author discusses three possible sources of uncertainty occurring in argumentation that can be addressed by quantifying the probability of attack: *Explicit uncertainty of attack*, *Implicit imprecision of argument*, and *Incompleteness in the set premises or the claims* made by the arguments. To investigate how the attachment of probability to attacks influences the semantic analysis in the abstract framework, the author considers a probability distribution over the spanning subgraphs of an argumentation graph. From this distribution, the probability that a set of arguments be admissible or included in an extension can be determined. Therefore, adding probabilities to attacks in abstract argumentation frameworks leads to a formalism where attacks might or might not be a part of the semantic analysis choosing a direction that differs from our approach.

Another proposal for making the possible consideration of attacks as effective something to be pondered, D. Kontarinis *et al.* in [15] advances an idea in the context of modeling online multi-agent debates involving multi-party argumentation. The introduction of agents in a debate with expertise on specific areas opens an interesting perspective: when a debate is deemed unresolved in a "controversial" manner, calling an additional expert may be a natural way to help make a decision. The expert then can analyze the situation from a more informed point of view and introduce a resolution. The authors analyze different application domains, such as constructing interactive forums on the Web, like DebateGraph [9]. In these systems, arguments can be represented, the attack relation defined, and additional information added. On the other hand, other proposals (for instance, the Parmenides [8] system and IMPACT [2]) include reasoning machinery, usually from argumentation theory, which provides a formal way to decide on the acceptability of the arguments represented. However, the conflicting relation between arguments presented in the debate has different importance levels according to the experts' votes. Note that these experts' familiarity with the point of contention varies according to the perceived topics tied to each argument; thus, the influence of an expert to judge an attack relation is not global but depends on the topics under discussion.

We have offered a formalization of an abstract argumentation framework that considers a set of interrelated topics that decorate the arguments in the framework. These topics are there to reflect what the arguments are addressing and provide a supporting structure for the analysis of multi-topic argumentation; one of the contributions is examining new argumentation semantics that consider these topics to obtain the accepted arguments. Topics are related to each other, configuring a graph structure representing that relationship; furthermore, from the graph, a notion of distance between topics is introduced naturally, which is used to study proximity-based semantics. The central aspect of these argumentation semantics is the initial idea that an argument should be defended by closely related arguments linked to the addressed topics. We explore this position by defining new elements such as neighborhood-bounded admissible sets. The relation between these new formalizations, the previous version of proximity-based admissibility, and the classical admissibility semantics has been analyzed. The addition of topics to abstract argumentation as a focusing device suggests several directions for future work; for instance, the role of *central* and *peripheral* arguments, in a similar sense as central and peripheral nodes in a graph or apply information retrieval concepts to establish the importance of arguments according to its own set of hashtags in a given hashcloud.

References

1. Bench-Capon, T.J.M.: Value-based argumentation frameworks. In: Benferhat, S., Giunchiglia, E. (eds.) Proceedings of NMR, pp. 443–454 (2002)

2. Benn, N., Macintosh, A.: Argument visualization for eParticipation: towards a research agenda and prototype tool. In: Tambouris, E., Macintosh, A., de Bruijn, H. (eds.) ePart 2011. LNCS, vol. 6847, pp. 60–73. Springer, Heidelberg (2011). https://doi.org/10.1007/978-3-642-23333-3_6

3. Buckley, F., Harary, F.: Distance in graphs. Addison-Wesley Publishing Company Advanced Book Program, Redwood (1990)

4. Budán, M.C., Cobo, M.L., Martinez, D.C., Simari, G.R.: Bipolarity in temporal argumentation frameworks. Int. J. Approx. Reason. **84**, 1–22 (2017)

5. Budán, M.C., Cobo, M.L., Martinez, D.C., Simari, G.R.: Proximity semantics for topic-based abstract argumentation. Inf. Sci. **508**, 135–153 (2020)

6. Budán, M.C., Lucero, M.G., Chesñevar, C., Simari, G.R.: Modeling time and valuation in structured argumentation frameworks. Inf. Sci. **290**, 22–44 (2015)

7. Budán, P.D., Escañuela Gonzalez, M.G., Budán, M.C.D., Martinez, M.V., Simari, G.R.: Similarity notions in bipolar abstract argumentation. Argument Comput. **11**(1–2), 103–149 (2020)

8. Cartwright, D., Atkinson, K.: Using computational argumentation to support e-participation. IEEE Intell. Syst. **24**(5), 42–52 (2009)

9. DebateGraph. https://www.debategraph.org/

10. Deza, M.M., Deza, E.: Encyclopedia of Distances, 2nd edn. Springer, Heidelberg (2013). https://doi.org/10.1007/978-3-642-30958-8

11. Dung, P.M.: On the acceptability of arguments and its fundamental role in nonmonotonic reasoning and logic programming and n-person games. Artif. Intell. **77**, 321–357 (1995)

12. Foucault, M., Smith, A., Sheridan, A.: The Archaeology of Knowledge; And. The Discourse on Language. Pantheon Books, Pantheon Books (1972)

13. Goddard, W., Oellermann, O.R.: Distance in graphs. In: Dehmer, M. (ed.) Structural Analysis of Complex Networks, chap. 3, pp. 49–72. Birkhäuser Basel (2011)

14. Hunter, A.: Probabilistic qualification of attack in abstract argumentation. Int. J. Approx. Reason. **55**(2), 607–638 (2014)

15. Kontarinis, D., Bonzon, E., Maudet, N., Moraitis, P.: Picking the right expert to make a debate uncontroversial. In: Verheij, B., Szeider, S., Woltran, S. (eds.) Computational Models of Argument - Proceedings of COMMA 2012, Austria. Frontiers in Artificial Intelligence and Applications, vol. 245, pp. 486–497. IOS Press (2012)

16. Leite, J., Martins, J.G.: Social abstract argumentation. In: Walsh, T. (ed.) IJCAI 2011, Proceedings of the 22nd International Joint Conference on Artificial Intelligence, Barcelona, pp. 2287–2292. IJCAI/AAAI (2011)

17. Visser, W., Hindriks, K.V., Jonker, C.M.: An argumentation framework for qualitative multi-criteria preferences. In: Modgil, S., Oren, N., Toni, F. (eds.) TAFA 2011. LNCS (LNAI), vol. 7132, pp. 85–98. Springer, Heidelberg (2012). https://doi.org/10.1007/978-3-642-29184-5_6

Burdens of Persuasion and Standards of Proof in Structured Argumentation

Roberta Calegari[1] and Giovanni Sartor[1,2(✉)]

[1] CIRFID-Alma AI, University of Bologna, Bologna, Italy
{roberta.calegari,giovanni.sartor}@unibo.it
[2] European University Institute of Florence, Fiesole, Italy

Abstract. In this paper we provide an account of the burden of persuasion, in the context of structured argumentation. First, burdens of proof in legal proceedings are discussed in general, distinguishing the burdens of production and the burdens of persuasion. Then, we focus on burdens of persuasion, illustrating their role in civil and criminal law.

A formal model for the burden of persuasion is then defined, discussed, and used to capture the role of the burden of persuasion in adjudicating conflicts between conflicting arguments and in determining the dialectical status of arguments. We consider how our model can also capture adversarial burdens of proof, namely, those cases in which failure to establish an argument for a proposition burdened with persuasion entails establishing the complementary proposition.

Finally, we examine how burdens of proofs can be integrated with standards of proof defining the extent to which an argument for a proposition burdened with persuasion has to be stronger than arguments to the contrary, in order to meet the burden.

Keywords: Burden of persuasion · Argumentation · Legal reasoning · Standard of proof

1 Introduction

The burden of proof is a central feature of many dialectical contexts. It is particularly relevant in those domains, such as legal disputations or political debates, in which controversial issues are discussed in order to adopt a decision (see [23] on burdens of proof in different dialogue types).

Generally speaking, we can say that burdens of proof distribute dialectical responsibilities between the parties in a dialogue. In other words, when a party has a burden of proof of a certain type relative to a claim ϕ, then, unless the party provides the kinds of arguments or evidence that is required by that type of burden, the party will lose on the claim. Losing on the burdened claim means

R. Calegari and G. Sartor have been supported by the H2020 ERC Project "Compu-Law" (G.A. 833647).

P. Baroni et al. (Eds.): CLAR 2021, LNAI 13040, pp. 40–59, 2021.
https://doi.org/10.1007/978-3-030-89391-0_3

that, for the purpose of the dialectic interaction at stake, it will be assumed that the claim has not been established, not even as a relevant possibility.

Burdens of proof complement the analysis of dialectical frameworks that are provided by argumentation systems. In particular, they are important in adversarial contexts: they facilitate the process of reaching a single outcome in contexts of doubt and lack of information. This is obtained, we shall argue, by ruling out (considering as unacceptable) those arguments which fail to meet any applicable burden.

Research in AI & law has devoted a number of contributions to the formal analysis of burdens of proof: models of defeasible legal reasoning have been criticised for not taking burdens of proof into account [11], the distinction between different standards of proof has been addressed [5], formal accounts of burdens of proof have been developed within models for formal argumentation [2,8,19]. However, it seems to us that a comprehensive model of burdens of proof in legal reasoning is still missing.

In the legal domain, two types of burdens can be distinguished: the *burden of production* (also called burden of providing evidence, or 'evidential' burden), and the *burden of persuasion* [19]. This terminology is used in common law systems [24], but the distinction is also recognised in civil law jurisdiction, possibly using a different terms [10]. The focus of this paper is on the burden of persuasion. We will show how an allocation of the burden of persuasion may induce single outcomes in contexts in which the assessment of conflicting arguments would, without such an allocation, remain undecided.

Our model builds upon the approach introduced in Prakken and Sartor [9,19,20], i.e., upon the view that burdens of persuasion complement argument priorities in deciding conflicts between arguments raising incompatible claims: unless priorities provide for a different outcome, the argument for a claim burdened with persuasion loses. This approach, however, does not address the cases in which the burden of persuasion concerns the conclusion of a multistep argument, which is subject to undecided challenges against earlier inference steps. We shall argue that in such cases too, the burdened argument has to be rejected: uncertainty upon non-final steps also entails failing to be persuasive.

The idea is related to the Carneades' approach [7,8], according to which the dialectical status of an argument determines whether a burden of persuasion is satisfied. This approach uses different types of premises (ordinary premises, assumptions, and exceptions) and information about the dialectical status of statements (stated, questioned, accepted, or rejected) to allocate burdens of proof and assess whether they have been met.

Hence our analysis combines Prakken and Sartor's [17,19] model with the insight from Carneades' [7], and takes into account the fact that the persuasiveness of an argument, in a dialectical context, is determined not only by the internal strength of the argument, as resulting from the strength of the inference rules used for building the argument (according, for instance, to the last link criterion), but also by the applicable counterarguments.

Our model originates from legal considerations and is applied to legal examples. However, the issue of the burden of proof has a significance that goes beyond the legal domain. It also concerns other domains – such as public discourse, risk management, etc. – in which evidence and arguments are needed, and corresponding responsibilities are allocated, according to types of dialogues and dialectical or organisational roles [22,23].

The novelty of this contribution consists of a new definition of defeat relations involving arguments burdened with persuasion, a corresponding definition of the criteria for labelling such argument, and a formalisation of the concept of standards of proof.

2   Burdens of Production and Burdens of Persuasion

Following the account in Prakken and Sartor [19], we distinguish the burden of production from the burden of persuasion. A party burdened with production needs to provide some support for the claim he or she is advancing. More exactly, we can say that the party has the burden of production for ϕ if the following is the case: unless relevant support for ϕ is provided – i.e., unless an argument for ϕ is presented that deserves to be taken into consideration – then ϕ will not be established (even in the absence of arguments against ϕ). When knowledge is represented through a set of rules and exceptions, the party interested in establishing the conclusion of a rule usually has the burden of production relative to the elements in the rule's antecedent, while the other party (who is interested in preventing the derivation of the rule's consequent) has the burden of production relative to the exceptions to the rule (as provided in a separate exception clause or in an unless-exception within the rule).

Meeting the burden of production for a claim ϕ is only a *necessary* condition, and not a sufficient one, for establishing ϕ, since the produced arguments may be defeated by counterarguments. This aspect is addressed by the burden of persuasion: the party looking to establish a claim burdened with persuasion needs to provide a 'convincing' argument for it—that is, an argument that prevails over arguments to the contrary to an extent that is determined by the applicable standard of proof. If there is a burden of persuasion on a proposition ϕ, and all arguments for ϕ fail to prevail over their counterarguments, then the party concerned will lose on ϕ.

Let us illustrate the way in which the burden of persuasion works through two examples, one from criminal law and one from civil law.

Burden of Persuasion in Criminal Law. In criminal law, the burden of production is distributed between prosecution and defence, while the burden of persuasion (in most legal systems) is always on prosecution. More exactly, in criminal law, the burden of production falls on the prosecution relative to the two constitutive elements of crime, namely, the criminal act (*actus reus*) and the required mental state (*mens rea*, be it intention/recklessness or negligence), while it falls to the defendant relative to justifications or exculpatory defences (e.g., self-defence, state of necessity, etc.). In other words, if both actus reus and mens rea are established, but no exculpatory evidence is provided, the decision should be a criminal conviction. On the other hand, the burden of persuasion falls on the prosecution for all determinants of criminal responsibility, including not only for the constitutive elements of a crime but also for the absence of justifications or exculpatory defences.

Example 1 (Criminal law example). Let us consider a case in which a woman, Hellen, has shot and killed an intruder in her home. The applicable law consists of *(a)* the rule according to which intentional killing constitutes murder, and *(b)* the exception according to which there is no murder if the victim was killed in self-defence. Assume that it has been established with certainty that Hellen shot the intruder and that she did so intentionally. However, it remains uncertain whether the intruder was threatening Hellen with a gun, as claimed by the defence, or had turned back and was running away on having been discovered, as claimed by prosecution. The burden of persuasion is on prosecution, who needs to provide a convincing argument for murder. Since, in this case, it remains uncertain whether there was self-defence, prosecution has failed to provide such an argument. Therefore, the legally correct solution is that there should be no conviction: Hellen needs to be acquitted.

Burden of Persuasion in Civil Law. In civil law, burdens of production and burdens of persuasion may be allocated in different ways. The general principle is that the plaintiff only has the burden of proof (both of production and persuasion) relatively to the operative facts that ground its claim, while the defendant has the burden of proof relative to those exceptions which may prevent the operative facts from delivering their usual outcomes, such as justifications with regard to torts, or incapability and vices of consent in contracts. However, derogations from this principle may be established by the law, in order to take into account various factors, such as the presumed ability of each party to provide evidence in favour of his or her claim, the need to protect weaker parties against abuses, etc.

In matters of civil liability, for example, it is usually the case that the plaintiff, who asks for compensation, has to prove both that the defendant caused him harm, and that this was done intentionally or negligently. However, in certain cases, the law establishes an inversion of the burden of proof for negligence (both the burden of production and the burden of persuasion). This means that in order to obtain compensation, the plaintiff only has to prove that he was harmed by the defendant. This will be sufficient to win the case unless the defendant provides a convincing argument that she was diligent (not negligent).

Example 2 (Civil law example). Let us consider a case in which a doctor caused harm to a patient by misdiagnosing his case. Assume that there is no doubt that the doctor harmed the patient: she failed to diagnose cancer, which consequently spread and became incurable. However, it is uncertain whether or not the doctor followed the guidelines governing this case: it is unclear whether she prescribed all the tests that were required by the guidelines, or whether she failed to prescribe some tests that would have enabled cancer to be detected. Assume that, under the applicable law, doctors are liable for any harm suffered by their patients, but they can avoid liability if they show that they were diligent (not negligent) in treating the patient, i.e., that they exercised due care. Thus, rather than the patients having the burden of proving that doctors have been negligent (as it should be the case according to the general principles), doctors have the burden of proving their diligence. Let us assume that the law also says that doctors are considered to be diligent if they followed the applicable medical guidelines. In this case, given that the doctor has the burden of persuasion on her diligence, and that she failed to provide a convincing argument for it, the legally correct solution is that she should be ordered to compensate the patient.

These two examples share a common feature. In both, uncertainty remains concerning a decisive issue, namely, the existence of self-defence in the first example and the doctor's diligence in the second. However, this uncertainty does not preclude the law from prescribing a single legal outcome in each case. This outcome can be achieved by discarding the arguments that fail to meet the required burden of persuasion, i.e., the prosecution's argument for murder and the doctor's argument for her diligence, respectively.

3   Argumentation Framework

We introduce a structured argumentation framework relying on a lightweight ASPIC$^+$-like argumentation system [14]. For the sake of simplicity, we assume that arguments only consist of defeasible rules, to the exclusion of strict rules, and of some constituents of a knowledge base—such as axioms, ordinary premises, assumptions, and issues—that can be found in the complete model [14]. A framework based on defeasible rules is sufficient for our purposes and can be extended as needed with further structures. In this section, we introduce arguments, preferences, and defeat relations.

3.1   Defeasible Theories

As usual, by a literal we mean an atomic proposition or its negation.

Notation 31. *For any literal ϕ, its complement is denoted by $\bar{\phi}$. That is, if ϕ is atom p, then $\bar{\phi} = \neg p$, while if ϕ is $\neg p$, then $\bar{\phi}$ is p.*

Literals are brought into relation through defeasible rules.

Definition 1 (Defeasible rule). *A **defeasible rule** r has the form: $\rho :$ $\phi_1, ..., \phi_n, \sim \phi'_1, ..., \sim \phi'_m \Rightarrow \psi$ with $0 \leq n$ and $0 \leq m$, and where*

- *ρ, an atom, is the unique identifier for r, denoted by $N(r)$;*
- *each $\phi_1, ... \phi_n, \phi'_1, ..., \phi'_m, \psi$ is a literal;*
- *$\phi_1, ... \phi_n, \sim \phi'_1, ..., \sim \phi'_m$ are denoted by Antecedent(r) and ψ by Consequent(r);*
- *$\sim \phi$ denotes the weak negation (negation by failure) of ϕ: ϕ is an exception that would block the application of the rule whose antecedent includes $\sim \phi$.*

The name of a rule can be used to specify that the named rule is applicable, and its negation correspondingly to specify that the rule is inapplicable [13].

A superiority relation $\succ$ is defined over rules: $s \succ r$ states that rule s prevails over rule r.

Definition 2 (Superiority relation). *A **superiority relation** $\succ$ over a set of rules Rules is an antireflexive and antisymmetric binary relation, i.e., $\succ \subseteq$ Rules $\times$ Rules.*

A defeasible theory consists of a set of rules and a superiority relation over the rules.

Definition 3 (Defeasible theory). *A **defeasible theory** is a tuple $\langle Rules, \succ \rangle$ where Rules is a set of rules, and $\succ$ is a superiority relation over Rules.*

Given a defeasible theory, by chaining rules from the theory we can construct arguments, as specified in the following definition; cf. [3,13,21].

Definition 4 (Argument). *An **argument** constructed from a defeasible theory $\langle Rules, \succ \rangle$ is a finite construct of the form: $A : A_1, \ldots A_n \Rightarrow_r \phi$ with $0 \leq n$, where*

- *A is the argument's unique identifier;*
- *$A_1, \ldots, A_n$ are arguments constructed from the defeasible theory $\langle Rules, \succ \rangle$;*
- *ϕ is the conclusion of the argument, denoted by $Conc(A)$;*
- *$r : Conc(A_1), \ldots, Conc(A_n) \Rightarrow \phi$ is the top rule of A, denoted by $TopRule(A)$.*

Notation 32. *Given an argument $A : A_1, \ldots A_n \Rightarrow_r \phi$ as in Definition 4, $Sub(A)$ denotes the **set of subarguments** of A, i.e., $Sub(A) = Sub(A_1) \cup \ldots \cup Sub(A_n) \cup \{A\}$. $DirectSub(A)$ denotes the **direct subarguments** of A, i.e., $DirectSub(A) = \{A_1, \ldots, A_n\}$.*

We assume that preferences over arguments are defined via a last-link ordering: an argument A is preferred over another argument B if the top rule of A is stronger than the top rule of B.

Definition 5 (Preference relation). *A **preference relation** $\succ$ is a binary relation over a set of arguments $\mathcal{A}$: an argument A is preferred to argument B, denoted by $A \succ B$, iff $TopRule(A) \succ TopRule(B)$.*

3.2   Defeat with Burdens of Persuasion

Let us first identify burdens of persuasion, i.e., those literals the proof of which requires a convincing argument. We assume that such literals are consistent (it cannot be the case that there is a burden of persuasion both on ϕ and $\overline{\phi}$).

Definition 6 (Burdens of persuasion). *Let BurdPers, the set of **burdens of persuasion**, be a set of literals such that if $\phi \in$ BurdPers then $\overline{\phi} \notin$ BurdPers. We say that an argument A is burdened with persuasion if $Conc(A) \in$ BurdPers.*

We now consider possible collisions between arguments, i.e., those cases in which an argument A challenges an argument B: *(a)* by contradicting the conclusion of a B' subargument (rebutting), or *(b)* by denying (the application of) the top rule of a B' subargument or by contradicting a weak negation in the body of the top rule of a B' subargument (undercutting).

Note that our notion of rebutting corresponds to the notion of successful rebutting in [14].

Definition 7 (bp-rebut). *Argument* A **bp-rebuts** *argument* B *iff* $\exists B' \in Sub(B)$ *such that* $Conc(A) = \overline{Conc(B')}$ *and*

1. $Conc(A) \notin BurdPers$, *and* $B' \not\succ A$, *or*
2. $Conc(A) \in BurdPers$ *and* $A \succ B'$.

According to Definition 7.1, for an unburdened argument A to rebut B by contradicting the latter's subargument B', it is sufficient that B' is non-superior to A. According to 7.2 for a burdened argument A to rebut B by contradicting B', it is necessary that A is superior to B'. Thus, burdens of persuasion supplement priorities in deciding conflicts between arguments having opposed conclusions. They dictate the outcome of such conflicts when priorities do not already determine which argument is to prevail: when two arguments contradict one another, the one burdened with persuasion will fail to bp-rebut the other, while the latter will succeed in bp-rebutting the first.

Undercutting is defined as usual, including both the case in which the attacker excludes the application of the top rule of the attacked argument (by denying the rule's name) and the case in which it contradicts a weakly negated literal in the body of that rule.

Definition 8 (bp-undercut). A **undercuts** B *iff* $\exists B' \in Sub(B)$ *such that:*

1. $Conc(A) = \neg N(r)$ *and* $TopRule(B') = r$; *or*
2. $Conc(A) = \phi$ *and* $\sim \phi \in Antecedent(TopRule(B'))$

Finally, we have the notions of bp-defeat and strict bp-defeat that are defined on the basis of bp-rebutting and undercutting. As you can see from the definition below the difference from the usual notion of defeat pertains to bp-rebuts.

Definition 9 (bp-defeat)

1. A **bp-defeats** B *iff* A *bp-rebuts* B *or* A *undercuts* B
2. A **strictly-bp-defeats** B *iff* A *bp-defeats* B *and* B *does not bp-defeats* A .

3.3   Example

To exemplify the notions just introduced, let us formalise Example 2 through a set of rules. Note that we assume that evidence is provided to establish the factual claims at issue, i.e., that the corresponding burdens of production are satisfied (facts e1, e2, e3).

Example 3 (Civil law example: rules and arguments)

e1 : ev_1 er1 : $ev_1 \Rightarrow \neg guidelines$
e2 : ev_2 er2 : $ev_2 \Rightarrow guidelines$
e3 : ev_3 er3 : $ev_3 \Rightarrow harm$
r1 : $\neg guidelines \Rightarrow \neg dueDiligence$ r2 : $guidelines \Rightarrow dueDiligence$
r3 : $harm, \sim dueDiligence \Rightarrow liable$

We can then build the following arguments:

A1 :$\Rightarrow ev_1$ A2 :$\Rightarrow ev_2$
A3 :$\Rightarrow ev_3$ A4 : $A1 \Rightarrow \neg guidelines$
A5 : $A2 \Rightarrow guidelines$ A6 : $A3 \Rightarrow harm$
A7 : $A4 \Rightarrow \neg dueDiligence$ A8 : $A5 \Rightarrow dueDiligence$
A9 : $A6 \Rightarrow liable$

If there were no burden of persuasion the defeat relation would be the following:

- arguments A4 and A5 defeat one another,
- A5 defeats A7,
- A4 defeats A8,
- A7 and A8 defeat one another,
- A8 strictly defeats A9.

If on the contrary, there is burden on the doctors' diligence ($dueDiligence \in$ BurdPers), then A8 fails to defeat A7, so that A7 strictly defeats A8.

4 A Labelling Semantic for Burdens of Persuasion

In this section, we show how arguments are linked through argumentation graphs. Then, we define a labelling semantics that takes burdens of persuasion into account.

4.1 Argumentation Graphs and Bp-Labelling

In an argumentation graph, arguments are connected according to the defeat relation.

Definition 10 (Argumentation graph). *An **argumentation graph** constructed from a defeasible theory T is a tuple $\langle \mathcal{A}, \rightsquigarrow \rangle$, where $\mathcal{A}$ is the set of all arguments constructed from T, and $\rightsquigarrow$ is defeat relation over $\mathcal{A}$.*

Notation 41. *Given an argumentation graph $G = \langle \mathcal{A}, \rightsquigarrow \rangle$, we write $\mathcal{A}_G$, and $\rightsquigarrow_G$ to denote the graph's arguments and attacks respectively.*

Now, let us introduce the notion of the {IN, OUT, UND}-labelling of an argumentation graph, where each argument in the graph is labelled IN, OUT, or UND, depending on whether it is accepted, rejected, or undecided, respectively.

Definition 11 (Labelling). *Let G be an argumentation graph. An* {IN, OUT, UND}*-labelling L of G is a total function* $\mathcal{A}_G \rightarrow$ {IN, OUT, UND}.

Notation 42. *Given a labelling L, we write* IN(L) *for* {$A|L(A) =$ IN}, OUT(L) *for* {$A|L(A) =$ OUT} *and* UND(L) *for* {$A|L(A) =$ UND}.

There are various ways to specify {IN, OUT, UND}-labelling functions [1]. For example, they can be *complete* or *grounded.*

Definition 12. *A* **complete** {IN, OUT, UND}*-labelling of an argumentation graph G is an* {IN, OUT, UND}*-labelling such that* $\forall A \in \mathcal{A}_G$

1. *A is labelled* IN *iff all defeaters of A are labelled* OUT, *and*
2. *A is labelled* OUT *iff A has a defeater which is labelled* IN.

Definition 13. *A* **grounded** {IN, OUT, UND}*-labelling of an argumentation graph G is a complete* {IN, OUT, UND}*-labelling L of G such that* IN(L) *is minimal.*

Remark that any argument not labelled IN or OUT must be labelled UND, since any {IN, OUT, UND}-labelling is a total function.

While common specifications of {IN, OUT, UND}-labellings define reasonable positions [1], they do not cater for burdens of persuasion. We now introduce the notion of bp-labelling, namely, a labelling which takes into account a set of burdens of persuasion.

Definition 14 (bp-labelling). *A* **bp-labelling** *of an argumentation graph G, relative to a set of burdens of persuasion* BurdPers, *is an* {IN, OUT, UND}*-labelling s.t.* $\forall A \in \mathcal{A}_G$ *with* Conc(A) = ϕ

1. $A \in$ IN(L) *iff* $\forall B \in \mathcal{A}_G$ *such that B bp-defeats* $A : B \in$ OUT(L)
2. $A \in$ OUT(L) *iff*
   (a) $\phi \in$ BurdPers *and* $\exists B \in \mathcal{A}_G$ *such that*
       – *B bp-defeats A and*
       – $B \in$ IN(L) *or* $B \in$ UND(L)
   (b) $\phi \notin$ BurdPers *and* $\exists B \in \mathcal{A}_G$ *such that*
       – *B bp-defeats A and*
       – $B \in$ IN(L)
3. $A \in$ UND(L) *otherwise.*

Burdens of persuasion affect conditions for rejection, as specified in Definition 14 (2) (a). The rejection (the OUT labelling) of an argument burdened of persuasion may be determined by any counterargument B that is accepted (IN) or also is uncertain (UND). On the contrary, as specified in 14 (2) (b) the rejection of an argument that is not burdened with persuasion requires a defeating counterargument B that is IN.

Note that the semantic just described does not always deliver a single labelling. Multiple labelling may exist when arguments rebut each other, none of them being burdened with persuasion. If one of these arguments is labelled IN the other is labelled OUT and vice versa. To address such a situation, we focus on IN-minimal labelling, i.e., on the labelling where both such arguments (rents are labelled UND. Let us call such a labelling a *grounded bp-labelling*.

Definition 15 (Grounded bp-labelling). *A **bp-labelling** L of an argumentation graph G is a **grounded bp-labelling** iff* UND(L) *is maximal.*

Proposition 1. *If BurdPers* $= \emptyset$, L_1 *is the grounded labelling of argumentation graph G, as defined by* [1] *and* L_2 *is the grounded bp-labelling of G, then* IN$(L_1) =$ IN(L_2).

Proof. It is easy to see that if condition 14(1) concerning arguments burdened with persuasion is removed from Definition 14, we obtain the definition of grounded labelling as characterised in [1].

4.2 Examples

Let us now apply the model just introduced to some legal examples.

Example 4 (Civil law example: graphs and bp-labelling). Let us consider again the Example 2 and the corresponding rules and arguments built in Example 3. The argumentation graph and its grounded $\{$IN, OUT, UND$\}$-labelling are depicted in Fig. 1 (left), in which all arguments are UND except arguments for undisputed facts.

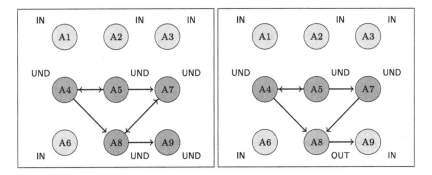

Fig. 1. Grounded $\{$IN, OUT, UND$\}$-labelling of Example 2 in the absence of burdens of persuasion (left) and its bp-labelling with BurdPers $= \{dueDiligence, liable\}$ (right).

The result is not satisfactory according to the law, since it does not take into account the applicable burdens of persuasion. The doctor should have lost the case – i.e., be found liable – since she failed to discharge her burden of proving that she was diligent (non-negligent). The doctor's failure results from the fact that it remains uncertain whether she followed the guidelines. To capture this aspect of the argument, we need to specify the burdens of persuasion. Let us assume that (as under Italian law) we have BurdPers = {*dueDiligence, liable*} (i.e., the doctor has to provide a convincing argument that she was diligent, the patient has to provide a convincing argument for the doctor's liability). As the burdened doctor's argument for *dueDiligence* is OUT, her liability can be established even though it remains uncertain whether the guidelines were followed. □

This example shows how the model here presented allows us to deal with the *inversion of the burden of proof*, i.e., a situation in which one argument A is presented for a claim ϕ being burdened with persuasion, and A (or a subargument of it) is attacked by a counterargument B, of which the conclusion ψ is also burdened with persuasion. If no convincing argument for ψ can be found, then the attack fails, and the uncertainty on ψ does not affect the status of A. In the example, the argument for the doctor's due diligence fails to meet its burden of persuasion. Consequently, it fails to defeat the argument for the doctor's liability, which succeeds, meeting its burden of persuasion.

Example 5 (Criminal law example: rules, graphs and bp-labelling). According to the description in Example 1, let us consider the following rules (for simplicity's sake, we will not specify the evidence here, but we assume that all factual claims are supported by evidence):

> f1: ⇒ *killed*
> f2: ⇒ *intention*
> f3: ⇒ *threatWithWeapon*
> f4: ⇒ ¬*threatWithWeapon*
> r1: *threatWithWeapon* ⇒ *selfDefence*
> r2: ¬*threatWithWeapon* ⇒ ¬*selfDefence*
> r3: *selfDefence* ⇒ ¬*murder*
> r4: *killed, intention* ⇒ *murder*

with $r3 \succ r4$. We can build the following arguments:

> C1 :⇒ ¬*threatWithWeapon* C2 : C1 ⇒ ¬*selfDefence*
> A1 :⇒ *killed*   B1 :⇒ *threatWithWeapon*
> A2 :⇒ *intention*   B2 : B1 ⇒ *selfDefence*
> A3 : A1, A2 ⇒ *murder*   B3 : B2 ⇒ ¬*murder*

In the {IN, OUT, UND}-labelling of Fig. 2 (left), all arguments are UND except for the undisputed facts. Thus, in the absence of burdens of persuasion, we do not obtain the legally correct answer, namely, acquittal. To obtain acquittal we need to introduce burdens of persuasion. Prosecution has the burden of persuasion on *murder*: it therefore falls to the prosecution to persuade the judge that there was killing, that it was intentional, and that the killer did not act in self-defence. The bp-labelling is depicted in Fig. 2 (right). The prosecution failed to meet its burden of proving murder, i.e., its argument is not convincing, since it remains undetermined whether there was self-defence. Therefore, murder is OUT and the presumed killer is to be acquitted. □

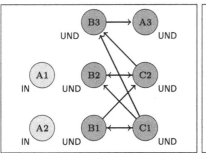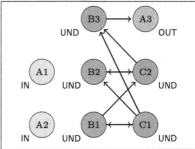

Fig. 2. Grounded {IN, OUT, UND}-labelling of Example 1 in the absence of burdens of persuasion (left) and bp-labelling with the burden of persuasion BurdPers = {*murder*} (right).

4.3   The Problem of Defeat Cycles

A complexity in argumentation graphs including arguments burdened of persuasion concerns what we may call defeat cycles, i.e., cycles of arguments that defeat one another. Cycles of defeats have been extensively in argumentation theory [1,4,6]. Here we just consider how the problem emerges in connection with burdens of persuasion.

Definition 16 (Defeat cycle). *A defeat cycle is a set of arguments S where $\forall$ argument $A \in S$, $\exists B \in S$ such that A defeats B and A is defeated by B.*

Note that this definition includes, beyond the usual case of head-to-head rebuttals, those cases in which arguments attack each other's subarguments, or undercut one another, as in Example 6.

Example 6 (Defeat cycle example). Let us consider the following rules, with $Conc(A1) \in$ BurdPers

$$Rules: \quad \text{r1} : \sim a \Rightarrow b \quad \text{r2} : \sim b \Rightarrow c \quad \text{r3} : \sim c \Rightarrow a$$
$$Args: \quad \text{A1} : \Rightarrow a \quad\quad \text{A2} : \Rightarrow b \quad\quad \text{A3} : \Rightarrow c$$

It's easy to see that A1 undercuts A2, which undercuts A3, which undercuts A1.

Determining the status of a burdened argument included in a defeat cycle, such as $A1$ in Example 6, is problematic (assuming that no argument in the cycle is defeated by external attackers). Consider for instance the case of argument $A1$ in Example 6. The argument cannot be IN, since there are no reasons for assuming that its attacker is OUT, not it can be UND because doubt should entail rejection for burdened arguments, not it can be OUT, since in such a case there would be no reason for it to be in such status, as its only attacker, $A3$ would be OUT as well. Among these three imperfect solutions, it seems that the second one may be preferable, in accordance with the idea that, in the absence of a

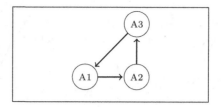

Fig. 3. Defeat cycle example

decisive reason to accepting it, an argument burdened with persuasion should be rejected (Fig. 3).

In conclusion, it seems that we have two approaches to deal with such (vicious) cycles. One approach consists in restricting the argumentation graphs we are considering to those that do not contain defeat cycles including arguments burdened with persuasion, i.e., in making this restriction a constraint on the construction of valid argumentation graphs with burdens of persuasion. In fact, we have not been able to find reasonable legal examples that may include such cycles.

The second approach consists of assuming that all arguments burdened with persuasion, which are included in a circular bp-defeat set are OUT. More formally, let us introduce the following definition, which is meant to capture circular defeat sets such that no external argument rules out any argument in the cycle: all external defeaters of burdened arguments in the set are OUT, and all external defeaters of non-burdened arguments are OUT or UND.

Definition 17 (Protected defeat cycle). *A defeat cycle $\mathcal{S}$ is **protected** in G iff $\forall A \in \mathcal{S}$ holds that*

- *if $Conc(A) \in BurdPers$, then $\forall B \in \mathcal{A}_G \backslash \mathcal{S}$ such that B bp-defeats A: $B \in$ OUT(L)*
- *if $Conc(B) \notin BurdPers$ then $\forall B \in \mathcal{A}_G \backslash \mathcal{S}$ such that B strictly bp-defeats A: $B \in$ OUT(L) or $B \in$ UND(L).*

Following the idea that all burdened arguments in a protected cycle set are OUT we can then modify Definition 14 as follows.

Definition 18 (bp-labelling with defeat cycles). *A **bp-labelling** of an argumentation graph G, relative to a set of burdens of persuasion BurdPers, is an $\{$IN, OUT, UND$\}$-labelling s.t. $\forall A \in \mathcal{A}_G$ with $Conc(A) = \phi$*

1. $A \in \text{IN}(L)$ *iff* $\forall B \in \mathcal{A}_G$ *such that* B *bp-defeats* $A : B \in \text{OUT}(L)$
2. $A \in \text{OUT}(L)$ *iff*
   (a) $\phi \in$ *BurdPers and*
       - $\exists B \in \mathcal{A}_G$ *such that bp-defeats* A *and* $B \in \text{IN}(L)$ *or* $B \in \text{UND}(L)$, *or*
       - $A \in \mathcal{S}$ *such that* $\mathcal{S}$ *is a protected circular defeat set in* G
   or
   (b) $\phi \notin$ *BurdPers and* $\exists B \in \mathcal{A}_G$ *such that* B *bp-defeats* A *and* $B \in \text{IN}(L)$
3. $A \in \text{UND}(L)$ *otherwise.*

5   Adversarial Burden of Persuasion

Adversarial burdens of persuasion expand a bp-labelling approach in order to capture those cases in which failure to meet a burden of persuasion on ϕ entails that $\overline{\phi}$ (ϕ's complement) is established.

For instance, failure to show that the accused is guilty entails that he should be found innocent. Similarly, the plaintiff's failure to provide a convincing argument that she has a right to compensation for a certain event entails that she has no right to be compensated. Or the burden of providing a convincing argument that a genetically modified crop is not harmful may entails – according to the so-called precautionary principle – that the crop is deemed to be harmful.

Thus, an adversarial burden of persuasion on a claim ϕ entails not only that arguments for ϕ will be OUT if they are not IN, but also that failure to establish ϕ entails ϕ's complement, according to a rule "$r :\sim \phi \Rightarrow \overline{\phi}$".

Example 7 (Criminal law example: adversarial bp). Let us consider again our example concerning criminal law (Example 5). Let us assume that we add the rule

$$\text{abp1} :\sim murder \Rightarrow \neg murder$$

This rule enables us to develop an argument for concluding that in the criminal law example above that there is no murder. This is indeed what generally happens in criminal and other legal cases: failure to establish the prosecution's claim that a murder was committed or the plaintiff's claim that a compensation is due leads to the conclusion that there was no crime or that no compensation is due according to an argument like the following.

$$B_4 = \{\} \Rightarrow \neg murder$$

The corresponding new argumentation graph is depicted in Fig. 4.

6   Standards of Proof

In this section, we complement burdens of proof with standards of proof. Following the approach by [20], we model standards of proof as the required bandwidth between competing arguments, i.e., as the extent to which one argument has to prevail over its counterargument in order to meet the applicable burden.

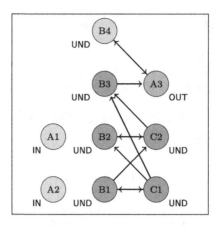

Fig. 4. Criminal law example with adversarial bp.

6.1   From Priorities to Bandwidths

As with priorities, we assume that bandwidths between arguments are determined by comparing their top rules. Given that $r_1 \succ r_2$, we indicate the bandwidth between r_1 and r_2 rules through a positive rational number, which expresses the positive extent to which r_1 prevails over r_2, i.e., the comparative superiority of r_1 over r_2. If $r_1 \not\succ r_2$ we assign 0 to the corresponding bandwidth (this holds both when r_2 prevails over r_1 and when there is no superiority between the two rules). Accordingly, we define the bandwidth function as follows.

Definition 19 (Bandwidth function). *Let $\succ$ be a superiority relation over a set of rules Rules. A bandwidth assignment over $\succ$ is a function* BW *which assigns to every pair $(r_i, rj) \in$ Rules a number as follows:*

- *if $(r_i, rj) \in \succ$, then* $\mathsf{BW}(r_i, rj) \in \mathbb{R}_{>0}$
- *otherwise,* $\mathsf{BW}(r_i, rj) = 0$

Notation 61. *We use $r_i \succ^n rj$ as an abbreviation for $\mathsf{BW}(r_i, rj) = n$, i.e., to express that rule r_i prevails over rule rj to the extent n.*

Note that we may want to impose some constraints over bandwidths, for instance to require that if $r_1 \succ^x r_2$ and $r_2 \succ^y r_3$ then $r_1 \succ^z r_3$ and $z \geq max(x, y)$ (or even $z = x + y$), but this is not needed for our purposes.

In our examples, for the sake of simplicity, we assume that bandwidths only take values 1, 2, or 3, denoting respectively that r_1 *barely prevails* over r_2 (as sufficient to meet the standard of preponderance of evidence), that it *significantly prevails* (as needed to meet the standard of clear and convincing evidence) and that *strongly prevails* (as needed to meet the standard of "beyond reasonable doubt"). Other ranges of possible values may however be considered, depending on the standards being modelled.

As above, the ordering over rules is transferred to the ordering over arguments: argument A is preferred to argument B to the extent x, denoted by $A \succ^x B$, iff $\mathsf{TopRule}(A) \succ^x \mathsf{TopRule}(B)$.

We are now in a condition to define the notion of rebutting with standard of proof, denoted as *bps-rebutting*. The idea is that the conflict between two arguments A and B such that A contradicts a subargument $B' \in Sub(B)$ is to be determined by the bandwidth between A and B'. We have three cases to consider:

- There is no burden of persuasion on both A and B'. Then, as usual, A bps-rebuts B, unless B' is superior to A.
- There is a burden of persuasion on A. Then A bps-rebuts B' only if it is superior to B' to an extent that at least reaches the applicable standard.
- There is a burden of persuasion on B. Then A bps-rebuts B unless B' superior to A to an extent that reaches the standard.

Definition 20 (bps-rebutting). *An argument A **bps-rebuts** an argument B relative to a standard $S \in \mathbb{R}_{>0}$ iff $\exists B' \in Sub(B)$ such that $Conc(A) = \overline{Conc(B')}$*

1. *$Conc(A), Conc(B') \notin BurdPers$, and $B' \not\succ A$*
2. *$Conc(A) \in BurdPers$, and $\mathsf{BW}(A, B') \geq S$*
   or
3. *$Conc(B') \in BurdPers$ and $\mathsf{BW}(B', A) \not\geq S$*

On this basis, we get the following definition for defeat relative to a standard of proof (bps-defeat).

Definition 21 (bps-defeat)

- *A **bps-defeats** B relative to standard of proof S iff A bps-rebuts B relatively to S or A undercuts B*
- *A **strictly bps-defeats** B relative to standard of proof S iff B iff A bps-defeats B relative to standard of proof S and B does not bps-defeats B relative to standard of proof S.*

We can now define the notion of bp-labelling with a standard of persuasion, which will be denoted as bps-labelling.

Definition 22 (bps-labelling). *A **bps-labelling** of a cycle-free argumentation graph G, relative to a set of burdens of persuasion $BurdPers$ and a standard of proof $S \in \mathbb{R}_{>0}$, is an $\{\mathsf{IN}, \mathsf{OUT}, \mathsf{UND}\}$-labelling s.t. $\forall A \in \mathcal{A}_G$ with $Conc(A) = \phi$.*

1. *$A \in \mathsf{IN}(L)$ iff $\forall B \in \mathcal{A}_G$ such that B bps-defeats A: $B \in L(\mathsf{OUT})$*
2. *$A \in \mathsf{OUT}(L)$ iff*
   (a) $\phi \in BurdPers$ and $\exists B \in \mathcal{A}_G$ such that B bps-defeats A: $B \notin L(\mathsf{OUT})$ or
   (b) $\phi \notin BurdPers$ and $\exists B \in \mathcal{A}_G$ such that B bps-defeats A: $B \in L(\mathsf{IN})$
3. *$A \in \mathsf{UND}(L)$ otherwise.*

Definition 23 (Grounded bps-labelling). *A **bps-labelling** L of an argumentation graph G is a **grounded bps-labelling** iff $\mathsf{UND}(L)$ is maximal.*

6.2   Examples

Let us now consider how different standards of proof may affect the outcome of a dispute, by comparing a criminal case from a civil case for the compensation of damages resulting from a crime.

Example 8 (Criminal law example with standards of proof). Let us first provide an example by modifying our criminal law example. In Example 5, the outcome was no conviction for Hellen, since a doubt remains whether she acted in self-defence, as a consequence of the doubt on whether she was threatened with a weapon. Let us now assume that the evidence against Hellen being *not* being threatened with weapons ($f4 :\Rightarrow \neg threatWithWeapon$) prevails over the evidence to the contrary ($f3 :\Rightarrow threatWithWeapon$), but only to a small extent (e.g.,1), i.e., $f4 \succ^1 f3$.

Given that the bandwidth 1 is inferior to the standard 3 for criminal law, we get that argument C1 for $\neg threatWithWeapon$ fails to strictly defeat B1 for *threatWithWeapon*. Consequently, both arguments are UND, as a consequence, also the argument B2 for self-defence is UND. Accordingly, the argument for A3 for murder is UND. Thus, the attempt to establish a conviction for murder fails. The resulting bps-labelling is depicted in Fig. 5 (left).

Let us now assume that the evidence for $\neg threatWithWeapon$ is stronger, i.e., $f4 \succ^3 f3$ and correspondingly C1 $\succ^3$ B1. It is easy to see that with this bandwidth, C1 strictly defeats B1, which is consequently OUT as also B2 and B3. As a consequence A3 is IN and conviction for murder is successfully established. The resulting bps-labelling is depicted in Fig. 5 (right).

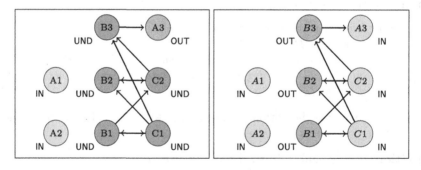

Fig. 5. bps-labelling relative to the murder case in a penal suit with $f4 \succ^1 f3$ (left) and with $f4 \succ^3 f3$ (right)

Example 9 (Civil law suit for damages resulting from a crime). Assume that the issue of murder is addressed in a civil suit, where the standard of proof is 1. Moreover, let us add one further rule to our framework, namely a rule which extends the previous example with the right to compensation:

$$r5 : murder \Rightarrow compensation$$

and accordingly, with the following argument:

$$A4 := A3 \Rightarrow compensation$$

It is easy to see that in such a case A3 would be IN, since $f4 \succ^1 f3$ and in civil suit the bandwidth is 1, so that also compensation for murder can be granted (A4 would be IN). This is what happens in those legal systems in which criminal and civil suits can be independently started for the same facts (as in the famous O.J. Simpson case). This result is depicted in Fig. 6.

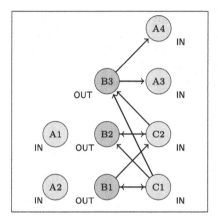

Fig. 6. bps-labelling relative to the compensation of a murder in a civil suit with $f4 \succ^1 f3$.

7 Conclusion

We have presented a formal model for the burden of persuasion. The model is based on the idea that arguments burdened with persuasion have to be rejected when there is uncertainty about them. Consequently, such arguments become irrelevant to the argumentation framework including them: not only they fail to be included in the set of the accepted arguments (the IN ones), but they also are unable to affect the status of the arguments they attack.

We have shown how an allocation of the burden of persuasion may lead to a single outcome (IN arguments) in contexts in which the assessment of conflicting arguments would otherwise remain undecided. We have also shown how our model is able to address inversions of burdens of proof, namely, those cases in which the burden shifts from one party to the other. In such cases, there is the burden of persuasion over the conclusion of a multistep argument, and at the same time a burden of persuasion over the conclusion of an attacker against a subargument of that multistep argument.

We have also modelled adversarial burdens of proofs, namely, those cases in which failure to meet a burden of proof for a claim ϕ entails the complementary claim $\overline{\phi}$.

Finally, we have shown how standards of proof can be captured in our model. This has been done by introducing the requirement that, in order to meet the applicable standard, a burdened argument must prevail at least to a certain extent (as specified by the standard) over the arguments to the contrary.

The model can be expanded in various ways, to capture further aspects of legal reasoning. For instance, it can also be supplemented with argumentation over burdens of persuasion [15,18], in a manner similar to the way in which argumentation systems can be expanded to include argumentation about priorities (see [12,16]). An open issue, that we plan to address in future research concerns how to deal with defeat circles including burdened arguments (see Sect. 4.3). More generally we plan to study the properties of our semantics and the connection of our semantics with the standard semantics for argumentation. We also plan to inquire about the way in which our model fits into legal procedures and enables a rational reconstruction of aspects of them. Connections with the handling of burdens in other formalisms, such as defeasible logic [9] have to be explored.

References

1. Baroni, P., Caminada, M., Giacomin, M.: An introduction to argumentation semantics. Knowl. Eng. Rev. **26**(4), 365–410 (2011). https://doi.org/10.1017/S0269888911000166
2. Calegari, R., Sartor, G.: A model for the burden of persuasion in argumentation. In: Villata, S., Harašta, J., Křemen, P. (eds.) Legal Knowledge and Information Systems. JURIX 2020: The Thirty-Third Annual Conference. Frontiers in Artificial Intelligence and Applications, Brno, Czech Republic, 9–11 December 2020, vol. 334, pp. 13–22. IOS (2020). https://doi.org/10.3233/FAIA200845
3. Caminada, M., Amgoud, L.: On the evaluation of argumentation formalisms. Artif. Intell. **171**(5–6), 286–310 (2007). https://doi.org/10.1016/j.artint.2007.02.003
4. Cramer, M., van der Torre, L.: SCF2-an argumentation semantics for rational human judgments on argument acceptability. In: Proceedings of the 8th Workshop on Dynamics of Knowledge and Belief (DKB-2019) and the 7th Workshop KI & Kognition (KIK-2019) co-located with 44nd German Conference on Artificial Intelligence (KI 2019), Kassel, Germany, 23 September 2019, pp. 24–35 (2019)
5. Farley, A.M., Freeman, K.: Burden of proof in legal argumentation. In: Proceedings of the 5th International Conference on Artificial Intelligence and Law, Maryland, USA, pp. 156–164. ACM (1995). https://doi.org/10.1145/222092.222227
6. Gabbay, D.: The handling of loops in argumentation networks. J. Logic Comput. **26**(4), 1065–1147 (2014). https://doi.org/10.1093/logcom/exu007
7. Gordon, T.F., Prakken, H., Walton, D.: The Carneades model of argument and burden of proof. Artif. Intell. **171**(10), 875–896 (2007). https://doi.org/10.1016/j.artint.2007.04.010
8. Gordon, T.F., Walton, D.N.: Proof burdens and standards. In: Simari, G., Rahwan, I. (eds.) Argumentation in Artificial Intelligence, pp. 239–258. Springer, Boston (2009). https://doi.org/10.1007/978-0-387-98197-0_12
9. Governatori, G., Sartor, G.: Burdens of proof in monological argumentation. In: Winkels, R. (ed.) Proceeding of JURIX 2010: The Twenty-Third Annual Conference on Legal Knowledge and Information Systems, pp. 57–66. IOS (2010)

10. Hahn, U., Oaksford, M.: The burden of proof and its role in argumentation. Argumentation **21**, 36–61 (2007). https://doi.org/10.1007/s10503-007-9022-6
11. Leenes, R.E.: Burden of proof in dialogue games and Dutch civil procedure. In: Proceedings of the 8th International Conference on Artificial Intelligence and Law, Missouri, USA, pp. 109–18. ACM (2001). https://doi.org/10.1145/383535.383549
12. Modgil, S., Prakken, H.: Reasoning about preferences in structured extended argumentation frameworks. In: Proceedings of COMMA 2010, Computational Models of Argumentation, Italy, pp. 347–58. IOS (2010). https://doi.org/10.3233/978-1-60750-619-5-347
13. Modgil, S., Prakken, H.: The ASPIC$^+$ framework for structured argumentation: a tutorial. Argument Comput. **5**(1), 31–62 (2014). https://doi.org/10.1080/19462166.2013.869766
14. Prakken, H.: An abstract framework for argumentation with structured arguments. Argument Comput. **1**, 93–124 (2010). https://doi.org/10.1080/19462160903564592
15. Prakken, H., Reed, C., Walton, D.N.: Dialogues about the burden of proof. In: Proceedings of the 10th International Conference on Artificial Intelligence and Law, Bologna, Italy, pp. 115–124. ACM (2005). https://doi.org/10.1145/1165485.1165503
16. Prakken, H., Sartor, G.: Rules about rules: assessing conflicting arguments in legal reasoning. Artif. Intell. Law **4**, 331–68 (1996). https://doi.org/10.1007/BF00118496
17. Prakken, H., Sartor, G.: Formalising arguments about the burden of persuasion. In: Proceedings of the 11th International Conference on Artificial Intelligence and Law (ICAIL 2007), pp. 97–106. ACM (2007)
18. Prakken, H., Sartor, G.: Formalising arguments about the burden of persuasion. In: 11th International Conference on Artificial Intelligence and Law, Stanford California, pp. 97–106. ACM, June 2007
19. Prakken, H., Sartor, G.: A logical analysis of burdens of proof. Legal Evidence Proof: Stat. Stories Logic **1**, 223–253 (2010)
20. Prakken, H., Sartor, G.: On modelling burdens and standards of proof in structured argumentation. In: 24th Annual Conference on Legal Knowledge and Information Systems, pp. 83–92. IOS (2011)
21. Vreeswijk, G.: Abstract argumentation systems. Artif. Intell. **90**(1–2), 225–279 (1997). https://doi.org/10.1016/S0004-3702(96)00041-0
22. Walton, D.: Arguments from Ignorance. Pennsylvania State University Press, Pennsylvania (1996). https://doi.org/10.1007/978-3-319-15013-03
23. Walton, D.: Burden of Proof, Presumption and Argumentation. Cambridge University Press, Cambridge (2014). https://doi.org/10.1017/CBO9781107110311
24. Williams, C.: Burdens and standards in civil litigation. Sydney Law Rev. **25**, 165–188 (2003)

Implementation of Choice of Jurisdiction and Law in Private International Law by PROLEG Meta-interpreter

Ken Satoh[1]([✉]), Laura Giordano[2], and Matteo Baldoni[3]

[1] National Institute of Informatics, Tokyo, Japan
ksatoh@nii.ac.jp
[2] Università del Piemonte Orientale, Vercelli, Italy
laura.giordano@uniupo.it
[3] Università di Torino, Turin, Italy
baldoni@di.unito.it

Abstract. Private International law (also called Conflict of laws) treats international affairs which involves legal systems of multiple countries. In the domain of private international law, *choice of jurisdiction* (the choice of country whose court can have a competence to treat the affairs) and *choice of law* (the choice of law on which the judgement of the affair is based) are main questions. In this paper, we give an implementation of both questions using extending PROLEG meta-interpreter. PROLEG is our legal knowledge representation language which consists of general rules and exceptions in one legal system. We extend PROLEG to handle different legal systems and reference of other legal systems within reasoning about international affairs.

1 Introduction

Private International law (also called Conflict of laws) is the body of jurisprudence that undertakes to reconcile a difference between the laws of different states or countries in a case in which a transaction or occurrence to the case has a connection to two or more jurisdictions (in Black's Law Dictionary, 9th edition). In this paper, we focus on reasoning about *choice of jurisdiction* (the choice of the state (or country) that should exercise jurisdiction over a case) and *choice of law* (the question of which jurisdiction's law should apply in a given case). These two reasoning problems are practically important if a judge solves international affairs in a litigation.

For example, we would like to reason about an international matter ("Taro is a legitimate child of Yoko" holds in Japan?), where Taro and Yoko are Japanese. At the first glance, there seems no problem. However, in Japan, we have the following rule to decide "legitimacy".

X is a legitimate child of Y if Y is married and X has a biological child relation with Y.

© Springer Nature Switzerland AG 2021
P. Baroni et al. (Eds.): CLAR 2021, LNAI 13040, pp. 60–75, 2021.
https://doi.org/10.1007/978-3-030-89391-0_4

Then, we need to check the marital status of Yoko and suppose that we have the following facts as well.

- John has a single nationality of Country1.
- John and Yoko agreed to get married and registered their marriage at Country1.
- John and Yoko have a son named Taro.

In this case, the marital status cannot be determined only by Japanese law and is somehow related with the law of Country1. Before this, we have to decide the Japanese court has a power of deciding the case (jurisdiction). Even if the Japanese court has a jurisdiction, this matter cannot be answered by only considering the legislation of Japan, but requires the determination of the choice of law which is the most suitable to solve the international affairs.

To solve the above question, we formalize PIL to decide "choice of law" for a legal issue: to determine an applicable law for an international legal matter in one country may require to refer to another law in another country which may result in a sequence of references of laws to different countries. We formalize this reasoning by a rule-based fragment of the modal language in [2], extended with context variables, and allows the interactions among contexts to be captured, context variables to occur within modalities and context names to be used as predicate arguments, thus supporting a simple combination of meta-predicates and modal constructs [3]. We then translate the formalism into a logic program (PROLOG) which reifies predicate to express legal matters with a variable to express the country of applicable law for the international legal matters [10].

As a related research, Dung and Sartor in [6] consider the issue of deciding the court having competence as well as the issue of establishing the legal system according to which the court has to decide (jurisdiction). Dung and Sartor provide an analysis of private international law and propose a formal model based on modular argumentation. Calegari [5] proposes an implementation of jurisdiction reasoning using argument-based logic programming based on the idea of Dung and Sartor. However, they do not consider "choice of law". As another related research the specificity of the rules in Conflict of Laws have been analyzed by Markovich [8] in the formalism of the input/output framework [7], where such rules assign a set of sets of norms (a legal system) to a given domain (a set of statements).

In this paper, we present a detailed implementation of PIL reasoning based on PROLEG [9] for choice of jurisdiction and choice of law. PROLEG is a logic programming language for rule-based legal knowledge representation and it represents laws in the form of "general rules" and "exceptions". This form of representation fits lawyers' reasoning patter and therefore is for lawyers easy to understand. In this work, we implement the choice of jurisdiction directly using PROLEG since the choice of jurisdiction does not involve considerations of other country's law and therefore, it is a direct application of PROLEG. However, to find out which jurisdiction accepts the case, we index PROLEG with the context of country so that we can reason about different jurisdictions in one system. For the choice of law, we need to extend a meta-interpreter of PROLEG written in

PROLOG so that a mechanism of choice of law for each legal conditions are introduced.

We put the source of extended PROLOG meta-interpreter for Modular-PROLEG with the choice of law function in the Appendix.

2 Reasoning About Jurisdiction

Since reasoning about competence in one country is done only by a domestic law where the litigation arises, usual PROLEG reasoning can be used. However to reason about jurisdiction for each country, we index PROLEG predicate with countries in the form of $P\#C$ (P: atom, C:country name). We call this version of PROLEG as *Modular-PROLEG* since C can be regarded as a module of PROLEG program.

2.1 Syntax of Modular-PROLEG

A Modular-PROLEG program $\mathcal{P}$ is a pair of a PROLEG rulebase $\mathcal{R}$ and a PROLEG factbase $\mathcal{F}$.

- PROLEG rulebase consists of the following expressions; a rule and an exception.
  - A **rule** of the form of Horn clauses:

    $$H\#C \Leftarrow B_1\#C_1, ..., B_n\#C_2.$$

    where $H\#C$ is called a head of the rules and $B_i\#C_i$'s is called a requisite.
  - An **exception** is an expression of the form $exception(H\#C, E\#C)$ or $exception(H, E)\#C$ where H, E are atoms each of which is the head of rule.

  The above rule means that $H\#C$ is satisfied in principle if all the requisites $B_i\#C_i$ are satisfied in each country C_i, whereas the exception means that"$H\#C$ is not satisfied if $E\#C$ is satisfied (even if all the requisites of a rule whose head is $H\#C$ are satisfied)".

  We sometimes write "$H\#C \Leftarrow B_1\#C, ..., B_n\#C.$" as "$(H \Leftarrow B_1, ..., B_n)\#C.$" if all the referred countries are same in the head and in the body of a rule and we write rules of "$(H \Leftarrow B_1, ..., B_n)\#C.$" for any country C as "$(H \Leftarrow B_1, ..., B_n)\#\_.$"
- PROLEG factbase consists of the following expression:

  $$fact(X\#C).$$

  where $X\#C$ is a prerequisite which is not any head of any rule in PROLEG rulebase. $fact(X\#C)$ means that X is the fact in the country C.

2.2   Modular-PROLEG Semantics a la Answer Set Programming

Let a Modular-PROLEG program $\mathcal{P}$ be $\langle \mathcal{R}, \mathcal{F} \rangle$ where $\mathcal{R}$ is a rulebase and $\mathcal{F}$ is a factbase. Let M be a set of atoms of the heads of rules, $H \# C$ plus a set of facts $\{F \# C | fact(F \# C) \in \mathcal{F}\}$. We define *a set of applicable rules w.r.t. M*, $\mathcal{R}^M$, as follows:

$$\{R \in \mathcal{R} | \text{there is no } E \# C \text{ s.t. } exception(head(R) \# C, E \# C) \in \mathcal{R} \text{ and } E \# C \in M\}.$$

This means that if some exception is found for a conclusion $head(R) \# C$ of a rule R, we do not consider such rule R for derivation. The semantics of $\mathcal{P}$ (called an *extension* of $\mathcal{P}$) is given as a set of ground atoms M s.t. $M = min(\mathcal{R}^M \cup \{F \# C | fact(F \# C) \in \mathcal{F}\})$ where $min(T)$ is the minimum model of a set of Horn clauses T where we regard $P \# C$ in T as an atom.

2.3   Meta Interpreter of Modular-PROLEG

Here is a meta-interpreter of Modular-PROLEG (Fig. 1. This is a non-deterministic algorithm in that we have a **select** operation. If we fail at some point in the algorithm, we assume that we backtrack to **select** operation and check other alternatives. We use the same algorithm with PROLEG meta-interpreter [9] except handling of the context of countries.

2.4   Example of Reasoning About Jurisdiction

Here is a part of Personal Status Litigation Act (LSA) in Japan. Article 3-2 of PSLA sets the rules for when actions can be filed in a Japanese court. Under the current rules, actions can be filed in a Japanese court where any of the following applies:

Article 3-2(1), PSLA: The defendant is domiciled in Japan.
Article 3-2(7), PSLA: The plaintiff lives in Japan and there are special circumstances that a family court in Japan should exercise jurisdiction to deliver equity between the parties or for due and prompt process of proceedings.

However, there is an exceptional situation of rejecting jurisdiction of Japan if the jurisdiction in Japan harms equity between the parties or leads to undue and delayed process of proceedings. (Article 3–5, PSLA).

Here is a PROLEG translation of the above rules and exception.

```
% PROLEG rules for Jurisdiction
% Personal Status Litigation Act.  (psla)

% (Article 3-2(1), PSLA)
(hasJuris(P,C) <= defendant(P,Def),domicile(Def,C))#C.
% (Article 3-2(7), PSLA)
(hasJuris(P,C) <= positive_special_circumstance(P))#C.
(positive_special_circumstance(P) <=
```

```
prove(S) goal set S
begin
  if S == ∅ then return(∅);
  forall an atom A#C ∈ S do
  if A#C is a fact s.t. fact(F#C) is in the factbase
    s.t. F#C is unifiable with A#C by most general unifier θ then
  begin
    S := (S − {A#C})θ; return(prove(S))
  end
  else % A#C should be a head in some rules
  begin
    select a rule (H ⇐ B₁, ..., Bₙ)#C in the rulebase
      whose head matches A#C with H#C by most general unifier θ;
    if such a rule does not exist then return(false);
    S := (S − {A#C} ∪ {B₁#C, ..., Bₙ#C})θ;
    if prove(S)==Sδ then
    begin
      for every exception(G,E)#c s.t. (A#C)θδ is unified with G#c
      by most general unifier η
        if prove({(E#c)θδη}) then return(false)
      return(Sθδ)
    end
    else if prove(S)==false then return(false)
  end
end
```

Fig. 1. Algorithm of Meta-Interpreter for Modular-PROLEG

```
   defendant(P,Def),plaintiff(P,Pla),
   deliver_equity(P,Def,Pla))#_.
(positive_special_circumstance(P) <=
   due_and_prompt_process(P))#_.

exception(hasJuris(P,C),negative_special_circumstance(P))#C.

% (Artcile 3-5, PSLA)
(negative_special_circumstance(P) <=
   defendant(P,Def),plaintiff(P,Pla),harm_equity(P,Def,Pla))#_.
(negative_special_circumstance(P) <=
   undue_and_delay_process(P))#_.
```

Suppose that we have the following facts.

```
% PROLEG facts for Jurisdiction
fact(plaintiff(cp_rel(taro,john),taro)#_).
fact(domicile(taro,japan)#_).
fact(defendant(cp_rel(taro,john),john)#_).
fact(domicile(john,country1)#_).
fact(due_and_prompt_process(cp_rel(taro,john))#japan).
```

```
fact(harm_equity(cp_rel(taro,john),john,taro)#country1).
```

Here is the output trace for hasJuris(cp_rel(taro,john), Country)#Country in which we can reason about which country has a competence (In this case, Japan) for the question "Taro is a child of John" (we call this relation "*cp_rel* between Taro and John"). For the Country1, although we can see that the defendant John lives in Country1, there is a negative special circumstance of having equity so the competence of the Country1 is rejected. For Japan, since there is a positive special circumstance of having due and prompt process, the competence of Japan is accepted.

```
% Reasoning about jurisdiction
  Starting to prove: hasJuris(cp_rel(taro,john),_3190)#_3190
  (hasJuris(cp_rel(taro,john),_3190)<=
    defendant(cp_rel(taro,john),_4370),
    domicile(_4370,_3190))#_3190 found.
   fact(defendant(cp_rel(taro,john),john)#_3190) found.
   fact(domicile(john,country1)#country1) found.
  hasJuris(cp_rel(taro,john),country1)#country1 succeeded.
  Exception check:negative_special_circumstance(cp_rel(taro,john))#country1
    Starting to prove: negative_special_circumstance(cp_rel(taro,john))#country1
    (negative_special_circumstance(cp_rel(taro,john))<=
      defendant(cp_rel(taro,john),_4618),
      plaintiff(cp_rel(taro,john),_4630),
      harm_equity(cp_rel(taro,john),_4618,_4630))#country1 found.
     fact(defendant(cp_rel(taro,john),john)#country1) found.
     fact(plaintiff(cp_rel(taro,john),taro)#country1) found.
     fact(harm_equity(cp_rel(taro,john),john,taro)#country1) found.
    negative_special_circumstance(cp_rel(taro,john))#country1 succeeded.
  Failed to deny negative_special_circumstance(cp_rel(taro,john))#country1
  (hasJuris(cp_rel(taro,john),_3190)<=
    positive_special_circumstance(cp_rel(taro,john)))#_3190 found.
   Starting to prove: positive_special_circumstance(cp_rel(taro,john))#_3190
   (positive_special_circumstance(cp_rel(taro,john))<=
     defendant(cp_rel(taro,john),_4398),
     plaintiff(cp_rel(taro,john),_4410),
     deliver_equity(cp_rel(taro,john),_4398,_4410))#_3190 found.
    fact(defendant(cp_rel(taro,john),john)#_3190) found.
    fact(plaintiff(cp_rel(taro,john),taro)#_3190) found.
    fact(deliver_equity(cp_rel(taro,john),john,taro)#_3190) not found.
   (positive_special_circumstance(cp_rel(taro,john))<=
     due_and_prompt_process(cp_rel(taro,john)))#_3190 found.
    fact(due_and_prompt_process(cp_rel(taro,john))#japan) found.
   positive_special_circumstance(cp_rel(taro,john))#japan succeeded.
  hasJuris(cp_rel(taro,john),japan)#japan succeeded.
  Exception check:negative_special_circumstance(cp_rel(taro,john))#japan
  No Exception: negative_special_circumstance(cp_rel(taro,john))#japan
************** Jurisdiction OK. **************
C = japan ;
```

3   Reasoning About Choice of Law

We review how to reason about international affairs involving choice of law defined in [3]. Given a legal matter P in one country, C, we would like to decide whether the matter is valid in the country in the following way.

1. We decide the country X whose law is applied to decide the matter P as follows.
   (a) There should be a rule in the private international law in C which indicates an applicable law in (possible another) country C' for the matter P in the country, C.
   (b) If $C' = C$, $X = C$.
   (c) Else ($C' \neq C$), we need to again decide the country X of the applicable law for P according to the private international law in C' (called "envoi" here)
   (d) If we detect a loop in the "envoi" (called "renvoi" here), we set the applicable law to the starting country of the loop. For example, if the private international laws makes this reference of applicable law, "$A \rightarrow B \rightarrow C \rightarrow D \rightarrow B$", then we decide an applicable law for the matter as country B.
2. We decompose the matter P into submatters according to a rule defined in the applicable law in X.
3. If a submatter is determined by a global fact and the global fact is in the fact base, the submatter is valid.
4. Otherwise, we iterate the process above (we decide an applicable law of the submatter and then check the submatter is valid in the applicable law).

In the following subsection, we show how to implement the above in Modular-PROLEG for PIL with the "envoi" mechanism.

3.1   Syntax of Modular-PROLEG for PIL

A Modular-PROLEG program for PIL $\mathcal{P}$ is a pair of a PROLEG rulebase $\mathcal{R}$ and a PROLEG factbase $\mathcal{F}$.

– PROLEG rulebase consists of two parts: *"choice of law" part $\mathcal{C}$* and *substantive part $\mathcal{S}$*. Both parts consist of rules and exceptions like Modular-PROLEG rule base.
   • In $\mathcal{C}$, the head of each rules are always of the form of a special atom $envoi(P\#C, AC)$ where $P\#C$ is a Modular-PROLEG atom and AC is a variable whose type is a country.
   • In $\mathcal{S}$, we do not use $envoi(\_, \_)$ anywhere.
– PROLEG factbase consists of the following expression:

$$fact(X)\#C.$$

3.2   Semantics for Modular-PROLEG for PIL

Let a Modular-PROLEG program for PIL $\mathcal{P}$ be $\langle \mathcal{R}, \mathcal{F} \rangle$. Let M be a set of atoms of the heads of rules, $H\#C$ plus a set of facts $\{F\#C|fact(F)\#C \in \mathcal{F}\}$. We define *a set of applicable rules w.r.t.* M, $\mathcal{R}^M$, as follows:

$\{R \in \mathcal{R}|$there is no $E\#C$ s.t. $exception(head(R)\#C, E\#C) \in \mathcal{R}$ and $E\#C \in M\}$.

The semantics of $\mathcal{P}$ (called an *extension* of $\mathcal{P}$) is given as a set of atoms M s.t. $M = min(\mathcal{R}^M \cup \{F\#C|fact(F)\#C \in \mathcal{F}\}) \cup$ $\{P\#C_0|envoi(P, C_1)\#C_0 \in M, envoi(P, C_2)\#C_1 \in M, ..., envoi(P, C_n)\#C_i \in M(i \leq n),$ and $P\#C_i \in M\}$.

The last set is the derived augmented international affairs based on the "envoi" mechanism.

3.3   Meta-interpreter of Modular-PROLEG for PIL

The meta-interpreter of Modular-PROLEG for PIL is the meta-interpreter of Modular-PROLEG augmented by the choice of law mechanism as follows (Figs. 2 and 3). Every time we decompose an international affair into sub international affairs, we reason about choice of law which applies to each sub international affairs.

3.4   Example of Reasoning About International Affairs

We show an example of reasoning about international affairs, namely the question whether "Taro is a legitimate child of Yoko" is valid in Japan? (we call this relation "*lcp_rel* between Taro and Yoko").

We firstly decide which country's law applicable to determine the above question. Suppose that we have the following rules in Japan for choice of law for legitimate child-parent relationship:

(*lcp_rel1*) We use law of the home country of a parent, or
(*lcp_rel2*) We use law of the home country of the nationality of a spouse of the parent.

We check rule (*lcp_rel1*), we need to decide the home country of the parent (in this case, Yoko) and deciding the home country could be an international affair. Note that inside the process of "choice of law", we might have a nested reasoning of solving the international affair and this deciding problem of home country is such a nested reasoning. So we firstly need to decide which country's law is applied for the home country problem. Suppose that we have the following rule for the choice of law for "home country" as follows (we assume this rule is valid in Japan and also in Country1).

– Home country will be determined in the law in the country of the court.

---

pilprove(S) goal set S
begin
  if $S == \emptyset$ **then return**($\emptyset$);
  forall an atom $A\#C \in S$ **do**
  if $A\#C$ is a fact s.t. `fact`($F\#C$) is in the factbase
    s.t. $F\#C$ is unifiable with $A\#C$ by most general unifier θ **then**
  begin
    $S := (S - \{A\#C\})\theta$; **return**(pilprove($S$))
  end
  else % $A\#C$ should be a head in some rules
  begin
    $AC :=$ choice_of_law($A\#C, \{\}$) % AC: Chosen law for A in C
    select a rule $(H \Leftarrow B_1, ..., B_n)\#AC$ in the rulebase
      whose head matches $A\#AC$ with $H\#AC$ by most general unifier θ;
    if such a rule does not exist **then return**(false);
    $S := (S - \{A\#C\} \cup \{B_1\#AC, ..., B_n\#AC\})\theta$;
    if pilprove(S)==$S\delta$ **then**
    begin
      for every exception(G,E)$\#c$ s.t. $(A\#C)\theta\delta$ is unified with $G\#c$
      by most general unifier η
        if pilprove($\{(E\#c)\theta\delta\eta\}$) **then return**(false)
      return($S\theta\delta$)
    end
    else if pilprove(S)==**false then return**(false)
  end
end

Fig. 2. Algorithm of modular-PROLEG meta-interpreter for PIL

---

choice_of_law($A\#C,ReferringHistory$) $A\#C$: a goal
begin
  if $C \in ReferringHistory$ **return**(C); %Renvoi
  else if $A == envoi(\_,\_)$ **then return**(C) % envoi's chosen law is always C's law.
  else
  begin
    $\{envoi(A\#C, EC)\theta\} :=$ **return**(solve($pil, \{envoi(A\#C, EC)\}$));
    return(choice_of_law(($A\#EC)\theta,EC\theta \cup ReferringHistory$)
  end
end

Fig. 3. Algorithm of choice of law

Since in this case, lcp_rel is raised in the Japanese court, we use Japanese law to determine the home country of the Yoko. Suppose that we have the following substantive law for deciding the home country (we assume this rule is valid in Japan and also in Country1).

- The home country is the person's nationality, if the person has only one nationality.

In this case, Yoko has a single nationality (Japanese) so her home country is Japan. Then, we use the following Japanese substantive law to determine *lcp_rel*.

- A child X and a parent Y has a legitimate child relationship if X is married (called "*mrg*" here) and X and Y have a biological child-parent relation (called "*bcp_rel*" here).

Then, we have to determine Yoko's marital status. To decide marital status, we need to decide which country's law is applicable for this. Suppose that there is the following universal rule (valid in Japan and Country1) for "choice of law":

- We use law of the home country of either spouse.

Suppose that we choose the law of Yoko's home country (Japan). Suppose that we have the following Japanese substantive law for marriage:

- A marriage relationship holds between Spouse 1 and Spouse 2 if there is an agreement on marriage between Spouse1 and Spouse 2 and they register their marriage in Japan.
- There is an exception for the above rule in that if divorce between Spouse 1 and Spouse 2 is made after the marriage, the marriage is no longer valid.

In this case, although there is an agreement between Yoko and John, the marriage was registered only in Country1 (See Introduction). We cannot prove the marital status for Yoko using Japanese law.

On the other hand, suppose that we choose the law of the home country of Yoko's spouse, John (Country1). Suppose that we have the following Country1's substantive law for marriage:

- A marriage relationship holds between Spouse 1 and Spouse 2 if there is an agreement on marriage between Spouse1 and Spouse 2 and they register their marriage in Country1.
- There is an exception for the above rule in that if divorce between Spouse 1 and Spouse 2 is made after the marriage, the marriage is no longer valid.

In this case, there is registration of marriage between Yoko and John in Country1 so the marriage between Yoko and John could be proved in Japan by default. However, suppose that John and Yoko made a divorce in Country1 after the marriage. In this case, the marriage between Yoko and John is not valid. Therefore, we cannot prove *mrg* status between Yoko and John so *lcp_rel* is not satisfied.

We show a program in Modular-PROLEG for PIL and the trace of reasoning as follows.

```
% PROLEG program for Private International Law
% RC: referred country
% lcp_rel: legitimate_child_parent_relation
% mrg: marriage
```

```
% hmc: home_country
% HMC: Home_Country
% agr: agreement
% rgst: registering
% Sp: Spouse
% Chld: Child
% Prnt: Parent
% s_nat: single_nationality
% CtznList: CitizenshipList
% bcp_rel: bilogical_child_parent_relation

(envoi(lcp_rel(_,Prnt),RC) <= hmc(Prnt,RC))#_.
(envoi(lcp_rel(_,Prnt),RC) <= mrg(Prnt,PrntSp), hmc(PrntSp,RC))#japan.
(envoi(lcp_rel(_,Prnt),RC) <= mrg(PrntSp,Prnt), hmc(PrntSp,RC))#japan.
(envoi(mrg(P,S),RC) <= claim(mrg,P,S),hmc(P,RC))#_.
(envoi(mrg(P,S),RC) <= claim(mrg,P,S),hmc(S,RC))#_.
(envoi(dvrc(P,S),RC) <= claim(dvrc,P,S),hmc(P,RC))#_.
(envoi(dvrc(P,S),RC) <= claim(dvrc,P,S),hmc(S,RC))#_.
% For every country, home country rule is always each country's rule.
(envoi(hmc(_,_),RC) <= call(RC=C))#C.

% Domestic Rules
(mrg(Sp1,Sp2) <= agr(mrg,Sp1,Sp2), rgst(mrg,Sp1,Sp2))#_.
exception(mrg(Sp1,Sp2),dvrc(Sp1,Sp2))#_. % (dvrc: divorce)
(dvrc(Sp1,Sp2) <= agr(dvrc,Sp1,Sp2), rgst(dvrc,Sp1,Sp2))#_.

(lcp_rel(Chld,Prnt) <= mrg(Prnt,_), bcp_rel(Chld,Prnt))#_.
(hmc(P,HMC) <= s_nat(P,HMC))#_.


% Substantive Facts
fact(s_nat(john,country1))#_.
fact(s_nat(yoko,japan))#_.
fact(bcp_rel(taro,john))#_.
fact(bcp_rel(taro,yoko))#_.
fact(agr(mrg,john,yoko))#_.
fact(agr(mrg,yoko,john))#_.
fact(rgst(mrg,john,yoko))#country1.
fact(rgst(mrg,yoko,john))#country1.
fact(agr(dvrc,john,yoko))#_.
fact(agr(dvrc,yoko,john))#_.
fact(rgst(dvrc,john,yoko))#country1.
fact(rgst(dvrc,yoko,john))#country1.
fact(claim(mrg,john,yoko))#_.
fact(claim(mrg,yoko,john))#_.
fact(claim(dvrc,john,yoko))#_.
fact(claim(dvrc,yoko,john))#_.


% Reasoning about international affairs
  Starting to prove: lcp_rel(taro,yoko)#japan
```

% Reasoning about choice of law for lcp_rel(taro,yoko) is started.
    Starting to prove: envoi(lcp_rel(taro,yoko),_9406)#japan
    (envoi(lcp_rel(taro,yoko),_9406)<=
      hmc(yoko,_9406))#japan found.
    Starting to prove: hmc(yoko,_9406)#japan
        Starting to prove: envoi(hmc(yoko,_9406),_9484)#japan
        (envoi(hmc(yoko,_9406),_9484)<=
          call(_9484=japan))#japan found.
    envoi(hmc(yoko,_9406),japan)#japan succeeded.
    Exception check: envoi(hmc(yoko,_9406),japan)#japan
    No Exception:envoi(hmc(yoko,_9406),japan)#japan
    applying_country_for(hmc(yoko,_9406)) found(japan)
    (hmc(yoko,_9406)<=
      s_nat(yoko,_9406))#japan found.
    fact(s_nat(yoko,japan)#japan) found.
    hmc(yoko,japan)#japan succeeded.
    Exception check: hmc(yoko,japan)#japan
    No Exception:hmc(yoko,japan)#japan
    envoi(lcp_rel(taro,yoko),japan)#japan succeeded.
    Exception check: envoi(lcp_rel(taro,yoko),japan)#japan
    No Exception:envoi(lcp_rel(taro,yoko),japan)#japan
    applying_country_for(lcp_rel(taro,yoko)) found(japan)
% Choice of law for lcp_rel(taro,yoko) is determined as Japan's law.
% Substantive reasoning for lcp_rel(taro,yoko) is started
    (lcp_rel(taro,yoko)<=
      mrg(yoko,_9760),
      bcp_rel(taro,yoko))#japan found.
    Starting to prove: mrg(yoko,_9760)#japan
% Reasoning about choice of law for mrg(yoko,_9760) is started.
    Starting to prove: envoi(mrg(yoko,_9760),_9826)#japan
    (envoi(mrg(yoko,_9760),_9826)<=
      claim(mrg,yoko,_9760),
      hmc(yoko,_9826))#japan found.
    fact(claim(mrg,yoko,john)#japan) found.
    Starting to prove: hmc(yoko,_9826)#japan
        Starting to prove: envoi(hmc(yoko,_9826),_9952)#japan
        (envoi(hmc(yoko,_9826),_9952)<=
          call(_9952=japan))#japan found.
    envoi(hmc(yoko,_9826),japan)#japan succeeded.
    Exception check: envoi(hmc(yoko,_9826),japan)#japan
    No Exception:envoi(hmc(yoko,_9826),japan)#japan
    applying_country_for(hmc(yoko,_9826)) found(japan)
    (hmc(yoko,_9826)<=
      s_nat(yoko,_9826))#japan found.
    fact(s_nat(yoko,japan)#japan) found.
    hmc(yoko,japan)#japan succeeded.
    Exception check: hmc(yoko,japan)#japan
    No Exception:hmc(yoko,japan)#japan
    envoi(mrg(yoko,john),japan)#japan succeeded.
    Exception check: envoi(mrg(yoko,john),japan)#japan

```
      No Exception:envoi(mrg(yoko,john),japan)#japan
      applying_country_for(mrg(yoko,john)) found(japan)
% Choice of law for mrg(yoko,john) is determined as Japan's law.
% Substantive reasoning for mrg(yoko,john) by Japan's law is started.
      (mrg(yoko,john)<=
         agr(mrg,yoko,john),
         rgst(mrg,yoko,john))#japan found.
      fact(agr(mrg,yoko,john)#japan) found.
      fact(rgst(mrg,yoko,john)#japan) not found.
% Substantive reasoning for mrg(yoko,john) by Japan's law is failed
%    since the condition is not satisfied.
% Another reasoning about choice of law for mrg(yoko,_9760) is started.
      (envoi(mrg(yoko,_9760),_9826)<=
         claim(mrg,yoko,_9760),
         hmc(_9760,_9826))#japan found.
      fact(claim(mrg,yoko,john)#japan) found.
      Starting to prove: hmc(john,_9826)#japan
         Starting to prove: envoi(hmc(john,_9826),_9952)#japan
         (envoi(hmc(john,_9826),_9952)<=
            call(_9952=japan))#japan found.
         envoi(hmc(john,_9826),japan)#japan succeeded.
         Exception check: envoi(hmc(john,_9826),japan)#japan
         No Exception:envoi(hmc(john,_9826),japan)#japan
         applying_country_for(hmc(john,_9826)) found(japan)
      (hmc(john,_9826)<=
         s_nat(john,_9826))#japan found.
      fact(s_nat(john,country1)#japan) found.
      hmc(john,country1)#japan succeeded.
      Exception check: hmc(john,country1)#japan
      No Exception:hmc(john,country1)#japan
   envoi(mrg(yoko,john),country1)#japan succeeded.
   Exception check: envoi(mrg(yoko,john),country1)#japan
   No Exception:envoi(mrg(yoko,john),country1)#japan
   applying_country_for(mrg(yoko,john)) found(country1)
% Choice of law for mrg(yoko,john) is determined as country1's law.
% Substantive reasoning for mrg(yoko,john) by country1's law is started
      (mrg(yoko,john)<=
         agr(mrg,yoko,john),
         rgst(mrg,yoko,john))#country1 found.
      fact(agr(mrg,yoko,john)#country1) found.
      fact(rgst(mrg,yoko,john)#country1) found.
   mrg(yoko,john)#country1 succeeded.
   Exception check: mrg(yoko,john)#country1
   Try to deny: dvrc(yoko,john)#country1
      Starting to prove: dvrc(yoko,john)#country1
% Reasoning about choice of law for dvrc(yoko,john) is started.
         Starting to prove: envoi(dvrc(yoko,john),_10552)#country1
         (envoi(dvrc(yoko,john),_10552)<=
            claim(dvrc,yoko,john),
            hmc(john,_10552))#country1 found.
```

```
fact(claim(dvrc,yoko,john)#country1) found.
Starting to prove: hmc(john,_10552)#country1
  Starting to prove: envoi(hmc(john,_10552),_10678)#country1
  (envoi(hmc(john,_10552),_10678)<=
    call(_10678=country1))#country1 found.
  envoi(hmc(john,_10552),country1)#country1 succeeded.
  Exception check: envoi(hmc(john,_10552),country1)#country1
  No Exception:envoi(hmc(john,_10552),country1)#country1
  applying_country_for(hmc(john,_10552)) found(country1)
  (hmc(john,_10552)<=
    s_nat(john,_10552))#country1 found.
  fact(s_nat(john,country1)#country1) found.
  hmc(john,country1)#country1 succeeded.
  Exception check: hmc(john,country1)#country1
  No Exception:hmc(john,country1)#country1
envoi(dvrc(yoko,john),country1)#country1 succeeded.
Exception check: envoi(dvrc(yoko,john),country1)#country1
No Exception:envoi(dvrc(yoko,john),country1)#country1
applying_country_for(dvrc(yoko,john)) found(country1)
% Choice of law for dvrc(yoko,john) is determined as country1's law.
% Substantive reasoning for dvrc(yoko,john) by country1's law is started
  (dvrc(yoko,john)<=
    agr(dvrc,yoko,john),
    rgst(dvrc,yoko,john))#country1 found.
  fact(agr(dvrc,yoko,john)#country1) found.
  fact(rgst(dvrc,yoko,john)#country1) found.
  dvrc(yoko,john)#country1 succeeded.
  Exception check: dvrc(yoko,john)#country1
  No Exception:dvrc(yoko,john)#country1
  Failed to deny dvrc(yoko,john)#country1
% Substantive reasoning for mrg(yoko,john) by country1's law is failed
%   since exception is found.
```

4   Conclusion

We give an implementation of reasoning about "choice of jurisdiction" and substantive international affairs based on Modular-PROLEG which involves "choice of law". For future works, we would like to develop more advanced man-machine interface to visualize reasoning process, and we would also aim at investigating comparison with other approaches for representing reasoning in private international law, especially in dealing with exceptions and contextual reasoning in the literature, including Defeasible Logic [1] and the CKR (Contextualized Knowledge Repositories) framework by Bozzato et al. [4].

Appendix

```
% Meta Interpreter for Modular-PROLEG (for PIL) program
% Top Level Goal is either
% solve(plain,P#Country) for a query of Modular-PROLEG.
% solve(pil,P#Country) for a query of Modular-PROLEG for PIL.

solve(Phase,(P,Q)#Country):-!,
    solve(Phase,P#Country), solve(Phase,Q#Country).
solve(_,call(P)#_):-!,   % for built_in predicate
    call(P).
solve(_,P#Country):-
    is_fact(P#Country),!,
    fact(P#Country).
solve(Phase,P#Country):- % This is a main part.
    (Phase = pil ->
        choice(P#Country,AC,[])); % For PIL, we firstly calculate choice of law.
        AC = Country  % For ordinary Modular-PROLEG, we do nothing.
    ),
    (P <= Q)#AC,
    solve(Phase,Q#AC),
    no_counter_argument(Phase,P#AC).

no_counter_argument(_,P#Country):-
    \+exception(P,_)#Country.
no_counter_argument(Phase,P#Country):-
    exception(P,R)#Country,
    unsolve(Phase,R#Country).

unsolve(Phase,R#Country):-
    groundize(R#Country), % We need this for correctness of NAF.
    solve(Phase,R#Country),
    !,
    fail.

choice(_#_,C,History):-  % If renvoi happens,
    member(C,History),!. % AC becomes the starting point of loop.
choice(envoi(_,_)#C,C,_):-!. % Envoi rule is always each country's rule
choice(P#C,AC,History):-
    !,
    solve(pil,envoi(P,RC)#C), % We compute one step forward for choice of law.
    choice(P#RC,AC,[RC|History]).

is_fact(P#_):-
    \+ (P<=_)#_.

groundize((P,Q)#Country):-!, groundize(P#Country), groundize(Q#Country).
groundize(P#Country):- is_fact(P#Country),!, fact(P#Country).
groundize(P#Country):- (P <= Q)#Country, groundize(Q#Country).
```

References

1. Antoniou, G., Billington, D., Governatori, G., Maher, M.J.: Representation results for defeasible logic. ACM Trans. Comput. Log. **2**(2), 255–287 (2001). https://doi.org/10.1145/371316.371517
2. Baldoni, M., Giordano, L., Martelli, A.: A modal extension of logic programming: modularity, beliefs and hypothetical reasoning. J. Log. Comput. **8**(5), 597–635 (1988)
3. Baldoni, M., Giordano, L., Satoh, K.: Renvoi in private international law: a formalization with modal context. In: Proceedings of JURIX 2019, pp. 157–162 (2019)
4. Bozzato, L., Eiter, T., Serafini, L.: Enhancing context knowledge repositories with justifiable exceptions. Artif. Intell. **257**, 72–126 (2018)
5. Calegari, R., Contissa, G., Pisano, G., Sartor, G., Sartor, G.: Arg-tuProlog: a modular logic argumentation tool for PIL. In: Profeedings of JURIX 2020, pp. 265–268 (2020)
6. Dung, P.M., Sartor, G.: The modular logic of private international law. Artif. Intell. Law **19**(2–3), 233–261 (2011). https://doi.org/10.1007/s10506-011-9112-5
7. Makinson, D., van der Torre, L.: What is input/output logic? In: Löwe, B., Malzkom, W., Räsch, T. (eds.) Foundations of the Formal Sciences II. Trends in Logic (Studia Logica Library), vol. 17, pp. 163–174. Springer, Heidelberg (2003). https://doi.org/10.1007/978-94-017-0395-6_12
8. Markovich, R.: On the formal structure of rules in conflict of laws. In: Proceedings of JURIX 2019, pp. 199–204 (2019)
9. Satoh, K., et al.: PROLEG: an implementation of the presupposed ultimate fact theory of Japanese civil code by PROLOG technology. In: Onada, T., Bekki, D., McCready, E. (eds.) JSAI-isAI 2010. LNCS (LNAI), vol. 6797, pp. 153–164. Springer, Heidelberg (2011). https://doi.org/10.1007/978-3-642-25655-4_14
10. Satoh, K., Baldoni, M., Giordano, L.: Reasoning about applicable law in private international law in logic programming. In: Proceedings of JURIX 2020, pp. 281–285 (2020)

Full Papers

Collective Argumentation
with Topological Restrictions

Weiwei Chen(✉) ⓘD

Institute of Logic and Cognition and Department of Philosophy,
Sun Yat-sen University, Guangzhou, China
chenww26@mail2.sysu.edu.cn

Abstract. Collective argumentation studies how to reach a collective decision that is acceptable to the group in a debate. I introduce the concept of topological restriction to enrich collective argumentation. Topological restrictions are rational constraints assumed to be satisfied by individual agents. We assume that in a debate, for every pair of arguments that are being considered, every agent indicates whether the first one attacks the second, i.e., an agent's argumentative stance is characterized as an argumentation framework, and only argumentation frameworks that satisfy topological restrictions are allowed. The topological constraints we consider in this paper include acyclicity, symmetry, as well as a newly defined topological property called t-self-defense. We show that when profiles of argumentation frameworks provided by agents satisfy topological restrictions, impossibility results during aggregation can be avoided. Furthermore, if a profile is topological-restricted with respect to t-self-defense, then the majority rule preserves admissibility during aggregation.

Keywords: Collective argumentation · Topological restriction · Social choice theory

1 Introduction

Abstract argumentation theory is a formalism that deals with the formalization of argumentation. It has been applied for over twenty years to analyze the argument justification. When there are several agents involved in a debate, such as juridical and parliamentary debates, they may have different opinions on the evaluation of the acceptability of arguments or the justification of attacks between arguments. Collective argumentation has been discussed extensively in the literature of formal argumentation (see [6,7]). Among them, some are dedicated to investigating the aggregation of arguments [9,12,13,23], while others study the aggregation of attacks [7,8,10,11,21].

The problem of aggregation of abstract argumentation frameworks has received attention in the literature in the last decade or so [7,12,13,23]. On aggregation rules, some study the performance of simple and straightforward rules, such as the majority rule, quota rules, while some other study rules with high

© Springer Nature Switzerland AG 2021
P. Baroni et al. (Eds.): CLAR 2021, LNAI 13040, pp. 79–93, 2021.
https://doi.org/10.1007/978-3-030-89391-0_5

complexity, such as distance-based rules. It is worth mentioning that while different aggregation mechanisms, different aggregation entities have been employed, a common feature of these work is that they study the aggregation of argumentation frameworks without restrictions. In other words, no restriction is imposed on the argumentation frameworks. Each individual agent provides an arbitrary argumentation framework that represents her argumentative stance in a debate. In this case, we assume that for every pair of arguments that are being considered in a debate, every agent indicates whether the first attack the second. Given a semantic property agreed upon by the individual agents, the output may or may not satisfy such property.

I propose the notion of topological restriction to enrich collective argumentation. Topological restrictions will help us to get rid of argumentation frameworks that are not desirable. For example, we may consider it irrational for an individual agent to support argumentation frameworks that contain odd-length cycles, with which an argument may indirectly attack and support another. In this case, the acceptance status of the second argument is controversial and we would like to avoid such controversy. In such circumstances, we can require that agents' argumentation frameworks satisfy acyclicity. For acyclic argumentation frameworks, the acceptance status of arguments is unambiguous as the grounded extension coincides with the unique preferred extension that is also stable. There are other topological properties that can help us avoid controversy, such as symmetry. For symmetric argumentation frameworks, the attack-relation is symmetric. As a consequence, every symmetric argumentation framework is coherent (which means that every preferred extension is stable) and relatively grounded (which means that the grounded extension is the intersection of all its preferred extensions).

Our contribution is two-fold: first, we introduce the notion of topological restriction to the aggregation of argumentation frameworks and study several topological restrictions during aggregation, including acyclicity, symmetry, and a newly defined topological property called t-self-defense. We show that with topological restrictions, impossibility results during aggregation of attack-relations can be avoided. To be specific, there are some aggregation rules that preserve demanding properties. Also, we show that, if a profile is topological-restricted with respect to t-self-defense, then the majority rule, a rule that is very appealing on normative grounds, as it treats all agents in a "fair" manner, preserves admissibility during aggregation.

The remainder of the paper is organized as follows. Section 2 presents relevant concepts from the theory of abstract argumentation, including some of the fundamentals of the model of abstract argumentation and topological. Section 3 introduces our model and Sect. 4 introduces the concept of topological restriction. Section 5 presents our preservation results with topological restrictions of acyclicity and symmetry. Section 6 introduces a topological property called t-self-defense and preservation results for admissibility with t-self-defense. Section 7 concludes the paper.

2   Argumentation Framework and Topological Property

An argumentation framework is a pair $AF = \langle Arg, \rightharpoonup \rangle$, in which Arg is a set of arguments and $\rightharpoonup$ is a set of binary relations called the attack relation built on Arg. Given two arguments $A, B \in Arg$, $A \rightharpoonup B$ if and only if A attacks B. Given a set of arguments $\Delta \subseteq Arg$, we say that Δ is *conflict-free* if there are no arguments $A, B \in Arg$ such that $A \rightharpoonup B$ is the case; we say that Δ defends $A \in Arg$ if for every argument $B \in Arg$ with $B \rightharpoonup A$ is the case, there is an argument $C \in \Delta$ such that $C \rightharpoonup B$; we say that Δ is self-defending if Δ defends every argument in Δ; we say that Δ is *admissible* if Δ is conflict-free and self-defending; furthermore, we say that:

- Δ is complete if Δ is admissible and every argument defended by Δ is included in Δ.
- Δ is grounded if Δ is the minimal complete extension (w.r.t. set inclusion)
- Δ is preferred if Δ is a maximal admissible set (w.r.t. set inclusion)
- Δ is stable if Δ is conflict-free and attacks every argument that is not in Δ.

A semantics defines which set of arguments can be accepted, which can be considered as a property of sets of arguments. We now present another family of properties considered in the literature in abstract argumentation, namely *topological properties* of argumentation frameworks. While topological properties of argumentation frameworks have no immediately apparent relationships with argumentation semantics, they play an important role in the study of such semantics. As early as in the seminal paper by Dung [16], well-foundedness has been identified as a topological properties and has been shown that it is a sufficient condition for agreement among grounded, preferred, and stable semantics, namely the grounded extension is the only preferred and stable extension.

Definition 1. *An argumentation framework is well-founded if and only if there exists no infinite sequence* $A_0, A_1, \cdots, A_n$ *of arguments such that for each i,* $A_{i+1} \rightharpoonup A_i$ *is the case.*

In the case of a finite argumentation framework, well-foundedness coincides with *acyclicity* of the attack relation.

Definition 2. *An argumentation framework* $AF = \langle Arg, \rightharpoonup \rangle$ *is coherent if every preferred extension of AF is stable.*

The absence of odd-length cycles is a sufficient condition to ensure that the argumentation framework is coherent, i.e., ensure that stable extensions exist and coincide with preferred extensions.

Definition 3. *An argumentation framework* $AF = \langle Arg, \rightharpoonup \rangle$ *is a symmetric argumentation framework if* $\rightharpoonup$ *is symmetric, nonempty and irreflexive.*

In other words, an argumentation framework $AF = \langle Arg, \rightharpoonup \rangle$ is symmetric if for any pair of argument $A, B \in Arg$ with A attacks B is the case, then B will be counter-attacked by A.

Other topological properties of argumentation frameworks in the literature include *antisymmetry* (i.e., the absence of mutual attack between arguments), *directionality property*, introduced in [4], *SCC-recursiveness property*, introduced in [5], *almost determinedness property*, introduced in [3], as well as *limited controversy* introduced by Dung in his seminal work [17].

3   The Aggregation Model

Fix a set of arguments Arg as well as a set of agents $N = \{1, \cdots, n\}$, suppose that each agent provides an argumentation framework, reflecting her individual views on the status of possible attacks between arguments. Thus, we are given a profile of attack-relations $\rightharpoonup = (\rightharpoonup_1, \ldots, \rightharpoonup_n)$. Sometimes we may want to aggregate individual argumentation frameworks to obtain a single argumentation framework that reflects the consensus of the group, what would be a good method to arrive at this goal? In this paper, we focus on the method from social choice theory, an aggregation rule is a function that maps any given profile of attack-relations into a single attack-relation $F : (2^{Arg \times Arg})^n \to 2^{Arg \times Arg}$. We use $N_{att}^{\rightharpoonup} := \{i \in N \mid att \in (\rightharpoonup_i)\}$ to denote the set of *supporters* of the attack att in profile $\rightharpoonup$.

Now we present several intuitively desirable property of aggregation rules. Such properties are called axioms in the literature on social choice theory [1]. All of these axioms are adapted of axioms formulated in the literature on graph aggregation [18] and have been defined in the work by Chen and Endriss [12].

Definition 4. *An aggregation rule is said to be* neutral *if $N_{att}^{\rightharpoonup} = N_{att'}^{\rightharpoonup}$ implies $att \in F(\rightharpoonup) \Leftrightarrow att' \in F(\rightharpoonup)$ for all profiles $\rightharpoonup$ and all attacks att, att'.*

Definition 5. *An aggregation rule is said to be* independent *if $N_{att}^{\rightharpoonup} = N_{att}^{\rightharpoonup'}$ implies $att \in F(\rightharpoonup) \Leftrightarrow att \in F(\rightharpoonup)$ for all attacks att and all profiles $\rightharpoonup, \rightharpoonup'$.*

Definition 6. *An aggregation rule is said to be* unanimous *if $F(\rightharpoonup) \supseteq (\rightharpoonup_1) \cap \cdots \cap (\rightharpoonup_n)$ is the case for all profiles $\rightharpoonup = (\rightharpoonup_1, \ldots, \rightharpoonup_n)$.*

Definition 7. *An aggregation rule is said to be* grounded *if $F(\rightharpoonup) \subseteq (\rightharpoonup_1) \cup \cdots \cup (\rightharpoonup_n)$ is the case for all profiles $\rightharpoonup = (\rightharpoonup_1, \ldots, \rightharpoonup_n)$.*

Thus, an aggregation rule is neutral if two attacks receive the same votes in a profile, then the acceptance status of them are the same in the outcome, i.e., attacks are treated symmetrically; an aggregation rule is independent if the acceptance of an attack only depends on its supporters; unanimity assumes that if an attack is accepted by everyone, then it should be accepted in the collective outcome; groundedness postulates that only attacks with at least one supporter can be collective accepted.

Two special families of aggregation we consider in this paper are the quota rules and the dictatorship rules. All of them are simple rules that are adaptations from other parts of social choice theory, such as judgment aggregation [19] and graph aggregation [18]. Notably, all of them are well defined in [12].

Definition 8. *Let* $q \in \{1, \ldots, n\}$. *The **quota rule** F_q with quota q accepts all those attacks that are supported by at least q agents:*

$$F_q(\rightarrowtail) = \{att \in Arg \times Arg \mid \#N^{\rightarrowtail}_{att} \geqslant q\}$$

The *majority rule* is the quota rule F_q with $q = \lceil \frac{n+1}{2} \rceil$. Two further quota rules are also of special interest. The *unanimity rule* only accepts attacks that are supported by everyone, i.e., this is F_q with $q = n$. The *nomination rule* is the quota rule F_q with $q = 1$. Despite being a somewhat extreme choice, the nomination rule has some intuitive appeal in the context of argumentation, as it reflects the idea that we should take seriously any conflict between arguments raised by at least one member of the group.

Definition 9. *The **dictatorship rule** F_{D_i} of dictator $i \in N$ accepts all those attacks that are accepted by agent i:*

$$F_{D_i}(\rightarrowtail) = \rightarrowtail_i$$

Thus, under a dictatorship, to compute the outcome, we simply copy the attack-relation of the dictator. Intuitively speaking, dictatorships in particular, are unattractive rules, as they unfairly exclude everyone except i from the decision process.

We consider the preservation of semantic properties of argumentation frameworks. An AF-property $P \subseteq 2^{Arg \times Arg}$ is the set of all attack-relations on Arg that satisfy P, we denote it by $P(\rightarrowtail)$. For example, non-emptiness of the grounded extension is a simple semantic property, an AF satisfies such property if there is at least one argument that is not attacked by any argument in AF.

Definition 10 (Preservation). *Fix a finite set Arg of arguments and a set of $N = \{1, \cdots, n\}$ agents. Suppose that each agent provides an argumentation framework, which reflects her individual views on the status of possible attacks between arguments. An aggregation rule F is said to preserve a property P if for every profile $\rightarrowtail$ it is the case that $P(\rightarrowtail_i)$ being the case for all agents $i \in N$ then $P(F(\rightarrowtail))$.*

Thus, in the case where all agents' attack-relations satisfy P, F preserves P if the outcome of F satisfies P as well. The AF-properties we will discuss in this paper include *conflict-freeness, admissibility, being an extension under a specific semantics, non-emptiness of the grounded extension*, and *coherence. Conflict-freeness* is a AF-property which requires that, if for all sets $\Delta \subseteq Arg$, whenever Δ is conflict-free in $\langle Arg, \rightarrowtail_i \rangle$ for all agents $i \in N$, we would like that Δ is conflict-free in $\langle Arg, F(\rightarrowtail) \rangle$. If it is the case, then we say that F preserves conflict-freeness. The AF-property of *admissibility* can be defined in the same way. *Being an extension under a specific semantics* require that, given a set of arguments Δ, Δ is an extension of a given semantics in $\langle Arg, \rightarrowtail_i \rangle$ for all agents $i \in N$, then Δ is also an extension of the semantics of $\langle Arg, F(\rightarrowtail) \rangle$. Finally, *coherence* is also an attractive properties, because-if satisfied by an argumentation framework-they ensure that preferred and stable extensions will coincide and result in the same recommendations about which arguments to accept, thereby making decisions less controversial. It is worth noting that topological properties are a special subset of AF-properties.

4 Topological Restriction

In this section, I introduce the notion of topological restriction for the aggregation of attack-relations of argumentation frameworks. What are the intuitions behind this notion? First, while it is easy to verify that most semantic properties cannot be preserved by the majority rule[1], we cannot get things going for any aggregation rule that satisfies desirable axiomatic requirements. As an example, we present the following impossibility theorem.

Theorem 1 (Chen and Endriss, 2019). *For* $|Arg| \geqslant 5$, *any unanimous, grounded, and independent aggregation rule F that preserves either complete or preferred extensions must be a dictatorship.*

To prove Theorem 1, Chen and Endriss have used a technique developed by Endriss and Grandi for the more general framework of graph aggregation, which in turn was inspired by the seminal work on preference aggregation of Arrow [2]. Clearly, Theorem 1 is an impossibility result. At the heart of Theorem 1 (as well as other impossibility results), there are three types of conditions: axioms of aggregation rules, semantic properties of argumentation frameworks, as well as argumentation frameworks allowed to input. To cope with such negative results, one direction is relaxing such conditions, requirements, or argumentation frameworks allowed.

Before going any further, we recall approaches that aim to deal with impossibility results in the literature on social choice theory. In the literature on judgment aggregation, there is an approach that proposes to restrict the range of agendas, namely restricting the range of agendas on which we can perform satisfactorily with aggregation rules. Another approach in judgment aggregation is *domain restriction*, namely restricting the profiles allowed to input. Introduced by List [20], *unidimensional alignment* is a widely known way of domain restriction. The idea of unidimensional alignment is that only profiles which are unidimensionally aligned are allowed to the aggregation rule. *Value restriction* is another type of domain restriction, for which the idea was first introduced by Sen [22] for preference aggregation and later generalized by Dietrich and List [15] for judgment aggregation. They show that if a profile is *value-restricted* in the sense that for every minimal inconsistent subset X of the agenda, there exists two formulas $\varphi, \psi \in X$ such that no agent accepts both φ and ψ, then the outcome of the majority rule will be consistent (meaning that no p and $\neg p$ get accepted at the same time).

---

[1] A notable exception is conflict-freeness, which can be preserved by the majority rule [12].

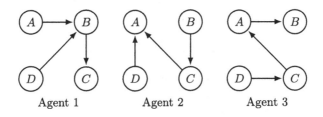

Fig. 1. Example for a profile with $Arg = \{A, B, C, D\}$.

Recently, Chen considers value-restriction during the aggregation of extensions of AFs [10]. He assumes that individual agents choose different extensions when confronted with the same abstract argumentation framework and study the preservation of properties of extensions. Chen uses a formula Γ to describe such a property of extensions, and refers to Γ as an integrity constraint. He shows that if for every prime implicates π of the integrity constraint Γ of a given semantic properties, there exists two distinct literals such that no agent rejects both, then the majority rule preserves admissible outcomes [10].

I propose to restrict the input of the aggregation rule in the sense that only argumentation frameworks with the specific feature are allowed to the aggregation rule. In the work by Chen and Endriss in which the model is the one we adopt in this paper, there is no restriction made to the argumentation frameworks put forward by individual agents. While there are many argumentation frameworks that contain undesirable features, it is very natural to restrict the inputs to the family of argumentation frameworks without such features.

Definition 11. *A profile* $\rightharpoonup\; = (\rightharpoonup_1, \ldots, \rightharpoonup_n)$ *is* topological-restricted *with respect to a constraint* Γ *if and only if* $\rightharpoonup_i$ *satisfies* Γ *for all* $i \in N$.

Thus, given a constraint Γ which is a topological property of argumentation frameworks, a profile is topological-restricted with respect to Γ if every individual argumentation framework satisfies Γ. When we perform aggregation on the profile, only argumentation frameworks satisfying Γ are allowed to aggregation rules. While most preservation results of demanding properties are negative [12], possible results may be obtained when restrictions are imposed. Consider the following example:

Example 1. Let us consider an example that illustrates the preservation of acyclicity with majority. Recall that the majority includes an attack if and only if a majority of the individual agents do. Consider three agents for which the first one supports $A \rightharpoonup B$ and $B \rightharpoonup C$, the second supports $B \rightharpoonup C$ and $C \rightharpoonup A$, and the third supports $C \rightharpoonup A$ and $A \rightharpoonup B$. Clearly, every individual argumentation framework in this profile satisfies acyclicity. If we apply this rule to the profile shown in Fig. 1, then we obtain the argumentation framework that contains three attacks $A \rightharpoonup B$, $B \rightharpoonup C$, and $C \rightharpoonup A$, which forms a cycle, violating acyclicity. But if no individual agent supports $A \rightharpoonup B$, for example, acyclicity will be preserved in this case. Thus, we can think that rejecting $A \rightarrowtail B$ is a topological restriction Γ. If a profile is topological-restricted with respect to Γ, the majority rule preserves acyclicity in this specific case.

Example 1 cares only about a specific profile. We now present a proposition which is more concrete, showing that if a profile is topological-restricted with respect to a constraint Γ, then every plausible aggregation rule preserves an AF-property. The AF-property is the nonemptiness of the grounded extension. Here we recall the work by Chen and Endriss, who present a preservation result for nonemptiness of the grounded extension.

Theorem 2 (Chen and Endriss, 2019). *If $|Arg| \geqslant n$, then under any neutral and independent aggregation rule F that preserves nonemptiness of the grounded extension at least one agent must have veto powers.*

Proposition 1. *Let Γ be a topological property that requires that there is an argument $A \in Arg$ that is unattacked in $\rightarrowtail_i$ for all $i \in N$. Given a profile $\rightarrowtail = (\rightarrowtail_1, \ldots, \rightarrowtail_n)$ which is topological-restricted with respect to Γ, then every aggregation rule that is grounded preserves the nonemptiness of the grounded extension.*

Proof. Let F be the aggregation rule that is grounded. Consider a profile of attack-relations $\rightarrowtail = (\rightarrowtail_1, \cdots, \rightarrowtail_n)$. Suppose that $A \in Arg$ is an unattacked argument in $\rightarrowtail_i$ for all $i \in N$. Clearly, as F is grounded, i.e., $F(\rightarrowtail) \subseteq \rightarrowtail_1 \cup, \cdots, \cup \rightarrowtail_n$, no argument attacks A in $F(\rightarrowtail)$. □

Thus, a positive result is obtained when the profile is topological-restricted with respect to a topological property that is weak and easy to satisfy. Proposition 1 provides a clue on how to overcome negative results during aggregation. In the following section, we study more topological restrictions, including notable topological properties in the literature, such as acyclicity, symmetry, as well as t-self-defense, a newly defined topological property, and we are going to show that the majority rule is well behaved with it.

5   Preservation Results with Topological Restrictions

In this section, we present preservation results for AF-properties with topological restrictions. The topological restrictions include acyclicity and symmetry. Most of our results have the following form: there is an aggregation rule preserving an AF-property, and the AF-property coincides with the second AF-property, if a profile of argumentation frameworks whose members satisfy a topological restriction, then the preservation result for one semantics can be extended to another.

5.1   Acyclicity

Acyclicity is an important property of argumentation frameworks. As we have mentioned in previous sections, if an argumentation framework is acyclic, then it contains a single extension which is the only complete, preferred and stable extension.

Definition 12. *A profile* $\rightarrowtail = (\rightarrowtail_1, \cdots, \rightarrowtail_n)$ *is topological-restricted with respect to acyclicity if* $\rightarrowtail_i$ *is acyclic for all* $i \in N$.

Thus, a profile is *topological-restricted* with respect to acyclicity if every argumentation framework in the profile satisfies acyclicity.

Fact 3. *In the case of a finite argumentation framework, well-foundedness coincides with acyclicity of the attack relation.*

Theorem 4 (Dung, 1995). *Every acyclic argumentation framework has exactly one complete extension which is grounded, preferred and stable.*

Proposition 2 (Chen and Endriss, 2019). *The nomination rule preserves stable extensions.*

Fact 5. *Every stable extension is preferred and complete.*

We now present a preservation results for preferred and complete extensions with topological restrictions. The preservation of both AF-properties has been discussed in-depth by Chen and Endriss in [12], who show that the preservation of extensions of either preferred or complete semantics is impossible by means of a "simple" aggregation rule (a rule that satisfies three "fair" axioms), unless the rule in use is a dictatorship.

Theorem 6 (Chen and Endriss, 2019). *For* $|Arg| \geq 5$, *any unanimous, grounded, and independent aggregation rule* F *that preserves either preferred or complete extensions must be a dictatorship.*

Proposition 3. *For any profile of attack-relations* $\rightarrowtail = (\rightarrowtail_1, \cdots, \rightarrowtail_n)$, *if* $\rightarrowtail$ *is topological-restricted with respect to acyclicity, then the nomination rule preserves preferred and complete extensions.*

Proof. Let F be the nomination rule. Suppose that $\Delta \subseteq Arg$ be the set of arguments that is preferred or complete in $\rightarrowtail_i$ for all $i \in N$. According to Theorem 4, Δ is stable in $\rightarrowtail_i$ for all $i \in N$. Thus, as F preserves stable extensions, Δ is stable in $F(\rightarrowtail)$. By the fact that every stable extension is preferred and complete, we get that Δ is preferred or complete in $F(\rightarrowtail)$, we are done.

5.2   Symmetry

In this section, we consider the topological restriction of symmetry.

Definition 13. *An argumentation framework* $AF = \langle Arg, \rightarrowtail \rangle$ *is a symmetric argumentation framework if* $\rightarrowtail$ *is symmetric, nonempty and irreflexive.*

Before going any further, we present a result regarding the preservation of conflict-freeness in [12], which shows that every plausible aggregation rule preserves it.

Theorem 7 (Chen and Endriss, 2019). *Every aggregation rule F that is grounded preserves conflict-freeness.*

We also present a result concerning the relation between admissibility and conflict-freeness in [14], which shows that admissible sets and conflict-free sets coincide in symmetric argumentation frameworks.

Proposition 4 (Coste-Marquis et al., 2005). *Let* $AF = \langle Arg, \rightarrowtail \rangle$ *be a symmetric argumentation framework, a set of arguments* $\Delta \in Arg$ *is admissible if and only if it is conflict-free.*

Definition 14. *A profile* $\rightarrowtail = (\rightarrowtail_1, \cdots, \rightarrowtail_n)$ *is topological-restricted with respect to symmetry if* $\rightarrowtail_i$ *is symmetric for all* $i \in N$.

With Theorem 7 and Proposition 4, we are ready to present a preservation result for admissibility with topological restrictions.

Theorem 8. *For any profile of attack-relations* $\rightarrowtail = (\rightarrowtail_1, \cdots, \rightarrowtail_n)$, *if* $\rightarrowtail$ *is topological-restricted with respect to symmetry, then every aggregation rule that is grounded and neutral preserves admissibility.*

Proof. Consider a profile of attack-relations $\rightarrowtail = (\rightarrowtail_1, \cdots, \rightarrowtail_n)$. Let F be an aggregation rule that is grounded and neutral. Let $\Delta \subseteq Arg$ be a set of arguments that is admissible in $\rightarrowtail_i$ for all $i \in N$. Clearly, Δ is conflict-free $\rightarrowtail_i$ for all $i \in N$. As F preserves conflict-freeness (cf. Theorem 7), we get that Δ is conflict-free in $F(\rightarrowtail)$. According to neutrality of F and the fact that the profile is topological-restricted with respect to symmetry, for every pair of arguments $A, B \in Arg$, $A \rightarrowtail B$ and $B \rightarrowtail A$ are treated symmetrically, and they receive the same votes, i.e., if $A \rightarrowtail B$ get accepted by F, so does $B \rightarrowtail A$. Thus, $F(\rightarrowtail)$ is symmetric. Combining with Proposition 4, we get that Δ is admissible in $F(\rightarrowtail)$, we are done.

Proposition 5 (Coste-Marquis et al., 2005). *Every symmetric argumentation framework is coherent.*

Recall that coherence is a property that ensures that the stable and the preferred semantics coincide. It is defined as the AF-property of every preferred extension being a stable extension. We say that an aggregation rule F preserves coherence if it is the case that, whenever $\langle Arg, \rightarrowtail_i \rangle$ is coherent for all $i \in N$, then $F(\rightarrowtail)$ is coherent. Chen and Endriss [12] have shown that preservation of coherence is impossible unless we use dictatorships.

Theorem 9 (Chen and Endriss, 2019). *For $|Arg| \geqslant 4$, any unanimous, grounded, and independent aggregation rule F that preserves coherence must be a dictatorship.*

When the profile under consideration is topological-restricted with respect to symmetry, the impossibility result can be avoided.

Proposition 6. *For any profile of attack-relations $\rightarrowtail = (\rightarrowtail_1, \cdots, \rightarrowtail_n)$, if $\rightarrowtail$ is topological-restricted with respect to symmetry, then any aggregation rule that is grounded and neutral preserves coherence.*

Proof. Let F be an aggregation rule that is grounded and neutral. Consider a pair of arguments $A, B \in Arg$ as well as the attacks $A \rightarrowtail B$, $B \rightarrowtail A$ between them. According to the fact that $\rightarrowtail$ is a profile that is topological-restricted with respect to symmetry and the fact that F is an aggregation rule that is grounded and neutral, we get that $A \rightarrowtail B$ and $B \rightarrowtail A$ receive the same votes and they are treated symmetrically by F. Thus, if $A \rightarrowtail B$ get accepted, then $B \rightarrowtail A$ get accepted as well. As a consequence, $F(\rightarrowtail)$ is a symmetric argumentation framework. Together with Proposition 5, we get that $F(\rightarrowtail)$ is coherent.

Recall that Theorem 1 has shown that only dictatorships preserve preferred extensions. Interestingly, with the topological restriction of symmetry, we obtain a much more positive result.

Theorem 10. *For any profile of attack-relations $\rightarrowtail = (\rightarrowtail_1, \cdots, \rightarrowtail_n)$, if $\rightarrowtail$ is topological-restricted with respect to symmetry, then the nomination rule preserves preferred extensions.*

Proof. Let F be the nomination rule. Suppose that $\Delta \subseteq Arg$ is a set of arguments that is preferred in $\rightarrowtail_i$ for all $i \in N$. According to Proposition 5, Δ is stable in $\rightarrowtail_i$ for all $i \in N$. Thus, as F preserves stable extensions (cf. Proposition 2), Δ is stable in $F(\rightarrowtail)$. By the fact that every stable extension is preferred, we get that Δ is preferred in $F(\rightarrowtail)$, we are done.

6 The Majority Rule and Topological Restrictions

In this section, we focus on the preservation of semantic properties with topological restrictions. The aggregation rule we pay particular attention to is the majority rule. We first show that the majority rule does not preserve admissibility, a property at the heart of all classical semantics. Then, we define a topological property, followed by a result that shows that if a profile of attack-relations is topological-restricted with respect to the property, then the majority rule preserves admissibility during aggregation.

Example 2. Consider the profile illustrated in Fig. 2, $\{A_1, A_2, A_3, C\}$ is admissible in every individual's argumentation framework, but it is not admissible in the outcome of the majority rule. Thus, the majority rule does not preserve admissibility.

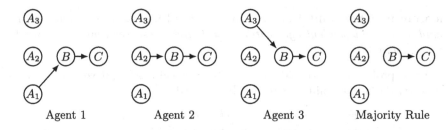

Fig. 2. Scenarios used in Example 2.

Next, we introduce the notion of *the union of attack-relations* of profiles of attack-relations.

Definition 15. *Given a profile* $\rightharpoonup = (\rightharpoonup_1, \ldots, \rightharpoonup_n)$, *we denote the union of attack-relations of* $\rightharpoonup$ *by* $\rightharpoonup_u$, *i.e.,* $\rightharpoonup_u = \rightharpoonup_i \cup \cdots \cup \rightharpoonup_n$.

In other words, the union of attack-relations of a profile if it includes those attacks that accepted by at least one agent. For instance, in Example 2, $\rightharpoonup_u = \{A_1 \rightharpoonup B, A_2 \rightharpoonup B, A_3 \rightharpoonup B, B \rightharpoonup C\}$.

Definition 16. *Given a profile of attack-relations* $\rightharpoonup = (\rightharpoonup_1, \ldots, \rightharpoonup_n)$. *We say that* $\rightharpoonup$ *is topological-restricted with respect to* t-self-defense *if for every attack* $B \rightharpoonup C \in \rightharpoonup_u$ *whose attacker* B *has two or more attackers in* $\langle Arg, \rightharpoonup_u \rangle$, *for every pair of attackers* A_i, A_j *of* B *no agent rejects both* $A_i \rightharpoonup B$ *and* $A_j \rightharpoonup B$.

In other words, for every attack $att = B \rightharpoonup C \in \rightharpoonup_u$, we denote the attackers of B by $A_1, \cdots, A_k$ with $k \geqslant 2$, i.e., $A_1 \rightharpoonup B, \cdots, A_k \rightharpoonup B \in \rightharpoonup_u$, there are at least two attackers A_i and A_j of B for which no agent rejects both $A_i \rightharpoonup B$ and $A_j \rightharpoonup B$.

Theorem 11. *If the number of agents is odd, then for any profile of attack-relations* $\rightharpoonup = (\rightharpoonup_1, \cdots, \rightharpoonup_n)$, *if* $\rightharpoonup$ *is a profile that is topological-restricted with respect to* t-self-defense, *then the majority rule preserves admissibility.*

Proof. Assume that $\Delta \subseteq Arg$ is admissible in $\rightharpoonup_i$ for all $i \in N$. Let F be the majority rule. According to Theorem 7, Δ is conflict-free in $F(\rightharpoonup)$. It remains to show that Δ is self-defending in $F(\rightharpoonup)$. To arrive at this goal, we need to show that for every argument $C \in \Delta$, if C is attacked by some argument B, then B is attacked by some argument in Δ in the outcome of the majority rule.

Suppose that $B \rightharpoonup C \in F(\rightharpoonup)$ is the case, then $B \rightharpoonup C \in \rightharpoonup_u$. If B has only one attacker in $\langle Arg, \rightharpoonup_u \rangle$, and we denote it by A, then any agent who supports $B \rightharpoonup C$ would be required to support $A \rightharpoonup B$, meaning that the majority of agents support $A \rightharpoonup B$. Thus, in this scenario, $B \rightharpoonup C$ and $A \rightharpoonup B$ receive the same votes, which is also a majority of supports from agents. If $A \notin \Delta$, then Δ is not self-defending in such agents' argumentation frameworks, contradicting our earlier assumption. Thus, $A \in \Delta$, meaning that C is defended by Δ.

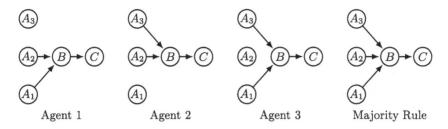

Fig. 3. Scenarios used in Example 3.

If B has two or more attackers in $\langle Arg, \rightharpoonup_u \rangle$, we denote the attackers of B by $A_1, \cdots, A_k$. According to the assumption that $\rightharpoonup$ is topological-restricted with respect to t-self-defense, for every pair of attackers A_i and A_j of B, no agent rejects both $A_i \rightharpoonup B$ and $A_j \rightharpoonup B$. We now show that C is defended by Δ in $F(\rightharpoonup)$. If there are two or more arguments in $A_1, \cdots, A_k$ that are included in Δ, we take two of them and denote by A_i and A_j. Clearly, one of $A_i \rightharpoonup B$ and $A_j \rightharpoonup B$ is supported by the majority of agents. Thus, A is defended by Δ in $F(\rightharpoonup)$. If there is only one argument in $A_1, \cdots, A_k$ that is included by Δ, and we denote it by A_i. Clearly, $A_i \rightharpoonup B$ is supported by agents who support $B \rightharpoonup C$, i.e., $A_i \rightharpoonup B$ is accepted by F, meaning that C is defended by Δ in $F(\rightharpoonup)$ as well. For the scenario that no argument in $A_1, \cdots, A_k$ that is included in Δ, we note that this is impossible as for agents who support $B \rightharpoonup C$, Δ is not self-defending in their individual argumentation frameworks.

Let us come back to Example 2, the union of attack-relations of the profile $\rightharpoonup_u = \{A_1 \rightharpoonup B, A_2 \rightharpoonup B, A_3 \rightharpoonup B, B \rightharpoonup C\}$. Clearly, the profile is not topological-restricted with respect to t-self-defense as $B \rightharpoonup C$, whose attacker B has three attackers, and for every pair of attackers of B in $\langle Arg, \rightharpoonup_u \rangle$ there is at least one agent who rejects both.

Example 3. Now we consider the profile illustrated in Fig. 3, in which $\rightharpoonup_1 = \{A_1 \rightharpoonup B, A_2 \rightharpoonup B\}, \rightharpoonup_2 = \{A_2 \rightharpoonup B, A_3 \rightharpoonup B\}, \rightharpoonup_3 = \{A_3 \rightharpoonup B, A_1 \rightharpoonup B\}$ and we want to know whether $\{A_1, A_2, A_3, C\}$ is admissible if the outcome of the majority rule. Clearly, the profile is topological-restricted with respect to t-self-defense. We can see that the union of attack-relations of the profile $\rightharpoonup_u = \{A_1 \rightharpoonup B, A_2 \rightharpoonup B, A_3 \rightharpoonup B, B \rightharpoonup C\}$, and for every attack in $B \rightharpoonup C$, for example, for every pair of attackers A_1, A_2, for example, no agent rejects both $A_1 \rightharpoonup B$ and $A_2 \rightharpoonup B$. While $\{A_1, A_2, A_3, C\}$ is admissible in every individual agent's argumentation framework, it is also admissible in the outcome of the majority rule, as expected.

7   Conclusion

In this paper, we have studied the preservation of semantic properties during the aggregation of argumentation frameworks with topological restrictions. The topological restrictions we consider in this paper include acyclicity, symmetry, as well as t-self-defense, and the semantic properties we consider include conflict-freeness, admissibility, being an extension under a specific semantics, nonemptiness of the grounded extension and coherence. Compared to the preservation results for several semantic properties by Chen and Endriss without restrictions showing that only dictatorships preserve them, there are aggregation rules that have some intuitive appeal preserve them with topological restrictions. When the restriction under consideration is t-self-defense, we can even preserve admissibility under the majority rule.

Acknowledgments. I would like to thank three anonymous reviewers of CLAR-2020 for their helpful comments. This work was supported by the China Postdoctoral Science Foundation Grant (No. 2019M663352) and the Key Project of National Social Science Foundation of China (No. 16AZX017).

References

1. Arrow, K.J., Sen, A.K., Suzumura, K. (eds.): Handbook of Social Choice and Welfare. North-Holland (2002)
2. Arrow, K.J.: Social Choice and Individual Values, 2nd edn. Wiley, Hoboken (1963). First edition published in 1951
3. Baroni, P., Giacomin, M.: Characterizing defeat graphs where argumentation semantics agree. In: Proceedings of the 1st International Workshop on Argumentation and Non-Monotonic Reasoning (ARGNMR07), pp. 33–48 (2007)
4. Baroni, P., Giacomin, M.: On principle-based evaluation of extension-based argumentation semantics. Artif. Intell. **171**(10–15), 675–700 (2007)
5. Baroni, P., Giacomin, M., Guida, G.: SCC-recursiveness: a general schema for argumentation semantics. Artif. Intell. **168**(1–2), 162–210 (2005)
6. Baumeister, D., Neugebauer, D., Rothe, J.: Collective acceptability in abstract argumentation. J. Appl. Log. **2631**(6), 1503 (2021)
7. Bodanza, G.A., Tohmé, F.A., Auday, M.R.: Collective argumentation: a survey of aggregation issues around argumentation frameworks. Argument Comput. **8**(1), 1–34 (2017)
8. Caminada, M., Pigozzi, G.: On judgment aggregation in abstract argumentation. J. Auton. Agents Multiagent Syst. **22**(1), 64–102 (2011)
9. Chen, W.: Collective argumentation: the case of aggregating support-relations of bipolar argumentation frameworks. In: Proceedings of the 18th Conference on Theoretical Aspects of Rationality and Knowledge (TARK), pp. 87–102 (2021)
10. Chen, W.: Guaranteeing admissibility of abstract argumentation frameworks with rationality and feasibility constraints. J. Log. Comput. (2021, to appear). https://doi.org/10.1093/logcom/exab011
11. Chen, W., Endriss, U.: Aggregating alternative extensions of abstract argumentation frameworks: preservation results for quota rules. In: Proceedings of the 7th International Conference on Computational Models of Argument (COMMA). IOS Press (2018)

12. Chen, W., Endriss, U.: Preservation of semantic properties in collective argumentation: the case of aggregating abstract argumentation frameworks. Artif. Intell. **269**, 27–48 (2019)

13. Coste-Marquis, S., Devred, C., Konieczny, S., Lagasquie-Schiex, M.C., Marquis, P.: On the merging of Dung's argumentation systems. Artif. Intell. **171**(10–15), 730–753 (2007)

14. Coste-Marquis, S., Devred, C., Marquis, P.: Symmetric argumentation frameworks. In: Godo, L. (ed.) ECSQARU 2005. LNCS (LNAI), vol. 3571, pp. 317–328. Springer, Heidelberg (2005). https://doi.org/10.1007/11518655_28

15. Dietrich, F., List, C.: Majority voting on restricted domains. J. Econ. Theory **145**(2), 512–543 (2010)

16. Dung, P.M.: On the acceptability of arguments and its fundamental role in nonmonotonic reasoning, logic programming and n-person games. Artif. Intell. **77**(2), 321–358 (1995)

17. Dung, P.M., Mancarella, P., Toni, F.: Computing ideal sceptical argumentation. Artif. Intell. **171**(10), 642–674 (2007)

18. Endriss, U., Grandi, U.: Graph aggregation. Artif. Intell. **245**, 86–114 (2017)

19. Grossi, D., Pigozzi, G.: Judgment Aggregation: A Primer. Synthesis Lectures on Artificial Intelligence and Machine Learning. Morgan & Claypool Publishers (2014)

20. List, C.: A possibility theorem on aggregation over multiple interconnected propositions. Math. Soc. Sci. **45**(1), 1–13 (2003)

21. Rahwan, I., Tohmé, F.A.: Collective argument evaluation as judgement aggregation. In: Proceedings of the 9th International Conference on Autonomous Agents and Multiagent Systems (AAMAS), pp. 417–424. IFAAMAS (2010)

22. Sen, A.K.: A possibility theorem on majority decisions. Econometrica: J. Econometric Soc. 491–499 (1966)

23. Tohmé, F.A., Bodanza, G.A., Simari, G.R.: Aggregation of attack relations: a social-choice theoretical analysis of defeasibility criteria. In: Hartmann, S., Kern-Isberner, G. (eds.) FoIKS 2008. LNCS, vol. 4932, pp. 8–23. Springer, Heidelberg (2008). https://doi.org/10.1007/978-3-540-77684-0_4

The Choice-Preferred Semantics for Relevance-Oriented Acceptance of Admissible Sets of Arguments

Marcos Cramer$^{(\boxtimes)}$ and Yannick Spörl

TU Dresden, Dresden, Germany
marcos.cramer@tu-dresden.de, yannick.spoerl@mailbox.tu-dresden.de

Abstract. In abstract argumentation, multiple argumentation semantics for choosing sets of jointly acceptable arguments have been defined. In the *principle-based approach*, multiple principles have been proposed and formalized in order to guide the choice for a semantics and the search for new semantics. *Admissibility* is a central principle satisfied by many semantics, including *complete*, *stable*, *grounded* and *preferred*. A more recently introduced principle is the *INRA* principle, motivated by considerations about the relevance of arguments and supported by a cognitive study. This paper additionally introduces and motivates the *SAF-WOC* principle in order to positively distinguish less abstention-friendly semantics like preferred and stable from more abstention-friendly semantics like grounded and complete. After observing that no existing semantics satisfies these three principles, we define the novel *choice-preferred* semantics that satisfies the three principles. Additionally we show that *choice-preferred* satisfies further desirable principles like *existence*, *directionality*, *SCC-recursiveness* and *completeness*.

1 Introduction

The formal study of argumentation is an important field of research within AI [12]. A central focus of this field has been the idea of Dung [9] that under some conditions, the acceptance of arguments depends only on a so-called *attack* relation among the arguments, and not on the internal structure of the arguments. This approach is called *abstract* argumentation and the directed graph that represents the arguments as well as the attack relation between them is called an *argumentation framework* (*AF*). In general, whether an argument is deemed acceptable depends on the decision about other arguments. Therefore the basic concept in abstract argumentation is a *set* of arguments that can be accepted together, called an *extension*. Crucially, there may be several of such extensions, and these extensions may be incompatible. An *extension-based argumentation semantics* takes as input an AF and produces as output a set of extensions.

The fact that many argumentation semantics have been proposed in the literature naturally gives rise to the question how to choose between these semantics

P. Baroni et al. (Eds.): CLAR 2021, LNAI 13040, pp. 94–111, 2021.
https://doi.org/10.1007/978-3-030-89391-0_6

for a given application as well as the question how to systematically search for new semantics that might be even more suitable to a given application than any of the semantics studied so far. Both of these questions are addressed by the *principle-based approach to abstract argumentation* [2,13], in which semantics are evaluated based on their satisfaction of various normatively desirable principles. One prominent example of a principle satisfied by many of the widely studied semantics is *admissibility*, according to which any extension should be free of internal conflicts and should defend each of its arguments against all outside attackers.

Cramer and van der Torre [7] have introduced the principle of *Irrelevance of Necessarily Rejected Arguments (INRA)*. Informally, INRA says that if an argument is attacked by every extension of an AF, then deleting this argument should not change the set of extensions. The idea here is that an argument that is attacked by every extension would be rejected by any party in a debate, and hence would never be brought up in a debate. Hence, it should be treated as irrelevant to the debate, i.e. just like if it did not exist.

Cramer and van der Torre [7] defined the novel SCF2 semantics, which satisfies INRA as well as some further desirable properties, and which is additionally supported by two empirical cognitive studies on argumentation semantics [5,6]. However, SCF2 does not satisfy admissibility. Among the widely studied semantics satisfying admissibility, grounded and complete semantics satisfy INRA, while preferred, stable and semi-stable do not.

Argumentation semantics can be broadly classified into the following two groups depending on how they treat attack cycles of even length that are not attacked from the outside: Some semantics, like *complete*, *grounded*, *ideal* and *eager*, allow (or even require) that no argument is accepted from such an even cycle, whereas other semantics, like *preferred*, *stable*, *semi-stable*, *stage*, *CF2*, *stage2* and *SCF2* require every second argument in the cycle to be accepted. Due to this feature, the semantics from the second class implement some form of reasoning by cases for arguments attacked by multiple arguments from an even cycle. While the semantics from the first satisfy the principle *Allowing Abstentions* [13] and the semantics from the second class do not satisfy this principle, so far no principle has been defined to positively differentiate the semantcis from the second class from the semantics of the first class. For this purpose we introduce and motivate the principle of *Some Acceptance for Frameworks Without Odd Cycles* (SAFWOC), which states that any argumentation framework without odd attack cycles does not have the empty set among its extensions.

We observe that none of the widely studied argumentation semantics satisfies the three principles Admissibility, INRA and SAFWOC. We therefore define the new *choice-preferred* semantics that satisfies these three principles. Furthermore, we show that choice-preferred also satisfies *existence*, *directionality*, *SCC-recursiveness* and *completeness*.

2   Preliminaries

In this section we define required notions from abstract argumentation theory [1,9]. We define eleven argumentation semantics (including seven widely studied admissibility-based semantics) as well as six principles from the literature on principle-based argumentation [2,7,13].

Definition 1. *An argumentation framework (AF) $F = \langle Ar, att \rangle$ is a finite directed graph in which the set Ar of vertices is considered to represent arguments and the set att of edges is considered to represent the attack relation between arguments, i.e. the relation between a counterargument and the argument that it counters.*

Given an argumentation framework, we want to choose sets of arguments for which it is rational and coherent to accept them together. Such a set of arguments that may be accepted together is called an *extension*. Multiple *argumentation semantics* have been defined in the literature, i.e. multiple different ways of defining extensions given an argumentation framework. Before we consider specific argumentation semantics, we first give a formal definition of the notion of an *argumentation semantics*:

Definition 2. *An argumentation semantics is a function σ that maps any AF $F = (Ar, att)$ to a set $\sigma(F) \subseteq 2^{Ar}$. The elements of $\sigma(F)$ are called σ-extensions of F.*

We usually define an argumentation semantics σ by specifying criteria which a subset of Ar has to satisfy in order to be a σ-extension of F. In this paper we consider the *complete, grounded, preferred, semi-stable, ideal, eager, stable, stage, CF2, stage2* and *SCF2 semantics*. The first seven are based on the notion of *admissibility* and are therefore called *admissibility-based semantics*. The last five always choose extensions that are *naive extensions*, i.e. subset-maximal conflict-free sets of arguments, which is why they are called *naive-based semantics*. Note that the stable semantics is the only semantics that belongs to both categories (at the price of not providing any extension at all in some scenarios). Apart from these eleven semantics, we also define *naive extensions* and *SCOOC-naive extensions*, as we need them for our definition of CF2 and SCF2 semantics respectively.

Definition 3. *An att-path is a sequence $\langle a_0, \ldots, a_n \rangle$ of arguments where $(a_i, a_{i+1}) \in att$ for $0 \le i < n$ and where $a_j \ne a_k$ for $0 \le j < k \le n$ with either $j \ne 0$ or $k \ne n$. An even att-cycle is an att-path $\langle a_0, \ldots, a_n \rangle$ where $a_0 = a_n$ and n is even; analogously for odd att-cycle. A simple unattacked cycle is an even or odd cycle $\langle a_0, \ldots, a_n \rangle$ in which a_{i+1} is only attacked by a_i for every $1 \le i \le n$.*

Definition 4. *Let $F = \langle Ar, att \rangle$ be an AF, and let $S \subseteq Ar$. We write $F|_S$ for the restricted AF $\langle S, att \cap (S \times S) \rangle$. The set S is called conflict-free iff there are no arguments $b, c \in S$ such that b attacks c (i.e. such that $(b, c) \in att$). Argument*

$a \in Ar$ is defended *by S iff for every $b \in Ar$ such that b attacks a there exists $c \in S$ such that c attacks b.* The set S is called admissible *iff it defends every argument in S and there are no arguments $b, c \in S$ such that b attacks c.* We say *that the set S* attacks *an argument $a \in Ar$ iff some argument in S attacks a.* We define $S^+ = \{a \in Ar \mid S \text{ attacks } a\}$ and $S^- = \{a \in Ar \mid a \text{ attacks some } b \in S\}$. We define S to be strongly complete outside odd cycles *iff for every argument $a \in Ar$, if no argument in $\{a\} \cup \{a\}^-$ is in an odd att-cycle and $S \cap \{a\}^- = \emptyset$, then $a \in S$.*

- S is a complete extension *of F iff it is admissible and it contains all the arguments it defends.*
- S is a stable extension *of F iff it is conflict-free and it attacks all the arguments of $Ar \setminus S$.*
- S is the grounded extension *of F iff it is a subset-minimal complete extension of F.*
- S is a preferred extension *of F iff it is a subset-maximal admissible extension of F.*
- S is a semi-stable extension *of F iff it is an admissible extension and there exists no admissible extension S_1 such that $S \cup S^+ \subset S_1 \cup S_1^+$.*
- S is an ideal extension *of F iff it is a subset-maximal admissible subset of every preferred extension of F.*
- S is an eager extension *of F iff it is a subset-maximal admissible subset of every semi-stable extension of F.*
- S is a stage extension *of F iff S is a conflict-free set and there exists no conflict-free set S_1 such that $S \cup S^+ \subset S_1 \cup S_1^+$.*
- S is a naive extension *of F iff S is a subset-maximal conflict-free set.*
- S is a SCOOC-naive extension *iff S is subset-maximal among the conflict-free subsets of Ar that are strongly complete outside odd cycles.*

We also need the notion of *skeptically accepting* an argument:

Definition 5. *Let $F = \langle Ar, att \rangle$ be an AF, let σ be an argumentation semantics, and let $a \in Ar$. We say that a is skeptically accepted in F with respect to σ iff for every $E \in \sigma(F)$, $a \in E$.*

The idea behind CF2, stage2 and SCF2 semantics is that we partition the AF into *strongly connected components* and recursively evaluate it, component by component, using a procedure called the *simplified SCC-recursive scheme*. This scheme was first defined in [3] and was first presented as an abstract function in the way we present it here in [7]. For defining this scheme, we first need some auxiliary notions:

Definition 6. *Let $F = \langle Ar, att \rangle$ be an AF, and let $a, b \in Ar$. We define $a \sim b$ iff either $a = b$ or there is an att-path from a to b and there is an att-path from b to a. The equivalence classes under the equivalence relation $\sim$ are called* strongly connected components *(SCCs) of F. We denote the set of SCCs of F by $SCCs(F)$. Given $S \subseteq Ar$, we define $D_F(S) := \{b \in Ar \mid \exists a \in S : (a, b) \in att \land a \not\sim b\}$.*

Definition 7. *Let σ be an argumentation semantics. The argumentation semantics $scc(\sigma)$ is defined as follows. Let $F = \langle Ar, att \rangle$ be an AF, and let $S \subseteq Ar$. Then S is an $scc(\sigma)$-extension of F iff either*

- *$|SCCs(F)| \leq 1$ and S is a σ-extension of F, or*
- *$|SCCs(F)| > 1$ and for each $C \in SCCs(F)$, $S \cap C$ is an $scc(\sigma)$-extension of $F|_{C \backslash D_F(S)}$.*

We are now ready to present definitions of CF2 semantics [3], stage2 semantics [10,11] and SCF2 semantics [7]:

Definition 8. *We define CF2, stage2 and SCF2 semantics as follows:*

- *CF2 semantics is defined to be $scc(naive)$.*
- *stage2 semantics is defined to be $scc(stage)$.*
- *Given an AF $F = \langle Ar, att \rangle$, a set $S \subseteq Ar$ is called a SCF2 extension of F iff S is a $scc(SCOOC\text{-}naive)$-extension of $F|_{Ar'}$, where $Ar' := \{a \in Ar \mid (a,a) \notin att\}$.*

We now turn towards defining principles for abstract argumentation, i.e. properties that argumentation semantics may or may not satisfy, and that have been proposed as being desirable for some applications of abstract argumentation.

The first principle is the *admissibility principle* introduced by Baroni and Giacomin [2]. It states that for every framework, all of its extensions should be admissible:

Definition 9. *A semantics σ satisfies the* admissibility principle *iff for every AF F, every $S \in \sigma(F)$ is admissible in F.*

The *completeness principle* is a strengthening of *admissibility* that requires extensions to be complete extensions:

Definition 10. *A semantics σ satisfies the* completeness principle *iff for every AF F, every $S \in \sigma(F)$ is a complete extension of F.*

The *principle of Irrelevance of Necessarily Rejected Arguments (INRA principle)* was introduced by Cramer and van der Torre [7]. It requires that if an argument is attacked by every extension of an AF, then deleting this argument should not change the set of extensions. In order to formally define the INRA principle, we first need to define a notation for an AF with one argument deleted:

Definition 11. *Let $F = \langle Ar, att \rangle$ be an AF and let $a \in Ar$ be an argument. Then F_{-a} denotes the restricted AF $F|_{Ar \backslash \{a\}}$.*

Definition 12. *A semantics σ satisfies* Irrelevance of Necessarily Rejected Arguments (INRA) *iff for every AF $F = \langle Ar, att \rangle$ and every argument $a \in Ar$, if every $E \in \sigma(F)$ attacks a, then $\sigma(F) = \sigma(F_{-a})$.*

The idea here is that an argument that is attacked by every extension would be rejected by any party in a debate, and hence would never be brought up in a debate. Hence, it should be treated as irrelevant to the debate, i.e. just like if it did not exist.

The *existence principle* requires that for every argumentation framework, there exists at least one extension:

Definition 13. *We say that a semantics σ satisfies the* existence principle *iff for every AF F, $\sigma(F) \neq \emptyset$.*

We now define the *directionality principle* introduced by Baroni and Giacomin [2]. For this, we first need an auxiliary notion:

Definition 14. *Let $F = \langle Ar, att \rangle$ be an AF. A set $U \subseteq Ar$ is* unattacked *iff there exists no $a \in Ar \setminus U$ such that a attacks some $b \in U$.*

Definition 15. *A semantics σ satisfies the* directionality principle *iff for every AF F and every unattacked set U, it holds that $\sigma(F|_U) = \{E \cap U \mid E \in \sigma(F)\}$.*

We now define the principle of *SCC-recursiveness* [13]. We modify the wording used by [13] a bit in order to make the definition formally more precise.

Intuitively this principle says that one can compute the extensions by first considering an unattacked SCC, compute the semantics on it, determine its impact on other SCCs and then recursively continue this computation. In order to formalize this intuition, we first need three auxiliary definitions:

Definition 16. *Given an argumentation framework $F = (Ar, att)$ and sets $S, E \subseteq Ar$, we define $U_F(S, E) := \{a \in S \mid \not\exists b : (b, a) \in att, b \not\rightarrow a$ and E does not attack $b\}$.*

Definition 17. *A binary function BF is called a* base function *iff for every AF $F = (Ar, att)$ such that $|SCCs(F)| \leq 1$ and every set $C \subseteq Ar$, $BF(F, C) \subseteq 2^{Ar}$.*

Definition 18. *Given a base function BF, an AF $F = (Ar, att)$ and a set $C \subseteq Ar$, we recursively define $GF(BF, F, C) \subseteq 2^{Ar}$ as follows: for every $E \subseteq Ar$, $E \in GF(BF, F, C)$ iff*

- *in case $|SCCs(F)| \leq 1$, $E \in BF(F, C)$,*
- *otherwise, for all $S \in SCCs(F)$, $(E \cap S) \in GF(BF, F|_{S \setminus D_F(E)}, U_F(S, E) \cap C)$.*

Definition 19. *A semantics σ satisfies the* SCC-recursiveness principle *iff there is a base function BF such that for every AF $F = (Ar, att)$ we have $\sigma(F) = GF(BF, F, Ar)$.*

Table 1 shows which semantics satisfies which principle. All results other than those for the SCF2 row, the completeness column and the INRA column are taken over from [13]. The SCF2 row is based on results from Cramer and van der Torre [7], apart from the non-satisfaction of admissibility and completeness, which follows trivially from the fact that in SCF2 the 3-cycle AF

$\langle\{a, b, c\}, \{(a, b), (b, c), (c, a)\}\rangle$ has non-empty extensions $\{a\}$, $\{b\}$ and $\{c\}$. For the semantics other than SCF2, the completeness column is based on well-known properties of those semantics. The INRA column is mostly taken over from Theorems 1 and 2 of Cramer and van der Torre [7], with the exception of the cases of the ideal and eager semantics. The fact that the ideal and eager semantics do not satisfy INRA follows from the same counterexample as the one given in Theorem 2 of Cramer and van der Torre [7] (this was pointed out by an anonymous reviewer of this paper).

Table 1. Satisfaction of the principles defined in this section by the semantics defined in this section

	Admissibility	Completeness	INRA	Existence	Directionality	SCC-recursiveness
complete	✓	✓	✓	✓	✓	✓
stable	✓	✓	✗	✗	✗	✓
grounded	✓	✓	✓	✓	✓	✓
preferred	✓	✓	✗	✓	✓	✓
semi-stable	✓	✓	✗	✓	✗	✗
ideal	✓	✓	✗	✓	✓	✗
eager	✓	✓	✗	✓	✓	✗
stage	✗	✗	✗	✓	✗	✗
CF2	✗	✗	✗	✓	✓	✓
stage2	✗	✗	✗	✓	✓	✓
SCF2	✗	✗	✓	✓	✓	✓

3   A Novel Principle: SAFWOC

In this section we introduce a new principle called *Some Acceptance for Frameworks Without Odd Cycles* (*SAFWOC*). In order to motivate this principle, let us first consider the argumentation framework F_0 depicted in Fig. 1.

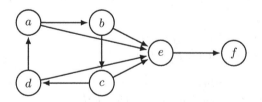

Fig. 1. Argumentation framework F_0.

Here there are two preferred extensions: $\{a, c, f\}$ and $\{b, d, f\}$. Note that both of these extensions accept argument f, so that f is skeptically accepted with respect to the preferred semantics. Intuitively, one can view the preferred semantics as coming to the conclusion f through a form of reasoning by cases: In the 4-cycle $\langle a, b, c, d, a \rangle$, one has to either accept $\{a, c\}$ or $\{b, d\}$. Either way, e will be attacked by an accepted argument, so f will be defended and therefore accepted. In this example, the stable, semi-stable, stage, CF2, stage2 and SCF2 semantics have the same extensions, so the same kind of reasoning by cases works there.

In the grounded, ideal, eager and complete semantics, however, $\emptyset$ is an extension (in grounded, ideal and eager semantics, $\emptyset$ is the only extension; in complete semantics the extensions are $\emptyset$ together with the two preferred extensions). Therefore f is not skeptically accepted with respect to these four semantics. The problem here is that these semantics allow (and grounded, ideal and eager semantics even require) that in a simple unattacked cycle like $\langle a, b, c, d, a \rangle$, no argument should be accepted. This behavior of grounded and complete semantics is certainly desirable for some applications, but for others it is desirable to have at least one argument in an even cycle accepted, so that reasoning by cases works as explained above.

Unattacked cycles of any even length will be treated similarly to the 4-cycle in F_0 in all eleven semantics considered in this paper (with some caveats in the case of CF2; see [11]).

The fact that many argumentation semantics allow for this kind of reasoning by cases over even cycles can be seen as a motivation for formulating a principle that captures what these semantics have in common with respect to such reasoning. We want to state this principle in as general terms as possible, so ideally we do not want to restrict ourselves just to even cycles. However, simple unattacked odd cycles expose a different behavior: Here no admissibility-based semantics can accept any argument. Intuitively, simple unattacked odd cycles correspond to paradoxical situations in which no defensible decision can be made.

Nevertheless, we can go beyond the case of even cycles: In preferred, stable, semi-stable, stage, CF2, stage2 and SCF2 semantics, every argumentation framework that does not involve any odd cycles will have at least one argument in each extension. This motivates the introduction of the principle of *Some Acceptance for Frameworks Without Odd Cycles* (*SAFWOC principle*), which states that any argumentation framework without odd attack cycles does not have the empty set among its extensions:

Definition 20. *Let $F = (Ar, att)$ be an argumentation framework. A semantics σ satisfies* Some Acceptance for Frameworks Without Odd Cycles *(SAFWOC) iff for every AF F, if F contains no odd cycle then $\emptyset \notin \sigma(F)$.*

Even though the formal definition of SAFWOC is rather technical, it ultimately rests on the important destinction between more skeptical semantics without reasoning by cases like grounded, ideal, eager and complete on the one hand and more credulous semantics with reasoning by cases like preferred, stable, semi-stable, stage, CF2, stage2 and SCF2. In applications calling for a semantics of the second kind, a semantics of the first kind may be highly inappropriate. The SAFWOC semantics is an attempt to formalize this distinction between semantics, which has already been made informally by many people working on abstract argumentation.

The SAFWOC principle can also be motivated by the desire to ensure that as long as there is no paradoxical argumentation, a semantics should not support complete absention, i.e. at least one argument should be accepted. The informal notion of paradoxical argumentation is formalized here through the requirement of having no odd cycles.

We now establish that preferred, stable, semi-stable, stage, CF2, stage2 and SCF2 semantics satisfy SAFWOC, while complete, grounded, ideal and eager do not.

Theorem 1. *Preferred, stable, semi-stable, stage, CF2, stage2 and SCF2 semantics satisfy SAFWOC.*

Proof. Let $F = (Ar, att)$ be an argumentation framework such that F contains no odd cycle. We first show that there exists a non-empty admissible subset of Ar.

Let $S \in SCCs(F)$ be an unattacked SCC of F. Choose $a \in S$. Since F does not contain any odd cycles, every element of S can be reached from a either only through paths of even length or only through paths of odd length. Let A be the set of all elements of S that are reachable from a through paths of even length. Then clearly A is admissible.

Suppose for a contradiction that $\emptyset \in preferred(F)$. Then $\emptyset$ is subset-maximal among the admissible sets. However, the admissible set A contradicts this maximality. So $\emptyset \notin preferred(F)$.

A stable extension must attack all arguments not contained in it, so it cannot be empty.

Suppose for a contradiction that $\emptyset \in semi\text{-}stable(F)$. Since $\emptyset \cup \emptyset^+ = \emptyset$, the maximality condition in the definition of semi-stable implies that $\emptyset$ is the only admissible sets. However, the non-empty admissible set A contradicts this. So $\emptyset \notin semi\text{-}stable(F)$.

Suppose for a contradiction that $\emptyset \in stage(F)$. Let $a \in Ar$. Since F contains no odd cycle, it contains no self-attacks, so $\{a\}$ is conflict-free. Furthermore, $\{a\} \cup \{a\}^+$ is non-empty, which is in contradiction with $\emptyset \in stage(F)$ due to the maximality condition in the definition of stage.

Suppose for a contradiction that $\emptyset \in CF2(F)$. Let S be an unattacked SCC of F. Then $\emptyset$ is a naive extension of S. Given that F contains no self-attacks, this is not possible.

Suppose for a contradiction that $\emptyset \in stage2(F)$. Let S be an unattacked SCC of F. Then $\emptyset$ is a stage extension of S. Given what we showed about stage semantics above, this is not possible.

Suppose for a contradiction that $\emptyset \in SCF2(F)$. Let S be an unattacked SCC of F. Then $\emptyset$ is a SCOOC-naive extension of S. Given that F contains no self-attacks, this is not possible. □

Theorem 2. *Complete, grounded, ideal and eager semantics do not satisfy SAFWOC.*

Proof. Consider the 2-cycle AF $\langle\{a,b\},\{(a,b),(b,a)\}\rangle$. One can easily see that $\emptyset$ is a complete, grounded, ideal and eager extension of this AF. □

4 Motivation for New Semantics

Most of the most widely studied argumentation semantics satisfy admissibility. The same holds true for SAFWOC, as it is satisfied by preferred, stable, semi-stable, stage, CF2, stage2 and SCF2 semantics. Furthermore, three very widely studied semantics, namely preferred, stable and semi-stable, satisfy both of these principles. For this reason it seems plausible to assume that these are principles that are relevant to many applications of abstract argumentation.

The INRA principle has been introduced by Cramer and van der Torre [7]. They argued that this principle is plausible for determining what humans consider a rational judgment on the acceptability of arguments. While some semantics are known to satisfy INRA, none of the eleven semantics defined in Sect. 2 satisfies INRA while also satisfying admissibility and SAFWOC. It seems desirable to fill this gap by defining a semantics that simultaneously satisfies admissibility, SAFWOC and INRA.

In the next two sections, we will first define the *choice-preferred* semantics and then show that it does indeed satisfy these principles. Furthermore, we will show that it also satisfies completeness, existence, directionality and SCC-recursiveness, thus making it a semantics with multiple desirable properties.

5 Choice-Preferred Semantics

Before we formally define the choice-preferred semantics, we first informally explain and motivate its functioning, starting from considerations about an example AF.

Consider the 2-3-cycle AF F_1 depicted in Fig. 2. Note that here the only preferred extension is $\{c\}$. So b is necessarily rejected, i.e. attacked by every extension. But when we delete b, then we get a second extension, namely $\{a\}$. Now the idea behind choice-preferred semantics is that in situations like these, we want to ensure that b is not necessarily rejected by having the choice not to reject b, i.e. by having an extension that does not attack b. In this case, the only admissible set that does not attack b is the empty set, so we want the empty set to be an extension.

More generally, we want to ensure that in any AF consisting of a single SCC, no argument is strongly rejected. This way the INRA principle will be trivially satisfied for such AFs. We then generalize this approach even further by defining the choice-preferred semantics through SCC-recursion, which will lead to the INRA principle being satisfied even for AFs consisting of multiple SCCs. In this case we can have strongly rejected arguments, but they will always be attacked from a previous SCC, so that deleting them from the AF does not change the SCC-recursive computation of the extensions.

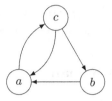

Fig. 2. The 2-3-cycle AF F_1

In order to ensure that no argument is strongly rejected in an AF consisting of a single SCC, we allow for any argument a from the SCC to be chosen, and then we choose a subset-maximal complete extension that does not attack a. There always exists at least one such subset-maximal complete extension, because the empty set is always a complete extension of the AF consisting of a single SCC. Thus we always choose at least one extension that does not attack a, so a is not strongly rejected.

After having given this informal motivation and explanation of the choice-preferred semantics, we now define the semantics formally. Since we define it through an SCC-recursion, we make use of the definition of $GF(BF, F, C)$ from Definition 18.

Definition 21. Let $F = (Ar, att)$ be an AF. We define choice-preferred(F) := $GF(BF_{cp}, F, Ar)$, where the base function BF_{cp} is defined as follows: For every $E \subseteq Ar$, $E \in BF_{cp}(AF, C)$ iff either $Ar = \emptyset$ and $E = \emptyset$ or $Ar \neq \emptyset$ and there is an $a \in Ar$ such that E is subset-maximal among the subsets of C that are complete and do not attack a.

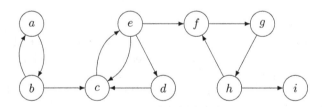

Fig. 3. A more complex argumentation framework F_2

Example 1. Consider the AF F_2 depicted in Fig. 3. We now explain how the extensions of F_2 can be computed in an SCC-recursive way. We start from the initial SCC $\{a, b\}$, for which there are two extensions, $\{a\}$ (because it is subset-maximal among the complete extensions of $F_2|_{\{a,b\}}$ that do not attack a) and $\{b\}$ (because it is subset-maximal among the complete extensions of $F_2|_{\{a,b\}}$ that do not attack b).

- If we choose the extension $\{b\}$ for the initial SCC, then c is attacked by b, i.e. it is in the set $D_{F_2}(E)$ of arguments that will be excluded from the AF in the SCC-recursive computation of the semantics. Then $\{e\}$ is an initial SCC, so e will be accepted, thus excluding d and f from further consideration. This makes $\{g\}$ an initial SCC, leading to the acceptance of g, thus excluding h from further consideration. So finally $\{i\}$ becomes an inital SCC, so i is accepted. In this way, we attain the extension $\{b, e, g, i\}$.

- If we choose the extension $\{a\}$ for the initial SCC, then $\{c, d, e\}$ becomes an initial SCC. Just like we discussed before for the AF F_1 from Fig. 2, we now have two options: We can choose $\{e\}$ from this SCC, or we can choose $\emptyset$. If we choose $\{e\}$ we proceed analogously as in the previous case, leading to the extension $\{a, e, g, i\}$. If we choose $\emptyset$, then we next consider the now initial SCC $\{f, g, h\}$, noting that f is not included in the set $U_{F_2}(\{f, g, h\}, E)$ of arguments that are unattacked by previous SCCs (because no accepted argument defends it against the attack from e). From this SCC we can only choose $\emptyset$. Finally we consider the now initial SCC $\{i\}$, noting that i is not included in the set $U_{F_2}(\{i\}, E)$ (because no accepted argument defends it against the attack from h). Since i is not in this set of arguments that are unattacked by previous SCCs, we cannot choose i, i.e. we can only choose $\emptyset$. This way we get the extension $\{a\}$.

Thus we see that the three choice-preferred extensions of F_2 are $\{a\}$, $\{a, e, g, i\}$ and $\{b, e, g, i\}$.

6 Satisfaction of Principles

In this section we show that the choice-preferred semantics does indeed satisfy the desired properties of admissibility, INRA and SAFWOC, as well as the further principles completeness, existence, directionality and SCC-recursiveness.

We start by showing that the choice-preferred semantics satisfies completeness.

Theorem 3. *The choice-preferred semantics satisfies completeness.*

Proof. We prove the theorem by proving through an induction over the number of arguments in F that for any AF $F = (Ar, att)$ and $C \subseteq Ar$, every set in $GF(BF_{cp}, F, C)$ is a complete extension of F. The base cases, in which there is at most one argument in the AF, are trivial, because such an AF consists of only one SCC and the base function BF_{cp} always chooses a complete extension from an SCC. So we assume for the inductive hypothesis that the required completeness property is satisfied by AFs of size less than n (i.e. with less than n arguments). Let $F = (Ar, att)$ be an AF of size n. If F consists of a single SCC, then the completeness property is again satisfied due to the base function BF_{cp}. So assume that $|SCCs(F)| > 1$. Let $C \subseteq Ar$ and let E be an element of $GF(BF_{cp}, F, C)$. We need to show that E is a complete extension of F. Since $|SCCs(F)| > 1$, Definition 18 ensures that for every $S \in SCCs(F)$,

$(E \cap S) \in GF(BF_{cp}, F|_{S \setminus D_F(E)}, U_F(S, E) \cap C)$. Since $E \cap S$ has less than n elements for every $S \in SCCs(F)$, the inductive hypothesis now implies that for every $S \in SCCs(F)$, $E \cap S$ is a complete extension of $F|_{S \setminus D_F(E)}$. Using this fact, we will now show that E is a complete extension of F:

- Suppose for a contradiction that E is not conflict-free. So there are $a, b \in E$ with $(a, b) \in att$. Let S_b be the SCC of F that contains b. Since $b \in E \cap S_b$ and $E \cap S_b$ is a complete extension of $F|_{S_b \setminus D_F(E)}$, we have that $a \notin S_b$. Thus $b \in D_F(E)$. Given that $b \in (E \cap S_b)$, this contradicts the fact that $(E \cap S_b) \in GF(BF_{cp}, F|_{S_b \setminus D_F(E)}, U_F(S^b, E) \cap C)$. Hence E is conflict-free.
- Suppose for a contradiction that E does not defend itself. So there are $a \in Ar$ and $b \in E$ such that $(a, b) \in att$ and E does not attack a. Let S_b be the SCC of F that contains b. Since $b \in E \cap S_b$ and $E \cap S_b$ is a complete extension of $F|_{S_b \setminus D_F(E)}$, $a \notin S_b$. Thus $b \notin U_F(S_b, E)$. Given Definition 18, this contradicts $b \in E$. Hence E defends itself.
- Suppose for a contradiction that E defends a but $a \notin E$. Since $a \notin E$, in the SCC-recursive computation of E, a gets removed at some step either due to a being in some $D_{F'}(E)$ for some subframework F' of F, or due to a not being in some $U_{F'}(S', E)$ for some subframework F' of F and some SCC S' of F' containing a, or due to a not being in the chosen complete extension E' of some single-SCC subframework $F' = (Ar', att')$ of F. The first case cannot occur due to the conflict-freeness of E. The second case cannot occur, since E defends a. The third case cannot occur, since $E' = E \cap Ar'$, so E' defends a against all attackers from within Ar', so $a \in E'$ by the completeness of E'. Thus we have arrived at a contradiction. Hence a is a complete extension of F.

$\square$

From this it directly follows that the choice-preferred semantics also satisfies admissibility:

Theorem 4. *The choice-preferred semantics satisfies admissibility.*

Next we show that the choice-preferred semantics satisfies the existence principle. For this we first establish a lemma that ensures that the existence principle holds on the level of a single SCC, independently of which set of arguments is assumed to be unattacked from the outside.

Lemma 1. *Let $F = (Ar, att)$ be an AF with $|SCCs(F)| = 1$, and let $C \subseteq Ar$. Then $BF_{cp}(F, C) \neq \emptyset$.*

Proof. If $Ar = \emptyset$, then $\emptyset \in BF_{cp}(F, C)$ by the first disjunct in the definition of BF_{cp} in Definition 21.

If $att = \emptyset$, then $|Ar| = 1$ due to the assumption that $|SCCs(F)| = 1$, and therefore $Ar \in BF_{cp}(F, C)$ by Definition 21.

Now suppose $Ar \neq \emptyset$ and $att \neq \emptyset$. Choose $a \in Ar$. Then $\emptyset$ is a complete set that is a subset of C and does not attack a. Hence there exists a subset-maximal complete set E that is a subset of C and does not attack a. Then $E \in BF_{cp}(F, C)$. $\square$

Due to the assumption that AFs are finite, every AF has at least one SCC that is not attacked by any other SCC. For each AF, we fix one such SCC and call it S_F^u. We can make the choice for S_F^u in such a way that when U is an unattacked set in F and $S_F^u \subseteq U$, then $S_{F|_U}^u = S_F^u$. The definition of choice-preferred semantics refers to an SCC-recursive computation of the extensions. Intuitively this means that we can compute the extensions by first considering an unattacked SCC, choose a choice-preferred extension from it, determine its impact on other SCCs and then recursively continue this computation. In order to formalize this intuition, we defined GF in Definition 18 based on the base function BF in line with the standard definition in the literature (e.g. [13]). However, this standard definition quantifies over all SCCs and therefore does not capture well the intuition that we can compute the extension by starting from an unattacked SCC. In the proof of Theorem 5, we will need to make use of this intuition. This intuition is captured by the following lemma, which directly follows from Definition 18 and the fact that AFs are finite:

Lemma 2. *Let BF be a base function, let $F = (Ar, att)$ and let $C \subseteq Ar$. Then $E \in GF(BF, F, C)$ iff either $Ar = E = \emptyset \in BF(F, C)$ or the following two properties are satisfied:*

- *$E \cap S_F^u \in BF(F|_{S_F^u}, S_F^u \cap C)$,*
- *$(E \setminus S_F^u) \in GF(BF, F|_{Ar \setminus (S_F^u \cup (S_F^u \cap E)^+)}, C \setminus (S_F^u \cup (S_F^u \setminus E^+)^+))$.*

Theorem 5. *The choice-preferred semantics satisfies existence.*

Proof. We prove the theorem by proving through an induction over the number of arguments in F that for any AF $F = (Ar, att)$ and $C \subseteq Ar$, $GF(BF_{cp}, F, C) \neq \emptyset$.

For the base cases we assume that there is at most one argument in the AF. Then $|SCCs(F)| \leq 1$, so $GF(BF_{cp}, F, C) = BF_{cp}(F, C)$, which is non-empty by Lemma 1.

For the inductive step, we assume the inductive hypothesis that any AF of size less than n satisfies the required property. Let $F = (Ar, att)$ be an AF of size n and let $C \subseteq Ar$. If $|SCCs(F)| = 1$, then the required property $GF(BF_{cp}, F, C) \neq \emptyset$ is satisfied based on Lemma 1, as in the base case. So assume that $|SCCs(F)| > 1$. By Lemma 1, there exists $E \in BF_{cp}(F|_{S_F^u}, S_F^u \cap C)$. By the inductive hypothesis, there exists $E' \in GF(BF_{cp}, F|_{Ar \setminus (S_F^u \cup (S_F^u \cap E)^+)}, C \setminus (S_F^u \cup (S_F^u \setminus E^+)^+))$. Now we show that $E \cup E' \in GF(BF_{cp}, F, C)$. For this we use Lemma 2, establishing the two propoerties listed in the lemma:

- By the choice of E, we know that $E = (E \cup E') \cap S_F^u$ and that $E \in BF_{cp}(F|_{S_F^u}, S_F^u \cap C)$. So $(E \cup E') \cap S_F^u \in BF_{cp}(F|_{S_F^u}, S_F^u \cap C)$, as required.
- By the choice of E', we know that $E' = (E \cup E') \setminus S_F^u$ and that $E' \in GF(BF_{cp}, F|_{Ar \setminus (S_F^u \cup (S_F^u \cap E)^+)}, C \setminus (S_F^u \cup (S_F^u \setminus E^+)^+))$. So $(E \cup E') \setminus S_F^u \in GF(BF_{cp}, F|_{Ar \setminus (S_F^u \cup (S_F^u \cap E)^+)}, C \setminus (S_F^u \cup (S_F^u \setminus E^+)^+))$, as required.

$\square$

Next we show that the choice-preferred semantics satisfies the directionality principle.

Theorem 6. *The choice-preferred semantics satisfies directionality.*

Proof. Let $F = (Ar, att)$ be an AF, and let U be an unattacked set in F.

Suppose E is a choice-preferred extension of $F|_U$. We need to show that there exists a choice-preferred extension E' of F such that $E = E' \cap U$. By the proof of Theorem 5, there exists some $E^* \in GF(BF_{cp}, F|_{Ar \setminus U}, Ar \setminus (U \cup (U \setminus E^+)^+))$. Define $E' := E \cup E^*$. Clearly $E = E' \cap U$, as required. Now one can easily see that Definition 18 implies that E' is a choice-preferred extension of F.

Conversely, suppose E is a choice-preferred extension of F. Now one can easily see that Definition 18 implies that $E \cap U$ is a choice-preferred extension of $F|_U$. $\square$

Next we show that the choice-preferred semantics satisfies the INRA principle.

Theorem 7. *The choice-preferred semantics satisfies the INRA principle.*

Proof. Write σ for *choice-preferred*. Let $F = (Ar, att)$ be an AF with an argument $a \in Ar$ such that every extension $E \in \sigma(F)$ attacks a. By the definition of choice-preferred we must have $|SCCs(F)| > 1$, because otherwise there would be an extension that does not attack a. We can now distinguish two possible structures of the framework F_{-a}:

$\underline{|SCCs(F_{-a})| = 1}$. Then F consists of exactly two SCCs: $Ar \setminus \{a\}$ and $\{a\}$, otherwise there would be multiple SCCs after the removal of a. $Ar \setminus \{a\}$ attacks a, so a can not also attack $Ar \setminus \{a\}$, i.e. $Ar \setminus \{a\}$ is an unattacked set. Now INRA follows from choice-preferred's satisfaction of the directionality principle.

$\underline{|SCCs(F_{-a})| > 1}$. We will make an induction over the number of arguments and assume INRA for strict subframeworks of F. Further we will call S_a the SCC in F that contains the argument a. First we will show $\sigma(F) \subseteq \sigma(F_{-a})$ by showing that for every extension E in $\sigma(F)$, we have $E \in \sigma(F_{-a})$. So assume $E \in \sigma(F)$, i.e. $E \in GF(BF_{cp}, F, Ar)$. Then for every $S \in SCCs(F)$, we have $(E \cap S) \in GF(BF_{cp}, F|_{S \setminus D_F(E)}, U_F(S, E) \cap Ar)$. It is easy to see that this implies $(E \cap S) \in \sigma(F|_{S \setminus D_F(E)})$. By the induction hypothesis, we get that $(E \cap S) \in GF(BF_{cp}, F|_{S \setminus (D_F(E) \cup \{a\})}, U_F(S, E) \cap Ar)$ (1). To show that $E \in \sigma(F_{-a})$ it remains to be shown that for every $S' \in SCCs(F_{-a})$, $(E \cap S') \in \sigma(F_{-a}|_{S' \setminus D_{F_{-a}}(E)})$ (*).

It is important to point out that either $S' \in SCCs(F)$ or $S' \subseteq S_a$, because the removal of a may only change the structure of S_a, while all other SCCs in F remain unchanged. If $S' \in SCCs(F)$ then $F|_{S' \setminus D_{F_{-a}}(E)} = F|_{S' \setminus (D_F(E) \cup \{a\})}$ and so the desired property (*) follows directly from (1).

If $S' \subseteq S_a$ we consider both possible structures of S_a:

– $|SCCs(F|_{S_a \setminus (D_F(E) \cup \{a\})})| = 1$.
  Then the only SCC in $F|_{S_a \setminus (D_F(E) \cup \{a\})}$ is either fully contained in S' or

fully disjoint with it. In the first case $S' = S_a \setminus \{a\}$, so $E \cap S' = E \cap S_a$ and $F|_{S_a \setminus (D_F(E) \cup \{a\})} = F_{-a}|_{S' \setminus D_{F_{-a}}(E)}$ and according to **(1)** (*) holds. In the second case $S' \subseteq D_{F_{-a}}(E)$, while $E \cap S' = \emptyset$, which holds, as $\emptyset$ is an extension for the empty framework.

- $|SCCs(F|_{S_a \setminus (D_F(E) \cup \{a\})})| > 1$.
  For each $S^* \in SCCs(F|_{S_a \setminus (D_F(E) \cup \{a\})})$, we have that $E \cap S^*$ is an extension for $F_{S^* \setminus D_{F|_{S_a \setminus (D_F(E) \cup \{a\})}}}$ **(2)**. For any $S'' \in SCCs(F|_{S' \setminus D_F(E)})$, we have that $S'' \in SCCs(F|_{S_a \setminus (D_F(E) \cup \{a\})})$ because $F|_{S' \setminus D_F(E)} \subseteq F|_{S_a \setminus (D_F(E) \cup \{a\})}$ and so S' dissolves into SCCs that are part of the framework reduced to S_a without a. So according to **(2)**, $E \cap S''$ is an extension for every S''.

This concludes the proof that $\sigma(F) \subseteq \sigma(F_{-a})$. The proof for $\sigma(F_{-a}) \subseteq \sigma(F)$ works similarly. □

Next we show that the choice-preferred semantics satisfies the SAFWOC principle.

Theorem 8. *The choice-preferred semantics satisfies the SAFWOC principle.*

Proof. Let $F = (Ar, att)$ be an argumentation framework such that F contains no odd cycle. Suppose for a contradiction that $\emptyset$ is a choice-preferred extension of F. Let $S \in SCCs(F)$ be an unattacked SCC of F. Then $\emptyset$ is a choice-preferred extension of $F|_S$. So there must be an argument $a \in S$ such that $\emptyset$ is a subset-maximal complete extension of $F|_S$ that does not attack a. Since F does not contain any odd cycles, every element of S can be reached from a either only through paths of even length or only through paths of odd length. Let A be the set of all elements of S that are reachable from a through paths of even length. Then clearly A is a complete extension of $F|_S$ and A does not attack a. This contradicts the subset-maximality of $\emptyset$. □

From the definition of the choice-preferred semantics, it directly follows that the choice-preferred semantics satisfies SCC-recursiveness.

Theorem 9. *The choice-preferred semantics satisfies SCC-recursiveness.*

7   Conclusion and Future Work

In this paper we have considered how to combine the recently introduced INRA principle, which ensures a relevance-oriented acceptance of arguments, with the admissibility principle, which is satisfied by all the argumentation semantics that are most widely used in applications of abstract argumentation. After noting that the grounded, ideal, eager and complete semantics satisfy both INRA and admissibility, we introduced and motivated a further principle, *Some Acceptance for Frameworks Without Odd Cycles* (SAFWOC), in order to positively distinguish less abstention-friendly semantics like preferred, stable, semi-stable, stage, CF2, stage2 and SCF2 from more abstention-friendly semantics like grounded, ideal, eager and complete. We then noted that no existing argumentation semantics

satisfies these three principles together, thus motivating the introduction of the novel *choice-preferred semantics* that does satisfy all three of these principles as well as several others.

This paper opens up several paths for future research. First, the principle-based analysis of the choice-preferred semantics can be extended further by considering other principles that go beyond the scope of this paper. Additionally, the relation between choice-preferred semantics and other existing semantics should be studied in more detail. We conjecture that every stable extension is a choice-preferred extension, that every choice-preferred extension is a preferred extension, and that choice-preferred semantics and semi-stable semantics are not comparable in this way, but the proofs for these conjectures are left to future work.

Furthermore, the complexity of reasoning tasks involving the choice-preferred semantics should be studied. We expect the choice-preferred semantics to behave similarly to the preferred semantics from a computational and complexity-theoretical point of view, but this will have to be confirmed in future work.

The INRA principle was originally introduced in combination with considerations about empirically tested human judgments about the acceptability of arguments. So this gives rise to the research question whether there are instances of human argumentation in which the choice-preferred predicts human judgments about the acceptability of arguments better than other existing semantics.

Dauphin, Rienstra and van der Torre [8] have introduced the *semi-qualified admissibility principle*, a weakening of admissibility motivated by the notion of *weak admissibility* introduced in [4]. For semi-qualified admissibility, an argument only needs to be defended against those attackers that appear in at least one extension. This weakening of admissibility allows for the acceptance of arguments attacked by odd cycles. Furthermore, they have defined analogs of standard admissible argumentation semantics that satisfy semi-qualified admissibility and allow for the acceptance of arguments attacked by odd cycles. These semantics are defined through a variant of SCC-recursion. In future work, one could similarly define an analog of the choice-preferred semantics and study its properties.

References

1. Baroni, P., Caminada, M., Giacomin, M.: An introduction to argumentation semantics. Knowl. Eng. Rev. **26**(4), 365–410 (2011). https://doi.org/10.1017/S0269888911000166
2. Baroni, P., Giacomin, M.: On principle-based evaluation of extension-based argumentation semantics. Artif. Intell. **171**(10), 675–700 (2007). https://doi.org/10.1016/j.artint.2007.04.004
3. Baroni, P., Giacomin, M., Guida, G.: SCC-recursiveness: a general schema for argumentation semantics. Artif. Intell. **168**(1), 162–210 (2005)
4. Baumann, R., Brewka, G., Ulbricht, M.: Revisiting the foundations of abstract argumentation-semantics based on weak admissibility and weak defense. In: Proceedings of the AAAI Conference on Artificial Intelligence, vol. 34, pp. 2742–2749 (2020)

5. Cramer, M., Guillaume, M.: Empirical cognitive study on abstract argumentation semantics. In: Frontiers in Artificial Intelligence and Applications, pp. 413–424 (2018)
6. Cramer, M., Guillaume, M.: Empirical study on human evaluation of complex argumentation frameworks. In: Calimeri, F., Leone, N., Manna, M. (eds.) JELIA 2019. LNCS (LNAI), vol. 11468, pp. 102–115. Springer, Cham (2019). https://doi.org/10.1007/978-3-030-19570-0_7
7. Cramer, M., van der Torre, L.: SCF2 - an argumentation semantics for rational human judgments on argument acceptability. In: Beierle, C., Ragni, M., Stolzenburg, F., Thimm, M. (eds.) Proceedings of the 8th Workshop on Dynamics of Knowledge and Belief (DKB'19) and the 7th Workshop KI & Kognition (KIK'19). CEUR Workshop Proceedings, vol. 2445, pp. 24–35. CEUR-WS.org (2019)
8. Dauphin, J., Rienstra, T., van der Torre, L.: A principle-based analysis of weakly admissible semantics. In: Prakken, H., Bistarelli, S., Santini, F., Taticchi, C. (eds.) Computational Models of Argument - Proceedings of COMMA 2020, Perugia, Italy, 4–11 September 2020. Frontiers in Artificial Intelligence and Applications, vol. 326, pp. 167–178. IOS Press (2020). https://doi.org/10.3233/FAIA200502
9. Dung, P.M.: On the acceptability of arguments and its fundamental role in non-monotonic reasoning, logic programming and n-person games. Artif. Intell. **77**(2), 321–357 (1995)
10. Dvořák, W., Gaggl, S.A.: Incorporating stage semantics in the SCC-recursive schema for argumentation semantics. In: In Proceedings of the 14th International Workshop on Non-Monotonic Reasoning (NMR 2012) (2012)
11. Dvořák, W., Gaggl, S.A.: Stage semantics and the SCC-recursive schema for argumentation semantics. J. Log. Comput. **26**(4), 1149–1202 (2016). https://doi.org/10.1093/logcom/exu006
12. Rahwan, I., Simari, G.R.: Argumentation in Artificial Intelligence, 1st edn. Springer, Heidelberg (2009). https://doi.org/10.1007/978-0-387-98197-0
13. van der Torre, L., Vesic, S.: The principle-based approach to abstract argumentation semantics. In: Baroni, P., Gabbay, D., Giacomin, M., van der Torre, L. (eds.) Handbook of Formal Argumentation. College Publications (2018)

New Weak Admissibility Semantics for Abstract Argumentation

Jérémie Dauphin[1]([✉]), Tjitze Rienstra[2], and Leendert van der Torre[1,3]

[1] University of Luxembourg, Esch-sur-Alzette, Luxembourg
{jeremie.dauphin,leon.vandertorre}@uni.lu
[2] Maastricht University, Maastricht, The Netherlands
t.rienstra@maastrichtuniversity.nl
[3] Zhejiang University, Hangzhou, China

Abstract. Baumann, Brewka and Ulbricht [3,4] recently introduced weak admissibility as an alternative to Dung's notion of admissibility [7], and they used it to define weakly preferred, weakly complete and weakly grounded semantics of argumentation frameworks. In earlier work, we introduced two variants of their new semantics which we called qualified and semi-qualified semantics. We analysed all known variants of weak admissibility semantics with respect to some of the principles discussed in the literature on abstract argumentation, as well as some new principles we introduced to distinguish them all. Such a principle-based analysis can be used not only for selecting a semantics for an application, or for algorithmic design, but also for further research into weak admissibility semantics. In this paper, we introduce six new kinds of semantics based on weak admissibility, and we provide an initial principle-based analysis. The analysis illustrates various ways in which the new semantics improve on existing ones.

Keywords: Formal argumentation · Abstract argumentation · Principle-based analysis · Weak admissibility

1 Introduction

There are three classes of abstract argumentation semantics, which can be illustrated by their behaviour on odd- and even-length cycles. Roughly, in Dung's admissibility-based semantics [7], the maximal extensions may contain arguments of even-length cycles but no arguments of odd-length cycles, unless the odd-length cycle is attacked by some accepted argument. In naïve-based semantics like CF2 semantics [2], arguments that are only attacked by self-attacking arguments are typically included in the extensions. In addition, odd-length cycles and even-length cycles are treated similarly, in the sense that naïve extensions may also contain arguments from odd-length cycles. Under the weak admissibility semantics recently introduced by Baumann, Brewka and Ulbricht (BBU) [3,4], the extensions typically include arguments that are only attacked

© Springer Nature Switzerland AG 2021
P. Baroni et al. (Eds.): CLAR 2021, LNAI 13040, pp. 112–126, 2021.
https://doi.org/10.1007/978-3-030-89391-0_7

by self-attacking arguments (as in naïve-based semantics), but the extensions typically do not contain arguments from odd-length cycles (as in admissibility-based semantics). In earlier work, we introduced two variants of BBU semantics which we called qualified and semi-qualified semantics [5]. The importance of these weak admissibility-based semantics is demonstrated by the fact that these papers obtained best paper awards at top conferences, the first [3] at the 17th International Conference on Principles of Knowledge Representation and Reasoning (KR20) and the second [5] at the 8th International Conference on Computational Models of Argument (COMMA 2020).

BBU semantics is compared to existing semantics not only in terms of their behaviour on a few examples, but also with a more systematic principle-based comparison [3,5]. All known variants of weak admissibility semantics have been analysed with respect to some of the principles discussed in the literature on abstract argumentation, as well as some new principles introduced to distinguish them all. It has been observed that such a principle-based analysis can be used for further research into weak admissibility semantics, for selecting a semantics for a particular application, or for the design of algorithms. We therefore raise the following research questions in this paper:

1. Which other semantics can be defined along the lines of weak admissibility?
2. How can these new semantics be distinguished from existing weak admissibility-based semantics? Which principles do these new semantics satisfy?

In this paper, we introduce six new kinds of semantics based on weak admissibility, and we provide an initial principle-based analysis. The analysis illustrates various ways in which the new semantics improve on existing ones. Let us illustrate these differences using the argumentation frameworks shown in Fig. 1 and 2. Table 1 lists seven kinds of complete semantics. Four are existing semantics: Dung's original complete semantics [7], BBU weakly complete semantics [4], and qualified as well as semi-qualified complete semantics [5]. Three are new semantics introduced in this paper: the weakly ∀-complete, the ∃-complete, and the ∀-complete semantics. Moreover, for each notion of complete semantics, there is a corresponding notion of minimal complete (or grounded) and maximal complete (or preferred) semantics, giving a total of nine new kinds of semantics. Since some of the semantics coincide, as we show later, there are only six new kinds of semantics.

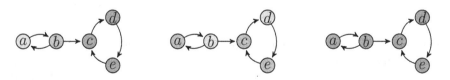

Fig. 1. A two-cycle attacking a three-cycle, with ∀-complete extensions in green, the arguments they attack in red and arguments that are neither in blue. (Color figure online)

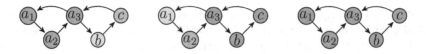

Fig. 2. Two connected three-cycles, with ∀-complete extensions in green, the arguments they attack in red and arguments that are neither in blue. (Color figure online)

Table 1. Various semantics applied to the frameworks depicted in Fig. 1 and 2.

Semantics	Fig. 1 extensions	Fig. 2 extensions
Complete [7]	$\emptyset$, $\{a\}$, $\{b,d\}$	$\emptyset$
Weakly complete [4]	$\{a\}$, $\{b,d\}$	$\{a_1\}$, $\{b\}$
Qualified complete [5]	$\emptyset$, $\{a\}$, $\{b,d\}$	$\emptyset$
Semi-qualified complete [5]	$\emptyset$, $\{a\}$, $\{b,d\}$	$\emptyset$
Weakly ∀-complete	$\{a\}$, $\{b,d\}$	$\emptyset$, $\{a_1\}$, $\{b\}$
∃-complete	$\emptyset$, $\{a\}$, $\{b,d\}$	$\{a_1\}$, $\{b\}$
∀-complete	$\emptyset$, $\{a\}$, $\{b,d\}$	$\emptyset$, $\{a_1\}$, $\{b\}$

Let us have a closer look at Table 1. Consider Fig. 1. Here, the weakly admissible sets are $\{b,d\}$ and $\{a\}$, $\{b\}$ and $\emptyset$. The weakly complete extensions are $\{b,d\}$ and $\{a\}$. Here, $\emptyset$ is not weakly complete since $\emptyset$ weakly defends $\{d\}$, even though $\{d\}$ is not weakly admissible. This is one way in which our new semantics differs from BBU weakly complete semantics [3,4].

Now consider Fig. 2. Here, we also have two minimal weakly complete extensions, $\{a_1\}$ and $\{b\}$. This is due to the fact that $\emptyset$ defends a_1 and b, but not both at the same time. So it seems strange to exclude $\emptyset$ as a weakly complete extension and be forced to choose either a_1 or b. We see that under weakly ∀-complete and ∀-complete semantics, this phenomenon does not occur.

To define our new semantics, we adopt the same inverted methodology as Baumann, Brewka and Ulbricht (BBU) [3,4], in the sense that we first define the notion of weak admissibility, and only then the notion of defence. In our case, we start from the notion of weak admissibility, but we define defence in a slightly different way. The difference is illustrated by the argumentation framework in Fig. 1. Whereas in BBU semantics, the empty set defends $\{d\}$, thereby preventing the empty set from being complete, that is not the case in some of our semantics.

Moreover, we distinguish between what we call some-things-considered (STC) and all-things-considered (ATC) defence. Consider the argumentation framework visualized in Fig. 2. In BBU semantics, $\emptyset$ defends $\{a_1\}$ and $\{b\}$, but not their union $\{a_1, b\}$. This is an example where BBU semantics does not satisfy Dung's so-called fundamental lemma, which says that we can add defended arguments in any order. For such cases, we say that the empty set STC defends $\{a_1\}$ and $\{b\}$, but it does not ATC defend them.

The layout of this paper is as follows. In Sect. 2, we introduce earlier work on weak admissibility. In Sect. 3, we introduce our new weak admissibility semantics.

In Sect. 4, we show which principles they satisfy. In Sect. 5, we discuss related and future work, and conclude in Sect. 6.

2 Preliminaries

We remind the reader of the basic notions of abstract argumentation introduced by Dung [7].

Definition 1. (Abstract argumentation and semantics). *An argumentation framework* (AF) *is a pair $F = (A, \rightarrow)$ where A is a set of abstract arguments and $\rightarrow$ is a relation of attack among them. Given a set $S \subseteq A$, we say that:*

- *S is conflict-free iff there are no $a, b \in S$ such that $a \rightarrow b$;*
- *$y \in A$ is an attacker of S iff $\exists a \in S$ such that $y \rightarrow a$;*
- *$S^+ := \{a \in A \mid \exists b \in S, b \rightarrow a\}$;*
- *S classically defends $S' \subseteq A$ iff for every attacker y of S', there is $a \in S$ such that $a \rightarrow y$;*
- *S is admissible iff S is conflict-free and defends itself;*
- *S is a complete extension of F iff S is admissible, and for every $S' \supseteq S$, if S defends S', then $S' \subseteq S$.*

The semantics introduced in this paper are based on the concept of *weak admissibility*, as introduced by Baumann, Brewka and Ulbricht [4]. Weak admissibility is based on the notion of a *reduct*, where one removes from the framework a set of arguments as well as every argument it attacks.

Definition 2 (Reduct [4]). *Let $F = (A, \rightarrow)$ be an AF and let $E \subseteq A$. The E-reduct of F is the AF $F^E = (E^*, \rightarrow \cap (E^* \times E^*))$, where $E^* = A \setminus (E \cup E^+)$.*

The notion of reduct is used to define weak admissibility. When checking whether a set is weakly admissible, one checks whether any of its attackers is weakly admissible in the reduct.

Definition 3 (Weak admissibility [4]). *Let $F = (A, \rightarrow)$ be an AF. The set of weakly admissible sets of F is denoted as $ad^w(F)$ and defined by $E \in ad^w(F)$ if and only if E is conflict-free and, for every attacker y of E, we have $y \notin \cup ad^w(F^E)$.*

As mentioned in the introduction, the methodology is the inverse of the methodology of Dung [7], where the concept of defence is defined first and then used to define admissibility. In the case of weak admissibility, the notion of weak admissibility is defined first and then used to define the notion of weak defence.

Definition 4 (Weak defence [4]). *Let $F = (A, \rightarrow)$ be an AF. A set $E \subseteq A$ weakly defends a set $X \subseteq A$ iff for any attacker y of X we have:*

- *E attacks y, or*

– $y \notin \cup ad^w(F^E)$, $y \notin E$, and $X \subseteq X' \in ad^w(F)$.

We show later in the paper that the notion of weak defence between weakly admissible sets can be defined in a manner that does not require one to recompute any reduct. For the reader's convenience, we provide an alternative definition here, and show in Sect. 4 that it is equivalent.

Proposition 1. *Let* $F = (A, \rightarrow)$ *be an AF,* $E \in ad^w(F)$, $X \supseteq E$ *and* $D = X \backslash E$. *E weakly defends* X *iff:*

1. *for any attacker* y *of* D, $y \notin \cup \{Z \in ad^w(F) \mid E \subseteq Z\}$, *and*
2. *there is a set* $X' \supseteq X$ *such that* $X' \in ad^w(F)$.

The notions of weak admissibility and weak defence are then used to define weakly complete, weakly grounded and weakly preferred semantics, in the same way that in Dung's work [7], the notions of admissibility and defence are used to define complete, grounded and preferred semantics.

Definition 5 (Weak admissibility semantics [4]). *Let* $F = (A, \rightarrow)$ *be an AF and* $E \subseteq A$. *We say that* E *is:*

– *a weakly complete extension of* F *iff* $E \in ad^w(F)$ *and for any* $E' \supseteq E$, *if* E *weakly defends* E', *then* $E' \subseteq E$;
– *a weakly grounded extension of* F *iff* E *is a* $\subseteq$-*minimal weakly complete extension of* F;
– *a weakly preferred extension of* F *iff* E *is a* $\subseteq$-*maximal weakly admissible set in* F.

3   New Weak Admissibility Semantics

In this section, we present new semantics inspired by weak admissibility. The main point is that if an argument is never accepted, then it should not prevent other arguments from being accepted. We thus base our semantics on the notion of weak admissibility, but revise the derived notion of defence into three variants: weak ∀-defence, ∃-defence and ∀-defence.

For the notion of weak ∀-defence, we look at all ⊆-maximal supersets of the extension that are weakly defended by it. If their intersection is the extension itself, then it is defended. This allows for the fact that when lifted to a notion of complete extensions, where the extension defends more arguments but in a disjoint manner, we allow the extension to abstain from including any of those arguments. We refer back to the discussion of Fig. 2 in the introduction, where the empty set defends $\{a_1\}$ and $\{b\}$, but not $\{a_1, b\}$. Arguments that are defended and are compatible with all other defended arguments must, on the other hand, still be included.

Definition 6 (Weak ∀-defence). *Let* $F = (A, \rightarrow)$ *be an AF. A set* $E \subseteq A$ *weakly ATC (all-things-considered) defends* $X \subseteq A$ *(E weak ∀-defends X) iff* E *weakly defends* X, *and* X *is a subset of the intersection of the* $\subseteq$-*maximal supersets of* E *that are weakly defended by* E.

For $\exists$-defence, we start again from the notion of weak defence, but now change $X \subseteq X' \in ad^w(F)$ into $X \cup E \in ad^w(F)$. Thus, for E to defend X, it is required that $E \cup X$ is weakly admissible, rather than some arbitrary superset of X being weakly admissible. This avoids the case where $\emptyset$ defends $\{d\}$ in the AF of Fig. 1.

Definition 7 ($\exists$-defence). *Let $F = (A, \to)$ be an AF. A set $E \subseteq A$ STC (some-things-considered) defends a set $X \subseteq A$ (E $\exists$-defends X) whenever, for every attacker y of X, either E attacks y, or $y \notin \cup ad^w(F^E)$ and $X \cup E \in ad^w(F)$.*

For the notion of $\forall$-defence, we take the modification made for weak $\forall$-defence, but use the notion of $\exists$-defence as a base instead of weak defence.

Definition 8 ($\forall$-defence). *Let $F = (A, \to)$ be an AF. A set $E \subseteq A$ ATC (all-things-considered) defends $X \subseteq A$ (E $\forall$-defends X) iff E $\exists$-defends X, and X is a subset of the intersection of the $\subseteq$-maximal supersets of E that are $\exists$-defended by E.*

We now lift these different notions of defence to notions of admissibility, in the same way that the classical notion of defence is lifted to provide the classical notion of admissibility.

Definition 9 (weak $\forall$-admissibility). *Let $F = (A, \to)$ be an AF. A set $E \subseteq A$ is weakly $\forall$-admissible iff E is conflict-free and weakly $\forall$-defends itself.*

Definition 10 ($\exists$-admissibility). *Let $F = (A, \to)$ be an AF. A set $E \subseteq A$ is $\exists$-admissible iff E is conflict-free and $\exists$-defends itself.*

Definition 11 ($\forall$-admissibility). *Let $F = (A, \to)$ be an AF. A set $E \subseteq A$ is $\forall$-admissible iff E is conflict-free and $\forall$-defends itself.*

It turns out that these three notions are all equivalent to weak admissibility. We show this in Sect. 4 with Theorem 1. For this reason, in the definitions to come, we work directly with weakly admissible sets. One should keep in mind that while the notions of weak admissibility arising from the different notions of weak defence are equivalent, the notions of weak defence are all different, and still give rise to different weak admissibility semantics, as we will see in the rest of this paper.

Example 1. In Fig. 1, the weak admissible, weak $\forall$-admissible, $\exists$-admissible and $\forall$-admissible semantics are all the same: $\emptyset$, $\{b\}$, $\{d, b\}$ and $\{a\}$. In Fig. 2, the weakly admissible, weak $\forall$-admissible, $\exists$-admissible and $\forall$-admissible sets are $\emptyset$, $\{b\}$ and $\{a_1\}$.

The new notions of defence can be lifted to complete and grounded semantics in the same way as classical defence is lifted to give rise to the complete and grounded semantics in Dung's work [7]. Contrary to the notions of admissibility which arise from the different notions of defence, the different notions of complete semantics are not equivalent. The differences arise from differences in the notions of defence. For example, some weakly admissible sets might $\exists$-defend some of their supersets, but not $\forall$-defend any of them, resulting in different complete extensions. For similar reasons, the resulting grounded semantics are also different.

Definition 12 (Weak $\forall$-complete semantics). *Let $F = (A, \rightarrow)$ be an AF and $E \subseteq A$. We say that E is a weak $\forall$-complete extension of F ($E \in co^{w\forall}(F)$) iff $E \in ad^w(F)$, and for any $E' \supseteq E$, if E weakly $\forall$-defends E', then $E' \subseteq E$.*

Definition 13 ($\exists$-complete semantics). *Let $F = (A, \rightarrow)$ be an AF and $E \subseteq A$. We say that E is an $\exists$-complete extension of F ($E \in co^{\exists}(F)$) iff $E \in ad^w(F)$ and for any $E' \supseteq E$, if E $\exists$-defends E', then $E' \subseteq E$.*

Definition 14 ($\forall$-complete semantics). *Let $F = (A, \rightarrow)$ be an AF and $E \subseteq A$. We say that E is a $\forall$-complete extension of F ($E \in co^{\forall}(F)$) iff $E \in ad^w(F)$, and for any $E' \supseteq E$, if E $\forall$-defends E', then $E' \subseteq E$.*

In order to illustrate the formal definitions, we provide examples of the different kinds of weakly complete semantics below, but remind the reader that these are also discussed in the introduction.

Example 2 (Difference between complete extensions in Fig. 1 and 2). In Fig. 1, the weak-complete and weak-$\forall$-complete extensions are $\{d, b\}$ and $\{a\}$. The $\exists$-complete and $\forall$-complete extensions are $\emptyset$, $\{d, b\}$ and $\{a\}$. In Fig. 2, the weak/$\exists$-complete extensions are $\{b\}$ and $\{a_1\}$. The $\forall$/weak-$\forall$ admissible sets are $\emptyset$, $\{b\}$ and $\{a_1\}$.

These two examples are enough to show that all four kinds of semantics are different, since the ones that agree on the first framework disagree on the second.

Definition 15 (Weak $\forall$-grounded semantics). *Let $F = (A, \rightarrow)$ be an AF and $E \subseteq A$. We say that E is a weak $\forall$-grounded extension of F iff E is a $\subseteq$-minimal weak $\forall$-complete extension of F.*

Definition 16 ($\exists$-grounded semantics). *Let $F = (A, \rightarrow)$ be an AF and $E \subseteq A$. We say that E is an $\exists$-grounded extension of F iff E is a $\subseteq$-minimal $\exists$-complete extension of F.*

Definition 17 ($\forall$-grounded semantics). *Let $F = (A, \rightarrow)$ be an AF and $E \subseteq A$. We say that E is a $\forall$-grounded extension of F iff E is a $\subseteq$-minimal $\forall$-complete extension of F.*

Example 3. Consider Fig. 3. In the framework depicted, the weakly $\forall$-grounded and $\forall$-grounded extension is $\{e\}$, whereas the $\exists$-grounded extensions are $\{a_1, e\}$ and $\{b, e\}$. It is interesting to see that since d is not weakly admissible, the empty set $\forall$-defends $\{e\}$. In addition, $\{e\}$ is weakly admissible since in its reduct, $F^{\{e\}}$, d is still not weakly admissible. Therefore, $\{e\}$ is the $\forall$-grounded extension.

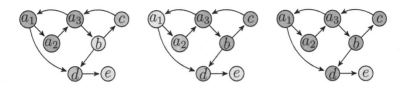

Fig. 3. Two connected 3-cycles defending an argument, with ∀-complete extensions in green, the arguments they attack in red and arguments that are neither in blue. (Color figure online)

4 Principles

In this section, we provide a preliminary analysis of the principles satisfied by these new semantics. We also provide a few properties for the different notions of weak defence, and explain how they are related. A complete overview of the results obtained is shown in Table 2. For comparison, this table also includes the qualified semantics (q-co, q-gr, q-pr) and semi-qualified semantics (sq-co, sq-pr) discussed by Dauphin, Rienstra, and van der Torre [5]. The results for co^w, pr^w, gr^w, as well as for the various qualified and semi-qualified semantics, have been demonstrated previously in [5], except for the result of directionality for pr^w, which is taken from the work of Baumann, Brewka and Ulbricht [3].

Table 2. Principles satisfied by the semantics discussed in this paper

	co^w	pr^w	gr^w	$co^{w\forall}$	$gr^{w\forall}$	$co^\exists$	$gr^\exists$	$co^\forall$	$gr^\forall$	q-co	q-gr	q-pr	sq-co	sq-pr
Abs.	✗	✗	✗	✗	✗	✗	✗	?	?	✗	✓	✗	✓	✗
Dir.	✗	✓	✗	✗	✗	?	?	?	?	✓	✓	✓	✓	✓
Red. adm.	✓	✓	✓	✓	✓	✓	✓	✓	✓	?	?	?	?	?

Definition 18. *A semantic function σ satisfies the principles of:*

- *allowing abstention iff for every AF $F = (A, \rightarrow)$, and $a \in A$, if there exists $E_1, E_2 \in \sigma(F)$ such that $a \in E_1$ and $a \in E_2^+$, then there exists E_3 such that $a \notin E_3 \cup E_3^+$;*
- *directionality iff for every AF $F = (A, \rightarrow)$ and unattacked set U of F we have $\sigma(F){\downarrow}_U = \sigma(F{\downarrow}_U)$, where an unattacked set U of F is any set $U \subseteq A$ such that there is no $x \in A\backslash U$ and $y \in U$ with $x \rightarrow y$, and $\sigma(F){\downarrow}_U = \{E \cap U | E \in \sigma(F)\}$, $F{\downarrow}_U = (U, \rightarrow \cap U \times U)$.*
- *reduct admissibility iff for every AF $F = (A, \rightarrow)$, for every $E \in \sigma(F)$, we have $\forall a \in E$, $\forall b \in A$, if $b \rightarrow a$, then $b \notin \cup \sigma(F^E)$.*

Proposition 2. *$co^{w\forall}$, $gr^{w\forall}$, $co^\exists$ and $gr^\exists$ do not satisfy the principle of allowing abstention.*

Proof. For $co^{w\forall}$ and $gr^{w\forall}$, the counter-example is in Fig. 1. We have two extensions for both semantics: $\{a\}$ and $\{b,d\}$. There is an extension including a and another one attacking it, but there is no extension where a is neither included nor attacked.

The counter-example for $co^{\exists}$ and $gr^{\exists}$ is depicted in Fig. 4. The $\exists$-complete and $\exists$-grounded extensions coincide, and are $\{b\}$ and $\{a_1,d\}$. So there is one extension where d is included and another where d is attacked, but no extension where neither is the case. □

Fig. 4. Two connected 3-cycles where one attacks another argument. This shows the failure of allowing abstention for $co^{\exists}$ and $gr^{\exists}$.

Proposition 3. $co^{w\forall}$ and $gr^{w\forall}$ do not satisfy the principle of directionality.

Proof. The counter-example is in Fig. 1. For both semantics, there are two extensions: $\{a\}$ and $\{b,d\}$. When restricted to the unattacked set $\{a,b\}$, we obtain $\{\{a\},\{b\}\}$. However, when applying the semantic function to this restricted framework, we obtain weak $\forall$-complete extensions $\{\emptyset,\{a\},\{b\}\}$ and weak $\forall$-grounded extension $\{\emptyset\}$, neither of which match $\{\{a\},\{b\}\}$. □

Conjecture 1. $co^{\exists}$, $gr^{\exists}$, $co^{\forall}$ and $gr^{\forall}$ satisfy the principle of directionality.

These four semantic functions handle the counter-example to directionality of $co^{w\forall}$ better, however it does not seem straightforward to prove that the principle holds in general. Further research in this direction should prove fruitful.

Proposition 4. $co^{\exists}$, $gr^{\exists}$, $co^{\forall}$, $gr^{\forall}$, $co^{w\forall}$ and $gr^{w\forall}$ all satisfy the principle of reduct admissibility.

Proof. This follows from the fact that each of these semantic functions are based on weak admissibility. □

We now analyse some properties of intermediate notions such as defence and admissible sets. An important observation is that the various notions of defence introduced in this paper all give rise to an equivalent notion of admissible sets. Additionally, these notions of defence are related, as described in the following proposition:

Proposition 5. Let $F = (A, \rightarrow)$ and $E, X \subseteq A$. If E $\forall$-defends X, then E $\exists$-defends X. If E $\exists$-defends X, then E weakly defends X. If E weakly $\forall$-defends X, then E weakly defends X.

Proof. It follows from the definition that $\forall$-defence implies $\exists$-defence, since $\exists$-defence is an explicit condition of $\forall$-defence.

$\exists$-defence implies weak defence follows from the fact that $X \cup E \in ad^w(F)$ implies that there exists $X' \in ad^w(F)$ with $X \subseteq X'$.

It follows from the definition that weak $\forall$-defence implies weak defence, since weak defence is an explicit condition of weak $\forall$-defence.   □

Theorem 1. *Let $F = (A, \rightarrow)$ be an AF, and $E \subseteq A$ a set of arguments. The following statements are equivalent:*

1. *E is weakly admissible;*
2. *E is $\exists$-admissible;*
3. *E is $\forall$-admissible;*
4. *E is weakly $\forall$-admissible.*

Proof. If E is not conflict-free, then none of the statements hold. We therefore only need to look at cases where E is conflict-free. We prove the equivalence by showing a cycle of implications between items 1, 2 and 3, then show equivalence between items 1 and 4.

- $1 \Rightarrow 2$ (*E* weakly admissible implies $\exists$-admissible): We have to show that E $\exists$-defends itself. By Proposition 4.4, item 3 of [4], E weakly defends itself. Additionally, $E \cup E$ is weakly admissible, so E $\exists$-defends itself.
- $2 \Rightarrow 3$ (*E* $\exists$-admissible implies $\forall$-admissible): We have to show that E $\forall$-defends itself. E $\exists$-defends itself. Since E $\exists$-defends at least itself, it is included in every $\subseteq$-maximal superset of itself which it $\exists$-defends. Therefore, it is included in the intersection of those sets, and so it $\forall$-defends itself.
- $3 \Rightarrow 1$ (*E* $\forall$-admissible implies weakly admissible): E $\forall$-defends itself, hence E weakly defends itself. E is also conflict-free since it is $\forall$-admissible. Therefore, by Proposition 4.4 item 4 of [4], E is weakly admissible.
- $4 \Rightarrow 1$ (*E* weakly $\forall$-admissible implies weakly admissible): E weakly $\forall$-defends itself, therefore E weakly defends itself by Proposition 5. Therefore, by Proposition 4.4 item 4 of [4], E is weakly admissible.
- $1 \Rightarrow 4$ (*E* weakly admissible implies weakly $\forall$-admissible): E is a subset of all its supersets, so we only have to show that E weakly defends itself. By Proposition 4.4 item 3 of [4], E being weakly admissible implies that it weakly defends itself. Therefore E is weakly $\forall$-admissible.   □

It is important to observe that the $\forall$-grounded extension is not always unique. The $\exists$-grounded extension is not always unique either.

Proposition 6. *The weak $\forall$-grounded and $\exists$-grounded extensions are not always unique.*

Proof. Consider Fig. 1. The weak $\forall$-grounded extensions are $\{a\}$ and $\{b, d\}$. The empty set is not weakly $\forall$-complete, since the only $\subseteq$-maximal superset of itself that it weakly defends is $\{d\}$, and therefore it weakly $\forall$-defends $\{d\}$, which it does not include.

Consider Fig. 2. The $\exists$-grounded extensions are $\{a_1\}$ and $\{b\}$. The empty set is not $\exists$-complete, since it defends both $\{a_1\}$ and $\{b\}$, as they are weakly admissible, and their only attacker is never admissible in the reduct by the empty set, i.e. the original framework.   □

On the other hand, in both of the frameworks depicted in Fig. 1 and 2, the $\forall$-grounded extension is unique. However, it remains to be proven that this is always the case.

Conjecture 2. The $\forall$-grounded extension is always unique.

We now interest ourselves in a few properties of the newly introduced notions, in particular $\exists$-defence. We show that $\exists$-defence satisfies a property which is reminiscent of the Fundamental lemma described in Dung's work [7].

Proposition 7. *(Generalisation of Theorem 3.11 from [4]) Let $F = (A, \rightarrow)$ be an AF. Let $E, X \subseteq A$. If E is weakly admissible and E classically defends X, then $E \cup X$ is weakly admissible.*

Proof. Repeated applications of Theorem 3.11 from [4], since classical defence is monotonic.   □

Proposition 8. *Let $F = (A, \rightarrow)$ be an AF. If $E \subseteq A$ is weakly admissible and $\exists$-defends $X \subseteq A$, then $E \cup X$ is weakly admissible.*

Proof. If E $\exists$-defends X, then by definition we have that for every attacker y of X, either (1) $y \notin \cup ad^w(F^E)$, $y \notin E$ and $X \cup E \in ad^w(F)$, or (2) E attacks y. If there is at least one y satisfying condition (1), we directly obtain that $E \cup X$ is weakly admissible. Otherwise, we obtain that every y satisfies condition (2), i.e. for every attacker y of X, E attacks y. Then E classically defends X. Using Proposition 7, it then follows that $E \cup X$ is weakly admissible.   □

It is worth mentioning that Proposition 8 does not hold for weak defence. That is, if a weakly admissible set E weakly defends a set X, it does not follow that $E \cup X$ is weakly admissible. To see why, consider Fig. 1, where $\emptyset$ is weakly admissible and weakly defends $\{d\}$, but $\{d\}$ is not weakly admissible.

On the other hand, Proposition 5 implies that this result holds for $\forall$-defence as well.

We now show a few more properties of $\forall$-complete extensions, in particular that $\subseteq$-maximal $\forall$-complete extensions coincide with weakly preferred extensions.

Proposition 9. *Let $F = (A, \rightarrow)$ be an AF. If E is weakly preferred, then it is $\forall$-complete.*

Proof. Suppose E is weakly preferred. Then E is weakly admissible, and the only superset of E that is $\forall$-defended by E is E itself, which implies that E equals the intersection of the $\subseteq$-maximal supersets of E that are $\forall$-defended by E. Hence it is $\forall$-complete.   □

Proposition 10. *Let $F = (A, \rightarrow)$ be an AF. If E is weakly admissible, then there is a $\forall$-complete set that includes E.*

Proof. Suppose E is weakly admissible. Then E is included in a weakly preferred extension, and using Proposition 9, it follows that it is $\forall$-complete. □

Proposition 11. *Let $F = (A, \rightarrow)$ be an AF. If $E \subseteq A$ is a $\subseteq$-maximal $\forall$-complete extension, then E is weakly preferred.*

Proof. Suppose E is a $\subseteq$-maximal $\forall$-complete extension of F. Then E is weakly admissible. Suppose E is not weakly preferred. Then there is an $E' \supsetneq E$ that is weakly admissible. But then using Proposition 10, E' is also included in a $\forall$-complete extension that is bigger than E. This contradicts the assumption that E is a $\subseteq$-maximal $\forall$-complete extension. □

From Propositions 9 and 11, we can deduce that the weakly preferred extensions are precisely the $\subseteq$-maximal $\forall$-complete extensions.

One can also provide alternative definitions for each of the notions of defence we have introduced. The main point to consider is that for the purpose of defining a semantics, the notion of defence only really matters between a weakly admissible set and its supersets. With these assumptions in place, the conditions for defence can be reformulated.

Proposition 12 (Alternative definition from [3]). *Let $F = (A, \rightarrow)$ be an AF, $E \in ad^w(F)$, $X \supseteq E$ and $D = X \setminus E$. We have that E weakly defends X iff:*

1. *for any attacker y of D, $y \notin \cup ad^w(F^E)$, and*
2. *there is a set $D' \supseteq D$ such that $D' \in ad^w(F^E)$.*

Theorem 2 (Theorem 4.1 from [3]). *Let $F = (A, \rightarrow)$ be an AF and $E \in ad^w(F)$. Suppose that $E \cap E' = \emptyset$. Then, $E' \in ad^w(F^E)$ if and only if $E \cup E' \in ad^w(F)$.*

From this theorem, we can infer more practical, yet equivalent conditions for weak defence.

Proposition 13. *Let $F = (A, \rightarrow)$ be an AF, $E \in ad^w(F)$, $X \supseteq E$ and $D = X \setminus E$. The following two statements are equivalent:*

1. *There is a set $D' \supseteq D$ such that $D' \in ad^w(F^E)$.*
2. *There is a set $X' \supseteq X$ such that $X' \in ad^w(F)$.*

Proof. 1. $\Rightarrow$ 2.
$D' \in ad^w(F^E)$ and $E \in ad^w(F)$, thus according to Theorem 2, $E \cup D' \in ad^w(F)$. So there exists such an X', namely $E \cup D'$.
2. $\Rightarrow$ 1.
$X' \supseteq X$ such that $X' \in ad^w(F)$. We also have $E \in ad^w(F)$, therefore by Theorem 2, we have $X' \setminus E \in ad^w(F^E)$. Since $D = X \setminus E$, then $D \subseteq X' \setminus E$. □

Proposition 14. *Let $F = (A, \rightarrow)$ be an AF, $E \in ad^w(F)$, $X \supseteq E$ and $D = X \setminus E$ such that there exists an $X' \supseteq X$ with $X' \in ad^w(F)$. The following two statements are equivalent:*

1. *For any attacker y of D, $y \notin \cup ad^w(F^E)$.*
2. *For any attacker y of D, $y \notin \cup \{Z \in ad^w(F) \mid E \subseteq Z\}$.*

Proof. We prove the proposition by showing the equivalence of the negation of both items, i.e. the equivalence of the existence of an attacker y of D from either (1.) the set $\cup ad^w(F^E)$ or from (2.) the set $\cup \{Z \in ad^w(F) \mid E \subseteq Z\}$.

1. $\Rightarrow$ 2.
Suppose there exists $y \in \cup ad^w(F^E)$ such that y attacks D. Then, there must be some $S \in ad^w(F^E)$ such that $y \in S$. By Theorem 2, $E \cup S \in ad^w(F)$. Therefore, there exists $y \in \cup \{Z \in ad^w(F) \mid E \subseteq Z\}$ with y attacks D.
2. $\Rightarrow$ 1.
Suppose there exists $y \in \cup \{Z \in ad^w(F) \mid E \subseteq Z\}$ such that y attacks D. Then there must be $Z \in ad^w(F)$ with $Z \supseteq E$ and $y \in Z$. Let $S = Z \setminus E$. Then, according to Theorem 2, $S \in ad^w(F^E)$. Suppose for a contradiction that $y \in E$. Then, X is not conflict-free and neither is any $X' \supseteq X$. Therefore, there is no $X' \supseteq X$ such that $X' \in ad^w(F)$. This contradicts our initial assumption that there exists such an X'. So $y \notin E$, and so $y \in S$. Therefore $y \in \cup ad^w(F^E)$. $\qquad\square$

From these results, we can infer an equivalent notion of weak defence where one does not have to compute weak admissibility again when computing defence. One only has to compute the weak admissible sets in the original framework, and for the purpose of computing defence, computing weak admissibility in some reducts is no longer necessary.

The notion only applies when considering weakly admissible sets and asking which of their supersets they defend. However, this is exactly the question that is of interest when asking whether a weakly admissible set is weakly complete. Therefore, for the purpose of computing weakly complete extensions, this notion is equivalent to the original definition of weak defence.

Proposition 15. *Let $F = (A, \rightarrow)$ be an AF, $E \in ad^w(F)$, $X \supseteq E$ and $D = X \setminus E$. E weakly-defends X iff:*

1. *for any attacker y of D, $y \notin \cup \{Z \in ad^w(F) \mid E \subseteq Z\}$, and*
2. *there is a set $X' \supseteq X$ such that $X' \in ad^w(F)$.*

The same can be done for the newly introduced notion of $\exists$-defence.

Proposition 16. *Let $F = (A, \rightarrow)$ be an AF, $E \in ad^w(F)$, $X \supseteq E$ and $D = X \setminus E$. E $\exists$-defends X iff:*

1. *for any attacker y of D, $y \notin \cup \{Z \in ad^w(F) \mid E \subseteq Z\}$, and*
2. *$X \in ad^w(F)$.*

5   Related and Future Work

In general, one of the main purposes of axiomatisation in formal logic is to understand the logic with an intuitively understandable small set of principles. In proposing axioms, care should be taken to ensure that each axiom is sufficiently reasonable and sufficiently independent of others. Ideally, there should be some degree of philosophical motivation behind them. However, in the principle-based analysis of abstract argumentation [1, 8], thus far the focus has been on the use of principles to differentiate between various semantics, and to assist with computational techniques using decomposability. Concerning the first issue, Baumann, Brewka and Ulbricht [4] show that the weakly grounded extensions are not necessarily unique, and the principle-based analysis by Dauphin, Rienstra and van der Torre [5] shows that weakly complete semantics does not satisfy the principles of directionality or SCC decomposability.

The *weakly complete* semantics of Dondio and Longo [6] (which, despite the name, is different from the weakly complete semantics of BBU) provides yet another way to deal with defence from arguments that are never accepted. Their labelling-based semantics is based on an "undecidedness blocking" mechanism where the undecided label is not always propagated to the arguments that are attacked. In future work, we plan to include their approach in our analysis.

6   Conclusion

The semantics of abstract argumentation frameworks has been an active area of research ever since Dung published his seminal'95 paper [7]. The topic deals with the question of how to determine the acceptable arguments of an argumentation framework, and forms the foundation of any form of reasoning using Dung's model of argumentation. The recent BBU proposal [3, 4] to define semantics in terms of their new notions of weak admissibility and weak defence is interesting because it leads to a third category of semantics besides the classically admissible and naïve categories. While these semantics overcome issues concerning self-attacking arguments and odd-length cycles, we have shown in earlier work that there are several principles, often considered desirable, that are violated by their semantics [5]. In this paper, we defined six new variants of weak admissible semantics, and provided an initial principle-based analysis to distinguish them from BBU semantics. While some questions remain (such as whether our new semantics satisfy the directionality principle, and whether ∀-grounded extensions are unique), our work shows that the intuitions behind weak defence and weak admissibility can be applied in different ways, leading to a wide range of new variants of weakly admissible semantics.

Acknowledgements. Leon van der Torre acknowledges financial support from the Fonds National de la Recherche Luxembourg (INTER/Mobility/19/13995684/DLAl/van der Torre).

References

1. Baroni, P., Giacomin, M.: On principle-based evaluation of extension-based argumentation semantics. Artif. Intell. **171**(10–15), 675–700 (2007)
2. Baroni, P., Giacomin, M., Guida, G.: SCC-recursiveness: a general schema for argumentation semantics. Artif. Intell. **168**(1–2), 162–210 (2005)
3. Baumann, R., Brewka, G., Ulbricht, M.: Comparing weak admissibility semantics to their dung-style counterparts - reduct, modularization, and strong equivalence in abstract argumentation. In: Proceedings of the the 17th International Conference on Principles of Knowledge Representation and Reasoning (KR2020) (2020)
4. Baumann, R., Brewka, G., Ulbricht, M.: Revisiting the foundations of abstract argumentation - semantics based on weak admissibility and weak defense. In: The Thirty-Fourth AAAI Conference on Artificial Intelligence, AAAI 2020, New York, USA, 7–12 February 2020. AAAI Press (2020). https://www.aaai.org/Library/AAAI/aaai20contents.php
5. Dauphin, J., Rienstra, T., van der Torre, L.: A principle-based analysis of weakly admissible semantics. In: Prakken, H., Bistarelli, S., Santini, F., Taticchi, C. (eds.) Computational Models of Argument - Proceedings of COMMA 2020, Perugia, Italy, September 4–11, 2020. Frontiers in Artificial Intelligence and Applications, vol. 326, pp. 167–178. IOS Press (2020). https://doi.org/10.3233/FAIA200502
6. Dondio, P., Longo, L.: Weakly complete semantics based on undecidedness blocking. arXiv preprint arXiv:2103.10701 (2021)
7. Dung, P.M.: On the acceptability of arguments and its fundamental role in non-monotonic reasoning, logic programming and n-person games. Artif. Intell. **77**(2), 321–357 (1995)
8. van der Torre, L., Vesic, S.: The principle-based approach to abstract argumentation semantics. In: Baroni, P., Gabbay, D., Giacomin, M., van der Torre, L. (eds.) Handbook of Formal Argumentation, chap. 12, pp. 2735–2778. College Publications, London (2018)

On Restricting the Impact of Self-attacking Arguments in Gradual Semantics

Vivien Beuselinck[1]📵, Jérôme Delobelle[2](✉)📵, and Srdjan Vesic[3]📵

[1] Aniti, Université Fédérale, Toulouse, France
vivien@beuselinck.fr
[2] LIPADE, Université de Paris, Paris, France
jerome.delobelle@u-paris.fr
[3] CNRS, Univ. Artois, CRIL, Lens, France
vesic@cril.fr

Abstract. The issue of how a semantics should deal with self-attacking arguments was always a subject of debate amongst argumentation scholars. A consensus exists for extension-based semantics because those arguments are always rejected (as soon as the semantics in question respect conflict-freeness). In case of gradual semantics, the question is more complex, since other criteria are taken into account. A way to check the impact of these arguments is to use the principles (i.e. desirable properties to be satisfied by a semantics) from the literature. Principles like Self-Contradiction and Strong Self-Contradiction prescribe how to deal with self-attacking arguments. We show that they are incompatible with the well-known Equivalence principle (which is satisfied by almost all the existing gradual semantics), as well as with some other principles (e.g. Counting). This incompatibility was not studied until now and the class of semantics satisfying Self-Contradiction is under-explored. In the present paper, we explore that class of semantics. We show links and incompatibilities between several principles. We define a semantics that satisfies (Strong) Self-Contradiction and a maximal number of compatible principles. We introduce an iterative algorithm to calculate our semantics and prove that it always converges. We also provide a characterisation of our semantics. Finally, we experimentally show that our semantics is computationally efficient.

Keywords: Abstract argumentation · Gradual semantics · Self-attack

1 Introduction

Theory of computational argumentation allows to model exchange of arguments and conflicts between them. Although in most cases a conflict occurs between two arguments, sometimes an argument may conflict with itself. Such an argument is called a self-attacking argument. Discussion on how to deal with self-attacking

© Springer Nature Switzerland AG 2021
P. Baroni et al. (Eds.): CLAR 2021, LNAI 13040, pp. 127–146, 2021.
https://doi.org/10.1007/978-3-030-89391-0_8

arguments is often indirectly included in the problems of dealing with odd-length cycles, because a self-attack is the smallest odd-length cycle. However, in contrast to greater odd-length cycles, the presence of a self-attack is due to inconsistency in an argument itself.

In order to reason in presence of these arguments, several methods have been defined in abstract argumentation by proposing to deal with them directly [8,9,11,16] or indirectly [7]. These methods essentially concern extension-based semantics. In the context of ranking-based and gradual argumentation semantics [2,5], little research was conducted to find out how self-attacking arguments should be dealt with and what is the impact they have on the acceptability of other arguments. Existing studies are essentially done through the principle-based study of these semantics. Indeed, defining and studying principles drew attention of many scholars in this area.

Consider Equivalence, which is one of the well-known principles, stating that the acceptability degree of an argument should only depend on acceptability degrees of its direct attackers and consider the argumentation graph $\mathcal{F}_{ex}$ containing two arguments a and b, and where b is attacked by a self-attacking argument a (i.e., $\mathcal{F}_{ex} = (\{a, b\}, \{(a, a), (a, b)\})$). Equivalence implies that a and b should be equally acceptable because a and b are both attacked by a self-attacking argument. However, this is debatable, since the intuition behind a self-attacking argument is that it is inconsistent in one way or another so we would tend to accept b being attacked by a (which is self-attacking) rather than accepting a. Note that, under all semantics returning conflict-free extensions, a self-attacking argument is always rejected, i.e. it does not belong to any extension. Also, regarding the ranking-based and gradual semantics, it was pointed out that it would be natural to attach the worst possible rank to self-attacking arguments [19]. Furthermore, two principles were defined to formalise this intuition.

The first one is called Strong Self-Contradiction, and introduced by Matt and Toni [19]. It says that the acceptability degree of an argument must be 0 if and only if that argument is self-attacking. The second principle, called Self-Contradiction, was introduced by Bonzon et al. [12] and states that every self-attacking argument is strictly less acceptable than every non self-attacking argument. Consider the argumentation graph $\mathcal{F}_{ex}$ again and note that, under every semantics that satisfies Self-Contradiction, b is strictly more acceptable than a. This example shows that Equivalence and Self-Contradiction are not compatible, i.e. there exists no semantics that satisfies both of them.

To the best of our knowledge, there exists only one semantics (known as M&T) that satisfies Self-Contradiction and Strong Self-Contradiction. That semantics was introduced by Matt and Toni [19]. However, this semantics has a limitation that makes it inapplicable in practice. Namely, as noted by Matt and Toni themselves, as the space used to calculate the scores grows exponentially with the number of arguments, even with the optimisation techniques they used it did not scale to more than a dozen of arguments.

The research objective of the present paper is to study the under-explored family of semantics that satisfy Strong Self-Contradiction. Our goals are thus to identify which principles are (in)compatible with Strong Self-Contradiction and to define a semantics, which we call nsa (no self-attacks), that satisfies Strong Self-Contradiction as well as a maximal number of compatible principles. After introducing the formal setting and recalling the existing principles from the literature, we prove the incompatibilities between some of the principles, and identify a maximal set of principles that contains (Strong) Self-Contradiction. We introduce an iterative algorithm in order to define a new semantics and prove that it always converges. The acceptability of degree of each argument with respect to nsa is then defined as the limit of the corresponding sequence. We provide a characterisation of nsa, i.e. a declarative (non-iterative) definition and show that the two are equivalent: each semantics satisfying the declarative definition coincides with nsa. We check which principles are satisfied by nsa and compare it with the h-categorizer semantics [10] and the M&T semantics in terms of principle satisfaction. We formally prove that no semantics can satisfy a strict super-set of the set of principles satisfied by nsa. We experimentally show that nsa is computationally efficient and compare it with the M&T semantics and the h-categorizer semantics. The results confirm the hypothesis that the M&T semantics does not scale.

2 Formal Setting and Existing Semantics

An argumentation graph (AG) [17] is a directed graph $\mathcal{F} = (\mathcal{A}, \mathcal{R})$ where $\mathcal{A}$ is a finite set of arguments and $\mathcal{R}$ a binary relation over $\mathcal{A}$, i.e. $\mathcal{R} \subseteq \mathcal{A} \times \mathcal{A}$. For $a, b \in \mathcal{A}$, $(a, b) \in \mathcal{R}$ means that a attacks b. The notation $\text{Att}_{\mathcal{F}}(a) = \{b \mid (b, a) \in \mathcal{R}\}$ represents the set of direct attackers of argument a. For two graphs $\mathcal{F} = (\mathcal{A}, \mathcal{R})$ and $\mathcal{F}' = (\mathcal{A}', \mathcal{R}')$, we denote by $\mathcal{F} \otimes \mathcal{F}'$ the argumentation graph $\mathcal{F}'' = (\mathcal{A} \cup \mathcal{A}', \mathcal{R} \cup \mathcal{R}')$.

Dung's framework comes equipped with various types of semantics used to evaluate the arguments. These include the extension-based semantics (see [6] for an overview), the labelling-based semantics [14], the ranking-based semantics (see [12] for an overview) and the gradual semantics. We refer the reader to [1,13] for a complete overview of the existing families of semantics in abstract argumentation and the differences between these approaches (e.g., definition, outcome, application). In this article, we focus on gradual semantics which assign to each argument in an argumentation graph a score, called *acceptability degree*. This degree belongs to the interval $[0, 1]$. Higher degrees correspond to stronger arguments.

Definition 1 (Gradual semantics). *A gradual semantics is a function S which associates to any argumentation graph $\mathcal{F} = (\mathcal{A}, \mathcal{R})$ a function $Deg_{\mathcal{F}}^{S} : \mathcal{A} \to [0, 1]$. Thus, $Deg_{\mathcal{F}}^{S}(x)$ represents the acceptability degree of $x \in \mathcal{A}$.*

In the rest of the section we recall two gradual semantics. We first introduce h-categorizer, which is one of the most studied gradual semantics and also satisfies a maximal compatible set of principles from the literature.[1] Then we introduce

---

[1] Formally: out of the principles from Sect. 3, no semantics satisfies a strict superset of the principles satisfied by h-categorizer.

M&T semantics which is, to the best of our knowledge, the only semantics known in the literature to satisfy Self-Contradiction.

2.1 h-categorizer Semantics

The h-categorizer semantics [10,20] uses a categorizer function to assign a value to each argument by taking into account the strength of its attackers, which itself takes into account the strength of its attackers, and so on.

Definition 2 (h-categorizer semantics). *Let* $\mathcal{F} = (\mathcal{A}, \mathcal{R})$ *be an argumentation graph. The h-categorizer semantics is a gradual semantics such that* $\forall x \in \mathcal{A}$*:*

$$Deg_{\mathcal{F}}^{h}(x) = \frac{1}{1 + \sum_{y \in \text{Att}_{\mathcal{F}}(x)} Deg_{\mathcal{F}}^{h}(y)}$$

2.2 M&T Semantics

The gradual semantics introduced by Matt and Toni [19] computes the acceptability degree of an argument using a two-person zero-sum strategic game. For an AG $\mathcal{F} = (\mathcal{A}, \mathcal{R})$ and an argument $x \in \mathcal{A}$, the set of strategies for the proponent is the set of all subsets of arguments that contain x: $S_P(x) = \{P \mid P \subseteq \mathcal{A}, x \in P\}$ and for the opponent it is the set of all subsets of arguments: $S_O = \{O \mid O \subseteq \mathcal{A}\}$. Given two strategies $X, Y \subseteq \mathcal{A}$, the set of attacks from X to Y is defined by $Y_{\mathcal{F}}^{\leftarrow X} = \{(x, y) \in X \times Y \mid (x, y) \in \mathcal{R}\}$. From this measurement, Matt and Toni define the notion of degree of acceptability of a set of arguments w.r.t. another one used to compute the reward of a proponent's strategy.

Definition 3 (Reward). *Let* $\mathcal{F} = (\mathcal{A}, \mathcal{R})$ *be an argumentation graph,* $x \in \mathcal{A}$ *be an argument,* $P \in S_P(x)$ *be a strategy chosen by the proponent and* $O \in S_O$ *be a strategy chosen by the opponent. The degree of acceptability of P w.r.t. O is* $\phi(P, O) = \frac{1}{2} \left[1 + f(|O_{\mathcal{F}}^{\leftarrow P}|) - f(|P_{\mathcal{F}}^{\leftarrow O}|) \right]$ *with* $f(n) = \frac{n}{n+1}$*. The reward of P over O, denoted by* $r_{\mathcal{F}}(P, O)$*, is defined by:*

$$r_{\mathcal{F}}(P, O) = \begin{cases} 0 & \text{iff } P \text{ is not conflict-free} \\ 1 & \text{iff } P \text{ is conflict-free and } |P_{\mathcal{F}}^{\leftarrow O}| = 0 \\ \phi(P, O) & \text{otherwise} \end{cases}$$

Proponent and opponent have the possibility of using a strategy according to some probability distributions, respectively $p = (p_1, p_2, \ldots, p_m)$ and $q = (q_1, q_2, \ldots, q_n)$, with $m = |S_P|$ and $n = |S_O|$. For each argument $x \in \mathcal{A}$, the proponent's expected payoff $E(x, p, q)$ is $E(x, p, q) = \sum_{j=1}^{n} \sum_{i=1}^{m} p_i q_j r_{i,j}$ with $r_{i,j} = r_{\mathcal{F}}(P_i, O_j)$ where P_i (respectively O_j) represents the ith (respectively j^{th}) strategy of $S_P(x)$ (respectively S_O). The proponent can expect to get at least $\min_q E(x, p, q)$, where the minimum is taken over all the probability distributions q available to the opponent. Hence the proponent can choose a strategy which will guarantee her a reward of $\max_p \min_q E(x, p, q)$. The opposite is also true with $\min_q \max_p E(x, p, q)$.

Definition 4 (M&T semantics). *The semantics M&T is a gradual semantics that assigns a score to each argument $x \in \mathcal{A}$ in $\mathcal{F}$ as follows:*

$$Deg_{\mathcal{F}}^{\text{MT}}(x) = \max_{p} \min_{q} E(x, p, q) = \min_{q} \max_{p} E(x, p, q)$$

3 Principles for Gradual Semantics

Principles have been introduced by [4] in order to better understand the behavior of the gradual semantics, choose a semantics for a particular application, guide the search for new semantics, compare semantics with each other, etc. We do not claim that all of these principles are mandatory (we will see later that some of them are incompatible). In the rest of this section, we introduce the principles.[2]

The first one, called Anonymity, states that the name of an argument should not impact its acceptability degree.

Principle 1 (Anonymity). *A semantics S satisfies Anonymity iff for any two AGs $\mathcal{F} = (\mathcal{A}, \mathcal{R})$ and $\mathcal{F}' = (\mathcal{A}', \mathcal{R}')$ for any isomorphism f from $\mathcal{F}$ to $\mathcal{F}'$, $\forall a \in \mathcal{A}, Deg_{\mathcal{F}}^{S}(a) = Deg_{\mathcal{F}'}^{S}(f(a))$.*

Independence says that the acceptability degree of an argument should be independent of unconnected arguments.

Principle 2 (Independence). *A semantics S satisfies Independence iff, for any two AGs $\mathcal{F} = (\mathcal{A}, \mathcal{R})$ and $\mathcal{F}' = (\mathcal{A}', \mathcal{R}')$ such that $\mathcal{A} \cap \mathcal{A}' = \emptyset$, $\forall a \in \mathcal{A}$, $Deg_{\mathcal{F}}^{S}(a) = Deg_{\mathcal{F} \otimes \mathcal{F}'}^{S}(a)$.*

Directionality states that the acceptability of argument x can depend on y only if there is a path from y to x.

Principle 3 (Directionality). *A semantics S satisfies Directionality iff, for any AG $\mathcal{F} = (\mathcal{A}, \mathcal{R})$ and $\mathcal{F}' = (\mathcal{A}, \mathcal{R}')$ such that $a, b \in \mathcal{A}$, $\mathcal{R}' = \mathcal{R} \cup \{(a, b)\}$ it holds that : $\forall x \in \mathcal{A}$, if there is no path from b to x, then $Deg_{\mathcal{F}}^{S}(x) = Deg_{\mathcal{F}'}^{S}(x)$.*

Neutrality states that an argument with an acceptability degree of 0 should have no impact on the arguments it attacks.

Principle 4 (Neutrality). *A semantics S satisfies Neutrality iff, for any AG $\mathcal{F} = (\mathcal{A}, \mathcal{R})$ if $\forall a, b \in \mathcal{A}$, $\text{Att}_{\mathcal{F}}(b) = \text{Att}_{\mathcal{F}}(a) \cup \{x\}$ with $x \in \mathcal{A} \backslash \text{Att}_{\mathcal{F}}(a)$ and $Deg_{\mathcal{F}}^{S}(x) = 0$ then $Deg_{\mathcal{F}}^{S}(a) = Deg_{\mathcal{F}}^{S}(b)$.*

Equivalence says that if two arguments have the same attackers, or more generally attackers of the same strength, they should have the same acceptability degree.

Principle 5 (Equivalence). *A semantics S satisfies Equivalence iff, for any AG $\mathcal{F} = (\mathcal{A}, \mathcal{R})$, $\forall a, b \in \mathcal{A}$, if there exists a bijective function f from $\text{Att}_{\mathcal{F}}(a)$ to $\text{Att}_{\mathcal{F}}(b)$ s.t. $\forall x \in \text{Att}_{\mathcal{F}}(a)$, $Deg_{\mathcal{F}}^{S}(x) = Deg_{\mathcal{F}}^{S}(f(x))$ then $Deg_{\mathcal{F}}^{S}(a) = Deg_{\mathcal{F}}^{S}(b)$.*

---

[2] We do not include the Proportionality principle since it is only applicable when arguments are attached intrinsic weights.

Maximality states that a non-attacked argument should have the highest acceptability degree.

Principle 6 (Maximality). *A semantics S satisfies Maximality iff, for any AG $\mathcal{F} = (\mathcal{A}, \mathcal{R})$, $\forall a \in \mathcal{A}$, if $\text{Att}_{\mathcal{F}}(a) = \emptyset$ then $Deg^S_{\mathcal{F}}(a) = 1$.*

Counting states that a non-zero degree attacker should impact the acceptability of the attacked argument.

Principle 7 (Counting). *A semantics S satisfies Counting iff for any AG $\mathcal{F} = (\mathcal{A}, \mathcal{R})$, $\forall a, b \in \mathcal{A}$, if i) $Deg^S_{\mathcal{F}}(a) > 0$ and ii) $\text{Att}_{\mathcal{F}}(b) = \text{Att}_{\mathcal{F}}(a) \cup \{y\}$ with $y \in \mathcal{A} \backslash \text{Att}_{\mathcal{F}}(a)$ and $Deg^S_{\mathcal{F}}(y) > 0$ then $Deg^S_{\mathcal{F}}(a) > Deg^S_{\mathcal{F}}(b)$.*

Weakening says that the acceptability of an argument should be strictly lower than 1 if it has at least one attacker with a non-zero acceptability degree.

Principle 8 (Weakening). *A semantics S satisfies Weakening iff for any AG $\mathcal{F} = (\mathcal{A}, \mathcal{R})$, $\forall a \in \mathcal{A}$, if $\exists b \in \text{Att}_{\mathcal{F}}(a)$ s.t. $Deg^S_{\mathcal{F}}(b) > 0$, then $Deg^S_{\mathcal{F}}(a) < 1$.*

Weakening Soundness states that if the acceptability degree of an argument is not maximal, it must be that it is attacked by at least one non-zero degree attacker.

Principle 9 (Weakening Soundness). *A semantics S satisfies Weakening Soundness iff, for any AG $\mathcal{F} = (\mathcal{A}, \mathcal{R})$, $\forall a \in \mathcal{A}$, if $Deg^S_{\mathcal{F}}(a) < 1$ then $\exists b \in \text{Att}_{\mathcal{F}}(a)$ such that $Deg^S_{\mathcal{F}}(b) > 0$.*

Reinforcement states that the acceptability degree increases if the acceptability degrees of attackers decrease.

Principle 10 (Reinforcement). *A semantics S satisfies Reinforcement iff for any AG $\mathcal{F} = (\mathcal{A}, \mathcal{R})$, $\forall a, b \in \mathcal{A}$, if i) $Deg^S_{\mathcal{F}}(a) > 0$ or $Deg^S_{\mathcal{F}}(b) > 0$, ii) $\text{Att}_{\mathcal{F}}(a) \backslash \text{Att}_{\mathcal{F}}(b) = \{x\}$, iii) $\text{Att}_{\mathcal{F}}(b) \backslash \text{Att}_{\mathcal{F}}(a) = \{y\}$, iv) $Deg^S_{\mathcal{F}}(y) > Deg^S_{\mathcal{F}}(x)$, then $Deg^S_{\mathcal{F}}(a) > Deg^S_{\mathcal{F}}(b)$.*

Resilience states that no argument in an argumentation graph can have a acceptability degree of 0. It is certainly not a mandatory principle.

Principle 11 (Resilience). *A semantics S satisfies Resilience if for any AG $\mathcal{F} = (\mathcal{A}, \mathcal{R})$, $\forall a \in \mathcal{A}$, $Deg^S_{\mathcal{F}}(a) > 0$.*

The last three principles are incompatible with each other. The first principle, called Cardinality Precedence states, roughly speaking, that the greater the number of direct attackers of an argument, the lower its acceptability degree.

Principle 12 (Cardinality Precedence). *A semantics S satisfies Cardinality Precedence iff for any AG $\mathcal{F} = (\mathcal{A}, \mathcal{R})$, $\forall a, b \in \mathcal{A}$, if i) $Deg^S_{\mathcal{F}}(b) > 0$, and ii) $|\{x \in \text{Att}_{\mathcal{F}}(a)$ s.t. $Deg^S_{\mathcal{F}}(x) > 0\}| > |\{y \in \text{Att}_{\mathcal{F}}(b)$ s.t. $Deg^S_{\mathcal{F}}(y) > 0\}|$ then $Deg^S_{\mathcal{F}}(a) < Deg^S_{\mathcal{F}}(b)$.*

Quality Precedence states, roughly speaking, that the greater the acceptability degree of the strongest attacker of an argument, the lower its acceptability degree.

Principle 13 (Quality Precedence). *A semantics S satisfies Quality Precedence if for any AG $\mathcal{F} = (\mathcal{A}, \mathcal{R})$, $\forall a, b \in \mathcal{A}$, if i) $Deg_{\mathcal{F}}^{S}(a) > 0$ and ii) $\exists y \in \text{Att}_{\mathcal{F}}(b)$ s.t. $\forall x \in \text{Att}_{\mathcal{F}}(a)$, $Deg_{\mathcal{F}}^{S}(y) > Deg_{\mathcal{F}}^{S}(x)$ then $Deg_{\mathcal{F}}^{S}(a) > Deg_{\mathcal{F}}^{S}(b)$.*

Compensation states that several attacks from arguments with a low acceptability degree may compensate one attack from an argument with high acceptability degree. [3]

Principle 14 (Compensation). *A semantics S satisfies Compensation iff both Cardinality Precedence and Quality Precedence are not satisfied.*

In the literature, two principles directly refer to the self-attacking arguments. The first one, called Self-Contradiction, was introduced by [12] and states that the degree of a self-attacking argument should be strictly lower than the degree of an argument that does not attack itself.

Principle 15 (Self-Contradiction). *A semantics S satisfies Self-Contradiction iff, for any AG $\mathcal{F} = (\mathcal{A}, \mathcal{R})$ with two arguments $a, b \in \mathcal{A}$, if $(a, a) \in \mathcal{R}$ and $(b, b) \notin \mathcal{R}$ then $Deg_{\mathcal{F}}^{S}(b) > Deg_{\mathcal{F}}^{S}(a)$.*

The second principle was introduced by Matt and Toni [19]. Its original name was "Self-contradiction must be avoided". We rename it for clarity reasons, namely in order to avoid the confusion with the name of Principle 15. This principle states that an argument that attacks itself should have the smallest acceptability degree (i.e. 0).

Principle 16 (Strong Self-Contradiction). *A semantics S satisfies Strong Self- Contradiction iff, for any AG $\mathcal{F} = (\mathcal{A}, \mathcal{R})$ with $a \in \mathcal{A}$, $Deg_{\mathcal{F}}^{S}(a) = 0$ iff $(a, a) \in \mathcal{R}$.*

4   Analysis of Principles and Links Between Them

In this section we analyse the links between principles and identify two maximal mutually compatible sets of principles. Let us first observe that Strong Self-Contradiction implies Self-Contradiction. The next proposition follows directly from the definitions of the respective principles.

Proposition 1. *If a gradual semantics S satisfies Strong Self-Contradiction, it satisfies Self-Contradiction.*

Proof. Let us suppose that Strong Self-Contradiction is satisfied by S. This means that those and only those arguments that have the minimum score are the self-attacking arguments ($\forall a \in \mathcal{A}$, $Deg_{\mathcal{F}}^{S}(a) = 0$ iff $(a, a) \in \mathcal{R}$). This implies that all arguments that do not attack themselves have an acceptability degree greater than 0. Formally, $\forall b \in \mathcal{A}$, $Deg_{\mathcal{F}}^{S}(b) > 0$ iff $(b, b) \notin \mathcal{R}$. Consequently, for two arguments $a, b \in \mathcal{A}$, if $(a, a) \in \mathcal{R}$ and $(b, b) \notin \mathcal{R}$ then $Deg_{\mathcal{F}}^{S}(b) > Deg_{\mathcal{F}}^{S}(a) = 0$. $\square$

---

[3] There are several version of this principle. We use the version that allows to clearly distinguish between the three cases (CP, QP, Compensation). Namely, each semantics satisfies *exactly* one of the three principles.

As discussed in the introduction, the next result shows that Equivalence and Self-Contradiction are incompatible.

Proposition 2. *There exists no gradual semantics S that satisfies both Equivalence and Self-Contradiction.*

Proof. We provide a proof by contradiction. Let us suppose that a gradual semantics S satisfies both Equivalence and Self-Contradiction and consider the argumentation graph $\mathcal{F} = (\mathcal{A}, \mathcal{R})$ with $\mathcal{A} = \{a, b\}$ and $\mathcal{R} = \{(a, a), (a, b)\}$.
From Self-Contradiction, we have $Deg_{\mathcal{F}}^{S}(a) < Deg_{\mathcal{F}}^{S}(b)$, while from Equivalence, we have $Deg_{\mathcal{F}}^{S}(a) = Deg_{\mathcal{F}}^{S}(b)$.
Contradiction. Hence, S does not satisfy both Equivalence and Self-Contradiction. Since S was arbitrary, we conclude that there exists no semantics that satisfies both Equivalence and Self-Contradiction. $\square$

However, the Equivalence principle is not the only one incompatible with Strong Self-Contradiction. Some other incompatibilities exist mainly because self-attacking arguments are treated differently from other arguments. Indeed, according to Strong Self-Contradiction, self-attacking arguments are directly classified as the worst arguments, whereas the other principles just consider a self-attack as an attack like any other (i.e. an attack between two distinct arguments).

Proposition 3. *There exists no gradual semantics S that satisfies both Strong Self-Contradiction and Resilience.*

Proof. We provide a proof by contradiction. Let us suppose that a gradual semantics S satisfies both Strong Self-Contradiction and Resilience, and consider the argumentation graph $\mathcal{F} = (\mathcal{A}, \mathcal{R})$ where $\mathcal{A} = \{a\}$ and $R = \{(a, a)\}$.
From Strong Self-Contradiction, we have $Deg_{\mathcal{F}}^{S}(a) = 0$, while from Resilience, we have $Deg_{\mathcal{F}}^{S}(a) > 0$.
Contradiction. Hence, S does not satisfy both Strong Self-Contradiction and Resilience. Since S was arbitrary, there exists no semantics that satisfies both Resilience and Strong Self-Contradiction. $\square$

Proposition 4. *There exists no gradual semantics S that satisfies both Strong Self-Contradiction and Weakening Soundness.*

Proof. We provide a proof by contradiction. Let us suppose that a gradual semantics S satisfies both Strong Self-Contradiction and Weakening Soundness, and consider the argumentation graph $\mathcal{F} = (\mathcal{A}, \mathcal{R})$ where $\mathcal{A} = \{a\}$ and $R = \{(a, a)\}$.
From Strong Self-Contradiction, we have $Deg_{\mathcal{F}}^{S}(a) = 0$, while from Weakening Soundness, we have $Deg_{\mathcal{F}}^{S}(a) > 0$ because a is the only attacker of a and $Deg_{\mathcal{F}}^{S}(a) = 0$.
Contradiction. Hence, S does not satisfy both Strong Self-Contradiction and Weakening Soundness. Since S was arbitrary, there exists no semantics that satisfies both Strong Self-Contradiction and Weakening Soundness. $\square$

Proposition 5. *There exists no gradual semantics S that satisfies both Strong Self-Contradiction and Reinforcement.*

Proof. We provide a proof by contradiction. Let us suppose that a gradual semantics S satisfies both Strong Self-Contradiction and Reinforcement, and consider the argumentation graph $\mathcal{F} = (\{a, b, c, d\}, \{(a, a), (c, c), (c, a), (a, b), (d, b)\})$. From Strong Self-Contradiction, we have $0 = Deg_{\mathcal{F}}^{S}(a) < Deg_{\mathcal{F}}^{S}(b)$.

From Reinforcement, we have $Deg_{\mathcal{F}}^{S}(a) > Deg_{\mathcal{F}}^{S}(b)$ because i) $Deg_{\mathcal{F}}^{S}(b) > 0$, ii) $\mathtt{Att}_{\mathcal{F}}(a)\backslash\mathtt{Att}_{\mathcal{F}}(b) = \{c\}$, iii) $\mathtt{Att}_{\mathcal{F}}(b)\backslash\mathtt{Att}_{\mathcal{F}}(a) = \{d\}$, and iv) $Deg_{\mathcal{F}}^{S}(d) > Deg_{\mathcal{F}}^{S}(c)$.

Contradiction. Hence, S does not satisfy both Strong Self-Contradiction and Reinforcement. Since S was arbitrary, there exists no semantics that satisfies both Strong Self-Contradiction and Reinforcement. $\square$

Proposition 6. *There exists no gradual semantics S that satisfies both Strong Self-Contradiction and Neutrality.*

Proof. We provide a proof by contradiction. Let us suppose that a gradual semantics S satisfies both Strong Self-Contradiction and Neutrality, and consider the argumentation graph $\mathcal{F} = (\{a, b, x\}, \{(x, x), (b, b), (x, b), (b, a)\})$. From Strong Self-Contradiction, we have $0 = Deg_{\mathcal{F}}^{S}(b) < Deg_{\mathcal{F}}^{S}(a)$. From Neutrality, we have $Deg_{\mathcal{F}}^{S}(a) = Deg_{\mathcal{F}}^{S}(b)$ because $\mathtt{Att}_{\mathcal{F}}(b) = \mathtt{Att}_{\mathcal{F}}(a) \cup \{x\}$ with $Deg_{\mathcal{F}}^{S}(x) = 0$.

Contradiction. Hence, S does not satisfy both Strong Self-Contradiction and Neutrality. Since S was arbitrary, there exists no semantics that satisfies both Strong Self-Contradiction and Neutrality. $\square$

Taking these incompatibilities into account, our goal is now to study two maximal mutually compatible sets of principles we are interested in. For this, we need the notion of dominance. A semantics S dominates a semantics S' on the set of principles P if the subset of principles from P satisfied by S is a strict superset of the subset of principles from P satisfied by S'. In the rest of the discussion, we suppose that P is the set of all principles studied in Sect. 3. Note that if a semantics S satisfies a maximal for set inclusion set of principles, it is not dominated by any semantics.

A first maximal (for set inclusion) set of principles has been identified by [4] and is a direct consequence of their Proposition 1. We define this set of principles as $P_{CREW} = \{$Anonymity, Independence, Directionality, Neutrality, Equivalence, Maximality, Weakening, Counting, Weakening Soundness, Reinforcement, Resilience and Compensation$\}$.

Theorem 1 ([4]). *P_{CREW} is a maximal for set inclusion set of principles.*

We can formally show that there is a unique maximal set of principles compatible with Compensation, Resilience, Equivalence and Weakening Soundness.

Theorem 2. *Let P be the set of all principles defined in Sect. 3 (Principles 1–16). Let S be a gradual semantics that satisfies Compensation, Resilience, Equivalence and Weakening Soundness. If S is not dominated w.r.t. P, then S satisfies exactly the principles from P_{CREW}.*

Proof. On one hand, we know from the work by [4] that h-categorizer satisfies all the principles from P_{CREW}. On the other hand, it is clear from the incompatibility results between the principles that S cannot satisfy Strong Self-Contradiction which is incompatible with Resilience (see Proposition 3), Self-Contradiction which is incompatible with Equivalence (see Proposition 2), Cardinality/Quality Precedence which are both incompatible with Compensation (see [4]). Thus, in order not to be dominated by h-categorizer, S must satisfy all the principles from P_{CREW}; due to the incompatibilities, S cannot satisfy any more principles.   □

In this paper we choose to explore the space of principles compatible with Strong Self-Contradiction (which is not in P_{CREW}). One naturally wants to maximise the set of satisfied principles. Can we satisfy Strong Self-Contradiction and all the other principles? The answer is negative (see Propositions 2–6). First, one has to choose between Cardinality Precedence, Quality Precedence and Compensation. In this paper, we explore the possibility of satisfying Compensation. This choice is based on the fact that this principle is satisfied by virtually all semantics, as showed by Amgoud et al. [4]. Indeed, Cardinality Precedence and Quality Precedence represent, roughly speaking, *drastic* or *extreme* cases and are satisfied only by the semantics specifically designed to satisfy them, like max-based semantics and card-based semantics [4] or by semantics having other specificities. For instance, iterative schema [18], which satisfies Quality Precedence, is a discrete semantics (it takes only three possible values). This yields another maximal set of principles which includes those two principles. We define this set of principles as P_{2S2C} = {Anonymity, Independence, Directionality, Maximality, Weakening, Counting, Compensation, Self-Contradiction, Strong Self-Contradiction}.

Theorem 3. *P_{2S2C} is a maximal for set inclusion set of principles.*

Proof. Firstly, all the principles in P_{2S2C} are compatible because nsa satisfies all of them (see Proposition 7). Secondly, P_{2S2C} is maximal because for each remaining principle $p \in$ {Equivalence, Weakening Soundness, Neutrality, Reinforcement, Cardinality Precedence, Quality Precedence and Resilience}, there exists (at least) one principle in P_{2S2C} which is incompatible with p, i.e. Equivalence and Self-Contradiction are incompatible (see Proposition 2); Neutrality and Strong Self-Contradiction are incompatible (see Proposition 6); Reinforcement and Strong Self-Contradiction are incompatible (see Proposition 5); Weakening Soundness and Strong Self-Contradiction are incompatible (see Proposition 4); Cardinality Precedence and Compensation are incompatible (see [4]); Quality Precedence and Compensation are incompatible (see [4]); and Resilience and Strong Self-Contradiction are incompatible (see Proposition 3).   □

We now show that there is a unique maximal set of principles compatible with Strong Self-Contradiction and Compensation. This follows from the fact that if a semantics satisfies Strong Self-Contradiction, it cannot satisfy several principles (see Propositions 2–6) but can satisfied all the others (as witnessed by the semantics we introduce in this paper).

Theorem 4. *Let P be the set of all principles defined in Sect. 3 (Principles 1–16). Let S be a gradual semantics that satisfies Strong Self-Contradiction and Compensation. If S is not dominated w.r.t. P, then S satisfies exactly the principles from P_{2S2C}.*

Proof. It is clear that from the incompatibility results between different principles, S cannot satisfy (i) Resilience, Equivalence and Weakening Soundness which are incompatible with Strong Self-Contradiction (or Self-Contradiction), and (ii) Cardinality Precedence and Quality Precedence which are both incompatible with Compensation. The set of remaining principles corresponds exactly to P_{2S2C} which is a maximal for set inclusion set of principles. However, S cannot satisfy exactly a subset of P_{2S2C} because, in this case, S will be dominated by a semantics that satisfies the principles of P_{2S2C}. Consequently, when S satisfies Strong Self-Contradiction and Compensation, the only way to ensure that S is not dominated is when S satisfies exactly the principles from P_{2S2C}.   □

To the best of our knowledge, no semantics that satisfy all the principles from P_{2S2C} has been presented in the literature. In the next section, we define a semantics that satisfies this set of principles.

Before doing that, let us comment on the non satisfaction of some principles. It is tempting to change the principles in order to treat the self-attacks in another way, and consequently make the principles fit some definitions or theorems. We argue that it is better to start by having a full picture of what happens with *existing* principles. Indeed, the principles should be the most stable part of a theory. We are not against introduction of new principles (or changing the existing ones). This might be part of future work.

5 No Self-Attack h-categorizer Semantics

In this section, we define a new gradual semantics, called no self-attack h-categorizer (**nsa**) semantics, inspired by the h-categorizer semantics. The main difference is that we assign 0 degree to the self-attacking arguments.

Definition 5 (nsa). *Let $\mathcal{F} = (\mathcal{A}, \mathcal{R})$ be an AG. We define $f_{\mathtt{nsa}}^{\mathcal{F},i} : \mathcal{A} \to [0, +\infty]$ as follows : for every argument $a \in \mathcal{A}$ for $i \in \{0, 1, 2, ..\}$,*

$$
f_{\mathtt{nsa}}^{\mathcal{F},i}(a) = \begin{cases} 0 & if \ (a, a) \in \mathcal{R} \\ 1 & if \ (a, a) \notin \mathcal{R} \ and \ i = 0 \\ \dfrac{1}{1 + \sum_{b \in \mathtt{Att}_{\mathcal{F}}(a)} f_{\mathtt{nsa}}^{\mathcal{F},i-1}(b)} & if \ (a, a) \notin \mathcal{R} \ and \ i > 0 \end{cases} \tag{1}
$$

By convention, if $\mathtt{Att}_{\mathcal{F}}(a) = \emptyset$, $\sum_{b \in \mathtt{Att}_{\mathcal{F}}(a)} f_{\mathtt{nsa}}^{\mathcal{F},i-1}(b) = 0$.

Although **nsa** is inspired by the h-categorizer semantics, the modifications made change the result obtained requiring the verification that **nsa** also converges to a unique result. Thus, in the next result, we show that for every argumentation graph $\mathcal{F} = (\mathcal{A}, \mathcal{R})$, for every argument $a \in \mathcal{A}$, $f_{nsa}^{\mathcal{F},i}(a)$ converges as i approaches infinity. Roughly speaking, the next theorem aims to formally check that assigning zero values to self-attacking arguments does not impact the convergence of the scores. Thus, applying **nsa** to the original argumentation graph $\mathcal{F}$ provides the same result as when the h-categorizer semantics is applied on a restricted version of $\mathcal{F}$ where the self-attacking arguments are deleted.

Theorem 5. *For every argumentation graph* $\mathcal{F} = (\mathcal{A}, \mathcal{R})$, *for every* $a \in \mathcal{A}$, *if* $(a, a) \notin \mathcal{R}$, *we have* $\lim_{i \to \infty} f_{nsa}^{\mathcal{F},i}(a) = Deg_{\mathcal{F}'}^{h}(a)$ *where* $\mathcal{F}' = (\mathcal{A}', \mathcal{R}')$ *with* $\mathcal{A}' = \{x \in \mathcal{A} | (x, x) \notin \mathcal{R}\}$ *and* $\mathcal{R}' = \{(x, y) \in \mathcal{R} \mid x \in \mathcal{A}' \text{ and } y \in \mathcal{A}'\}$.

Proof. Let $\mathcal{F} = (\mathcal{A}, \mathcal{R})$ be an AG and $\mathcal{F}' = (\mathcal{A}', \mathcal{R}')$ be an AG such that $\mathcal{A}' = \{x \in \mathcal{A}|(x, x) \notin \mathcal{R}\}$ and $\mathcal{R}' = \{(x, y) \in \mathcal{R} \mid x \in \mathcal{A}' \text{ and } y \in \mathcal{A}'\}$. Without loss of generality, let us denote $\mathcal{A} = \{a_0, a_1, \ldots, a_n\}$.

Let us recall the iterative version of h-categorizer, that can be used to calculate the scores of arguments [20]: for every a, for $i \in \mathbb{N}$

$$f_h^{\mathcal{F},i}(a) = \begin{cases} 1 & if \ i = 0 \\ \dfrac{1}{1 + \sum_{b \in \text{Att}_\mathcal{F}(a)} f_h^{\mathcal{F},i-1}(b)} & if \ i > 0 \end{cases} \tag{2}$$

We prove by induction on i that for each $a \in \mathcal{A}'$:

$$f_{nsa}^{\mathcal{F},i}(a) = f_h^{\mathcal{F}',i}(a)$$

<u>Base</u>: Let $i = 0$. From the formal definition of **nsa** (Definition 5) and Eq. (2), we have $f_{nsa}^{\mathcal{F},0}(a) = f_h^{\mathcal{F}',0}(a) = 1$. Thus, the inductive base holds.

<u>Step</u>: Let us suppose that the inductive hypothesis is true for every $k \in \{0, \overline{1}, \ldots i\}$ and let us show that it is true for $i + 1$. We need to prove :

$$f_{nsa}^{\mathcal{F},i+1}(a) = f_h^{\mathcal{F}',i+1}(a)$$

From the inductive hypothesis, we know that for each argument $a \in \mathcal{A}'$, $f_{nsa}^{\mathcal{F},i}(a) = f_h^{\mathcal{F}',i}(a)$. Thus, from Eq. (1), we have:

$$f_{nsa}^{\mathcal{F},i+1}(a) = \frac{1}{1 + \sum_{b \in \text{Att}_\mathcal{F}(a)} f_{nsa}^{\mathcal{F},i}(b)}$$

From Eq. (2), we have

$$f_h^{\mathcal{F}',i+1}(a) = \frac{1}{1 + \sum_{b \in \text{Att}_{\mathcal{F}'}(a)} f_h^{\mathcal{F}',i}(b)}$$

Let us note $\text{Att}_{\mathcal{F}}(a) = \text{Att}_{\mathcal{F}'}(a) \cup \{b_0, \ldots, b_m\}$ with $m \geq 0$ and remark that $\forall b \in \{b_0, \ldots, b_m\}$, we have $(b, b) \in \mathcal{R}$. According to Eq. (1), $\forall b \in \{b_0, \ldots, b_m\}$, $f_{\text{nsa}}^{\mathcal{F},i}(b) = 0$. Consequently, as 0 is the neutral element of the addition, we have $\forall a \in \mathcal{A}'$, $f_{\text{nsa}}^{\mathcal{F},i+1}(a) = f_h^{\mathcal{F}',i+1}(a)$.

By induction, we conclude that for every $i \in \mathbb{N}$ and for every $a \in \mathcal{A}'$

$$f_{\text{nsa}}^{\mathcal{F},i}(a) = f_h^{\mathcal{F}',i}(a)$$

Since f_h converges when $i \to \infty$ and f_{nsa} coincides with f_h for every argument of $\mathcal{A}'$, we conclude that f_{nsa} converges too. Formally, $\forall a \in A'$, $\lim_{i \to \infty} f_{\text{nsa}}^{\mathcal{F},i}(a) = \lim_{i \to \infty} f_h^{\mathcal{F}',i}(a) = Deg_{\mathcal{F}'}^h(a)$. □

We can now introduce the formal definition of nsa.

Definition 6 (nsa). *The no self-attack h-categorizer semantics is a function* nsa *which associates to any argumentation framework* $\mathcal{F} = (\mathcal{A}, \mathcal{R})$ *a function* $Deg_{\mathcal{F}}^{\text{nsa}}(a) : A \to [0,1]$ *as follows:* $Deg_{\mathcal{F}}^{\text{nsa}}(a) = \lim_{i \to \infty} f_{nsa}^{\mathcal{F},i}(a)$.

We can now show that the acceptability degrees attributed to arguments by nsa satisfy the equation from Definition 5 (naturally, not taking into account the second line of the equation, since it considers the case $i = 0$).

Theorem 6. *For any* $\mathcal{F} = (\mathcal{A}, \mathcal{R})$, *for any* $a \in \mathcal{A}$,

$$Deg_{\mathcal{F}}^{\text{nsa}}(a) = \begin{cases} 0 & \text{if } (a, a) \in \mathcal{R} \\ \dfrac{1}{1 + \sum_{b \in \text{Att}_{\mathcal{F}}(a)} Deg_{\mathcal{F}}^{\text{nsa}}(b)} & \text{otherwise} \end{cases}$$

Proof. Let $\mathcal{F} = (A, R)$ be an argumentation graph and $a \in A$.
The case where a is a self-attacking argument is trivial.
In the rest of the proof we consider the case where a is not a self-attacking argument. Letting $\lim_{i \to \infty}$ in the following equality

$$f_{\text{nsa}}^{i+1}(a) = \frac{1}{1 + \sum_{b \in \text{Att}_{\mathcal{F}}(a)} f_{\text{nsa}}^i(b)}$$

and using the fact that arithmetical operations and sum are continuous functions, we obtain :

$$\lim_{i \to \infty} f_{\text{nsa}}^{i+1}(a) = \frac{1}{1 + \sum_{b \in \text{Att}_{\mathcal{F}}(a)} \lim_{i \to \infty} f_{\text{nsa}}^i(b)}$$

then

$$Deg_{\mathcal{F}}^{\text{nsa}}(a) = \frac{1}{1 + \sum_{b \in \text{Att}_{\mathcal{F}}(a)} Deg_{\mathcal{F}}^{\text{nsa}}(a)}$$

□

We now show that the equation from Theorem 6 is not only satisfied by **nsa**, but is also its characterization. More precisely, the next result proves that if an arbitrary semantics D satisfies that equation, it must be that D coincides with **nsa**.

Theorem 7. *Let $\mathcal{F} = (\mathcal{A}, \mathcal{R})$ be an AG with $a \in \mathcal{A}$ and $D : \mathcal{A} \to [0,1]$ be a function with the following formula:*

$$D(a) = \begin{cases} 0 & if (a,a) \in \mathcal{R} \\ \dfrac{1}{1 + \sum_{b \in Att_{\mathcal{F}}(a)} D(b)} & otherwise \end{cases} \tag{3}$$

then $D \equiv Deg_{\mathcal{F}}^{\text{nsa}}$.

Proof. Let $\mathcal{F} = (\mathcal{A}, \mathcal{R})$ be an AG and suppose that $D : \mathcal{A} \to [0,1]$ is the function from Eq. (3).

Let $A = \{a_1, .., a_n\}$ and let $F : [0,1]^n \to [0,1]^n$ be the function such that $F(x_1, .., x_n) = (F_1(x_1, .., x_n), ..., F_n(x_1, ..., x_n))$ where the functions F_i are defined by the following equality:

$$F_i(x_1, \ldots, x_n) = \begin{cases} 0 & if (a_i, a_i) \in \mathcal{R} \\ \dfrac{1}{1 + \displaystyle\sum_{j : a_j \in Att_{\mathcal{F}}(a_i)} x_j} & otherwise \end{cases} \tag{4}$$

We also define the partial order $\leq$ on $\mathbb{R}^n$ in the following way: if $x = (x_1, \ldots, x_n)$ and $y = (y_1, \ldots, y_n)$ then $x \leq y$ iff for every i it holds that $x_i \leq y_i$. Thus, from Eq. (3), it follows that $F(D(a_1), ..., D(a_n)) = (D(a_1), ..., D(a_n))$.

Observe that F is a non-increasing function and that $G = F \circ F$ is a non-decreasing function, and that :

$$(f_{\text{nsa}}^{i+1}(a_1), ..., f_{\text{nsa}}^{i+1}(a_n)) = F((f_{\text{nsa}}^i(a_1), ..., f_{\text{nsa}}^i(a_n)))$$

for every $i \in \mathbb{N}$. Since $(f_{\text{nsa}}^0(a_1), ..., f_{\text{nsa}}^0(a_n)) \in [0,1]^n$ with $f_{\text{nsa}}^0(a_i) = 0$ iff $(a_i, a_i) \in \mathcal{R}$ and $f_{\text{nsa}}^0(a_i) = 1$ otherwise, by the inequalities, we obtain

$$(f_{\text{nsa}}^0(a_1), ..., f_{\text{nsa}}^0(a_n)) \geq (D(a_1), ..., D(a_n)) \tag{5}$$

From (5), and since F is non-increasing, we have:

$$(f_{\text{nsa}}^1(a_1), ..., f_{\text{nsa}}^1(a_n)) \leq (D(a_1), ..., D(a_n)) \tag{6}$$

From (6), and since $G = F \circ F$ is non-decreasing, we have:

$$(f_{\text{nsa}}^{2i}(a_1), ..., f_{\text{nsa}}^{2i}(a_n)) \geq (D(a_1), ..., D(a_n)) \tag{7}$$

and

$$(f_{\text{nsa}}^{2i+1}(a_1), ..., f_{\text{nsa}}^{2i+1}(a_n)) \leq (D(a_1), ..., D(a_n)) \tag{8}$$

for every $i \in \mathbb{N}$.

Since all f^i converge, from (7) and (8) we obtain

$$(Deg_{\mathcal{F}}^{\text{nsa}}(a_1), \ldots, Deg_{\mathcal{F}}^{\text{nsa}}(a_n)) \geq (D(a_1), \ldots, D(a_n))$$

and

$$(Deg_{\mathcal{F}}^{\text{nsa}}(a_1), \ldots, Deg_{\mathcal{F}}^{\text{nsa}}(a_n)) \leq (D(a_1), \ldots, D(a_n))$$

and thus $\forall a \in \mathcal{A}, Deg_{\mathcal{F}}^{\text{nsa}}(a) = D(a)$. $\qquad \square$

Below is an example of the **nsa** semantics applied on an argumentation graph.

Example 1. *Let us apply the no self-attack h-categorizer semantics (nsa) on the argumentation graph illustrated in Fig. 1. By definition, the self-attacking arguments have an acceptability degree of 0: $Deg_{\mathcal{F}}^{\text{nsa}}(a_0) = Deg_{\mathcal{F}}^{\text{nsa}}(a_2) = 0$. The non-attacked arguments or the arguments only attacked by self-attacking arguments have, by definition, the maximum score: $Deg_{\mathcal{F}}^{\text{nsa}}(a_5) = 1$. Applying the formula from Theorem 6, we obtain the following acceptability degrees for a_1 and a_4: $Deg_{\mathcal{F}}^{\text{nsa}}(a_1) = 0.732$ and $Deg_{\mathcal{F}}^{\text{nsa}}(a_4) = 0.399$. Finally, following the same method, here are the details concerning a_3 :*

$$Deg_{\mathcal{F}}^{\text{nsa}}(a_3) = \frac{1}{1 + Deg_{\mathcal{F}}^{\text{nsa}}(a_1) + Deg_{\mathcal{F}}^{\text{nsa}}(a_2) + Deg_{\mathcal{F}}^{\text{nsa}}(a_4)} = 0.477$$

In order to have an overview of the difference between **nsa** *and the gradual semantics introduced in Sect. 2, the degrees of acceptability of arguments w.r.t. the h-categorizer semantics and the M&T semantics have also been added in the table of Fig. 1. This comparison clearly shows that nullifying the impact of self-attacking arguments more or less significantly changes the degree of acceptability of other arguments (e.g. a_1 and a_3).*

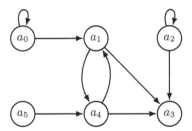

$Deg_{\mathcal{F}}^{S}$	nsa	h	MT
a_0	0	0.618	0
a_1	0.732	0.495	0.25
a_2	0	0.618	0
a_3	0.477	0.398	0.167
a_4	0.399	0.401	0.25
a_5	1	1	1

Fig. 1. On the left, an argumentation graph $\mathcal{F}$ and, on the right, the table containing the degrees of acceptability of each argument of $\mathcal{F}$ w.r.t. the no self-attack h-categorizer semantics (**nsa**), the h-categorizer semantics (**h**) and the semantics M&T (**MT**).

6   Principle-Based Evaluation of Semantics

In this section we evaluate the **nsa** semantics with respect to principle compliance, and compare the results with two existing semantics, namely M&T and *h*-categorizer (Table 1). We first show that **nsa** satisfies all the principles from P_{2S2C}, and thus cannot be dominated by any semantics.

Proposition 7. *The gradual semantics* **nsa** *satisfies all principles from* P_{2S2C}. *The other principles are not satisfied.*

In order to axiomatically compare **nsa** with the two other gradual semantics, let us check for the principles studied in this paper those that are satisfied by M&T and recall those satisfied by the *h*-categorizer semantics.

Proposition 8. *The gradual semantics M&T satisfies Anonymity, Maximality, Independence, Directionality, Weakening, Compensation, Self-Contradiction and Strong Self-Contradiction. The other principles are not satisfied.*

Proposition 9 ([3]). *The gradual semantics h-categorizer satisfies all the principles from* P_{CREW}. *The other principles are not satisfied.*

Note that **nsa** dominates M&T, i.e. it satisfies strictly more principles. Observe that **nsa** and *h*-categorizer are incomparable in terms of principles satisfaction. Indeed, **nsa** represents one choice, i.e. the position to satisfy Strong Self-Contradiction and Compensation. It also satisfies all the compatible principles. *h*-categorizer represents another choice, namely that to satisfy Compensation, Resilience, Equivalence and Weakening Soundness. Concretely, a semantics satisfying P_{CREW} considers that a self-attacking argument is a path like the other ones. So an argument which attacks itself (and is not attacked by any other argument) can be stronger than an argument which is attacked by several arguments. On the contrary, a semantics which satisfies P_{2S2C} considers that a self-attacking argument is intrinsically flawed, without even requiring other arguments to defeat it. Note that there exist other maximal sets of compatible principles, for example the one containing Resilience and Self-Contradiction. We leave a detailed study of these maximal sets of compatible principles for future work.

7   Experimental Results

We now empirically compare **nsa** with M&T and h-categoriser semantics. We consider a large experimental setting representing three different models used during the ICCMA competition (http://argumentationcompetition.org/) as a way to generate random argumentation graphs: i) the Erdös-Rényi model (ER) which generates graphs by randomly selecting attacks between arguments, ii) the Barabasi-Albert model (BA) which provides networks, called scale-free networks, with a structure in which some nodes have a huge number of links, but in which nearly all nodes are connected to only a few other nodes, and iii)

Table 1. Principles satisfied by the M&T, h-categorizer and **nsa** semantics. The shaded cells contain the results already proved in the literature.

Principles	M&T	h-cat	nsa
Anonymity	✓	✓	✓
Independence	✓	✓	✓
Directionality	✓	✓	✓
Neutrality	×	✓	×
Equivalence	×	✓	×
Maximality	✓	✓	✓
Weakening	✓	✓	✓
Counting	×	✓	✓
Weakening Soundness	×	✓	×
Reinforcement	×	✓	×
Resilience	×	✓	×
Cardinality Precedence	×	×	×
Quality Precedence	×	×	×
Compensation	✓	✓	✓
Self-Contradiction	✓	×	✓
Strong Self-Contradiction	✓	×	✓

the Watts-Strogatz model (WS) which produces graphs which have small-world network properties, such as high clustering and short average path lengths. The generation of these three types of AGs was done by the AFBenchGen2 generator [15]. We generated a total of 2160 AGs evenly distributed between the three models. For each model, the number of arguments varies among $Arg = \{5, 10, 15, 25, 50, 100, 250, 500\}$ with 90 AGs for each of these values. The parameters used to generate graphs are as follows: for ER, 10 random instances for each (numArg, probAttacks) in $Arg \times \{0.2, 0.3, \ldots, 1\}$; for BA, 9 random instances for each (numArg, probCycles) in $Arg \times \{0, 0.1, \ldots, 0.9\}$; for WS, (numArg, probCycles, β, $\mathcal{K}$) in $Arg \times \{0.25, 0.5, 0.75\} \times \{0, 0.25, 0.5, 0.75, 1\} \times \{k \in 2\mathbb{N} \ s.t. \ 2 \leq k \leq |Arg| - 1\}$. We refer the reader to [15] for the meaning of the parameters.

In order to compare the execution times of the three semantics studied in this paper, we have implemented them in C and ran the program on a cluster of identical computers with dual quad-core processors with 128 GB RAM.[4]

---

[4] The code and benchmarks are available online at https://github.com/jeris90/nsa_code.git.

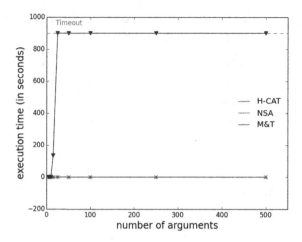

Fig. 2. Execution speed for the nsa (in green), the M&T (in blue) and the h-categorizer (in red) semantics. x-axis shows the number of arguments of the instances ($Arg = \{5, 10, 15, 25, 50, 100, 250, 500\}$). y-axis shows the execution time in seconds (with a timeout of 900 s). (Color figure online)

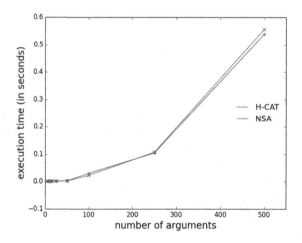

Fig. 3. A zoomed-in version of the graph from Fig. 2 to better see the difference between the execution speed for the nsa and the h-categorizer semantics.

Figure 2 shows the average execution time obtained by each semantics for the instances classified according to the number of arguments. A first remark is that, unlike the other two semantics, the M&T semantics quickly explodes in time since it systematically reaches the timeout (900 s) when the number of arguments is greater than 15. A second remark is that, unsurprisingly, the nsa and h-categorizer semantics have very similar execution times for each of the instances. Figure 3 shows the difference between nsa and h-categorizer semantics more precisely. Moreover, they allow us to quickly compute (with an average smaller than one second) the degree of acceptability of each argument even for large AGs. Only a few very dense instances (i.e. those with a high probability of cycles) require between 1 and 2 s when numArg = 500.

8   Summary

We studied the question of the treatment of self-attacks by gradual semantics following a principle-based approach. We showed links and incompatibilities between principles, defined a new semantics called no self-attack h-categorizer semantics and proved that it dominates the only existing semantics satisfying Self-Contradiction principle. Moreover, we showed that our semantics satisfies a maximal possible amount of principles (i.e. no semantics satisfying Self-Contradiction can satisfy more principles) and is usable in practice as it returns results very quickly (on average less than 1 s) even on large and dense AGs.

In addition to the future work already discussed in the paper, we think it would be interesting to extend the approach we used for the h-categorizer semantics to other gradual semantics (if possible). Finally, the work presented in this paper concerns "classic" argumentation graphs but one could naturally ask the same question about AGs containing more information (support relation, weight on arguments and/or attacks, etc.).

Acknowledgements. Vivien Beuselinck was supported by the ANR-3IA Artificial and Natural Intelligence Toulouse Institute. Srdjan Vesic was supported by Responsible AI Chair a chair in Artificial Intelligence (https://ia-responsable.eu/).

References

1. Amgoud, L.: A replication study of semantics in argumentation. In: Proceedings of the 28th International Joint Conference on Artificial Intelligence (IJCAI'19) (2019)
2. Amgoud, L., Ben-Naim, J.: Ranking-based semantics for argumentation frameworks. In: Liu, W., Subrahmanian, V.S., Wijsen, J. (eds.) SUM 2013. LNCS (LNAI), vol. 8078, pp. 134–147. Springer, Heidelberg (2013). https://doi.org/10.1007/978-3-642-40381-1_11
3. Amgoud, L., Ben-Naim, J.: Axiomatic foundations of acceptability semantics. In: Principles of Knowledge Representation and Reasoning: Proceedings of the Fifteenth International Conference, KR 2016, pp. 2–11. AAAI Press (2016)
4. Amgoud, L., Ben-Naim, J., Doder, D., Vesic, S.: Acceptability semantics for weighted argumentation frameworks. In: Sierra, C. (ed.) Proceedings of the 26th International Joint Conference on Artificial Intelligence, (IJCAI'17), pp. 56–62 (2017)
5. Amgoud, L., Doder, D.: Gradual semantics accounting for varied-strength attacks. In: Proceedings of the 18th International Conference on Autonomous Agents and MultiAgent Systems, (AAMAS'19). pp. 1270–1278 (2019)
6. Baroni, P., Caminada, M., Giacomin, M.: An introduction to argumentation semantics. Knowl. Eng. Rev. **26**(4), 365–410 (2011)

7. Baroni, P., Giacomin, M.: Solving semantic problems with odd-length cycles in argumentation. In: Nielsen, T.D., Zhang, N.L. (eds.) ECSQARU 2003. LNCS (LNAI), vol. 2711, pp. 440–451. Springer, Heidelberg (2003). https://doi.org/10. 1007/978-3-540-45062-7_36

8. Baumann, R., Brewka, G., Ulbricht, M.: Comparing weak admissibility semantics to their dung-style counterparts - reduct, modularization, and strong equivalence in abstract argumentation. In: Calvanese, D., Erdem, E., Thielscher, M. (eds.) Proc. of the 17th International Conference on Principles of Knowledge Representation and Reasoning, (KR'20), pp. 79–88 (2020)

9. Baumann, R., Brewka, G., Ulbricht, M.: Revisiting the foundations of abstract argumentation - semantics based on weak admissibility and weak defense. In: Proceedings of the 34th AAAI Conference on Artificial Intelligence, (AAAI'20), pp. 2742–2749 (2020)

10. Besnard, P., Hunter, A.: A logic-based theory of deductive arguments. Artif. Intell. **128**(1–2), 203–235 (2001)

11. Bodanza, G.A., Tohmé, F.A.: Two approaches to the problems of self-attacking arguments and general odd-length cycles of attack. J. Appl. Log. **7**(4), 403–420 (2009)

12. Bonzon, E., Delobelle, J., Konieczny, S., Maudet, N.: A comparative study of ranking-based semantics for abstract argumentation. In: Proceedings of the 30th AAAI Conference on Artificial Intelligence (AAAI'16), pp. 914–920 (2016)

13. Bonzon, E., Delobelle, J., Konieczny, S., Maudet, N.: Combining extension-based semantics and ranking-based semantics for abstract argumentation. In: Proceedings of the 16th International Conference on Principles of Knowledge Representation and Reasoning (KR'18), pp. 118–127 (2018)

14. Caminada, M.: On the issue of reinstatement in argumentation. In: Fisher, M., van der Hoek, W., Konev, B., Lisitsa, A. (eds.) JELIA 2006. LNCS (LNAI), vol. 4160, pp. 111–123. Springer, Heidelberg (2006). https://doi.org/10.1007/11853886_11

15. Cerutti, F., Vallati, M., Giacomin, M.: Afbenchgen2: a generator for random argumentation frameworks (2017). http://argumentationcompetition.org/2017/ AFBenchGen2.pdf

16. Dauphin, J., Rienstra, T., van der Torre, L.: A principle-based analysis of weakly admissible semantics. In: Proceedings of the 8th International Conference on Computational Models of Argument, (COMMA'20), Frontiers in Artificial Intelligence and Applications, vol. 326, pp. 167–178 (2020)

17. Dung, P.M.: On the acceptability of arguments and its fundamental role in non-monotonic reasoning, logic programming and n-person games. Artif. Intell. **77**(2), 321–358 (1995)

18. Gabbay, D.M., Rodrigues, O.: Equilibrium states in numerical argumentation networks. Log. Univers. **9**(4), 411–473 (2015). https://doi.org/10.1007/s11787-015-0119-7

19. Matt, P.-A., Toni, F.: A game-theoretic measure of argument strength for abstract argumentation. In: Hölldobler, S., Lutz, C., Wansing, H. (eds.) JELIA 2008. LNCS (LNAI), vol. 5293, pp. 285–297. Springer, Heidelberg (2008). https://doi.org/10. 1007/978-3-540-87803-2_24

20. Pu, F., Luo, J., Zhang, Y., Luo, G.: Argument ranking with categoriser function. In: Buchmann, R., Kifor, C.V., Yu, J. (eds.) KSEM 2014. LNCS (LNAI), vol. 8793, pp. 290–301. Springer, Cham (2014). https://doi.org/10.1007/978-3-319-12096-6_26

Flexible Dispute Derivations with Forward and Backward Arguments for Assumption-Based Argumentation

Martin Diller$^{(\boxtimes)}$ (ID), Sarah Alice Gaggl (ID), and Piotr Gorczyca

Logic Programming and Argumentation Group, Faculty of Computer Science,
Technische Universität Dresden, Dresden, Germany
martin.diller@tu-dresden.de

Abstract. Assumption-based argumentation (ABA) is one of the main general frameworks for structured argumentation. Dispute derivations for ABA allow for evaluating claims in a dialectical manner: i.e. on the basis of an exchange of arguments and counter-arguments for a claim between a proponent and an opponent of the claim. Current versions of dispute derivations are geared towards determining (credulous) acceptance of claims w.r.t. the admissibility-based semantics that ABA inherits from abstract argumentation. Relatedly, they make use of backwards or top down reasoning for constructing arguments. In this work we define flexible dispute derivations with forward as well as backward reasoning allowing us, in particular, to also have dispute derivations for finding admissible, complete, and stable assumption sets rather than only determine acceptability of claims. We give an argumentation-based definition of such dispute derivations and a more implementation friendly alternative representation in which disputes involve exchange of claims and rules rather than arguments. These can be seen as elaborations on, in particular, existing graph-based dispute derivations on two fronts: first, in also allowing for forward reasoning; second, in that all arguments put forward in the dispute are represented by a graph and not only the proponents.

Keywords: Argumentation · Assumption-based argumentation · Dispute derivations

1 Introduction

Assumption-based argumentation [3,4,12,16,34] (ABA) is one of the main formalisms for structured argumentation [2], also very much related to ASPIC+ [18,27,28]. ABA frameworks are built from a deductive system consisting of a language and set of rules. ABA arguments are then proofs in such a deductive system. Certain elements of the language are singled out as assumptions and a total mapping is provided associating each assumption to its so called contrary. Assumptions, and thus arguments using such

---

This research was partially funded by the Deutsche Forschungsgemeinschaft (DFG, German Research Foundation) – project number 389792660 – TRR 248, and by the Bundesministerium für Bildung und Forschung (BMBF) Förderkennzeichen 01IS20056_NAVAS.

© Springer Nature Switzerland AG 2021
P. Baroni et al. (Eds.): CLAR 2021, LNAI 13040, pp. 147–168, 2021.
https://doi.org/10.1007/978-3-030-89391-0_9

assumptions, can be attacked by arguments for their contraries. For flat ABA, which we will be focusing on this work (and has, as far as we are aware, also been the focus of all other work on reasoning methods for ABA), semantics can be equivalently defined at the level of assumption sets as well as arguments. In either case one ultimately obtains sets of assumptions which can be deemed reasonable to the same degree that the arguments that can be built from them are reasonable according to the classical admissibility-based semantics of abstract argumentation [14].

One of the main reasoning methods which has been devised for (flat) ABA is that of dispute derivations [10,11,15,17,20,33]. These build on one of if not *the* main native (vs reduction-based [9]) method for reasoning in abstract argumentation; namely, argumentation games (see e.g. [5,7,8,13,21–23,26,29,31,35]). Dispute derivations are conceived of as a game between a proponent and opponent, where starting from some goal claim the proponent searches for an argument proving the goal. This search reveals assumptions on which the proof depends, which can be attacked by the opponent by arguments for their contraries. Such arguments from the opponent can in turn be attacked by the proponent by searching for further arguments and so on. Dispute derivations can be seen as hybrid syntactic-semantic methods for searching for only those arguments needed to answer a query and are thus related to the issue of selecting such relevant arguments in structured argumentation more general [1,6,19,30,32,36].

Although reduction-based methods also for reasoning in ABA (as for abstract argumentation) have to date proved to be much more efficient than dispute derivations [24,25], dispute derivations remain interesting for a number of reasons. The main of these is that reducing argumentation to other formalisms often undermines the purpose of using argumentation in the first place; which is presumably to allow for a dialectic evaluation of claims in terms of arguments and counter-arguments. Dispute derivations deliver such "dialectic explications". This makes them especially suitable when information is limited and unreliable; also, for approximate, dynamic, and interactive reasoning.

As detailed, there have been several versions of dispute derivations to date. But all have in common that they are conceived primarily as decision procedures for determining credulous acceptance of a claim w.r.t. the admissible-based semantics (in the first versions of dispute derivations focus was on grounded, admissible, and ideal semantics; in later [10,11] versions the ideal semantics is dropped); i.e. whether there is an admissible (and hence complete and preferred) assumption set from which the claim can be proven. Related to this, they make use of backwards reasoning: both the proponent and opponent make use of top down or backwards reasoning to search for their arguments.

Top down reasoning is often enough. In particular, for the focused task of determining credulous acceptance of claims; yet, another fundamental paradigm in reasoning is forward or bottom up from established claims to further claims. In the context of dispute derivations such reasoning becomes relevant for more global tasks as e.g. determining acceptance of several claims or, relatedly, determining complete assumption sets rather than only credulous acceptance. Moreover, while for determining credulous acceptance computing e.g. complete assumption sets is not necessary, more revealing explications can often be obtained. In particular, computing complete assumption sets allows, as the name of the semantics suggests, a more "complete" picture of sets of assumptions which are congruous with a claim of interest. Furthermore, forward reasoning allows a straightforward generalisation of dispute derivations also for the stable semantics, this semantics not having been considered in previous work on disputes for ABA.

So in this work we add forward reasoning to dispute derivations. This allows us, in particular, to define dispute derivations for finding admissible, complete, and stable assumption sets as well as for determining acceptance of claims w.r.t. these semantics. We do so in several steps. We start in Sect. 3 by considering dispute derivations from an implementation independent and purely argumentation-based perspective: i.e. in terms of the arguments that are exchanged by the proponent and opponent. In particular, especially for forward reasoning how much of a dispute is "remembered" and made use of in further dispute steps is crucial. We provide a definition of flexible dispute derivations (with forward and backward arguments) based on structured dispute derivations from [33] and then graph-based dispute derivations from [10] in Sect. 3.2. The only thing that distinguishes these variants of dispute derivations is precisely how much of previous dispute steps is made use of in further steps. We note that there is room for improvement in this regard, particularly for the purpose of forward reasoning, and thus propose a novel variant of flexible dispute derivations in Sect. 3.3.

We then in Sect. 4 change gear to a more implementation focused perspective more in line with existing work on ABA disputes and give an alternative representation of our novel variant of dispute derivations from Sect. 3.3. In this version disputes involve the exchange of claims and rules rather than arguments; in particular, the opponents and proponents arguments are represented in a shared graph consisting in the dependency relations between rules and statements put forward during the dispute. Thus we further generalise [10] in which only the proponents arguments are represented as a graph, while the opponents are not. In Sect. 5 we then provide details on an interactive interface we implemented for our dispute derivations that is freely available. Section 2 contains the background needed for our work and Sect. 6 the conclusions.

2   Formal Background

Definition 1. *An ABA framework is a tuple* $\mathscr{F} = (\mathscr{L}, \mathscr{R}, \mathscr{A}, ^-)$ *where*

- $(\mathscr{L}, \mathscr{R})$ *is a deductive system, with a language* $\mathscr{L}$ *and a set of inference rules* $\mathscr{R}$,
- $\mathscr{A} \subseteq \mathscr{L}$ *is a (non-empty) set, whose elements are referred to as* assumptions,
- $^-$ *is a total mapping from* $\mathscr{A}$ *into* $\mathscr{L}$, *where* $\bar{a}$ *is the* contrary *of a.*

We also define for a set of statements $S \subseteq \mathscr{L}$, $\bar{S} = \{\bar{u} \in \mathscr{L} \mid u \in (S \cap \mathscr{A})\}$. As in previous work on dispute derivations, here we also restrict our attention to flat ABA: i.e. frameworks where there is no rule $h \leftarrow B \in \mathscr{R}$ s.t. $h \in \mathscr{A}$. In all of this work we will consider the ABA framework to be fixed and thus not define notions relative to an ABA framework. Elements of $\mathscr{L}$ we will refer to as statements, sometimes as claims.

Arguments have been defined in several different ways for ABA. For a comprehensive definition we define arguments in ASPIC+ [27] style:

Definition 2. *For an ABA* $\mathscr{F} = (\mathscr{L}, \mathscr{R}, \mathscr{A}, ^-)$, *an* argument *is defined as follows.*

(i) $a = s$ *is an argument if* $s \in \mathcal{L}$. *Then* $Prem(a) = \{s\}$, $Asm(a) = \{s\} \cap \mathscr{A}$, $Conc(a) = s$,
$TopSub(a) = \{s\}$, $Sub(a) = \{s\}$.

(ii) $a = s \leftarrow a_1, \ldots, a_n$ *is an argument if* $a_1, \ldots, a_n$ *are arguments such that there
exists* $s \leftarrow Conc(a_1), \ldots, Conc(a_n) \in \mathscr{R}$. *Then* $Prem(a) = Prem(a_1) \cup \ldots \cup Prem(a_n)$,
$Asm(a) = Asm(a_1) \cup \ldots \cup Asm(a_n) \cup (\{s\} \cap \mathscr{A})$, $Conc(a) = s$, $TopSub(a) = \{s\} \cup$
$\{s \leftarrow a'_1, \ldots, a'_n \mid a'_1 \in TopSub(a_1), \ldots, a'_n \in TopSub(a_n)\}$, $Sub(a) = Sub(a_1) \cup \ldots \cup$
$Sub(a_n) \cup TopSub(a)$.

For instance let $a = p \leftarrow b, [q \leftarrow r, s]$ be an argument built from rules $p \leftarrow b, q$
and $q \leftarrow r, s$ with only $b \in \mathscr{A}$. Then we have that the premisses of the argument are
$Prem(a) = \{b, r, s\}$, the assumptions $Asm(a) = \{b\}$, the conclusion $Conc(a) = p$, the
top-sub-arguments $TopSub(a) = \{p; \ p \leftarrow b, q; \ p \leftarrow b, [q \leftarrow r, s]\}$, and the sub-arguments
$Sub(a) = \{b; \ r; \ s; \ q \leftarrow r, s\} \cup TopSub(a)$. We extend the above notions to sets of arguments in the obvious manner; e.g. for a set of arguments A, $Prem(A) = \bigcup_{a \in A} Prem(a)$.

We denote all arguments in $\mathscr{F}$ as *Args*. An argument a is complete if $Prem(a) \subseteq \mathscr{A}$.
This is what is usually called an argument for ABA; what we have defined are "potential
arguments". The reason for the latter being that these are what dispute derivations work
on. Related to this, note that our notion of sub-arguments, differently to what is the
case in ASPIC+, includes all sub-arguments; not only those with the same premisses
as the main argument. Given that statements and rules can be thought of as (potential)
simple arguments we notationally and otherwise will usually not distinguish between
such simple arguments and the statements and rules underlying them.

Attacks in (flat) ABA can be defined between assumption sets, between arguments,
as well as in the form of hybrid attacks between assumptions and arguments. This leads
to equivalent assumption, argument, and hybrid views respectively of the semantics.
Dispute derivations are based on a hybrid view and so we here review this perspective.

Definition 3. *The notions of attack we need are:*

- *An argument a attacks a set of assumptions U' if $Conc(a) = \overline{u'}$ for a $u' \in U'$.*
- *A set of assumptions U attacks a set of assumptions U' if there is a (complete) argument a with $Prem(a) \subseteq U$ that attacks U'. In particular, if $U' = \{u'\}$ (i.e. U' is a
  singleton set with only the assumption u') we say simply that U attacks u'.*
- *A set of assumptions U attacks an argument a' if there is a (complete) argument a
  with $Prem(a) \subseteq U$ that attacks $Asm(a')$.*

Definition 4. *The definitions of the semantics we mainly consider in this work are:*

- *A set of assumptions is* admissible *if it does not attack itself and it attacks all complete arguments that attack it.*
- *A set of assumptions is* complete *if it is admissible and contains all assumptions
  it defends, where $U \subseteq \mathscr{A}$ defends $u \in \mathscr{A}$ if U attacks all complete arguments that
  attack u.*
- *A set of assumptions is* stable *if it does not attack itself and attacks all assumptions
  it does not contain.*

A set of statements S is (credulously) acceptable w.r.t. a semantics σ if there is a σ
assumption set U w.r.t. which $S \subseteq Conc(A)$ for $A \subseteq Args$ with $Asm(A) \subseteq U$.

3 Argument-Based Flexible Dispute Derivations

In this section we develop rather abstract (not implementation focused) definitions of flexible dispute derivations, first of all, following structured dispute derivations [33] and then graph-based dispute derivations [10] (Sect. 3.2). We call these StFlexDDs and GrFlexDDs for short. We focus on the common aspects of these, at first sight, rather different looking versions of dispute derivations by considering how the disputes evolve in terms of the arguments put forward by the proponent and opponent.

We identify certain shortcomings (inherited from their non-flexible counterparts) in the manner in which StFlexDDs and GrFlexDDs make use of the arguments constructed in previous steps in the disputes. These shortcomings are particularly relevant for incorporating forward reasoning into dispute derivations, since forward reasoning builds on established claims. We thus then propose a different form of dispute derivations which we call simply flexible dispute derivations or FlexDDs for short (Sect. 3.3). Although from an argument-based perspective FlexDDs seem quite complex, we will see in Sect. 4 that in fact they lead to an equally natural yet implementation friendly alternative representation where claims and rules are put forward rather than arguments.

3.1 Argument and Dispute State Expansions

Basic moves both from the proponent and opponent in flexible dispute derivations involve expansions of arguments which we define as follows:

Definition 5. *An* expansion *of $A = \{a_1, \ldots, a_n\} \subseteq Args$ w.r.t. an argument $a' \in Args$ with $Conc(a_1) \cup \ldots \cup Conc(a_n) \subseteq Prem(a')$ is obtained from a' by replacing at least one $s_i \in Prem(a')$ for which $s_i = Conc(a_i)$ with a_i for each $1 \leq i \leq n$. We denote it $a' \lessdot A$. When $n = 1$, we will often denote the expansion as $a' \lessdot a_1$.*

Thus a *forward expansion* of a set of arguments A w.r.t. $\mathscr{R}$ (now taken as a set of 1-step arguments) is of the form $r \lessdot A$ with $r \in \mathscr{R}$. A *backward expansion* of an argument a w.r.t. $\mathscr{R}$ amounts to an expansion of the form $a \lessdot r$ with $r \in \mathscr{R}$.

Disputes consist of sequences of dispute states which we define simply as tuples $(\mathscr{B}, \mathscr{P})$ where $\mathscr{B} \subseteq Args$ are the arguments considered by the opponent and $\mathscr{P} \subseteq Args$ those considered by the proponent. The different types of moves which the proponent and opponent can make in a dispute amount to "expanding" either $\mathscr{B}$ or $\mathscr{P}$. The expansion is by an argument a with i) $a = u \in \mathscr{A}$, ii) $a = h \leftarrow B$, iii) $a = h \leftarrow B \lessdot A'$ or iv) $a = a' \lessdot h \leftarrow B$ for $A' \subseteq \mathscr{B}$ and $a' \in \mathscr{B}$, or $A' \subseteq \mathscr{P}$, $a' \in \mathscr{P}$ respectively, $h \leftarrow B \in \mathscr{R}$.

There are several viable options for defining such expansions. These correspond to differences in how much of the arguments put forward during a dispute is "remembered" and considered in future expansions by the proponent and opponent. The different variants of flexible dispute derivations we consider in this work, i.e. StFlexDDs, GrFlexDDs, and FlexDDs will differ precisely on the underlying notion of expansion.

Table 1. Auxiliary notation for argument-based flexible dispute derivations. All defined w.r.t. a dispute state $(\mathcal{B}, \mathcal{P})$.

Notation	Description
$\mathcal{D} = Asm(\mathcal{P})$	Defenses
$\mathcal{C} = \{u \in \mathcal{A} \mid \bar{u} \in Conc(\mathcal{P})\}$	Culprits
$\mathcal{R}^- = \{h \leftarrow B \in \mathcal{R} \mid B \cap \mathcal{C} \neq \emptyset\}$	Blocked rules (culprits in bodies)
$\mathcal{R}^\sim = \{h \leftarrow B \in \mathcal{R} \mid (\{h\} \cup B) \cap (\overline{B} \cup \mathcal{C} \cup \overline{\mathcal{D}}) \neq \emptyset\}$	Rules blocked for the proponent (either inconsistent; otherwise culprits or contraries of defenses in head or body)
$\mathcal{P}^* = \{a \in \mathcal{P} \mid Prem(a) \subseteq \mathcal{A}\}$	Proponents complete arguments
$\mathcal{B}^{*/-} = \{a \in \mathcal{B} \mid Prem(a) \subseteq (\mathcal{A} \setminus \mathcal{C})\}$	Opponents complete unblocked arguments
$\mathcal{P}^+ = \{a \in \mathcal{P} \setminus \mathcal{P}^* \mid \neg \exists a' \neq a \in \mathcal{P}$ s.t. $Conc(a') = Conc(a)$ and $a' \in \mathcal{P}^*$ or $a \in Sub(a')\}$	Maximal incomplete proponent arguments
$\mathcal{P}^{\#}_{\gamma \cup \overline{\mathcal{C}}} = \{a \in \mathcal{P}^+ \mid Conc(a) \in \gamma \cup \overline{\mathcal{C}}\}$	Maximal incomplete proponent arguments for goals and contraries of culprits
$\mathcal{B}^{!/-}_S = \{a \in \mathcal{B} \mid Asm(a) \cap \mathcal{C} = \emptyset, Conc(a) \in S\}$	Unblocked arguments with conclusions in $S \subseteq \mathcal{L}$
$\mathcal{A}^! = \{u \in \mathcal{A} \mid u \in Asm(\mathcal{B}^{!/-}_{\overline{\mathcal{D}}})\}$	Candidates for culprits
$\mathcal{J} = \{u \in \mathcal{A} \setminus \mathcal{C} \mid \bar{u} \notin Conc(\mathcal{B}^{*/-})\}$	Assumptions defended at the dispute state

3.2 Argument-Based Flexible Dispute Derivations Following Structured and Graph-Based Dispute Derivations

Flexible Structured Dispute Derivations. Dispute derivations consist of a sequence of dispute states which are tuples of the form $(\mathcal{B}, \mathcal{P})$ where $\mathcal{B} \subseteq Args$ are the opponents and $\mathcal{P} \subseteq Args$ the proponents arguments. Dispute derivations are also defined for a set of goals $\gamma \subseteq \mathcal{L}$ which we assume to be consistent; i.e. $\gamma \cap \overline{\gamma} = \emptyset$. Note that we consider a set of goals here rather than a single goal as in previous versions of dispute derivations.

In Table 1 we give definitions of several auxiliary notions needed to define the possible moves in dispute derivations. These are all defined w.r.t. a dispute state $(\mathcal{B}, \mathcal{P})$.

Dispute derivations consist of a sequence of dispute advancements either by the proponent or the opponent and a termination condition indicating when the dispute has concluded. Each of the advancements consist of a move by the proponent or opponent, there being several conceivable "backward" and "forward" moves that accord with ABA semantics. We give thus a very general definition of dispute advancements including all such conceivable moves in what follows. The moves can be restricted in several ways to obtain, together with tailored termination conditions, restricted dispute variants which, for instance, are sound w.r.t. the admissible, complete, or stable semantics.

For StFlexDDs[1] a proponent dispute state advancement from a dispute state $(\mathcal{B}, \mathcal{P})$ is a dispute state $(\mathcal{B}, \mathcal{P}')$ with $\mathcal{P}' = \mathcal{P} \cup \{a\} \neq \mathcal{P}$, $X_1 \subseteq \overline{\mathcal{A}}$, $X_2 \subseteq \mathcal{A}$ where either

---

[1] Note that in [10,33] the rules blocked for the proponent and opponent are identical (i.e. $\mathcal{R}^-$), while we use the stronger notion of blocked rules for the proponent $\mathcal{R}^\sim$.

P-B-$\langle \overline{\mathscr{A}^!} \cup X_1 \rangle$:   i) $a = a' \lessdot h \leftarrow B$ for $h \leftarrow B \in \mathscr{R} \setminus \mathscr{R}^\sim$, $a' \in \mathscr{P}^{\#}_{\gamma \cup \mathscr{C}}$; or

ii) $a = h \leftarrow B$ for $h \leftarrow B \in \mathscr{R} \setminus \mathscr{R}^\sim$ with $h \in (\overline{\mathscr{A}^!} \cup X_1) \setminus \overline{\mathscr{D}}$;

P-F-$\langle (\overline{\mathscr{A}^!} \cap \mathscr{A}) \cup X_2 \rangle$: i) $a = h \leftarrow B \lessdot A$ for $A \subseteq \mathscr{P}^*$, $h \leftarrow B \in \mathscr{R} \setminus \mathscr{R}^\sim$; or

ii) $a = u$ for $u \in ((\overline{\mathscr{A}^!} \cap \mathscr{A}) \cup X_2) \setminus (\{\overline{u}\} \cup \mathscr{C} \cup \overline{\mathscr{D}})$.

An opponent dispute state advancement from a dispute state $(\mathscr{B}, \mathscr{P})$ is a dispute state $(\mathscr{B}', \mathscr{P})$ with $\mathscr{B}' = \mathscr{B} \cup \{a\} \neq \mathscr{B}$, $Y_1 \subseteq \overline{\mathscr{A}}$, and $Y_2 \subseteq \mathscr{A}$ where either

O-B-$\langle \overline{\mathscr{D}} \cup Y_1 \rangle$:   i) $a = a' \lessdot h \leftarrow B$ for $a' \in \mathscr{B}^{!/-}_{\overline{\mathscr{D}} \cup Y_1}$, $h \leftarrow B \in \mathscr{R} \setminus \mathscr{R}^-$; or

ii) $a = h \leftarrow B$ for a $h \leftarrow B \in \mathscr{R} \setminus \mathscr{R}^-$ with $h \in \overline{\mathscr{D}} \cup Y_1$;

O-F-$\langle (\overline{\mathscr{D}} \cap \mathscr{A}) \cup Y_2 \rangle$: i) $a = h \leftarrow B \lessdot A$ for $A \subseteq \mathscr{B}^{*/-}$, $h \leftarrow B \in \mathscr{R} \setminus \mathscr{R}^-$; or

ii) $a = u$ for $u \in (\overline{\mathscr{D}} \cap \mathscr{A}) \cup Y_2 \setminus \mathscr{C}$.

Each of the types of moves in disputes, e.g. P-B-$\langle \overline{\mathscr{A}^!} \cup X_1 \rangle$ which represents a backward move from the proponent, depend on a parameter, here $X_1 \subseteq \overline{\mathscr{A}}$. When $X_1 = \overline{\mathscr{A}}$, the move P-B is "least constrained". P-B is "most constrained" when $X_1 = \{\}$. The latter we denote as P-B-$\langle \overline{\mathscr{A}^!} \rangle$. The least constrained moves give us the most general possible dispute advancements, which we denote "free style" (DF) dispute advancements. The most constrained moves gives us dispute advancements which are sound and complete (when $\mathscr{L}$ is finite and $\mathscr{R}$ is acyclic) for credulous acceptance w.r.t. the admissible semantics. These, which we denote DAB, follow previous versions of dispute derivations as in [33] and [10]. The dispute advancements we consider in this work, including also for complete and stable semantics, are summarised in Table 2. Here e.g. for dispute advancements of type DAB, the proponent can move in P-B-$\langle \overline{\mathscr{A}^!} \rangle$ manner: both making P-B-$\langle \overline{\mathscr{A}^!} \rangle$-i or P-B-$\langle \overline{\mathscr{A}^!} \rangle$-ii moves. On the other hand, the proponent can move in P-F-$\langle \overline{\mathscr{A}^!} \cap \mathscr{A} \rangle$-ii but not in P-F-$\langle \overline{\mathscr{A}^!} \cap \mathscr{A} \rangle$-i manner. The dispute advancement types listed in Table 2 are just a few of the most obvious of several possible combinations. Note that DAB $\subseteq$ DABF (i.e. DAB moves are DABF moves), DABF $\subseteq$ DC, DABF $\subseteq$ DS, DC $\subseteq$ DF, and DS $\subseteq$ DF (also, usually $\subsetneq$).

Table 2. Dispute advancements with DAB for credulous acceptance w.r.t. the admissible semantics, DABF for credulous acceptance w.r.t. the admissible semantics but including "conservative" forward moves of the proponent, DC for the complete semantics, DS for the stable semantics, and DF for "free style". Columns "Proponent" and "Opponent" represent allowed moves by the proponent and opponent respectively.

Advancement	Proponent	Opponent
DAB	P-B-$\langle \overline{\mathscr{A}^!} \rangle$, P-F-$\langle \overline{\mathscr{A}^!} \cap \mathscr{A} \rangle$-ii	O-B-$\langle \overline{\mathscr{D}} \rangle$, O-F-$\langle \overline{\mathscr{D}} \cap \mathscr{A} \rangle$-ii
DABF	P-B-$\langle \overline{\mathscr{A}^!} \rangle$, P-F-$\langle \overline{\mathscr{A}^!} \cap \mathscr{A} \rangle$	O-B-$\langle \overline{\mathscr{D}} \rangle$, O-F-$\langle \overline{\mathscr{D}} \cap \mathscr{A} \rangle$-ii
DC	P-B-$\langle \overline{\mathscr{A}^!} \rangle$, P-F-$\langle (\overline{\mathscr{A}^!} \cap \mathscr{A}) \cup \mathscr{I} \rangle$	O-B-$\langle \overline{\mathscr{D}} \cup \overline{\mathscr{I}} \rangle$, O-F-$\langle (\overline{\mathscr{D}} \cup \overline{\mathscr{I}}) \cap \mathscr{A} \rangle$-ii
DS	P-B-$\langle \overline{\mathscr{A}^!} \rangle$, P-F-$\langle \mathscr{A} \rangle$	O-B-$\langle \overline{\mathscr{D}} \rangle$, O-F-$\langle \overline{\mathscr{D}} \cap \mathscr{A} \rangle$-ii
DF	P-B-$\langle \overline{\mathscr{A}} \rangle$, P-F-$\langle \mathscr{A} \rangle$	O-B-$\langle \overline{\mathscr{A}} \rangle$, O-F-$\langle \mathscr{A} \rangle$

Table 3. Termination conditions. TA for admissible, TC for complete, and TS for stable.

Cond.	Proponent winning	Opponent cannot move	Proponent cannot move
TA	$\gamma\cup\overline{\mathscr{C}}\subseteq Conc(\mathscr{P}^*)$, $\mathscr{B}^{!/-}_{\overline{\mathscr{D}}}\cap\mathscr{B}^{*/-}=\emptyset$	O-B-$\langle\overline{\mathscr{D}}\rangle$ + O-F-$\langle\overline{\mathscr{D}}\cap\mathscr{A}\rangle$-ii or O-F-$\langle\mathscr{A}\rangle$	P-B-$\langle\overline{\mathscr{A}^!}\rangle$ + P-F-$\langle\mathscr{A}^!\cap\mathscr{A}\rangle$-ii or P-F-$\langle\mathscr{A}\rangle$
TC	$\gamma\cup\overline{\mathscr{C}}\subseteq Conc(\mathscr{P}^*)$, $\mathscr{B}^{!/-}_{\overline{\mathscr{D}}}\cap\mathscr{B}^{*/-}=\emptyset$, $\mathscr{I}\setminus\mathscr{D}=\emptyset$	O-B-$\langle\overline{\mathscr{D}}\rangle$ + O-F-$\langle\overline{\mathscr{D}}\cap\mathscr{A}\rangle$-ii or O-F-$\langle\mathscr{A}\rangle$	P-B-$\langle\overline{\mathscr{A}^!}\rangle$ + P-F-$\langle(\overline{\mathscr{A}^!}\cap\mathscr{A})\cup\mathscr{I}\rangle$ or P-F-$\langle\mathscr{A}\rangle$
TS	$\gamma\cup\overline{\mathscr{C}}\subseteq Conc(\mathscr{P}^*)$, $\mathscr{B}^{!/-}_{\overline{\mathscr{D}}}\cap\mathscr{B}^{*/-}=\emptyset$, $\overline{\mathscr{D}}\cup\mathscr{C}=\mathscr{A}$	O-B-$\langle\overline{\mathscr{D}}\rangle$ + O-F-$\langle\overline{\mathscr{D}}\cap\mathscr{A}\rangle$-ii or O-F-$\langle\mathscr{A}\rangle$	P-B-$\langle\overline{\mathscr{A}^!}\rangle$ + P-F-$\langle\mathscr{A}\rangle$

The termination conditions we consider in this work are summarised in Table 3. There is, first of all, a condition that has to be satisfied at a dispute state $(\mathscr{B},\mathscr{P})$ for the proponent to be winning. This is in the column "Proponent winning". Then the proponent wins if this condition is satisfied and the opponent cannot move in either of the two possible combinations of moves in the column "Opponent cannot move". The opponent wins if the "Proponent winning" condition is not satisfied and the proponent cannot move in either of the two possible combinations of moves in the column "Proponent moves". So, for the termination condition for the admissible semantics TA, we have that the proponent wins if $\gamma\cup\overline{\mathscr{C}}\subseteq Conc(\mathscr{P}^*)$, $\mathscr{B}^{!/-}_{\overline{\mathscr{D}}}\cap\mathscr{B}^{*/-}=\emptyset$ and the opponent cannot advance further either in DAB manner: O-B-$\langle\overline{\mathscr{D}}\rangle$+O-F-$\langle\overline{\mathscr{D}}\cap\mathscr{A}\rangle$-ii; or in forwards DF manner: O-F-$\langle\mathscr{A}\rangle$. The opponent wins if $\gamma\cup\overline{\mathscr{C}}\setminus Conc(\mathscr{P}^*)\neq\emptyset$ or $\mathscr{B}^{!/-}_{\overline{\mathscr{D}}}\cap\mathscr{B}^{*/-}\neq\emptyset$ and the proponent cannot advance further either in DAB manner: P-B-$\langle\overline{\mathscr{A}^!}\rangle$+P-F-$\langle\mathscr{A}^!\cap\mathscr{A}\rangle$-ii or in forwards DF manner: P-F-$\langle\mathscr{A}\rangle$.

A dispute derivation variant then depends on allowed moves M and termination criteria C. For simplicity we allow that termination criteria make reference to moves which may not be allowed at a specific dispute variant; i.e. although moves are restricted these are all conceived as subsets of dispute variants where advancements are as in DF and hence checking for DF moves (and any other subset) is possible. As already indicated, dispute variants are defined for a set of goals $\gamma\subseteq\mathscr{L}$ (s.t. $\gamma\cap\overline{\gamma}=\emptyset$). They consist of a sequence of dispute states starting at $(\{\},\gamma)$. At each step the last dispute state is selected and advanced either according to the proponent or opponent and the allowed moves M. The dispute derivation ends at a dispute state satisfying the termination criteria C.

Example 1. Consider the ABA framework from Example 6.2 in [33] with $\mathscr{A}=\{a,b,c,d,e,f\}$, where $\overline{a}=q,\overline{b}=f,\overline{c}=u,\overline{d}=v,\overline{e}=v,\overline{f}=v$. Also:

$$\mathscr{R}=\{p\leftarrow a,u;\ q\leftarrow b,r;\ q\leftarrow c,s;\ q\leftarrow c,t;\ u\leftarrow a;\ s\leftarrow;\ t\leftarrow d;\ t\leftarrow e\}.$$

A DAB + TA StFlexDD following the structured dispute derivation of Fig. 7 in [33] is shown in Table 4. Note first of all, that in order to follow structured dispute derivations as in [33] the opponent must, for every statement that it (backward-) expands

Table 4. A DAB + TA StFlexDD for Example 1. Labels $-$, $*$, #, ! are used to distinguish blocked, complete, maximal incomplete, and opposing arguments respectively. Only complete and maximal incomplete arguments for goals and contraries of culprits of the proponent are shown. The dispute derivation ends with the opponent not being able to advance further in O-B-$\langle \overline{\mathscr{D}} \rangle$+O-F-$\langle \overline{\mathscr{D}} \cap \mathscr{A} \rangle$-ii manner.

Step and move type	$\mathscr{P}$	$\mathscr{B}$	$(\gamma \cup \overline{\mathscr{C}}) \setminus Conc(\mathscr{P}^*)$	$\mathscr{D}$	$\mathscr{C}$
0	$\{^{\#}p\}$	$\{\}$	$\{p\}$	$\{\}$	$\{\}$
1 (P-B-i, $p \leftarrow a, u$)	$\{^{\#}p \leftarrow a, u\}$	$\{\}$	$\{p\}$	$\{a\}$	$\{\}$
2 (O-B-ii, $q \leftarrow b, r$)	$\{^{\#}p \leftarrow a, u\}$	$\{^!q \leftarrow b, r\}$	$\{p\}$	$\{a\}$	$\{\}$
3 (O-B-ii, $q \leftarrow c, s$)	$\{^{\#}p \leftarrow a, u\}$	$\{^!q \leftarrow b, r; \,^!q \leftarrow c, s\}$	$\{p\}$	$\{a\}$	$\{\}$
4 (O-B-ii, $q \leftarrow c, t$)	$\{^{\#}p \leftarrow a, u\}$	$\{^!q \leftarrow b, r; \,^!q \leftarrow c, s; \,^!q \leftarrow c, t\}$	$\{p\}$	$\{a\}$	$\{\}$
5 (P-B-ii, $u \leftarrow a$)	$\{^{\#}p \leftarrow a, u; \,^*u \leftarrow a\}$	$\{^!q \leftarrow b, r; \,^{-!}q \leftarrow c, s; \,^{-!}q \leftarrow c, t\}$	$\{p\}$	$\{a\}$	$\{c\}$
6 (P-B-i, $u \leftarrow a$)	$\{^*u \leftarrow a; \,^*p \leftarrow a, [u \leftarrow a]\}$	$\{^!q \leftarrow b, r; \,^{-!}q \leftarrow c, s; \,^{-!}q \leftarrow c, t\}$	$\{\}$	$\{a\}$	$\{c\}$
7 (P-F-ii, f)	$\{^*u \leftarrow a; \,^*p \leftarrow a, [u \leftarrow a]; \,^*f\}$	$\{^{-!}q \leftarrow b, r; \,^{-!}q \leftarrow c, s; \,^{-!}q \leftarrow c, t\}$	$\{\}$	$\{a, f\}$	$\{b, c\}$

Table 5. A DF + TA StFlexDD for Example 2. Only complete and maximal incomplete arguments of the proponent are shown. The dispute derivation ends with the opponent not being able to advance further in O-F-$\langle \mathscr{A} \rangle$ manner.

Step and move type	$\mathscr{P}$	$\mathscr{B}$	$(\gamma \cup \overline{\mathscr{C}}) \setminus Conc(\mathscr{P}^*)$	$\mathscr{D}$	$\mathscr{C}$
0	$\{^{\#}p\}$	$\{\}$	$\{p\}$	$\{\}$	$\{b, c\}$
1 (P-B-i, $p \leftarrow a$)	$\{^*p \leftarrow a\}$	$\{\}$	$\{\}$	$\{a\}$	$\{b, c\}$
2 (O-F-ii, a)	$\{^*p \leftarrow a\}$	$\{^*a\}$	$\{\}$	$\{a\}$	$\{b, c\}$
3 (O-F-i, $p \leftarrow a$)	$\{^*p \leftarrow a\}$	$\{^*a; \,^*p \leftarrow a\}$	$\{\}$	$\{a\}$	$\{b, c\}$

on (e.g. q in the example in steps 2–4), expand the statement with every non-blocked rule. This is not necessary in StFlexDDs. Secondly, note that structured dispute derivations from [33] include a tracking mechanism whereby arguments that are not necessary for further evolution of the dispute derivation are discarded. As we strive for a general definition which allows us to consider several manners of expanding the opponents and proponents argument we do not do this here. For a direct implementation of StFlexDDs one could e.g. only store complete and maximal incomplete arguments of the proponent; also, one could remove arguments from the opponent which have been fully backward expanded. In fact, to simplify the example, we do not show all the proponents arguments in Table 4.

Nevertheless, we note in the dispute derivation from Table 4 redundancy in the moves. In particular, $u \leftarrow a$ is used twice by the proponent and it is only the second use that makes c a culprit. The reason is that following [33] the proponent is only "aware" of its arguments, but not of their internal structure.

Example 2. Consider the ABA framework with $\mathscr{A} = \{a, b, c\}$, where $\overline{a} = t, \overline{b} = p, \overline{c} = p$; and

$$\mathscr{R} = \{p \leftarrow a; \ t \leftarrow b; \ t \leftarrow c; \ t \leftarrow u; \ u \leftarrow v; \ v \leftarrow u\}.$$

A DF + TA StFlexDD (which also satisfies TC and TS) is shown in Table 5. Note that any DAB + TA dispute derivation for the same example will not terminate because of the circularity in the rules $u \leftarrow v$ and $v \leftarrow u$. Even when replacing these circular rules with a very long chain of rules starting at $t \leftarrow u$ and ending e.g. with a rule with one of b or c in the body, one gets a much shorter dispute derivation using forward moves. Note nevertheless again here the redundancy in particular in the need for the opponent to essentially repeat the moves by the proponent.

For flexible dispute derivations following structured dispute derivations and the variants we consider in this section we have the following results generalising the results for structured dispute derivations (for credulous reasoning w.r.t. the admissible semantics; i.e. DAB+TA in our context) from [33] in our more flexible setting:

Theorem 1. *DF +* {*TA, TC, TS*} *StFlexDDs are sound for the admissible, complete, and stable semantics respectively. This means e.g. for DF + TA that if there is a DF + TA StFlexDD ending with a dispute state* $(\mathcal{B}, \mathcal{P})$ *and the proponent as winner, then* $\mathcal{D}$ *is an admissible assumption set w.r.t. which* γ *is acceptable.*

Corollary 1. {*DAB, DABF, DC, DS*}+{*TA, TC, TS*} *StFlexDDs are sound for the admissible, complete, and stable semantics respectively.*

Theorem 2. *If* $\mathscr{L}$ *is finite and* $\mathscr{R}$ *is acyclic, DAB + TA StFlexDDs are complete for credulous acceptance w.r.t. the admissible semantics. I.e. if* γ *is acceptable for some admissible assumption set, then there is a DAB + TA StFlexDD ending with a dispute state* $(\mathcal{B}, \mathcal{P})$ *and the proponent as winner, s.t.* $\mathcal{D}$ *is an admissible assumption set w.r.t. which* γ *is acceptable. Moreover, DC + TC StFlexDDs are complete for the complete semantics and DS + TS StFlexDDs are complete for the stable semantics. E.g. for the complete semantics: if* γ *is acceptable for some complete assumption set U, then there is a DC + TC StFlexDD ending with a dispute state* $(\mathcal{B}, \mathcal{P})$ *and the proponent as winner, s.t.* $\mathcal{D} = U$. *Finally,* {*DC, DS, DF*} *+ TA StFlexDDs are complete for the admissible semantics.*

Corollary 2. *If* $\mathscr{L}$ *is finite and* $\mathscr{R}$ *is acyclic,* {*DABF, DC, DS, DF*} *+ TA StFlexDDs are complete for credulous acceptance w.r.t. the admissible semantics. Also, DF + TC StFlexDDs are complete for the complete semantics and DF + TS StFlexDDs are complete for the stable semantics.*

Flexible Graph-Based Dispute Derivations. We only need to change the notion of expansion of the opponents, respectively proponents arguments in the definition of dispute advancements to get GrFlexDDs. Specifically, we need the following notions:

Definition 6. *Let* $A \subseteq Args$ *and* $a \in Args$. *Then* $A \bowtie \{a\}$ *is the rule minimal (also called non bloated in [10]) closure of* $A \cup \{a\}$ *under sub-arguments and argument expansions. Here, first of all,* $A' \subseteq Args$ *is closed under sub-arguments if* $A' = Sub(A')$. *Moreover,* A' *is closed under expansions if* $a' = a'' \lessdot A''$ *for some* $a'' \in A'$, $A'' \subseteq A'$, *then also* $a' \in A'$. *Also,* A' *is rule minimal if there are no* $h \leftarrow B, h' \leftarrow B' \in Sub(A')$ *s.t.* $h = h'$ *but* $B \neq B'$. *Then, assuming A is closed under sub-arguments, closed under argument expansions,*

Table 6. A DAB + TA GrFlexDD for Example 3 (ABA framework from Example 1). Only maximal arguments of the proponent (for goals and contraries of culprits) and the opponent (for contraries of defenses) are shown. The dispute derivation ends with the opponent not being able to advance further in O-B-$\langle\overline{\mathscr{D}}\rangle$+O-F-$\langle\overline{\mathscr{D}}\cap\mathscr{A}\rangle$-ii manner.

Step and move type	$\mathscr{P}$	$\mathscr{B}$	$\gamma\cup\overline{\mathscr{C}}\setminus Conc(\mathscr{P}^*)$	$\mathscr{D}$	$\mathscr{C}$
0	$\{^{\#}p\}$	$\{\}$	$\{p\}$	$\{\}$	$\{\}$
1 (P-B-i, $p\leftarrow a,u$)	$\{^{\#}p\leftarrow a,u\}$	$\{\}$	$\{p,u\}$	$\{a\}$	$\{c\}$
2 (O-B-ii, $q\leftarrow b,r$)	$\{^{\#}p\leftarrow a,u\}$	$\{\,^{1}q\leftarrow b,r\}$	$\{p,u\}$	$\{a\}$	$\{c\}$
3 (P-B-i, $u\leftarrow a$)	$\{^{*}u\leftarrow a;\ ^{*}p\leftarrow a,[u\leftarrow a]\}$	$\{\,^{1}q\leftarrow b,r\}$	$\{\}$	$\{a\}$	$\{c\}$
4 (P-F-ii, f)	$\{^{*}u\leftarrow a;\ ^{*}p\leftarrow a,[u\leftarrow a];\ ^{*}f\}$	$\{^{-1}q\leftarrow b,r\}$	$\{\}$	$\{a,f\}$	$\{b,c\}$

and rule minimal, $A\bowtie\{a\}$ is the closure under sub-arguments and argument expansions of $A\cup\{a\}$ if this closure is also rule minimal, while otherwise $A\bowtie\{a\}=A$ (i.e. expansions which bloat the argument set are disallowed).

On the other hand, $A:\{a\}$ is the argument rule minimal union of A and a. Here $A'\subseteq Args$ is argument rule minimal if for each $a'\in A'$, $\{a'\}$ is rule minimal (such an a' is also called non-flabby in [10]). Then, assuming A is argument rule minimal, $A:\{a\}=A\cup\{a\}$ if $A\cup\{a\}$ is argument rule minimal, while otherwise $A:\{a\}=A$ (i.e. a must be rule minimal, aka non-flabby).

In GrFlexDDs a proponent dispute state advancement from a dispute state $(\mathscr{B},\mathscr{P})$ is a dispute state $(\mathscr{B},\mathscr{P}')$ with $\mathscr{P}'=\mathscr{P}\bowtie\{a\}\neq\mathscr{P}$, $X_1\subseteq\overline{\mathscr{A}}$, $X_2\subseteq\mathscr{A}$ with P-B-$\langle\overline{\mathscr{A}^{!}}\cup X_1\rangle$ and P-F-$\langle(\overline{\mathscr{A}^{!}}\cap\mathscr{A})\cup X_2\rangle$ moves defined as before. An opponent dispute state advancement from a dispute state $(\mathscr{B},\mathscr{P})$ is a dispute state $(\mathscr{B}',\mathscr{P})$ with $\mathscr{B}'=\mathscr{B}:\{a\}\neq\mathscr{B}$, $Y_1\subseteq\overline{\mathscr{A}}$, and $Y_2\subseteq\mathscr{A}$ with O-B-$\langle\overline{\mathscr{D}}\cup Y_1\rangle$ and O-F-$\langle(\overline{\mathscr{D}}\cap\mathscr{A})\cup Y_2\rangle$ moves defined as previously.

Example 3. Consider again the ABA framework from Example 1. To compare, a DAB + TA GrFlexDD following more or less that in Table 4 is shown in Table 6. Note that here c becomes a culprit already at step 1, while in the DAB + TA StFlexDD of Table 4 this happens at step 5 (since only then is there an argument in $\mathscr{P}$ with conclusion $\overline{c}=u$). Also, $u\leftarrow a$ only needs to be used once by the proponent, while in the dispute derivation of Table 4 this occurs twice. In the end the dispute becomes shorter by 3 steps.

Example 4. Consider a slightly more complex version of the ABA framework from Example 16 in [10] with $\mathscr{A}=\{a,b,c,d\}$, where $\overline{a}=t,\overline{b}=r,\overline{c}=t,\overline{d}=c$. Also:

$$\mathscr{R}=\{p\leftarrow q;\ q\leftarrow a;\ r\leftarrow p;\ t\leftarrow b;\ t\leftarrow p,s;\ t\leftarrow q,u,d\}.$$

A DAB + TA GrFlexDD based on the graph-based dispute derivation of Table 8 in [10] (the first 4 steps correspond to the whole dispute derivation in [10], except that here $t\leftarrow b$ is invoked by the opponent rather than simply b) is shown in Table 7. Note the redundancy in steps 6–7 of the opponent where the argument $p\leftarrow[q\leftarrow a]$ is constructed again. Also $q\leftarrow a$ is used in step 7 and then again in step 9.

Table 7. A DAB + TA GrFlexDD for Example 4. Only maximal arguments of the proponent (for goals and contraries of culprits) and the opponent (for contraries of defenses) are shown. The dispute derivation ends with the opponent not being able to advance further in O-B-$\langle \overline{\mathscr{D}} \rangle$+O-F-$\langle \overline{\mathscr{D}} \cap \mathscr{A} \rangle$-ii manner.

Step and move type	$\mathscr{P}$	$\mathscr{B}$	$\gamma \cup \overline{\mathscr{C}} \setminus Conc(\mathscr{P}^*)$	$\mathscr{D}$	$\mathscr{C}$
0	$\{^{\#}p\}$	{}	$\{p\}$	{}	{}
1 (P-B-i, $p \leftarrow q$)	$\{^{\#}p \leftarrow q\}$	{}	$\{p\}$	{}	{}
2 (P-B-i, $q \leftarrow a$)	$\{^{*}p \leftarrow [q \leftarrow a]\}$	{}		$\{a\}$	{}
3 (O-B-ii, $t \leftarrow b$)	$\{^{*}p \leftarrow [q \leftarrow a]\}$	$\{^{*!}t \leftarrow b\}$		$\{a\}$	{}
4 (P-B-ii, $r \leftarrow p$)	$\{^{*}p \leftarrow [q \leftarrow a];$ $^{*}r \leftarrow [p \leftarrow [q \leftarrow a]]\}$	$\{^{-*!}t \leftarrow b\}$		$\{a\}$	$\{b\}$
5 (O-B-ii, $t \leftarrow p,s$)	$\{^{*}p \leftarrow [q \leftarrow a];$ $^{*}r \leftarrow [p \leftarrow [q \leftarrow a]]\}$	$\{^{-*!}t \leftarrow b;\, ^{!}t \leftarrow p,s\}$		$\{a\}$	$\{b\}$
6 (O-B-i, $p \leftarrow q$)	$\{^{*}p \leftarrow [q \leftarrow a];$ $^{*}r \leftarrow [p \leftarrow [q \leftarrow a]]\}$	$\{^{-*!}t \leftarrow b;\, ^{!}t \leftarrow [p \leftarrow q],s\}$		$\{a\}$	$\{b\}$
7 (O-B-i, $q \leftarrow a$)	$\{^{*}p \leftarrow [q \leftarrow a];$ $^{*}r \leftarrow [p \leftarrow [q \leftarrow a]]\}$	$\{^{-*!}t \leftarrow b;$ $^{!}t \leftarrow [p \leftarrow [q \leftarrow a]],s\}$		$\{a\}$	$\{b\}$
8 (O-B-ii, $t \leftarrow q,u,d$)	$\{^{*}p \leftarrow [q \leftarrow a];$ $^{*}r \leftarrow [p \leftarrow [q \leftarrow a]]\}$	$\{^{-*!}t \leftarrow b;$ $^{!}t \leftarrow [p \leftarrow [q \leftarrow a]],s;$ $^{!}t \leftarrow q,u,d\}$		$\{a\}$	$\{b\}$
9 (O-B-ii, $q \leftarrow a$)	$\{^{*}p \leftarrow [q \leftarrow a];$ $^{*}r \leftarrow [p \leftarrow [q \leftarrow a]]\}$	$\{^{-*!}t \leftarrow b;$ $^{!}t \leftarrow [p \leftarrow [q \leftarrow a]],s;$ $^{!}t \leftarrow [q \leftarrow a],u,d\}$		$\{a\}$	$\{b\}$

We again obtain soundness and completeness results generalising the results for graph-based dispute derivations (for credulous reasoning) from [10]:

Theorem 3. $DF + \{TA, TC, TS\}$ *GrFlexDDs are sound for the admissible, complete, and stable semantics respectively.*

Corollary 3. $\{DAB, DABF, DC, DS\} + \{TA, TC, TS\}$ *GrFlexDDs are sound for the admissible, complete, and stable semantics respectively.*

Theorem 4. *If $\mathscr{L}$ is finite $DAB + TA$ GrFlexDDs are complete for credulous acceptance w.r.t. the admissible semantics. Moreover, $DC + TC$ GrFlexDDs are complete for the complete semantics and $DS + TS$ GrFlexDDs are complete for the stable semantics. Finally, $\{DC, DS, DF\} + TA$ GrFlexDDs are complete for the admissible semantics.*

Corollary 4. *If $\mathscr{L}$ is finite, $\{DABF, DC, DS, DF\} + TA$ GrFlexDDs are complete for credulous acceptance w.r.t. the admissible semantics. Also, $DF + TC$ GrFlexDDs are complete for the complete semantics and $DF + TS$ GrFlexDDs are complete for the stable semantics.*

3.3   Flexible Dispute Derivations

In the previous section we presented definitions of argument-based flexible variants of structured and graph-based dispute derivations. The objective was, first of all, to give a general definition showing the common aspects between the, at the first sight, different looking forms of dispute derivations while also incorporating flexibility in the order and types of moves allowed. At the same time, our definition allows to make clear the differences between structured and graph-based dispute derivations (and their flexible variants) in terms of how much of the arguments put forward during a dispute is stored and made use of in later steps of the dispute. We have seen that in this regard GrFlexDDs, while improving on StFlexDDs, still have some redundancy in that, firstly, the opponent does not make use of the proponents arguments when putting forward its own arguments. Also, there is redundancy in the moves of the opponent w.r.t. previous moves of itself (see in particular Example 4). These issues become especially pressing in the context of dispute derivations with forward moves as forward reasoning, more than backward reasoning, relies on previous moves.

We now propose FlexDDs to remedy the above mentioned issues. Again, we only need to change the definition of expansions of the opponents and proponents arguments in dispute advancements. Once more, we first need a definition:

Definition 7. *Let $A \subseteq Args$, $a \in Args$. Then $A \bowtie \{a\}$ is the closure of $A \cup \{a\}$ under sub-arguments and argument expansions.*

Thus $A \bowtie \{a\}$ is a more relaxed version of $A \rtimes \{a\}$ used in the definition of GrFlexDDs for the proponents dispute advancements.

In FlexDDs a proponent dispute state advancement from a dispute state $(\mathscr{B}, \mathscr{P})$ is a dispute state $(\mathscr{B}', \mathscr{P}')$ with $\mathscr{P}' = \mathscr{P} \rtimes \{a\} \neq \mathscr{P}$, $\mathscr{B}' = \mathscr{B} \bowtie \{a\}$, $X_1 \subseteq \overline{\mathscr{A}}$, $X_2 \subseteq \mathscr{A}$ with P-B-$\langle \overline{\mathscr{A}^!} \cup X_1 \rangle$ and P-F-$\langle (\overline{\mathscr{A}^!} \cap \mathscr{A}) \cup X_2 \rangle$ moves defined as before. An opponent dispute state advancement from a dispute state $(\mathscr{B}, \mathscr{P})$ is a dispute state $(\mathscr{B}', \mathscr{P})$ with $\mathscr{B}' = \mathscr{B} \bowtie \{a\} \neq \mathscr{B}$, $Y_1 \subseteq \overline{\mathscr{A}}$, $Y_2 \subseteq \mathscr{A}$ with O-B-$\langle \overline{\mathscr{D}} \cup Y_1 \rangle$ and O-F-$\langle (\overline{\mathscr{D}} \cap \mathscr{A}) \cup Y_2 \rangle$ moves defined as previously. So, main changes w.r.t. GrFlexDDs are that the proponents moves also have an effect on the opponents arguments. Also, $\mathscr{B}' = \mathscr{B} \bowtie \{a\}$ rather than $\mathscr{B}' = \mathscr{B} : \{a\}$ is used for updating the opponents arguments. We thus, first of all, follow [10] in restricting the set of arguments of the proponent to be rule minimal. This has been argued for convincingly in [10] for both conceptual reasons (why have more than one justification line for a claim?) as well as computational reasons (guarantees completeness of disputes when $\mathscr{L}$ is finite even if $\mathscr{R}$ contains cycles).

In [10] then the authors have also argued for the opponents arguments to be rule minimal partly again for conceptual reasons but even more so for computational reasons. Regarding the conceptual arguments of the authors, we note that, in any case, all possible rule minimal arguments attacking the defenses of the proponent need to be considered in dispute derivations. Thus the opponents arguments are not globally rule minimal (as the proponents are). Regarding the computational reasons, while it is true that restricting attention to the arguments of the opponent that are rule minimal guarantees completeness also if $\mathscr{R}$ contains cycles (assuming $\mathscr{L}$ is finite), we will show that this is not necessary. In fact, treatment of the proponents and opponents expansions in an (almost) symmetric way leads to a definition of dispute derivations which avoids some of the remaining redundancy in moves of GrFlexDDs while staying complete when $\mathscr{L}$ is finite and $\mathscr{R}$ contains cycles. Moreover, as we will show in Sect. 4, our definition of FlexDDs leads naturally to an implementation where all arguments in dispute derivations are represented as a graph rather than only the proponents as in the implementation of [10].

Table 8. A DAB + TA FlexDD for Example 5 (ABA framework from Example 4). Here $ labels arguments which are held by the proponent as well as the opponent. Only complete and maximal arguments for goals and contraries of culprits as well as maximal arguments for contraries of defenses are shown. The dispute derivation ends with the opponent not being able to advance further in O-B-$\langle \overline{\mathscr{D}} \rangle$+O-F-$\langle \overline{\mathscr{D}} \cap \mathscr{A} \rangle$-ii manner.

Step and move type	$\mathscr{B}$	$\gamma \cup \overline{\mathscr{C}} \setminus Conc(\mathscr{P}^*)$	$\mathscr{D}$	$\mathscr{C}$
0	$\{ {}^{\#\$}p \}$	$\{p\}$	$\{\}$	$\{\}$
1 (P-B-i, $p \leftarrow q$)	$\{ {}^{\#\$}p \leftarrow q \}$	$\{p\}$	$\{\}$	$\{\}$
2 (P-B-i, $q \leftarrow a$)	$\{ {}^{*\$}p \leftarrow [q \leftarrow a] \}$	$\{\}$	$\{a\}$	$\{\}$
3 (O-B-ii, $t \leftarrow b$)	$\{ {}^{*\$}p \leftarrow [q \leftarrow a]; \ {}^{*!}t \leftarrow b \}$	$\{\}$	$\{a\}$	$\{\}$
4 (P-B-ii, $r \leftarrow p$)	$\{ {}^{*\$}p \leftarrow [q \leftarrow a]; \ {}^{*\$}r \leftarrow [p \leftarrow [q \leftarrow a]]; \ {}^{-*!}t \leftarrow b \}$	$\{\}$	$\{a\}$	$\{b\}$
5 (O-B-ii, $t \leftarrow p,s$)	$\{ {}^{*\$}p \leftarrow [q \leftarrow a]; \ {}^{*\$}r \leftarrow [p \leftarrow [q \leftarrow a]]; \ {}^{-*!}t \leftarrow b; \ {}^{!}t \leftarrow [p \leftarrow [q \leftarrow a]],s \}$	$\{\}$	$\{a\}$	$\{b\}$
6 (O-B-ii, $t \leftarrow q,u,d$)	$\{ {}^{*\$}p \leftarrow [q \leftarrow a]; \ {}^{*\$}r \leftarrow [p \leftarrow [q \leftarrow a]]; \ {}^{-*!}t \leftarrow b; \ {}^{!}t \leftarrow [p \leftarrow [q \leftarrow a]],s; \ {}^{!}t \leftarrow [q \leftarrow a],u,d \}$	$\{\}$	$\{a\}$	$\{b\}$

Example 5. Consider again the ABA framework from Example 4. A DAB + TA FlexDD following more or less the DAB + TA GrFlexDD from Table 7 is shown in Table 8. Note that here the steps 5–7 from Table 7 are performed in one step: step 5. Also, steps 8–9 from Table 7 are completed in step 6. A DC + TC (and DS + TS) FlexDD for the same example is shown in Table 9.

For FlexDDs we have the following results:

Theorem 5. *DF + {TA, TC, TS} FlexDDs are sound for the admissible, complete, and stable semantics respectively.*

Corollary 5. *{DAB, DABF, DC, DS} + {TA, TC, TS} FlexDDs are sound for the admissible, complete, and stable semantics respectively.*

Lemma 1. *If $\mathscr{L}$ is finite, the number of possible DF and hence also {DAB, DABF, DC, DS} moves of the proponent and opponent in FlexDDs is also finite.*

Proof. We give the proof for the opponent. For the proponent it is analogous. Note first that the opponents moves involve adding an assumption (O-F-$\langle \mathscr{A} \rangle$-ii) or a rule to $\mathscr{B}$ (O-B-$\langle \mathscr{A} \rangle$-ii), or expanding arguments backwards or forwards (O-B-$\langle \mathscr{A} \rangle$-i or O-F-$\langle \mathscr{A} \rangle$-i) w.r.t. some rule. Now, once an assumption is put in $\mathscr{B}$ it cannot be added again by the requirement $\mathscr{B}' = \mathscr{B} \bowtie \{a\} \neq \mathscr{B}$. Also, if some rule r is used in one step (either by adding it to $\mathscr{B}$ or expanding some argument w.r.t. it, which means by closure under sub-arguments that then also r is in $\mathscr{B}'$), then r cannot be used in any other step. For O-B-$\langle \overline{\mathscr{A}} \rangle$-ii this is clear by the requirement $\mathscr{B}' = \mathscr{B} \bowtie \{a\} \neq \mathscr{B}$. For O-B-$\langle \overline{\mathscr{A}} \rangle$-i note that if $a' \in \mathscr{B}$ and $h \leftarrow B \in \mathscr{B}$ then $a' \lessdot h \leftarrow B$ is also already in $\mathscr{B}$ because $\mathscr{B}$ is required to be closed by argument expansions. Analogously for O-F-$\langle \mathscr{A} \rangle$-i moves.

Table 9. A DC + TC (and DS + TS) FlexDD for Example 5 (ABA framework from Example 4). Only complete and maximal arguments for goals and contraries of culprits as well as maximal arguments for contraries of defenses are shown. The dispute derivation ends with the opponent not being able to advance further in O-F-$\langle \mathscr{A} \rangle$ manner.

Step and move type	$\mathscr{B}$	$\gamma \cup \overline{\mathscr{C}} \setminus Conc(\mathscr{P}^*)$	$\mathscr{D}$	$\mathscr{C}$	$\mathscr{I} \setminus \mathscr{D}$
0	$\{ {}^{\#\$}p \}$	$\{p\}$	$\{\}$	$\{\}$	$\{a,b,c,d\}$
1 (P-B-i, $p \leftarrow q$)	$\{ {}^{\#\$}p \leftarrow q \}$	$\{p\}$	$\{\}$	$\{\}$	$\{a,b,c,d\}$
2 (P-B-i, $q \leftarrow a$)	$\{ {}^{*\$}p \leftarrow [q \leftarrow a] \}$	$\{\}$	$\{a\}$	$\{\}$	$\{b,c,d\}$
3 (O-B-ii, $t \leftarrow b$)	$\{ {}^{*\$}p \leftarrow [q \leftarrow a];\ {}^{*!}t \leftarrow b \}$	$\{\}$	$\{a\}$	$\{\}$	$\{b,d\}$
4 (P-B-ii \ P-F-i, $r \leftarrow p$)	$\{{}^{*\$}p \leftarrow [q \leftarrow a];$ ${}^{*\$}r \leftarrow [p \leftarrow [q \leftarrow a]];$ ${}^{-*!}t \leftarrow b\}$	$\{\}$	$\{a\}$	$\{b\}$	$\{c,d\}$
5 (P-F-ii, c)	$\{{}^{*\$}p \leftarrow [q \leftarrow a];$ ${}^{*\$}r \leftarrow [p \leftarrow [q \leftarrow a]];$ ${}^{-*!}t \leftarrow b;\ {}^{*\$}c\}$	$\{\}$	$\{a,c\}$	$\{b,d\}$	$\{\}$

Theorem 6. *If $\mathscr{L}$ is finite DAB + TA FlexDDs are complete for credulous acceptance w.r.t. the admissible semantics. Moreover, DC + TC FlexDDs are complete for the complete semantics and DS + TS FlexDDs are complete for the stable semantics. Finally, $\{DC, DS, DF\} + TA$ FlexDDs are complete for the admissible semantics.*

Corollary 6. *If $\mathscr{L}$ is finite, $\{DABF, DC, DS, DF\} + TA$ FlexDDs are complete for credulous acceptance w.r.t. the admissible semantics. Also, $DF + TC$ FlexDDs are complete for the complete semantics and $DF + TS$ FlexDDs are complete for the stable semantics.*

4 Rule-Based Flexible Dispute Derivations

Rule-based flexible dispute derivations, or RlFlexDDs for short, provide an alternative representation and implementation of FlexDDs. Relying on the observation contained in the proof of Lemma 1 (on which Theorem 6 depends), in RlFlexDDs the proponent and opponent put forward claims and rules rather than arguments. Moreover, they make use of the underlying (labelled) graph of the dependencies between statements and rules put forward by the proponent and opponent during a dispute. RlFlexDDs thus generalise the work of [10] which implements DAB+TA GrFlexDD disputes. As we have already indicated, in the dispute derivations of [10] the proponents arguments are represented as graph, while the opponents are not. Also, the opponent does not make use of the proponents arguments.

So, in RlFlexDDs a dispute state for a set of goals $\gamma \subseteq \mathscr{L}$ (s.t. $\gamma \cap \overline{\gamma} = \emptyset$) is a tuple $(\mathbb{B}, \mathbb{P})$ where $\mathbb{B} \subseteq (\mathscr{L} \cup \mathscr{R})$, and $\mathbb{P} \subseteq \mathbb{B}$. To define rule-based dispute advancements we define the auxiliary notation in Table 10; in large part encoding the analogous notions from Sect. 3.3 in the rule setting. Concretely, we have that e.g. $s \in \mathbb{P}^* \cap \mathscr{L}$ iff there is a complete argument for s using rules in $\mathbb{P}$. Also, $s \in \mathbb{B}^{*/-} \cap \mathscr{L}$ iff there is a complete argument for s using rules in $\mathbb{B}$ that does not use any culprit. On the other hand, $s \in \mathbb{B}^- \cap \mathscr{L}$ implies first of all that all arguments for s using non-blocked (i.e. without culprits in bodies) rules use rules only in $\mathbb{B}$. Also, that all such arguments (using rules only in $\mathbb{B}$) which are complete are blocked (i.e. make use of some culprit). As a consequence then, $s \in \mathbb{B}_S^{!/-} \cap \mathscr{L}$ if s is used in an argument for some $s' \in S$ (with $S \subseteq \mathscr{L}$) and the latter two conditions (for $s \in \mathbb{B}^-$) do not hold.

Table 10. Auxiliary notation for rule-based flexible dispute derivations. All notions w.r.t. a dispute state $(\mathbb{B}, \mathbb{P})$.

Notation	Description
$\mathscr{D} = \mathbb{P} \cap \mathscr{A}$	Defenses
$\mathscr{C} = \{u \in \mathscr{A} \mid \bar{u} \in \mathbb{P}\}$	Culprits
$\mathscr{J}_{\mathbb{B}} = \mathscr{R} \setminus \mathbb{B}$	Remaining rules for the opponent
$\mathscr{J}_{\mathbb{P}} = \mathscr{R} \setminus \mathbb{P}$	Remaining rules for the proponent
$\mathscr{J}_{\mathbb{B}}^- = \{h \leftarrow B \in \mathscr{J}_{\mathbb{B}} \mid B \cap \mathscr{C} \neq \emptyset\}$	Blocked remaining rules
$\mathscr{J}_{\mathbb{P}}^{\sim} = \{h \leftarrow B \in \mathscr{J}_{\mathbb{P}} \mid$ $(\{h\} \cup B) \cap (\bar{B} \cup \mathscr{C} \cup \bar{\mathscr{D}}) \neq \emptyset\}$	Remaining rules blocked for the proponent
$(\mathbb{P} \cap \mathscr{L})^{\downarrow} = \{s \in \mathbb{P} \cap \mathscr{L} \mid \neg \exists h \leftarrow B \in \mathbb{P}$ with $h = s\}$	Played unexpanded statements of the proponent
$(\mathbb{B} \cap \mathscr{L})^{\uparrow\uparrow} = \{s \in (\mathbb{B} \cap \mathscr{L}) \mid \neg \exists h \leftarrow B \in$ $(\mathscr{J}_{\mathbb{B}} \setminus \mathscr{J}_{\mathbb{B}}^-)$ with $h = s\}$	Played fully expanded statements
$\mathbb{B}^- = (\mathbb{B} \cap \mathscr{C}) \cup \{s \in (\mathbb{B} \cap \mathscr{L})^{\uparrow\uparrow} \setminus \mathscr{A} \mid \neg \exists h \leftarrow$ $B \in (\mathbb{B} \cap \mathscr{R}) \setminus \mathbb{B}^-$ with $h = s\} \cup \{h \leftarrow B \in \mathbb{B} \cap \mathscr{R} \mid$ $B \cap \mathbb{B}^- \neq \emptyset\}$	Played blocked pieces
$\mathbb{P}^* = (\mathbb{P} \cap \mathscr{A}) \cup \{h \leftarrow B \in (\mathbb{P} \cap \mathscr{R}) \mid B \subseteq \mathbb{P}^*\} \cup \{s \in$ $(\mathbb{P} \cap (\mathscr{L} \setminus \mathscr{A})) \mid \exists h \leftarrow B \in \mathbb{P}^*$ with $h = s\}$	Complete played pieces of the proponent
$\mathbb{B}^{*/-} = (\mathbb{B} \cap (\mathscr{A} \setminus \mathscr{C})) \cup \{h \leftarrow B \in (\mathbb{B} \setminus \mathbb{B}^-) \cap \mathscr{R} \mid$ $B \subseteq \mathbb{B}^{*/-}\} \cup \{s \in (\mathbb{B} \setminus \mathbb{B}^-) \cap (\mathscr{L} \setminus \mathscr{A}) \mid \exists h \leftarrow$ $B \in \mathbb{B}^{*/-}$ with $h = s\}$	Unblocked complete played pieces of the opponent
$\mathbb{B}_S^{!/-} = ((\mathbb{B} \setminus \mathbb{B}^-) \cap S) \cup \{s \in (\mathbb{B} \setminus \mathbb{B}^-) \cap \mathscr{L} \mid$ $\exists h \leftarrow B \in \mathbb{B}_S^{!/-} \cap \mathscr{R}$ with $s \in B\} \cup \{h \leftarrow B \in$ $(\mathbb{B} \setminus \mathbb{B}^-) \cap \mathscr{R} \mid h \in \mathbb{B}_S^{!/-}\}$	Unblocked pieces supporting statements in $S \subseteq \mathscr{L}$
$\mathscr{A}' = \mathscr{A} \cap \mathbb{B}_{\bar{\mathscr{D}}}^{!/-}$	Candidates for culprits
$\mathscr{I} = \{u \in \mathscr{A} \setminus \mathscr{C} \mid \bar{u} \notin \mathbb{B}^{*/-}\}$	Currently defended assumptions

Note that $\mathbb{B}^-$ and $\mathbb{P}^*$ are monotonic; i.e. once some element is in the set they remain in the set. This means these sets can be computed incrementally as the dispute evolves. On the other hand, $\mathbb{B}^{*/-}$, and $\mathbb{B}_S^{!/-}$ are not monotonic; but once some element becomes blocked (is in $\mathbb{B}^-$) it cannot be in either $\mathbb{B}^{*/-}$ or $\mathbb{B}_S^{!/-}$ anymore. This means as elements become blocked, they do not need to be considered for computation of $\mathbb{B}^{*/-}$ and $\mathbb{B}_S^{!/-}$.

Now to the definition of dispute advancements for RlFlexDDs. First of all, a proponent dispute state advancement from a dispute state $(\mathbb{B}, \mathbb{P})$ is a dispute state $(\mathbb{B}', \mathbb{P}')$ with $\mathbb{P}' = \mathbb{P} \cup T$, $\mathbb{B}' = \mathbb{B} \cup T$, $X_1 \subseteq \overline{\mathscr{A}}$, and $X_2 \subseteq \mathscr{A}$ where either

$$P\text{-}B\text{-}\langle \overline{\mathscr{A}^!} \cup X_1 \rangle: \quad \text{i) } T = \{h \leftarrow B\} \cup B \text{ for } h \leftarrow B \in \mathscr{J}_{\mathbb{P}} \setminus \mathscr{J}_{\mathbb{P}}^{\sim} \text{ with } h \in (\mathbb{P} \cap \mathscr{L})^{\downarrow};$$

or

$$\text{ii) } T = \{h\} \cup \{h \leftarrow B\} \cup B \text{ for } h \leftarrow B \in \mathscr{J}_{\mathbb{P}} \setminus \mathscr{J}_{\mathbb{P}}^{\sim} \text{ with } h \in (\overline{\mathscr{A}^!} \cup X_1) \setminus (\mathbb{P} \cup \overline{\mathscr{D}});$$

$$P\text{-}F\text{-}\langle (\overline{\mathscr{A}^!} \cap \mathscr{A}) \cup X_2 \rangle: \text{ i) } T = \{h\} \cup \{h \leftarrow B\} \text{ with } h \leftarrow B \in \mathscr{J}_{\mathbb{P}} \setminus \mathscr{J}_{\mathbb{P}}^{\sim} \text{ with } h \notin \mathbb{P} \text{ or}$$
$$h \in (\mathbb{P} \cap \mathscr{L})^{\downarrow}, \ b \in \mathbb{P}^* \text{ for each } b \in B; \text{ or}$$

$$\text{ii) } T = \{u\} \text{ for } u \in ((\overline{\mathscr{A}^!} \cap \mathscr{A}) \cup X_2) \setminus (\mathbb{P} \cup \{\overline{u}\} \cup \mathscr{C} \cup \overline{\mathscr{D}}).$$

An opponent dispute state advancement from a dispute state $(\mathbb{B}, \mathbb{P})$ is a dispute state $(\mathbb{B}', \mathbb{P})$ with $\mathbb{B}' = \mathbb{B} \cup T$, $Y_1 \subseteq \overline{\mathscr{A}}$, and $Y_2 \subseteq \mathscr{A}$ where either

$$O\text{-}B\text{-}\langle \overline{\mathscr{D}} \cup Y_1 \rangle: \quad \text{i) } T = \{h \leftarrow B\} \cup B \text{ for } h \leftarrow B \in \mathscr{J}_{\mathbb{B}} \setminus \mathscr{J}_{\mathbb{B}}^{-} \text{ with } h \in \mathbb{B}_{\overline{\mathscr{D}} \cup Y_1}^{!/-} \cap \mathscr{L};$$

or

$$\text{ii) } T = (\{h\} \cup \{h \leftarrow B\} \cup B) \text{ for a } h \leftarrow B \in \mathscr{J}_{\mathbb{B}} \setminus \mathscr{J}_{\mathbb{B}}^{-} \text{ with } h \in \overline{\mathscr{D}} \cup Y_1;$$

$$O\text{-}F\text{-}\langle (\overline{\mathscr{D}} \cap \mathscr{A}) \cup Y_2 \rangle: \text{ i) } T = \{h\} \cup \{h \leftarrow B\} \text{ for } h \leftarrow B \in \mathscr{J}_{\mathbb{B}} \setminus \mathscr{J}_{\mathbb{B}}^{-} \text{ with } b \in \mathbb{B}^{*/-} \text{ for}$$
$$\text{each } b \in B; \text{ or}$$

$$\text{ii) } T = \{u\} \text{ for } u \in ((\overline{\mathscr{D}} \cap \mathscr{A}) \cup Y_2) \setminus (\mathscr{A} \cap \mathbb{B}).$$

Different types of dispute advancements for RlFlexDDs are defined as for StFlexDDs, GrFlexDDs, and FlexDDs (i.e., with some abuse of notation, as in Table 2). Only for the termination conditions the definition needs to change slightly (concretely, the notion of "proponent winning") to reflect the change in notation. See Table 11.

Table 11. Termination conditions for RlFlexDDs. TA for admissible, TC for complete, and TS for stable.

Cond.	Proponent winning	Opponent cannot move	Proponent cannot move
TA	$\gamma \cup \mathscr{C} \subseteq \mathscr{P}^*$, $(\overline{\mathscr{D}} \cap \mathbb{B}^{*/-}) = \emptyset$	$O\text{-}B\text{-}\langle \overline{\mathscr{D}} \rangle$ + $O\text{-}F\text{-}\langle \overline{\mathscr{D}} \cap \mathscr{A} \rangle$-ii or $O\text{-}F\text{-}\langle \mathscr{A} \rangle$	$P\text{-}B\text{-}\langle \overline{\mathscr{A}^!} \rangle$ + $P\text{-}F\text{-}\langle \overline{\mathscr{A}^!} \cap \mathscr{A} \rangle$-ii or $P\text{-}F\text{-}\langle \mathscr{A} \rangle$
TC	$\gamma \cup \mathscr{C} \subseteq \mathscr{P}^*$, $(\overline{\mathscr{D}} \cap \mathbb{B}^{*/-}) = \emptyset$, $\mathscr{I} \setminus \mathscr{D} = \emptyset$	$O\text{-}B\text{-}\langle \overline{\mathscr{D}} \rangle$ + $O\text{-}F\text{-}\langle \overline{\mathscr{D}} \cap \mathscr{A} \rangle$-ii or $O\text{-}F\text{-}\langle \mathscr{A} \rangle$	$P\text{-}B\text{-}\langle \overline{\mathscr{A}^!} \rangle$ + $P\text{-}F\text{-}\langle (\overline{\mathscr{A}^!} \cap \mathscr{A}) \cup \mathscr{I} \rangle$ or $P\text{-}F\text{-}\langle \mathscr{A} \rangle$
TS	$\gamma \cup \mathscr{C} \subseteq \mathscr{P}^*$, $(\overline{\mathscr{D}} \cap \mathbb{B}^{*/-}) = \emptyset$, $\mathscr{D} \cup \mathscr{C} = \mathscr{A}$	$O\text{-}B\text{-}\langle \overline{\mathscr{D}} \rangle$ + $O\text{-}F\text{-}\langle \overline{\mathscr{D}} \cap \mathscr{A} \rangle$-ii or $O\text{-}F\text{-}\langle \mathscr{A} \rangle$	$P\text{-}B\text{-}\langle \overline{\mathscr{A}^!} \rangle$ + $P\text{-}F\text{-}\langle \mathscr{A} \rangle$

Table 12. A DC + TC (and DS + TS) RlFlexDD for Example 6 (ABA framework from Example 4). Label − represents played blocked pieces, label ∗ complete played pieces, label " unexpanded statements of the proponent, label ∧ fully expanded statements (non assumptions), and label ! represents opposing pieces. The dispute derivation ends with the opponent not being able to advance further in O-F-$\langle \mathscr{A} \rangle$ manner.

Step and move type	$\mathbb{B}$	$\gamma \cup \overline{\mathscr{C}} \setminus \mathbb{P}^*$	$\mathscr{D}$	$\mathscr{C}$	$\mathscr{I} \setminus \mathscr{D}$
0	$\{\,^{"\$}p\,\}$	$\{p\}$	$\{\}$	$\{\}$	$\{a,b,c,d\}$
1 (P-B-i, $p \leftarrow q$)	$\{\,^{\wedge\$}p;\ ^{"\$}q;\ ^{\$}p \leftarrow q\,\}$	$\{p\}$	$\{\}$	$\{\}$	$\{a,b,c,d\}$
2 (P-B-i, $q \leftarrow a$)	$\{\,^{**\$}a;\ ^{**\wedge\$}p;\ ^{**\wedge\$}q;\ ^{**\$}p \leftarrow q;\ ^{**\$}q \leftarrow a\,\}$	$\{\}$	$\{a\}$	$\{\}$	$\{b,c,d\}$
3 (O-B-ii, $t \leftarrow b$)	$\{\,^{**\$}a;\ ^{*!}b;\ ^{**\wedge\$}p;\ ^{**\wedge\$}q;\ ^{*!}t;\ ^{**\$}p \leftarrow q;\ ^{**\$}q \leftarrow a;\ ^{*}t \leftarrow b\,\}$	$\{\}$	$\{a\}$	$\{\}$	$\{b,d\}$
4 (P-B-ii \ P-F-i, $r \leftarrow p$)	$\{\,^{**\$}a;\ ^{-*!}b;\ ^{**\wedge\$}p;\ ^{**\wedge\$}q;\ ^{**\wedge\$}r;\ ^{*!}t;\ ^{**\$}p \leftarrow q;\ ^{**\$}q \leftarrow a;\ ^{-*}t \leftarrow b;\ ^{**\$}r \leftarrow p\,\}$	$\{\}$	$\{a\}$	$\{b\}$	$\{c,d\}$
5 (P-F-ii, c)	$\{\,^{**\$}a;\ ^{-*!}b;\ ^{**\$}c;\ ^{**\wedge\$}p;\ ^{**\wedge\$}q;\ ^{**\wedge\$}r;\ ^{*!}t;\ ^{**\$}p \leftarrow q;\ ^{**\$}q \leftarrow a;\ ^{-*}t \leftarrow b;\ ^{**\$}r \leftarrow p\,\}$	$\{\}$	$\{a,c\}$	$\{b,d\}$	$\{\}$

Example 6. Consider again the ABA framework from Examples 4 and 5. A DC + TC (and DS + TS) RlFlexDD following the DC + TC FlexDD from Table 9 is in Table 12.

Based on the results for FlexDDs from Sect. 3.3 and the fact that RlFlexDDs essentially implement FlexDDs we obtain the following results for RlFlexDDs:

Corollary 7. $\{DAB, DABF, DC, DS, DF\} + \{TA, TC, TS\}$ *RlFlexDDs are sound for the admissible, complete, and stable semantics respectively.*

Corollary 8. *If $\mathscr{L}$ is finite $\{DAB, DABF, DC, DS, DF\} + TA$ RlFlexDDs are complete for credulous acceptance w.r.t. the admissible semantics. Moreover, $\{DC, DF\} + TC$ RlFlexDDs are complete for the complete semantics and $\{DS, DF\} + TS$ RlFlexDDs are complete for the stable semantics. Finally, $\{DC, DS, DF\} + TA$ RlFlexDDs are complete for the admissible semantics.*

5   Implementation

We have implemented an interactive reasoner, `aba-dd-rule-based`, for all variants of RlFlexDDs considered in this work. At the moment the system is conceived mainly for didactic and research purposes. The code is freely available[2]. The system allows for choosing a combination of dispute advancement type and termination criteria and then guiding the user through an RlFlexDD of that nature (advancement types and termination criteria can also be changed on the fly). At each step the user can choose which move to make from the list of allowed moves provided by the system. See Fig. 1 for a screenshot of the interface for step 4 of the RlFlexDD from Table 12. Limited automatisation is also possible in that the user can choose that the system move forward a

---

[2] https://github.com/gorczyca/aba-dd-rule-based.

```
«« 4. PF1: r ← p »»»
B:
    {$***^a; *^!--b; $***p; $**p ← q; $**q ← a; $***^q; $**r ← p; $**^r; *--t ← b; *!t}
Goals & culprit contraries (w/o complete pieces):
    {}
Defences:
    {a}
Culprits:
    {b}

?
Possible moves:
PF2:
        0: Assumption: c
        1: Assumption: d
OB1:
        0: Rule: t ← p,s
        1: Rule: t ← q,u,d
OB2:
        0: Rule: t ← p,s
        1: Rule: t ← q,u,d
OF2:
        0: Assumption: c
```

Fig. 1. Interface of `aba-dd-rule-based` at step 4 of the RlFlexDD from Table 12

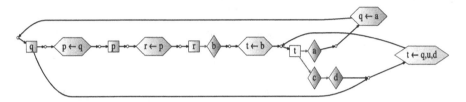

Fig. 2. Graphical output of `aba-dd-rule-based` at step 5 (end state) of the RlFlexDD from Table 12. Here green nodes represents the proponents pieces. The goal is in blue. Yellow is for the opponents pieces, while those in orange are blocked. Red is for culprits. Grey nodes represent remaining rules which are blocked but whose heads have been made use of in the dispute. Black arrows represent support, while red ones denote attacks. (Color figure online)

random number of steps (of some type) and the system can also backtrack a number of steps. The system can also produce a graphical representation of the statements and rules put forward during the dispute until that point. See Fig. 2 for the graphical output of `aba-dd-rule-based` at step 5 (end state) of the RlFlexDD from Table 12. We refer to the webpage for many other features of `aba-dd-rule-based` as well as larger and more realistic examples on which to experiment with RlFlexDDs.

6 Conclusions and Future Work

We have defined a variant of dispute derivations which allows for forward in addition to backward reasoning and thus for computing admissible, complete, and stable assumption sets in addition to reasoning about credulous acceptance of statements. We have given an abstract argument-based definition of such dispute derivations which we have derived from similarly abstract representations of flexible variants of dispute derivations from [10,33]. We have then provided a more implementation focused rule-based definition. For this version we also implemented an interactive system. Ultimately, we have generalised graph-based dispute derivations from [10] on two fronts: incorporating forward reasoning, as well as in that both the proponents and opponents arguments are represented in a shared graph rather than only the proponents arguments being represented in a graph.

While the most immediate benefits of dispute derivations lie in the domain of interactive reasoning, investigating to what extent some of the variants of dispute derivations we have defined in this work can be turned into fully automated reasoning procedures (even if only to support interactive reasoning) is of interest. In particular, DABF + TA is an obvious candidate for obtaining more efficient procedures for credulous reasoning. Also, with forward reasoning giving at least argument-based flexible dispute derivations for non-flat ABA as well as for sceptical acceptance of statements should be in reach. We also would like to improve our interactive system, in particular for making the whole interface graphical and also for allowing switching between argument-based and rule-based views.

References

1. Amgoud, L., Besnard, P., Vesic, S.: Equivalence in logic-based argumentation. J. Appl. Non Class. Logics **24**(3), 181–208 (2014)
2. Besnard, P., et al.: Introduction to structured argumentation. Argum. Comput. **5**(1), 1–4 (2014)
3. Bondarenko, A., Dung, P.M., Kowalski, R.A., Toni, F.: An abstract, argumentation-theoretic approach to default reasoning. Artif. Intell. **93**, 63–101 (1997)
4. Bondarenko, A., Toni, F., Kowalski, R.A.: An assumption-based framework for non-monotonic reasoning. In: LPNMR, pp. 171–189. MIT Press (1993)
5. Booth, R., Caminada, M., Marshall, B.: DISCO: a web-based implementation of discussion games for grounded and preferred semantics. In: COMMA. Frontiers in Artificial Intelligence and Applications, vol. 305, pp. 453–454. IOS Press (2018)
6. Borg, A., Straßer, C.: Relevance in structured argumentation. In: IJCAI, pp. 1753–1759. ijcai.org (2018)
7. Caminada, M.: A discussion game for grounded semantics. In: Black, E., Modgil, S., Oren, N. (eds.) TAFA 2015. LNCS (LNAI), vol. 9524, pp. 59–73. Springer, Cham (2015). https://doi.org/10.1007/978-3-319-28460-6_4
8. Caminada, M.: Argumentation semantics as formal discussion. In: Baroni, P., Gabbay, D., Giacomin, M. (eds.) Handbook of Formal Argumentation, pp. 487–518. College Publications (2018)
9. Cerutti, F., Gaggl, S.A., Thimm, M., Wallner, J.P.: Foundations of implementations for formal argumentation. In: Baroni, P., Gabbay, D., Giacomin, M. (eds.) Handbook of Formal Argumentation, pp. 689–768. College Publications (2018)
10. Craven, R., Toni, F.: Argument graphs and assumption-based argumentation. Artif. Intell. **233**, 1–59 (2016)
11. Craven, R., Toni, F., Williams, M.: Graph-based dispute derivations in assumption-based argumentation. In: Black, E., Modgil, S., Oren, N. (eds.) TAFA 2013. LNCS (LNAI), vol. 8306, pp. 46–62. Springer, Heidelberg (2014). https://doi.org/10.1007/978-3-642-54373-9_4
12. Cyras, K., Fan, X., Schulz, C., Toni, F.: Assumption-based argumentation: disputes, explanations, preferences. In: Baroni, P., Gabbay, D., Giacomin, M. (eds.) Handbook of Formal Argumentation, pp. 365–408. College Publications (2018)
13. Doutre, S., Mengin, J.: On sceptical versus credulous acceptance for abstract argument systems. In: Alferes, J.J., Leite, J. (eds.) JELIA 2004. LNCS (LNAI), vol. 3229, pp. 462–473. Springer, Heidelberg (2004). https://doi.org/10.1007/978-3-540-30227-8_39

14. Dung, P.M.: On the acceptability of arguments and its fundamental role in nonmonotonic reasoning, logic programming and n-person games. Artif. Intell. **77**(2), 321–358 (1995)
15. Dung, P.M., Kowalski, R.A., Toni, F.: Dialectic proof procedures for assumption-based, admissible argumentation. Artif. Intell. **170**(2), 114–159 (2006)
16. Dung, P.M., Kowalski, R.A., Toni, F.: Assumption-based argumentation. In: Simari, G.R., Rahwan, I. (eds.) Argumentation in Artificial Intelligence, pp. 199–218. Springer, Heidelberg (2009). https://doi.org/10.1007/978-0-387-98197-0_10
17. Dung, P.M., Mancarella, P., Toni, F.: Computing ideal sceptical argumentation. Artif. Intell. **171**(10–15), 642–674 (2007)
18. Dung, P.M., Thang, P.M.: Closure and consistency in logic-associated argumentation. J. Artif. Intell. Res. **49**, 79–109 (2014)
19. Efstathiou, V., Hunter, A.: Algorithms for generating arguments and counterarguments in propositional logic. Int. J. Approx. Reason. **52**(6), 672–704 (2011)
20. Gaertner, D., Toni, F.: Hybrid argumentation and its properties. In: COMMA. Frontiers in Artificial Intelligence and Applications, vol. 172, pp. 183–195. IOS Press (2008)
21. Jakobovits, H., Vermeir, D.: Dialectic semantics for argumentation frameworks. In: ICAIL, pp. 53–62. ACM (1999)
22. Keshavarzi Zafarghandi, A., Verbrugge, R., Verheij, B.: Discussion games for preferred semantics of abstract dialectical frameworks. In: Kern-Isberner, G., Ognjanović, Z. (eds.) ECSQARU 2019. LNCS (LNAI), vol. 11726, pp. 62–73. Springer, Cham (2019). https://doi.org/10.1007/978-3-030-29765-7_6
23. Keshavarzi Zafarghandi, A., Verbrugge, R., Verheij, B.: A discussion game for the grounded semantics of abstract dialectical frameworks. In: COMMA. Frontiers in Artificial Intelligence and Applications, vol. 326, pp. 431–442. IOS Press (2020)
24. Lehtonen, T., Wallner, J.P., Järvisalo, M.: From structured to abstract argumentation: assumption-based acceptance via AF reasoning. In: Antonucci, A., Cholvy, L., Papini, O. (eds.) ECSQARU 2017. LNCS (LNAI), vol. 10369, pp. 57–68. Springer, Cham (2017). https://doi.org/10.1007/978-3-319-61581-3_6
25. Lehtonen, T., Wallner, J.P., Järvisalo, M.: Reasoning over assumption-based argumentation frameworks via direct answer set programming encodings. In: AAAI, pp. 2938–2945. AAAI Press (2019)
26. Modgil, S., Caminada, M.: Proof theories and algorithms for abstract argumentation frameworks. In: Simari, G.R., Rahwan, I. (eds.) Argumentation in Artificial Intelligence, pp. 105–129. Springer, Boston (2009). https://doi.org/10.1007/978-0-387-98197-0_6
27. Modgil, S., Prakken, H.: Abstract rule-based argumentation. In: Baroni, P., Gabbay, D., Giacomin, M. (eds.) Handbook of Formal Argumentation, pp. 287–364. College Publications (2018)
28. Prakken, H.: An abstract framework for argumentation with structured arguments. Argum. Comput. **1**(2), 93–124 (2010)
29. Prakken, H., Sartor, G.: Argument-based extended logic programming with defeasible priorities. J. Appl. Non Class. Logics **7**(1), 25–75 (1997)
30. Strass, H., Wyner, A., Diller, M.: EMIL: extracting meaning from inconsistent language: towards argumentation using a controlled natural language interface. Int. J. Approx. Reason. **112**, 55–84 (2019)
31. Thang, P.M., Dung, P.M., Hung, N.D.: Towards a common framework for dialectical proof procedures in abstract argumentation. J. Log. Comput. **19**(6), 1071–1109 (2009)
32. Thimm, M., Rienstra, T.: Approximate reasoning with ASPIC+ by argument sampling. In: SAFA@COMMA. CEUR Workshop Proceedings, vol. 2672, pp. 22–33. CEUR-WS.org (2020)
33. Toni, F.: A generalised framework for dispute derivations in assumption-based argumentation. Artif. Intell. **195**, 1–43 (2013)

34. Toni, F.: A tutorial on assumption-based argumentation. Argum. Comput. **5**(1), 89–117 (2014)
35. Vreeswik, G.A.W., Prakken, H.: Credulous and sceptical argument games for preferred semantics. In: Ojeda-Aciego, M., de Guzmán, I.P., Brewka, G., Moniz Pereira, L. (eds.) JELIA 2000. LNCS (LNAI), vol. 1919, pp. 239–253. Springer, Heidelberg (2000). https://doi.org/10.1007/3-540-40006-0_17
36. Yun, B., Oren, N., Croitoru, M.: Efficient construction of structured argumentation systems. In: COMMA. Frontiers in Artificial Intelligence and Applications, vol. 326, pp. 411–418. IOS Press (2020)

Towards a General Theory of Decomposability in Abstract Argumentation

Massimiliano Giacomin[1]([✉])[ID], Pietro Baroni[1]([✉])[ID], and Federico Cerutti[1,2][ID]

[1] University of Brescia, Brescia, Italy
{massimiliano.giacomin,pietro.baroni,federico.cerutti}@unibs.it
[2] Cardiff University, Cardiff, UK

Abstract. The paper introduces a general model for the study of decomposability in abstract argumentation, i.e. the possibility of determining the semantics outcome based on local evaluations in subframeworks. As such, the paper extends a previous work by generalizing over the kind of information locally exploited. While not concerned with specific semantics, the paper shows the range of decomposable semantics with varying degrees of local information. It also introduces the notion of a canonical local function, which can enforce decomposability whenever this is possible.

Keywords: Abstract argumentation · Argumentation semantics · Decomposability.

1 Introduction

Dung's model provides an abstract account of argumentation where arguments are simply represented as nodes of a directed graph, called *argumentation framework*, and binary attacks between them correspond to the graph's edges [13]. This formalism turns out to capture several approaches in nonmonotonic reasoning and structured argumentation. Its importance lies in the formal methods, called *argumentation semantics*, to assess a set of arguments in order to determine their justification status, and thus the status of the relevant conclusions in structured instances of the abstract model. This is necessary since conflicts between arguments prevent them from being accepted altogether, and a formal method is needed to solve the conflict [1].

While in the original definitions of argumentation semantics an argumentation framework is considered as a monolithic structure and arguments are evaluated at a global level, in recent years attention has been devoted to defining semantics in a modular fashion, i.e. determining the semantics outcome based on local evaluations in subframeworks [3,8,16]. Several motivations underlie this research interest. First, a local approach can save computation time [7,11] possibly applying parallel computation techniques [12] or exploiting incremental

© Springer Nature Switzerland AG 2021
P. Baroni et al. (Eds.): CLAR 2021, LNAI 13040, pp. 169–189, 2021.
https://doi.org/10.1007/978-3-030-89391-0_10

computation in a dynamic context [17]. Second,various equivalence relations [6,14,19] heavily rely on modules and can also help summarizing (possibly complex) argumentation frameworks [4]. Furthermore, this research issue is a starting point to tackle the problem of combining different argumentation semantics, i.e. regarding a global argumentation framework as composed of a set of interacting parts each associated with a (possibly) different semantics [15,18], e.g. to model a multi-agent context or to integrate different kinds of reasoning [5].

In a previous paper [4], the modular definition of argumentation semantics has been investigated without any restriction on how an argumentation framework is partitioned into subframeworks. In particular, the property of *decomposability* of argumentation semantics has been introduced concerning the correspondences between semantics outcome at global and local level. A semantics **S** is decomposable if, given a partition of an argumentation framework into a set of sub-frameworks, the outcomes produced by **S** can be obtained as a combination of the outcomes produced by a local counterpart of **S** applied separately on each sub-framework, and vice versa.

While we are not aware of other investigations at this level of generality, the framework proposed in [4] assumes that the local computation in each subframework can have access only to a specific kind of information about the outcome of the computations in the outside components. In particular, the available information is relatively limited, including the set of outside attackers, the labels assigned to them by the computations in other subframeworks and the attacks directed from such arguments to inner arguments. It turns out that, among the most common semantics proposed in the literature, full decomposability with respect to every arbitrary partition is satisfied by some semantics. In contrast, others require the partition to be based on the strongly connected components of the argumentation framework. A few semantics then lack the decomposability property.

An interesting issue is whether exploiting further information would be useful and lead more semantics to be decomposable. For instance, we may consider attacks from inner arguments to outside arguments, or we may consider a larger set of outside arguments, such as the attackers of attackers, and so on.

This paper aims at providing a model for the investigation of the above issue at a general level, without relying on the specific argumentation semantics definitions (which is left for future work). More specifically, this paper aims at providing some answers to the following research issues:

1. How to model in general the diverse kinds of information that can be exploited in local computations, and the relevant functions representing the local counterparts of argumentation semantics;
2. Determining the range of semantics that are decomposable under different degrees of local information exploited, investigating in particular the extreme cases of null and complete information, respectively;
3. How to determine, in general, the local counterpart of an argumentation semantics to guarantee decomposability.

After some background provided in Sect. 2, the first question is dealt with in Sect. 3, by introducing the notions of local information function and local function. On this basis, a generalized notion of decomposability w.r.t. [4] is provided. Sections 4 and 5 are devoted to the second and third questions, respectively, while Sect. 6 discusses and concludes the paper.

2 Background

We follow the traditional definition of argumentation framework introduced by Dung [13] and define its restriction to a subset of arguments.

Definition 1. *An* argumentation framework *is a pair* $AF = (\mathcal{A}, att)$ *in which* $\mathcal{A}$ *is a finite[1] set of arguments and* $att \subseteq \mathcal{A} \times \mathcal{A}$. *An argument* α *such that* $(\alpha, \alpha) \in att$ *is called* self-attacking. *Given a set* $Args \subseteq \mathcal{A}$, *the restriction of* AF *to* $Args$, *denoted as* $AF{\downarrow}_{Args}$, *is the argumentation framework* $(Args, att \cap (Args \times Args))$. *The (infinite) set of all possible argumentation frameworks is denoted as* SAF.

We will also need two relations and two operators between argumentation frameworks.

Definition 2. *Given two argumentation frameworks* $AF_1 = (\mathcal{A}_1, att_1)$ *and* $AF_2 = (\mathcal{A}_2, att_2)$:

- $AF_1 \subseteq AF_2$ *iff* $\mathcal{A}_1 \subseteq \mathcal{A}_2$ *and* $att_1 \subseteq att_2$
- $AF_1 \sqsubseteq AF_2$ *iff* $\mathcal{A}_1 \subseteq \mathcal{A}_2$ *and* $AF_2{\downarrow}_{\mathcal{A}_1} = AF_1$
- $AF_1 \ominus AF_2 \triangleq \mathcal{A}_1 \backslash \mathcal{A}_2$
- $AF_1 \backslash AF_2 \triangleq AF_1{\downarrow}_{AF_1 \ominus AF_2}$

The relation $\subseteq$ extends set inclusion to argumentation frameworks, while $AF_1 \sqsubseteq AF_2$ holds if AF_1 is a subframework[2] of AF_2. In this case, $AF_2 \ominus AF_1$ returns the set of arguments of AF_2 outside AF_1, while $AF_2 \backslash AF_1$ returns the corresponding argumentation framework.

Proposition 1 shows that $\subseteq$ and $\sqsubseteq$ are partial orders.

Proposition 1. *The relations* $\subseteq$ *and* $\sqsubseteq$ *between argumentation frameworks are reflexive, antisymmetric and transitive.*

Proof. The proof that $\subseteq$ and $\sqsubseteq$ are reflexive is immediate from the relevant definitions. The fact that $\subseteq$ is antisymmetric directly follows from the fact that the set-inclusion relation $\subseteq$ is antisymmetric, and since $\sqsubseteq$ is stricter than $\subseteq$ it is antisymmetric in turn. As to transitivity, the proof for $\subseteq$ is immediate taking into account that the set-inclusion relation $\subseteq$ is transitive. As to $\sqsubseteq$, if $AF_1 \sqsubseteq AF_2$ and $AF_2 \sqsubseteq AF_3$ then by transitivity of $\subseteq$ and the fact that $\sqsubseteq$ is stricter than $\subseteq$ it holds that $AF_1 \subseteq AF_3$, and in particular $\mathcal{A}_1 \subseteq \mathcal{A}_3$. Since $AF_3{\downarrow}_{\mathcal{A}_2} = AF_2$ and $AF_2{\downarrow}_{\mathcal{A}_1} = AF_1$, we have that $AF_3{\downarrow}_{\mathcal{A}_1} = AF_1$, thus $AF_1 \sqsubseteq AF_3$. □

---

[1] In the general definition, the set of arguments may be infinite.
[2] It is immediate to see that $\sqsubseteq$ is stricter than $\subseteq$, i.e. $AF_1 \sqsubseteq AF_2$ entails $AF_1 \subseteq AF_2$.

In this paper we adopt the labelling-based approach to the definition of argumentation semantics. As shown in [2,9], for the semantics considered in this paper there is a direct correspondence with the "traditional" extension-based approach.

A labelling assigns to each argument of an argumentation framework a label taken from a predefined set Λ. We adopt the most common choice for Λ, i.e. $\{\mathtt{in}, \mathtt{out}, \mathtt{undec}\}$, where the label $\mathtt{in}$ means that the argument is accepted, the label $\mathtt{out}$ means that the argument is rejected, and the label $\mathtt{undec}$ means that the status of the argument is undecided. For technical reasons, we define labellings both for argumentation frameworks and for arbitrary sets of arguments.

Definition 3. *Given a set of arguments Args, a labelling of Args is a total function Lab : Args $\rightarrow$ $\{\mathtt{in}, \mathtt{out}, \mathtt{undec}\}$. The set of all labellings of Args is denoted as $\mathfrak{L}_{Args}$. Given an argumentation framework $AF = (\mathcal{A}, att)$, a labelling of AF is a labelling of $\mathcal{A}$. The set of all labellings of AF is denoted as $\mathfrak{L}(AF)$. For a labelling Lab of Args, the restriction of Lab to a set of arguments $Args' \subseteq Args$, denoted as $Lab{\downarrow}_{Args'}$, is defined as $Lab \cap (Args' \times \{\mathtt{in}, \mathtt{out}, \mathtt{undec}\})$. We extend this notation to sets of labellings, i.e. given a set of a labellings $\mathfrak{L} \subseteq \mathfrak{L}_{Args}$, $\mathfrak{L}{\downarrow}_{Args'} \triangleq \{Lab{\downarrow}_{Args'} \mid Lab \in \mathfrak{L}\}$. Moreover, if $Lab \in \mathfrak{L}(AF)$ and $AF' \subseteq AF$, where $AF' = (\mathcal{A}', att')$, $Lab{\downarrow}_{AF'}$ will denote $Lab{\downarrow}_{\mathcal{A}'}$.*

A labelling-based semantics prescribes a set of labellings for each argumentation framework.

Definition 4. *Given an argumentation framework $AF = (\mathcal{A}, att)$, a labelling-based semantics S associates with AF a subset of $\mathfrak{L}(AF)$, denoted as $\mathbf{L_S}(AF)$.*

Various notions of justification can be considered for arguments. The most common one considers an argument *skeptically justified* in an argumentation framework AF according to a semantics **S** if it is assigned the label $\mathtt{in}$ by all labellings of $\mathbf{L_S}(AF)$.

In general, a semantics encompasses a set of alternative labellings for a single argumentation framework. If a semantics **S** is defined in such a way that the set of labellings is always non empty, i.e. $\forall AF, \mathbf{L_S}(AF) \neq \emptyset$, then **S** is said to be *universally defined*. Moreover, a semantics may be defined so that a unique labelling is always prescribed, i.e. for every argumentation framework AF, $|\mathbf{L_S}(AF)| = 1$. In this case the semantics is said to be *single-status*, while in the general case it is said to be *multiple-status*.

As an extreme case of semantics corresponding to the most skeptical one, which has a theoretical, rather than practical, interest, we consider the semantics **UND**, a single-status semantics which assigns to all arguments the label $\mathtt{undec}$.

Definition 5. *The semantics* **UND** *is such that $\forall AF = (\mathcal{A}, att) \in SAF$, $\mathbf{L_{UND}}(AF) = \{Lab\}$, where $\forall \alpha \in \mathcal{A}, Lab(\alpha) = \mathtt{undec}$.*

Many other semantics exist, corresponding to different criteria to select labellings. While in this paper we are *not* concerned with the relevant definitions, we consider as a basic requirement for a semantics **S** to satisfy *conflict-freeness*, i.e. $\forall AF \in SAF$ and $\forall Lab \in \mathbf{L_S}(AF)$, *Lab* is conflict-free according to the following definition, taken from [10].

Definition 6. *Let Lab be a labelling of an argumentation framework* $AF = (\mathcal{A}, att)$. *Lab is conflict-free if for each* $\alpha \in \mathcal{A}$ *it holds that*

- *if* α *is labelled* in *then it does not have an attacker that is labelled* in
- *if* α *is labelled* out *then it has at least an attacker that is labelled* in.

3   A General Model for Decomposability

The proposed model for the analysis of decomposability of argumentation semantics is articulated in two layers. The first layer deals with the representation, in a general way, of the information locally used for the computation of labellings in subframeworks. The second layer focuses on the modelling of this computation through the notion of the local function.

3.1   Modelling Local Information

Given a subframework of the global argumentation framework, the information needed for the local computation of the labellings in this subframework should include the topology of the subframework itself. Still, in general, it has also some information from the outside. On the one hand, some knowledge of the topology of the neighboring part of the graph is needed. On the other hand, the labelling assigned to this part by the local computations on external subframeworks is required in order to extend it with a local labelling of the subgraph.

The topological information specifically available depends on the kind of information exploited for the local computation. For instance, one might decide to consider external attackers with the unidirectional attacks from them, or one might also take into account the external nodes attacked by the subframework, or the attackers of the attackers might also be considered, and so on. To model all these possibilities we introduce the notion of *local information function*, which takes in input a "global" argumentation framework AF^* and one of its subframeworks AF, and returns as output the portion of AF^* which can be taken into account to compute the labellings of AF (note that this portion of course must extend AF). Some constraints are also introduced concerning the role of AF^* (see the relevant explanation later).

Definition 7. *A local information function is a function* $\mathcal{LI} : \{(AF^*, AF) \mid AF^*, AF \in SAF \wedge AF \sqsubseteq AF^*\} \to SAF$ *such that* $\forall AF^*, AF \in SAF : AF \sqsubseteq AF^*$

- $AF \sqsubseteq \mathcal{LI}(AF^*, AF)$ *and* $\mathcal{LI}(AF^*, AF) \subseteq AF^*$

– if $AF^* \subseteq AF^{**}$ then either $\mathcal{LI}(AF^{**}, AF) = \mathcal{LI}(AF^*, AF)$ or it is not the case that $\mathcal{LI}(AF^{**}, AF) \subseteq AF^*$

For ease of notation, in the following $\mathcal{LI}(AF^*, AF)$ will be denoted as $\mathcal{LI}_{AF^*}(AF)$.

Some explanation on the constraints introduced in the above definition is in order.

As to the first item, $AF \sqsubseteq \mathcal{LI}(AF^*, AF)$ means that the local subframework must be known, and thus is part of the available information, to compute the appropriate labellings. The other condition $\mathcal{LI}(AF^*, AF) \subseteq AF^*$ expresses that the neighboring part of AF returned by the function is taken from AF^*. Here the use of $\subseteq$ rather than $\sqsubseteq$ gives more freedom in the choice of the local information, since it makes it possible to neglect some attacks that otherwise should be taken into account (e.g. one might consider external attackers with the relevant attacks directed towards AF but neglect the attacks directed from AF to such attackers).

The second item concerns the role of AF^*, which must be used only to identify the neighboring part of the subframework available locally. However, in principle there might be some further information hidden in the way the output of the function, say AF', is selected depending on AF^*, e.g. subtle dependencies could be introduced where part of the external topology might be artificially excluded to take into account the topology of $AF^* \setminus AF'$. To avoid this possibility, the constraint requires that if AF^* is enlarged, then either AF' does not change, or the additional elements of the enlarged global framework play an explicit role, i.e. some appear in the novel output of the local information function.

Definition 7 encompasses various local information functions corresponding to different criteria to select the local information taken into account.

As two extreme cases, we introduce the local information functions $m\mathcal{LI}$ and $M\mathcal{LI}$. The first function models the case where no external information is available, i.e. $m\mathcal{LI}$ returns as output just the subframework where local labellings are computed. The second function models the case where all external topological information is available, i.e. $M\mathcal{LI}$ returns as output the whole global argumentation framework.

Definition 8. $m\mathcal{LI}$ is the local information function such that $\forall AF^*, AF \in SAF : AF \sqsubseteq AF^*, m\mathcal{LI}_{AF^*}(AF) = AF$. $M\mathcal{LI}$ is the local information function such that $\forall AF^*, AF \in SAF : AF \sqsubseteq AF^*, M\mathcal{LI}_{AF^*}(AF) = AF^*$.

There are plenty of other local information functions between the two extreme cases described above, and in the following we introduce some of them just for the sake of the example. In order to make their definitions easier, we first introduce some notations.

Definition 9. Given an argumentation framework $AF = (\mathcal{A}, att)$ and a set of arguments $Args \subseteq \mathcal{A}$:

– $Args_{AF}^{inp} = \{\alpha \in \mathcal{A} \setminus Args \mid \exists \beta \in Args, (\alpha, \beta) \in att\}$
– $Args_{AF}^{att-inp} = att \cap (Args_{AF}^{inp} \times Args)$

$$- Args_{AF}^{Batt-inp} = Args_{AF}^{att-inp} \cup (att \cap (Args \times Args_{AF}^{inp}))$$
$$- Args_{AF}^{out} = \{\alpha \in \mathcal{A}\backslash Args \mid \exists \beta \in Args, (\beta, \alpha) \in att\}$$
$$- Args_{AF}^{att-out} = att \cap (Args \times Args_{AF}^{out})$$
$$- Args_{AF}^{Batt-out} = Args_{AF}^{att-out} \cup (att \cap (Args_{AF}^{out} \times Args))$$

In words, $Args_{AF}^{inp}$ includes the arguments attacking $Args$ from the outside, $Args_{AF}^{att-inp}$ includes the attacks from $Args_{AF}^{inp}$ to $Args$ (but not vice versa), $Args_{AF}^{Batt-inp}$ includes the attacks from $Args_{AF}^{inp}$ to $Args$ and vice versa. $Args_{AF}^{out}$ includes the outside arguments attacked by $Args$, $Args_{AF}^{att-out}$ includes the attacks from $Args$ to $Args_{AF}^{out}$, while $Args_{AF}^{Batt-out}$ also includes the existing reverse attacks.

Definition 10. *The following functions from* $\{(AF^*, AF) \mid AF^*, AF \in SAF \wedge AF \sqsubseteq AF^*\}$ *to* SAF *are defined:*

$$- inp\mathcal{LI}_{AF^*}(AF) = (\mathcal{A} \cup \mathcal{A}_{AF^*}^{inp}, att \cup \mathcal{A}_{AF^*}^{att-inp})$$
$$- Binp\mathcal{LI}_{AF^*}(AF) = (\mathcal{A} \cup \mathcal{A}_{AF^*}^{inp}, att \cup \mathcal{A}_{AF^*}^{Batt-inp})$$
$$- inpout\mathcal{LI}_{AF^*}(AF) = (\mathcal{A} \cup \mathcal{A}_{AF^*}^{inp} \cup \mathcal{A}_{AF^*}^{out}, att \cup \mathcal{A}_{AF^*}^{att-inp} \cup \mathcal{A}_{AF^*}^{att-out})$$
$$- Binpout\mathcal{LI}_{AF^*}(AF) = (\mathcal{A} \cup \mathcal{A}_{AF^*}^{inp} \cup \mathcal{A}_{AF^*}^{out}, att \cup \mathcal{A}_{AF^*}^{Batt-inp} \cup \mathcal{A}_{AF^*}^{Batt-out})$$

where $AF = (\mathcal{A}, att)$.

In words, $inp\mathcal{LI}$ selects as external information[3] the set of outside attackers and the unidirectional attacks from them to AF, $Binp\mathcal{LI}$ is similar but considers both possible directions for the attacks, $inpout\mathcal{LI}$ extends $inp\mathcal{LI}$ with the set of outside arguments that are attacked by AF as well as the relevant attacks from AF, while $Binpout\mathcal{LI}$ is similar but considers both directions for the attack relations.

One may also consider a larger neighboring part w.r.t. direct attackers and attacked arguments. For instance, besides the direct attackers the local information may involve also their attackers, the attackers of their attackers, and so on until a level k.

Definition 11. *Given an argumentation framework* $AF = (\mathcal{A}, att)$, *a path in* AF *of length* n *from* α_0 *to* α_n *is a sequence of arguments* $\alpha_0, \ldots, \alpha_n$ *such that* $(\alpha_i, \alpha_{i+1}) \in att$ *for each* $i \in \{0, \ldots, n-1\}$. *We indicate that a path of length* n *exists from* α_0 *to* α_n *as* $p_{AF}^n(\alpha_0, \alpha_n)$. *Given a set of arguments* $Args \subseteq AF$ *and an integer* $k > 0$, $Args_{AF}^{inp-k} \equiv \{\alpha \in \mathcal{A}\backslash Args \mid \exists \beta \in \mathcal{A}, p_{AF}^n(\alpha, \beta), n \leq k\}$.

The following function considers all the ancestors of the arguments in AF (w.r.t. the attack relation) of distance less that or equal to a constant k as well as all involved attacks.

Definition 12. $inp - k - \mathcal{LI}$ *is the function from* $\{(AF^*, AF) \mid AF^*, AF \in SAF \wedge AF \sqsubseteq AF^*\}$ *to* SAF *such that* $inp - k - \mathcal{LI}_{AF^*}(AF) \equiv AF^* \downarrow_{(\mathcal{A} \cup \mathcal{A}_{AF^*}^{inp-k})}$.

---

[3] This local information function is the one implicitly adopted in [4].

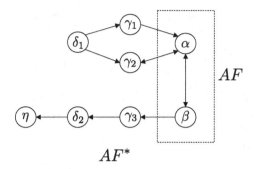

Fig. 1. Argumentation frameworks AF^* and AF, with $AF \sqsubseteq AF^*$.

Example 1. Consider the argumentation frameworks $AF^* = (\{\alpha, \beta, \gamma_1, \gamma_2, \gamma_3, \delta_1, \delta_2, \eta\}, \{(\delta_1, \gamma_1), (\delta_1, \gamma_2), (\gamma_1, \alpha), (\gamma_2, \alpha), (\alpha, \gamma_2), (\alpha, \beta), (\beta, \alpha), (\beta, \gamma_3), (\gamma_3, \delta_2), (\delta_2, \eta)\})$ and $AF = AF^*\!\downarrow_{\{\alpha,\beta\}}$, depicted in Fig. 1. It turns out that:

- $inp\mathcal{LI}_{AF^*}(AF) = (\{\alpha, \beta, \gamma_1, \gamma_2\}, \{(\alpha, \beta), (\beta, \alpha), (\gamma_1, \alpha), (\gamma_2, \alpha)\})$
- $Binp\mathcal{LI}_{AF^*}(AF) = (\{\alpha, \beta, \gamma_1, \gamma_2\}, \{(\alpha, \beta), (\beta, \alpha), (\gamma_1, \alpha), (\gamma_2, \alpha), (\alpha, \gamma_2)\})$
- $inpout\mathcal{LI}_{AF^*}(AF) = (\{\alpha, \beta, \gamma_1, \gamma_2, \gamma_3\}, \{(\alpha, \beta), (\beta, \alpha), (\gamma_1, \alpha), (\gamma_2, \alpha), (\beta, \gamma_3)\})$
- $Binpout\mathcal{LI}_{AF^*}(AF) = (\{\alpha, \beta, \gamma_1, \gamma_2, \gamma_3\}, \{(\alpha, \beta), (\beta, \alpha), (\gamma_1, \alpha), (\gamma_2, \alpha), (\alpha, \gamma_2), (\beta, \gamma_3)\})$
- $inp - 2 - \mathcal{LI}_{AF^*}(AF) = AF^*\!\downarrow_{\{\delta_1, \gamma_1, \gamma_2, \alpha, \beta\}}$

To show that the above functions are actually local information functions, we have to prove that they satisfy the constraints of Definition 7. The following proposition introduces sufficient conditions that might be easier to verify w.r.t. those of Definition 7. In particular, the constraint concerning the role of the global framework AF^* (second item in Definition 7) holds if a function is monotone w.r.t. AF^* and its output does not change if AF^* is replaced with the same argumentation framework returned as output.

Proposition 2. *Let $\mathcal{LI}$ be a function from $\{(AF^*, AF) \mid AF^*, AF \in SAF \wedge AF \sqsubseteq AF^*\}$ to SAF. If $\forall AF^*, AF \in SAF : AF \sqsubseteq AF^*$ the following conditions are satisfied*

- *$AF \sqsubseteq \mathcal{LI}_{AF^*}(AF)$ and $\mathcal{LI}_{AF^*}(AF) \subseteq AF^*$*
- *for every $AF^{**} \in SAF$ such that $AF^* \subseteq AF^{**}$, it holds that $\mathcal{LI}_{AF^*}(AF) \subseteq \mathcal{LI}_{AF^{**}}(AF)$*
- *$\mathcal{LI}_{\mathcal{LI}_{AF^*}(AF)}(AF) = \mathcal{LI}_{AF^*}(AF)$*

then $\mathcal{LI}$ is a local information function.

Proof. Referring to Definition 7, only the second item has to be proved since the first one holds by the first hypothesis. For this purpose, we show that for every

$AF, AF^*, AF^{**} \in SAF$ such that $AF^* \subseteq AF^{**}$, if $\mathcal{LI}_{AF^{**}}(AF) \subseteq AF^*$ then $\mathcal{LI}_{AF^{**}}(AF) = \mathcal{LI}_{AF^*}(AF)$.

If $\mathcal{LI}_{AF^{**}}(AF) \subseteq AF^*$, by the second hypothesis (monotony w.r.t. the global framework) $\mathcal{LI}_{\mathcal{LI}_{AF^{**}}(AF)}(AF) \subseteq \mathcal{LI}_{AF^*}(AF)$. According to the third hypothesis $\mathcal{LI}_{\mathcal{LI}_{AF^{**}}(AF)}(AF) = \mathcal{LI}_{AF^{**}}(AF)$, thus $\mathcal{LI}_{AF^{**}}(AF) \subseteq \mathcal{LI}_{AF^*}(AF)$. Since $AF^* \subseteq AF^{**}$, the second hypothesis yields $\mathcal{LI}_{AF^*}(AF) \subseteq \mathcal{LI}_{AF^{**}}(AF)$. Thus by antisymmetry of $\subseteq$ we get $\mathcal{LI}_{AF^{**}}(AF) = \mathcal{LI}_{AF^*}(AF)$. □

We can then show that the functions introduced above are local information functions.

Proposition 3. *The functions* $m\mathcal{LI}$, $M\mathcal{LI}$, $inp\mathcal{LI}$, $Binp\mathcal{LI}$, $inpout\mathcal{LI}$, $Binpout\mathcal{LI}$, $inp - k - \mathcal{LI}$ *are local information functions.*

Proof. For all of the functions the proof is based on Proposition 2.

As to $m\mathcal{LI}$, if $AF \sqsubseteq AF^*$ then it is immediate to see that $AF \sqsubseteq m\mathcal{LI}_{AF^*}(AF)$ and $m\mathcal{LI}_{AF^*}(AF) \subseteq AF^*$, since $m\mathcal{LI}_{AF^*}(AF) = AF$. Also the second required constraint that $m\mathcal{LI}_{AF^*}(AF) \subseteq m\mathcal{LI}_{AF^{**}}(AF)$ trivially holds, since $m\mathcal{LI}_{AF^*}(AF) = m\mathcal{LI}_{AF^{**}}(AF) = AF$. Finally, as to the third constraint $m\mathcal{LI}_{m\mathcal{LI}_{AF^*}(AF)}(AF) = m\mathcal{LI}_{AF}(AF) = AF = m\mathcal{LI}_{AF^*}(AF)$.

As to $M\mathcal{LI}$, if $AF \sqsubseteq AF^*$ then $AF \sqsubseteq M\mathcal{LI}_{AF^*}(AF)$ and $M\mathcal{LI}_{AF^*}(AF) \subseteq AF^*$ trivially hold, since $M\mathcal{LI}_{AF^*}(AF) = AF^*$. The second constraint holds since $M\mathcal{LI}_{AF^*}(AF) \subseteq M\mathcal{LI}_{AF^{**}}(AF)$ equates to $AF^* \subseteq AF^{**}$. As to the third constraint, by the definition of $M\mathcal{LI}$ we directly get $M\mathcal{LI}_{M\mathcal{LI}_{AF^*}(AF)}(AF) = M\mathcal{LI}_{AF^*}(AF)$.

As to the other functions, by inspection of their definitions it is easy to see that for each $\mathcal{LI} \in \{inp\mathcal{LI}, Binp\mathcal{LI}, inpout\mathcal{LI}, Binpout\mathcal{LI}, inp - k - \mathcal{LI}\}$ $\mathcal{LI}_{AF^*}(AF)$ is obtained by adding to AF elements (arguments and attacks) from $AF^* \ominus AF$. Thus the first item of Proposition 2 is verified. It is also easy to see that all elements of $\mathcal{LI}_{AF^*}(AF)$ are still present in the output obtained with AF^* enlarged, thus also the second item holds. As to the third item, let $\mathcal{LI}_{AF^*}(AF) = AF'$. According to the definitions of the functions, each element included in $\mathcal{LI}_{AF^*}(AF)$ is still an element of $\mathcal{LI}_{AF'}(AF)$, thus also the last item of Proposition 2 is verified. □

Local information functions can be partially ordered based on the amount of information returned as output.

Definition 13. *Given two local information functions* $\mathcal{LI}_1$ *and* $\mathcal{LI}_2$, $\mathcal{LI}_1 \preceq \mathcal{LI}_2$ *iff* $\forall AF^*, AF \in SAF$: $AF \sqsubseteq AF^*$ *it holds that* $\mathcal{LI}_{1 AF^*}(AF) \subseteq \mathcal{LI}_{2 AF^*}(AF)$.

In words, if $\mathcal{LI}_1 \preceq \mathcal{LI}_2$ then $\mathcal{LI}_1$ always returns an argumentation framework which is contained in that returned by $\mathcal{LI}_2$. For instance, the local information function $inp\mathcal{LI}$, that returns as output the outside attackers of AF and the relevant (unidirectional) attacks, is less informative than $inpout\mathcal{LI}$ that also includes outside attacked nodes and the relevant unidirectional attacks, and $inpout\mathcal{LI}$ is in turn less informative than $Binpout\mathcal{LI}$.

It is easy to see that $\preceq$ is a partial order with the least and the greatest elements.

Proposition 4. $\preceq$ *is reflexive, transitive and antisymmetric. $m\mathcal{L}\mathcal{I}$ and $M\mathcal{L}\mathcal{I}$ are the least and greatest element, respectively, w.r.t. $\preceq$ of the set of local information functions.*

Proof. The proof that $\preceq$ is a partial order is immediate taking into account that by Proposition 1 the relation $\subseteq$ between argumentation frameworks is a partial order.

By definition of local information function (see Definition 7) $\forall \mathcal{L}\mathcal{I}$, $\forall AF^*, AF \in SAF : AF \sqsubseteq AF^*$, it holds that $AF \sqsubseteq \mathcal{L}\mathcal{I}_{AF^*}(AF)$ and $\mathcal{L}\mathcal{I}_{AF^*}(AF) \subseteq AF^*$. Since $AF \sqsubseteq \mathcal{L}\mathcal{I}_{AF^*}(AF)$ entails $AF \subseteq \mathcal{L}\mathcal{I}_{AF^*}(AF)$, it holds that $\forall \mathcal{L}\mathcal{I}$, $m\mathcal{L}\mathcal{I} \preceq \mathcal{L}\mathcal{I}$ and $\mathcal{L}\mathcal{I} \preceq M\mathcal{L}\mathcal{I}$. $\qquad\square$

While local information functions model the identification criterion of available topological information for all possible subframeworks of all global argumentation frameworks, the information available for a specific subframework of a given framework is represented by an *argumentation framework with input*, which besides topological information includes the labelling externally assigned to the neighboring part of the subframework. The next definition introduces this notion in a generalized form w.r.t. [4].

Definition 14. *Given $AF, AF' \in SAF$ such that $AF \sqsubseteq AF'$, an argumentation framework with input is a tuple (AF, AF', Lab) where $Lab \in \mathcal{L}_{AF' \ominus AF}$.*

Intuitively, AF plays the role of a subframework, while AF' and Lab are the elements affecting the computation of the labellings of AF. In particular, AF' represents the portion of the global argumentation framework which is taken into account, including AF itself, while Lab is the labelling assigned to the relevant arguments outside AF, i.e. those belonging to $AF' \ominus AF$.

The relationships between the notions of local information function and argumentation framework with input are described in the following definitions.

Definition 15. *An argumentation framework with input (AF, AF', Lab) is derived from a local information function $\mathcal{L}\mathcal{I}$ in AF^*, written $(AF, AF', Lab) \in AF^{inp}_{\mathcal{L}\mathcal{I},AF^*}$, if $AF' = \mathcal{L}\mathcal{I}_{AF^*}(AF)$.*

(AF, AF', Lab) is derived from $\mathcal{L}\mathcal{I}$, written $(AF, AF', Lab) \in AF^{inp}_{\mathcal{L}\mathcal{I}}$, if $\exists AF^*$ such that $(AF, AF', Lab) \in AF^{inp}_{\mathcal{L}\mathcal{I},AF^*}$.

Intuitively, given a subframework AF of AF^*, one can derive in AF^* an argumentation framework with input by applying a local information function to AF and AF^*, obtaining $(AF, \mathcal{L}\mathcal{I}_{AF^*}(AF), Lab)$. The second part of the definition removes the reference to a specific global argumentation framework AF^*, by defining an argumentation framework with input as derived from $\mathcal{L}\mathcal{I}$ if there is AF^* where it can be derived from $\mathcal{L}\mathcal{I}$.

While in the notions introduced above the labelling component of argumentation frameworks with input is not constrained, the notion of realizability introduced in the following definition requires the labelling component to be enforced by a labelling prescribed by the semantics.

Definition 16. *An argumentation framework with input* (AF, AF', Lab) *is realized from a local information function* $\mathcal{LI}$ *in an argumentation framework* AF^* *under a semantics* **S**, *written* $(AF, AF', Lab) \in RAF_{\mathcal{LI},AF^*,\mathbf{S}}^{inp}$, *if* $(AF, AF', Lab) \in AF_{\mathcal{LI},AF^*}^{inp}$ *and* $\exists Lab^* \in \mathbf{L_S}(AF^*)$ *such that* $Lab^* \downarrow_{AF' \ominus AF} = Lab$.

(AF, AF', Lab) *is realized from a local information function* $\mathcal{LI}$ *under a semantics* **S**, *written* $(AF, AF', Lab) \in RAF_{\mathcal{LI},\mathbf{S}}^{inp}$, *if* $\exists AF^* \in SAF$ *such that* $(AF, AF', Lab) \in RAF_{\mathcal{LI},AF^*,\mathbf{S}}^{inp}$.

3.2   The Notions of Local Function and Decomposability

We are now able to define the notion of decomposability of an argumentation semantics, which corresponds to a generalization to the setting devised above of the notion introduced in [4] with the same name.

The first step is defining a local function, representing a local counterpart of the notion of semantics, since it takes as input an argumentation framework with input (rather than a standard argumentation framework) and produces as output a set of labellings for the inner local argumentation framework. It makes sense to define a local function with reference to a local information function, since only the argumentation frameworks with input derived from the adopted local information function can play a role (see Definition 15).

Definition 17. *A local function* F *for a local information function* $\mathcal{LI}$ *assigns to any* $(AF, AF', Lab) \in AF_{\mathcal{LI}}^{inp}$ *a (possibly empty) set of labellings of* AF, *i.e.* $F(AF, AF', Lab) \in 2^{\mathfrak{L}(AF)}$.

As in [4], decomposability may hold for a specific family of partitions of the argumentation frameworks. A family of partitions is captured by the following notion from [4].

Definition 18. *A partition selector* $\mathcal{F}$ *is a function receiving as input an argumentation framework* $AF = (\mathcal{A}, att)$ *and returning a set of partitions of* $\mathcal{A}$.

A semantics **S** is *decomposable* (also called fully decomposable) if the labellings prescribed on an argumentation framework AF correspond to the possible combinations of *compatible* labellings obtained by applying a local function F in the subframeworks that partition the global framework.

Definition 19. *A local function* F *for a local information function* $\mathcal{LI}$ *enforces decomposability of a semantics* **S** *under* $\mathcal{LI}$ *w.r.t. a partition selector* $\mathcal{F}$ *iff for every argumentation framework* $AF = (\mathcal{A}, att)$ *and for every partition* $\mathcal{P} = \{P_1, \ldots, P_n\} \in \mathcal{F}(AF)$, *the following condition holds:* $\mathbf{L_S}(AF) = \{L_{P_1} \cup \ldots \cup$

$L_{Pn} \mid L_{P_i} \in F(AF{\downarrow}_{P_i}, \mathcal{LI}_{AF}(AF{\downarrow}_{P_i}), (\bigcup_{j=1...n, j\neq i} L_{Pj}){\downarrow}_{\mathcal{LI}_{AF}(AF{\downarrow}_{P_i})\ominus AF{\downarrow}_{P_i}})\}$.
A semantics **S** *is decomposable (or equivalently fully decomposable) under* $\mathcal{LI}$
w.r.t. $\mathcal{F}$ *iff there is a local function* F *which enforces decomposability of* **S** *under*
$\mathcal{LI}$ *w.r.t.* $\mathcal{F}$. *In case the reference to* $\mathcal{F}$ *is omitted, the property holds for every*
partition, i.e. w.r.t. the partition selector which returns the set of all possible
partitions of an argumentation framework.

In the above definition, each subframework enriched with the locally available external information is modelled by the argumentation framework with input $(AF{\downarrow}_{P_i}, \mathcal{LI}_{AF}(AF{\downarrow}_{P_i}), (\bigcup_{j=1...n, j\neq i} L_{Pj}){\downarrow}_{\mathcal{LI}_{AF}(AF{\downarrow}_{P_i})\ominus AF{\downarrow}_{P_i}})$. The first component is the subframework of AF on the partition element P_i. The second component is the available topological information on the neighboring part. The third component is the labelling assigned to the available arguments outside the subframework $AF{\downarrow}_{P_i}$, i.e. those included in the set $\mathcal{LI}_{AF}(AF{\downarrow}_{P_i}) \ominus AF{\downarrow}_{P_i}$. Compatibility refers to the fact that any labelling of a subframework is used by F to compute other labellings in other subframeworks. More specifically, each local labelling L_{Pi} depends on the other ones since the labelling component taken as input by F is obtained from the labellings L_{Pj} (with $j \neq i$) computed in external subframeworks.

4   On the Power of Local Information Functions

Intuitively, the more local information is available, the easier it is to determine the global labellings from local computation. Therefore, we expect a more expressive local information function to foster the correct identification of the global labellings, yielding a larger set of decomposable semantics.

Proposition 5. *If a semantics* **S** *is decomposable under* $\mathcal{LI}$ *w.r.t.* $\mathcal{F}$ *then for*
any $\mathcal{LI}'$ *such that* $\mathcal{LI} \preceq \mathcal{LI}'$, **S** *is decomposable under* $\mathcal{LI}'$ *w.r.t.* $\mathcal{F}$.

Proof. By the hypothesis, there is a local function F for $\mathcal{LI}$ such that for every argumentation framework $AF = (\mathcal{A}, att)$ and for every partition $\mathcal{P} = \{P_1, \ldots, P_n\} \in \mathcal{F}(AF)$

$$\mathbf{L_S}(AF) = \{L_{P1} \cup \ldots \cup L_{Pn} \mid$$
$$L_{Pi} \in F(AF{\downarrow}_{P_i}, \mathcal{LI}_{AF}(AF{\downarrow}_{P_i}), (\bigcup_{j=1...n, j\neq i} L_{Pj}){\downarrow}_{\mathcal{LI}_{AF}(AF{\downarrow}_{P_i})\ominus AF{\downarrow}_{P_i}})\} \quad (1)$$

Let us define the local function F' for $\mathcal{LI}'$ such that for $(AF, AF', Lab) \in AF_{\mathcal{LI}'}^{inp}$,
$F'(AF, AF', Lab) \equiv F(AF, \mathcal{LI}_{AF'}(AF), Lab{\downarrow}_{\mathcal{LI}_{AF'}(AF)\ominus AF})$.

We prove that F' enforces decomposability of **S** under $\mathcal{LI}'$ w.r.t. $\mathcal{F}$, i.e. for every argumentation framework $AF = (\mathcal{A}, att)$ and for every partition $\mathcal{P} = \{P_1, \ldots, P_n\} \in \mathcal{F}(AF)$

$$\mathbf{L_S}(AF) = \{L_{P1} \cup \ldots \cup L_{Pn} \mid$$
$$L_{Pi} \in F'(AF{\downarrow}_{P_i}, \mathcal{LI}'_{AF}(AF{\downarrow}_{P_i}), (\bigcup_{j=1...n, j\neq i} L_{Pj}){\downarrow}_{\mathcal{LI}'_{AF}(AF{\downarrow}_{P_i})\ominus AF{\downarrow}_{P_i}})\}$$

This directly derives from (1) if

$$F'(AF{\downarrow}_{P_i}, \mathcal{LI}'_{AF}(AF{\downarrow}_{P_i}), (\bigcup_{j=1...n, j\neq i} L_{Pj}){\downarrow}_{\mathcal{LI}'_{AF}(AF{\downarrow}_{P_i})\ominus AF{\downarrow}_{P_i}})$$

$$= F(AF{\downarrow}_{P_i}, \mathcal{LI}_{AF}(AF{\downarrow}_{P_i}), (\bigcup_{j=1...n, j\neq i} L_{Pj}){\downarrow}_{\mathcal{LI}_{AF}(AF{\downarrow}_{P_i})\ominus AF{\downarrow}_{P_i}})$$

In order to prove this condition, for the sake of clarity we introduce the following substitutions:

$$AF \to AF^*$$
$$AF{\downarrow}_{P_i} \to AF$$
$$\mathcal{LI}_{AF}(AF{\downarrow}_{P_i}) \to AF'$$
$$\mathcal{LI}'_{AF}(AF{\downarrow}_{P_i}) \to AF''$$
$$(\bigcup_{j=1...n, j\neq i} L_{Pj}) \to Lab$$

Under these substitutions, it is easy to see that the following conditions hold:

$$AF' = \mathcal{LI}_{AF^*}(AF) \tag{2}$$

$$AF'' = \mathcal{LI}'_{AF^*}(AF) \tag{3}$$

$$AF'' \subseteq AF^* \tag{4}$$

where the last condition is due to the definition of local information function referring to $\mathcal{LI}'$.

Taking into account the substitutions above, the thesis becomes

$$F'(AF, AF'', Lab{\downarrow}_{AF''\ominus AF}) = F(AF, AF', Lab{\downarrow}_{AF'\ominus AF})$$

According to the definition of F', the first term can be expressed as

$$F(AF, \mathcal{LI}_{AF''}(AF), (Lab{\downarrow}_{AF''\ominus AF}){\downarrow}_{\mathcal{LI}_{AF''}(AF)\ominus AF})$$

Since by definition of local information function $\mathcal{LI}_{AF''}(AF) \subseteq AF''$, it holds that $(Lab{\downarrow}_{AF''\ominus AF}){\downarrow}_{\mathcal{LI}_{AF''}(AF)\ominus AF} = Lab{\downarrow}_{\mathcal{LI}_{AF''}(AF)\ominus AF}$ and thus the same term can be expressed as

$$F(AF, \mathcal{LI}_{AF''}(AF), Lab{\downarrow}_{\mathcal{LI}_{AF''}(AF)\ominus AF})$$

Now, since by (4) $AF'' \subseteq AF^*$, by definition of local information function either $\mathcal{LI}_{AF''}(AF) = \mathcal{LI}_{AF^*}(AF)$ or it is not the case that $\mathcal{LI}_{AF^*}(AF) \subseteq AF''$. On the other hand, by the hypothesis that $\mathcal{LI} \preceq \mathcal{LI}'$, $\mathcal{LI}_{AF^*}(AF) \subseteq \mathcal{LI}'_{AF^*}(AF)$ which by (3) yields $\mathcal{LI}_{AF^*}(AF) \subseteq AF''$. Thus the first option holds, yielding the following expression for the term:

$$F(AF, \mathcal{LI}_{AF^*}(AF), Lab{\downarrow}_{\mathcal{LI}_{AF^*}(AF)\ominus AF})$$

which by (2) is equivalent to $F(AF, AF', Lab{\downarrow}_{AF'\ominus AF})$, and we are done. $\square$

Note that the constraints introduced in Definition 7 are crucial in the above proof.

Summing up, the partial order $\preceq$ between local information functions has a direct impact on the capability of capturing the global labellings through local computations. It is then interesting to determine the sets of semantics that are decomposable under the minimum and maximum (w.r.t. $\preceq$) local information functions, i.e. $m\mathcal{LI}$ and $M\mathcal{LI}$, respectively.

Proposition 6. *There are only four semantics satisfying conflict-freeness that are decomposable under* $m\mathcal{LI}$:

- *The semantics* **UND**
- *The semantics* **S** *such that* $\forall AF \in SAF$, $\mathbf{L_S}(AF) = \emptyset$
- *The semantics* **S** *such that* $\mathbf{L_S}(AF) = \emptyset$ *if there is a self-attacking argument in* AF, $\mathbf{L_S}(AF) = \mathbf{L_{UND}}(AF)$ *otherwise*
- *The semantics* **S** *such that* $\mathbf{L_S}(AF) = \emptyset$ *if there is an argument which is not self-attacking in* AF, $\mathbf{L_S}(AF) = \mathbf{L_{UND}}(AF)$ *otherwise.*

Among these semantics, only **UND** *is universally defined.*

Proof. First, to show that the four semantics are fully decomposable, we select for each semantics **S** the local function F such that $F(AF, AF, \emptyset) = \mathbf{L_S}(AF)$ as defined above (note in particular that all argumentation frameworks with input in $AF_{m\mathcal{LI}}^{inp}$ have the form $(AF, AF, \emptyset)$). It is then easy to see that F enforces decomposability of **S** under $m\mathcal{LI}$.

It is also immediate to verify that all of the four semantics satisfy conflict-freeness, and among them only **UND** is universally defined.

To show that there are no other semantics satisfying conflict-freeness that are decomposable under $m\mathcal{LI}$, for any $AF = (\mathcal{A}, att) \in SAF$, consider the partition $\mathcal{P} = \{\{\alpha\} \mid \alpha \in \mathcal{A}\}$, i.e. consisting of all sets including exactly a single argument. If **S** is decomposable under $m\mathcal{LI}$, according to Definition 19 we must have, letting $\mathcal{A} = \{\alpha_1, \ldots, \alpha_n\}$,

$$\mathbf{L_S}(AF) = \{L_{P1} \cup \ldots \cup L_{Pn} \mid L_{Pi} \in F(AF\!\downarrow_{\{\alpha_i\}}, AF\!\downarrow_{\{\alpha_i\}}, \emptyset)\} \quad (5)$$

Note that given an argument α there are only two possibilities for $AF\!\downarrow_{\{\alpha\}}$, i.e. $AF_1 = (\{\alpha\}, \emptyset)$ if α is not self-attacking and $AF_2 = (\{\alpha\}, \{(\alpha, \alpha)\})$ otherwise. Let us then evaluate the possible outcomes for $F(AF_1, AF_1, \emptyset)$ and $F(AF_2, AF_2, \emptyset)$. First, the labelling $\{(\alpha, \mathtt{out})\}$ can be ruled out for both $F(AF_1, AF_1, \emptyset)$ and $F(AF_2, AF_2, \emptyset)$ by considering the condition (5) applied to AF_1 and AF_2, since the resulting labelling $\{(\alpha, \mathtt{out})\}$ would violate the second condition of Definition 6. Also the labelling $\{(\alpha, \mathtt{in})\}$ can be ruled out. In particular, as to $F(AF_2, AF_2, \emptyset)$ it is again sufficient to consider the condition (5) applied to AF_2, since the resulting labelling $\{(\alpha, \mathtt{in})\}$ would violate the first condition of Definition 6. As to $F(AF_1, AF_1, \emptyset)$, in the argumentation framework $AF = (\{\alpha_1, \alpha_2\}, \{(\alpha_1, \alpha_2)\})$ the condition (5) would prescribe (possibly among others) the labelling $\{(\alpha_1, \mathtt{in}), (\alpha_2, \mathtt{in})\}$, violating the first condition of Definition 6. As a consequence, only four cases are possible, and according to (5) they correspond to the four semantics above in the relevant order, i.e.

- $F(AF_1, AF_1, \emptyset) = \{\{(\alpha, \mathtt{undec})\}\}$ and $F(AF_2, AF_2, \emptyset) = \{\{(\alpha, \mathtt{undec})\}\}$
- $F(AF_1, AF_1, \emptyset) = \emptyset$ and $F(AF_2, AF_2, \emptyset) = \emptyset$
- $F(AF_1, AF_1, \emptyset) = \{\{(\alpha, \mathtt{undec})\}\}$ and $F(AF_2, AF_2, \emptyset) = \emptyset$
- $F(AF_1, AF_1, \emptyset) = \emptyset$ and $F(AF_2, AF_2, \emptyset) = \{\{(\alpha, \mathtt{undec})\}\}$

$\square$

Proposition 7. *Every semantics* **S** *is decomposable under* $M\mathcal{LI}$.

Proof. For a semantics **S**, we consider the local function F for $M\mathcal{LI}$ defined as $F(AF, AF', Lab) \equiv \{Lab'\!\downarrow_{\mathcal{A}} \mid Lab' \in \mathbf{L_S}(AF') \wedge Lab'\!\downarrow_{AF' \ominus AF} = Lab\}$, where $\mathcal{A}$ denotes the set of arguments of AF.

We have to prove that for every argumentation framework $AF = (\mathcal{A}, att)$ and for every partition $\mathcal{P} = \{P_1, \ldots, P_n\}$, it holds that $\mathbf{L_S}(AF) = \{L_{P_1} \cup \ldots \cup L_{P_n} \mid L_{P_i} \in F(AF\!\downarrow_{P_i}, M\mathcal{LI}_{AF}(AF\!\downarrow_{P_i}), (\bigcup_{j=1\ldots n, j \neq i} L_{P_j})\!\downarrow_{M\mathcal{LI}_{AF}(AF\!\downarrow_{P_i}) \ominus AF\!\downarrow_{P_i})\} = \{L_{P_1} \cup \ldots \cup L_{P_n} \mid L_{P_i} \in F(AF\!\downarrow_{P_i}, AF, (\bigcup_{j=1\ldots n, j \neq i} L_{P_j})\!\downarrow_{AF \ominus AF\!\downarrow_{P_i}})\}$, where by the definition of F and taking into account that $AF = (\mathcal{A}, att)$ we have that $F(AF\!\downarrow_{P_i}, AF, (\bigcup_{j=1\ldots n, j \neq i} L_{P_j})\!\downarrow_{AF \ominus AF\!\downarrow_{P_i}}) = \{Lab\!\downarrow_{P_i} \mid Lab \in \mathbf{L_S}(AF) \wedge Lab\!\downarrow_{\mathcal{A} \setminus P_i} = (\bigcup_{j=1\ldots n, j \neq i} L_{P_j})\!\downarrow_{\mathcal{A} \setminus P_i}\}$.

Let us first consider a labelling $Lab \in \mathbf{L_S}(AF)$. Since $\mathcal{P}$ is a partition, it obviously holds that $Lab = L_{P_1} \cup \ldots \cup L_{P_n}$ with $L_{P_i} = Lab\!\downarrow_{P_i}$, and $Lab\!\downarrow_{\mathcal{A} \setminus P_i} = (\bigcup_{j=1\ldots n, j \neq i} L_{P_j})\!\downarrow_{\mathcal{A} \setminus P_i}$, thus $L_{P_i} \in F(AF\!\downarrow_{P_i}, AF, (\bigcup_{j=1\ldots n, j \neq i} L_{P_j})\!\downarrow_{AF \ominus AF\!\downarrow_{P_i}})$.

Let us then consider a collection of labellings L_{P_i} for $i = 1 \ldots n$ such that $L_{P_i} \in F(AF\!\downarrow_{P_i}, AF, (\bigcup_{j=1\ldots n, j \neq i} L_{P_j})\!\downarrow_{AF \ominus AF\!\downarrow_{P_i}})$. By the expression above, $L_{P_i} = Lab^i\!\downarrow_{P_i}$ with $Lab^i \in \mathbf{L_S}(AF)$ and $Lab^i\!\downarrow_{\mathcal{A} \setminus P_i} = (\bigcup_{j=1\ldots n, j \neq i} L_{P_j})\!\downarrow_{\mathcal{A} \setminus P_i}$. The last condition entails that, for any $i, j = 1 \ldots n$, $Lab_i\!\downarrow_{P_j} = L_{P_j}$, thus in particular $Lab^1 = \ldots = Lab^n$. As a consequence, $L_{P_1} \cup \ldots \cup L_{P_n} \in \mathbf{L_S}(AF)$. $\square$

Summing up, if complete information on the global argumentation framework is available to the local computations, then all semantics become decomposable. If no external information is available, decomposable semantics are only those that are maximally undecided (i.e. those leaving all arguments undecided). This seems to be perfectly reasonable behavior, confirming the suitability of our model and the adopted definition of decomposability.

5   The Canonical Local Function

Once the general model has been designed, the next step is to identify a way to determine a suitable local function for an argumentation semantics **S**. By 'suitable' we mean being able to enforce decomposability of **S** if this is possible, i.e. if **S** is decomposable. Inspired by the notion of standard argumentation framework of [4], the idea is to consider, for any argumentation framework with input (AF, AF', Lab) *derived* from $\mathcal{LI}$, the labellings prescribed by **S** in an argumentation framework AF^* in which the argumentation framework with input is *realized* from $\mathcal{LI}$. Consequently, any local function enforcing decomposability must include as output the restriction of the labellings of AF^* to the subframework AF. This is shown in the following proposition, whose proof is omitted due to space limitations.

Proposition 8. *Let $\mathbf{S}$ be a fully decomposable semantics under $\mathcal{LI}$, and let $(AF, AF', Lab) \in AF_{\mathcal{LI}}^{inp}$ be an argumentation framework with input derived from $\mathcal{LI}$. Let AF^* be an argumentation framework such that $AF' = \mathcal{LI}_{AF^*}(AF)$, and $Lab^* \in \mathbf{L_S}(AF^*)$ be a labelling of AF^* such that $Lab^* \downarrow_{AF' \ominus AF} = Lab$. Then, for any local function F which enforces decomposability of $\mathbf{S}$ under $\mathcal{LI}$, $Lab^* \downarrow_{AF} \in F(AF, AF', Lab)$.*

We should note that the reverse of the above proposition does not hold, i.e. F may require additional labellings w.r.t. those mentioned in the proposition. A labelling included in $F(AF, AF', Lab)$ may not play a role in forming the labellings of AF^* due to the compatibility conditions, but it may be required in a different argumentation framework. This suggests adopting the following definition of the *canonical local function*, which includes all possible labellings that play a role in some argumentation framework.

Definition 20. *Given a semantics $\mathbf{S}$ and a local information function $\mathcal{LI}$, the canonical local function $F_{\mathbf{S}}^{\mathcal{LI}}$ of $\mathbf{S}$ associated to $\mathcal{LI}$ is defined as follows. For any $(AF, AF', Lab) \in AF_{\mathcal{LI}}^{inp}$, $F_{\mathbf{S}}^{\mathcal{LI}}(AF, AF', Lab) = \{Lab^* \downarrow_{AF} \mid \exists AF^* \in SAF, AF' = \mathcal{LI}_{AF^*}(AF), Lab^* \in \mathbf{L_S}(AF^*) \wedge Lab^* \downarrow_{AF' \ominus AF} = Lab\}.*

Example 2. Consider (AF, AF', Lab) with $AF = (\{\alpha, \beta\}, \{(\alpha, \beta), (\beta, \alpha)\})$, $AF' = (\{\alpha, \beta, \gamma_1, \gamma_2\}, \{(\alpha, \beta), (\beta, \alpha), (\gamma_1, \alpha), (\gamma_2, \alpha)\})$ and $Lab = \{(\gamma_1, \mathsf{out}), (\gamma_2, \mathsf{out})\}$. Since in Example 1 $AF' = inp\mathcal{LI}_{AF^*}(AF)$, it holds that $(AF, AF', Lab) \in AF_{inp\mathcal{LI}}^{inp}$. We determine $F_{\mathbf{S}}^{\mathcal{LI}}(AF, AF', Lab)$ where $\mathbf{S}$ is the *preferred semantics*, a well-known multiple-status semantics [13]. To this purpose, we consider all $AF^* \in SAF$ such that $AF' = inp\mathcal{LI}_{AF^*}(AF)$ and $\exists Lab^* \in \mathbf{L_S}(AF^*)$ with $Lab^* \downarrow_{\{\gamma_1, \gamma_2\}} = \{(\gamma_1, \mathsf{out}), (\gamma_2, \mathsf{out})\}$. Referring again to Example 1, there are two preferred labellings in AF^*, both assigning the label in to δ_1 and the label out to γ_1 and γ_2. One of this labellings assigns in to α and out to β, the other assigns out to α and in to β, thus $\{(\alpha, \mathsf{in}), (\beta, \mathsf{out})\}$ and $\{(\alpha, \mathsf{out}), (\beta, \mathsf{in})\}$ belong to $F_{\mathbf{S}}^{\mathcal{LI}}(AF, AF', Lab)$. Finally, it can be proved that for any AF^* satisfying the conditions above there are no preferred labellings assigning different labellings to $\{\alpha, \beta\}$, thus $F_{\mathbf{S}}^{\mathcal{LI}}(AF, AF', Lab) = \{\{(\alpha, \mathsf{in}), (\beta, \mathsf{out})\}, \{(\alpha, \mathsf{out}), (\beta, \mathsf{in})\}\}$.

The following proposition shows that the output of the canonical local function is necessary to enforce decomposability (if possible).

Proposition 9. *Let $\mathbf{S}$ be a decomposable semantics under $\mathcal{LI}$ and let F be a local function which enforces decomposability of $\mathbf{S}$ under $\mathcal{LI}$. Then, $\forall (AF, AF', Lab) \in AF_{\mathcal{LI}}^{inp}$, $F_{\mathbf{S}}^{\mathcal{LI}}(AF, AF', Lab) \subseteq F(AF, AF', Lab)$.*

Proof. The proof is an immediate consequence of Proposition 8.

The reverse of this proposition does not hold since a local function F enforcing decomposability can prescribe for a subframework spurious labellings that are not compatible with those of the other subframeworks and thus do not alter the set of labellings obtained by joining the results of local computations.

On the other hand, the output of $F_S^{\mathcal{LI}}$ includes all labellings sufficient to enforce decomposability, if this is possible.

Proposition 10. *If a semantics* **S** *is fully decomposable under a local information function* $\mathcal{LI}$, *then* $F_S^{\mathcal{LI}}$ *enforces decomposability of* **S** *under* $\mathcal{LI}$.

Proof. By the hypothesis there is a local function F for $\mathcal{LI}$ such that for every argumentation framework $AF = (\mathcal{A}, att)$ and for every partition $\mathcal{P} = \{P_1, \ldots, P_n\}$

$$\mathbf{L_S}(AF) = \{L_{P_1} \cup \ldots \cup L_{P_n} \mid$$
$$L_{P_i} \in F(AF{\downarrow}_{P_i}, \mathcal{LI}_{AF}(AF{\downarrow}_{P_i}), (\textstyle\bigcup_{j=1\ldots n, j \neq i} L_{P_j}){\downarrow}_{\mathcal{LI}_{AF}(AF{\downarrow}_{P_i}) \ominus AF{\downarrow}_{P_i}})\} \, (6)$$

and we have to prove that for every $AF = (\mathcal{A}, att)$ and for every partition $\mathcal{P} = \{P_1, \ldots, P_n\}$

$$\mathbf{L_S}(AF) = \{L_{P_1} \cup \ldots \cup L_{P_n} \mid$$
$$L_{P_i} \in F_S^{\mathcal{LI}}(AF{\downarrow}_{P_i}, \mathcal{LI}_{AF}(AF{\downarrow}_{P_i}), (\textstyle\bigcup_{j=1\ldots n, j \neq i} L_{P_j}){\downarrow}_{\mathcal{LI}_{AF}(AF{\downarrow}_{P_i}) \ominus AF{\downarrow}_{P_i}})\} \, (7)$$

First, consider $Lab \equiv L_{P_1} \cup \ldots \cup L_{P_n}$ such that for every $i \in \{1, \ldots, n\}$ $L_{P_i} \in$ $F_S^{\mathcal{LI}}(AF{\downarrow}_{P_i}, \mathcal{LI}_{AF}(AF{\downarrow}_{P_i}), (\bigcup_{j=1\ldots n, j \neq i} L_{P_j}){\downarrow}_{\mathcal{LI}_{AF}(AF{\downarrow}_{P_i}) \ominus AF{\downarrow}_{P_i}})$. By Proposition 9, $F_S^{\mathcal{LI}}(AF{\downarrow}_{P_i}, \mathcal{LI}_{AF}(AF{\downarrow}_{P_i}), (\bigcup_{j=1\ldots n, j \neq i} L_{P_j}){\downarrow}_{\mathcal{LI}_{AF}(AF{\downarrow}_{P_i}) \ominus AF{\downarrow}_{P_i}}) \subseteq$ $F(AF{\downarrow}_{P_i}, \mathcal{LI}_{AF}(AF{\downarrow}_{P_i}), (\bigcup_{j=1\ldots n, j \neq i} L_{P_j}){\downarrow}_{\mathcal{LI}_{AF}(AF{\downarrow}_{P_i}) \ominus AF{\downarrow}_{P_i}})$. Thus by (6) it holds that $Lab \in \mathbf{L_S}(AF)$.

As to the other direction of the proof, take a labelling $Lab \in \mathbf{L_S}(AF)$. According to (6) $\mathbf{L_S}(AF) = L_{P_1} \cup \ldots \cup L_{P_n}$, where for each $i \in \{1, \ldots, n\}$ $L_{P_i} \in F(AF{\downarrow}_{P_i}, \mathcal{LI}_{AF}(AF{\downarrow}_{P_i}), (\bigcup_{j=1\ldots n, j \neq i} L_{P_j}){\downarrow}_{\mathcal{LI}_{AF}(AF{\downarrow}_{P_i}) \ominus AF{\downarrow}_{P_i}})$. Note in particular that $L_{P_i} = Lab{\downarrow}_{P_i}$. In order to prove condition (7) we show that $L_{P_i} \in F_S^{\mathcal{LI}}(AF{\downarrow}_{P_i}, \mathcal{LI}_{AF}(AF{\downarrow}_{P_i}), (\bigcup_{j=1\ldots n, j \neq i} L_{P_j}){\downarrow}_{\mathcal{LI}_{AF}(AF{\downarrow}_{P_i}) \ominus AF{\downarrow}_{P_i}})$.

According to the definition of canonical local function (see Definition 20) $F_S^{\mathcal{LI}}(AF{\downarrow}_{P_i}, \mathcal{LI}_{AF}(AF{\downarrow}_{P_i}), (\bigcup_{j=1\ldots n, j \neq i} L_{P_j}){\downarrow}_{\mathcal{LI}_{AF}(AF{\downarrow}_{P_i}) \ominus AF{\downarrow}_{P_i}}) =$ $\{Lab^*{\downarrow}_{AF{\downarrow}_{P_i}} \mid \exists AF^*, \mathcal{LI}_{AF}(AF{\downarrow}_{P_i}) = \mathcal{LI}_{AF^*}(AF{\downarrow}_{P_i}), Lab^* \in \mathbf{L_S}(AF^*) \wedge$ $Lab^*{\downarrow}_{\mathcal{LI}_{AF}(AF{\downarrow}_{P_i}) \ominus AF{\downarrow}_{P_i}} = (\bigcup_{j=1\ldots n, j \neq i} L_{P_j}){\downarrow}_{\mathcal{LI}_{AF}(AF{\downarrow}_{P_i}) \ominus AF{\downarrow}_{P_i}}\}$. Choosing in the last expression $AF^* = AF$, we note that letting $Lab^* = Lab$ yields all the relevant conditions to be satisfied. In particular, $\mathcal{LI}_{AF}(AF{\downarrow}_{P_i}) =$ $\mathcal{LI}_{AF^*}(AF{\downarrow}_{P_i})$ trivially holds, $Lab \in \mathbf{L_S}(AF)$ holds by assumption, and finally the condition $Lab{\downarrow}_{\mathcal{LI}_{AF}(AF{\downarrow}_{P_i}) \ominus AF{\downarrow}_{P_i}} = (\bigcup_{j=1\ldots n, j \neq i} L_{P_j}){\downarrow}_{\mathcal{LI}_{AF}(AF{\downarrow}_{P_i}) \ominus AF{\downarrow}_{P_i}}$ holds because for any i $L_{P_i} = Lab{\downarrow}_{P_i}$. Thus we get $Lab{\downarrow}_{AF{\downarrow}_{P_i}} \in$ $F_S^{\mathcal{LI}}(AF{\downarrow}_{P_i}, \mathcal{LI}_{AF}(AF{\downarrow}_{P_i}), (\bigcup_{j=1\ldots n, j \neq i} L_{P_j}){\downarrow}_{\mathcal{LI}_{AF}(AF{\downarrow}_{P_i}) \ominus AF{\downarrow}_{P_i}})$. The conclusion follows noting that $Lab{\downarrow}_{AF{\downarrow}_{P_i}} = Lab{\downarrow}_{P_i} = L_{P_i}$. $\square$

The canonical local function is pivotal for investigating the decomposability property of a semantics, since it allows one to fix without loss of generality the local function in the condition of Definition 19. In particular, according to Proposition 10 the proof that a semantics **S** is fully decomposable under $\mathcal{LI}$ can focus on this condition with $F = F_{\mathbf{S}}^{\mathcal{LI}}$, and conversely to show that a semantics is not decomposable it is sufficient to identify an argumentation framework and a partition where the same condition is not satisfied by $F_{\mathbf{S}}^{\mathcal{LI}}$.

An important question is then how to identify the definition of the canonical local function. To answer this question, one needs to consider the specific semantics definition, which is outside the scope of the present paper. Here we prove that such a function can be generated by a *standard argumentation framework function*, which associates to any realized argumentation framework with input a finite set of argumentation frameworks in which this argumentation framework with input is realized.

Definition 21. *Given a local information function $\mathcal{LI}$ and a semantics **S**, a standard argumentation framework function f_{ST} from $\mathcal{LI}$ under **S** is a (possibly partial) function which associates to any argumentation framework with input $(AF, AF', Lab) \in AF_{\mathcal{LI}}^{inp}$ a finite set of argumentation frameworks such that $f_{ST}(AF, AF', Lab) \subseteq \{AF^* \mid (AF, AF', Lab) \in RAF_{\mathcal{LI}, AF^*, \mathbf{S}}^{inp}\}$.*

Note that $f_{ST}(AF, AF', Lab)$ is not defined, i.e. returns the empty set, if $(AF, AF', Lab) \notin RAF_{\mathcal{LI}, \mathbf{S}}^{inp}$.

The following definition clarifies the relationship between standard argumentation framework functions and local functions. Intuitively, a local function F is generated by a standard argumentation framework function f_{ST} if the argumentation frameworks returned by f_{ST} for any argumentation framework with input allows one to construct the output of F, thus providing in a sense a complete characterization of the argumentation framework with input.

Definition 22. *A local function F for a local information function $\mathcal{LI}$ is generated by a standard argumentation framework function f_{ST} from $\mathcal{LI}$ under **S** if for any $(AF, AF', Lab) \in AF_{\mathcal{LI}}^{inp}$ it holds that*

$$F(AF, AF', Lab) = \{Lab^* \downarrow_{AF} \mid \exists AF^* \in f_{ST}(AF, AF', Lab), Lab^* \in \mathbf{L_S}(AF^*),$$
$$Lab^* \downarrow_{AF' \ominus AF} = Lab\}$$

There is always a standard argumentation framework function that generates the canonical local function.

Proposition 11. *Given a semantics **S** and a local information function $\mathcal{LI}$, there exists a standard argumentation framework function f_{ST} from $\mathcal{LI}$ under **S** which generates the canonical local function $F_{\mathbf{S}}^{\mathcal{LI}}$.*

Proof. We construct f_{ST} as follows. Taking into account Definition 20, for any $(AF, AF', Lab) \in AF_{\mathcal{LI}}^{inp}$ the output of $F_{\mathbf{S}}^{\mathcal{LI}}(AF, AF', Lab)$ can be expressed as

$$\bigcup_{AF^*:AF'=\mathcal{LI}_{AF^*}(AF)} \{Lab^* \downarrow_{AF} \mid Lab^* \in \mathbf{L_S}(AF^*) \wedge Lab^* \downarrow_{AF' \ominus AF} = Lab\}$$

Since the number of labellings of AF, i.e. the cardinality of $\mathfrak{L}(AF)$, is 3^n where n is the number of arguments in AF, obviously the number of distinct labellings $Lab^* \downarrow_{AF}$ in the set above is finite as well. Thus there is a finite set of argumentation frameworks, that we let as $f_{ST}(AF, AF', Lab)$, such that

$$F_S^{\mathcal{L}\mathcal{I}}(AF, AF', Lab) =$$
$$\bigcup_{AF^* \in f_{ST}(AF, AF', Lab)} \{Lab^* \downarrow_{AF} \mid Lab^* \in \mathbf{L_S}(AF^*) \wedge Lab^* \downarrow_{AF' \ominus AF} = Lab\}$$

This corresponds to our desired f_{ST} (see Definition 22).   □

6   Discussion and Conclusion

In this paper, we have devised a model for studying the decomposability of argumentation semantics in Dung's abstract argumentation setting. The model corresponds to a generalization of the definitions introduced in a previous paper: it encompasses all possible kinds of local information available for the local computations, under some mild constraints. In this general model, we have proved a monotone relationship between the degree of information available locally and the set of decomposable semantics, and we have investigated the range of capabilities of local information in allowing decomposability of semantics, by determining the sets of decomposable semantics in the two extreme situations concerning the availability of local information. Furthermore, we have identified in general terms a local function for any semantics that enforces decomposability whenever possible, i.e. when the semantics is decomposable. This represents a reference point to prove or disprove the decomposability of a specific semantics.

Many future directions of this work can be envisaged, both at the level of the general model and its instantiation with specific semantics.

At the abstract level, an interesting issue concerns the possible relationship between decomposability w.r.t. a partition selector and decomposability under a local information function. For instance, the fact that a semantics is decomposable when the partition elements coincide with the strongly connected components of the argumentation framework may imply that, if the available local information includes such components (and possibly some neighboring part), the semantics is decomposable. This relation could be investigated in general terms.

Moreover, further investigation may be devoted to the notion of the canonical local function. For a semantics, there might be various standard argumentation framework functions that generate the canonical local function. An interesting issue is to identify a minimal one, i.e. minimizing the number of argumentation frameworks associated with each argumentation framework with input. A related issue concerns the identification of particular conditions on the local information function that allows one to identify a local function able to enforce decomposability (if this is possible) and that can be generated by a standard argumentation framework function which associates to any argumentation framework with input a singleton, i.e. an argumentation framework only. This happens for some semantics in [4], where the local information involves direct attackers only.

Turning to the level of specific semantics, a first issue is to identify for the semantics available in the literature the canonical local function (or one of its variations as described above) in an explicit form. This will be useful for studying decomposability under different local information functions and, possibly, determining the minimal local information sufficient to guarantee decomposability.

References

1. Atkinson, K., et al.: Towards artificial argumentation. AI Mag. **38**(3), 25–36 (2017)
2. Baroni, P., Caminada, M., Giacomin, M.: An introduction to argumentation semantics. Knowl. Eng. Rev. **26**(4), 365–410 (2011)
3. Baroni, P., Giacomin, M.: On principle-based evaluation of extension-based argumentation semantics. Artif. Intell. (Spec. Issue Argument. A.I.) **171**(10/15), 675–700 (2007)
4. Baroni, P., Boella, G., Cerutti, F., Giacomin, M., van der Torre, L.W.N., Villata, S.: On the input/output behavior of argumentation frameworks. Artif. Intell. **217**, 144–197 (2014)
5. Baroni, P., Giacomin, M.: Some considerations on epistemic and practical reasoning in abstract argumentation. In: Proceedings of the 2nd Workshop on Advances in Argumentation In Artificial Intelligence, pp. 1–5 (2018)
6. Baumann, R., Brewka, G.: Analyzing the equivalence zoo in abstract argumentation. In: Leite, J., Son, T.C., Torroni, P., van der Torre, L., Woltran, S. (eds.) CLIMA 2013. LNCS (LNAI), vol. 8143, pp. 18–33. Springer, Heidelberg (2013). https://doi.org/10.1007/978-3-642-40624-9_2
7. Baumann, R., Brewka, G., Wong, R.: Splitting argumentation frameworks: an empirical evaluation. In: Modgil, S., Oren, N., Toni, F. (eds.) TAFA 2011. LNCS (LNAI), vol. 7132, pp. 17–31. Springer, Heidelberg (2012). https://doi.org/10.1007/978-3-642-29184-5_2
8. Baumann, R.: Splitting an argumentation framework. In: Delgrande, J.P., Faber, W. (eds.) LPNMR 2011. LNCS (LNAI), vol. 6645, pp. 40–53. Springer, Heidelberg (2011). https://doi.org/10.1007/978-3-642-20895-9_6
9. Caminada, M.: On the issue of reinstatement in argumentation. In: Fisher, M., van der Hoek, W., Konev, B., Lisitsa, A. (eds.) JELIA 2006. LNCS (LNAI), vol. 4160, pp. 111–123. Springer, Heidelberg (2006). https://doi.org/10.1007/11853886_11
10. Caminada, M.W.A.: A labelling approach for ideal and stage semantics. Argument Comput. **2**(1), 1–21 (2011)
11. Cerutti, F., Giacomin, M., Vallati, M., Zanella, M.: A SCC recursive meta-algorithm for computing preferred labellings in abstract argumentation. In: Proceedings of the 14th International Conference on Principles of Knowledge Representation and Reasoning (KR 2014) (2014, to appear)
12. Cerutti, F., Tachmazidis, I., Vallati, M., Batsakis, S., Giacomin, M., Antoniou, G.: Exploiting parallelism for hard problems in abstract argumentation. In: Proceedings of the 29th AAAI Conference on Artificial Intelligence, vol. 29 (2015)
13. Dung, P.M.: On the acceptability of arguments and its fundamental role in non-monotonic reasoning, logic programming and n-person games. Artif. Intell. **77**, 321–357 (1995)
14. Gabbay, D.M.: Fibring argumentation frames. Stud. Log. **93**(2–3), 231–295 (2009)

15. Giacomin, M.: Handling heterogeneous disagreements through abstract argumentation (extended abstract). In: An, B., Bazzan, A., Leite, J., Villata, S., van der Torre, L. (eds.) PRIMA 2017. LNCS (LNAI), vol. 10621, pp. 3–11. Springer, Cham (2017). https://doi.org/10.1007/978-3-319-69131-2_1

16. Liao, B., Huang, H.: Partial semantics of argumentation: basic properties and empirical results. J. Log. Comput. **23**(3), 541–562 (2013)

17. Liao, B., Jin, L., Koons, R.C.: Dynamics of argumentation systems: a division-based method. Artif. Intell. **175**, 1790–1814 (2011)

18. Rienstra, T., Perotti, A., Villata, S., Gabbay, D.M., van der Torre, L.: Multi-sorted argumentation. In: Modgil, S., Oren, N., Toni, F. (eds.) TAFA 2011. LNCS (LNAI), vol. 7132, pp. 215–231. Springer, Heidelberg (2012). https://doi.org/10.1007/978-3-642-29184-5_14

19. Villata, S., Boella, G., van Der Torre, L.: Argumentation patterns. In: Proceedings of ARGMAS 2011 8th International Workshop on Argumentation in Multi-Agent Systems, pp. 133–150 (2011)

Abstract Argumentation with Qualitative Uncertainty: An Analysis in Dynamic Logic

Andreas Herzig[1] and Antonio Yuste-Ginel[2(✉)]

[1] IRIT, Toulouse, France
herzig@irit.fr
[2] Departamento de Filosofía, Universidad de Málaga, Málaga, Spain

Abstract. We extend the existing encoding of abstract argumentation frameworks in DL-PA (Dynamic Logic of Propositional Assignments) in order to capture different formalisms for arguing with qualitative forms of uncertainty. More in particular, we encode the main reasoning tasks of (rich) incomplete argumentation frameworks and control argumentation frameworks. After that, and inspired by our encoding, we define and study a new class of structures that are shown to be maximally expressive: *constrained incomplete argumentation frameworks*.

Keywords: Incomplete argumentation frameworks · Dynamic logic of propositional assignments · Control argumentation frameworks

1 Introduction

Formal argumentation has been proved to be a successful approach to non-monotonic reasoning (see e.g. [15]), among many other applications [2,12]. Within the studies directed to provide a formal model for argument-based inference, abstract models of argumentation play a crucial role, as they answer a rather fundamental question: how should a rational agent choose among a conflicting set of arguments those that are better justified? The adjective *abstract* stresses that these models disregard the nature and structure of arguments, in order to focus on the different semantics through which one could give a precise answer to the question above. The foremost abstract model of argumentation is the use of directed graphs, first proposed by Dung in [23] under the name of *argumentation frameworks* (AFs), where nodes stand for arguments and arrows stand for attacks among arguments.

Andreas Herzig is partially supported by the EU ICT-48 2020 project TAILOR (No. 952215). Antonio Yuste-Ginel gratefully acknowledges funding received from the PhD grant No. MECDFPU 2016/04113. We thank Sylvie Doutre and Jean-Guy Mailly for previous discussions on the topic of this paper, specially for triggering the idea of constrained incomplete argumentation frameworks.

© Springer Nature Switzerland AG 2021
P. Baroni et al. (Eds.): CLAR 2021, LNAI 13040, pp. 190–208, 2021.
https://doi.org/10.1007/978-3-030-89391-0_11

Despite being an elegant and powerful tool, AFs have limited modelling capabilities for many purposes. Consequently, many extensions of Dung's model have been proposed in the literature since its publication. Examples of such extensions are the addition of a support relation [16], of recursive forms of attacks [6] and of preferences among arguments [1]. An essential limitation that AFs come equipped with is the assumption that the formalized agent has perfect knowledge about the relevant arguments and attacks of the debate (that is, about the structure of the AF). This turns out to be an important shortcoming in adversarial contexts, where usually one wants to model the information (i.e., the part of an AF) that an agent thinks that her opponent entertains, and thus uncertainty naturally pops up into the picture. However, the assumption of perfect knowledge has been relaxed through the study of extensions of AFs that include different forms of uncertainty, either through the use of probability [28] or through qualitative methods. Among the second group of approaches, *incomplete argumentation frameworks* (IAFs) [8–11,24] and *control argumentation frameworks* (CAFs) [18,31] have recently received a lot of attention, resulting in a precise complexity map of the different associated reasoning tasks as well as some applications [19].

Concurrently, a large number of works within formal argumentation have focused on building a suitable logical theory for reasoning about argumentation formalisms, with a special focus on AFs and their dynamics (see [13] for a recent survey on the topic). The *dynamic logic of propositional assignments* (DL-PA) [4] has been shown to be a useful tool for this enterprise [20–22]. DL-PA is a well-behaved variant of *propositional dynamic logic* (PDL) [26], where atomic programs are restricted to assignments of propositional variables to either Truth or Falsity. It is expressive enough to capture all standard argumentation semantics. When compared to encodings in propositional logic, DL-PA can capture semantics that incorporate minimality or maximality criteria more succinctly. Moreover, its advantages over other encodings of AFs in equally succinct languages (e.g. *quantified Boolean formulas*) have also been highlighted [21].

Contribution and Structure. In this paper, we explain how to extend the machinery of [20–22] so as to use DL-PA for reasoning about different formalisms for arguing with qualitative uncertainty. In particular, and after introducing the basic tools (Sects. 2 and 3) we encode in DL-PA programs the main reasoning tasks concerning *incomplete argumentation frameworks* (Sect. 4), their enriched version (called *rich incomplete argumentation frameworks* [29]) (Sect. 5), and *control argumentation frameworks* (Sect. 6). After that, and inspired by our encoding, we define and study the expressive power of a new class of structures for arguing with qualitative uncertainty: *constrained incomplete argumentation frameworks*, whose naturally associated reasoning tasks are also encodable in DL-PA (Sect. 7). We close the paper by discussing related work and pointing out paths for future research in Sect. 8. Most of the proofs are merely sketched for space reasons, details are left to the reader.

2 Background

General Notation for Sets of Arguments and Attack Relations. We assume a finite, non-empty set of arguments $\mathcal{U}$ (the *universe*) as fixed from now on. We moreover assume that $\mathcal{U}$ is big enough to accommodate our examples. Sets of arguments (denoted A, sometimes with a superscript) are supposed to be subsets of $\mathcal{U}$; and all conflict relations (denoted R, sometimes with a superscript) are supposed to be defined over $\mathcal{U}$ (i.e., $R \subseteq \mathcal{U} \times \mathcal{U}$). Given $A \subseteq \mathcal{U}$ and $R \subseteq \mathcal{U} \times \mathcal{U}$, we use $R_{|A}$ to abbreviate $R \cap (A \times A)$ (the restriction of R to A).

2.1 Abstract Argumentation Frameworks and Their Stable Semantics

An **argumentation framework** (AF) is a directed graph (A, R) [23], where A stands for a set of arguments and R stands for a conflict-based relation among them (typically, an attack relation).[1] Argumentation semantics are meant to capture the informal notion of a reasonable position in a debate (i.e. in an AF). There is a large number of available semantics studied in the literature (see [5]). For the sake of presentation we stick to stable semantics, but our approach can be straightforwardly extended to the rest of standard semantics defined by Dung [23], namely admissible, complete, grounded and preferred: it suffices to combine our results with those of [20]. A set of arguments $E \subseteq A$ is a **stable extension** if (i) $(E \times E) \cap R = \emptyset$ ('E is conflict-free') and (ii) $x \in A \setminus E$ implies that there is a $y \in E$ such that $(y, x) \in R$ ('E attacks every argument outside itself'). We note $\mathsf{st}(A, R)$ the set of all stable extensions of (A, R). An argument $x \in E$ is said to be credulously (resp. sceptically) **accepted** if it belongs to at least one (resp. every) extension.

As an example, for the AF (A_0, R_0) represented in the picture below we have $\mathsf{st}(A_0, R_0) = \{\{b, e\}, \{c, d\}\}$.

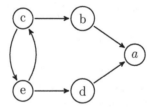

2.2 Dynamic Logic of Propositional Assignments (DL-PA)

We shall use DL-PA as a the general logical framework of this paper. We start by associating several kinds of propositional variables to arguments. To every

---

[1] As $A \subseteq \mathcal{U}$, we actually focus on *finite* AFs, as most of the literature does. This is an essential limitation of our approach, as our encodings use formulas parametrised by $\mathcal{U}$, which makes finiteness of $\mathcal{U}$ necessary. Capturing some argumentation semantics for the general case has been shown to require powerful logical languages, such as modal μ-calculus for the grounded semantics [25].

set of arguments $A \subseteq \mathcal{U}$ we associate the set of awareness variables $\mathsf{AW}_A = \{\mathsf{aw}_x \mid x \in A\}$, and the set of acceptance variables $\mathsf{IN}_A = \{\mathsf{in}_x \mid x \in A\}$. Furthermore, to every relation $R \subseteq \mathcal{U} \times \mathcal{U}$ we associate the set of attack variables $\mathsf{ATT}_R = \{\mathsf{r}_{x,y} \mid (x,y) \in R\}$. The set of propositional variables of our logic is then

$$\mathsf{Prp}_\mathcal{U} = \mathsf{AW}_\mathcal{U} \cup \mathsf{IN}_\mathcal{U} \cup \mathsf{ATT}_{\mathcal{U} \times \mathcal{U}}$$
$$= \{\mathsf{aw}_x \mid x \in \mathcal{U}\} \cup \{\mathsf{in}_x \mid x \in \mathcal{U}\} \cup \{\mathsf{r}_{x,y} \mid (x,y) \in \mathcal{U}^2\}.$$

Then formulas and programs of DL-PA are defined by mutual recursion:

$$\varphi ::= p \mid \neg\varphi \mid (\varphi \wedge \varphi) \mid [\pi]\varphi$$
$$\pi ::= +p \mid -p \mid \varphi? \mid (\pi;\pi) \mid (\pi \cup \pi) \mid \pi^{\smile}$$

where p ranges over $\mathsf{Prp}_\mathcal{U}$. The formula $[\pi]\varphi$ reads "φ is true after every possible execution of π". The program $+p$ makes p true and $-p$ makes p false. The program $\varphi?$ tests that φ is true (and fails when it is false). The program $\pi_1;\pi_2$ is the sequential composition of π_1 and π_2, and $\pi_1 \cup \pi_2$ is their nondeterministic composition. Finally, $\pi^{\smile}$ is the execution of π 'the other way round'. As usual, skip abbreviates the program $\top?$.

Formulas of DL-PA are interpreted over classical propositional valuations, i.e., subsets of $\mathsf{Prp}_\mathcal{U}$. Programs are interpreted as binary relations on the set of all valuations. We use v, v', v'' to denote valuations. Again by mutual recursion, the interpretation of modal formulas is:

$$v \models [\pi]\varphi \text{ if } (v,v') \in ||\pi|| \text{ implies } v' \models \varphi,$$

and the interpretation of programs $||\pi|| \subseteq 2^{\mathsf{Prp}_\mathcal{U}} \times 2^{\mathsf{Prp}_\mathcal{U}}$ is:

$$||+p|| = \{(v,v') \mid v' = v \cup \{p\}\}$$
$$||-p|| = \{(v,v') \mid v' = v \setminus \{p\}\}$$
$$||\varphi?|| = \{(v,v) \mid v \models \varphi\}$$
$$||\pi;\pi'|| = ||\pi|| \circ ||\pi'||$$
$$||\pi \cup \pi'|| = ||\pi|| \cup ||\pi'||$$
$$||\pi^{\smile}|| = ||\pi||^{-1}$$

A formula φ is DL-PA satisfiable if $v \models \varphi$ for some v, and it is valid if $v \models \varphi$ for every v. It is known that satisfiability, validity, and model-checking are all PSPACE complete decision problems [3].

From Valuations to AFs and Backward. Each propositional valuation $v \subseteq \mathsf{Prp}_\mathcal{U}$ represents an AF (A_v, R_v), where $A_v = \{x \in \mathcal{U} \mid \mathsf{aw}_x \in v\}$ and $R_v = \{(x,y) \in \mathcal{U}^2 \mid \mathsf{r}_{x,y} \in v\}_{|A_v}$. The other way round, each AF (A, R) can be represented as a propositional valuation $v_{(A,R)} = \{\mathsf{aw}_x \mid x \in A\} \cup \{\mathsf{r}_{x,y} \mid (x,y) \in R\}$. Note that if we start with a valuation v' we have that $v_{(A_{v'}, R_{v'})} = v'$ does not generally hold (because a valuation can contain an attack variable $\mathsf{r}_{a,b}$ with neither aw_a nor aw_b being members of it). If we, however, start with an AF (A', R') we have that $(A_{v_{(A',R')}}, R_{v_{(A',R')}}) = (A', R')$ is always the case.

3 Formalisms for Arguing with Qualitative Uncertainty

We now review three formalisms for representing qualitative uncertainty about abstract argumentation frameworks. We start by presenting *control argumentation frameworks* (CAFs) [18], which besides uncertainty, also include a dynamic component. After that, we introduce *rich incomplete argumentation frameworks* (rIAFs) [29] and *incomplete argumentation frameworks* (IAFs) [8] as special cases of CAFs.

A **control argumentation framework** is a triple $\mathsf{CAF} = (F, C, U)$ where:

- $F = (A^F, R^F)$ is the *fixed part*, with $R^F \subseteq (A^F \cup A^?) \times (A^F \cup A^?)$, and both A^F and $A^?$ being two finite sets of arguments;
- $U = (A^?, (R^? \cup R^{\leftrightarrow}))$ is the *uncertain part*, where

$$R^?, R^{\leftrightarrow} \subseteq (A^F \cup A^?) \times (A^F \cup A^?)$$

and $R^{\leftrightarrow}$ is symmetric and irreflexive;[2]
- $C = (A^C, R^C)$ is the *control part* where A^C is yet another finite set of arguments and

$$R^C \subseteq (A^C \times (A^F \cup A^? \cup A^C)) \cup ((A^F \cup A^? \cup A^C) \times A^C);$$

- A^F, $A^?$, and A^C are pairwise disjoint; and
- $R^F, R^?, R^{\leftrightarrow}$, and R^C are pairwise disjoint.

Standard AFs can be viewed as CAFs with empty uncertain and control parts: CAFs where $A^?$, $R^?$, $R^{\leftrightarrow}$, and A^C are empty (and therefore R^C is empty by definition too).

Given a $\mathsf{CAF} = (F, C, U)$, a **control configuration** is a subset of control arguments $\mathsf{CFG} \subseteq A^C$. The *CAF associated to* CFG is $\mathsf{CAF_{CFG}} = (F, C_{\mathsf{CFG}}, U)$ where $C_{\mathsf{CFG}} = (\mathsf{CFG}, R^C \mid_{A^F \cup A^? \cup A_{\mathsf{CFG}}})$.

Epistemic Interpretation of CAFs. In order to throw some intuition, let us briefly recall the epistemic interpretation of CAFs provided in [32]. A CAF can be thought as modelling an agent (the proponent) who is trying to convince another agent (the opponent) to accept certain argument(s). Under this interpretation, F represents the arguments and attacks that the proponent knows the opponent knows. U represents the argument and attacks such that the proponent is not sure about how the opponent perceives them. In particular, $R^{\leftrightarrow}$ is an conflict relation such that the proponent knows that the opponent knows that these attacks hold, but the direction of the attack according to the opponent's perception is unknown to the proponent. This makes perfect sense if we understand conflict relations as defeat relations (as done in the field of structured argumentation [14]). In this picture, the proponent can be sure about the opponent's perception of at least one of the attacks between a and b (for instance, because

---

[2] Symmetry and irreflexivity of $R^{\leftrightarrow}$ are not assumed in the original paper [18], but as pointed out by [30,31], both assumptions can be made without loss of generality.

they have contradictory conclusions), but the proponent still lacks information about the opponent's knowledge so as to know how he (the opponent) perceives the relative strength of a and b, and hence the direction of the defeat. As for $C = (A^C, R^C)$, it is supposed to be the part of the framework that depends on the actions of the proponent. More precisely, it can be interpreted as private, communicable knowledge of the proponent, i.e., the arguments and attacks such that (i) they are known to the proponent, (ii) they are unknown to the opponent (and the proponent knows this). Moreover, CAFs make a strong assumption about control arguments: (iii) the proponent is completely sure about the effects of communicating each of them.

Example 1. With the above interpretation in mind, consider the CAF $\mathsf{CAF}_0 = (F_0, C_0, U_0)$ where $A_0^F = \{a\}$, $R_0^F = \{(f, e)\}$, $A_0^U = \{c, e, f\}$, $R^U = \{(f, c)\}$, $R^{\leftrightarrow} = \{(c, e), (e, c)\}$, $A_0^C = \{b, d\}$ and $R_0^C = \{(b, a), (d, a), (c, b), (e, d)\}$.
We represent CAF_0 graphically as follows:

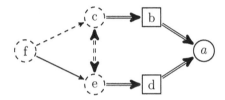

where solid circles stand for fixed arguments, normal arrows stand for fixed attacks, dashed circles stand for uncertain arguments, dashed arrows stand for uncertain attacks, dashed double arrows stand for symmetric attacks, squares stand for control arguments, and double arrows for control attacks.

A fundamental notion for reasoning about CAFs (and the rest of formalisms for qualitative uncertainty that will be studied here) is that of completion.

A **completion** of $\mathsf{CAF} = (F, C, U)$ is any AF (A^*, R^*) such that:

– $(A^F \cup A^C) \subseteq A^* \subseteq (A^F \cup A^C \cup A^?)$;
– $(R^F \cup R^C)_{|A^*} \subseteq R^* \subseteq (R^F \cup R^C \cup R^? \cup R^{\leftrightarrow})_{|A^*}$; and
– for every x, y: $(x, y) \in R^{\leftrightarrow}$ and $x, y \in A^*$ implies $(x, y) \in R^*$ or $(y, x) \in R^*$.

A completion can be seen as a provisional removal of uncertainty or, in epistemic terms, as a possible world (cf. [27,32]). This removal lets the proponent reason under the assumption that the opponent's AF is such-and-such. If we identify standard AFs (A, R) with CAFs with empty uncertain and control parts then (A, R) is the unique completion of itself.

The completions of CAF_0 are depicted in Table 1.

A **rich incomplete AF** [29] is a pair $\mathsf{rIAF} = (F, U)$ where F and U are exactly as in a CAF. A rich incomplete AF can be informally understood as a CAF with empty A^C and R^C, i.e., where we abstract away from the dynamics. We sometimes unravel F and U and represent rich incomplete AFs as tuples of the form $(A^F, A^?, R^F, R^?, R^{\leftrightarrow})$. The notion of completion is easily adapted to rIAFs.

Table 1. Completions of CAF_0. The column [**1, 2,..., 6**] and the row [**A, B, C**] are just included for numbering purposes. Empty cells do *not* represent the empty completion $(\emptyset, \emptyset)$.

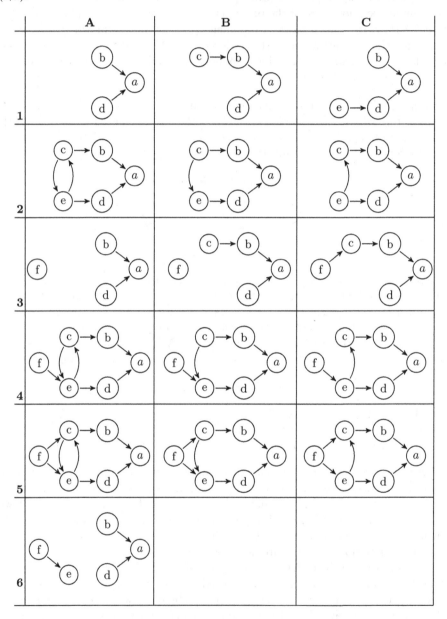

Example 2. Let $\mathsf{rIAF}_0 = (A_0^F, A_0^U, R_0^F, R_0^U, R_0^\leftrightarrow)$ where $A_0^F = \{a, b, d\}$, $A_0^U = \{c, e, f\}$, $R_0^F = \{(b,a), (d,a), (c,b), (e,d), (f,e)\}$, $R_0^U = \{(f,c)\}$, and $R_0^\leftrightarrow = \{(c,e), (e,c)\}$. Note that rIAF_0 has exactly the same set of completions as CAF_0 (from Example 1), that is, all those depicted in Table 1. Actually rIAF_0 can be seen as the full development of CAF_0, i.e., CAF_0 where all the control arguments have been used by the proponent.

We represent rIAF_0 graphically as follows:

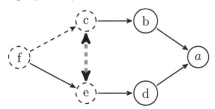

An **incomplete AF** [8] (IAF), is a rich IAF with empty $R^\leftrightarrow$. We represent IAFs as tuples of the form $(A, A^?, R, R^?)$. There are some notable subclasses of IAFs, well-studied in the literature, namely **attack-incomplete AFs** (att-IAFs, for short), which are IAFs with empty $A^?$; and **argument-incomplete** AFs (arg-IAFs, for short), which are IAFs with empty $R^?$. The notion of completion is again straightforwardly relativised to IAFs.

Example 3. Let us consider $\mathsf{IAF}_0 = (A_0^F, A_0^U, R_0^F, R_0^U)$, where $A_0^F = \{a, b, d\}$, $A_0^U = \{c, e, f\}$, $R_0^F = \{(b,a), (d,a), (c,b), (e,d), (c,e), (e,c), (f,e)\}$ and $R_0^U = \{(f,c)\}$, graphically represented below. The set of completions of IAF_0 is the one depicted in Table 1 except for the cells **B2**, **C2**, **B4**, **C4**, **B5** and **C5** (as the symmetric attack $c \leftrightarrow e$ is now fixed).

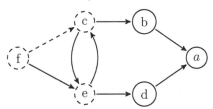

Given a control AF, CAF, we note completions(CAF) its set of completions (and we do the same for IAFs and rIAFs).

Classic reasoning tasks such as extension enumeration or argument acceptance have been generalized from AFs to both IAFs and rIAFs. As an example, let us consider the following one:

stable-Necessary-Credulous-Acceptance (st-NCA)
Given: A rich IAF $\mathsf{rIAF} = (A^F, A^?, R^F, R^?, R^\leftrightarrow)$ and an argument $a \in A^F$.
Question: Is it true that for every $(A^*, R^*) \in$ completions(rIAF) there is an $E \in \mathsf{st}(A^*, R^*)$ such that $a \in E$?

We can replace st by any other semantics as well as switch quantifiers in the definition above in order to obtain different variants of the problem.

Regarding CAFs, defining relevant reasoning tasks gets slightly more complicated, since we have to take into account their dynamic aspect (the control part). In this context, a natural reasoning task is finding a control configuration (that is, a set of control arguments) such that a certain argument gets accepted by the opponent after the latter learns about them. Just as before, acceptability is then relativised to quantification over completions and extensions. As an example, let us consider:

---

stable-Necessary-Sceptical-Controllability (st-NSCon)

Given: A control argumentation framework
$CAF = (F, C, U)$ and an argument $a \in A^F$.
Question: Is it true that there is a configuration
$CFG \subseteq A_C$ such that for every completion (A^*, R^*)
of CAF_{CFG} and for every $E \in st(A^*, R^*), a \in E$?

Expressivity via Sets of Completions. Following [29], we can compare the modelling power of each of the previous formalisms for arguing with uncertainty (IAFs, rIAFs and possibly others) using the sets of completions that they can represent. Let $(att\text{-}, arg\text{-})\mathcal{IAF}$ (resp. $\mathcal{RIAF}, \mathcal{CAF}$) denote the class of all (att-,arg-)IAFs (resp. rIAFs, CAFs), and let $\mathcal{X}$ and $\mathcal{Y}$ be metavariables denoting arbitrary classes of the previous list. We say that $\mathcal{X}$ is **at least as expressive as** $\mathcal{Y}$ (in symbols, $\mathcal{X} \succeq \mathcal{Y}$) if, for every $Y \in \mathcal{Y}$ there is a $X \in \mathcal{X}$ such that completions(X) = completions(Y). We use $\succ$ to denote the strict counterpart of $\succeq$, we use $\preceq$ to denote the inverse of $\succeq$, and we use $\equiv$ to abbreviate $\succeq \cap \preceq$. For instance, in [29], it was proved that $\mathcal{RIAF} \succ \mathcal{IAF}$.

4   Incomplete AFs in DL-PA

Our first aim is to capture incomplete AFs using DL-PA. More precisely, given an incomplete argumentation framework $IAF = (A, A^?, R, R^?)$, we want to design a program $makeComp^{IAF}$ such that every valuation that is $makeComp^{IAF}$-accessible from the valuation v_{IAF} associated to IAF represents a completion of IAF and, vice versa, every completion of IAF is represented by at least one $makeComp^{IAF}$-successor of v_{IAF}.

First of all, we **associate to IAF its valuation**

$$v_{IAF} = v_{(A^F, R^F)}$$
$$= AW_{A^F} \cup ATT_{R^F}$$
$$= \{aw_x \mid x \in A^F\} \cup \{r_{x,y} \mid (x, y) \in R^F\}.$$

Note that $(A_{v_{IAF}}, R_{v_{IAF}})$ is already a completion of IAF: it is the smallest one, where only fixed arguments and fixed attacks between them are considered. What we need to do in order to compute all the completions of IAF is varying the value of propositional variables representing arguments in $A^?$ and attacks in $R^?$. Let us first define the DL-PA program that computes all possible combinations of variables in a given set. Let $P = \{p_1, ..., p_n\}$ be a subset of $\mathtt{Prp}_\mathcal{U}$ and define

$$\mathsf{vary}(\mathsf{P}) = (+p_1 \cup -p_1); ...; (+p_n \cup -p_n).$$

(Note that the order of the propositional variables does not matter.) With this abbreviation at hand we are able to define the program to compute the completions we are after:

$$\mathsf{makeComp}^{\mathsf{IAF}} = \mathsf{vary}(\mathsf{AW}_{A^?}); \mathsf{vary}(\mathsf{ATT}_{R^?}).$$

The next proposition shows that our original target is reached.

Proposition 1. *Let* $\mathsf{IAF} = (A, A^?, R, R^?)$, *then*

- *If* $(v_{\mathsf{IAF}}, v) \in ||\mathsf{makeComp}^{\mathsf{IAF}}||$, *then* $(A_v, R_v) \in \mathsf{completions}(\mathsf{IAF})$.
- *If* $(A^*, R^*) \in \mathsf{completions}(\mathsf{IAF})$, *then* $(v_{\mathsf{IAF}}, v_{(A^*,R^*)}) \in ||\mathsf{makeComp}^{\mathsf{IAF}}||$.

Proof. For the first item, suppose $(v_{\mathsf{IAF}}, v) \in ||\mathsf{makeComp}^{\mathsf{IAF}}||$. We recall that $||\mathsf{vary}(P)|| = \{(v', v'') \mid (v' \setminus v'') \cup (v'' \setminus v') \subseteq P\}$ for any set of atoms P [21].[3] Hence, by the semantics of the sequential composition operator ;, we have that $(v_{\mathsf{IAF}}, v) \in ||\mathsf{makeComp}^{\mathsf{IAF}}||$ amounts to saying that the set of variables whose truth values differs from v_{IAF} to v, formally the set $(v \setminus v_{\mathsf{IAF}}) \cup (v_{\mathsf{IAF}} \setminus v)$, must be a subset of $\mathsf{AW}_{A^?} \cup \mathsf{ATT}_{R^?}$. But, since all variables from $\mathsf{AW}_{A^?} \cup \mathsf{ATT}_{R^?}$ are false in v_{IAF} by definition, we have that $v = v_{\mathsf{IAF}} \cup P$ for some $P \subseteq \mathsf{AW}_{A^?} \cup \mathsf{ATT}_{R^?}$. From this statement, and applying the definition of (A_v, R_v) and the one of completion, we obtain that $(A_v, R_v) \in \mathsf{completions}(\mathsf{IAF})$.

For the second item, suppose that $(A^*, R^*) \in \mathsf{completions}(\mathsf{IAF})$, which amounts to $A^F \subseteq A^* \subseteq A^F \cup A^?$ and $R^F_{|A^*} \subseteq R^* \subseteq (R^F \cup R^?)_{|A^*}$. Now, remember that $v_{(A^*,R^*)} = \mathsf{AW}_{A^*} \cup \mathsf{ATT}_{R^*}$. From the two previous statements and the definition of v_{IAF}, we can deduce that the set of variables whose truth values differ from v to $v_{(A^*,R^*)}$ must be a subset of $\mathsf{AW}_{A^?} \cup \mathsf{ATT}_{R^?}$, which, as argued before, amounts to saying that $(v_{\mathsf{IAF}}, v_{(A^*,R^*)}) \in ||\mathsf{makeComp}^{\mathsf{IAF}}||$.

Using this result together with the general technique to compute extensions provided in [20, 22], we can reduce reasoning problems in IAFs to model-checking problems in DL-PA. Note that we need an encoding of argumentation semantics that takes into account our "awareness" variables. As shown in [22], the following propositional schema characterizes the stable semantics in awareness-relativised AFs:

$$\mathsf{Stable} = \bigwedge_{x \in \mathcal{U}} \Big((\mathsf{in}_x \rightarrow \mathsf{aw}_x) \wedge$$

$$\big(\mathsf{aw}_x \rightarrow (\mathsf{in}_x \leftrightarrow \neg \bigvee_{y \in \mathcal{U}} (\mathsf{in}_y \wedge \mathsf{r}_{y,x} \wedge \mathsf{aw}_x \wedge \mathsf{aw}_y))\big)\Big).$$

---

[3] Note that vary is noted flipSome in [21].

The authors show that v is a model of Stable if and only if $\{x \in \mathcal{U} \mid \text{in}_x \in v\}$ is a stable extension of (A_v, R_v). Note that Stable is actually parametrised by $\mathcal{U}$, but we drop it to simplify notation.

The program $\text{makeExt}^{\text{st}} = \text{vary}(\text{IN}_\mathcal{U}); \text{Stable?}$ nondeterministically builds all possible stable extensions by first varying the values of the 'in' variables and then checking that a stable valuation has been obtained [20,22]. Our general technique is then illustrated by the following result.

Proposition 2. *Let* $\text{IAF} = (A, A^?, R, R^?)$, *and* $a \in A^F$, *then the answer to* st-NCA *with input* IAF *and* a *is yes iff* $v_{\text{IAF}} \models [\text{makeComp}^{\text{IAF}}]\langle\text{makeExt}^{\text{st}}\rangle\text{in}_a$.

Proof (Sketched). The result follows from the definition of the reasoning task, the correctness of $\text{makeExt}^{\text{st}}$ ([20,21]), Proposition 1, and the semantics of DL-PA. $\square$

5   Rich Incomplete AFs in DL-PA

Things get slightly more complicated when computing the completions of a rich IAF in DL-PA, since the program vary does not suffice to compute the symmetric attacks of $R^{\leftrightarrow}$. We can, however, find a specific program for this purpose.

First of all, given $\text{rIAF} = (A^F, A^?, R^F, R^?, R^{\leftrightarrow})$, we **associate to** rIAF **its valuation**

$$
\begin{aligned}
v_{\text{rIAF}} &= v_{(A^F, R^F)} \\
&= \text{AW}_{A^F} \cup \text{ATT}_{R^F} \\
&= \{\text{aw}_x \mid x \in A^F\} \cup \{r_{x,y} \mid (x,y) \in R^F\}.
\end{aligned}
$$

Note that, contrarily to what happened with IAFs, $(A_{v_{\text{rIAF}}}, R_{v_{\text{rIAF}}})$ is *not* always a completion of rIAF (this is false as soon as $R^{\leftrightarrow} \cap (A^F \times A^F)$ is not empty). Let us now define the program that will be used to compute the presence of elements of $R^{\leftrightarrow}$ in each completion. Let $\text{ATT}_R = \{r_{x_1,y_1}, ..., r_{x_n,y_n}\}$ be a set of attack variables, and define

$$
\text{dis}(\text{ATT}_R) = (+r_{x_1,y_1} \cup +r_{y_1,x_1}) ; \ldots ; (+r_{x_n,y_n} \cup +r_{y_n,x_n}).
$$

Intuitively, dis makes true at least one of the pairs from the set $\{(x_i, y_i), (y_i, x_i)\}$, for each $1 \leq i \leq n$. Moreover, when applied to symmetric relations, dis makes true either (x_i, y_i), or (y_i, x_i), or both. We have now the tools to define the program makeComp in its version for rIAFs. Let $\text{rIAF} = (A^F, A^?, R^F, R^?, R^{\leftrightarrow})$, and define

$$
\text{makeComp}^{\text{rIAF}} = \text{vary}(\text{AW}_{A^?}); \text{vary}(\text{ATT}_{R^?}); \text{dis}(\text{ATT}_{R^{\leftrightarrow}}).
$$

The following proposition shows that the above program is correct.

Proposition 3. *Let* $\text{rIAF} = (A^F, A^?, R^F, R^?, R^{\leftrightarrow})$, *then:*

- *If* $(v_{\text{rIAF}}, v) \in \|\text{makeComp}^{\text{rIAF}}\|$, *then* $(A_v, R_v) \in \text{completions}(\text{rIAF})$.

- If $(A^*, R^*) \in$ completions(rIAF), *then* $(v_{\text{rIAF}}, v_{(A^*,R^*)}) \in \|\text{makeComp}^{\text{rIAF}}\|$.

Proof (Sketched). The proof is analogous to the one of Proposition 1, but taking into account the observation that, when applied to the *symmetric* relation $R^{\leftrightarrow} = \{(x_1, y_1), (y_1, x_1), ..., (x_n, y_n), (y_n, x_n)\}$, every execution of dis(ATT$_{R^{\leftrightarrow}}$) makes true either r_{x_i,y_i}, or r_{y_i,x_i} or both, for every $1 \leq i \leq n$.

Again, acceptance problems can be reduced to model-checking problems. As an example, consider the following reduction, where st-PSA stands for *stable-Possible-Sceptical Acceptance*.

Proposition 4. *Let* rIAF $= (A^F, A^?, R^F, R^?, R^{\leftrightarrow})$, *and let* $a \in A^F$, *then the answer to* st-*PSA with input* rIAF *and* a *is yes iff*

$$v_{\text{rIAF}} \models \langle \text{makeComp}^{\text{rIAF}} \rangle [\text{makeExt}^{\text{st}}] \text{in}_a.$$

Proof (Sketched). The result follows from the definition of the reasoning problem, the correctness of makeExtst [20,21], Proposition 3, and the semantics of DL-PA.

6   Control AFs in DL-PA

We now move to control argumentation frameworks. Regarding uncertainty, control argumentation frameworks are essentially rich incomplete argumentation frameworks; however, the delicate part is their dynamic component, i.e., the control part.

First, given a CAF CAF $= (F, C, U)$, we define its **associated valuation** as

$$v_{\text{CAF}} = v_{(A^F, R^F \cup R^C)}$$
$$= \text{AW}_{A^F} \cup \text{ATT}_{R^F} \cup \text{ATT}_{R^C}$$
$$= \{\text{aw}_x \mid x \in A^F\} \cup \{r_{x,y} \mid (x,y) \in R^F\} \cup \{r_{x,y} \mid (x,y) \in R^C\}.$$

Note that v_{CAF} contains all attack variables corresponding to control attacks, but none of them appear in $(A_{v_{\text{CAF}}}, R_{v_{\text{CAF}}})$, since none of the control arguments has been communicated yet. This highlights the fact that in the epistemic interpretation of CAFs, the proponent knows how the opponent will perceive the attack relations regarding all communicable arguments (a point that might be subject to criticism).

To capture the dynamic component of CAF we define the following program:

$$\text{control}^{\text{CAF}} = \text{vary}(\text{AW}_{A^C}).$$

Intuitively, control^{CAF} nondeterministically chooses some of the possible control configurations of CAF (i.e., some subset of control arguments).

What about completions? As mentioned, if we restrict to uncertainty, CAFs are essentially rIAFs [29]. Hence, once we have computed some control configuration, it suffices to use the same program as for rIAFs:

$$\text{makeComp}^{\text{CAF}} = \text{vary}(\text{AW}_{A^?}); \text{vary}(\text{ATT}_{R^?}); \text{dis}(\text{ATT}_{R^{\leftrightarrow}}).$$

We again state a correctness result:

Proposition 5. *Let* $\mathsf{CAF} = (F, C, U)$.

- *If* $(v_{\mathsf{CAF}}, v) \in \|\mathsf{control}^{\mathsf{CAF}}; \mathsf{makeComp}^{\mathsf{CAF}}\|$, *then there is a control configuration* $\mathsf{CFG} \subseteq A^C$ *and a completion* (A^*, R^*) *of* $\mathsf{CAF}_{\mathsf{CFG}}$ *such that* $(A_v, R_v) = (A^*, R^*)$.

- *For every control configuration* $\mathsf{CFG} \subseteq A^C$ *and every* $(A^*, R^*) \in$ $\mathsf{completions}(\mathsf{CAF}_{\mathsf{CFG}})$ *there is a valuation* $v \in 2^{\mathsf{Prp}_U}$ *such that* $(v_{\mathsf{CAF}}, v) \in$ $\|\mathsf{control}^{\mathsf{CAF}}; \mathsf{makeComp}^{\mathsf{CAF}}\|$ *and* $(A_v, R_v) = (A^*, R^*)$.

Proof (Sketched). The proof is analogous to those of Propositions 1 and 3. The essential difference lies in the fact that the previous execution of $\mathsf{control}^{\mathsf{CAF}}$ is needed to nondeterministically choose a control configuration of CAF. Also, note that $\mathsf{ATT}_{R^C} \subseteq v_{\mathsf{CAF}}$ is essential for obtaining the needed control attacks in the corresponding completion.

We can then combine the previous programs with $\mathsf{makeExt}$ in order to reduce controllability problems to model-checking problems in DL-PA. As an example, consider the following.

Proposition 6. *Let* $\mathsf{CAF} = (F, C, U)$ *and* $a \in A^F$. *The answer to* st-*NSCon with input* CAF *and* a *is yes if and only if*

$$v_{\mathsf{CAF}} \models \langle \mathsf{control}^{\mathsf{CAF}} \rangle [\mathsf{makeComp}^{\mathsf{CAF}}; \mathsf{makeExt}^{st}] \mathsf{in}_a.$$

Proof (Sketched). The result follows from the definition of the reasoning task, the correctness of $\mathsf{makeExt}^{st}$ [20,21], Proposition 5, and the semantics of DL-PA.

7   Constrained Incomplete AFs and Their Encoding in DL-PA

We now move to study a very general class of structures for modelling qualitative uncertainty about AFs: *constrained incomplete AFs*. To the best of our knowledge, these structures have not been studied before in the literature. They are however inspired by the notion of *constrained AF* [17], and by the encoding of other structures in DL-PA as undertaken in this paper.

Let U be given, a **constrained incomplete AF** (cIAF) is a pair $\mathsf{cIAF} = (U, \varphi)$ where φ is a Boolean formula built over the set of propositional variables $\mathsf{AW}_U \cup \mathsf{ATT}_{U \times U}$. The set of **completions** of a given cIAF is defined as

$$\mathsf{completions}(U, \varphi) = \{(A_v, R_v) \mid v \subseteq \mathsf{Prp}_U \text{ and } v \models \varphi\}.$$

We note $c\text{-}\mathcal{IAF}$ the class of all constrained incomplete argumentations frameworks.

Example 4. Let us consider $\mathsf{cIAF}_1 = (U, \varphi)$ with $U = \{a, b\}$ and $\varphi = (\mathsf{aw}_a \wedge \mathsf{aw}_b) \wedge (\mathsf{r}_{a,b} \vee \mathsf{r}_{b,a}) \wedge \neg(\mathsf{r}_{a,b} \wedge \mathsf{r}_{b,a}) \wedge \neg\mathsf{r}_{a,a} \wedge \neg\mathsf{r}_{b,b}$. The completions of cIAF_1 are:

$$a \bullet \longrightarrow \bullet b \qquad\qquad a \bullet \longleftarrow \bullet b$$

Proposition 7. *cIAFs are strictly more expressive than IAFs and rIAFs. In other words, for every (r)IAF, there is a cIAF with the same set of completions; but there is a cIAF such that no (r)IAF has the same set of completions.*

Proof. We only have to prove $c\text{-}\mathcal{IAF} \succ \mathcal{RIAF}$ (as $c\text{-}\mathcal{IAF} \succ \mathcal{IAF}$ follows from $\mathcal{RIAF} \succ \mathcal{IAF}$ [29] and the transitivity of $\succ$).

For the first part of the statement (for every rIAF there is a cIAF with the same set of completions), let rIAF be a rIAF with completions(rIAF) = $\{(A_1^*, R_1^*), ..., (A_n^*, R_n^*)\}$. Note that, for any AF (A, R) defined over $\mathcal{U}$, we can write its *theory* (see e.g. [22]), that is, the formula

$$\mathsf{Th}(A, R) = \bigwedge_{x \in A} \mathsf{aw}_x \wedge \bigwedge_{x \in \mathcal{U} \setminus A} \neg\mathsf{aw}_x \wedge \bigwedge_{(x,y) \in R} \mathsf{r}_{x,y} \wedge \bigwedge_{(x,y) \in \mathcal{U}^2 \setminus R} \neg\mathsf{r}_{x,y}.$$

It is then easy to show that for any valuation $v \subseteq \mathsf{Prp}_{\mathcal{U}}$, we have that $v \models \mathsf{Th}(A, R)$ iff $(A_v, R_v) = (A, R)$. Now, letting $\rho = \bigvee_{1 \leq i \leq n} \mathsf{Th}(A_i^*, R_i^*)$, we have that

$$\mathsf{completions}(\mathcal{U}, \rho) = \mathsf{completions}(\mathsf{rIAF}).$$

In order to prove the second half of the proposition, it suffices to use the cIAF of Example 4 (called cIAF_0). Reasoning towards contradiction, suppose that there is a rIAF rIAF $= (A^F, A^?, R^F, R^?, R^{\leftrightarrow})$ with the same set of completions as cIAF_0. Then $(a, b) \in R^F \cup R^? \cup R^{\leftrightarrow}$ (since (a, b) appears in a completion of rIAF). We show that the last statement is absurd. If $(a, b) \in R^F$, then (a, b) should appear in all completions of rIAF where a and b are present, but this is not true. If $(a, b) \in R^?$, we reason by cases on $(b, a) \in R^F \cup R^? \cup R^{\leftrightarrow}$: the first one is impossible, since (b, a) would be in every completion where a and b appear, and that is not the case; the second one is absurd because we would have an extension with neither (a, b) nor (b, a), and this is not the case; the third one is impossible because it would imply $(a, b) \in R^{\leftrightarrow}$, but we have assumed that $(a, b) \in R^?$, and we know that $R^? \cap R^{\leftrightarrow} = \emptyset$ by definition. Finally, suppose that $(a, b) \in R^{\leftrightarrow}$, which implies $(b, a) \in R^{\leftrightarrow}$ (by symmetry of $R^{\leftrightarrow}$), which is impossible because we would have a completion with both (a, b) and (b, a), but this is not the case.

Note that in the first part of the proof we have used an argument that works for *any* set of directed graphs with domain $\mathcal{U}$ (and not only for the completions of a given rIAF), hence we can state that:

Corollary 1. *For any set S of directed graphs with domain $\mathcal{U}$, there is a cIAF cIAF such that $\mathsf{S} = \mathsf{completions}(\mathsf{cIAF})$.*

In words, cIAFs are a maximally expressive formalism for representing qualitative uncertainty about AFs. Figure 1 depicts the relative expressivity of the different formalisms adding qualitative uncertainty to abstract argumentation that we have discussed in this paper.

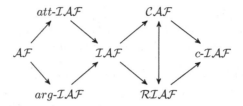

Fig. 1. Relative expressivity of formalisms for qualitative uncertainty in formal argumentation. An arrow from $\mathcal{X}$ to $\mathcal{Y}$ means that $\mathcal{X} \preceq \mathcal{Y}$. Transitive and reflexive arrows are omitted.

The Need of cIAFs. Besides being mathematically interesting, one may wonder why one should use cIAFs. Our main motivation is that, while the computational complexity of reasoning tasks associated to the previously introduced formalisms ((r)IAFs and subclasses) is well-known and relatively low, their modelling power is rather limited. Consider, for instance, a proponent reasoning about the view of her opponent on a very simple debate, containing only two arguments $\{a, b\}$. Suppose that a is an argument about public health policies stated by the right-wing presidential candidate. Similarly, b is an argument stated by the left-wing candidate. Imagine that a and b have contradictory conclusions, so they are mutually incompatible. Let us informally understand R as a *defeat* relation here, that is, a relation based on logical incompatibility plus some kind of epistemic-based assessment of the involved arguments (for instance, regarding the reliability of their premises), as it is usually done in structured argumentation. Now, suppose our proponent knows that her opponent is polarized, in the sense that he (the opponent) is already inclined towards one side of the political spectrum, but she does not know which one; then the possible AFs that the agent attributes to her opponent are exactly the completions of cIAF$_1$ (see Example 4). As we have shown in the proof of Proposition 7, there is no rIAF (and therefore no IAF) with that exact set of completions as cIAF$_1$.

Let us now show how cIAFs can be captured using DL-PA. Let cIAF $= (\mathcal{U}, \varphi)$, and define its associated valuation simply as the empty set, that is, $v_{\text{cIAF}} = \emptyset$. (Actually any valuation over $\text{Prp}_{\mathcal{U}}$ will do the job.) The program that generates all completions of cIAF is defined as

$$\text{makeComp}^{\text{cIAF}} = \text{vary}(\text{AW}_{\mathcal{U}}); \text{vary}(\text{ATT}_{\mathcal{U} \times \mathcal{U}}); \varphi?.$$

Proposition 8. *Let* cIAF $= (\mathcal{U}, \varphi)$, *then:*

- *If* $(v_{\text{cIAF}}, v) \in \|\text{makeComp}^{\text{cIAF}}\|$, *then* $(A_v, R_v) \in \text{completions(cIAF)}$.
- *If* $(A^*, R^*) \in \text{completions(cIAF)}$, *then* $(v_{\text{cIAF}}, v_{(A^*, R^*)}) \in \|\text{makeComp}^{\text{cIAF}}\|$.

Proof (Sketched). Note that the interpretation of $\text{vary}(\text{AW}_{\mathcal{U}}); \text{vary}(\text{ATT}_{\mathcal{U} \times \mathcal{U}})$, when restricted to $2^{\text{Prp}_{\mathcal{U}} \setminus \text{IN}_{\mathcal{U}}}$, is actually the total relation $2^{\text{Prp}_{\mathcal{U}} \setminus \text{IN}_{\mathcal{U}}} \times 2^{\text{Prp}_{\mathcal{U}} \setminus \text{IN}_{\mathcal{U}}}$. Hence from $v_{\text{cIAF}} = \emptyset$ we have an execution of $\text{vary}(\text{AW}_{\mathcal{U}}); \text{vary}(\text{ATT}_{\mathcal{U} \times \mathcal{U}})$ that goes to *any* valuation in $2^{\text{Prp}_{\mathcal{U}} \setminus \text{IN}_{\mathcal{U}}}$. Then, the execution of φ? filters those valuations of $2^{\text{Prp}_{\mathcal{U}} \setminus \text{IN}_{\mathcal{U}}}$ that satisfy the constraint of cIAF, i.e. the set of valuations of $2^{\text{Prp}_{\mathcal{U}} \setminus \text{IN}_{\mathcal{U}}}$ representing the set of completions of cIAF. As an illustration of the proof, consider Fig. 2.

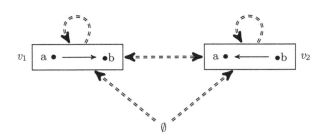

Fig. 2. Completions of cIAF_1 seen as valuations over $\text{Prp}_{\{a,b\}}$. Dashed double arrows represent the interpretation of $\text{makeComp}^{\text{cIAF}}$ (the other valuations over $\text{Prp}_{\{a,b\}}$ are omitted).

Reasoning problems for IAFs can be easily adapted to cIAFs: we just have to ensure that the argument about which we formulate the query belongs to all completions. As an example, consider:

stable-Necessary-Credulous-Acceptance (st-NCA)
Given: A constrained IAF cIAF $= (\mathcal{U}, \varphi)$ and an argument $a \in \mathcal{U}$ such that $\models \varphi \to \text{aw}_a$. **Question:** Is it true that for every $(A^*, R^*) \in \text{completions(cIAF)}$ there is an $E \in \text{st}(A^*, R^*)$ such that $a \in E$?

Note that requiring $\models \varphi \to \text{aw}_a$ amounts to requiring $a \in A$ for all $(A, R) \in$ completions$(\mathcal{U}, \varphi)$. Once again, we can reduce acceptability problems in cIAFs to DL-PA model-checking problems. As an example, we have the following:

Proposition 9. *Let* cIAF $= (\mathcal{U}, \varphi)$ *and let* $a \in \mathcal{U}$ *such that* $\models \varphi \to \text{aw}_a$, *then the answer to* st-*PSA with input* cIAF *and* a *is yes if and only if*

$$v_{\text{cIAF}} \models \langle \text{makeComp}^{\text{cIAF}} \rangle [\text{makeExt}^{\text{st}}] \text{in}_a.$$

Proof (Sketched). The result follows from from the definition of the reasoning task, the correctness of $\text{makeExt}^{\text{st}}$ ([20,21]), Proposition 8, and the semantics of DL-PA.

8   Discussion and Future Work

Getting Closer to the Model-Checking Approach. Our encoding of formalisms for arguing with qualitative uncertainty can be qualified as *hybrid*, since it combines some previous semantic reasoning with reasoning inside DL-PA. For instance, in order to compute the completions of an IAF, one first needs to find its associated valuation (reasoning outside the logic, using semantic objects), then has to write down the makeComp program, and finally reasoning in DL-PA to find the makeComp-successors of the associated valuation. We followed this hybrid method because we found intuitive the identification of directed graphs with propositional valuations over $\mathtt{Prp}_{\mathcal{U}}$. However, we can adopt results from [20–22] to get a more homogeneous method here. For instance, let $\mathsf{IAF} = (A, A^?, R, R^?)$ be an IAF, instead of computing its associated valuation, we can write down a propositional formula that characterizes its fixed elements (similarly to what is done in [20] for standard AFs):

$$\mathsf{Th}(\mathsf{IAF}) = \bigwedge_{x \in A^F} \mathsf{aw}_x \wedge \bigwedge_{x \in \mathcal{U} \backslash A^F} \neg \mathsf{aw}_x \wedge \bigwedge_{(x,y) \in R^F} \mathsf{r}_{x,y} \bigwedge_{(x,y) \in \mathcal{U}^2 \backslash R^F} \neg \mathsf{r}_{x,y}.$$

If we combine this formula with the makeComp program and the inverse operator we obtain a formula whose models completely characterize the set of completions of IAF:

$$\mathsf{completions}(\mathsf{IAF}) = \{(A_v, R_v) \mid v \in \|\langle (\mathsf{Th}(\mathsf{IAF})?; \mathsf{makeComp}^{\mathsf{IAF}})^{\smile} \rangle \top \| \}.$$

Comparison to QBF Encodings. As mentioned before, all we have done in DL-PA can as well be done in equally expressive logical frameworks like propositional logic or *quantified Boolean formulas* (QBF). The advantage over the former is that (1) some semantics can be expressed more compactly in DL-PA, and (2) the reasoning problems can be expressed directly as DL-PA programs. The advantage over QBFs is that the DL-PA encoding of reasoning problems by means of programs is more natural than the rather complex QBF encodings that one can find in the literature. Actually, most of the works on arguing with qualitative uncertainty use QBF encodings and algorithms for determining the complexity of associated reasoning tasks (see e.g. [8] or [31]). All advantages already pointed out by [21] of using DL-PA instead of QBF for encoding argumentative semantics are preserved by our encodings. In particular, "extension construction programs such as makeExt$^\sigma$ capture things in a more general, flexible and natural way than a QBF encoding". This enables a straightforward extension of our results to all semantics that have been encoded in DL-PA (admissible, complete, grounded, preferred) and potentially others.

Dynamics and Uncertainty. The dynamic nature of our approach also paves the way for a systematic study of the different dynamic extensions of IAFs (e.g. in order to enforce arguments, as done in [7]) and the rest of formalisms studied here, which we leave for future work.

References

1. Amgoud, L., Vesic, S.: A new approach for preference-based argumentation frameworks. Ann. Math. Artif. Intell. **63**(2), 149–183 (2011). https://doi.org/10.1007/s10472-011-9271-9

2. Atkinson, K., et al.: Towards artificial argumentation. AI Mag. **38**(3), 25–36 (2017). https://doi.org/10.1609/aimag.v38i3.2704

3. Balbiani, P., Herzig, A., Schwarzentruber, F., Troquard, N.: DL-PA and DCL-PC: model checking and satisfiability problem are indeed in PSPACE. CoRR abs/1411.7825 (2014). http://arxiv.org/abs/1411.7825

4. Balbiani, P., Herzig, A., Troquard, N.: Dynamic logic of propositional assignments: a well-behaved variant of PDL. In: 2013 28th Annual ACM/IEEE Symposium on Logic in Computer Science, pp. 143–152. IEEE (2013). https://doi.org/10.1109/LICS.2013.20

5. Baroni, P., Caminada, M., Giacomin, M.: Abstract argumentation frameworks and their semantics. In: Handbook of Formal Argumentation, pp. 159–236. College Publications (2018)

6. Baroni, P., Cerutti, F., Giacomin, M., Guida, G.: Encompassing attacks to attacks in abstract argumentation frameworks. In: Sossai, C., Chemello, G. (eds.) ECSQARU 2009. LNCS (LNAI), vol. 5590, pp. 83–94. Springer, Heidelberg (2009). https://doi.org/10.1007/978-3-642-02906-6_9

7. Baumann, R., Brewka, G.: Expanding argumentation frameworks: enforcing and monotonicity results. In: Baroni, P., Cerutti, F., Giacomin, M., Simari, G.R. (eds.) Proceedings of the COMMA 2010, vol. 216, pp. 75–86. IOS Press (2010). https://doi.org/10.3233/978-1-60750-619-5-75

8. Baumeister, D., Järvisalo, M., Neugebauer, D., Niskanen, A., Rothe, J.: Acceptance in incomplete argumentation frameworks. Artif. Intell. **295**, 103470 (2021). https://doi.org/10.1016/j.artint.2021.103470

9. Baumeister, D., Neugebauer, D., Rothe, J.: Credulous and skeptical acceptance in incomplete argumentation frameworks. In: Proceedings of the COMMA 2018. Frontiers in AI and Applications, vol. 305, pp. 181–192. IOS Press (2018). https://doi.org/10.3233/978-1-61499-906-5-181

10. Baumeister, D., Neugebauer, D., Rothe, J., Schadrack, H.: Complexity of verification in incomplete argumentation frameworks. In: McIlraith, S.A., Weinberger, K.Q. (eds.) Proceedings of the Thirty-Second AAAI Conference on Artificial Intelligence, (AAAI 2018), pp. 1753–1760. AAAI Press (2018)

11. Baumeister, D., Neugebauer, D., Rothe, J., Schadrack, H.: Verification in incomplete argumentation frameworks. Artif. Intell. **264**, 1–26 (2018). https://doi.org/10.1016/j.artint.2018.08.001

12. Bench-Capon, T.J., Dunne, P.E.: Argumentation in artificial intelligence. Artif. Intell. **171**(10–15), 619–641 (2007). https://doi.org/10.1016/j.artint.2007.05.001

13. Besnard, P., Cayrol, C., Lagasquie-Schiex, M.C.: Logical theories and abstract argumentation: a survey of existing works. Argument Comput. **11**(1–2), 41–102 (2020). https://doi.org/10.3233/AAC-190476

14. Besnard, P., et al.: Introduction to structured argumentation. Argument Comput. **5**(1), 1–4 (2014). https://doi.org/10.1080/19462166.2013.869764

15. Caminada, M.: Rationality postulates: applying argumentation theory for non-monotonic reasoning. J. Appl. Log. **4**(8), 2707–2734 (2017)

16. Cayrol, C., Lagasquie-Schiex, M.C.: On the acceptability of arguments in bipolar argumentation frameworks. In: Godo, L. (ed.) ECSQARU 2005. LNCS (LNAI), vol. 3571, pp. 378–389. Springer, Heidelberg (2005). https://doi.org/10.1007/11518655_33

17. Coste-Marquis, S., Devred, C., Marquis, P.: Constrained argumentation frameworks. In: Proceedings of the Tenth International Conference on Principles of Knowledge Representation and Reasoning, pp. 112–122. AAAI Press (2006)

18. Dimopoulos, Y., Mailly, J., Moraitis, P.: Control argumentation frameworks. In: McIlraith, S.A., Weinberger, K.Q. (eds.) Proceedings of the Thirty-Second AAAI Conference on Artificial Intelligence, (AAAI 2018), The 30th innovative Applications of Artificial Intelligence (IAAI 2018), and the 8th AAAI Symposium on Educational Advances in Artificial Intelligence (EAAI 2018), New Orleans, Louisiana, USA, 2–7 February 2018, pp. 4678–4685. AAAI Press (2018). https://www.aaai.org/ocs/index.php/AAAI/AAAI18/paper/view/16639

19. Dimopoulos, Y., Mailly, J.G., Moraitis, P.: Argumentation-based negotiation with incomplete opponent profiles. In: 13èmes Journées d'Intelligence Artificielle Fondamentale (JIAF 2019), pp. 91–100 (2019)

20. Doutre, S., Herzig, A., Perrussel, L.: A dynamic logic framework for abstract argumentation. In: Baral, C., De Giacomo, G., Eiter, T. (eds.) Fourteenth International Conference on the Principles of Knowledge Representation and Reasoning. AAAI Press (2014)

21. Doutre, S., Herzig, A., Perrussel, L.: Abstract argumentation in dynamic logic: representation, reasoning and change. In: Liao, B., Ågotnes, T., Wang, Y.N. (eds.) CLAR 2018. LASLL, pp. 153–185. Springer, Singapore (2019). https://doi.org/10.1007/978-981-13-7791-4_8

22. Doutre, S., Maffre, F., McBurney, P.: A dynamic logic framework for abstract argumentation: adding and removing arguments. In: Benferhat, S., Tabia, K., Ali, M. (eds.) IEA/AIE 2017. LNCS (LNAI), vol. 10351, pp. 295–305. Springer, Cham (2017). https://doi.org/10.1007/978-3-319-60045-1_32

23. Dung, P.M.: On the acceptability of arguments and its fundamental role in nonmonotonic reasoning, logic programming and n-person games. Artif. Intell. **77**(2), 321–357 (1995). https://doi.org/10.1016/0004-3702(94)00041-X

24. Fazzinga, B., Flesca, S., Furfaro, F.: Revisiting the notion of extension over incomplete abstract argumentation frameworks. In: Proceedings of IJCAI 2020, pp. 1712–1718. IJCAI Organization, July 2020. https://doi.org/10.24963/ijcai.2020/237

25. Grossi, D.: On the logic of argumentation theory. In: Proceedings of the 9th International Conference on Autonomous Agents and Multiagent Systems, pp. 409–416. IFAMA (2010)

26. Harel, D., Kozen, D., Tiuryn, J.: Dynamic Logic. MIT Press, Cambridge (2000)

27. Herzig, A., Yuste-Ginel, A.: On the epistemic logic of incomplete argumentation frameworks. In: Proceedings of International Conference on Principles of Knowledge Representation and Reasoning. AAAI Press (2021)

28. Li, H., Oren, N., Norman, T.J.: Probabilistic argumentation frameworks. In: Modgil, S., Oren, N., Toni, F. (eds.) TAFA 2011. LNCS (LNAI), vol. 7132, pp. 1–16. Springer, Heidelberg (2012). https://doi.org/10.1007/978-3-642-29184-5_1

29. Mailly, J.G.: A note on rich incomplete argumentation frameworks. arXiv preprint arXiv:2009.04869 (2020)

30. Niskanen, A.: Computational approaches to dynamics and uncertainty in abstract argumentation. Ph.D. thesis, Helsingin yliopisto (2020)

31. Niskanen, A., Neugebauer, D., Järvisalo, M., et al.: Controllability of control argumentation frameworks. In: Proceedings of the Twenty-Ninth International Joint Conference on Artificial Intelligence (IJCAI 2020). IJCAI Organization (2021). https://doi.org/10.24963/ijcai.2020/257

32. Proietti, C., Yuste-Ginel, A.: Dynamic epistemic logics for abstract argumentation. Synthese 1–60 (2021). https://doi.org/10.1007/s11229-021-03178-5

Explanations of Non-monotonic Inference in Admissibility-Based Abstract Argumentation

Timotheus Kampik[1]([⊠]) and Kristijonas Čyras[2]

[1] Umeå University, Umeå, Sweden
tkampik@cs.umu.se
[2] Ericsson Research, Stockholm, Sweden
kristijonas.cyras@ericsson.com

Abstract. In this paper, we introduce a formal framework for explaining change of inference in abstract argumentation, in particular in the context of iteratively drawing inferences from a sequence of normal expansions, with a focus on admissible set-based semantics. We then conduct a formal analysis, showing that given an initial argumentation framework and an extension that has been inferred from it, we can guarantee the existence of explanation arguments for the violation of monotony when inferring an extension from a normal expansion of the initial argumentation framework.

Keywords: Formal argumentation · Explainable artificial intelligence · Non-monotonic reasoning

1 Introduction

Recently, formal argumentation approaches have received increasing attention in the Artificial Intelligence (AI) community, partly because argumentation is considered an enabler of *explainable* AI. However, claiming that argumentation-based inference is in itself always explainable is naive; indeed, a range of approaches that facilitate explainability in argumentation have been introduced in recent years [11,26]. In this paper, we advance the research direction of explainable argumentation by introducing a formal approach that explains the violation of monotony in *sequential* argumentation, where we draw inferences from an argumentation framework, then update it with new arguments and attacks, draw new inferences and so on. In particular, we introduce the notion of *monotony violation explanations*, *i.e.* sets of arguments that can explain the violation of monotony, given an argumentation semantics that satisfies a newly introduced relaxed monotony principle; we prove that three of Dung's initial admissible set-based semantics[1] satisfy this principle. With this approach, our

---

[1] The exception among the four semantics that Dung introduces in his seminal paper is stable semantics, which is not universally defined.

© Springer Nature Switzerland AG 2021
P. Baroni et al. (Eds.): CLAR 2021, LNAI 13040, pp. 209–223, 2021.
https://doi.org/10.1007/978-3-030-89391-0_12

work extends the body of research on explainable formal argumentation by enabling the explanation of dynamic inference.

Let us provide an example that gives an intuition of the approach this paper introduces.

Example 1. Assume we have a machine reasoner $\mathcal{R}$ that draws inferences from a belief base (that may contain conflicting beliefs). The belief base *expands* with time, and $\mathcal{R}$ draws new inferences after every expansion. Several IT systems subscribe to $\mathcal{R}$'s inferences and update their configurations based on the conclusions that $\mathcal{R}$ serves. Updating a configuration may be costly (imply down-time, manual effort, and the re-routing of workflow instances); hence, $\mathcal{R}$ needs to provide an *explanation* every time *monotony is violated*, *i.e.* when a previous recommendation about a system configuration is withdrawn.

For instance, let us assume an abstract argumentation-based model, in which $\mathcal{R}$ starts with the initial argumentation framework $AF = (AR, AT)$ – where AR is a set of statements ("arguments") and $AT \subseteq AR \times AR$ ("attacks") – such that $AF = (\{a\}, \{\})$; *i.e.*, we have only one statement and no attacks. From this framework, $\mathcal{R}$ infers[2] $\{a\}$. Then, AF *normally expands* to $AF' = (AR', AT') = (\{a, b, c, d\}, \{(a, b), (b, a)\})$: new arguments and attacks are added to AF, but the attacks between arguments in AR remain unaffected[3]. From AF', $\mathcal{R}$'s inference function allows to infer either $\{a, c, d\}$ or $\{b, c, d\}$. $\mathcal{R}$ opts to infer $\{a, c, d\}$ because it is monotonic w.r.t. the previous inference $\{a\}$ and no explanations need to be provided.

However, things get more tricky when AF' is normally expanded to $AF'' = (AR'', AT'') = (\{a, b, c, d, e, f, g\}, \{(a, b), (b, a), (e, c), (e, d), (e, f), (f, a), (f, e), (f, g), (g, f)\})$. $\mathcal{R}$'s inference function allows to infer either $\{a, e, g\}$, or $\{b, e, g\}$, or $\{b, c, d, f\}$. Now, $\mathcal{R}$ is forced to violate monotony in order to comply with the constraints the inference function imposes. Intuitively, a reasonable decision is to infer $\{b, c, d, f\}$ because it minimizes the number of arguments (w.r.t cardinality) that are part of the previous conclusion but not part of the current conclusion, *i.e.* $|\{a, c, d\} \setminus \{b, c, d, f\}| < |\{a, c, d\} \setminus \{a, e, g\}| < |\{a, c, d\} \setminus \{b, e, g\}|$. (While more nuanced variants of monotony-maximizing extension-selection are introduced in [19], in this paper, we focus on cardinality-based monotony maximization with respect to a particular previous inference, which – self-evidently – may but does not necessarily have to be the most recently drawn inference from a temporal perspective.) To *explain* the violation of monotony, $\mathcal{R}$ may proceed by highlighting *monotony violation explanations*, *i.e.* arguments that satisfy the following constraints:

– The argument has been newly added.
– The argument attacks an argument that was in the previous conclusion.

---

[2] In this example, the behavior of $\mathcal{R}$'s inference function coincides with preferred semantics [13], to be defined later.

[3] We focus on normal expansions because we consider it a reasonable assumption that in an argumentation context, dynamic scenarios are modeled by adding arguments to an argumentation framework without deleting arguments (instead, arguments can be defeated) and without changing the attack relations between existing arguments.

– The argument is not attacked by any subset of arguments in the new conclusion that defends itself against all attackers and is not in conflict with the previous conclusion.

Figure 1 depicts the example's argumentation frameworks. The *monotony violation explanations* of the conclusion $\{b, c, d, f\}$ as inferred from AF'' w.r.t. the previous conclusion $\{a, c, d\}$ that has been inferred from AF' are the arguments comprising the set $\{e, f\}$. Intuitively, the fact that we infer f explains that we can no longer infer a; in turn, e explains why we have to infer f, *i.e.* to still be able to infer c and d.

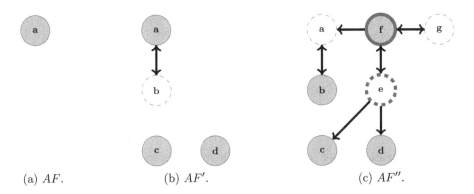

(a) AF.   (b) AF'.   (c) AF''.

Fig. 1. Explaining the violation of monotony. Here and henceforth, the gray arguments in each argumentation framework comprise the inferred extension; arguments with a dashed border are rejected and arguments with a bold border are monotony violation explanations.

The rest of this paper is organized as follows. Section 2 provides the necessary theoretical preliminaries. Then, Sect. 3 introduces and analyzes the monotony violation explainability framework. An implementation of the framework is described in Sect. 4. Section 5 discusses the framework in the context of related work, before Sect. 6 concludes the paper.

2   Preliminaries

The central model that this paper makes use of is the notion of an abstract argumentation framework.

Definition 1 (Argumentation Framework [13]). *An argumentation framework AF is a tuple (AR, AT), such that AR is a set of elements (called arguments) and $AT \subseteq AR \times AR$ (called attacks).*

We assume that the arguments in an argumentation framework are finite. Given an argumentation framework $AF = (AR, AT)$, we say for two arguments

$a, b \in AR$ that a attacks b if and only if $(a, b) \in AT$. Given $S \subseteq AR$, we say that S attacks a if and only if there exists an argument $c \in S$, such that c attacks a and we say that a attacks S if and only if there exists an argument $d \in S$, such that a attacks d; we say that S attacks $P \subseteq AR$ if and only if there exists an argument $e \in S$, such that e attacks P. We say that S defends a if and only if for every argument $g \in AR$, such that g attacks a it holds true that S attacks g.

In abstract argumentation, admissible and conflict-free sets are important notions.

Definition 2 Conflict-free and Admissible Sets [13]). *Let $AF = (AR, AT)$ be an argumentation framework. A set $S \subseteq AR$:*

- *is conflict-free (in AF) iff $\nexists a, b \in S$ such that a attacks b;*
- *is admissible (in AF) iff S is conflict-free and $\forall a \in S$, it holds true that S defends a.*

Let us now introduce some argumentation semantics, *i.e.* functions that infer sets of *extensions* from an argumentation framework, where each extension is a subset of the argumentation framework's arguments.

Definition 3 (Dung's Admissibility-based Semantics [13]). *Let $AF = (AR, AT)$ be an argumentation framework. An admissible set $S \subseteq AR$ is a:*

- *stable extension of AF iff S attacks each argument that does not belong to S. Stable semantics $\sigma_{st}(AF)$ denotes all stable extensions of AF;*
- *complete extension of AF iff each argument that is defended by S belongs to S. Complete semantics $\sigma_{co}(AF)$ denotes all complete extensions of AF;*
- *preferred extension of AF iff S is a maximal (w.r.t. set inclusion) admissible subset of AR. Preferred semantics $\sigma_{pr}(AF)$ denotes all preferred extensions of AF;*
- *grounded extension of AF iff S is the minimal (w.r.t. set inclusion) complete extension of AF. Grounded semantics $\sigma_{gr}(AF)$ denotes all grounded extensions of AF.*

Given an argumentation semantics σ and an argumentation framework AF, we call every $E \in \sigma(AF)$ a σ-extension of AF. Colloquially speaking, argumentation framework *expansions* constrain how an argumentation framework is manipulated: (simple) expansions specify that no arguments or attacks can be removed, whereas normal expansions demand that in addition, no new attacks can be added between existing arguments.

Definition 4 (Argumentation Framework Expansions [4]). *Let $AF = (AR, AT)$ and $AF' = (AR', AT')$ be argumentation frameworks.*

- *AF' is an expansion of AF (denoted by $AF \preceq AF'$) iff $AR \subseteq AR'$ and $AT \subseteq AT'$.*
- *AF' is a normal expansion of AF (denoted by $AF \preceq_N AF'$) iff $AF \preceq AF'$ and $(AR \times AR) \cap (AT' \setminus AT) = \emptyset$.*

To facilitate the design and analysis of argumentation semantics, formal argumentation *principles* have been introduced in the literature [25]. The universality principle describes whether an argumentation semantics always returns at least one extension [3].

Definition 5 (Universality). *Let σ be an argumentation semantics. σ is universally defined (σ satisfies universality) iff for every argumentation framework AF it holds true that $|\sigma(AF)| \geq 1$.*

A particularly relevant principle in the context of this work is *weak cautious monotony*, which stipulates that normally expanding an argumentation framework must allow us to infer any set of arguments contained in any of the original argumentation framework's extensions, given this extension is not attacked by any of the newly added arguments.

Definition 6 (Weak Cautious Monotony [20]**).** *Let σ be an argumentation semantics. σ satisfies weak cautious monotony iff for every two argumentation frameworks $AF = (AR, AT)$ and $AF' = (AR', AT')$, such that $AF \preceq_N AF'$, and $\forall E \in \sigma(AF)$, it holds true that if $\{(a, b) \mid (a, b) \in AT', a \in AR' \setminus AR, b \in E\} = \emptyset$ then $\exists E' \in \sigma(AF')$ such that $E \subseteq E'$.*

As a measure of how much an inference result violates monotony w.r.t. a previous inference, we have defined the notion of a *degree of monotony* in a recent work.

Definition 7 (Degree of Monotony [19]**).** *Let E and E' be two finite sets of arguments. We define the degree of monotony of E' w.r.t. E, denoted by $deg_{mon}(E', E)$, as follows:*

$$deg_{mon}(E', E) = \begin{cases} 1 & \text{if } |E| = 0; \\ \frac{|E' \cap E|}{|E|} & \text{otherwise.} \end{cases}$$

The degree of monotony allows us to guide extension selection when first picking an extension that a semantics infers from an argumentation framework and then determining the extensions a semantics returns from an update of this argumentation framework, such that these extensions maximize the degree of monotony w.r.t. the previously inferred extension.

Definition 8 (Degree of Monotony-Maximizing Extensions [19]**).** *Let $AF' = (AR', AT')$ be an argumentation framework. Let σ be a universally defined argumentation semantics, and let E be a finite set of arguments. We define the monotony-maximizing σ-extensions of AF' w.r.t. E, denoted by $Exts_{mon}(E, AF', \sigma)$, as $\{E'|E' \in \sigma(AF'), \nexists E'' \in \sigma(AF')$, such that $deg_{mon}(E', E) < deg_{mon}(E'', E)\}$.*

Let us illustrate the notion of degree of monotony-maximizing extensions by introducing an example.

Example 2. Consider the argumentation frameworks $AF = (AR, AT) = (\{a, b, c\}, \{(a, b), (b, a)\})$ and $AF' = (AR', AT') = (\{a, b, c, d\}, \{(a, b), (b, a), (d, c)\})$, as well as preferred semantics. Note that $AF \preceq_N AF'$. $\sigma_{pr}(AF) = \{\{a, c\}, \{b, c\}\}$ and $\sigma_{pr}(AF') = \{\{a, d\}, \{b, d\}\}$. Let us assume we first select $E = \{a, c\}$ from $\sigma_{pr}(AF)$ and then normally expand AF to AF'. No matter which extension we select from $\sigma_{pr}(AF')$, we will violate monotony. However, intuitively, it does not make sense to "switch" from an inference that entails a to an inference that entails b. The degree of monotony-maximizing extensions support this intuition: $deg_{mon}(\{a, d\}, E) = \frac{1}{2}$ and $deg_{mon}(\{b, d\}, E) = 0$; $Exts_{mon}(E, AF', \sigma_{pr}) = \{\{a, d\}\}$.

3 Explainability Framework

Let us now provide a formal explainability framework for the intuition we have outlined in the introduction. We call the central principle of our framework the Relaxed Monotony Explainability (RME) principle, as it helps us explain the relaxation (or: the constrained violation) of monotony.

Definition 9 (Relaxed Monotony Explainability (RME) Principle). *Let σ be an argumentation semantics. σ satisfies the Relaxed Monotony Explainability (RME) principle iff for every two argumentation frameworks $AF = (AR, AT)$ and $AF' = (AR', AT')$, such that $AF \preceq_N AF'$, the following statement holds true:*

$$\forall E \in \sigma(AF), \exists E' \in \sigma(AF'), \text{ such that if } E \nsubseteq E'$$
$$\text{Then } \exists a \in AR' \setminus AR, \text{ such that}$$
$$a \text{ attacks } E \text{ and } \nexists S \subseteq E', \text{ such that}$$
$$S \text{ is admissible in } AF', S \cup E \text{ is conflict-free and } S \text{ attacks } a$$

Intuitively, the principle says that after a normal expansion, an originally inferred extension must be entailed by some extension of the normal expansion unless the original extension is attacked by some new arguments that in turn are not attacked by a set of arguments in the new extension that defends itself and is not in conflict with arguments in the original extension. We can show that the satisfaction of the RME principle implies the satisfaction of weak cautious monotony.

Proposition 1. *Let σ be an argumentation semantics. If σ satisfies the RME principle then σ satisfies weak cautious monotony.*

Proof. 1. By definition of weak cautious monotony (Definition 6), σ satisfies weak cautious monotony iff the following statement holds true for every two argumentation frameworks $AF = (AR, AT)$ and $AF' = (AR', AT')$, such that $AF \preceq_N AF'$:

$$\forall E \in \sigma(AF), \text{ if } \nexists E' \in \sigma(AF'), \text{ such that } E \subseteq E'$$
$$\text{Then } \exists a \in AR' \setminus AR, \text{ such that}$$
$$a \text{ attacks } E$$

2. By definition of the RME principle (Definition 9) it follows that σ satisfies the RME principle iff the following statement holds true for every two argumentation frameworks $AF = (AR, AT)$ and $AF' = (AR', AT')$, such that $AF \preceq_N AF'$:

$\forall E \in \sigma(AF)$, if $\nexists E' \in \sigma(AF')$, such that $E \subseteq E'$

Then $\exists E'' \in \sigma(AF'), \exists a \in AR' \setminus AR$, such that

a attacks E and $\nexists S \subseteq E''$, such that

S is admissible in $AF', S \cup E$ is conflict-free and S attacks a

3. From 2. and 3. it follows that if σ satisfies the RME principle then σ satisfies weak cautious monotony. □

Also, let us show that complete, preferred, and grounded semantics satisfy the RME principle.

Proposition 2. *Let σ_x be an argumentation semantics such that $x \in \{co, pr, gr\}$. σ_x satisfies the RME principle.*

Proof. For every two argumentation frameworks $AF = (AR, AT)$ and $AF' = (AR', AT')$, such that $AF \preceq_N AF'$, for every $E \in \sigma_x(AF)$, we have two cases.

Case 1: If $\exists E' \in \sigma_x(AF')$, such that $E \subseteq E'$, it follows from the definition of the RME principle (Definition 9) that the proposition holds true.

Case 2: If $\nexists E' \in \sigma_x(AF')$, such that $E \subseteq E'$, we have two sub-cases.

Sub-case 2.1: $x \in \{co, pr\}$. Because $E \in \sigma_x(AF)$ and $\nexists E' \in \sigma_x(AF')$, such that $E \subseteq E'$, by definition of σ_x (Definition 3), it holds true that E attacks all arguments that attack E in AF and $\nexists S' \subseteq AR'$, such that S' is conflict-free, $E \subseteq S'$ and S' attacks all arguments that attack S' in AF'. It follows that $\exists a \in AR' \setminus AR$, such that a attacks E and a is not attacked by any set $S \subseteq AR$, such that $E \subseteq S$ and S is admissible in AF'. Hence, from the definition of an admissible set (Definition 2) and the definition of σ_x (Definition 3), it follows that $\exists a \in AR' \setminus AR$, $\exists E'' \in \sigma_x(AF')$, such that a attacks E and a is not attacked by any set $S \subseteq E''$, such that S is admissible in AF', and $S \cup E$ is conflict-free; consequently, σ_x satisfies the RME principle as stipulated in Definition 9 and the proposition holds true for this sub-case.

Sub-case 2.2: $x = gr$. Note that σ_{gr} is universally uniquely defined, *i.e.* $|\sigma_{gr}(AF')| = 1$. Let E' be the grounded extension of AF'. Suppose for a contradiction that $E \nsubseteq E'$ and $\forall a \in AR' \setminus AR$, such that a attacks E it holds true that a is attacked by some set $S \subseteq E'$, such that S is admissible in AF' and $S \cup E$ is conflict-free. It follows that because E is the grounded extension of AF (and hence by definition the $\subseteq$-minimal complete extension of AF), E is defended by the $\subseteq$-minimal complete extension (and hence the grounded extension) of AF', from which it follows that $E \subseteq E'$. This is a contradiction, which means that if $E \nsubseteq E'$, then there must be

$a \in AR' \setminus AR$, such that a attacks E and a is not attacked by $S \subseteq E'$, such that S is admissible in AF' and $S \cup E$ is conflict-free. Hence, from the definition of the RME principle (Definition 9), it follows that the proposition holds true for $x = gr$. □

In contrast, we can show that stable semantics violates the RME principle.

Proposition 3. *Stable semantics σ_{st} violates the RME principle.*

Proof. We provide a proof by counter-example. Let us consider the argumentation frameworks $AF = (\{b\}, \{\})$ and $AF' = (\{a, b\}, \{(a, a)\})$. Let us observe that $AF \preceq_N AF'$, $\sigma_{st}(AF) = \{\{b\}\}$, and $\sigma_{st}(AF') = \emptyset$. It follows that the following statement does not hold true:

$\forall E \in \sigma(AF), \exists E' \in \sigma(AF')$, such that if $E \not\subseteq E'$

Then $\exists a \in AR' \setminus AR$, such that

a attacks E and and $\nexists S \subseteq E'$, such that

S is admissible in $AF', S \cup E$ is conflict-free and S attacks a

By definition (Definition 9), this violates the RME principle, which proves the proposition. □

It makes sense to combine the RME principle with the *degree of monotony*-maximizing extension selection approach. Let us motivate this using an example.

Example 3. We go back to AF and AF' as introduced in Example 2 (also, see Fig. 2) and consider preferred semantics. Again, we select $\{a, c\}$ as our preferred extension of AF. No matter which extension we select from $\sigma_{pr}(AF') = \{\{a, d\}, \{b, d\}\}$, we will violate monotony and $\{d\}$ will be our explanation. However, $\{d\}$ can hardly explain why we no longer infer a; this change in inference is certainly counter-intuitive, and can be prevented by determining $Exts_{mon}(E, AF', \sigma) = \{\{a, d\}\}$ as a filter when selecting the extension we want to infer from AF'.

Let us introduce the RME$_{max}$ principle, a stricter variant of the RME principle that ensures we can apply the approach outlined by Example 3.

Definition 10 (RME $_{max}$ Principle). *Let σ be an argumentation semantics. σ satisfies the RME_{max} principle iff σ is universally defined and for every two argumentation frameworks $AF = (AR, AT)$ and $AF' = (AR', AT')$, such that $AF \preceq_N AF'$, the following statement holds true:*

$\forall E \in \sigma(AF), \forall E' \in Exts_{mon}(E, AF', \sigma)$, *if* $E \not\subseteq E'$

Then $\exists a \in AR' \setminus AR$, *such that*

a *attacks* E *and* $\nexists S \subseteq E'$, *such that*

S *is admissible in* $AF', S \cup E$ *is conflict-free and* S *attacks* a

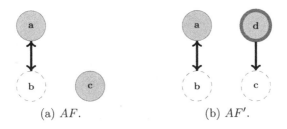

(a) AF.   (b) AF'.

Fig. 2. $\{d\}$ explains the violation of monotony when first inferring $\{a, c\}$ from AF and then inferring $\{d, c\}$ from AF'. Intuitively, d better explains losing only c when the selected extension is monotony maximizing (*i.e.* $\{a, d\}$) as opposed to losing a and c when the selected extension is not monotony maximizing (*i.e.* $\{b, d\}$).

Let us highlight that the difference to the RME principle (Definition 9) is that if monotony is violated, the *then* condition must hold true not merely for at least one extension of the expanded argumentation framework, but for all maximally monotonic extensions. Note that by definition, if one maximally monotonic extension violates monotony, then all maximally monotonic extensions violate monotony.

Also note that – as a potential alternative to the RME$_{max}$ principle – it is not possible to require an attack from a "new" argument to at least one (or every) previously inferred argument that is no longer inferred after the update as a necessary condition for the violation of monotony (at least not if we want to select a newly inferred extension that is maximally monotonic w.r.t. the previous inference result). We can illustrate this using another example.

Example 4. Consider $AF = (AR, AT) = (\{a, b, c, d\}, \{(a, b), (b, a)\}), AF' = (\{a, b, c, d, e\}, \{(a, b), (b, a), (b, e), (e, c), (e, d)\})$ – see Fig. 3 – and preferred semantics σ_{pr}. Note that $AF \preceq_N AF'$ and $\sigma_{pr}(AF) = \{\{a, c, d\}, \{b, c, d\}\}$. Assume that before expanding AF to AF', we have selected $\{a, c, d\}$ from $\sigma_{pr}(AF)$. Given $\sigma_{pr}(AF') = \{\{a, e\}, \{b, c, d\}\}$, let us select $\{b, c, d\}$ as our conclusion, assuming that we want to maximize monotony, *i.e.* to reject as few of the previously inferred arguments as possible. However, $AR' \backslash AR = \{e\}$ does not attack $\{a, c, d\} \backslash \{b, c, d\} = \{a\}$; it merely dictates that to maintain a maximal degree of monotony, our conclusion needs to entail b, which in turn attacks a; *i.e.*, it is *not necessary* to require the "new" argument e to attack some previously, but no longer inferred argument, namely a, to violate monotony.

Now, let us prove that the RME principle can indeed be combined with the degree of monotony-maximizing extension selection approach, *i.e.* that complete, preferred, and grounded semantics satisfy the RME$_{max}$ principle.

Proposition 4. *Let σ_x be an argumentation semantics, such that $x \in \{co, pr, gr\}$. σ_x satisfies the RME$_{max}$ principle.*

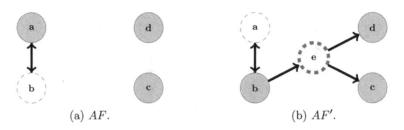

(a) AF.   (b) AF'.

Fig. 3. e, which is the only argument in $AR' \setminus AR$, does not attack any argument accepted in AF but rejected in AF' after selecting maximally monotonic extensions.

Proof. Let us note that σ_x is universally defined [3]. Because for every argumentation framework, there exists exactly one grounded extension, for $x = gr$ we conclude that $|Exts_{mon}(E, AF', \sigma_x)| = |\sigma_x(AF')| = 1$ and the proof follows from Proposition 2. For $x \in \{co, pr\}$, we have two cases $\forall E \in \sigma_x(AF), \forall E' \in Exts_{mon}(E, AF', \sigma_x)$:

Case 1: $E \subseteq E'$. By definition of RME_{max}, the proposition holds true for this case.

Case 2: $E \not\subseteq E'$. By definition of $Exts_{mon}$ (Definition 8), $\forall E'' \in \sigma_x(AF')$ it holds that $E \not\subseteq E''$ (because otherwise, if $E \subseteq E''$, then $deg_{mon}(E'', E) = 1$, *i.e.* $deg_{mon}(E'', E)$ is maximal, and hence $deg_{mon}(E'', E) > deg_{mon}(E', E)$ (since $E \not\subseteq E'$), which contradicts $E' \in Exts_{mon}(E, AF', \sigma_x)$). Hence, from Proposition 2 it follows that $\exists E^* \in \sigma_x(AF')$ such that $\exists a \in AR' \setminus AR$, such that a is not attacked by any set $S \subseteq E^*$, such that S is admissible in AF' and $S \cup E$ is conflict-free. Suppose for a contradiction that $\forall a' \in AR' \setminus AR$, such that a' attacks E it holds true that a' is attacked by some set $S' \subseteq E^*$, such that S' is admissible in AF' and $S' \cup E$ is conflict-free. It follows that by definition of σ_x (Definition 3), $S' \cup E$ is an admissible set in AF' and hence, (again by definition of σ_x), $\exists E'' \in \sigma_x(AF')$, such that $E \subseteq E''$. This contradicts that $E \not\subseteq E''$ as noted above, after the premise of the case (Case 2), and proves the proposition. □

Finally, let us define the notion of *monotony violation explanations*, *i.e.* arguments whose attacks on arguments in a previously inferred extension explain – in a normal expansion scenario – the violation of monotony, given a semantics that satisfies the RME_{max} principle.

Definition 11 (Monotony Violation Explanations). *Let $AF = (AR, AT)$ and $AF' = (AR', AT')$ be argumentation frameworks, such that $AF \preceq_N AF'$ and let σ be an argumentation semantics that satisfies the RME_{max} principle. Let $E \in \sigma(AF)$ and $E' \in \sigma(AF')$, such that $E' \in Exts_{mon}(E, AF', \sigma)$. The monotony violation explanations of E' w.r.t. E, σ, AF and AF' (denoted by $EXPS_{E,E'}(AF, AF, \sigma)$ are $\{a | a \in AR' \setminus AR, a$ attacks E, a is not attacked by any set $S \subseteq E'$, such that S is admissible in AF', $S \cup E$ is conflict-free}.*

Let us go back to the examples and identify the monotony violation explanations.

Example 5. Consider the following examples:

- Consider the argumentation frameworks AF' and AF'' as depicted by Fig. 1, preferred semantics and $E = \{a, c, d\}, E \in \sigma_{pr}(AF'), E' = \{b, c, d, f\}, E' \in Exts_{mon}(E, AF'', \sigma_{pr})$. $EXPS_{E,E'}(AF', AF'', \sigma_{pr}) = \{e, f\}$.
- Consider the argumentation frameworks AF and AF' as depicted by Fig. 2, preferred semantics and $E = \{b, c\}, E \in \sigma_{pr}(AF), E' = \{b, d\}, E' \in Exts_{mon}(E, AF', \sigma_{pr})$. $EXPS_{E,E'}(AF, AF', \sigma_{pr}) = \{d\}$.
- Consider the argumentation frameworks AF and AF' as depicted by Fig. 3, preferred semantics and $E = \{a, c, d\}, E \in \sigma_{pr}(AF), E' = \{b, c, d\}, E' \in Exts_{mon}(E, AF', \sigma_{pr})$. $EXPS_{E,E'}(AF, AF', \sigma_{pr}) = \{e\}$.

Finally, let us show that given complete, preferred or grounded semantics, for every argumentation frameworks, one of its extensions, and any of its normal expansions, for all extensions of the normal expansion that entail the originally inferred extension (if there are any), the set of monotony violation explanations of any of these new extensions w.r.t. the originally inferred extension is empty.

Proposition 5. *Let σ_x be an argumentation semantics such that $x \in \{co, pr, gr\}$. For every two argumentation frameworks $AF = (AR, AT)$, $AF' = (AR', AT')$ such that $AF \preceq_N AF'$, $\forall E \in \sigma_x(AF), E' \in \sigma_x(AF')$, such that $E \subseteq E'$, it holds true that $EXPS_{E,E'}(AF, AF', \sigma_x) = \emptyset$.*

Proof. Suppose for a contradiction that there exist two argumentation frameworks $AF = (AR, AT), AF' = (AR', AT')$, such that $AF \preceq_N AF'$ and $\exists E \in \sigma_x(AF), E' \in \sigma_x(AF')$, such that $E \subseteq E'$ and $EXPS_{E,E'}(AF, AF', \sigma_x) \neq \emptyset$. By definition of σ_x (Definition 3), it holds true that E' is conflict-free and $\forall b \in E'$, E' defends b (in AF'). Because $E \subseteq E'$, it follows that E' is admissible in AF', $E' \cup E$ is conflict-free and E' attacks all arguments that attack E. Consequently, it holds true that $\nexists a \in AR' \setminus AR$, such that a attacks E and a is not attacked by any set $S \subseteq E'$, such that S is admissible in AF' and $S \cup E$ is conflict-free. From the definition of monotony violation explanations (Definition 11), it follows that $EXPS_{E,E'}(AF, AF', \sigma_x) = \emptyset$, which contradicts $EXPS_{E,E'}(AF, AF', \sigma_x) \neq \emptyset$ as noted above and proves the proposition. □

4   Implementation

A Java implementation, including documentation (tutorial and application programming interface documentation) of the explainability framework is available at https://git.io/JOizF. The source code is openly available and the software can be installed using Java dependency management and build tools such as Maven[4] and Gradle[5]. The implementation is part of the DiArg argumentation-based dialog reasoner, which in turn is based on the abstract argumentation libraries that are provided by the Tweety project [24]. As the implementation

---

[4] https://maven.apache.org/.
[5] https://gradle.org/.

can – to a large extent – rely on existing argumentation reasoners, we consider an analysis of algorithmic implementation details (which depend on the implementation of these dependencies) out of the scope of this paper, yet potentially relevant future work.

5 Discussion

Our explainability framework makes use of research results on *argumentation dynamics* (see [12] for a survey), and in particular relies on notions that have been introduced in the context of monotony analysis, *i.e.* on Baumann's and Brewka's *normal expansions* [4][6] and our recently introduced weak cautious monotony abstract argumentation principle [20]. By extending the weak cautious monotony principle, we make the aforementioned results applicable to the domain for explainable argumentation. From the perspective of explainable automated reasoning (see [10] for a survey), our research can be considered a novel contribution at the intersection of principle-based [25] and explainable [26] argumentation.

Argumentation-based explanations take many forms (see *e.g.* [11] for a recent survey). A common approach to explaining argument acceptability – *i.e.* membership in extensions, or inference – in argumentation frameworks essentially amounts to traversing the argument graph and can be formalized by extracting graphs that satisfy some formal properties [8]. A popular example of explanations as sub-graphs with desirable properties uses the concept of a dispute tree [14,15], which commonly, but not exclusively, gives rise to conversational explanations, often by means of a dialogue (game). Explanations in argumentation frameworks can also come in the form of extensions themselves, *e.g.* [18,21], as well as by means of the structure of the extensions' arguments and relationships, where applicable in structured argumentation frameworks.

Notions of argumentation-based explanations that are most related to our work are approaches that modify the argument graph to make an argument (non-)acceptable. Commonly, addition or removal of arguments and/or relations that change the acceptability status of some pre-specified argument is a form of explanation, *e.g.* [17,22,23]. Such changes typically presuppose some "universal" space of argument graph modification [6,22,28]. Instead, our Monotony Violation Explanations amount to sets of arguments that best explain the differences between inferences in an abstract argumentation framework before and after a change – a (normal) expansion – of the argument graph. Importantly, our explanations consider the aspect of monotony maximization when selecting extensions for inference after the change. This roughly pertains to indicating changes that

---

[6] Let us highlight that we make use of normal expansions and not of the change operations for abstract argumentation frameworks that were introduced by Cayrol *et al.* [7] because the latter do not support the addition of arbitrarily many arguments as part of a single operation, which makes Baumann's and Brewka's normal expansions slightly more convenient in our case.

led to altered inferences and indirectly explain why some new inferences are preferred over others. Consequently, our approach can be seen as the reverse of the kind of explanations that indicate what changes could be applied to an argumentation framework to achieve desirable inferences, as in the works discussed above.

Future work can extend the formal framework we provide in this paper, for example as follows.

- Analyses of RME and RME_{max} principle satisfaction for naive set-based [1] and weak admissible set-based [5] argumentation semantics can be conducted. Let us claim that some naive set-based semantics like stage [27], CF2 [1], and stage2 [16] semantics do not satisfy the RME and RME_{max} principles: consider the argumentation frameworks $AF = (\{a,b,c\}, \{(a,b),(b,c),(c,a)\})$, $AF' = (\{a,b,c,d\}, \{(a,b),(b,c),(c,a),(d,c)\})$ for a counter-example. Consequently, new principles are required to explain the violation of monotony for these semantics, and potentially, the identification of additional relaxed monotony explainability principles can apply a principle-based analysis instead of proving the satisfaction with/violation of a principle semantics-by-semantics.
- Analogous principles can potentially be introduced to other formal argumentation approaches, such as gradual (bipolar) argumentation (see e.g. [2]). For instance, one could define monotony with respect to the relative order of argument final strengths after either some expansion of the argument graph or a change in the initial strengths of arguments. The degree of monotony could then be based on some of the many similarity measures over ordered sequences. Instead of looking at monotony-maximizing extensions then, one could look at arguments that changed their relative ordering, and define and extract explanatory arguments (or changes in their initial strengths) that best explain those changes, potentially by also referring to other properties studied in [2].
- Human-Computer Interaction (HCI) studies that assess the effectiveness of the explanations can be conducted. Let us highlight that at the current stage, we consider an HCI evaluation premature. The behavior of Dung-style admissible set-based semantics is in many cases counter-intuitive (see [9], and consider, for instance, the argumentation framework $AF = (\{a,b\}, \{(a,a),(a,b)\})$ and preferred semantics); hence, an HCI study is likely to yield rather "noisy" results, considering that technically correct explanation of counter-intuitive semantics behavior may confuse study participants.

6 Conclusion

In this paper, we have introduced explanations for the acceptability dynamics in dynamic systems, where explanations attribute changes to argumentation frameworks with reference to a desirable relaxed monotony property. Based on this property, we have constructed a theoretical framework for explaining the violation of monotony in the context of *Dung-style* admissible set-based semantics.

While a software implementation of this theoretical framework is provided, we consider this work primarily an initial stepping stone towards real-world applicable explainability of monotony violations of non-monotonic machine reasoners.

Acknowledgments. We thank the anonymous reviewers for their thoughtful and useful feedback. This work was partially supported by the Wallenberg AI, Autonomous Systems and Software Program (WASP) funded by the Knut and Alice Wallenberg Foundation.

References

1. Baroni, P., Caminada, M., Giacomin, M.: Abstract argumentation frameworks and their semantics (chap. 4). In: Baroni, P., Gabbay, D., Massimiliano, G., van der Torre, L. (eds.) Handbook of Formal Argumentation, pp. 159–236. College Publications (2018)
2. Baroni, P., Rago, A., Toni, F.: From fine-grained properties to broad principles for gradual argumentation: a principled spectrum. Int. J. Approximate Reasoning **105**, 252–286 (2019). https://doi.org/10.1016/j.ijar.2018.11.019
3. Baumann, R.: On the nature of argumentation semantics: existence and uniqueness, expressibility, and replaceability. J. Appl. Log. **4**(8), 2779–2886 (2017)
4. Baumann, R., Brewka, G.: Expanding argumentation frameworks: enforcing and monotonicity results. COMMA **10**, 75–86 (2010)
5. Baumann, R., Brewka, G., Ulbricht, M.: Revisiting the foundations of abstract argumentation-semantics based on weak admissibility and weak defense. In: AAAI, pp. 2742–2749 (2020)
6. Booth, R., Gabbay, D.M., Kaci, S., Rienstra, T., van der Torre, L.: Abduction and dialogical proof in argumentation and logic programming. In: Schaub, T., Friedrich, G., O'Sullivan, B. (eds.) 21st European Conference on Artificial Intelligence. Frontiers in Artificial Intelligence and Applications, vol. 263, pp. 117–122. IOS Press, Prague (2014). https://doi.org/10.3233/978-1-61499-419-0-117
7. Cayrol, C., de Saint-Cyr, F.D., Lagasquie-Schiex, M.C.: Change in abstract argumentation frameworks: adding an argument. J. Arti. Intell. Res. **38**, 49–84 (2010)
8. Cocarascu, O., Čyras, K., Rago, A., Toni, F.: Explaining with argumentation frameworks mined from data. In: 1st International Workshop on Dialogue, Explanation and Argumentation in Human-Agent Interaction (DEXAHAI), Southampton (2018)
9. Cramer, M., Guillaume, M.: Empirical study on human evaluation of complex argumentation frameworks. In: Calimeri, F., Leone, N., Manna, M. (eds.) JELIA 2019. LNCS (LNAI), vol. 11468, pp. 102–115. Springer, Cham (2019). https://doi.org/10.1007/978-3-030-19570-0_7
10. Čyras, K., et al.: Machine reasoning explainability. arXiv preprint arXiv:2009.00418 (2020)
11. Čyras, K., Rago, A., Albini, E., Baroni, P., Toni, F.: Argumentative XAI: a survey. In: Zhou, Z.H. (ed.) 30th International Joint Conference on Artificial Intelligence, pp. 4392–4399. IJCAI, Montreal (2021). https://doi.org/10.24963/ijcai.2021/600
12. Doutre, S., Mailly, J.G.: Constraints and changes: a survey of abstract argumentation dynamics. Argum. Comput. **9**, 223–248 (2018). https://doi.org/10.3233/AAC-180425

13. Dung, P.M.: On the acceptability of arguments and its fundamental role in non-monotonic reasoning, logic programming and n-person games. Artif. Intell. **77**(2), 321–357 (1995)
14. Dung, P.M., Kowalski, R., Toni, F.: Dialectic proof procedures for assumption-based, admissible argumentation. Artif. Intell. **170**(2), 114–159 (2006). https://doi.org/10.1016/j.artint.2005.07.002
15. Dung, P.M., Mancarella, P., Toni, F.: Computing ideal sceptical argumentation. Artif. Intell. **171**(10–15), 642–674 (2007). https://doi.org/10.1016/j.artint.2007.05.003
16. Dvořák, W., Gaggl, S.A.: Stage semantics and the SCC-recursive schema for argumentation semantics. J. Log. Comput. **26**(4), 1149–1202 (2014). https://doi.org/10.1093/logcom/exu006
17. Fan, X., Toni, F.: On explanations for non-acceptable arguments. In: Black, E., Modgil, S., Oren, N. (eds.) TAFA 2015. LNCS (LNAI), vol. 9524, pp. 112–127. Springer, Cham (2015). https://doi.org/10.1007/978-3-319-28460-6_7
18. Fan, X., Toni, F.: On computing explanations in argumentation. In: Bonet, B., Koenig, S. (eds.) 29th AAAI Conference on Artificial Intelligence, pp. 1496–1502. AAAI Press, Austin (2015)
19. Kampik, T., Gabbay, D.: The "degrees of monotony" - dilemma in abstract argumentation. In: Symbolic and Quantitative Approaches to Reasoning with Uncertainty 2021 (2021, to appear)
20. Kampik, T., Nieves, J.C.: Abstract argumentation and the rational man. J. Log. Comput. **31**(2), 654–699 (2021). https://doi.org/10.1093/logcom/exab003
21. Liao, B., van der Torre, L.: Explanation semantics for abstract argumentation. In: Prakken, H. (ed.) Computational Models of Argument, vol. 326, pp. 271–282. IOS Press (2020). https://doi.org/10.3233/FAIA200511
22. Sakama, C.: Abduction in argumentation frameworks. J. Appl. Non-Class. Log. **28**(2–3), 218–239 (2018). https://doi.org/10.1080/11663081.2018.1487241
23. Saribatur, Z.G., Wallner, J.P., Woltran, S.: Explaining non-acceptability in abstract argumentation. In: Giacomo, G.D., et al. (eds.) 24th European Conference on Artificial Intelligence, pp. 881–888. IOS Press, Santiago de Compostela (2020). https://doi.org/10.3233/FAIA200179
24. Thimm, M.: Tweety: a comprehensive collection of Java libraries for logical aspects of artificial intelligence and knowledge representation. In: Proceedings of the Fourteenth International Conference on Principles of Knowledge Representation and Reasoning. KR 2014, pp. 528–537. AAAI Press (2014)
25. van der Torre, L., Vesic, S.: The principle-based approach to abstract argumentation semantics. IfCoLog J. Log. Appl. **4**(8), 2735–2778 (2017)
26. Vassiliades, A., Bassiliades, N., Patkos, T.: Argumentation and explainable artificial intelligence: a survey. Knowl. Eng. Rev. **36**, e5 (2021). https://doi.org/10.1017/S0269888921000011
27. Verheij, B.: Two approaches to dialectical argumentation: admissible sets and argumentation stages. In: Proceedings of the NAIC 1996, pp. 357–368 (1996)
28. Wakaki, T., Nitta, K., Sawamura, H.: Computing abductive argumentation in answer set programming. In: McBurney, P., Rahwan, I., Parsons, S., Maudet, N. (eds.) ArgMAS 2009. LNCS (LNAI), vol. 6057, pp. 195–215. Springer, Heidelberg (2010). https://doi.org/10.1007/978-3-642-12805-9_12

The Burden of Persuasion in Abstract Argumentation

Timotheus Kampik[1(✉)], Dov Gabbay[2,3,4], and Giovanni Sartor[5,6]

[1] Umeå University, Umeå, Sweden
tkampik@cs.umu.se
[2] King's College London, London, UK
dov.gabbay@kcl.ac.uk
[3] University of Luxembourg, Esch-sur-Alzette, Luxembourg
[4] Bar Ilan University, Ramat Gan, Israel
[5] European University Institute, Florence, Italy
giovanni.sartor@eui.eu
[6] Università di Bologna, Bologna, Italy

Abstract. In this paper, we provide a formal framework for modeling the *burden of persuasion* in legal reasoning. The framework is based on abstract argumentation, a frequently studied method of non-monotonic reasoning, and can be applied to different argumentation semantics; it supports burdens of persuasion with arbitrary many levels, and allows for the placement of a burden of persuasion on any subset of an argumentation framework's arguments. Our framework can be considered an extension of related works that raise questions on how burdens of persuasion should be handled in some conflict scenarios that can be modeled with abstract argumentation. An open source software implementation of the introduced formal notions is available as an extension of an argumentation reasoning library.

Keywords: Formal argumentation · Non-monotonic reasoning · Legal reasoning

1 Introduction

Over the past decades, formal argumentation has emerged as a promising collection of methods for reasoning under uncertainty [4]. A particularly relevant application domain that can benefit from argumentation-based models of conflicts and contradictions is legal reasoning [9]. An important notion in legal argumentation – but also in other domains in which an outcome has to be reached under time and resource constraints, such as political debates – is the *burden of persuasion* [20]. By saying that an argument is burdened with persuasion we mean that the argument only is relevant when it is convincing, *i.e.* when it overcomes all relevant objections against it. If this is not the case, the argument has to be rejected for failing to meet its burden of persuasion. In an argumentation-based theory, the burden of persuasion may be placed on some of the arguments

© Springer Nature Switzerland AG 2021
P. Baroni et al. (Eds.): CLAR 2021, LNAI 13040, pp. 224–243, 2021.
https://doi.org/10.1007/978-3-030-89391-0_13

in the theory. Roughly speaking, if there are several conflicting conclusions (here and henceforth referred to as *extensions* to align with formal argumentation terminology), we can infer from the theory (considering constraints imposed by a basic inference function), the burden of persuasion dictates that we must be *less skeptical* towards unburdened arguments than towards burdened ones. If we are faced with conflicting extensions, one being only supported by burdened arguments and one being only supported by unburdened arguments, we select the latter. Moreover, any successful attacks against a burdened argument entail that the burdened argument is to be rejected[1]. In a recent paper, Calegari *et al.* present a model of the burden of persuasion that is based on a structured argumentation approach [11]; in their paper, the authors also highlight some limitations of their model, such as the inability to meaningfully model burdened arguments that are part of cyclic structures. This paper aims to address these limitations by introducing a model of the burden of persuasion that only relies on abstract argumentation and supports any abstract argumentation framework (where the burden of persuasion may be placed on any subset of the argumentation framework's arguments), as well as arbitrary many *levels of burdens*.

Let us introduce an example that gives an intuition of our approach.

Example 1. Usually patients have the burden of persuasion on the liability of medical doctors in order to be compensated for the harm they suffered as a consequence of an unsuccessful treatment. This follows from the general principle that the plaintiffs in a legal case should persuade the judge in order to get a favorable decision. Should the outcome remain uncertain, their claim has to be rejected. However, doctors do not have to pay compensation in case they were diligent in treating the patient and the failure of the treatment was not due to incompetence or carelessness. The possibility of doctors to avoid liability is limited by the fact that – at least in some legal systems – they have the burden of persuasion with regard to their diligence. Their arguments to this effect must be convincing. Otherwise they will be rejected: in case uncertainty remains on whether they were diligent or not, their liability will consequently be established. Note that this is a simplified representation of the matter at stake, since other aspects of the case may have to be considered, such as the difficulty or extraordinary nature of the case of the patient.

Let us assume however, that under the given normative framework a patient asks for compensation. The patient's argument l for the doctors' liability is based on the fact that the doctor subjected him to an unsuccessful and harmful therapy. Argument l is attacked by an expert witness in favor of the doctor, whose argument a claims that the doctor was diligent, since the adopted therapy is successful in the vast majority of cases; this was argued in a leading top scientific journal, the evidence of this journal being sufficient to guarantee the truth of the claim. The patient's expert witness attacks argument a through argument b, according to which a therapy with a higher success rate is available. The high success rate of the adopted treatment is insufficient to establish diligence, if an even more effective treatment is state-of-the art. The Court's expert witness

---

[1] Here, we assume a model where an argument is either burdened or unburdened.

attacks argument b through one further argument c, according to which the scientific evidence in favor of b is insufficient, being based on a restricted set of the scientific literature. Finally, argument c is attacked by argument a, which includes the claim that one single journal was sufficient to establish a scientific claim.

We end up with the following *argumentation framework* – a tuple consisting of a set of *arguments* AR and a set of *attacks* $AT \subseteq AR \times AR$ (Fig. 1):

$$AF' = (AR', AT') = (\{l, a, b, c\}, \{(a, c), (a, l), (b, a), (c, b)\})$$

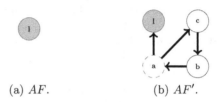

(a) AF.   (b) AF'.

Fig. 1. We restrict AF' to $\{l\}$, generating AF, to reflect that the burden of persuasion rests on the rejection of l. Then, we infer $\{l\}$ from AF and check if we can infer an extension that entails $\{l\}$ from AF'. Since this is the case, we have to consider $\{l\}$ as valid. In the example, arguments with a gray background are unambiguously inferred; arguments with a white background and a solid border may be inferred (are part of at least one extension, considering the burden of persuasion approach); arguments with a dashed border are unambiguously rejected.

Intuitively, it is not clear which of the arguments are *valid* in this framework, so that their conclusion (extension) has to be endorsed, and in particular whether l is valid or not. As noted above, the patient should have the burden of persuasion on liability, but the doctor has the burden of persuasion on her diligence. We assume that it is uncontroversial that the patient has been harmed by the wrong therapy: there is no doubt that the patient has satisfied his burden of persuasion on this point. The issue is whether the doctor has satisfied her burden of persuasion relative to her diligence. She has no benefit of doubt in this regard: in case doubts remain on her diligence, her argument has to be rejected, and so her liability toward the patient will have to be established. The crucial point is then to establish whether there is doubt on her diligence based on the circle of arguments $\{a, b, c\}$.

Hence, we generate the following *argumentation framework sequence* from AF': $AFS = \langle AF, AF' \rangle$, where $AF = (\{l\}, \{\})$; we call AF the *restriction of AF' to $\{l\}$*. We first determine all possible extensions of AF, and trivially, there is only one, which is $\{l\}$. Then, we determine all extensions of AF'. Here, we have different options.

1. Assuming that the cycle of arguments "a attacks c attacks b attacks a" is a self-contradiction, we can say that the only extension is the empty set; the

traditional abstract argumentation semantics as introduced in Dung's seminal paper [14] behave accordingly. However, from a legal reasoning perspective, we need to employ a more credulous approach.

2. Again considering the cycle of arguments "a attacks c attacks b attacks c" as a self-contradiction, we can discard the arguments in this cycle, but then conclude that surely, l cannot be rejected; the recently introduced weak admissible set-based argumentation semantics family [8] formalizes this intuition, and allows us to again infer $\{l\}$ as the only extension. This result is aligned with common legal notions of the burden of persuasion *in our case*, because the practitioner's diligence is not beyond doubt[2].

3. We can assume that any of the arguments a, b, or c could be part of an extension, but that these three arguments are mutually exclusive, and hence infer that $\{a\}$, $\{b, l\}$ and $\{c, l\}$ are extensions. This intuition is formalized (for example) by CF2 [6] and SCF2 [12] semantics; not all extensions reject l; hence, the notion of the burden of persuasion constrains us to select one of the extensions that entail l, *i.e.* either $\{b, l\}$ or $\{c, l\}$. This means we have to accept l and we conclude that the doctor has not successfully persuaded the court that she has acted without negligence.

Let us highlight that our framework for modeling the burden of persuasion is not merely determining whether a set of arguments is *credulously accepted* – whether it is entailed by at least one extension – or *skeptically accepted, i.e.* whether it is entailed by all extensions. For this, we introduce an additional (abstract) example, which also illustrates how we can manage multiple levels of the burden of persuasion.

Example 2. Consider the following argumentation framework:

$$AF'' = (\{a, b, c, d, e\}, \{(a, b), (a, e), (b, a), (b, e), (c, d), (d, c), (e, a), (e, b)\})$$

and the following burdens of persuasion: *i)* a and b are unburdened; *ii)* c is burdened with a "light-weight" level 1 burden; *iii)* d and e are burdened with a "heavier" level 2 burden. Let us assume a credulous inference function allows for the following extensions[3] (given only AF'' and no burden of persuasion model):

$$\{a, c\}, \{a, d\}, \{b, c\}, \{b, d\}, \{e, c\}, \{e, d\}$$

We take a look at the unburdened arguments and their attacks among each other, which gives us the argumentation framework $AF = (\{a, b\}, \{(a, b), (b, a)\})$. We

---

[2] For the sake of conciseness, we do not consider weak admissibility-based semantics in detail. However, let us claim that the simple example $AF = (\{a, b, c\}, \{(a, b), (b, c), (c, a)\})$ illustrates that all weak admissible set-based semantics Baumann *et al.* may not be sufficiently credulous for many applications that require a model of the burden of persuasion.

[3] In this example, the inferences we draw from the abstract argumentation frameworks coincide, for example, with the *extensions* (sets of arguments) returned by CF2 [6] and SCF2 [12] semantics.

assume that from AF, we can infer either $\{a\}$ or $\{b\}$. This means that we need to consider all extensions that can be inferred from AF''', given they entail either $\{a\}$ or $\{b\}$. We "filter" the extensions accordingly and remain with the following sets[4]:

$$\{a, c\}, \{a, d\}, \{b, c\}, \{b, d\}$$

Now, we consider the arguments that carry the first-level burden of persuasion, i.e. $\{c\}$ and $AF' = (\{a, b, c\}, \{(a, b), (b; a)\})$. Because of the unburdened arguments, we have to be able to infer either $\{a\}$ or $\{b\}$. But surely, we can allow for this inference and still guarantee that we can infer $\{c\}$: we merely need to remove the extensions $\{a, d\}$ and $\{b, d\}$:

$$\{a, c\}, \{b, c\}$$

It follows that $\{a, c\}$ and $\{b, c\}$ are our final extensions; the arguments that carry the second-level burden of persuasion – d and e – are rejected. No unambiguous conclusion can be reached, as our final inference result is "either $\{a, c\}$ or $\{b, c\}$" (Fig. 2).

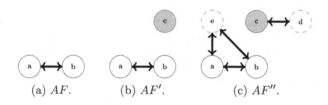

(a) AF.   (b) AF'.   (c) AF''.

Fig. 2. Multiple levels of burdens of persuasion.

A software implementation of the formal concepts we introduce in this paper is available at https://git.io/JGueN. The implementation relies on the abstract argumentation reasoner provided by the *Tweety* project [21].

The rest of this paper is organized as follows. Section 2 provides relevant theoretical preliminaries. Then, Sect. 3 introduces our formal framework for modeling the burden of persuasion in abstract argumentation. The suitability of applying different argumentation semantics, as well as the relevance of skeptical acceptance are discussed in Sect. 4. Finally, Sect. 5 discusses the framework in the context of related research, before Sect. 6 concludes the paper.

2   Preliminaries

This section introduces the preliminaries that our work is based upon. The central notion this paper uses is Dung's (abstract) argumentation framework [14].

---

[4] Let us note that there are some intricate details in the filtering approach that this example does not cover.

An argumentation framework AF is a tuple (AR, AT), such that AR is a set of *arguments* and AT is a set of *attacks*, $AT \subseteq AR \times AR$. We assume that the set of arguments in an argumentation framework is finite. For $(a, b) \in AT$, we say that "a attacks b". For $S \subseteq AR$, $b \in S$, and $a \in AR$, iff $(b, a) \in AT$, we say that "S attacks a" and iff $(a, b) \in AT$, we say that "a attacks S"; we denote $\{a | a \in AR, a$ attacks $S\}$ by S^- and $\{b | b \in AR, S$ attacks $b\}$ by S^+. For $S \subseteq AR$, $P \subseteq AR$ such that $\exists (a, b) \in AT, a \in S, b \in P$, we say that "$S$ attacks P". For $S \subseteq AR, a \in AR$, we say that "S defends a" iff $\forall b \in AR$, such that b attacks a it holds true that S attacks b. Given $S \subseteq AR$, we define $AF \downarrow_S = (S, AT \cap S \times S)$. We call $AF \downarrow_S$ the *restriction of AF to S*. Let us introduce some properties of sets of arguments in an argumentation framework.

Definition 1 (Conflict-free, Unattacked, and Admissible Sets [3]). *Let $AF = (AR, AT)$ be an argumentation framework. A set $S \subseteq AR$: i) is conflict-free iff $\nexists a, b \in S$ such that a attacks b; ii) is unattacked iff $\nexists a \in AR \setminus S$ such that a attacks S; iii) is admissible iff S is conflict-free and $\forall a \in S$, it holds true that S defends a.*

Argumentation framework expansions model the addition of new arguments and attacks to an argumentation framework.

Definition 2 (Argumentation Framework Expansions [7]). *Let $AF = (AR, AT)$ and $AF' = (AR', AT')$ be argumentation frameworks. AF' is an expansion of AF (denoted by $AF \preceq_E AF'$) iff $AR \subseteq AR'$ and $AT \subseteq AT'$. AF' is a normal expansion of AF (denoted by $AF \preceq_N AF'$) iff $AF \preceq_E AF'$ and $(AR \times AR) \cap (AT' \setminus AT) = \{\}$.*

While our formal framework does not rely on expansions or normal expansions, these notions can be used to establish the connection between our work and the research direction of *dynamics* in formal argumentation (see Sect. 5).

An argumentation semantics σ takes an argumentation framework as its input and determines sets of arguments (*extensions*) that can be considered valid conclusions. Dung's seminal paper introduces stable, preferred, complete, and grounded argumentation semantics.

Definition 3 (Dung's Argumentation Semantics [14]). *Let $AF = (AR, AT)$ be an argumentation framework. An* admissible *set $S \subseteq AR$ is a:*

- stable extension *of AF iff S attacks each argument that does not belong to S.* $\sigma_{st}(AF)$ *denotes all stable extensions of AF.*
- preferred extension *of AF iff S is a maximal (w.r.t. set inclusion) admissible subset of AR.* $\sigma_{pr}(AF)$ *denotes all preferred extensions of AF.*
- complete extension *of AF iff each argument that is defended by S belongs to S.* $\sigma_{co}(AF)$ *denotes all complete extensions of AF.*
- grounded extension *of AF iff S is the minimal (w.r.t. set inclusion) complete extension of AF.* $\sigma_{gr}(AF)$ *denotes all grounded extensions of AF.*

Given any argumentation semantics σ and any argumentation framework AF, we call a set $S \in \sigma(AF)$ a σ-extension of AF. If and only if for every argumentation framework AF it holds true that $|\sigma(AF)| \geq 1$ we say that σ is universally defined; if and only if for every argumentation framework AF it holds true that $|\sigma(AF)| = 1$ we say that σ is universally uniquely defined. Dung's semantics are all based on the notion of an admissible set. Later works introduce semantics based on naive ($\subseteq$-maximal conflict-free) sets.

Definition 4 (Naive and Stage Semantics [23]). *Let $AF = (AR, AT)$ be an argumentation framework and let $S \subseteq AR$.*

- *S is a naive extension of AF iff S is a maximal conflict-free subset of AR w.r.t. set inclusion. $\sigma_{naive}(AF)$ denotes all naive extensions of AF.*
- *S is a stage extension of AF iff S is conflict-free and $S \cup S^+$ is maximal w.r.t. set inclusion, i.e. $\nexists S' \subseteq AR$, such that S' is a conflict-free set and $S \cup S^+ \subset S' \cup S'^+$. $\sigma_{stage}(AF)$ denotes the stage extensions of AF.*

Given an argumentation framework AF and an argumentation semantics σ, the skeptically accepted set of arguments is the intersection of the σ-extensions of AF.

Definition 5 (Skeptical Acceptance). *Let $AF = (AR, AT)$ be an argumentation framework and let σ be an argumentation semantics. We call $\bigcap_{E \in \sigma(AF)} E$ the skeptically accepted set of arguments of AF given σ and denote it by $\sigma^{\cap}(AF)$.*

Let us introduce some preliminaries for so-called *SCC-recursive semantics*, starting with the notion of a path between arguments.

Definition 6 (Path between Arguments). *Let $AF = (AR, AT)$ be an argumentation framework. A path from an argument $a_0 \in AR$ to another argument $a_n \in AR$ is a sequence of arguments $P_{a_0,a_n} = \langle a_0, ..., a_n \rangle$, such that for $0 \leq i < n$, a_i attacks a_{i+1}.*

Based on this definition, we can define the notion of reachability.

Definition 7 (Reachability). *Let $AF = (AR, AT)$ be an argumentation framework. We say that given two arguments $a, b \in AR$, "b is reachable from a" iff there exists a path $P_{a,b}$ or $a = b$.*

Based on the notion of reachability, we can define *strongly connected components*.

Definition 8 (Strongly Connected Components (SCC)). *Let $AF = (AR, AT)$ be an argumentation framework. $S \subseteq AR$ is a strongly connected component of AF iff $\forall a, b \in S$, a is reachable from b and b is reachable from a and $\nexists c \in AR \setminus S$, such that a is reachable from c and c is reachable from a. Let us denote the strongly connected components of AF by $SCCS(AF)$.*

Another preliminary for SCC-recursive semantics is the UP function.

Definition 9 (UP [6]**).** *Let* $AF = (AR, AT)$ *be an argumentation framework and let* $E \subseteq AR$, $S \subseteq AR$. *We define* $UP_{AF}(S, E) = \{a | a \in S, \nexists b \in E \setminus S \text{ such that } (b, a) \in AT\}$.

Now, we can introduce the SCC-recursive and naive set-based CF2 semantics.

Definition 10 (CF2 Semantics [6]**).** *Let* $AF = (AR, AT)$ *be an argumentation framework and let* $E \subseteq AR$. E *is a CF2 extension iff:*

- E *is a naive extension of* AF *if* $|SCCS(AF)| = 1$;
- $\forall S \in SCCS(AF)$, $(E \cap S)$ *is a CF2 extension of* $AF \downarrow_{UP_{AF}(S,E)}$, *otherwise.*

$\sigma_{CF2}(AF)$ *denotes all CF2 extensions of* AF.

To give a rough intuition of how SCC-recursive semantics (and in particular: CF2 semantics) work, let us introduce an example.

Example 3. Consider $AF = (\{a, b, c\}, \{(a, b), (b, a), (a, c), (b, c)\})$. We have two SCCs: $\{a, b\}$ and $\{c\}$. Colloquially speaking, we traverse the SCC graph, starting with unattacked ("top-level") SCCs: first, we take the top-level SCC $\{a, b\}$ and determine $\sigma_{naive}(AF \downarrow_{\{a,b\}}) = \{\{a\}, \{b\}\}$. Then, $\forall E \in \{\{a\}, \{b\}\}$, we determine $UP_{AF}(S, E)$, where $S = \{c\}$, because $\{c\}$ is the "next" and only remaining SCC. Because $UP_{AF}(\{c\}, \{a\}) = UP_{AF}(\{c\}, \{b\}) = \{\}$ and $\sigma_{naive}((\{\}, \{\})) = \{\{\}\}$, we remain with $\{a\}$ and $\{b\}$ as our CF2 extensions.

Stage2 is an SCC-recursive semantics that has been introduced to address some shortcomings of CF2 semantics, notably unintuitive behavior when resolving even-length cycles of length ≥ 6, roughly speaking (see Example 4, argumentation framework AF^{**}).

Definition 11 (Stage2 Semantics [15]**).** *Let* $AF = (AR, AT)$ *be an argumentation framework and let* $E \subseteq AR$. E *is a stage2 extension iff:*

- E *is a stage extension of* AF *if* $|SCCS(AF)| = 1$;
- $\forall S \in SCCS(AF)$, $(E \cap S)$ *is a stage2 extension of* $AF \downarrow_{UP_{AF}(S,E)}$, *otherwise.*

$\sigma_{stage2}(AF)$ *denotes all stage2 extensions of* AF.

Another "CF2 improvement attempt" is made by Cramer's and Van der Torre's SCF2 semantics [12]. The authors start by defining a notion that ignores self-attacking arguments.

Definition 12 (nsa(AF) [12]**).** *Let* $AF = (AR, AT)$ *be an argumentation framework. We define* $nsa(AF) = AF \downarrow_{\{a | a \in AR \text{ and } (a,a) \notin AT\}}$.

Based on this notion, Cramer and Van der Torre introduce nsa(CF2) semantics as an intermediate step on the way to SCF2 semantics.

Definition 13 (nsa(CF2) Semantics [12]**).** *Let* $AF = (AR, AT)$ *be an argumentation framework. A set* $E \subseteq AR$ *is an nsa(CF2)-extension of* AF *iff* $E \in \sigma_{CF2}(nsa(AF))$. $\sigma_{nsa(CF2)}(AF)$ *denotes all nsa(CF2) extensions of* AF.

This approach fixes some issues with CF2 semantics and self-attacking arguments. To tackle the problem with even-length cycles, we need to define some preliminaries.

Definition 14 (Attack Cycles). *Let $AF = (AR, AT)$ be an argumentation framework. An attack cycle C is a sequence of arguments $\langle a_0, ..., a_n \rangle$ where $(a_i, a_{i+1}) \in AT$ for $0 \leq i < n$ and $a_j \neq a_k$ for $0 \leq j < k \leq n$ if not $j = 0$ and $k = n$, and where $a_0 = a_n$. An attack cycle is odd iff n is odd and even iff n is even.*

Cramer and Van der Torre introduce a specific property to describe how a CF2-like semantics should ideally behave in the case of even cycles that are not "affected" by odd cycles, roughly speaking.

Definition 15 (Strong Completeness Outside Odd Cycles (Set) [12]**).** *Let $AF = (AR, AT)$ be an argumentation framework. A set $S \subseteq AR$ is strongly complete outside odd cycles iff $\forall a \in AR$, if no argument in $\{a\} \cup \{a\}^-$ is in an odd attack cycle and $S \cap \{a\}^- = \{\}$ then $a \in S$.*

To systematically analyze argumentation semantics, a range of formal argumentation principles have been defined [5, 22]. Cramer and Van der Torre turn the *strong completeness outside odd cycles* property into a principle to "catch" unintuitive CF2 behavior.

Definition 16 (SCOOC Principle [12]**).** *An argumentation semantics σ is Strongly Complete Outside Odd Cycles (SCOOC) iff for every argumentation framework $AF, \forall E \in \sigma(AF), E$ is strongly complete outside odd cycles.*

Based on this principle and the notion of $nsa(CF2)$ semantics, SCF2 semantics is defined.

Definition 17 (SCF2 Semantics [12]**).** *Let $AF = (AR, AT)$ be an argumentation framework and let E be a set such that $E \subseteq AR$. E is an SCF2 extension iff:*

- *E is a naive extension of $nsa(AF)$ and E is strongly complete outside odd cycles if $|SCCS(nsa(AF))| = 1$;*
- *$\forall S \in SCCS(nsa(AF)), (E \cap S)$ is an SCF2 extension of $AF \downarrow_{UP_{nsa(AF)}(S,E)}$, otherwise.*

$\sigma_{SCF2}(AF)$ *denotes all SCF2 extensions of AF.*

Let us introduce some examples that illustrate the behaviors of – and highlights the difference between – stage, CF2, stage2, and SCF2 semantics. However, let us note that a detailed explanation of the semantics is beyond the scope of this paper and the reader may consult the original works instead.

Example 4. Let us consider the following argumentation frameworks: *i)* $AF' = (\{a, b, c\}, \{(a, b), (b, c), (c, c)\})$; *ii)* $AF'' = (\{a, b, c\}, \{(a, b), (a, c), (b, c), (c, a)\})$; *iii)* $AF^* = (\{a, b, c\}, \{(a, b), (b, c), (c, a), (c, c)\})$; *iv)* $AF^{**} = (\{a, b, c, d, e, f\}, \{(a, b), (b, c), (c, d), (d, e), (e, f), (f, a)\})$. Table 1 displays the extensions stage, CF2, stage2, and SCF2 semantics yield for these argumentation frameworks.

Table 1. Differences between stage, CF2, stage2, and SCF2 semantics (examples).

	Stage	CF2	Stage2	SCF2
AF'	$\{a\},\{b\}$	$\{a\}$	$\{a\}$	$\{a\}$
AF''	$\{a\}$	$\{a\},\{b\},\{c\}$	$\{a\}$	$\{a\},\{b\},\{c\}$
AF^*	$\{a\},\{b\}$	$\{a\},\{b\}$	$\{a\},\{b\}$	$\{a\}$
AF^{**}	$\{a,c,e\},\{b,d,f\}$	$\{a,c,e\},$ $\{b,d,f\}$ $\{a,d\},\{b,e\},$ $\{c,f\}$	$\{a,c,e\},\{b,d,f\}$	$\{a,c,e\},\{b,d,f\}$

Argumentation principles that are relevant in the context of this paper are the admissibility and naivety principles.

Definition 18 (Admissibility and Naivety Principles [5]). *Let σ be an argumentation semantics. σ satisfies the admissibility principle iff for every argumentation framework $AF = (AR, AT)$, $\forall E \in \sigma(AF)$, E is an admissible set. σ satisfies the naivety principle iff for every argumentation framework $AF = (AR, AT)$, $\forall E \in \sigma(AF)$, E is a maximal conflict-free subset (w.r.t. set inclusion) of AR.*

3   An Abstract Argumentation-Based Burden of Persuasion

In this section, we introduce our formal framework for modeling burdens of persuasion in abstract argumentation.

Definition 19 (Burden of Persuasion-Framework (BPF)). *A Burden of Persuasion Framework (BPF) is a tuple $AF_{BP} = (ARS, AT)$, where:*

- *$ARS = \langle S_0, ..., S_n \rangle$ and each $S_i, 0 \leq i \leq n$ is a non-empty set of arguments, such that for each $S_j, 0 \leq j \leq n, i \neq j$, it holds true that $S_i \cap S_j = \{\}$;*
- *We denote $\bigcup_{0 \leq k \leq n} S_k$ by $ARGS(ARS)$;*
- *$AT \subseteq ARGS(ARS) \times ARGS(ARS)$.*

We assume that given a BPF $AF_{BPF}(ARS, AT)$, $ARGS(ARS)$ is finite. Let us introduce some short-hand notation that makes it easier to work with BPFs.

Definition 20 (BPF Short-hand Notation). *Let $AF_{BP} = (ARS, AT)$ be a BPF, such that $ARS = \langle S_0, ..., S_n \rangle$. Given $0 \leq i \leq n$, we denote $\bigcup_{0 \leq j < i} S_j$ by AR_i and $(AR_i, AT \cap (AR_i \times AR_i))$ by AF_i. Also, for any $AF_{BP} = (ARS, AT)$, such that $ARS = \langle S_0, ..., S_n \rangle$, we denote:*

$$AF_{BP-1} = \begin{cases} AF_{BP} & \text{if } n = 0; \\ (\langle S_0 \cup S_n \rangle, AT) & \text{if } n = 1; \\ (\langle S_0, ..., S_{n-2}, S_{n-1} \cup S_n \rangle, AT) & \text{otherwise.} \end{cases}$$

For a set of arguments $S \subseteq S_0$ we say that S is unburdened *and for any argument $a \in S_0$ we say that a is unburdened. For a set of arguments $S' \subseteq S_k, 0 < k \leq n$, we say that S' is* burdened *or that S' is level k-burdened, and for an argument $a' \in S_k$ we say that a' is* burdened *or that a' is level k-burdened.*

Let us introduce an example of a BPF.

Example 5. Consider Example 2. When modeling the argumentation frameworks that we have in the example as a BPF, we get:

- AF_{BP} = $(\langle\{a,b\},\{c\},\{d,e\}\rangle, \{(a,b),(a,e),(b,a),(b,e),(c,d),(d,c),(e,a),(e,b)\})$;
- $AF_2 = (\{a,b,c,d,e\},\{(a,b),(a,e),(b,a),(b,e),(c,d),(d,c),(e,a),(e,b)\})$;
- $AF_1 = (\{a,b,c\},\{a,b),(b,a)\})$;
- $AF_0 = (\{a,b\},\{(a,b),(b,a)\})$;
- AF_{BP-1} = $(\langle\{a,b\},\{c,d,e\}\rangle, \{(a,b),(a,e),(b,a),(b,e),(c,d),(d,c),(e,a),(e,b)\})$.

The set of arguments $\{a,b\}$ is unburdened, $\{c\}$ is level 1-burdened and $\{d,e\}$ is level 2-burdened.

Before we can define a way to determine the extensions of BPFs, let us introduce the notion of $\subseteq$-maximal monotonic extensions.

Definition 21 ($\subseteq$-Maximal Monotonic Extensions). *Let AR and A be finite sets of arguments (extensions) and let $EXTS \subseteq 2^{AR}$ and $ES \subseteq 2^A$. We define the $\subseteq$-maximal monotonic extensions of $EXTS$ w.r.t. ES, denoted by $EXTS_{mon}^{\subseteq-max}(EXTS, ES)$, as follows:*

$$EXTS_{mon}^{\subseteq-max}(EXTS, ES) =$$
$$\{E | E \in EXTS, \exists S \in ES \text{ such that } \forall E' \in EXTS, E' \cap S \subseteq E \cap S\}$$

Let us highlight that the notion of $\subseteq$-maximal monotonic extensions is purposefully different from the cardinality-based monotony measure and optimization approach [19] that we have recently introduced. Colloquially speaking, we can say that the $\subseteq$-maximal approach is more credulous. As an example, consider the argumentation frameworks $AF = (\{a,b,c\},\{\})$ and $AF' = (\{a,b,c,d,e\},\{(d,a),(d,e),(e,b),(e,c),(e,d)\})$ and preferred semantics. $\sigma_{pr}(AF) = \{\{a,b,c\}\}$; the only cardinality-maximal monotonic extension of $\sigma_{pr}(AF')$ w.r.t. to $\{\{a,b,c\}\}$ is $\{b,d,c\}$, whereas we have two $\subseteq$-maximal monotonic extensions of $\sigma_{pr}(AF')$ w.r.t. to $\{\{a,b,c\}\}$, *i.e.* $\{b,d,c\}$ and $\{a,e\}$. Hence, $\subseteq$-maximal monotonic extensions are better aligned with the notion of the *burden of persuasion* in legal reasoning: intuitively, we cannot eliminate doubt in this scenario. However, we want to avoid the inclusion of extensions that are not Pareto optimal. Let us provide an example to illustrate this problem.

Example 6. Consider $EXTS = \{\{a,b\},\{\}\}$ and $ES = \{\{a\},\{c\}\}$. $EXTS_{mon}^{\subseteq-max}(EXTS, ES) = \{\{a,b\},\{\}\}$. However, intuitively, it makes sense to "drop" $\{\}$, because its absence does not affect the fact that c is not entailed by any set of arguments in $EXTS$, but its presence implies that we *may* select a set of arguments from $EXTS$ that does not entail a.

To address this issue, we define *Pareto optimal* $\subseteq$-maximal monotonic extensions.

Definition 22 (Pareto Optimal $\subseteq$ -Maximal Monotonic Extensions).
Let AR and A be finite sets of arguments (extensions), let $EXTS \subseteq 2^{AR}$ and $ES \subseteq 2^A$. We define the Pareto optimal $\subseteq$-maximal monotonic extensions of $EXTS$ w.r.t. ES, denoted by $EXTS_{po-mon}^{\subseteq-max}(EXTS, ES)$, as follows:

$$EXTS_{po-mon}^{\subseteq-max}(EXTS, ES) = \{E | E \in EXTS \text{ and}$$
$$\nexists E' \in EXTS, \text{ such that}$$
$$\forall S \in ES, S \cap E \subseteq S \cap E' \text{ and}$$
$$\exists S' \in ES, \text{ such that } S' \cap E \subset S' \cap E'\}$$

Let us continue the previous example to illustrate the difference between the previous two definitions.

Example 7. Consider again $EXTS = \{\{a, b\}, \{\}\}$ and $ES = \{\{a\}, \{c\}\}$.
$EXTS_{po-mon}^{\subseteq-max}(EXTS, ES) = \{\{a, b\}\}$.

Now, let us define a way to determine the extension of a BPF, given any universally defined argumentation semantics.

Definition 23 (BP Semantics and Extensions). *Let $AF_{BP} = (ARS, AT)$ be a BPF, such that $ARS = \langle S_0, ..., S_n \rangle$, and let σ be an argumentation semantics. We define the σ-extensions of AF_{BP} as returned by the BP semantics σ^{BP}, denoted by $\sigma^{BP}(AF_{BP})$, as follows:*

$$\sigma^{BP}(AF_{BP}) =$$
$$\begin{cases} \sigma(AF_0) & \text{if } n = 0; \\ EXTS_{po-mon}^{\subseteq-max}(\sigma^{BP}(AF_{BP-1}), \sigma(AF_0) \cup ... \cup \sigma(AF_{n-1})) & \text{otherwise.} \end{cases}$$

Let us provide an example of how BPF extensions are determined.

Example 8. Consider the BPF $AF_{BP} = (ARS, AT) = (\langle \{a, b\}, \{c, d, e\}, \{f\} \rangle, \{(a, c), (a, e), (c, d), (d, b), (d, f), (e, a), (e, c), (f, b), (f, d)\})$. Let us assume we apply SCF2 semantics[5] and first provide an intuition that strays from the recursive definition (Definition 23). Based on AF_{BP}, we generate the following argumentation frameworks: $AF_0 = (\{a, b\}, \{\})$; $AF_1 = (\{a, b, c, d, e\}, \{(a, c), (a, e), (c, d), (d, b), (e, a), (e, c)\})$; $AF_2 = (\{a, b, c, d, e, f\}, \{(a, c), (a, e), (c, d), (d, b), (d, f), (e, a), (e, c), (f, b), (f, d)\})$. Figure 3 depicts AF_0, AF_1, and AF_2. Then, we determine the CF2 extensions of AF_2 and AF_0: $\sigma_{SCF2}(AF_2) = \{\{a, d\}, \{a, f\}, \{e, d\}, \{e, f\}\}$ and $\sigma_{SCF2}(AF_0) = \{\{a, b\}\}$. $EXTS_{po-mon}^{\subseteq-max}(\sigma_{SCF2}(AF_2), \sigma_{SCF2}(AF_0)) = \{\{a, d\}, \{a, f\}\}$. Next, we determine the SCF2 extensions of AF_1: $\sigma_{SCF2}(AF_1) = \{\{a, d\}, \{e, d\}\}$. $EXTS_{po-mon}^{\subseteq-max}$

---

[5] Let us note that for this BPF, applying preferred semantics would not make a difference at any of the steps that follow. This may help the reader follow along.

$(\sigma_{SCF2}(AF_2), \sigma_{SCF2}(AF_0) \cup \sigma_{SCF2}(AF_1)) = \{\{a,d\}\}$; hence our final result is $\sigma^{BP}_{SCF2}(AF_{BP}) = \{\{a,d\}\}$.

Following the recursive definition (Definition 23), we proceed as follows.

1. $\sigma^{BP}_{SCF2}(AF_{BP}) =$
   $EXTS^{\subseteq-max}_{po-mon}(\sigma^{BP}_{SCF2}(AF_{BP-1}), \sigma_{SCF2}(AF_0) \cup \sigma_{SCF2}(AF_1))$;
2. $AF_{BP-1} = (\langle\{a,b\},\{c,d,e,f\}\rangle, AT)$;
3. $\sigma^{BP}_{SCF2}(AF_{BP-1}) = EXTS^{\subseteq-max}_{po-mon}(\sigma^{BP}_{SCF2}(AF_{(BP-1)-1}), \sigma_{SCF2}(AF_0))$;
4. $AF_{(BP-1)-1} = (\langle\{a,b,c,d,e,f\}\rangle, AT)$;
5. $\sigma^{BP}_{SCF2}(AF_{(BP-1)-1}) = \sigma_{SCF2}(AF_2) = \{\{a,d\},\{a,f\},\{e,d\},\{e,f\}\}$;
6. $\sigma_{SCF2}(AF_0) = \{\{a,b\}\}$;
7. $\sigma^{BP}_{SCF2}(AF_{BP-1}) = EXTS^{\subseteq-max}_{po-mon}(\sigma^{BP}_{SCF2}(AF_{(BP-1)-1}), \sigma_{SCF2}(AF_0)) =$
   $\{\{a,d\},\{a,f\}\}$;
8. $\sigma^{BP}_{SCF2}(AF_{BP}) =$
   $EXTS^{\subseteq-max}_{po-mon}(\sigma^{BP}_{SCF2}(AF_{BP-1}), \sigma_{SCF2}(AF_0) \cup \sigma_{SCF2}(AF_1)) =$
   $EXTS^{\subseteq-max}_{po-mon}(\{\{a,d\},\{a,f\}\}, \{\{a,b\}\} \cup \{\{a,d\},\{e,d\}\}) = \{\{a,d\}\}$.

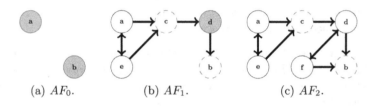

(a) AF_0.   (b) AF_1.   (c) AF_2.

Fig. 3. Example: given the $AF_{BP} = (\langle\{a,b\},\{c,d,e\},\{f\}\rangle, \{(a,c),(a,e),(c,d),(d,b),$ $(d,f),(e,a),(e,c),(f,b),(f,d)\})$, the figure depicts AF_0, AF_1, and AF_2.

We can show that given an argumentation semantics σ that is universally defined, the corresponding BPF semantics σ^{BP} is universally defined as well.

Proposition 1. *Let σ be an argumentation semantics. If σ is universally defined then σ^{BP} is universally defined.*

Similarly, given an argumentation semantics σ that is universally uniquely defined, the corresponding BP semantics σ^{BP} is universally uniquely defined.

Proposition 2. *Let σ be an argumentation semantics. If σ is universally uniquely defined then σ^{BP} is universally uniquely defined.*

We provide the proofs in the Appendix. Let us claim that for every universally uniquely defined argumentation semantics σ, for every burden of persuasion-framework $AF_{BP} = (\langle S_0, ..., S_n\rangle, AT)$ it holds true that $\sigma^{BP}(AF_{BP}) = \sigma(AF_n)$. We call any argumentation semantics for which this condition holds true *burden agnostic* – every universally uniquely defined argumentation semantics is burden agnostic and for burden agnostic semantics, it does not make sense to construct burden of persuasion-frameworks.

4   Semantics Selection and Skeptical Acceptance

The formal framework we have introduced in the previous section can be applied together with any universally defined argumentation semantics (see Proposition 1)[6]. To analyze the feasibility of different argumentation semantics in the context of our framework, let us first give an overview of the three main abstract argumentation semantics families, using the argumentation framework $AF = (\{a, b, c, d\}, \{(a, b), (b, c), (c, a), (a, d)\})$ as an example that highlights key differences[7].

Admissible Set-Based Semantics. The four argumentation semantics (stable, complete, preferred and grounded, see Definition 3) that Dung introduces in his seminal paper all satisfy the principle of admissibility (see Definition 18): any extension such a semantics yields must be an admissible set. Considering the example argumentation framework AF, the only set in 2^{AR} that is admissible is $\{\}$. Hence, we suggest that typically, admissible set-based semantics are too skeptical to be useful when applied to burden of persuasion frameworks. In the example, no matter where we place burdens of persuasion, we always have to infer the empty set. In case this skepticism is considered adequate in face of odd cycles, users may consider applying a universally defined admissible set-based semantics that is relatively credulous, such as preferred or complete semantics and should then consider ignoring self-attacking arguments (or abstaining from constructing argumentation frameworks that contain self-attacking arguments). However, let us note that even then, applying weak admissible set based semantics (see below) may be more suitable.

Weak Admissible Set-Based Semantics. Baumann *et al.* introduce the weak admissible set-based semantics family [8] to address a long-standing problem with admissible set-based semantics that Dung observes in his seminal paper. Consider the example argumentation framework AF, or the even simpler framework $AF' = (\{a, d\}, \{(a, a), (a, d)\})$ and assume that an argument that – roughly speaking – defeats itself should be rejected (which is, arguably, an intuition that motivates admissibility). According to this assumption, we want to reject a when considering AF', and a, b and c, when considering AF. Consequently, we should, for sure, be able to infer d from AF (and AF'). Weak admissible set-based semantics achieve this behavior by systematically relaxing admissibility. For the sake of conciseness, we do not introduce a formal perspective on weak admissible set-based semantics. Still, let us speculate that the application of weak admissible set-based semantics may be useful in the context of burden of persuasion frameworks, given we want to ensure skepticism in face of odd cycles.

---

[6] However, it does not make sense to apply the approach using universally uniquely defined semantics, see the previous section.

[7] Note that in this section, we merely provide intuitions that can guide a practical selection of argumentation semantics. These intuitions are informed by more thorough, overviews and principle-based analyses of abstract argumentation semantics, as for example surveyed by Baroni *et al.* [3] (argumentation semantics overview) and Van der Torre and Vesic [22] (overview of argumentation principles).

Naive Set-Based Semantics. Naive set-based semantics, as initially introduced by Verheij [23] form the most credulous of the three semantics families; the naivety principle (see Definition 18) merely requires that every extension a semantics infers is a ⊆-maximal conflict-free (*naive*) set. By definition, every extension that an admissible set-based or weak admissible set-based semantics yields is conflict-free and hence entailed by a naive set. Any of the naive set-based semantics whose definitions we provide in Sect. 2 infers the following three extensions from the example framework AF: $\{a\}$, $\{b, d\}$, and $\{c, d\}$. Naive set-based semantics start off with the naivety principle, and then typically formalize further constraints that are related to the notions of SCC-recursiveness (see Sect. 2) or *range*, *i.e.* ⊆-maximality of an extension in union with the arguments the extension attacks. Among the four "reasonable" naive set-based semantics (not considering naive semantics, which does not impose any further constraint besides naivety), the two semantics that employ the notion of *range*, *i.e.* stage and stage2 semantics, can be considered more skeptical than the two semantics that are SCC-recursively defined, but do not use range (CF2 and SCF2 semantics). Consider AF'' as introduced by Example 4. Also, Example 4 highlights that stage, stage2, and CF2 semantics may behave counter-intuitively when self-attacking arguments are present; hence, self-attacking arguments should be avoided or ignored. Because of the well-known limitations (see Example 4 and also Dvorak and Gaggl [15], as well as Cramer and Van der Torre [12]), there is most likely no use-case that justifies the application of CF2 semantics; instead SCF2 semantics should be applied, or – if SCF2 semantics is deemed too complex – a stage semantics variant that ignores self-attacking arguments may be a reasonable and slightly more skeptical approximation.

In the context of our burden of persuasion framework, naive set-based semantics are arguably the most interesting abstract argumentation family, due to their relatively credulous behavior. This behavior can then be further constrained by the burden of persuasion model in a BPF. Still, in many scenarios, a naive set-based semantics yields several extensions for a given BPF, and hence is inconclusive. Then, we can use the notion of credulous and skeptical acceptance as an additional assessment layer; in particular, we may ask the following questions. *i)* Given a set of arguments that includes burdened arguments (or, in the case of multiple levels of burdens: arguments with a high level of burden), are these arguments entailed by the skeptical extension we can infer? *ii)* Given a set of arguments that are unburdened (or, in the case of multiple levels of burdens: unburdened arguments or arguments with a low level of burden), are these arguments entailed by at least one extension we can infer? Let us claim that in the case of naive set-based semantics, the notions of credulous and skeptical acceptance are more useful than the notion of *undecided* arguments in traditional labeling-based approaches (see, *e.g.*, Wu and Caminada [24]); all arguments that are not entailed by a naive-based extension are in conflict with this extension and hence, it is counter-intuitive to consider arguments that are not attacked by the extension – and consequently, are attackers of the extension – as undecided.

5 Discussion

From a formal theory perspective, our framework for modeling burdens of persuasion can be considered a contribution to the research area of *argumentation dynamics* (see Doutre and Mailly [13] for a survey). At first glance, this connection may not be obvious. However, let us observe that we can model a BPF $AF_{BP} = (\langle S_0, ..., S_1 \rangle, AT)$ as a sequence of normal expansions (see Definition 2) $\langle AF_0, ..., AF_n \rangle$, such that for $AF_i, 0 < i \leq n, AF_{i-1} \preceq_N AF_i$. For example, given the BPF $AF_{BP} = (\langle \{a\}, \{b\}, \{c\} \rangle, \{(a, b), (b, a), (b, c), (c, b)\})$, we have the sequence of normally expanding argumentation frameworks $\langle AF_0, AF_1, AF_2 \rangle = \langle (\{a\}, \{\}), (\{a, b\}, \{(a, b), (b, a)\}), (\{a, b, c\}, \{(a, b), (b, a), (b, c), (c, b)\}) \rangle$. Given this sequence (and an argumentation semantics σ), BP semantics applies an abstract argumentation semantics and returns $EXTS_{po-mon}^{\subseteq-max}(EXTS_{po-mon}^{\subseteq-max}(\sigma(AF_2), \sigma(AF_0)), \sigma(AF_0) \cup \sigma(AF_1))$.

Let us note that the formal framework we provide is fundamentally different from traditional approaches to model preferences in formal argumentation, such as preference-based [1] and value-based [10] argumentation (where value-based argumentation is a generalization of preference-based argumentation). While the sequence of sets of arguments in a BPF can be considered as a total preference order on non-intersecting sets of arguments, the way this order is interpreted by BP semantics does not allow for the inference of sets of arguments that entail conflicts; the order merely gives us a way to treat uncertainty ("doubt") that is inherent in the corresponding abstract argumentation framework. In contrast, in preference-based argumentation, preferences may lead to a disregard of conflicts. Colloquially speaking, we can summarize that value-based and preference-based argumentation favor preferred arguments no matter what when drawing inferences in face of contradictions, whereas our burden of persuasion approach merely favors preferred sets of arguments *if in doubt*.

Still, let us note that our burden of persuasion frameworks and semantics reflect the idea of using preferences on the set of arguments in an argumentation framework to "narrow down" the extensions that an abstract argumentation semantics returns. Work in this direction has been conducted by Kaci *et al.* [18], as well as by Amgoud and Vesic [2]. For the sake of conciseness, let us informally claim here that each BPF can be mapped to a preference-based argumentation framework, but that the aforementioned approaches are fundamentally different to ours. For instance, let us claim that when considering the BPF $AF_{BP} = \langle \{a, c\}, \{b, d\} \rangle, \{(a, b), (a, c), (b, a), (b, d)\})$ and preferred semantics, neither Kaci *et al.*'s approach, nor the two approaches (*democratic* and *elitist*) introduced by Amgoud and Vesic allow for inferring only the extension $\{a, d\}$ but also infer the extension $\{b, c\}$. However, as b carries the burden of persuasion, it should not be able to defeat a, which then in turn can defeat the unburdened argument c. A formal, detailed comparison can be considered promising future work.

Similarly, our approach is different from *argumentation with many lives* in which arguments and attacks have numeric weights and an argument is defeated iff the sum of the weights of successful attacks on the argument exceeds the number of *lives* of the argument (roughly speaking) [17]. Similarly to value-based argumentation, argumentation with many lives allows for the inference of sets of arguments that are not conflict-free; also, it requires the assignment of weights (quantification) of arguments and attacks, which is not feasible in many legal use cases.

From a legal perspective, let us note that the burden of persuasion is related to, but different from, the *standard of persuasion* [16] which, from a formal argumentation perspective, relates more directly to the required strength of one or several attackers to defeat an argument. Modeling standards of persuasion in formal argumentation is certainly interesting future work, but not within the scope of this paper.

Considering previous research on formal models of burdens of persuasion, our work can be considered a continuation of recent research that introduces the burden of persuasion to structured argumentation [11]. This model of the burden of persuasion is based on grounded semantics and can be described – from an abstract argumentation perspective – as follows.

1. Given an abstract argumentation framework $AF = (AR, AT)$, we place the burden of persuasion on the arguments in a set $S \subseteq AR$.
2. We determine the grounded extension E_{gr} of AF and say that an argument $a \in AR$ is labeled as follows. IN if $a \in E_{gr}$; OUT if $a \in E_{gr}^+$; UND, otherwise. We denote all arguments labeled IN by $IN_{gr}(AF)$; all arguments labeled OUT by $OUT_{gr}(AF)$; all arguments labeled UND by $UND_{gr}(AF)$.
3. Based on the grounded labeling, we create the grounded burden of persuasion labeling (BP labeling). A BP-labeling is a 3-tuple $(IN^{BP}(AF), OUT^{BP}(AF), UND^{BP})$, such that $\forall a \in AR$, the following holds:
   If $a \in S$. $a \in IN^{BP}(AF)$ if $a \in E_{gr}$; $a \in OUT^{BP}(AF)$ if $a \in E_{gr}^+$ or $a \in (UND_{gr}(AF) \setminus S)^+$; $a \in UND^{BP}(AF)$, otherwise.
   If $a \notin S$.) $a \in IN^{BP}(AF)$ if $a \notin E_{gr}^+$ and $\forall b \in IN^{BP}(AF), b$ does not attack a; $a \in OUT^{BP}(AF)$, otherwise.

This approach has shortcomings (even when only considering one burden of persuasion level as above). Below we give two examples that also illustrate how our framework addresses the issues.

Self-attacking Arguments. Consider the argumentation framework $AF = (AR, AT) = (\{a, b, c,\}, \{(a, a), (a, b), (b, c)\})$ with the burden of persuasion placed on $\{b\}$. Considering the approach by Calegari *et al.*, we have: *i)* a is UND; *ii)* b is initially undecided, and because it carries the burden of persuasion, it is finally out; *iii)* hence, c is in. This is problematic, because a as a self-defeating argument should arguably not defeat b, even if the burden of persuasion lies on b. In contrast, when using our approach we have the following BPF: $AF_{BP} = (\langle \{a, c\}, \{b\} \rangle, AT)$. $\sigma_{SCF2}^{BP}(AF_{BP}) = \{\{b\}\}$; *i.e.*, we infer $\{b\}$ because the burden of persuasion is not strong enough to allow for the defeat of b by a self-attacking argument.

Consistent Defeat from Inconsistent Arguments. Consider the abstract argumentation framework $AF' = (AR', AT') = (\{a, b, c, d, e\}, \{(a, b), (b, a),$

$(a,c),(b,c),(c,d),(d,e)\}$). What we have in this framework is a phenomenon that we can colloquially describe as *consistent defeat from inconsistent arguments*. We place the burden of persuasion on argument $\{d\}$. Let us apply the approach by Calegari *et al.* a and b attack each other and are hence undecided, but both arguments *consistently* attack c. Again considering three-valued labeling and grounded semantics, we have d is out and e is in. However, we claim that we should conclude that c is out, because it is attacked by both a and b, and that consequently, d is in and e is out. Let us highlight the difference to the previous example. In the previous example, we maintain it should be impossible to infer a because a is inconsistent with itself. However, in this example, we maintain it should be impossible to infer "not d", because we have to infer "either a or b", which implies the defeat of c. Our approach supports this intuition: $AF'_{BP} = (\langle\{a,b,c,d\},\{e\}\rangle, AT')$ and $\sigma^{BP}_{SCF2}(AF'_{BP}) = \{\{a,d\},\{b,d\}\}$.

6 Conclusion

In this paper, we have introduced a formal framework for modeling the burden of persuasion in abstract argumentation, which is accompanied by an open source software implementation. The framework supports arbitrary many levels of burdens, can be combined with any universally defined argumentation semantics, and addresses some open issues that previous works have identified in models of burdens of persuasion for structured argumentation. By abstracting from structured argumentation specifics, the framework can be applied to a range of formal argumentation variants.

Acknowledgments. We thank the anonymous reviewers for their thoughtful and useful feedback. This work was partially supported by the Wallenberg AI, Autonomous Systems and Software Program (WASP) funded by the Knut and Alice Wallenberg Foundation.

Appendix - Proofs

Proposition 1. *Let σ be an argumentation semantics. If σ is universally defined then σ^{BP} is universally defined.*

Proof. Let $AF_{BP} = (ARS, AT)$ be a BPF and $ARS = \langle S_0, ..., S_n\rangle$. If $n = 0$, by definition of σ^{BP} (Definition 23) it holds true that $\sigma^{BP}(AF_{BP}) = \sigma(AF_0)$. Hence, the proposition holds true for $n = 0$. For $n > 0$, we provide a proof by induction on n.

Base Case: $n = 1$. By definition of σ^{BP}, it holds true that $\sigma^{BP}(AF_{BP}) = EXTS^{\subseteq-max}_{po-mon}(\sigma(AF_1), \sigma(AF_0))$. Because σ is universally defined, by definition of $EXTS^{\subseteq-max}_{po-mon}$ (Definition 22), it holds true that $|EXTS^{\subseteq-max}_{po-mon}(\sigma(AF_1), \sigma(AF_0))| \geq 1$. Hence, the proposition holds true for the base case.

Inductive Case: $n = k + 1$. By definition of σ^{BP}, it holds true that $\sigma^{BP}.(AF_{BP}) = EXTS_{po-mon}^{\subseteq-max}(\sigma(AF_{BP-1}), \sigma(AF_0) \cup ... \cup \sigma(AF_{k+1}))$. Because σ is universally defined it holds true that $|\sigma(AF_0) \cup ... \cup \sigma(AF_{k+1})| \geq 1$ and from the base case and from the definition of $EXTS_{po-mon}^{\subseteq-max}$ it follows that $|\sigma(AF_{BP-1})| \geq 1$. Hence, $\sigma^{BP}(AF_{BP})$ is universally defined for $n = k + 1$ and the proof follows from the inductive case. □

Proposition 2. *Let σ be an argumentation semantics. If σ is universally uniquely defined then σ^{BP} is universally uniquely defined.*

Proof. Let $AF_{BP} = (ARS, AT)$ be a BPF and $ARS = \langle S_0, ..., S_n \rangle$. If $n = 0$, by definition of σ^{BP} (Definition 23) it holds true that $\sigma^{BP}(AF_{BP}) = \sigma(AF_0)$. Hence, the proposition holds true for $n = 0$. For $n > 0$, we provide a proof by induction on n.

Base case: $n = 1$. By definition of σ^{BP}, it holds true that $\sigma^{BP}(AF_{BP}) = EXTS_{po-mon}^{\subseteq-max}(\sigma(AF_1), \sigma(AF_0))$. Because σ is universally uniquely defined, by definition of $EXTS_{po-mon}^{\subseteq-max}$ (Definition 22), it holds true that $|EXTS_{po-mon}^{\subseteq-max}(\sigma(AF_1), \sigma(AF_0))| = 1$. Hence, the proposition holds true for the base case.

Inductive Case: $n = k + 1$. By definition of σ^{BP}, it holds true that $\sigma^{BP}(AF_{BP}) = EXTS_{po-mon}^{\subseteq-max}(\sigma(AF_{BP-1}), \sigma(AF_0) \cup ... \cup \sigma(AF_{k+1}))$. Because σ is universally uniquely defined it holds true that $|\sigma(AF_0) \cup ... \cup \sigma(AF_{k+1})| \geq 1$ and from the base case and from the definition of $EXTS_{po-mon}^{\subseteq-max}$ it follows that $|\sigma(AF_{BP-1})| = 1$. Hence, $\sigma^{BP}(AF_{BP})$ is universally uniquely defined for $n = k + 1$ and the proof follows from the inductive case. □

References

1. Amgoud, L., Cayrol, C.: Inferring from inconsistency in preference-based argumentation frameworks. J. Autom. Reason. **29**(2), 125–169 (2002). https://doi.org/10.1023/A:1021603608656
2. Amgoud, L., Vesic, S.: Rich preference-based argumentation frameworks. Int. J. Approx. Reason. **55**(2), 585–606 (2014)
3. Baroni, P., Caminada, M., Giacomin, M.: Abstract argumentation frameworks and their semantics. In: Baroni, P., Gabbay, D., Massimiliano, G., van der Torre, L. (eds.) Handbook of Formal Argumentation. College Publications, chap. 4, pp. 159–236. College Publications (2018)
4. Baroni, P., Gabbay, D.M., Giacomin, M., van der Torre, L.: Handbook of Formal Argumentation. College Publications (2018)
5. Baroni, P., Giacomin, M.: On principle-based evaluation of extension-based argumentation semantics. Artif. Intell. **171**(10), 675–700 (2007)
6. Baroni, P., Giacomin, M., Guida, G.: SCC-recursiveness: a general schema for argumentation semantics. Artif. Intell. **168**(1), 162–210 (2005). https://doi.org/10.1016/j.artint.2005.05.006

7. Baumann, R., Brewka, G.: Expanding argumentation frameworks: enforcing and monotonicity results. COMMA **10**, 75–86 (2010)
8. Baumann, R., Brewka, G., Ulbricht, M.: Revisiting the foundations of abstract argumentation-semantics based on weak admissibility and weak defense. In: AAAI, pp. 2742–2749 (2020)
9. Bench-Capon, T., Prakken, H., Sartor, G.: Argumentation in legal reasoning. In: Simari, G., Rahwan, I. (eds.) Argumentation in Artificial Intelligence, pp. 363–382. Springer, Heidelberg (2009). https://doi.org/10.1007/978-0-387-98197-0_18
10. Bench-Capon, T.J.: Persuasion in practical argument using value-based argumentation frameworks. J. Log. Comput. **13**(3), 429–448 (2003)
11. Calegari, R., Riveret, R., Sartor, G.: The burden of persuasion in structured argumentation. In: Proceedings of the Nineteenth International Conference on Artificial Intelligence and Law, ICAIL '21. Association for Computing Machinery, New York (2021)
12. Cramer, M., van der Torre, L.: SCF2-an argumentation semantics for rational human judgments on argument acceptability. In: Proceedings of the 8th Workshop on Dynamics of Knowledge and Belief (DKB-2019) and the 7th Workshop KI\ & Kognition (KIK-2019) co-located with 44nd German Conference on Artificial Intelligence (KI 2019), Kassel, Germany, 23 September 2019, pp. 24–35 (2019)
13. Doutre, S., Mailly, J.G.: Constraints and changes: a survey of abstract argumentation dynamics. Argum. Comput. **9**, 223–248 (2018). https://doi.org/10.3233/AAC-180425
14. Dung, P.M.: On the acceptability of arguments and its fundamental role in non-monotonic reasoning, logic programming and n-person games. Artif. Intell. **77**(2), 321–357 (1995)
15. Dvořák, W., Gaggl, S.A.: Stage semantics and the SCC-recursive schema for argumentation semantics. J. Logic Comput. **26**(4), 1149–1202 (2014). https://doi.org/10.1093/logcom/exu006
16. Friedman, R.D.: Standards of persuasion and the distinction between fact and law. Northwest. Univ. Law Rev. **86**, 916 (1991)
17. Gabbay, D.M., Rozenberg, G.: Introducing abstract argumentation with many lives. FLAP **7**(3), 295–336 (2020)
18. Kaci, S., van der Torre, L., Villata, S.: Preference in abstract argumentation. In: Computational Models of Argument, pp. 405–412. IOS Press (2018)
19. Kampik, T., Gabbay, D.: The "Degrees of Monotony"-dilemma in abstract argumentation. In: Vejnarová, J., Wilson, N. (eds.) Symbolic and Quantitative Approaches to Reasoning with Uncertainty 2021. Springer, Cham (2021, to appear)
20. Prakken, H., Sartor, G.: A logical analysis of burdens of proof. In: Legal Evidence and Proof: Statistics, Stories, Logic, pp. 223–253 (2009)
21. Thimm, M.: Tweety: a comprehensive collection of java libraries for logical aspects of artificial intelligence and knowledge representation. In: Proceedings of the Fourteenth International Conference on Principles of Knowledge Representation and Reasoning, KR 2014, pp. 528–537. AAAI Press (2014)
22. van der Torre, L., Vesic, S.: The principle-based approach to abstract argumentation semantics. IfCoLog J. Log. Appl. **4**(8), 2735–2778 (2017)
23. Verheij, B.: Two approaches to dialectical argumentation: admissible sets and argumentation stages. Proc. NAIC **96**, 357–368 (1996)
24. Wu, Y., Caminada, M.: A labelling-based justification status of arguments. Stud. Logic **3**(4), 12–29 (2010)

Handling Support Cycles and Collective Interactions in the Logical Encoding of Higher-Order Bipolar Argumentation Frameworks

Marie-Christine Lagasquie-Schiex[(✉)]

Université de Toulouse, IRIT, 118 route de Narbonne, 31062 Toulouse, France
lagasq@irit.fr

Abstract. In our paper [13], we have proposed a logical encoding of argumentation frameworks with higher-order interactions (*i.e.* attacks or supports whose targets are arguments or other attacks or supports) with an evidential meaning for supports, such frameworks are called REBAF. With this encoding, we are able to characterize the semantics of REBAF under the form of specific logical models. Nevertheless this encoding has two important drawbacks: first the handling of support cycles has some weaknesses and secondly the collective interactions (*i.e.* attacks or supports whose source is a set of arguments and not only one argument) are not taken into account. The current paper proposes an improvement of this encoding for solving these drawbacks.

Keywords: Abstract argumentation · Logical translation · Higher-order interactions · Bipolar interactions

1 Introduction

Formal argumentation has become an essential paradigm in Artificial Intelligence (see for instance [24]) and the original Dung's argumentation framework (AF) [15] is the cornerstone of this domain. An AF is a collection of *arguments* interacting with each other through a relation reflecting conflicts between them, called *attack*, and enables to determine *acceptable* sets of arguments called *extensions*. Then AF have been extended along different lines, *e.g.* by enriching them with positive interactions between arguments (usually expressed by a *support relation*, see for instance [9,17,25]), or *higher-order interactions* (*i.e.* interactions whose targets are other interactions, see for instance [3,4,14,16,20,26]). Note that there exist several interpretations of the support (deductive support [5], necessary support [22], evidential support [23]). Here is an example of such frameworks in the legal field (this example is an extension of an example presented in [2]).

Example 1. *The prosecutor says that the defendant had intention to kill the victim (argument b). A witness says that she saw the defendant throwing a sharp*

© Springer Nature Switzerland AG 2021
P. Baroni et al. (Eds.): CLAR 2021, LNAI 13040, pp. 244–265, 2021.
https://doi.org/10.1007/978-3-030-89391-0_14

knife towards the victim (argument a). Argument a can be considered as a support for argument b. The lawyer argues back that the defendant was in a habit of throwing the knife at his wife's foot once drunk (argument c). This latter argument is better considered attacking the support from a to b, than attacking or supporting arguments a or b themselves. So, the prosecutor's argumentation seems no longer sufficient for proving the intention to kill.   □

Such frameworks are of interest when one wants to keep an abstract point of view but with an enriched context. In [13], a logical encoding of argumentation frameworks with higher-order attacks and supports has been proposed considering that the support meaning is the evidential one [23][1] (so we talk about *REBAF*) and the acceptability semantics are defined as in [7]. This encoding is able to take into account REBAF but with two important drawbacks; first we will show that the handing of support cycles is unsufficient, and secondly the collective interactions (those whose source is not a single argument but a set of arguments) are not taken into account. So our aim is to propose a solution to these two drawbacks. The paper is organized as follows: the necessary background about argumentation frameworks is given in Sect. 2; the logical encoding for frameworks with higher-order attacks and evidential supports (REBAF) is recalled in Sect. 3; an analysis of the case of REBAF with support cycles is presented and a new proposition that can properly handle supports cycles is given in Sect. 4; Sect. 5 is dedicated to the treatment of the collective interactions; and Sect. 6 concludes the paper. Sketch of proof are given in Appendix A (complete proofs and many examples can be found in [18,19]).

2   Background on REBAF Given in [7]

We recalled here the main definitions and properties concerning REBAF.

Definition 1 [7]. *An evidence-based recursive argumentation framework (REBAF) is a sextuple $\langle \mathbf{A}, \mathbf{R}_a, \mathbf{R}_e, \mathbf{s}, \mathbf{t}, \mathbf{P} \rangle$ where $\mathbf{A}$, $\mathbf{R}_a$ and $\mathbf{R}_e$ are three (possible infinite) pairwise disjunct sets respectively representing arguments, attacks and supports names, and where $\mathbf{P} \subseteq \mathbf{A} \cup \mathbf{R}_a \cup \mathbf{R}_e$ is a set representing the prima-facie elements that do not need to be supported. Functions $\mathbf{s} : (\mathbf{R}_a \cup \mathbf{R}_e) \longrightarrow 2^{\mathbf{A}} \backslash \varnothing$ and $\mathbf{t} : (\mathbf{R}_a \cup \mathbf{R}_e) \longrightarrow (\mathbf{A} \cup \mathbf{R}_a \cup \mathbf{R}_e)$ respectively map each attack and support to its source and its target.*

Note that the source of attacks and supports is a set of arguments (so any interaction is a *collective* one),[2] the set $\mathbf{P}$ may contain arguments, attacks or supports and no constraint on the prima-facie elements is assumed (they can be

---

[1] This meaning allows to distinguish between two different kinds of arguments: *prima-facie* (those that are justified whenever they are not defeated) and *standard arguments* (those that are not directly assumed to be justified and must inherit support from prima-facie arguments through a chain of supports).

[2] This kind of interactions has been introduced by [21] in the context of SETAF: argumentation frameworks with attacks whose source is a set of arguments.

attacked or supported). Note also that no constraint is given about the existence or not of cycles; so support cycles, attack cycles or mixed cycles (with attacks and supports) can appear in a REBAF.

Semantics of REBAF are defined in [7] using the notion of *structure*: a structure plays the same role as an *extension* in the Dung framework, *i.e.* gives a set of elements (arguments and interactions) that are "acceptable together".

Definition 2 [7]. *Let* **REBAF** $= \langle \mathbf{A}, \mathbf{R}_a, \mathbf{R}_e, \mathbf{s}, \mathbf{t}, \mathbf{P} \rangle$. *A triple* $U = (S, \Gamma, \Delta)$ *is a structure of* **REBAF** *iff* $S \subseteq \mathbf{A}$, $\Gamma \subseteq \mathbf{R}_a$ *and* $\Delta \subseteq \mathbf{R}_e$. *Moreover, for any pair of structures* $U = (S, \Gamma, \Delta)$ *and* $U' = (S', \Gamma', \Delta')$, $U \subseteq U'$ *iff* $(S \cup \Gamma \cup \Delta) \subseteq (S' \cup \Gamma' \cup \Delta')$. *A structure* U *is* $\subseteq$-*maximal (resp.* $\subseteq$-*minimal) iff every* U' *that satisfies* $U \subseteq U'$ *(resp.* $U' \subseteq U$) *also satisfies* $U' \subseteq U$ *(resp.* $U \subseteq U'$).

Some specific sets of elements w.r.t. a structure can be defined:

Definition 3 [7]. *Let* **REBAF** $= \langle \mathbf{A}, \mathbf{R}_a, \mathbf{R}_e, \mathbf{s}, \mathbf{t}, \mathbf{P} \rangle$ *and given a structure* $U = (S, \Gamma, \Delta)$,

- *The sets of defeated elements w.r.t. U:*
  $Def_X(U) \stackrel{\text{def}}{=} \{x \in X | \exists \alpha \in \Gamma, \mathbf{s}(\alpha) \subseteq S \text{ and } \mathbf{t}(\alpha) = x\}$ *with* $X \in \{\mathbf{A}, \mathbf{R}_a, \mathbf{R}_e\}$
  $Def(U) \stackrel{\text{def}}{=} Def_{\mathbf{A}}(U) \cup Def_{\mathbf{R}_a}(U) \cup Def_{\mathbf{R}_e}(U)$
- *The set of supported elements* $Sup(U)$ *is recursively defined as follows:*[3]
  $Sup(U) \stackrel{\text{def}}{=} \mathbf{P} \cup \{\mathbf{t}(\alpha) | \exists \alpha \in \Delta \cap Sup(U \backslash \{\mathbf{t}(\alpha)\}), \mathbf{s}(\alpha) \subseteq (S \cap Sup(U \backslash \{\mathbf{t}(\alpha)\}))\}$
- *The set of* unsupportable *elements w.r.t.* U:[4]
  $UnSupp(U) \stackrel{\text{def}}{=} \overline{Sup(U')}$ *with* $U' = (\overline{Def_{\mathbf{A}}(U)}, \mathbf{R}_a, \overline{Def_{\mathbf{R}_e}(U)})$
- *The set of* unacceptable *elements w.r.t.* U: $UnAcc(U) \stackrel{\text{def}}{=} Def(U) \cup UnSupp(U)$
- *The set of* unactivable *attacks w.r.t.* U:
  $UnAct(U) \stackrel{\text{def}}{=} \{\alpha \in \mathbf{R}_a | \alpha \in UnAcc(U) \text{ or } \mathbf{s}(\alpha) \cap UnAcc(U) \neq \varnothing\}$
- *The set of* acceptable *elements w.r.t.* U: $Acc(U) \stackrel{\text{def}}{=} \{x \in \mathbf{A} \cup \mathbf{R}_a \cup \mathbf{R}_e \mid x \in Sup(U) \text{ and } \forall \alpha \in \mathbf{R}_a \text{ st } \mathbf{t}(\alpha) = x, \alpha \in UnAct(U)\}$

Then using these sets, REBAF semantics can be defined:

Definition 4 [7]. *Let* **REBAF** $= \langle \mathbf{A}, \mathbf{R}_a, \mathbf{R}_e, \mathbf{s}, \mathbf{t}, \mathbf{P} \rangle$. *Let* $U = (S, \Gamma, \Delta)$, U *is*

- self-supporting *iff* $(S \cup \Gamma \cup \Delta) \subseteq Sup(U)$
- conflict-free *iff* $X \cap Def_Y(U) = \varnothing$ *for any* $(X, Y) \in \{(S, \mathbf{A}), (\Gamma, \mathbf{R}_a), (\Delta, \mathbf{R}_e)\}$
- U *is* admissible *iff it is conflict-free and* $S \cup \Gamma \cup \Delta \subseteq Acc(U)$
- complete *iff it is conflict-free and* $Acc(U) = S \cup \Gamma \cup \Delta$
- grounded *iff it is a* $\subseteq$-*minimal complete structure*
- preferred *iff it is a* $\subseteq$-*maximal admissible structure*
- stable *iff* $(S \cup \Gamma \cup \Delta) = \overline{UnAcc(U)}$

---

[3] By abuse of notation, we write $U \backslash T$ instead of $(S \backslash T, \Gamma \backslash T, \Delta \backslash T)$ with $T \subseteq (\mathbf{A} \cup \mathbf{R}_a \cup \mathbf{R}_e)$.

[4] Let X be a subset of a set Y, $\overline{X}$ denotes the set complement of X w.r.t. Y. Here Y will be $\mathbf{A}$, $\mathbf{R}_a$, $\mathbf{R}_e$ or their union, depending of the context.

Example 1 (cont'd): The argumentation framework corresponding to the example given in the introduction can be represented as follows (argument names are given in circular nodes, interaction names in square nodes, prima-facie elements are in grey nodes and non prima-facie element in white nodes; attacks are represented by simple edges and supports by double edges):

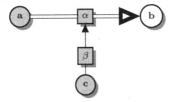

In this framework, neither β nor its source is attacked and β and its source are prima-facie. So, for any structure U, it holds that neither β nor its source c is unacceptable w.r.t. U. As a consequence, for any structure U, α is not acceptable w.r.t. U as α is attacked by β and β is not unactivable w.r.t. U. As b is not prima-facie, and α is the only support to b, no admissible structure contains b. As a consequence, there is a unique complete, grounded, preferred and stable structure $U = (\{a, c\}, \{\beta\}, \varnothing)$. □

3   Background on the Logical Description of a REBAF Given in [13]

The logical description of a REBAF proposed in [13] allows an explicit representation of arguments, attacks, evidential supports and their properties using first-order logics with the binary equality predicate.

Note that, in [13], only a variant of REBAF has been considered in which *interactions are restricted to binary interactions* (that is for any interaction α, $s(\alpha)$ is a singleton). This restriction is one of the drawbacks we are interested in and will be removed in Sect. 5.

Note also that the quantifiers $\exists$ and $\forall$ range over some domain D. To restrict them to subsets of D, bounded quantifiers are used: $\forall x \in E \ (P(x))$ means $\forall x (E(x) \rightarrow P(x))$.

The following tables give respectively the used vocabulary, the formulae describing a given REBAF and those describing the four different principles used in REBAF semantics[5] and the logical bases built using the previous formulae.

---

[5] Note that the conflict-freeness principle is expressed by the formulae **(1)**, **(2)**, **(3)**, **(2bis)**, **(3bis)**.

Vocabulary for the logical description of a REBAF

Predicate symbol	Meaning
$Arg(x)$	x is an argument
$Attack(x)$ (resp. $ESupport(x)$)	x is an attack (resp. evidential support)
$PrimaFacie(x)$	x is a prima-facie element
$Acc(x)$	x is accepted, with $x \in \mathbf{A}$
$NAcc(x)$	x cannot be accepted, with $x \in \mathbf{A}$
$Val(\alpha)$	α is valid, with $\alpha \in (\mathbf{R}_a \cap \mathbf{R}_e)$
$Supp(x)$	x is supported, with $x \in (\mathbf{A} \cup \mathbf{R}_a \cap \mathbf{R}_e)$
$UnSupp(x)$	x is unsupportable, with $x \in (\mathbf{A} \cup \mathbf{R}_a \cap \mathbf{R}_e)$
$eAcc(x)$	x is accepted and supported, with $x \in \mathbf{A}$
$eVal(\alpha)$	α is valid and supported, with $\alpha \in (\mathbf{R}_a \cap \mathbf{R}_e)$
Function symbol	Meaning
$T(\alpha)$ (resp. $S(\alpha)$)	denotes the target (resp. source) of α, with $\alpha \in (\mathbf{R}_a \cap \mathbf{R}_e)$

Note that the word "accepted" used for giving the meaning of the predicat Acc is a relic of a previous work in which only attacks have been taken into account (see [12]). Here, considering that an argument must also be supported (see Definition 3), the meaning of Acc is so closer to the notion of defence, whereas the predicate $eAcc$ corresponds to the acceptability in the sense of Definition 3 (defence and support).

Logical Theory for Describing any REBAF: Description of the impact of an attack or a support to its target; and constraint on the variables: any variable must correspond either to an argument, or an attack, or a support (exclusive or)

(1)	$\forall x \in (Attack \cup ESupport) \; \forall y \in Attack$
	$\quad ((eVal(y) \wedge (T(y) = x) \wedge eAcc(S(y))) \rightarrow \neg Val(x))$
(2)	$\forall x \in Arg \; \forall y \in Attack \;\; ((eVal(y) \wedge (T(y) = x) \wedge eAcc(S(y))) \rightarrow NAcc(x))$
(3)	$\forall x \in Arg \; (NAcc(x) \rightarrow \neg Acc(x))$
(1bis)	$\forall x \in (Attack \cup ESupport \cup Arg) \;\; ((PrimaFacie(x) \vee$
	$\quad \exists y \in ESupport \; (eVal(y) \wedge (T(y) = x) \wedge eAcc(S(y)))) \rightarrow Supp(x))$
(2bis)	$\forall x \in Arg \; ((Acc(x) \wedge Supp(x)) \leftrightarrow eAcc(x))$
(3bis)	$\forall x \in (Attack \cup ESupport) \;\; ((Val(x) \wedge Supp(x)) \leftrightarrow eVal(x))$
(4)	$\forall x \; (Attack(x) \rightarrow \neg Arg(x))$
(4bis)	$\forall x \; (Attack(x) \rightarrow \neg ESupport(x))$
(4ter)	$\forall x \; (ESupport(x) \rightarrow \neg Arg(x))$
(5)	$\forall x \; (Arg(x) \vee Attack(x) \vee ESupport(x))$

Logical Encoding of Specificities of a Given REBAF $= \langle \mathbf{A}, \mathbf{R}_a, \mathbf{R}_e, \mathbf{s}, \mathbf{t}, \mathbf{P} \rangle$, $\mathbf{A} = \{a_1, \ldots a_n\}$, $\mathbf{R}_a = \{\alpha_1, \ldots, \alpha_k\}$, $\mathbf{R}_e = \{\alpha_{k+1}, \ldots, \alpha_m\}$, $\mathbf{P} = \{x_1, \ldots x_l\}$

(6)	$(S(\alpha) = a) \wedge (T(\alpha) = b)$ for all $\alpha \in \mathbf{R}_a \cup \mathbf{R}_e$ with $\mathbf{s}(\alpha) = a$ and $\mathbf{t}(\alpha) = b$
(7)	$\forall x \; (Arg(x) \leftrightarrow (x = a_1) \vee \ldots \vee (x = a_n))$
(8)	$\forall x \; (Attack(x) \leftrightarrow (x = \alpha_1) \vee \ldots \vee (x = \alpha_k))$
(8bis)	$\forall x \; (ESupport(x) \leftrightarrow (x = \alpha_{k+1}) \vee \ldots \vee (x = \alpha_m))$
(8ter)	$\forall x \; (PrimaFacie(x) \leftrightarrow (x = x_1) \vee \ldots \vee (x = x_l))$
(9)	$a_i \neq a_j$ for all $a_i, a_j \in \mathbf{A}$ with $i \neq j$
(10)	$\alpha_i \neq \alpha_j$ for all $\alpha_i, \alpha_j \in \mathbf{R}_a \cup \mathbf{R}_e$ with $i \neq j$

Logical formalisation of REBAF semantics (4 principles)

Self-supporting principle: Each supported element must receive evidential support (so either it is prima-facie, or it is the target of an e-valid support from an e-accepted source). And elements that are unsupportable cannot be supported.

$$(17) \quad \forall x \in (Attack \cup ESupport \cup Arg)$$
$$\left(\begin{array}{l} Supp(x) \rightarrow \\ \left(\begin{array}{l} PrimaFacie(x) \vee \\ \exists y \in ESupport \\ (eVal(y) \wedge (T(y) = x) \wedge eAcc(S(y))) \end{array} \right) \end{array} \right)$$

$$(18) \quad \forall x \in (Attack \cup ESupport \cup Arg)$$
$$\left(\begin{array}{l} UnSupp(x) \leftrightarrow \\ \left(\begin{array}{l} \neg PrimaFacie(x) \wedge \\ \forall y \in ESupport(T(y) = x \rightarrow \\ \left(\begin{array}{l} \exists \beta \in Attack(T(\beta) \in \{S(y), y\} \wedge \\ eVal(\beta) \wedge eAcc(S(\beta)))) \end{array} \right) \\ \vee UnSupp(S(y)) \\ \vee UnSupp(y)) \end{array} \right) \end{array} \right)$$

Defence Principle: An attacked element is "accepted" *only if* for each attack against it, either the source or the attack itself is defeated (by an e-valid attack from an e-accepted argument), or the source or the attack itself is unsupportable (w.r.t. e-valid elements and e-accepted arguments).

$$(11) \quad \forall \alpha \in Attack$$
$$\left(\begin{array}{l} Acc(T(\alpha)) \rightarrow \\ \left(\begin{array}{l} \exists \beta \in Attack(T(\beta) \in \{S(\alpha), \alpha\} \\ \wedge eVal(\beta) \wedge eAcc(S(\beta))) \\ \vee UnSupp(S(\alpha)) \\ \vee UnSupp(\alpha) \end{array} \right) \end{array} \right)$$

$$(12) \quad \forall \alpha \in Attack \; \forall \delta \in (Attack \cup ESupport)$$
$$\left(\begin{array}{l} ((\delta = T(\alpha)) \wedge Val(\delta)) \rightarrow \\ \left(\begin{array}{l} \exists \beta \in Attack(T(\beta) \in \{S(\alpha), \alpha\} \\ \wedge eVal(\beta) \wedge eAcc(S(\beta))) \\ \vee UnSupp(S(\alpha)) \\ \vee UnSupp(\alpha) \end{array} \right) \end{array} \right)$$

Reinstatement Principle: This is a dual principle of that of defence. So an attacked element is "accepted" *if* for each attack against it, either the source or the attack itself is defeated (by an e-valid attack from an e-accepted argument), or the source or the attack itself is unsupportable

$$(13) \quad \forall c \in Arg \; ($$
$$\left(\begin{array}{l} \forall \alpha \in Attack \\ \left(\begin{array}{l} T(\alpha) = c \rightarrow \\ \left(\begin{array}{l} \exists \beta \in Attack(T(\beta) \in \{S(\alpha), \alpha\} \wedge \\ eVal(\beta) \wedge eAcc(S(\beta))) \\ \vee UnSupp(S(\alpha)) \\ \vee UnSupp(\alpha) \end{array} \right) \end{array} \right) \\ \rightarrow Acc(c)) \end{array} \right)$$

$$(14) \quad \forall \delta \in (Attack \cup ESupport) \; ($$
$$\left(\begin{array}{l} (\forall \alpha \in Attack \\ \left(\begin{array}{l} T(\alpha) = \delta \rightarrow \\ \left(\begin{array}{l} \exists \beta \in Attack(T(\beta) \in \{S(\alpha), \alpha\} \wedge \\ eVal(\beta) \wedge eAcc(S(\beta))) \\ \vee UnSupp(S(\alpha)) \\ \vee UnSupp(\alpha) \end{array} \right) \end{array} \right) \\ \rightarrow Val(\delta)) \end{array} \right)$$

Stability Principle: If an element is not "accepted" (resp. supported) then it must be attacked by the structure (resp. unsupportable w.r.t. the structure)

$$(15) \quad \forall c \in Arg \; (\neg Acc(c)$$
$$\rightarrow \left(\begin{array}{l} \exists \beta \in Attack(T(\beta) = c \wedge \\ eVal(\beta) \wedge eAcc(S(\beta))) \end{array} \right))$$

$$(16) \quad \forall \alpha \in (Attack \cup ESupport) \; (\neg Val(\alpha)$$
$$\rightarrow \left(\begin{array}{l} \exists \beta \in Attack(T(\beta) = \alpha \wedge \\ eVal(\beta) \wedge eAcc(S(\beta))) \end{array} \right))$$

$$(19) \quad \forall x \in (Arg \cup Attack \cup ESupport) \; (\neg Supp(x) \rightarrow UnSupp(x))$$

Five Logical Bases for Encoding a REBAF and Its Semantics

$\Sigma(\textbf{REBAF}) = \{(1), \ldots, (10)\}$	$\Sigma_{ss}(\textbf{REBAF}) = \Sigma(\textbf{REBAF}) \cup \{(17), (18)\}$
$\Sigma_d(\textbf{REBAF}) = \Sigma_{ss}(\textbf{REBAF}) \cup \{(11), (12)\}$	
$\Sigma_r(\textbf{REBAF}) = \Sigma_{ss}(\textbf{REBAF}) \cup \{(13), (14)\}$	
$\Sigma_s(\textbf{REBAF}) = \Sigma_{ss}(\textbf{REBAF}) \cup \{(15), (16), (19)\}$	

[13] proposed characterizations of the REBAF structures under different semantics in terms of models of the previous bases. Let **REBAF** = $\langle \textbf{A}, \textbf{R}_a, \textbf{R}_e, \textbf{s}, \textbf{t}, \textbf{P} \rangle$. Let Σ_x be one of these bases. Given $\mathcal{I}$ an interpretation of Σ_x, we define $U_{\mathcal{I}} = (S_{\mathcal{I}}, \Gamma_{\mathcal{I}}, \Delta_{\mathcal{I}})$ with: $S_{\mathcal{I}} = \{x \in \textbf{A} | \mathcal{I}(eAcc(x)) = true\}$,

$\Gamma_{\mathcal{I}} = \{x \in \mathbf{R}_a | \mathcal{I}(eVal(x)) = true\}$ and $\Delta_{\mathcal{I}} = \{x \in \mathbf{R}_e | \mathcal{I}(eVal(x)) = true\}$. Moreover, let $\mathcal{I}$ be a model of Σ_x, $\mathcal{I}$ is a $\subseteq$-maximal (resp. minimal) model of Σ_x iff there is no model $\mathcal{I}'$ of Σ_x with $(S_{\mathcal{I}} \cup \Gamma_{\mathcal{I}} \cup \Delta_{\mathcal{I}}) \subset$ (resp. $\supset$) $(S_{\mathcal{I}'} \cup \Gamma_{\mathcal{I}'} \cup \Delta_{\mathcal{I}'})$.

Two different characterizations are given in [13], one for REBAF without support cycles and another for REBAF with support cycles. In both cases, the idea is that a structure gathers the acceptable elements w.r.t. it. In this paper, we are interested in the second one in which only some models must be considered.

Definition 5 (Def. 6.1 in [13]). $\mathcal{I}$ *is a* support-founded interpretation *iff for each argument (resp. support) x s.t. $\Sigma_{ss}(\mathbf{REBAF}) \models Supp(x) \rightarrow eAcc(x)$ (resp. $eVal(x)$), it holds that $\mathcal{I}(eAcc(x))$ (resp. $\mathcal{I}(eVal(x)))) = false$, $\mathcal{I}(UnSupp(x)) = true$. Then a* support-founded model *of $\Sigma_d(\mathbf{REBAF})$ is a support-founded interpretation which is a model of $\Sigma_d(\mathbf{REBAF})$.*

In [13], this definition has been used for characterizing admissible structures (and some other kinds of structures) of a given **REBAF** with support cycles by a subclass of models of $\Sigma_d(\mathbf{REBAF})$:

Proposition 1 (Prop. 6.2 in [13]). *Let* $\mathbf{REBAF} = \langle \mathbf{A}, \mathbf{R}_a, \mathbf{R}_e, \mathbf{s}, \mathbf{t}, \mathbf{P} \rangle$ *with only binary interactions. Let* $U = (S, \Gamma, \Delta)$ *be a structure on* **REBAF**.

- *U is admissible iff there exists a support-founded model $\mathcal{I}$ of $\Sigma_d(\mathbf{REBAF})$ with $U = U_{\mathcal{I}}$.*
- *U is complete iff there exists a support-founded model $\mathcal{I}$ of $(\Sigma_d(\mathbf{REBAF}) \cup \Sigma_r(\mathbf{REBAF}))$ with $U = U_{\mathcal{I}}$.*
- *U is a preferred structure iff there exists a $\subseteq$-maximal support-founded model $\mathcal{I}$ of $\Sigma_d(\mathbf{REBAF})$ with $U = U_{\mathcal{I}}$.*
- *U is the grounded structure iff $U = U_{\mathcal{I}}$ where $\mathcal{I}$ is a $\subseteq$-minimal support-founded model of $(\Sigma_d(\mathbf{REBAF}) \cup \Sigma_r(\mathbf{REBAF}))$.*

4   REBAF with Support Cycles: Analysis and New Proposition

In this section, the definition of support-founded models is discussed using examples and we show that it leads to a characterisation of REBAF semantics that only holds when considering REBAF with specific cycles. First of all, some definitions about supports cycles must be given before analysing the impact of such support cycles in the logical computation of structures for the REBAF.

Definition 6. *Let* $\mathbf{REBAF} = \langle \mathbf{A}, \mathbf{R}_a, \mathbf{R}_e, \mathbf{s}, \mathbf{t}, \mathbf{P} \rangle$. *A directed cycle of supports (DCS) in this REBAF is a sequence* $\mathbf{C} = (x_0, \ldots, x_{n-1}, x_n)$, $n > 0$, *such that:*[6]

---

[6] By abuse of language, the set of the elements composing **C** will be also denoted by **C**. So **C** will be used with set operators as $\cap$ ou $\cup$ and will be comparable with other sets.

- $\forall i = 0 \ldots n$, $x_i \in \mathbf{A} \cup \mathbf{R}_e$ and $x_n = x_0$ (n is the size of the DCS),
- $\forall i = 0 \ldots n - 1$, if $x_i \in \mathbf{A}$ then $x_{i+1} \in \mathbf{R}_e$ and $\mathsf{s}(x_{i+1}) = x_i$,
- $\forall i = 0 \ldots n - 1$, if $x_i \in \mathbf{R}_e$ then $x_{i+1} = \mathsf{t}(x_i)$.

A simple DCS $\mathbf{C} = (x_0, \ldots, x_{n-1}, x_n)$ is a DCS in which $\forall i, j = 0 \ldots n - 1$, if $i \neq j$ then $x_i \neq x_j$.
Let $\mathbf{C} = (x_0, \ldots, x_{n-1}, x_n)$ and $\mathbf{C}' = (x'_0, \ldots, x'_{m-1}, x'_m)$ be two DCS of this REBAF s.t. there exist $x_i \in \mathbf{C}$ and $x'_j \in \mathbf{C}'$ and $x_i = x'_j$. The aggregation of $\mathbf{C}$ and $\mathbf{C}'$, denoted by $\mathbf{C} \cup \mathbf{C}'$, is the directed cycle corresponding to the union of the sets $\{x_0, \ldots, x_{n-1}\}$ and $\{x'_0, \ldots, x'_{m-1}\}$.
Let $\mathbf{C} = (x_0, \ldots, x_{n-1}, x_n)$ be a DCS. $\mathbf{C}$ is a maximal DCS iff there does not exist another DCS that could be aggregated with $\mathbf{C}$.

Two counterexamples of Prop. 6.2 in [13] (numbered 1 here) can be exhibited showing that the definition given for support founded models (Definition 5) is not sufficient to avoid some problematic models.

Example 2. Consider 3 simple DCS that can be agglomerated into a non-simple DCS with $\mathbf{P} = \{\alpha_1, \alpha_2, \alpha_3, \beta_1, \beta_2, \beta_3\}$.

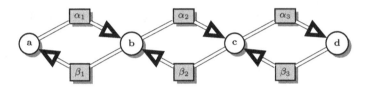

Here Σ_{ss} does not entail $Supp(x) \rightarrow eAcc(x)$ for $x \in \{a, b, c, d\}$. So Definition 5 cannot be used in order to remove models in which a (resp. b, c, d) is supported by itself. The origin of this problem is the fact that, following Formula (17), the existence of several supporters for b and c prevents the entailment described in Definition 5: $\Sigma_{ss} \models Supp(c) \rightarrow (eAcc(c) \vee eAcc(b))$ and not $\Sigma_{ss} \models Supp(c) \rightarrow eAcc(c)$. □

Example 3. Consider an attacked argument that supports an even-length support cycle $\mathbf{C} = (a, \alpha, b, \beta, a)$ with $\mathbf{P} = \{c, d, \pi, \mu, \alpha, \beta\}$.

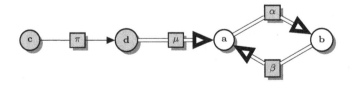

Once again Definition 5 is not enough for removing the model $\mathcal{I}$ of Σ_d with $S_{\mathcal{I}} = \{a, b, c\}$, $\Gamma_{\mathcal{I}} = \{\pi\}$ and $\Delta_{\mathcal{I}} = \{\alpha, \beta, \mu\}$. And the structure $(S_{\mathcal{I}}, \Gamma_{\mathcal{I}}, \Delta_{\mathcal{I}})$ is not admissible since it is not self-supporting in the sense of Definition 3: there is no chain of supported supports leading to a (resp. to b) rooted in a prima-facie argument that belongs to the structure (since d is attacked and not defended). □

Thus, Definition 5 is not sufficient in the general case. In order to identify the elements that cannot be supported without themselves, the main point must be to find the elements of the REBAF that would be able to play a role for supporting the elements of a cycle. That leads us to define the *impacting support chains* for an element of a REBAF. Informally an impacting support chain for an element x is a sequence targeting x, originated in a prima-facie argument and composed alternatively by "an argument, a support, an argument, a support, ...". Moreover no repetition is authorized (so any element appears only one time in the sequence); and x cannot belong to the sequence. Note that the existence of such a chain for an element x does not imply that x is supported (it is just a necessary condition for this supportability).

Definition 7. *Let* **REBAF** $= \langle \mathbf{A}, \mathbf{R}_a, \mathbf{R}_e, \mathbf{s}, \mathbf{t}, \mathbf{P} \rangle$. *Let* x *be an element of this REBAF. An* impacting support chain *for* x *is a sequence* **ISC** $= (x_0, \ldots, x_n)$ *with* $n > 0$ *and:*

- $\forall i \in [0 \ldots n]$, $x_i \in (\mathbf{A} \cup \mathbf{R}_e) \setminus \{x\}$, $x_0 \in \mathbf{A} \cap \mathbf{P}$, $x_n \in \mathbf{R}_e$ *s.t.* $\mathbf{t}(x_n) = x$,
- $\forall i, j \in [0 \ldots n]$, *if* $i \neq j$, *then* $x_i \neq x_j$,
- $\forall i \in [1 \ldots n]$, *if* $x_i \in \mathbf{R}_e$ *then* $x_{i-1} = \mathbf{s}(x_i)$ *and if* $x_i \in \mathbf{A}$ *then* $x_i = \mathbf{t}(x_{i-1})$.

Example 2 (cont'd): Here, for any element, there is no impacting support chain. $\square$

Example 3 (cont'd): Considering the arguments in the cycle, argument a has one ISC, (d, μ), and argument b has also one ISC, (d, μ, a, α). $\square$

Example 4. *Here 2 simple DCS are interconnected and can be aggregated:* $\mathbf{C} = (a, \alpha, \beta, c, \gamma, d, \delta, a)$ *and* $\mathbf{C}' = (b, \beta, c, \gamma, d, \mu, b)$ *with* $\mathbf{P} = \{e, \pi, \mu, \alpha, \delta, \gamma\}$.

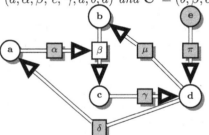

Considering the impacting support chains of some elements of the DCS, we have for instance:

- *The ISC for d:* (e, π).
- *The ISC for c:* $(e, \pi, d, \mu, b, \beta)$.
- *The ISC for a:* (e, π, d, δ).
- *The ISC for β:* $(e, \pi, d, \delta, a, \alpha)$. $\square$

Moreover we must also take into account the fact that the existence of support cycles has an impact on the *UnSupp* predicate. Considering for instance a REBAF reduced to a simple DCS (a, α, b, β, a) with $\mathbf{P} = \{\alpha, \beta\}$, for any structure U, $UnSupp(U) = \{a, b\}$, whereas a model $\mathcal{I}$ of Σ_{ss} exists in which $\mathcal{I}(UnSupp(a)) = \mathcal{I}(UnSupp(b)) = false$ that does not reflect the reality concerning the "unsupportable" status of a and b.

All the previous remarks lead to the following improvement of the notion of *support-founded interpretation* given in [13]:

Definition 8. *Let* **REBAF** $= \langle \mathbf{A}, \mathbf{R}_a, \mathbf{R}_e, \mathbf{s}, \mathbf{t}, \mathbf{P} \rangle$. $\mathcal{I}$ *is a* support-founded interpretation *iff the two following conditions hold:*

1. *for each argument (resp. support) x non prima-facie, belonging to a maximal DCS and s.t. $\mathcal{I}(eAcc(x)) = true$ (resp. $\mathcal{I}(eVal(x)) = true$), there exists at least one impacting support chain $\mathbf{ISC} = (x_0, \ldots, x_n)$ for x that is satisfied by $\mathcal{I}$, i.e. $\forall x_i \in \mathbf{ISC}$, if $x_i \in \mathbf{A}$ then $\mathcal{I}(eAcc(x_i)) = true$, otherwise $\mathcal{I}(eVal(x_i)) = true$;*
2. *for each element x of $\mathbf{REBAF}$, $\mathcal{I}(UnSupp(x)) = true$ iff $x \in UnSupp(U_\mathcal{I})$.*

Let Σ_x be a base of formulae built over $\mathbf{REBAF}$. A support-founded model of Σ_x is a support-founded interpretation which is a model of Σ_x.

Using Definition 8, the characterization of REBAF semantics becomes:[7]

Proposition 2. *Let $\mathbf{REBAF} = \langle \mathbf{A}, \mathbf{R}_a, \mathbf{R}_e, \mathbf{s}, \mathbf{t}, \mathbf{P} \rangle$ with only binary interactions. Let $U = (S, \Gamma, \Delta)$ be a structure on $\mathbf{REBAF}$.*

1. *U is admissible iff there exists a support-founded model $\mathcal{I}$ of $\Sigma_d(\mathbf{REBAF})$ (in the sense of Definition 8) with $U = U_\mathcal{I}$.*
2. *U is complete iff there exists a support-founded model $\mathcal{I}$ of $(\Sigma_d(\mathbf{REBAF}) \cup \Sigma_r(\mathbf{REBAF}))$ (in the sense of Definition 8) with $U = U_\mathcal{I}$.*
3. *U is a preferred structure iff there exists a $\subseteq$-maximal support-founded model $\mathcal{I}$ of $\Sigma_d(\mathbf{REBAF})$ (in the sense of Definition 8) with $U = U_\mathcal{I}$.*
4. *U is the grounded structure iff $U = U_\mathcal{I}$ where $\mathcal{I}$ is a $\subseteq$-minimal support-founded model of $(\Sigma_d(\mathbf{REBAF}) \cup \Sigma_r(\mathbf{REBAF}))$ (in the sense of Definition 8).*
5. *U is stable iff there exists $\mathcal{I}$ support-founded model of $\Sigma_s(\mathbf{REBAF})$ (in the sense of Definition 8) with $U = U_\mathcal{I}$.*

Let us illustrate the above results on the previous examples:

Example 2 (cont'd): Apply Proposition 2 leads to the unique complete, preferred, stable and grounded structure $(\varnothing, \varnothing, \{\alpha_1, \alpha_2, \alpha_3, \beta_1, \beta_2, \beta_3\})$.   □

Example 3 (cont'd): Apply Proposition 2 leads to the unique complete, preferred, stable and grounded structure $(\{c\}, \{\pi\}, \{\alpha, \beta, \mu\})$.   □

Example 4 (cont'd): Apply Proposition 2 leads to the unique complete, preferred, stable and grounded structure $(\{a, b, c, d, e\}, \varnothing, \{\alpha, \beta, \gamma, \delta, \pi, \mu\})$.   □

5   Collective Interactions in REBAF: Impact on the Logical Encoding

Considering the logical translation of a REBAF, it remains a constraint given in [13] that must be relaxed since, here, we want to handle collective interactions. First consider an example that shows how the source of a collective interaction that is not reduced to a singleton can impact the computation of structures.

---

[7] Note that this proposition is more complete that Prop. 6.2 in [13] (numbered Proposition 1 here) since stable semantics is also taken into account.

Example 5. *In this example, there are a collective attack and a collective sup-port using the same source (this source is graphically represented by a "dotted diamond" containing the elements composing the source). Arguments c and e are the only elements that are not prima-facie.*

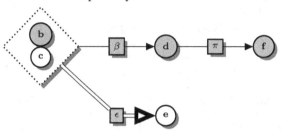

Since c is unsupportable, then neither β nor ϵ can be activable and there is one preferred structure that is: $(\{b, d\}, \{\beta, \pi\}, \{\epsilon\})$*. Trivially, an interaction can be activable w.r.t. a structure only if all the arguments in its source are in this structure.*

Consider now the 3 types of changes that must be done in the encoding in order to handle collective interactions: a change in the vocabulary, a change in the formulae, and a change related to the impact of support cycles.

Vocabulary. We must now express the fact that the source of an interaction can be a set of arguments and so that a given argument belongs to the source of a given interaction. So the old unary function S becomes now a binary predicate: $S(a, \alpha)$ means that "the argument a belongs to the source of α"

Formulae. What happens to the formulae in which sources appear? Three cases occur and each case corresponds to a particular behaviour:[8]

- The source is used as a parameter in the predicate *eAcc*; in this case, the idea is that the source of an interaction is e-accepted iff *all the arguments* belonging to this source are also e-accepted; so the old formula $eAcc(s_\alpha)$ corresponds to: $\forall a \in Arg(S(a, \alpha) \to eAcc(a))$
- The source is used as a parameter in the predicate *UnSupp*; in this case, the idea is that the source of an interaction is unsupportable iff *at least one argument* belonging to this source is also unsupportable; so the old formula $UnSupp(s_\alpha)$ corresponds to: $\exists a \in Arg(S(a, \alpha) \land UnSupp(a))$
- The source is used as a parameter in the equality predicate; here two subcases are possible depending of the aim of this equality in the formulae:
  - either this equality is used for testing if a given argument a belongs to the source of an interaction α and so the old equality $s_\alpha = a$ becomes a *logical or* between all the elements of the source:
    $(a_1 = a) \lor (a_2 = a), \lor \ldots \lor (a_n = a)$, for $\mathbf{s}(\alpha) = \{a_1, a_2, \ldots, a_n\}$
    that is equivalent to: $\exists x \in Arg(S(x, \alpha) \land x = a)$

---

[8] Note that a formula as $x \in \{s_y, y\}$ is just a shortcut for $(x = s_y) \lor (x = y)$ (see for instance formulae **(18)** and **(11)** to **(14)**).

- or this equality is used for defining the source of an interaction α with a given argument a and so the old equality $s_\alpha = a$ becomes a *logical and* between all the elements of the source:

$$S(a_1, \alpha) \wedge S(a_2, \alpha), \wedge \ldots \wedge S(a_n, \alpha), \text{ for } \mathbf{s}(\alpha) = \{a_1, a_2, \ldots, a_n\}$$

This last case appears only in formula **(6)**. In the other formulae, the first case applies when an equality appears.

Of course formulae **(1)** to **(19)** could be rewritten using the new formalism but the result becomes hard to read. So, our choice is to keep the old formulae in which the predicates applied to a source are considered as the shortcut defined as previously. For instance, formula **(2)** can be kept (shortcuts shown in a box):

$$\forall x \in Arg \ \forall y \in Attack \ \left(\left(eVal(y) \wedge (t_y = x) \wedge \boxed{eAcc(s_y)} \right) \rightarrow NAcc(x) \right)$$

but that means (formulae corresponding to the shortcuts shown in a box):

$$\forall x \in Arg \ \forall y \in Attack$$
$$\left(\left(eVal(y) \wedge (t_y = x) \wedge \boxed{\forall x_i \in Arg(S(x_i, y) \rightarrow eAcc(x_i))} \right) \rightarrow NAcc(x) \right)$$

Another example is formula **(11)**, we keep:

$$\forall \alpha \in Attack \left(\begin{array}{l} Acc(t_\alpha) \\ \left(\begin{array}{l} \exists \beta \in Attack \\ ((t_\beta = \alpha \vee \boxed{t_\beta = s_\alpha}) \wedge eVal(\beta) \wedge \boxed{eAcc(s_\beta)}) \\ \vee \boxed{UnSupp(s_\alpha)} \\ \vee UnSupp(\alpha) \end{array} \right) \end{array} \right)$$

but that means:

$$\forall \alpha \in Attack \left(\begin{array}{l} Acc(t_\alpha) \\ \left(\begin{array}{l} \exists \beta \in Attack \\ ((t_\beta = \alpha \vee \boxed{\exists x \in Arg(S(x, \alpha) \wedge t_\beta = x)}) \\ \wedge eVal(\beta) \wedge \boxed{\forall x \in Arg(S(x, \beta) \rightarrow eAcc(x))}) \\ \vee \boxed{\exists x \in Arg(S(x, \alpha) \wedge UnSupp(x))} \\ \vee UnSupp(\alpha) \end{array} \right) \end{array} \right)$$

As it has already been said, the only exception of this use of shortcut is formula **(6)** that is very specific and must be rewritten; the old formula

$$(s_\alpha = a) \wedge (t_\alpha = b) \text{ for all } \alpha \in \mathbf{R}_a \cup \mathbf{R}_e \text{ with } \mathbf{s}(\alpha) = a \text{ and } \mathbf{t}(\alpha) = b$$

becomes:

$$S(a_1, \alpha) \wedge \ldots \wedge S(a_n, \alpha) \wedge (t_\alpha = b) \text{ for all } \alpha \in \mathbf{R}_a \cup \mathbf{R}_e$$
$$\text{with } \mathbf{s}(\alpha) = \{a_1, \ldots, a_n\} \text{ and } \mathbf{t}(\alpha) = b$$

Note that the definition of the bases of formulae remains unchanged.

At this point, it is worth to note that if there is no support cycles in the REBAF then the use of the formulae bases is enough for characterizing the REBAF semantics without the removal of some models. So the difficulty comes with the existence of these cycles and implies that we are able to remove the models in which an element is supported only because it is satisfied by these models (so with no supported supports without itself contrary to what is required in Definition 3). The detection of such models was exactly the aim of Definition 8. Nevertheless, since we now want to take into account collective supports, some questions appear:

- "Is Definition 8 enough for characterizing support-founded models when collective supports exist in the REBAF?"
- and more generally "How to take into account support cycles when we have collective supports?".

The answer to these questions implies new definitions for DCS and support-founded interpretations.

Support Cycles and Collective Interactions. First we must adapt the previous definitions about support cycles in order to take into account collective interactions. Concerning the definition of DCS, the important point is the fact that, in a cycle, the targets and the sources must be clearly identified since they could be different (an interaction can only target one element of the source of another interaction):

Definition 9. *Let* **REBAF** $= \langle \mathbf{A}, \mathbf{R}_a, \mathbf{R}_e, \mathbf{s}, \mathbf{t}, \mathbf{P} \rangle$. *A directed cycle of supports (DCS) in this REBAF is a sequence* $\mathbf{C} = (x_0, \dots, x_{n-1}, x_n)$ *such that:*[9]

- $n > 0$ *and* n *is the* size *of the DCS*
- $\forall i = 0 \dots n$, *either* $x_i \in \mathbf{R}_e$, *or* $x_i = (a, S)$ *with* $S \in 2^{\mathbf{A}} \setminus \varnothing$ *and* $a \in \mathbf{A} \cap S$ *(a is called the "target field" of* x_i *and* S *is called the "source field" of* x_i*),*
- $x_n = x_0$
- $\forall i = 0 \dots n - 1$, *if* $x_i = (a, S) \in (\mathbf{A}, 2^{\mathbf{A}} \setminus \varnothing)$ *then* $x_{i+1} \in \mathbf{R}_e$ *and* $\mathbf{s}(x_{i+1}) = S$,
- $\forall i = 0 \dots n - 1$, *if* $x_i \in \mathbf{R}_e$ *then*
  - *if* $x_{i+1} \in \mathbf{R}_e$ *then* $\mathbf{t}(x_i) = x_{i+1}$
  - *if* $x_{i+1} = (a, S) \in (\mathbf{A}, 2^{\mathbf{A}} \setminus \varnothing)$ *then* $\mathbf{t}(x_i) = a$.

A simple DCS $\mathbf{C} = (x_0, \dots, x_{n-1}, x_n)$ *is a DCS in which* $\forall i, j = 0 \dots n - 1$, *if* $i \neq j$ *then* $x_i \neq x_j$.

Note that a DCS is now an "hybrid" sequence composed either with interactions, or with pairs (an argument, a non-empty set of arguments). The other definitions (for aggregation and maximal DSC) remain unchanged.

Example 6. *This example gives an example of support cycles with an higher-order support. Here* β, d *and* e *are not prima-facie.*

---

[9] We use the same notation as the one given in Definition 6. So here too, by abuse of language, the set of the elements composing $\mathbf{C}$ will be also denoted by $\mathbf{C}$ and $\mathbf{C}$ will be used with set operators as $\cap$ ou $\cup$ and will be comparable with other sets.

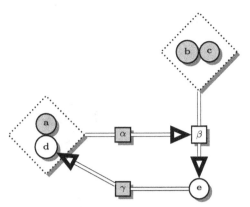

Here there is one DCS: $((d, \{a, d\}), \alpha, \beta, (e, \{e\}), \gamma, (d, \{a, d\}))$.
Note that the only preferred structure is $(\{a, b, c\}, \varnothing, \{\alpha, \gamma\})$.

It is also interesting to notice that a DCS can be represented by several sequences (n sequences if n is the size of the DCS, each sequence being obtained by shifting to the right – or to the left). For instance, the DCS of this REBAF can also be expressed with: $(\beta, (e, \{e\}), \gamma, (d, \{a, d\}), \alpha, \beta)$.

Example 7. *This example gives an example of several support cycles that can be aggregated*

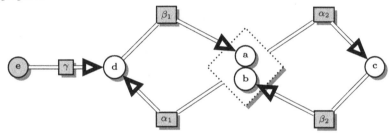

Here there are three DCS (only the last one is a maximal DCS):

- $((d, \{d\}), \beta_1, (a, \{a, b\}), \alpha_1, (d, \{d\}))$
- $((c, \{c\}), \beta_2, (b, \{a, b\}), \alpha_2, (c, \{c\}))$
- $((d, \{d\}), \beta_1, (a, \{a, b\}), \alpha_2, (c, \{c\}), \beta_2, (b, \{a, b\}), \alpha_1, (d, \{d\}))$

The interesting point is the fact that the set $\{a, b\}$ that is the source of α_1 and α_2 corresponds to two distinct elements in a DCS: $(a, \{a, b\})$ and $(b, \{a, b\})$; and each of them can be used as the preceding element of the supports α_1 or α_2 in the DCS.

Note that the only preferred structure is $(\{e, d, a\}, \varnothing, \{\alpha_1, \alpha_2, \beta_1, \beta_2, \gamma\})$.

Consider now the notion of impacting support chain. The following example shows that this notion must also be improved:

Example 8. *Consider the following REBAF with only arguments and supports; among these, there exist 2 collective supports (one from $\{a, b\}$ to x and the another one from $\{c, d, e\}$ to y).*

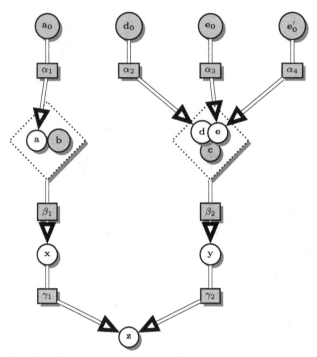

Let consider the elements that impact the supported status of argument z. Clearly simple chains are not enough and we must use the notion of "trees"; indeed, any element of the source of a collective support must be supported if we want the target of this support to be also supported. Here, three "trees" must be taken into account for computing the supported status of z:

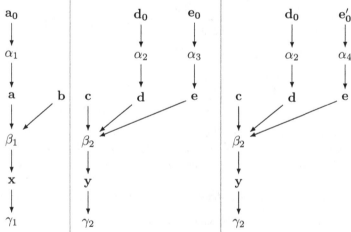

The previous example gives the main ideas for defining the notion of impacting support tree for an element of the REBAF:

Definition 10. *Let* **REBAF** $= \langle \mathbf{A}, \mathbf{R}_a, \mathbf{R}_e, \mathbf{s}, \mathbf{t}, \mathbf{P} \rangle$. *Let* x *be an element of this REBAF. An* impacting support tree *for* x *is a set* **IST** $= \{x_0, \ldots, x_n\}$ *with* $n > 0$ *s.t.:*

- $\forall x_i, i \in [0 \ldots n]$, $x_i \in (\mathbf{A} \cup \mathbf{R}_e) \setminus \{x\}$ *and is called a* node *of the tree;*
- *Let* $\mathbf{IST_P} = (\mathbf{IST} \cap \mathbf{P} \cap \mathbf{A})$. $\mathbf{IST_P} \neq \varnothing$;
- $!\exists x_i \in \mathbf{IST}$ *s.t.* $x_i \in \mathbf{R}_e$ *and* $\mathbf{t}(x_i) = x$; x_i *is called the* root *of the tree;*[10]
- $\forall i, j \in [0 \ldots n]$, *if* $i \neq j$, *then* $x_i \neq x_j$;
- $\forall x_i \in \mathbf{IST} \cap \mathbf{A}$, *either* $\exists x_j \in \mathbf{IST} \cap \mathbf{R}_e$ *s.t.* $x_i = \mathbf{t}(x_j)$, *or* $x_i \in \mathbf{IST_P}$ *(in this case* x_i *is called a* leaf *of the tree);*
- $\forall x_i \in \mathbf{IST} \cap \mathbf{R}_e$, $\forall x_j \in \mathbf{s}(x_i)$, $x_j \in \mathbf{IST}$.

Note that, as in Definition 7, an element x cannot belong to its impacting support tree, and by definition non repetition is authorized.

Example 5 (cont'd): There is no **IST** for any interaction or argument. Indeed the only element that is the target of a support is e and e has no **IST**, because the support ϵ cannot belong to an **IST** for e (one argument of its source, c, cannot belong to an **IST**; it is neither prima-facie, nor targeted by a support).   □

Example 6 (cont'd): Considering the existence of the DCS and the fact that d in this DCS needs to be supported without itself, there is no **IST** for d (idem for β and e).   □

Example 7 (cont'd): In this example, considering the non prima-facie elements, there are an **IST** for d ($\{\gamma, e\}$) and another for a ($\{\beta_1, d, \gamma, e\}$), but nothing for c, nor b. Indeed, c needs the support of b and b needs the support of c, so its own support that is forbidden by Definition 3.   □

Example 8 (cont'd): Considering a, there is one **IST** $= \{\alpha_1, a_0\}$. Considering d, there is one **IST** $= \{\alpha_2, d_0\}$. Considering e, there are two **IST**, $\{\alpha_3, e_0\}$ and $\{\alpha_4, e_0'\}$. Considering z, there are three **IST**:

- $\{\gamma_1, x, \beta_1, a, b, \alpha_1, a_0\}$ (root: γ_1, leaves: a_0 and b),
- $\{\gamma_2, y, \beta_2, c, d, e, \alpha_2, d_0, \alpha_3, e_0\}$ (root: γ_2, leaves: c, d_0 and e_0),
- $\{\gamma_2, y, \beta_2, c, d, e, \alpha_2, d_0, \alpha_4, e_0'\}$ (root: γ_2, leaves: c, d_0 and e_0').

The other elements of the REBAF have no **IST**.   □

Characterization: A New Proposition. The previous definition completed by the constraint concerning the unsupportable status of the element[11] leads to the following new definition for support-founded interpretations and models:

Definition 11. *Let* **REBAF** $= \langle \mathbf{A}, \mathbf{R}_a, \mathbf{R}_e, \mathbf{s}, \mathbf{t}, \mathbf{P} \rangle$. $\mathcal{I}$ *is a support-founded interpretation iff the two following conditions hold:*

---

[10] $!\exists x_i \in \mathbf{IST}$ means "there exists *only one* $x_i \in \mathbf{IST}$.
[11] See Definition 7.

1. *for each argument (resp. support) x non prima-facie, belonging to a maximal DCS and s.t. $\mathcal{I}(eAcc(x)) = true$ (resp. $\mathcal{I}(eVal(x)) = true$), there exists at least one impacting support tree $\text{IST} = (x_0, \ldots, x_n)$ for x that is satisfied by $\mathcal{I}$, i.e. $\forall x_i \in \text{IST}$, if $x_i \in \mathbf{A}$ then $\mathcal{I}(eAcc(x_i)) = true$, otherwise $\mathcal{I}(eVal(x_i)) = true$;*
2. *for each element x of REBAF, $\mathcal{I}(UnSupp(x)) = true$ iff $x \in UnSupp(U_{\mathcal{I}})$ with $U_{\mathcal{I}} = (S_{\mathcal{I}}, \Gamma_{\mathcal{I}}, \Delta_{\mathcal{I}})$.*

Let Σ_x be a base of formulae built over REBAF. A support-founded model of Σ_x is a support-founded interpretation which is a model of Σ_x.

Then using these support-founded models, the following characterization of REBAF semantics can be given for any kind of REBAF:

Proposition 3. *Let $\text{REBAF} = \langle \mathbf{A}, \mathbf{R}_a, \mathbf{R}_e, \mathbf{s}, \mathbf{t}, \mathbf{P} \rangle$. Let $U = (S, \Gamma, \Delta)$ be a structure on REBAF.*

1. *U is admissible iff there exists $\mathcal{I}$ support-founded model of $\Sigma_d(\text{REBAF})$ (in the sense of Definition 11) with $S_{\mathcal{I}} = S$, $\Gamma_{\mathcal{I}} = \Gamma$ and $\Delta_{\mathcal{I}} = \Delta$.*
2. *U is complete iff there exists $\mathcal{I}$ support-founded model of $(\Sigma_d(\text{REBAF}) \cup \Sigma_r(\text{REBAF}))$ (in the sense of Definition 11) with $S_{\mathcal{I}} = S$, $\Gamma_{\mathcal{I}} = \Gamma$ and $\Delta_{\mathcal{I}} = \Delta$.*
3. *U is a preferred structure iff there exists $\mathcal{I} \subseteq$-maximal support-founded model of $\Sigma_d(\text{REBAF})$ (in the sense of Definition 11) with $S_{\mathcal{I}} = S$, $\Gamma_{\mathcal{I}} = \Gamma$ and $\Delta_{\mathcal{I}} = \Delta$.*
4. *U is the grounded structure iff $S = S_{\mathcal{I}}$, $\Gamma_{\mathcal{I}} = \Gamma$ and $\Delta_{\mathcal{I}} = \Delta$ where $\mathcal{I}$ is a $\subseteq$-minimal support-founded model of $(\Sigma_d(\text{REBAF}) \cup \Sigma_r(\text{REBAF}))$ (in the sense of Definition 11).*
5. *U is stable iff there exists $\mathcal{I}$ support-founded model of $\Sigma_s(\text{REBAF})$ (in the sense of Definition 11) with $S_{\mathcal{I}} = S$, $\Gamma_{\mathcal{I}} = \Gamma$ and $\Delta_{\mathcal{I}} = \Delta$.*

Using Proposition 3, consider the previous examples and the preferred semantics:

Example 5 (cont'd): The $\subseteq$-maximal support-founded models $\mathcal{I}$ of $\Sigma_d(\text{REBAF})$ (in the sense of Definition 11) correspond to the preferred structure $(\{b, d\}, \{\beta, \pi\}, \{\epsilon\})$. □

Example 6 (cont'd): The $\subseteq$-maximal support-founded models $\mathcal{I}$ of $\Sigma_d(\text{REBAF})$ (in the sense of Definition 11) correspond to the preferred structure $(\{a, b, c\}, \varnothing, \{\alpha, \gamma\})$. The models that satisfy $eAcc(d)$ (resp. $eAcc(e)$, $eVal(\beta)$) are not kept since they are not support-founded (no **IST** for these arguments or this interaction that could be satisfied). □

Example 7 (cont'd): The $\subseteq$-maximal support-founded models $\mathcal{I}$ of $\Sigma_d(\text{REBAF})$ (in the sense of Definition 11) correspond to the preferred structure $(\{e, d, a\}, \varnothing, \{\alpha_1, \alpha_2, \beta_1, \beta_2, \gamma\})$. □

Example 8 (cont'd): The $\subseteq$-maximal support-founded models $\mathcal{I}$ of $\Sigma_d(\text{REBAF})$ (in the sense of Definition 11) correspond to the preferred structure $(\mathbf{A}, \mathbf{R}_a, \mathbf{R}_e)$. □

6   Conclusion and Future Works

This paper presents two improvements of the logical translation of argumentation frameworks with higher-order attacks and evidential supports (REBAF) described initially in [13]. First, we have proven that the attempt done for handling the support cycles in REBAF in [13] does not hold in the general case. So a new definition for the notion of support-founded models is proposed in this paper. Note that, as a side-effect, we have also defined an additional notion: the *Directed Cycles of Supports (DCS)* (and their possible aggregation); this notion is not simple in the case of higher-order argumentation frameworks, since the graphical representation of such frameworks is not a "directed graph" as defined in Graph Theory (unlike what happens for Dung argumentation frameworks). Secondly, in order to respect the general definition of REBAF, we have proposed an extension of the original encoding given in [13] that deals with collective interactions (attacks or supports whose source is a set of arguments). These improvements provide characterizations of admissible (resp. complete, preferred, grounded but also stable) structures in the presence of all kinds of support cycles and of collective interactions, so for all types of REBAF.

Considering future works, several possibilities appear. The first one is the implementation of this work for obtaining an efficient solver for the computation of REBAF semantics.[12] This point is related with the existence of the International Competition on Computational Models of Argumentation (ICCMA, see [1]), currently only centered around Dung framework, and so this could be the opportunity for this competition to open up to enriched frameworks as RAF and REBAF, for instance. A second future work could be an extension of this work to other argumentation frameworks also using bipolar and higher-order interactions. Indeed, there exist at least two other meanings of the support relation (the deductive and the necessary supports) and it could be interesting to study the impact of these other meanings on our modelization, particularly knowing that some links exist between the evidential support and the necessary support, and that deductive and necessary supports are dual notions (see [8,10]). And a third future work could be a comparative study with some other existing works also using logics for argumentation encoding and computation (see for instance ADS - Abstract Dialectical Frameworks - in [6]).

A   Sketchs of Proof

The proofs of Proposition 3 (or 2) are done using the following lemmas.

Lemma 1 (Lemma Appendix A.1 in [13]). *Any conflict-free self-supporting structure U satisfies: $Acc(U) \subseteq \overline{UnAcc(U)} \subseteq \overline{Def(U)}$.*

Lemma 2 (Lemma Appendix A.2 in [13]). *Any stable structure U satisfies: $\overline{Sup(U)} = UnSupp(U)$.*

---

[12] A basic implementation has already been done but without any code optimization, see [11].

Lemma 3 (Lemma Appendix A.3, in [13]). *Let $U = (S, \Gamma, \Delta)$ be a structure and $x \notin \mathbf{P}$ be the target of a support y s.t. $y \in \Delta \cap Sup(U)$ and $s_y \in S \cap Sup(U)$. Then, there exists a support z s.t. $t_z = x$, $z \in \Delta \cap Sup(U \setminus \{x\})$ and $s_z \in S \cap Sup(U \setminus \{x\})$ and so $x \in Sup(U)$.*

The preceding lemma can be adapted for collective interactions with a similar proof (the $\in$ of the source being replaced by a $\subseteq$).

Lemma 4. *Let $U = (S, \Gamma, \Delta)$ be a structure and $x \notin \mathbf{P}$ be the target of a support y s.t. $y \in \Delta \cap Sup(U)$ and $s_y \subseteq S \cap Sup(U)$. Then, there exists a support z s.t. $t_z = x$, $z \in \Delta \cap Sup(U \setminus \{x\})$ and $s_z \subseteq S \cap Sup(U \setminus \{x\})$ and so $x \in Sup(U)$.*

Sketchs of Proof of Proposition 3 (or 2). These proofs are strongly inspired by the proofs of props 6.1 and 6.2 in [13]. The only differences concern the nature of the source (now a set, so the $\in$ of the source will be replaced by a $\subseteq$ for proving Proposition 3) and the use of specific support-founded models.

For the $\Rightarrow$ direction and for each semantics, given a structure $U = (S, \Gamma, \Delta)$ that is an extension of this semantics, an interpretation $\mathcal{I}$ is built s.t. $U_\mathcal{I} = U$ (as in the proofs of propositions 6.1 and 6.2 in [13]); then we prove that $\mathcal{I}$ is a model of the corresponding logical bases, so a model of any formula in these bases (for instance when the semantics is the admissibility, $\mathcal{I}$ must be a model of Σ_d so a model of formulae **(1)** to **(12)**, plus formulae **(17)** and **(18)**); and finally we prove that $\mathcal{I}$ is a support-founded model. We give here only proofs for formulae **(17)**, **(18)** and **(19)**, and for the fact that $\mathcal{I}$ is a support-founded model since they are the most impacted by our changes.

- Let us first consider formula **(17)** (for all semantics). Let x s.t. $\mathcal{I}(Supp(x)) = true$. By definition of $\mathcal{I}(Supp)$, $x \in Sup(U)$. By definition of $Sup(U)$, either $x \in \mathbf{P}$ or x is the target of a support α s.t. $\alpha \in \Delta$, $\alpha \in Sup(U \setminus \{x\})$, $s_\alpha \subseteq S$ (or $s_\alpha \in S$) and $s_\alpha \subseteq Sup(U \setminus \{x\})$ (or $s_\alpha \in Sup(U \setminus \{x\})$). In the first case, formula **(17)** is trivially satisfied by $\mathcal{I}$ (following the building of $\mathcal{I}$). In the second case, as $S = S_\mathcal{I}$ and $\Delta = \Delta_\mathcal{I}$ it holds that $\mathcal{I}(eAcc(s_\alpha)) = true$ and $\mathcal{I}(eVal(\alpha)) = true$. Hence formula **(17)** is satisfied by $\mathcal{I}$.
- Let us now consider formula **(18)** (for all semantics). Let x s.t. $\mathcal{I}(UnSupp(x)) = true$. By definition of $\mathcal{I}(UnSupp)$, $x \in UnSupp(U)$. And, since $UnSupp(U) = \overline{Sup(U')}$ (where $U' = (\overline{Def_\mathbf{A}(U)}, \mathbf{R}_a, \overline{Def_{\mathbf{R}_e}(U)})$), $x \in \overline{Sup(U')}$. So $x \notin \mathbf{P}$ and using the contrapositive of Lemma 4 (or Lemma 3 for Proposition 2), applied to the structure U', it follows that for each support leading to x, either the support or its source[13] is defeated by U, or the support or its source is itself not supported by U', hence belongs to $UnSupp(U)$. So $\mathcal{I}$ satisfies the "only if" part of formula **(18)**. For the "if" part, let us consider x s.t. $x \notin \mathbf{P}$ and for each support leading to x, either the support or its source is defeated by U, or the support or at least one component of its source belongs to $UnSupp(U) = \overline{Sup(U')}$. As $U' \setminus \{x\} \subseteq U'$, it holds that $\overline{Sup(U')}$

---

[13] If the source is defeated by U, that means that at least one of its components is defeated by U (idem for the unsupportability of the source).

$\subseteq \overline{Sup(U' \setminus \{x\})}$. Hence, from Definition 3, it holds that $x \notin Sup(U')$, that is $x \in UnSupp(U)$ and so $\mathcal{I}(UnSupp(x)) = true$. So $\mathcal{I}$ satisfies formula **(18)**.

- Consider now formula **(19)** (for stable semantics). Let $x \in \mathbf{A} \cup \mathbf{R}_a \cup \mathbf{R}_e$ s.t. $\mathcal{I}(Supp(x)) = false$. By definition of $\mathcal{I}(Supp)$, $x \notin Sup(u)$. Due to Lemma 2, it follows that $x \in UnSupp(U)$, hence $\mathcal{I}(UnSupp(x)) = true$, by definition of $\mathcal{I}(UnSupp)$. We have proved that $\mathcal{I}$ satisfies formula **(19)**. So $\mathcal{I}$ is a model of $\Sigma_s(\mathbf{REBAF})$.

- And finally, we have to prove that $\mathcal{I}$ is support-founded (for all semantics). Condition 2 of Definition 11 (or Definition 8) is trivially satisfied (following the building of $\mathcal{I}$). Consider now Condition 1. Let $x \in \mathbf{A}$ s.t. x is non prima-facie and there exists a DCS $\mathbf{C}$ containing x. Assume that $\mathcal{I}(eAcc(x)) = true$. So $x \in U$ and, since U is admissible (so self-supporting) and x non prima-facie, then there exists at least one tree (or chain for Proposition 2) of supported supports $(x_0, \dots, x_n)$ leading to x with any x_i belonging to U. Moreover, for all x_i, we have $x_i \in Sup(U)$. So following the definition of $\mathcal{I}$ we have either $\mathcal{I}(eAcc(x_i)) = true$ or $\mathcal{I}(eVal(x_i)) = true$ depending of the nature of x_i (argument or support). Thus there exists an impacting support tree (or chain for Proposition 2) $(x_0, \dots, x_n)$ for x that is satisfied by $\mathcal{I}$. So $\mathcal{I}$ is a support-founded model. The proof for $x \in \mathbf{R}_e$ is similar.

For the $\Leftarrow$ direction and for each semantics, given a support-founded interpretation $\mathcal{I}$ that is a model of the corresponding logical bases, we show that $U_\mathcal{I}$ is a structure of the semantics (for instance, for the admissible semantics, $U_\mathcal{I}$ must be conflict-free, self-supporting and any element of the structure must be acceptable wrt $U_\mathcal{I}$). Of course the proofs for the preferred (or grounded) semantics are simpler since we only use the maximality (or minimality) property (as in the proofs of props 6.1 and 6.2 in [13]).

References

1. International Competition on Computational Models of Argumentation (ICCMA). http://argumentationcompetition.org/
2. Arisaka, R., Satoh, K.: Voluntary manslaughter? A case study with meta-argumentation with supports. In: Kurahashi, S., Ohta, Y., Arai, S., Satoh, K., Bekki, D. (eds.) JSAI-isAI 2016. LNCS (LNAI), vol. 10247, pp. 241–252. Springer, Cham (2017). https://doi.org/10.1007/978-3-319-61572-1_16
3. Baroni, P., Cerutti, F., Giacomin, M., Guida, G.: AFRA: argumentation framework with recursive attacks. Int. J. Approx. Reason. **52**, 19–37 (2011)
4. Barringer, H., Gabbay, D., Woods, J.: Temporal dynamics of support and attack networks: from argumentation to zoology. In: Hutter, D., Stephan, W. (eds.) Mechanizing Mathematical Reasoning. LNCS (LNAI), vol. 2605, pp. 59–98. Springer, Heidelberg (2005). https://doi.org/10.1007/978-3-540-32254-2_5
5. Boella, G., Gabbay, D.M., van der Torre, L., Villata, S.: Support in abstract argumentation. In: Proceedings of COMMA, pp. 111–122. IOS Press (2010)
6. Brewka, G., Ellmauthaler, S., Strass, H., Wallner, J.P., Woltran, S.: Abstract dialectical frameworks. In: Baroni, P., Gabbay, D., Giacomin, M., van der Torre, L. (eds.) Handbook of Formal Argumentation, chap. 5, pp. 237–286. College Publications (2018)

7. Cayrol, C., Fandinno, J., Fariñas del Cerro, L., Lagasquie-Schiex, M.-C.: Argumentation frameworks with recursive attacks and evidence-based supports. In: Ferrarotti, F., Woltran, S. (eds.) FoIKS 2018. LNCS, vol. 10833, pp. 150–169. Springer, Cham (2018). https://doi.org/10.1007/978-3-319-90050-6_9
8. Cayrol, C., Fandinno, J., Fariñas del Cerro, L., Lagasquie-Schiex, M.C.: Structure-based semantics of argumentation frameworks with higher-order attacks and supports (short paper). In: Modgil, S., Budzynska, K., Lawrence, J. (eds.) Proceedings of COMMA, pp. 29–36. IOS Press (2018)
9. Cayrol, C., Lagasquie-Schiex, M.C.: Gradual valuation for bipolar argumentation frameworks. In: Godo, L. (ed.) ECSQARU 2005. LNCS (LNAI), vol. 3571, pp. 366–377. Springer, Heidelberg (2005). https://doi.org/10.1007/11518655_32
10. Cayrol, C., Lagasquie-Schiex, M.C.: Bipolarity in argumentation graphs: towards a better understanding. Intl. J. Approx. Reason. 54(7), 876–899 (2013)
11. Cayrol, C., Lagasquie-Schiex, M.C.: The Grafix website. http://www.irit.fr/grafix
12. Cayrol, C., Lagasquie-Schiex, M.C.: Logical encoding of argumentation frameworks with higher-order attacks. In: Proceedings of the 30th International Conference on Tools with Artificial Intelligence (ICTAI). IEEE (2018)
13. Cayrol, C., Lagasquie-Schiex, M.C.: Logical encoding of argumentation frameworks with higher-order attacks and evidential supports. Int. J. Artif. Intell. Tools 29(3–4), 2060003:1–2060003:50 (2020). https://doi.org/10.1142/s0218213020600039
14. Cohen, A., Gottifredi, S., García, A.J., Simari, G.R.: An approach to abstract argumentation with recursive attack and support. J. Appl. Logic 13(4), 509–533 (2015)
15. Dung, P.M.: On the acceptability of arguments and its fundamental role in non-monotonic reasoning, logic programming and n-person games. Artif. Intell. 77, 321–357 (1995)
16. Gabbay, D.M.: Fibring argumentation frames. Stud. Logica. 93, 231–295 (2009)
17. Karacapilidis, N., Papadias, D.: Computer supported argumentation and collaborative decision making: the Hermes system. Inf. Syst. 26(4), 259–277 (2001)
18. Lagasquie-Schiex, M.C.: Handling support cycles in the logical encoding of argumentation frameworks with higher-order attacks and evidential supports. Rapport de recherche IRIT/RR-2021-04-FR, IRIT, France (2021). http://www.irit.fr/publis/ADRIA/PapersMCL/Rapport-IRIT-2021-04.pdf
19. Lagasquie-Schiex, M.C.: Logical encoding of argumentation frameworks with higher-order attacks and evidential supports: taking into account the collective interactions. Rapport de recherche IRIT/RR-2021-05-FR, IRIT, France (2021). http://www.irit.fr/publis/ADRIA/PapersMCL/Rapport-IRIT-2021-05.pdf
20. Modgil, S.: Reasoning about preferences in argumentation frameworks. Artif. Intell. 173, 901–934 (2009)
21. Nielsen, S.H., Parsons, S.: A generalization of Dung's abstract framework for argumentation: arguing with sets of attacking arguments. In: Maudet, N., Parsons, S., Rahwan, I. (eds.) ArgMAS 2006. LNCS (LNAI), vol. 4766, pp. 54–73. Springer, Heidelberg (2007). https://doi.org/10.1007/978-3-540-75526-5_4
22. Nouioua, F., Risch, V.: Argumentation frameworks with necessities. In: Benferhat, S., Grant, J. (eds.) SUM 2011. LNCS (LNAI), vol. 6929, pp. 163–176. Springer, Heidelberg (2011). https://doi.org/10.1007/978-3-642-23963-2_14
23. Oren, N., Reed, C., Luck, M.: Moving between argumentation frameworks. In: Proceedings of COMMA, pp. 379–390. IOS Press (2010)
24. Rahwan, I., Simari, G.: Argumentation in Artificial Intelligence. Springer, Boston (2009). https://doi.org/10.1007/978-0-387-98197-0

25. Verheij, B.: DefLog: on the logical interpretation of prima facie justified assumptions. J. Logic Comput. **13**, 319–346 (2003)
26. Villata, S., Boella, G., Gabbay, D.M., van der Torre, L.: Modelling defeasible and prioritized support in bipolar argumentation. AMAI **66**(1–4), 163–197 (2012)

Tableau-Based Decision Procedure for Logic of Knowing-How via Simple Plans

Yanjun Li[(⊠)]

College of Philosophy, Nankai University, Tianjin, China

Abstract. Recently, there has been an increasing interest in studying logic of knowing-how based on the idea of planning. In literature, it is shown that knowing-how logics based on 10 different types of plans, including simple plans, share the same proof system. In this paper, we present a tableau system for the knowing-how logic via simple plans, and we show that there is an algorithm that runs in polynomial space for deciding whether a formula of the knowing-how logic is satisfiable. Since the knowing-how logic is an extension of epistemic logic which is PSPACE-hard for multi-agent version, it follows that the multi-agent knowing-how logic via simple plans is PSPACE-complete.

Keywords: Epistemic logic · Knowing-how logic · Tableau

1 Introduction

Standard epistemic logic proposed by von Wright and Hintikka concerns with reasoning about propositional knowledge which is expressed by *knowing that* φ [7,14]. However, beyond *knowing that*, there are other expressions of knowledge in natural language, such as *knowing whether, knowing what, knowing how, knowing why*, and so on. All of them are usually called knowledge of *knowing-wh*. Recently, there has been an increasing interest on the logics of these knowing-wh (cf. e.g., [3–5,8,9,15,17]). Among the logics of *knowing-wh*, the logics of knowing-how received the most attention (cf. [4,10,13,16]).

The discussion about formalizing knowing-how can date back to [11,12]. In [15,16], Wang proposed a new way of formalizing knowing-how motivated by the idea of planning under uncertainty in artificial intelligence (AI). Planning under uncertainty is to find a plan that is always executable to the end to guarantee achieving the goal, given that the agent is uncertain about the exact state where he is. Take the following example presented in [10]. The map of a hotel's floor is illustrated below, where rooms (denoted by s_i) are connected by (one-way) corridors (r arrows) or stairs (u arrows). The proposition p is true at rooms only s_2 and s_3, and q is true at only s_4, s_7, and s_8.

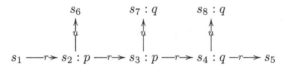

© Springer Nature Switzerland AG 2021
P. Baroni et al. (Eds.): CLAR 2021, LNAI 13040, pp. 266–283, 2021.
https://doi.org/10.1007/978-3-030-89391-0_15

An agent now is lost in the floor. He only knows that he is in a p-room, but he is not sure whether he is in s_2 or s_3. However, with the map in hand, he does have a plan to guarantee achieving a q-room by first moving right (r) and then moving up (u). Inspired by this idea, Wang interpreted the notion of *knowing how to achieve* φ as there exists a *linear plan* (i.e. a sequence of actions) such that the agent knows that performing the plan can guarantee achieving φ.

Along with this approach of formalizing knowing-how based on planning, [4] proposed a knowing-how logic based on a different notion of plan, a uniform strategy, which is a partial function from belief states to actions. Besides linear plan and uniform strategy, there are other intuitive notions of plan. For example, in the example above, the action sequence rr is a *weaker linear* plan for achieving a $\neg q$-state since the agent will always terminate on s_5 even though it cannot alway fully executable to the end. In [10], they use a programming language to specify 10 types of plans, such as simple plans, linear plans, unbounded linear plans, conditional plans, knowledge-based plans, and so on. They show that all these 10 types of plans lead to the same knowing-how logic in the sense that they share the same proof system.

In this paper, we present a tableau-based decision procedure for the knowing-how logic via simple plans, and so a decision procedure for the proof system presented in [10]. A simple plan is an at most one step plan, that is, a single action a or the empty sequence ϵ. Based on the semantic tableau method for epistemic logic which is proposed in [6] and developed in [2], we present a tableau calculus for the knowing-how logic via simple plans. Moreover, we show that there is an algorithm that runs in polynomial space for deciding whether there is a closed tableau. With other known results, this leads to the result that multi-agent knowing-how logic via simple plans is PSPACE-complete.

The structure of this paper are as follows: Sect. 2 introduces the knowing-how logic based on simple plans; Sect. 3 presents the tableau system; Sect. 4 shows the completeness of the tableau system. Section 5 presents a decision procedure based on the tableau system. Finally, we conclude with some remarks in Sect. 6.

2 Preliminaries

In this section, we introduce the knowing-how logic via simple plans. Let $\mathbf{P}$ be a countable set of propositional symbols, and let $\mathbf{I}$ be a set of agents.

Definition 1 (ELKh Language). *The Epistemic Language $\mathcal{L}$ of Knowing How is defined by the following BNF where $p \in \mathbf{P}$ and $i \in \mathbf{I}$:*

$$\varphi ::= \bot \mid p \mid \neg\varphi \mid (\varphi \wedge \varphi) \mid \mathcal{K}_i\varphi \mid \mathcal{K}h_i\varphi.$$

We use $\top, \vee, \rightarrow$ as usual abbreviations and write $\widehat{\mathcal{K}}_i\varphi$ for $\neg\mathcal{K}_i\neg\varphi$. The formula $\mathcal{K}_i\varphi$ means that the agent i knows that φ, and the formula $\mathcal{K}h_i\varphi$ means that the agent knows how to achieve φ.

Formulas are interpreted on models defined as follows.

Definition 2 (Model). *An Epistemic Transition System (or, a model) $\mathcal{M}$ is a quintuple $\langle W, \{\sim_i| i \in \mathbf{I}\}, \{\mathbf{A}_i \mid i \in \mathbf{I}\}, \{R(a) \mid a \in \mathbf{A}_i, i \in \mathbf{I}\}, V \rangle$ where:*

- *W is a non-empty set of states,*
- *$\sim_i \subseteq W \times W$ is an equivalence relation for each $i \in \mathbf{I}$,*
- *$\mathbf{A}_i$ is a set of actions for each $i \in \mathbf{I}$,*
- *$R(a) \subseteq W \times W$ is a binary relation for each $i \in \mathbf{I}$ and each $a \in \mathbf{A}_i$,*
- *$V : W \to 2^{\mathbf{P}}$ is a valuation function.*

Notations. For each $s \in W$, $[s]^i \subseteq W$ denotes the equivalence class $\{t \in W \mid s \sim_i t\}$, and $[W]^i$ denotes the collection of all the equivalence classes on W for $\sim_i$. The binary relation $R(a)$ on W also can be seen as a function from W to the power set of W, such that for each $s \in W$, $R(a)(s) = \{t \in W \mid (s,t) \in R(a)\}$. Thus, by abusing the notation, we sometimes also write $(s,t) \in R(a)$ as $t \in R(a)(s)$. We use $\mathbf{A}_i^\epsilon$ to denote the set $\mathbf{A}_i \cup \{\epsilon\}$. If $\sigma = \epsilon$, let $R(\sigma)(s) = \{s\}$. Given a set of states X and $\sigma \in \mathbf{A}_i^\epsilon$, we use $R(\sigma)(X)$ to denote the set $\bigcup_{s \in X} R(\sigma)(s)$.

Before we introduce the semantics, we firstly introduce the following auxiliary notion of strong executability.

Definition 3 (Strong executability). *Let A be a set of actions. Let X be a set of states. We say that an action $a \in A$ is strongly executable on X if for each $s \in X$, there exists t such that $(s,t) \in R(a)$. In particular, the empty ϵ is strongly executable on all sets of states.*

Now we are ready to introduce the semantics.

Definition 4 (Semantics $\vDash$). *The satisfaction relation $\vDash$ is defined as follows between formulas and pointed models:*

$$
\begin{array}{ll}
\mathcal{M}, s \nvDash \bot & always \\
\mathcal{M}, s \vDash p & \Longleftrightarrow p \in V(s) \\
\mathcal{M}, s \vDash \neg\varphi & \Longleftrightarrow \mathcal{M}, s \nvDash \varphi \\
\mathcal{M}, s \vDash \varphi \wedge \psi & \Longleftrightarrow \mathcal{M}, s \vDash \varphi \text{ and } \mathcal{M}, s \vDash \psi \\
\mathcal{M}, s \vDash \mathcal{K}_i\varphi & \Longleftrightarrow \text{ for all } s' : s \sim_i s' \text{ implies } \mathcal{M}, s' \vDash \varphi \\
\mathcal{M}, s \vDash \mathcal{K}h_i\varphi & \Longleftrightarrow \text{ there exists } \sigma \in \mathbf{A}_i^\epsilon \text{ such that} \\
& \quad 1.\ \sigma \text{ is strongly executable on } [s]^i, \text{ and} \\
& \quad 2.\ \mathcal{M}, t \vDash \varphi \text{ for all } t \in R(\sigma)([s]^i).
\end{array}
$$

In [10], an atom action or the empty sequence ϵ is called a simple plan. Besides simple plans, there also discusses knowing-how based on other types of plans, such as linear plans, conditional plans, knowledge-based plans, and so on.

Example 1. Let the model $\mathcal{M}$ be depicted as below, where there are two agents i and j, and $\mathbf{A}_i = \mathbf{A}_j = \{a\}$. Dash dot lines below represent equivalence relations, and reflexive dash dot lines are omitted.

We then have the followings:

- $\mathcal{M}, s_2 \vDash \mathcal{K}h_i p$. At the state s_2, the agent i knows how to achieve p-states, since he can achieve that goal by doing ϵ, namely staying where he is.
- $\mathcal{M}, s_2 \vDash \mathcal{K}h_j q$. At the state s_2, the agent j knows how to achieve the q-state, since he can achieve that goal by doing the action a.

Proposition 1. *The following formulas are valid:*

1. $\neg \mathcal{K}h_i \bot$
2. $\mathcal{K}_i \varphi \to \mathcal{K}h_i \varphi$
3. $\mathcal{K}h_i \varphi \to \mathcal{K}_i \mathcal{K}h_i \varphi$
4. $\neg \mathcal{K}h_i \varphi \to \mathcal{K} \neg \mathcal{K}h_i \varphi$

Proof. 1. Assume that there is a pointed model $(\mathcal{M}, s)$ such that $\mathcal{M}, s \vDash \mathcal{K}h_i \bot$. This follows that there is $\sigma \in \mathbf{A}_i^\epsilon$ such that σ is strongly executable on $[s]^i$ and $\mathcal{M}, t \vDash \bot$ for all $t \in R(\sigma)([s]^i)$. Since $s \in [s]^i$, this follows that σ is strongly executable on s. We then have that $R(\sigma)(s) \neq \emptyset$. Since we have shown that $\mathcal{M}, t \vDash \bot$ for all $t \in R(\sigma)([s]^i)$, this follows that there is $\mathcal{M}, t \vDash \bot$ for some t. Contradiction! Therefore, there is no pointed model $(\mathcal{M}, s)$ such that $\mathcal{M}, s \vDash \mathcal{K}h_i \bot$, namely, $\vDash \neg \mathcal{K}h_i \bot$.

2. Let $(\mathcal{M}, s)$ be a pointed model such that $\mathcal{M}, s \vDash \mathcal{K}_i \varphi$. Next we will show that $\mathcal{M}, s \vDash \mathcal{K}h_i \varphi$. Since $\mathcal{M}, s \vDash \mathcal{K}_i \varphi$, this follows that $\mathcal{M}, t \vDash \varphi$ for all $t \in [s]^i$. Please note that $R(\epsilon)([s]^i) = [s]^i$ and that ϵ is strongly executable on $[s]^i$. Thus, we know that ϵ is a good plan for $\mathcal{M}, s \vDash \mathcal{K}h_i \varphi$.

3. Let $(\mathcal{M}, s)$ be a pointed model such that $\mathcal{M}, s \vDash \mathcal{K}h_i \varphi$. Next we will show that $\mathcal{M}, s \vDash \mathcal{K}_i \mathcal{K}h_i \varphi$. Since $\mathcal{M}, s \vDash \mathcal{K}h_i \varphi$, this follows that there is $\sigma \in \mathbf{A}_i^\epsilon$ such that σ is strongly executable on $[s]^i$ and $\mathcal{M}, t \vDash \varphi$ for all $t \in R(\sigma)([s]^i)$. For each $s' \in [s]^i$, since $\sim_i$ is an equivalence relation, we have that $[s]^i = [s']^i$ and then that $R(\sigma)([s]^i) = R(\sigma)([s']^i)$. Thus, σ also is a good plan for $\mathcal{M}, s' \vDash \mathcal{K}h_i \varphi$. Therefore, we have shown that $\mathcal{M}, s' \vDash \mathcal{K}h_i \varphi$ for each $s' \in [s]^i$. Thus, we have that $\mathcal{M}, s \vDash \mathcal{K}_i \mathcal{K}h_i \varphi$.

4. Let $(\mathcal{M}, s)$ be a pointed model such that $\mathcal{M}, s \vDash \neg \mathcal{K}h_i \varphi$. Next we will show that $\mathcal{M}, s \vDash \mathcal{K}_i \neg \mathcal{K}h_i \varphi$. Assume that $\mathcal{M}, s \nvDash \mathcal{K}_i \neg \mathcal{K}h_i \varphi$. This follows that $\mathcal{M}, s' \vDash \mathcal{K}h_i \varphi$ for some $s' \in [s]^i$. Since we have shown above that $\vDash \mathcal{K}h_i \varphi \to \mathcal{K}_i \mathcal{K}h_i \varphi$, this follows that $\mathcal{M}, s' \vDash \mathcal{K}_i \mathcal{K}h_i \varphi$. Since $s' \in [s]^i$, this follows that $s \in [s']^i$ due to the fact that $\sim_i$ is an equivalence relation. We then have that $\mathcal{M}, s \vDash \mathcal{K}h_i \varphi$. This is contradictory with the fact that $\mathcal{M}, s \vDash \neg \mathcal{K}h_i \varphi$. Thus, $\mathcal{M}, s \vDash \mathcal{K}_i \neg \mathcal{K}h_i \varphi$.

The proof system $\mathbb{SLKH}$ is presented in Table 1. It is shown in [10] that $\mathbb{SLKH}$ is sound and complete with respect to knowing-how via simple plans.

Table 1. Proof System SLKH

Axioms	
TAUT	all axioms of propositional logic
DISTK	$\mathcal{K}_i p \wedge \mathcal{K}_i(p \to q) \to \mathcal{K}_i q$
T	$\mathcal{K}_i p \to p$
4	$\mathcal{K}_i p \to \mathcal{K}_i \mathcal{K}_i p$
5	$\neg \mathcal{K}_i p \to \mathcal{K}_i \neg \mathcal{K}_i p$
AxKtoKh	$\mathcal{K}_i p \to \mathcal{K}h_i p$
AxKhtoKhK	$\mathcal{K}h_i p \to \mathcal{K}h_i \mathcal{K}_i p$
AxKhtoKKh	$\mathcal{K}h_i p \to \mathcal{K}_i \mathcal{K}h_i p$
AxKhKh	$\mathcal{K}h_i \mathcal{K}h_i p \to \mathcal{K}h_i p$
AxKhbot	$\mathcal{K}h_i \bot \to \bot$

Rules			
MP	$\dfrac{\varphi, \varphi \to \psi}{\psi}$	NECK	$\dfrac{\varphi}{\mathcal{K}_i \varphi}$
MONOKh	$\dfrac{\varphi \to \psi}{\mathcal{K}h_i \varphi \to \mathcal{K}h_i \psi}$	SUB	$\dfrac{\varphi(p)}{\varphi[\psi/p]}$

3 Tableau System for **ELKh**

In this section, we present the tableau system. Intuitively, a tableau is a tree with additional information about models. Nodes of tableau tree represent states of models.

Before we formally define tableaux, we firstly introduce two auxiliary notions below.

Definition 5 (Labelled formula). *A labelled formula is a pair of the form $\langle n, \varphi \rangle$ where $n \in \mathbb{N}$ and $\varphi \in \mathcal{L}$.*

The label n in a labelled formula $\langle n, \varphi \rangle$ is a node of tableau trees. The labelled formula $\langle n, \varphi \rangle$ represents that the state that the node n represents satisfies the formula φ.

Moreover, there are two kinds of relations in models: epistemic relations $\sim_i$ and action relation $R(a)$. These information about $\sim_i$ and $R(a)$ will also be attached on tableau trees.

Definition 6 (Branch). *A branch is a pair of the form $\langle L, S \rangle$ where L is a set of labelled formulas and $S \subseteq ((\mathbf{I} \cup \mathcal{L}|_{\mathcal{K}h}) \times \mathbb{N} \times \mathbb{N})$ where $\mathcal{L}|_{\mathcal{K}h} = \{\mathcal{K}h_i \varphi \in \mathcal{L} \mid i \in \mathbf{I}, \varphi \in \mathcal{L}\}$.*

The set S carries information about relations $\sim_i$ and $R(a)$. If $\langle i, n, m \rangle \in S$, it represents that the pair of the states n and m are in the relation $\sim_i$, namely, $n \sim_i m$. If $\langle \mathcal{K}h_i \varphi, n, m \rangle \in S$, it represents that there is an action a such that $R(a)$ connects n and m (namely $(n, m) \in R(a)$) and that a is a good plan for the state n satisfies $\mathcal{K}h_i\varphi$. The relation S in the branch represents a part of the relations $\sim_i$ and $R(a)$ in models. This will be more clear when we construct models from tableau branches in the proof of Proposition 7.

Now we are ready to define tableaux.

Definition 7 (Tableau). *A tableau for φ is a set of branches T inductively defined as follows:*

- $T = \{\langle\{\langle 0, \varphi\rangle\}, \emptyset\rangle\}$. *This is called the initial tableau for φ.*
- $T = (T'\backslash\{b\}) \cup B$, *where T' is a tableau for φ that contains the branch $b = \langle L, S\rangle$, and B is a finite set of branches generated by one of the tableau rules defined below:*
  - $R\neg$: *if* $\langle n, \neg\neg\varphi\rangle \in L$ *then* $B = \{\langle L \cup \{\langle n, \varphi\rangle\}, S\rangle\}$.
  - $R\wedge$: *if* $\langle n, \varphi_1 \wedge \varphi_2\rangle \in L$ *then* $B = \{\langle L \cup \{\langle n, \varphi_1\rangle, \langle n, \varphi_2\rangle\}, S\rangle\}$.
  - $R\vee$: *if* $\langle n, \neg(\varphi_1 \wedge \varphi_2)\rangle \in L$ *then* $B = \{\langle L \cup \{\langle n, \neg\varphi_1\rangle, \langle n, \neg\varphi_2\rangle\}, S\rangle, \langle L \cup \{\langle n, \neg\varphi_1\rangle, \langle n, \varphi_2\rangle\}, S\rangle, \langle L \cup \{\langle n, \varphi_1\rangle, \langle n, \neg\varphi_2\rangle\}, S\rangle\}$.
  - $Cut\text{-}\mathcal{K}$: *if* $\langle n, \neg\mathcal{K}_i\varphi\rangle \in L$ *then* $B = \{\langle L \cup \{\langle n, \neg\varphi\rangle\}, S\rangle, \langle L \cup \{\langle n, \varphi\rangle\}, S\rangle\}$.
  - $\mathcal{K}T$: *if* $\langle n, \mathcal{K}_i\varphi\rangle \in L$ *then* $B = \{\langle L \cup \{\langle n, \varphi\rangle\}, S\rangle\}$.
  - $Cut\text{-}\mathcal{K}h$: *if* $\langle n, \mathcal{K}h_i\varphi\rangle \in L$, *we have that* $B = \{b_1, b_2\}$ *where* $b_1 = \langle L \cup \{\langle n, \neg\mathcal{K}_i\varphi\rangle, \langle n, \neg\mathcal{K}h_i\bot\rangle\}, S\rangle$ *and* $b_2 = \langle L \cup \{\langle n, \mathcal{K}_i\varphi\rangle, \langle n, \neg\mathcal{K}h_i\bot\rangle\}, S\rangle$.
  - $Cut\text{-}\neg\mathcal{K}h$: *if* $\langle n, \neg\mathcal{K}h_i\varphi\rangle \in L$ *then* $B = \{\langle L \cup \{\langle n, \neg\mathcal{K}_i\varphi\rangle\}, S\rangle\}$.
  - $R\mathcal{K}$: *if* $\langle n, \mathcal{K}_i\varphi\rangle \in L$ *and* $(i, n, n') \in S$ *then* $B = \{\langle L \cup \{\langle n', \varphi\rangle\}, S\rangle\}$.
  - $\mathcal{K}4$: *if* $\langle n, \mathcal{K}_i\varphi\rangle \in L$ *and* $(i, n, n') \in S$ *then* $B = \{\langle L \cup \{\langle n', \mathcal{K}_i\varphi\rangle\}, S\rangle\}$.
  - $\mathcal{K}5$: *if* $\langle n, \neg\mathcal{K}_i\varphi\rangle \in L$ *and* $(i, n, n') \in S$ *then* $B = \{\langle L \cup \{\langle n', \neg\mathcal{K}_i\varphi\rangle\}, S\rangle\}$.
  - $R\neg\mathcal{K}$: *if* $\langle n, \neg\mathcal{K}_i\varphi\rangle \in L$ *then* $B = \{\langle L \cup \{\langle n', \neg\varphi\rangle\}, S \cup \{(i, n, n')\}\rangle\}$ *for some $n' \in \mathbb{N}$ not occurring in b.*
  - $\mathcal{K}h4$: *if* $\langle n, \mathcal{K}h_i\varphi\rangle \in L$ *and* $(i, n, n') \in S$ *then* $B = \{\langle L \cup \{\langle n', \mathcal{K}h_i\varphi\rangle\}, S\rangle\}$.
  - $\mathcal{K}h5$: *if* $\langle n, \neg\mathcal{K}h_i\varphi\rangle \in L$ *and* $(i, n, n') \in S$ *then we have that* $B = \{\langle L \cup \{\langle n', \neg\mathcal{K}h_i\varphi\rangle\}, S\rangle\}$.
  - $R\pm\mathcal{K}h$: *if* $\{\langle n, \neg\mathcal{K}h_i\varphi\rangle, \langle n, \mathcal{K}h_i\psi\rangle, \langle n, \neg\mathcal{K}_i\psi\rangle\} \subseteq L$ *then* $B = \{\langle L \cup \{\langle n', \neg\varphi\rangle, \langle n', \psi\rangle\}, S \cup \{(\mathcal{K}h_i\psi, n, n')\}\rangle\}$ *for some $n' \in \mathbb{N}$ not occurring in b.*

Tableau rules in 'nominator/denominator' form are presented in Table 2. Please note that we use the colon ':' to distinguish elements of L and elements of S. For example, in the rule $\mathcal{K}4$, the notation $\langle n, \mathcal{K}h_i\varphi\rangle : \langle i, n, n'\rangle$ means that $\langle n, \mathcal{K}h_i\varphi\rangle$ is an element in L and that $\langle i, n, n'\rangle$ is an element in S. When there is no need to mention elements of S, we will omit the colon.

There is no cut rule for $\mathcal{K}$, since the rule $\mathcal{K}T$ plays the same role. The cut rules and the rules $R\neg$, $R\vee$ and $R\wedge$ together will make sure that in fully expanded tableaux, it is closed over subformulas (see Proposition 3). This is also the reason why our rule $R\vee$ is different from standard one, which is normally as follows:

$$\frac{\neg(\varphi_1 \wedge \varphi_2)}{\neg\varphi_1 \mid \neg\varphi_2}$$

Table 2. Tableau rules

$$(R\neg) \; \frac{\langle n, \neg\neg\varphi\rangle}{\langle n, \varphi\rangle}$$

$$(R\vee) \; \frac{\langle n, \neg(\varphi_1 \wedge \varphi_2)\rangle}{\begin{array}{c|c|c} \langle n, \neg\varphi_1\rangle & \langle n, \neg\varphi_1\rangle & \langle n, \varphi_1\rangle \\ \langle n, \neg\varphi_2\rangle & \langle n, \varphi_2\rangle & \langle n, \neg\varphi_2\rangle \end{array}} \qquad\qquad (R\wedge) \; \frac{\langle n, \varphi_1 \wedge \varphi_2\rangle}{\begin{array}{c} \langle n, \varphi_1\rangle \\ \langle n, \varphi_2\rangle \end{array}}$$

$$(\text{Cut-}\neg\mathcal{K}) \; \frac{\langle n, \neg\mathcal{K}_i\varphi\rangle}{\langle n, \neg\varphi\rangle \mid \langle n, \varphi\rangle} \qquad\qquad (\mathcal{K}T) \; \frac{\langle n, \mathcal{K}_i\varphi\rangle}{\langle n, \varphi\rangle}$$

$$(\text{Cut-}\mathcal{K}h) \; \frac{\langle n, \mathcal{K}h_i\varphi\rangle}{\begin{array}{c|c} \langle n, \neg\mathcal{K}_i\varphi\rangle & \langle n, \mathcal{K}_i\varphi\rangle \\ \langle n, \neg\mathcal{K}h_i\bot\rangle & \langle n, \neg\mathcal{K}h_i\bot\rangle \end{array}} \qquad\qquad (\text{Cut-}\neg\mathcal{K}h) \; \frac{\langle n, \neg\mathcal{K}h_i\varphi\rangle}{\langle n, \neg\mathcal{K}_i\varphi\rangle}$$

$$(R\neg\mathcal{K}) \; \frac{\langle n, \neg\mathcal{K}_i\varphi\rangle}{\langle n', \neg\varphi\rangle : \langle i, n, n'\rangle} \; n' \text{ is new} \qquad\qquad (R\mathcal{K}) \; \frac{\langle n, \mathcal{K}_i\varphi\rangle : \langle i, n, n'\rangle}{\langle n', \varphi\rangle}$$

$$(\mathcal{K}4) \; \frac{\langle n, \mathcal{K}_i\varphi\rangle : \langle i, n, n'\rangle}{\langle n', \mathcal{K}_i\varphi\rangle} \qquad\qquad (\mathcal{K}5) \; \frac{\langle n, \neg\mathcal{K}_i\varphi\rangle : \langle i, n, n'\rangle}{\langle n', \neg\mathcal{K}_i\varphi\rangle}$$

$$(\mathcal{K}h4) \; \frac{\langle n, \mathcal{K}h_i\varphi\rangle : \langle i, n, n'\rangle}{\langle n', \mathcal{K}h_i\varphi\rangle} \qquad\qquad (\mathcal{K}h5) \; \frac{\langle n, \neg\mathcal{K}h_i\varphi\rangle : \langle i, n, n'\rangle}{\langle n', \neg\mathcal{K}h_i\varphi\rangle}$$

$$(R\pm\mathcal{K}h) \; \frac{\begin{array}{c} \langle n, \neg\mathcal{K}h_i\varphi\rangle \\ \langle n, \mathcal{K}h_i\psi\rangle \\ \langle n, \neg\mathcal{K}_i\psi\rangle \end{array}}{\begin{array}{c} \langle n', \neg\varphi\rangle \\ \langle n', \psi\rangle : \langle \mathcal{K}h_i\psi, n, n'\rangle \end{array}} \; n' \text{ is new}$$

The property of closing over subformulas together with rules $\mathcal{K}4$, $\mathcal{K}5$, $\mathcal{K}h4$ and $\mathcal{K}h5$ plays an important role in showing that all epistemic accessible nodes share the same epistemic formulas (see Proposition 6). All these are standard for epistemic logic.

The real characteristic rule of our tableau system for knowing-how logic is the rule $R\pm\mathcal{K}h$. (Of cours, the rules $\mathcal{K}h4$ and $\mathcal{K}h5$ are important for all epistemic accessible states having the same $\mathcal{K}h$- and $\neg\mathcal{K}h$-formulas, but these can be done by imitating rules for $\mathcal{K}$.) Firstly, if among formulas attached on n, there are only formulas of the form $\neg\mathcal{K}h_i\varphi$ but without any formula of the form $\mathcal{K}h_i\psi$, then we only need to ensure that n satisfies $\neg\mathcal{K}_i\varphi$ but need not to add any action-successor n' of n. This is why both $\mathcal{K}h$- and $\neg\mathcal{K}h$-formulas are involved in the rule $R{\pm}\mathcal{K}h$. Secondly, if there is indeed a formula $\mathcal{K}h_i\psi$ attached on n, by the rule Cut-$\mathcal{K}h$, we have either $\langle n, \mathcal{K}_i\psi \rangle$ or $\langle n, \neg\mathcal{K}_i\psi \rangle$ and $\langle n, \neg\mathcal{K}h_i\bot \rangle$. If n satisfies $\mathcal{K}_i\psi$, it follows that n satisfied $\mathcal{K}h_i\psi$. Otherwise, the rule $R{\pm}\mathcal{K}h$ will be triggered.

Definition 8 (Closed tableau). *Let $b = \langle L, S \rangle$ be a branch. The set L is closed if and only if for some n and φ, either $\{\langle n, \varphi \rangle, \langle n, \neg\varphi \rangle\} \subseteq L$ or $\langle n, \bot \rangle \in L$. The branch b is closed if and only if L is closed. The branch b is open if and only if it is not closed. A tableau is closed if and only if all its branches are closed. A tableau is open if and only if it is not closed.*

In the remaining section, we will show the soundness of the tableau system.

Definition 9 (Interpretation of branch). *Given a model $\mathcal{M}$ and a branch $b = \langle L, S \rangle$, let f be a function which assigns a state in $\mathcal{M}$ to each n occurring in b and assigns an action in $\mathbf{A}_i$ to each $(\mathcal{K}h_i\varphi, n, n')$ in S. We say that f is an interpretation of b in $\mathcal{M}$ if and only if the following conditions hold:*

- *$\mathcal{M}, f(n) \vDash \varphi$ for all $\langle n, \varphi \rangle \in L$;*
- *$f(n) \sim_i f(n')$ for all $(i, n, n') \in S$;*
- *$f(n') \in R(f(\mathcal{K}h_i\varphi, n, n'))([f(n)]^i)$ for all $(\mathcal{K}h_i\varphi, n, n') \in S$.*

Proposition 2. *Let f be an interpretation of a branch $b = \langle L, S \rangle$ in a model $\mathcal{M}$. If B is a set of branches generated by applying one of the tableau rules to b, then there exists a branch $b' \in B$ that has an interpretation in $\mathcal{M}$.*

Proof. If the rule applied is $R\neg$, $R\vee$, $R\wedge$, or Cut-$\neg\mathcal{K}$, it is straightforward. We restrict our attention to the other rules.

- Cut-$\mathcal{K}h$: We then have that $\langle n, \mathcal{K}h_i\varphi \rangle \in L$ and $B = \{b_1, b_2\}$ where $b_1 = \langle L \cup \{\langle n, \neg\mathcal{K}_i\varphi \rangle, \langle n, \neg\mathcal{K}h_i\bot \rangle\}, S \rangle$ and $b_2 = \langle L \cup \{\langle n, \mathcal{K}_i\varphi \rangle, \langle n, \neg\mathcal{K}h_i\bot \rangle\}, S \rangle$. Since f is an interpretation of b in $\mathcal{M}$, this implies that $\mathcal{M}, f(n) \vDash \mathcal{K}h_i\varphi$. By Proposition 1, we know that $\mathcal{M}, f(n) \vDash \neg\mathcal{K}h_i\bot$. Please note that either $\mathcal{M}, f(n) \vDash \mathcal{K}_i\varphi$ or $\mathcal{M}, f(n) \vDash \neg\mathcal{K}_i\varphi$. Therefore, if $\mathcal{M}, f(n) \vDash \mathcal{K}_i\varphi$, this follows that f is an interpretation of b_2. If $\mathcal{M}, f(n) \vDash \neg\mathcal{K}_i\varphi$, this follows that f is an interpretation of b_1.
- $\mathcal{K}T$: We then have that $\langle n, \mathcal{K}_i\varphi \rangle \in L$ and $B = \{\langle L \cup \{\langle n, \varphi \rangle\}, S \rangle\}$. Since f is an interpretation of b in $\mathcal{M}$, this implies that $\mathcal{M}, f(n) \vDash \mathcal{K}_i\varphi$. Moreover, since the relation $\sim_i$ in $\mathcal{M}$ is reflexive, this implies that $\mathcal{M}, f(n) \vDash \varphi$. Therefore, f is also an interpretation of the branch in B.
- Cut-$\neg\mathcal{K}h$: We then have that $\langle n, \neg\mathcal{K}h_i\varphi \rangle \in L$ and $B = \{\langle L \cup \{\langle n, \neg\mathcal{K}_i\varphi \rangle\}, S \rangle\}$. Since f is an interpretation of b in $\mathcal{M}$, this implies that $\mathcal{M}, f(n) \vDash \neg\mathcal{K}h_i\varphi$. Suppose that $\mathcal{M}, f(n) \vDash \mathcal{K}_i\varphi$. This implies that $\epsilon \in \mathbf{A}_i^\epsilon$ would be a witness plan for $\mathcal{M}, f(n) \vDash \mathcal{K}h_i\varphi$. Contradiction! Thus, we have that $\mathcal{M}, f(n) \vDash \neg\mathcal{K}_i\varphi$. Therefore, f is also an interpretation of the branch in B.
- $R\neg\mathcal{K}$: We then have that $\langle n, \neg\mathcal{K}_i\varphi \rangle \in L$ and $B = \{\langle L \cup \{\langle n', \neg\varphi \rangle\}, S \cup \{(i, n, n')\} \rangle\}$ where $n' \in \mathbb{N}$ does not occur in b. Since f is an interpretation of b, this implies that $\mathcal{M}, f(n) \vDash \neg\mathcal{K}_i\varphi$. Thus, there is a state s in $\mathcal{M}$ such that

$f(n) \sim_i s$ and $\mathcal{M}, s \vDash \neg\varphi$. We define f' as $f' = f \cup \{n' \mapsto s\}$. Since n' does not occur in b, f' is a well-defined function. Therefore, f' is an interpretation of the branch in B.

- $R\mathcal{K}$: We then have $\langle n, \mathcal{K}_i\varphi \rangle \in L$, $(i, n, n') \in S$ and $B = \{\langle L \cup \{\langle n', \varphi \rangle\}, S \rangle\}$. Since f is an interpretation of b in $\mathcal{M}$, this implies that $\mathcal{M}, f(n) \vDash \mathcal{K}_i\varphi$ and $f(n) \sim_i f(n')$. Thus, we have have that $\mathcal{M}, f(n') \vDash \varphi$. Therefore, f is also an interpretation of the branch in B.

- $\mathcal{K}4$: We then have $\langle n, \mathcal{K}_i\varphi \rangle \in L$, $(i, n, n') \in S$ and $B = \{\langle L \cup \{\langle n', \mathcal{K}_i\varphi \rangle\}, S \rangle\}$. Since f is an interpretation of b, this implies that $\mathcal{M}, f(n) \vDash \mathcal{K}_i\varphi$ and $f(n) \sim_i f(n')$. Since $\sim_i$ is transitive, we then have that $f(n) \sim_i s$ for all s with $f(n') \sim_i s$. This implies that $\mathcal{M}, s \vDash \varphi$ for all s with $f(n') \sim_i s$. Thus, we have that $\mathcal{M}, f(n') \vDash \mathcal{K}_i\varphi$. Therefore, f is also an interpretation of the branch in B.

- $\mathcal{K}5$: We have $\langle n, \neg\mathcal{K}_i\varphi \rangle \in L$, $(i, n, n') \in S$ and $B = \{\langle L \cup \{\langle n', \neg\mathcal{K}_i\varphi \rangle\}, S \rangle\}$. Since f is an interpretation of b, this implies that $\mathcal{M}, f(n) \vDash \neg\mathcal{K}_i\varphi$ and $f(n) \sim_i f(n')$. Due to $\mathcal{M}, f(n) \vDash \neg\mathcal{K}_i\varphi$, we then have that $\mathcal{M}, s \vDash \neg\varphi$ for some s with $f(n) \sim_i s$. Since $\sim_i$ is an equivalence relation and $f(n) \sim_i f(n')$, this implies that $f(n') \sim_i s$. Thus, we have that $\mathcal{M}, f(n') \vDash \neg\mathcal{K}_i\varphi$. Therefore, f is also an interpretation of the branch in B.

- $\mathcal{K}h4$: We then have that $\langle n, \mathcal{K}h_i\varphi \rangle \in L$, $(i, n, n') \in S$ and $B = \{\langle L \cup \{\langle n', \mathcal{K}h_i\varphi \rangle\}, S \rangle\}$. Since f is an interpretation of b, this implies $\mathcal{M}, f(n) \vDash \mathcal{K}h_i\varphi$ and $f(n) \sim_i f(n')$. By the semantics $\vDash$, this implies $\mathcal{M}, f(n') \vDash \mathcal{K}h_i\varphi$. Therefore, f is also an interpretation of the branch in B.

- $\mathcal{K}h5$: We then have that $\langle n, \neg\mathcal{K}h_i\varphi \rangle \in L$, $(i, n, n') \in S$ and $B = \{\langle L \cup \{\langle n', \neg\mathcal{K}h_i\varphi \rangle\}, S \rangle\}$. Since f is an interpretation of b, it follows that $\mathcal{M}, f(n) \vDash \neg\mathcal{K}h_i\varphi$ and $f(n) \sim_i f(n')$. Suppose that $\mathcal{M}, f(n') \vDash \mathcal{K}h_i\varphi$. This implies that there exists a witness plan $\sigma \in \mathbf{A}_i^\epsilon$ for $\mathcal{M}, f(n') \vDash \mathcal{K}h_i\varphi$. Since $f(n) \sim_i f(n')$, this implies that $[f(n)]^i = [f(n')]^i$. By the semantics $\vDash$, we then have that σ is also a witness plan for $\mathcal{M}, f(n) \vDash \mathcal{K}h_i\varphi$. This is contradictory with that $\mathcal{M}, f(n) \vDash \neg\mathcal{K}h_i\varphi$. Thus, we have that $\mathcal{M}, f(n') \nvDash \mathcal{K}h_i\varphi$ and then $\mathcal{M}, f(n') \vDash \neg\mathcal{K}h_i\varphi$. Therefore, f is also an interpretation of the branch in B.

- $R\pm\mathcal{K}h$: We then have that $\{\langle n, \neg\mathcal{K}h_i\varphi \rangle, \langle n, \mathcal{K}h_i\psi \rangle, \langle n, \neg\mathcal{K}_i\psi \rangle\} \subseteq L$ and $B = \{\langle L \cup \{\langle n', \neg\varphi \rangle, \langle n', \psi \rangle\}, S \cup \{\mathcal{K}h_i\psi, n, n'\} \rangle\}$. Since f is an interpretation of b, this implies that $\mathcal{M}, f(n) \vDash \neg\mathcal{K}h_i\varphi$, $\mathcal{M}, f(n) \vDash \mathcal{K}h_i\psi$, and $\mathcal{M}, f(n) \vDash \neg\mathcal{K}_i\psi$. Due to $\mathcal{M}, f(n) \vDash \mathcal{K}h_i\psi$, there exists $\sigma \in \mathbf{A}_i^\epsilon$ such that σ is strongly executable on $[f(n)]^i$ and that $\mathcal{M}, t \vDash \psi$ for all $t \in R(\sigma)([f(n)]^i)$. Since $\mathcal{M}, f(n) \vDash \neg\mathcal{K}_i\psi$, this implies that $\sigma \neq \epsilon$, i.e., $\sigma \in \mathbf{A}_i$. Moreover, since $\mathcal{M}, f(n) \vDash \neg\mathcal{K}h_i\varphi$ and σ is strongly executable on $[f(n)]^i$, this implies that $\mathcal{M}, v \nvDash \varphi$ for some $v \in R(\sigma)([f(n)]^i)$. Thus, we have that there exists $v \in R(\sigma)([f(n)]^i)$ such that $\mathcal{M}, v \vDash \psi$ and $\mathcal{M}, v \vDash \neg\varphi$. We then define f' as $f' = f \cup \{n' \mapsto v, (\mathcal{K}h_i\varphi, n, n') \mapsto \sigma\}$. Since n' does not occur in b, this implies that f' is well-defined. Thus, f' is an interpretation of the branch b_2.

Theorem 1 (Soundness). *If φ_0 is satisfiable, then there are no closed tableaux for φ_0.*

Proof. Since φ_0 is satisfiable, this implies that there exists a pointed model $(\mathcal{M}, s)$ such that $\mathcal{M}, s \vDash \varphi_0$. Suppose that T is a closed tableau for φ_0. By Definition 7, we know that T is an extension of the initial tableau $\{\langle \{\langle 0, \varphi_0 \rangle\}, \emptyset \rangle\}$. We define a function f as $f = \{0 \mapsto s\}$. Then f is an interpretation of the initial tableau. By Proposition 2, there exists a branch $b \in T$ which has an interpretation in $\mathcal{M}$. Since T is closed, this implies that b is closed. Contradiction! Therefore, we have that there are no closed tableaux for φ_0.

4   Completeness

In this section, we show the completeness of the tableau system. The key is to show that there is a model satisfying φ if there is an open saturated tableau for φ.

Definition 10 (Saturated tableau). *Let T be a tableau for φ. T is saturated if and only if T is saturated under all tableau rules, as defined below:*

1. *T is saturated under rule $R\neg$ if and only if for all $b = \langle L, S \rangle \in T$, if $\langle n, \neg\neg\varphi \rangle \in L$, then $\langle n, \varphi \rangle \in L$.*
2. *T is saturated under rule $R\wedge$ if and only if for all $b = \langle L, S \rangle \in T$, if $\langle n, \varphi_1 \wedge \varphi_2 \rangle \in L$, then $\{\langle n, \varphi_1 \rangle, \langle n, \varphi_2 \rangle\} \subseteq L$.*
3. *T is saturated under rule $R\vee$ if and only if for all $b = \langle L, S \rangle \in T$, if $\langle n, \neg(\varphi_1 \wedge \varphi_2) \rangle \in L$, then $\{\langle n, \neg\varphi_1 \rangle, \langle n, \neg\varphi_2 \rangle\} \subseteq L$, or $\{\langle n, \neg\varphi_1 \rangle, \langle n, \varphi_2 \rangle\} \subseteq L$, or $\{\langle n, \varphi_1 \rangle, \langle n, \neg\varphi_2 \rangle\} \subseteq L$.*
4. *T is saturated under rule $\mathcal{K}T$ if and only if for all $b = \langle L, S \rangle \in T$, if $\langle n, \mathcal{K}_i\varphi \rangle \in L$, then $\langle n, \varphi \rangle \in L$.*
5. *T is saturated under rule $Cut\text{-}\neg\mathcal{K}$ if and only if for all $b = \langle L, S \rangle \in T$, if $\langle n, \neg\mathcal{K}_i\varphi \rangle \in L$, then either $\langle n, \neg\varphi \rangle \in L$ or $\langle n, \varphi \rangle \in L$.*
6. *T is saturated under rule $Cut\text{-}\mathcal{K}h$ if and only if for all $b = \langle L, S \rangle \in T$, if $\langle n, \mathcal{K}h_i\varphi \rangle \in L$, then either we have that $\{\langle n, \neg\mathcal{K}_i\varphi \rangle, \langle n, \neg\mathcal{K}h_i\bot \rangle\} \subseteq L$, or we have that $\{\langle n, \mathcal{K}_i\varphi \rangle, \langle n, \neg\mathcal{K}h_i\bot \rangle\} \subseteq L$.*
7. *T is saturated under rule $Cut\text{-}\neg\mathcal{K}h$ if and only if for all $b = \langle L, S \rangle \in T$, if $\langle n, \neg\mathcal{K}h_i\varphi \rangle \in L$, then $\langle n, \neg\mathcal{K}_i\varphi \rangle \in L$.*
8. *T is saturated under rule $R\neg\mathcal{K}$ if and only if for all $b = \langle L, S \rangle \in T$, if $\langle n, \neg\mathcal{K}_i\varphi \rangle \in L$, then $(i, n, n') \in S$ and $\langle n', \neg\varphi \rangle \in L$ for some $n' \in \mathbb{N}$.*
9. *T is saturated under rule $R\mathcal{K}$ if and only if for all $b = \langle L, S \rangle \in T$, if $\langle n, \mathcal{K}_i\varphi \rangle \in L$ and $(i, n, n') \in S$, then $\langle n', \varphi \rangle \in L$.*
10. *T is saturated under rule $\mathcal{K}4$ if and only if for all $b = \langle L, S \rangle \in T$, if $\langle n, \mathcal{K}_i\varphi \rangle \in L$ and $(i, n, n') \in S$, then $\langle n', \mathcal{K}_i\varphi \rangle \in L$.*
11. *T is saturated under rule $\mathcal{K}5$ if and only if for all $b = \langle L, S \rangle \in T$, if $\langle n, \neg\mathcal{K}_i\varphi \rangle \in L$ and $(i, n, n') \in S$, then $\langle n', \neg\mathcal{K}_i\varphi \rangle \in L$.*
12. *T is saturated under rule $\mathcal{K}h4$ if and only if for all $b = \langle L, S \rangle \in T$, if $\langle n, \mathcal{K}h_i\varphi \rangle \in L$ and $(i, n, n') \in S$, then $\langle n', \mathcal{K}h_i\varphi \rangle \in L$.*
13. *T is saturated under rule $\mathcal{K}h5$ if and only if for all $b = \langle L, S \rangle \in T$, if $\langle n, \neg\mathcal{K}h_i\varphi \rangle \in L$ and $(i, n, n') \in S$, then $\langle n', \neg\mathcal{K}h_i\varphi \rangle \in L$.*

14. *T is saturated under rule R±Kh if and only if for all $b = \langle L, S \rangle \in T$, if $\{\langle n, \neg Kh_i\varphi \rangle, \langle n, Kh_i\psi \rangle, \langle n, \neg K_i\psi \rangle\} \subseteq L$, then $\{\langle n', \neg\varphi \rangle, \langle n', \psi \rangle\} \subseteq L$ and $(Kh_i\psi, n, n') \in S$ for some $n' \in \mathbb{N}$.*

Before we construct a model for φ from an open saturated tableau, we first introduce some auxiliary notions.

Definition 11 (Subformulas). *The function sub : $\mathcal{L} \to \mathcal{P}(\mathcal{L})$ is defined as follows:*

$$sub(\bot) = \{\bot\}$$
$$sub(p) = \{p\}$$
$$sub(\neg\varphi) = sub(\varphi) \cup \{\neg\varphi\}$$
$$sub(\varphi \wedge \psi) = sub(\varphi) \cup sub(\psi) \cup \{\varphi \wedge \psi\}$$
$$sub(K_i\varphi) = sub(\varphi) \cup \{K_i\varphi\}$$
$$sub(Kh_i\varphi) = sub(\varphi) \cup \{Kh_i\varphi, K_i\varphi, Kh_i\bot\}$$

Each $\psi \in sub(\varphi)$ is called a subformula of φ. Particularly, ψ is called a proper subformula if $\psi \neq \varphi$. Let $sub^+(\varphi) = sub(\varphi) \cup \{\neg\psi \mid \psi \in sub(\varphi)\}$.

The definition of subformulas here is a little different from the common definition of subformulas, since here we call $K_i\varphi$ and $Kh_i\bot$ subformulas of $Kh_i\varphi$. The reason is the following: in constructing the tableau, we need to apply the rule $R±Kh$ if we must build a witness plan for $Kh_i\psi$. To trigger the rule $R±Kh$, besides the formula $Kh_i\psi$, we still need the formula $\neg K_i\psi$ and a negation of Kh_i-formula. Moreover, to keep the size of tableau for φ as small as possible, we normally use only subformulas of φ. Therefore, in this paper, we call $K_i\varphi$ and $Kh_i\bot$ subformulas of $Kh_i\varphi$.

Definition 12 (Length of formulas). *The length of formulas $len(\varphi)$ is defined as follows:*

$$len(\bot) = 1$$
$$len(p) = 1$$
$$len(\neg\varphi) = len(\varphi) + 1$$
$$len(\varphi \wedge \psi) = len(\varphi) + len(\psi) + 1$$
$$len(K_i\varphi) = len(\varphi) + 1$$
$$len(Kh_i\varphi) = len(\varphi) + 3$$

Please note that applying the rule Cut-Kh will generates $\neg K_i\varphi$ for $Kh_i\varphi$. To ensure that the length of formulas will be shrunk during application of rules, we need the length of $\neg K_i\varphi$ to be less than that of $Kh_i\varphi$. This is the reason that $len(Kh_i\varphi) = len(\varphi) + 3$.

It can be shown that $|sub(\varphi)| \leq len(\varphi)$ and $|sub^+(\varphi)| \leq 2 \cdot len(\varphi)$.

The following proposition says that formulas labelled on a node n are closed under subformulas.

Proposition 3. *Let $b = \langle L, S \rangle$ be a branch of a saturated tableau for φ_0. If $\langle n, \varphi \rangle \in L$, then for each subformula ψ of φ, either $\langle n, \psi \rangle \in L$ or $\langle n, \neg\psi \rangle \in L$.*

Proof. We prove it by induction on the length of φ. If $len(\varphi) = 1$, it implies that φ is a proposition letter p or $\bot$, then the claim holds trivially. Before moving on, we would like to make it clear that the claim holds trivially if the subformula ψ is φ, i.e., $\psi := \varphi$. If $len(\varphi) = k + 1$ where $k \geq 1$, we then have the following cases:

- $\varphi := \neg p$ for some p, or $\varphi := \neg\bot$. It is obvious.
- $\varphi := \neg\neg\chi$. Except for $\psi := \neg\chi$, each proper subformula ψ of φ is a subformula of χ. Since the tableau is saturated, by the rule $\langle n, \chi \rangle \in L$. By induction on the length, we then have that either $\langle n, \psi \rangle \in L$ or $\langle n, \neg\psi \rangle \in L$.
- $\varphi := \neg(\varphi_1 \wedge \varphi_2)$. Let ψ be a proper subformula of φ. We then have that $\psi := (\varphi_1 \wedge \varphi_2)$, or ψ is a subformula of either φ_1 or φ_2. If $\psi := (\varphi_1 \wedge \varphi_2)$, we then have that $\langle n, \neg\psi \rangle \in L$. Let ψ be a subformula of φ_1. Since the tableau is saturated, by the rule $R\vee$, it implies that either $\langle n, \neg\varphi_1 \rangle \in L$ or $\langle n, \varphi_1 \rangle \in L$. By induction on the length, we have that either $\langle n, \psi \rangle \in L$ or $\langle n, \neg\psi \rangle \in L$. The proof is similar if ψ is a subformula of φ_2.
- $\varphi := \neg\mathcal{K}_i\chi$. Except for $\psi := \mathcal{K}_i\chi$, each proper subformula ψ of φ is a subformula of χ. Since the tableau is saturated, by the rule Cut-$\neg\mathcal{K}$, it implies that either $\langle n, \neg\chi \rangle \in L$ or $\langle n, \chi \rangle \in L$. By induction on the length, we then have that either $\langle n, \psi \rangle \in L$ or $\langle n, \neg\psi \rangle \in L$.
- $\varphi := \neg\mathcal{K}h_i\chi$. Except for $\psi := \mathcal{K}h_i\chi$, each proper subformula ψ of φ is a subformula of $\mathcal{K}_i\chi$. Since the tableau is saturated, by the rules Cut-$\neg\mathcal{K}h$, implies that $\langle n, \neg\mathcal{K}_i\chi \rangle \in L$. By induction on the length, we then have that either $\langle n, \psi \rangle \in L$ or $\langle n, \neg\psi \rangle \in L$.
- $\varphi := (\varphi_1 \wedge \varphi_2)$. Each proper subformula ψ of φ is a subformula of either φ_1 or φ_2. By the rule $R\wedge$, we then have that both $\langle n, \varphi_1 \rangle \in L$ and $\langle n, \varphi_2 \rangle \in L$. By induction, we then have that either $\langle n, \psi \rangle \in L$ or $\langle n, \neg\psi \rangle \in L$.
- $\varphi := \mathcal{K}_i\chi$. Each proper subformula ψ of φ is a subformula of χ. By the rule $\mathcal{K}T$, we then have that $\langle n, \chi \rangle \in L$. By induction, we then have that either $\langle n, \psi \rangle \in L$ or $\langle n, \neg\psi \rangle \in L$.
- $\varphi := \mathcal{K}h_i\chi$. If the subformula of $\mathcal{K}h_i\chi$ is either $\mathcal{K}_i\chi$ or $\mathcal{K}h_i\bot$, by the rule Cut-$\mathcal{K}h$, we have that $\neg\mathcal{K}h_i\bot \in L$ and either $\mathcal{K}h_i\chi \in L$ or $\neg\mathcal{K}_i\chi \in L$. Except $\mathcal{K}_i\chi$ and $\mathcal{K}h_i\bot$, each proper subformula ψ of φ is a subformula of χ. By the rules Cut-$\mathcal{K}h$, Cut-$\neg\mathcal{K}$, and $\mathcal{K}T$, we then have that either $\langle n, \neg\chi \rangle \in L$ or $\langle n, \chi \rangle \in L$. By induction, we then have that either $\langle n, \psi \rangle \in L$ or $\langle n, \neg\psi \rangle \in L$.

Next, we will show that if n and n' are linked by the epistemic relation $\sim_i$, then they share the same epistemic formulas and knowing-how formulas. Before that, we first show two auxiliary propositions.

Proposition 4. *Let $b = \langle L, S \rangle$ be a branch of a tableau T. If $\langle i, n, n' \rangle \in S$ and $\langle n', \psi \rangle \in L$, then there exists $\langle n, \varphi \rangle \in L$ such that ψ is either a subformula of φ or a negation of some subformula of φ.*

Proof. For the branch in the initial tableau, the claim holds trivially, since the set S in the branch of the initial tableau is $\emptyset$. We can observe that all the tableau rules preserve the claim. Thus, the claim holds for all branches.

Proposition 5. *Let $b = \langle L, S \rangle$ be a branch of a saturated tableau T. If we have that $\{\langle i, n_0, n_1 \rangle, \cdots, \langle i, n_k, n_{k+1} \rangle\} \subseteq S$ and $\langle n_{k+1}, \psi \rangle \in L$, we then have that either $\langle n_0, \psi \rangle \in L$ or $\langle n_0, \neg\psi \rangle \in L$.*

Proof. It follows from Propositions 3 and 4.

Proposition 6. *Let $b = \langle L, S \rangle$ be an open branch of a saturated tableau T, and let $\{\langle i, n_0, n_1 \rangle, \cdots, \langle i, n_k, n_{k+1} \rangle\} \subseteq S$. We have that $\langle n_0, \psi \rangle \in L$ iff $\langle n_{k+1}, \psi \rangle \in L$ if ψ is either an epistemic formula $\mathcal{K}_i \chi$ or a knowing-how formula $\mathcal{K}h_i \chi$.*

Proof. If $\langle n_0, \psi \rangle \in L$, by the rule $\mathcal{K}4$ or $\mathcal{K}h4$, we then have that $\langle n_{k+1}, \psi \rangle \in L$. If $\langle n_{k+1}, \psi \rangle \in L$, by Proposition 5, we have that either $\langle n_0, \psi \rangle \in L$ or $\langle n_0, \neg\psi \rangle \in L$. Suppose that $\langle n_0, \neg\psi \rangle \in L$, by the rule $\mathcal{K}5$ or $\mathcal{K}h5$, we then have that $\langle n_{k+1}, \neg\psi \rangle \in L$. This is contradictory with the fact that b is open. Thus, we have that $\langle n_0, \psi \rangle \in L$.

Now we are ready to show the key proposition of this section.

Proposition 7. *Let T be a saturated tableau for φ_0. If T is open, then φ_0 is satisfiable.*

Proof. Since T is open, there exists a branch $b = \langle L, S \rangle \in T$ that is open. Next, we will build a model for φ from the branch b. The model $\mathcal{M} = \langle W, \{\sim_i | i \in \mathbf{I}\}, \{\mathbf{A}_i | i \in \mathbf{I}\}, \{R(a) | a \in \mathbf{A}_i, i \in \mathbf{I}\}, V \rangle$ is defined as follows:

- W is the set of n occurring in b,
- for each $i \in \mathbf{I}$, $\sim_i$ is the reflexive, transitive and symmetric closure of the binary relation $\{\langle n, n' \rangle | \langle i, n, n' \rangle \in S\}$ on W,
- for each $i \in \mathbf{I}$, $\mathbf{A}_i = \{a_{\mathcal{K}h_i\varphi} | \langle n, \mathcal{K}h_i\varphi \rangle \in L \text{ for some } n\}$,
- for each $i \in \mathbf{I}$ and each $a_{\mathcal{K}h_i\varphi} \in \mathbf{A}_i$, $R(a_{\mathcal{K}h_i\varphi}) = \{\langle n, n' \rangle | (\mathcal{K}h_i\varphi, n, n') \in S\}$,
- for each $n \in W$, $V(n) = \{p | \langle n, p \rangle \in L\}$.

Since T is a saturated tableau for φ_0, this implies that $\langle 0, \varphi_0 \rangle \in L$. To show that φ_0 is satisfiable, we will show the following more general claim:

$$\mathcal{M}, n \vDash \varphi \text{ for all } \langle n, \varphi \rangle \in L.$$

We prove the claim by induction on $len(\varphi)$. If $len(\varphi) = 1$, since b is open, this implies that $\varphi := p$. By the definition of $\mathcal{M}$, we then have that $\mathcal{M}, n \vDash p$. If $len(\varphi) = k + 1$ where $k \geq 1$, we then have the following cases:

- $\varphi := \neg\bot$. It is obvious.
- $\varphi := \neg p$. Since b is open and $\langle n, \neg p \rangle \in L$, this implies that $\langle n, p \rangle \notin L$. By the definition of $\mathcal{M}$, we then have that $\mathcal{M}, n \vDash \neg p$.
- $\varphi := \neg\neg\chi$. Since T is saturated, by the rule $R\neg$, we have that $\langle n, \chi \rangle \in L$. By induction, we have that $\mathcal{M}, n \vDash \chi$, and then $\mathcal{M}, n \vDash \neg\neg\chi$.
- $\varphi := \neg(\varphi_1 \wedge \varphi_2)$. By the rule $R\vee$, we have that $\langle n, \neg\varphi_1 \rangle \in L$ or $\langle n, \neg\varphi_2 \rangle \in L$. By induction, we have that $\mathcal{M}, n \vDash \neg\varphi_1$ or $\mathcal{M}, n \vDash \neg\varphi_2$. Thus, we have $\mathcal{M}, n \vDash \neg(\varphi_1 \wedge \varphi_2)$.

- $\varphi := \neg\mathcal{K}_i\chi$. By the rule $R\neg\mathcal{K}$, there is n' such that $(i, n, n') \in S$ and $\langle n', \neg\chi\rangle \in L$. By induction, we have $\mathcal{M}, n' \vDash \neg\chi$. By the definition of $\mathcal{M}$, we have that $n \sim_i n'$. Thus, we have that $\mathcal{M}, n \vDash \neg\mathcal{K}_i\chi$.

- $\varphi := \neg\mathcal{K}h_i\chi$. Firstly, by the rule Cut-$\neg\mathcal{K}h$, we have that $\langle n, \neg\mathcal{K}_i\chi\rangle \in L$. By induction, we have that $\mathcal{M}, n \vDash \neg\mathcal{K}_i\chi$. This implies that ϵ cannot be a witness plan for $\mathcal{M}, n \vDash \mathcal{K}h_i\chi$.

  We continue to show that every action in $\mathbf{A}_i$ cannot not be a witness plan. If there is some $a_{\mathcal{K}h_i\psi} \in \mathbf{A}_i$ such that it is strongly executable on $[n]^i$. It implies that there is some n' such that $(n, n') \in R(a_{\mathcal{K}h_i\psi})$ in $\mathcal{M}$. By the definition of $\mathcal{M}$, we have that $(\mathcal{K}h_i\psi, n, n') \in S$. Such triples can only be generated by the rule $R\pm\mathcal{K}h$. Thus, we have that $\langle n', \neg\chi\rangle \in L$. By induction, we have that $\mathcal{M}, n' \vDash \neg\chi$. Thus, $a_{\mathcal{K}h_i\psi}$ is not a witness plan for $\mathcal{M}, n \vDash \mathcal{K}h_i\chi$. Therefore, we have shown that for each $\sigma \in \mathbf{A}_i^\epsilon$, if it is strongly executable on $[n]^i$ then there is some $n' \in R(\sigma)([n]^i)$ such that $\mathcal{M}, n' \vDash \neg\chi$. Thus, we have $\mathcal{M}, n \vDash \neg\mathcal{K}h_i\chi$.

- $\varphi := (\varphi_1 \wedge \varphi_2)$. By the rule $R\wedge$, we have that both $\langle n, \varphi_1\rangle \in L$ and $\langle n, \varphi_2\rangle \in L$. By induction, we have that both $\mathcal{M}, n \vDash \varphi_1$ and $\mathcal{M}, n \vDash \varphi_2$. Thus, we have that $\mathcal{M}, n \vDash \varphi_1 \wedge \varphi_2$.

- $\varphi := \mathcal{K}_i\chi$. By the definition of $\sim_i$, for each $n' \in [n]^i$, there are three cases: (1) $n = n'$; (2) there are $(i, n_0, n_1), \cdots, (i, n_k, n_{k+1})$ in S such that $n_0 = n$ and $n_{k+1} = n'$; (3) there are $(i, n_0, n_1), \cdots, (i, n_k, n_{k+1})$ in S such that $n_0 = n'$ and $n_{k+1} = n$.
  For (1), by the rule $\mathcal{K}T$, we have $\langle n', \chi\rangle \in L$. For (2) and (3), by Proposition 6, we have that $\langle n', \mathcal{K}_i\chi\rangle \in L$. By the rule $\mathcal{K}T$ again, we have $\langle n', \chi\rangle \in L$. Thus, we have shown that $\langle n', \chi\rangle$ is in L in all cases. By induction, we have $\mathcal{M}, n' \vDash \chi$. Thus, we have $\mathcal{M}, n \vDash \mathcal{K}_i\chi$.

- $\varphi := \mathcal{K}h_i\chi$. By the rule Cut-$\mathcal{K}h$, we have that either $\langle n, \mathcal{K}_i\chi\rangle \in L$ or $\langle n, \neg\mathcal{K}_i\chi\rangle \in L$. If $\langle n, \mathcal{K}_i\chi\rangle \in L$, by induction, we have that $\mathcal{M}, n \vDash \mathcal{K}_i\chi$. This means that ϵ can be a witness plan for $\mathcal{M}, n \vDash \mathcal{K}h_i\chi$. Therefore, we have $\mathcal{M}, n \vDash \mathcal{K}h_i\chi$.
  Next we focus on the case of $\langle n, \neg\mathcal{K}_i\chi\rangle \in L$. Since $\langle n, \mathcal{K}h_i\chi\rangle \in L$, by the rule Cut-$\mathcal{K}h$, we have that $\langle n, \neg\mathcal{K}h_i\bot\rangle \in L$. Thus, we now have that $\{\langle n, \mathcal{K}h_i\chi\rangle, \langle n, \neg\mathcal{K}_i\chi\rangle, \langle n, \neg\mathcal{K}h_i\bot\rangle\} \subseteq L$. Furthermore, by Proposition 6, we have that for each $m \in [n]^i$, there is $\{\langle m, \mathcal{K}h_i\chi\rangle, \langle m, \neg\mathcal{K}_i\chi\rangle, \langle m, \neg\mathcal{K}h_i\bot\rangle\} \subseteq L$. By the rule $R\pm\mathcal{K}h$, we know that for each $m \in [n]^i$, there is n_m such that $(\mathcal{K}h_i\chi, n, n_m) \in S$. By the definition of $\mathcal{M}$, we know that $a_{\mathcal{K}h_i\chi}$ is strongly executable on $[n]^i$. Moreover, for each $n' \in R(a_{\mathcal{K}h_i\chi})([n]^i)$, we have by the definition of $\mathcal{M}$ that $(\mathcal{K}h_i\chi, m, n') \in S$ where $m \in [n]^i$. By the tableau rules, we know that there is $\langle n', \chi\rangle \in L$ whenever a triple like $(\mathcal{K}h_i\chi, m, n')$ is generated. Thus, by induction, we have that $\mathcal{M}, n' \vDash \chi$. Therefore, we have that $\mathcal{M}, n \vDash \mathcal{K}h_i\chi$.

Now we are ready to show the completeness of the tableau system.

Theorem 2 (Completeness). *If there are no closed tableaux for φ_0, then φ_0 is Satisfiable.*

Proof. If there are no closed tableaux for φ_0, it means that all tableaux for φ_0 are open. We then can extend the initial tableau for φ_0 to be an open saturated tableau for φ_0. By Proposition 7, φ_0 is satisfiable.

5   Decision Procedure

In this section we present a procedure of the tableau calculus defined in Sect. 3. The procedure below will construct a tree and define a function L that labels each node of the tree with a set of formulas. There are three types of successors: normal tree successors, i-successors, and $\mathcal{K}h_i\psi$-successors. Moreover, for each inner node s of the tree, either it has only normal tree successors, or it has i-successors for each $\neg\mathcal{K}_i\varphi \in L(s)$ and $\mathcal{K}h_i\psi$-successors for each $\mathcal{K}h_i\psi \in L(s)$ but $\mathcal{K}_i\psi \notin L(s)$.

The procedure for constructing a tableau tree for φ:

1. Construct a tree consisting of a single node s_0 (the "root"), with $L(s_0) = \{\varphi_0\}$.
2. Repeat until none of below applies:
    (a) *Forming a subformula-closed tableau*: if s is a leaf of the tree, $L(s)$ is not closed, and ψ is a witness to one of the following rules (we call them 'static rules'): $R\neg$, $R\wedge$, $\mathcal{K}T$, Cut-$\mathcal{K}h$, Cut-$\neg\mathcal{K}$, Cut-$\neg\mathcal{K}h$, and $R\vee$, then:
        * if ψ is the witness of $R\neg$, $R\wedge$, $\mathcal{K}T$, Cut-$\neg\mathcal{K}h$, then create a successor node s' of s and set $L(s') = L(s) \cup \Psi$ where Ψ is the set of formulas generated by applying the corresponding rule;
        * if ψ is the witness of Cut-$\neg\mathcal{K}$ or Cut-$\mathcal{K}h$, then create two successors s_1 and s_2 of s and set $L(s_1) = L(s) \cup \Psi_1$ and $L(s_2) = L(s) \cup \Psi_2$ where Ψ_1 and Ψ_2 are the set of generated formulas by applying the corresponding rule;
        * if ψ is the witness of $R\vee$, such as $\neg(\psi_1 \wedge \psi_2) \in L(s)$, then create three successors s_1, s_2, s_3 of s and set $L(s_1) = L(s) \cup \{\neg\psi_1, \neg\psi_2\}$, $L(s_2) = L(s) \cup \{\neg\psi_1, \psi_2\}$, and $L(s_3) = L(s) \cup \{\psi_1, \neg\psi_2\}$.
    (b) *Creating $\mathcal{K}$ and $\mathcal{K}h$ successor nodes*: if s is a leaf of the tree, $L(s)$ is not closed, and no static rules are applicable, then:
        i. for each witness of the rule $R\neg\mathcal{K}$, such as $\neg\mathcal{K}_i\chi \in L(s)$, if there is no ancestor s'' of s in the tree such that

        $$L(s'') = \{\neg\chi\} \cup L(s)|\mathcal{K}_i \cup L(s)|\neg\mathcal{K}_i \cup L(s)|\mathcal{K}h_i \cup L(s)|\neg\mathcal{K}h_i$$

        (where $L(s)|K_i$ is the set of formulas $\mathcal{K}_i\psi'$ such that $\mathcal{K}_i\psi' \in L(s)$ and the sets $L(s)|\neg\mathcal{K}_i, L(s)|\mathcal{K}h_i, L(s)|\neg\mathcal{K}h_i$ are similarly defined), then create an i-successor node s' (i.e., add node s' th the tree and an edge from s to s' labelled i) and set $L(s') = \{\neg\chi\} \cup L(s)|\mathcal{K}_i \cup L(s)|\neg\mathcal{K}_i \cup L(s)|\mathcal{K}h_i \cup L(s)|\neg\mathcal{K}h_i$.
        ii. for each witness of the rule $R\pm\mathcal{K}h$, such as $\{\neg\mathcal{K}h_i\chi, \mathcal{K}h_i\psi, \neg\mathcal{K}_i\psi\} \subseteq L(s)$, create a $\mathcal{K}h_i\psi$-successor s' and set $L(s') = \{\neg\chi, \psi\}$.

In the remaining section, we will show that the procedure can be done in polynomial spaces. Firstly, we show that the size of the tree constructed by the procedure is of polynomial.

Proposition 8. *The final tree for φ constructed by the procedure above is an $O(m^3)$-ary tree whose height is at most m^3, where $m = |sub^+(\varphi)|$.*

Proof. First, let us make an observation that for each node s of the tree, the set $L(s)$ is a subset of the set $sub^+(\varphi)$. This implies $|L(s)| \leq m$ for each node s.

In step 2(a), we at most create three successors for a leaf. In step 2(b), there are at most m witnesses for the rule $R\neg\mathcal{K}$ because of $|L(s)| \leq m$. Since each witness for the rule $R\pm\mathcal{K}h$ is a set of three formulas, there are at most $\binom{m}{3}$ witnesses for this rule. Thus, in step 2(b), we at most create $\binom{m}{3} + m$ successors for a leaf. Therefore, the final tree is an $O(m^3)$-ary tree.

Next we show that the height of the final tree is at most m^3. Before that, we introduce some notations. We use $len(L(s))$ to denote the biggest length of formulas in $L(s)$. Because of $|L(s)| \leq m$ for each node s, this implies that we can apply step 2(a) at most m times before we reach a node s' such that either $L(s')$ is closed or there are no static rules applicable to $L(s')$. In step 2(b), for each successor node s' created in 2(b)ii, we have that $len(L(s')) < len(L(s))$. However, this is not the case if the successor s' is created in 2(b)i. For successor node s' created in 2(b)i, we have that $len(L(s')) \leq len(L(s))$. As it is shown in [6], there are at most m^2 consecutive successors of s before the length of formulas becomes strictly less. Thus, the height of the final tree at most m^3.

Please note that the final tree for φ is an and-or tree, and each node is attached a subset of $sub^+(\varphi)$. With a depth-first exploration of an and-or tree, we have the following:

Theorem 3. *There is an algorithm that runs in polynomial space for deciding whether there is a closed tableau for a formula.*

Theorem 4. *The satisfiability of multi-agent knowing-how logic is PSPACE-complete.*

Proof. Multi-agent epistemic logic is a fragment of multi-agent knowing-how logic. Since the multi-agent epistemic logic is PSPACE-hard (cf. [6]), this implies that multi-agent knowing how logic is also PSPACE-hard. Moreover, to check whether a formula φ is satisfiable, by Theorems 1 and 2, we only need to check whether there is a closed tableau for φ. By Theorem 3, we know that checking the satisfiability of a formula $\varphi \in \mathcal{L}$ is in PSPACE. Thus, it is PSPACE-complete.

6   Conclusion

In this paper, we presented a tableau system for the knowing-how logic via simple plans which is an extension of the standard epistemic logic. The tableau system is an adaption of that proposed in [2]. We also presented a tableau-based decision procedure that runs in polynomial space, which is an extension of the decision procedure proposed in [6] for the standard epistemic logic. Since the multi-agent epistemic logic is PSPACE-hard, it follows that the multi-agent knowing-how logic via simple plans is PSPACE-complete.

A direct future work is to show the complexity of single-agent knowing-how logic via simple plans. We know that the complexity of single-agent epistemic logic is NP-complete while the complexity of multi-agent epistemic logic is PSPACE-complete. We guess that this is not the case for knowing-how logic via simple plans. We conjecture the complexity of single-agent and multi-agent knowing how logic via simple plans is the same. It is also interesting to discuss the complexity for other knowing-how logics. In [1], they show that a knowing-how logic with binary $\mathcal{K}h_i$-modalities is NP-complete.

Acknowledgment. This work is supported by the National Social Science Foundation for Young Scholars of China (Grant No. 18CZX062). The author thanks three anonymous reviewers for their useful comments, which helped the author to improve the presentation of the paper.

References

1. Areces, C., Fervari, R., Saravia, A.R., Velázquez-Quesada, F.R.: Uncertainty-based semantics for multi-agent knowing how logics. In: Halpern, J., Perea, A. (eds.) Proceedings Eighteenth Conference on Theoretical Aspects of Rationality and Knowledge, Beijing, China, 25–27 June 2021. Electronic Proceedings in Theoretical Computer Science, vol. 335, pp. 23–37. Open Publishing Association (2021). https://doi.org/10.4204/EPTCS.335.3
2. Balbiani, P., van Ditmarsch, H., Herzig, A., De Lima, T.: Tableaux for public announcement logic. J. Log. Comput. **20**(1), 55–76 (2010). https://doi.org/10.1093/logcom/exn060
3. Fan, J., Wang, Y., van Ditmarsch, H.: Contingency and knowing whether. Rev. Symb. Log. **8**(01), 75–107 (2015)
4. Fervari, R., Herzig, A., Li, Y., Wang, Y.: Strategically knowing how. In: IJCAI International Joint Conference on Artificial Intelligence, pp. 1031–1038 (2017). https://doi.org/10.24963/ijcai.2017/143
5. Gu, T., Wang, Y.: "Knowing value" logic as a normal modal logic. In: Proceedings of AiML, vol. 11 (2016)
6. Halpern, J.Y., Moses, Y.: A guide to completeness and complexity for modal logics of knowledge and belief. Artif. Intell. **54**(2), 319–379 (1992)
7. Hintikka, J.: Knowledge and Belief: An Introduction to the Logic of the Two Notions. Cornell University Press, Ithaca (1962)
8. Li, Y., Wang, Y.: Achieving while maintaining: a logic of knowing how with intermediate constraints. In: Proceedings of ICLA 2017, pp. 154–167 (2017)
9. Li, Y., Wang, Y.: Multi-agent knowing how via multi-step plans: a dynamic epistemic planning based approach. In: Blackburn, P., Lorini, E., Guo, M. (eds.) LORI 2019. LNCS, vol. 11813, pp. 126–139. Springer, Heidelberg (2019). https://doi.org/10.1007/978-3-662-60292-8_10
10. Li, Y., Wang, Y.: Planning-based knowing how: a unified approach. Artif. Intell. **296**, 103487 (2021)

11. McCarthy, J.: First order theories of individual concepts and propositions. Mach. Intell. **9**, 129–147 (1979)
12. Moore, R.C.: A formal theory of knowledge and action. Technical report, DTIC Document (1984)
13. Naumov, P., Tao, J.: Together we know how to achieve: an epistemic logic of know-how. Artif. Intell. **262**, 279–300 (2018)
14. Von Wright, G.H.: An Essay in Modal Logic. North Holland, Amsterdam (1951)
15. Wang, Y.: A logic of knowing how. In: van der Hoek, W., Holliday, W.H., Wang, W. (eds.) LORI 2015. LNCS, vol. 9394, pp. 392–405. Springer, Heidelberg (2015). https://doi.org/10.1007/978-3-662-48561-3_32
16. Wang, Y.: A logic of goal-directed knowing how. Synthese **195**(10), 4419–4439 (2016). https://doi.org/10.1007/s11229-016-1272-0
17. Wang, Y., Fan, J.: Knowing that, knowing what, and public communication: public announcement logic with Kv operators. In: Proceedings of IJCAI 2013, pp. 1147–1154 (2013)

Integrating Individual Preferences into Collective Argumentation

Chonghui Li(✉) and Beishui Liao

Institute of Logic and Cognition, Zhejiang University, Hangzhou, China
{lisabell,baiseliao}@zju.edu.cn

Abstract. In the field of collective argumentation, multiple agents may have distinct knowledge representations and individual preferences. In order to obtain reasonable collective outcome for the group, either individual frameworks should be merged or individual preference should be aggregated. However, framework merging and preference aggregation are different procedures, leading to disagreements on collective outcome. In this paper, we figure out a solution to combine framework merging, argumentative reasoning and incomplete preference aggregation together. Furthermore, a couple of rational postulates are proposed to be the criteria for the reasonability of collective outcome obtained based on our approach.

Keywords: Collective argumentation · Framework merging · Incomplete preference aggregation · Concordance

1 Introduction

Based on abstract argumentation, collective argumentation deals with the scenarios in which multiple agents have distinct individual frameworks representing their observed information and reasoning knowledge, aiming to obtain a reasonable reasoning outcome for the group [1]. For this purpose, an operation called *framework merging* is adopted to form representative collective frameworks first and then jointly accepted arguments can be obtained by argumentative reasoning with the collective frameworks. The criteria for the reasonability lie in the representativeness of collective frameworks and the acceptability of arguments at the group level. Existing literatures [2–6] are along with this line. However, if we extend individual frameworks to include individual preferences, what influences do they have on collective outcome? And what are the renewed criteria for the reasonability of collective outcome? Let us illustrate the questions with an example: Three Detectives.

Example 1. There are four suspects A, B, C and D in a stolen jewellery case. Each of them has an argument as follows.

– A: B is the criminal, because I saw B sold the jewellery to D two days ago. (argument a)

© Springer Nature Switzerland AG 2021
P. Baroni et al. (Eds.): CLAR 2021, LNAI 13040, pp. 284–301, 2021.
https://doi.org/10.1007/978-3-030-89391-0_16

- B: It's none of my business. The truth is A, C and D conspired the stealing. (argument b)
- C: I saw B wore a jewellery very similar to the stolen one yesterday. (argument c)
- D: I know nothing about this incident. (argument d)

Assume there is a committee of three detectives (subscript indexed as 1, 2, 3) in charge of the case. They need to identify the conflicting arguments with their own knowledge and reason with the case independently. Three individual frameworks representing detectives' distinct observed information are shown in Fig. 1. Here each detective represents the arguments (the dots) which have attack relation (the directed edges) in a di-graph, excluding the arguments which he/she personally supposes to be irrelevant. Apart from this, three detectives have their own preferences over the conflicting arguments, based on their personal credences on the suspects' arguments. Assume that each detective is a rational agent, whose preference is always *coherent* with his/her cognition. That is to say, if a detective supposes that argument a attacks argument b, then it is impossible for him/her to suppose b is more credible than a.

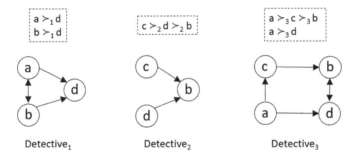

Fig. 1. The profile for three detectives

Note that the modelling of knowledge representations for three detectives may not be unique. Due to the vagueness of natural language and the subjectivity of personal cognition, multiple agents may have a variety of options for their knowledge representations. Now based on the example, our research question becomes more explicit: among four arguments, what are those arguments accepted by the committee as a reasonable collective choice? And what are the reasons for the choice?

Before the response, we need to make a further analysis on the nature of these questions. On one hand, if individual preferences were not considered, through the operations of framework merging and argumentative reasoning, three detectives may reach a reasonable collective outcome. On the other hand, if we were only informed with individual preferences over arguments, then through a procedure of preference aggregation, three detectives would agree on a social preference which leads to a reasonable collective choice too. It is obvious that framework merging and preference aggregation are different operations, they deviate from each other in at least three points: different inputs, different measurements on social agreement, and as a result, different outputs. However, in the scenario of Three Detectives, both individual frameworks and individual preferences are provided as given information, we need to figure out an approach to combine framework merging, argumentative reasoning and preference aggregation together and find an updated reasonable choice for the committee. Since individual preferences indicate the credence on arguments and are always coherent with the structure of individual frameworks, if they are aggregated to a reasonable social preference, it is supposed to have dominant influences on collective reasoning outcome. That is to say, an argument with greater credence according to social preference should be more acceptable than the ones with less credences for the group. Therefore, a solution for the combination could be: the collective outcome obtained from framework merging and argumentative reasoning is in *concordance* with social preference.

In this paper, we propose a novel method for framework merging which can form representative collective frameworks and has less complexity in computation and better explainability, compared to Coste-Marquis' method [2]. As individual preferences might be incomplete with respect to the profile, we adopt a pairwise majority based procedure for incomplete preference aggregation, proposed by Koncazk in [7]. Considering that the winner(s) of social preference is possibly discarded in the stage of argumentative reasoning, we apply social preference as modification of collective frameworks before argumentative reasoning. Then the criteria for the reasonability of collective outcome are renewed: it is the result obtained from reasoning with representative collective frameworks and in concordance with majority-based social preference.

The layout of the paper is as follows. Section 2 recalls some preliminaries of abstract argumentation, preference-based abstract argumentation, framework merging, preference aggregation. In Sect. 3, we propose a novel method for framework merging and evaluate the advantages of our method. In Sect. 4, we introduce a procedure of incomplete preference aggregation, define a method to obtain social preference over arguments and verify the reasonability of it. We establish the concordance between collective framework and social preference and have it evaluated in Sect. 5. Finally we conclude the paper in Sect. 6.

2   Preliminaries

First, let's recall some key elements of abstract argumentation frameworks as proposed by Dung in [8].

Definition 1. *An abstract argumentation framework (AF) is a pair $\mathcal{F} = (\mathcal{A}, \mathcal{D})$ where $\mathcal{A}$ is a set of arguments and $\mathcal{D} \subseteq \mathcal{A} \times \mathcal{A}$ is a defeat relation.*

The key problem is to determine the sets of arguments that can be accepted together. According to some criteria, a set of accepted arguments is called an *extension.* Let us first introduce two basic criteria: conflict-freeness and acceptability.

Definition 2. *Given an AF* $\mathcal{F} = (\mathcal{A}, \mathcal{D})$ *and a set of arguments* $S \subseteq \mathcal{A}$*, we say that* S *is conflict-free iff* $\nexists A, B \in S$ *such that* $(A, B) \in \mathcal{D}$*. We say that an argument* $A \in \mathcal{A}$ *is acceptable w.r.t.* S *iff* $\forall B \in \mathcal{A}$*, if* $(B, A) \in \mathcal{D}$ *then* $\exists C \in S$ *such that* $(C, B) \in \mathcal{D}$*.*

A set of arguments S is *admissible* when it is conflict-free and each argument in the set is acceptable w.r.t. S. Several semantics have been proposed based on admissible sets. In this paper, we only focus on the standard semantics defined in [8]. We say S is a *complete* extension of $\mathcal{F}$ iff it is admissible and each argument acceptable w.r.t. S belongs to S. S is a *preferred* extension of $\mathcal{F}$ iff it is a maximal(w.r.t. set inclusion) complete extension of $\mathcal{F}$. S is a *grounded* extension of $\mathcal{F}$ iff it is the minimal (w.r.t. set inclusion) complete extension of $\mathcal{F}$. S is a *stable* extension of $\mathcal{F}$ iff it is conflict-free and it attacks all the arguments that do not belong to S. We denote $\mathcal{E}_\sigma(\mathcal{F})$ the set of extensions of $\mathcal{F}$ for the semantics $\sigma \in \{\mathbf{co}(mplete), \mathbf{pr}(eferred), \mathbf{gr}(ounded), \mathbf{st}(able)\}$.

Preference-based argumentation framework is first proposed by [9] as a extended framework of abstract argumentation framework.

Definition 3. *A preference-based argumentation framework (PAF) is a triple* $\mathcal{F}_p = (\mathcal{A}, \mathcal{R}, \succ)$*, where* $\mathcal{A}$ *is a set of arguments,* $\mathcal{R} \subseteq \mathcal{A} \times \mathcal{A}$ *is a binary attack relation and* $\succ$ *is a strict partial order(irreflexive and transitive) over* $\mathcal{A}$*, called preference relation.*

Definition 4. *Let* $(\mathcal{A}, \mathcal{R}, \succ)$ *be a PAF and the reduction of PAF is an AF* $\mathcal{F} = (\mathcal{A}, \mathcal{D})$ *s.t.* $\forall a, b \in \mathcal{A}$*:*

- *Reduction 1 [9]:* $(a, b) \in \mathcal{D}$ *iff* $(a, b) \in \mathcal{R}$ *and* $b \nsucc a$*;*
- *Reduction 2 [10]:* $(a, b) \in \mathcal{D}$ *iff* $((a, b) \in \mathcal{R}, b \nsucc a)$ *or* $((b, a) \in \mathcal{R}, (a, b) \notin \mathcal{R}, a \succ b)$*.*
- *Reduction 3 [11]:* $(a, b) \in \mathcal{D}$ *iff* $((a, b) \in \mathcal{R}, b \nsucc a)$ *or* $((a, b) \in \mathcal{R}, (b, a) \notin \mathcal{R}))$
- *Reduction 4 [11]:* $(a, b) \in \mathcal{D}$ *iff* $((a, b) \in \mathcal{R}, b \nsucc a)$ *or* $((a, b) \in \mathcal{R}, (b, a) \notin \mathcal{R}))$ *or* $((b, a) \in \mathcal{R}, (a, b) \notin \mathcal{R}, a \succ b)$*.*

Note that if preference is not included, a PAF is exactly an AF since each attack in PAF is successfully converted to a defeat in AF. When preference is given, there exists a relationship between PAF and AF, called *reduction*. Definition 4 introduces four kinds of reduction in the existing literature. It is intuitive that an attack is successful (i.e. converted to a defeat) if and only if the attacked argument is not stronger than the attacker. It is exactly what Reduction 1 states. However, if a class of attacks which is called *critical attack* exists, namely $(a, b) \in \mathcal{R}$ and $b \succ a$, they won't be kept as defeats in AF. As a result, conflicting arguments may be all accepted which violates conflict-freeness of extensions. Critical attack is reversed in Reduction 2, deleted by Reduction 3 only if the opposite attack $(b, a) \in \mathcal{R}$ exists and made to be a symmetric attack by Reduction 4.

Next, we introduce basic definitions of framework merging and preference aggregation within the scope of collective argumentation.

Definition 5. *Given* $\{1,\ldots,n\}$ *a set of agents and a profile of AFs* $\hat{\mathcal{F}} = (\mathcal{F}_1,\ldots,\mathcal{F}_n)$, *where* $\mathcal{F}_i = (\mathcal{A}_i, \mathcal{R}_i)$. *Framework merging is an operation* Mer : $\hat{\mathcal{F}} \to \mathcal{F}_{coll}$, *where* $\mathcal{F}_{coll} = (\mathcal{A}_{coll}, \mathcal{R}_{coll})$.

Note that different operations may give rise to different outputs and as a result, collective framework may not be unique.

Definition 6. *Given* $\{1,\ldots,n\}$ *is a set of agents,* $\mathcal{A}_1,\ldots,\mathcal{A}_n$ *are sets of arguments which belong correspondingly to agents* $\{1,\ldots,n\}$ *and a profile of individual preferences is* $\hat{\mathcal{P}} = (\succ_1,\ldots,\succ_n)$, *where* $\succ_i$ *is agent i's preference over* $\mathcal{A}_i$. *Then preference aggregation is a procedure* $Agg : \hat{\mathcal{P}} \to \succsim_s$. *When* $\mathcal{A}_1 = \cdots = \mathcal{A}_n$, *it is called complete preference aggregation, otherwise we say it is incomplete preference aggregation.*

Previous work [12–14] focuses on complete preference aggregation in the area of collective argumentation. However, based on the settings of this paper, we consider the more complicated situation, namely incomplete preference aggregation.

3 A Novel Method for Framework Merging

Given distinct individual frameworks and individual preferences, in this section we temporarily put individual preferences aside and focus on obtaining collective frameworks from individual frameworks through the operation of framework merging. In the vein of framework merging, quantitative approach and qualitative approach tackle the problem differently. While the former treats the appearances of an attack in individual frameworks as *weight* [4–6], the latter treats it in a qualitative way. In extant literatures, Coste-Marquis proposes a qualitative approach [2]. There are three steps: consensual expansion, distance-based framework merging and argumentative reasoning. The main idea is to form representative collective frameworks first and then obtain collective reasoning outcome. However, it has high complexity in computation, limited capacity in explanation and difficulty in including individual preference.

As preference is regarded as a qualitative force influencing argument strength, we adopt qualitative approach to merging individual frameworks. We propose a novel method for framework merging. First of all, we define a class of relation in collective framework.

Definition 7. *Given a profile of AFs* $\hat{\mathcal{F}} = (\mathcal{F}_1,\ldots,\mathcal{F}_n)$, *where* $\mathcal{F}_i = (\mathcal{A}_i, \mathcal{R}_i)$. *We say a relation* (a, b) *is exclusive w.r.t.* $\hat{\mathcal{F}}$ *iff* $a, b \in \mathcal{A}_i$ *and* $\nexists \mathcal{F}_k = (\mathcal{A}_k, \mathcal{R}_k)$ *where* $i \neq k$ *s.t.* $a \in \mathcal{A}_k$ *and* $b \in \mathcal{A}_k$.

Definition 7 identifies a special class of binary relation, which appears only once in the profile of individual frameworks. Note that exclusive relations includes either attack or non-attack. Based on it, we define our method of framework merging.

Definition 8. *Given a profile of AFs* $\hat{\mathcal{F}} = (\mathcal{F}_1,\ldots,\mathcal{F}_n)$, *where* $\mathcal{F}_i = (\mathcal{A}_i, \mathcal{R}_i)$. *Our method of framework merging is the operation giving rise to a set of collective framework, denoted as* $\Gamma = \{\mathcal{F}_{coll_1},\ldots,\mathcal{F}_{coll_k}\}$, *where* $\mathcal{F}_{coll_j} = (\mathcal{A}_{coll_j}, \mathcal{R}_{coll_j})$. Γ *is defined as:*

- $\mathcal{A}_{coll_1} = \cdots = \mathcal{A}_{coll_k} = \bigcup_i \mathcal{A}_i$;
- $\mathcal{R}_{coll_1}, \ldots, \mathcal{R}_{coll_k}$ are exactly the members in $R_1 \bigcup R_2 \bigcup R_3^*$, where[1]:
  - $R_1 = \{(a,b)|(a,b)$ is an exclusive attack w.r.t. $\hat{\mathcal{F}}\}$;
  - $R_2 = \{(a,b)|\#(\{i|(a,b) \in \mathcal{R}_i\}) > \#(\{j|(a,b) \notin \mathcal{R}_j\})$, where $\mathcal{F}_i = (\mathcal{A}_i, \mathcal{R}_i), \mathcal{F}_j = (\mathcal{A}_j, \mathcal{R}_j)$ and $a, b \in \mathcal{A}_i \cap \mathcal{A}_j\}$;
  - $R_3^* \in 2^{R_3}$, where $R_3 = \{(a,b)|\#(\{i|(a,b) \in \mathcal{R}_i\}) = \#(\{j|(a,b) \notin \mathcal{R}_j\})$, where $\mathcal{F}_i = (\mathcal{A}_i, \mathcal{R}_i), \mathcal{F}_j = (\mathcal{A}_j, \mathcal{R}_j)$ and $a, b \in \mathcal{A}_i \cap \mathcal{A}_j\}$.

Let's proceed with some elaborations on Definition 8. In each collective framework, the set of attacks is corresponding to each member in the union of: R_1, R_2 and R_3^*. R_1 is the set of attacks which are exclusive w.r.t the profile of individual frameworks. R_2 and R_3 are sets of attacks involving pairs of arguments which are in common in the profile of individual frameworks. For any attack, only if the votes of its appearance in the profile of individual frameworks are strictly greater than the ones of its absence can it be preserved in R_2. Therefore, R_2 is based on strict majority. R_3 deals with the attacks which have equal votes for their appearances and absences in the profile of individual frameworks. Each member of 2^{R_3} has equal possibility to appear in the set of attack in collective frameworks. For instance, if $R_3 = \{(a,b)\}$, then we have two collective frameworks: one includes the pair in its set of attack and the other denies the pair as its attack.

In the following, we illustrate two basic properties of our approach of framework merging.

Proposition 1. $\#(\Gamma) = 2^{\#(R_3)}$.

Proof. The cardinality of set Γ is the number of collective frameworks we obtained from framework merging operation Mer. According to Definition 8, the number of collective frameworks is determined by $\#(\{\mathcal{A}_{coll}\})$ and $\#(\{\mathcal{R}_{coll}\})$. Due to $\#(\{\mathcal{A}_{coll}\}) = 1$, the number of collective frameworks is determined by $\#(\{\mathcal{R}_{coll}\})$, i.e. $\#(\{R_1 \bigcup R_2 \bigcup R_3^*\})$. As $R_3^* \in 2^{R_3}$, $\#(\Gamma) = \#(2^{R_3})$, i.e. equals to $2^{\#(R_3)}$.

Corollary 1. If $R_3 = \emptyset$, then the collective framework is unique.

Let us illustrate the method with the running example.

Example 2. Given the profile of three detectives' individual frameworks as Fig. 1 shows, if we exclude individual preferences in this stage, we obtain four collective frameworks $\mathcal{F}_{coll_1}, \mathcal{F}_{coll_2}, \mathcal{F}_{coll_3}, \mathcal{F}_{coll_4}$ according to Definition 8, shown in Fig. 2. Here, $R_1 = \{(a,c)\}, R_2 = \{(c,b), (b,d), (d,b)(a,d)\}, R_3 = \{(a,b), (b,a)\}$. Hence according to Proposition 1, $\#(\Gamma) = 2^2 = 4$.

Our approach forms collective frameworks on the basis of classifying the attacks in the profile of individual frameworks into three categories. It is one-step operation and has better explainability on how we merge individual frameworks. Another benefit is that we are informed the number of collective frameworks as soon as R_3 is calculated. For the evaluation, we define five rational postulates, referring some of them to [15] and [16].

---

[1] For any set $S, \#(S)$ denotes the cardinality of S.

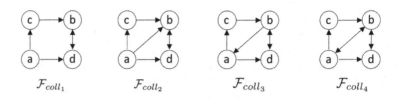

$\mathcal{F}_{coll_1}$ $\qquad$ $\mathcal{F}_{coll_2}$ $\qquad$ $\mathcal{F}_{coll_3}$ $\qquad$ $\mathcal{F}_{coll_4}$

Fig. 2. Four collective frameworks for Three Detectives example

Definition 9. *Given a profile of AFs* $\hat{\mathcal{F}} = (\mathcal{F}_1, \ldots, \mathcal{F}_n)$, *where* $\mathcal{F}_i = (\mathcal{A}_i, \mathcal{R}_i)$. *Through a framework merging operation* Mer, *we obtain the set of collective frameworks* $\Gamma = \{\mathcal{F}_{coll_1}, \ldots, \mathcal{F}_{coll_k}\}$, *where* $\mathcal{F}_{coll_j} = (\mathcal{A}_{coll_j}, \mathcal{R}_{coll_j})$. *Five rational postulates on attack are defined as:*

- **Nomination** [15] *(P1). If* $\#(\{i \in n | (a,b) \in \mathcal{R}_i\}) = 1$, *then* $(a,b) \in \bigcap_j \mathcal{R}_{coll_j}$.
- **Unanimity** [16] *(P2). If* $\#(\{i \in n | (a,b) \in \mathcal{R}_i\}) = n$, *then* $(a,b) \in \bigcap_j \mathcal{R}_{coll_j}$.
- **Strict majority** *(P3). Let* $\#(\{i \in n | a \in \mathcal{A}_i, b \in \mathcal{A}_i\}) = m$. *If* $\#(\{i \in m | (a,b) \in \mathcal{R}_i\}) > \frac{m}{2}$, *then* $(a,b) \in \bigcap_j \mathcal{R}_{coll_j}$.
- **Weak majority** *(P4). Let* $\#(\{i \in n | a \in \mathcal{A}_i, b \in \mathcal{A}_i\}) = m$. *If* $\#(\{i \in m | (a,b) \in \mathcal{R}_i\}) = \frac{m}{2}$, *then* $\exists \mathcal{F}_{coll_j} \in \Gamma$ *s.t.* $(a,b) \in \mathcal{R}_{coll_j}$.
- **Closure** [16] *(P5).* $\bigcup_j \mathcal{R}_{coll_j} \subseteq \bigcup_i \mathcal{R}_i$.

Nomination (P1) means once the attack appears in individual frameworks it will appear in collective frameworks. According to Definition 8, it is obvious that: P1 is satisfied by R_1; unanimity (P2) and strict majority (P3) are satisfied by R_2; weak majority (P4) is satisfied by R_3. Note that strict minority of attacks in the profile of individual frameworks will not preserved in the set of attack of collective frameworks but closure (P5) on attack is held. In short, our method satisfies above five rational postulates and the collective frameworks obtained from the method is representative for the profile of individual frameworks.

Proposition 2. *The collective frameworks obtained according to Definition 3 satisfies P1, P2, P3, P4 and P5.*

Now we introduce argumentative reasoning. To obtain a collective outcome for the group, we need to find the acceptability for arguments in collective frameworks. As we introduced in Sect. 2, acceptability of arguments is determined by abstract argumentation semantics (refer as Definition 2). If collective framework is unique, we can figure out the extensions instantly. If there are multiple collective frameworks, how to find out the joint acceptability of arguments? Here, we adopt Coste-Marquis' proposal in [2].

Definition 10. *Given a set of collective frameworks* $\Gamma = \{\mathcal{F}_{coll_1}, \ldots, \mathcal{F}_{coll_k}\}$, *obtained from* $\hat{\mathcal{F}}$ *according to Definitions 8, where* $\mathcal{F}_{coll_j} = (\mathcal{A}_{coll_j}, \mathcal{R}_{coll_j})$. *For any subset* $S \subseteq \mathcal{A}_{coll_j}$:
S is sceptically jointly accepted for Γ *iff* $\forall \mathcal{F}_{coll_i} \in \Gamma, \exists E \in \mathcal{E}_\sigma(\mathcal{F}_{coll_i})$ *and* $S \subseteq E$.
S is credulously jointly accepted for Γ *iff* $\exists \mathcal{F}_{coll_i} \in \Gamma, \exists E \in \mathcal{E}_\sigma(\mathcal{F}_{coll_i})$ *and* $S \subseteq E$.
The sets of arguments which are sceptically and credulously jointly accepted under a certain semantics σ *are denoted respectively as* $Sa_\sigma(\Gamma), Ca_\sigma(\Gamma)$.

4   Incomplete Preference Aggregation

In this section, we deal with individual preferences. In order to find a reasonable social preference for the group, a procedure for preference aggregation is needed. Since each individual framework is distinct, individual preferences are incomplete with respect to the profile. Thus a procedure of incomplete preference aggregation should be considered. In this section, we adopt *pairwise majority* based procedure to obtain Condorcet winners for the profile of incomplete individual preferences, proposed by Konczak in [7] and define a social preference over arguments of collective frameworks based on Condorcet winners. We evaluate the social preference obtained based on our method with three rational postulates.

In the following, we provide the basic notion of Condorcet winner in traditional preference aggregation, introduce the extended notions of necessary Condorcet winner and possible Condorcet winner, and the algorithms to compute two kinds of Condorcet winner. These are already introduced in [7]. We adapt the definitions in the context of collective argumentation.

Definition 11. *Given $\hat{\mathcal{P}} = (\succ_1, \ldots, \succ_n)$ is a profile of complete individual preferences, where $\succ_i$ is a strict total order over a set of alternatives: $\{a, b, \ldots\}$. An alternative x is defined as a Condorcet winner iff $\forall y \neq x$, $\#(\{i | x \succ_i y\}) > \frac{n}{2}$.*

Definition 12. *Given a profile of AFs $\hat{\mathcal{F}} = (\mathcal{F}_1, \ldots, \mathcal{F}_n)$, where $\mathcal{F}_i = (\mathcal{A}_i, \mathcal{R}_i)$ and $\hat{\mathcal{P}} = (\succ_1, \ldots, \succ_n)$ is a profile of incomplete individual preferences w.r.t. $\bigcup_i \mathcal{A}_i$, where $\succ_i$ is a strict total order over $\mathcal{A}_i$, we say $\succ_i'$ is a completion of $\succ_i$ w.r.t. $\hat{\mathcal{P}}$ iff $\succ_i'$ is a strict total order over $\bigcup_i \mathcal{A}_i$ and $\succ_i'$ extends $\succ_i$. The set of all completions of $\succ_i$ is denoted as $Com(\succ_i)$.*

Definition 13. *Given a profile of AFs $\hat{\mathcal{F}} = (\mathcal{F}_1, \ldots, \mathcal{F}_n)$, where $\mathcal{F}_i = (\mathcal{A}_i, \mathcal{R}_i)$ and $\hat{\mathcal{P}} = (\succ_1, \ldots, \succ_n)$ is a profile of incomplete individual preferences w.r.t. $\bigcup_i \mathcal{A}_i$, let $Com(\hat{\mathcal{P}}) = Com(\succ_1) \times \ldots \times Com(\succ_n)$, for any $a \in \bigcup_i \mathcal{A}_i$ we define:*

- *a is a necessary Condorcet winner iff $\forall \hat{\mathcal{P}}' \in Com(\hat{\mathcal{P}})$, a is a Condorcet winner for $\hat{\mathcal{P}}'$;*
- *a is a possible Condorcet winner iff $\exists \hat{\mathcal{P}}' \in Com(\hat{\mathcal{P}})$, a is a Condorcet winner for $\hat{\mathcal{P}}'$.*

Definition 14. *Given a profile of AFs $\hat{\mathcal{F}} = (\mathcal{F}_1, \ldots, \mathcal{F}_n)$, where $\mathcal{F}_i = (\mathcal{A}_i, \mathcal{R}_i)$ and $\hat{\mathcal{P}} = (\succ_1, \ldots, \succ_n)$ is a profile of incomplete individual preferences w.r.t. $\bigcup_i \mathcal{A}_i$, for $x, y \in \bigcup_i \mathcal{A}_i$, we denote $N_{\hat{\mathcal{P}}}(x, y) = \#(\{i | x \succ_i y\}) - \#(\{i | y \succ_i x\})$, then we define:*

$$N_{\succ_i}^{max}(x, y) = \begin{cases} +1 & \text{if not } (y \succ_i x) \\ -1 & \text{if } y \succ_i x \end{cases} \text{ and } N_{\succ_i}^{min}(x, y) = \begin{cases} +1 & \text{if } x \succ_i y \\ -1 & \text{if not } (x \succ_i y) \end{cases}$$

$$N_{\hat{\mathcal{P}}}^{max}(x, y) = \sum_{i=1}^{n} N_{\succ_i}^{max}(x, y) \text{ and } N_{\hat{\mathcal{P}}}^{min}(x, y) = \sum_{i=1}^{n} N_{\succ_i}^{min}(x, y)$$

Argument a is a necessary Condorcet winner iff $\forall y \neq a$, $N_{\hat{\mathcal{P}}}^{min}(a, y) > 0$. The set of necessary winners for $\hat{\mathcal{P}}$ is denoted as $NW(\hat{\mathcal{P}})$.

Argument a is a possible Condorcet winner iff $\forall y \neq a$, $N_{\hat{\mathcal{P}}}^{max}(a, y) > 0$. The set of possible winners for $\hat{\mathcal{P}}$ is denoted as $PW(\hat{\mathcal{P}})$.

Note that due to $x, y \in \bigcup_i \mathcal{A}_i$, $y \succ_i x$ implies that $x, y \in \mathcal{A}_i$ and hence "not $y \succ_i x$" indicates the situations as follows: (1)$x, y \in \mathcal{A}_i$ but $x \succ_i y$; (2)either x or y is not in $\mathcal{A}_i$; (3)neither x nor y is in $\mathcal{A}_i$. The intuition of the algorithms is that for any pair of arguments (x, y), $N_{\hat{\mathcal{P}}}^{max}(x, y)$ covers the "best" case and $N_{\hat{\mathcal{P}}}^{min}(x, y)$ covers the "worst" case among all completions of individual preferences. If an argument is superior to any other arguments in the "worst" case, it is a necessary Condorcet winner for $\hat{\mathcal{P}}$.

In [7], Konczak states that possible Condorcet winners surely exist while necessary Condorcet winners do not. However, our question is: based on necessary and possible Condorcet winners, how to form a social preference over arguments of collective frameworks? Next, we propose a method.

Definition 15. *Given a profile of AFs $\hat{\mathcal{F}} = (\mathcal{F}_1, \ldots, \mathcal{F}_n)$, where $\mathcal{F}_i = (\mathcal{A}_i, \mathcal{R}_i)$ and $\hat{\mathcal{P}} = (\succ_1, \ldots, \succ_n)$ is a profile of incomplete individual preferences over $\bigcup_i \mathcal{A}_i$. Let $NW(\hat{\mathcal{P}})$ and $PW(\hat{\mathcal{P}})$ be the set of necessary and possible winners for $\hat{\mathcal{P}}$, then an aggregated social preference over $\bigcup_i \mathcal{A}_i$ (i.e. the set of arguments of collective frameworks), denoted as $\succsim_s$, is defined based on a strict partition $\gg$ on the sets of arguments:*

- *If $NW(\hat{\mathcal{P}}) \neq \emptyset$, then $NW(\hat{\mathcal{P}}) \gg PW(\hat{\mathcal{P}}) \setminus NW(\hat{\mathcal{P}}) \gg \bigcup_i \mathcal{A}_i \setminus (NW(\hat{\mathcal{P}}) \cup PW(\hat{\mathcal{P}}))$;*
- *If $NW(\hat{\mathcal{P}}) = \emptyset$, then $PW(\hat{\mathcal{P}}) \gg \bigcup_i \mathcal{A}_i \setminus PW(\hat{\mathcal{P}})$.*

Then for any two arguments $a, b \in \bigcup_i \mathcal{A}_i$:

- *If a, b belong to the same partition, then: $a \sim_s b$;*
- *If a, b belong to different partitions, then $a \succ_s b$ iff a is in the former partition and b is in the latter.*

We illustrate the operation for incomplete preference aggregation defined above with Three Detectives example.

Example 3. Proceed with Example 1. The AFs profile is $\hat{\mathcal{F}}^3 = (\mathcal{F}_1', \mathcal{F}_2', \mathcal{F}_3')$ as shown in Fig. 1. The profile of incomplete individual preferences w.r.t $\{a, b, c, d\}$ is $\hat{\mathcal{P}}^3 = (\succ_1, \succ_2, \succ_3)$, where:

- $\succ_1$: $a \succ_1 d$ and $b \succ_1 d$,
- $\succ_2$: $c \succ_2 b \succ_2 d$,
- $\succ_3$: $a \succ_3 c \succ_3 b$ and $a \succ_3 d$.

According to Definition 14, $N_{\hat{\mathcal{P}}}^{min}(x, y)$ and $N_{\hat{\mathcal{P}}}^{max}(x, y)$ are shown in Table 1, where $x, y \in \{a, b, c, d\}$. As $\nexists y \neq x$, $N_{\hat{\mathcal{P}}}^{min}(x, y) > 0$, $NW(\hat{\mathcal{P}}^3) = \emptyset$; As $\forall y \neq x$, when $x = a$ and c, $N_{\hat{\mathcal{P}}}^{max}(x, y) > 0$, $PW(\hat{\mathcal{P}}^3) = \{a, c\}$. Thus there is no necessary Condorcet winner and the possible Condorcet winners for $\hat{\mathcal{P}}^3$ are arguments a, c. According to Definition 15, we obtain a social preference: $a \sim_s c \succ_s b \sim_s d$.

Table 1. $N_{\hat{\mathcal{P}}}^{min}(x,y)$ and $N_{\hat{\mathcal{P}}}^{max}(x,y)$ for $\hat{\mathcal{P}}^3$

$N_{\hat{\mathcal{P}}}^{min}(x,y)$	a	b	c	d
a	$-$	-1	-1	1
b	-3	$-$	-3	-1
c	-3	1	$-$	-1
d	-3	-1	-3	$-$

$N_{\hat{\mathcal{P}}}^{max}(x,y)$	a	b	c	d
a	$-$	3	3	3
b	1	$-$	-1	1
c	1	3	$-$	3
d	-1	1	1	$-$

To evaluate social preference obtained according to Definition 14 and 15, we propose three postulates as follows.

Definition 16. *Given a profile of AFs $\hat{\mathcal{F}} = (\mathcal{F}_1, \ldots, \mathcal{F}_n)$, where $\mathcal{F}_i = (\mathcal{A}_i, \mathcal{R}_i)$ and $\hat{\mathcal{P}} = (\succ_1, \ldots, \succ_n)$ is a profile of incomplete individual preferences over $\bigcup_i \mathcal{A}_i$. Let Γ be the set of collective frameworks, the social preference for $\hat{\mathcal{P}}$ be $\succsim_s$ and σ be a certain semantics. Three rational postulates on social preference are defined as:*

- *Completeness (P6). $\succsim_s$ is complete and transitive.*
- *Pairwise strict majority (P7). If $a \succ_s b$, then: $\#(\{i \in n | a \succ_i b\}) > \#(\{i \in n | b \succ_i a\})$ or $\#(\{i \in n | \text{ not } (b \succ_i a)\}) > \#(\{i \in n | \text{ not } (a \succ_i b)\})$.*
- *Decisiveness in joint acceptance (P8). If $NW(\hat{\mathcal{P}}) = \{a\}$, then $a \in Sa_\sigma(\Gamma)$.*

First of all, let us explain the implications of these rational postulates. *Completeness* means each argument in collective framework can be compared w.r.t. social preference. As individual preferences are partial orders which means some of arguments are incomparable w.r.t. individual preferences. Our method contributes the total comparability of arguments at the collective level. *Pairwise strict majority* indicates social preference has two characteristics of pairwise-majority-based consensus among agents, which actually maximises the agreement for the group. *Decisiveness in joint acceptance* states the necessary Condorcet winner always sceptically jointly accepted under a certain semantics as a collective outcome.

The satisfaction of P6 can be obtained instantly according to Definition 15 and the satisfaction of P7 are given in the following proposition.

Proposition 3. *Given a profile of AFs $\hat{\mathcal{F}} = (\mathcal{F}_1, \ldots, \mathcal{F}_n)$, where $\mathcal{F}_i = (\mathcal{A}_i, \mathcal{R}_i)$ and $\hat{\mathcal{P}} = (\succ_1, \ldots, \succ_n)$ is a profile of incomplete individual preferences over $\bigcup_i \mathcal{A}_i$. Let the social preference for $\hat{\mathcal{P}}$ be $\succsim_s$, if $a \succ_s b$, then: $\#(\{i \in n | a \succ_i b\}) > \#(\{i \in n | b \succ_i a\})$ or $\#(\{i \in n | \text{ not } (b \succ_i a)\}) > \#(\{i \in n | \text{ not } (a \succ_i b)\})$.*

Proof. According to [7], if necessary Condorcet winner exists, it is also a possible Condorcet winner and $PW(\hat{\mathcal{P}}) \setminus NW(\hat{\mathcal{P}}) = \emptyset$. Then according to Definition 15, if $a \succ_s b$, we have two possible situations:(1) a is a necessary Condorcet winner and b is neither a necessary Condorcet winner nor a possible Condorcet winner. If we want to prove $\#(\{i \in n | a \succ_i b\}) > \#(\{i \in n | b \succ_i a\})$ holds for this situation, we need to prove $N_{\hat{\mathcal{P}}}^{min}(a, b) > 0$. It is always held, since a is a necessary Condorcet winner and $\forall x \neq a$, $N_{\hat{\mathcal{P}}}^{min}(a, x) > 0$. (2) a is a possible Condorcet winner and b is neither a necessary Condorcet winner nor a possible Condorcet winner. If we want to prove $\#(\{i \in n| \text{ not } (b \succ_i a)\}) > \#(\{i \in n| \text{ not } (a \succ_i b)\})$, we need to prove $N_{\hat{\mathcal{P}}}^{max}(a, b) > 0$. It is always held, since a is a possible Condorcet winner and $\forall x \neq a$, $N_{\hat{\mathcal{P}}}^{max}(a, x) > 0$.

The verification for our method on P8 is based on the definition *preference-coherent*, which is a reasonable assumption to require agents to be rational. That is to say, an argument with less credence should not attack the argument more credible than it. Note that symmetric attack possibly exists when two arguments are incomparable w.r.t a partial order.

Definition 17. *Given a PAF $\mathcal{F}_P = (\mathcal{A}, \mathcal{R}, \succ)$, where $\succ$ is a strict partial order over $\mathcal{A}$. We say $\mathcal{F}_p$ is preference-coherent iff for any $a, b \in \mathcal{A}$: $(a, b) \in \mathcal{R}, (b, a) \notin \mathcal{R}$ iff $a \succ b$; $(a, b) \in \mathcal{R}, (b, a) \in \mathcal{R}$ only if a, b is incomparable w.r.t $\succ$.*

Theorem 1. *Given a profile of AFs $\hat{\mathcal{F}} = (\mathcal{F}_1, \ldots, \mathcal{F}_n)$ and $\hat{\mathcal{P}} = (\succ_1, \ldots, \succ_n)$ is a profile of individual preferences, where $\mathcal{F}_i = (\mathcal{A}_i, \mathcal{R}_i)$ and $\succ_i$ is an individual preference over $\mathcal{A}_i$. Let each AF in $\hat{\mathcal{F}}$ be preference-coherent w.r.t. its individual preference, Γ be the set of collective frameworks, $\succsim_s$ be social preference for $\hat{\mathcal{P}}$ and $\sigma = gr$. If $NW(\hat{\mathcal{P}}) = \{b\}$, then $b \in Sa_\sigma(\Gamma)$.*

Proof. Given $NW(\hat{\mathcal{P}}) = \{b\}$, we know that b is on the top rank of $\succsim_s$ and it is the unique winner. $b \in Sa_{gr}(\Gamma)$ means b is not attacked in all collective frameworks. Assume the contrary, that is to say b is attacked in some of collective frameworks and we need to prove a contradiction with $NW(\hat{\mathcal{P}}) = \{b\}$. Let the attacker of b in some of collective frameworks be argument c, we have $b \succ_s c$. According to P7, the characteristic of pairwise majority for necessary winner b is held as: $\#(\{i \in n|b \succ_i c\}) > \#(\{i \in n|c \succ_i b\})$ (equation (i)). As each AF in $\hat{\mathcal{F}}$ is preference-coherent w.r.t. its individual preference, the set of individual frameworks which has individual preference $b \succ_i c$ has two situations: let the cardinalities of two situations be $k_1 = \#(\{i|(b, c) \in \mathcal{R}_i \text{ and } (c, b) \notin \mathcal{R}_i\}), k_2 = \#(\{i|(b, c), (c, b) \notin \mathcal{R}_i\})$; the set of individual frameworks which has individual preference $c \succ_i b$ also has two situations: let the cardinalities of two situations be $k_3 = \#(\{i|(c, b) \in \mathcal{R}_i \text{ and } (b, c) \notin \mathcal{R}_i, k_4 = \#(\{i|(b, c), (c, b) \notin \mathcal{R}_i\})$; There are two situations left for individual preference in which b and c are incomparable, let the cardinalities of two situations be $k_5 = \#(\{i|(b, c), (c, b) \in \mathcal{R}_i\}), k_6 = \#(\{i|(b, c), (c, b) \notin \mathcal{R}_i\})$. Then according to equation (i), we have: $k_1 + k_2 > k_3 + k_4 + k_5 + k_6$ (equation (ii)). Since c is the attacker of b in some of collective frameworks and (c, b) can't be an exclusive attack in R_1 since b is a necessary Condorcet winner, according to Definition 8, we have $(c, b) \in R_3$ or $(c, b) \in R_2$, which means $k_3 + k_5 \geq k_1 + k_2 + k_4 + k_6$ (equation (iii)), contradicting to equation (ii), which means b is not a necessary Condorcet winner. Contradiction. Hence the conclusion is held.

Three postulates consist of criteria for the reasonability of social preference. As discussed above, we reach the conclusion that our method satisfies all of them and the social preference is reasonable.

Proposition 4. *The Social preference obtained from the method according to Definition 14 and Definition 15 satisfies P6, P7 and P8.*

5 The Concordance Between Collective Framework and Social Preference

In Sect. 3 we define a method for framework merging and in Sect. 4 we provide a method for obtaining social preference based on Konczak's definitions of necessary and possible Condorcet winners. Furthermore, we evaluate the reasonabilities of two methods respectively with a couple of postulates. The results are positive, showing that they are both reasonable according to the criteria. However, in our scenario, individual preferences are provided as given information as well as individual frameworks. A unified reasonable collective outcome is expected for the group of agents. Since framework merging and preference aggregation are different operations with different inputs, it is supposed that collective outcomes obtained respectively may not agree with each other. Although in Theorem 1, we have already proved that the necessary Condorcet winner is always sceptically jointly accepted under grounded semantics as a collective outcome, the disagreement on the joint acceptability of other arguments could still exist. Let us check it with the running example Three Detectives.

Example 4. First we perform argumentative reasoning according to Definition 10 with four collective frameworks obtained in Example 2. Let $\sigma = pr$, we have: $\mathcal{E}_{pr}(\mathcal{F}_{coll_1}) = \{\{a,b\}\}, \mathcal{E}_{pr}(\mathcal{F}_{coll_2}) = \{\{a\}\}, \mathcal{E}_{pr}(\mathcal{F}_{coll_3}) = \{\emptyset\}, \mathcal{E}_{pr}(\mathcal{F}_{coll_4}) = \{\{a\}, \emptyset\}$. Therefore, we don't have sceptically jointly accepted arguments under preferred semantics and credulously jointly accepted arguments under preferred semantics are a, b. While the result of social preference obtained in Example 3 shows that a, c should be mostly acceptable. The results of two operations agree on one argument but disagree with each other on two arguments!

Now the question comes: how to obtain a renewed reasonable collective outcome with more agreements? Since social preference stands for majority based consensus on the credence over arguments in collective frameworks, it should have dominance on the acceptability of arguments. For this reason, shall we only take the result of social preference into account and disregard the reasoning result from collective frameworks? It is unreasonable. Take the running example for illustration, there is an attack between the winners of social preference according to each collective framework, which means argument a and c can not be both accepted. Therefore, we need to find a solution which integrates social preference into collective frameworks or collective extensions. As proposed in [10,11,17], preference may have two roles in single-framework argumentation: one role as modification of framework and the other role as refinement of extensions. In our scenario, after framework merging, we obtain a set of representative collective frameworks. To some extent, each of them can be seen as a single framework representing for the group as a whole. Thus we may consider the application of two roles for social preference. If we apply it as refinement on collective extensions, a possible situation could be that the winners of social preference are discarded in the stage of argumentative reasoning. Hence the option left for us is to apply social preference as modification of collective frameworks, which is also called *reduction* in [9–11]. In the background of collective argumentation, we call it the *concordance* between collective framework and social preference. We distinguish two forms of concordance, namely strong concordance and weak concordance. Their definitions are based on Reduction 2 and Reduction 4 in Definition 4. Formally, we define them as follows.

Definition 18. *Given a profile of AFs $\hat{\mathcal{F}} = (\mathcal{F}_1, \ldots, \mathcal{F}_n)$, where $\mathcal{F}_i = (\mathcal{A}_i, \mathcal{R}_i)$ and $\hat{\mathcal{P}} = (\succ_1, \ldots, \succ_n)$ is a profile of incomplete individual preferences over $\bigcup_i \mathcal{A}_i$. Let $\Gamma = \{\mathcal{F}_{coll_1} \ldots \mathcal{F}_{coll_k}\}$ be the set of collective frameworks, where $\mathcal{F}_{coll_j} = (\mathcal{A}_{coll_j}, \mathcal{R}_{coll_j})$ and the social preference for $\hat{\mathcal{P}}$ be $\succsim_s$.*

- *Strong concordance is a mapping $Con_{st} : \Gamma \to \Gamma'_{st}$, where $\Gamma'_{st} = \{\mathcal{F}'_{coll_1} \ldots \mathcal{F}'_{coll_k}\}$ and $\mathcal{F}'_{coll_j} = (\mathcal{A}_{coll_j}, \mathcal{D}_{coll_j})$, defined as: $\forall \mathcal{F}_{coll_j} \in \Gamma$ s.t. $(b, a) \in \mathcal{R}_{coll_j}, (a, b) \notin \mathcal{R}_{coll_j}$, if $a \succ_s b$, then: $(a, b) \in \mathcal{D}_{coll_j}$.*
- *Weak concordance is a mapping $Con_{we} : \Gamma \to \Gamma'_{we}$, where $\Gamma'_{we} = \{\mathcal{F}'_{coll_1} \ldots \mathcal{F}'_{coll_k}\}$ and $\mathcal{F}'_{coll_j} = (\mathcal{A}_{coll_j}, \mathcal{D}_{coll_j})$, defined as: $\forall \mathcal{F}_{coll_j} \in \Gamma$ s.t. $(b, a) \in \mathcal{R}_{coll_j}, (a, b) \notin \mathcal{R}_{coll_j}$, if $a \succ_s b$, then: $(b, a) \in \mathcal{D}_{coll_j}, (a, b) \in \mathcal{D}_{coll_j}$.*

We apply two concordances with Three Detectives example and check whether the disagreement is diminished.

Example 5. Proceed with Example 4. Let $\sigma = gr$, according to Definition 18:

- If we require a strong concordance between collective framework and social preference, $\Gamma'_{st} = \{\mathcal{F}'_{coll_1}, \mathcal{F}'_{coll_2}\}$, where $\mathcal{F}'_{coll_1}$ and $\mathcal{F}'_{coll_2}$ are shown in Fig. 3. $\mathcal{E}_{gr}(\mathcal{F}'_{coll_1}) = \{\{a, b\}\}$ and $\mathcal{E}_{gr}(\mathcal{F}'_{coll_2}) = \{\{a\}\}$. Therefore, argument a is sceptically jointly accepted under grounded semantics as collective outcome.
- If we require a weak concordance between collective framework and social preference, $\Gamma'_{we} = \{\mathcal{F}'_{coll_1}, \mathcal{F}'_{coll_2}, \mathcal{F}'_{coll_3}\}$, where $\mathcal{F}'_{coll_1}, \mathcal{F}'_{coll_2}$ and $\mathcal{F}'_{coll_3}$ are shown in Fig. 3. $\mathcal{E}_{gr}(\mathcal{F}'_{coll_1}) = \{\{a, b\}\}, \mathcal{E}_{gr}(\mathcal{F}'_{coll_2}) = \{\{a\}\}$ and $\mathcal{E}_{gr}(\mathcal{F}'_{coll_3}) = \{\emptyset\}$. Therefore, argument a is credulously jointly accepted under grounded semantics as collective outcome.

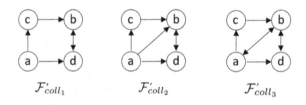

$$\mathcal{F}'_{coll_1} \qquad \mathcal{F}'_{coll_2} \qquad \mathcal{F}'_{coll_3}$$

Fig. 3. Collective frameworks after concordance in Three Detectives

From Example 5 we can see that after the operation of concordance, under grounded semantics (which is the most sceptical of all), argument a can be sceptically (with strong concordance) or credulously (with weak concordance) jointly accepted as a collective outcome. Actually, if we choose preferred semantics (which is the most credulous of all), argument a will be sceptically jointly accepted with both strong and weak concordance. After the operation of concordance, an agreement (i.e. the sceptical joint acceptability of arguments under a certain semantics) has been reached between the reasoning result from framework merging and one of social winners!

To evaluate the operation of concordance and provide new criteria for the reasonability of collective outcome, we propose three postulates as follows.

Definition 19. *Let* $\Gamma = \{\mathcal{F}_{coll_1} \dots \mathcal{F}_{coll_k}\}$ *be the set of collective frameworks, where* $\mathcal{F}_{coll_j} = (\mathcal{A}_{coll_j}, \mathcal{R}_{coll_j})$ *and the social preference for* $\hat{\mathcal{P}}$ *be* $\succsim_s$*. Let the operation of concordance be* Con_x *where* $x \in \{st, we\}$*. Let the sets of collective frameworks obtained after concordance be* Γ'_x*. Let* $\sigma \in \{co, pr, gr, st\}$ *and the sets of sceptically and credulously jointly accepted arguments after concordance be* $Sa_\sigma(\Gamma'_x)$ *and* $Ca_\sigma(\Gamma'_x)$*. Let* $win(\succsim_s) = \{a | \forall b \in \mathcal{A}_{coll_j} \ s.t. \ a \succ_s b \ or \ a \sim_s b$ *but not the case* $b \succ_s a\}$ *denote the set of social winners.*

- *Collective cardinality decline (P9).* $\#(\Gamma'_x) \subseteq \#(\Gamma)$.
- *Joint acceptance growth (P10).* $Sa_\sigma(\Gamma) \subseteq Sa_\sigma(\Gamma'_x)$ *and* $Ca_\sigma(\Gamma) \subseteq Ca_\sigma(\Gamma'_x)$.
- *Social winner(s) dominance (P11).* $\exists a \in win(\succsim_s) \ s.t. \ a \in Sa_\sigma(\Gamma'_x)$.

Let us elaborate the implications of these postulates. P9 states that after concordance, the cardinality of collective frameworks declines which means representative frameworks for the group become more concentrated and complexity of computation is reduced. P10 indicates that another benefit of concordance is more arguments are possible to be jointly accepted. P11 says although it seems that the group are less prudent on the acceptance of arguments than before according P10, we make sure that at least one of social winners is sceptically accepted under a certain semantics as collective outcome, which implies non-emptiness of collective outcome. Next, we verify our methods with three postulates.

Proposition 5. *The operations of strong concordance and weak concordance satisfy collective cardinality decline (P9).*

Proof. Only if $\exists a, b \in \mathcal{A}_{coll}$ s.t. $(a, b), (b, a) \in R_3$ and a, b is not indifferent according to $\succsim_s$, we have $\#(\Gamma'_x) \subset \#(\Gamma)$ and in other situations we have $\#(\Gamma'_x) = \#(\Gamma)$. Thus the conclusion is held.

Corollary 2. $\#(\Gamma'_{st}) \subseteq \#(\Gamma'_{we})$.

Proof. When $\exists a, b \in \mathcal{A}_{coll}$ s.t. $(a, b), (b, a) \in R_3$ and a, b is not indifferent according to $\succsim_s$, we have at least four collective frameworks. According to strict concordance, $\emptyset, (a, b)$ or $\emptyset, (b, a)$ will preserved as a result while symmetric attack $(a, b)(b, a)$ will be excluded. According to weak concordance, $(a, b)(b, a)$ will also preserved, which means $\#(\Gamma'_{st}) \subset \#(\Gamma'_{we})$. In other situations we have $\#(\Gamma'_x) = \#(\Gamma)$. Thus the conclusion is held.

Proposition 6. *The operation of strong concordance doesn't satisfy joint acceptance growth (P10) while the operation of weak concordance satisfies it only if under complete, preferred and stable semantics.*

Proof. First we prove the violation of strong concordance. According to the definition, $\forall \mathcal{F}_{coll_j} \in \Gamma$, if $a \succ_s b, (b,a) \in \mathcal{R}_{coll_j}, (a,b) \notin \mathcal{R}_{coll_j}$, then $(a,b) \in \mathcal{D}_{coll_j}$. It means argument a will take the place of argument b appearing in the set of sceptically jointly accepted arguments if a is not defeated by other arguments. $\exists b \in Sa_\sigma(\Gamma)$ and $b \notin Sa_\sigma(\Gamma'_{st})$, thus $Sa_\sigma(\Gamma) \not\subseteq Sa_\sigma(\Gamma'_{st})$. The proof of $Ca_\sigma(\Gamma) \not\subseteq Ca_\sigma(\Gamma'_{st})$ is the same. Next we prove the operation of weak concordance satisfies P10 only if under complete, preferred and stable semantics. According to the definition, $\forall \mathcal{F}_{coll_j} \in \Gamma$, if $a \succ_s b, (b,a) \in \mathcal{R}_{coll_j}, (a,b) \notin \mathcal{R}_{coll_j}$, weak concordance make the attack (b,a) to be symmetric. It means if argument a and b are not defeated by other arguments, under grounded semantics neither of them can be sceptically jointly accepted. $\exists b \in Sa_{gr}(\Gamma)$ and $b \notin Sa_{gr}(\Gamma'_{we})$. Thus $Sa_{gr}(\Gamma) \not\subseteq Sa_{gr}(\Gamma'_{we})$. The proof of $Ca_{gr}(\Gamma) \not\subseteq Ca_{gr}(\Gamma'_x)$ is the same. Let $\sigma \in \{co, pr, st\}$, $\forall \mathcal{F}_{coll_j} \in \Gamma$, if argument a and b are not defeated by other arguments and after weak concordance, $(a,b)(b,a) \in \mathcal{D}_{coll_j}$, we have $b \in Sa_\sigma(\Gamma)$ and $a, b \in Sa_\sigma(\Gamma'_{we})$. Thus $Sa_\sigma(\Gamma) \subseteq Sa_\sigma(\Gamma'_{we})$. The proof of $Ca_\sigma(\Gamma) \subseteq Ca_\sigma(\Gamma'_{we})$ is the same.

Proposition 7. *The operation of strong concordance satisfies social winner(s) dominance (P11) and the operation of weak concordance satisfies it only if under complete, preferred and stable semantics.*

Proof. As proved in Theorem 1, if social winner is the necessary Condorcet winner, without the operation of concordance, it will be sceptically jointly accepted. Here we only need to prove that if $NW(\hat{\mathcal{P}}) = \emptyset$ and $\exists a \in PW(\hat{\mathcal{P}})$ then $a \in Sa_\sigma(\Gamma'_x)$. (1) If a is attacked by a possible Condorcet winner b, since $a \sim_s b$ there is no concordance, i.e. $\Gamma = \Gamma'_x$. b will be sceptically jointly accepted. Thus $b \in win(\succsim_s)$ s.t. $b \in Sa_\sigma(\Gamma)$. (2)$\forall \mathcal{F}_{coll_j} \in \Gamma$, if a is attacked by an argument $b \in \bigcup_i \mathcal{A}_i \setminus PW(\hat{\mathcal{P}})$, since $a \succ_s b$ concordance is needed. The operation of strong concordance will reverse the attack and then $\forall \mathcal{F}'_{coll_j} \in \Gamma'_{st}, a \in \mathcal{E}_\sigma(\mathcal{F}'_{coll_j})$, i.e. $a \in Sa_\sigma(\Gamma'_{st})$. Let $\sigma \in \{co, pr, st\}$, the operation of weak concordance will make the attack be symmetric so that $\forall \mathcal{F}'_{coll_j} \in \Gamma'_{we}, a \in \mathcal{E}_\sigma(\mathcal{F}'_{coll_j})$, i.e. $a \in Sa_\sigma(\Gamma'_{we})$. Since when $\sigma = gr$, $\forall \mathcal{F}'_{coll_j} \in \Gamma'_{we}, a \notin \mathcal{E}_{gr}(\mathcal{F}_{coll_j})$, i.e. $a \notin Sa_{gr}(\Gamma'_{we})$. Therefore under grounded semantics, the conclusion is not held.

Table 2. The evaluation on two concordances

Concordance	P1-P5	P9	P10	P11
Con_{st}	✓	✓	×	✓
Con_{we}	✓	✓	✓$^{\sigma \in \{pr,st,co\}}$	✓$^{\sigma \in \{pr,st,co\}}$

For clarification, we list all above results in Table 2. From the table, we can see that both strong and weak concordances satisfy P1-P5 since the operation of framework merging is same for them and it satisfies all of five postulates.

Further, weak concordance satisfies all of three postulates under complete, preferred and stable semantics, including grounded semantics in P9. Although strong concordance doesn't satisfy P10, it satisfies both P9 and P11 under all standard semantics. Note that the collective outcome obtained after the operation of concordance, not only preserves majority based consensus among individual frameworks, but also modifies collective frameworks to ensure at least one of social winners will be accepted by the group. Therefore, it is more reasonable than the results obtained from framework merging or incomplete preference aggregation, since it reflects the interplayed consensus on reasoning result and social credence.

6   Conclusion

Individual preferences give rise to argument strength in collective argumentation and may have influences on collective outcome correspondingly. In order to tackle individual preferences as well as distinct individual frameworks in a multi-agent scenario, in this paper we first propose a method for the operation of framework merging and then define a method to obtain social preference through the operation of incomplete preference aggregation. However, two different operations may not agree with each other on the joint acceptability of arguments. Aiming to find a solution to reach more agreements between the results from framework merging and incomplete preference aggregation, we define an operation called concordance, which is actually the modification of collective frameworks according to social preference. As a result, the collective outcome obtained from argumentative reasoning with modified collective frameworks is renewed to reflect the dominance of social preference. We propose a couple of rational postulates and verify that the methods we propose are equipped with reasonability.

6.1   Related Work

Preference has been studied in single-framework argumentation [9–11,17]. [10,17] proposes two roles for preference and the following paper [11] agrees with them but proposes four methods for reduction. We adopt two reductions proposed in [10] and [11] for the reason that they can preserve conflicting relation between pairs of arguments and strengthen the argument strength of social winners. Although these previous work hasn't studied preference in the background of collective argumentation, they genuinely construct basis for the research in this paper.

In the perspective of framework merging, Coste-Marquis' approach [2] is close to us. Since distance-based framework merging always gives rise to majority-based results, we define two subsets of attack for collective framework based on the majority and adopt Coste-Marquis' proposal in argumentative reasoning. However, our approach is more concise on the definition and more explainable on the results. Another qualitative approach for framework merging is Delobelle's work [3]. He propose an approach for framework merging based on belief revision [18] and represent the expected extensions as formula consisting of arguments. His approach is deviated from ours and each individual framework in his settings shares the same set of arguments. Apart from these, Delobelle [6], Gabbay [5] and Cayrol [4] adopt a quantitative way for framework merging, treating the appearances of an argument or an attack in individual frameworks as weights. Delobelle selects collective extensions based on weights. In Gabbay's approach, weights can be propogated in the collective framework and the acceptability of arguments is determined by a threshold. Cayrol's approach only defines a quasi-semantics named vs-defend to justify a successful defense between pairs of arguments.

Based on Bench-Capon's innovative VAF [12–14,19] study value preference in the field of multi-agent systems. Airiau [12] discusses the criteria for rationalisation of the profile of individual frameworks. The rationalisation actually comes from transitivity and acyclicity of strict total ordering. Lisowski [13] concerns about the correspondence between the reasoning results obtained from value preference aggregation and framework merging. They figure out a method to construct the correspondence. Liao [14] studies value preference's influences on the reasoning results based on different aggregation rules and ordering-lifting principles. However, preference aggregation in both [13] and [14] is dealing with complete preference according to their settings and the approach for framework merging adopted in [13] is a quota rule which is unable to tackle framework merging of distinct individual frameworks.

6.2   Future Work

First, as studied in [14], different aggregation rules may give rise to different results with certain properties. We'd like to adopt other incomplete preference aggregation procedures, such as Borda procedure proposed in [7] and minmax regret approximation [20], and evaluate the reasonability of them respectively. Second, as proposed by Baumeister in [21], there is a class of argumentation framework with uncertainty called incomplete argumentation framework. In future, we can extend our research to integrate incomplete individual preferences into the profile of incomplete individual frameworks. Third, since individual preference can be quantitatively represented as personal degree of belief, in other words, we can treat it as a probability. Then we can connect this area with probabilistic argumentation framework.

Acknowledgments. The research reported in this paper was supported in part by the "2030 Megaproject"—New Generation Artificial Intelligence of China under Grant 2018AAA0100904, the Natural Science Foundation of Zhejiang Province under Grant No. LY20F030014, and the National Social Science Foundation Major Project of China under grant No. 20 & ZD047.

References

1. Bodanza, G., Tohmé, F., Auday, M.: Collective argumentation: a survey of aggregation issues around argumentation frameworks. Argument Comput. **8**, 1–34 (2017)
2. Coste-Marquis, S., Devred, C., Konieczny, S., Lagasquie-Schiex, M.-C., Marquis, P.: On the merging of Dung's argumentation systems. Artif. Intell. **171**, 730–753 (2007)

3. Delobelle, J., Haret, A., Konieczny, S., Mailly, J.G., Rossit, J., Woltran, S.: Merging of abstract argumentation frameworks. In: KR, pp. 33–42 (2016)
4. Cayrol, C., Lagasquie-Schiex, M.-C.: Weighted argumentation systems: a tool for merging argumentation systems. In: 2011 IEEE 23rd International Conference on Tools with Artificial Intelligence, pp. 629–632 (2011)
5. Gabbay, D., Rodrigues, O.: A numerical approach to the merging of argumentation networks. In: Fisher, M., van der Torre, L., Dastani, M., Governatori, G. (eds.) CLIMA 2012. LNCS (LNAI), vol. 7486, pp. 195–212. Springer, Heidelberg (2012). https://doi.org/10.1007/978-3-642-32897-8_14
6. Delobelle, J., Konieczny, S., Vesic, S.: On the aggregation of argumentation frameworks: operators and postulates. J. Log. Comput. **28**, 1671–1699 (2018)
7. Konczak, K., Lang, J.: Voting procedures with incomplete preferences. In: Proceedings of the IJCAI 2005 Multidisciplinary Workshop on Advances in Preference Handling, vol. 20 (2005)
8. Dung, P.M.: On the acceptability of arguments and its fundamental role in nonmonotonic reasoning, logic programming and n-person games. Artif. Intell. **77**, 321–357 (1995)
9. Amgoud, L., Cayrol, C.: Inferring from inconsistency in preference-based argumentation frameworks. J. Autom. Reason. **29**, 125–169 (2002)
10. Amgoud, L., Vesic, S.: Rich preference-based argumentation frameworks. Int. J. Approximate Reasoning **55**, 585–606 (2014)
11. Kaci, S., van der Torre, L., Villata, S.: Preference in abstract argumentation. In: 7th International Conference on Computational Models of Argument (COMMA), vol. 305, pp. 405–412 (2018)
12. Airiau, S., Bonzon, E., Endriss, U., Maudet, N., Rossit, J.: Rationalisation of profiles of abstract argumentation frameworks: characterisation and complexity. J. Artif. Intell. Res. **60**, 149–177 (2017)
13. Lisowski, G., Doutre, S., Grandi, U.: Aggregation in value-based argumentation frameworks. arXiv preprint arXiv:1907.09113 (2019)
14. Liao, B., Li, C.: A solution to ethical dilemmas based on preference aggregation and formal argumentation. J. Hunan Univ. Sci. Technol. (Soc. Sci. Ed.) **23**(3), 33–49 (2020)
15. Chen, W., Endriss, U.: Preservation of semantic properties in collective argumentation: the case of aggregating abstract argumentation frameworks. Artif. Intell. **269**, 27–48 (2019)
16. Dunne, P.E., Marquis, P., Wooldridge, M.: Argument aggregation: basic axioms and complexity results. In: Computational Models of Argument, vol. 129–140. IOS Press (2012)
17. Amgoud, L., Vesic, S.: Two roles of preferences in argumentation frameworks. In: Liu, W. (ed.) ECSQARU 2011. LNCS (LNAI), vol. 6717, pp. 86–97. Springer, Heidelberg (2011). https://doi.org/10.1007/978-3-642-22152-1_8
18. Coste-Marquis, S., Konieczny, S., Mailly, J.G., Marquis P.: On the revision of argumentation systems: minimal change of arguments statuses. In: KR, pp. 52–61 (2014)
19. Bench-Capon, T.J.: Persuasion in practical argument using value-based argumentation frameworks. J. Log. Comput. **13**, 429–448 (2003)
20. Lu, T., Boutilier, C.: Robust approximation and incremental elicitation in voting protocols. In: IJCAI, pp. 287–293 (2011)
21. Baumeister, D., Neugebauer, D., Rothe, J., Schadrack, H.: Verification in incomplete argumentation frameworks. Artif. Intell. **264**, 1–26 (2018)

A Logic for Binary Classifiers and Their Explanation

Xinghan Liu[1(✉)] and Emiliano Lorini[2]

[1] ANITI, Toulouse University, Toulouse, France
xinghan.liu@univ-toulouse.fr
[2] IRIT-CNRS, Toulouse University, Toulouse, France
Emiliano.Lorini@irit.fr

Abstract. Recent years have witnessed a renewed interest in Boolean functions in explaining binary classifiers in the field of explainable AI (XAI). The standard approach to Boolean functions is based on propositional logic. We present a modal language of a ceteris paribus nature which supports reasoning about binary classifiers and their properties. We study a family of classifier models, axiomatize it and show completeness of our axiomatics. Moreover, we prove that satisfiability checking for our modal language relative to such a class of models is NP-complete. We leverage the language to formalize counterfactual conditional as well as a variety of notions of explanation including abductive, contrastive and counterfactual explanations, and biases. Finally, we present two extensions of our language: a dynamic extension by the notion of assignment enabling classifier change and an epistemic extension in which the classifier's uncertainty about the actual input can be represented.

Keywords: Boolean classifier · Explainable AI · Modal logic · Ceteris paribus logic · Epistemic logic

1 Introduction

The notions of explanation and explainability have been extensively investigated by philosophers [13,19] and are key aspects of AI-based systems given the importance of explaining the behavior and prediction of an artificial intelligent system. A variety of notions of explanations have been discussed in the area of explainable AI (XAI) including abductive, contrastive and counterfactual explanation [1,8,18,21–23]. Recently, there has been a renewed interest for the notion of explanation in the context of classifier systems, i.e., explaining why a classifier has classified a given input instance in a certain way [7,17,18,25]. Classifier systems can be seen as "black boxes" computing a given (Boolean) function in the context of a classification or prediction task. Artificial feedforward neural networks are special kinds of classifier systems aimed at learning or, at least approximating, the function mapping instances of the input data to their corresponding outputs. Explaining why the system has classified a given instance in

© Springer Nature Switzerland AG 2021
P. Baroni et al. (Eds.): CLAR 2021, LNAI 13040, pp. 302–321, 2021.
https://doi.org/10.1007/978-3-030-89391-0_17

a certain way and identifying the set of features that is necessary (minimally) sufficient for the classification is crucial for making the system intelligible and for finding biases in the classification process.

In this paper we introduce a modal language for representing classifiers with binary input data.[1] It extends propositional logic by a finite set of atomic formulas of type $t(x), t(y), \ldots$, which we call *decision atoms*. Moreover, it includes *ceteris paribus* (CP) modal operators of the form $[X]$ to represent that a formula is necessarily true regardless of the truth or the falsity of the atomic propositions outside the set of atomic propositions X.

A question may come immediately: why bother us by a modal language? A classifier is nothing but a function. A Boolean classifier is thus a function whose inputs are valuations of atomic propositions and outputs are True or False, which can in turn be expressed as some propositional formula, particularly in disjunctive normal form (DNF). This is already known since the seminal work of Boole on propositional logic. Our answer is that extending to modal logic is both a natural and a fruitful move.

To see why a modal logic viewpoint is natural, first notice that a classifier can be viewed as a partition of all possible inputs. Figure 1 illustrates a classifier, which can be expressed as $\{((\{p, q\}, \texttt{yellow})\} \cup \{((\{\neg p, q\}, \texttt{red})\} \cup \{((\{p, \neg q\}, \texttt{blue})\} \cup \{((\{\neg p, \neg q\}, \texttt{blue})\}$, or equivalently $(p \wedge q \wedge t(\texttt{yellow})) \vee (\neg p \wedge q \wedge t(\texttt{red})) \vee (p \wedge \neg q \wedge t(\texttt{blue})) \vee (\neg p \wedge \neg q \wedge t(\texttt{blue}))$ in propositional logic. But clearly, it can also be seen as an S5 Kripke model, where each world represents a possible valuation of atoms.

Moreover, as Quine [24] found, a Boolean classifier can be uniquely characterized by a DNF consisting of its *prime implicants* which will be introduced later. Intuitively, it means that if a data point is classified as True by a classifier f, then we can perturb it by changing values of some of its variables, and it keeps being True, as long as some of its prime implicants stays invariant. Obviously, this understanding contains a *ceteris paribus* reading of modality. For example, in our language we will be allowed to write the formula $(\neg p \wedge \neg q) \rightarrow [\{q\}]t(\texttt{blue})$. It says that any input which evaluates atom q in the same way as the input $\{\neg p, \neg q\}$ is necessarily classified as blue. In other words, when atom q is false the input is classified as blue regardless of the other atoms' truth values, which indicates that $\neg q$ is an implicant of $t(\texttt{blue})$.[2]

As for fruitfulness, extending the logical framework to modal logic and more generally to non-classical logics, opens up new vistas including (i) defining counterfactual conditional and studying its relationship with the notions of abductive and contrastive explanation, (ii) modeling classifier dynamics through the use of formal semantics for logics of communication and change [27,30], and (iii) rep-

---

[1] So the classifier we model here is slightly more expressive than Boolean classifier. Introducing decision atoms $t(x), t(y), \ldots$ below allows us to encode more than two decision values (classifications). Sometime we also use binary/Boolean classifier in this more general sense. Notice that we cannot use the term *psuedo-Boolean*, since in Boolean function it means $Val = \mathfrak{R}$ [5], but we need our Val staying finite.

[2] In fact it appears to be a prime implicant, when we formally introduce this notion.

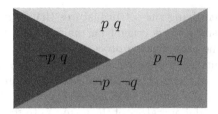

Fig. 1. A classifier as a function is a partition on an S5 model

resenting the classifier's uncertainty about the actual instance to be classified through the use of epistemic logic [10].

To sum up, the paper offers a unified logical framework for modeling and comparing different notions of explanation and bias in classifier systems. It is structured as follows. In Sect. 2 we introduce the *ceteris paribus* language and the notion of classifier model which is used to interpret it. Moreover, we investigate some extra properties of classifier models to capture interesting subclasses of classifier models for the sake of classifier explanation. In Sect. 3 a counterfactual conditional operator will be defined and its relevance for understanding the behavior of a classifier will be highlighted. Section 4 is devoted to classifier explanation, where notions of abductive explanation (AXp), contrastive explanation (CXp) and bias in terms of classifier will be represented in the classifier model.[3] Besides, the connection between CXp and counterfactual are elucidated. Finally, in Sect. 5 we present two extensions of our language: (i) a dynamic extension by the notion of assignment enabling classifier change and (ii) an epistemic extension in which the classifier's uncertainty about the actual input can be represented.

2 A Language for Binary Classifiers

In this section we introduce a language for modeling binary classifiers and present its semantics. The language has a *ceteris paribus* nature. It contains *ceteris paribus* operators of the form $[X]$ that allow us to express the fact that the classifier's actual decision (or classification) does not depend on the features of the input in the complementary set $Atm \setminus X$, with Atm the set of atomic propositions and X a subset of it. Such operators were introduced for the first time in [12].

2.1 Basic Language and Classifier Model

Let Atm be a finite set of atomic propositions with elements noted $p, q, \ldots$ We define $AtmSet = 2^{Atm}$.

---

[3] The notations AXp and CXp are credited to [17,18].

Let us assume the set Atm includes special atomic formulas of type $t(x)$, where $x \in Val$ and Val is a finite set of decision values with elements noted $x, y, \ldots$ We call them decision atoms and note $Dec = \{t(x) : x \in Val\}$ the corresponding set. The decision atom $t(x)$ has to be read "the actual decision takes value x".

The modal language $\mathcal{L}(Atm)$ is defined by the following grammar:

$$\varphi ::= p \mid \neg\varphi \mid \varphi_1 \wedge \varphi_2 \mid [X]\varphi,$$

where p ranges over Atm and X ranges over $AtmSet$. The set of atomic propositions occurring in a formula φ is noted $Atm(\varphi)$. It should be clear that x and X refer to different things in our setting.

The formula $[X]\varphi$ has a *ceteris paribus* (CP) reading: "φ is necessary all features in X being equal" or "φ is necessary regardless of the truth or falsity of the atoms in $Atm \setminus X$". Operator $\langle X \rangle$ is the dual of $[X]$ and is defined as usual: $\langle X \rangle \varphi =_{def} \neg[X]\neg\varphi$.

The language $\mathcal{L}(Atm)$ is interpreted relative to classifier models whose class is defined as follows.

Definition 1 (Classifier model). *A classifier model (CM) is a tuple $C = (S, f)$ where:*

- $S = 2^{Atm \setminus Dec}$ *is the set of states, and*
- $f : S \longrightarrow Val$ *is a decision (or classification) function.*

The class of classifier models is noted **CM**.

A pointed classifier model is a pair (C, s) with $C = (S, f)$ a classifier model and $s \in S$.

Formulas in $\mathcal{L}(Atm)$ are interpreted relative to a pointed classifier model, as follows.

Definition 2 (Satisfaction relation). *Let (C, s) be a pointed classifier model with $C = (S, f)$ and $s \in S$. Then:*

$$(C, s) \models p \Longleftrightarrow p \in s \text{ for } p \in (Atm \setminus Dec),$$
$$(C, s) \models t(x) \Longleftrightarrow f(s) = x \text{ for } t(x) \in Dec,$$
$$(C, s) \models \neg\varphi \Longleftrightarrow (C, s) \not\models \varphi,$$
$$(C, s) \models \varphi \wedge \psi \Longleftrightarrow (C, s) \models \varphi \text{ and } (C, s) \models \psi,$$
$$(C, s) \models [X]\varphi \Longleftrightarrow \forall s' \in S : \text{ if } (s \cap X) = (s' \cap X)$$
$$\text{then } (C, s') \models \varphi.$$

Note in particular the *ceteris paribus* interpretation of the modal operator $[X]$. The formula $[X]\varphi$ is true at a state s if φ is true at all states that are modulo-X equivalent to state s. The condition $(s \cap X) = (s' \cap X)$ indeed stipulates that s and s' are indistinguishable with regard to the atoms (the features) in X. We abbreviate $(C, s) \models \varphi$ as $s \models \varphi$ when the context is clear.

Notions of satisfiability and validity for formulas in $\mathcal{L}(Atm)$ relative to the class **CM** as well as classifier model validity are defined in the usual way. Specifically, a formula φ of $\mathcal{L}(Atm)$ is said to be satisfiable relative to the class **CM** if there exists a pointed classifier model (C, s) with $C \in$ **CM** such that $(C, s) \models \varphi$. It is said to be valid relative to **CM**, noted $\models_{\mathbf{CM}} \varphi$, if $\neg\varphi$ is not satisfiable relative to **CM**. Moreover, we say that that φ is valid in the classifier model $C = (S, f)$, noted $C \models \varphi$, if $(C, s) \models \varphi$ for every $s \in S$.

Let us close this part by forecasting how we will use classifier models to represent explanations and bias in Sect. 4 with the following example.

Example 1 (Applicant Alice). Given the language $\mathcal{L}(Atm)$ with $Atm = \{p_1, p_2, q_1, q_2, \mathsf{t}(x), \mathsf{t}(y)\}$. Let us have a CM $C = (S, f)$ s.t. $C \models \mathsf{t}(x) \leftrightarrow ((q_1 \wedge q_2) \vee (p_1 \wedge q_1))$. Consider a pointed CM (C, s) where $s = \{p_2, q_1\}$, $f(s) = y$.

We interpret p_1, p_2, q_1, q_2 in the example above as gender (male p_1 or female $\neg p_1$), postcode (inner city p_2 or suburb $\neg p_2$), employment situation (employed q_1 or unemployed $\neg q_1$) and property ownership (possess q_2 or rent $\neg q_2$), respectively; f as a classifier of loan; x, y as acceptance and rejection by the bank, respectively; s as the state of an applicant, say, Alice. So this models a scenario that Alice is applying for a loan from her bank. She is female, employed, rents an apartment in the inner city. The bank decides to reject Alice's application.

Now Alice is asking for explanations of the decision/classification, e.g., 1) which of her features (necessarily) lead to the current decision, 2) changing which features would make a difference, 3) perhaps most importantly, whether the decision for her is biased. In Sect. 4 we will show how to use the language $\mathcal{L}(Atm)$ and its semantics to answer these questions.

2.2 Properties of Classifier Models

Though the correspondence between classifier models and classifiers is salient, things are subtler than they seem. In this section, we are going to study interesting subclasses of classifier models satisfying extra properties which are relevant in some domains of application.

Definition 3 (Properties). *Let $X \subseteq (Atm \setminus Dec)$ be finite and let $C = (S, f)$ be a classifier model. Then, C is said to be*

- *X-definite (i.e., $def(X)$) if, $\forall s, s' \in S$, if $(s \cap X) = (s' \cap X)$ then $f(s) = f(s')$,*
- *X-essential (i.e. $ess(X)$), if $\forall p \in X$, C is not $Atm \setminus (Dec \cup \{p\})$-definite, and $\forall p \notin X$, C is $Atm \setminus (Dec \cup \{p\})$-definite;*
- *X-non trivial (i.e., $ntr(X)$) if $\exists s, s' \in S$ such that $(s \cap X) \neq (s' \cap X)$ and $f(s) \neq f(s')$.*

Let $P \subseteq Prop$ with

$$Prop = \{def(X), ess(X), ntr(X) : X \subseteq (Atm \setminus Dec)\}.$$

We denote by $\mathbf{CM}_P$ the class of classifier models satisfying each property in P.

The following proposition captures the interesting aspects of certain X-property and connections between different properties.

Proposition 1. *Let $X, X' \subseteq (Atm \setminus Dec)$ and let $C = (S, f)$ be any classifier model. Then,*

1. $C \in \mathbf{CM}_{\{def(Atm \setminus Dec)\}}$,
2. *if* $C \in \mathbf{CM}_{\{def(X)\}}$ *and* $X \subseteq X'$ *then* $C \in \mathbf{CM}_{\{def(X')\}}$,
3. $\exists! Y \subseteq (Atm \setminus Dec)$ *such that* $C \in \mathbf{CM}_{\{ess(Y)\}}$,
4. *if* $C \in \mathbf{CM}_{\{ess(Y), def(X)\}}$ *for some* $Y \subseteq (Atm \setminus Dec)$, *then* $Y \subseteq X$,
5. *if* $C \in \mathbf{CM}_{\{ntr(X)\}}$, *then* $C \in \mathbf{CM}_{\{ntr(Y)\}}$ *for all* $Y \subseteq (Atm \setminus Dec)$,
6. *if* $C \in \mathbf{CM}_{\{ntr(Y), def(X)\}}$ *for some* $Y \subseteq (Atm \setminus Dec)$, *and* $X \cap X' = \emptyset$, *then* $C \notin \mathbf{CM}_{\{def(X')\}}$

The proposition states that a classifier model always has definite set(s) and a unique essential set, which is also the minimal definite set. Non-triviality is an "all or all not" property, i.e., knowing whether C is X-non trivial or not for some X is enough to know whether C is Y-non trivial or Y-trivial for any $Y \subseteq (Atm \setminus Dec)$. The last item highlights that there are cases in which the class of classifier models crushes, i.e., for some set of semantic properties P, the model class $\mathbf{CM}_P$ is empty.

The fact that not all variables in a function are essential plays an important role in explaining classifiers. Actually, when an intelligent agent, human or artificial, makes a classification, she only takes a (finite) subset of all possible features into account. Take human eyes for instance. It is quite common that we perceive a lot, but not all of them are recognized with awareness. Dretske hence distinguished between *sensual perception,* and *meaningful perception* or *perceptual recognition* (for more discussion see [9,14]). Figure 2 illustrates this idea.

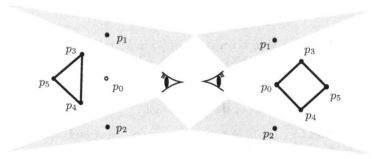

Fig. 2. Two pointed models of the Eye Model

Example 2 (Eye Model). Figure 2 gives two pointed classifier models, call them $(C^{\preccurlyeq}, s_l)$ and $(C^{\preccurlyeq}, s_r)$, where $C^{\preccurlyeq} = (S, f)$. We have $s_l = \{p_1, p_2, p_3, p_4, p_5\}$, $f(s_l) = \{\texttt{triangle}\}$, and $s_r = \{p_0, p_1, p_2, p_3, p_4, p_5\}$, $f(s_r) = \{\texttt{quadrilateral}\}$. Moreover, we have:

$$C^{\preccurlyeq} \models \texttt{t(triangle)} \leftrightarrow \bigvee_{X \subseteq Atm \backslash (Dec \cup \{p_1, p_2\}):|X|=3} \left(\bigwedge_{p \in X} p \wedge \bigwedge_{p \in Atm \backslash (Dec \cup \{p_1, p_2\} \cup X)} \neg p \right),$$

$C^{\preccurlyeq} \models \texttt{t(quadrilateral)} \leftrightarrow (p_0 \wedge p_3 \wedge p_4 \wedge p_5)$, and $C^{\preccurlyeq} \in \mathbf{CM}_{\{ess(\{p_0, p_3, p_4, p_5\})\}}$.

Thus, the eye classifies an input as "triangle" if exactly three of $\{p_0.p_3, p_4, p_5\}$ are true in the input, and as "quadrilateral" when all four of them are true in the input. The inessential variables p_1 and p_2 are put in the grey zone, which indicates that they are out of the perceptual recognition/awareness.

One last thing to introduce, before eventually representing classifier explanation in our model, is a conditional operator.

3 Counterfactual Conditional

In this section we investigate a simple notion of counterfactual conditional for binary classifiers, inspired from Lewis' notion [20]. In Sect. 4, we will elucidate its connection with the notion of explanation.

We start our analysis by defining the following notion of similarity between worlds in a model relative to a finite set of features X.

Definition 4. *Let* $C = (S, f)$ *be a classifier model,* $s, s' \in S$ *and* $X \subseteq (Atm \backslash Dec)$. *The similarity between* s *and* s' *in* S *relative to the set of features* X, *noted* $sim_C(s, s', X)$, *is defined as follows:*

$$sim_C(s, s', X) = |\{p \in X : (C, s) \models p \text{ iff } (C, s') \models p\}|.$$

A dual notion of distance between worlds can defined from the previous notion of similarity:

$$dist_C(s, s', X) = |X| - sim_C(s, s', X).$$

This notion of distance is in accordance of [6] in knowledge revision.[4] The following definition introduces the concept of conditional. Following Lewis' view, we evaluate a conditional at a state of a classifier model and stipulate that the conditional holds if all closest worlds to the actual world in which the antecedent is true satisfy the consequent of the conditional.

Definition 5. *Let* $C = (S, f)$ *be a classifier model,* $s \in S$ *and* $X \subseteq (Atm \backslash Dec)$. *We say that "if* φ *was true then* ψ *would be true, relative to the set of features* X" *at* s, *noted* $(C, s) \models \varphi \Rightarrow_X \psi$, *if and only if* $closest_C(s, \varphi, X) \subseteq ||\psi||_C$ *where*

$$closest_C(s, \varphi, X) = \arg\max_{s' \in ||\varphi||_C} sim_C(s, s', X),$$

and for every $\varphi \in \mathcal{L}(Atm)$:

$$||\varphi||_C = \{s \in S : (C, s) \models \varphi\}.$$

---

[4] There are other options besides measuring distance by cardinality, e.g., distance in sense of subset relation as [2]. We will consider them in further research.

As the following proposition highlights the previous notion of counterfactual conditional is expressible in the language $\mathcal{L}(Atm)$.

Proposition 2. *Let $C = (S, f)$ be a classifier model, $s \in S$ and $X \subseteq (Atm \setminus Dec)$. Then,*

$$(C, s) \models \varphi \Rightarrow_X \psi \text{ if and only if}$$

$$(C, s) \models \bigwedge_{0 \leq k \leq |X|} \left(\mathsf{maxSim}(\varphi, X, k) \rightarrow \bigwedge_{Y \subseteq X : |Y| = k} [Y](\varphi \rightarrow \psi) \right),$$

with

$$\mathsf{maxSim}(\varphi, X, k) =_{def} \bigvee_{Y \subseteq X : |Y| = k} \langle Y \rangle \varphi \wedge \bigwedge_{Y \subseteq X : k < |Y|} [Y] \neg \varphi.$$

In light of the previous proposition, we can see $\varphi \Rightarrow_X \psi$ as an abbreviation of its corresponding $\mathcal{L}(Atm)$-formula.[5] For notational convenience, we simply write $\varphi \Rightarrow \psi$ instead of $\varphi \Rightarrow_{(Atm \setminus Dec)} \psi$. Formula $\varphi \Rightarrow \psi$ captures the standard notion of conditional of conditional logic. One can show that $\Rightarrow$ satisfies all semantic conditions of Lewis' logic VC.[6]

The interesting aspect of the previous notion of counterfactual conditional is that it can be used to represent a binary classifier's approximate decision for a given instance. Let us suppose the set of decision values Val includes a special symbol ? meaning that the classifier has no sufficient information enabling it to classify an instance in a precise way. More compactly, ? means that the classifier abstains from making a precise decision. In this situation, the classifier can try to make an approximate decision: it considers the closest instances to the actual instance for which it has sufficient information to make a decision and checks whether the decision is uniform among all such instances. In other words, x is the classifier's approximate classification of (or decision for) the actual instance, noted $\mathsf{apprDec}(x)$ if and only if "if a precise decision was made for the input then this decision would be x". Formally:

$$\mathsf{apprDec}(x) =_{def} \left(\bigvee_{y \in Val : y \neq ?} \mathsf{t}(y) \right) \Rightarrow \mathsf{t}(x).$$

The following proposition provides two interesting validities.

---

[5] A similar approach of ceteris paribus is [11]. They also refine Lewis' semantics for counterfactual by selecting the closest worlds according to not only the actual world and antecedent, but also a set of formulas where they note as Γ. The main technical difference is that they allow any counterfactual-free formula as a member of Γ, while in our setting X only contains atomic formulas.

[6] A remarkable fact is that not all $\Rightarrow_X$ satisfy the *strong centering* condition, which says that the actual world is the only closest world when the antecedent is already true here. To see it, consider a toy classifier model (C, s) such that $S = \{s, s', s'', s'''\}$ with $s = \{p, q\}$, $s' = \{p\}$, $s'' = \{q\}$, $s''' = \emptyset$. We have $closest_C(s, p, \emptyset) = \{s, s'\}$, rather than $closest_C(s, p, \emptyset) = \{s\}$. All the rest of conditions in VC are satisfied regardless of what X is.

Proposition 3. *Let* $x, y \in Val \setminus \{?\}$. *Then,*

$$\models_{\mathbf{CM}} \mathsf{apprDec}(x) \rightarrow \neg\mathsf{apprDec}(y) \text{ if } x \neq y,$$
$$\models_{\mathbf{CM}} \mathsf{t}(x) \rightarrow \mathsf{apprDec}(x).$$

According to the first validity, a classifier cannot make two different approximate decisions. According to the second validity, if the classifier is able to make a precise decision for a given instance, then its approximate decision coincides with it.

It is worth noting that the following formula is not valid relative to the class **CM**

$$\bigvee_{x \in Val \setminus \{?\}} \mathsf{apprDec}(x).$$

This means that a classifier may be unable to approximately classify the actual instance.

4 Explanations and Biases

We will formalize some existing notions of explanation of classifier in our model, and deepen the current study. For this purpose it is necessary to introduce the following notations. Given a classifier model $C = (S, f)$, for any $s \in S$, call $\hat{s} =_{def} \bigwedge_{p \in s} p \wedge \bigwedge_{p \notin s} \neg p$ an *instance*. Instances are special *terms*, a.k.a. *properties*, where a term $\lambda =_{def} \bigwedge_{p \in X} p \wedge \bigwedge_{p \in Y} \neg p$ for some $X, Y \subseteq (Atm \setminus Dec)$ such that $X \cap Y = \emptyset$; and by $\overline{\lambda}$ we mean $\bigwedge_{p \in X} \neg p \wedge \bigwedge_{p \in Y} p$. By convention $\top$ is a term of zero conjuncts. We say $\lambda \subseteq \lambda'$ when the set of literals included in λ is a subset of the set of literals included in λ', and $\lambda \subset \lambda'$ when $\lambda \subseteq \lambda'$ but $\lambda' \not\subseteq \lambda$. In this case we may say λ' is a part of λ. Additionally, to define bias we may distinguish the set of protected features PF, like gender and race, and the set of non-protected features NF, such that $\mathsf{PF} \cup \mathsf{NF} = (Atm \setminus Dec)$ and $\mathsf{PF} \cap \mathsf{NF} = \emptyset$.

4.1 Prime Implicant Expressed in CM

Now we are in position to formalize *prime implicant*, which plays a fundamental role in Boolean functions and in classifier explanations.

Definition 6 (Prime Implicant (PImp)). *Let* $C = (S, f) \in \mathbf{CM}$. *We call property* λ *an* implicant *of* x *w.r.t.* f *at* s, *if* $\forall s' \in S$, *if* $(C, s') \models \lambda$ *then* $f(s') = x$.

Moreover, we call property λ *a* prime implicant *of* x *w.r.t.* f *at* s, *noted* $(C, s) \models \mathsf{PImp}(\lambda, x)$, *if* λ *is an implicant of* x *w.r.t.* f *at* s, *and there is no* λ', *s.t.* $\lambda' \subseteq \lambda$, *and* λ' *is an implicant of* x *w.r.t.* f *at* s.

Notice that being a prime implicant is a global property of the classifier, though we formalize it by means of a pointed model. Obviously Definition 6 generalizes the definition of prime implicant of the pure Boolean function. If we take $Val = \{\texttt{True}, \texttt{False}\}$ and interpret x as $\texttt{True}$, we will recover the definition in e.g., [5].

As the following proposition highlights, the notion of prime implicant is expressible in the language $\mathcal{L}(Atm)$. Thus, like counterfactual conditional, we will conceive $\mathsf{PImp}(\lambda, x)$ as an abbreviation of its corresponding $\mathcal{L}(Atm)$-formula. We will do the same for the notions of abductive explanation, contrastive explanation and bias which will also be seen as abbreviations of corresponding $\mathcal{L}(Atm)$-formulas.

Proposition 4. *Let $C = (S, f) \in \mathbf{CM}$ and $s \in S$. We have $(C, s) \models \mathsf{PImp}(\lambda, x)$ iff*

$$(C, s) \models [\emptyset]\big(\lambda \to (\mathsf{t}(x) \land \bigwedge_{p \in Atm(\lambda)} \langle Atm(\lambda) \setminus \{p\}\rangle \neg \mathsf{t}(x))\big)$$

The following proposition shows the relation between prime implicants of a classifier and the essential set of its model.

Proposition 5. *Let $C = (S, f) \in \mathbf{CM}$. C is X-essential, if $\forall p \in (Atm \setminus Dec)$, $p \in X$ iff for some $x \in Val$ there is a prime implicant λ of x w.r.t. f and $p \in Atm(\lambda)$.*

4.2   Abductive Explanation (AXp)

Theoretically, knowing all prime implicants helps make the classifier transparent and understandable to humans. However, prime implicants are hard to list. Therefore, many researchers focus on prime implicants of a given input [7,17]. In such a way the explanation stays "local".

Definition 7 (Abductive Explanation (AXp)). *Let $C = (S, f) \in \mathbf{CM}$ and $s \in S$. We say property λ abductively explains the decision x of f at s, noted $(C, s) \models \mathsf{AXp}(\lambda, x)$, if $(C, s) \models \lambda \land \mathsf{PImp}(\lambda, x)$.*

The two conjuncts indicate respectively that 1) λ is a part of instance $\widehat{s}$, i.e. $\lambda \subseteq \widehat{s}$, since λ is true at s; 2) λ is a prime implicant of x. Notice that 1) uses the fact that $(C, s) \models \lambda$ iff $\widehat{s} \to \lambda$ is a propositional logical tautology.

Many names besides AXp are found in literature, e.g. *PI-explanation* and *sufficient reason* [7]. We prefer the name AXp used by Ignatiev et al. [17,18] because of its connection with CXp in the next subsection. Darwiche and Hirth in [7] proved that any decision has a sufficient reason, in our setting:

Proposition 6. *Let $C = (S, f) \in \mathbf{CM}$, $s \in S$ and $f(s) = x$. We have $(C, s) \models \mathsf{AXp}(\lambda, x)$ for some property $\lambda \subseteq \widehat{s}$.*

We can show it by Proposition 1.3 that C is always X-essential for some X, which means $\bigwedge_{p \in s \cap X} p \wedge \bigwedge_{p \notin s \& p \in X} \neg p$ contain all AXps that we look for. Notice that when C is trivial, $X = \emptyset$ and λ is $\top$, which by convention is the conjunction of zero literal.

Last, let us continue with the Alice example.

Example 3. In Alice's case, since $\widehat{s}$ is the instance $\neg p_1 \wedge p_2 \wedge q_1 \wedge \neg q_2$, (recall $s = \{p_2, q_1\}$), we have $(C, s) \models \mathsf{AXp}(\neg p_1 \wedge \neg q_2, y)$, namely that Alice's being female and not owning a property abductively explains the rejection.

4.3   Contrastive Explanation (CXp)

AXp is a minimal part of a given instance $\widehat{s}$ verifying the current decision. A natural counterpart of AXp, contrastive explanation (CXp, named in [17]), is a minimal part of $\widehat{s}$ which falsifies the current decision.

Definition 8 (Contrastive Explanation (CXp)). *Let* $C = (S, f) \in \mathbf{CM}$, $s \in S$, *and* $f(s) = x$. *We say that* λ *contrastively explains the decision* x *of* f *at* s, *noted* $(C, s) \models \mathsf{CXp}(\lambda, x)$, *if* $\lambda \subseteq \widehat{s}$; $\exists s' \in S$, *s.t.* $s \triangle s' = Atm(\lambda)$, *and* $f(s') \neq x$; *and* $\forall s'' \in S$, $s \triangle s'' \subset Atm(\lambda)$ *implies* $f(s'') = x$.[7]

In plain words, λ is a CXp of x at s, if λ is a part of $\widehat{s}$; changing the valuation of every atom in λ falsifies the current decision; and no falsification happens when we only consider changing the valuation of a proper part of λ. Like prime implicant and abductive explanation, the language $\mathcal{L}(Atm)$ is expressive enough to capture contrastive explanation.

Proposition 7. *Let* $C = (S, f) \in \mathbf{CM}$ *and* $s \in S$. $(C, s) \models \mathsf{CXp}(\lambda, x)$ *iff*

$$(C, s) \models \lambda \wedge \mathsf{t}(x) \wedge \langle Atm \setminus Atm(\lambda) \rangle \neg \mathsf{t}(x) \wedge \bigwedge_{p \in Atm(\lambda)} [(Atm \setminus Atm(\lambda)) \cup \{p\}] \mathsf{t}(x).$$

We define CXp by minimizing the change from the current input, while in defining counterfactual conditional we maximize the similarity. It makes one question whether these are two paths towards the same end. Actually in XAI, many researchers consider contrastive explanations and counterfactual explanations either closely related [32], or even interchangeable [26]. Our framework agrees that CXp has a counterfactual nature in light of the next proposition.

Proposition 8. *We have the following validity:*

$$\models_{\mathbf{CM}} \mathsf{CXp}(\lambda, x) \to (\overline{\lambda} \Rightarrow \neg \mathsf{t}(x)).$$

Proof. For any $C = (S, f) \in \mathbf{CM}$ and $s \in S$, suppose $(C, s) \models \mathsf{CXp}(\lambda, x)$, we need to show $(C, s) \models \overline{\lambda} \Rightarrow \neg \mathsf{t}(x)$. By the antecedent, $\exists s' \in S$, s.t. $s \triangle s' = Atm(\lambda)$ and $f(s') \neq x$. It is not hard to show that $closest_C(s, \overline{\lambda}, Atm) = \{s'\}$. Therefore $(C, s) \models \overline{\lambda} \Rightarrow \neg \mathsf{t}(x)$, since $closest_C(s, \overline{\lambda}, Atm) \subseteq \|\neg \mathsf{t}(x)\|_C$.   ∎

---

[7] The symbol $\triangle$ denotes symmetric difference.

Notice that $\models_{\mathbf{CM}} (\overline{\lambda} \Rightarrow \neg t(x)) \rightarrow \mathsf{CXp}(\lambda, x)$ does not hold. Consider the pointed model in the proof above: for any property λ' s.t. $\lambda \subset \lambda' \subseteq \hat{s}$, we have $(C, s) \models \overline{\lambda}' \Rightarrow \neg t(x)$, but $(C, s) \models \neg\mathsf{CXp}(\lambda', x)$. Hence, we view CXp as a special kind of counterfactual, whose antecedent needs to be minimal.

Example 4. In Alice's case, $(C, s) \models \mathsf{CXp}(\neg p_1, y) \wedge \mathsf{CXp}(\neg q_2, y)$, namely both Alice's being female and not owning property contrastively explain the rejection.

Moreover, since gender is hard to change, owing a property is the (relatively) *actionable* explanation for Alice[8], if she wants to follow the rule of f. But surely Alice has another option, i.e. alleging the classifier as biased. As we will see in the next subsection, an application of CXp is to detect decision bias.

4.4   Decision Bias

A primary goal of XAI is to detect and avoid biases. Bias is understood as making decision w.r.t. some protected features, e.g. race, gender and age.

A widely accepted notion of decision bias, see e.g. [7,16], can be expressed in our setting as follows. Intuitively, the rejection for Alice is biased, if there is a Bob, who only differs from Alice on some protected feature, but gets accepted.

Definition 9 (Decision Bias). *Let* $C = (S, f) \in \mathbf{CM}$, $s \in S$, *and* $f(s) = x$. *We say that the decision* x *of* f *at* s *is biased, noted* $(C, s) \models \mathsf{Bias}(x)$, *if* $\exists s' \in S$, *s.t.* $s \triangle s' \subseteq \mathsf{PF}$ *and* $f(s') \neq x$.

The notion of bias is also expressible in our language.

Proposition 9. *Let* $C = (S, f) \in \mathbf{CM}$ *and* $s \in S$. *Then,* $(C, s) \models \mathsf{Bias}(x)$ *iff*

$$(C, s) \models t(x) \wedge \bigvee_{X \subseteq \mathsf{PF}} \langle Atm \setminus X \rangle \neg t(x).$$

Let us answer the last question regarding Alice raised at the end of Sect. 2.1.

Example 5. Split $(Atm \setminus Dec)$ in Example 1 into $\mathsf{PF} = \{p_1, p_2\}$ and $\mathsf{NF} = \{q_1, q_2\}$. We then have $(C, s) \models \mathsf{Bias}(y)$. The decision for Alice is biased, since gender is the protected feature responsible for the rejection, a bias as we want to model.

As we stated, CXp can be used to detect decision bias. Actually, we have $(C, s) \models \mathsf{CXp}(\neg p_1, y)$, i.e. being female contrastively explains Alice's rejection; and $(C, s) \models p_1 \Rightarrow t(x)$, namely if Alice were male, she would get accepted. The following result makes the statement precise.

Proposition 10. *We have the following validity:*

$$\models_{\mathbf{CM}} \mathsf{Bias}(x) \leftrightarrow \bigvee_{Atm(\lambda) \subseteq \mathsf{PF}} \mathsf{CXp}(\lambda, x).$$

---

[8] For the significance of actionablility in XAI, see e.g. [26].

Proof. We show that for any $C = (S, f) \in \mathbf{CM}$ and $s \in S$, both directions are satisfied in (C, s). The right to left direction is obvious, since from the antecedent we know there is a property λ' s.t. $\exists s' \in S, s \triangle s' = Atm(\lambda') \subseteq \mathsf{PF}$ and $(C, s') \models \neg\mathsf{t}(x)$, which means $(C, s) \models \mathsf{Bias}(x)$. The other direction is proven by contraposition. Suppose for any λ s.t. $Atm(\lambda) \subseteq \mathsf{PF}$, $(C, s) \models \neg\mathsf{CXp}(\lambda, x)$, then it means $\forall s' \in S$, if $s \triangle s' = Atm(\lambda)$, then $f(s') = x$, which means $(C, s) \models \neg\mathsf{Bias}(x)$.   ∎

5   Axiomatization and Complexity

In this section we provide a sound and complete axiomatics for the language $\mathcal{L}(Atm)$ relative to the formal semantics defined above. The following abbreviation is given for the sake of compactness, for every finite $X, Y \subseteq Atm$:

$$\mathsf{cn}_{Y,X} =_{def} \bigwedge_{p \in Y} p \wedge \bigwedge_{p \in X \setminus Y} \neg p.$$

Definition 10 (Logic BCL). *We define* BCL *(Binary Classifier Logic) to be the extension of classical propositional logic given by the following axioms and rules of inference:*

$$([\emptyset]\varphi \wedge [\emptyset](\varphi \to \psi)) \to [\emptyset]\psi \tag{$\mathbf{K}_{[\emptyset]}$}$$

$$[\emptyset]\varphi \to \varphi \tag{$\mathbf{T}_{[\emptyset]}$}$$

$$[\emptyset]\varphi \to [\emptyset][\emptyset]\varphi \tag{$\mathbf{4}_{[\emptyset]}$}$$

$$\varphi \to [\emptyset]\langle\emptyset\rangle\varphi \tag{$\mathbf{B}_{[\emptyset]}$}$$

$$[X]\varphi \leftrightarrow \bigwedge_{Y \subseteq X} \left(\mathsf{cn}_{Y,X} \to [\emptyset](\mathsf{cn}_{Y,X} \to \varphi)\right) \tag{$\mathbf{Red}_{[\emptyset]}$}$$

$$\bigvee_{x \in Val} \mathsf{t}(x) \tag{$\mathbf{AtLeast}_{\mathsf{t}(x)}$}$$

$$\mathsf{t}(x) \to \neg\mathsf{t}(y) \; \textit{if } x \neq y \tag{$\mathbf{AtMost}_{\mathsf{t}(x)}$}$$

$$\bigwedge_{Y \subseteq (Atm \setminus Dec)} \left((\mathsf{cn}_{Y,(Atm \setminus Dec)} \wedge \mathsf{t}(x)) \to [\emptyset](\mathsf{cn}_{Y,(Atm \setminus Dec)} \to \mathsf{t}(x))\right) \tag{$\mathbf{Def}$}$$

$$\bigwedge_{X \subseteq (Atm \setminus Dec)} \langle\emptyset\rangle\mathsf{cn}_{X,(Atm \setminus Dec)} \tag{$\mathbf{Comp}$}$$

$$\frac{\varphi \to \psi \quad \varphi}{\psi} \tag{$\mathbf{MP}$}$$

$$\frac{\varphi}{[\emptyset]\varphi} \tag{$\mathbf{Nec}_{[\emptyset]}$}$$

It can be seen that $[\emptyset]$ is an S5 style modal operator, $\mathbf{Red}_{[\emptyset]}$ reduces any $[X]$ to $[\emptyset]$. $\mathbf{AtLeast}_{\mathsf{t}(x)}$, $\mathbf{AtMost}_{\mathsf{t}(x)}$, $\mathbf{Def}$ represent the decision function syntactically, that every $cn_{Y, Atm \backslash Dec}$ maps to some unique $t(x)$.[9] **Comp** ensures the function is total.

The following theorem highlights that the logic BCL is sound and complete relative to its corresponding semantics. The proof is entirely standard and based on a canonical model argument.

Theorem 1. *The logic* BCL *is sound and complete relative to the class* **CM**.

The following theorem provides a complexity result for checking satisfiability of formulas in $\mathcal{L}(Atm)$ relative to the class **CM**. The proof of the complexity result is based on three steps. First, we have that validity relative to the class **CM** is equivalent to validity relative to the class of *ceteris paribus* models presented in [12] that "globally" satisfy a finite set of formulas corresponding to the axioms in $\{$**AtLeast**$_{t(x)}$, **AtMost**$_{t(x)}$, **Def**, **Comp**$\}$. The size of such a set of formulas is constant and does not depend on the size of the formula to be checked. Therefore, we can polynomially reduce satisfiability checking relative to class **CM** to satisfiability checking relative to such a model class. In [12] it is shown that, if the set of atomic propositions is finite, then the latter problem is in NP. This gives NP-membership for our logic. NP-hardness follows from NP-hardness of propositional logic.

Theorem 2. *Checking satisfiability of formulas in* $\mathcal{L}(Atm)$ *relative to* **CM** *is NP-complete.*

6   Extensions

In this section, we briefly discuss two interesting extensions of our logical framework and analysis of binary classifiers. Their full development is left for future work.

6.1   Dynamic Extension

The first extension we want to discuss consists in adding to the language $\mathcal{L}(Atm)$ dynamic operators of the form $[x := \varphi]$ with $x \in Dec$, where $x := \varphi$ is a kind of assignment in the sense of [27,31] and the formula $[x := \varphi]\psi$ has to be read "ψ holds after every decision is set to x in context φ". The resulting language, noted $\mathcal{L}^{dyn}(Atm)$, is defined by the following grammar:

$$\varphi ::= p \mid \neg\varphi \mid \varphi_1 \wedge \varphi_2 \mid [X]\varphi \mid [x := \varphi]\psi$$

where p ranges over Atm, X ranges over $AtmSet$ and x ranges over Dec. The interpretation of formula $[x := \varphi]\psi$ relative to a pointed classifier model (C, s) with $C = (S, f)$ goes as follows:

$$(C, s) \models [x := \varphi]\psi \Longleftrightarrow (C^{x := \varphi}, s) \models \psi,$$

---

[9] Notice that $cn_{Y, Atm \backslash Dec}$ is just another expression of $\widehat{s}$ where $s = Y$.

where $C^{x:=\varphi} = (S, f^{x:=\varphi})$ is the updated classifier model where, for every $s' \in S$:

$$f^{x:=\varphi}(s') = \begin{cases} x \text{ if } (C, s') \models \varphi, \\ f(s') \text{ otherwise.} \end{cases}$$

Intuitively, the operation $x := \varphi$ consists in globally classifying all instances satisfying φ with value x.

Dynamic operators $[x := \varphi]$ are useful for modeling a classifier's revision. Specifically, new knowledge can be injected into the classifier thereby leading to a change in its classification. For example, the classifier could learn that if an object is a furniture, has one or more legs and has a flat top, then it is a table. This is captured by the following assignment:

$$\text{table} := objIsFurniture \wedge objHasLegs \wedge objHasFlatTop.$$

An application of dynamic change is to model the training process of a classifier, together with counterfactual conditionals with ? in Sect. 3. Suppose at the beginning we have a CM $C = (S, f)$ which is totally ignorant, i.e. $\forall s \in S, f(s) =?$. We then prepare to train the classifier. The training set consists of pairs $(s_1, x_1), (s_2, x_2) \ldots (s_n, x_n)$ where $\forall i \in \{1, \ldots, n\}, s_i \in S, x_i \in (Val \backslash \{?\})$ and $\forall j \in \{1, \ldots, n\}, i \neq j$ implies $s_i \neq s_j$. We train the classifier by revising it with $[x_1 = \hat{s}_1] \ldots [x_n = \hat{s}_n]$ one by one. Obviously the order does not matter here. In other words, we re-classify some states. With a bit abuse of notation, let $C^{train} = (S, f^{train})$ denote the model resulting from the series of revisions. We finish training by inducing the final model $C^\dagger = (S, f^\dagger)$ from C^{train}, where $\forall s \in S, f^\dagger(s) = x$, if $(C^{train}, s) \models \text{apprDec}(x)$, otherwise $f^\dagger(s) = f^{train}(s)$.

The logic BCL−DC (BCL with Decision Change) extends the logic BCL by the dynamic operators $[x := \varphi]$. It is defined as follows.

Definition 11 (Logic BCL−DC). *We define* BCL−DC *(BCL with Decision Change) to be the extension of* BCL *of Definition 10 generated by the following reduction axioms for the dynamic operators* $[x := \varphi]$:

$$[x := \varphi]\text{t}(x) \leftrightarrow (\varphi \vee \text{t}(x))$$
$$[x := \varphi]\text{t}(y) \leftrightarrow (\neg\varphi \wedge \text{t}(y)) \text{ if } x \neq y$$
$$[x := \varphi]p \leftrightarrow p \text{ if } p \notin Dec$$
$$[x := \varphi]\neg\psi \leftrightarrow \neg[x := \varphi]\psi$$
$$[x := \varphi](\psi_1 \wedge \psi_2) \leftrightarrow ([x := \varphi]\psi_1 \wedge [x := \varphi]\psi_2)$$
$$[x := \varphi][X]\psi \leftrightarrow [X][x := \varphi]\psi$$

and the following rule of inference:

$$\frac{\varphi_1 \leftrightarrow \varphi_2}{\psi \leftrightarrow \psi[\varphi_1/\varphi_2]} \tag{RE}$$

It is routine exercise to verify that the equivalences in Definition 11 are valid for the class **CM** and that the rule of replacement of equivalents (RE) preserves validity. The completeness of $\mathsf{BCL-DC}$ for this class of models follows from Theorem 1, in view of the fact that the reduction axioms and the rule of replacement of proved equivalents can be used to find, for any $\mathcal{L}^{dyn}$-formula, a provably equivalent $\mathcal{L}$-formula.

Theorem 3. *The logic* $\mathsf{BCL-DC}$ *is sound and complete relative to the class* **CM**.

The following complexity result is a consequence of Theorem 2 and the fact that via the reduction axioms in Definition 11 we can find a polynomial reduction of satisfiability checking for formulas in $\mathcal{L}^{dyn}$ to satisfiability checking for formulas in $\mathcal{L}$.

Theorem 4. *Checking satisfiability of formulas in* $\mathcal{L}^{dyn}(Atm)$ *relative to* **CM** *is NP-complete.*

6.2 Epistemic Extension

In the second extension we consider that, a classifier is conceived as an agent which has to classify what it perceives. The agent could have uncertainty about the actual instance to be classified since it cannot see all its features.

In order to represent the agent's epistemic state and uncertainty, we slightly redefine the set of atomic formulas Atm. We note Atm_0 the set of basic atoms and assume that $Dec \cap Atm_0 = \emptyset$, where Dec is the set of decision atoms defined in Sect. 2.1. Then, we define:

$$Atm = Atm_0 \cup Dec \cup \{\mathsf{o}(p) : p \in Atm_0\},$$

where $\mathsf{o}(p)$ is a 'observability' (or 'visibility') atom in the sense of [4,15,28,29] which has to be read "the agent can see the truth value of p". For notational convenience, we note $ObsAtm = \{\mathsf{o}(p) : p \in Atm_0\}$.

The language for our epistemic extension is noted $\mathcal{L}^{epi}(Atm)$ and defined by the following grammar:

$$\varphi ::= p \mid \neg\varphi \mid \varphi_1 \wedge \varphi_2 \mid [X]\varphi \mid \mathsf{K}\varphi,$$

where p ranges over Atm and X ranges over $AtmSet$.

The epistemic operator K is used to represent what agent i knows in the light of what it sees. In order to interpret this new modality, we have to enrich classifier models with an epistemic component.

Definition 12 (Epistemic classifier model). *An epistemic classifier model (ECM) is a tuple* $C = (S, f, \sim)$ *where* $C = (S, f)$ *is a classifier model such that, for all* $s, s' \in S$:

$$\text{if } (s \cap Atm_0) = (s' \cap Atm_0) \text{ then } f(s) = f(s'),$$

and ~ is a binary relation on S such that, for all s, s' ∈ S:

$$s \sim s' \text{ if and only if } (i) \; Obs(s) = Obs(s') \text{ and}$$
$$(ii) \; (s \cap ObsAtm) = (s' \cap ObsAtm),$$

where, for every s ∈ S, Obs(s) = {p ∈ Atm₀ : o(p) ∈ s} is the set of atomic propositions that are visible to the agent at s.

The class of ECMs is noted **ECM**.

According to Definition 12, the classification of a given input instance should only depend on its features captured by basic atoms. In other words, observability atoms are irrelevant for classification. Furthermore, the agent cannot distinguish between two states s and s' if and only if (i) the truth values of the visible variables are the same at s and s', and (ii) what the agent can see is the same at s and s'. The way the epistemic accessibility relation $\sim$ is defined guarantees that it is an equivalence relation.

Proposition 11. *Let C = (S, f, ~) be a ECM. Then, the relation ~ is reflexive, transitive and symmetric.*

The interpretation for formulas in $\mathcal{L}^{epi}(Atm)$ extends the interpretation for formulas in $\mathcal{L}(Atm)$ given in Definition 2 by the following condition for the epistemic operator:

$$(C, s) \models \mathsf{K}\varphi \Longleftrightarrow \forall s' \in S : \text{ if } s \sim s' \text{ then } (C, s') \models \varphi.$$

The following are three interesting validities of our epistemic extension:

$$\models_{\mathbf{ECM}} \mathsf{o}(p) \rightarrow \big((p \rightarrow \mathsf{K}p) \wedge (\neg p \rightarrow \mathsf{K}\neg p)\big), \tag{1}$$

$$\models_{\mathbf{ECM}} \mathsf{o}(p) \leftrightarrow \mathsf{K} \, \mathsf{o}(p), \tag{2}$$

$$\models_{\mathbf{ECM}} \Big(\bigwedge_{p \in Atm_0} \mathsf{o}(p) \wedge \mathsf{t}(x) \Big) \rightarrow \mathsf{K} \, \mathsf{t}(x). \tag{3}$$

According to the first validity, the agent knows the truth value of each variable it can see. According to the second validity, the agent knows what it can see. Finally, according to the third validity, if the agent can see all features of the input, then it has no uncertainty about the classification of the actual instance. Indeed, the agent's uncertainty about the classification is only determined by the imperfect visibility of the input features (if all features are visible, then the agent has no uncertainty about how the input should be classified).

As the following theorem indicates, the complexity result of Sect. 5 generalizes to the epistemic extension. It is based on (i) the fact that for every formula in $\mathcal{L}^{epi}(Atm)$ we can find an equivalent formula in $\mathcal{L}(Atm)$ with no epistemic operators, (ii) the adaptation of the polynomial satisfiability preserving translation from $\mathcal{L}(Atm)$ to the modal logic S5 given in [12].

Theorem 5. *Checking satisfiability of formulas in $\mathcal{L}^{epi}(Atm)$ relative to **ECM** is NP-complete.*

7   Conclusion

We have introduced a modal language and a formal semantics that allow us to capture the *ceteris paribus* nature of binary classifiers. We have formalized in the language a variety of notions which are relevant for understanding a classifier's behavior including counterfactual conditional, abductive and contrastive explanation, bias. We have provided two extensions that support reasoning about classifier change and a classifier's uncertainty about the actual instance to be classified. We have also offered axiomatics and complexity results for our logical setting.

We believe that the complexity results presented in the paper are exploitable in practice. We have shown that satisfiability checking in the basic *ceteris paribus* setting and in its epistemic extension are NP-complete. Indeed, both problems are polynomially reducible to satisfiability checking in the modal logic S5 for which a polynomial satisfiability preserving translation into propositional logic exists [3]. This opens up the possibility of using SAT solvers for automated verification and generation of explanation and bias in binary classifiers. We plan to focus on this topic in future research.

Another direction of future research is the generalization of the epistemic extension given in Sect. 6.2 to the multi-agent case. The idea is to conceive classifiers as agents and to be able to represent both the agents' uncertainty about the instance to be classified and their knowledge and uncertainty about other agents' knowledge and uncertainty (i.e., higher-order knowledge and uncertainty).

Finally, we plan to investigate more in depth classifier dynamics we briefly discussed in Sect. 6.1. The idea is to see them as learning dynamics. Based on this idea, we plan to study the problem of finding a sequence of update operations guaranteeing that the classifier will be able to make approximate decisions for a given set of instances.

Acknowledgements. Support from the ANR-3IA Artificial and Natural Intelligence Toulouse Institute is gratefully acknowledged.

References

1. Biran, O., Cotton, C.: Explanation and justification in machine learning: a survey. In: IJCAI 2017 Workshop on Explainable AI (XAI), vol. 8, no. 1, pp. 8–13 (2017)
2. Borgida, A.: Language features for flexible handling of exceptions in information systems. ACM Trans. Database Syst. (TODS) 10(4), 565–603 (1985)
3. Caridroit, T., Lagniez, J.-M., Le Berre, D., de Lima, T., Montmirail, V.: A SAT-based approach for solving the modal logic S5-satisfiability problem. In: Proceedings of the Thirty-First AAAI Conference on Artificial Intelligence (AAAI 2017), pp. 3864–3870. AAAI Press (2017)
4. Charrier, T., Herzig, A., Lorini, E., Maffre, F., Schwarzentruber, F.: Building epistemic logic from observations and public announcements. In: Proceedings of the Fifteenth International Conference on Principles of Knowledge Representation and Reasoning (KR 2016), pp. 268–277. AAAI Press (2016)

5. Crama, Y., Hammer, P.L.: Boolean Functions: Theory, Algorithms, and Applications. Cambridge University Press, Cambridge (2011)
6. Dalal, M.: Investigations into a theory of knowledge base revision: preliminary report. In: Proceedings of the Seventh National Conference on Artificial Intelligence, vol. 2, pp. 475–479. Citeseer (1988)
7. Darwiche, A., Hirth, A.: On the reasons behind decisions. In: 24th European Conference on Artificial Intelligence, ECAI 2020. Frontiers in Artificial Intelligence and Applications, vol. 325, pp. 712–720. IOS Press (2020)
8. Dhurandhar, A., et al.: Explanations based on the missing: towards contrastive explanations with pertinent negatives. In: Advances in Neural Information Processing Systems, pp. 592–603 (2018)
9. Dretske, F: Meaningful perception. An Invitation to Cognitive Science: Visual Cognition, pp. 331–352 (1995)
10. Fagin, R., Moses, Y., Halpern, J.Y., Vardi, M.Y.: Reasoning about Knowledge. MIT Press, Cambridge (1995)
11. Girard, P., Triplett, M.A.: Ceteris paribus logic in counterfactual reasoning. In: TARK 2015, pp. 176–193 (2016)
12. Grossi, D., Lorini, E., Schwarzentruber, F.: The ceteris paribus structure of logics of game forms. J. Artif. Intell. Res. **53**, 91–126 (2015)
13. Hempel, C.G., Oppenheim, P.: Studies in the logic of explanation. Philos. Sci. **15**(2), 135–175 (1948)
14. Herzig, A., Lorini, E.: A modal logic of perceptual belief. In: Lihoreau, F., Rebuschi, M. (eds.) Epistemology, Context, and Formalism. SL, vol. 369, pp. 197–211. Springer, Cham (2014). https://doi.org/10.1007/978-3-319-02943-6_12
15. Herzig, A., Lorini, E., Maffre, F.: A poor man's epistemic logic based on propositional assignment and higher-order observation. In: van der Hoek, W., Holliday, W.H., Wang, W. (eds.) LORI 2015. LNCS, vol. 9394, pp. 156–168. Springer, Heidelberg (2015). https://doi.org/10.1007/978-3-662-48561-3_13
16. Ignatiev, A., Cooper, M.C., Siala, M., Hebrard, E., Marques-Silva, J.: Towards formal fairness in machine learning. In: Simonis, H. (ed.) CP 2020. LNCS, vol. 12333, pp. 846–867. Springer, Cham (2020). https://doi.org/10.1007/978-3-030-58475-7_49
17. Ignatiev, A., Narodytska, N., Asher, N., Marques-Silva, J.: From contrastive to abductive explanations and back again. In: Baldoni, M., Bandini, S. (eds.) AIxIA 2020. LNCS (LNAI), vol. 12414, pp. 335–355. Springer, Cham (2021). https://doi.org/10.1007/978-3-030-77091-4_21
18. Ignatiev, A., Narodytska, N., Marques-Silva, J.: Abduction-based explanations for machine learning models. In: Proceedings of the AAAI Conference on Artificial Intelligence, vol. 33, pp. 1511–1519 (2019)
19. Kment, B.: Counterfactuals and explanation. Mind **115**(458), 261–310 (2006)
20. Lewis, D.: Counterfactuals. Harvard University Press, Cambridge (1973)
21. Martens, D., Provost, F.: Explaining data-driven document classifications. MIS Q. **38**(1), 73–100 (2014)
22. Mittelstadt, B., Russell, C., Wachter, S.: Explaining explanations in AI. In: Proceedings of the Conference on Fairness, Accountability, and Transparency, pp. 279–288 (2019)
23. Mothilal, R.K., Sharma, A., Tan, C.: Explaining machine learning classifiers through diverse counterfactual explanations. In: Proceedings of the 2020 Conference on Fairness, Accountability, and Transparency, pp. 607–617 (2020)
24. Quine, W.V.: A way to simplify truth functions. Am. Math. Mon. **62**(9), 627–631 (1955)

25. Shi, W., Shih, A., Darwiche, A., Choi, A.: On tractable representations of binary neural networks. arXiv preprint arXiv:2004.02082 (2020)
26. Sokol, K., Flach, P.A.: Counterfactual explanations of machine learning predictions: opportunities and challenges for AI safety. In: SafeAI@ AAAI (2019)
27. Van Benthem, J., Van Eijck, J., Kooi, B.: Logics of communication and change. Inf. Comput. **204**(11), 1620–1662 (2006)
28. van der Hoek, W., Iliev, P., Wooldridge, M.J.: A logic of revelation and concealment. In: Proceedings of the International Conference on Autonomous Agents and Multiagent Systems, (AAMAS 2012), pp. 1115–1122. IFAAMAS (2012)
29. Van Der Hoek, W., Troquard, N., Wooldridge, M.J.: Knowledge and control. In: Proceedings of the 10th International Conference on Autonomous Agents and Multiagent Systems (AAMAS 2021), pp. 719–726. IFAAMAS (2011)
30. van Ditmarsch, H., van Der Hoek, W., Kooi, B.: Dynamic Epistemic Logic. Synthese Library, vol. 337. Springer, Heidelberg (2007)
31. van Ditmarsch, H.P., van der Hoek, W., Kooi, B.P.: Dynamic epistemic logic with assignment. In: Proceedings of the 4th International Joint Conference on Autonomous Agents and Multiagent Systems (AAMAS 2005), pp. 141–148. ACM (2005)
32. Verma, S., Dickerson, J., Hines, K.: Counterfactual explanations for machine learning: a review. arXiv preprint arXiv:2010.10596 (2020)

Extension-Based Semantics for Incomplete Argumentation Frameworks

Jean-Guy Mailly$^{(\boxtimes)}$ iD

LIPADE, University of Paris, Paris, France
jean-guy.mailly@u-paris.fr

Abstract. Incomplete Argumentation Frameworks (IAFs) have been defined to incorporate some qualitative uncertainty in abstract argumentation: information such as "I am not sure whether this argument exists" or "I am not sure whether this argument attacks that one" can be expressed. Reasoning with IAFs is classically based on a set of completions, *i.e.* standard argumentation frameworks that represent the possible worlds encoded in the IAF. The number of these completions may be exponential with respect to the number of arguments in the IAF. This leads, in some cases, to an increase of the complexity of reasoning, compared to the complexity of standard AFs. In this paper, we follow an approach that was initiated for Partial AFs (a subclass of IAFs), which consists in defining new forms of conflict-freeness and defense, the properties that underly the definition of Dung's semantics for AFs. We generalize these semantics from PAFs to IAFs. We show that, among three possible types of admissibility, only two of them satisfy some desirable properties. We use them to define two new families of extension-based semantics. We study the properties of these semantics, and in particular we show that their complexity remains the same as in the case of Dung's AFs. Finally, we propose a logical encoding of these semantics, that paves the way to the development of SAT-based solvers for reasoning with our new semantics for IAFs.

Keywords: Abstract argumentation · Uncertainty

1 Introduction

Abstract argumentation has been a major subfield of Knowledge Representation and Reasoning since the seminal paper by Dung [14]. However, although it is very appealing, Dung's framework is limited in the kind of information that can be modeled: only (abstract) arguments and attacks between them. For this reason, many generalization of this framework have been proposed, introducing the notion of support between arguments [2], weighted attacks [15] or arguments [26], preferences between arguments [1], and so on.

Among these generalizations of Dung's framework, a very natural research direction is the introduction of uncertainty in the model. Indeed, uncertainty

© Springer Nature Switzerland AG 2021
P. Baroni et al. (Eds.): CLAR 2021, LNAI 13040, pp. 322–341, 2021.
https://doi.org/10.1007/978-3-030-89391-0_18

is omnipresent in real world, and must be taken into account in the modeling of agents that reason about their environment or about other agents. Moreover, when arguments are generated from natural language processing [21], the nuances that exist in natural language are likely to be sources of uncertainty [5] that should appear in the formal model. Two directions have been followed for integrating uncertainty in abstract argumentation: quantitative representation of uncertainties (*e.g.* probabilities [19,22]) and qualitative ones [6,11,12]. While quantitative representation of uncertainty is valuable when it is available, allowing fine grained reasoning about uncertainty, it may not be available in many realistic cases. The study of qualitative models of uncertainty is thus of utter importance for the design of AI systems.

In this paper, we follow this direction. Qualitative uncertainty in abstract argumentation was originally studied in a context of Argumentation Framework (AF) merging [12]: Partial Argumentation Frameworks (PAFs) are AFs with possible ignorance about the existence of some attacks. Semantics dedicated to these PAFs were then defined in [11]. However, most of the work in this field focuses on a generalization of PAFs, namely Incomplete AFs (IAFs), and reasoning is based on *completions*. A completion is an argumentation framework that represents one of the (uncertain) options encoded in the IAF. Classical reasoning tasks are then adapted in two versions: the possible view (is some property true for some completion?) and the necessary view (is some property true for each completion?). However, the number of completions is (in the worst case) exponential in the number of arguments. This means that various reasoning problems are harder for IAFs than their counterpart for standard AFs [6,8,18].

In this paper, we follow the approach initiated by [11]: we define new forms of conflict-freeness and defense based on the different types of information in an IAF. The combination of a notion of conflict-freeness and a notion of defense yields a notion of admissibility; we show that among the three possible variants of admissibility, only two of them satisfy some desirable property, namely Dung's Fundamental Lemma. This lemma states, in classical AFs, that an admissible set remains admissible if an argument defended by it is added to the set. From the two "fundamental" notions of admissibility for IAFs, we define variants of the classical complete, preferred and stable semantics. We study some properties of these semantics, and we show that their complexity remains the same as in the standard AF case. Finally, we propose logical encodings, in the same vein as [9], that pave the way to SAT-based implementations for reasoning with our new semantics.

The rest of the paper is organized as follows. Section 2 describes the background notions on abstract argumentation. In Sect. 3, we define our new semantics and study some of their properties, in particular the satisfaction of the Fundamental Lemma, and some inclusion relations between them. In Sect. 4, we show that the complexity remains the same as in the standard AF case,[1] and we provide a logical encoding for our semantics. Finally, Sect. 5 describes some related work, and Sect. 6 concludes the paper.

---

[1] At the exception of skeptical acceptability under the complete semantics, for which we do not have a tight complexity result yet.

2   Background

2.1   Abstract Argumentation Frameworks

Abstract argumentation is the study of relations between abstract pieces of information called *arguments*; the internal nature of arguments, as well as their origin, is considered as irrelevant. Only the interactions between arguments are considered in order to determine which arguments are acceptable or not. The most classical type of relationship is the so-called *attack* relation, that expresses a contradiction between arguments. An attack is generally directed from one argument to another one, meaning that the first one somehow *defeats* the second one. The seminal paper [14] has launched the strong interest for abstract argumentation in the last 25 years. In this section, we formally introduce this abstract framework and how it is used for reasoning.

We suppose the existence of a finite set of arguments $\mathbf{A}$.

Definition 1 (Argumentation Framework). *An argumentation framework (AF) is a pair $\mathcal{F} = \langle \mathcal{A}, \mathcal{R} \rangle$ with $\mathcal{A} \subseteq \mathbf{A}$ the set of arguments and $\mathcal{R} \subseteq \mathcal{A} \times \mathcal{A}$ the set of attacks.*

For $a, b \in \mathcal{A}$, we say that a *attacks* b if $(a, b) \in \mathcal{R}$. If b attacks some $c \in \mathcal{A}$, then a *defends* c against b. Similarly, a set $S \subseteq \mathcal{A}$ attacks (resp. defends) an argument b if there is some $a \in S$ that attacks (resp. defends) b.

Example 1. Figure 1 depicts an AF $\mathcal{F} = \langle \mathcal{A}, \mathcal{R} \rangle$, with $\mathcal{A} = \{a, b, c\}$ (*i.e.* the nodes of the graph) and $\mathcal{R} = \{(b, a), (b, c), (c, b)\}$ (*i.e.* the edges of the graph).

Fig. 1. An example of AF $\mathcal{F}$

The acceptability of arguments is classically evaluated through the concept of *extensions*, *i.e.* sets of arguments that are jointly acceptable. This form of joint acceptance can be interpreted as defining a coherent point of view about the argumentative scenario that is represented by the AF. Different semantics have been defined, that yield different sets of extensions. The usual semantics are based on two main principles: conflict-freeness and admissibility.

Definition 2 (Conflict-freeness and Admissibility). *Given $\mathcal{F} = \langle \mathcal{A}, \mathcal{R} \rangle$ an AF, the set $S \subseteq \mathcal{A}$ is*

- *conflict-free iff $\forall a, b \in S$, $(a, b) \notin \mathcal{R}$;*
- *admissible iff it is conflict-free and $\forall a \in S$, $\forall b \in \mathcal{A}$ s.t. $(b, a) \in \mathcal{R}$, $\exists c \in S$ s.t. $(c, b) \in \mathcal{R}$.*

The meaning of conflict-freeness is quite easy to understand: we do not want to accept together arguments that are conflicting. Admissibility corresponds to a notion of "self-defense": a (conflict-free) set of arguments must be able to defend itself against external attacks in order to be considered as a valid point of view. We use $cf(\mathcal{F})$ (resp. $ad(\mathcal{F})$) to denote the set of conflict-free (resp. admissible) sets of an AF $\mathcal{F}$.

These principles are usually considered to be too weak to define semantics, but the classical semantics are based on them.[2] We recall now the definition of these semantics:

Definition 3 (Admissibility-based Semantics). *Given* $\mathcal{F} = \langle \mathcal{A}, \mathcal{R} \rangle$ *an AF, the admissible set* $S \subseteq \mathcal{A}$ *is*

- a complete *extension iff S contains all the arguments that it defends;*
- a preferred *extension iff S is a $\subseteq$-maximal admissible set;*
- a grounded *extension iff S is a $\subseteq$-minimal complete extension.*

A fourth semantics is defined by Dung, that does not directly rely on the notion of admissibility:

Definition 4 (Stable Semantics). *Given* $\mathcal{F} = \langle \mathcal{A}, \mathcal{R} \rangle$ *an AF, the conflict-free set* $S \subseteq \mathcal{A}$ *is a* stable extension *iff* $\forall a \in \mathcal{A} \backslash S$, S *attacks* a.

We use $co(\mathcal{F})$, $pr(\mathcal{F})$, $gr(\mathcal{F})$ and $st(\mathcal{F})$ for the sets of (respectively) complete, preferred, grounded and stable extensions. Among their basic properties:

- $\forall \mathcal{F}, |\sigma(\mathcal{F})| \geq 1$ for $\sigma \in \{co, pr, gr\}$;
- $\forall \mathcal{F}, |gr(\mathcal{F})| = 1$;
- $\forall \mathcal{F}, st(\mathcal{F}) \subseteq pr(\mathcal{F}) \subseteq co(\mathcal{F})$.

The last point implies that stable extensions are admissible sets as well, even if they are not explicitly defined through admissibility.

Example 2. Considering again $\mathcal{F}$ from Example 1; its extensions for the four semantics defined previously are given in Table 1 (second column).

For further details about these semantics, as well as other semantics that have been defined subsequently, we refer the reader to [4,14].

Given an argumentation framework and a semantics, classical reasoning tasks include the verification that a given set of arguments is an extension, and that a given argument is credulously or skeptically acceptable, *i.e.* belongs to some or each extension. Formally:

σ-Ver Given an AF $\mathcal{F} = \langle \mathcal{A}, \mathcal{R} \rangle$ and $S \subseteq \mathcal{A}$, is S a σ-extension of $\mathcal{F}$?
σ-Cred Given an AF $\mathcal{F} = \langle \mathcal{A}, \mathcal{R} \rangle$ and $a \in \mathcal{A}$, does a belong to some σ-extension of $\mathcal{F}$?

---

[2] However, let us notice that we will sometimes include them in the family of studied semantics, for homogeneity of the presentation, *e.g.* in the complexity results (see Sect. 4.1).

σ-Skep Given an AF $\mathcal{F} = \langle \mathcal{A}, \mathcal{R} \rangle$ and $a \in \mathcal{A}$, does a belong to each σ-extension of $\mathcal{F}$?

We use $\mathsf{Cred}_\sigma(\mathcal{F})$ (resp. $\mathsf{Skep}_\sigma(\mathcal{F})$) to denote the set of credulously (resp. skeptically) accepted arguments of $\mathcal{F}$, *i.e.* those for which the answer to σ-Cred (resp. σ-Skep) is "YES".

Example 3. The credulously and skeptically accepted arguments in $\mathcal{F}$ from Example 1 are given in Table 1 (third and fourth columns).

Table 1. Extensions and acceptable arguments of $\mathcal{F}$, for $\sigma \in \{\mathsf{gr}, \mathsf{st}, \mathsf{co}, \mathsf{pr}\}$.

Semantics σ	$\sigma(\mathcal{F})$	$\mathsf{Cred}_\sigma(\mathcal{F})$	$\mathsf{Skep}_\sigma(\mathcal{F})$
gr	$\{\emptyset\}$	$\emptyset$	$\emptyset$
st	$\{\{b\}, \{a,c\}\}$	$\{a,b,c\}$	$\emptyset$
co	$\{\emptyset, \{b\}, \{a,c\}\}$	$\{a,b,c\}$	$\emptyset$
pr	$\{\{b\}, \{a,c\}\}$	$\{a,b,c\}$	$\emptyset$

The complexity of these problems for various semantics has been established, see *e.g.* [16] for an overview. The relevant results for this paper are summarized in Table 2. We assume that the reader is familiar with basic notions of complexity theory, otherwise see *e.g.* [3].

Table 2. Complexity of σ-Ver, σ-Cred and σ-Skep, for $\sigma \in \{\mathsf{cf}, \mathsf{ad}, \mathsf{gr}, \mathsf{st}, \mathsf{co}, \mathsf{pr}\}$. $\mathcal{C}$-c means $\mathcal{C}$-complete.

Semantics σ	σ-Ver	σ-Cred	σ-Skep
cf	in L	in L	Trivial
ad	in L	NP-c	Trivial
gr	P-c	P-c	P-c
st	in L	NP-c	coNP-c
co	in L	NP-c	P-c
pr	coNP-c	NP-c	Π_2^P-c

2.2 Qualitative Uncertainty in AFs

Now we present the existing models that incorporate qualitative uncertainty in abstract argumentation.

Incomplete Argumentation Frameworks

Definition 5 (Incomplete Argumentation Framework). *An incomplete argumentation framework (IAF) is a tuple $\mathcal{I} = \langle \mathcal{A}, \mathcal{A}^?, \mathcal{R}, \mathcal{R}^? \rangle$ where*

- $\mathcal{A} \subseteq \mathbf{A}$ *is the set of* certain arguments;
- $\mathcal{A}^? \subseteq \mathbf{A}$ *is the set of* uncertain arguments;
- $\mathcal{R} \subseteq (\mathcal{A} \cup \mathcal{A}^?) \times (\mathcal{A} \cup \mathcal{A}^?)$ *the set of* certain attacks;
- $\mathcal{R}^? \subseteq (\mathcal{A} \cup \mathcal{A}^?) \times (\mathcal{A} \cup \mathcal{A}^?)$ *the set of* uncertain attacks.

$\mathcal{A}$ *and* $\mathcal{A}^?$ *are disjoint sets of arguments, and* $\mathcal{R}$, $\mathcal{R}^?$ *are disjoint sets of attacks.*

Intuitively, $\mathcal{A}$ and $\mathcal{R}$ correspond, respectively, to arguments and attacks that certainly exist, while $\mathcal{A}^?$ and $\mathcal{R}^?$ are those that may (or may not) actually exist.

Example 4. Figure 2 depicts an IAF $\mathcal{I} = \langle \mathcal{A}, \mathcal{A}^?, \mathcal{R}, \mathcal{R}^? \rangle$ with $\mathcal{A} = \{a, b\}$ (plain nodes), $\mathcal{A}^? = \{c\}$ (square dashed node), $\mathcal{R} = \{(c, b)\}$ (plain edge) and $\mathcal{R}^? = \{(b, a)\}$ (dotted edge). It means that the arguments a and b certainly exist, and there is an uncertainty regarding the existence of the attack (b, a). Then, the argument c is uncertain, but if it exists then the attack (c, d) certainly exists as well.

Fig. 2. An example of IAF $\mathcal{I}$

Reasoning with such IAFs is generally made through the notion of completion:

Definition 6 (Completion). *Let* $\mathcal{I} = \langle \mathcal{A}, \mathcal{A}^?, \mathcal{R}, \mathcal{R}^? \rangle$ *be an IAF. A completion of* $\mathcal{I}$ *is a pair* $\langle \mathcal{A}_c, \mathcal{R}_c \rangle$ *such that*

- $\mathcal{A} \subseteq \mathcal{A}_c \subseteq \mathcal{A} \cup \mathcal{A}^?$;
- $\mathcal{R} \cap (\mathcal{A}_c \times \mathcal{A}_c) \subseteq \mathcal{R}_c \subseteq (\mathcal{R} \cup \mathcal{R}^?) \cap (\mathcal{A}_c \times \mathcal{A}_c)$.

Example 5. Figure 3 depicts the completions of $\mathcal{I}$ from Example 4. $\mathcal{F}_1$ shows the situation where none of the uncertain elements actually exists, while $\mathcal{F}_4$ shows the opposite situation (all the uncertain elements appear). $\mathcal{F}_2$ and $\mathcal{F}_3$ shows the intermediate situations, where only one uncertain element (either the argument c, or the attack (b, a)) exists.

(a) $\mathcal{F}_1$	(b) $\mathcal{F}_2$	(c) $\mathcal{F}_3$	(d) $\mathcal{F}_4$

Fig. 3. The completions of $\mathcal{I}$

As seen with the previous example, the number of completions is generally exponential in the size of the IAF. More precisely, it is bounded by $2^{|\mathcal{A}^?|+|\mathcal{R}^?|}$.

Finally, reasoning tasks like credulous acceptance, skeptical acceptance or verification are defined with respect to some or each completion [6,8]: each classical reasoning task has two variants, following the possible view (the property holds in some completion) and the necessary view (the property holds in each completion). These reasoning tasks are, in most cases, computationally harder than their counterpart for standard AFs (under the usual assumption that the polynomial hierarchy does not collapse) [6,8]. This can be explained by the exponential number of completions.

Partial Argumentation Frameworks. Partial Argumentation Frameworks were initially defined as tool in a merging process [12]. They are tuples $\langle A, R, I, N \rangle$ with three binary relations over the set of arguments A: R is the (certain) attack relation, I the ignorance relation, and N the (certain) non-attack relation. Since $N = (A \times A) \backslash (R \cup I)$, a PAF can be identified with only $\langle A, R, I \rangle$. Since the meaning of I is exactly the same as the meaning of $\mathcal{R}^?$, PAFs actually form a subclass of IAFs:[3] any PAF $\langle A, R, I \rangle$ is an IAF $\langle \mathcal{A}, \emptyset, \mathcal{R}, \mathcal{R}^? \rangle$ with $\mathcal{A} = A$, $\mathcal{R} = R$, $\mathcal{R}^? = I$.

Extension-based semantics for PAFs have been defined in [11]. Intuitively, the idea consists in defining different forms of conflict-freeness and defense, and then combine them for defining three types of admissibility. From these new notions of admissibility, the authors define three variants of the preferred semantics, and study their properties. An interesting point is the fact that the complexity remains the same as in Dung's setting, contrary to the other reasoning methods for IAFs. These are the notions that are generalized from PAFs to IAFs in the next section.

3 Generalizing Extension-Based Semantics from PAFs to IAFs

In this section, we follow the same approach as [11] for defining semantics for IAFs. Instead of defining the extensions with respect to the set of completions of the IAF, we will generalize the basic concepts of conflict-freeness and defense to take into account the uncertainty in the IAF. Then, the usual admissibility-based semantics can be defined.

3.1 Conflict-Free and Admissible Sets of IAFs

We follow two approaches for defining conflict-freeness and defense for IAFs:

- Optimistic view: we consider that only certain arguments and attacks are harmful, so keep the definition of conflict-freeness and defense as in Dung's frameworks;
- Pessimistic view: we consider that all attacks are harmful, and must be defended by certain arguments and attacks only.

---

[3] This subclass was studied under the name *Attack-Incomplete AFs* [7].

By optimistic, we mean that the agent considers (*e.g.*) that $(a, b) \in \mathcal{R}^?$ does not make a a real "threat" against the acceptance of b. Roughly speaking, it means that the agent is tolerant to conflicts if they are uncertain. On the opposite, the pessimistic view means that the agent considers that all uncertain attacks against an argument are real threats against the acceptance of b, and that b must be defended by certain elements only in order to be accepted. Let us formally define the corresponding versions of conflict-freeness and defense.

Definition 7 (Weak and Strong Conflict-freeness). *Let* $\mathcal{I} = \langle \mathcal{A}, \mathcal{A}^?, \mathcal{R}, \mathcal{R}^? \rangle$ *be an IAF. The set* $S \subseteq \mathcal{A} \cup \mathcal{A}^?$ *is*

- *weakly conflict-free iff* $\forall a, b \in S \cap \mathcal{A}$, $(a, b) \notin \mathcal{R}$;
- *strongly conflict-free iff* $\forall a, b \in S$, $(a, b) \notin \mathcal{R} \cup \mathcal{R}^?$.

We use $\mathsf{cf}_w(\mathcal{I})$ and $\mathsf{cf}_s(\mathcal{I})$ to denote, respectively, the weakly and strongly conflict-free sets of an IAF $\mathcal{I}$.

Example 6. Figure 4 depicts an IAF $\mathcal{I}_2 = \langle \mathcal{A}, \mathcal{A}^?, \mathcal{R}, \mathcal{R}^? \rangle$, with $\mathcal{A} = \{a, b, d, e\}$, $\mathcal{A}^? = \{c, f\}$, $\mathcal{R} = \{(c, b), (e, b), (e, f)\}$ and $\mathcal{R}^? = \{(b, a), (b, e), (d, e)\}$. The set $\{a, b, c\}$ is weakly conflict-free: the attack from b to a does not violate the weak conflict-freeness since it is uncertain, and the attack from c to b does not violate it either because the attacker (c) is uncertain. It is not strongly conflict-free because of the same two attacks.

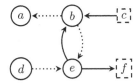

Fig. 4. An example of IAF $\mathcal{I}_2$

Strong conflict-freeness can be regarded as conflict-freeness applied on the "full" graph $\mathcal{F}_{full} = \langle \mathcal{A} \cup \mathcal{A}^?, \mathcal{R} \cup \mathcal{R}^? \rangle$, *i.e.* an AF made from the same arguments and attacks than the IAF, but without any uncertainty. However, weakly conflict-free sets do not correspond to the conflict-free sets of the "minimal" graph $\mathcal{F}_{min} = \langle \mathcal{A}, \mathcal{R} \cap (\mathcal{A} \times \mathcal{A}) \rangle$ (*i.e.* the AF obtained by simply ignoring the uncertain elements): see *e.g.* $\{a, b, c\}$ exhibited in Example 6, which is not a set of arguments in $\mathcal{F}_{min}$ (since $c \notin \mathcal{A}$).

Definition 8 (Weak and Strong Defense). *Let* $\mathcal{I} = \langle \mathcal{A}, \mathcal{A}^?, \mathcal{R}, \mathcal{R}^? \rangle$ *be an IAF. Given a set of arguments* $S \subseteq \mathcal{A} \cup \mathcal{A}^?$ *and an argument* $a \in \mathcal{A} \cup \mathcal{A}^?$,

- S *weakly defends* a *iff* $\forall b \in \mathcal{A}$ *such that* $(b, a) \in \mathcal{R}$, $\exists c \in S \cap \mathcal{A}$ *s.t.* $(c, b) \in \mathcal{R}$;
- S *strongly defends* a *iff* $\forall b \in \mathcal{A} \cup \mathcal{A}^?$ *such that* $(b, a) \in \mathcal{R} \cup \mathcal{R}^?$, $\exists c \in S \cap \mathcal{A}$ *s.t.* $(c, b) \in \mathcal{R}$.

Example 7. Considering again $\mathcal{I}_2$ from Example 6, we observe that $S = \{a\}$ weakly defends a, since there is no $x \in \mathcal{A}$ s.t. $(x, a) \in \mathcal{R}$. On the contrary, a is not strongly defended by S, because there is no argument in $S \cap \mathcal{A}$ that attacks b. But $S' = \{a, e\}$ strongly defends a: $e \in S' \cap \mathcal{A}$ (certainly) attacks b.

We observe that in the case where $\mathcal{A}^? = \emptyset$, then weak conflict-freeness and defense correspond to the notions of $\mathcal{R}$-conflict-freeness and $\mathcal{R}$-acceptability defined in [11], while the strong versions correspond to $\mathcal{RI}$-conflict-freeness and $\mathcal{RI}$-acceptability. Then, if $\mathcal{R}^? = \emptyset$ also holds, then both weak conflict-freeness and strong conflict-freeness coincide with the classical conflict-freeness [14], while both forms of defense defined here correspond with the classical defense.

For defining a notion of admissibility, we must combine conflict-freeness and defense. In theory, Definitions 7 and 8 induce four notions of admissibility. However, the following result shows that weak conflict-freeness and strong conflict-freeness induce the same notion of admissibility when combined with strong defense.

Proposition 1. *Let $\mathcal{I} = \langle \mathcal{A}, \mathcal{A}^?, \mathcal{R}, \mathcal{R}^? \rangle$ be an IAF. Let $S \subseteq \mathcal{A} \cup \mathcal{A}^?$ be a set of arguments such that S is weakly conflict-free and $\forall a \in S$, S strongly defends a. Then S is strongly conflict-free.*

The proof is similar to the proof of [11, Property 1].

Proof. Reasoning towards a contradiction, let us suppose that S is not strongly conflict-free, *i.e.* $\exists a, b \in S$ such that $(a, b) \in \mathcal{R}^?$ (we can exclude the option $(a, b) \in \mathcal{R}$ because S is assumed to be weakly conflict-free). Then, since S strongly defends all its elements, in particular it strongly defends b, so $\exists c \in S$ such that $(c, a) \in \mathcal{R}$. This is a contradiction with the weak conflict-freeness of S. So we can conclude that S is strongly conflict-free.

Now we define the three variants of admissibility.[4]

Definition 9 (Weak, Mixed and Strong Admissibility). *Given $\mathcal{I} = \langle \mathcal{A}, \mathcal{A}^?, \mathcal{R}, \mathcal{R}^? \rangle$ an IAF, a set of arguments $S \subseteq \mathcal{A} \cup \mathcal{A}^?$ is*

- *weakly admissible iff S is weakly conflict-free and weakly defends all its elements;*
- *mixedly admissible iff S is strongly conflict-free and weakly defends all its elements;*
- *strongly admissible iff S is strongly conflict-free and strongly defends all its elements.*

The weakly (resp. mixedly, strongly) admissible sets of an IAF $\mathcal{I}$ are denoted by $\mathsf{ad}_w(\mathcal{I})$ (resp. $\mathsf{ad}_m(\mathcal{I})$, $\mathsf{ad}_s(\mathcal{I})$).

The definitions imply that $\mathsf{ad}_s(\mathcal{I}) \subseteq \mathsf{ad}_m(\mathcal{I}) \subseteq \mathsf{ad}_w(\mathcal{I})$, for any IAF $\mathcal{I}$. Also, as in the standard Dung's framework, every IAF has at least one admissible set,

---

[4] The terminology "strong defense" and "strong admissibility" has been used with another meaning in [10], where it applies to classical AFs, not IAFs.

for all the variations of admissibility. Indeed, for any IAF $\mathcal{I}$, $\emptyset \in \mathsf{ad}_s(\mathcal{I})$. This fact will be useful later to guarantee the existence of extensions for the semantics based on admissibility.

Before going further with the definition of semantics based on these new notions of admissibility, we briefly discuss a property of classical semantics that we believe is important. It is called the *Fundamental Lemma* by Dung [14, Lemma 10]. This lemma states that if a set of arguments S is admissible, and defends an argument a, then $S \cup \{a\}$ is admissible. Besides its technical interest for proving some further results, this lemma describes an intuitive property of argumentation in general: if a point of view (*i.e.* a set of arguments) is seen as valid, then it should be jointly acceptable with any argument that it success-fully defends. We thus consider this property as necessary for defining reason-able semantics. With the following lemma, we determine which of the notions of admissibility given in Definition 9 satisfy a notion of "fundamentality" similar to Dung's lemma. More precisely, we show that only weak and strong admissibility are suitable for defining semantics.

Lemma 1 (Fundamental Lemma). *Given $\mathcal{I} = \langle \mathcal{A}, \mathcal{A}^?, \mathcal{R}, \mathcal{R}^? \rangle$ an IAF, and $S \subseteq \mathcal{A} \cup \mathcal{A}^?$ a weakly (resp. strongly) admissible set, if S weakly (resp. strongly) defends some $a \in \mathcal{A} \cup \mathcal{A}^?$, then $S \cup \{a\}$ is weakly (resp. strongly) admissible.*

Proof. We first consider weak admissibility. Let us prove that $S \cup \{a\}$ is weakly conflict-free. First of all, notice that if $a \in \mathcal{A}^?$ then the set $S \cup \{a\}$ is weakly conflict-free iff S is weakly conflict-free, since only certain attacks between cer-tain arguments violate weak conflict-freeness. So in the rest of the reasoning we suppose that $a \in \mathcal{A}$. Towards a contradiction, suppose that $S \cup \{a\}$ is not weakly conflict-free. Then, $\exists b \in S \cap \mathcal{A}$ such that, either $(b, a) \in \mathcal{R}$ or $(a, b) \in \mathcal{R}$. In the former case, since S weakly defends a, then there must be a $c \in S \cap \mathcal{A}$ with $(c, b) \in \mathcal{R}$, which is impossible since S is weakly conflict-free. Hence the contradiction. In the latter case $((a, b) \in \mathcal{R})$, since S is weakly admissible, it must defend b against a, and the same reasoning applies for concluding the impossibility. Thus $S \cup \{a\}$ is weakly conflict-free.

The fact that $S \cup \{a\}$ weakly defends all its elements comes from the fact that S weakly defends all its elements, as well as a. So we conclude that $S \cup \{a\}$ is weakly admissible.

Now, consider S a strongly admissible set that strongly defends some $a \in \mathcal{A} \cup \mathcal{A}^?$. Suppose that $S \cup \{a\}$ is not strongly conflict-free. It means that some $b \in S$ is such that $(b, a) \in \mathcal{R} \cup \mathcal{R}^?$ or $(a, b) \in \mathcal{R} \cup \mathcal{R}^?$. In the first case, the fact that S strongly defends a (against b) means that some $c \in S \cap \mathcal{A}$ attacks b, which violates strong conflict-freeness of S. In the second case, since S strongly defends all its elements, there is a $c \in S \cap \mathcal{A}$ such that $(c, a) \in \mathcal{R}$, which is impossible for similar reasons to the first case. Hence $S \cup \{a\}$ is strongly conflict-free. Finally, the fact that $S \cup \{a\}$ strongly defends all its elements follows the fact that S strongly defends all its elements and a. So we conclude that $S \cup \{a\}$ is strongly admissible.

On the contrary, mixed admissibility does not satisfy a property of fundamentality.

Proposition 2. *There is an IAF* $\mathcal{I} = \langle \mathcal{A}, \mathcal{A}^?, \mathcal{R}, \mathcal{R}^? \rangle$, $S \subseteq \mathcal{A} \cup \mathcal{A}^?$ *and an argument* $a \in \mathcal{A} \cup \mathcal{A}^?$ *such that* S *is mixedly admissible,* S *weakly defends* a, *and* $S \cup \{a\}$ *is not mixedly admissible.*

Proof. The IAF given at Fig. 5 provides an example. The set $S = \{b\}$ is mixedly admissible (it is strongly conflict-free, and it has no attacker). S weakly defends a (since there is no $x \in \mathcal{A}$ such that $(x, a) \in \mathcal{R}$, there is actually no need to weakly defend a). But $S \cup \{a\}$ is not strongly conflict-free, hence not mixedly admissible.

Fig. 5. A counter-example about fundamentality of mixed admissibility

Because of this reason, we do not consider mixed admissibility as suitable for defining semantics (*e.g.* mixed preferred or mixed complete semantics).

Example 8. Based on Example 6 and 7, we observe that, in $\mathcal{I}_2$ from Fig. 4, $\{a\}$ is weakly admissible but not strongly admissible. $\{a, e\}$ is not strongly admissible either, because it does not strongly defend e (against the uncertain attack (d, e)). The full sets of weakly and strongly admissible sets of $\mathcal{I}_2$ are given in Table 3.

Table 3. Weakly and Strongly Admissible Sets of $\mathcal{I}_2$.

$\mathsf{ad}_w(\mathcal{I}_2)$	$\emptyset$, $\{a\}$, $\{c\}$, $\{d\}$, $\{e\}$, $\{a, c\}$, $\{a, d\}$, $\{a, e\}$, $\{c, d\}$, $\{c, e\}$, $\{d, e\}$, $\{a, c, d\}$, $\{a, c, e\}$, $\{a, d, e\}$, $\{c, d, e\}$, $\{a, c, d, e\}$
$\mathsf{ad}_s(\mathcal{I}_2)$	$\emptyset$, $\{c\}$, $\{d\}$, $\{c, d\}$

3.2   Admissibility-Based Semantics for IAFs

The classical definitions of Dung's semantics can be adapted to IAFs, based on the two different notions of admissibility identified as suitable in Lemma 1.

Definition 10 (Admissibility-based Semantics). *Given* $\mathcal{I} = \langle \mathcal{A}, \mathcal{A}^?, \mathcal{R}, \mathcal{R}^? \rangle$ *an IAF, a weakly (resp. strongly) admissible set of arguments* $S \subseteq \mathcal{A} \cup \mathcal{A}^?$ *is*

- a weakly (resp. strongly) complete *extension iff S contains all the arguments that it weakly (resp. strongly) defends;*
- a weakly (resp. strongly) preferred *extension iff it is a* $\subseteq$-maximal weakly *(resp. strongly) admissible set.*

For $x \in \{w, s\}$ and $\sigma \in \{\text{co}, \text{pr}\}$, the set of x-σ extensions of an IAF $\mathcal{I}$ is denoted $\sigma_x(\mathcal{I})$. In the definition of the versions of complete semantics, the notion of defense used is the same as in the underlying notion of admissibility.

Example 9. We continue Example 8. From the weakly and strongly admissible sets described in Table 3, we deduce $\text{co}_w(\mathcal{I}_2) = \text{pr}_w(\mathcal{I}_2) = \{\{a, c, d, e\}\}$, and $\text{co}_s(\mathcal{I}_2) = \text{pr}_s(\mathcal{I}_2) = \{\{c, d\}\}$.

We observe some usual properties regarding these semantics.

Proposition 3. *Given* $\mathcal{I} = \langle \mathcal{A}, \mathcal{A}^?, \mathcal{R}, \mathcal{R}^? \rangle$ *an IAF, and* $x \in \{w, s\}$,

- $\text{pr}_x(\mathcal{I}) \neq \emptyset$;
- $\text{pr}_x(\mathcal{I}) \subseteq \text{co}_x(\mathcal{I})$.

Proof. The first item is a direct consequence of the fact that $\text{ad}_x(\mathcal{I}) \neq \emptyset$, as seen previously. The existence of (finitely many) admissible sets implies the existence of $\subseteq$-maximal admissible sets.

Now, let S be a x-preferred extension of $\mathcal{I}$. Reasoning towards a contradiction, let us suppose that $S \not\subseteq \text{co}_x(\mathcal{I})$. Since S is x-admissible, it means that S x-defends some argument a that it does not contain. According to Lemma 1, $S \cup \{a\}$ is x-admissible. This means that we have identified a proper superset of S which is x-admissible, thus S is not a $\subseteq$-maximal x-admissible set. This contradicts the fact that S is x-preferred. So we can conclude $S \in \text{co}_x(\mathcal{I})$.

3.3 Stable Semantics for IAFs

Now we focus on a counterpart of stable semantics for IAFs.

Definition 11 (Stable Semantics). *Given* $\mathcal{I} = \langle \mathcal{A}, \mathcal{A}^?, \mathcal{R}, \mathcal{R}^? \rangle$ *an IAF,*

- *a weakly conflict-free set of arguments* $S \subseteq \mathcal{A} \cup \mathcal{A}^?$ *is a* weakly stable *extension iff* $\forall a \in \mathcal{A} \backslash S$, *there is some* $b \in S \cap \mathcal{A}$ *such that* $(b, a) \in \mathcal{R}$;
- *a strongly conflict-free set of arguments* $S \subseteq \mathcal{A} \cup \mathcal{A}^?$ *is a* strongly stable *extension iff* $\forall a \in (\mathcal{A} \cup \mathcal{A}^?) \backslash S$, *there is some* $b \in S \cap \mathcal{A}$ *such that* $(b, a) \in \mathcal{R}$.

Weakly and strongly stable extensions of an IAF $\mathcal{I}$ are denoted by $\text{st}_x(\mathcal{I})$, where $x \in \{w, s\}$.

Example 10. Continuing Example 9, we observe that the weakly preferred extension $S = \{a, c, d, e\}$ is weakly stable as well: the argument $e \in S \cap \mathcal{A}$ (certainly) attacks all the arguments in $\mathcal{A} \backslash S$. It is not strongly stable, since it is not strongly conflict-free.

On the contrary, the strongly preferred extension $S' = \{c, d\}$ is not strongly stable, since it does not attack all the arguments in $(\mathcal{A} \cup \mathcal{A}^?) \backslash S$ (*e.g.* a is not attacked by S').

In Dung's framework, although admissibility is not directly involved in the definition of the stable semantics, any stable extension is actually an admissible set. We show here that it is also the case for strong and weak stable semantics of IAFs.

Proposition 4 (Admissibility of Stable Extensions). *For any IAF* $\mathcal{I} = \langle \mathcal{A}, \mathcal{A}^?, \mathcal{R}, \mathcal{R}^? \rangle$, $\mathsf{st}_x \subseteq \mathsf{ad}_x(\mathcal{I})$, *with* $x \in \{w, s\}$.

Proof. Consider S a weakly stable extension of $\mathcal{I}$. By definition of weakly stable semantics, S is weakly conflict-free. Let us prove that it weakly defends all its elements. Consider any $a \in \mathcal{A} \backslash S$ such that $(a, b) \in \mathcal{R}$ for some $b \in S$. By definition of the weakly stable semantics, there is a $c \in S \cap \mathcal{A}$ such that $(c, a) \in \mathcal{R}$, so S weakly defends b. Thus, S weakly defends all its elements, hence it is weakly admissible.

Now we consider S a strongly stable extension of $\mathcal{I}$. Again, strong conflict-freeness is implied by the definition, so we just need to prove that S strongly defends all its elements. Consider any $a \in \mathcal{A} \cup \mathcal{A}^?$ such that $(a, b) \in \mathcal{R} \cup \mathcal{R}^?$, for some $b \in S$. By definition of strongly stable extensions, there is some $c \in S \cap \mathcal{A}$ such that $(c, a) \in \mathcal{R}$. Thus S strongly defends a, and then all its elements. We can conclude that it is strongly admissible. □

Another classical results that still holds for our new semantics is the relationship between (weakly or strongly) stable and (weakly or strongly) preferred extensions.

Proposition 5 (Preferredness of Stable Extensions). *For any IAF* $\mathcal{I} = \langle \mathcal{A}, \mathcal{A}^?, \mathcal{R}, \mathcal{R}^? \rangle$, $\mathsf{st}_x \subseteq \mathsf{pr}_x(\mathcal{I})$, *with* $x \in \{w, s\}$.

Proof. Consider $S \in \mathsf{st}_w(\mathcal{I})$. From Proposition 4, we know that S is weakly admissible. Towards a contradiction, suppose that S is not weakly preferred, *i.e.* $\exists S' \in \mathsf{ad}_w(\mathcal{I})$ such that $S \subset S'$. This implies the existence of an argument $a \in S' \backslash S$. The weak stability of S implies the existence of some $b \in S \cap \mathcal{A}$ such that $(b, a) \in \mathcal{R}$, which violates the weak admissibility of S'. We reach a contradiction, and thus we conclude that $S \in \mathsf{pr}_w(af)$.

Now consider $S \in \mathsf{st}_s(\mathcal{I})$. Again, Proposition 4 implies the strong admissibility of S. Suppose the existence of $S' \in \mathsf{ad}_s(\mathcal{I})$ with $S \subset S'$. Take $a \in S' \backslash S$; the strong stability of S implies the existence of $b \in S \cap \mathcal{A}$ such that $(b, a) \in \mathcal{R}$, thus violating the strong admissibility of S'. We reach a contradiction, and conclude that S' does not exist, hence $S \in \mathsf{pr}_s(\mathcal{I})$. □

Example 10 and Proposition 5 imply that $\mathsf{st}_s(\mathcal{I}_2) = \emptyset$. The non-existence of stable extensions in Dung's framework is one of the main differences between this semantics and the ones based on admissibility. We can simply show a similar example for the weakly stable semantics as well: add a certain argument g to $\mathcal{A}$ and $(g, g) \in \mathcal{R}$. The set $\{a, c, d, e\}$ remains the single weakly preferred extension, but it does not attack g, so it is not weakly stable in the new IAF.

4 Computational Issues

4.1 Computational Complexity

In this section, we study the complexity of the variants of verification, credulous acceptability and skeptical acceptability for IAFs. Formally, for $\sigma \in \{\mathsf{cf}, \mathsf{ad}, \mathsf{co}, \mathsf{pr}, \mathsf{st}\}$ and $x \in \{w, s\}$:

σ_x-Ver Given an IAF $\mathcal{I} = \langle \mathcal{A}, \mathcal{A}^?, \mathcal{R}, \mathcal{R}^? \rangle$ and $S \subseteq \mathcal{A}$, is S a x-σ-extension of $\mathcal{F}$?

σ_x-Cred Given an IAF $\mathcal{I} = \langle \mathcal{A}, \mathcal{A}^?, \mathcal{R}, \mathcal{R}^? \rangle$ and $a \in \mathcal{A} \cup \mathcal{A}^?$, does a belong to some x-σ-extension of $\mathcal{F}$?

σ_x-Skep Given an IAF $\mathcal{I} = \langle \mathcal{A}, \mathcal{A}^?, \mathcal{R}, \mathcal{R}^? \rangle$ and $a \in \mathcal{A} \cup \mathcal{A}^?$, does a belong to each x-σ-extension of $\mathcal{F}$?

Lower Bounds. We can prove that reasoning with our semantics for IAFs is (at least) as hard as reasoning with the corresponding semantics for AFs. This can be done by showing that any AF $\mathcal{F} = \langle \mathcal{A}, \mathcal{R} \rangle$ can be transformed into an IAF $\mathcal{I}_{\mathcal{F}}$ that has the same extensions.

Definition 12 (IAF Associated with an AF). *Given $\mathcal{F} = \langle \mathcal{A}, \mathcal{R} \rangle$ an AF, the IAF associated with $\mathcal{F}$ is $\mathcal{I}_{\mathcal{F}} = \langle \mathcal{A}, \emptyset, \mathcal{R}, \emptyset \rangle$.*

Now we prove the correspondance of extensions, *i.e.* $\sigma(\mathcal{F}) = \sigma_w(\mathcal{I}_{\mathcal{F}}) = \sigma_s(\mathcal{I}_{\mathcal{F}})$, for any $\sigma \in \{\mathsf{cf}, \mathsf{ad}, \mathsf{pr}, \mathsf{co}, \mathsf{st}\}$.

Proposition 6 (Dung Compatibility). *Given $\mathcal{F} = \langle \mathcal{A}, \mathcal{R} \rangle$ an AF, $\sigma \in \{\mathsf{cf}, \mathsf{ad}, \mathsf{pr}, \mathsf{co}, \mathsf{st}\}$ and $x \in \{w, s\}$, $\sigma(\mathcal{F}) = \sigma_x(\mathcal{I}_{\mathcal{F}})$, where $\mathcal{I}_{\mathcal{F}}$ follows Definition 12.*

Proof. Observe that a set $S \subseteq \mathcal{A}$ is conflict-free (in $\mathcal{F}$) iff it is weakly and strongly conflict-free (in $\mathcal{I}_{\mathcal{F}}$). Then, a set $S \subseteq \mathcal{A}$ defends an argument $a \in \mathcal{A}$ against all it attackers (in $\mathcal{F}$) iff it weakly and strongly defends a against all its attackers (in $\mathcal{I}_{\mathcal{F}}$). These facts imply $\mathsf{ad}(\mathcal{F}) = \mathsf{ad}_w(\mathcal{I}_{\mathcal{F}}) = \mathsf{ad}_s(\mathcal{I}_{\mathcal{F}})$, which in turn imply the equivalence of complete and preferred extensions of $\mathcal{F}$ with the (weak and strong) complete and preferred extensions of $\mathcal{I}_{\mathcal{F}}$. Given $S \subseteq \mathcal{A}$, the equivalence between the conditions for S being stable in $\mathcal{F}$ and (weakly or strongly) stable in $\mathcal{I}_{\mathcal{F}}$ is straightforward.

This allows to prove that the complexity of reasoning with AFs provides a lower bound of the complexity of reasoning with IAFs.

Proposition 7. *Given $\sigma \in \{\mathsf{cf}, \mathsf{ad}, \mathsf{pr}, \mathsf{co}, \mathsf{st}\}$, $x \in \{w, s\}$, and $\mathcal{P} \in \{\mathsf{Ver}, \mathsf{Cred}, \mathsf{Skep}\}$, if σ-$\mathcal{P}$ is $\mathcal{C}$-hard, then σ_x-$\mathcal{P}$ is $\mathcal{C}$-hard.*

Proof. Proposition 6 provides a polynomial-time reduction from σ-$\mathcal{P}$ to σ_x-$\mathcal{P}$.

Upper Bounds for Extension Verification. Similarly to Dung's classical setting, most of the properties of extensions can be verified in polynomial time for our IAF semantics.

Lemma 2. *Given an IAF $\mathcal{I} = \langle \mathcal{A}, \mathcal{A}^?, \mathcal{R}, \mathcal{R}^? \rangle$ and a set of arguments $S \subseteq \mathcal{A} \cup \mathcal{A}^?$, the following tasks are doable in polynomial time:*

1. *check whether S is weakly (resp. strongly) conflict-free,*
2. *check whether S weakly (resp. strongly) defends some argument $a \in \mathcal{A}$ (resp. $a \in \mathcal{A} \cup \mathcal{A}^?$),*
3. *check whether each argument in $\mathcal{A} \backslash S$ (resp. $(\mathcal{A} \cup \mathcal{A}^?) \backslash S$) is attacked by an argument in $S \cap \mathcal{A}$.*

Proof. For item 1., weak (resp. strong) conflict-freeness is checked by enumerating every $(a, b) \in S \times S$, and verifying whether $(a, b) \in \mathcal{R}$ (resp. $(a, b) \in \mathcal{R} \cup \mathcal{R}^?$). There are $|S|^2$ such pairs (a, b), and verifying the membership to $\mathcal{R}$ (resp. $\mathcal{R} \cup \mathcal{R}^?$) is bounded by $|\mathcal{A} \cup \mathcal{A}^?|^2$ (*i.e.* the maximal number of possible attacks in an IAF).

For item 2., identifying the arguments $b \in \mathcal{A}$ (resp. $b \in \mathcal{A} \cup \mathcal{A}^?$) such that $(b, a) \in \mathcal{R}$ (resp. $(b, a) \in \mathcal{R} \cup \mathcal{R}^?$) only requires to enumerate all the arguments in $\mathcal{A}$ (resp. $\mathcal{A} \cup \mathcal{A}^?$), and then polynomially check the membership to $\mathcal{R}$ (resp. $\mathcal{R} \cup \mathcal{R}^?$). Then, for each of these attackers b, enumerate all the arguments $c \in S \cap \mathcal{A}$ and check the membership of (c, b) to $\mathcal{R}$ (resp. $\mathcal{R} \cup \mathcal{R}^?$). All the enumerations are polynomially bounded.

Finally, for item 3., enumerate all the pairs (a, b) such that $a \in S \cap \mathcal{A}$ and $b \in \mathcal{A} \backslash S$ (resp. $b \in (\mathcal{A} \cup \mathcal{A}^?) \backslash S$), and then check whether $(a, b) \in \mathcal{R}$.

Combining these polynomial operations allows to check whether a set of arguments is an extension, for most of the semantics studied in this paper.

Proposition 8. *For $\sigma \in \{\mathsf{cf}, \mathsf{ad}, \mathsf{co}, \mathsf{st}\}$ and $x \in \{w, s\}$, σ_x-Ver is polynomial.*

Proof. The result straightforwardly follows Lemma 2.

Following Proposition 7, the verification of (weakly or strongly) preferred extensions is intractable (under the usual assumptions of complexity theory). The following results proves that it remains at the first level of the polynomial hierarchy, similarly to Dung's preferred semantics.

Proposition 9. *For $x \in \{w, s\}$, pr_x-Ver is in coNP.*

Proof. Given $S \subseteq \mathcal{A} \cup \mathcal{A}^?$, proving that S is not a weakly (resp. strongly) preferred extension is doable with the following non-deterministic polynomial algorithm:

1. Check whether S is weakly (resp. strongly) admissible. If not, then S is not weakly (resp. strongly) preferred.
2. Otherwise, guess a proper superset of S, *i.e.* $S \subset S' \subseteq \mathcal{A} \cup \mathcal{A}^?$. Verifying whether S' is a weakly (resp. strongly) admissible set is doable in polynomial time with a deterministic algorithm. If S' is weakly (resp. strongly) admissible, then S is not a weakly (resp. strong) preferred extension.

This algorithm proves that the complementary problem is in NP, thus we conclude that pr_x-Ver $\in$ coNP for $x \in \{w, s\}$.

Upper Bounds for Acceptability. First, consider the case of cf_x, for $x \in \{w, s\}$. An argument a is credulously accepted w.r.t. cf_x iff $\{a\} \in \mathsf{cf}_x(\mathcal{I})$. This can be easily checked, by verifying that $(a, a) \notin \mathcal{R}$ and $(a, a) \notin \mathcal{R}^?$. This is doable in polynomial time and logarithmic space. Thus cf_x-Cred $\in$ L, for $x \in \{w, s\}$. Skeptical acceptability is even easier: since $\emptyset$ is weakly (resp. strongly) conflict-free, there is no skeptically acceptable argument w.r.t. cf_x for any IAF. The reasoning is the same for ad_x-Skep.

Proposition 10. *For $\sigma \in \{\mathsf{ad}, \mathsf{co}, \mathsf{st}, \mathsf{pr}\}$ and $x \in \{w, s\}$, σ_x-Cred is in* NP.

Proof. For $\sigma \in \{\mathsf{ad}, \mathsf{co}, \mathsf{st}\}$, guess a set of arguments that contains the queried argument a, and check (in polynomial time, see Proposition 8) whether it is a x-σ-extension. This is a NP algorithm for deciding σ_x-Cred.

For $\sigma = \mathsf{pr}$, notice that an argument belongs to some weakly (resp. strongly) preferred extension iff it belongs to some weakly (resp. strongly) admissible set, hence the result.

Proposition 11. *For $\sigma \in \{\mathsf{co}, \mathsf{st}\}$ and $x \in \{w, s\}$, σ_x-Skep is in* coNP.

Proof. Guess a set of arguments that does not contain the queried argument a and check (in polynomial time) whether it is a x-σ-extension, *i.e.* a is not skeptically accepted w.r.t. σ_x. This is a NP algorithm, thus σ_x-Skep is in coNP.

Proposition 12. *For $x \in \{w, s\}$, pr_x-Skep is in Π_2^P.*

Proof. Analogous to Proposition 11, except that the higher complexity of verification under the (weakly or strongly) preferred semantics yields a higher complexity upper bound for skeptical acceptability as well.

Discussion. We have proved that, in spite of the higher expressivity of IAFs compared to standard AFs, the complexity of most classical reasoning tasks remains the same. The only exception is skeptical acceptability under (weakly or strongly) complete semantics, for which we only have a coNP upper bound, while it is polynomial in standard Dung's AFs. We plan to study a counterpart of the grounded semantics for IAFs, which could bring new insights for the complete semantics. Finally, notice that using the weak or strong counterpart of our semantics does not have an impact on the complexity of reasoning.

4.2 SAT-Based Computational Approach

We follow the classical approach, initiated by [9], which consists in associating an AF with a propositional formula such that there is a bijection between the extensions of the AF and the models of the formula. Its has been applied with success for developing argumentation solvers [20,24].

In the following, we consider an IAF $\mathcal{I} = \langle \mathcal{A}, \mathcal{A}^?, \mathcal{R}, \mathcal{R}^? \rangle$, and we define a set of propositional variables $X_{\mathcal{A} \cup \mathcal{A}^?} = \{x_a \mid a \in \mathcal{A} \cup \mathcal{A}^?\}$. Intuitively, an interpretation ω corresponds to the set of arguments $S = \{a \in \mathcal{A} \cup \mathcal{A}^? \mid \omega(x_a) = \top\}$. We will provide in the rest of this section propositional formulas such that their models correspond to desirable sets of arguments (*e.g.* weakly or strongly conflict-free sets or extensions).

Conflict-Freeness. Recall that a set of arguments is weakly conflict-free if there is no certain attack between two certain arguments in it, while it is strongly conflict-free if there is no attack at all (neither certain nor uncertain) between any element of the set. This is encoded, respectively, by the following formulas ϕ_{cf}^w and ϕ_{cf}^s:

$$\phi_{\text{cf}}^w = \bigwedge_{a,b\in\mathcal{A},(a,b)\in\mathcal{R}} (\neg x_a \vee \neg x_b)$$

$$\phi_{\text{cf}}^s = \bigwedge_{a,b\in\mathcal{A}\cup\mathcal{A}^?,(a,b)\in\mathcal{R}\cup\mathcal{R}^?} (\neg x_a \vee \neg x_b)$$

Admissibility. Weak (resp. strong) admissibility is based on weak (resp. strong) conflict-freeness, and weak (resp. strong) defense. We introduce a formula δ_w (resp. δ_s) which characterizes sets of arguments that weakly (resp. strongly) defend all their elements.

$$\delta_w = \bigwedge_{a\in\mathcal{A}\cup\mathcal{A}^?} x_a \rightarrow \bigwedge_{b\in\mathcal{A},(b,a)\in\mathcal{R}} \bigvee_{c\in\mathcal{A},(c,b)\in\mathcal{R}} x_c$$

$$\delta_s = \bigwedge_{a\in\mathcal{A}\cup\mathcal{A}^?} x_a \rightarrow \bigwedge_{b\in\mathcal{A}\cup\mathcal{A}^?,(b,a)\in\mathcal{R}\cup\mathcal{R}^?} \bigvee_{c\in\mathcal{A},(c,b)\in\mathcal{R}} x_c$$

Then, weak and strong admissibility are encoded in

$$\phi_{\text{ad}}^x = \phi_{\text{cf}}^x \wedge \delta_x$$

where $x \in \{w, s\}$.

Complete Extensions. The formulas δ_w and δ_s characterize sets of arguments that (weakly or strongly) defend all their elements. To characterize complete extensions, we just need to replace the implication by an equivalence, which yields sets of arguments that defend all their elements and contain everything they defend. Formally,

$$\phi_{\text{co}}^x = \phi_{\text{cf}}^x \wedge \delta_x'$$

where $x \in \{w, s\}$, and

$$\delta_w' = \bigwedge_{a\in\mathcal{A}\cup\mathcal{A}^?} x_a \leftrightarrow \bigwedge_{b\in\mathcal{A},(b,a)\in\mathcal{R}} \bigvee_{c\in\mathcal{A},(c,b)\in\mathcal{R}} x_c$$

$$\delta_s' = \bigwedge_{a\in\mathcal{A}\cup\mathcal{A}^?} x_a \leftrightarrow \bigwedge_{b\in\mathcal{A}\cup\mathcal{A}^?,(b,a)\in\mathcal{R}\cup\mathcal{R}^?} \bigvee_{c\in\mathcal{A},(c,b)\in\mathcal{R}} x_c$$

Stable Extensions. Weakly (resp. strongly) stable extensions are weakly (resp. strongly) conflict-free sets that attack all the certain arguments (resp. all the arguments) that they do not contain. Said otherwise, it means that an argument which is not attacked by (a certain argument in) the extension belongs to the extension. It can be characterized as follows:

$$\phi_{\mathsf{st}}^{w} = \phi_{\mathsf{cf}}^{w} \wedge \bigwedge_{a \in \mathcal{A}} ((\bigwedge_{b \in \mathcal{A}, (b,a) \in \mathcal{R}} \neg x_b) \rightarrow x_a)$$

$$\phi_{\mathsf{st}}^{s} = \phi_{\mathsf{cf}}^{s} \wedge \bigwedge_{a \in \mathcal{A} \cup \mathcal{A}^?} ((\bigwedge_{b \in \mathcal{A}, (b,a) \in \mathcal{R}} \neg x_b) \rightarrow x_a)$$

Preferred Extensions. Finally, weakly and strongly preferred semantics cannot (under the usual assumptions of complexity theory) be directly encoded as propositional formulas, since the complexity of reasoning with weak and strong preferred semantics is higher than the complexity of Boolean satisfiability (especially, skeptical acceptability is Π_2^{P}-complete). However, other techniques related to propositional logic have been used in the past for computing preferred extensions, *e.g.* quantified Boolean formulas [17], maximal satisfiable subsets [20] or CEGAR (CounterExample Guided Abstraction Refinement) [24]. These techniques could be adapted for computing weakly or strongly preferred extensions.

5   Related Work

Control Argumentation Frameworks (CAFs) [13,23,25] are highly related to IAFs. They add another kind of uncertainty (about the direction of an attack), and a "control part", which is a set of arguments and attacks that must be selected by the agent, the goal being to enforce the acceptability of a set of arguments in each (or some) completion, by means of the selected control arguments. Reasoning with CAFs is only based on completions, and generally the computational complexity is high (at least the same as reasoning with completions of IAFs, and sometimes higher).

Reasoning with weighted AFs (*i.e.* AFs with weights on the attacks) [15] consists, somehow, in relaxing conflict-freeness in order to jointly accept conflicting arguments, as soon as the total amount of conflict (*i.e.* the sum of the weights of the attacks) is lower than a given inconsistency budget. We could adapt this principle for IAFs, by accepting only a given amount of uncertain attacks in extensions.

6   Conclusion

In this paper, we have continued an effort started by [11], and defined extension-based semantics for Incomplete Argumentation Frameworks that do not rely on the completions of the IAF. We have studied the properties of our new semantics, and provided complexity results and logical encoding that pave the way to SAT-based computation.

Future work include, naturally, missing complexity results (*i.e.* tight results for the skeptical acceptability under weakly and strongly complete semantics) and implementation of our encodings. In particular, the comparison of the various methods that reach the second level of the polynomial hierarchy for computing the preferred extensions is an enthralling question. The study of the grounded semantics will fulfill our study of Dung-style semantics for IAFs. We also plan to apply this kind of semantics to Control Argumentation Frameworks, which would decrease the complexity of controllability. This requires to take into account the additional type of information, namely the uncertainty about the direction of attacks. The link with weighted AFs, *i.e.* integrating an inconsistency budget in the weak variants of our semantics, is also a promising line for future research.

References

1. Amgoud, L., Cayrol, C.: A reasoning model based on the production of acceptable arguments. Ann. Math. Artif. Intell. **34**(1–3), 197–215 (2002)
2. Amgoud, L., Cayrol, C., Lagasquie-Schiex, M., Livet, P.: On bipolarity in argumentation frameworks. Int. J. Intell. Syst. **23**(10), 1062–1093 (2008)
3. Arora, S., Barak, B.: Computational Complexity - A Modern Approach. Cambridge University Press, Cambridge (2009)
4. Baroni, P., Caminada, M., Giacomin, M.: Abstract argumentation frameworks and their semantics. In: Baroni, P., Gabbay, D., Giacomin, M., van der Torre, L. (eds.) Handbook of Formal Argumentation, pp. 159–236. College Publications (2018)
5. Baroni, P., Giacomin, M., Liao, B., van der Torre, L.: Encompassing uncertainty in argumentation schemes. In: Proceedings of the Workshop on Frontiers and Connections between Argumentation Theory and Natural Language Processing, Forlì-Cesena, Italy, 21–25 July 2014 (2014)
6. Baumeister, D., Järvisalo, M., Neugebauer, D., Niskanen, A., Rothe, J.: Acceptance in incomplete argumentation frameworks. Artif. Intell. **295**, 103470 (2021)
7. Baumeister, D., Neugebauer, D., Rothe, J.: Verification in attack-incomplete argumentation frameworks. In: Walsh, T. (ed.) ADT 2015. LNCS (LNAI), vol. 9346, pp. 341–358. Springer, Cham (2015). https://doi.org/10.1007/978-3-319-23114-3_21
8. Baumeister, D., Neugebauer, D., Rothe, J., Schadrack, H.: Verification in incomplete argumentation frameworks. Artif. Intell. **264**, 1–26 (2018)
9. Besnard, P., Doutre, S.: Checking the acceptability of a set of arguments. In: 10th International Workshop on Non-Monotonic Reasoning (NMR 2004), pp. 59–64 (2004)
10. Caminada, M., Dunne, P.E.: Strong admissibility revisited: theory and applications. Argument Comput. **10**(3), 277–300 (2019)
11. Cayrol, C., Devred, C., Lagasquie-Schiex, M.C.: Handling ignorance in argumentation: semantics of partial argumentation frameworks. In: Mellouli, K. (ed.) ECSQARU 2007. LNCS (LNAI), vol. 4724, pp. 259–270. Springer, Heidelberg (2007). https://doi.org/10.1007/978-3-540-75256-1_25
12. Coste-Marquis, S., Devred, C., Konieczny, S., Lagasquie-Schiex, M., Marquis, P.: On the merging of Dung's argumentation systems. Artif. Intell. **171**(10–15), 730–753 (2007)

13. Dimopoulos, Y., Mailly, J.G., Moraitis, P.: Control argumentation frameworks. In: 32nd AAAI Conference on Artificial Intelligence (AAAI 2018), pp. 4678–4685 (2018)

14. Dung, P.M.: On the acceptability of arguments and its fundamental role in non-monotonic reasoning, logic programming and n-person games. Artif. Intell. **77**(2), 321–358 (1995)

15. Dunne, P.E., Hunter, A., McBurney, P., Parsons, S., Wooldridge, M.J.: Weighted argument systems: basic definitions, algorithms, and complexity results. Artif. Intell. **175**(2), 457–486 (2011)

16. Dvořák, W., Dunne, P.E.: Computational problems in formal argumentation and their complexity. In: Baroni, P., Gabbay, D., Giacomin, M., van der Torre, L. (eds.) Handbook of Formal Argumentation, pp. 631–688. College Publications (2018)

17. Egly, U., Woltran, S.: Reasoning in argumentation frameworks using quantified boolean formulas. In: Computational Models of Argument: Proceedings of COMMA 2006, 11–12 September 2006, Liverpool, UK, vol. 144, pp. 133–144 (2006)

18. Fazzinga, B., Flesca, S., Furfaro, F.: Revisiting the notion of extension over incomplete abstract argumentation frameworks. In: 29th International Joint Conference on Artificial Intelligence (IJCAI 2020), pp. 1712–1718 (2020)

19. Hunter, A.: Some foundations for probabilistic abstract argumentation. In: Verheij, B., Szeider, S., Woltran, S. (eds.) Computational Models of Argument - Proceedings of COMMA 2012, Vienna, Austria, 10–12 September 2012. Frontiers in Artificial Intelligence and Applications, vol. 245, pp. 117–128. IOS Press (2012)

20. Lagniez, J.M., Lonca, E., Mailly, J.G.: CoQuiAAS: a constraint-based quick abstract argumentation solver. In: 27th IEEE International Conference on Tools with Artificial Intelligence, ICTAI 2015, Vietri sul Mare, Italy, 9–11 November 2015, pp. 928–935. IEEE Computer Society (2015)

21. Lawrence, J., Reed, C.: Argument mining: a survey. Comput. Linguist. **45**(4), 765–818 (2019)

22. Li, H., Oren, N., Norman, T.J.: Probabilistic argumentation frameworks. In: Proceedings of the First International Workshop on Theory and Applications of Formal Argumentation (TAFA 2011), pp. 1–16 (2011)

23. Mailly, J.G.: Possible controllability of control argumentation frameworks. In: 8th International Conference on Computational Models of Argument (COMMA 2020), pp. 283–294 (2020)

24. Niskanen, A., Järvisalo, M.: μ-toksia: an efficient abstract argumentation reasoner. In: Calvanese, D., Erdem, E., Thielscher, M. (eds.) Proceedings of the 17th International Conference on Principles of Knowledge Representation and Reasoning, KR 2020, Rhodes, Greece, 12–18 September 2020, pp. 800–804 (2020)

25. Niskanen, A., Neugebauer, D., Järvisalo, M.: Controllability of control argumentation frameworks. In: Proceedings of the Twenty-Ninth International Joint Conference on Artificial Intelligence, IJCAI 2020, pp. 1855–1861 (2020)

26. Rossit, J., Mailly, J.G., Dimopoulos, Y., Moraitis, P.: United we stand: accruals in strength-based argumentation. Argument Comput. **12**(1), 87–113 (2021)

Relevant Epistemic Logic with Public Announcements and Common Knowledge

Vít Punčochář and Igor Sedlár(✉)

Institute of Computer Science, Czech Academy of Sciences,
Prague, Czech Republic
vit.puncochar@centrum.cz, sedlar@cs.cas.cz

Abstract. Building on our previous work in non-classical dynamic epistemic logic, we add common knowledge operators to a version of public announcement logic based on the relevant logic R. We prove a completeness result with respect to a relational semantics, and we show that an alternative semantics based on information states is dual to the relational one. We add a question-forming inquisitive disjunction operator to the language and prove a completeness result with respect to the information semantics. It is argued that relevant public announcements are particularly suitable for modelling public argumentation.

1 Introduction

Various problematic closure properties of epistemic operators in classical epistemic logic led to the exploration of a number of alternatives to the classical framework; see [9]. One approach to avoiding closure under classical consequence is to represent epistemic states of agents as sets of *abstract situations*, roughly in the sense of Barwise and Perry [2], instead of representing them as sets of possible worlds. This approach leads naturally to epistemic logics based on paraconsistent and substructural propositional logics; see [3,10,19,21,22] for example. Combining these logics with an account of information dynamics is a topic of recent interest: [1,11] explore versions of intuitionistic public announcement logic, [18,20] study paraconsistent bilattice public announcement logic, and [4] outlines a fuzzy version of public announcement logic. Authors of the present paper explored versions of public announcement logic based on relevant and substructural logics in [14] and [25]. The latter paper focuses on modelling epistemic updates in the standard relational semantics for relevant modal logic and the former paper used a more general information-state semantics. All papers mentioned so far use languages without *common knowledge*, a concept linked to information dynamics in a number of important ways.

The aim of this paper is to (i) extend the frameworks presented in [14] and [25] with common knowledge and provide a complete axiomatization, and (ii) explore the relationship between these frameworks. In Sect. 2 we add common knowledge to the relational semantics introduced in [25]. We argue that the notion of update embodied in the semantics has a natural link to the notion of

© Springer Nature Switzerland AG 2021
P. Baroni et al. (Eds.): CLAR 2021, LNAI 13040, pp. 342–361, 2021.
https://doi.org/10.1007/978-3-030-89391-0_19

public argumentation. In Sect. 3 we prove a completeness result for the relational semantics. Then, in Sect. 4, we introduce an informational semantics following the approach of [14]. The main result here is that informational and relational models are dual, implying that the sound and complete axiomatization of Sect. 3 is sound and complete with respect to information models as well. In Sect. 5 we add questions to our object language in the style of inquisitive semantics [7] and show that the completeness proof of Sect. 3 can be extended to completeness of this enriched language with respect to informational semantics.

2 Relational Semantics

Definition 1. *Fix a countable set of propositional variables* Pr *and a finite set of agent indices* G. *The language* $\mathcal{L}$ *contains operators* t *(zero-ary),* $\wedge, \rightarrow, \otimes,$ [] *(binary),* $\neg$ *and* B_a, C_A *for all* $a \in G$ *and non-empty* $A \subseteq G$ *(unary). The set of formulas of* $\mathcal{L}$, *denoted as* $Fm_{\mathcal{L}}$, *is generated by* Pr *using the operators of* $\mathcal{L}$ *in the usual way.*

We define $\varphi \leftrightarrow \psi := (\varphi \rightarrow \psi) \wedge (\psi \rightarrow \varphi)$, $\varphi \vee \psi := \neg(\neg\varphi \wedge \neg\psi)$, $B_A\varphi := \bigwedge_{a \in A} B_a\varphi$, $B_A^+\varphi := B_A C_A\varphi$, and $K_a\varphi := C_{\{a\}}\varphi$. Operators t, $\neg, \wedge, \otimes, \rightarrow$ are *propositional*, all B_a and C_A are *epistemic operators* and [] is the *dynamic operator*. We use r to range over propositional operators, r_i over i-ary propositional operators and $r_{>0}$ over propositional operators of non-zero arity.

We read "$B_a\varphi$" as "Agent a *believes* that φ", although what we mean is, more generally, that a has information that supports (or allows a to conclude that) φ. $B_A\varphi$ means that all agents in the group $A \subseteq G$ believe that φ. We read "$C_A\varphi$" as "φ is *common knowledge* in the group of agents A". $K_a\varphi$ is read "Agent a *knows* that φ" and $B_A^+\varphi$ as "it is *common belief* in group A that φ". Our choice of primitive epistemic operators may seem a bit odd, but it can be shown that belief, knowledge, common belief and common knowledge interact in expected ways. In particular, $B_A^+\varphi$ holds in s iff $B_A\varphi$ holds in s, $B_A B_A\varphi$ holds in s, and so on, which corresponds to the usual semantics of common belief. K_a is an "S4-type" knowledge operator, that is, $K_a\varphi \rightarrow \varphi$ and $K_a\varphi \rightarrow K_a K_a\varphi$ are valid, as we will see below.

The dynamic operator [] expresses effects of *public announcement* of a piece of information: we read $[\varphi]\psi$ as "ψ is the case after φ is publicly announced to all agents". Our notion of public announcement differs somewhat from the notion embodied in Public Announcement Logic [12,26]: we do not assume that the announced piece of information is *truthful*, nor is it implied that the information is *accepted* by the agents upon the announcement; we also allow the possibility that the announcement may cause some agents to drop some of the previously accepted information.[1]

---

[1] We note that while "announcement" seem to us to best express the notion we have in mind, we have hesitated because of its technical connotations. Another term that may be used is "reception" – upon an announcement agents receive a piece of information, but nothing is implied about the nature of the information nor about what the agents make of it.

A natural informal interpretation of such a general notion of public announcement is in terms of *public argumentation*. Imagine a group of agents, engaged in a public discussion. Public announcements can be seen as acts of putting forward arguments for or against claims in the discussion. These arguments do not have to be truthful and they do not have to be persuasive, meaning that the agents do not always accept the arguments. Moreover, arguments can cause agents to reject some of the information they accepted before. All of these features are characteristic aspects of our general rendering of public announcement. We will return to these aspects after introducing the semantics.

We note that our semantics extends the semantic framework of relevant logic introduced by Routley and Meyer in the 1970s. Our axiomatization extends the axiomatization of the relevant logic R, introduced by Anderson and Belnap in the 1960s. We do not have the space to review relevant logic in detail. The reader is referred to [8] or [17], for example.

Definition 2. *A* relevant epistemic model for G *is* $\mathfrak{M} = (S, \sqsubseteq, L, R, C, E, V)$ *where* $(S, \sqsubseteq, L, R, C, V)$ *is a Routley–Meyer model for the relevant logic* R*, i.e.*

- $(S, \sqsubseteq)$ *is a partially ordered set;*
- L *is an up-set in* $(S, \sqsubseteq)$;
- R *is a ternary relation on* $(S, \sqsubseteq)$ *that is anti-monotonic in the first two coordinates and monotonic in the third coordinate, and satisfies the following frame conditions (we use the standard notation* $Rstuw := \exists x (Rstx \,\&\, Rxuw)$ *and* $Rs(tu)w := \exists x (Rtux \,\&\, Rsxw)$*)*

$$Rstuw \implies Rs(tu)w \quad (1) \qquad Rstu \implies Rsttu \quad (3)$$

$$Rstuw \implies Rt(su)w \quad (2) \qquad Rstu \implies Rtsu \quad (4)$$

- $s \sqsubseteq t$ *iff there is* $x \in L$ *such that* $Rsxt$;
- C *is a symmetric binary relation on* $(S, \sqsubseteq)$ *that is anti-monotonic in both coordinates such that for all* s *there is a unique maximal element* $\bar{s}$ *of the set* $C(s) = \{t \mid Cst\}$ *and*

$$\bar{\bar{s}} = s \quad (5) \qquad Rstu \implies Rs\bar{u}\bar{t} \quad (6)$$

- V *is a function from* Pr *to up-sets in* $(S, \sqsubseteq)$;

and E *is a function from* G *to binary relations on* $(S, \sqsubseteq)$ *that are anti-monotonic in the first coordinate and monotonic in the second coordinate.*

Informally, $E(a)$ represents the information about the epistemic state of a provided by situations in the model as follows. For each $s \in S$ there is a body of information, denote it as $s(a)$, such that s provides information that $s(a)$ is the epistemic state of a ($s(a)$ may be empty). $E(a)st$ represents the assumption that $s(a)$ is contained in t. Hence, $E(a)(s) = \{t \mid E(a)st\}$ can be seen as the representation of $s(a)$.

We define $E(A) := \bigcup_{a \in A} E(a)$ and $E^*(A)$ as the reflexive transitive closure of $(\sqsubseteq \cup E(A))$.[2] $E^+(A)$ is the transitive closure of $E(A)$. We will usually write the agent (group) indices in a subscript.

Remark 1. We note that each relevant epistemic model is *fully associative*:

$$Rstuw \iff Rs(tu)w \tag{7}$$

The full associativity condition will be required in our completeness proof, in particular in the steps for $[\varphi][\psi]\chi$. Without common knowledge in the language, these cases are dealt with implicitly using the monotonicity rule R5; however, in the present context they have to be dealt with explicitly. This means that our present approach is limited to logics based on fully associative frames, for example the R-based logics we focus on here. An extension of our results to weaker logics is an open problem.

Definition 3. *The* satisfaction relation *between pointed models (that is, pairs of the form $(\mathfrak{M}, s)$ where s is in $\mathfrak{M}$) and $\mathcal{L}$-formulas is induced by V of $\mathfrak{M}$ as follows:*

- $(\mathfrak{M}, s) \models p$ *iff* $s \in V(p)$;
- $(\mathfrak{M}, s) \models t$ *iff* $s \in L$;
- $(\mathfrak{M}, s) \models \neg\varphi$ *iff* $\forall t$, Cst *implies* $(\mathfrak{M}, t) \not\models \varphi$;
- $(\mathfrak{M}, s) \models \varphi \wedge \psi$ *iff* $(\mathfrak{M}, s) \models \varphi$ *and* $(\mathfrak{M}, s) \models \psi$;
- $(\mathfrak{M}, s) \models \varphi \rightarrow \psi$ *iff,* $\forall tu$, *if* $Rstu$ *and* $(\mathfrak{M}, t) \models \varphi$, *then* $(\mathfrak{M}, u) \models \psi$;
- $(\mathfrak{M}, s) \models \varphi \otimes \psi$ *iff* $\exists tu$ *such that* $Rtus$ *and* $(\mathfrak{M}, t) \models \varphi$ *and* $(\mathfrak{M}, u) \models \psi$;
- $(\mathfrak{M}, s) \models B_a\varphi$ *iff* $\forall t$, $E_a st$ *only if* $(\mathfrak{M}, t) \models \varphi$;
- $(\mathfrak{M}, s) \models C_A\varphi$ *iff* $\forall t$, $E_A^* st$ *only if* $(\mathfrak{M}, t) \models \psi$;
- $(\mathfrak{M}, s) \models [\varphi]\psi$ *iff* $(\mathfrak{M}^{[\varphi]}, s) \models \psi$, *where* $\mathfrak{M}^{[\varphi]}$ *differs from* $\mathfrak{M}$ *only in that* $E_a^{[\varphi]} st$ *iff there are* u, v *such that* $E_a su$, $Ruvt$ *and* $(\mathfrak{M}, v) \models \varphi$.

A formula φ is valid in $\mathfrak{M}$ iff $(\mathfrak{M}, s) \models \varphi$ for all $s \in L$. We define $\mathfrak{M}(\varphi) := \{s \mid (\mathfrak{M}, s) \models \varphi\}$.

$\mathfrak{M}^{[\varphi]}$ is the model that results from $\mathfrak{M}$ after the public announcement of φ. Intuitively, $\mathfrak{M}^{[\varphi]}$ results from $\mathfrak{M}$ by extending all situations in $\mathfrak{M}$ with the information that φ has been publicly announced. This transformation of the model $\mathfrak{M}$ does not affect the "non-epistemic" structure consisting of the underlying Routley–Meyer model, but it does affect the epistemic accessibility relations since, intuitively, $s(a)$ for each s and a is modified by the announcement. Our semantics reflects the idea that this modification can be represented using the ternary relation R. We take R to represent the effects of "*merging*" situations: $Rstu$ iff the result of "merging" the information in s with the information in t

---

[2] Note that this notation is somewhat misleading as $E^*(A)$ does not denote the reflexive transitive closure of $E(A)$.

is contained in u. Crucially, "merging" is not necessarily monotonic.[3] Merging is lifted to sets of situations X, Y (representing arbitrary pieces of information) using the standard construction

$$X \otimes Y = \{u \mid \exists st(s \in X \ \& \ t \in Y \ \& \ Rstu\}. \tag{8}$$

After the information that φ *has been announced to* a is added to s, the epistemic state $s(a)$ is transformed into a new epistemic state $s(a)^{[\varphi]}$. Intuitively, announcing φ triggers a "merge" of the epistemic state of the given agent with the information expressed by φ. Using (8), we obtain

$$E_a^{[\varphi]}(s) = E_a(s) \otimes \mathfrak{M}(\varphi) = \{u \mid \exists tv(E_a st \ \& \ (\mathfrak{M}, v) \models \varphi \ \& \ Rtvu\}. \tag{9}$$

Hence, $s(a)^{[\varphi]}$ is contained in u iff u contains the result of merging $s(a)$ with the information that φ. This is exactly how $\mathfrak{M}^{[\varphi]}$ is defined.

Proposition 1. *Formulas of the following forms are not valid: 1.* $\neg\varphi \to [\varphi]\psi$; *2.* $[\varphi]B_a\varphi$; *3.* $B_a\varphi \to [\psi]B_a\varphi$.

We leave the construction of counterexamples to the reader. The fact that $\neg\varphi \to [\varphi]\psi$ is not valid means that announcements are not necessarily truthful: announcing a false formula does not lead to "explosion". The failure of $[\varphi]B_a\varphi$ means that announced information is not necessarily accepted by agents. This feature is related in spirit to well-known *unsuccessful updates* of classical public announcement logic, but the mechanism underlying the feature is more general than the so-called Moorean phenomena at work in the classical case. The failure of $B_a\varphi \to [\psi]B_a\varphi$ shows that announcements in our setting are *non-monotonic:* after an announcement of ψ, agents may abandon previously held beliefs. As mentioned above, all three aspects are typical features of public argumentation.

Definition 4. *For any* $\mathfrak{M}$, φ *and non-empty* $A \subseteq G$:

- *an* A-*path in* $\mathfrak{M}$ *is a finite sequence* $\langle s_i \mid i < n \rangle$ *of situations in* $\mathfrak{M}$, *for some* $n \geq 0$, *such that for all* $j < n - 1$, *either* $s_j \sqsubseteq s_{j+1}$ *or* $E_A s_j s_{j+1}$;
- *an* $A^{[\varphi]}$-*path in* $\mathfrak{M}$ *is a finite sequence* $\langle s_i \mid i < n \rangle$ *of situations in* $\mathfrak{M}$, *for some* $n \geq 0$, *such that for all* $j < n - 1$, *either* $s_j \sqsubseteq s_{j+1}$ *or* $E_A^{[\varphi]} s_j s_{j+1}$.

A path (A-path or an $A^{[\varphi]}$*-path) is a path* from s *iff it is non empty and its first element is* s; *it is a path* ending in t *iff it is non-empty and its last element is* t.

Note that $(\mathfrak{M}, s) \models C_A\varphi$ iff $(\mathfrak{M}, t) \models \varphi$ for all t such that there is an A-path in $\mathfrak{M}$ starting with s and ending in t; similarly $(\mathfrak{M}, s) \models [\psi]C_A\varphi$ iff $(\mathfrak{M}, t) \models [\psi]\varphi$ for all t such that there is an $A^{[\psi]}$-path in $\mathfrak{M}$ starting with s and ending in t.

---

[3] This reading is related to a number of interpretations of R popular in the relevant logic literature. For instance, Dunn and Restall point out that "perhaps the best reading [of $Rstu$] is to say that the combination of the pieces of information s and t (not necessarily the union) is a piece of information in u" [8, p. 67]. Restall adds that "a body of information warrants $\varphi \to \psi$ if and only if whenever you *update* that information with new information which warrants φ, the resulting (perhaps new) body of information warrants ψ" [17, p. 362] (notation adjusted).

3   A Relational Completeness Result

In this section we provide a complete axiomatization of the set of formulas valid in all relevant epistemic models. The axiom system RPAC, shown in Fig. 1, is a combination of the proof system for the relevant logic R, axioms and rules specifying that B_a are regular and monotonic modalities, the usual axioms and rules for the common knowledge operator, and the so-called *reduction axioms* for the update operator.

The completeness proof will combine the method of "partial filtration", used to prove completeness for versions of Propositional Dynamic Logic based on relevant logics [23,24], the standard canonical model argument for R, and the completeness argument for Public Announcement Logic using reduction axioms. Our proof follows the usual strategy of proving completeness for Public Announcement Logic with common knowledge, but we use a different notion of filtration (the "filtrated model" is infinite, only epistemic accessibility relations are defined in terms of a finite set of formulas) and our models are more general. We note that, unlike in [23,24], our proof does not require the presence of "extensional truth constants" $\top, \bot$. (We will specify the reason for this in Remark 2 below).

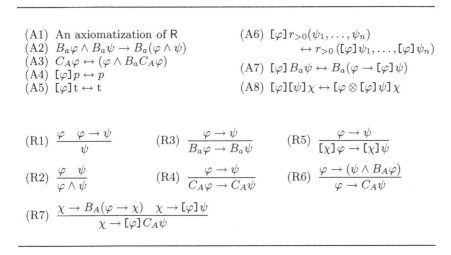

(A1) An axiomatization of R

(A2) $B_a\varphi \wedge B_a\psi \rightarrow B_a(\varphi \wedge \psi)$

(A3) $C_A\varphi \leftrightarrow (\varphi \wedge B_a C_A\varphi)$

(A4) $[\varphi]p \leftrightarrow p$

(A5) $[\varphi]t \leftrightarrow t$

(A6) $[\varphi]r_{>0}(\psi_1, \ldots, \psi_n)$
$\leftrightarrow r_{>0}([\varphi]\psi_1, \ldots, [\varphi]\psi_n)$

(A7) $[\varphi]B_a\psi \leftrightarrow B_a(\varphi \rightarrow [\varphi]\psi)$

(A8) $[\varphi][\psi]\chi \leftrightarrow [\varphi \otimes [\varphi]\psi]\chi$

(R1) $\dfrac{\varphi \quad \varphi \rightarrow \psi}{\psi}$

(R2) $\dfrac{\varphi \quad \psi}{\varphi \wedge \psi}$

(R3) $\dfrac{\varphi \rightarrow \psi}{B_a\varphi \rightarrow B_a\psi}$

(R4) $\dfrac{\varphi \rightarrow \psi}{C_A\varphi \rightarrow C_A\psi}$

(R5) $\dfrac{\varphi \rightarrow \psi}{[\chi]\varphi \rightarrow [\chi]\psi}$

(R6) $\dfrac{\varphi \rightarrow (\psi \wedge B_A\varphi)}{\varphi \rightarrow C_A\psi}$

(R7) $\dfrac{\chi \rightarrow B_A(\varphi \rightarrow \chi) \quad \chi \rightarrow [\varphi]\psi}{\chi \rightarrow [\varphi]C_A\psi}$

Fig. 1. The axiom system RPAC.

Lemma 1. *All theorems of* RPAC *are valid in all relevant epistemic models.*

Proof. We prove only the cases for A7 and R7 explicitly. First, $(\mathfrak{M}, s) \not\models [\varphi]B_a\psi$ iff there is t such that $E_a^{[\varphi]} st$ and $(\mathfrak{M}^{[\varphi]}, t) \not\models \psi$ iff there are t, u, v such that $E_a su$ and $Ruvt$ and $(\mathfrak{M}, v) \models \varphi$ and $(\mathfrak{M}, t) \not\models [\varphi]\psi$ iff $(\mathfrak{M}, s) \not\models B_a(\varphi \rightarrow [\varphi]\psi)$.

Second, to show that R7 preserves validity, assume that $\mathfrak{M}(\chi) \subseteq \mathfrak{M}(B_a(\varphi \rightarrow \chi))$ and $\mathfrak{M}(\chi) \subseteq \mathfrak{M}([\varphi]\psi)$. Let $(\mathfrak{M}, s) \models \chi$. To prove that $(\mathfrak{M}, s) \models [\varphi]C_A\psi$, we prove that for all $A^{[\varphi]}$-paths from s ending in t, $(\mathfrak{M}, t) \models [\varphi]\psi$; using the second assumption of the rule, this can be established by showing that $(\mathfrak{M}, t) \models \chi$ for each such t. We show this by induction on the length of $A^{[\varphi]}$-paths from s ending in t. The base case $s = t$ follows directly from our assumptions. Now assume that we have a path $(t_1, \ldots, t_m, t)$ such that $t_1 = s$ and that $(\mathfrak{M}, t_m) \models \chi$. If $t_m \sqsubseteq t$, then we are done. If $E_A^{[\varphi]} t_m t$, then we reason as follows. $(\mathfrak{M}, t_m) \models \chi$ entails that $(\mathfrak{M}, t_m) \models B_A(\varphi \to \chi)$ and $E_A^{[\varphi]} t_m t$ entails that there are u, v such that $E_A t_m u$, $Ruvt$ and $(\mathfrak{M}, v) \models \varphi$. Hence, $(\mathfrak{M}, t) \models \chi$.   □

Definition 5. *A set of formulas Γ is closed iff $\varphi \in \Gamma$ implies $\psi \in \Gamma$ for all subformulas ψ of φ, and*

- $C_A\varphi \in \Gamma$ only if $\{B_A C_A\varphi, B_A\varphi\} \subseteq \Gamma$;
- $[\varphi]r_{>0}(\psi_1, \ldots, \psi_n) \in \Gamma$ only if $\{[\varphi]\psi_i \mid i \leq n\} \subseteq \Gamma$;
- $[\varphi]B_A\psi \in \Gamma$ only if $B_A(\varphi \to [\varphi]\psi) \in \Gamma$;
- $[\varphi]C_A\psi \in \Gamma$ only if $[\varphi]B_A C_A\psi \in \Gamma$ and $[\varphi]\psi \in \Gamma$;
- $[\varphi][\psi]\chi \in \Gamma$ only if $[\varphi \otimes [\varphi]\psi]\chi \in \Gamma$.

A set of formulas is a prime RPAC-theory iff it is closed under forming conjunctions, closed under RPAC-provable implications, and satisfies the property that if $\varphi \vee \psi$ is in the set, then φ or ψ is in the set.

Definition 6. *Let Φ be a finite closed set. The canonical model for Φ is a structure $\mathfrak{M}_\Phi = (S, \sqsubseteq, L, R, C, E, V)$ where*

- S *is the set of all prime RPAC-theories;*
- $\sqsubseteq$ *is set inclusion;*
- $\Gamma \in L$ *iff Γ contains all theorems of L;*
- $R\Gamma\Delta\Sigma$ *iff, for all $\varphi \to \psi \in \Gamma$, if $\varphi \in \Delta$, then $\psi \in \Sigma$;*
- $C\Gamma\Delta$ *iff, for all $\neg\varphi \in \Gamma$, $\varphi \notin \Delta$;*
- $E(a)\Gamma\Delta$ *iff, for all $B_a\varphi \in \Phi \cap \Gamma$, $\varphi \in \Delta$;*
- $V(p) = \{\Gamma \mid p \in \Gamma\}$.

We define $F(a)\Gamma\Delta$ iff, $\varphi \in \Delta$ for all $B_a\varphi \in \Gamma$. The satisfaction relation is defined just as for epistemic models.

Note that the canonical epistemic accessibility relations $E(a)$ are defined using $B_a\varphi \in \Phi$, not arbitrary $B_a\varphi$; the latter defines the auxiliary relations $F(a)$. As in epistemic models, E_A denotes the union of $E(a)$ for $a \in A$. $E^*(A)$ is the reflexive transitive closure of the union of $\sqsubseteq$ with $E(A)$. Note that $F(a) \subseteq E(a)$ for all a, but the converse inclusion does not hold.

The notation $\vdash_{\mathsf{RPAC}} \varphi$ means that φ is a theorem of RPAC; we will use only $\vdash \varphi$ in this paper. We call a pair of sets of formulas (Γ, Δ) *independent* iff there are no finite non-empty $\Gamma' \subseteq \Gamma$ and $\Delta' \subseteq \Delta$ such that $\vdash \bigwedge \Gamma' \to \bigvee \Delta'$.

Lemma 2 (Pair Extension). *If (Γ, Δ) is independent, then there is a prime theory $\Sigma \supseteq \Gamma$ disjoint from Δ.*

Proof. This is a corollary of the well-known fact that each non-overlapping filter-ideal pair in a distributive lattice is extended by a non-overlapping prime filter-ideal pair. This result is usually stated for non-empty filters and ideals. However, if Γ is empty, then we can set $\Sigma := \emptyset$ and if Γ is non-empty but Δ is empty, then we set $\Sigma := Fm$. It is clear that both Fm and $\emptyset$ are prime theories.   □

Lemma 3. *For all Φ, $\mathfrak{M}_\Phi$ is a relevant epistemic model.*

Definition 7. *For all finite Φ, we define the following:*

- *If Γ is a prime theory not disjoint from Φ, then $\underline{\Gamma_\Phi} := \bigwedge(\Gamma \cap \Phi)$;*
- *if X is a non-empty set of prime theories, then $\underline{X_\Phi} := \bigvee_{\Gamma \in X} \underline{\Gamma_\Phi}$.*

If Φ is clear from the context, then we write just $\underline{\Gamma}$ and $\underline{X}$.

Note that $\underline{X}$ is well-defined even for infinite X since Φ is finite. Note also that $\Gamma \in X$ implies $\underline{X} \in \Gamma$ (since if the assumption holds then $\underline{\Gamma} \to \underline{X}$ is a theorem and obviously $\underline{\Gamma} \in \Gamma$).

Remark 2. Formulas of the form $\underline{\Gamma_\Phi}$ and $\underline{X_\Phi}$ will be used in the proof of the Truth Lemma, in the cases for $C_A \varphi$ and $[\varphi]C_A\psi$. In that particular context, each Γ we will need to "characterize" by $\underline{\Gamma_\Phi}$ will have a non-empty intersection with Φ and each X considered will be non-empty. For this reason, we do not need to account for empty conjunctions and disjunctions and so, unlike in [23,24], we do not need the presence of the "extensional" truth constants $\top$ and $\bot$ in the language.

Definition 8 (Complexity). *We define the following complexity function c : $Fm \to \mathbb{N}$:*

1. $c(p) = 1$ *for all $p \in Pr$;*
2. $c(\mathsf{t}) = 1$;
3. $c(f(\varphi_1, \ldots, \varphi_n)) = (\sum_{i=1}^n c(\varphi_i)) + 1$ *for all $f \in \{\neg, \wedge, \to, \otimes, B_a, C_A\}$;*
4. $c([\varphi]\psi) = (4 + c(\varphi)) \cdot c(\psi)$.

The closure of Γ is the smallest closed superset of Γ.

It can be shown that the closure of any finite set is finite. Our definition of the complexity function is virtually the same as the definition used in [26], for example.

Lemma 4. *For all φ, ψ and χ:*

1. $c(\varphi) > c(\psi)$ *if ψ is a proper subformula of φ;*
2. $c([\varphi]r_{>0}(\psi_1, \ldots, \psi_n\psi_n)) > r_{>0}([\varphi]\psi_1, \ldots, [\varphi]\psi_n)$;
3. $c([\varphi]B_a\psi) > c(\varphi \to [\varphi]\psi) + 1$;
4. $c([\varphi]C_A\psi) > c([\varphi]\psi)$;
5. $c([\varphi][\psi]\chi) > c([\varphi \otimes [\varphi]\psi]\chi)$.

Lemma 5 (Truth Lemma). *For all $\mathfrak{M}$, all finite closed Φ, all formulas $\varphi \in \Phi$ and all prime theories Γ:*

$$\varphi \in \Gamma \iff (\mathfrak{M}_\Phi, \Gamma) \models \varphi. \tag{10}$$

Proof. Induction on $c(\varphi)$. The base case is trivial. The rest of the cases are established as follows. Our induction hypothesis is that (10) holds for all φ such that $c(\varphi) < c(\theta)$ for some fixed θ. We prove that (10) holds for θ. We reason by cases.

The cases where the main connective of θ is $r_{>0}$ are established as usual in completeness proofs for R (these cases use the assumption that Φ is closed under subformulas), and the case for $\theta = B_a\varphi$ is established as usual in modal logic.

If $\theta = C_A\varphi$, then we reason as follows. To prove the left-to-right implication, we will use the following facts:

(i) if $C_A\varphi \in \Gamma \cap \Phi$ and $E_A\Gamma\Delta$, then $C_A\varphi \in \Delta$; and
(ii) if $C_A\varphi \in \Gamma \cap \Phi$, then each A-path from Γ ends with Δ such that $C_A\varphi \in \Delta$.

Fact (i) is established as follows: If $C_A\varphi \in \Phi$, then $B_A C_A\varphi \in \Phi$ and so $B_a C_A\varphi \in \Phi$ for all $a \in A$. If $E_A\Gamma\Delta$, then $E_a\Gamma\Delta$ for some $a \in A$. Hence, if $C_A\varphi \in \Gamma$, then $B_a C_A\varphi \in \Gamma$ using A3 and R3. Hence, $C_A\varphi \in \Delta$ by the definition of E_a and properties of prime theories.

Fact (ii) is established by induction on the length of A-paths from Γ. The base case of the one-element path is trivial: $C_A\varphi \in \Gamma$ by assumption and $\varphi \in \Gamma$ by A3. Now assume that we have a path $(\Delta_1, \ldots, \Delta_m, \Delta)$ such that $\Delta_1 = \Gamma$ and that the claim holds for $(\Delta_1, \ldots, \Delta_m)$. Then $C_A\varphi \in \Delta_m$. If $\Delta_m \subseteq \Delta$, then clearly $C_A\varphi \in \Delta$ and so $\varphi \in \Delta$ by A3. If $E_A\Delta_m\Delta$, then $C_A\varphi \wedge \varphi \in \Delta$ by (i).

Now assume that $C_A\varphi \in \Gamma \cap \Phi$ and $E_A^+\Gamma\Delta$. The latter means that there is an A-path from Γ ending with Δ. Hence, $\varphi \in \Delta$ by (ii). Since Δ was arbitrary, we obtain $(\mathfrak{M}, \Gamma) \models C_A\varphi$.

Conversely, let X be the set of Δ such that there is an A-path $(\Gamma, \ldots, \Delta)$. Assume that $(\mathfrak{M}, \Delta) \models \varphi$ for all $\Delta \in X$. By the induction hypothesis, $\varphi \in \Delta$ for all $\Delta \in X$. Since $\varphi \in \Phi$, Γ and indeed $\underline{\Delta}$ for all $\Delta \in X$ and $\underline{X}$ are defined. (We know that at least $\Gamma \in X$.) We prove that

(iii) $\vdash \underline{\Gamma} \to \underline{X}$;
(iv) $\vdash \underline{X} \to \varphi$;
(v) $\vdash \underline{X} \to B_A\underline{X}$.

Using R6, (iv) and (v) entail $\vdash \underline{X} \to C_A\varphi$, which together with (iii) gives $\vdash \underline{\Gamma} \to C_A\varphi$. Hence, $C_A\varphi \in \Gamma$.

Claims (iii) and (iv) are obvious. Claim (v) is established as follows. If $\not\vdash \underline{X} \to B_A\underline{X}$, then there are $\Delta \in X$ and Θ such that $\underline{\Delta} \in \Theta$ and $B_A\underline{X} \notin \Theta$. Using the Pair Extension Lemma, there is Σ such that $F_A\Theta\Sigma$ and $\underline{X} \notin \Sigma$. But since $\underline{\Delta} \in \Theta$, $F_A\Theta\Sigma$ implies that $E_A\Delta\Sigma$. ($F_A\Theta\Sigma$ entails that $E_a\Theta\Sigma$ for some $a \in A$. Assume that $B_a\chi \in \Delta \cap \Phi$. Then $\vdash \underline{\Delta} \to B_a\chi$ and so $B_a\chi \in \Theta$. This means that $\chi \in \Sigma$.) Hence, $\Delta \in X$ implies $\Sigma \in X$, contradicting $\underline{X} \notin \Sigma$.

Now we consider the case $\theta = [\varphi]\psi$. We reason by cases, depending on the form of ψ:

Case 1. $\theta = [\varphi]p$. Then $\theta \in \Gamma$ iff $p \in \Gamma$ (using A4) iff $(\mathfrak{M}, \Gamma) \models p$ (using the induction hypothesis) iff $(\mathfrak{M}^{[\varphi]}, \Gamma) \models p$ (using the definition of $\mathfrak{M}^{[\varphi]}$) iff $(\mathfrak{M}, \Gamma) \models [\varphi]p$ (using the definition of $\models$).

Case 2. $\theta = [\varphi]r(\psi_1, \ldots, \psi_n)$. All sub-cases of this form are established using the definition of a closed set (closure under subformulas), Lemma 4, and the fact that update with φ does not modify the underlying Routley–Meyer model $(S, \sqsubseteq, L, R, C, V)$, just the epistemic accessibility relations E_a.

Case 3. $\theta = [\varphi]B_a\psi$. Then $\theta \in \Gamma$ iff $B_a(\varphi \to [\varphi]\psi) \in \Gamma$ (using A7) iff $(\mathfrak{M}, \Gamma) \models B_a(\varphi \to [\varphi]\psi)$ (using the induction hypothesis, relying on the definition of a closed set and item 3 of Lemma 4) iff for all Σ, Σ' and Δ, $E_A\Gamma\Sigma$ & $R\Sigma\Sigma'\Delta$ and $(\mathfrak{M}, \Sigma') \models \varphi$ only if $(\mathfrak{M}^{[\varphi]}, \Delta) \models \psi$ (definition of $\models$) iff, for all Δ, $E_A^{[\varphi]}\Gamma\Delta$ only if $(\mathfrak{M}^{[\varphi]}, \Delta) \models \psi$ (definition of $E_A^{[\varphi]}$) iff $(\mathfrak{M}^{[\varphi]}, \Gamma) \models B_a\psi$ (definition of $\models$) iff $(\mathfrak{M}, \Gamma) \models [\varphi]B_a\psi$ (definition of $\models$).

Case 4. $\theta = [\varphi]C_A\psi$. We will use the following two facts:

(vi) If $[\varphi]C_A\psi \in \Phi \cap \Gamma$ and $E_A^{[\varphi]}\Gamma\Delta$, then $[\varphi]C_A\psi \in \Delta$ and $[\varphi]\psi \in \Delta$; and

(vii) if $[\varphi]C_A\psi \in \Phi \cap \Gamma$, then each $A^{[\varphi]}$-path from Γ ends with Δ such that $[\varphi]C_A\psi \in \Delta$ and $[\varphi]\psi \in \Delta$.

Fact (vi) is established as follows. If $E_A^{[\varphi]}\Gamma\Delta$, then there is $a \in A$ such that $E_a^{[\varphi]}\Gamma\Delta$, which means that there are Σ_1, Σ_2 such that $E_a\Gamma\Sigma_1$, $R\Sigma_1\Sigma_2\Delta$ and $(\mathfrak{M}, \Sigma_2) \models \varphi$ (note that $E_a^{[\varphi]}$ is defined using $\models$). Using the induction hypothesis (φ is a subformula of θ), we get $\varphi \in \Sigma_2$. Now $[\varphi]C_A\psi \in \Gamma$ entails $[\varphi]B_aC_A\psi \in \Gamma$ and $[\varphi]B_a\psi \in \Gamma$ (using A3 and R5) and this entails $B_a(\varphi \to [\varphi]C_A\psi) \in \Gamma$ and $B_a(\varphi \to [\varphi]\psi) \in \Gamma$ (using A7). It follows from the definition of a closed set that $\{B_a(\varphi \to [\varphi]C_A\psi), B_a(\varphi \to [\varphi]\psi)\} \subseteq \Phi$, and so we can infer that $\varphi \to [\varphi]C_A\psi \in \Sigma_1$ and $\varphi \to [\varphi]\psi \in \Sigma_1$, which also means that $[\varphi]C_A\psi \in \Delta$ and $[\varphi]\psi \in \Delta$.

Fact (vii) is established by induction on the length of $A^{[\varphi]}$-paths from Γ. The base case of a one-element path is trivial: $[\varphi]C_A\psi$ is assumed to be in Γ and $[\varphi]\psi \in \Gamma$ by A3. Now assume that (vii) holds for all $A^{[\varphi]}$-paths of length m, where $2 \leq m < n$ and take $(\Delta_1, \ldots, \Delta_n)$, where $\Delta_1 = \Gamma$. We know that $C_A\varphi \in \Delta_{n-1}$. If $\Delta_n \subseteq \Delta_{n-1}$, then we are done. If $E_A^{[\varphi]}\Delta_{n-1}\Delta_n$, then $[\varphi]C_A\varphi \in \Delta_n$ thanks to (vi).

Now assume that $[\varphi]C_A\psi \in \Gamma$ and that $E_A^{[\varphi]}\Gamma\Delta$. The latter means that there is a $A^{[\varphi]}$-path $(\Gamma_1, \ldots, \Gamma_n)$ such that $\Gamma_1 = \Gamma$ and $\Gamma_n = \Delta$. By (vii), $[\varphi]\psi \in \Delta$. By the induction hypothesis, $(\mathfrak{M}, \Delta) \models [\varphi]\psi$ (see item 5 of Lemma 4) and so $(\mathfrak{M}^{[\varphi]}, \Delta) \models \psi$. Since Δ was arbitrary, we obtain $(\mathfrak{M}^{[\varphi]}, \Gamma) \models C_A\varphi$. This means that $(\mathfrak{M}, \Gamma) \models [\varphi]C_A\psi$.

Conversely, let X be the set of Δ such that there is an $A^{[\varphi]}$-path $(\Gamma, \ldots, \Delta)$. Assume that $(\mathfrak{M}, \Gamma) \models [\varphi]C_A\psi$, which means that $(\mathfrak{M}^{[\varphi]}, \Delta) \models \psi$ for all $\Delta \in X$. By the induction hypothesis, $[\varphi]\psi \in \Delta$ for all $\Delta \in X$. Since $[\varphi]\psi \in \Phi$,

$\underline{\Gamma}$ and indeed $\underline{\Delta}$ for all $\Delta \in X$ and $\underline{X}$ are defined. (We know that at least $\Gamma \in X$.) We prove that

(viii) $\vdash \underline{\Gamma} \to \underline{X}$;
  (ix) $\vdash \underline{X} \to [\varphi]\psi$;
  (x) $\vdash \underline{X} \to B_A(\varphi \to \underline{X})$.

Using R7, (ix) and (x) entail that $\vdash \underline{X} \to [\varphi]C_A\psi$, which together with (viii) entails $\vdash \underline{\Gamma} \to [\varphi]C_A\psi$. This means that $[\varphi]C_A\psi \in \Gamma$.

Claim (viii) follows from $\Gamma \in X$. Claim (ix) follows from the assumption that $[\varphi]\psi \in \bigcap X$. Claim (x) is established as follows. If $\nvdash \underline{X} \to B_A(\varphi \to \underline{X})$, then there is $\Delta \in X$ such that $\nvdash \underline{\Delta} \to B_A(\varphi \to \underline{X})$. Hence, by the Pair Extension Lemma, there is Θ such that $\underline{\Delta} \in \Theta$ and $B_A(\varphi \to \underline{X}) \notin \Theta$. The latter means that there is $a \in A$ and Σ such that $F_a\Theta\Sigma$ and $\varphi \to \underline{X} \notin \Sigma$. The latter here means that there are Π, Ω such that $R\Sigma\Pi\Omega$, $\varphi \in \Pi$ and $\underline{X} \notin \Omega$. Using the induction hypothesis, we obtain $(\mathfrak{M}, \Pi) \models \varphi$, and so $E_A^{[\varphi]}\Delta\Omega$ (since $F_A\Theta\Sigma$ and $\underline{\Delta} \in \Theta$ imply that $E_A\Delta\Sigma$). Since $\Delta \in X$, it follows that $\Omega \in X$, contradicting $\underline{X} \notin \Omega$.

Case 5. $\theta = [\varphi][\psi]\chi$. We will use the following fact:

(xi) For $a \in G$ and all formulas α, β: $E_a^{[\alpha][\beta]} = E_a^{[\alpha \otimes [\alpha]\beta]}$.

(xi) needs the assumption of full associativity (7):

$$
\begin{aligned}
E_a^{[\alpha][\beta]}\Delta\Sigma \iff & \exists \Sigma_1\Sigma_2(E_a^{[\alpha]}\Delta\Sigma_1 \ \& \ R\Sigma_1\Sigma_2\Sigma \ \& \ (\mathfrak{M}^{[\alpha]}, \Sigma_2) \models \beta) \\
\iff & \exists \Theta_1\Theta_2\Sigma_2(E_a\Delta\Theta_1 \ \& \ R\Theta_1\Theta_2\Sigma_2\Sigma \ \& \\
& \qquad (\mathfrak{M}, \Theta_2) \models \alpha \ \& \ (\mathfrak{M}, \Sigma_2) \models [\alpha]\beta) \\
\iff & \exists \Theta_1\Theta_2\Sigma_2(E_a\Delta\Theta_1 \ \& \ R\Theta_1(\Theta_2\Sigma_2)\Sigma \ \& \\
& \qquad (\mathfrak{M}, \Theta_2) \models \alpha \ \& \ (\mathfrak{M}, \Sigma_2) \models [\alpha]\beta) \\
\iff & \exists \Theta_1\Theta_3(E_a\Delta\Theta_1 \ \& \ R\Theta_1\Theta_3\Sigma \ \& \ (\mathfrak{M}, \Theta_3) \models \alpha \otimes [\alpha]\beta) \\
\iff & E_a^{[\alpha \otimes [\alpha]\beta]}\Delta\Sigma
\end{aligned}
$$

Now we reason as follows: $\theta \in \Gamma$ iff $[\varphi \otimes [\varphi]\psi]\chi \in \Gamma$ (using A8) iff $(\mathfrak{M}, \Gamma) \models [\varphi \otimes [\varphi]\psi]\chi$ (induction hypothesis, relying on item 6 of Lemma 4 and the definition of a closed set) iff $(\mathfrak{M}^{[\varphi \otimes [\varphi]\psi]}, \Gamma) \models \chi$ iff $(\mathfrak{M}^{[\varphi][\psi]}, \Gamma) \models \chi$ (since $\mathfrak{M}^{[\varphi \otimes [\varphi]\psi]} = \mathfrak{M}^{[\varphi][\psi]}$ by (xi)) iff $(\mathfrak{M}, \Gamma) \models [\varphi][\psi]\chi$. $\square$

Theorem 1. φ *is a theorem of* RPAC *iff* φ *is valid in all relevant epistemic models.*

Proof. Soundness follows from Lemma 1. Completeness is established using the Pair Extension Lemma, the Truth Lemma and Lemma 3: If φ is not a theorem, then neither is $t \to \varphi$. Take Φ the closure of $\{t \to \varphi\}$ and consider $\mathfrak{M}_\Phi$, which is a relevant epistemic model by Lemma 3. By the Pair Extension Lemma, there is a $\Gamma \in L$ such that $\varphi \notin \Gamma$. By the Truth Lemma, φ is not valid in $\mathfrak{M}_\Phi$. $\square$

4   Information Models

The semantics used in the previous sections builds on the framework introduced in [25], which has been in this paper adjusted to the background logic R and extended with common knowledge. Another approach to a public announcement logic with a substructural basis was developed in [14]. It turns out that these two approaches are closely related, which will be discussed in detail in this section. The merit of the alternative perspective that we will now describe is that it will allow us in the next section to enrich our logic with a further dimension that forms a crucial ingredient of informational dynamics. In particular, this perspective will allow us to express in the object language not only statements but also questions. For definition of the semantic models of this alternative framework we will need the following notion of a situation.

Definition 9. *Let $(P, \leq)$ be a complete lattice, where for any $X \subseteq P$, $\bigsqcup X$ denotes the join of X. An element $s \in P$ is called a* situation *in $(P, \leq)$ iff it is completely join-irreducible, i.e. iff for every $X \subseteq P$, $s = \bigsqcup X$ only if $s = x$, for some $x \in X$. The set of situations in $(P, \leq)$ will be denoted as $Sit(P)$. For any $x \in P$, the set of situations below x, i.e. the set $\{s \in Sit(P) \mid s \leq x\}$, will be denoted as $Sit(x)$.*

Note that if meet distributes over arbitrary joins in a complete lattice $(P, \leq)$ then for every situation $s \in Sit(P)$ and every $X \subseteq P$, if $s \leq \bigsqcup X$ then $s \leq x$ for some $x \in X$.

Definition 10. *An* information model *for G is $\mathfrak{N} = (P, \leq, 1, \cdot, C, \sigma, V)$ such that (a) $\langle P, \leq \rangle$ is a complete lattice; (b) every state from P is identical to the join of a set of situations, that is, for any $x \in P$, $x = \bigsqcup Sit(x)$; (c) 1 is an identity with respect to the binary operation $\cdot$ on P, i.e. $1 \cdot x = x$; (d) $\sqcap$ (i.e. the finite meet) and $\cdot$ distribute over arbitrary joins from both directions; (e) C is symmetric binary relation on P, and $Cx \bigsqcup Y$ iff there is $y \in Y$ such that Cxy; (f) σ is a map that assigns to each agent $a \in G$ a function $\sigma(a)$ (we will often write σ_a) from situations to states; (g) if s, t are situations such that $s \leq t$ then $\sigma_a(s) \leq \sigma_a(t)$; (h) $V(p) \in S$, for every atomic formula p.*

P represents a set of *information states*, $x \leq y$ expresses that the state x is an informational *refinement* of the state y (i.e. x is informationally stronger than y), 1 is called a *logical state*, $x \cdot y$ is called *fusion* of the states x and y, Cxy says that x is *compatible* with y, σ called an *information state map*, V is a *valuation* that assigns to every atomic formula an informational content, represented as a state in P.

Note that distributivity of fusion over joins implies its monotonicity, i.e. $x_1 \leq x_2$ and $y_1 \leq y_2$ only if $x_1 \cdot y_1 \leq x_2 \cdot y_2$. Moreover, there is the least element 0 in $\mathfrak{N}$ that can be defined as $\bigsqcup \emptyset$.

Definition 11. *A* relevant information model *for G is an information model $\mathfrak{N} = (P, \leq, 1, \cdot, C, \sigma, V)$ for G where (i) fusion is associative, commutative, and $x \leq x \cdot x$, (ii) for every situation $s \in Sit(P)$ there is a state $x \in P$ such that Cxy if and only if $s \leq y$, (iii) for all states $x, y, z \in S$, if $Cx(y \cdot z)$ then $C(x \cdot y)z$.*

Let σ be an inquisitive state map, $A \subseteq G$ a set of agents, and s a situation. We define $\sigma_A(s) = \bigsqcup_{a \in A} \sigma_a(s)$. Moreover, we define:

$$\sigma_A^*(s) = \bigsqcup \{t \in S \mid \exists t_1, \ldots, t_n \in Sit(S): t_1 = s,\ t_{i+1} \leq \sigma_A(t_i),\ t_n = t \}.$$

The support relation between pointed relevant information models and formulas from $\mathcal{L}$ is defined as follows:

- $(\mathfrak{N}, x) \Vdash p$ iff $x \leq V(p)$;
- $(\mathfrak{N}, x) \Vdash \mathbf{t}$ iff $x \leq 1$;
- $(\mathfrak{N}, x) \Vdash \neg\varphi$ iff, $\forall y$, if Cxy, then $(\mathfrak{N}, y) \not\Vdash \varphi$;
- $(\mathfrak{N}, x) \Vdash \varphi \wedge \psi$ iff $(\mathfrak{N}, x) \Vdash \varphi$ and $(\mathfrak{N}, x) \Vdash \psi$;
- $(\mathfrak{N}, x) \Vdash \varphi \rightarrow \psi$ iff, $\forall y$, if $(\mathfrak{N}, y) \Vdash \varphi$, then $(\mathfrak{N}, x \cdot y) \Vdash \psi$;
- $(\mathfrak{N}, x) \Vdash \varphi \otimes \psi$ iff, $\exists yz$, $(\mathfrak{N}, y) \Vdash \varphi$, $(\mathfrak{N}, z) \Vdash \psi$, and $x \leq y \cdot z$;
- $(\mathfrak{N}, x) \Vdash B_a\varphi$ iff, for all $s \in Sit(x)$, $(\mathfrak{N}, \sigma_a(s)) \Vdash \varphi$;
- $(\mathfrak{N}, x) \Vdash C_A\varphi$ iff, for all $s \in Sit(x)$, $(\mathfrak{N}, \sigma_A^*(s)) \Vdash \varphi$;
- $(\mathfrak{N}, x) \Vdash [\varphi]\psi$ iff $(\mathfrak{N}^{[\varphi]}, x) \Vdash \psi$, where $\mathfrak{N}^{[\varphi]}$ differs from $\mathfrak{N}$ only in that $\sigma_a^{[\varphi]}(s) = \bigsqcup \{\sigma_a(s) \cdot y \mid (\mathfrak{N}, y) \Vdash \varphi\}$.

A formula φ is valid in a relevant information model $\mathfrak{N}$ if $(\mathfrak{N}, 1) \Vdash \varphi$. Note that since 1 is an identity for fusion an implication $\varphi \rightarrow \psi$ is valid in $\mathfrak{N}$ iff ψ is supported by all states of $\mathfrak{N}$ that support φ.

Lemma 6. *For any relevant information model $\mathfrak{N}$ and any formula φ from $\mathcal{L}$, there is a state $info^{\mathfrak{N}}(\varphi)$ in $\mathfrak{N}$ such that $\mathfrak{N}, x \Vdash \varphi$ iff $x \leq info^{\mathfrak{N}}(\varphi)$.*

Proof. The claim follows from the fact that for any φ from $\mathcal{L}$ the set of states supporting φ contains 0, is downward closed and closed under $\bigsqcup$. This can be shown by induction on φ. We will consider only the inductive steps for modal operators. The inductive steps for $\neg, \wedge, \rightarrow$ are discussed in [15]. Support by 0 and downward persistence for the operators $B_a, C_A, [\varphi]$ is straightforward. Let us prove that the set of states supporting $B_a\varphi$ is closed under $\bigsqcup$. Assume $(\mathfrak{N}, x_i) \Vdash B_a\varphi$, for each $i \in I$. Take any $s \in Sit(\bigsqcup_{i \in I} x_i)$. Since s is a situation, we obtain $s \in Sit(x_i)$, for some $i \in I$. It follows that $(\mathfrak{N}, \sigma_a(s)) \Vdash \varphi$. Hence $(\mathfrak{N}, \bigsqcup_{i \in I} x_i) \Vdash B_a\varphi$. The inductive step for C_A is analogous and the step for $[\varphi]$ is straightforward. $\square$

The state $info^{\mathfrak{N}}(\varphi)$, the existence of which is guaranteed by the previous lemma, represents the informational content of the formula φ in $\mathfrak{N}$. (If no confusion arises the superscript will be omitted.) Its existence allows us to characterize update of states in the following simplified way.

Lemma 7. $\sigma_a^{[\varphi]}(s) = \sigma_a(s) \cdot info(\varphi)$.

The semantics based on relevant information models is closely related to the semantics based on relevant epistemic models. In order to spell out the exact connection we will use the notion of duality of two semantic frameworks introduced in [15]. Let S_1 and S_2 be two semantic frameworks based respectively on some classes of models C_1 and C_2 and equipped with semantic clauses determining which formulas are valid in which models. We say that models $\mathfrak{M} \in C_1$ and $\mathfrak{N} \in C_2$ are $\mathcal{L}$-equivalent if they validate exactly the same formulas from $\mathcal{L}$. We say that the semantic system S_2 is a dual counterpart of S_1 w.r.t. the language $\mathcal{L}$ if there are two maps $f : C_1 \to C_2$ and $g : C_2 \to C_1$ such that (a) every $\mathfrak{M} \in C_1$ is $\mathcal{L}$-equivalent to $f(\mathfrak{M})$, and (b) for every $\mathfrak{M} \in C_1$ and $\mathfrak{N} \in C_2$ it holds that $g(f(\mathfrak{M}))$ is isomorphic to $\mathfrak{M}$ and $f(g(\mathfrak{N}))$ is isomorphic to $\mathfrak{N}$.

The main goal of this section is to show that the semantics based on relevant information models is a dual counterpart of the semantics based on relevant epistemic models. (As already pointed out, the added value of this dual counterpart is that it will allow us to capture not only statements but also questions.) This result extends the results from [15] that established similar duality between information models and Routley–Meyer models for a basic propositional language involving only the operators $\{\wedge, \to, \neg\}$.

We will now describe an operation that transforms relevant epistemic models into relevant information models. We will use the following notation: Let $(S, \sqsubseteq)$ be a partial order and $s \in S$. Then UpS denotes the set of all up-sets of S, and $s^\uparrow$ denotes the set $\{t \in S \mid s \sqsubseteq t\}$. Note that the sets of the form $s^\uparrow$ are exactly the situations in the complete lattice $(UpS, \subseteq)$.

Definition 12. *Let $\mathfrak{M} = (S, \sqsubseteq, L, R, C, E, V)$ be a relevant epistemic model. We define a corresponding structure $\mathfrak{M}^i = (P^i, \leq^i, 1^i, \cdot^i, C^i, \sigma^i, V^i)$, where $P^i = UpS$; $\leq^i = \subseteq$; $1^i = L$; $x \cdot^i y = \{s \in S \mid \exists t \in x, u \in y \text{ such that } Rtus\}$; $C^i xy$ iff there are $s \in x$ and $t \in y$ such that Cst; $\sigma_a^i(s^\uparrow) = E_a(s)$; $V^i = V$.*

Lemma 8. *If $\mathfrak{M}$ is a relevant epistemic model then $\mathfrak{M}^i$ is a relevant information model.*

Theorem 2. *$\mathfrak{M}^i$ is $\mathcal{L}$-equivalent to $\mathfrak{M}$, for every relevant epistemic model $\mathfrak{M}$.*

Proof. Let $\mathfrak{M} = (S, \sqsubseteq, L, R, C, E, V)$ be a relevant epistemic model, and $\mathfrak{M}^i = (P^i, \leq^i, 1^i, \cdot^i, C^i, \sigma^i, V^i)$ the corresponding relevant information model. We have to show that for any θ from $\mathcal{L}$, $(\mathfrak{M}^i, L) \Vdash \theta$ iff for all $s \in L$, $(\mathfrak{M}, s) \models \theta$. We prove something more general:

(*) For any $X \in UpS$, $(\mathfrak{M}^i, X) \Vdash \theta$ iff, for all $s \in X$, $(\mathfrak{M}, s) \models \theta$.

This can be proved by induction on θ. We will go only through the inductive steps for the operators B_a, C_A, and $[\varphi]$. Take any $X \in UpS$. As the induction hypothesis, assume that the claim (*) holds for some given formulas φ, ψ.

Assume that $\theta = B_a\varphi$. Then it holds: $(\mathfrak{M}^i, X) \Vdash B_a\varphi$ iff, for all $s \in X$, $(\mathfrak{M}^i, \sigma_a^i(s^\uparrow)) \Vdash \varphi$ iff, for all $s \in X$, $(\mathfrak{M}^i, E_a(s)) \Vdash \varphi$ iff (by induction hypothesis), for all $s \in X$ and for all $t \in E_a(s)$, $(\mathfrak{M}, t) \models \varphi$ iff, for all $s \in X$, $(\mathfrak{M}, s) \models B_a\varphi$.

Assume that $\theta = C_A\varphi$. It holds that $(\sigma_A^i)^*(s^\uparrow) = E_A^*(s)$ so we can proceed in the same way as in the case of $B_a\varphi$.

Finally assume that $\theta = [\varphi]\psi$. It can be shown that $(\mathfrak{M}^i)^{[\varphi]} = (\mathfrak{M}^{[\varphi]})^i$. So, we can proceed as follows: $(\mathfrak{M}^i, X) \Vdash [\varphi]\psi$ iff $((\mathfrak{M}^i)^{[\varphi]}, X) \Vdash \psi$ iff $((\mathfrak{M}^{[\varphi]})^i, X) \Vdash \psi$ iff, for all $s \in X$, $(\mathfrak{M}^{[\varphi]}, s) \models \psi$ iff, for all $s \in X$, $(\mathfrak{M}, s) \models [\varphi]\psi$.

Now we will define an inverse operation that transforms relevant information models into relevant epistemic models.

Definition 13. *Let* $\mathfrak{N} = (P, \leq, 1, \cdot, C, \sigma, V)$ *be a relevant information model. We define a corresponding structure* $\mathfrak{N}^e = (S^e, \sqsubseteq^e, L^e, R^e, C^e, E^e, V^e)$, *where* $S^e = Sit(P)$; $s \sqsubseteq^e t$ *iff* $t \leq s$; $L^e = Sit(1)$; $R^e stu$ *iff* $u \leq s \cdot t$; $C^e st$ *iff* Cst; $E_a^e(s) = Sit(\sigma_a(s))$; $V^e(p) = Sit(V(p))$.

Lemma 9. *If* $\mathfrak{N}$ *is a relevant information model then* $\mathfrak{N}^e$ *is a relevant epistemic model.*

Lemma 10. *Let* $\mathfrak{M} = (S, \sqsubseteq, L, R, C, E, V)$ *be a relevant epistemic model and let* $\mathfrak{M}^{ie} = (S^{ie}, \sqsubseteq^{ie}, L^{ie}, R^{ie}, C^{ie}, E^{ie}, V^{ie})$. *Then the map assigning to any* $s \in S$ *the set* $s^{\uparrow}$ *is a bijection between* S *and* S^{ie}. *Moreover, the following holds: (a)* $s \sqsubseteq t$ *iff* $s^{\uparrow} \sqsubseteq^{ie} t^{\uparrow}$, *(b)* $s \in L$ *iff* $s^{\uparrow} \in L^{ie}$, *(c)* $Rstu$ *iff* $R^{ie} s^{\uparrow} t^{\uparrow} u^{\uparrow}$, *(d)* Cst *iff* $C^{ie} s^{\uparrow} t^{\uparrow}$, *(e)* $E_a st$ *iff* $E_a^{ie} s^{\uparrow} t^{\uparrow}$, *(f)* $s \in V(p)$ *iff* $s^{\uparrow} \in V^{ie}(p)$.

Proof. For an illustration, we will just show how to prove (c) and (e). The proof of (c) goes as follows: $R^{ie} s^{\uparrow} t^{\uparrow} u^{\uparrow}$ iff $u^{\uparrow} \leq^i s^{\uparrow} \cdot^i t^{\uparrow}$ iff $u^{\uparrow} \subseteq s^{\uparrow} \cdot^i t^{\uparrow}$ iff $u \in s^{\uparrow} \cdot^i t^{\uparrow}$ iff $\exists v \in s^{\uparrow} \exists w \in t^{\uparrow} : Rvwu$ iff $Rstu$. (e) can be proved in the following way: $E_a st$ iff $t \in \sigma_a^i(s^{\uparrow})$ iff $t^{\uparrow} \leq^i \sigma_a^i(s^{\uparrow})$ iff $E_a^{ie} s^{\uparrow} t^{\uparrow}$.

Lemma 11. *Let* $\mathfrak{N} = (P, \leq, 1, \cdot, C, \sigma, V)$ *be a relevant information model and let* $\mathfrak{N}^{ei} = (P^{ei}, \leq^{ei}, 1^{ei}, \cdot^{ei}, C^{ei}, \sigma^{ei}, V^{ei})$. *The map assigning to any* $x \in P$ *the set* $Sit(x)$ *is a bijection between* P *and* P^{ei}. *Moreover, the following holds: (a)* $x \leq y$ *iff* $Sit(x) \leq^{ei} Sit(y)$, *(b)* $Sit(1) = 1^{ei}$, *(c)* $Sit(x \cdot y) = Sit(x) \cdot^{ei} Sit(y)$, *(d)* Cxy *iff* $C^{ei} Sit(x) Sit(y)$, *(e)* $Sit(\sigma_a(s)) = \sigma_a^{ei}(Sit(s))$, *(f)* $Sit(V(p)) = V^{ei}(p)$.

Lemmas 10 and 11 lead directly to the following theorem.

Theorem 3. $\mathfrak{M}$ *is isomorphic to* $\mathfrak{M}^{ie}$, *for every relevant epistemic model* $\mathfrak{M}$, *and* $\mathfrak{N}$ *is isomorphic to* $\mathfrak{N}^{ei}$, *for every relevant information model* $\mathfrak{N}$.

Theorems 3 and 2 together show that the the semantics based on relevant information models is indeed a dual counterpart of the semantics based on relevant epistemic models. As a consequence, RPAC is also complete with respect to relevant information models.

5   Questions

In this section we will extend the language $\mathcal{L}$ so that it will be possible to express not only statements but also questions. To this end, we will borrow some techniques from inquisitive semantics (see, e.g., [5,7]). Let $\mathcal{L}^{inq}$ denote the language $\mathcal{L}$ enriched with a binary connective $\mathbb{W}$ called *inquisitive disjunction*. The operator $\mathbb{W}$ can be embedded arbitrarily under any operator with the exception of the public announcement modality. We will assume that $[\varphi]\nu$ is in the language $\mathcal{L}^{inq}$ only if φ is a formula of the language $\mathcal{L}$ (but ν may contain inquisitive disjunction).

The formulas of the language $\mathcal{L}$ will be called *declarative*. The connective $\mathbb{W}$ produces questions from declarative formulas. Given declarative formulas φ, ψ, the formula $\varphi\mathbb{W}\psi$ expresses the question *whether φ or ψ*. This can be contrasted with $\varphi \vee \psi$ which expresses the statement *that φ or ψ*. (Recall that $\varphi \vee \psi$ is defined as $\neg(\neg\varphi \wedge \neg\psi)$.) The support condition for this additional connective is defined as follows:

$$(\mathfrak{N}, x) \Vdash \nu \mathbb{W} \mu \text{ iff } (\mathfrak{N}, x) \Vdash \nu \text{ or } (\mathfrak{N}, x) \Vdash \mu.$$

This captures the idea that an information state resolves a question if it provides some answer to the question. Compare the clause to the support condition for the declarative disjunction $\vee$ spelled out in the following lemma.

Lemma 12. $(\mathfrak{N}, x) \Vdash \nu \vee \mu$ *iff for all* $s \in Sit(x)$, $(\mathfrak{N}, s) \Vdash \nu$ *or* $(\mathfrak{N}, s) \Vdash \mu$.

In the language $\mathcal{L}^{inq}$ we can express directly, for example, that the agent's information state resolves the question ν $(B_a\nu)$, that the question is resolved by the common knowledge in a group $(C_A\nu)$, or that ν would be resolved after the public announcement of φ $([\varphi]\nu)$.

It is obvious from the semantic clause for inquisitive disjunction that the set of states supporting $\nu \mathbb{W} \mu$ is the union of the set of states supporting ν and the set of states supporting μ. As a consequence, Lemma 6 cannot be formulated for the whole language $\mathcal{L}^{inq}$. Sets of states supporting formulas of $\mathcal{L}^{inq}$ are not in general closed under join, though they are always downward closed and nonempty (contain always the least element).

Let InqRPAC be the logic consisting of all formulas from the language $\mathcal{L}^{inq}$ that are valid in all relevant information models. In formulation of an axiomatic system for InqRPAC we have to be careful to specify which schemata of RPAC are semantically valid for the whole language $\mathcal{L}^{inq}$ and which must be restricted to the declarative language $\mathcal{L}$. In particular, we can take the axiomatization of RPAC as specified in Fig. 1 and assume that we can substitute any formulas of $\mathcal{L}^{inq}$ for the variables in the axiom and rule schemata, with the exception of the variables occurring in the scope of the public announcement modality and in the double negation axiom (which is among the axioms of R), the reduction axiom for the belief modality (A7), and the rules (R6) and (R7). That is, the exception concerns the public announcement modality and the following axioms and rules:

(DN) $\neg\neg\varphi \to \varphi$ \qquad\qquad (A7) $[\varphi]B_a\psi \leftrightarrow B_a(\varphi \to [\varphi]\psi)$

(R6) $\dfrac{\nu \to (\varphi \wedge B_A\nu)}{\nu \to C_A\varphi}$ \qquad\qquad (R7) $\dfrac{\nu \to B_A(\varphi \to \nu) \quad \nu \to [\varphi]\psi}{\nu \to [\varphi]C_A\psi}$

To secure soundness we must assume that only declarative formulas can be substituted for φ and ψ in these four schemata (but any formula of $\mathcal{L}^{inq}$ can be substituted for ν). Let us illustrate the reason behind this restriction on the rule R6. Assume that $\nu \to (\varphi \wedge B_A\nu)$ is valid in a relevant information model $\mathfrak{N}$ and assume that $\mathfrak{N}, x \Vdash \nu$. Then $\mathfrak{N}, x \Vdash \varphi \wedge B_A\nu$. Let $s \in Sit(x)$. Then φ is supported by every state in $\{t \in P \mid \exists t_1, \ldots, t_n \in Sit(P): t_1 = s, t_{i+1} \le \sigma_A(t_i), t_n = t \}$.

Since we assume that φ is in $\mathcal{L}$, it is supported also by the join of this set, i.e. by $\sigma_A^*(s)$. Since this holds for every $s \in Sit(x)$, we obtain $\mathfrak{N}, x \Vdash C_A\varphi$ as desired. Hence, $\nu \to C_A\varphi$ is valid in $\mathfrak{N}$.

The system for InqRPAC consists of the system for RPAC, adjusted to the language $\mathcal{L}^{inq}$ in the just described way, and extended with the axioms in Fig. 2 that characterize inquisitive disjunction. Note that while ν, μ, θ range over arbitrary formulas of $\mathcal{L}^{inq}$, φ (in the axioms Inq7 and Inq10) is again restricted to formulas of $\mathcal{L}$. The axioms Inq1-Inq3 are the standard (introduction and elimination) axioms for disjunction. The axioms Inq4-Inq10 specify how the other operators of the language distribute over inquisitive disjunction. Note that the inverse implications of Inq4-Inq10 are provable from the other axioms.

(Inq1) $\nu \to \nu \mathbin{\wedge\!\!\!\vee} \mu$
(Inq2) $\mu \to \nu \mathbin{\wedge\!\!\!\vee} \mu$
(Inq3) $((\nu \to \theta) \wedge (\mu \to \theta)) \to ((\nu \mathbin{\wedge\!\!\!\vee} \mu) \to \theta)$
(Inq4) $\neg(\nu \mathbin{\wedge\!\!\!\vee} \mu) \to (\neg\nu \wedge \neg\mu)$
(Inq5) $(\theta \wedge (\nu \mathbin{\wedge\!\!\!\vee} \mu)) \to ((\theta \wedge \nu) \mathbin{\wedge\!\!\!\vee} (\theta \wedge \mu))$
(Inq6) $(\theta \otimes (\nu \mathbin{\wedge\!\!\!\vee} \mu)) \to ((\theta \otimes \nu) \mathbin{\wedge\!\!\!\vee} (\theta \otimes \mu))$
(Inq7) $(\varphi \to (\nu \mathbin{\wedge\!\!\!\vee} \mu)) \to ((\varphi \to \nu) \mathbin{\wedge\!\!\!\vee} (\varphi \to \mu))$ (for declarative φ)
(Inq8) $B_a(\nu \mathbin{\wedge\!\!\!\vee} \mu) \to (B_a\nu \vee B_a\mu)$
(Inq9) $C_A(\nu \mathbin{\wedge\!\!\!\vee} \mu) \to (C_A\nu \vee C_A\mu)$
(Inq10) $[\varphi](\nu \mathbin{\wedge\!\!\!\vee} \mu) \to ([\varphi]\nu \mathbin{\wedge\!\!\!\vee} [\varphi]\mu)$ (for declarative φ)

Fig. 2. The axioms for inquisitive disjunction in the system for InqRPAC.

Lemma 13. *The system for InqRPAC is sound with respect to all relevant information models.*

We can prove completeness of the system InqRPAC using a strategy that is common in inquisitive logic (see, e.g., [15]). In our specific setting this strategy amounts to the reduction of completeness for InqRPAC to completeness for RPAC (which was proved in Sect. 3). Such a reduction is possible due to two characteristic properties of the logic that need to be proved: (1) disjunctive normal form, and (2) disjunction property.

Lemma 14. *For any formula ν of $\mathcal{L}^{inq}$ there are formulas $\varphi_1, \ldots, \varphi_n$ of $\mathcal{L}$ such that $\nu \leftrightarrow (\varphi_1 \mathbin{\wedge\!\!\!\vee} \ldots \mathbin{\wedge\!\!\!\vee} \varphi_n)$ is a theorem of InqRPAC.*

Proof. This is a straightforward extension of a standard theorem in inquisitive logic. (For more details, see, e.g., [13].) One can proceed by induction on the complexity of ν using the distributive axioms Inq4-Inq10 and their converses.

Lemma 15. *Let ν, μ be formulas of $\mathcal{L}^{inq}$. Then $\nu \mathbin{\wedge\!\!\!\vee} \mu$ is valid in every relevant information model only if ν is valid in every relevant information model or μ is valid in every relevant information model.*

Proof. To prove this claim, we will adapt to our current setting a technique developed in [13]. For any relevant information models $\mathfrak{N}_1 = (P_1, \leq_1, 1_1, \cdot_1, C_1, \sigma_1, V_1)$ and $\mathfrak{N}_2 = (P_2, \leq_2, 1_2, \cdot_2, C_2, \sigma_2, V_2)$ we can define their product $\mathfrak{N}_1 \times \mathfrak{N}_2 = (P, \leq, 1, \cdot, C, \sigma, V)$ where $P = P_1 \times P_2$ (the Cartesian product of P_1 and P_2); $(x, y) \leq (v, w)$ iff $x \leq_1 v$ and $y \leq_2 w$; $1 = (1_1, 1_2)$; $(x, y) \cdot (v, w) = (x \cdot_1 v, y \cdot_2 w)$; $C(x, y)(v, w)$ iff $C_1 x v$ or $C_2 y w$; $\sigma_a((s, t)) = (\sigma_1(a)(s), \sigma_2(a)(t))$; $V(p) = (V_1(p), V_2(p))$. It can be shown that $\mathfrak{N}_1 \times \mathfrak{N}_2$ is again a relevant information model. Assume that 0_1 is the least element of $\mathfrak{N}_1$ and 0_2 is the least element of $\mathfrak{N}_2$. The following holds for any formula ν of $\mathcal{L}^{inq}$:

  (a) $(\mathfrak{N}_1 \times \mathfrak{N}_2, (x, 0_2)) \Vdash \nu$ iff $(\mathfrak{N}_1, x) \Vdash \nu$,
  (b) $(\mathfrak{N}_1 \times \mathfrak{N}_2, (0_1, y)) \Vdash \nu$ iff $(\mathfrak{N}_2, y) \Vdash \nu$.

These claims can be proved by induction on the complexity of ν. For an illustration, let us consider the inductive step for $[\varphi]$. Assume that (a) and (b) hold for some φ from $\mathcal{L}$ and μ from $\mathcal{L}^{inq}$. Using the induction hypothesis it can be shown that $(\mathfrak{N}_1 \times \mathfrak{N}_2)^{[\varphi]} = \mathfrak{N}_1^{[\varphi]} \times \mathfrak{N}_2^{[\varphi]}$. Using this fact we can prove the inductive step for $[\varphi]$ as follows: $(\mathfrak{N}_1 \times \mathfrak{N}_2, (x, 0_2)) \Vdash [\varphi]\mu$ iff $((\mathfrak{N}_1 \times \mathfrak{N}_2)^{[\varphi]}, (x, 0_2)) \Vdash \mu$ iff $(\mathfrak{N}_1^{[\varphi]} \times \mathfrak{N}_2^{[\varphi]}, (x, 0_2)) \Vdash \mu$ iff $(\mathfrak{N}_1^{[\varphi]}, x) \Vdash \mu$ iff $(\mathfrak{N}_1, x) \Vdash [\varphi]\mu$. The step for (b) is analogous.

Assuming that we have proved (a) and (b) we can prove disjunction property as follows. Assume that there is a relevant information model $\mathfrak{N}_1$ in which ν is not valid, and a relevant information model $\mathfrak{N}_2$ in which μ is not valid. Then $(\mathfrak{N}_1, 1_1) \nVdash \nu$ and $(\mathfrak{N}_2, 1_2) \nVdash \mu$. If follows from (a) and (b) that $(\mathfrak{N}_1 \times \mathfrak{N}_2, (1_1, 0_2)) \nVdash \nu$ and $(\mathfrak{N}_1 \times \mathfrak{N}_2, (0_1, 1_2)) \nVdash \mu$. By persistence, $(\mathfrak{N}_1 \times \mathfrak{N}_2, (1_1, 1_2)) \nVdash \nu \mathbin{\mathpalette\@vee\relax} \mu$ and thus $\nu \mathbin{\mathpalette\@vee\relax} \mu$ is not valid in $\mathfrak{N}_1 \times \mathfrak{N}_2$.

Theorem 4. *ν is a theorem of* InqRPAC *iff ν is valid in all relevant information models.*

Proof. The left-to-right direction amounts to Lemma 13. For the right-to-left direction assume that ν is valid in all relevant information models. Then, by disjunctive normal form (Lemma 14), there are $\varphi_1, \ldots, \varphi_n$ in $\mathcal{L}$ such that $\nu \leftrightarrow (\varphi_1 \mathbin{\mathpalette\@vee\relax} \ldots \mathbin{\mathpalette\@vee\relax} \varphi_n)$ is a theorem of InqRPAC. By soundness (Lemma 13), $\varphi_1 \mathbin{\mathpalette\@vee\relax} \ldots \mathbin{\mathpalette\@vee\relax} \varphi_n$ is valid in all relevant information models. By disjunction property (Lemma 15), for some i, φ_i is valid in all relevant information models. By duality between relevant information models and relevant epistemic models for $\mathcal{L}$ (Theorems 3 and 2) we obtain that φ_i is valid in every relevant epistemic model. By completeness of RPAC w.r.t. relevant epistemic models (Theorem 1), φ_i is a theorem of RPAC. Since InqRPAC is an extension of RPAC, φ_i is also a theorem of InqRPAC. It follows that $\varphi_1 \mathbin{\mathpalette\@vee\relax} \ldots \mathbin{\mathpalette\@vee\relax} \varphi_n$ is a theorem of InqRPAC. Hence, ν is a theorem of InqRPAC.

The semantics based on information models allows us to equip agents not only with information states but also with issues.[4] Then one can define also

---

[4] In [6] issues were introduced in the context of standard inquisitive epistemic logic based on classical logic. In [16] issues were introduced in the semantics of substructural inquisitive epistemic logic.

a public utterance of questions and the inquisitive analogues of the modalities B_a and C_A.[5] This would be an interesting further extension of the language $\mathcal{L}^{inq}$. However, the methods employed in this paper cannot be directly applied to this extension. The reason is that completeness for such a language cannot be straightforwardly reduced to completeness of its non-inquisitive fragment, which was possible in the case of the language $\mathcal{L}^{inq}$. The inquisitive analogue of B_a was studied in the context of substructural inquisitive logics in [16]. The investigation of the inquisitive analogue of C_A is left for future research.

6   Conclusion

This paper can be seen as a further expansion of our previous work on modal and inquisitive substructural logics [13–16,24,25]. In particular, we have extended the relevant logic R with various epistemic operators and studied their interactions. The main novelty of the paper is the incorporation of common knowledge into this rich context. The main result of the paper is a completeness of R, extended with a belief modality, public announcement and common knowledge, with respect to a suitable relational semantics (Theorem 1). We also considered an alternative semantics that allowed us to express also questions in the object language and we presented a completeness proof also for this enriched language (Theorem 4).

Acknowledgement. This work is supported by the Czech Science Foundation grant number GJ18-19162Y. We thank three anonymous reviewers for their valuable comments.

References

1. Balbiani, P., Galmiche, D.: About intuitionistic public announcement logic. In: Beklemishev, L., Demri, S., Máté, A. (eds.) Proceedings of 11th International Conference on Advances in Modal Logic (AiML 2016), pp. 97–116. College Publications (2016)
2. Barwise, J., Perry, J.: Situations and Attitudes. MIT Press, Cambridge (1983)
3. Bílková, M., Majer, O., Peliš, M.: Epistemic logics for sceptical agents. J. Log. Comput. **26**(6), 1815–1841 (2016)
4. Cabrer, L., Rivieccio, U., Rodriguez, R.O.: Lukasiewicz public announcement logic. In: Carvalho, J.P., Lesot, M.-J., Kaymak, U., Vieira, S., Bouchon-Meunier, B., Yager, R.R. (eds.) IPMU 2016. CCIS, vol. 611, pp. 108–122. Springer, Cham (2016). https://doi.org/10.1007/978-3-319-40581-0_10
5. Ciardelli, I.: Questions in logic. Ph.D. thesis, University of Amsterdam (2016)
6. Ciardelli, I., Roelofsen, F.: Inquisitive dynamic epistemic logic. Synthese **192**(6), 1643–1687 (2015)

---

[5] The inquisitive analogue of B_a is a standard modality in inquisitive epistemic logic usually denoted as E_a (see [6]). The inquisitive analogue of C_A was introduced semantically in [5] in the context of standard inquisitive epistemic logic without an axiomatic characterization.

7. Ciardelli, I., Groenendijk, J., Roelofsen, F.: Inquisitive Semantics. Oxford University Press, Oxford (2019)
8. Dunn, J.M., Restall, G.: Relevance logic. In: Gabbay, D.M., Guenthner, F. (eds.) Handbook of Philosophical Logic, 2nd edn., vol. 6, pp. 1–128. Kluwer (2002)
9. Fagin, R., Halpern, J.Y., Moses, Y., Vardi, M.Y.: Reasoning About Knowledge. MIT Press, Cambridge (1995)
10. Levesque, H.: A logic of implicit and explicit belief. In: Proceedings of AAAI 1984, pp. 198–202 (1984)
11. Ma, M., Palmigiano, A., Sadrzadeh, M.: Algebraic semantics and model completeness for intuitionistic public announcement logic. Ann. Pure Appl. Log. **165**(4), 963–995 (2014)
12. Plaza, J.: Logics of public communications. In: Emrich, M.L., Pfeifer, M.S., Hadzikadic, M., Ras, W.Z. (eds.) Proceedings of 4th International Symposium on Methodologies for Intelligent Systems: Poster Session Program, pp. 201–216. Oak Ridge National Laboratory (1989)
13. Punčochář, V.: Substructural inquisitive logics. Rev. Symb. Log. **12**, 296–330 (2019)
14. Punčochář, V.: Inquisitive dynamic epistemic logic in a non-classical setting. In: Martins, M.A., Sedlár, I. (eds.) DaLi 2020. LNCS, vol. 12569, pp. 205–221. Springer, Cham (2020). https://doi.org/10.1007/978-3-030-65840-3_13
15. Punčochář, V.: A relevant logic of questions. J. Philos. Log. **49**(5), 905–939 (2020)
16. Punčochář, V., Sedlár, I.: Epistemic extensions of substructural inquisitive logics. J. Log. Comput. (2020). First Online
17. Restall, G.: Relevant and substructural logics. In: Hanbook of the History of Logic, vol. 7, pp. 289–398. Elsevier (2006)
18. Rivieccio, U.: Bilattice public announcement logic. In: Goré, R., Kooi, B., Kurucz, A. (eds.) Advances in Modal Logic 2014, pp. 459–477. College Publications (2014)
19. Routley, R., Routley, V.: The role of inconsistent and incomplete theories in the logic of belief. Comm. Cogn. **8**(2/4), 185–235 (1975)
20. Santos, Y.D.: A four-valued dynamic epistemic logic. J. Log. Lang. Inf. **29**(4), 451–489 (2020)
21. Sedlár, I.: Substructural epistemic logics. J. Appl. Non-Classical Log. **25**(3), 256–285 (2015)
22. Sedlár, I.: Epistemic extensions of modal distributive substructural logics. J. Log. Comput. **26**(6), 1787–1813 (2016)
23. Sedlár, I.: A general completeness argument for propositional dynamic logic. In: Advances in Modal Logic 2020, Short Papers, pp. 102–106 (2020)
24. Sedlár, I.: Relational semantics for propositional dynamic logics. Submitted manuscript, June 2021
25. Sedlár, I., Tedder, A.: Situated epistemic updates. In: Proceedings of LORI-VIII (2021, to appear)
26. van Ditmarsch, H., van der Hoek, W., Kooi, B.: Dynamic Epistemic Logic. Springer, Heidelberg (2008). https://doi.org/10.1007/978-1-4020-5839-4

A Variant with the Variable-Sharing Property of Brady's 4-Valued Implicative Expansion BN4 of Anderson and Belnap's Logic FDE

Gemma Robles[(✉)][iD]

Dpto. de Psicología, Sociología y Filosofía, Universidad de León,
Campus de Vegazana, s/n, 24071 León, Spain
gemma.robles@unileon.es
http://grobv.unileon.es

Abstract. A logic L has the "variable-sharing property" (VSP) if in all L-theorems of conditional form antecedent and consequent share at least a propositional variable. Anderson and Belnap consider the VSP as a necessary property any relevance logic has to fulfil. Now, among relevance logicians, Brady's logic BN4 is widely viewed as the adequate implicative 4-valued logic. But BN4 does not have the VSP. The aim of this paper is to define a variant of BN4 having, in addition to the VSP, some properties that do not support its consideration as a mere artificial construct.

Keywords: Relevant logics · 4-valued relevant logics · Two-valued Belnap-Dunn semantics · Variable-sharing property · Brady's 4-valued logic BN4

1 Introduction

A logic L has the "variable-sharing property" (VSP) if in all L-theorems of the form $A \rightarrow B$, A and B share at least a propositional variable. Anderson and Belnap consider the VSP as a necessary condition any relevance logic worthy of the name has to fulfil (cf. [1]). On the other hand, Anderson and Belnap's *First degree entailment logic*, FDE, is the minimal logic in their De Morgan family of relevant logics (cf. [1], §15.2). FDE is also known as Belnap and Dunn's 4-valued logic BD4 (our label). BD4 can be viewed as a 4-valued logic in which formulas can be both true and false or neither true nor false, in addition to being true and false (cf. [1,5,6,9,10]).

The question of expanding FDE with a full implicative connective poses itself, since as the name of the logic suggests, formulas of the form $A \rightarrow B$ are

This work is supported by the Spanish Ministry of Science and Innovation under Grant [PID2020-116502GB-I00]. We thank three referees of CLAR 2021 for their comments and suggestions on a previous draft of this paper.

© Springer Nature Switzerland AG 2021
P. Baroni et al. (Eds.): CLAR 2021, LNAI 13040, pp. 362–376, 2021.
https://doi.org/10.1007/978-3-030-89391-0_20

not considered in FDE if either A or B contains $\rightarrow$ (cf. [1], p. 158 where the postulates of the system are given together with the note "the variables range over truth-functions of variables"). Some full implicative expansions of FDE have been given in the literature (cf. [7,13–15,17,18,21] and references in the last two items), but there is still a lot of investigation to be done in the topic (cf. [17]).

Among the implicative expansions of FDE, Brady's 4-valued logic BN4 (cf. [7]) seems to be regarded as the adequate implicative 4-valued logic. In this sense, Meyer et al. note: "BN4 is the correct logic for the 4-valued situation where extra values are to be interpreted in the *both* and *neither* senses" (cf. [16], p. 25). On his part, Slaney thinks that BN4 has the truth-functional implication most naturally associated with FDE (cf. [24], p. 289). And, nevertheless, BN4 lacks the VSP (cf. [21][1]), as it is the case with all the implicative expansions of FDE proposed so far, to the best of our knowledge.

The aim of this paper is then to define a variant of BN4, the logic BN4^{VSP}, enjoying the variable-sharing property. It will be proved that, in addition to the VSP, BN4^{VSP} has other interesting properties such as paraconsistency and paracompleteness. Moreover, BN4^{VSP} has a *natural conditional* in a sense akin to that defined in [25] (cf. Definition 5 and Remark 4 below), and last but not least, it fulfils all conditions required of implicative logics in the classical Polish logical tradition except, of course, that of complying with the rule VEQ, $A \Rightarrow B \rightarrow A$ (cf. Definition 9 below)[2].

Before explaining the structure of the paper, let us note a last remark. It is known that there are infinitely many logics with the VSP (cf. [11]). Furthermore, some many-valued logics with the VSP have been studied in the literature. For example, the logic characterized by Belnap's eigth-element matrix $\mathrm{M_0}$ (cf. [4]), axiomatized in [8]; or the logic determined by Meyer's six-element crystal lattice CL, also axiomatized in [8]. But it does not seem possible to interpret in a intuitive clear way the meaning of the logical values in these matrices. However, the meaning of the four values in FDE (or BD4) and its expansions is crystalline.

The paper is organized as follows.

In Sect. 2, the matrix MBN4^{VSP}, a variant of Brady's matrix MBN4 is defined. Let L be the logic defined by using the consequence relation associated with MBN4^{VSP}: for any set of wffs Γ and wff A, $\Gamma \vDash_{\mathrm{MBN4^{VSP}}} A$ iff A is assigned a designated value whenever Γ is assigned a designated value for any MBN4^{VSP}-interpretation (cf. Definition 1). It is proved that L has a natural conditional and also that L (and so any logic included in it) has the variable-sharing property. In Sect. 3, a Hilbert-type system equivalent to L is given. Let us call this system BN4^{VSP}. Of course, we could have used the methods in [2,3]

---

[1] Actually, in [21] it is stated that BN4 has the "quasi relevance property" (QRP) The QRP reads: if $A \rightarrow B$ is a theorem, then either A and B share at least a propositional variable or both $\neg A$ and B are theorems. But BN4 lacks the VSP: $\neg(A \rightarrow A) \rightarrow (B \rightarrow B)$ is MBN4-valid.

[2] Notice that the rule VEQ encloses an infinity of paradoxes of relevance, the simplest of which may be $q \rightarrow (p \rightarrow p)$. Consequently, it cannot be a rule of a logic with the VSP.

(resp., those in [18]), in order to define a Gentzen-type system (resp., a natural deduction system) equivalent to L. Instead, we shall use two-valued Belnap-Dunn semantics to formulate BN4^{VSP}. But let us stress that the aim of this paper *is not* to axiomatize MBN4^{VSP}, but to highlight this matrix and the properties the logic it determines enjoys when defined from a Hilbert-style point of view. No doubt, other properties of this logic can be emphasized when defined as a Gentzen-type system or a natural deduction one. Concerning the relative merits of these three methods just mentioned, cf. [20], §6 and [18], §8. Anyway, the one used here has been employed in other works by us (cf. [14,15,21]). As pointed out in the referred papers, this method is based upon [7] as applied in said papers. Thus, it will not be necessary to go to each detail in the soundness and completeness proofs, and some of the general ideas or strategies in these proofs will be referred to the items mentioned above. In Sect. 3, we prove some of the proof-theoretical properties of BN4^{VSP}, that is, some of the properties of the logic determined by MBN4^{VSP} when formulated as a Hilbert-type system. In Sect. 4, we prove the (strong) soundness and completeness of BN4^{VSP} w.r.t. the two-valued Belnap-Dunn semantics defined in Sect. 3. Finally, the paper is ended in Sect. 5 with some concluding remarks on the results obtained and a couple of suggestions on future work on the topic.

2   The Matrix MBN4^{VSP}

In this section the matrix MBN4^{VSP} is defined.

MBN4^{VSP} is an implicative expansion of Belnap and Dunn's matrix $\mathcal{FOUR}$ characterizing Anderson and Belnap's *First degree entailment logic*, FDE (cf. [1], §15.2, [5,6,9,10]). But MBN4^{VSP} actually originates as a modification of Brady's matrix MBN4, also an implicative expansion of $\mathcal{FOUR}$ (cf. [7]). It will be proved that the implicative expansion of FDE, BN4^{VSP}, enjoying the VSP is determined by the matrix MBN4^{VSP}.

Definition 1 (Preliminary notions). *The propositional language consists of a denumerable set of propositional variables $p_0, p_1, ..., p_n, ...,$ and the following connectives: $\rightarrow$ (conditional), $\wedge$ (conjunction), $\vee$ (disjunction) and $\neg$ (negation). The biconditional and the set of wffs is defined in the customary way. A, B, C, etc. are metalinguistic variables. Then logics are formulated as Hilbert-type axiomatic systems, the notions of 'theorem' and 'proof from a set of premises' being the usual ones, while the following notions are understood in a fairly standard sense (cf., e.g., [14,15,21]): extension and expansion of a given logic, logical matrix M and M-interpretation, M-consequence, M-validity and, finally, M-determined logic.*

Definition 2 (Belnap and Dunn's matrix $\mathcal{FOUR}$). *The propositional language consists of the connectives $\wedge, \vee$ and $\neg$. Belnap and Dunn's matrix $\mathcal{FOUR}$ is the structure $(\mathcal{V}, D, \mathbf{F})$ where (1) $\mathcal{V}$ is $\{0, 1, 2, 3\}$ and is partially ordered as shown in the following lattice:*

(2) $D = \{2,3\}$; $F = \{f_\wedge, f_\vee, f_\neg\}$ *where* $f_\wedge$ *and* $f_\vee$ *are defined as the glb (or lattice meet) and the lub (or lattice joint), respectively. Finally,* $f_\neg$ *is an involution with* $f_\neg(0) = 3, f_\neg(3) = 0, f_\neg(1) = 1, f_\neg(2) = 2$ *(cf. [5,6,9,10]). We display the tables for* $\wedge, \vee$ *and* $\neg$:

$\wedge$	0 1 2 3	$\vee$	0 1 2 3	$\neg$	
0	0 0 0 0	0	0 1 2 3	0	3
1	0 1 0 1	1	1 1 3 3	1	1
2	0 0 2 2	2	2 3 2 3	2	2
3	0 1 2 3	3	3 3 3 3	3	0

Remark 1 (On the symbols for referring to the four truth-values). It is customary to use f, n, b and t instead of $0, 1, 2$ and 3, respectively (cf., e.g., [17]). The former stand for false only, neither true or false, both true and false and true only, respectively. The latter have been chosen in order to use the tester in [12], in case one is needed. Also, to put in connection the results in the present paper with previous work by us.

Definition 3 (Brady's matrix MBN4). *The propositional language consists of the connectives* $\rightarrow, \wedge, \vee$ *and* $\neg$. *The matrix MBN4 is the structure* $(\mathcal{V}, D, F)$ *where (1)* $\mathcal{V}$ *and* D *are defined as in* $\mathcal{FOUR}$ *and* $F = \{f_\rightarrow, f_\wedge, f_\vee, f_\neg\}$ *where* $f_\wedge$ *and* $f_\vee$ *and* $f_\neg$ *are defined as in* $\mathcal{FOUR}$, *and* $f_\rightarrow$ *is defined according to the following truth-table (cf. [7]):*

$\rightarrow$	0 1 2 3
0	3 3 3 3
1	1 3 1 3
2	0 1 2 3
3	0 1 0 3

Definition 4 (The matrix MBN4^{VSP}). *The matrix MBN4^{VSP} is defined similarly as MBN4, except that the truth-table according to which* $\rightarrow$ *is interpreted in MBN4 is replaced by the following one:*

$\rightarrow$	0 1 2 3
0	3 3 1 3
1	1 3 1 3
2	0 1 2 1
3	0 1 0 3

Remark 2 (The table for ↔). Below, the truth-table of the biconditional (↔) is displayed since this connective plays a role more significant in BN4^{VSP} than in most propositional logics (cf. Propositions 5 and 6 below).

↔	0	1	2	3
0	3	1	0	0
1	1	3	1	1
2	0	1	2	0
3	0	1	0	3

Remark 3 (On the conditional table in MBN4^{VSP}). We note that the condition $0 \to 2 = 1$ is not strictly necessary in order to prove the VSP. Nevertheless, if $0 \to 2 = 3$ is maintained, then the rule Contraposition (i.e., $A \to B \Rightarrow \neg B \to \neg A$) would not preserve MBN4^{VSP}-validity (consider any MBN4^{VSP}-interpretation I such that for different propositional variables p, q, we have $I(p) = 0$ and $I(q) = 2$. Then, $I(p \to q) = 3$, but $I(\neg q \to \neg p) = 1$).

We remark that the conditional defined by MBN4^{VSP} is a natural conditional in accordance with the following definition (cf. Definition 2.5 in [22]).

Definition 5 (Natural conditionals). *Let $\mathcal{V}$ and D be defined as in Definition 2. Then an $f_\to$-function on $\mathcal{V}$ defines a natural conditional if the following conditions are satisfied:*

1. *$f_\to$ coincides with (the $f_\to$-function for) the classical conditional when restricted to the subset $\{0, 3\}$ of $\mathcal{V}$.*
2. *$f_\to$ satisfies Modus Ponens, that is, for any $a, b \in \mathcal{V}$, if $a \to b \in D$ and $a \in D$, then $b \in D$.*
3. *For any $a, b \in \mathcal{V}$, $a \to b \in D$ if $a = b$.*

Remark 4 (Natural conditionals in Tomova's original paper). We note that natural conditionals are defined in [25] exactly as in Definition 5 except for condition (3), which reads there as follows: For any $a, b \in \mathcal{V}$, $a \to b \in D$ if $a \leq b$. (Notice that the conditional defined by Brady's MBN4 is a natural conditional in Tomova's sense.)

In the following section, it is proved that the logic BN4^{VSP}, shown MBN4^{VSP}-determined in Sect. 4, fulfils all conditions required of an implicative logic in the classical Polish logical tradition (cf., e.g., [19] or [26]), except, of course, that of complying with VEQ (cf. Sect. 1 above). For now, it is proved that BN4^{VSP} enjoys (an adapted to the matrix-determined logics version of) the *variable-sharing property* (VSP).

Definition 6 (VSP for matrix-determined logics). *Let L be a logic determined by the matrix M. L has the variable-sharing property (VSP) if A and B share at least a propositional variable in all M-valid wffs of the form $A \to B$.*

Definition 7 (VSP standard definition). *A logic L has the VSP if A and B share at least a propositional variable in all L-theorems of the form $A \to B$.*

Of course, once L has been shown M-determined via a soundness and completeness theorem, L has the VSP in the sense of Definition 6 iff L has the VSP in the sense of Definition 7. Next, it is proved that the logic determined by MBN4^{VSP} we have referred to by BN4^{VSP} has the VSP as this property is rendered in Definition 6.

Proposition 1 (BN4^{VSP} has the VSP). *Let $A \to B$ be an MBN4^{VSP}-valid wff. Then A and B share at least a propositional variable.*

Proof. Suppose that A and B do not share propositional variables. It is proved that $A \to B$ is not MBN4^{VSP}-valid. Let I be an MBN4^{VSP}-interpretation assigning 2 (resp., 0) to each propositional variable in A (resp., B). Then, $I(A) = 2$ and $I(B) \in \{0,3\}$ since $\{2\}$ and $\{0,3\}$ are closed under $\to, \wedge, \vee$ and $\neg$. Consequently, $I(A \to B) \in \{0,1\}$.

3 The Logic BN4^{VSP}

The logic BN4^{VSP}, that is, the logic determined by the matrix MBN4^{VSP}, can be formulated in a Hilbert-style way as follows.

Definition 8 (The logic BN4^{VSP}). *The logic BN4^{VSP} can be formulated with the following axioms, rules of inference and metarule ($A_1, ..., A_n \Rightarrow B$ means 'if $A_1, ..., A_n$, then B')[3]:*
Axioms:

> A1. $A \to A$
> A2. $(A \wedge B) \to (B \wedge A)$
> A3. $[A \wedge (B \wedge C)] \to [(A \wedge B) \wedge C]$
> A4. $[A \wedge (B \vee C)] \leftrightarrow [(A \wedge B) \vee (A \wedge C)]$
> A5. $\neg(A \vee B) \leftrightarrow (\neg A \wedge \neg B)$
> A6. $(A \to \neg B) \to (B \to \neg A)$
> A7. $\neg\neg A \to A$
> A8. $(A \vee \neg B) \vee (A \to B)$
> A9. $[(A \wedge B) \wedge (\neg A \wedge \neg B)] \to (A \to B)$

---

[3] A referee of CLAR 2021 worries about many-valued extensions because of the presence of such formulas as A8. This is an interesting question we cannot discuss in detail here. Let us only remark that the type of formulas the referee is concerned about is not the only fault of many-valued extensions; actually, they do not seem to collide with the VSP. For example, it is shown in "A general characterization of the variable-sharing property by means of logical matrices" (G. Robles and J. M. Méndez, *Notre Dame Journal of Formal Logic*, 53(2), 223–244, 2012) that relatively strong logics with the VSP have Dummett's axiom for the intermediate logic LC (i.e., $(A \to B) \vee (B \to A)$) as one of their theorems. The conclusion seems inescapable: the VSP and the disjunction property are independent of each other.

Rules of inference:

$$R1 \ (Adj). \ A, B \Rightarrow A \wedge B$$
$$R2 \ (MP). \ A \to B, A \Rightarrow B$$
$$R3 \ (E\wedge). \ A \wedge B \Rightarrow A, B$$
$$R4 \ (I\vee). \ A \Rightarrow A \vee B, B \vee A$$
$$R5 \ (CI\wedge). \ A \to B, A \to C \Rightarrow A \to (B \wedge C)$$
$$R6 \ (Fac \leftrightarrow). \ A \leftrightarrow B \Rightarrow (A \wedge C) \leftrightarrow (B \wedge C)$$
$$R7 \ (Pref). \ B \to C \Rightarrow (A \to B) \to (A \to C)$$
$$R8. \ \neg A \wedge \neg B \Rightarrow (A \vee B) \vee (A \to B)$$
$$R9. \ A \wedge B \Rightarrow (\neg A \vee \neg B) \vee (A \to B)$$
$$R10. \ A \to B, A \wedge \neg A \Rightarrow \neg B$$
$$R11. \ A \to B, B \wedge \neg B \Rightarrow \neg A$$
$$R12. \ \neg(A \to B) \Rightarrow A \wedge \neg B$$
$$R13. \ A \wedge \neg B \Rightarrow \neg(A \to B)$$

Metarule:

$$(MR). \ \text{If } A, B \Rightarrow C, \text{ then } D \vee A, D \vee B \Rightarrow D \vee C$$

Remark 5 (On the axiomatization of $BN4^{VSP}$). CI$\wedge$, Fac$\leftrightarrow$ and Pref abbreviate "conditioned introduction of conjunction", "factor w.r.t. $\leftrightarrow$" and "Prefixing", respectively. The metarule MR can be dropped if a "disjunctive version" of each rule is added. (The disjunctive version of, e.g., MP is the following rule: $C \vee (A \to B), C \vee A \Rightarrow C \vee B$. On the role of disjunctive rules in certain logics, cf. [8, 23] and references therein.)

Remark 6 (On $BN4^{VSP}$ and the logic DW). Routley and Meyer's basic logic B is axiomatized as follows (cf. [23], Chapter 4). Axioms: (a1) $A \to A$; (a2) $(A \wedge B) \to A$, $(A \wedge B) \to B$; (a3) $A \to (A \vee B)$, $B \to (A \vee B)$; (a4) $[(A \to B) \wedge (A \to C)] \to [A \to (B \wedge C)]$; (a5) $[(A \to C) \wedge (B \to C)] \to [(A \vee B) \to C]$; (a6) $[A \wedge (B \vee C)] \to [(A \wedge B) \vee (A \wedge C)]$; (a7) $A \to \neg\neg A$; (a8) $\neg\neg A \to A$. Rules of inference: Adj; MP; Pref; Suffixing (Suf) $A \to B \Rightarrow (B \to C) \to (A \to C)$ and contraposition (Con) $A \to B \Rightarrow \neg B \to \neg A$. Then the logic DW is an important weak relevant logic extending B, which is axiomatized when deleting A7 and Con, while adding the axiom (a7$'$) $(A \to \neg B) \to (B \to \neg A)$ (cf. [23], Chapter 4). Well then, consider now the logic DW$'$ axiomatized with A1-A7 and R1-R5, Evee (T16), Pref and Suf. This is a sublogic of DW obtained by restricting a2, a3, a4 and a5 to their respective rule form. Thus, BN4^{VSP} can intuitively be considered as a 4-valued extension of DW$'$ enjoying the "relevance principle", i.e., the VSP. Axioms A8 and A9 and R8-R13 are characteristic features of this 4-valued extension.

Remark 7 (The axiomatization of BN4). Brady's BN4 can be axiomatized as a 4-valued extension of contractionless relevant logic RW. Given DW (cf. Remark

6), RW can be axiomatized by deleting the rules Pref and Suf, while adding the axioms (a8) $(A \to B) \to [(B \to C) \to (A \to B)]$, (a9) $A \to [(A \to B) \to B]$ and the rule Disjunctive Modus Ponens (dMP), $C \lor (A \to B), C \lor A \Rightarrow C \lor B$. Then, BN4 can be axiomatized by adding the following axioms to RW. (a10) $(\neg A \land B) \to (A \to B)$; (a11) $\neg A \to [A \lor (A \to B)]$, (a12) $(A \lor \neg B) \lor (A \to B)$ and (a13) $A \lor [\neg(A \to B) \to A]$ (cf. [15,21]). So a10-a13 are the characteristic axioms of BN4, a 4-valued extension of relevant logic RW, while BN4^{VSP} is a 4-valued extension of the (weaker) relevant logic DW.

On the other hand, all axioms and rules of BN4^{VSP}, except R10, are provable in BN4, while a10, a11 and a13 of BN4 fail in BN4^{VSP}, and a9 holds only as a rule of inference.

In what follows, we prove some proof-theoretical properties of BN4^{VSP}.

Proposition 2 (Some theorems and rules of BN4^{VSP}). *The following are provable in BN4^{VSP}:*

$$T1.\ A \leftrightarrow A$$

$$T2.\ (A \leftrightarrow B) \to (B \leftrightarrow A)$$

$$T3\ (Trans).\ A \to B, B \to C \Rightarrow A \to C$$

$$T4\ (Trans \leftrightarrow).\ A \leftrightarrow B, B \leftrightarrow C \Rightarrow A \leftrightarrow C$$

$$T5.\ A \to \neg\neg A$$

$$T6.\ A \leftrightarrow \neg\neg A$$

$$T7.\ (A \to B) \to (\neg B \to \neg A)$$

$$T8.\ (\neg A \to \neg B) \to (B \to A)$$

$$T9.\ (A \to B) \leftrightarrow (\neg B \to \neg A)$$

$$T10.\ (\neg A \to B) \to (\neg B \to \neg A)$$

$$T11\ (Con \leftrightarrow).\ A \leftrightarrow B \Rightarrow \neg B \leftrightarrow \neg A$$

$$T12\ (Suf).\ A \to B \Rightarrow (B \to C) \to (A \to C)$$

$$T13\ (Pref \leftrightarrow).\ A \leftrightarrow B \Rightarrow (C \to A) \leftrightarrow (C \to B)$$

$$T14\ (Suf \leftrightarrow).\ A \to B \Rightarrow (B \to C) \leftrightarrow (A \to C)$$

$$T15.\ (A \lor B) \leftrightarrow \neg(\neg A \land \neg B)$$

$$T16\ (E \lor).\ A \to C, B \to C \Rightarrow (A \lor B) \to C$$

$$T17\ (Sum \leftrightarrow).\ A \leftrightarrow B \Rightarrow (A \lor C) \leftrightarrow (B \lor C)$$

$$T18.\ (A \land B) \leftrightarrow (B \land A)$$

$$T19.\ [(A \land B) \land C] \to [A \land (B \land C)]$$

$$T20.\ [(A \land B) \land C] \leftrightarrow [A \land (B \land C)]$$

$$T21.\ (A \lor B) \leftrightarrow (B \lor A)$$

$$T22.\ (A \lor A) \to A$$

$$T23.\ A \to (A \land A)$$

$$T24 \; (Fac' \leftrightarrow). \; A \leftrightarrow B \Rightarrow (C \wedge A) \leftrightarrow (C \wedge B)$$
$$T25 \; (Sum' \leftrightarrow). \; A \leftrightarrow B \Rightarrow (C \vee A) \leftrightarrow (C \vee B)$$

Trans, Trans↔, Con↔, Suf, Pref↔, Suf↔ and Sum↔ abbreviate Transitivity, Transitivity w.r.t. ↔, Contraposition w.r.t. ↔, Suffixing, Prefixing w.r.t. ↔, Suffixing w.r.t. ↔ and Summation w.r.t. ↔, respectively. Fac' ↔ and Sum' ↔ are alternative versions of Fac↔ and Sum↔.

Proof. It is easy and it is left to the reader.

Proposition 3 (Replacement). *For any wffs A, B, $A \leftrightarrow B \Rightarrow C[A] \leftrightarrow C[A/B]$ where $C[A]$ is a wff in which A appears and $C[A/B]$ is the result of substituting A by B in $C[A]$ in one or more places where A occurs.*

Proof. By induction on the structure of $C[A]$ using Fac↔ (R6), Trans↔ (T4), Con↔ (T11), Pref↔ (T13), Suf↔ (T14), Sum↔ (T17), Fac' ↔ (T24) and Sum' ↔ (T25).

Proposition 4 (Additional theorems and rules of BN4^VSP). *The following are provable in $BN4^{VSP}$:*

$$T26. \; (A \wedge B) \leftrightarrow \neg(\neg A \vee \neg B)$$
$$T27. \; \neg(A \wedge B) \leftrightarrow (\neg A \vee \neg B)$$
$$T28. \; [A \vee (B \vee C)] \leftrightarrow [(A \vee B) \vee C]$$
$$T29. \; [A \vee (B \wedge C)] \leftrightarrow [(A \vee B) \wedge (A \vee C)]$$
$$T30 \; (Modus \; Tollens \; -MT). \; A \rightarrow B, \neg B \Rightarrow \neg A$$
$$T31. \; A \rightarrow B, B \wedge \neg B \Rightarrow A$$

Proof. Easy by using Replacement (Proposition 3).

Proposition 5 (Arrangement in conjunctive and disjunctive wffs). *Let A be a wff of the form $B_1 \wedge ... \wedge B_n$ (resp., $B_1 \vee ... \vee B_n$) where the n wffs are arranged in a given way. And let A' be the result of associating $B_1, ..., B_n$ in any way whichever. Then, $\vdash_{BN4^{VSP}} A \leftrightarrow A'$.*

Proof. By Replacement and the commutative and associative properties of $\wedge$ and $\vee$ (T18, T20, T21 and T28).

Proposition 6 (Summation w.r.t. ⇒ —Sum⇒). *For any wffs $A, B_1, ..., B_n$, if $B_1, ..., B_n \Rightarrow A$, then $C \vee B_1, ..., C \vee B_n \Rightarrow C \vee A$.*

Proof. By induction on the length of the proof $B_1, ..., B_n \Rightarrow A$. We remark that in [15], §3, it is noted that the modest strength of FDE suffices to carry out the proof of the *Extension Lemma* provided Proposition 6 is at our disposal. Now, Proposition 6 does not follow if the facts in Proposition 5 have not been proved previously. But said facts can be elusive in certain weak logics, hence our interest in proving Replacement and the commutative and associative properties of $\wedge$ (those of $\vee$ are not necessary, although T22 certainly is (cf. [14,15,21]).

The section is ended noting that BN4^{VSP} complies with the requirements imposed to "implicative logics" in the classical Polish logical tradition, except, of course, VEQ (cf. [19], pp. 179–180 or [26], p. 228). Consider the following definition:

Definition 9 (Implicative logics). *A logic L is implicative if the following properties (C1)-(C5) are predicable of L:*

$$C1.\ A \rightarrow A \qquad\qquad\qquad\qquad \text{Reflexivity}$$
$$C2.\ A \rightarrow B, A \Rightarrow B \qquad\qquad\qquad \text{Modus Ponens}$$
$$C3.\ A \Rightarrow B \rightarrow A \qquad\qquad\qquad\qquad \text{VEQ}$$
$$C4.\ A \rightarrow B, B \rightarrow C \Rightarrow A \rightarrow C \qquad\qquad \text{Transitivity}$$
$$C5.\ A \leftrightarrow B \rightarrow\ C[A] \leftrightarrow\ C[A/B] \qquad\quad \text{Replacement}$$

Now, BN4^{VSP} has properties C1, C2, C4 and C5 (cf. Definition 8 and Propositions 2 and 3).

4   Belnap-Dunn Semantics for BN4^{VSP}

As it is well-known, Belnap-Dunn two-valued semantics (BD-semantics) is characterized by the possibility of assigning T, F, both T and F or neither T nor F to the formulas of a given logical language (cf. [5,6,9,10]; T represents truth and F represents falsity).

Given an implicative expansion of $\mathcal{FOUR}$ (Definition 2), M, the idea for defining a BD-semantics, M′, equivalent to the matrix semantics based upon M is simple: a wff A is assigned both T and F in M′ iff it is assigned 2 in M; A is assigned neither T nor F in M′ iff it is assigned 1 in M; finally, A is assigned T but not F (resp., F but not T) in M′ iff it is assigned 3 (resp., 0) in M.

The BD-semantics for BN4^{VSP}, equivalent to the matrix semantics based upon MBN4^{VSP} (Definition 4), to be defined below has been built by following the simple intuitive ideas just exposed.

In the sequel, the notion of a BN4^{VSP}-model and the accompanying notions of BN4^{VSP}-consequence and BN4^{VSP}-validity are defined. BN4^{VSP}-models and said annexed notions constitute a BD-semantics for BN4^{VSP} (a BN4^{VSP}-semantics) equivalent to the one based upon the matrix MBN4^{VSP}, in the sense explained above. It will be proved that the logic BN4^{VSP} is sound and complete w.r.t. BN4^{VSP}-semantics.

Definition 10 (BN4^{VSP}-models). *A BN4^{VSP}-model is a structure (K, I), where (i) $K = \{\{T\}, \{F\}, \{T, F\}, \emptyset\}$, and (ii) I is a BN4^{VSP}-interpretation from the set of all wffs to K, this notion being defined according to the following conditions for each propositional variable p and wffs A, B:*

    1. $I(p) \in K$

    2a. $T \in I(\neg A)$ iff $F \in I(A)$

    2b. $F \in I(\neg A)$ iff $T \in I(A)$

    3a. $T \in I(A \wedge B)$ iff $T \in I(A)$ & $T \in I(B)$

    3b. $F \in I(A \wedge B)$ iff $F \in I(A)$ or $F \in I(B)$

    4a. $T \in I(A \vee B)$ iff $T \in I(A)$ or $T \in I(B)$

    4b. $F \in I(A \vee B)$ iff $F \in I(A)$ & $F \in I(B)$

    5a. $T \in I(A \rightarrow B)$ iff $[T \notin I(A)$ & $F \notin I(B)]$ or

        $[T \notin I(A)$ & $F \in I(A)$ & $T \notin I(B)$ & $F \in I(B)]$ or

        $[T \in I(A)$ & $F \in I(A)$ & $T \in I(B)$ & $F \in I(B)]$ or

        $[T \in I(A)$ & $F \notin I(A)$ & $T \in I(B)$ & $F \notin I(B)]$

    5b. $F \in I(A \rightarrow B)$ iff $T \in I(A)$ & $F \in I(B)$

Definition 11 (BN4$^{\mathbf{VSP}}$-consequence, BN4$^{\mathbf{VSP}}$-validity). *Let M be a $BN4^{VSP}$-model. For any set of wffs Γ and wff A:*

1. *$\Gamma \vDash_M A$ (A is a consequence of Γ in M) iff $T \in I(A)$ whenever $T \in I(\Gamma)$.*
2. *$\Gamma \vDash_{BN4^{VSP}} A$ (A is a consequence of Γ in $BN4^{VSP}$-semantics) iff $\Gamma \vDash_M A$ for each $BN4^{VSP}$-model M ($T \in I(\Gamma)$ iff $\forall A \in \Gamma(T \in I(A))$; $F \in I(\Gamma)$ iff $\exists A \in \Gamma(F \in I(A))$).*
3. *In particular, $\vDash_{BN4^{VSP}} A$ (A is valid in $BN4^{VSP}$-semantics) iff $\vDash_M A$ for each $BN4^{VSP}$-model M (i.e., iff $T \in I(A)$ for each $BN4^{VSP}$-model M).*

(By $\vDash_{BN4^{VSP}}$ we shall refer to the relation just defined.)

Now, given Definition 4 together with the adjoined notions of MBN4^{VSP}-interpretation and MBN4^{VSP}-validity (cf. Definition 1), and Definitions 10 and 11, we easily prove:

Proposition 7 (Coextensiveness of $\vDash_{\mathbf{MBN4^{VSP}}}$ and $\vDash_{\mathbf{BN4^{VSP}}}$). *For any set of wffs Γ and wff A, $\Gamma \vDash_{MBN4^{VSP}} A$ iff $\Gamma \vDash_{BN4^{VSP}} A$. In particular, $\vDash_{MBN4^{VSP}} A$ iff $\vDash_{BN4^{VSP}} A$. (By $\vDash_{MBN4^{VSP}}$, we refer to the consequence relation definable in $MBN4^{VSP}$ —cf. Definitions 1 and 4)[4]*

Proof. Cf., e.g., the proof of Theorem 8 in [7] or Proposition 4.4 in [14], where the simple proof procedure is exemplified in the cases of the logics BN4 and Sm4, respectively.

Proposition 7 simply formalizes the intuitive translation (explained above) of the matrix semantics based upon MBN4^{VSP} into Belnap and Dunn's two-valued type BN4^{VSP}-semantics. Nevertheless, Proposition 7 is a most useful proposition:

---

[4] A referee of CLAR 2021 remarks that this result can be obtained as a special case of the general procedure described in §2 of "Generalizing functional completeness in Belnap-Dunn logic" (H. Omori and K. Sano, *Studia Logica*, 103(5), 883–917, 2015).

it gives us the possibility of easily proving soundness of BN4^{VSP} w.r.t. $\vDash_{MBN4^{VSP}}$, while proving completeness w.r.t. $\vdash_{BN4^{VSP}}$ by using a canonical model construction.

Theorem 1 (Soundness of BN4^{VSP}). *For any set of wffs Γ and wff A, if $\Gamma \vdash_{BN4^{VSP}} A$, then (1) $\Gamma \vDash_{MBN4^{VSP}} A$ and (2) $\Gamma \vDash_{BN4^{VSP}} A$.*

Proof. Let I be an MBN4^{VSP}-interpretation (defined in the MBN4^{VSP}-model M). (1) It is easy to check the following facts: (i) I assigns a designated value to the conclusion of rules R1-R13 if it assigns a designated value to the premise(s) of said rules; (ii) A1-A9 are assigned 2 or 3 by I; (iii) concerning the metarule MR, let $I(D \vee A) = I(D \vee B) = 2$ or 3 but $I(D \vee C) = 0$ or 1 for some wffs A, B and C. Then, it is clear that C is not a M-consequence of A, B (i.e., $A, B \Rightarrow C$ is falsified). (2) It is immediate from (1) and Proposition 7 (in case a tester is needed, the one in [12] can be used).

As has just been pointed out, completeness is proved by a canonical model construction, similarly as in, e.g., [14,15] or [21]. Let us see how this proof proceeds. Firstly, the notion of a BN4^{VSP}-theory and the classes of BN4^{VSP}-theories of interest in the present paper are introduced. Then, the concept of a canonical model is defined.

Definition 12 (BN4^{VSP}-theories. Classes of BN4^{VSP}-theories). *A BN4^{VSP}-theory (theory, for short) is a set of formulas closed under BN4^{VSP}-entailment (BN4^{VSP}-ent), all the rules of BN4^{VSP} and the metarule MR (a theory t is closed under BN4^{VSP}-ent iff whenever $A \to B$ is a BN4^{VSP}-theorem and $A \in t$, then $B \in t$). Then, a theory t is regular iff it contains all BN4^{VSP}-theorems, and it is prime iff it has the disjunction property (i.e., if $A \vee B \in t$, then $A \in t$ or $B \in t$).*

The following lemma is instrumental in the completeness proof.

Lemma 1 (The conditional in prime, regular theories). *Let t be a regular and prime theory. For any wffs A, B, we have:*

(a) $A \to B \in t$ iff $[A \notin t$ & $\neg B \notin t]$ or $[A \notin t$ & $\neg A \in t$ & $B \notin t$ & $\neg B \in t]$ or $[A \in t$ & $\neg A \in t$ & $B \in t$ & $\neg B \in t]$ or $[A \in t$ & $\neg A \notin t$ & $B \in t$ & $\neg B \notin t]$

(b) $\neg(A \to B) \in t$ iff $A \in t$ & $\neg B \in t$

Proof. Similar to those of Theorem 10 in [7], Lemma 2.3 in [14], Lemma 3.6 in [15] or Lemma 5.7 in [21]. In order to prove (a), we can use A8, A9, MP, R8, R9, R10, R11, T30 and T31 (cf. Proposition 4). The proof of (b) is obtained by using R12 and R13.

(a) ($\Rightarrow$) Suppose (1) $A \to B \in t$ and, for reductio, (2) $[A \in t$ or $\neg B \in t]$ & $[A \in t$ or $\neg A \notin t$ or $B \in t$ or $\neg B \notin t]$ & $[A \notin t$ or $\neg A \notin t$ or $B \notin t$ or $\neg B \notin t]$ & $[A \notin t$ or $\neg A \in t$ or $B \notin t$ or $\neg B \in t]$. Suppose (3) $A \in t$. Then, we have 64 possibilities to consider. But each one of them belongs to one of the following categories. (i) It contains a contradiction (e.g., $A \in t$ & $A \notin t$); (ii) it contains $A \in t$ and $B \in t$; (iii) it contains $\neg A \notin t$ and $\neg B \in t$; (iv) it contains $A \in t$, $\neg A \in t$ and $\neg B \notin t$; (v) it contains $B \in t$, $\neg B \in t$ and $\neg A \notin t$. Now, the situations in (ii)-(v) also lead to contradiction by using (1) and the rules MP, MT, T30, R10 and R11, respectively. (4) $\neg B \in t$. We have also 64 possibilities to consider, which are proved similarly as case (3) was solved. (We use MP, MT, T30 and T31.)

(a) ($\Leftarrow$) $A \rightarrow B$ follows by A8, R8, A9 and R9, respectively. Let us prove, for example, the first of the cases. Suppose $A \notin t$ and $\neg B \notin t$. By A8, $(A \vee \neg B) \vee (A \rightarrow B)$, and primeness of t, $A \in t$ or $\neg B \in t$ or $A \rightarrow B \in t$. Consequently, $A \rightarrow B \in t$, as it was to be proved.

Next, (b) is immediate by R10 and R11.

Next, we sketch the framework of the completeness proof. A canonical model is a structure (K, I_t) where K is defined as in Definition 10 and I_t is a t-interpretation built upon a regular and prime theory t. A t-interpretation is a function from the set of all wffs to K defined as follows: for each wff A, $T \in I_t(A)$ iff $A \in t$ and $F \in I_t(A)$ iff $\neg A \in t$. Canonical models are shown BN4^{VSP}-models by proving that I_t fulfils the conditions listed in Definition 10. But it is obvious that A5, A7, T5 and T27 guarantee that clauses (1a) to (4b) hold canonically (cf. Propositions 3 and 4) while Lemma 1 takes care of clauses (5a) and (5b). Once canonical models are shown BN4^{VSP}-models, completeness is proved as follows. Suppose that Γ is a set off wffs and A a wff such that $\Gamma \nvDash_{\text{BN4}^{\text{VSP}}} A$. Then A does not belong to the set of consequences derivable in BN4^{VSP} from Γ (in symbols, $A \notin Cn\Gamma[\text{BN4}^{\text{VSP}}]$). Next, the regular theory $Cn\Gamma[\text{BN4}^{\text{VSP}}]$ is extended to a prime theory t such that $A \notin t$. Then t generates a t-interpretation I_t such that $T \in I_t(\Gamma)$ (since $T \in I_t(Cn\Gamma[\text{BN4}^{\text{VSP}}])$: $Cn[\text{BN4}^{\text{VSP}}] \subseteq t$) but $T \notin I_t(A)$, whence A does not follow from Γ in the canonical BN4^{VSP}-model built upon t. So, $\Gamma \nvDash_{\text{BN4}^{\text{VSP}}} A$. (Notice that we have not needed consistent theories in any sense of the term "consistent".)

Remark 8 (On the Extension Lemma). Once the instrumental Propositions 5 and 6 have been shown to hold for BN4^{VSP}, the Extension Lemma can be proved similarly as, e.g., in [7], Lemma 9; [14], Lemma 24; [15], Lemma 3.11.

Leaning upon the argumentation just developed, I think that I am entitled to state the following completeness theorem w.r.t. both $\vDash_{\text{MBN4}^{\text{VSP}}}$ and $\vDash_{\text{BN4}^{\text{VSP}}}$.

Theorem 2 (Completeness of BN4^{VSP}). *For any set of wffs Γ and wff A, $\Gamma \vdash_{\text{BN4}^{\text{VSP}}} A$ if (1) $\Gamma \vDash_{\text{MBN4}^{\text{VSP}}} A$ or (2) $\Gamma \vDash_{\text{BN4}^{\text{VSP}}} A$.*

The paper is ended with some suggestions for future work on the topic.

5   Concluding Remarks

According to Anderson and Belnap, the variable-sharing property (VSP) is a property a logic has to enjoy in order to deserve being named a relevance logic. As pointed out in the introduction to the paper, Brady's BN4 is widely considered the correct 4-valued logic among relevant logicians. But BN4 lacks the VSP. The initial impetus of the investigation reported in the present paper was to find a significant 4-valued implicative expansion of FDE with the VSP worthy of consideration. The logic $BN4^{VSP}$, a variant of BN4, does have the VSP, in addition to sporting some properties that do not support its consideration as a mere artificial construct.

There is a number of ways in which the investigation carried out in this paper can be pursued. We limit ourselves to remark two of them.

1. Is $BN4^{VSP}$ just one of a class of significant 4-valued implicative expansions of FDE having the VSP?[5]
2. According to Anderson and Belnap, two properties need to be predicable of a logic of entailment: one of them is the VSP, the other one is the Ackermann Property (AP). The AP reads as follows: a logic L has the AP if in all L-theorems of the form $A \rightarrow (B \rightarrow C)$, $\rightarrow$ appears in A (cf. [1]). Well then, is there a significant 4-valued expansion of FDE with both the VSP and the AP?

References

1. Anderson, A.R., Belnap, N.D., Jr., Dunn, J.M.: Entailment, the Logic of Relevance and Necessity, vol. II. Princeton University Press, Princeton (1992)
2. Avron, A., Ben-Naim, J., Konikowska, B.: Cut-free ordinary sequent calculi for logics having generalized finite-valued semantics. Logica Universalis **1**(1), 41–70 (2007). https://doi.org/10.1007/s11787-006-0003-6
3. Avron, A., Konikowska, B., Zamansky, A.: Cut-free sequent calculi for C-systems with generalized finite-valued semantics. J. Log. Comput. **23**(3), 517–540 (2013). https://doi.org/10.1093/logcom/exs039
4. Belnap, N.D., Jr.: Entailment and relevance. J. Symb. Log. **25**(2), 144–146 (1960)
5. Belnap, N.D., Jr.: A useful four-valued logic. In: Epstein, G., Dunn, J.M. (eds.) Modern Uses of Multiple-Valued Logic, pp. 8–37. D. Reidel Publishing Co., Dordrecht (1977)
6. Belnap, N.D., Jr.: How a computer should think. In: Ryle, G. (ed.) Contemporary Aspects of Philosophy, pp. 30–55. Oriel Press Ltd., Stocksfield (1977)
7. Brady, R.T.: Completeness proofs for the systems RM3 and BN4. Logique et Anal. (N.S.) **25**, 9–32 (1982)
8. Brady, R.T. (ed.): Relevant Logics and Their Rivals, vol. II. Ashgate, Aldershot (2003)
9. Dunn, J.M.: Intuitive semantics for first-degree entailments and "coupled trees". Philos. Stud. **29**, 149–168 (1976)

---

[5] A referee of CLAR 2021 remarks that there are 2^{17} different matrices with natural conditionals (in the sense of Definition 5) complying with the VSP. Well then, since this paper was written, we have pursued the topic it introduces and almost all the 2^{17} variants are non-significant in the sense that they lack one or more of the properties $MBN4^{VSP}$ exhibits (actually, only 24 of said matrices share the properties $MBN4^{VSP}$ has).

10. Dunn, J.M.: Partiality and its dual. Studia Logica **66**, 5–40 (2000)
11. Dziobiak, W.: There are $2^{\aleph_0}$ logics with the relevance principle between R and RM. Studia Logica **42**(1), 49–61 (1983). https://doi.org/10.1007/BF01418759
12. González, C.: MaTest (2011). https://sites.google.com/site/sefusmendez/matest. Accessed 27 June 2021
13. López, S.M.: Belnap-Dunn semantics for the variants of BN4 and E4 which contain Routley and Meyer's logic B. Logic Logical Philos. 1–28 (2021). https://doi.org/10.12775/LLP.2021.004
14. Méndez, J.M., Robles, G.: The logic determined by Smiley's matrix for Anderson and Belnap's First Degree Entailment Logic. J. Appl. Non-Classical Log. **26**(1), 47–68 (2016). https://doi.org/10.1080/11663081.2016.1153930
15. Méndez, J.M., Robles, G.: Strengthening Brady's paraconsistent 4-valued logic BN4 with truth-functional modal operators. J. Log. Lang. Inf. **25**(2), 163–189 (2016). https://doi.org/10.1007/s10849-016-9237-8
16. Meyer, R.K., Giambrone, S., Brady, R.T.: Where gamma fails. Studia Logica **43**, 247–256 (1984). https://doi.org/10.1007/BF02429841
17. Omori, H., Wansing, H.: 40 years of FDE: an introductory overview. Studia Logica **105**(6), 1021–1049 (2017). https://doi.org/10.1007/s11225-017-9748-6
18. Petrukhin, Y., Shangin, V.: Correspondence analysis and automated proof-searching for first degree entailment. Eur. J. Math. **6**, 1452–1495 (2020). https://doi.org/10.1007/s40879-019-00344-5
19. Rasiowa, H.: An Algebraic Approach to Non-classical Logics, vol. 78. North-Holland Publishing Company, Amsterdam (1974)
20. Robles, G.: The class of all 3-valued implicative expansions of Kleene's strong logic containing Anderson and Belnap's First degree entailment logic. J. Appl. Log. **8**(7), 2035–2071 (2021)
21. Robles, G., Méndez, J.M.: A companion to Brady's 4-valued relevant logic BN4: the 4-valued logic of entailment E4. Log. J. IGPL **24**(5), 838–858 (2016). https://doi.org/10.1093/jigpal/jzw011
22. Robles, G., Méndez, J.M.: The class of all natural implicative expansions of Kleene's strong logic functionally equivalent to Łukasiewicz's 3-valued logic Ł3. J. Log. Lang. Inf. **29**(3), 349–374 (2020). https://doi.org/10.1007/s10849-019-09306-2
23. Routley, R., Meyer, R.K., Plumwood, V., Brady, R.T.: Relevant Logics and Their Rivals, vol. 1. Ridgeview Publishing Co., Atascadero (1982)
24. Slaney, J.: Relevant logic and paraconsistency. In: Bertossi, L., Hunter, A., Schaub, T. (eds.) Inconsistency Tolerance. LNCS, vol. 3300, pp. 270–293. Springer, Heidelberg (2005). https://doi.org/10.1007/978-3-540-30597-2_9
25. Tomova, N.: A Lattice of implicative extensions of regular Kleene's logics. Rep. Math. Log. **47**, 173–182 (2012). https://doi.org/10.4467/20842589RM.12.008.0689
26. Wójcicki, R.: Theory of Logical Calculi: Basic Theory of Consequence Operations. Springer, Dordrecht (1988). https://doi.org/10.1007/978-94-015-6942-2

Intrinsic Argument Strength in Structured Argumentation: A Principled Approach

Jeroen Paul Spaans[(✉)] [iD]

Utrecht University, Utrecht, The Netherlands

Abstract. Abstract argumentation provides us with methods such as gradual and Dung semantics with which to evaluate arguments after potential attacks by other arguments. Some of these methods can take intrinsic strengths of arguments as input, with which to modulate the effects of attacks between arguments. Coming from abstract argumentation, these methods look only at the relations between arguments and not at the structure of the arguments themselves. In structured argumentation the way an argument is constructed, by chaining inference rules starting from premises, is taken into consideration. In this paper we study methods for assigning an argument its intrinsic strength, based on the strengths of the premises and inference rules used to form said argument. We first define a set of principles, which are properties that strength assigning methods might satisfy. We then propose two such methods and analyse which principles they satisfy. Finally, we present a generalised system for creating novel strength assigning methods and speak to the properties of this system regarding the proposed principles.

Keywords: Intrinsic argument strength · Structured argumentation · Principles · Weight aggregation · Aggregation method

1 Introduction

Argumentation is used in Artificial Intelligence to aid in solving many varied problems; for example, it is used to help with nonmonotonic reasoning [6], to help in making and explaining decisions [13] and to develop architectures for agents in a multi-agent setting [8]. Argumentation's core concept is justifying claims by use of arguments. These arguments are reasons to believe or accept a claim.

Arguments might not agree with one another, such as when two arguments support contradicting claims or when one argument contradicts a premise of another. In these cases we speak of one argument standing in an attack relation to another. To help draw conclusions about which arguments to accept Dung introduced abstract argumentation frameworks [6] in which arguments and the binary attack relations between them are modelled in a directed graph. Different semantics may then be used to determine the status of each argument.

© Springer Nature Switzerland AG 2021
P. Baroni et al. (Eds.): CLAR 2021, LNAI 13040, pp. 377–396, 2021.
https://doi.org/10.1007/978-3-030-89391-0_21

Dung's semantics [6] and those in the same family, such as those researched in [2], define extensions of arguments such that every argument is *in* (accepted), *out* (rejected) or, in some cases, *undecided.*

Gradual semantics, introduced by Cayrol and Lagasquie-Schiex [5] and further researched in [1], do not seek to accept or reject arguments like the aforementioned *Dung-* or *extension semantics* but rather to compute their overall strength.

Arguments will often have a base weight, or *intrinsic strength,* representing, for example, the certainty of the argument's premises [4]. To determine the overall strength of an argument, the attacks against it are taken into account. These attacks may also be weighted, for example to represent their degree of relevance [7].

Gradual semantics have been proposed both for semi-weighted abstract argumentation frameworks (i.e. those frameworks where only the arguments have a base weight) [1] and for weighted abstract argumentation frameworks (i.e. those frameworks where arguments and attacks are weighted) [3], each based on different ways of aggregating attacks, considering the strength of each attacker and (where applicable) the strength of each attack, to lower the weight or strength of the argument under attack.

The aforementioned falls under what is known as *abstract argumentation.* Here the internal structure of an argument and the nature of attacks is not considered. When we do take these factors into consideration, such as in [11,12] and this paper, we speak of *structured argumentation.*

An argument, in structured argumentation, can intuitively be seen as the application of one or more *strict* or *defeasible* inference rules, starting from a set of premises. We might apply the strict inference rule *if X is a bird, then X is an animal* (strict, because this inference is based on a definition and is therefore not open to attack) to the premise *Tweety is a bird* to form an argument for the claim *Tweety is an animal.* Similarly we might apply the defeasible inference rule *if X is a bird, then X can most likely fly* (defeasible because X might be a penguin or a baby bird, in which case they cannot fly, leaving the inference open to attack) to the same premise to form an argument for the claim *Tweety can fly.* It is plain to see how inference rules can be combined to form more complex arguments in the shape of an inference tree. If conflict arises between the conclusion of an argument A and some part of an argument B we speak of an attack from A to B. we may specify such an attack to, for example, be a *rebuttal* when A attacks B on its conclusion or an *undermining* when it attacks B on a premise.

While gradual semantics allow us to determine the overall strength of arguments after attacks when we have been given the intrinsic strength of each argument, no standard has arisen in the literature for deriving these intrinsic strengths from the structure of the arguments. Such a standard is what we hope to work toward with this paper. The aim is to investigate different methods for aggregating given weights of the premises and inference rules used to form the argument to derive the intrinsic strength of the argument as a whole.

The paper is structured as follows. We first introduce the basic concepts used in structured argumentation. Then we will define a series of principles, each of which will be a property a method for assigning an argument its intrinsic strength can satisfy. We then propose two intrinsic strength assigning methods and evaluate which principles they satisfy. Next we introduce the aggregation method, a framework for creating new strength assigning methods. Lastly, we speak to the properties of an aggregation method, especially in regard to the earlier-proposed principles.

2   Basic Concepts

In argumentation à la Dung, we look at arguments in an argumentation graph, which consists of a set of arguments and a binary attack relation on this set. In gradual argumentation, as in [3] which is where we take the following definition from, we often assign weights in the interval $[0, 1]$ (lower is weaker) to both the arguments and attacks in our argumentation graph, resulting in a *weighted argumentation graphs*.

Definition 1 (Weighted Argumentation Graph). *A weighted argumentation graph (WAG) is an ordered tuple $G = \langle \mathcal{A}, \sigma, \mathcal{R}, \pi \rangle$, where $\mathcal{A}$ is a non-empty finite set of arguments, $\mathcal{R} \subseteq \mathcal{A} \times \mathcal{A}$, $\sigma : \mathcal{A} \to [0, 1]$ and $\pi : \mathcal{R} \to [0, 1]$.*

Here $\sigma(a)$ is the base weight of argument a, $(a, b) \in \mathcal{R}$ means a attacks b and $\pi((a, b))$ is the weight of the attack from a to b. In this paper we are looking to formulate σ such that it represents an argument's intrinsic strength, where $\sigma(a)$ is an aggregation of the strengths of the premises and inference rules used in a over the structure of a.

Example 1. Take the argumentation graph in Fig. 1. Here $\mathcal{A} = \{a, b, c, d, e\}$ and $\mathcal{R} = \{(a, b), (b, c), (b, e), (d, c)\}$. Assume the weight of all arguments and attacks in the graph is 1.

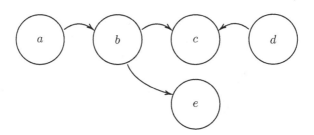

Fig. 1. An argumentation graph

Grounded Dung semantics [6] would give us the set of arguments, called an extension, to accept. *Grounded* semantics, specifically, would give the smallest complete extension. To find this extension we need a few concepts:

- an argument $a \in \mathcal{A}$ is acceptable with respect to $E \subseteq \mathcal{A}$ iff E defends a. That is, $\forall b \in \mathcal{A}$ s.t. $(b, a) \in \mathcal{R}$, $\exists c \in E$ s.t. $(c, b) \in \mathcal{R}$.
- A set of arguments E is conflict free iff $\forall a, b \in E$, $(a, b) \notin \mathcal{R}$.
- A set of arguments E is admissible iff it is conflict-free and all arguments in E are acceptable with respect to E.
- A set of arguments E is a complete extension iff it is an admissible set and every acceptable argument with respect to E belongs to E.

Following these concepts we see that b and c cannot be included in a complete extension, since a and d have no attackers and as such a set containing b and c could never defend them from the attacks of a and d. From here we get the unique grounded extension $E_g = \{a, d, e\}$.

The gradual Weighted h-Categorizer Semantics [1] (which we can use because all attack weights are 1) would assign each argument x an acceptability degree $\mathrm{Deg}(x) = \lim_{i \to \infty} f^i(x)$ where

$$f^i(x) = \begin{cases} \sigma(x) & \text{if } i = 0 \\ \dfrac{\sigma(x)}{1 + \sum_{b_i \in \mathrm{Att}(x)} f^{i-1}(b_i)} & \text{otherwise} \end{cases}$$

and $\mathrm{Att}(x)$ denotes the attackers of x. This would result in $\mathrm{Deg}(a) = 1$, $\mathrm{Deg}(b) = \frac{1}{2}$, $\mathrm{Deg}(c) = \frac{2}{5}$, $\mathrm{Deg}(d) = 1$ and $\mathrm{Deg}(e) = \frac{2}{3}$.

Having seen how arguments can relate to one another, we now look to how arguments are formed. In doing so, we introduce a modified variant of the ASPIC+ framework [11].

To construct an argument, we must first know the building blocks that are at our disposal. In an argument we make inferences based on inference rules with antecedents and consequents that are all well-formed formulae in some logical language.

Definition 2 (Argumentation System). *An argumentation system is a pair* $AS = (\mathcal{L}, \mathcal{R})$ *where:*

- $\mathcal{L}$ *is a logical language consisting of propositional or ground predicate-logic literals that is closed under negation.*
- $\mathcal{R} = \mathcal{R}_d \cup \mathcal{R}_s$ *with* $\mathcal{R}_d \cap \mathcal{R}_s = \emptyset$, *where* $\mathcal{R}_d$ *is a finite set of defeasible inference rules of the form* $\{\varphi_1, \ldots, \varphi_n\} \Rightarrow \varphi$, $\mathcal{R}_s$ *is a finite set of strict inference rules of the form* $\{\varphi_1, \ldots, \varphi_n\} \to \varphi$ *and* φ, φ_i *are meta-variables ranging over well-formed formulae in* $\mathcal{L}$. *We call* $\varphi_1, \ldots, \varphi_n$ *the antecedents of the rule and* φ *its consequent.*

Just in case $\psi = \neg\varphi$ or $\varphi = \neg\psi$, we write $\psi = -\varphi$. Here $-$ is not a member of $\mathcal{L}$ but rather a metalinguistic symbol used to simplify notation.

In any argument we start our reasoning from one or more *premises*. These are the pieces of knowledge from which we infer other information. What is important to notice, is that a premise may be *fallible* or *infallible*. Fallible premises are open to attack. Suppose we combine our belief that we saw Robin in Rotterdam this morning with the knowledge that Rotterdam is in the Netherlands to argue Robin was in the Netherlands this morning. This argument is deductively valid but still open to attack. Suppose our friend Alex informs us they saw Robin in Berlin at the same time we believe to have seen them in Rotterdam. Since our friends usually tell us the truth, this allows us to form an argument that attacks the original premise that we saw Robin in Rotterdam. Infallible premises, such as *1 is a natural number*, are not open to attack. In accordance with [11] we will call these infallible premises *axiom* premises and we will refer to premises that are open to attack as *ordinary* premises. We call the body of information from which premises may be taken a knowledge base.

Definition 3 (Consistency). *For any $S \subseteq \mathcal{L}$, let the closure of S under strict rules, denoted $Cl_{\mathcal{R}_S}(S)$, be the smallest set containing S and the consequent of any strict rule in $\mathcal{R}_s$ whose antecedents are in $Cl_{\mathcal{R}_S}(S)$. Then a set $S \subseteq \mathcal{L}$ is directly consistent iff there are no $\psi, \varphi \in S$ such that $\psi = -\varphi$ and indirectly consistent iff $Cl_{\mathcal{R}_S}(S)$ is directly consistent. [12]*

Definition 4 (Knowledge Base). *A knowledge base in an $AS = (\mathcal{L}, \mathcal{R})$ is a set $\mathcal{K} \subseteq \mathcal{L}$, where $\mathcal{K} = \mathcal{K}_n \cup \mathcal{K}_p$, $\mathcal{K}_n$ is a set of axioms, $\mathcal{K}_p$ is a set of ordinary premises, $\mathcal{K}_n$ is indirectly consistent and $\mathcal{K}_n \cap \mathcal{K}_p = \emptyset$.*

With an argumentation system and a knowledge base we could create an argument, but we would still be missing the rule and premise weights. To codify these we introduce the *weighted argumentation theory*.

Definition 5 (Weighted Argumentation Theory). *A weighted argumentation theory is a tuple $WAT = (AS, \mathcal{K}, s)$ where:*

- *$AS = (\mathcal{L}, \mathcal{R})$ is an argumentation system.*
- *$\mathcal{K}$ is a knowledge base.*
- *s is a function assigning weights to rules and premises, such that $\forall r \in \mathcal{R}_s$, $s(r) = 1$; $\forall p \in \mathcal{K}_n$, $s(p) = 1$; $\forall r' \in \mathcal{R}_d$, $s(r') \in [0, 1)$; $\forall p' \in \mathcal{K}_p$, $s(p') \in [0, 1)$ and a higher weight is assigned to stronger premises and inference rules.*

Example 2. Continuing with the *Tweety is a bird* example from the introduction to this paper, we might have:

- s(Tweety is a bird $\rightarrow$ Tweety is an animal) $= 1$; because all birds are, by definition, animals and as such this is a strict inference rule.
- s(Tweety is a bird $\Rightarrow$ Tweety can fly) $= 0.95$; because most birds can fly, so this is a strong defeasible inference rule.
- s(Tweety is a bird $\Rightarrow$ Tweety is yellow) $= 0.05$; because, while existent, yellow birds are quite rare, so this is a weak defeasible inference rule.

We can now define an argument over a WAT $= (AS, \mathcal{K}, s)$. As in ASPIC+ [11] we chain together applications of inference rules from AS into inference trees, starting from premises in $\mathcal{K}$.

For a given argument A, $\texttt{Conc}(A)$ returns the conclusion of A, $\texttt{TopRule}(A)$ returns the last inference rule used in the argument, $\texttt{Ant}(A)$ returns the argument's set of antecedent arguments, $\texttt{Sub}(A)$ returns the subarguments of A, $\texttt{DefRules}(A)$ returns all the defeasible rules used in A, $\texttt{StrRules}(A)$ returns all the used strict rules and $\texttt{OrdPrem}(A)$ and $\texttt{Axioms}(A)$ return the ordinary and axiomatic premises used to construct the argument respectively.

The structure of an argument defined like this is the same as in ASPIC+, but there are two differences between the functions we define over an argument and those commonly used in ASPIC+. Firstly, we split up the function $\texttt{Prem}$, which returns all of the premises used in an argument, into $\texttt{Axioms}$ and $\texttt{OrdPrem}$ to more easily distinguish between the strict and defeasible parts of an argument. Secondly and more notably, while ASPIC+ uses ordinary sets for the values of $\texttt{Prem}$, $\texttt{StrRules}$ and $\texttt{DefRules}$, we use multisets for the values of the four premise and rule functions. A multiset, also called a bag, is much like an ordinary set but, contrary to a normal set, is able to contain an element more than once [10]. The use of multisets allows us to more easily determine the strength of an argument in later sections of this paper because, intuitively, each use of a defeasible premise or inference rule should affect the strength of an argument and these multisets allow us to easily iterate over each occurence.

Definition 6 (Multiset). *A multiset is a modification of a set that allows multiple instances of its elements. Like an ordinary set, a multiset is unordered. e.g. $[a, a, a, b, b]$ is a multiset containing a and b where a has multiplicity $m(a) = 3$ and b has multiplicity $m(b) = 2$. This multiset may also be denoted $[a^3, b^2]$ or $\{(a, 3), (b, 2)\}$.*

We often say the elements of a multiset come from a fixed set U called the universe, such that the support of a multiset A is the multiset's underlying set $\mathbf{Supp}(A) = \{x \in U | m_A(x) > 0\}$. For readability, we say $A = \emptyset$ when $\mathbf{Supp}(A) = \emptyset$.

We use the following functions on multisets:

- *Union: the union of multisets A and B, $A \cup B$ is the multiset C with multiplicity function $m_C(x) = max(m_A(x), m_B(x)), \forall x \in U$.*
- *Sum: the sum of of multisets A and B, $A \uplus B$ is the multiset C with multiplicity function $m_C(x) = m_A(x) + m_B(x), \forall x \in U$.*

When using multisets in product or sum notation we assume to iterate over each occurrence of an element; for instance $\prod_{a \in [b,b,c]} a = b \cdot b \cdot c$. The same assumption is made for set builder notation, such that $\{f(x) | x \in [a, a, b]\} = [f(a), f(a), f(b)]$.

Definition 7 ((General) Argument). *A general argument A over a WAT $= (AS, \mathcal{K}, s)$ is defined recursively. It can be obtained by applying one or more of the following steps a finite amount of times;*

1. premise φ, if $\varphi \in \mathcal{K}_n$, where:
   $\texttt{Conc}(A) = \varphi$;
   $\texttt{TopRule}(A) = undefined$;

$Ant(A) = \emptyset$;
$Sub(A) = \{\varphi\}$;
$DefRules(A) = \emptyset$;
$StrRules(A) = \emptyset$;
$OrdPrem(A) = \emptyset$;
$Axioms(A) = [\varphi]$.

2. premise φ, if $\varphi \in \mathcal{K}_p$, where:
$Conc(A) = \varphi$;
$TopRule(A) = undefined$;
$Ant(A) = \emptyset$;
$Sub(A) = \{\varphi\}$;
$DefRules(A) = \emptyset$;
$StrRules(A) = \emptyset$;
$OrdPrem(A) = [\varphi]$;
$Axioms(A) = \emptyset$.

3. $\{A_1, \ldots, A_n\} \rightarrow \varphi$, if $A_1, \ldots, A_n$ are arguments and
$\{Conc(A_1), \ldots, Conc(A_n)\} \rightarrow \varphi \in \mathcal{R}_s$, where:
$Conc(A) = \varphi$;
$TopRule(A) = \{Conc(A_1), \ldots, Conc(A_n)\} \rightarrow \varphi$;
$Ant(A) = \{A_1, \ldots, A_n\}$;
$Sub(A) = Sub(A_1) \cup \cdots \cup Sub(A_n) \cup \{A\}$;
$DefRules(A) = DefRules(A_1) \uplus \cdots \uplus DefRules(A_n)$;
$StrRules(A) = StrRules(A_1) \uplus \cdots \uplus StrRules(A_n) \uplus [\{Conc(A_1), \ldots, Conc(A_n)\} \rightarrow \varphi]$;
$OrdPrem(A) = OrdPrem(A_1) \uplus \cdots \uplus OrdPrem(A_n)$;
$Axioms(A) = Axioms(A_1) \uplus \cdots \uplus Axioms(A_n)$

4. $\{A_1, \ldots, A_n\} \Rightarrow \varphi$, if $A_1, \ldots, A_n$ are arguments and
$\{Conc(A_1), \ldots, Conc(A_n)\} \Rightarrow \varphi \in \mathcal{R}_d$, where:
$Conc(A) = \varphi$;
$TopRule(A) = \{Conc(A_1), \ldots, Conc(A_n)\} \Rightarrow \varphi$;
$Ant(A) = \{A_1, \ldots, A_n\}$;
$Sub(A) = Sub(A_1) \cup \cdots \cup Sub(A_n) \cup \{A\}$;
$DefRules(A) = DefRules(A_1) \uplus \cdots \uplus DefRules(A_n) \uplus [\{Conc(A_1), \ldots, Conc(A_n)\} \Rightarrow \varphi]$;
$StrRules(A) = StrRules(A_1) \uplus \cdots \uplus StrRules(A_n)$;
$OrdPrem(A) = OrdPrem(A_1) \uplus \cdots \uplus OrdPrem(A_n)$;
$Axioms(A) = Axioms(A_1) \uplus \cdots \uplus Axioms(A_n)$.

A general argument A is an argument iff:

1. $Sub(A)$ *is indirectly consistent; and*
2. *If A contains non-strict subarguments A' and A'' such that $Conc(A') = Conc(A'')$, then $A' = A''$.*

An argument A is called strict when $DefRules(A) = OrdPrem(A) = \emptyset$. Else it is called defeasible.

Later in this paper, we will use the premises and inference rules used in an argument as the input of functions to determine the argument's strength. To simplify notation we introduce the *basis* of an argument.

Definition 8 ((Defeasible/Strict) Basis). *For an argument A the defeasible basis of A, written $DefBasis(A)$ is the multiset of all ordinary premises and defeasible inference rules used in A. i.e. $DefBasis(A) = OrdPrem(A) \uplus DefRules(A)$.*

The strict basis of A, $StrBasis(A) = Axioms(A) \uplus StrRules(A)$, is the multiset of all axiomatic premises and strict inference rules used in A.

The basis of A is the sum of its strict and defeasible bases, s.t. $Basis(A) = DefBasis \uplus StrBasis$.

For ease of notation we also introduce the `Rules` and `Prem` functions which return the multisets of all inference rules and premises used in an argument respectively.

Definition 9 (Rules). *For an argument A,*

$$Rules(A) = StrRules(A) \uplus DefRules(A).$$

Definition 10 (Prem). *For an argument A,*

$$Prem(A) = Axioms(A) \uplus OrdPrem(A).$$

We say two arguments are isomorphic if they have the same structure (or shape) and have the same weights for the equivalently positioned premises and inference rules.

Definition 11 (Isomorphism). *Take arguments A over $WAT = (AS, \mathcal{K}, s)$ and A' over a $WAT' = (AS', \mathcal{K}', s')$. There exists an isomorphism between A and A' when:*

– *If the arguments state a premise (Items 1, 2; Definition 7),*

$$s(Conc(A)) = s'(Conc(A')).$$

– *If the arguments make an inference (Items 3, 4; Definition 7),*

$$s(TopRule(A)) = s'(TopRule(A')) \text{ and}$$
$$\text{there exists a bijective function } f : Ant(A) \rightarrow Ant(A') \text{ such that}$$
$$\forall A'' \in Ant(A), f(A'') \in Ant(A') \text{ is an isomorphic image of } A''.$$

With our arguments defined, we are looking to assign each argument an intrinsic strength, based on its structure.

Definition 12 (Intrinsic Strength). *Str is a function that assigns numbers in $[0, 1]$ to arguments, such that for an argument A over a $WAT = (AS, \mathcal{K}, s)$, $Str(A)$ is the intrinsic strength of A where stronger arguments are assigned higher values.*

3   Principles

When assigning intrinsic strength to arguments, we may wish to look to certain principles our method of assigning these strengths might adhere to. This aids us in understanding the method we use to assign strengths, in comparing different strength-assigning methods, in proposing sensible methods for assigning strengths, and in selecting a suitable method for assigning strength for a certain application.

In this section we propose 13 such principles, which describe the way the weights of premises and inference rules and the intrinsic strengths of antecedent arguments affect the intrinsic strength of an argument. Most of these principles are intended to be intuitively desirable traits for the assigning of a strength value to an argument.

A similar approach is taken in [1] and later in [3] in the exploration of semantics that assign acceptability degrees to arguments after attacks by other arguments in (semi-)weighted argumentation graphs by aggregating attacks, (their weights,) and the base argument weights. Many of the principles proposed in this section resemble those used in the aforementioned papers.

Our first principle states that the identity, that is the name and meaning, of an argument A should not affect the strength assigned to it. Only its structure should.

Principle 1 (Anonymity)

$\forall WAT = (AS, \mathcal{K}, s), \ \forall A \, A' \text{ over } WAT,$
$$\text{if an isomorphism exists between } A \text{ and } A', \ Str(A) = Str(A')$$

The second principle says that when an argument A only states a premise, the argument should have a strength equal to the weight of its premise.

Principle 2 (Premising)

$\forall WAT = (AS, \mathcal{K}, s), \ \forall A \text{ over } WAT,$
$$TopRule(A) = \ undefined \ \rightarrow Str(A) = s(Conc(A))$$

Our next principle prescribes that when all of an argument A's premises are certain and its inferences are strict, the argument's strength should be 1.

Principle 3 (Strict Argument)

$$\forall WAT = (AS, \mathcal{K}, s), \ \forall A \text{ over } WAT, \ DefBasis(A) = \emptyset \rightarrow Str(A) = 1$$

The Resilience principle states that when all premises and inference rules used in an argument have a weight higher than 0, the argument's strength should also be higher than 0.

Principle 4 (Resilience)

$$\forall WAT = (AS, \mathcal{K}, s), \ \forall A \text{ over } WAT, \ (\forall b \in Basis(A), \ s(b) > 0) \rightarrow Str(A) > 0$$

According to the next principle, if any of the premises or inference rules used in argument A has weight 0, the intrinsic strength of A should also be 0.

Principle 5 (Argument Death)

$$\forall WAT = (AS, \mathcal{K}, s), \ \forall A \ over \ WAT, \ (\exists b \in \textbf{\textit{Basis}}(A), \ s(b) = 0) \rightarrow \textbf{\textit{Str}}(A) = 0$$

The next principle says that when all antecedents of an argument A have intrinsic strength 1, the intrinsic strength of A should equal the weight of its top rule.

Principle 6 (Antecedent Maximality)

$$\forall WAT = (AS, \mathcal{K}, s), \ \forall A \ over \ WAT, \ \forall A' \in \textbf{\textit{Ant}}(A),$$
$$\textbf{\textit{Str}}(A') = 1 \wedge \textbf{\textit{TopRule}}(A) \neq \ undefined \ \rightarrow \textbf{\textit{Str}}(A) = s(\textbf{\textit{TopRule}}(A))$$

Next, Antecedent Neutrality says that any antecedents of an argument A with intrinsic strength 1 should not affect the intrinsic strength of A.

Principle 7 (Antecedent Neutrality)

$$\forall WAT = (AS, \mathcal{K}, s), \ \forall A \, A' \, A'' \ over \ WAT,$$
$$s(\textbf{\textit{TopRule}}(A)) = s(\textbf{\textit{TopRule}}(A')) \wedge \textbf{\textit{Ant}}(A') = \textbf{\textit{Ant}}(A) \cup \{A''\} \wedge \textbf{\textit{Str}}(A'') = 1$$
$$\rightarrow \textbf{\textit{Str}}(A) = \textbf{\textit{Str}}(A')$$

Dual to Antecedent Neutrality, Antecedent Weakening says that any antecedents of an argument A with intrinsic strength lower than 1 should lower the intrinsic strength of A if it is not already 0.

Principle 8 (Antecedent Weakening)

$$\forall WAT = (AS, \mathcal{K}, s), \ \forall A \, A' \, A'' \ over \ WAT,$$
$$s(\textbf{\textit{TopRule}}(A)) = s(\textbf{\textit{TopRule}}(A')) \wedge \textbf{\textit{Ant}}(A') = \textbf{\textit{Ant}}(A) \cup \{A''\}$$
$$\wedge \textbf{\textit{Str}}(A'') < 1 \wedge \textbf{\textit{Str}}(A) > 0$$
$$\rightarrow \textbf{\textit{Str}}(A) > \textbf{\textit{Str}}(A')$$

To satisfy Inferential Weakening, applying a defeasible inference rule should result in an argument with an intrinsic strength lower than that of any of its antecedent arguments, so long as none of the antecedent arguments have strength 0.

Principle 9 (Inferential Weakening)

$$\forall WAT = (AS, \mathcal{K}, s), \ \forall A \ over \ WAT,$$
$$TopRule(A) \in \mathcal{R}_d \wedge (\forall A' \in \textbf{\textit{Ant}}(A), Str(A') > 0)$$
$$\rightarrow Str(A) < min\{Str(A')|A' \in \textbf{\textit{Ant}}(A)\}$$

For Inference Weight Sensitivity to apply, applying a weaker defeasible inference rule to a set of antecedent arguments should result in a weaker argument than applying a stronger rule to the same antecedents would, so long as none of the antecedent arguments have strength 0.

Principle 10 (Inference Weight Sensitivity)

$$\forall WAT = (AS, \mathcal{K}, s), \ \forall A \, A' \ over \ WAT,$$
$$Ant(A) = Ant(A') \wedge s(TopRule(A)) < s(TopRule(A'))$$
$$\wedge \, (\forall A'' \in Ant(A), \ Str(A'') > 0)$$
$$\rightarrow Str(A) < Str(A')$$

The Proportionality principle says that when two arguments have equally strong top rules and for each of the first argument's antecedents the second argument has a distinct antecedent with a lower strength, the first argument's overall strength should be higher.

Principle 11 (Proportionality)

$$\forall WAT = (AS, \mathcal{K}, s), \ \forall A \, A' \ over \ WAT,$$
$$s(TopRule(A)) = s(TopRule(A'))$$
$$\wedge \ there \ exists \ an \ injective \ function \ f : Ant(A) \rightarrow Ant(A')$$
$$such \ that \ \forall A'' \in Ant(A), Str(A'') > Str(f(A''))$$
$$\rightarrow Str(A) > Str(A')$$

Prescribing a single correct valuation, Weakest Link says an argument A's strength should be equal to the weight of its weakest premise or inference rule.

Principle 12 (Weakest Link)

$$\forall WAT = (AS, \mathcal{K}, s), \ \forall A \ over \ WAT, \ Str(A) = min(\{s(b)|b \in Basis(A)\})$$

The Weakest Link principle is so restrictive in what strengths it allows that most methods of assigning strength will not satisfy it. Still, limiting the strength of an argument to the weight of its weakest link seems to be a desirable property. To accommodate this we introduce the Weakest-Link Limiting principle, which states the intrinsic strength should be no higher than the weight of its weakest premise or inference rule.

Principle 13 (Weakest-Link Limiting)

$$\forall WAT = (AS, \mathcal{K}, s), \ \forall A \ over \ WAT, \ Str(A) \leq min(\{s(b)|b \in Basis(A)\})$$

4 Assigning Intrinsic Strength

Having defined a series of principles by which to evaluate methods for assigning intrinsic strength to arguments, we now look to what said methods might be. Two methods that come to mind are the *simple product* method, where we multiply the weights of all the premises and inference rules used in an argument (adding a factor for each time a premise or rule is used) to determine this arguments strength, and the *weakest link* method, where we equate the intrinsic strength of an argument to the lowest weight of any premise or inference rule used in it.

Definition 13 (Simple Product Method). *The simple product method (SP) assigns any argument A over any $WAT = (AS, \mathcal{K}, s)$ an intrinsic strength equal to the product of the weights of all members of $Basis(A)$, such that:*

$$Str_{sp}(A) = \prod_{b \in Basis(A)} s(b)$$

Because $Basis(A) = DefBasis(A) \uplus StrBasis(A)$, $\forall b \in StrBasis(A), s(b) = 1$ (Definitions 5, 7 and 8) and 1 is the identity element for multiplication, this is equivalent to:

$$Str_{sp}(A) = \prod_{b \in DefBasis(A)} s(b)$$

Definition 14 (Weakest Link Method). *The weakest link method (WL) assigns any argument A over any $WAT = (AS, \mathcal{K}, s)$ an intrinsic strength equal to the minimum of the weights of all members of $Basis(A)$, such that:*

$$Str_{wl}(A) = min\{s(b) | b \in Basis(A)\}$$

Example 3. We look at an example argument A_4 with subarguments A_1, A_2 and A_3, shown in Fig. 2. Argument A_1 states an axiomatic premise with weight 1.

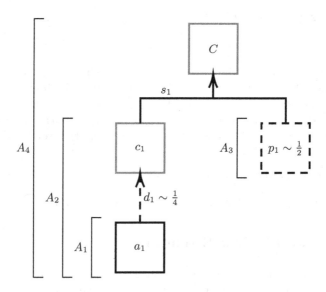

Fig. 2. An argument

A_2 makes an inference from the premise stated in A_1 using defeasible inference rule d_1 with strength $\frac{1}{4}$. Argument A_3 states an ordinary premise with weight $\frac{1}{2}$. Finally, argument A_4 uses strict inference rule s_1 to infer its conclusion from the conclusion of A_2 and the premise stated in A_3.

If we were to use the simple product method to assign strengths to A_4 and its subarguments, we would have:

- $Str_{sp}(A_1) = 1$ as it uses no rules and states an axiomatic premise.
- $Str_{sp}(A_2) = 1 \cdot \frac{1}{4} = \frac{1}{4}$; multiplying the weight of its one premise and its one defeasible inference rule.
- $Str_{sp}(A_3) = \frac{1}{2}$; the weight of the ordinary premise it states.
- $Str_{sp}(A_4) = 1 \cdot 1 \cdot \frac{1}{4} \cdot \frac{1}{2} = \frac{1}{8}$; the product of the weights of all the inference rules and premises used in the argument.

If we were to use the weakest link method instead, we would have:

- $Str_{wl}(A_1) = 1$ as it uses no rules and states an axiomatic premise.
- $Str_{wl}(A_2) = \min(1, \frac{1}{4}) = \frac{1}{4}$; the smallest weight of its one premise and its one defeasible inference rule.
- $Str_{wl}(A_3) = \frac{1}{2}$; the weight of the ordinary premise it states.
- $Str_{wl}(A_4) = \min(1, \frac{1}{4}, \frac{1}{2}) = \frac{1}{4}$; the smallest of the weights of all the inference rules and premises used in the argument.

Note that for SP, because of the commutative and associative properties of multiplication, instead of assigning strength equal to the product of the weights of all the premises and inference rules used in an argument, we can equivalently assign the weight of the premise for arguments just stating a premise and multiply the weight of the inference rule used with the strengths of the antecedent arguments for an argument making an inference. This method better matches the recursive nature of an argument. Similarly, we can keep the weight of the premise for arguments just stating a premise and take the minimum of the weight of the inference rule used and the strengths of the antecedent arguments for an argument making an inference when using WL.

Theorem 1 (SP Works Recursively). *For an argument A over a WAT $= (AS, \mathcal{K}, s)$:*

- *if $TopRule(A) = undefined$, $Str_{sp}(A) = s(Conc(A))$*
- *else, $Str_{sp}(A) = s(TopRule(A)) \cdot \prod_{a \in Ant(A)} Str_{sp}(a)$*

Theorem 2 (WL Works Recursively). *For an argument A over a WAT $= (AS, \mathcal{K}, s)$:*

- *if $TopRule(A) = undefined$, $Str_{wl}(A) = s(Conc(A))$*
- *else, $Str_{wl}(A) = min(s(TopRule(A)), m)$*
  where $m = min(\{Str_{wl}(a)|a \in Ant(A)\})$

Note 1. A proof for Theorem 1 is provided in the appendix. A proof for Theorem 2 can be constructed in the same fashion.

We now look to each of the principles defined in the previous section and determine which are satisfied by the simple product method and the weakest link method respectively:

Theorem 3. *SP satisfies Anonymity, Premising, Strict Argument, Resilience, Argument Death, Antecedent Maximality, Antecedent Neutrality, Antecedent Weakening, Inferential Weakening, Inference Weight Sensitivity, Proportionality and Weakest-Link Limiting. SP does not satisfy Weakest Link.*

Theorem 4. *WL satisfies Anonymity, Premising, Strict Argument, Resilience, Argument Death, Antecedent Maximality, Antecedent Neutrality, Weakest Link and Weakest-Link Limiting.*
WL does not satisfy Antecedent Weakening, Inferential Weakening, Inference Weight Sensitivity or Proportionality.

A full formal proof for every element of Theorem 3 can be found in the appendix. Many of the proofs to support Theorem 4 are very similar to those used for Theorem 3. Because of this, combined with the fact that in Sect. 6 we take a closer look at the class WL belongs to and how this class relates to our principles, we take a more informal approach with Theorem 4 and offer a proof sketch in the appendix instead.

5   Aggregation Methods

In the previous section we proposed two methods for assigning intrinsic strength to arguments. We saw that the simple product method satisfies most of the principles proposed in Sect. 3. The weakest link method satisfies significantly fewer of the principles, but nevertheless represents an intuitive concept. We also saw that both methods can be rewritten to not derive the assigned strength directly from the basis of an argument as a whole, but rather to assign arguments that state a premise a strength based on the weight of that premise and to assign arguments that make an inference a strength based on an aggregation of the strengths of the argument's antecedents combined with the weight of the applied inference rule.

In this section we introduce a technique that we may use to come up with new methods for assigning strength, based on the rewriting of our previous methods. We combine two functions, one to aggregate the strengths of the antecedents of the argument we are assessing and the other to combine this aggregate with the weight of the top rule used or inference made by the argument. This structure allows us to easily mix and match these two components to fine-tune the behaviour of our strength assigning method.

Definition 15 (Aggregation Method). *An aggregation method $M = (f, g)$ is a pair of functions $g : \bigcup_{n=0}^{\infty}[0,1]^n \to [0,1]$ and $f : [0,1] \times [0,1] \to [0,1]$ such that g is symmetric, used to evaluate the intrinsic strength of an argument A over a $WAT = (AS, \mathcal{K}, s)$ such that, when $\{A_1, \ldots, A_n\} = \mathbf{Ant}(A)$:*

– If $TopRule(A)$ is defined, $Str(A) = f(s(TopRule(A)), g(Str(A_1), \ldots, Str(A_n)))$.

– Else, $Str(A) = f(s(Conc(A)), g(Str(A_1), \ldots, Str(A_n)))$.

Here g aggregates the strengths of the antecedents of A and f combines the weight of the inference or premise with the aggregated antecedent strengths.

This definition of an aggregation method is inspired by [3], where a similar method is used to assign arguments an acceptability degree after attacks by other arguments in a fully weighted argumentation graph.[1]

Using our new definition of an aggregation method, we can construct a method that replicates the behaviour of our simple product method; take $M_{sp} = (f_{\text{prod}}, g_{\text{prod}})$ where:

$$f_{\text{prod}}(x, y) = x \cdot y$$

$$g_{\text{prod}}(x_1, \ldots, x_n) = \prod_{i=1}^{n} x_i$$

Similarly we can replicate the weakest link method with $M_{wl} = (f_{\text{min}}, g_{\text{min}})$, where:

$$f_{\text{min}}(x, y) = \min\{x, y\}$$

$$g_{\text{min}}(x_1, \ldots, x_n) = \begin{cases} 1 & \text{if } n = 0 \\ \min\{x_1, \ldots, x_n\} & \text{otherwise} \end{cases}$$

We may now also recombine the functions we used to construct M_{sp} and M_{wl} to create other aggregation methods. For instance we might make a method $M_{wm} = (f_{\text{prod}}, g_{\text{min}})$ that looks at the weakest antecedent of an argument and returns the product of said antecedent's strength and the argument's top rule or premise, which we might call the weakening minimum method.

We want the user of the aggregation methods to be free to choose aggregation functions that suit their use case. Therefore we deliberately left the choice of aggregation functions in the definition of an aggregation method unconstrained beyond the required symmetry of g. There are, however, some intuitive properties we want our aggregation methods to satisfy. To ensure they do we introduce the notion of a *well-behaved aggregation method*:

Definition 16 (Well-Behaved Aggregation Method). *An aggregation method $M = (f, g)$ is considered well-behaved iff:*

1. f *is non-decreasing in both variables whenever neither variable is 0.*
2. $f(0, x) = f(x, 0) = 0$

---

[1] In [3], a function is used to aggregate the weight of an attack with the weight of the attacker, a second function is used to aggregate the results of the first function for all attacks and a third function is used to combine this second aggregate with the initial weight of the argument under attack.

3. $f(x, 1) = f(1, x) = x$
4. $g() = 1$
5. $g(x) = x$
6. $g(x_1, \ldots, x_n, 0) = 0$
7. $g(x_1, \ldots, x_n) = g(x_1, \ldots, x_n, 1)$
8. $g(x_1, \ldots, x_n, y) \leq g(x_1, \ldots, x_n, z)$ *if* $y \leq z$

We considered adding two requirements, being $f(x, y) > 0$ *whenever* $x, y > 0$ and $g(x_1, \ldots, x_n) > 0$ *whenever* $x_1, \ldots, x_n > 0$, that correspond to the Resilience principle to the definition of a well-behaved aggregation method. We finally decided against this, because we feel it should be permissible for an aggregation method to 'kill' an argument if its components are too weak. It should be noted, however, that an aggregation method that kills off arguments in this way is precluded from satisfying Resilience.

It is plain to see how both M_{sp} and M_{wl} satisfy all the requirements presented in Definition 16 and, as such, are considered well-behaved aggregation methods.

Note how both f-functions we proposed are t-norms and both g-functions make use of t-norms [9]. It would seem that when one is looking to create a novel aggregation method, t-norms are a good place to look, at least for functions f. For functions g one might be tempted to also look to common aggregate functions such as the mean or median, but using these often results in a non-well-behaved aggregation method (specifically violating Definition 16 Point 7).

What follow are a few more examples of functions we could use to construct an aggregation method. For function f we might also use the Hamacher product f_{Ham} or the Łukasiewicz t-norm f_{Luk}, both being t-norms:

$$f_{\text{Ham}}(x, y) = \begin{cases} 0 & \text{if } x = y = 0 \\ \frac{xy}{x+y-xy} & \text{otherwise} \end{cases}$$

$$f_{\text{Luk}}(x, y) = \max(0, x + y - 1)$$

We might base our function g on the same two t-norms, adding special cases for when an argument has no or just one antecedent, giving us g_{Ham} and g_{Luk}:

$$g_{\text{Ham}}(x_1, \ldots, x_n) = \begin{cases} 1 & \text{if } n = 0 \\ x_1 & \text{if } n = 1 \\ x_1 \oplus \cdots \oplus x_n & \text{otherwise} \end{cases}$$

$$\text{where } x_1 \oplus x_2 = \begin{cases} 0 & \text{if } x = y = 0 \\ \frac{xy}{x+y-xy} & \text{otherwise} \end{cases}$$

$$g_{\text{Luk}}(x_1, \ldots, x_n) = \begin{cases} 1 & \text{if } n = 0 \\ x_1 & \text{if } n = 1 \\ x_1 \oplus \cdots \oplus x_n & \text{otherwise} \end{cases}$$

$$\text{where } x_1 \oplus x_2 = \max(0, x + y - 1)$$

Like the functions making up M_{sp} and M_{wl}, the functions f and g proposed here satisfy their respective requirements for an aggregation method based on them to be well-behaved.

6   Properties of Aggregation Methods

When choosing functions to construct an aggregation method, t-norms have the clear benefits of being commutative, monotonic and associative, as well as having 1 as their identity element and 0 as a null-element. These properties make it so that when we pick a t-norm for f and we base our g on a t-norm as we did for g_{Ham}, making sure an empty input results in value 1 and a single input value x results in output value x, we are guaranteed to have a well-behaved aggregation method.

We now look at the principles proposed in Sect. 3 to see how they relate to (well-behaved) aggregation methods.

Our first observation is that all aggregation methods satisfy Anonymity. This is because two isomorphic arguments have the same shape and the same weights for the premises and inference rules in the same places and an aggregation method only considers these two factors. A formal proof for this can be found in the appendix.

Theorem 5. *Any aggregation method satisfies Anonymity.*

The other principles are not necessarily satisfied by any aggregation method. We see that a well-behaved aggregation method is guaranteed to satisfy seven out of our thirteen principles, including Anonymity. This, however, does not mean the other principles cannot be satisfied by an aggregation method. Take, for instance, the well-behaved aggregation method M_{sp} which, as demonstrated in Sect. 4, satisfies five of the non-guaranteed principles.

Theorem 6. *Beyond Anonymity, any well-behaved aggregation method is guaranteed to satisfy Premising, Strict Argument, Argument Death, Antecedent Maximality, Antecedent Neutrality and Weakest-Link Limiting.*
The satisfaction of Resilience, Antecedent Weakening, Inferential Weakening, Inference Weight Sensitivity, Proportionality, or Weakest Link is not guaranteed.

Once again, many of the proofs for Theorem 6 closely resemble those presented in Sect. 4. Some others are simple counterexamples. Because of this we present only a proof sketch, which can be found in the Appendix.

7   Conclusion

In the field of argumentation, the focus of much of the research done has been on finding sensible ways of interpreting conflicts between arguments. The fruits of this labour can be found in Dung semantics that accept or reject arguments

based on the attack relations between them [6] and in the many gradual semantics that assign these arguments acceptability degrees [3]. Both of these types
of semantics belong to what we call abstract argumentation. That is, they do
away with the internal structure of the arguments under consideration and look
only at the relations between arguments. While gradual semantics have emerged
that can take into consideration the weights of attacks and base weights of arguments when determining arguments' final acceptability degree, no standard had
emerged for relating these weights to the structure of an argument.

What we set out to do in writing this paper is to investigate how to create
suitable methods for taking the structure of an argument and using it, combined with weights for the premises and inference rules used in the argument, to
determine the intrinsic strength of an argument. Throughout this investigation
we related the method for assigning strength under inspection to a set of principles corresponding to traits we deemed desirable, or at the least intuitive, in a
strength-assigning method.

The fact that we take the weights of premises and inference weights to correspond to a degree of defeasibility, with strict rules and premises having weight
1 and defeasible rules and premises having weight <1, gives rise to a possible
criticism to our approach. Some might object to the idea of an argument being
'punished' twice for being defeasible: once by having a lowered intrinsic strength
and a second time by being opened up to attacks from other arguments.

The first strength-assigning methods we looked at, the simple product
method (SP) and the weakest link method (WL), both take the weights of every
occurrence of a premise or inference rule in an argument as input when determining said argument's intrinsic strength. We found SP to satisfy many of our
principles. WL satisfied fewer of our principles but nevertheless represents an
important concept, in that any argument can only be so strong as its weakest
link.

Our definition of an argument closely resembles that used in ASPIC+, the
system for structured argumentation introduced by Modgil and Prakken [11].
This definition allows for an argument to state a premise or to apply an inference
rule to the conclusions of a set of antecedent arguments. We saw how both SP
and WL can be equivalently redefined to not take the strengths of the members
of the basis of an argument as input, but rather to assign an argument stating
a premise an intrinsic strength equal to the weight of said premise and for an
argument making an inference to combine the weight of the applied inference
rule with an aggregation of the strengths of its antecedent arguments. This
observation led to the introduction of aggregation methods.

An aggregation method is a combination of two functions that are used to
assign an argument an intrinsic strength; one function g to aggregate antecedent
argument strengths and another function f to combine the resulting aggregate
with the weight of the last applied inference rule or the stated premise. Aggregation methods allow us to mix and match these two functions to easily create
new methods of assigning intrinsic strength to an argument.

To capture what behaviours we wanted aggregation methods to express, we introduced the notion of a well-behaved aggregation method. One compelling result here is that we found that whenever one picks a t-norm for f and bases their g on a t-norm, the resulting aggregation method is guaranteed to be well-behaved. A possible criticism to our definition of an aggregation method is that the way it is used to assign an intrinsic strength to an argument is perhaps needlessly complicated. We define special cases for arguments making an inference and those stating a premise, both using functions f and g, but what follows from our notion of a well-behaved aggregation method is that we always want premising arguments to get assigned a strength equal to the weight of the premise they state. It might have been more clear to change the case for premising arguments to reflect this directly.

When relating well-behaved aggregation methods to the principles we defined earlier in the paper, we found that a well-behaved aggregation method is only guaranteed to satisfy half of our principles. This finding might give rise to the criticism that when the methods we ourselves deem well-behaved do not necessarily satisfy our own principles, the principles may be too strict. We, however, believe that this result is acceptable as our principles are intended not as requirements, but rather as formalisations of options.

We see a bright future for aggregation methods in structured argumentation. Future work we would specifically like to see done is an exploration of the weakening of the proposed principles that are not guaranteed to be satisfied by a well-behaved aggregation method, such that they still express the same ideas, but might be satisfied by all well-behaved aggregation methods. Another avenue for future work we believe to be promising is an exploration of the relationships between the proposed principles; we would, for instance, be interested to see whether certain principles follow from (a combination of) other principles or whether there are other properties, such as the guarantee that any subargument of an argument A is at least as strong as A, that hold as a consequence of satisfying certain principles. Finally, we feel interesting prospects lie in the development of aggregation methods tailored to specific use cases, making use of the aggregation method's easily adaptable nature.

Acknowledgements. Special thanks go out to Dragan Doder, for his expert guidance in writing this paper, for introducing us to many of the topics we discuss and for always being there to discuss new ideas. This paper would not have existed without his help.

Appendix

For a full version of this paper, including proofs and proof sketches, please refer to https://arxiv.org/abs/2109.00318.

References

1. Amgoud, L., Ben-Naim, J., Doder, D., Vesic, S.: Acceptability semantics for weighted argumentation frameworks. In: Sierra, C. (ed.) Proceedings of the

Twenty-Sixth International Joint Conference on Artificial Intelligence, IJCAI 2017, Melbourne, Australia, 19–25 August 2017, pp. 56–62. ijcai.org (2017). https://doi.org/10.24963/ijcai.2017/9

2. Amgoud, L., Cayrol, C.: A reasoning model based on the production of acceptable arguments. Ann. Math. Artif. Intell. **34**(1–3), 197–215 (2002). https://doi.org/10.1023/A:1014490210693

3. Amgoud, L., Doder, D.: Gradual semantics accounting for varied-strength attacks. In: Elkind, E., Veloso, M., Agmon, N., Taylor, M.E. (eds.) Proceedings of the 18th International Conference on Autonomous Agents and MultiAgent Systems, AAMAS 2019, Montreal, QC, Canada, 13–17 May 2019, pp. 1270–1278. International Foundation for Autonomous Agents and Multiagent Systems (2019). http://dl.acm.org/citation.cfm?id=3331831

4. Benferhat, S., Dubois, D., Prade, H.: Argumentative inference in uncertain and inconsistent knowledge bases. In: Heckerman, D., Mamdani, E.H. (eds.) UAI 1993: Proceedings of the Ninth Annual Conference on Uncertainty in Artificial Intelligence, The Catholic University of America, Providence, Washington, DC, USA, 9–11 July 1993, pp. 411–419. Morgan Kaufmann (1993). https://dslpitt.org/uai/displayArticleDetails.jsp?mmnu=1&smnu=2&article_id=606&proceeding_id=9

5. Cayrol, C., Lagasquie-Schiex, M.: Graduality in argumentation. J. Artif. Intell. Res. **23**, 245–297 (2005). https://doi.org/10.1613/jair.1411

6. Dung, P.M.: On the acceptability of arguments and its fundamental role in non-monotonic reasoning, logic programming and n-person games. Artif. Intell. **77**(2), 321–358 (1995). https://doi.org/10.1016/0004-3702(94)00041-X

7. Dunne, P.E., Hunter, A., McBurney, P., Parsons, S., Wooldridge, M.J.: Weighted argument systems: basic definitions, algorithms, and complexity results. Artif. Intell. **175**(2), 457–486 (2011). https://doi.org/10.1016/j.artint.2010.09.005

8. Kakas, A., Amgoud, L., Kern-Isberner, G., Maudet, N., Moraitis, P.: ABA: argumentation based agents. In: McBurney, P., Parsons, S., Rahwan, I. (eds.) ArgMAS 2011. LNCS (LNAI), vol. 7543, pp. 9–27. Springer, Heidelberg (2012). https://doi.org/10.1007/978-3-642-33152-7_2

9. Klement, E., Mesiar, R., Pap, E.: Triangular Norms, Trends in Logic, vol. 8. Springer, Heidelberg (2000). https://doi.org/10.1007/978-94-015-9540-7

10. Knuth, D.E.: The Art of Computer Programming, Volume II: Seminumerical Algorithms, 3rd edn. Addison-Wesley (1998). https://www.worldcat.org/oclc/312898417

11. Modgil, S., Prakken, H.: The $ASPIC^+$ framework for structured argumentation: a tutorial. Argument Comput. **5**(1), 31–62 (2014). https://doi.org/10.1080/19462166.2013.869766

12. Prakken, H.: Probabilistic strength of arguments with structure. In: Thielscher, M., Toni, F., Wolter, F. (eds.) Principles of Knowledge Representation and Reasoning: Proceedings of the Sixteenth International Conference, KR 2018, Tempe, Arizona, 30 October–2 November 2018, pp. 158–167. AAAI Press (2018). https://aaai.org/ocs/index.php/KR/KR18/paper/view/17978

13. Zhong, Q., Fan, X., Luo, X., Toni, F.: An explainable multi-attribute decision model based on argumentation. Expert Syst. Appl. **117**, 42–61 (2019). https://doi.org/10.1016/j.eswa.2018.09.038

How Can You Resolve a Trilemma?
- A Topological Approach -

Kazuko Takahashi$^{(\boxtimes)}$ and Tamon Okubo

Kwansei Gakuin University, 2-1, Gakuen, Sanda 669-1338, Japan
ktaka@kwansei.ac.jp

Abstract. This paper discusses how to escape a state in which argumentation can reach no conclusion, by offering a new argument. We formalize our approach based on Dung's abstract argumentation framework (AF). When an AF has no stable extension, we have no meaningful conclusion. We address the problem of whether it is possible to revise this situation by adding an argument that attacks an existing one. If possible, how many solutions can we generate and at what position should it be added? We discuss this problem using an AF consisting of a trilemma and show conditions depending on the topology of the AF. We also address the point that a specific argument can be accepted or not by this action. We extend the discussion into two possible directions: a general N-lemma case and a set of AFs, each of which consists of several trilemmas. It follows that when a large argumentation becomes stuck in a practical situation, the position to which a counter-argument should be added can be detected by a check of the topology of the AF.

Keywords: Abstract argumentation · Computational argumentation · Revision of argumentation · Graph topology

1 Introduction

Argumentation appears in many scenes in our daily life and has been studied from various perspectives. In the field of artificial intelligence and logic programming, the Abstract Argumentation Framework (AF) introduced by Dung [15] has been regarded as a strong framework to handle inconsistency and has generated considerable work on computational argumentation [17].

An AF can be represented as a directed graph in which a node corresponds to an argument, and an edge to an attack relation. When we consider an argumentation as a graph, we find several topological types. One type that attracts our interest is that including a cycle, which means that arguments are attacked by each other.

When two arguments A and B are attacked by each other, we cannot arrive at a unique outcome that each agent can accept. In this case, either A or B is

This work was supported by JSPS KAKENHI Grant Number JP17H06103.

T. Okubo—Currently, Fuji Soft Incorporated.

P. Baroni et al. (Eds.): CLAR 2021, LNAI 13040, pp. 397–416, 2021.
https://doi.org/10.1007/978-3-030-89391-0_22

Fig. 1. A trilemma in argumentation.

acceptable. Furthermore, consider what happens when three arguments, A, B, and C, attack in such an order that A attacks B, B attacks C, and C attacks A. We call this a *trilemma*. In this case, either one of A, B or C is acceptable. However, this result is weak in the sense that each single argument does not attack all of the other arguments. According to Dung's semantics, such an AF does not have a stable extension, and no argument is skeptically or credulously accepted. In practical argumentation, the argumentation becomes stuck, and no meaningful result is possible. We can escape from this sticky state by providing a new counter-argument. Moreover, if we want a specific argument to be accepted, we have to choose an appropriate position.

For example, consider the situation in which three agents give their arguments:

a: We should go to Okinawa; it is cold in Hokkaido.

b: We should go to Tokyo because it costs a lot to go to Okinawa.

c: We should go to Hokkaido because we cannot find beautiful scenery in Tokyo.

In this case, these arguments constitute a trilemma (Fig. 1). If an agent adds a new argument d, "It is risky to go to Tokyo now because of COVID-19," then the argument b is defeated, and as a result, a and d are accepted. Therefore, if an agent wants her claim a to be accepted, she needs to offer such an argument.

If the entire argumentation is larger, trilemmas may appear in many locations, and they may interact in complicated ways. In such a case, how can one agent find a way to persuade the others?

Changes in argumentation systems have been discussed in several works [14]. In these works, the authors consider the properties depending on the patterns of change in extensions and do not discuss the position to which a new attack is added. Here, we do not address the problem based on a principle of change in extension types but in terms of positions where an argument will be added.

In this paper, we consider AFs consisting of trilemmas that share one or two nodes. We investigate the properties of such an argument graph according to each topology and formalize them. We focus on stable semantics, since this is considered most suitable in a practical situation for drawing a plausible conclusion that is admitted by all agents and that attacks every argument against the conclusion.

More specifically, we discuss the problem of whether we can get an AF with a stable extension by adding one argument and an attack to the AF without it. If it is possible, we show the position to be added. We consider such a change based on the topology. Starting from a simple trilemma, we discuss extensions of the result in two directions: the N-lemma case and the meta-AF case.

Our aim is to resolve a stuck argumentation by offering a counter-argument for a practical situation, rather than to find a general method that can be applied to any argument graph including the ones that seldom appear in practical situations.

This paper is organized as follows. In Sect. 2, we describe basic concepts. In Sect. 3 and in Sect. 4, we consider the stable extension in the case of an AF including a single trilemma and an AF constructed by more than one trilemma, respectively, as well as one including the N-lemma. In Sect. 5, we consider a case of a meta-AF. In Sect. 6, we compare our approach with related works. Finally, in Sect. 7, we present conclusions and directions for future research.

2 Basic Concepts

The abstract argumentation framework (AF), proposed by Dung [15], is a representation of an argumentation structure, ignoring its content.

Definition 1 (argumentation framework (AF)). Argumentation Framework (AF) *is defined as a pair* $\langle \mathcal{A}, \mathcal{R} \rangle$ *where* $\mathcal{A}$ *is a set of arguments and* $\mathcal{R} \subseteq \mathcal{A} \times \mathcal{A}$.

A pair $(A, B) \in \mathcal{R}$ is called *an attack*, and it is said that A *attacks* B.

AF can be represented as a graph in which each node corresponds to an argument, and each edge corresponds to an attack. In this paper, we consider a finite AF.

Definition 2 (sub-AF). *Let* $AF_1 = \langle \mathcal{A}_1, \mathcal{R}_1 \rangle$ *and* $AF_2 = \langle \mathcal{A}_2, \mathcal{R}_2 \rangle$ *be AFs. An* AF_1 *is said to be a* sub-AF *of* AF_2 *if* $\mathcal{A}_1 \subseteq \mathcal{A}_2$ *and* $\mathcal{R}_1 \subseteq \mathcal{R}_2$*, and is denoted by* $AF_1 \subseteq AF_2$.

Semantics is defined either by an extension or labeling, which has a one-to-one relation [2]. In this paper, we consider stable semantics.

Definition 3 (stable extension). *Let* $\langle \mathcal{A}, \mathcal{R} \rangle$ *be an AF.* $S \subseteq \mathcal{A}$ *is said to be a* stable extension *if the following two conditions hold.*

- $\neg \exists A, B \in S; (A, B) \in \mathcal{R}$ *(There is no pair of arguments that attacks each other (conflict-freeness).)*
- $\forall B \in \mathcal{A} \setminus S, \exists A \in S; (A, B) \in \mathcal{R}$ *(Each argument outside the set is attacked by some argument in the set (stability).)*

Definition 4 (labeling, complete labeling). *Let* $\langle \mathcal{A}, \mathcal{R} \rangle$ *be an AF. Labeling is a total function from a set of arguments to a set* $\{\text{in}, \text{out}, \text{undec}\}$*. Labeling* $\mathcal{L}$ *is said to be* complete *if the following conditions are satisfied for any argument* $A \in \mathcal{A}$.

- $\mathcal{L}(A) = \text{in}$ *iff* $\forall B \in \mathcal{A}; (B, A) \in \mathcal{R} \Rightarrow \mathcal{L}(B) = \text{out}$.
- $\mathcal{L}(A) = \text{out}$ *iff* $\exists B \in \mathcal{A}; \mathcal{L}(B) = \text{in} \wedge (B, A) \in \mathcal{R}$.

Definition 5 (stable labeling). *Let* $\langle \mathcal{A}, \mathcal{R} \rangle$ *be an AF. For a complete labeling* $\mathcal{L}$, *if* $\{A|A \in \mathcal{A}, \mathcal{L}(A) = \text{undec}\} = \emptyset$, *then it is called* stable labeling.

It has been proven that stable extension and stable labeling coincide, that is, a stable extension corresponds to exactly one stable labeling and vice versa [2].

In addition to these concepts, we introduce several new concepts and terminology.

An AF with three arguments that constitutes a cycle is called a triangular unit.

Definition 6 (triangular unit(TU)). *An AF of the form* $\langle \{A, B, C\}, \{(A, B), (B, C), (C, A)\} \rangle$ *is called* a triangular unit (TU), *and is denoted by* $t(A, B, C)$. *When a TU is a sub-AF of an AF, then it is said that* the AF includes a triangular unit.

Definition 7 (connector, faucet). *Let* $\langle \mathcal{A}, \mathcal{R} \rangle$ *be an AF that includes a triangular unit* $\mathcal{T} = \langle \mathcal{A}_\mathcal{T}, \mathcal{R}_\mathcal{T} \rangle$. *If* $(A, B) \in \mathcal{R}, A \in \mathcal{A} \setminus \mathcal{A}_\mathcal{T}, B \in \mathcal{A}_\mathcal{T}$, *then B is said to be a* connector *of* $\mathcal{T}$; *if* $(A, B) \in \mathcal{R}, A \in \mathcal{A}_\mathcal{T}, B \in \mathcal{A} \setminus \mathcal{A}_\mathcal{T}$, *then A is said to be a* faucet *of* $\mathcal{T}$.

Example 1. In Fig. 2, a is the connector, and b and c are faucets of $t(a, b, c)$, respectively.

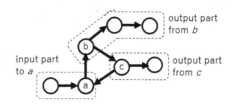

Fig. 2. Example of a triangular unit (TU).

For a TU, a sub-AF connected to C, which includes C itself, from the outside of the TU is called an *input part to* C and that connected from F, which includes F itself, to the outside of the TU is called an *output part from* F (Fig. 2).

Definition 8 (input part, output part). *(1) For an AF* $\langle \mathcal{A}, \mathcal{R} \rangle$ *including TU* $\langle \mathcal{A}_\mathcal{T}, \mathcal{R}_\mathcal{T} \rangle$, *its sub-AF* $\langle \mathcal{A}_1, \mathcal{R}_1 \rangle$ *such that* $\mathcal{A}_1 = \{A \mid \exists \sigma = (A_1, \ldots, A_{n-1}); \forall i (1 \leq i \leq n-1)(A_i, A_{i+1}) \in \mathcal{R} \setminus \mathcal{R}_\mathcal{T}$, *where* $A_1 = A, A_n = C \in \mathcal{A}_\mathcal{T}\} \cup \{C\}$, *and* $\mathcal{R}_1 = \{(A, B)|A, B \in \mathcal{A}_1\}$, *is called an* input part to C.
(2) For an AF $\langle \mathcal{A}, \mathcal{R} \rangle$ *including TU* $\langle \mathcal{A}_\mathcal{T}, \mathcal{R}_\mathcal{T} \rangle$, *its sub-AF* $\langle \mathcal{A}_2, \mathcal{R}_2 \rangle$ *such that* $\mathcal{A}_2 = \{B \mid \exists \sigma = (A_1, \ldots, A_{n-1}); \forall i (1 \leq i \leq n-1)(A_i, A_{i+1}) \in \mathcal{R} \setminus \mathcal{R}_\mathcal{T}$, *where* $A_1 = F \in \mathcal{A}_\mathcal{T}, A_n = B\} \cup \{F\}$, *and* $\mathcal{R}_2 = \{(A, B)|A, B \in \mathcal{A}_2\}$, *is called an* output part from F.

Note that if a node C is not a connector, then *input part to C* consists of only C. An AF may have several input parts or output parts.

Definition 9 (start-TU). *A triangular unit included by an AF without a connector is said to be a* start-TU.

Definition 10 (whisker). *For a new argument P and an attack I from P, a pair $\langle P, I \rangle$ is said to be a* whisker, *and P is said to be a* whisker node.

Definition 11 (stable AF, repair.[1]) *An AF with a stable extension is called a* stable AF, *and one without a stable extension is called an* unstable AF. *For an unstable AF, the act of revising it by adding a single whisker to get a stable AF is called a* repair.

The node to which a whisker is added is always labeled out when repaired, from the definition of stable labeling.

Definition 12 (entrance, acceptance set). *If we repair an unstable AF by adding a whisker to a node E, then the node is called an* entrance of AF *and their set is denoted by $ent(AF)$, and the obtained stable extension is called an* acceptance set.

3 AF Including One Triangular Unit

We pick up a triangular unit as the simplest odd-length cycle, and consider a finite AF that includes at most three TUs sharing their nodes. We assume that the entire AF has no cycle other than TUs and that it is uncontroversial, that is, there exists no arguments A and B connected by two different paths of even-length and odd-length. From this assumption, we have only one stable extension as a result of repair, and we denote the acceptance set on the entrance E for AF by $acc(AF, E)$.

We address the following problems:

1. When an AF is unstable, is it possible to repair it?
2. If so, how many solutions are possible, and where are the entrances?

In this section, we discuss the case in which an AF includes TUs sharing their nodes.

First, we discuss the case in which an AF includes only one TU.

When the TU has a faucet, the output part can be labeled without using undec if TU can be labeled without using undec. Therefore, we investigate only the case without a faucet.

---

[1] The meaning of "repair" is not exactly the same as that used in [4].

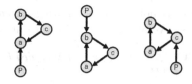

Fig. 3. An AF with one TU.

3.1   No Connector

If a TU has no connector, it is a start-TU, and it is trivial that a start-TU is unstable.

Proposition 1. *If AF includes only one start-TU, then it is unstable.*

In this case, we can repair it.

Proposition 2. *If an AF has only one start-TU, then we can repair it by taking any node as an entrance, yielding three solutions.*

Proof. Let AF be a triangular unit $t(a, b, c)$. Assume that we add a whisker node P to a without losing generality. Then, a becomes a connector of this TU. We get a labeling $\mathcal{L}$ such that $\mathcal{L}(P) = $ in, $\mathcal{L}(a) = $ out, $\mathcal{L}(b) = $ in, $\mathcal{L}(c) = $ out, and $acc(AF, a) = \{P, b\}$.   □

We show three solutions in Fig. 3. Hereafter, in the figures, the pink nodes and blue nodes show the arguments labeled in and out, respectively.

3.2   One Connector

When a TU has one connector, the AF has a stable extension depending on the topology. We divide the AF into the TU and the input part to the connector (both of which share the connector), and we consider labeling in each sub-AF. If two labelings can give the same value to the connector, then the AF is stable.

Proposition 3. *Let AF be an AF that includes a TU $t(a, b, c)$ with the unique connector a. Let $\mathcal{L}$ and $\mathcal{L}_C$ be labelings of the AF and the input part to a, respectively. Then, $\mathcal{L}_C(a) = $ in iff AF has no stable extension.*

Proof. ($\Rightarrow$) Assume that $\mathcal{L}_C(a) = $ in. Then, $\mathcal{L}(a)$ should be in, and $\mathcal{L}(b) = $ out, $\mathcal{L}(c) = $ in, which means that (c, a) is an attack from the node labeled in to the node labeled in. This is a contradiction.

($\Leftarrow$) Assume that $\mathcal{L}_C(a) = $ out. Then, $\mathcal{L}(a)$ should be out. $\mathcal{L}(a)$ is out, regardless of the value of $\mathcal{L}(c)$, from the definition of stable labeling. Therefore, there exists a labeling $\mathcal{L}(a) = $ out, $\mathcal{L}(b) = $ in, $\mathcal{L}(c) = $ out, which means that there exists a stable extension.   □

If we add a whisker to an arbitrary node a in the TU, then that node becomes a connector. Therefore, if the AF has no stable extension, then we add a whisker to any node in the TU or any node in the input part so that $\mathcal{L}_C(a) = $ out holds.

Proposition 4. *Let AF be an unstable AF that includes a TU $t(a, b, c)$ with the unique connector a. Let $\mathcal{L}_C$ be labelings of the input part to a. If there is no branch in the input part to a, that is, no node in the input part is attacked by more than one node, then we can repair it if we take a node in $\mathcal{T}$ or any node x in the input part such that $\mathcal{L}_C(x) = $ in holds as an entrance, and there are at least three solutions.*

Proof. Let $\mathcal{L}'$ be a labeling of the AF obtained by adding a whisker.

Assume that we add a whisker to a. Then, $\mathcal{L}'(a) = $ out, and then, $\mathcal{L}'(b) = $ in, $\mathcal{L}'(c) = $ out, which is stable.

Assume that we add a whisker to an arbitrary node x in the input part such that $\mathcal{L}_C(x) = $ in holds. Let $\mathcal{L}'_C$ be a label of the input part to a after the whisker is added. Then we get $\mathcal{L}'_C(x) = $ out and $\mathcal{L}'_C(a) = $ out. Therefore, we have $\mathcal{L}'(a) = $ out, $\mathcal{L}'(b) = $ in, $\mathcal{L}'(c) = $ out, which is stable. Note that if there is a branch, then we need more than one whisker to make $\mathcal{L}_C(a) = $ out, depending on the number of edges from the connector to the branching point, and there is no solution by adding only one whisker to the input part other than the connector.

Assume that we add a whisker to b. Then, $\mathcal{L}'(b) = $ out, and then, $\mathcal{L}'(c) = $ in, $\mathcal{L}'(a) = $ out, which is stable.

Assume that we add a whisker to c. Then, $\mathcal{L}'(c) = $ out, and $\mathcal{L}'(a) = $ in, $\mathcal{L}'(b) = $ out, which is stable.

Conversely, if we add a whisker to the other nodes, then we cannot repair the AF.

Therefore, there are at least three solutions. □

3.3 k Connectors

We generalize the case in which the number of connectors is k $(k = 0, 1, 2, 3)$.

Theorem 1. *Let AF be an AF that includes a TU $t(a, b, c)$. Let $\mathcal{L}_A$, $\mathcal{L}_B$ and $\mathcal{L}_C$ be labelings to input part to a, input part to b, and input part to c, respectively. Then, $\mathcal{L}_A(a) = \mathcal{L}_B(b) = \mathcal{L}_C(c) = $ in iff AF has no stable extension.*

Proof. ($\Rightarrow$) We show that we cannot define a stable labeling $\mathcal{L}$ to the AF. Assume that $\mathcal{L}(a) = $ in. As such, $\mathcal{L}(b) = $ out, and then, $\mathcal{L}(c) = $ in. This indicates an attack from the node labeled in to the one labeled in, which is a contradiction. Assume that $\mathcal{L}(a) = $ out. Then, $\mathcal{L}(b) = \mathcal{L}_B(b) = $ in, $\mathcal{L}(c) = $ out, and $\mathcal{L}(a) = \mathcal{L}_A(a) = $ in, which is a contradiction. Hence, AF has no stable extension.

($\Leftarrow$) We prove the contraposition by assuming that $\mathcal{L}_A(a) = $ out, without losing generality. Assume that $\mathcal{L}(a) = $ out. Then, $\mathcal{L}(b) = $ in, and then, $\mathcal{L}(c) = $ out and $\mathcal{L}(a) = \mathcal{L}_A(a) = $ out, which is consistent. Therefore, AF has a stable extension. □

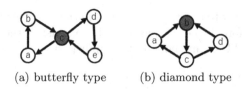

(a) butterfly type   (b) diamond type

Fig. 4. AF with two TUs.

If AF has no stable extension, we can repair it.

Theorem 2. *Let AF be an AF that includes a TU $t(a,b,c)$. Let $\mathcal{L}_A$, $\mathcal{L}_B$, and $\mathcal{L}_C$ be labelings to input part to a, input part to b, and input part to c, respectively. If the AF is unstable and each input part has no branch, then we can repair it iff we take any of the following nodes as an entrance:*

1. *any node x of input part to a such that $\mathcal{L}_A(x) = $ in.*
2. *any node y of input part to b such that $\mathcal{L}_B(y) = $ in.*
3. *any node z of input part to c such that $\mathcal{L}_C(z) = $ in.*

There are at least three solutions.

Proof. This can be proven, similarly to Proposition 4.   □

4   Triangular Units Sharing Nodes

4.1   AF Including Two triangular units

Assume that AF includes two TUs that share their nodes. For simplicity, we assume that each node in AF is included in at least one TU.

There are two topologies, depending on the number of nodes shared with the two TUs. If only one node is shared, we call it the Butterfly type (B-type), and if two nodes are shared, the Diamond type (D-type) (Fig. 4). In both types, TUs have only one common connector. In B-type (Fig. 4(a)), both TUs have the common connector c, and in D-type (Fig. 4(b)), both TUs have the common connector b. The connectors are shown as red nodes in the figures. A node that is not a connector is attacked by exactly one node. Neither of these AFs has a stable extension, and we can repair them. We have three solutions in the case of B-type (Fig. 5) and two solutions in the case of D-type (Fig. 6).

4.2   AF Including Three triangular units

Assume that AF includes three TUs that share their nodes. For simplicity, we assume that each node in the AF is included in at least one TU. There are three types of topology: BB-type (Fig. 7), BD-type (Fig. 10), and DD-type (Fig. 14), depending on the types sharing nodes. None of these AFs have a stable extension, and we can repair them.

Fig. 5. Solutions of B-type: $ent(AF) = \{a, c, e\}$.

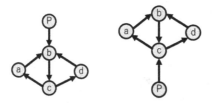

Fig. 6. Solutions of D-type: $ent(AF) = \{b, c\}$.

In this case, there exist one or two connectors. If two connectors exist, the position of the entrance is determined depending on the direction of an attack between the connectors. For each topology, we show that we can repair it by adding a whisker so that all the connectors are labeled out.

In the BB-type, each pair of TUs shares a single node. There are two topologies of the BB-type (Fig. 7).

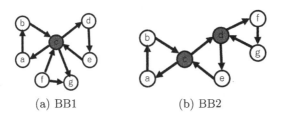

(a) BB1   (b) BB2

Fig. 7. BB-type.

For the BB1-type, there are four solutions: $ent(AF) = \{c, d, a, g\}$ (Fig. 8), and for BB2-type, there are two solutions: $ent(AF) = \{d, f\}$ (Fig. 9).

In the BD-type, a pair of TUs share a single node, and another pair of TUs share an edge. There are three BD-type topologies (Fig. 10).

For the BD1-type, there are three solutions: $ent(AF) = \{b, c, e\}$ (Fig. 11), for the BD2-type, there are two solutions: $ent(AF) = \{c, e\}$ (Fig. 12), and for the BD3-type, there is one solution: $ent(AF) = \{b\}$ (Fig. 13).

In the DD-type, two pairs of TUs share an edge. There are three DD-type topologies (Fig. 14).

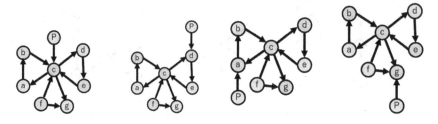

Fig. 8. Solutions of BB1: $ent(AF) = \{c, d, a, g\}$.

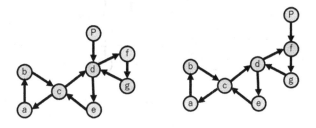

Fig. 9. Solutions of BB2: $ent(AF) = \{d, f\}$.

For DD1-type, there are two solutions: $ent(AF) = \{b, c\}$ (Fig. 15), for DD2-type, there is one solution: $ent(AF) = \{b\}$ (Fig. 16), and for DD3-type, there is one solution: $ent(AF) = \{c\}$ (Fig. 17).

4.3 AF Including k triangular units

From the investigation in Subsect. 4.1 and Subsect. 4.2, we show that the positions of the entrances can be determined generally for any topology presented in these previous sections.

We restrict the target AF to the one that satisfies the following conditions, since we want to clarify the properties of a trilemma itself, avoiding the AF that does not frequently appear in a practical argumentation from our target.

Definition 13 (module). *We call the AF that satisfies the following conditions* **Cond** *a module.*
[Cond]

1. *The AF consists of at most three TUs sharing their nodes.*
2. *Each node in the AF is included in at least one TU.*
3. *It has no cycle other than TUs.*
4. *It is uncontroversial.*

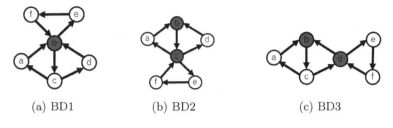

(a) BD1   (b) BD2   (c) BD3

Fig. 10. BD-type.

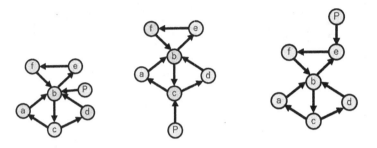

Fig. 11. Solutions of BD1: $ent(AF) = \{b, c, e\}$.

Theorem 3. *1. A module AF has no stable extension.*
2. When $AF = \langle \mathcal{A}, \mathcal{R} \rangle$ has one connector C, it can be repaired iff the common connector C or any node A that satisfies $(C, A) \in \mathcal{R}$ is taken as an entrance.
3. When $AF = \langle \mathcal{A}, \mathcal{R} \rangle$ has two connectors C_A and C_B such that $(C_A, C_B) \in \mathcal{R}$, it can be repaired iff C_B or any node B that satisfies $(C_B, B) \in \mathcal{R}$ and $(B, C_A) \notin \mathcal{R}$ is taken as an entrance.

Proof. 1. Since any TU included in AF is unstable, AF is unstable.
2. Assume that AF has one connector C. Let an arbitrary TU in AF be $t(A, B, C)$.
   (a) If we add a whisker to the node C, then C is labeled out. Node A is attacked only by C in AF. Therefore, if C is labeled out, then A is labeled in. Then, B, which is attacked by A, should be labeled out. All TUs can be labeled similarly, since the connector is common. Therefore, AF can be repaired.
   (b) If we add a whisker to the node A such that $(C, A) \in \mathcal{R}$, then A is labeled out, B attacked only by A is labeled in and as a result, C is labeled out. Therefore, AF can be repaired.
   (c) In contrast, assume that we add a whisker to B. Then B is labeled out. Let $t'(C, A', B')$ be another TU that shares the connector C. If C is labeled out, then A' is labeled in, since A' is attacked only by C; B' is labeled out, since B' is attacked only by A'; and C is labeled in, since both its attackers B and B' are labeled out, which is a contradiction. If C is labeled in, then A' is labeled out and B' is labeled in, and then C should be out, which is a contradiction.

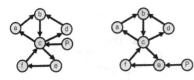
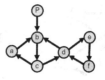

Fig. 12. Solutions of BD2: *ent*(*AF*) = {*c*, *e*}.

Fig. 13. Solution of BD3: *ent*(*AF*) = {*b*}.

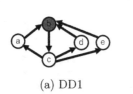

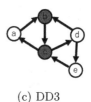

(a) DD1   (b) DD2   (c) DD3

Fig. 14. DD-type.

3. Assume that AF has two connectors C_A and C_B such that $(C_A, C_B) \in \mathcal{R}$. Let $t(A, C_A, C_B)$ be an arbitrary TU in AF that has two connectors, and $t(C_A, D, E)$ be an arbitrary TU in AF that has one connector C_A.

(a) If we add a whisker to C_B, then C_B is labeled out. Node A is attacked only by C_B. Therefore, if C_B is labeled out, then A is labeled in. Then, C_A which is attacked by A, should be labeled out. As for $t(C_A, D, E)$, node D is labeled in since it is attacked only by C_A, and node E is labeled out since it is attacked only by D. A TU that shares only C_B can be labeled without a contradiction for the same reason as that in the case of one connector. Therefore, AF can be repaired.

(b) If we add a whisker to the node B that satisfies $(C_B, B) \in \mathcal{R}$ and $(B, C_A) \notin \mathcal{R}$, then B is labeled out. Let $t(C_B, B, F)$ be a TU that has only one connector C_B. Then B is labeled out, regardless of the label of its other attacker. And F, attacked only by B, is labeled in, and C_B is labeled out. Therefore, AF can be repaired.

(c) In contrast, assume that we add a whisker to C_A. Then, C_A is labeled out. Let $t(C_B, B, F)$ be another TU that has only one connector C_B. If C_B is labeled in, then B is labeled out, and then F is labeled in. Therefore, C_B is labeled out, since C_B is attacked by F, which is a contradiction. If C_B is labeled out, then B is labeled in, and then F is labeled out. Therefore, C_B should be in, since C_B is attacked by F and C_A, both of which are labeled out, which is a contradiction. When we add a whisker to the other node, a similar discussion follows.   □

This theorem shows that we can find an entrance by simply checking the topology of an AF.

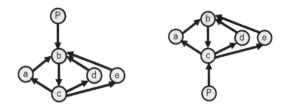

Fig. 15. Solutions of DD1: $ent(AF) = \{b, c\}$.

Fig. 16. Solution of DD2: $ent(AF) = \{b\}$.

Fig. 17. Solution of DD3: $ent(AF) = \{c\}$.

Example 2. The BB2-type AF $\langle \mathcal{A}, \mathcal{R} \rangle$, shown in Fig. 7(b), has connectors c and d such that $(c, d) \in \mathcal{R}$, $(d, f) \in \mathcal{R}$, and $(f, c) \notin \mathcal{R}$ hold. Therefore, d and f are entrances (Fig. 9).

In contrast, the BD3-type AF $\langle \mathcal{A}, \mathcal{R} \rangle$, shown in Fig. 10(c), has connectors b and d such that $(d, b) \in \mathcal{R}$, $(b, c) \in \mathcal{R}$, and $(c, d) \in \mathcal{R}$ hold. Therefore, b is an entrance, but c is not (Fig. 13).

Theorem 3 does not always hold if the AF consists of more than three TUs. For example, the AF shown in Fig. 18, which has three connectors, c, e and f, cannot be repaired.

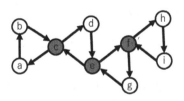

Fig. 18. AF that cannot be repaired.

4.4   Acceptance of a Specific Argument

We have discussed the entrances to obtain a stable AF. The next question is whether we can find a solution in which a specific argument can be accepted, that is, find an entrance on which an acceptance set includes the argument. The above investigation shows that it is impossible to make the connector be an accepted argument in the case of a trilemma. How about the arguments other than the connector? Unfortunately, it is impossible to ensure that some specific arguments will be accepted, even if any position is selected as an entrance in some topology. For example, see the solutions for BB2-type shown in Fig. 9. In this case, $\neg \exists E; b \in acc(AF, E)$, and we have to add more than one whisker to the graph to make b accepted.

4.5 N-Lemma

Theorem 3 holds not only for a trilemma but also N-lemma for any finite $N = 2m + 1$.

Definition 14 (odd-unit). *An AF of the form* $\langle \{A_1, \ldots, A_{2m+1}\}, \{(A_1, A_2), (A_2, A_3), \ldots, (A_{2m}, A_{2m+1}), (A_{2m+1}, A_1)\} \rangle$ *is called* an odd-unit *and is denoted by* $t(A_1, \ldots, A_{2m+1})$.

We set the **Cond_N** by replacing the term 'TU' in **Cond** by 'odd-unit', and obtain the following theorem.

Theorem 4. *1. The AF that satisfies* **Cond_N** *has no stable extension.*
2. When $AF = \langle \mathcal{A}, \mathcal{R} \rangle$ *has one connector* C, *it can be repaired iff the common connector* C *or any node* B *such that there exists a sequence of attacks* $(B_i, B_{i+1}) \in \mathcal{R}$ $(1 \le i \le 2s - 1)$ *where* $B_1 = C$ *and* $B_{2s} = B$ *is taken as an entrance.*
3. When AF has two connectors C_A *and* C_B *such that there exists a sequence of attacks* $(A_i, A_{i+1}) \in \mathcal{R}$ $(1 \le i \le 2h-1)$ *where* $A_1 = C_A$ *and* $A_{2h} = C_B$. *Then, it can be repaired iff a node* B *that satisfies one of the following conditions is taken as an entrance:*
(i) $B = C_B$
(ii) B *is a node of an odd-unit including both* C_A *and* C_B *and there exists a sequence of attacks* $(B_i, B_{i+1}) \in \mathcal{R}$ $(1 \le i \le 2s - 1)$ *where* $B_1 = C_A$ *and* $B_{2s} = B$.
(iii) B *is a node of an odd-unit including* C_B *but not* C_A, *and there exists a sequence of attacks* $(B_i, B_{i+1}) \in \mathcal{R}$ $(1 \le i \le 2s - 1)$ *where* $B_1 = B$ *and* $B_{2s} = C_B$ *and each* B_i $(1 \le i \le 2s - 1)$ *is not shared with the other odd-units.*

The theorem can be proved using the properties that all the nodes but for the connectors are attacked only by one node, respectively, and that the label of the entrance is always out.

Sketch of Proof. Due to space constraints, here we discuss the case in which AF has one connector. Let $t(A_1, \ldots, A_{2m+1})$ be an arbitrary odd-unit.

Assume that it shares an odd number of nodes $A_1, A_2, \ldots, A_{2t-1}$ where $(A_i, A_{i+1}) \in \mathcal{R}$ $(\forall i; 1 \le i \le 2t, t \le m)$. Then, $A_1, A_3, \ldots, A_{2t-1}$ have the same label, since each of them is attacked only by one node. Thus, we can consider labeling by reducing $A_1, A_2, \ldots, A_{2t-1}$ to one node. Then, the number of shared nodes can be considered as one. Similarly, since non-shared nodes

$A_{2t}, A_{2t+2}, \ldots, A_{2m}$ have the same label, we can consider labeling by reducing $A_{2t}, A_{2t+1}, \ldots, A_{2m}$ to one node. Then, the number of the non-shared nodes can be considered as two. As a result, the problem is reduced to the one in the case of a trilemma.

If an odd-unit $t(A_1, \ldots, A_{2m+1})$ shares an even number of nodes $A_1, A_2, \ldots, A_{2t}$, the problem is reduced to the one of a trilemma consisting of two shared nodes and one non-shared node.   □

Note that different from the case of a trilemma, the connector is not necessarily labeled out when repaired (Fig. 19).

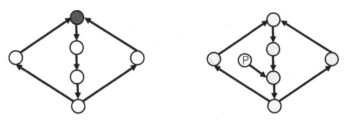

(a) unstable AF including 5-lemmas (b) labeling when a whisker is added

Fig. 19. Repaired AF in which the connector is not labeled in.

5   Connected Modules

In this section, we consider an AF consisting of modules connected by edges that are not included in any TU.

Definition 15 (meta-AF). *Let $\mathcal{M}$ be a set of modules $\{M_1, \ldots, M_k\}$, where $M_i = \langle \mathcal{A}_i, \mathcal{R}_i \rangle$. Let $AF(\mathcal{M})$ be an AF $\langle \mathcal{A}, \mathcal{R} \rangle$ where $\mathcal{A} = \bigcup_{i=1}^{k} \mathcal{A}_i, \mathcal{R} = \bigcup_{i=1}^{k} \mathcal{R}_i \cup \{(A_i, B_j) | A_i \in \mathcal{A}_i, B_j \in \mathcal{A}_j (1 \leq i \neq j \leq k)\}$. Then, $AF(\mathcal{M})$ is said to be a meta-AF of $\mathcal{M}$.*

We define the terms connector, faucet, and start-module for meta-AF, similarly with the case of a single triangular unit.

Definition 16 (connector, faucet, start-module). *Let $\mathcal{M}$ be a set of modules $\{M_1, \ldots, M_k\}$, where $M_i = \langle \mathcal{A}_i, \mathcal{R}_i \rangle$. Let $AF(\mathcal{M})$ be a meta-AF of $\mathcal{M}$.*

If $(A, B) \in \mathcal{R}, A \in \mathcal{A} \setminus \mathcal{A}_i, B \in \mathcal{A}_i$, then B is said to be a connector of M_i; if $(A, B) \in \mathcal{R}, A \in \mathcal{A}_i, B \in \mathcal{A} \setminus \mathcal{A}_i$, then A is said to be a faucet of M_i. $conn(M_i)$ and $faucet(M_i)$ denote the set of connectors and that of faucets of M_i, respectively. A module without a connector is said to be a start-module.

For simplicity, we assume that no module is isolated and that each pair of modules is connected by at most one edge. Note that $\{M_1, \ldots, M_k\}$ is not necessarily connected linearly. Each M_i may have more than one connector and/or faucet.

Example 3. Figure 20 shows an AF that consists of four modules. M_1 is a start-module. The connector and faucets of these modules are: $conn(M_1) = \{\}$, $faucet(M_1) = \{d, f\}$, $conn(M_2) = \{h\}$, $faucet(M_2) = \{j\}$, $conn(M_3) = \{p\}$, $faucet(M_3) = \{q\}$, and $conn(M_4) = \{k, m\}$, $faucet(M_4) = \{\}$.

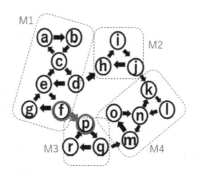

Fig. 20. Connected modules without a meta-cycle.

$AF(\mathcal{M})$ is unstable since each module is unstable.

Proposition 5. *$AF(\mathcal{M})$ is unstable.*

Let $\mathcal{M}$ be a set of modules $\{M_1, \ldots, M_k\}$, where $M_i = \langle \mathcal{A}_i, \mathcal{R}_i \rangle$. Let $AF(\mathcal{M})$ be a meta-AF of $\mathcal{M}$. In the following, we discuss its *repair*.

If there exists more than one start-module, then we have no solution since we have to add a whisker to each start-module so that each of them is stable. If there is one start-module, a configuration of modules should satisfy some condition so that it is possible to be repaired.

Proposition 6. *Let $\mathcal{M} = \{M_1, \ldots, M_k\}$ and $AF(\mathcal{M}) = \langle \mathcal{A}, \mathcal{R} \rangle$. Assume that $AF(\mathcal{M})$ has exactly one start-module.*

We can repair $AF(\mathcal{M})$ by setting the connector E of the start-module as an entrance iff the following three conditions hold for each $M_i \in \mathcal{M}$:

1. *If M_i is a start-module, then $\exists E, F; (E \in ent(M) \wedge F \in acc(M_i, E))$.*
2. *If M_i is not a start-module, let $(F_l, C_i) \in \mathcal{R}$ $(1 \leq l \neq i \leq k)$ where $F_l \in faucet(M_l)$,*
   then $\exists C_i; (C_i \in conn(M_i) \Rightarrow C_i \in ent(M_i) \wedge F_l \in acc(M_l, C_l))$.
3. *If M_i is not a start-module and if $\exists D_i; D_i \neq C_i, D_i \in conn(M_i)$, let $(F_j, C_i) \in \mathcal{R}$ $(1 \leq j \neq i, l \leq k)$ where $F_j \in faucet(M_j)$, then $D_i \in acc(M_i, C_i) \Leftrightarrow F_j \notin acc(M_j, C_j)$.*

Sketch of Proof. First, let M be a start-module. If we add a whisker to an entrance E of M, then we can repair M.

Next, let M not be a start-module. Then, it has a connector.

Assume that M_i ($1 \leq i \leq k$) has only one connector C_i. From the second condition, C_i is labeled out since the faucet F_l is labeled in, and it is an entrance of M_i. Therefore, M_i has a stable labeling. Let $\mathcal{L}$ be this labeling.

Assume that M_i ($1 \leq i \leq k$) has a connector D_i different from C_i. From the third condition, $\mathcal{L}(D_i) = \text{in}$ iff $\mathcal{L}(F_j) = \text{out}$, and $\mathcal{L}$ is a consistent labeling to M_i.

Therefore, $AF(\mathcal{M})$ can be repaired.   □

Example 4. Consider the AF shown in Fig. 20.

For a start-module M_1, it is a BB2-type module where $ent(M_1) = \{a, c\}$ and $acc(M_1, c) = \{a, d, f\}$. Since $c \in ent(M_1)$ and $d \in acc(M_1, c)$, the first condition is satisfied.

For M_2, $ent(M_2) = \{h, i, j\}$ and $acc(M_2, h) = \{i\}$. For the connector h of M_2 where $(d, h) \in \mathcal{R}$, $h \in ent(M_2) \wedge d \in acc(M_1, c)$ holds. For M_3, $ent(M_3) = \{p, q, r\}$ and $acc(M_3, p) = \{q\}$. For the connector p of M_3 where $(f, p) \in \mathcal{R}$, $p \in ent(M_3) \wedge f \in acc(M_1, c)$ holds. For M_4, $ent(M_4) = \{k, m, n\}$ and $acc(M_4, m) = \{k, o\}$. For the connector m of M_4 where $(q, m) \in \mathcal{R}$, $m \in ent(M_4) \wedge q \in acc(M_3, p)$ holds. Therefore, the second condition is satisfied.

M_4 has one more connector k where $(j, k) \in \mathcal{R}, j \in faucet(M_2)$. $j \notin acc(M_2, h) \wedge k \in acc(M_4, m)$ holds. Therefore, the third condition is satisfied.

Hence, we can repair it by adding a whisker node P to c, and the obtained stable extension is $\{P, a, d, f, i, k, o, q\}$.

Example 5. For the AF in Fig. 20, assume that an attack (f, p) is replaced by (f, r).

For M_3, $conn(M_3)$ is changed to $\{r\}$, and $acc(M_3, r) = \{p\}$. As a result, in M_4, $q \notin acc(M_3, r)$, which breaks the second condition.

Therefore, we cannot repair it.

Proposition 6 can be extended for an $AF(\mathcal{M})$ that has a meta-cycle. In this case, we must consider the connections between modules.

Example 6. Figure 21 presents an AF consisting of four modules that constitute a meta-cycle. In this case, we regard an arbitrary module as a start-module.

We take M_1 as a start-module where $ent(M_1) = \{a, c\}$ and $acc(M_1, a) = \{b, d, f\}$. Since $a \in ent(M_1) \wedge d \in acc(M_1, a)$, the first condition is satisfied.

It can be checked that the second condition is satisfied for each module.

In this case, it can be considered that M_1 has a connector f in addition to a, where $(p, f) \in \mathcal{R}$, $p \in faucet(M_4)$. And $p \notin acc(M_4, q) \wedge f \in acc(M_1, a)$ holds. Therefore, the third condition is satisfied.

Therefore, we can repair it by adding a whisker node P to a, and the obtained stable extension is $\{P, b, d, f, i, l, m, r\}$.

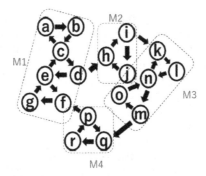

Fig. 21. Connected modules with a meta-cycle.

6   Related Works

In general, the main issue in changing an argumentation framework is the possibility of modification so that a set of arguments becomes a subset of an extension. This issue was introduced as an *enforcing problem* and was first discussed in [4]. Subsequently, considerable work has been done on this problem [14].

Boella et al. discussed the change in grounded semantics if we add or remove an attack relation [8,9]. They investigated the properties of the grounded extensions, such as expansive change or narrowing change.

Cayrol et al. expanded this discussion to several kinds of semantics including stable semantics. They investigated the properties of the change in extensions with regard to the addition and removal of an argument with an attack. They first investigated a single attack and then extended the procedure to addition and removal of multiple attacks [10–12]. They showed that some propositions depend on the changing type of extensions, but they did not address the classification of topological features, and not all topological patterns were covered.

Coste-Marquis et al. addressed the revision of extension on changing an attack relation between existing arguments as well as adding an argument with an attack [13].

Alfono et al. developed an efficient algorithm to compute the extension of the revised AF by adding an attack between existing arguments [1].

Baumann et al. showed the minimal change required in an extension to accept a given set of arguments [4], specifically, the change in extensions under several semantics for addition and removal of arguments and attacks [6,7]. They investigated the change in extensions in various cases. The complexity for the revision was also discussed [5,19].

These works focused mainly on how to find a solution to realize a minimal change in an extension and the type of properties involved in changes in extensions. In contrast, we did not focus on the properties of changes in extensions. Instead, we investigated the position to which an attack from a new argument is added. Specifically, we considered the AF consisting of TUs that has no stable extension and discussed the problem of how to modify it, depending on the topology. We also attempted to resolve the case of general odd-length cycles.

Some works have utilized the topological features of an argument graph for the treatment of dynamic argumentation frameworks [3,16]. They used simple topological features such as symmetry and similarity to reduce the complexity of computing changes in extensions, whereas we investigated the relationship of the topological feature and the possibility of repair.

A repair shown in our work can be regarded as an abduction in logic programming, in the sense of finding a minimal change in the knowledge base by adding a fact and a rule. Šefránek described the relationship between a dynamic argumentation framework and revision of logic programming [18]. It would be interesting to relate our approach to an abduction of logic programming.

7   Conclusion

We investigated the conditions under which an unstable AF consisting of a triangular unit can be revised to be stable by adding a new attack from a new argument. We have shown the positions to be added and the number of solutions.

The main contribution of our work is showing a uniform treatment of a trilemma in AFs using its topological features. We also discussed how the result can be extended in two possible directions. One is an extension from the trilemma to N-lemma for any odd-number $N \geq 3$, and the other is the case in which multiple triangular units are connected by edges that are not included in any triangular unit.

The results suggest that we can use topological features, such as connection patterns and the direction of edges, to obtain a stable AF. It follows that when a large argumentation falls into a sticky state, the position to which a counter-argument should be added can be detected by checking the topology of the AF.

Three main problems remain for future research. First, we should investigate the case in which a module includes more than three trilemmas (or N-lemmas). Second, we would like to explore other types of topology, such as those including even-length cycles and other semantics. Third, we plan to discuss the complexity of finding a position. It is not expensive to detect the connectors and the entrances for each topology, but a high computational cost may be incurred to identify its topology.

References

1. Alfaso, G., Greco, S., Parisi, F.: Incremental computation in dynamic argumentation frameworks. IEEE Intell. Syst. **36**(2), 6–12 (2021)
2. Baroni, P., Caminada, M., Giacomin, M.: An introduction to argumentation semantics. Knowl. Eng. Rev. **26**(4), 365–410 (2011)
3. Baroni, P., Giacomin, M., Liao, B.: On topology-related properties of abstract argumentation semantics. A correction and extension to dynamics of argumentation systems: a division-based method. Artif. Intell. **212**, 104–115 (2014)

4. Baumann, R., Brewka, G.: Expanding argumentation frameworks: enforcing and monotonicity results. In: COMMA 2010, pp. 75–86 (2010)
5. Baumann, R., Ulbricht, M.: If nothing is accepted - repairing argumentation frameworks. In: KR 2018, pp. 108–117 (2018)
6. Baumann, R., Brewka, G.: Extension removal in abstract argumentation - an axiomatic approach. In: AAAI 2019, pp. 2670–2677 (2019)
7. Baumann, R., Gabbay, D.M., Rodrigues, O.: Forgetting an argument. In: AAAI 2020, pp. 2750–2757 (2020)
8. Boella, G., Kaci, S., van der Torre, L.: Dynamics in argumentation with single extensions: abstraction principles and the grounded extension. In: Sossai, C., Chemello, G. (eds.) ECSQARU 2009. LNCS (LNAI), vol. 5590, pp. 107–118. Springer, Heidelberg (2009). https://doi.org/10.1007/978-3-642-02906-6_11
9. Boella, G., Kaci, S., van der Torre, L.W.N.: Dynamics in argumentation with single extensions: attack refinement and the grounded extension. In: AAMAS 2009, pp. 1213–1214 (2009)
10. Cayrol, C., de Saint-Cyr, F.D., Lagasquie-Schiex, M.-C.: Change in abstract argumentation frameworks: adding an argument. J. Artif. Intell. Res. **38**, 49–84 (2010)
11. Cayrol, C., de Saint-Cyr, F.D., Lagasquie-Schiex, M.-C.: Revision of an argumentation system. In: KR 2008, pp. 124–134 (2011)
12. Cayrol, C., Lagasquie-Schiex, M.-C.: Weighted argumentation systems: a tool for merging argumentation systems. In: ICAI 2011, pp. 629–632 (2011)
13. Coste-Marquis, S., Konieczny, S., Mailly, J.-G., Marquis, P.: Extension enforcement in abstract argumentation as an optimization problem. In: IJCAI 2015, pp. 2876–2882 (2015)
14. Doutre, S., Mailly, J.-G.: Constraints and changes: a survey of abstract argumentation dynamics. Argum. Comput. **9**(3), 223–248 (2018)
15. Dung, P.M.: On the acceptability of arguments and its fundamental role in nonmonotonic reasoning, logic programming and n-person games. Artif. Intell. **77**, 321–357 (1995)
16. Liao, B., Jin, L., Koons, R.C.: Dynamics of argumentation systems: a division-based method. Artif. Intell. **175**(11), 1790–1814 (2011)
17. Rahwan, I., Simari, G.R. (eds.): Argumentation in Artificial Intelligence. Springer, Heidelberg (2009)
18. Šefránek, J.: Updates of argumentation frameworks. In: NMR 2012 (2012)
19. Wallner, J.P., Niskanen, A., Järvisalo, M.: Complexity results and algorithms for extension enforcement in abstract argumentation. J. Artif. Intell. Res. **60**, 1–40 (2017)

A Multi Attack Argumentation Framework

Alexandros Vassiliades[1,2(✉)], Giorgos Flouris[2], Theodore Patkos[2],
Antonis Bikakis[3], Nick Bassiliades[1], and Dimitris Plexousakis[2]

[1] School of Informatics, Aristotle University of Thessaloniki, Thessaloniki, Greece
{valexande,nbassili}@csd.auth.gr
[2] Institute of Computer Science, Foundation for Research and Technology, Hellas,
Heraklion, Greece
{fgeo,patkos,dp}@ics.forth.gr
[3] Department of Information Studies, University College London, London, UK
a.bikakis@ucl.ac.uk

Abstract. This paper presents a novel abstract argumentation framework, called Multi-Attack Argumentation Framework (MAAF), which supports different types of attacks. The introduction of types gives rise to a new family of non-standard semantics which can support applications that classical approaches cannot, while also allowing classical semantics as a special case. The main novelty of the proposed semantics is the discrimination among two different roles that attacks play, namely an attack as a generator of conflicts, and an attack as a means to defend an argument. These two roles have traditionally been considered together in the argumentation literature. Allowing some attack types to serve one of those roles only, gives rise to the different semantics presented here.

1 Introduction

Many models for reasoning with arguments are grounded on Dung's abstract argumentation framework (AAF) [8], where the only ingredients are a set of arguments and a binary attack relation on that set. The simplicity and intuitiveness of this model led to its wide acceptance, and, at the same time, helped reveal additional features that needed to be devised, in order to accommodate the requirements of diverse domains. For instance, AAFs are based on the strong assumption that all arguments and all attacks have the same strength; many variations have been proposed in order to overcome this limitation, which consider preferences on arguments [2] or attacks [11], add weights to arguments [1] or attacks [9], associate arguments with values [5], or impose hierarchies on arguments [12].

In this paper, we focus on accommodating a different need, namely to support a reasoning argumentation model where the attack relation among arguments can be of different types. This gives rise to a new class of semantics, which is based on a treatment of different attack types. Note that an attack, in the standard argumentation literature, is used both as a *conflict-generator* (i.e., creating conflicts which disallow conflicting arguments to be put in the same extension and which create the need for defense) and as a *defender* (i.e., defending other arguments against attacks). Separating these two roles, and allowing certain attacks to be treated in the non-classical way (e.g., allowing them to play only one of these two roles), gives rise to various non-classical semantics which may find applications in different settings.

Consider, for example, the process of a trial. The presumption of innocence is so important that only specific types of attacks on the defendant's claims should be taken into consideration by the jury, e.g., claims by eye witnesses, experts etc. Other attacks, e.g., on the defendant's credibility, prior life choices etc., that generate doubts, should not be accounted for as evidence for conviction and need to be ignored. Interestingly, these latter types of attacks should still be considered relevant when placed against the claims of eye witnesses, experts etc., in order to ensure that the benefit of the doubt is given to the claimant. Figure 1 provides such an example. Intuitively, A_1, A_3 and A_4 should all be acceptable; the latter two, because they do not receive any attacks so there is no reason not to accept them, and A_1 because questioning the credibility of the defendant (attack from A_3) should not be enough to lead to conviction. The same type of attack (i.e., credibility), however, should still be sufficient to defend the defendant's claims from other attacks; in this case, for example, questioning the credibility of the witness (attack from A_4 to A_2) should be enough to defend the defendant from the witness' testimony (attack from A_2 to A_1).

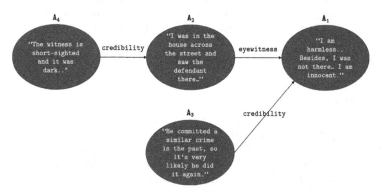

Fig. 1. Credibility attacks should be treated differently when they may lead to conviction than when they protect from it.

Notice that modeling different attack types is not always the same as modeling different argument types; while many of the existing AFs that characterize arguments and certain argument relations can indeed transfer this information to the attack relation, in the form of a strength value or a preference relation (see for example [7]), the inverse is not always possible. Attack types, such as rebuttals, undermines or undercuts, do not characterize the argument *per se*, but rather the relation between two arguments. Similarly, characterizing an attack as being of type irrelevant, i.e., arguing that a given argument is irrelevant in a given context, is not information inherent in the formulation of the argument, but, in a sense, on the placement of the argument in the argumentation tree. Eliminating (filtering) attacks made by irrelevant arguments, before generating the sets of acceptable extensions of a dialogue, can therefore be considered a beneficial pre-processing step.

The objective of this paper is to provide a framework that supports the above scenarios, by introducing two important novelties. The first is the introduction of attack types, that allows treating different attacks in a different manner. The second is the separation among the two roles of attacks, namely as conflict-generators and as defenders. In particular, by seeing these two functions of attacks as separate, and allowing some of the attacks to be used for only one, or both, of these roles, we get three different semantics:

- *Loose semantics*, where certain attack types are used only as defenders, as e.g., in the case of credibility attacks in Fig. 1.
- *Restricted semantics*, where certain attack types are ignored altogether (i.e., they have none of the two roles).
- *Firm semantics*, where certain attack types are used only as conflict-generators.

Following a related work analysis (Sect. 2), we formalise (Sect. 3) the three semantics explained above; the formalisation results to various types of extensions, in a manner similar to standard frameworks [8]. Then, we explore the properties of such semantics (Sect. 4), such as the existence of the different extensions, relationships among themselves and with the Dung semantics and others, and conclude in Sect. 5.

2   Related Work

The need to further refine the notion of attack in argumentation frameworks has led to several different extensions of Abstract Argumentation Frameworks. For example, Abstract Argumentation Frameworks with Recursive Attacks (AFRA) [3] and Extended Argumentation Frameworks (EAF) [12] extend the definition of attack, allowing attacks to be directed not only to arguments but also to other attacks. The difference between the two is that, while in EAFs only attacks whose target is an argument can be attacked, in AFRA any attack can be attacked. This idea is orthogonal to our approach that considers different types of attack, which are, however, all directed to arguments, and studying the combination of these two approaches, e.g. by allowing different types of attack that can be directed to arguments or attacks is an interesting research direction.

Commonsense Argumentation Frameworks [16], on the other hand, include two types of attacks, which differ in the type of arguments they are directed to, i.e. deductive arguments and commonsense arguments. They can therefore be considered as specializations of Multi-Attack Argumentation Frameworks, which we propose in this paper.

Some other studies have introduced weights or preferences on attacks following quantitative or qualitative approaches. For example, Weighted Argumentation Systems [9] assign weights to attacks as a way to describe their strength and use the idea of an inconsistency budget as a way to disregard attacks up to a certain weight. The idea of weighted attacks is also used in [10], where the acceptability of arguments is not defined in terms of the standard Dung-style extensions, but in terms of numerical values derived from a set of equations describing the arguments and their attack relations. While social networks is indeed a domain where numerical weights can be derived from the reactions of the users, in many other domains (for example, the legal domain) such types of data may not be available.

A qualitative approach to represent preferences among attacks was proposed in [11]. Similarly to our approach, they define a framework with (an arbitrary number of) types of attack. These are partially ordered, and each attack is assigned one of these types. This allows for a finer grained definition of defence (compared to AAFs), which can roughly be described as follows: an argument is defended against an attack from a counter-argument, if the latter receives a stronger attack from another argument. It also allows for a finer definition of acceptability semantics, which take into account the relative difference of strength between defensive and offensive attacks.

All such preference-based approaches, which use either numerical values or priorities to represent the (relative) strength of attacks, have a common characteristic: any non-preferred attack is either ignored or invalidated. Our approach offers alternative ways to treat attacks, which take into account their roles in an argumentation system, i.e. whether they are used as offensive or defensive attacks. For example, according to the firm semantics, a defense is effective only if it is from an argument of a specific type, while according to the loose semantics, an offensive attack is effective if the attacker is of a specific type. Choosing the right semantics depends on the specific requirements and characteristics of the application domain.

Another approach that also considers different types of attack in abstract argumentation was proposed in [15]. The motivation is similar to ours, namely that each attack relation can represent a different criterion according to which the arguments can be evaluated one against another. The evaluation of arguments, however, is based on the aggregation of the different relations using methods from social choice theory, such as majority voting, and the use of the standard acceptability semantics in the aggregate argumentation framework. They do not, therefore, provide ways to treat certain criteria differently than others, which is one of the main characteristics of Multi-Attack Argumentation Frameworks.

Different types of attack are common in structured argumentation frameworks. For example, in $ASPIC^+$ [13] arguments can be attacked in three different ways: on their uncertain premises (undermining), on their defeasible inferences (undercutting), or on the conclusions of their defeasible inferences (rebutting). Deductive argumentation [6] also supports different types of attack, which depend on the underlying logic. For example, choosing classical logic as the base logic provides seven different types of attack. The different types of attack in such frameworks are associated with the internal structure of arguments and cannot therefore be directly compared with Multi-Attack Argumentation Frameworks in which arguments are abstract. They can, however, easily be mapped to the representation model of Multi-Attack Argumentation Frameworks, i.e. by mapping each of the different types of attack they support to a different attack type of MAAF. This mapping enables alternative ways to reason with structured arguments by treating differently the different types of attack, which may be meaningful in some domains.

3   Multi Attack Argumentation Frameworks (MAAFs)

We define a multi-attack argumentation framework as an argumentation framework where attacks are of multiple types. Formally:

Definition 1. *A* multi-attack argumentation framework *(MAAF for short) is a tuple* $\langle \mathcal{A}, \mathcal{T}, \mathcal{R} \rangle$, *such that:*

- *$\mathcal{A}$ is a set of* arguments
- *$\mathcal{T}$ is a set of* attack types
- *$\mathcal{R} \subseteq \mathcal{A} \times \mathcal{A} \times \mathcal{T}$ is a set of type-annotated* attacks *among arguments*

Note that $\mathcal{A}$ and/or $\mathcal{T}$ can be infinite, so $\mathcal{R}$ can be infinite too. Intuitively an attack $(a, b, \tau) \in \mathcal{R}$ represents that a attacks b, and that the attack is of type τ. Note that the same two arguments may be related with attacks of different types, in which case each attack type is represented as a different triple in $\mathcal{R}$.

For any given set of types $\mathcal{T}_0 \subseteq \mathcal{T}$, we say that a *attacks* b w.r.t. $\mathcal{T}_0$ (denoted by $a \rightarrow_{\mathcal{T}_0} b$) if there exists $\tau \in \mathcal{T}_0$, such that $(a, b, \tau) \in \mathcal{R}$. For simplicity, we often write $\rightarrow_\tau$ to denote $\rightarrow_{\{\tau\}}$, and $\rightarrow$ to denote $\rightarrow_{\mathcal{T}}$. We extend notation to sets of arguments, and, for $B, C \subseteq \mathcal{A}$, we write $B \rightarrow_{\mathcal{T}_0} C$ if and only if $\exists b \in B$, $c \in C$ such that $b \rightarrow_{\mathcal{T}_0} c$. For singleton sets, we often write $b \rightarrow_{\mathcal{T}_0} C$ and $B \rightarrow_{\mathcal{T}_0} c$ instead of $\{b\} \rightarrow_{\mathcal{T}_0} C$ and $B \rightarrow_{\mathcal{T}_0} \{c\}$, respectively.

The *restriction* of an MAAF to a specific set of types $\mathcal{T}_0$ is the AAF that is generated from the MAAF by considering only the attacks in $\mathcal{T}_0$. Formally, given an MAAF $\langle \mathcal{A}, \mathcal{T}, \mathcal{R} \rangle$, the *restriction* of $\langle \mathcal{A}, \mathcal{T}, \mathcal{R} \rangle$ to $\mathcal{T}_0$ is an AAF $\langle \mathcal{A}', \mathcal{R}' \rangle$, where $\mathcal{A}' = \mathcal{A}$ and $\mathcal{R}' = \{(a, b) \mid (a, b, \tau) \in \mathcal{R}$ for some $\tau \in \mathcal{T}_0\}$.

The *flattening* of an MAAF is the AAF that is generated from the MAAF by ignoring types. Formally, for an MAAF $\mathcal{F} = \langle \mathcal{A}, \mathcal{T}, \mathcal{R} \rangle$, the *flattening* of $\mathcal{F}$ is an AAF $\langle \mathcal{A}', \mathcal{R}' \rangle$, where $\mathcal{A}' = \mathcal{A}$ and $\mathcal{R}' = \{(a, b) \mid (a, b, \tau) \in \mathcal{R}$ for some $\tau \in \mathcal{T}\}$. Note that the flattening of $\mathcal{F}$ is the same as the restriction of $\mathcal{F}$ to $\mathcal{T}$.

3.1   Classes of Extensions for MAAFs

To define MAAF extensions, we introduce three new classes of semantics: *firm*, *restricted* and *loose*. For each type of semantics defined in [8] (e.g., admissible, complete, etc.), we define its counterpart for each class (e.g., firmly admissible, restrictedly stable, loosely complete, etc.). The three classes differ in how certain types of attack are considered. As already mentioned, the idea behind our semantics is the treatment of certain types of attacks as being conflict-generators only or attackers only. To do this, we consider a certain set of types, say $\mathcal{T}_0$, which are treated in the "normal" manner. Different types of semantics can now result depending on the exact behaviour of the attacks in $\mathcal{T} \setminus \mathcal{T}_0$. In particular:

1. *Firm semantics* (e.g., admissible, complete etc.) w.r.t. a certain set of attack types (say $\mathcal{T}_0$) requires a candidate extension to be defended against all types of attacks, and an attack can be defended only by attacks from $\mathcal{T}_0$. In other words, attacks in $\mathcal{T}_0$ have the standard behaviour, but attacks in $\mathcal{T} \setminus \mathcal{T}_0$ act as conflict-generators only, not as defenders. We call them firm because, while they allow any type of argument to unleash offensive attacks, they only allow certain types of attack (those in $\mathcal{T}_0$) to defend an argument, making its defense more difficult.

2. *Restricted semantics* (e.g., admissible, complete etc.) w.r.t. a certain set of attack types (say $\mathcal{T}_0$) require a candidate extension to be defended against attacks from $\mathcal{T}_0$ only, and an attack can be defended only by attacks from $\mathcal{T}_0$. Thus, restricted semantics essentially consider only the attacks in $\mathcal{T}_0$, both for the attacks and for defending against them, i.e., attacks in $\mathcal{T} \setminus \mathcal{T}_0$ are totally ignored. This brings them quite close to the notion of the restriction of an MAAF, a statement that will be made precise in Proposition 4.

3. *Loose semantics* (e.g., admissible, complete etc.) w.r.t. a certain set of attack types (say $\mathcal{T}_0$) are the most "relaxed" ones, as they require a candidate extension to be defended only against attacks from $\mathcal{T}_0$, while defense can happen by any type of attack. In other words, in loose semantics, attacks in $\mathcal{T} \setminus \mathcal{T}_0$ are treated as defenders only, and cannot generate attacks. Loose semantics allows attacks to be ignored, so they may result to extensions that are not defended against all attacks, specifically against attacks that are of types not in $\mathcal{T}_0$.

In the following, we use shorthands to refer to the various types and classes of semantics. In particular, for the three classes of semantics, we use **fr** for firm, **re** for restricted, and **lo** for loose semantics. We also use θ as a catch-all variable that refers to any of these classes. Similarly, for types of extensions, we use **cf** for conflict-free, **ad** for admissible, **co** for complete, **pr** for preferred, **gr** for grounded, and **st** for stable. We also use σ as a catch-all variable to indicate any of these extension types. For example, we write **fr-co**-extension to refer to a firmly complete extension, and θ-σ-extension to refer to an extension of class θ and the type denoted by σ.

To formalise the above ideas, we first refine the notion of defense:

Definition 2. *Consider an MAAF $\langle \mathcal{A}, \mathcal{T}, \mathcal{R} \rangle$, some $\mathcal{T}_0 \subseteq \mathcal{T}$, some $a \in \mathcal{A}$ and some set $\mathcal{E} \subseteq \mathcal{A}$. We define the notion of defense for the different classes of semantics as follows:*

- *$\mathcal{E}$ firmly defends a (or **fr**-defends a) w.r.t. $\mathcal{T}_0$ if and only if $\mathcal{E} \rightarrow_{\mathcal{T}_0} b$ whenever $b \rightarrow a$*
- *$\mathcal{E}$ restrictedly defends a (or **re**-defends a) w.r.t. $\mathcal{T}_0$ if and only if $\mathcal{E} \rightarrow_{\mathcal{T}_0} b$ whenever $b \rightarrow_{\mathcal{T}_0} a$*
- *$\mathcal{E}$ loosely defends a (or **lo**-defends a) w.r.t. $\mathcal{T}_0$ if and only if $\mathcal{E} \rightarrow b$ whenever $b \rightarrow_{\mathcal{T}_0} a$*

Figure 2 visualises the notion of defense for various cases.

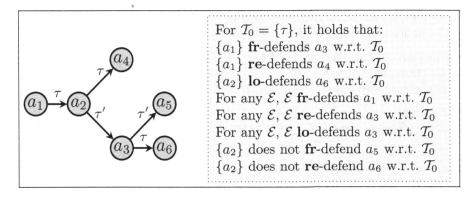

Fig. 2. The concept of fr/re/lo-defense visualised

3.2   Firm, Restricted and Loose Extensions

Now we can recast the standard definitions for the different types of semantics given in [8], using the above ideas:

Definition 3. *Consider an MAAF $\langle \mathcal{A}, \mathcal{T}, \mathcal{R} \rangle$ and some $\mathcal{T}_0 \subseteq \mathcal{T}$. A set $\mathcal{E} \subseteq \mathcal{A}$ is:*

- *Firmly conflict-free (**fr-cf**) w.r.t. $\mathcal{T}_0$ if and only if it is not the case that $\mathcal{E} \to \mathcal{E}$*
- *Restrictedly conflict-free (**re-cf**) w.r.t. $\mathcal{T}_0$ if and only if it is not the case that $\mathcal{E} \to_{\mathcal{T}_0} \mathcal{E}$*
- *Loose conflict-free (**lo-cf**) w.r.t. $\mathcal{T}_0$ if and only if it is not the case that $\mathcal{E} \to_{\mathcal{T}_0} \mathcal{E}$*

Note how the intuition behind the different classes of semantics are applied in Definition 3: **lo-cf** and **re-cf** sets may include self-attacks, as long as they are not of types in $\mathcal{T}_0$ (because attacks in $\mathcal{T} \setminus \mathcal{T}_0$ are not conflict-generators in these semantics), whereas **fr-cf** sets cannot include any self-attack. As a result, the definition of **re-cf** and **lo-cf** coincides, since the notion of defense (where the two classes of semantics differ) is not relevant to that of conflict-freeness. Nevertheless, for purposes of uniformity and symmetry, we decided to include both definitions.

The same ideas are applied to admissible extensions, whose definition essentially mimics the ones typically used in AAFs, but considers the alternative notions of defense (Definition 2) for each case:

Definition 4. *Consider an MAAF $\langle \mathcal{A}, \mathcal{T}, \mathcal{R} \rangle$ and some $\mathcal{T}_0 \subseteq \mathcal{T}$. For $\theta \in \{ \mathbf{fr}, \mathbf{re}, \mathbf{lo} \}$, a set $\mathcal{E} \subseteq \mathcal{A}$ is a θ-**ad** extension w.r.t. $\mathcal{T}_0$ (in words: firmly/restrictedly/loosely admissible) if and only if:*

- *$\mathcal{E}$ is θ-**cf***
- *If $a \in \mathcal{E}$, then $\mathcal{E}$ θ-defends a w.r.t. $\mathcal{T}_0$*

Complete semantics' definition slightly deviates from the respective one in AAFs to accommodate the differences in the definition of conflict-freeness.

Definition 5. *Consider an MAAF $\langle \mathcal{A}, \mathcal{T}, \mathcal{R} \rangle$ and some $\mathcal{T}_0 \subseteq \mathcal{T}$. For $\theta \in \{\mathbf{fr}, \mathbf{re}, \mathbf{lo}\}$, a set $\mathcal{E} \subseteq \mathcal{A}$ is a θ-$\mathbf{co}$ extension w.r.t. $\mathcal{T}_0$ (in words: firmly/restrictedly/loosely complete) if and only if:*

- *$\mathcal{E}$ is θ-$\mathbf{ad}$*
- *If $\mathcal{E}$ θ-defends a w.r.t. $\mathcal{T}_0$, and $\mathcal{E} \cup \{a\}$ is θ-$\mathbf{cf}$ w.r.t. $\mathcal{T}_0$, then $a \in \mathcal{E}$*

Note that, in the above definition, instead of only requiring that $a \in \mathcal{E}$ whenever $\mathcal{E}$ θ-defends a, we have included the additional requirement that $\mathcal{E} \cup \{a\}$ is θ-$\mathbf{cf}$, thereby deviating somewhat from the definition pattern used in AAFs for $\mathbf{co}$-semantics [8]. This additional requirement is redundant in the AAF setting, because it results as a corollary of the weaker definition. The same is true in the MAAF setting, but only for the $\mathbf{fr}$ and $\mathbf{re}$ semantics (see Proposition 2 and the analysis that follows it). For this reason, and for purposes of uniformity and symmetry, we decided to include this extra requirement in Definition 5.

Grounded and preferred semantics are defined analogously:

Definition 6. *Consider an MAAF $\langle \mathcal{A}, \mathcal{T}, \mathcal{R} \rangle$ and some $\mathcal{T}_0 \subseteq \mathcal{T}$. A set $\mathcal{E} \subseteq \mathcal{A}$ is a θ-$\mathbf{gr}$ extension w.r.t. $\mathcal{T}_0$ (in words: firmly/restrictedly/loosely grounded) if and only if $\mathcal{E}$ is a minimal with respect to set inclusion θ-$\mathbf{co}$ extension w.r.t. $\mathcal{T}_0$.*

Definition 7. *Consider an MAAF $\langle \mathcal{A}, \mathcal{T}, \mathcal{R} \rangle$ and some $\mathcal{T}_0 \subseteq \mathcal{T}$. A set $\mathcal{E} \subseteq \mathcal{A}$ is a θ-$\mathbf{pr}$ extension w.r.t. $\mathcal{T}_0$ (in words: firmly/restrictedly/loosely preferred) if and only if $\mathcal{E}$ is a maximal with respect to set inclusion θ-$\mathbf{ad}$ extension w.r.t. $\mathcal{T}_0$.*

Stable semantics also follow a similar pattern:

Definition 8. *Consider an MAAF $\langle \mathcal{A}, \mathcal{T}, \mathcal{R} \rangle$ and some $\mathcal{T}_0 \subseteq \mathcal{T}$. A set $\mathcal{E} \subseteq \mathcal{A}$ is:*

- *A firmly stable extension ($\mathbf{fr}$-$\mathbf{st}$) w.r.t. $\mathcal{T}_0$ if and only if:*
  - *$\mathcal{E}$ is maximally $\mathbf{fr}$-$\mathbf{cf}$ w.r.t. $\mathcal{T}_0$*
  - *$\mathcal{E} \rightarrow_{\mathcal{T}_0} a$ whenever $a \notin \mathcal{E}$*
- *A restrictedly stable extension ($\mathbf{re}$-$\mathbf{st}$) w.r.t. $\mathcal{T}_0$ if and only if:*
  - *$\mathcal{E}$ is maximally $\mathbf{re}$-$\mathbf{cf}$ w.r.t. $\mathcal{T}_0$*
  - *$\mathcal{E} \rightarrow_{\mathcal{T}_0} a$ whenever $a \notin \mathcal{E}$*
- *A loosely stable extension ($\mathbf{lo}$-$\mathbf{st}$) w.r.t. $\mathcal{T}_0$ if and only if:*
  - *$\mathcal{E}$ is maximally $\mathbf{lo}$-$\mathbf{cf}$ w.r.t. $\mathcal{T}_0$*
  - *$\mathcal{E} \rightarrow a$ whenever $a \notin \mathcal{E}$*

Note that Definition 8 also deviates somewhat from the definition pattern of $\mathbf{st}$ semantics in standard AAFs. In particular, instead of requiring that $\mathcal{E}$ is θ-$\mathbf{cf}$ (for the various θ), we have required that it is maximally θ-$\mathbf{cf}$, i.e., a θ-$\mathbf{cf}$ set that is maximal among all other θ-$\mathbf{cf}$ sets. As with the $\mathbf{co}$ semantics, this stronger requirement is redundant in the AAF setting, and also in the MAAF setting for $\mathbf{fr}$ and $\mathbf{re}$ semantics (we have, however, included it in their definitions for uniformity), but is necessary for $\mathbf{lo}$ semantics (see Proposition 3 and the analysis that follows it).

4   Properties of MAAFs

We can show several properties with regards to the interplay among various types of θ-σ-extensions. To simplify presentation, all the following results assume an arbitrary MAAF $\mathcal{F} = \langle \mathcal{A}, \mathcal{T}, \mathcal{R} \rangle$ and some $\mathcal{T}_0 \subseteq \mathcal{T}$. Also, the reference to $\mathcal{T}_0$ is often omitted when obvious; e.g., we write that $\mathcal{E}$ is a **lo-co** extension, to signify that $\mathcal{E}$ is a **lo-co** extension w.r.t. $\mathcal{T}_0$.

4.1   Initial Results and Special Cases

We first show the analogous of Dung's fundamental lemma (Lemma 10 in [8]). Note the different formulation of this result for **lo** semantics[1]:

Proposition 1. *For any given $\mathcal{E} \subseteq \mathcal{A}$, $a \in \mathcal{A}$, it holds that:*

*1. If $\mathcal{E}$ is θ-**ad**, and $\mathcal{E}$ θ-defends a, then $\mathcal{E} \cup \{a\}$ is θ-**ad**, for $\theta \in \{\mathbf{fr}, \mathbf{re}\}$*
*2. If $\mathcal{E}$ is **lo-ad**, $\mathcal{E}$ **lo**-defends a, and $\mathcal{E} \cup \{a\}$ is **lo-cf**, then $\mathcal{E} \cup \{a\}$ is **lo-ad***

Proposition 2 shows that the extra requirement of Definition 5 (compared to its counterpart in AAFs) is redundant for **fr** and **re** semantics:

Proposition 2. *For $\theta \in \{\mathbf{fr}, \mathbf{re}\}$, $\mathcal{E} \subseteq \mathcal{A}$, the following are equivalent:*

- *$\mathcal{E}$ is a θ-**co**-extension w.r.t. $\mathcal{T}_0$*
- *The following hold for $\mathcal{E}$:*
  - *$\mathcal{E}$ is θ-**ad** w.r.t. $\mathcal{T}_0$*
  - *If $\mathcal{E}$ θ-defends a w.r.t. $\mathcal{T}_0$, then $a \in \mathcal{E}$*

Note that the above equivalence does not hold for loose semantics. Indeed, the different formulation of Proposition 1 does not allow its use in the proof of Proposition 2. The MAAF visualised in Fig. 3 provides a counter-example: $\{a, b\}$ is **lo-co**, despite the fact that $\{a, b\}$ **lo**-defends c and $c \notin \{a, b\}$. This is due to the extra requirement that we added in Definition 5; without it, neither $\{a, b\}$, nor $\{a, b, c\}$ would be **lo-co**, i.e., we would end up having a maximal **lo-ad** extension ($\{a, b\}$), that is not **lo-co**, which is against the intuition behind complete extensions.

Similarly, Proposition 3 shows that the extra requirement of Definition 8 (compared to its AAF counterpart) is redundant for **fr-st** and **re-st** semantics:

Proposition 3. *For $\theta \in \{\mathbf{fr}, \mathbf{re}\}$, $\mathcal{E} \subseteq \mathcal{A}$, the following are equivalent:*

- *$\mathcal{E}$ is a θ-**st**-extension*
- *The following hold for $\mathcal{E}$:*
  - *$\mathcal{E}$ is θ-**cf***
  - *$\mathcal{E} \rightarrow_{\mathcal{T}_0} a$ whenever $a \notin \mathcal{E}$*

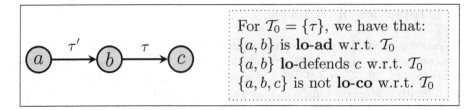

For $\mathcal{T}_0 = \{\tau\}$, we have that:
$\{a, b\}$ is **lo-ad** w.r.t. $\mathcal{T}_0$
$\{a, b\}$ **lo**-defends c w.r.t. $\mathcal{T}_0$
$\{a, b, c\}$ is not **lo-co** w.r.t. $\mathcal{T}_0$

Fig. 3. Counter-example for the counterpart of Proposition 2 for **lo** semantics

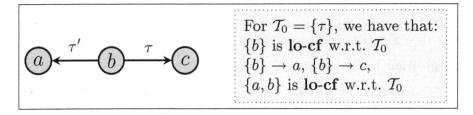

For $\mathcal{T}_0 = \{\tau\}$, we have that:
$\{b\}$ is **lo-cf** w.r.t. $\mathcal{T}_0$
$\{b\} \to a$, $\{b\} \to c$,
$\{a, b\}$ is **lo-cf** w.r.t. $\mathcal{T}_0$

Fig. 4. Counter-example for the counterpart of Proposition 3 for **lo** semantics

The example of Fig. 4 shows a case where the counterpart of Proposition 3 would fail for **lo** semantics. The set $\{b\}$ attacks all other arguments, and is **lo-cf**, but not maximally so. Thus, it is not **lo-st**. On the contrary, $\{a, b\}$ is **lo-st**. This shows why the extra maximality condition that was added to Definition 8 (compared to its counterpart in AAFs) is necessary: without it, both $\{a, b\}$ and $\{b\}$ would be **lo-st**.

The next result shows that restricted semantics can be computed using the restriction of an MAAF:

Proposition 4. *Consider an MAAF* $\mathcal{F} = \langle \mathcal{A}, \mathcal{T}, \mathcal{R} \rangle$ *and some* $\mathcal{T}_0 \subseteq \mathcal{T}$. *Set* $\mathcal{F}' = \langle \mathcal{A}', \mathcal{R}' \rangle$ *the restriction of* $\mathcal{F}$ *to* $\mathcal{T}_0$. *For any given* $\sigma \in \{\mathbf{cf}, \mathbf{ad}, \mathbf{co}, \mathbf{gr}, \mathbf{pr}, \mathbf{st}\}$ *and* $\mathcal{E} \subseteq \mathcal{A}$, $\mathcal{E}$ *is a* re-σ-*extension w.r.t.* $\mathcal{T}_0$ *if and only if* $\mathcal{E}$ *is a* σ-*extension of* $\mathcal{F}$.

The following result describes a special case, showing essentially that our semantics is a generalisation of Dung's (i.e., that AAF semantics emerge as a special case of MAAFs):

Proposition 5. *Consider an MAAF* $\mathcal{F} = \langle \mathcal{A}, \mathcal{T}, \mathcal{R} \rangle$ *and set* $\mathcal{T}_0 = \mathcal{T}$. *Consider also the MAAF's flattening* $\mathcal{F}' = \langle \mathcal{A}', \mathcal{R}' \rangle$, *and its restriction to* $\mathcal{T}_0$, $\mathcal{F}'' = \langle \mathcal{A}'', \mathcal{R}'' \rangle$. *Then, for any* $\sigma \in \{\mathbf{cf}, \mathbf{ad}, \mathbf{co}, \mathbf{gr}, \mathbf{pr}, \mathbf{st}\}$, $\mathcal{E} \subseteq \mathcal{A}$ *the following are equivalent:*

1. $\mathcal{E}$ *is a* lo-σ-*extension w.r.t.* $\mathcal{T}_0$
2. $\mathcal{E}$ *is a* re-σ-*extension w.r.t.* $\mathcal{T}_0$

---

[1] The proofs of all results appear in the Appendix.

3. $\mathcal{E}$ is a fr-σ-extension w.r.t. $\mathcal{T}_0$
4. $\mathcal{E}$ is a σ-extension of $\mathcal{F}'$
5. $\mathcal{E}$ is a σ-extension of $\mathcal{F}''$

4.2 Relations Among Extension Types, and Existence Results

The next proposition shows that the hierarchy of extensions that holds in the Dung setting, also holds for each class of extensions:

Proposition 6. *For any $\mathcal{E} \subseteq \mathcal{A}$:*

*1. If $\mathcal{E}$ is a θ-**ad**-extension w.r.t. $\mathcal{T}_0$, then $\mathcal{E}$ is a θ-**cf**-extension w.r.t. $\mathcal{T}_0$*
*2. If $\mathcal{E}$ is a θ-**co**-extension w.r.t. $\mathcal{T}_0$, then $\mathcal{E}$ is a θ-**ad**-extension w.r.t. $\mathcal{T}_0$*
*3. If $\mathcal{E}$ is a θ-**gr**-extension w.r.t. $\mathcal{T}_0$, then $\mathcal{E}$ is a θ-**co**-extension w.r.t. $\mathcal{T}_0$*
*4. If $\mathcal{E}$ is a θ-**pr**-extension w.r.t. $\mathcal{T}_0$, then $\mathcal{E}$ is a θ-**co**-extension w.r.t. $\mathcal{T}_0$*
*5. If $\mathcal{E}$ is a θ-**st**-extension w.r.t. $\mathcal{T}_0$, then $\mathcal{E}$ is a θ-**pr**-extension w.r.t. $\mathcal{T}_0$*

Our next result shows that we can "incrementally" construct minimally-complete extensions starting from an **ad** one. The proof follows an iterative function, similar to the function F_{AF} used by Dung in [8]. However, for MAAFs, there are two subtleties.

First, F_{AF} (as defined in [8]) adds all acceptable arguments in each iteration; for the **lo** case, this could lead to a set that is not **lo-cf** (see, e.g., Fig. 5: both b and c are acceptable by $\{a\}$, but $\{a, b, c\}$ is not **lo-cf**); thus, a more elaborate construction is needed.

Second, for infinite frameworks, the existence of a minimal fixpoint for F_{AF} (in [8]) is guaranteed by the implicit use of the Knaster-Tarski theorem ([14]), which requires an order preserving function. Although F_{AF} is order-preserving, our alternative is not.

To overcome these problems, the proof of Proposition 7 uses a more complex iterative function, employing ordinals. Importantly, this construction applies to all our semantics, as well as to standard AAFs, so it can be viewed also as an alternative proof for a well-known property of AAFs. Note also that the proof employs the Axiom of Choice.

Proposition 7. *Take any MAAF $\mathcal{F} = \langle \mathcal{A}, \mathcal{T}, \mathcal{R} \rangle$, some $\mathcal{T}_0 \subseteq \mathcal{T}$, and some $\mathcal{E}_* \subseteq \mathcal{A}$ such that $\mathcal{E}_*$ is θ-**ad** (for $\theta \in \{$**fr**, **re**, **lo**$\}$). Then, there exists some $\mathcal{E}$ such that $\mathcal{E} \supseteq \mathcal{E}_*$, and the following hold:*

*1. $\mathcal{E}$ is θ-**co**.*
*2. For any $\mathcal{E}'$ such that $\mathcal{E}_* \subseteq \mathcal{E}' \subset \mathcal{E}$, there exists $a \in \mathcal{E} \setminus \mathcal{E}'$ which is θ-defended by $\mathcal{E}'$ and $\mathcal{E}' \cup \{a\}$ is θ-**cf**.*
*3. For any $\mathcal{E}'$ such that $\mathcal{E}_* \subseteq \mathcal{E}' \subset \mathcal{E}$, $\mathcal{E}'$ is not θ-**co**.*

We next show that the existence of θ-σ extensions is guaranteed (except from θ-**st**), for all θ, analogously to the AAF case (see [8], [4]). Note that the proof for the infinite case in some of the semantics requires the Axiom of Choice:

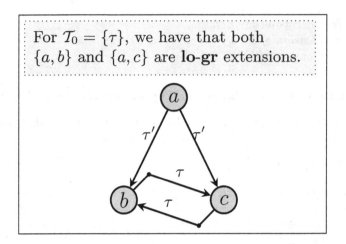

For $\mathcal{T}_0 = \{\tau\}$, we have that both $\{a, b\}$ and $\{a, c\}$ are **lo-gr** extensions.

Fig. 5. An MAAF with two **lo-gr** extensions

Proposition 8. *For any MAAF* $\mathcal{F} = \langle \mathcal{A}, \mathcal{T}, \mathcal{R} \rangle$, $\theta \in \{\mathbf{fr}, \mathbf{re}, \mathbf{lo}\}$, $\sigma \in \{\mathbf{cf}, \mathbf{ad}, \mathbf{co}, \mathbf{gr}, \mathbf{pr}\}$ *and* $\mathcal{T}_0 \subseteq \mathcal{T}$, *there exists a* θ-σ *extension w.r.t.* $\mathcal{T}_0$ *in* $\mathcal{F}$.

In AAFs, a **gr** extension is unique. The counter-example of Fig. 5 shows that this is not the case for **lo-gr** extensions. However, for the other semantics (**fr**, **re**), the uniqueness of **gr** extensions is guaranteed:

Proposition 9. *For any MAAF* $\mathcal{F} = \langle \mathcal{A}, \mathcal{T}, \mathcal{R} \rangle$, $\theta \in \{\mathbf{fr}, \mathbf{re}\}$ *and* $\mathcal{T}_0 \subseteq \mathcal{T}$, *there exists a unique* θ-**gr** *extension w.r.t.* $\mathcal{T}_0$ *in* $\mathcal{F}$.

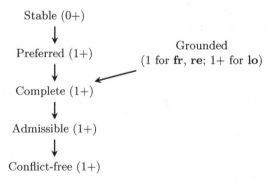

Fig. 6. Properties of MAAF extensions (apply to **fr**, **re**, **lo**, unless mentioned otherwise)

Propositions 6, 8 and 9 are summarised in Fig. 6.

4.3   Relations Among Extension Classes

The following propositions show the relation among **fr**, **re** and **lo** extensions, as well as the relation between these extensions and the extensions of the flattened AAF. This, along with Proposition 4, completes the picture with regards to the relationship among the different extension classes. We provide one proposition for each extension type (**cf**, **ad**, etc.), starting with the simple case of **cf**:

Proposition 10. *Take an MAAF $\mathcal{F} = \langle \mathcal{A}, \mathcal{T}, \mathcal{R} \rangle$, its flattened AAF $\mathcal{F}_F = \langle \mathcal{A}, \mathcal{R}' \rangle$ and some $\mathcal{E} \subseteq \mathcal{A}$. Then:*

1. *$\mathcal{E}$ is **fr-cf** if and only if $\mathcal{E}$ is **cf** in $\mathcal{F}_F$.*
2. *If $\mathcal{E}$ is **fr-cf** then $\mathcal{E}$ is **re-cf**.*
3. *$\mathcal{E}$ is **re-cf** if and only if $\mathcal{E}$ is **lo-cf**.*

Interestingly, the direction of inference for the case of defense reverses (compared to the **cf** case) for the flattened AAF and the **re** class:

Proposition 11. *Take an MAAF $\mathcal{F} = \langle \mathcal{A}, \mathcal{T}, \mathcal{R} \rangle$, its flattened AAF $\mathcal{F}_F = \langle \mathcal{A}, \mathcal{R}_F \rangle$, some $\mathcal{E} \subseteq \mathcal{A}$ and some $a \in \mathcal{A}$. Then:*

1. *If $\mathcal{E}$ **fr**-defends a, then $\mathcal{E}$ **re**-defends a.*
2. *If $\mathcal{E}$ **re**-defends a, then $\mathcal{E}$ defends a in $\mathcal{F}_F$.*
3. *If $\mathcal{E}$ defends a in $\mathcal{F}_F$, then $\mathcal{E}$ **lo**-defends a.*

This reversal of the direction of inference (in Propositions 10, 11) leads to the following proposition:

Proposition 12. *Take an MAAF $\mathcal{F} = \langle \mathcal{A}, \mathcal{T}, \mathcal{R} \rangle$, its flattened AAF $\mathcal{F}_F = \langle \mathcal{A}, \mathcal{R}_F \rangle$ and some $\mathcal{E} \subseteq \mathcal{A}$. Then:*

1. *If $\mathcal{E}$ is **fr-ad**, then $\mathcal{E}$ is **re-ad**.*
2. *If $\mathcal{E}$ is **fr-ad**, then $\mathcal{E}$ is **ad** in $\mathcal{F}_F$.*
3. *If $\mathcal{E}$ is **re-ad**, then $\mathcal{E}$ is **lo-ad**.*
4. *If $\mathcal{E}$ is **ad** in $\mathcal{F}_F$, then $\mathcal{E}$ is **lo-ad**.*
5. *If $\mathcal{E}$ is **re-ad** and **cf** in $\mathcal{F}_F$, then $\mathcal{E}$ is **ad** in $\mathcal{F}_F$.*

For complete, grounded and preferred semantics, the situation is more complex:

Proposition 13. *Take an MAAF $\mathcal{F} = \langle \mathcal{A}, \mathcal{T}, \mathcal{R} \rangle$, its flattened AAF $\mathcal{F}_F = \langle \mathcal{A}, \mathcal{R}_F \rangle$ and some $\mathcal{E} \subseteq \mathcal{A}$. Then:*

1. *If $\mathcal{E}$ is **re-co** and **fr-ad**, then $\mathcal{E}$ is **fr-co**.*
2. *If $\mathcal{E}$ is **co** in $\mathcal{F}_F$ and **re-ad**, then $\mathcal{E}$ is **re-co**.*
3. *If $\mathcal{E}$ is **lo-co** and **ad** in $\mathcal{F}_F$, then $\mathcal{E}$ is **co** in $\mathcal{F}_F$.*

Proposition 14. *Take an MAAF $\mathcal{F} = \langle \mathcal{A}, \mathcal{T}, \mathcal{R} \rangle$, its flattened AAF $\mathcal{F}_F = \langle \mathcal{A}, \mathcal{R}_F \rangle$ and some $\mathcal{E} \subseteq \mathcal{A}$. Then:*

1. *If $\mathcal{E}$ is* **fr-gr** *and* **re-co***, then $\mathcal{E}$ is* **re-gr***.*
2. *If $\mathcal{E}$ is* **re-gr** *and* **co** *in $\mathcal{F}_F$, then $\mathcal{E}$ is* **gr** *in $\mathcal{F}_F$.*
3. *If $\mathcal{E}$ is* **gr** *in $\mathcal{F}_F$ and* **lo-co***, then $\mathcal{E}$ is* **lo-gr***.*

Proposition 15. *Take an MAAF $\mathcal{F} = \langle \mathcal{A}, \mathcal{T}, \mathcal{R} \rangle$, its flattened AAF $\mathcal{F}_F = \langle \mathcal{A}, \mathcal{R}_F \rangle$ and some $\mathcal{E} \subseteq \mathcal{A}$. Then:*

1. *If $\mathcal{E}$ is* **re-pr** *and* **fr-ad***, then $\mathcal{E}$ is* **fr-pr***.*
2. *If $\mathcal{E}$ is* **pr** *in $\mathcal{F}_F$ and* **re-ad***, then $\mathcal{E}$ is* **re-pr***.*
3. *If $\mathcal{E}$ is* **lo-pr** *and* **ad** *in $\mathcal{F}_F$, then $\mathcal{E}$ is* **pr** *in $\mathcal{F}_F$.*

Finally, for stable semantics, the situation is similar to the case of admissible semantics:

Proposition 16. *Take an MAAF $\mathcal{F} = \langle \mathcal{A}, \mathcal{T}, \mathcal{R} \rangle$, its flattened AAF $\mathcal{F}_F = \langle \mathcal{A}, \mathcal{R}_F \rangle$ and some $\mathcal{E} \subseteq \mathcal{A}$. Then:*

1. *If $\mathcal{E}$ is* **fr-st***, then $\mathcal{E}$ is* **re-st***.*
2. *If $\mathcal{E}$ is* **fr-st***, then $\mathcal{E}$ is* **st** *in $\mathcal{F}_F$.*
3. *$\mathcal{E}$ is* **re-st***, if and only if $\mathcal{E}$ is* **lo-st***.*
4. *If $\mathcal{E}$ is* **re-st** *and* **cf** *in $\mathcal{F}_F$, then $\mathcal{E}$ is* **st** *in $\mathcal{F}_F$.*

Further corollaries can be derived by combining the above results (Propositions 10, 11, 12, 13, 14, 15, 16) with Propositions 4 and 6, to connect the various types and classes of semantics among themselves, and with the semantics of restricted/flattened AAF. These are direct and omitted.

5   Discussion and Conclusion

In this paper we presented the semantics of multi-attack argumentation frameworks, i.e., frameworks which support multiple attack types among arguments. The important novelty of our semantics is the discrimination between two roles of attacks that have traditionally been considered inseparably: the role of conflict-generator, and the role of defender. The combination of these two aspects allowed us to define new classes of semantics, which model interesting real-life situations, have nice formal properties, and engulf standard models as a special case. An AAF cannot capture the aforementioned aspects to the extent that an MAAF does.

Note that, although MAAFs admit several types of attacks, during the computation of semantics, all attack types are split into two classes: those that are in $\mathcal{T}_0$, and those that are not. Thus, we could define the same semantics by just allowing two different types. However, such a solution, albeit simpler, would have two disadvantages. The first is that it is intuitively better for the modeller to have several attack types, and then decide which ones are "normal" (to be placed in $\mathcal{T}_0$), and which ones are "special" (to be placed in $\mathcal{T} \setminus \mathcal{T}_0$). This approach has the additional advantage that the modeller can choose a different $\mathcal{T}_0$ depending on the application at hand. Second, our modelling allows more sophisticated semantics to be developed, e.g., by defining sets $\mathcal{T}_1, \mathcal{T}_2$ and treating the attacks in $\mathcal{T}_1$ as defenders only, and attacks in $\mathcal{T}_2$ as conflict-generators only. This extension is part of our future work.

Acknowledgments. This project has received funding from the Hellenic Foundation for Research and Innovation (HFRI) and the General Secretariat for Research and Technology (GSRT), under grant agreement No 188.

A   Appendix

Proof of Proposition 1

For the first result, $\mathcal{E} \cup \{a\}$ θ-defends $\mathcal{E} \cup \{a\}$, since, by our assumptions, $\mathcal{E}$ θ-defends $\mathcal{E}$, and $\mathcal{E}$ θ-defends a. So it suffices to show that, $\mathcal{E} \cup \{a\}$ is θ-**cf**.

Let us consider the case of firm semantics first. Suppose that $\mathcal{E} \cup \{a\}$ is not **fr-cf**. Then, there exist $a_1, a_2 \in \mathcal{E} \cup \{a\}$ such that $a_1 \to a_2$. We consider four cases, all of which lead to a contradiction, thus proving the point:

1. If $a_1, a_2 \in \mathcal{E}$, then $\mathcal{E}$ is not **fr-cf**, a contradiction.
2. If $a_1 \in \mathcal{E}, a_2 = a$, then, since $\mathcal{E}$ **fr**-defends a, it follows that there exists some $a_3 \in \mathcal{E}$ such that $a_3 \to_{\mathcal{T}_0} a_1$, a contradiction by case #1.
3. If $a_1 = a, a_2 \in \mathcal{E}$, then, since $\mathcal{E}$ is an **fr-ad**-extension, it follows that there exists $a_3 \in \mathcal{E}$, such that $a_3 \to_{\mathcal{T}_0} a$, i.e., $a_3 \to a$, a contradiction by case #2.
4. If $a_1 = a_2 = a$, then, since $\mathcal{E}$ **fr**-defends a, it follows that there exists some $a_3 \in \mathcal{E}$ such that $a_3 \to_{\mathcal{T}_0} a$, i.e., $a_3 \to a$, a contradiction by case #2.

The case of restricted semantics is completely analogous and omitted.

For the second result, using the same reasoning we note that $\mathcal{E} \cup \{a\}$ **lo**-defends $\mathcal{E} \cup \{a\}$. Given that $\mathcal{E} \cup \{a\}$ is **lo-cf** by our assumptions, the result follows.   □

Proof of Proposition 2

By Proposition 1 when $\mathcal{E}$ is θ-**ad**, and $\mathcal{E}$ θ-defends a, then $\mathcal{E} \cup \{a\}$ is θ-**cf**, for $\theta \in \{\mathbf{fr}, \mathbf{re}\}$. The result then follows trivially.   □

Proof of Proposition 3

It suffices to show that when $\mathcal{E}$ is θ-**cf**, and $\mathcal{E} \to_{\mathcal{T}_0} a$ whenever $a \notin \mathcal{E}$, then $\mathcal{E}$ is maximally θ-**cf**. Indeed, suppose that $\mathcal{E}'$ is θ-**cf** and $\mathcal{E}' \supset \mathcal{E}$. Then, take some $a \in \mathcal{E}' \setminus \mathcal{E}$. By our hypothesis, $\mathcal{E} \to_{\mathcal{T}_0} a$, i.e., $\mathcal{E}' \to_{\mathcal{T}_0} \mathcal{E}'$, a contradiction by our hypothesis that $\mathcal{E}'$ is θ-**cf**.   □

Proof of Proposition 4

Since $\mathcal{A} = \mathcal{A}'$, take any $a, b \in \mathcal{A}$, $\mathcal{E} \subseteq \mathcal{A}$. Then, apparently:

- a attacks b in $\mathcal{F}'$ if and only if $a \to_{\mathcal{T}_0} b$ in $\mathcal{F}$
- $\mathcal{E}$ defends a in $\mathcal{F}'$ if and only if $\mathcal{E}$ **re**-defends a in $\mathcal{F}$

Using the above two statements and Propositions 2, 3 (necessary for the case of **co**- and **st**-extensions respectively), it is easy to show the result.   □

Proof of Proposition 5

Since $\mathcal{T}_0 = \mathcal{T}$, we note that $a \to_{\mathcal{T}_0} b$ if and only if $a \to b$. The equivalence among #1, #2, #3 is then obvious by the respective definitions on θ-extensions. Moreover, the equivalence among #2 and #4 is obvious from Proposition 4, whereas the equivalence among #4 and #5 follows from the fact that $\mathcal{F}' = \mathcal{F}''$.

□

Proof of Proposition 6

For **re** semantics, all results follow from Proposition 4 and the corresponding results on the AAF (e.g., [8]), so let us consider the case of **fr** and **lo** semantics. #1, #2 and #3 are obvious by the respective definitions.

For #4, let $\theta \in \{\mathbf{fr}, \mathbf{lo}\}$, and take $\mathcal{E}$ to be a θ-**pr**-extension. Then it is θ-**ad**. Suppose that it is not θ-**co**. Then, there is some $a \notin \mathcal{E}$, such that $\mathcal{E}$ θ-defends a and $\mathcal{E} \cup \{a\}$ is θ-**cf**. But then, it is easy to see that $\mathcal{E} \cup \{a\}$ is θ-**ad**, which is a contradiction by the definition of θ-**pr**-extensions and the fact that $\mathcal{E} \cup \{a\} \supset \mathcal{E}$.

For #5, let us consider the case of firm semantics first, and take $\mathcal{E}$ to be an **fr**-**st**-extension. Then, it is **fr**-**cf** (and maximally so). We will show that it is also **fr**-**ad**. Indeed, take some $a, b \in \mathcal{A}$, such that $a \in \mathcal{E}$ and $b \to a$. Then $b \notin \mathcal{E}$ (since $\mathcal{E}$ is **fr**-**cf**), thus $\mathcal{E} \to_{T_0} b$ (since $\mathcal{E}$ is **fr**-**st**), which implies that $\mathcal{E}$ **fr**-defends a. Thus, $\mathcal{E}$ is also **fr**-**ad**. It is also maximal, because $\mathcal{E}$ is maximally **fr**-**cf**. Therefore, $\mathcal{E}$ is an **fr**-**pr**-extension.

For the **lo** case, take $\mathcal{E}$ to be a **lo**-**st**-extension. Then, it is **lo**-**cf** (and maximally so). We will show that it is also **lo**-**ad**. Indeed, take some $a, b \in \mathcal{A}$, such that $a \in \mathcal{E}$ and $b \to_{T_0} a$. Then $b \notin \mathcal{E}$ (since $\mathcal{E}$ is **lo**-**cf**), thus $\mathcal{E} \to b$ (since $\mathcal{E}$ is **lo**-**st**), which implies that $\mathcal{E}$ **lo**-defends a. Thus, $\mathcal{E}$ is also **lo**-**ad**. It is also maximal, because $\mathcal{E}$ is maximally **lo**-**cf**. Therefore, $\mathcal{E}$ is a **lo**-**pr**-extension. □

Proof of Proposition 7

We will prove the claim constructively. First, we will describe a construction over $\mathcal{F}$, and then we will show that this construction generates some $\mathcal{E}$ with the above properties. The proof is broken down in steps, represented as claims proved individually below. The last claim (Claim 5) shows the result.

Construction. We assume a well-order $<$ over $\mathcal{A}$ (its existence is guaranteed by the Axiom of Choice). For a given set $E \subseteq \mathcal{A}$, we denote by $\min_< E$ the minimal element of E according to $<$.

Moreover, for $E \subseteq \mathcal{A}$, set $E^{\mathbf{U}} = \{a \in \mathcal{A} \setminus E \mid E: \theta\text{-defends } a,\ E \cup \{a\}: \theta\text{-}\mathbf{cf}\}$, i.e., the arguments that are defended by E, and do not conflict with E.

We define the function: $\phi : 2^{\mathcal{A}} \mapsto 2^{\mathcal{A}}$ as follows:

$$\phi(E) = \begin{cases} E & , \text{when } E^{\mathbf{U}} = \emptyset \\ E \cup \{\min_<(E^{\mathbf{U}})\} & , \text{when } E^{\mathbf{U}} \neq \emptyset \end{cases}$$

Finally, we define a function $\mathcal{G}$ recursively on the ordinals as follows:

$$\begin{array}{ll} \mathcal{G}(\beta) = \mathcal{E}[*] & , \text{when } \beta = 0 \\ \mathcal{G}(\beta + 1) = \phi(\mathcal{G}(\beta)) & , \text{when } \beta \text{ is a successor ordinal} \\ \mathcal{G}(\beta) = \bigcup \{\mathcal{G}(\gamma) \mid \gamma < \beta\} & , \text{when } \beta \text{ is a limit ordinal} \end{array}$$

Claim 1. For two ordinals β, γ, if $\beta < \gamma$, then $\mathcal{G}(\beta) \subseteq \mathcal{G}(\gamma)$.

Proof of Claim 1. We will use transfinite induction on γ.

If $\gamma = 0$, then the result holds trivially as there is no β for which $\beta < \gamma$. Suppose that the result holds for all $\gamma < \delta$; we will show that it holds for $\gamma = \delta$.

If δ is a successor ordinal, then there exists some δ^- such that $\delta = \delta^- + 1$. Clearly, by the definition of $\mathcal{G}$ and ϕ, $\mathcal{G}(\delta) \supseteq \mathcal{G}(\delta^-)$. Furthermore, by the inductive hypothesis, $\mathcal{G}(\delta^-) \supseteq \mathcal{G}(\beta)$, which shows the result.

If δ is a limit ordinal, then the result follows directly by the definition of $\mathcal{G}$. ○

Claim 2. For any ordinals β, $\mathcal{G}(\beta) \supseteq \mathcal{E}_*$.

Proof of Claim 2. If $\beta = 0$ the result follows by the definition of $\mathcal{G}$. If $\beta > 0$, the result follows by Claim 1. ○

Claim 3. For any ordinal β, $\mathcal{G}(\beta)$ is θ-**ad**.

Proof of Claim 3. We will use transfinite induction over β. For $\beta = 0$, the result follows by our assumption on $\mathcal{E}_*$. Now suppose that it holds for all $\beta < \gamma$. We will show that it holds for $\beta = \gamma$.

If γ is a successor ordinal, then take γ^- such that $\gamma = \gamma^- + 1$. Then, by definition, $\mathcal{G}(\gamma) = \phi(\mathcal{G}(\gamma^-))$. By the inductive hypothesis $\mathcal{G}(\gamma^-)$ is θ-**ad**. Moreover, by the definition of ϕ, $\phi(E)$ is θ-**ad** whenever E is θ-**ad**, so $\mathcal{G}(\gamma)$ is θ-**ad**.

If γ is a limit ordinal, then suppose that $\mathcal{G}(\gamma)$ is not θ-**cf**. Then, there exist $a_1, a_2 \in \mathcal{G}(\gamma)$ such that $\{a_1, a_2\}$ is not θ-**cf**, and, thus, there exist ordinals δ_1, δ_2 such that $\delta_1 < \gamma$, $\delta_2 < \gamma$, $a_1 \in \mathcal{G}(\delta_1)$, $a_2 \in \mathcal{G}(\delta_2)$. If $\delta_1 = \delta_2$ then $\mathcal{G}(\delta_1)$ is not θ-**cf**, a contradiction by the inductive hypothesis. If $\delta_1 < \delta_2$ then $\mathcal{G}(\delta_2) \supseteq \mathcal{G}(\delta_1)$ (by Claim 1), so $a_1, a_2 \in \mathcal{G}(\delta_2)$, a contradiction by the inductive hypothesis. The case of $\delta_2 < \delta_1$ is analogous. Thus, $\mathcal{G}(\gamma)$ is θ-**cf**.

Now consider some $a \in \mathcal{G}(\gamma)$. Then, by the definition of $\mathcal{G}$, there exists some $\delta < \gamma$ such that $a \in \mathcal{G}(\delta)$. Since $\mathcal{G}(\delta)$ is θ-**ad** by the inductive hypothesis, it follows that $\mathcal{G}(\delta)$ θ-defends a, so, given that $\mathcal{G}(\gamma) \supseteq \mathcal{G}(\delta)$ (Claim 1), we conclude that $\mathcal{G}(\gamma)$ θ-defends a. Thus, $\mathcal{G}(\gamma)$ is θ-**ad**. ○

Claim 4. There exists ordinal β such that $\mathcal{G}(\beta) = \mathcal{G}(\beta + 1)$.

Proof of Claim 4. By Claim 1, we conclude that $\mathcal{G}$ is an increasing function from the ordinals into 2^A. It cannot be strictly increasing, as if it were we would have an injective function from the ordinals into a set, violating Hartogs' lemma. Therefore the function must be eventually constant, so for some β, $\mathcal{G}(\beta) = \mathcal{G}(\beta + 1)$. ○

Claim 5. There exists some $\mathcal{E}$ such that $\mathcal{E} \supseteq \mathcal{E}_*$, and the following hold:

1. $\mathcal{E}$ is θ-**co**.
2. For any $\mathcal{E}'$ such that $\mathcal{E}_* \subseteq \mathcal{E}' \subset \mathcal{E}$, there exists $a \in \mathcal{E} \setminus \mathcal{E}'$ which is θ-defended by $\mathcal{E}'$ and $\mathcal{E}' \cup \{a\}$ is θ-**cf**.
3. For any $\mathcal{E}'$ such that $\mathcal{E}_* \subseteq \mathcal{E}' \subset \mathcal{E}$, $\mathcal{E}'$ is not θ-**co**.

Proof of Claim 5. By Claim 4, there exists ordinal β such that $\mathcal{G}(\beta) = \mathcal{G}(\beta + 1)$. Set $\mathcal{E} = \mathcal{G}(\beta)$. By Claim 2, $\mathcal{E} \supseteq \mathcal{E}_*$, so it is an adequate choice. We will show that $\mathcal{E}$ satisfies the required properties.

For the first result, note that by Claim 3, $\mathcal{E}$ is θ-**ad**. Moreover, $\mathcal{E} = \mathcal{G}(\beta) = \mathcal{G}(\beta+1) = \phi(\mathcal{G}(\beta)) = \phi(\mathcal{E})$, which implies that $\mathcal{E}^{\textcircled{v}} = \emptyset$, which, in tandem with the fact that $\mathcal{E}$ is θ-**ad** leads to the conclusion that $\mathcal{E}$ is θ-**co**.

For the second result, take some $\mathcal{E}'$ such that $\mathcal{E}_* \subseteq \mathcal{E}' \subset \mathcal{E}$.
Set $S = \{\gamma \mid \mathcal{G}(\gamma) \nsubseteq \mathcal{E}'\}$. We observe that $\beta \in S$, so $S \neq \emptyset$. Set $\delta = \min_< S$. Obviously, $\delta = \beta$ or $\delta < \beta$.

If $\delta = 0$, then $\mathcal{G}(\delta) = \mathcal{E}_* \subseteq \mathcal{E}'$, a contradiction.

If δ is a successor ordinal, then take δ^- such that $\delta = \delta^- + 1$. Thus, $\mathcal{G}(\delta) = \phi(\mathcal{G}(\delta^-))$. By construction, $\mathcal{G}(\delta^-) \subseteq \mathcal{E}'$ and $\mathcal{G}(\delta) \nsubseteq \mathcal{E}'$, therefore $\mathcal{G}(\delta) = \mathcal{G}(\delta^-) \cup \{a\}$, for some a for which $\mathcal{G}(\delta^-)$ θ-defends a and $\mathcal{G}(\delta^-) \cup \{a\}$ is θ-**cf**. If $a \in \mathcal{E}'$, then $\mathcal{G}(\delta) \subseteq \mathcal{E}'$, a contradiction by the choice of δ, so $a \notin \mathcal{E}'$. Moreover, $a \in \mathcal{G}(\delta)$. If $\delta = \beta$ then $\mathcal{G}(\delta) = \mathcal{E}$, so $a \in \mathcal{E}$. If $\delta < \beta$ then $a \in \mathcal{G}(\delta) \subseteq \mathcal{G}(\beta)$ (by Claim 1), so $a \in \mathcal{E}$. We conclude that $a \in \mathcal{E} \setminus \mathcal{E}'$. Thus, we have found some a with the required properties.

If δ is a limit ordinal, then, by the definition of δ, $\mathcal{G}(\delta') \subseteq \mathcal{E}'$ for all $\delta' < \delta$. Therefore, $\mathcal{G}(\delta) = \bigcup_{\delta' < \delta} \mathcal{G}(\delta') \subseteq \mathcal{E}'$, a contradiction by the choice of δ.

The third result follows from the second: indeed, as there exists $a \in \mathcal{E} \setminus \mathcal{E}'$ which is θ-defended by $\mathcal{E}'$ and $\mathcal{E}' \cup \{a\}$ is θ-**cf**, it cannot be the case that $\mathcal{E}'$ is θ-**co**. ○
□

Proof of Proposition 8

For the case where $\theta = \mathbf{re}$, the proof follows directly by Proposition 4 and the related results from the AAF literature. So suppose that $\theta \in \{\mathbf{fr}, \mathbf{lo}\}$.

We first note that $\emptyset$ is θ-**cf** and θ-**ad** w.r.t. $\mathcal{T}_0$, so the claim is true for $\sigma \in \{\mathbf{cf}, \mathbf{ad}\}$.

Let us now turn our attention to the case where $\sigma = \mathbf{pr}$. Our proof follows the lines of the respective proof in [4]. Set $\mathcal{AD} = \{\mathcal{E} \mid \mathcal{E} \text{ is } \theta\text{-}\mathbf{ad}\}$ ($\mathcal{AD} \neq \emptyset$, as shown above). We will show that, any $\subseteq$-chain $(\mathcal{E}_i)_{i \in I}$ in $\mathcal{AD}$ possesses an upper bound. Indeed, set $\mathcal{E} = \bigcup \mathcal{E}_i$. Obviously $\mathcal{E} \supseteq \mathcal{E}_i$, so it is an upper bound; it remains to show that $\mathcal{E} \in \mathcal{AD}$, i.e., that $\mathcal{E}$ is θ-**ad**.

Now suppose that $\mathcal{E}$ is not θ-**cf**. Then there exist $a_1, a_2 \in \mathcal{E}$ that attack each other ($a \to b$ for $\theta = \mathbf{fr}$, $a \to_{\mathcal{T}_0} b$ for $\theta = \mathbf{lo}$). By the definition of $\mathcal{E}$, there exist $\mathcal{E}_i, \mathcal{E}_j$ such that $a_1 \in \mathcal{E}_i$, $a_2 \in \mathcal{E}_j$ for some $i, j \in I$. It is the case that $\mathcal{E}_i \subseteq \mathcal{E}_j$ or $\mathcal{E}_i \subseteq \mathcal{E}_j$, so suppose, without loss of generality, that $\mathcal{E}_i \subseteq \mathcal{E}_j$. Then $a_1, a_2 \in \mathcal{E}_j$, a contradiction, since $\mathcal{E}_j$ is θ-**ad** (thus θ-**cf**). Thus, $\mathcal{E}$ is θ-**cf**. It remains to show that $\mathcal{E}$ defends all $a \in \mathcal{E}$. Indeed, take some $a \in \mathcal{E}$. Then, $a \in \mathcal{E}_i$ for some $i \in I$, and, thus $\mathcal{E}_i$ θ-defends a, which implies that $\mathcal{E}$ θ-defends a, since $\mathcal{E} \supseteq \mathcal{E}_i$. Thus, any $\subseteq$-chain $(\mathcal{E}_i)_{i \in I}$ in $\mathcal{AD}$ possesses an upper bound, which, by Zorn's Lemma, implies that $\mathcal{AD}$ has a maximal element, i.e., that there exists a θ-**pr** extension. By proposition 6, this implies that there exists a θ-**co** extension as well.

For θ-**gr** extensions, note that $\emptyset$ is θ-**ad**, so applying Proposition 7 for $\mathcal{E}_* = \emptyset$ we ensure the existence of some $\mathcal{E}$ which is minimally θ-**co**, i.e., $\mathcal{E}$ is θ-**gr**.   □

Proof of Proposition 9

Given that $\emptyset$ is θ-**ad**, we can apply Proposition 7 for $\mathcal{E}_* = \emptyset$ to get some $\mathcal{E}$ which is minimally θ-**co**, i.e., $\mathcal{E}$ is θ-**gr**. Now suppose that there is a second θ-**gr** extension, say $\mathcal{E}'$ ($\mathcal{E}' \neq \mathcal{E}$). Obviously, $\mathcal{E} \nsubseteq \mathcal{E}'$ and $\mathcal{E}' \nsubseteq \mathcal{E}$. Set $\mathcal{E}_0 = \mathcal{E} \cap \mathcal{E}'$. It follows that $\emptyset \subseteq \mathcal{E}_0 \subset \mathcal{E}$, so by Proposition 7 again there exists some $a \in \mathcal{E} \setminus \mathcal{E}_0$ which is θ-defended by $\mathcal{E}_0$ and $\mathcal{E}_0 \cup \{a\}$ θ-**cf**. Moreover, $\mathcal{E}_0 \subset \mathcal{E}'$, so a is θ-defended by $\mathcal{E}'$. Thus, $\mathcal{E}'$ is θ-**gr**, thus θ-**co**, and also $\mathcal{E}'$ θ-defends a, so by Proposition 2, $a \in \mathcal{E}'$, a contradiction by the choice of a. $\square$

Proof of Proposition 10

The first case is direct from Definition 3 and the definition of $\mathcal{F}_F$. The second case is direct using proof by contradiction and the fact that $\mathcal{E} \rightarrow_{\mathcal{T}_0} \mathcal{E}$ implies $\mathcal{E} \rightarrow \mathcal{E}$. The third is direct from Definition 3. $\square$

Proof of Proposition 11

The first case follows from the fact that $b \rightarrow_{\mathcal{T}_0} c$ implies that $b \rightarrow c$ for any $b, c \in \mathcal{A}$. For the second and third cases, note that $a \rightarrow b$ if and only if $(a, b) \in \mathcal{R}_F$, and that $a \rightarrow_{\mathcal{T}_0} b$ implies that $a \rightarrow b$. From these, and the definition of defense in AAFs and MAAFs, the results follow easily. $\square$

Proof of Proposition 12

The first four cases are direct from Propositions 10, 11. For the fifth case, note that, since $\mathcal{E}$ is **re-ad**, it follows that for all $a \in \mathcal{E}$, $\mathcal{E}$ **re**-defends a for $\mathcal{T}_0$, and, thus, by Proposition 11, $\mathcal{E}$ defends a in $\mathcal{F}_F$. Combining this with the fact that $\mathcal{E}$ is **cf** in $\mathcal{F}_F$, we get the result. $\square$

Proof of Proposition 13

For the first case, it suffices to show that, if $\mathcal{E}$ **fr**-defends a w.r.t. $\mathcal{T}_0$, then $a \in \mathcal{E}$. Indeed, if $\mathcal{E}$ **fr**-defends a, then, by Proposition 11, $\mathcal{E}$ **re**-defends a, so, given that $\mathcal{E}$ is **re-co**, it follows that $a \in \mathcal{E}$. The proofs for the other cases are analogous. $\square$

Proof of Proposition 14

For the first case, we note that $\emptyset$ is **fr**-ad, so applying Proposition 7 for $\mathcal{E}_* = \emptyset$, we will get a **fr-co** extension (say $\mathcal{E}$) that is minimal among **fr-co** extensions, thus it is the (only) **fr-gr** extension of $\mathcal{F}$. By Proposition 7 again, we observe that, for any $\mathcal{E}' \subset \mathcal{E}$, there exists some $a \in \mathcal{E} \setminus \mathcal{E}'$ such that $\mathcal{E}'$ **fr**-defends a, i.e., $\mathcal{E}'$ **re**-defends a, i.e., $\mathcal{E}'$ is not **re-co**. Thus, $\mathcal{E}$ is **re-gr**.

The second case is totally analogous.

The third case uses a similar proof (and the same reasoning, except that the existence of a is guaranteed by the results in [8] (instead of Proposition 7). $\square$

Proof of Proposition 15

For the first case, suppose that $\mathcal{E}$ is not **fr-pr**. Then, there exists some $\mathcal{E}' \supset \mathcal{E}$ such that $\mathcal{E}'$ is **fr-pr**. But then, $\mathcal{E}'$ is **fr-ad** so (by Proposition 12) $\mathcal{E}'$ is **re-ad**, a contradiction by the fact that $\mathcal{E}$ is **re-pr**. The other cases are analogous. $\square$

Proof of Proposition 16

For the first: observe that, by Proposition 10, $\mathcal{E}$ is maximally **fr-cf** if and only if $\mathcal{E}$ is maximally **re-cf**. Then, the result is obvious by Definition 8.

For the second: we obtain by Proposition 10 that $\mathcal{E}$ is **cf** in $\mathcal{F}_F$. Also, since $\mathcal{E}$ is **fr-st**, $\mathcal{E} \rightarrow_{\mathcal{T}_0} a$ for all $a \notin \mathcal{E}$, thus $\mathcal{E} \rightarrow a$ in $\mathcal{F}_F$. We conclude that $\mathcal{E}$ is **st** in $\mathcal{F}_F$.

For the third: we observe that, by Proposition 10, $\mathcal{E}$ is maximally **re-cf** if and only if it is maximally **lo-cf**. Now take some $a \notin \mathcal{E}$. If $\mathcal{E}$ is **re-st**, then $ext \rightarrow_{\mathcal{T}_0} a$,

so $\mathcal{E} \to a$, so $\mathcal{E}$ is **lo-st**. If $\mathcal{E}$ is **lo-st**, then $\mathcal{E} \to a$, and suppose that it is not the case that $\mathcal{E} \to_{\mathcal{T}_0} a$. Then, $\mathcal{E} \cup \{a\} \supset \mathcal{E}$ and **lo-cf**, a contradiction.
For the fourth: since $\mathcal{E}$ is **re-st**, we get that $\mathcal{E} \to_{\mathcal{T}_0} a$ whenever $a \notin \mathcal{E}$, thus $\mathcal{E} \to a$ in $\mathcal{F}_F$ for all $a \notin \mathcal{E}$, and $\mathcal{E}$ is **cf** in $\mathcal{F}_F$ by the hypothesis, so $\mathcal{E}$ is **st** in $\mathcal{F}_F$.   □

References

1. Amgoud, L., Ben-Naim, J., Doder, D., Vesic, S.: Acceptability semantics for weighted argumentation frameworks. In: IJCAI 2017, pp. 56–62 (2017)
2. Amgoud, L., Vesic, S.: Rich preference-based argumentation frameworks. Int. J. Approximate Reasoning **55**(2), 585–606 (2014)
3. Baroni, P., Cerutti, F., Giacomin, M., Guida, G.: AFRA: argumentation framework with recursive attacks. IJAR **52**(1), 19–37 (2011)
4. Baumann, R., Spanring, C.: Infinite argumentation frameworks. In: Eiter, T., Strass, H., Truszczyński, M., Woltran, S. (eds.) Advances in Knowledge Representation, Logic Programming, and Abstract Argumentation. LNCS (LNAI), vol. 9060, pp. 281–295. Springer, Cham (2015). https://doi.org/10.1007/978-3-319-14726-0_19
5. Bench-Capon, T.J.M.: Persuasion in practical argument using value-based argumentation frameworks. J. Log. Comput. **13**(3), 429–448 (2003)
6. Besnard, P., Hunter, A.: A logic-based theory of deductive arguments. Artif. Intell. **128**(1–2), 203–235 (2001)
7. Cayrol, C., Lagasquie-Schiex, M.: From preferences over arguments to preferences over attacks in abstract argumentation: a comparative study. In: 25th IEEE International Conference on Tools with Artificial Intelligence, pp. 588–595 (2013)
8. Dung, P.M.: On the acceptability of arguments and its fundamental role in nonmonotonic reasoning, logic programming and n-person games. Artif. Intell. **77**(2), 321–357 (1995)
9. Dunne, P.E., Hunter, A., McBurney, P., Parsons, S., Wooldridge, M.: Weighted argument systems: basic definitions, algorithms, and complexity results. Artif. Intell. **175**(2), 457–486 (2011)
10. Eğilmez, S., Martins, J., Leite, J.: Extending social abstract argumentation with votes on attacks. In: Black, E., Modgil, S., Oren, N. (eds.) TAFA 2013. LNCS (LNAI), vol. 8306, pp. 16–31. Springer, Heidelberg (2014). https://doi.org/10.1007/978-3-642-54373-9_2
11. Martınez, D.C., Garcıa, A.J., Simari, G.R.: An abstract argumentation framework with varied-strength attacks. In: KR 2008, pp. 135–144 (2008)
12. Modgil, S.: Reasoning about preferences in argumentation frameworks. Artif. Intell. **173**(9–10), 901–934 (2009)
13. Modgil, S., Prakken, H.: A general account of argumentation with preferences. Artif. Intell. **195**, 361–397 (2013)
14. Tarski, A.: A lattice-theoretical fixpoint theorem and its applications. Pac. J. Math. **5**(2), 285–309 (1955)
15. Tohmé, F.A., Bodanza, G.A., Simari, G.R.: Aggregation of attack relations: a social-choice theoretical analysis of defeasibility criteria. In: Hartmann, S., Kern-Isberner, G. (eds.) FoIKS 2008. LNCS, vol. 4932, pp. 8–23. Springer, Heidelberg (2008). https://doi.org/10.1007/978-3-540-77684-0_4
16. Vassiliades, A., Patkos, T., Bikakis, A., Flouris, G., Bassiliades, N., Plexousakis, D.: Preliminary notions of arguments from commonsense knowledge. In: 11th Hellenic Conference on Artificial Intelligence, pp. 211–214 (2020)

Towards a Sound and Complete Dialogue System for Handling Enthymemes

Andreas Xydis$^{(\boxtimes)}$, Christopher Hampson, Sanjay Modgil, and Elizabeth Black

Department of Informatics, King's College London, London, UK
{andreas.xydis,christopher.hampson,sanjay.modgil,
elizabeth.black}@kcl.ac.uk

Abstract. A common assumption for argumentation-based dialogues is that any argument exchanged is complete, in the sense that its premises entail its claim. However, in real world dialogues, agents commonly exchange enthymemes—arguments with incomplete logical structure. This paper formalises the dialogical exchange of enthymemes that are missing some constituent elements, such that it is not possible to directly entail the claim of the intended argument from the premises of the enthymeme exchanged. This can lead to misunderstandings between agents; we provide a rich set of locutions for identifying and resolving such misunderstandings, and a protocol that governs the use of these. We show that, under certain conditions, the status of moves made during a dialogue conforming to our system corresponds with the status of arguments in the Dung argument framework instantiated by the contents of the moves made at that stage in the dialogue. This is significant since it ensures that the use of enthymemes does not prevent the agents from reaching the appropriate decision according to the information they have shared.

Keywords: Argumentation · Enthymemes · Dialogue · Framework

1 Introduction

Context. Structured approaches to argumentation [1] define binary attack (or defeat) relations amongst arguments constructed from a belief base of logical formulae $\mathcal{B}$. The claims of the winning (acceptable) arguments in the defined graph or 'argument framework' (AF) identify the non-monotonic inferences from $\mathcal{B}$. These approaches, initially defined for single agent (monological) reasoning, can be generalised to dialogical models of distributed reasoning in which agents exchange arguments and other locutions (e.g., [4,7,13]). One then aims at showing that the dialogue establishes a topic α as acceptable iff α is the claim of a justified argument in the AF defined by the contents $\mathcal{B}$ of the locutions exchanged (i.e., α is non-monotonically inferred from $\mathcal{B}$). These models are motivated by requirements for normatively scaffolding integration of human-AI and human-human reasoning via dialogue [6], and thus need to account for features of real-world dialogue.

© Springer Nature Switzerland AG 2021
P. Baroni et al. (Eds.): CLAR 2021, LNAI 13040, pp. 437–456, 2021.
https://doi.org/10.1007/978-3-030-89391-0_24

In structured argumentation, arguments typically consist of a conclusion (claim) deductively and/or defeasibly inferred from some premises. However, the aforementioned scaffolding requires that dialogues accommodate human agents' ubiquitous use of 'incomplete' arguments known as *enthymemes* [18]. Most works dealing with enthymemes focus on how an enthymeme can be constructed from the intended argument and how the intended argument can be reconstructed from a received enthymeme, based on assumptions that the sender and the receiver make about their shared knowledge and context, e.g. [2,3,7–9]. Few works that consider enthymemes additionally examine how enthymemes can be handled during dialogues between human and/or computational agents.

Suppose that two agents Ag_1 and Ag_2 have a dialogue to decide whether information about Blojo's affair should be published, where the intended argument of Ag_1 is A = "If Blojo is no longer a public figure ($\neg pf$), information about his affair is not in the public interest ($\neg pi$), *and* the information is private (pr), then the information should not be published ($\neg pub$). Blojo is no longer a public figure. Affairs do not concern the public ($\neg ap$), *hence* information about Blojo's affair is not in the public interest. Romantic preferences are private (rp), *hence* the information about Blojo's affair is private. Therefore the information about Blojo's affair should not be published." (see Fig. 1(i)). Ag_1 may move the enthymeme E_1 = "$\neg pf$, $\neg pi$, and pr, *hence* $\neg pub$", holding back from communicating the supports for the intermediate conclusions $\neg pi$ and pr. Ag_2 might then query $\neg pi$ and pr (separately), eliciting Ag_1's arguments "$\neg ap$ *hence* $\neg pi$" and "rp *hence* pr" (A' and A'' respectively; see Fig. 1(i)) which together 'backward extend' E_1 to yield the complete argument A.

In [10,11] and [13], the locutions formalised allow for the backward extension of enthymemes where agents can ask for further information to justify what appears as a premise in the enthymeme (as described in the above example). However, these works do not support the use of enthymemes that require forward extending in order to arrive at the claim, and which are commonly seen in real world dialogues. Consider that argument B = "Blojo is UN envoy for the Middle East (en), *hence* Blojo is a public figure (pf)." is the intended argument of Ag_2, but Ag_2 attacks E_1 with the enthymeme E_2 = en. It is not immediately clear why E_2 attacks E_1 (since en does not directly challenge any element of E_1). As discussed in [5], to avoid misunderstanding and so ensure a fully rational exchange, normative scaffolding would prompt Ag_1 to seek clarification—"what is implied by en such that your intended argument attacks E_1?"—to which Ag_2 might reply that en implies pf, thus *forward extending* E_2 to yield B which negates a premise in E_1.[1]

---

[1] Notice that before Ag_1 seeks clarification, although it appears that Ag_2 wins the dialogue (since she *moves* E_2 against A), E_2 does not formally attack A (since E_2 does not negate any element of A) and so Ag_1's argument A is determined acceptable according to the AF constructed by the contents of the enthymemes revealed by the agents. In other words, a mismatch can exist between the pragmatic and the logical conclusions implied by a dialogue in which enthymemes are used.

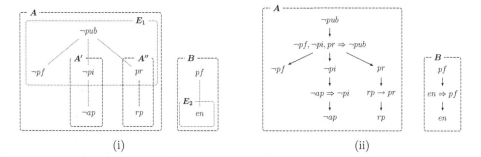

Fig. 1. (i) shows a formal representation of the arguments and enthymemes in the Blojo example from Sect. 1: arguments A and B (enclosed by a dashed line) as typically represented in the $ASPIC^+$ framework where a node is a claim (or intermediate claim) and the node's children are the premises that either strictly (if they are connected with a solid line) or defeasibly (if they are connected with a dotted line) infer this claim (or intermediate claim); the sub-arguments A' and A'' of A, which backward extend A on $\neg pi$ and pr, respectively, are enclosed by a dashed line; the enthymemes E_1 of A and E_2 of B are enclosed by a dotted line; B forward extends E_2. (ii) shows A and B as we represent arguments in this paper, where the inference rules applied ($\Rightarrow$ and $\rightarrow$ denoting the defeasible and strict inference, respectively) are explicitly provided and a claim (or intermediate claim) is connected to its premises via the inference rule applied.

Observe that [12] allows for both backward and forward extending of enthymemes, as does the dialogue system in [14], which additionally enables resolution of misunderstandings that arise due to use of enthymemes. However, these and the above mentioned works do not consider how the outcome of the dialogue relates to the AF that is instantiated based on contents of the enthymemes moved during a dialogue, meaning that there is no guarantee that the dialogue outcome respects the underlying argumentation theory. A notable exception is [13], but this work only addresses backward extension of enthymemes.

Contributions. Our primary contribution is the development of a dialogue system in which agents can move enthymemes and seek clarification to elicit forward extension of enthymemes, such that under certain conditions, the dialogical status of the moves made during the dialogue—determined by what we call the *dialogue framework*—corresponds to the acceptability of the arguments in the Dung AF instantiated from the contents of the moves made at that stage in the dialogue. This correspondence—not shown previously for dialogue systems that support forward extension of enthymemes—is significant since it demonstrates that the dialogue system we propose respects the logic and semantics of the underlying argumentation theory. Additionally, our results verify that when enthymemes are implemented in a dialogue, participants can still reach the same outcome as they would have done if they used their complete intended arguments (as shown in the Blojo example described above). This is important as we therefore show that there is no disadvantage to the use of enthymemes in dialogues, a common real-world feature of dialogues that supports efficient inter-agent communication. If we are to enable effective human-computer interaction and provide normative support for human-human dialogue, we need to account for the ubiquitous use of enthymemes in real-world dialogues and make sure that agents can still reach the "correct" conclusions based on the knowledge they have shared.

Moreover, we formalise enthymemes in the $ASPIC^+$ framework [16]—a general framework that subsumes other argumentation formalisms, and that has been shown to provide argumentative formalisations of a wide range of non-monotonic logics. To the best of our knowledge, this paper is the first to show soundness and completeness results for dialogical generalisations of $ASPIC^+$ (since complete arguments are a special case of enthymemes)[2]. Due to lack of space, we do not here account for the backward extension of enthymemes nor for the full range of misunderstandings that may occur due to use of enthymemes (as done in [14]). However, our work paves the way for a sound and complete dialogue system that accommodates use of any kind of enthymeme, and where any kind of uncertainty that arises from their use can be resolved.

Paper Outline. In Sect. 2 we review relevant background and formalise enthymemes within $ASPIC^+$. In Sect. 3 we define our dialogue system, instantiation of a dialogue framework from the moves made during a dialogue, and the evaluation of these moves. In Sect. 4 we prove soundness and completeness. Finally, we conclude and review directions for future work in Sect. 5.

2   Preliminaries

The $ASPIC^+$ framework [16] abstracts from the particularities of the underlying language, the nature of conflict, the defeasible inference rules, and strict inference rules (which can encode a deductive logic of one's choosing) that are used to chain inferences from premises to an argument's conclusion. $ASPIC^+$ arguments are evaluated in a Dung AF [15], and $ASPIC^+$ provides guidelines for ensuring that the outcome of evaluation yields rational outcomes.

An $ASPIC^+$ *argumentation theory* AT is a tuple $\langle AS, K \rangle$ consisting of an *argumentation system* AS and a *knowledge base* K. AS is a tuple $\langle L, (\bar{\cdot}), R, nom \rangle$ where L is a logical language and $(\bar{\cdot}) : L \to (2^L - \{\emptyset\})$ is a function that generalises the notion of negation, so as to declare that two formulae are in conflict (e.g., $\overline{married} = \{single, unmarried\}$). Additionally, $R = R_s \cup R_{def}$ is a set of strict (R_s) and defeasible (R_{def}) inference rules and $nom : R_{def}^* \to L$ (where R_{def}^* is the class of all defeasible rules) is a naming function which assigns a name (or nominal) to each defeasible rule (so that rules can be referenced in the object language). Lastly, $R = R_s \cup R_{def}$ is the (disjoint) union of a set of *strict*

---

[2] [4] formalises a dialogical generalisation of $ASPIC^+$ extended to accommodate reasoning about preferences; however soundness and completeness results are not shown.

rules R_s of the form $p_1, \ldots, p_n \rightarrow p$, and a set of *defeasible rules* R_{def} of the form $p_1, \ldots, p_n \Rightarrow p$, for $p, p_1, \ldots, p_n \in L$. For each rule $r \in R$ let antecedents$(r) = \{p_1, \ldots, p_n\}$ denote the set of antecedents of r and consequent$(r) = p$ denote the consequent of r. Finally, a knowledge base $K \subseteq L$ is a set of premises.[3]

Definition 1. *Given an argumentation system* $AS = \langle L, (\bar{\cdot}), R, nom \rangle$ *and an argumentation theory* $AT = \langle AS, K \rangle$, *an* **argument** *is a labelled (downward directed) tree* $A = \langle \text{Nodes}(A), \text{Edges}(A), \text{lab}_A \rangle$ *such that:*

1. $\text{lab}_A : \text{Nodes}(A) \rightarrow L \cup R$ *is a node labelling;*
2. $\text{Edges}(A) \subseteq \text{Nodes}(A) \times \text{Nodes}(A)$ *such that if* $(n_i, n_j) \in \text{Edges}(A)$, *then either:*
   (a) $\text{lab}_A(n_i) \in L$, $\text{lab}_A(n_j) \in R$ *and* consequent$(\text{lab}_A(n_j)) = \text{lab}_A(n_i)$, *or*
   (b) $\text{lab}_A(n_i) \in R$ *and* antecedents$(\text{lab}_A(n_i)) = \{\text{lab}_A(n_j) \mid (n_i, n_j) \in \text{Edges}(A)\} \subseteq L$,
   and if $(n_i, n_j), (n_i, n_k) \in \text{Edges}(A)$ *and* $n_j \neq n_k$ *then* $\text{lab}_A(n_j) \neq \text{lab}_A(n_k)$;
3. *for every node* $n \in \text{Leaves}(A)$, *we have* $\text{lab}_A(n) \in K$;
4. $|\text{Roots}(A)| = 1$;
5. $\text{lab}_A(\text{Conc}(A)) \in L$, *where* Conc$(A)$ *is the unique element in* Roots(A);

where $\text{Leaves}(A) = \{n_i \in \text{Nodes}(A) \mid \nexists(n_i, n_j) \in \text{Edges}(A)\}$, *and* $\text{Roots}(A) = \{n_i \in \text{Nodes}(A) \mid \nexists(n_j, n_i) \in \text{Edges}(A)\}$. *Let* $\mathcal{A}_{AT}$ *denote the set of arguments instantiated using the elements in* AT. *Let* $\mathcal{A}^*$ *denote the class of all arguments, and define* $\text{Rules}(A) = \{n \in \text{Nodes}(A) \mid \text{lab}_A(n) \in R\}$, *for all* $A \in \mathcal{A}^*$.

In the above definition of an *argument*, a strict/defeasible inference rule is incorporated as a node, intermediating between the parent node (the rule's conclusion) and the child node(s) (the rule's antecedent(s)). This contrasts with the standard $ASPIC^+$ notion of an argument in which the rules are represented by undirected edges (where solid lines represent strict rules and dotted lines represent defeasible rules) linking the conclusion to the rule's antecedents (see Fig. 1(i) and 1(ii)).

The binary *attack* and *defeat* relations over arguments are defined as for $ASPIC^+$ arguments. An attack from argument X to argument Y may succeed as a *defeat*, contingent on preferences defined over the argument X and the targeted sub-argument of Y, if X's claim conflicts with an ordinary premise or the consequent or name of a defeasible rule in Y (see [16] for more details).

Definition 2. *The* **argument framework** AF **instantiated by an argumentation theory** AT *is a tuple* $\langle \mathcal{A}_{AT}, Dfs \rangle$ *where* $Dfs \subseteq \mathcal{A}_{AT} \times \mathcal{A}_{AT}$ *is the* $ASPIC^+$ *defeat relation.*

In the definition below, we define a *complete labelling* on the argument framework instantiated by an argumentation theory [17].

---

[3] Note that in this paper we do not utilise the $ASPIC^+$ distinction between the disjoint sets of axiom (K_n) and ordinary (K_p) premises $(K = K_n \cup K_p)$, whereby only ordinary premises are fallible and so can be challenged/attacked.

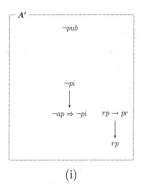
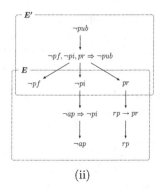

(i)   (ii)

Fig. 2. (i) shows a valid enthymeme in this paper, which is generated by removing multiple elements of A in Fig. 1(ii) such as inference rules, premises, and intermediate conclusions of A. (ii) Shows an *upwards extendable* enthymeme E of A and the *upwards extension E'* of E that yields A.

Definition 3. *Let $AF = \langle \mathcal{A}_{AT}, Dfs \rangle$ be instantiated by AT. We define a com-plete labelling on AF to be a (total) function $\mathsf{L} : \mathcal{A}_{AT} \to \{\text{IN}, \text{OUT}, \text{UNDEC}\}$ such that for every $X \in \mathcal{A}_{AT}$:*

1. $\mathsf{L}(X) = \text{IN}$ *iff for all $Y \in \mathcal{A}_{AT}$, if $(Y, X) \in Dfs$ then $\mathsf{L}(Y) = \text{OUT}$;*
2. $\mathsf{L}(X) = \text{OUT}$ *iff there exists $Y \in \mathcal{A}_{AT}$ such that $(Y, X) \in Dfs$ and $\mathsf{L}(Y) = \text{IN}$;*
3. $\mathsf{L}(X) = \text{UNDEC}$ *iff $\mathsf{L}(X) \neq \text{IN}$ and $\mathsf{L}(X) \neq \text{OUT}$.*

This paper does not adopt the standard figurative representations of $ASPIC^+$ arguments (e.g., Fig. 1(i)) because when an *enthymeme E* is constructed from an intended argument A, one may choose to remove the conclusion of an inference rule while retaining the inference rule, or remove a sub-argument whose conclu-sion is the antecedent of a strict/defeasible rule (see Fig. 2(i)). So an enthymeme E of an argument A is a forest of trees (i.e. a disjoint union of trees), whose nodes and edges are a subset of the nodes and edges of A, and the label of each node in E is the same label of the corresponding node in A.

Definition 4. *Let $AT = \langle AS, K \rangle$ and $A \in \mathcal{A}_{AT}$. An enthymeme E of an argument A (written $E \leq A$) is a labelled (downward directed) tree $E = \langle \mathsf{Nodes}(E), \mathsf{Edges}(E), \mathsf{lab}_E \rangle$ such that $\emptyset \neq \mathsf{Nodes}(E) \subseteq \mathsf{Nodes}(A)$ and $\mathsf{Edges}(E) \subseteq \mathsf{Edges}(A) \cap (\mathsf{Nodes}(E) \times \mathsf{Nodes}(E))$ and for every node $n \in \mathsf{Nodes}(E)$, $\mathsf{lab}_E(n) = \mathsf{lab}_A(n)$.*

As for arguments, we define $\mathsf{Roots}(E) = \{n_i \in \mathsf{Nodes}(E) \mid \nexists (n_j, n_i) \in \mathsf{Edges}(E)\}$ and $\mathsf{Leaves}(E) = \{n_i \in \mathsf{Nodes}(E) \mid \nexists (n_i, n_j) \in \mathsf{Edges}(E)\}$.

Note that the union of two enthymemes E_1 and E_2, defined in the obvi-ous way, is itself an enthymeme (denoted $E_1 \cup E_2$) and that an argument A is an enthymeme of itself, where $\mathsf{Roots}(A) = \{\mathsf{Conc}(A)\}$ and $\{\mathsf{lab}_A(n) : n \in \mathsf{Leaves}(A)\} \subseteq K$. The class of all enthymemes is denoted $\mathcal{E}^*$ and so includes the class of all arguments $(\mathcal{A}^* \subseteq \mathcal{E}^*)$.

As mentioned earlier, this paper only focuses on the forward extension of enthymemes. In other words, we are interested in enthymemes for which the only missing information needed to reconstruct the complete argument (from which an enthymeme was generated) is the information between the roots of the trees of the enthymeme and the root (claim) of the intended argument. Therefore, we define an *upwards extendable enthymeme* E of an argument A as an enthymeme which includes the premises (leaves) of A, and for each root rt of a tree in E, the label of rt is an element of L, i.e. that either it is a premise, in the case that rt is also a leaf, or it is the consequent of a rule used in E (e.g., see Fig. 2(ii)).

Definition 5. *We say that* $E = \langle \mathsf{Nodes}(E), \mathsf{Edges}(E), \mathsf{lab}_E \rangle$ *is an **upwards extendable enthymeme of** $A = \langle \mathsf{Nodes}(A), \mathsf{Edges}(A), \mathsf{lab}_A \rangle$ iff (i) $\mathsf{Leaves}(E) = \mathsf{Leaves}(A)$, and (ii) $\mathsf{lab}_E(n) \in L$, for every $n \in \mathsf{Roots}(E)$.*

*If E is an upwards extendable enthymeme of A, then we define the **upwards extension** of E that yields A to be the enthymeme E' (unique up to isomorphism) of A such that $A = E \cup E'$ and $\mathsf{Roots}(E) = \mathsf{Leaves}(E')$ (e.g., see Fig. 2(ii)).*

Notice that if $\mathsf{Conc}(A) \in \mathsf{Roots}(E)$, then $\mathsf{Roots}(E) = \{\mathsf{Conc}(A)\}$ and $E = A$.

3 Dialogue System

In this section we present a dialogue system that handles enthymemes, and define how its dialogues can be represented by a dialogue framework (i.e., a graph whose nodes correspond to the moves made during the dialogue and whose edges represent the relationships between those moves). A complete labelling function on the dialogue framework evaluates the dialogical status of a move; in Sect. 4 we show that this evaluation is sound and complete with reference to the argument framework AF instantiated from the contents of all the moves made during the dialogue. That is to say, an argument moved in the dialogue is judged to be winning in the dialogue under Dung's complete semantics iff the claim of the corresponding argument is justified (under Dung's complete semantics) in the AF instantiated from the contents of the moves of the dialogue.

An *enthymeme dialogue* d between *Prop* and *Op* is a sequence of moves, where each move is a 5-tuple that comprises the move's *sender, locution, content, target* and *reply*. The sender of each move is either *Prop* or *Op* (the participants of the dialogue). The locution of a move can be assert (used to posit upwards extendable enthymemes), and-so (used to request an upwards extension to an enthymeme) or hence (used to provide an upwards extension to an enthymeme). The *content* of a move depends on its locution: if a move's locution is assert or hence, its content is an enthymeme; if a move's locution is and-so, its content is $\emptyset$. The and-so and hence moves are made in explicit response to a previous move made: if a move's locution is and-so or hence, its *reply* is a natural number that is the index of the move to which it replies, otherwise its *reply* is $\emptyset$. When assertions are made, the enthymeme being asserted is being moved as a defeat against an enthymeme previously moved—the *target* of the assertion. If a move's locution is assert, its *target* is the natural number that indexes the move whose content is the asserted enthymeme that is being moved against otherwise its target is $\emptyset$.

When an agent assert an enthymeme, or moves an upwards extension to an enthymeme with a hence move, it has in mind a complete argument and this is the *intended argument* of the move. Note, since we may be dealing with nefarious agents, we do not insist here that the intended argument of a move must indeed extend the enthymeme moved; in Sect. 4 we consider *honest* agents, whose intended arguments do indeed extend the enthymemes moved and can be constructed from the sender's belief base. Similarly, when an agent asserts an enthymeme as a defeat against some target enthymeme, the agent has in mind a particular argument that it believes was intended as the complete argument of the target enthymeme: this is the *intended target argument* of the assert move. Section 4 considers *understanding* agents, whose intended targeted arguments match the intended argument of the target.

Definition 6. *An **enthymeme dialogue** between two participants Prop and Op is a sequence of **moves** $d = [m_0, m_1, \ldots, m_\ell]$, where each move $m_i = \langle s(m_i), l(m_i), c(m_i), re(m_i), t(m_i) \rangle$ is a 5-tuple comprising the following:*

- Sender: $s(m_i) \in \{Prop, Op\}$;
- Location: $l(m_i) \in \{\text{assert}, \text{and-so}, \text{hence}\}$;
- Content: *if* $l(m_i) \in \{\text{assert}, \text{hence}\}$ *then* $c(m_i) \in \mathcal{E}^*$, *otherwise* $c(m_i) = \emptyset$;
- Reply: *if* $l(m_i) \in \{\text{and-so}, \text{hence}\}$ *then* $re(m_i) \in \{0, \ldots, (i-1)\}$, *otherwise* $re(m_i) = \emptyset$;
- Target: *if* $l(m_i) \in \{\text{assert}\}$ *then* $t(m_i) \in \{0, \ldots, (i-1)\} \cup \{\emptyset\}$, *otherwise* $t(m_i) = \emptyset$.

If $l(m) \in \{\text{assert}, \text{hence}\}$, $\mathsf{IntArg}(m) \in \mathcal{A}^*$ *is the **intended argument** of m and if* $l(m) = \text{assert}$, $\mathsf{IntTarArg}(m) \in (\mathcal{A}^* \cup \{\emptyset\})$ *is the **intended target argument**.*

We now define a *well-formed enthymeme dialogue* d with two participants, *Prop* and *Op*. We assume that the agents share the same underlying argumentation system, ensuring they can understand each other, except that the defeasible rules they are each aware of may differ (and of course they may each have different belief bases, which are not defined by the argumentation system). The participants alternate turns and cannot repeat moves. *Prop* must start by asserting an *argument* (the conclusion of which we call the *topic* of the dialogue) and so we disallow a participant to ask for a forward extension of this argument with an and-so move.

An assert move puts forward an upwards extendable enthymeme[4] that targets (i.e., is moved as a defeat against) an enthymeme that has been moved previously (except for the first assert move, which has no target). Note that, while the target m' of a move m consists of the enthymeme E' (E' = content of m') this does not necessarily imply a valid defeat relation from the content E of m

---

[4] Recall, here we deal only with *forward extension* of enthymemes, so that an 'upwards extendable enthymeme' is an enthymeme that can potentially be forward extended.

Table 1. A well-formed enthymeme dialogue $d = [m_0, \ldots, m_6]$. The internal structure of enthymemes and intended arguments of moves are shown in Fig. 3.

Step	Dialogue d	$\mathsf{IntArg}(m_i)$	$\mathsf{IntTarArg}(m_i)$
1	$m_0 = (Prop, \mathsf{assert}, E, \emptyset, \emptyset)$	E	$\emptyset$
2	$m_1 = (Op, \mathsf{assert}, A', \emptyset, 0)$	A	E
3	$m_2 = (Prop, \mathsf{and\text{-}so}, \emptyset, 1, \emptyset)$	$-$	$-$
4	$m_3 = (Op, \mathsf{hence}, A'', 2, \emptyset)$	A	$-$
5	$m_4 = (Prop, \mathsf{assert}, B', \emptyset, 1)$	B	A
6	$m_5 = (Op, \mathsf{assert}, C, \emptyset, 4)$	C	B
7	$m_6 = (Prop, \mathsf{assert}, D, \emptyset, 3)$	D	A

(i.e. while m's enthymeme E purportedly defeats E' in m', E may not validly defeat E' according to the $ASPIC^+$ definition of defeat). Since we are dealing with enthymemes, the existence of valid defeat relations cannot necessarily be determined and our definition of well-formed enthymeme dialogues does not enforce them—the participants may be mistaken in the assumptions they have made regarding the other's intended arguments (i.e. E may not legitimately defeat the intended argument of m'), or may dishonestly target a move, even knowing that their enthymeme does not defeat it, for strategic purposes.

An and-so move is used to request an upwards extension of a previously asserted upwards extendable enthymeme, while a hence move replies to a previous and-so move and provides an upwards extension of the questioned upwards extendable enthymeme. Table 1 shows a well-formed enthymeme dialogue d and Fig. 3 shows the internal structure of enthymemes and intended arguments of moves made in d together with a natural language translation.

Definition 7. *Let* $AS_{\mathsf{Ag}} = \langle L, (\overline{\cdot}), R_{\mathsf{Ag}}, nom \rangle$ *be an argumentation system for* $\mathsf{Ag} \in \{Prop, Op\}$ *such that* $R_{\mathsf{Ag}} = R_s \cup R_{def}^{\mathsf{Ag}}$, *where* R_{def}^{Ag} *is* Ag's *defeasible rules. An enthymeme dialogue* $d = [m_0, \ldots, m_\ell]$ *between* $Prop$ *and* Op *is said to be* **well-formed** *if* $m_i \neq m_j$ *for all* $i \neq j$, *and for all* $i \leq \ell$:

1. $\mathsf{s}(m_i) = Prop$ *if* i *is even, otherwise* $\mathsf{s}(m_i) = Op$;
2. *If* $i = 0$, *then* $\mathsf{l}(m_i) = \mathsf{assert}$, $\mathsf{c}(m_i) \in \mathcal{A}^*$, *and* $\mathsf{t}(m_i) = \emptyset$;
3. *If* $i > 0$ *and* $\mathsf{l}(m_i) = \mathsf{assert}$, *then* $\mathsf{c}(m_i)$ *is an upwards extendable enthymeme of an argument* $A \in \mathcal{A}^*$ *and* $\mathsf{t}(m_i) = j$ *such that* $\mathsf{l}(m_j) \in \{\mathsf{assert}, \mathsf{hence}\}$;
4. *If* $\mathsf{l}(m_i) = \mathsf{and\text{-}so}$, *then* $\mathsf{re}(m_i) = j > 0$ *and* $\mathsf{l}(m_j) = \mathsf{assert}$;
5. *If* $\mathsf{l}(m_i) = \mathsf{hence}$, *then there exists* $A \in \mathcal{A}^*$ *such that* $A = \mathsf{c}(m_i) \cup \mathsf{c}(m_k)$ *and* $\mathsf{re}(m_i) = j$ *such that* $\mathsf{l}(m_j) = \mathsf{and\text{-}so}$ *and* $\mathsf{re}(m_j) = k$.

*The **topic** of d (denoted $\mathsf{Topic}(d)$) is the label of the conclusion of the argument moved in m_0.*

Henceforth, we use 'dialogue' as a shorthand for a well-formed enthymeme dialogue, and write d_i to refer to a dialogue whose last move is m_i (i.e.

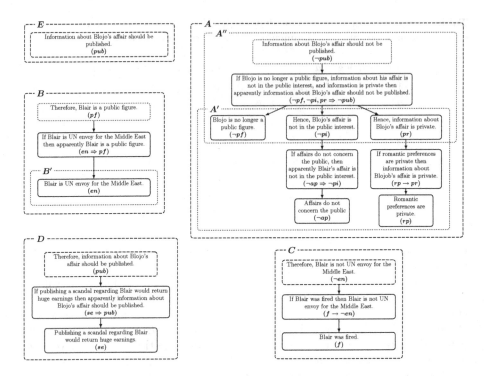

Fig. 3. The internal structure of enthymemes (enclosed by a dotted line) and intended arguments of moves in d (enclosed by a dashed line) described in Table 1, with *pub* being the topic of the dialogue. We, also, show the natural language translation of each premise (green), inference rule (purple), intermediate conclusion (orange) and claim of intended argument (red). (Color figure online)

$d_i = [m_0, \ldots, m_i])$. We define a *dialogue framework* of a dialogue d as a 4-tuple $DF = \langle \mathcal{M}, \mathcal{T}, \mathcal{R}, \mathcal{S} \rangle$ where $\mathcal{M}$ is the set of moves made in d, $\mathcal{T}$ is a binary defeat relationship between moves that is determined by the target relationship between moves, $\mathcal{R}$ is a binary reply relationship that is determined by the reply relationship between moves, and $\mathcal{S}$ is a binary support relationship that is determined by the reply relationship (m_i supports m_j iff there is some m such that m_i replies to m and m replies to m_j). Intuitively, the content E' of m_i is used as a response to m, where m questions the sender of m_j to provide an upwards extension of the enthymeme E in m_j. Hence E' upward extends E and so m_i supports m_j. Finally, we let $m_i \sim_{\mathcal{S}} m_j$ denote that either $m_i = m_j$, or that m_i supports m_j, or that m_j supports m_i. For example, Fig. 4 depicts the dialogue framework of the dialogue presented in Table 1.

Definition 8. *The **dialogue framework** of a dialogue $d = [m_0, \ldots, m_\ell]$ is a tuple $DF = \langle \mathcal{M}, \mathcal{T}, \mathcal{R}, \mathcal{S} \rangle$ where:*

- *$\mathcal{M} = \{m_0, \ldots, m_\ell\}$ is the set of moves of d,*
- *$\mathcal{T} \subseteq \mathcal{M} \times \mathcal{M}$ is a binary defeat relation such that $m_i \mathcal{T} m_j \iff \mathsf{t}(m_i) = j$,*

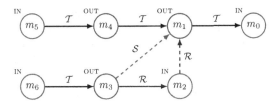

Fig. 4. The dialogue framework DF instantiated by d presented in Table 1. According to the complete labelling L on DF, $\mathsf{L}(m_0) = \mathsf{L}(m_2) = \mathsf{L}(m_5) = \mathsf{L}(m_6) = $ IN and $\mathsf{L}(m_1) = \mathsf{L}(m_3) = \mathsf{L}(m_4) = $ OUT.

- $\mathcal{R} \subseteq \mathcal{M} \times \mathcal{M}$ *is a binary* reply *relation such that* $m_i \mathcal{R} m_j \iff \mathtt{re}(m_i) = j$,
- $\mathcal{S} \subseteq \mathcal{M} \times \mathcal{M}$ *is a binary* support *relation such that* $m_i \mathcal{S} m_j \iff \exists m \in \mathcal{M} :$ $m_i \mathcal{R} m$ *and* $m \mathcal{R} m_j$.

Take $\sim_{\mathcal{S}} \subseteq \mathcal{M} \times \mathcal{M}$ *to be the smallest equivalence relation containing* $\mathcal{S}$.

We define a *complete labelling* on a dialogue framework $DF = \langle \mathcal{M}, \mathcal{T}, \mathcal{R}, \mathcal{S} \rangle$ such that the label of a move $m \in \mathcal{M}$ is IN iff a) for every move m' that targets or replies to m, m' is labelled OUT; and b) if m supports a move m'' and there is a move m''' targeting m'', then for every such move m''', m''' is labelled OUT (intuitively, since m's enthymeme forward extends m''''s enthymeme, then any challenge on m'' is a challenge on m, and so must be OUT in order that m be IN). Additionally, $m \in \mathcal{M}$ is labelled OUT iff a) there is a move m' that targets or replies to m such that m' is labelled IN; or b) there is a move m'' that m supports (i.e., m's enthymeme forward extends m''''s enthymeme) such that there is a move m''' that targets m'' and m''' is labelled IN. Figure 4 shows a complete labelling on a DF. A move $m \in \mathcal{M}$ is labelled UNDEC iff it is not labelled IN or OUT.

Definition 9. *Let* $DF = \langle \mathcal{M}, \mathcal{T}, \mathcal{R}, \mathcal{S} \rangle$ *be the dialogue framework of a dialogue* d. *We define a* **complete labelling** *on* DF *to be a (total) function* $\mathsf{L} : \mathcal{M} \to$ $\{$IN, OUT, UNDEC$\}$ *such that, for every* $m_i \in \mathcal{M}$:

1. $\mathsf{L}(m_i) = $ IN *iff for all* $m_j, m_k \in \mathcal{M}$:
   (a) *if* $(m_j, m_i) \in \mathcal{T} \cup \mathcal{R}$ *then* $\mathsf{L}(m_j) = $ OUT, *and*
   (b) *if* $(m_i, m_j) \in \mathcal{S}$ *and* $(m_k, m_j) \in \mathcal{T}$ *then* $\mathsf{L}(m_k) = $ OUT;
2. $\mathsf{L}(m_i) = $ OUT *iff there is some* $m_j, m_k \in \mathcal{M}$ *such that:*
   (a) $(m_j, m_i) \in \mathcal{T} \cup \mathcal{R}$ *and* $\mathsf{L}(m_j) = $ IN, *or*
   (b) $(m_i, m_j) \in \mathcal{S}$, $(m_k, m_j) \in \mathcal{T}$ *and* $\mathsf{L}(m_k) = $ IN.

We define an *argumentation theory instantiated by a dialogue* d as a tuple $AT_d = \langle AS_d, K_d \rangle$, where the logical language L, the contrariness function $(\bar{\ })$, the naming function nom, and the strict rules R_s of AS_d are those shared by the participants of d (as assumed in Definition 7). The *defeasible rules* of AS_d is the set of all the defeasible rules revealed during d. The *premises* in AT_d (i.e., K_d) is the set of the labels of the leaves of the enthymemes that have been moved during d with an assert move; this is because, as described earlier, the content E of an assert move is an upwards extendable enthymeme and so its leaves are the premises of the argument A from which E was constructed (according to Definition 5), whereas all the other elements of L in E and in the content E' of every hence move in d are the conclusions of inference rules. Lastly, we define an *argumentation theory of an agent* Ag *instantiated by a dialogue* d as a tuple $AT_d^{\text{Ag}} = \langle AS_d^{\text{Ag}}, K_d^{\text{Ag}} \rangle$ where $L, (\bar{\cdot}), nom$ and R_s are the same elements as explained earlier, the defeasible rules of AS_d^{Ag} is the set of defeasible rules revealed during d together with the defeasible rules that Ag knows, and K_d^{Ag} is the set of premises revealed during d together with the premises that Ag knows.

Definition 10. *Let* $d = [m_0, \dots, m_\ell]$ *be a dialogue between Prop and Op, where* $AS_{\text{Ag}} = \langle L, (\bar{\cdot}), R_{\text{Ag}}, nom \rangle$ *is the argumentation system for* Ag $\in \{Prop, Op\}$ *and* $R_{\text{Ag}} = R_s \cup R_{def}^{\text{Ag}}$. *The* **set of defeasible rules in** d *is given by:*

$$\mathsf{DefDRules}(d) = \bigcup_{i=0}^{\ell} \left\{ \mathsf{lab}_{\mathsf{c}(m_i)}(n) \in R_{def}^* \mid \mathsf{c}(m_i) \in \mathcal{E}^* \text{ and } n \in \mathsf{Nodes}(\mathsf{c}(m_i)) \right\}.$$

The **set of premises in** d *is:*

$$\mathsf{DPrem}(d) = \bigcup_{i=0}^{\ell} \left\{ \mathsf{lab}_{\mathsf{c}(m_i)}(n) \in L \mid \mathsf{l}(m_i) = \mathsf{assert} \text{ and } n \in \mathsf{Leaves}(\mathsf{c}(m_i)) \right\}.$$

The **argumentation theory instantiated by dialogue** d *is* $AT_d = \langle AS_d, K_d \rangle$, *where* $AS_d = \langle L, (\bar{\cdot}), R_s \cup \mathsf{DefDRules}(d), nom \rangle$ *and* $K_d = \mathsf{DPrem}(d)$.
The **argumentation theory of** Ag **instantiated by dialogue** d *is* $AT_d^{\text{Ag}} = \langle AS_d^{\text{Ag}}, K_d^{\text{Ag}} \rangle$, *where* $AS_d = \langle L, (\bar{\cdot}), R_s \cup \mathsf{DefDRules}(d) \cup R_{def}^{\text{Ag}}, nom \rangle$ *and* $K_d = \mathsf{DPrem}(d) \cup K_{\text{Ag}}$.

Example 1. From Table 1 and Fig. 3, $K_d = \{pub; \neg pf; \neg ap; rp; en; f; se\}$ and $\mathsf{DefDRules}(d) = \{\neg ap \Rightarrow \neg pi; \neg pf, \neg pi, pr \Rightarrow \neg pub; en \Rightarrow pf; se \Rightarrow pub\}$.

4   Soundness and Completeness

In this section we show a soundness and completeness correspondence between the status of moves made in a dialogue (as determined by a complete labelling on the dialogue framework) and the status of the intended arguments of those moves in the argument framework instantiated by the dialogue (as determined by a complete labelling on the argument framework). This correspondence depends on agents being *honest* and *understanding*, and on the dialogue being *exhaustive*.

If the participants of a dialogue are *honest* then the content of the first move is the same as its intended argument and there is no intended targeted argument (since the first move does not have a target). It also means that the intended argument of a move, whose content is an enthymeme, is an argument that the sender can construct based on their own private knowledge and the knowledge shared so far during the dialogue. If the participants of a dialogue are honest, this ensures that whenever they **assert** an enthymeme, this can indeed be upwards extended to provide the intended argument of the move, and the intended argument does defeat the intended targeted argument of the move (i.e., what the sender assumes to be the target move's intended argument) according to the $ASPIC^+$ definition of defeat.[5] An honest agent will only make an **and-so** move requesting an upwards extension to a previously asserted enthymeme, if that enthymeme does not defeat the content of its target (the intuition here is that an honest agent will not make spurious **and-so** moves when it is clear from the publicly moved information why an enthymeme has been moved). Finally, if an honest agent makes a **hence** move to supply an upwards extension to a previously asserted (and subsequently questioned with an **and-so**) enthymeme, then the intended argument of the **hence** move is the same as the intended argument of the questioned enthymeme, and the content of the **hence** move is the upwards extension to the enthymeme that yields this intended argument.

Definition 11. *Let* $d = [m_0, \ldots, m_\ell]$ *be a dialogue between Prop and Op, and* $DF = \langle \mathcal{M}, \mathcal{T}, \mathcal{R}, \mathcal{S} \rangle$ *the dialogue framework of d. Then* $\mathsf{Ag} \in \{Prop, Op\}$ *is* ***honest*** *with respect to d iff for every* $i \le \ell$ *such that* $\mathsf{s}(m_i) = \mathsf{Ag}$:

1. *If* $i = 0$, *then* $\mathsf{c}(m_i) = \mathsf{IntArg}(m_i)$ *and* $\mathsf{IntTarArg}(m_i) = \emptyset$;
2. *If* $\mathsf{c}(m_i) \in \mathcal{E}^*$, *then* $\mathsf{IntArg}(m_i) \in \mathcal{A}_{AT^{Ag}_{d_i}}$;
3. *If* $\mathsf{l}(m_i) = \mathsf{assert}$ *and* $m_i \mathcal{T} m_j$, *then* $\mathsf{c}(m_i) \le \mathsf{IntArg}(m_i)$, $\mathsf{c}(m_j) \le \mathsf{IntTarArg}(m_i)$, *and* $\mathsf{IntArg}(m_i)$ *defeats* $\mathsf{IntTarArg}(m_i)$;
4. *If* $\mathsf{l}(m_i) = \mathsf{and\text{-}so}$, $m_i \mathcal{R} m_j$ *and* $m_j \mathcal{T} m_k$, *then* $\mathsf{c}(m_j)$ *does not defeat* $\mathsf{IntArg}(m_k)$;
5. *If* $\mathsf{l}(m_i) = \mathsf{hence}$, $m_i \mathcal{R} m_j$ *and* $m_j \mathcal{R} m_k$, *then* $\mathsf{IntArg}(m_i) = \mathsf{IntArg}(m_k)$, *and* $\mathsf{IntArg}(m_i) = \mathsf{c}(m_i) \cup \mathsf{c}(m_k)$.

Example 2. Based on Table 1 and Fig. 3, we assume A is preferred to E since E is just a statement, whereas A is an argument whose claim is supported by some rationale. We also assume D is preferred to A since in the example's assumed context (the editorial board of a newspaper) financial considerations take precedence. Therefore, *Prop* and *Op* are honest.

Suppose an honest agent asserts an enthymeme E, their counterpart replies to E with an **and-so** move and the agent replies with a **hence** move whose content is an enthymeme E'. We know that E and E' are enthymemes of the same intended argument A (essentially, if there are two moves m and m' in d such that their contents are enthymemes and either $m = m'$ or there is a support relationship between m and m' then their intended arguments are the same).

Lemma 1. *Let* $d = [m_0, \ldots, m_\ell]$ *be a dialogue between Prop and Op who are honest with respect to d. If* $m_i \sim_{\mathcal{S}} m_j$ $(j, i \le \ell)$ *then* $\mathsf{IntArg}(m_i) = \mathsf{IntArg}(m_j)$.

---

[5] We assume that the participants of a dialogue have the same preferences and so they agree to whether an argument A defeats an argument B or not.

Proof. The proof is straightforward and follows from Definitions 7, 8 and 11.5.
□

When an honest participant moves an enthymeme E against an enthymeme E', their belief is that their intended argument of E defeats the intended argument of E'. However, they may be mistaken about the intended argument of E'. To deal with the full range of misunderstandings that can ensure thorough use of enthymemes, a large number of locutions is needed (as shown in [14]). For reasons of space, in this paper we assume that these misunderstandings do not arise so that we can restrict the locutions we require to a small set. We thus assume *understanding* participants; i.e., the intended targeted arguments of the moves they make correctly match each other. For example, *Prop* and *Op* from Table 1 are understanding.

Definition 12. *Let* $d = [m_0, \ldots, m_\ell]$ *be a dialogue between Prop and Op. Prop and Op are* **understanding agents** *(with respect to d) iff for every* $i = 0, \ldots, \ell$, *if* $1(m_i) = $ assert, *then* $\mathsf{IntTarArg}(m_i) = \mathsf{IntArg}(m_j)$ *where* $\mathsf{t}(m_i) = j$.

A dialogue d with honest and understanding participants is *exhaustive* iff: if there is an argument that can be constructed from the argument framework instantiated by d and that argument defeats the intended argument of some move m, then that argument has been asserted to target m', where either $m' = m$, or there is a support relation between m and m' (since the participants are honest, by Lemma 1, m and m' have the same intended argument and so an agent can target either one of the two moves); if an enthymeme has been asserted and does not defeat its target, then an and-so has been moved as a reply to the assertion (requesting that the enthymeme be extended to make the defeat explicit); and if an and-so is moved, then it is responded to. This is similar to Prakken's [13] notion of logical completeness.

Definition 13. *Let* $d = [m_0, \ldots, m_\ell]$ *be a dialogue with participants who are both honest and understanding with respect to d. Let* $DF = \langle \mathcal{M}, \mathcal{T}, \mathcal{R}, \mathcal{S} \rangle$ *be the dialogue framework of d and* $AF = \langle \mathcal{A}_{AT_d}, Dfs \rangle$ *be the argument framework instantiated by the argumentation theory* AT_d. *We say that d is* **exhaustive** *iff for every* $i \leq \ell$:

1. *if there are* $A, B \in \mathcal{A}_{AT_d}$ *such that* $\mathsf{IntArg}(m_i) = A$ *and* B *defeats* A, *then there are moves* $m_j, m_k \in \mathcal{M}$ *such that* $\mathsf{IntArg}(m_j) = B$, $m_i \sim_S m_k$ *and* $\mathsf{t}(m_j) = k$;
2. *if* $1(m_i) = $ assert *and* $\mathsf{c}(m_i)$ *does not defeat* $\mathsf{IntTarArg}(m_i)$, *then there is a move* m_j *where* $j > i$ *such that* $1(m_j) = $ and-so *and* $\mathsf{re}(m_j) = i$;
3. *if* $1(m_i) = $ and-so, *then there is a move* m_j *where* $j > i$, *such that* $1(m_j) = $ hence *and* $\mathsf{re}(m_j) = i$;

Example 3. The dialogue given in Table 1 is not exhaustive since there is no and-so move that replies to m_4.

If a dialogue d is exhaustive with honest and understanding participants, then for every move made whose content is an enthymeme, its intended argument can be instantiated by the argumentation theory instantiated by d. In what follows, let $d = [m_0, \ldots, m_l]$ be an exhaustive dialogue between agents *Prop* and *Op* who are both honest and understanding with respect to d, and let $DF = \langle \mathcal{M}, \mathcal{T}, \mathcal{R}, \mathcal{S} \rangle$ and $AF = \langle \mathcal{A}_{AT_d}, Dfs \rangle$ be, respectively, the dialogue framework of d and the argument framework instantiated by AT_d.

Lemma 2. *For every $m_i \in \mathcal{M}$, if $\mathsf{c}(m_i) \in \mathcal{E}^*$ then $\mathsf{IntArg}(m_i) \in \mathcal{A}_{AT_d}$.*

Proof. Let $m_i \in \mathcal{M}$ be such that $\mathsf{c}(m_i) \in \mathcal{E}^*$, and let $E_i = \mathsf{c}(m_i)$. If $E_i = \mathsf{IntArg}(m_i)$ then, by Definition 10, the premises of E_i belong to K_d and the defeasible rules of E_i belong to $\mathsf{DefDRules}(d)$ so $\mathsf{IntArg}(m_i) \in \mathcal{A}_{AT_d}$. Otherwise $E_i \neq \mathsf{IntArg}(m_i)$ and, by Definitions 11.3 and 11.5, we must have that $E_i \leq \mathsf{IntArg}(m_i)$. We have two cases:

Case 1) Suppose that $\mathsf{l}(m_i) = \mathsf{assert}$. So by Definition 11.3, $E_i \leq \mathsf{IntArg}(m_i)$ and $\mathsf{IntArg}(m_i)$ defeats $\mathsf{IntTarArg}(m_i)$. By Definition 7.3, and since $E_i \neq \mathsf{IntArg}(m_i)$ and $E_i \leq \mathsf{IntArg}(m_i)$, E_i is an upwards extendable enthymeme of $\mathsf{IntArg}(m_i)$ and $\mathsf{Conc}(E_i) \neq \mathsf{Conc}(\mathsf{IntArg}(m_i))$, so E_i does not defeat $\mathsf{IntTarArg}(m_i)$. Thus, by Definitions 13.2 and 13.3, there are moves $m, m_j \in \mathcal{M}$ such that $m_j \mathcal{R} m \mathcal{R} m_i$. By Definition 11.5, $\mathsf{IntArg}(m_i) = \mathsf{c}(m_i) \cup \mathsf{c}(m_j)$. Therefore, $\mathsf{IntArg}(m_i) \in \mathcal{A}_{AT_d}$.

Case 2) Suppose that $\mathsf{l}(m_i) = \mathsf{hence}$. So by Definition 7.5, there are moves $m, m_j \in \mathcal{M}$ such that $m_i \mathcal{R} m \mathcal{R} m_j$ and, by Definition 11.5, $\mathsf{IntArg}(m_i) = \mathsf{c}(m_i) \cup \mathsf{c}(m_j)$. Therefore, $\mathsf{IntArg}(m_i) \in \mathcal{A}_{AT_d}$. $\quad\square$

If a dialogue d is exhaustive, with honest and understanding participants, and includes a move m_i that targets m_j, then the intended argument of m_i defeats the intended argument of m_j in the AF instantiated by d (i.e., if there is a targeting relationship between two moves in the DF then there is also a defeat relationship between their intended arguments in the AF instantiated by d).

Lemma 3. *If there are moves $m_i, m_j \in \mathcal{M}$ such that $(m_i, m_j) \in \mathcal{T}$ then it holds that $(\mathsf{IntArg}(m_i), \mathsf{IntArg}(m_j)) \in Dfs$.*

Proof. By Lemma 2, for every $m_i \in \mathcal{M}$ such that $\mathsf{c}(m_i) \in \mathcal{E}^*$, $\mathsf{IntArg}(m_i) \in \mathcal{A}_{AT_d}$. By Definitions 11.3 and 12, $\mathsf{IntArg}(m_i)$ defeats $\mathsf{IntArg}(m_j)$.
$\quad\square$

We now show our main result. If a dialogue is exhaustive, with participants who are honest and understanding, then the dialectical status of the moves in the DF (determined by a complete labelling) is sound and complete in relation to the dialectical status of the arguments in the AF instantiated by the contents of the moves made in the dialogue (determined by a complete labelling).

Theorem 1. *Let $d = [m_0, \ldots, m_\ell]$ be an exhaustive dialogue between Prop and Op, who are honest and understanding with respect to d. Let $DF = \langle \mathcal{M}, \mathcal{T}, \mathcal{R}, \mathcal{S} \rangle$ be the dialogue framework of d, and $AF = \langle \mathcal{A}_{AT_d}, Dfs \rangle$ the argument framework instantiated by the argumentation theory AT_d. It follows that:*

(i) *For every complete labelling function* L_{AF} *on AF, there exists a complete labelling function* L_{DF} *on DF such that for every* $m_i \in \mathcal{M}$*, if* $\mathsf{c}(m_i) \in \mathcal{E}^*$ *then:*

$$\mathsf{L}_{DF}(m_i) = \mathsf{L}_{AF}(\mathsf{IntArg}(m_i)).$$

(ii) *For every complete labelling function* L_{DF} *on DF, there exists a complete labelling function* L_{AF} *on AF such that for every* $A \in \mathcal{A}_{AT_d}$*, if there is some* $m_i \in \mathcal{M}$ *such that* $A = \mathsf{IntArg}(m_i)$ *then:*

$$\mathsf{L}_{AF}(A) = \mathsf{L}_{DF}(m_i).$$

Proof. (i) Let L_{AF} be a complete labelling on AF and define a new function L_{DF} on DF such that for all $m_i \in \mathcal{M}$,

$$\mathsf{L}_{DF}(m_i) = \mathsf{L}_{AF}(\mathsf{IntArg}(m_i)) \tag{1}$$

if $\mathsf{c}(m_i) \in \mathcal{E}^*$ and the usual

$$\mathsf{L}_{DF}(m_i) = \begin{cases} \text{IN} & \text{if } \forall m_j \in \mathcal{M}; m_j \mathcal{R} m_i \text{ implies } \mathsf{L}_{DF}(m_j) = \text{OUT}, \\ \text{OUT} & \text{if } \exists m_j \in \mathcal{M}; m_j \mathcal{R} m_i \text{ and } \mathsf{L}_{DF}(m_j) = \text{IN}, \\ \text{UNDEC} & \text{otherwise} \end{cases} \tag{2}$$

if $\mathsf{c}(m_i) \notin \mathcal{E}^*$, which is to say, when $\mathsf{l}(m_i) = \text{and-so}$.

We claim that L_{DF} is a complete labelling on DF, so suppose $m_i \in \mathcal{M}$:

   Case 1) Suppose that $\mathsf{L}_{DF}(m_i) = \text{IN}$.

   – Suppose to the contrary that there is some $m_j \in \mathcal{M}$ such that $(m_j, m_i) \in \mathcal{T}$ and $\mathsf{L}_{DF}(m_j) \neq \text{OUT}$. It follows that $\mathsf{c}(m_i), \mathsf{c}(m_j) \in \mathcal{E}^*$ and $\mathsf{L}_{AF}(\mathsf{IntArg}(m_j)) \neq \text{OUT}$. Based on Lemma 3, we have that $(\mathsf{IntArg}(m_j), \mathsf{IntArg}(m_i)) \in \mathit{Dfs}$ in AF and since $\mathsf{L}_{AF}(\mathsf{IntArg}(m_j)) \neq \text{OUT}$, we have that $\mathsf{L}_{AF}(\mathsf{IntArg}(m_i)) \neq \text{IN}$, contrary to (1).

   – Suppose to the contrary that there is some $m_j \in \mathcal{M}$ such that $(m_j, m_i) \in \mathcal{R}$ and $\mathsf{L}_{DF}(m_j) \neq \text{OUT}$. From (2) we must have that $\mathsf{c}(m_i) \in \mathcal{E}^*$ and hence $\mathsf{l}(m_j) = \text{and-so}$. By Definition 13.3, there is some $m_k \in \mathcal{M}$ such that $\mathsf{c}(m_k) \in \mathcal{E}^*$ and $(m_k, m_j) \in \mathcal{R}$. By (2) we must have that $\mathsf{L}_{DF}(m_k) \neq \text{IN}$ and so by (1), $\mathsf{L}_{AF}(\mathsf{IntArg}(m_k)) \neq \text{IN}$. By Lemma 1, we then have that $\mathsf{IntArg}(m_i) = \mathsf{IntArg}(m_k)$ and so $\mathsf{L}_{AF}(\mathsf{IntArg}(m_i)) \neq \text{IN}$, contrary to (1).

   – Suppose to the contrary that there is some $m_j, m_k \in \mathcal{M}$ such that $(m_i, m_j) \in \mathcal{S}$, $(m_k, m_j) \in \mathcal{T}$ and $\mathsf{L}_{DF}(m_k) \neq \text{OUT}$, and so we have that $\mathsf{L}_{DF}(m_j) \neq \text{IN}$. Then $\mathsf{c}(m_i), \mathsf{c}(m_k) \in \mathcal{E}^*$ and by (1), we have that $\mathsf{L}_{AF}(\mathsf{IntArg}(m_k)) \neq \text{IN}$. Then by Lemma 1, we have that $\mathsf{IntArg}(m_i) = \mathsf{IntArg}(m_k)$ and so $\mathsf{L}_{AF}(\mathsf{IntArg}(m_i)) \neq \text{IN}$, contrary to (1).

Conversely, suppose that $\mathsf{L}_{DF}(m_i) \neq \text{IN}$. If $\mathsf{c}(m_i) \notin \mathcal{E}^*$ then by (2), there is some $m_j \in \mathcal{M}$ such that $(m_j, m_i) \in \mathcal{R}$ and $\mathsf{L}_{DF}(m_j) \neq \text{OUT}$, as required. Otherwise, by (1), $\mathsf{L}_{AF}(\mathsf{IntArg}(m_i)) \neq \text{IN}$. Hence, according to Definition 3 there is some $A \in \mathcal{A}_{AT_d}$ such that $(A, \mathsf{IntArg}(m_i)) \in \mathit{Dfs}$ and $\mathsf{L}_{AF}(A) \neq \text{OUT}$. By Definition 13.1, there are moves $m_i', m_j \in \mathcal{M}$

such that $m_i \sim_S m_i'$, $(m_j, m_i') \in \mathcal{T}$ and $\mathsf{IntArg}(m_j) = A$. It follows from (1) that $\mathsf{L}_{DF}(m_j) = \mathsf{L}_{AF}(\mathsf{IntArg}(m_j)) \neq \text{OUT}$. While by Lemma 1 we have that $\mathsf{IntArg}(m_i') = \mathsf{IntArg}(m_i)$, and so again from (1), $\mathsf{L}_{DF}(m_i') = \mathsf{L}_{AF}(\mathsf{IntArg}(m_i')) \neq \text{IN}$. Then, by Definition 8, we have three cases:

- If $m_i = m_i'$ then we are done since $(m_j, m_i') \in \mathcal{T}$ and $\mathsf{L}_{DF}(m_j) \neq \text{OUT}$.
- If $(m_i', m_i) \in \mathcal{S}$ then, by Definition 8, there is some $m \in \mathcal{M}$ such that $(m_i', m), (m, m_i) \in \mathcal{R}$. Since $\mathsf{L}_{DF}(m_i') \neq \text{IN}$, by (1), we then have that $\mathsf{L}_{DF}(m) \neq \text{OUT}$, so we are done.
- If $(m_i, m_i') \in \mathcal{S}$ then we are done, since $\mathsf{L}_{DF}(m_j) \neq \text{OUT}$ and also $(m_j, m_i') \in \mathcal{T}$.

Case 2) This case is analogous to Case 1 and is proved similarly.

(ii) Let L_{DF} be a complete labelling on DF. According to Lemma 2, we have that $\mathsf{IntArg}(m_i) \in \mathcal{A}_{AT_d}$ for every $m_i \in \mathcal{M}$ with $c(m_i) \in \mathcal{E}^*$, and so for each $m_i \in \mathcal{M}$ let $IntArgs = \{\mathsf{IntArg}(m_i) \mid m_i \in \mathcal{M}\}$, and define a function L_{AF} on AF by taking

$$\mathsf{L}_{AF}(A_i) = \mathsf{L}_{DF}(m_i) \tag{3}$$

for all $A_i = \mathsf{IntArg}(m_i) \in IntArgs$—since the dialogue is exhaustive we have that for every move m_i, m_j of the dialogue if $\mathsf{IntArg}(m_i) = \mathsf{IntArg}(m_j)$ then $\mathsf{L}_{DF}(m_i) = \mathsf{L}_{DF}(m_j)$ and so this function is well-defined. For $A \notin IntArgs$ we have the usual

$$\mathsf{L}_{AF}(A) = \begin{cases} \text{IN} & \text{if } \forall B \in \mathcal{A}_{AT_d}; (B, A) \in Dfs \text{ implies } \mathsf{L}_{AF}(B) = \text{OUT}, \\ \text{OUT} & \text{if } \exists B \in \mathcal{A}_{AT_d}; (B, A) \in Dfs \text{ and } \mathsf{L}_{AF}(B) = \text{IN}, \\ \text{UNDEC} & \text{otherwise.} \end{cases} \tag{4}$$

We claim that L_{AF} is a complete labelling on AF, so suppose $A \in \mathcal{A}_{AT_d}$:

Case 1) Suppose that $\mathsf{L}_{AF}(A) = \text{IN}$ and suppose to the contrary that there is some $B \in \mathcal{A}_{AT_d}$ such that $(B, A) \in Dfs$ and $\mathsf{L}_{AF}(B) \neq \text{OUT}$. It follows from (4) that $A \in IntArgs$ so let $m_i \in \mathcal{M}$ be a move such that $A = \mathsf{IntArg}(m_i)$. By Definition 13.1, there are some $m_j, m_k \in \mathcal{M}$ such that $B = \mathsf{IntArg}(m_j)$, $m_i \sim_S m_k$ and $(m_j, m_k) \in \mathcal{T}$. By Lemma 1, $\mathsf{IntArg}(m_i) = \mathsf{IntArg}(m_k) = A$. It then follows from (3) that $\mathsf{L}_{DF}(m_k) = \mathsf{L}_{AF}(A) = \text{IN}$ and $\mathsf{L}_{DF}(m_j) = \mathsf{L}_{AF}(B) \neq \text{OUT}$, contrary to Definition 9. Conversely, suppose that $\mathsf{L}_{AF}(A) \neq \text{IN}$. If $A \notin IntArgs$ then there is some $B \in \mathcal{A}_{AT_d}$ such that $(B, A) \in Dfs$ and $\mathsf{L}_{AF}(B) \neq \text{OUT}$, as required. So suppose that $A = \mathsf{IntArg}(m_i)$ for some $m_i \in \mathcal{M}$. By (3) we have that $\mathsf{L}_{DF}(m_i) = \mathsf{L}_{AF}(\mathsf{IntArg}(m_i)) \neq \text{IN}$. So there are three cases:

- Suppose there is an $m_j \in \mathcal{M}$ such that $(m_j, m_i) \in \mathcal{T}$ and $\mathsf{L}_{DF}(m_j) \neq \text{OUT}$. Hence, by Lemma 3, there is some $B = \mathsf{IntArg}(m_j) \in \mathcal{A}_{AT_d}$ such that $(B, A) \in Dfs$ and $\mathsf{L}_{AF}(B) = \mathsf{L}_{DF}(m_j) \neq \text{OUT}$.
- Suppose there is an $m_j \in \mathcal{M}$ such that $(m_j, m_i) \in \mathcal{R}$ and that $\mathsf{L}_{DF}(m_j) \neq \text{OUT}$. It follows from Definitions 9 and 13.3 that there is some $m_k \in \mathcal{M}$ such that $(m_k, m_j) \in \mathcal{R}$ and $\mathsf{L}_{DF}(m_k) \neq \text{IN}$. It then follows that there is some $m_j' \in \mathcal{M}$ such that $(m_j', m_k) \in \mathcal{T}$ and $\mathsf{L}_{DF}(m_j') \neq \text{OUT}$. Hence, by Lemma 3, there is some $B =$

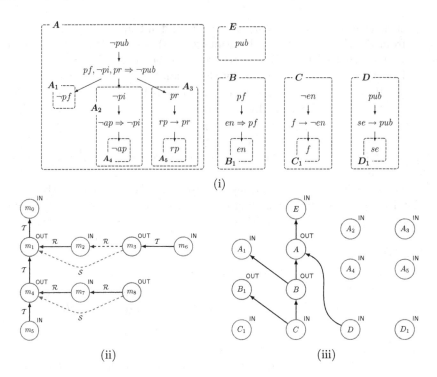

Fig. 5. (i). The arguments instantiated by $AT_{d'}$ enclosed by a dashed line. (ii) The dialogue framework $DF_{d'}$ of d'. (iii) The argument framework $AF_{d'}$ instantiated by $AT_{d'}$.

$\mathsf{IntArg}(m_j') \in \mathcal{A}_{AT_d}$ such that $(B, \mathsf{IntArg}(m_k)) \in Dfs$ and $\mathsf{L}_{AF}(B) = \mathsf{L}_{DF}(m_j') \neq \text{OUT}$. However, we have that $(m_k, m_i) \in S$ and so it follows from Lemma 1 that $\mathsf{IntArg}(m_k) = \mathsf{IntArg}(m_i) = A$, as required.

- Suppose there is some $m_j, m_k \in \mathcal{M}$ such that $(m_i, m_k) \in S$ and $(m_j, m_k) \in T$ and $\mathsf{L}_{DF}(m_j) \neq \text{OUT}$. Hence, by Lemma 3, there is some $B = \mathsf{IntArg}(m_j) \in \mathcal{A}_{AT_d}$ such that $(B, \mathsf{IntArg}(m_k)) \in Dfs$ and $\mathsf{L}_{AF}(B) = \mathsf{L}_{DF}(m_j) \neq \text{OUT}$. However, we have that $(m_i, m_k) \in S$ and so it follows from Lemma 1 that $\mathsf{IntArg}(m_k) = \mathsf{IntArg}(m_i) = A$, as required.

Case 2) This case is analogous to Case 1 and is proved similarly.

It is easy to understand that for any dialogue d, the label of the first move on DF shows the dialogical status of the topic t of d, since t is the conclusion of the argument moved by m_0. So, if d is exhaustive and its participants are honest and understanding (by Theorem 1) the acceptability of t in DF corresponds to the acceptability of t in the AF instantiated by d.

Example 4. Suppose d in Table 1 continues such that $d' = [m_0, \ldots, m_7, m_8]$ where $m_7 = \langle Op, \text{and-so}, \emptyset, 4, \emptyset \rangle$ and $m_8 = \langle Prop, \text{hence}, B, 7, \emptyset \rangle$ (see Fig. 5(i) for the internal structure of B). Suppose also that there are no other intended arguments that the participants can move in d' and that defeats have been calculated according to preferences. In other words, d' is exhaustive and its participants are honest and understanding. Figure 5(i) shows the arguments instantiated by $AT_{d'}$, whereas Fig. 5(ii) and 5(iii) show the $DF_{d'}$ and the $AF_{d'}$, respectively. In both frameworks the topic pub of d' is labelled IN, since m_0 is labelled IN in $DF_{d'}$ and $\mathsf{IntArg}(m_0)$ is labelled IN in $AF_{d'}$.

5 Conclusion

This paper introduces a novel dialogue system that handles upwards extendable enthymemes and instantiates a dialogue framework that is used to determine the dialogical status of the dialogue moves. As far as we are aware, there are no other works that handle upwards extendable enthymemes and also propose a mechanism for determining the status of the dialogue moves. Most importantly, we have shown that, for exhaustive dialogues with honest and understanding participants, there is a correspondence (under the complete semantics [15]) between the acceptability of the moves made during a dialogue and the acceptability of the intended arguments of those moves in the argument framework instantiated by the contents moved in the dialogue; similar to Prakken's [13] soundness and fairness results (which apply to a system that supports backwards extension of arguments, through a why move, but does not support upwards extendable enthymemes). This is important since it ensures the dialogue can be played out such that an enthymeme moved in the dialogue is only justified in the case that its intended argument is justified by the contents of the moves made in the dialogue. It is also worth highlighting that our paper is the first to formalise a sound and complete dialogical generalisation of the $ASPIC^+$ framework (soundness and completeness has not been shown for [4]).

This work is an important step towards defining how a dialogue framework is constructed for a more general dialogue system for handling enthymemes [14] that deals with both backward and forward extension of enthymemes—as well as the full range of misunderstandings that can occur as a result—such that there is a similar equivalence with the argument framework instantiated from the contents of the dialogue moves.

Note, the grounded and preferred labellings of an argument framework are the minimal and maximal complete labellings, respectively, whereas stable labellings are complete labellings with no arguments labelled as undecided [17]. Therefore, correspondence between complete labellings on the AF and DF as shown here can be extended to the grounded, preferred and stable labellings on the AF and DF, although we lack the space here to do so.

Our protocol allows participants to attack and reply to their own moves, request a forward extension for their own enthymemes and forward extend their interlocutor's enthymemes. This allows for cooperative, inquiry-style, dialogues where the participants jointly reason to determine the dialogical status of the topic, where it is natural to assume that the participants are honest. Our system also allows for more adversarial interactions, where the participants may act strategically to try to persuade one another; we will explore in future work how enthymemes might be used to give a strategic advantage to a participant (for example, an agent may omit some elements of its intended argument to make it harder for the receiver to identify counter arguments, or to make it harder for the receiver to identify whether the enthymeme does indeed defeat the argument it has been moved against).

References

1. Besnard, P., et al.: Introduction to structured argumentation. Argum. Comput. **5**, 1–4 (2014)
2. Black, E., Hunter, A.: A relevance-theoretic framework for constructing and deconstructing enthymemes. J. Log. Comput. **22**, 55–78 (2012)
3. Hosseini, S.-A., Modgil, S., Rodrigues, O.: Enthymeme construction in dialogues using shared knowledge. In: Proceedings of Computational Models of Argument, pp. 325–332 (2014)
4. Modgil, S.: Towards a general framework for dialogues that accommodate reasoning about preferences. In: Black, E., Modgil, S., Oren, N. (eds.) TAFA 2017. LNCS (LNAI), vol. 10757, pp. 175–191. Springer, Cham (2018). https://doi.org/10.1007/978-3-319-75553-3_13
5. Modgil, S.: Revisiting abstract argumentation. In: Proceedings of Theory and Applications of Formal Argumentation, pp. 1–15 (2013)
6. Modgil, S.: Dialogical scaffolding for human and artificial agent reasoning. In: Proceedings of Workshop on AI and Cognition, pp. 58–71 (2017)
7. Fan, X., Toni, F.: A general framework for sound assumption-based argumentation dialogues. Artif. Intell. **216**, 20–54 (2014)
8. Hunter, A.: Real arguments are approximate arguments. In: Proceedings of AAAI Conference on Artificial Intelligence, pp. 66–71 (2007)
9. Walton, D., Reed, C.: Argumentation schemes and enthymemes. Synthese **145**(3), 339–370 (2005)
10. Black, E., Hunter, A.: A generative inquiry dialogue system. In: Proceedings of Autonomous Agents and Multiagent Systems, pp. 1–8 (2007)
11. Hosseini, S-A.: Dialogues Incorporating Enthymemes and Modelling of Other Agents' Beliefs. PhD Thesis, King's College London (2017)
12. Dupin de Saint-Cyr, F.: Handling enthymemes in time-limited persuasion dialogs. In: Proceedings of International Conference on Scalable Uncertainty Management, pp. 149–162 (2011)
13. Prakken, H.: Coherence and flexibility in dialogue games for argumentation. J. Log. Comput. **15**, 1009–1040 (2005)
14. Xydis, A., Hampson, C., Modgil, S., Black, E.: Enthymemes in dialogues. In: Proceedings of Computational Models of Argument, pp. 395–402 (2020)
15. Dung, P.-M.: On the acceptability of arguments and its fundamental role in nonmonotonic reasoning, logic programming and n-person games. Artif. Intell. **77**(2), 321–357 (1995)
16. Modgil, S., Prakken, H.: Abstract rule-based argumentation. Handbook of Formal Argumentation, pp. 286–361 (2018)
17. Caminada, M.: On the issue of reinstatement in argumentation. In: Fisher, M., van der Hoek, W., Konev, B., Lisitsa, A. (eds.) JELIA 2006. LNCS (LNAI), vol. 4160, pp. 111–123. Springer, Heidelberg (2006). https://doi.org/10.1007/11853886_11
18. Walton, D.: Informal Logic: A Handbook for Critical Argumentation. Cambridge University Press, Cambridge (1989)

Short Papers and Extended Abstracts

A Henkin-Style Completeness Proof
for the Modal Logic S5

Bruno Bentzen[✉][iD]

Carnegie Mellon University, Pittsburgh, PA, USA

Abstract. This paper presents a recent formalization of a Henkin-style completeness proof for the propositional modal logic S5 using the Lean theorem prover. The proof formalized is close to that of Hughes and Cresswell [8], but the system, based on a different choice of axioms, is better described as a Mendelson system augmented with axiom schemes for K, T, S4, and B, and the necessitation rule as a rule of inference. The language has the false and implication as the only primitive logical connectives and necessity as the only primitive modal operator. The full source code is available online and has been typechecked with Lean 3.4.2.

Keywords: Modal logic · Completeness · Formal methods · Lean

1 Introduction

A proof of the completeness theorem for a given logic conforms to the Henkin style when it applies nonconstructive methods to build models out of maximal consistent sets of formulas (possibly after a Henkin language extension) using the deductive system itself. Henkin-style completeness proofs for modal logics have been around for over five decades [9] but the formal verification of completeness with respect to Kripke semantics is comparatively recent.

We present a formalization of a Henkin-style completeness proof for the propositional modal logic S5 using the Lean theorem prover. Although the proof is specific to S5, the same techniques can be applied to weaker normal modal systems such as K, T, S4, and B, by forgetting the appropriate extra accessibility conditions (as described in [8]). The formalization covers the syntax and semantics of S5, the deduction theorem, structural rules (weakening, contraction, exchange), the recursive enumerability of the language, and the soundness and completeness theorems. It has approximately 1,500 lines of code (but only two thirds of the development is required for the completeness proof). The full source code is available online. It has been typechecked with Lean 3.4.2.

The author thanks Jeremy Avigad, Mario Carneiro, Rajeev Goré, and Minchao Wu for helpful suggestions. An early version of this work was presented at the Lean Together 2019, Amsterdam, January 7–11, 2019. The source code described in this paper is publicly available online at: https://github.com/bbentzen/mpl/. An extended version is available at https://arxiv.org/abs/1910.01697.

© Springer Nature Switzerland AG 2021
P. Baroni et al. (Eds.): CLAR 2021, LNAI 13040, pp. 459–467, 2021.
https://doi.org/10.1007/978-3-030-89391-0_25

1.1   Related Work

The use of proof assistants in the mechanization of completeness proofs in the context of Kripke semantics has been recently studied in the literature for a variety of formal systems. Coquand [2] uses ALF to give a constructive formal proof of soundness and completeness w.r.t. Kripke models for intuitionistic propositional logic with implication as the sole logical constant. Building on Coquand's work, a constructive completeness proof w.r.t Kripke semantics for intuitionistic logic with implication and universal quantification has been verified with Coq by Heberlin and Lee [7]. Also using Coq, Doczal and Smolka present a constructive formal proof of completeness w.r.t. Kripke semantics and decidability of the forcing relation for an extension of modal logic K [4] and a variety of temporal logic [5]. In his formal verification of cut elimination for coalgebraic logics, Tews [13] provides a formalization of soundness and completeness proofs covering many different logics, including modal logic K.

To the best of our knowledge, our formalization of a Henkin-style completeness proof for propositional modal logic S5 is the first of its kind.[1] Our proof is close to that of Hughes and Cresswell [8], but given for a system based on a different choice of axioms. In Hughes and Cresswell's book, the basis of S5 is that of T plus an additional axiom. Here S5 is built on axiom schemes for K, T, S4 and B. This has the advantage that we can easily adapt the proof for different weaker systems. Another choice had to be made between using a deep or a shallow embedding for the formalization. Because our aim is metatheoretical, we use a deep embedding for the encoding of the syntax, as it allows us to prove metatheorems by structural induction on formulas or derivations.

1.2   Lean

Lean is an interactive theorem prover developed principally by Leonardo de Moura based on a version of dependent type theory known as the Calculus of Inductive Constructions [3,11]. Theorem proving in Lean can be done by constructing proof terms directly, as in Agda [10], by using tactics, imperative commands that describe how to construct a proof term, as in Coq [12], or by mixing them together in the same environment. Lean also supports classical reasoning, which is employed in the formalization along with the declaration of noncomputable constructions. The formalization also presupposes a few basic results on data structures which are not in the standard library, so, our development makes use of `mathlib`, the library of formalized mathematics for Lean [1].

In the remainder of this paper, Lean code will be used to illustrate design choices and give an overview of the proof method, not to discuss the proof itself. Interested readers are encouraged to consult `completeness.lean`, the main file

---

[1]   In independent work done roughly at the same time the author first completed this formalization in 2018, Wu and Goré [14] have described a formalization in Lean of modal tableaux for modal logics K, KT, and S4 with decision procedures with proofs of soundness and completeness. Also in 2018, but unknown to the author, From [6] formalized a Henkin-style completeness proof for system K in Isabelle.

of the formalization where the crucial proof steps are given in detail. We shall also give an informal proof sketch of the completeness theorem using mathematical notation to convey the key ideas of the proof.

2   Modal Logic

2.1   The Language

For simplicity, we shall work with a language which has implication ($\supset$) and the false ($\bot$) as the only primitive logical connectives, and necessity ($\Box$) as the only primitive modal operator. This language can be conveniently defined using inductive types in Lean:

```
inductive form {σ :nat} : Type
| atom : fin σ → form
| bot  : form
| impl : form → form → form
| box  : form → form
```

Using one of the four constructors displayed above (`atom`, `bot`, `impl`, `box`) is the only way to construct a term of type `form`. The elimination rule of this type is precisely the principle of induction on the structure of a formula.

While newly-defined terms are always exhibited in Polish notation by default, Lean supports unicode characters and has an extensible parser which allows the declaration of customized prefix or infix notations for terms and types.

```
prefix   '#'         := form.atom
notation '⊥'         := form.bot _
infix    '⊃'         := form.impl
notation '∼':40 p    := form.impl p (form.bot _)
prefix   '□':80      := form.box
prefix   '◇':80      := λ p, ∼(□ (∼ p))
```

Contexts are just sets of formulas. In Lean, sets are functions of type `A → Prop`:

```
def ctx : Type := set (form σ)
notation '·' := {}
notation Γ '·' p := set.insert p Γ
```

2.2   The Proof System

We define a Mendelson system augmented with axiom schemes for K, T, S4, and B, and the necessitation rule as a rule of inference. The proof system is implemented with a type of proofs, which is inductively defined as follows:

```
inductive prf : ctx σ → form σ → Prop
| ax {Γ} {p} (h :p∈ Γ): prf Γ p
| pl1 {Γ} {p q}        : prf Γ (p ⊃ (q ⊃ p))
| pl2 {Γ} {p q r}      : prf Γ ((p ⊃ (q ⊃ r)) ⊃ ((p ⊃ q) ⊃ (
    p ⊃ r)))
```

```
| p13 {Γ} {p q}                    : prf Γ (((~p) ⊃ ~q) ⊃ (((~p) ⊃ q) ⊃
    p)
| k  {Γ} {p q}                     : prf Γ (□(p ⊃ q) ⊃ (□p ⊃ □q))
| t  {Γ} {p}                       : prf Γ (□p ⊃ p)
| s4 {Γ} {p}                       : prf Γ (□p ⊃ □□p)
| b  {Γ} {p}                       : prf Γ (p ⊃ □◇p)
| mp {Γ} {p q} (hpq: prf Γ (p ⊃ q)) (hp :prf Γ p) :prf Γ q
| nec {Γ} {p} (h :prf · p) : prf Γ (□p)

notation Γ ' ⊢ₛ₅ ' p :=prf Γ p
notation Γ ' ⊬ₛ₅ ' p :=prf Γ p → false
```

2.3   Semantics

Kripke Models. The semantics for S5 are given by Kripke semantics. A model
$\mathcal{M}$ is a triple $\langle \mathcal{W}, \mathcal{R}, v \rangle$ where

- $\mathcal{W}$ is a non-empty set of objects called possible worlds;
- $\mathcal{R}$ is a binary, equivalence relation on possible worlds;
- v specifies the truth value of a formula at a world.

It is useful to let the members of $\mathcal{W}$ (possible worlds) be sets of formulas:

```
def wrld (σ :nat) := set (form σ)
```

Kripke models can be implemented as structures (inductive types with only one
constructor). This can be done using the **structure** command in Lean. We define
a 6-tuple composed of a domain, an accessibility relation, a valuation function,
and reflexivity, symmetry and transitivity proofs for the given relation:

```
structure model :=
(wrlds : set (wrld σ))
(access : wrld σ → wrld σ → bool)
(val : fin σ → wrld σ → bool)
(refl : ∀ w ∈ wrlds , access w w =tt)
(symm : ∀ w ∈ wrlds , ∀ v ∈ wrlds , access w v =tt → access v
    w =tt)
(trans : ∀ w ∈ wrlds , ∀ v ∈ wrlds , ∀ u ∈ wrlds ,
access w v = tt → access v u = tt → access w u = tt)
```

The Boolean type **bool** is used for truth values (i.e. either **tt** or **ff**).

Semantic Consequence. We have a forcing function which takes a model, a
formula, and a world as inputs and returns a boolean value. Non-modal connectives are given truth-functionally and a formula $\Box p$ is true at a world w iff if
$\mathcal{R}(w, v)$ then p is true at v, for all $v \in \mathcal{W}$:

```
def forces_form (M : model) : form σ → wrld σ → bool
| (#p)    := λ w, M.val p w
| (bot σ) := λ w, ff
```

```
|  (p ⊃ q)  := λ w, (bnot (forces_form p w)) ||(forces_form q w)
|  (□p)     := λ w, if (∀ v ∈ M.wrlds, w ∈ M.wrlds →
M.access w v = tt → forces_form p v =tt) then tt else ff
```

This function can be extended to contexts in the obvious way:

```
def forces_ctx (M : model) (Γ :ctx σ) :wrld σ → bool :=
λ w, if (∀ p, p ∈ Γ → forces_form M p w =tt) then tt else ff
```

A formula p is a semantic consequence of a context Γ iff, for all $\mathcal{M}$ and $w \in \mathcal{W}$, Γ being true at w in $\mathcal{M}$ implies p being true at w in $\mathcal{M}$.

```
inductive sem_csq (Γ :ctx σ) (p :form σ) :Prop
|  is_true (m : ∀ (M :model) (w : wrld σ),
forces_ctx M Γ w =tt → forces_form M p w =tt) : sem_csq

notation Γ '⊨_{s5}' p :=sem_csq Γ p
```

3   The Completeness Theorem

In this section we formalize a proof of completeness with respect to the proof system and semantics developed in the previous sections.

Theorem 1 (Completeness). *For every context Γ, any formula p that follows semantically from Γ is also derivable from Γ in the modal logic S5. In symbols:*

$$\Gamma \vDash_{S5} p \implies \Gamma \vdash_{S5} p$$

That is, every semantic consequence is also a syntactic consequence in S5.

The proof requires a non-constructive use of contraposition. We assume that both $\Gamma \vDash_{S5} p$ and $\Gamma \nvdash_{S5} p$ hold, and then derive a contradiction using the syntax to build a model $\mathcal{M} = \langle \mathcal{W}, \mathcal{R}, v \rangle$ (the canonical model) where Γ is true but p is false at a specific world in the domain.

We shall focus on sketching the formal argument for the following facts:

1. $\Gamma \cup \{\sim p\}$ has a maximal consistent extension $\Delta = \bigcup_{n \in \mathbb{N}} \Delta_n$, for

$$\Delta_0 := \Gamma \cup \{\sim p\}$$

$$\Delta_{n+1} := \begin{cases} \Delta_n \cup \{\varphi_{n+1}\} & \text{if } \Delta_n \cup \{\varphi_{n+1}\} \text{ is consistent} \\ \Delta_n \cup \{\sim\varphi_{n+1}\} & \text{otherwise} \end{cases}$$

2. There exists a canonical model where p is true at w iff $p \in w$;

Maximal Consistent Sets. We say that a context is maximal consistent if it is consistent and, moreover, for every formula expressible in the language, either it or its negation is contained in that context.

```
def is_max (Γ :ctx σ) :=is_consist Γ ∧ (∀ p, p ∈ Γ ∨ (∼p) ∈ Γ)
```

Our language is countable, so we can construct each Δ_{n+1} using natural numbers to run through the set of all formulas, deciding whether or not a number's corresponding formula (when it exists) is consistent with Δ_n or not. The enumerability of the language is expressed using `encodable` types, which are constructively countable types in Lean. Essentially, a type α is encodable when it has an injection `encode` : $\alpha \to$ `nat` and a (partial) inverse `decode` : `nat` $\to$ `option` α .

```
def insert_form (Γ :ctx σ) (p :form σ) :ctx σ :=
if is_consist (Γ , p) then , p else , ∼p

def insert_code (Γ :ctx σ) (n :nat) : ctx σ :=
match encodable.decode (form σ) n with
| none    := Γ
| some p := insert_form p
end

def maxn (Γ :ctx σ) :nat → ctx σ
| 0       := Γ
| (n+1) := insert_code (maxn n) n

def max (Γ :ctx σ) :ctx σ :=⋃ n, maxn Γ n
```

Before proceeding any further, we must show that Γ in contained in `max` Γ and that `max` Γ is maximal and consistent. For each `maxn` Γ n of the family of sets, we have Γ ⊆ `maxn` Γ n. So Γ must also be contained in their union, `max` Γ. This proof argument produces a term of type:

```
lemma subset_max_self {Γ :ctx σ} :Γ ⊆ max Γ
```

Now, every formula must be in the enumeration somewhere, so suppose that the formula p has index i. By the definition of `maxn` Γ i, either p or $\sim p$ is a member of `maxn` Γ i, so one of them is a member of `max` Γ. Thus, we have a term

```
theorem mem_or_mem_max {Γ :ctx σ} (p :form σ) :p ∈ max Γ ∨ (∼p)
    ∈ max Γ
```

Assume for the sake of contradiction that Γ is consistent but `max` Γ is not. By structural induction on the proof tree, we prove that there exists an i such that `maxn` Γ i is inconsistent. However, each `maxn` Γ i preserves consistency. This gives a function

```
lemma is_consist_max {Γ :ctx σ} :is_consist Γ → is_consist (
    max Γ)
```

The above proof sketches are implemented purely by unfolding definitions and inductive reasoning. They consist of approximately 150 lines of code in `completeness.lean`. There is even a one-line short case-reasoning proof that maximal consistent sets are closed under derivability:

```
lemma mem_max_of_prf {Γ :ctx σ} {p :form σ} (h₁ :is_max Γ)
(h₂ :Γ ⊢S5 p) :p ∈ Γ :=
(h₁.2 p).resolve_right (λ hn, h₁.1 (prf.mp (prf.ax hn) h₂))
```

The Canonical Model Construction. We build the model as follows:

- $\mathcal{W}$ is the set of all maximal consistent sets of formulas;
- $\mathcal{R}(w, v)$ iff $\Box p \in w$ implies $p \in v$;
- $\mathsf{v}(w, p) = 1$ if $w \in \mathcal{W}$ and $p \in w$, for a propositional letter p.

We have to show that $\mathcal{R}$ is an equivalence relation. Reflexivity translates as follows: $\Box p \in w$ implies $p \in w$ for a given world $w \in \mathcal{W}$. But this is easy because w is closed under derivability (it is a maximal consistent set of formulas) and our proof system has modus ponens and axiom schema (t).

Proving symmetry requires more work. Given any worlds $w, v \in \mathcal{W}$, suppose first that $\Box\varphi \in w$ implies $\varphi \in v$ for all formulas φ, and suppose that $\Box p \in v$. We want to show that $p \in w$. Since $\Diamond\Box p \supset p$ is a theorem of S5 (see `syntax/lemmas.lean`) we just have to prove that $\Diamond\Box p \in w$, or, equivalently, that $\Box\sim\Box p \notin w$. By contraposition on our initial hypothesis, it suffices to show that $\sim\Box p \notin v$. But $\Box p \in v$ and v is consistent.

For transitivity, we must show that $p \in u$, on the assumptions that $\Box p \in w$, that $\Box\varphi \in w$ implies $\varphi \in v$, and that $\Box\varphi \in v$ implies $\varphi \in u$, for any formula φ. In other words, we want to show that $\Box\Box p \in w$. But this follows from modus ponens and axiom scheme (s4).

This model construction is represented by the Lean code

```
def domain (σ :nat) : set (wrld σ) :={w | ctx.is_max w}

def unbox (w : wrld σ) :wrld σ :={p | (□p) ∈ w}

def access : wrld σ → wrld σ → bool :=
λ w v, if (unbox w ⊆ v) then tt else ff

def val : fin σ → wrld σ → bool :=
λ p w, if w ∈ domain σ ∧ (#p) ∈ w then tt else ff

lemma mem_unbox_iff_mem_box {p : form σ} {w :wrld σ} :
p ∈ unbox w ↔ (□p) ∈ w :=⟨ id, id ⟩
```

What is here called **unbox** is a set operation which takes a set of formulas w as an input and returns the set of formulas p such that $\Box p$ is a member of w.

A useful lemma about this operation is that if p is deducible from **unbox** w then actually $\Box p \in w$. It can be proved by structural induction on the derivation using the necessitation rule, giving us a term:

```
lemma mem_box_of_unbox_prf {p : form σ} {w :wrld σ}
(H : w ∈ domain σ) :(unbox w ⊢ₛ₅ p) → (□p) ∈ w
```

Truth and Membership. To prove completeness, we first show that a formula is true at a world in the canonical model iff it is a member of that world:

```
lemma form_tt_iff_mem_wrld {p : form σ} :
∀ (w ∈ domain σ), (forces_form model w p) = tt ↔ p ∈ w
```

Here model is the canonical model defined in the previous section. To prove this, we use induction on the structure of the formula p.

In the proof mechanization, we use the induction tactic in the tactic mode. This tactic produces four goals, of which the fourth is the most relevant one. To prove it, we begin by assuming the inductive hypothesis for p. If w is a world, and, if it is a maximal consistent set of formulas, then, by unfolding the definition of truth of a formula at a world in a model, the biconditional statement becomes

```
⊢ (∀ (v : wrld σ),
v ∈ model.wrlds → w ∈ model.wrlds → model.access w v = tt →
    forces_form model w p = tt) ↔ (□p) ∈ w)
```

In the forwards direction, we assume that $\Box p$ is true at w in the canonical model and that $\sim\Box p \in w$. But then, by lemma mem_box_of_unbox_prf, the context unbox $w \cup \{\sim p\}$ is consistent and can be extended to a maximal consistent set (i.e. a world in the domain). It is accessible to w because unbox $w \subseteq$ max (unbox $w \cup \{\sim p\}$), so p should be true at w. But $p \notin$ max (unbox $w \cup \{\sim p\}$) because it is consistent.

For the backwards direction, assume that $\Box p \in w$. Given a maximal consistent set of formulas v and assuming that $\Box\varphi \in w$ then $\varphi \in v$ for all φ, we have to show that p is true at v in the model. By the inductive hypothesis, however, it suffices to show that $p \in v$, but this follows from $\Box p \in w$.

The Completeness Proof. We now complete our proof by putting together all the above pieces into 24 lines of code. Since we know by hypothesis that $\Gamma \nvdash_{S5} p$, it follows that $\Gamma \cup \{\sim p\}$ is consistent–otherwise, if the false were deducible from it, we would have a contradiction by double negation elimination.

```
lemma consist_not_of_not_prf {Γ : form σ} {p : form σ} :
(Γ ⊬ₛ₅ p) → is_consist (Γ , ~p) :=λ hnp hc, hnp (mp dne (
    deduction hc))
```

Now assuming that $\Gamma \vDash_{S5} p$, the basic idea for deriving the contradiction is that, as max $\Gamma \cup \{\sim p\}$ is a world in the canonical model, and each formula $\varphi \in \Gamma$ is true at that world, Γ is true as well. Clearly, p is not consistent with $\Gamma \cup \{\sim p\}$, so $p \notin$ max $\Gamma \cup \{\sim p\}$, meaning that p must be false at that world.

This allows us to prove the desired theorem

```
theorem completenss {Γ : form σ} {p : form σ} :(Γ ⊨ₛ₅ p) → Γ ⊢ₛ₅
```

Acknowledgments. Work supported in part by the AFOSR grant FA9550-18-1-0120. Any opinions, findings and conclusions or recommendations expressed in this material are those of the author(s) and do not necessarily reflect the views of the AFOSR.

References

1. Carneiro, M.: The lean 3 mathematical library (mathlib) (2018). https:// robertylewis.com/files/icms/Carneiro_mathlib.pdf. International Congress on Mathematical Software
2. Coquand, C.: A formalised proof of the soundness and completeness of a simply typed lambda-calculus with explicit substitutions. Higher-Order Symb. Comput. **15**(1), 57–90 (2002)
3. Coquand, T., Huet, G.: The calculus of constructions. Inf. Comput. **76**(2–3), 95–120 (1988)
4. Doczkal, C., Smolka, G.: Constructive completeness for modal logic with transitive closure. In: Hawblitzel, C., Miller, D. (eds.) CPP 2012. LNCS, vol. 7679, pp. 224–239. Springer, Heidelberg (2012). https://doi.org/10.1007/978-3-642-35308-6_18
5. Doczkal, C., Smolka, G.: Completeness and decidability results for CTL in coq. In: Klein, G., Gamboa, R. (eds.) ITP 2014. LNCS, vol. 8558, pp. 226–241. Springer, Cham (2014). https://doi.org/10.1007/978-3-319-08970-6_15
6. From, A.H.: Epistemic logic. Archive of Formal Proofs, October 2018. https:// devel.isa-afp.org/entries/Epistemic_Logic.html. Formal proof development
7. Herbelin, H., Lee, G.: Forcing-based cut-elimination for Gentzen-style intuitionistic sequent calculus. In: Ono, H., Kanazawa, M., de Queiroz, R. (eds.) WoLLIC 2009. LNCS (LNAI), vol. 5514, pp. 209–217. Springer, Heidelberg (2009). https://doi. org/10.1007/978-3-642-02261-6_17
8. Hughes, G.E., Cresswell, M.J.: A New Introduction to Modal Logic. Psychology Press (1996)
9. Negri, S.: Kripke completeness revisited. In: Acts of Knowledge: History, Philosophy and Logic: Essays Dedicated to Göran Sundholm, pp. 247–282 (2009)
10. Norell, U.: Dependently typed programming in Agda. In: Koopman, P., Plasmeijer, R., Swierstra, D. (eds.) AFP 2008. LNCS, vol. 5832, pp. 230–266. Springer, Heidelberg (2009). https://doi.org/10.1007/978-3-642-04652-0_5
11. Pfenning, F., Paulin-Mohring, C.: Inductively defined types in the calculus of constructions. In: Main, M., Melton, A., Mislove, M., Schmidt, D. (eds.) MFPS 1989. LNCS, vol. 442, pp. 209–228. Springer, New York (1990). https://doi.org/10.1007/ BFb0040259
12. The Coq project: The coq proof assistant. http://www.coq.inria.fr (2017)
13. Tews, H.: Formalizing cut elimination of coalgebraic logics in Coq. In: Galmiche, D., Larchey-Wendling, D. (eds.) TABLEAUX 2013. LNCS (LNAI), vol. 8123, pp. 257–272. Springer, Heidelberg (2013). https://doi.org/10.1007/978-3-642-40537-2_22
14. Wu, M., Goré, R.: Verified decision procedures for modal logics. In: Harrison, J., O'Leary, J., Tolmach, A. (eds.) 10th International Conference on Interactive Theorem Proving (ITP 2019). Leibniz International Proceedings in Informatics (LIPIcs), vol. 141, pp. 31:1–31:19. Schloss Dagstuhl-Leibniz-Zentrum fuer Informatik, Dagstuhl (2019). https://doi.org/10.4230/LIPIcs.ITP.2019.31. http:// drops.dagstuhl.de/opus/volltexte/2019/11086

Base Argumentation as an Abstraction of Deductive Argumentation

Jinsheng Chen[1]([✉]), Beishui Liao[1], and Leendert van der Torre[2]

[1] Department of Philosophy, Zhejiang University, Hangzhou, China
[2] Department of Computer Science, University of Luxembourg,
Esch-sur-Alzette, Luxembourg

Abstract. Base argumentation is a logic-based instantiation of abstract argumentation. Each base argument is a subset of the given knowledge base. In this paper, we show that base argumentation satisfies some rationality postulates, and that base argumentation is equivalent to deductive argumentation under complete semantics. Due to its simplicity, base argumentation can be seen as an abstraction of deductive argumentation.

Keywords: Abstract argumentation · Deductive argumentation · Assumption-based argumentation

1 Introduction

Dung's abstract argumentation (AA) [9] is a formalism that provides many important insights into the nature of argumentation. A situation involving argumentation is represented by a directed graph, with each node representing an argument and each arc denoting an attack by one argument on another. Some general criteria are given to determining which arguments are acceptable. Even though the unspecified notions of argument and attack can be seen as a great advantage of the framework, they do not capture every interesting aspect of argumentation.

Structured argumentation provides more detailed formalisations of arguments than is available with abstract argumentation. These formalisations include assumption-based argumentation (ABA), a surplus-production model incorporating covariates (ASPIC+), Defeasible Logic Programming (DeLP), deductive argumentation and so on. The relationship between these formalisms has attracted the attention of researchers.

A formalism $\mathcal{F}_1$ is claimed to be an *instance* of formalism $\mathcal{F}_2$ if there exists a correspondence between $\mathcal{F}_1$-frameworks and $\mathcal{F}_2$-frameworks and correspondence between their extensions. Formally, let $\mathcal{F}_1, \mathcal{F}_2$ be argumentation formalisms, σ_1 a semantics in $\mathcal{F}_1$, and σ_2 a semantics in $\mathcal{F}_2$. We say that $\mathcal{F}_1$ is an instance of $\mathcal{F}_2$ under (σ_1, σ_2)-semantics if for each $\mathcal{F}_1$-framework F_1, we can form a $\mathcal{F}_2$-framework $(F_1)_\bullet$ and for each σ_1-extension of F_1, we can form a σ_2-extension of

© Springer Nature Switzerland AG 2021
P. Baroni et al. (Eds.): CLAR 2021, LNAI 13040, pp. 468–476, 2021.
https://doi.org/10.1007/978-3-030-89391-0_26

$(F_1)_\bullet$. When σ_1 and σ_2 are the same, we simply say that $\mathcal{F}_1$ is an instance of $\mathcal{F}_2$ under σ_1-semantics. If $\mathcal{F}_1$ and $\mathcal{F}_2$ are instances of each other under σ-semantics, we say that $\mathcal{F}_1$ and $\mathcal{F}_2$ are *equivalent* under σ-semantics.

For ABA and AA, Dung, Mancarella and Toni [8] show that flat ABA is an instance of AA under admissible, grounded and ideal extensions. Toni [14] proves this result for stable semantics, and Caminada et al. [6] for complete and preferred extensions. A negative result is shown in [6] that flat ABA is not an instance of AA under semi-stable and eager semantics. Conversely, Toni [14] shows that AA is an instance of flat ABA under admissible extensions, and claims that the proof for other semantics is similar. Therefore, flat ABA and AA are equivalent under admissible, grounded, ideal, stable, complete and preferred semantics, but are not equivalent under semi-stable and eager semantics. For a general overview of the correspondence between AA and ABA, we refer the reader to [7].

For ABA and ASPIC+, Modgil and Prakken [12] claim that ABA is a special case of ASPIC+. However, Caminada et al. [6] provide counter-examples to this claim in the context of semi-stable and eager semantics.

In this paper, we investigate the relationship between deductive argumentation and a new formalism called *base argumentation*. We show that base argumentation is equivalent to deductive argumentation under complete semantics. As will be illustrated below, base argumentation is simpler than deductive argumentation. Therefore, base argumentation can be seen as an abstraction of deductive argumentation.

Deductive argumentation [2,4] is an instantiation of abstract argumentation, and provides a more detailed formalisation of arguments and attacks. In deductive argumentation, a formal language and a base logic for representing knowledge and constructing arguments and counter-arguments is assumed. Formally, deductive arguments are premises-conclusion pairs such that the premises are, according to the base logic, consistent and subset-minimal sets logically implying their conclusions. Various options for specifying when one argument attacks another are defined based on the base logic and the notion of inconsistency.

In base argumentation, arguments are defined to be consistent subsets of the knowledge base. We call such arguments *base arguments*. The base logic is Tarski's abstract logic [13]. Argument Γ attacks argument Δ if Γ can logically deduce the negation of a formula in Δ.

In this paper, we: (1) show that base argumentation satisfies two rationality postulates adapted from [5] (Proposition 15); and (2) prove a correspondence between the attack relation of base argumentation frameworks and the attack relation of deductive argumentation frameworks (Proposition 16) with a bijective map between the sets of complete extensions of these frameworks (Proposition 18). With these results, base argumentation is equivalent to deductive argumentation under complete semantics.

Base argumentation is valued for its simplicity compared to deductive argumentation. Amgoud et al. [3] show that for a deductive argumentation system with a propositional logic base and a finite knowledge base, an infinite set of arguments and an infinite set of attacks among them can be generated. By contrast, since a finite knowledge base has a finite number of consistent subsets, the number of arguments in base argumentation is finite. Since base argumentation is equivalent to deductive argumentation under complete semantics, base argumentation can be seen as an abstraction of deductive argumentation.

The remainder of this paper is structured as follows. Section 2 presents some basic notions and concepts. Section 3 provides the formal definition of base argumentation frameworks and shows that they satisfy two rationality postulates. Section 4 shows a correspondence between the attack relation of base argumentation frameworks and the attack relation of deductive argumentation frameworks with a bijective map between the set of complete extensions of these frameworks. Section 5 concludes the paper and discusses some future work.

2   Preliminaries

2.1   Abstract Argumentation Framework

Central to the theory of abstract argumentation is the notion of an *abstract argumentation framework*, which is essentially a directed graph in which the arguments are represented by nodes and the attack relation is represented by arrows.

Definition 1. *An abstract argumentation framework T is a pair $(\mathcal{A}, \mathcal{R})$ where $\mathcal{A}$ is a set and $\mathcal{R} \subseteq \mathcal{A} \times \mathcal{A}$. Each element $A \in \mathcal{A}$ is called an* argument *and $(A, B) \in \mathcal{R}$ means that A* attacks *B.*

Let $T = (\mathcal{A}, \mathcal{R})$ be an argumentation framework. A set of arguments $S \subseteq \mathcal{A}$ *attacks* argument $A \in \mathcal{A}$ if there is an argument $A' \in S$ such that A' attacks A. S defends A if for each argument $B \in \mathcal{A}$, if B attacks A, then S attacks B.

Various proposals have been proposed in the literature for argumentation semantics to decide which arguments in an abstract argumentation framework are acceptable. In this paper, we consider the following semantics:

Definition 2. *Let $T = (\mathcal{A}, \mathcal{R})$ be an argumentation framework and $S \subseteq \mathcal{A}$.*

1. *S is a* conflict-free *extension iff there is no argument $A \in S$ such that S attacks A.*
2. *S is an* admissible *extension iff S is conflict-free and S defends each of its elements.*
3. *S is a* complete *extension iff S is admissible and contains each argument it defends.*

Argument φ is scentically or credulously justified under complete semantics in T if φ belongs to all or at least one complete extension.

2.2   Tarski's Abstract Logic

Logic-based instantiations of abstract argumentation frameworks rely on an underlying logic for generating logical arguments and for defining the attack relation, using inference of conflict or existence of inconsistency. In this paper, the base logic under consideration is Tarski's *abstract logic*, which is defined with the notion of an *abstract consequence relation*.

Definition 3. *Let $\mathcal{L}$ be a denumerable logical language containing a unary connective $\neg$ for negation. A relation $\vdash\ \subseteq \mathcal{P}(\mathcal{L}) \times \mathcal{L}$ is an* abstract consequence *relation if it satisfies the following conditions: for any $\Gamma, \Delta \subseteq \mathcal{L}$ and $\varphi, \psi \in \mathcal{L}$:*

1. *if $\varphi \in \Gamma$, then $\Gamma \vdash \varphi$.*
2. *if $\Gamma \vdash \varphi$ and $\Gamma \subseteq \Delta$, then $\Delta \vdash \varphi$.*
3. *if $\Gamma \vdash \varphi$ and for every $\psi \in \Gamma$, $\Delta \vdash \psi$, then $\Delta \vdash \varphi$.*

An abstract logic is a pair $(\mathcal{L}, \vdash)$ where $\vdash$ is an abstract consequence relation.

Note that almost all well-known monotonic logics (classical logics, intuitionistic logics, modal logics, etc.) are special cases of Tarski's abstract logic.

The notion of inconsistency is important for defining the attack relation.

Definition 4. *Let $(\mathcal{L}, \vdash)$ be an abstract logic. A set of formulas Γ is* inconsistent *if there exists a formula φ such that $\Gamma \vdash \varphi$ and $\Gamma \vdash \neg\varphi$. It is* consistent *otherwise.*

We make the following assumption on negation in this paper[1], which holds in most logics with negation[2]:

– If $\Gamma \cup \{\varphi\}$ is inconsistent, then $\Gamma \vdash \neg\varphi$.

Note that the above assumption is implied by the contraposition of the underlying logic.

2.3   Deductive Argumentation Framework

Having defined the base logic and the notion of inconsistency, we are ready to present the notion of deductive argumentation frameworks. The presentation is adapted from [2]. We start with the notion of a knowledge base.

---

[1] In the literature, the following condition of contraposition is considered:

$$\text{If } \Gamma \cup \{\varphi\} \vdash \psi, \text{ then } \Gamma \cup \{\neg\psi\} \vdash \neg\varphi.$$

If an abstract logic contains falsehood $\bot$, contrapostion implies the above assumption: Since $\Gamma \cup \{\varphi\}$ is inconsistent, $\Gamma \cup \{\varphi\} \vdash \bot$. By contraposition, $\Gamma \cup \{\neg\bot\} \vdash \neg\varphi$. Since $\neg\bot$ is equivalent to a tautology, $\Gamma \vdash \neg\varphi$.

[2] For propositional logic, the proof is as follows: Since $\Gamma \cup \{\varphi\}$ is inconsistent, $\Gamma \cup \{\varphi\} \vdash \bot$. By Deduction Theorem, $\Gamma \vdash \varphi \rightarrow \bot$. Since $(\varphi \rightarrow \bot) \leftrightarrow \neg\varphi$ is a tautology, $\Gamma \vdash \neg\varphi$.

Definition 5. *Let* $(\mathcal{L}, \vdash)$ *be an abstract logic. A knowledge base* Σ *is a subset of* $\mathcal{L}$ *such that* Σ *is free of tautologies: for all* $\varphi \in \Sigma$, *it is not the case that* $\emptyset \vdash \varphi$.

Deductive arguments are premises-conclusion pairs such that the premises are, according to the base logic, consistent and subset-minimal sets logically implying their conclusion.

Definition 6. *Let* $(\mathcal{L}, \vdash)$ *be an abstract logic and* Σ *a knowledge base. A deductive argument is a pair* (Γ, φ) *such that (1)* $\Gamma \subseteq \Sigma$ *and* Γ *is consistent, (2)* $\Gamma \vdash \varphi$ *and (3) there is no* $\Gamma' \subset \Gamma$ *such that* $\Gamma' \vdash \varphi$. *We use* α, β *etc. to denote deductive arguments.* (Γ, φ) *is a* sub-argument *of* (Δ, ψ) *if* $\Gamma \subseteq \Delta$.

Assumption 7. This paper makes the following assumption about the existence of deductive arguments:

– For any consistent set $\Gamma \subseteq \Sigma$, there exists φ such that (Γ, φ) is a deductive argument.

This assumption is natural since if we have the conjunction $\wedge$ in our language and Γ is finite, the desired φ is $\bigwedge \{\psi \mid \psi \in \Gamma\}$. Note that we assume Σ to be free of tautologies. Therefore, it is not the case that $\vdash \bigwedge \{\psi \mid \psi \in \Gamma\}$.

Now we define the attack relation on deductive arguments.

Definition 8. *Let* $(\mathcal{L}, \vdash)$ *be an abstract logic and* Σ *a knowledge base. Let* (Γ, φ) *and* (Δ, ψ) *be deductive arguments. Then* (Γ, φ) *attacks* (Δ, ψ) *iff there exists a formula* $\phi \in \Delta$ *such that* $\{\varphi, \phi\}$ *is inconsistent.*

The attack relation defined above is called an *assumption attack* in [10]. It follows directly that (Γ, φ) attacks (Δ, ψ) iff $\Gamma \vdash \neg\phi$ for some $\phi \in \Delta$.

Definition 9. *Let* $(\mathcal{L}, \vdash)$ *be an abstract logic and* Σ *a knowledge base. A deductive argumentation framework* $\mathcal{T}_d$ *is a pair* $(Ar_d(\Sigma), \mathcal{R}_d)$ *where* $Ar_d(\Sigma)$ *is the set of deductive arguments based on* Σ, *and* $\mathcal{R}_d$ *is the attack relation defined in Definition 8.*

Rationality postulates require that extensions of argumentation frameworks satisfy certain conditions. Amgoud [1] shows that any deductive argumentation framework satisfies the following proposition:

Proposition 10. *Let* $\mathcal{T}_d = (Ar_d(\Sigma), \mathcal{R}_d)$ *be a deductive argumentation framework. Then for any complete extension* $\mathcal{E}$ *of* $\mathcal{T}_d$,

1. $\mathcal{E}$ *is closed under sub-arguments, that is, for any deductive arguments* (Γ, φ) *and* (Δ, ψ), *if* $(\Gamma, \varphi) \in \mathcal{E}$ *and* $\Delta \subseteq \Gamma$, *then* $(\Delta, \psi) \in \mathcal{E}$.
2. $\mathcal{E}$ *satisfies the consistency postulate, that is,* $\bigcup \{\Gamma \mid (\Gamma, \varphi) \in \mathcal{E}\}$ *is consistent.*

Deductive argumentation frameworks also satisfy other rationality postulates, but that is outside the scope of this paper.

3   Base Argumentation Frameworks

In this section, we introduce the formalism of *base argumentation*. Each *base argument* is a consistent subset of the knowledge base. The attack relation on base arguments is similar to the assumption attack in Definition 8. The satisfaction of two rationality postulates adapted from [5] and [2] is proven.

Definition 11. *Let* $(\mathcal{L}, \vdash)$ *be an abstract logic and* Σ *a knowledge base. A base argument is a consistent subset of* Σ. *We use* Γ, Δ *etc. to denote base arguments. Base argument* Γ *is a* sub-argument *of* Δ *if* $\Gamma \subseteq \Delta$.

Definition 12. *Let* $(\mathcal{L}, \vdash)$ *be an abstract logic and* Σ *a knowledge base. Let* Γ *and* Δ *be deductive arguments.* Γ attacks Δ *iff there exists a formula* $\phi \in \Delta$ *such that* $\Gamma \vdash \neg\phi$.

Definition 13. *Let* $(\mathcal{L}, \vdash)$ *be an abstract logic and* Σ *a knowledge base. A base argumentation framework* $\mathcal{T}_b$ *is a pair* $(Ar_b(\Sigma), \mathcal{R}_b)$ *where* $Ar_b(\Sigma)$ *is the set of base arguments based on* Σ, *and* $\mathcal{R}_b$ *is the attack relation defined in Definition 12.*

Now we show that base argumentation satisfies two rationality postulates.

Definition 14. *Let* $(\mathcal{L}, \vdash)$ *be an abstract logic,* Σ *a knowledge base and* $\mathcal{T}_b = (Ar_b(\Sigma), \mathcal{R}_b)$ *a base argumentation framework.*

- $\mathcal{T}_b$ *is* closed under sub-arguments *iff for each complete extension* $\mathcal{E}$ *of* $\mathcal{T}_b$, *if* $\Gamma \in \mathcal{E}$ *and* $\Delta \subseteq \Gamma$, *then* $\Delta \in \mathcal{E}$.
- $\mathcal{T}_b$ *satisfies the* consistency *postulate iff for each complete extension* $\mathcal{E}$ *of* $\mathcal{T}_b$, $\bigcup_{\Gamma \in \mathcal{E}} \Gamma$ *is consistent.*

Proposition 15. *Let* $(\mathcal{L}, \vdash)$ *be an abstract logic,* Σ *a knowledge base and* $\mathcal{T}_b = (Ar_b(\Sigma), \mathcal{R}_b)$ *a base argumentation framework. Then* $\mathcal{T}_b$ *is closed under sub-arguments and satisfies the consistency postulate.*

4   Correspondence Between Base and Deductive Argumentation Frameworks

In this section, we prove some correspondence results between a base argumentation framework $\mathcal{T}_b = (Ar_b(\Sigma), \mathcal{R}_b)$ and a deductive argumentation framework $\mathcal{T}_d = (Ar_d(\Sigma), \mathcal{R}_d)$ obtained from the same abstract logic and knowledge base Σ. The correspondence results include a correspondence between $\mathcal{R}_b$ and $\mathcal{R}_d$ with a bijective map between the set of complete extensions of $\mathcal{T}_b$ and that of $\mathcal{T}_d$.

For simplicity, we say that Γ attacks Δ instead of $(\Gamma, \Delta) \in \mathcal{R}_b$ for base arguments Γ, Δ, and that (Γ, φ) attacks (Δ, ψ) instead of $((\Gamma, \varphi), (\Delta, \psi)) \in \mathcal{R}_d$ for deductive arguments $(\Gamma, \varphi), (\Delta, \psi)$.

The following proposition is about the correspondence between $\mathcal{R}_b$ and $\mathcal{R}_d$:

Proposition 16. *Let $(\mathcal{L}, \vdash)$ be an abstract logic, Σ a knowledge base, $\mathcal{T}_b = (Ar_b(\Sigma), \mathcal{R}_b)$ a base argumentation framework and $\mathcal{T}_d = (Ar_d(\Sigma), \mathcal{R}_d)$ a deductive argumentation framework. Then,*

1. *For $\Gamma, \Delta \in Ar_b(\Sigma)$, if Γ attacks Δ, then there exist deductive arguments (Γ', φ) and (Δ', ψ) such that (a) (Γ', φ) attacks (Δ', ψ) and (b) $\Gamma' \subseteq \Gamma$ and $\Delta' \subseteq \Delta$.*
2. *For $(\Gamma, \varphi), (\Delta, \psi) \in Ar_d(\Sigma)$, if (Γ, φ) attacks (Δ, ψ), then Γ attacks Δ.*

Denote by $\mathrm{COM}(\mathcal{T}_b)$ the set of complete extensions of $\mathcal{T}_b$ and by $\mathrm{COM}(\mathcal{T}_d)$ the set of complete extensions of $\mathcal{T}_d$. The following proposition defines and justifies functions $(.)_\bullet : \mathrm{COM}(\mathcal{T}_b) \to \mathrm{COM}(\mathcal{T}_d)$ and $(.)^\bullet : \mathrm{COM}(\mathcal{T}_d) \to \mathrm{COM}(\mathcal{T}_b)$.

Proposition 17. *Let $(\mathcal{L}, \vdash)$ be an abstract logic and Σ a knowledge base. Let $\mathcal{T}_b = (Ar_b(\Sigma), \mathcal{R}_b)$ be a base argumentation framework and $\mathcal{T}_d = (Ar_d(\Sigma), \mathcal{R}_d)$ a deductive argumentation framework.*

1. *If $\mathcal{E}$ is a complete extension of $\mathcal{T}_b$, then $\mathcal{E}_\bullet$, defined as follows, is a complete extension of $\mathcal{T}_d$.*

$$\mathcal{E}_\bullet := \{(\Gamma, \varphi) \mid (\Gamma, \varphi) \text{ is a deductive argument and } \Gamma \subseteq \Gamma' \text{ for some } \Gamma \in \mathcal{E}\}$$

2. *If $\mathcal{E}_d$ is a complete extension of $\mathcal{T}_d$ and $(\Gamma, \varphi) \in \mathcal{E}$, then $\mathcal{E}_d^\bullet$, defined as follows, is a complete extension of $\mathcal{T}_b$.*

$$\mathcal{E}_d^\bullet := \{\Gamma \mid (\Gamma, \varphi) \in \mathcal{E}_d\}$$

Next, we show that functions $(.)_\bullet$ and $(.)^\bullet$ are bijective.

Proposition 18. *Let $(\mathcal{L}, \vdash)$ be an abstract logic and Σ a knowledge base. Let $\mathcal{T}_b = (Ar_b(\Sigma), \mathcal{R}_b)$ be a base argumentation framework and $\mathcal{T}_d = (Ar_d(\Sigma), \mathcal{R}_d)$ a deductive argumentation framework.*

1. *$(.)_\bullet : \mathrm{COM}(\mathcal{T}_b) \to \mathrm{COM}(\mathcal{T}_d)$ is bijective.*
2. *$(.)^\bullet : \mathrm{COM}(\mathcal{T}_d) \to \mathrm{COM}(\mathcal{T}_b)$ is bijective.*

5   Conclusion and Future Work

This paper presented a preliminary formalism of base argumentation. It can be seen as an abstraction of deductive argumentation.

There are some possibilities for further research:

1. This paper only considers assumption attacks in deductive argumentation and then only for complete semantics. There are other settings in the literature.
2. We might investigate the relationship between extensions of base argumentation frameworks under different semantics and maximal consistent sets.

3. Base argumentation is similar to ABA. Both base argumentation and ABA treat the subsets of the knowledge base as the basic entities, which are called base arguments in base argumentation and sets of assumptions in ABA. The deductive mechanism in base argumentation is Tarski's logic, and ABA uses a deductive system. Extensions in base argumentation are sets of subsets of the knowledge base, while extensions in ABA are subsets of the knowledge base. Because of these similarities, we expect to find some connections between base argumentation and ABA.
4. Logic-based instantiations of ABA is studied by Heyninck and Arieli [11]. We will compare base argumentation with their work in the extended version of this paper.

Acknowledgements. The research reported in this paper was supported by the National Social Science Foundation Major Project of China under grants No. 20& ZD047 and No.18ZDA290. Leon van der Torre acknowledges financial support from the Fonds National de la Recherche Luxembourg (INTER/Mobility/19/1399 5684/DLAl/van der Torre).

References

1. Amgoud, L.: Postulates for logic-based argumentation systems. Int. J. Approx. Reason. **55**(9), 2028–2048 (2014)
2. Amgoud, L., Besnard, P.: Logical limits of abstract argumentation frameworks. J. Appl. Non-Classical Log. **23**(3), 229–267 (2013)
3. Amgoud, L., Besnard, P., Vesic, S.: Identifying the core of logic-based argumentation systems. In: 2011 IEEE 23rd International Conference on Tools with Artificial Intelligence, pp. 633–636. IEEE (2011)
4. Besnard, P., Hunter, A.: A review of argumentation based on deductive arguments. Handbook of Formal Argumentation, pp. 437–484 (2018)
5. Caminada, M., Amgoud, L.: On the evaluation of argumentation formalisms. Artif. Intell. **171**(5–6), 286–310 (2007)
6. Caminada, M., Sá, S., Alcântara, J., Dvořák, W.: On the difference between assumption-based argumentation and abstract argumentation. IfCoLog J. Log. Appl. **2**(1), 15–34 (2015)
7. Čyras, K., Schulz, C., Toni, F., Fan, X.: Assumption-based argumentation: disputes, explanations, preferences. IFCoLog J. Log. Appl. **4**(8), 2407–2456 (2017)
8. Dung, P.M., Mancarella, P., Toni, F.: Computing ideal sceptical argumentation. Artif. Intell. **171**(10–15), 642–674 (2007)
9. Dung, P.M.: On the acceptability of arguments and its fundamental role in non-monotonic reasoning, logic programming and n-person games. Artif. Intell. **77**(2), 321–357 (1995)
10. Elvang-Gøransson, M., Krause, P.J., Fox, J.: Acceptability of arguments as 'logical uncertainty'. In: Clarke, M., Kruse, R., Moral, S. (eds.) ECSQARU 1993. LNCS, vol. 747, pp. 85–90. Springer, Heidelberg (1993). https://doi.org/10.1007/BFb0028186
11. Heyninck, J., Arieli, O.: Simple contrapositive assumption-based argumentation frameworks. Int. J. Approx. Reason. **121**, 103–124 (2020)

12. Modgil, S., Prakken, H.: A general account of argumentation with preferences. Artif. Intell. **195**, 361–397 (2013)
13. Tarski, A.: On some fundamental concepts of metamathematics. Oxford (1956)
14. Toni, F.: Reasoning on the web with assumption-based argumentation. In: Eiter, T., Krennwallner, T. (eds.) Reasoning Web 2012. LNCS, vol. 7487, pp. 370–386. Springer, Heidelberg (2012). https://doi.org/10.1007/978-3-642-33158-9_10

An Argumentative Dialogue System for COVID-19 Vaccine Information

Bettina Fazzinga[1,2] , Andrea Galassi[3(✉)] , and Paolo Torroni[3]

[1] ICAR-CNR, Rende, Italy
bettina.fazzinga@icar.cnr.it
[2] DICES, University of Calabria, Rende, Italy
[3] DISI, University of Bologna, Bologna, Italy
{a.galassi,paolo.torroni}@unibo.it

Abstract. Dialogue systems are widely used in AI to support timely and interactive communication with users. We propose a general-purpose dialogue system architecture that leverages computational argumentation to perform reasoning and provide consistent and explainable answers. We illustrate the system using a COVID-19 vaccine information case study.

Keywords: Computational argumentation · Dialogue systems · Explainability · Expert systems · Chatbots

1 Introduction

Since the early days of AI, research has been inspired by the idea of developing programs that can communicate with users in natural language. With the advent of language technologies able to reach human performance in various tasks, AI chatbots and dialogue systems are starting to mature and this vision seems nearer than ever. As a result, more organizations are investing in chatbot development and deployment. In the 2019 Gartner CIO Survey, CIOs identified chatbots as the main AI-based application used in their enterprises,[1] with a global market valued in the billions of USD.[2]

In fact, chatbots are one example of the extent AI technologies are becoming ever more pervasive, both in addressing global challenges, and in the day-to-day routine. Public administrations too are adopting chatbots for key actions such as helping citizens in requesting services[3] and providing updates and information, for example, in relation with COVID-19 [13].[4]

---

[1] https://www.gartner.com/smarterwithgartner/chatbots-will-appeal-to-modern-workers/.

[2] https://www.mordorintelligence.com/industry-reports/chatbot-market.

[3] https://www.canada.ca/en/employment-social-development/services/my-account/terms-use-chatbot.html.

[4] https://government.economictimes.indiatimes.com/news/digital-india/covid-19-govt-launches-facebook-and-messenger-chatbot/74843125.

B. Fazzinga, A. Galassi, and P. Torroni—Equal contribution.

© Springer Nature Switzerland AG 2021
P. Baroni et al. (Eds.): CLAR 2021, LNAI 13040, pp. 477–485, 2021.
https://doi.org/10.1007/978-3-030-89391-0_27

However, the expansion of intelligent technologies has been met by growing concerns about possible misuses, motivating a need to develop AI systems that are *trustworthy*. On the one hand, governments are pressured for gaining or preserving an edge in intelligent technologies, which make intensive use of large amounts of data. On the other hand, there is an increasing awareness of the need for trustworthy AI systems.[5]

In the context of information-providing chatbots and assistive dialogue systems, especially in the public sector, we believe that trustworthiness demands transparency, explainability, correctness, and it requires architectural choices that take data access into account from the very beginning. Arguably, this kind of chatbot should not only use transparent and verifiable methods and be so conceived as to respect relevant data protection regulations, but it should also be able to explain its outputs or recommendations in a manner adapted to the intended (human) user.

We thus propose an architecture for AI dialogue systems where user interaction is carried out *in natural language*, not only for providing information to the user, but also to answer user queries about the *reasons* leading to the system output (explainability). The system selects answers based on a *transparent reasoning module*, built on top of a computational argumentation framework with a *rigorous, verifiable semantics* (transparency, auditability). Additionally, the system has a modular architecture, so as to decouple the natural language interface, where user data is processed, from the reasoning module, where expert knowledge is used to generate outputs (privacy and data governance).

Our work is positioned at the intersection of two areas: computational argumentation and natural language understanding. While computational argumentation has had significant applications in the context of automated dialogues among software agents, its combination with systems able to interact in natural language in socio-technical systems has been more recent. The most related proposal in this domain is a recent one by Chalaguine and Hunter [4]. With respect to such work, our focus is not on persuading the user but on offering correct information. Accordingly, we put greater emphasis on the correctness and justification of system outputs, and on the system's ability to reason with every relevant user input, as opposed to reacting to the last input. Our modular architecture enables a separation between language understanding and argumentative reasoning, which enables significant generality. In particular, our dialogue system architecture can be applied to multiple domains, without requiring any expensive retraining.

In this article we focus on the system's architecture and on the knowledge representation and reasoning module. We start with a brief overview of related approaches (Sect. 2). Next, we give a high-level description of the system architecture (Sect. 3) and then zoom in on the argumentation module supporting knowledge representation and reasoning and dialogue strategies (Sect. 4). To illustrate, we sketch a dialogue between chatbot and human in the context of

---

[5] https://ec.europa.eu/digital-single-market/en/news/ethics-guidelines-trustworthy-ai.

COVID-19 vaccines (Sect. 5), showing how background knowledge and user data can be formalized and jointly used to provide correct answers, and how the system output can be challenged by the user. Section 6 concludes.

2   Related Work

In the field of computational argumentation, significant work has been devoted to defining and reasoning over the argumentation graphs [1,5,10], leading to several ways of identifying "robust" arguments or sets of arguments [7,8]. However, the practical combination of computational argumentation and dialogue systems based on natural language has not been much explored. Among the few existing approaches, Rosenfeld and Kraus [16] combine theoretical argumentation with reinforcement learning to develop persuasive agents, while Rach et al. [14] extract a debate's argument structure and envision the dialogue as a game, structuring the answers as moves along a previously defined scheme. In both cases the agents are limited in their inputs and outputs to sentences "hard-coded" in the knowledge base.

An interesting approach in this direction is by Chalaguine and Hunter [4], who exploit sentence similarity to retrieve an answer from a knowledge base expressed in the form of a graph. No conversation history is kept, therefore the answers produced by the system do not take into account previous user inputs. We believe that this approach is inappropriate for complex scenarios where multiple pieces of information must be considered at the same time, since the user would have to include all of them in the same sentence. Moreover, this approach does not involve reasoning, but relevance-based answer retrieval. Our approach, instead, aims to output replies 'consistent' with *all* the information provided thus far by the user, and that will not be proven wrong later on. In particular, what we do is we *enforce* the condition of *acceptance* of some arguments, by eliciting specific user input. This can be seen as a practical application of the concepts defined by Baumann and Brewka [2]. In particular, our system relies on an argumentation module that maintains a history of the concepts expressed by the user and performs reasoning over an argumentation graph to compute the answer. It is therefore possible for the user to consider multiple information at the same time, to ask for more information if they are needed, and also to provide an explanation for the previous answers.

3   System Architecture

Our chatbot architecture consists of two core modules: the *language module* and the *argumentation module*. The former provides a natural language interface to the user input, while the latter deals with the problem of computing correct replies to be provided to the user, and it relies on computational argumentation. In this work, we will focus on the argumentation module, leaving the specific implementation of the language module for future developments.

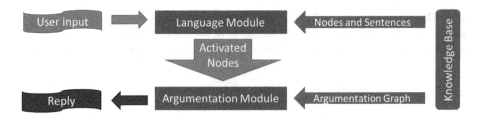

Fig. 1. System architecture.

We assume the presence of a scenario-specific *knowledge base* (KB) created by experts, in the form of an argumentation graph (see Sect. 3) with two kinds of nodes. Nodes are either *status* arguments or *reply* arguments. The former encode *facts* that correspond to the possible user sentences. Each status node is linked to one or more *reply* arguments it *supports*[6], and that represent replies to the facts stated by the user. Status nodes may also attack other status or reply nodes, typically because the facts they represent are incompatible with one another. Additionally, a set of natural language sentences is associated with each status node and represents some possible ways a user would express the facts the node encodes. These different representations of facts could be produced by domain experts or crowd-sourced.

The behaviour of the system and the interaction between the modules is illustrated in Fig. 1. The language module compares each user sentence against the sentences embedded in the KB. In particular, like Chalaguine and Hunter [4], we propose to use a sentence similarity measure to identify KB sentences matching the user input. Since each KB sentence is associated with a status node, a list of related status nodes can be computed from the list of sentences in the KB identified by the language module as a match. Accordingly, when a user writes a sentence, a set of status nodes N is 'activated', in the sense that they are recognized as matching with the user's input. However, differently from Chalaguine and Hunter [4], *all* the status arguments activated during the chat with the user are stored in a set S.

The fundamental principle that characterizes our approach is that a reply R among those supported by N is given to the user only if it is acceptable w.r.t. S. This means that the information given by the user needs to support and defend R from its attacks. If there is no acceptable reply with respect to S, the chatbot selects anyway a candidate reply R, but instead of offering R immediately, it prompts the user in order to acquire new information that could activate new status arguments which, added to S, could make R acceptable w.r.t. S. This *elicitation* process aims to guarantee that R is not proven wrong in the continuation of the chat. In fact, all the information that can be in contrast with R (i.e., that attack R) are asked to the user, in order to be sure to defeat any potential attackers.

---

[6] We point out that our concept of support is a new notion linking status nodes to reply nodes, and its semantics is different from the standard one [3,9].

This underlying *strategic reasoning* marks a significant difference from previous approaches. Another distinguishing feature is our system's ability to provide users with online, *on-demand explanations*. In particular, besides providing information and getting replies, users can also require an explanation for a given reply r. An explanation for r consists of a sequence of natural language sentences built from (i) descriptions of the status nodes of S supporting r and ii) motivations against other possible conflicting replies that the system discarded.

4   Argumentation Module

The argumentation module is based on a knowledge base expressed as an argument graph.

Definition 1 (Argumentation graph). *An argumentation graph is a tuple* $\langle A, R, D, T \rangle$, *where A and R are the arguments of the graph and are called* status *arguments and* reply *arguments, respectively, $D \subseteq A \times (A \cup R)$ encodes the attack/defeat relation, and $T \subseteq A \times R$ encodes the support relation.*

Each argument a in A is annotated with a set of natural language sentences, as described in the previous section. We say that a *attacks* (resp., *supports*) a reply node r iff $(a, r) \in D$ (resp., $(a, r) \in T$). By extension, we say that a set S attacks (resp., supports) r, or equivalently that r is attacked by (resp., supported by) S, iff there exists an argument $a \in S$ s.t. a attacks (resp., supports) r.

The aim of the argumentation module is to identify the reply nodes in response to the user sentences. To this end, in addition to the KB, each dialogue session relies on *dynamically acquired knowledge*, expressed as a set of facts or *status arguments* S. The dialogue strategy is to provide the user with a reply that is supported and defended by S. However, differently from other proposals, our system does not simply select a consistent reply at each turn. On the contrary, it strategizes in order to provide only robust replies, possibly delaying replies that need further fact-checking. To that end, the two following definitions distinguish between *consistent* and *potentially consistent* reply. The former can be given to the user right away, as it can not possibly be proven wrong in the future.[7] The latter, albeit consistent with the current known facts, may still be defeated by future user input, and therefore it should be delayed until a successful elicitation process is completed.

The formal definitions are based on the KB and on a representation of the state of the dialogue consisting of two sets: S and N. In particular, $S \subseteq A$ contains the arguments activated during the conversation so far, whereas $N \subseteq S$ contains arguments in support of the system's possible replies to the user. We recall that an argument a is *acceptable* w.r.t. a set S iff S defends a from every attack towards a.

---

[7] The implicit assumption here is that the user does not enter conflicting information, and that the language model correctly interprets the user input. Clearly, if this is not the case, the system's output becomes unreliable. But that wouldn't depend on the underlying reasoning framework. The definition of fall-back strategies able to handle such exceptions would be an important extension to the system.

Definition 2 (Consistent   reply).   *Given   an   argumentation   graph* $\langle A, R, D, T \rangle$ *and two sets* $S \subseteq A$ *and* $N \subseteq S$, *a reply* $r \in R$ *is* consistent *iff* N *supports* r *and* r *is acceptable w.r.t.* S.

Definition 3 (Potentially   consistent   reply).   *Given an argumentation graph* $\langle A, R, D, T \rangle$ *and two sets* $S \subseteq A$ *and* $N \subseteq S$, *a reply* $r \in R$ *is* poten-tially consistent *iff* N *supports* r, S *does not attack* r *and* r *is not acceptable w.r.t.* S.

Finally, users can challenge the system output. An *explanation* of a reply r consists of two parts. The first one contains the arguments leading to r, i.e., those belonging to a set S that supports r. The second one encodes the *why not*s, to explain why the chatbot did not give other replies.

Definition 4 (Explanation). *Given an argumentation graph* $\langle A, R, D, T \rangle$, *a set* $S \subseteq A$ *and a reply* $r \in R$, *an* explanation *for* r *is a pair* $\langle Supp, NotGiven \rangle$, *where Supp contains the arguments* $a \in S$ *s.t.* $(a, r) \in T$ *and NotGiven is a set of pairs* $\langle r', N' \rangle$, *where* $r' \neq r$, r' *is supported by* S *and* $N' \subseteq S$ *contains the arguments* b *attacking* r'.

In the next section we briefly explain how our strategy works to provide the user with consistent replies, by means of an example in the context of the COVID-19 vaccines.

5   Case Study

Disclaimer. The illustration that follows is based on a (simplistic) representa-tion of the domain knowledge. Its purpose is to show a proof of concept of our approach–not to offer sound advice about vaccines. We base our example on the content of the AIFA website.[8]

We consider the context of the vaccines for COVID-19, where we aim to create a dialogue system able to answer user inquiries about vaccination procedures, vaccine safety, and so on. Figure 2 shows an excerpt of the argumentation graph encoding the KB, in particular the part related to options for getting vaccinated.

Yellow rectangles represent status arguments, blue ovals reply arguments, green solid arrows support relations, pointing to the possible replies to user sen-tences, and red dotted arrows denote attack relations. It is worthwhile noticing that the graph contains both the positive and negative version of each status argument. This is a key modeling feature in the context at hand, as it enables the chatbot to properly capture and encode all the information provided by the user about their health conditions.

Let us consider this example: the user writes "Hi, I am Morgan and I suffer from latex allergy, can I get vaccinated?" The language module processes the user sentence and compares it against all the sentences provided by the knowledge base, resulting in a single positive match with the sentence "I have latex allergy"

---

[8] Italian medicines agency, https://www.aifa.gov.it/en/vaccini-covid-19.

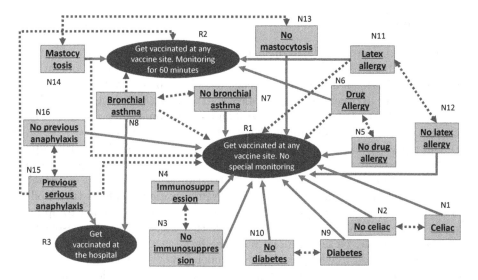

Fig. 2. An excerpt of an argumentation graph encoding knowledge about COVID-19 vaccines.

associated with node N_{11}. At this point, the argumentation module deals with the computation of the replies, finding that the only reply supported by $S = \{N_{11}\}$ is R_2 and that it is not a consistent reply, because it is attacked by both N_8 and N_{15}. It is, however, a potentially consistent reply: thus, although we cannot give it yet to the user, what we can do is acquire new information that would make it consistent. To make R_2 consistent, S must be augmented with both N_7 and N_{16}. This means that the user must tell that they do not suffer from bronchial asthma and that they had no previous anaphylaxis. Then, our strategy is to query the user whether they suffer from bronchial asthma and/or whether they had any previous anaphylaxis. Assume at this point that the user replies are $U_1 =$ *I do not suffer from bronchial asthma* and $U_2 =$ *I have never had any anaphylaxis*. Then, we can extend S with the new corroborating bits of information, obtaining $S = \{N_{11}, N_7, N_{16}\}$. Because R_2 is now a consistent reply, we can return R_2 to the user.

Alternatively, suppose that the user writes that they do suffer from bronchial asthma. In that case, we would have $S = \{N_{11}, N_8, N_{16}\}$, hence R_2 would not be a consistent reply. Accordingly, the only consistent reply that can be given to the user would be R_3.

Finally, suppose that, upon getting R_3 as a reply, the user asks for an explanation. In that case, $\langle Supp, NotGiven \rangle$ is such that $Supp = \{N_8\}$, and $NotGiven$ consists of the unique pair $\langle R_2, \{N_8\} \rangle$, meaning that R_2 was not given due to N_8, that is, due to the fact that the user suffers from bronchial asthma.

6 Conclusion

We presented a new modular dialogue system architecture based on computational argumentation and language technologies. In particular, our system exploits both user input and a knowledge base built by domain experts to perform reasoning in order to compute answers and identify missing bits of information. We illustrated our proposal with an information-seeking scenario, where a user requires information about COVID-19 vaccines.

Our proposal has multiple advantages over previous approaches. With respect to corpus-based dialogue systems, it can use expert knowledge. This is especially important in domains that require trustworthy, correct and explainable solutions. Indeed, a remarkable feature of argumentation graphs is their ability to support reasoning over the conflicts between arguments, leading to approving or discarding some responses. We believe that highlighting the reasons why a response can not be given, along with the facts that rule out other possible responses, is a good way to make the user understand the response and trust the system. Importantly, the architecture is general-purpose and does not require domain-specific training or reference corpora. With respect to prior work on argumentation-based dialogue systems, its major advantage is its ability to reason with multiple elements of user information, in order to provide focused and sound answers, by eventually performing the elicitation of missing data.

In this paper we focused on the argumentation module, leaving the implementation of the language module for future works. In this regard, we plan to explore the use of recent attention-based neural architectures [11] by representing the user input using BERT-based [6] sentence embeddings [15] and by comparing them using advanced similarity measures [12].

Since our proposal is general and not limited to a specific domain, it will be interesting to test our approach on new scenarios and also to consider languages other than English. Another important aspect we plan to address in the future is the management of conflicting information provided by the user, and the possibility to revise previously submitted information.

Acknowledgments. The research reported in this work was partially supported by the EU H2020 ICT48 project "Humane AI Net" under contract #952026.

References

1. Baroni, P., Giacomin, M.: Semantics of abstract argument systems. In: Simari, G., Rahwan, I. (eds.) Argumentation in Artificial Intelligence, pp. 25–44. Springer, Boston, MA (2009). https://doi.org/10.1007/978-0-387-98197-0_2
2. Baumann, R., Brewka, G.: Expanding argumentation frameworks: enforcing and monotonicity results. In: COMMA, vol. 216, pp. 75–86. IOS Press (2010). https://doi.org/10.3233/978-1-60750-619-5-75
3. Cayrol, C., Lagasquie-Schiex, M.C.: On the acceptability of arguments in bipolar argumentation frameworks. In: Godo, L. (ed.) ECSQARU 2005. LNCS (LNAI), vol. 3571, pp. 378–389. Springer, Heidelberg (2005). https://doi.org/10.1007/11518655_33

4. Chalaguine, L.A., Hunter, A.: A persuasive chatbot using a crowd-sourced argument graph and concerns. In: COMMA, vol. 326, pp. 9–20. IOS Press (2020). https://doi.org/10.3233/FAIA200487
5. Charwat, G., Dvorák, W., Gaggl, S.A., Wallner, J.P., Woltran, S.: Methods for solving reasoning problems in abstract argumentation - a survey. Artif. Intell. **220**, 28–63 (2015). https://doi.org/10.1016/j.artint.2014.11.008
6. Devlin, J., Chang, M., Lee, K., Toutanova, K.: BERT: pre-training of deep bidirectional transformers for language understanding. In: NAACL-HLT, no. 1, pp. 4171–4186. Association for Computational Linguistics (2019). https://doi.org/10.18653/v1/n19-1423
7. Dung, P.M.: On the acceptability of arguments and its fundamental role in nonmonotonic reasoning, logic programming and n-person games. Artif. Intell. **77**(2), 321–358 (1995). https://doi.org/10.1016/0004-3702(94)00041-X
8. Dung, P.M., Mancarella, P., Toni, F.: Computing ideal sceptical argumentation. Artif. Intell. **171**(10–15), 642–674 (2007). https://doi.org/10.1016/j.artint.2007.05.003
9. Fazzinga, B., Flesca, S., Furfaro, F.: Probabilistic bipolar abstract argumentation frameworks: complexity results. In: IJCAI, pp. 1803–1809. ijcai.org (2018). https://doi.org/10.24963/ijcai.2018/249
10. Fazzinga, B., Flesca, S., Furfaro, F.: Complexity of fundamental problems in probabilistic abstract argumentation: beyond independence. Artif. Intell. **268**, 1–29 (2019). https://doi.org/10.1016/j.artint.2018.11.003
11. Galassi, A., Lippi, M., Torroni, P.: Attention in natural language processing. IEEE Trans. Neural Netw. Learn. Syst. 1–18 (2020). https://doi.org/10.1109/TNNLS.2020.3019893
12. Galassi, A., Drazewski, K., Lippi, M., Torroni, P.: Cross-lingual annotation projection in legal texts. In: COLING, pp. 915–926. International Committee on Computational Linguistics, Barcelona, Spain (Online) (December 2020). https://doi.org/10.18653/v1/2020.coling-main.79
13. Miner, A.S., Laranjo, L., Kocaballi, A.B.: Chatbots in the fight against the COVID-19 pandemic. NPJ Digit. Med. **3**(1), 1–4 (2020). https://doi.org/10.1038/s41746-020-0280-0
14. Rach, N., Langhammer, S., Minker, W., Ultes, S.: Utilizing argument mining techniques for argumentative dialogue systems. In: D'Haro, L.F., Banchs, R.E., Li, H. (eds.) 9th International Workshop on Spoken Dialogue System Technology. LNEE, vol. 579, pp. 131–142. Springer, Singapore (2019). https://doi.org/10.1007/978-981-13-9443-0_12
15. Reimers, N., Gurevych, I.: Sentence-BERT: sentence embeddings using Siamese BERT-networks. In: EMNLP/IJCNLP, no. 1, pp. 3982–3992. Association for Computational Linguistics, Hong Kong, China (November 2019). https://doi.org/10.18653/v1/D19-1410
16. Rosenfeld, A., Kraus, S.: Strategical argumentative agent for human persuasion. In: ECAI, pp. 320–328. IOS Press, NLD (2016). https://doi.org/10.3233/978-1-61499-672-9-320

Extractive-Abstractive Summarization of Judgment Documents Using Multiple Attention Networks

Yan Gao[1] , Zhengtao Liu[1] , Juan Li[2](✉) , Fan Guo[1,2], and Fei Xiao[1,2]

[1] School of Automation, Central South University, Changsha 410083, China
[2] School of Law, Central South University, Changsha, China

Abstract. Judgment documents contain rich legal information, they are simultaneously lengthy with complex structure. This requires summarizing judgment documents in an effective way. By analyzing the structural features of Chinese judgment documents, we propose an automatic summarization method, which consists of an extraction model and an abstraction model. In the extraction model, all the sentences are encoded by a Self-Attention network and are classified into key sentences and non-key sentences. In the abstraction model, the initial summarization is refined into a final summarization by a unidirectional-bidirectional attention network. Such a summarization could help improve the efficiency in case handling and make judgment documents more accessible to the general readers. The experimental results on CAIL2020 dataset are satisfactory.

Keywords: Judgment documents · Automatic summarization · Attention network · Encoder-decoder

1 Introduction

Judgment documents contain a wealth of information. They record the processes and results of legal cases, which is an important means for the courts to opening the trial activities and publishing the reasons and results of their decisions. The judgment document is the only evidence for the courts to determine and allocate the substantive rights and obligations of the parties. However, the judgment documents use domain knowledge in a lengthy way and their structure tend to be complex, which set reading obstacles to the general readers. The summarization of judgment documents is compression of court decisions, reflecting the adjudication process, facts, reasons and judgment basis in the process of trial. A summarization of judgment documents with a short, simple sentence structure can help legal practitioners improve the efficiency of handling cases and enhance the public acceptance of the law.

A novel Extractive-Abstractive summarization method for Chinese judgment documents is proposed in this paper. The method includes an extraction model and an abstraction model. For a complete judgment document, key sentences are

© Springer Nature Switzerland AG 2021
P. Baroni et al. (Eds.): CLAR 2021, LNAI 13040, pp. 486–494, 2021.
https://doi.org/10.1007/978-3-030-89391-0_28

extracted by the extraction model and combined into an initial summarization. Then, the initial summarization is refined into a final summarization through the abstraction model. Summarization generated in this way contains almost all relevant information in a legal case in a brief way. Such a model could help to improve the efficiency of judicial professionals in handling cases and make judgment documents more accessible to the general readers.

2   Related Work

How to employ computers to process legal texts is a core problem in the AI&Law domain [1–3]. Automatic summarization of legal texts is to apply technology in natural language processing (NLP) to compress the legal texts automatically.

At present, automatic text summarization (ATS) broadly employs two approaches: extractive and abstractive. Extractive summarization refers to select key sentences from the original text as summarization, which is usually regarded as a sequence labeling task. For example, Kageback et al. [4] defined an objective function on the text to be compressed. They regarded extractive summarization as a problem of optimal selection of sentence sequences. Cao et al. [5] sought to make the selection more accurate. They predicted the score of each sentence and sorted them, then judged whether to add sentences to the summary according to the principle of redundancy. Cheng et al. [6] used LSTM (Long Short-Term Memory) [7] as a decoder for each sentence, whose input was the embedding of the previous sentence and its output was classified to determine whether the sentence should be included in the summary.

Abstractive summarization is to generate new sentences through the fusion of the original information, with stronger coherence and readability. Rush et al. [8] and Chopra et al. [9] combined the attention mechanism [10] with neural network, and constructed an automatic text summarization model based on Seq2Seq (sequence-to-sequence) [11] framework. They achieved good results on general text data sets. With the introduction of the pre-trained language model BERT [12], subsequent works [13,14] tried to combine Bert with Seq2Seq, which provided a new method for our task of summarizing judgment documents.

3   Proposed Model

In this section, we will describe our Extractive-Abstractive summarization model for judgment documents in detail. A summary of the judgment document should be logical, readable and consistent. This requires to extract the key sentences accurately, then refine and rewrite them. The whole model consists of two parts: key sentences extraction based on Self-Attention mechanism and summary abstraction based on attention mask mechanism.

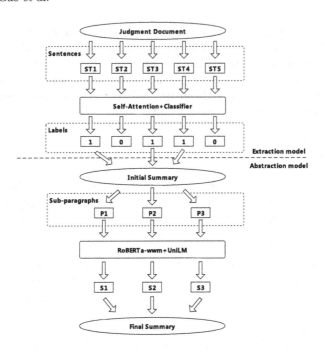

Fig. 1. Overall framework of our model.

3.1   Overview

Figure 1 shows the framework of our model. **Extraction model**: a complete judgment document is preprocessed and divided into a sentence set $\{ST_1, ST_2, ST_3...ST_n\}$. Then a pre-trained language model with Self-Attention mechanism is used as an encoder to obtain the feature embedding of the whole sentence. A trained classifier is combined to get the label of each sentence ("1" represents key sentence, "0" represents non-key sentence). **Abstraction model**: all the sentences labeled "1" are merged into an initial summarization, which is segmented into a sub-paragraph set $\{P_1, P_2, P_3...P_n\}$. Sub-paragraphs are sent into a generation model model based on RoBERTa-wwm[1] and unified language model (UniLM) [14] training method to generate corresponding summary set $\{S_1, S_2, S_3...S_n\}$. Finally, summary set is merged into a final summary of the whole judgment document.

3.2   Key Sentences Extraction Model

According to People's Court Civil Judgment Document Production Standards[2], cause of action, facts, issue, ratio of the decision, ruling basis and final judgment are important components in a judgment document. They are described in detail as follows:

---

[1] https://github.com/ymcui/Chinese-BERT-wwm.
[2] https://m.lawtime.cn/info/wenshu/pjmscpwsyishen/201607073334851.html.

- Cause of action: the source of the case and the category of legal disputes
- Facts: the chronological events that led to the lawsuit, including the legal claims and defenses of contending parties and the facts repeated in the court's opinion.
- Issue: legal issues being discussed
- Ratio of the decision: rationale of the Court for the final ruling
- Ruling basis: citations to established laws by the current case
- Final judgment: conclusion of the court

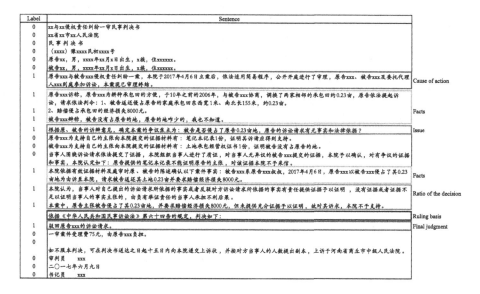

Fig. 2. Sentences in a Chinese judgment document and corresponding label.

As the Chinese judgment document shown in Fig. 2, there are many formal structural sentences labeled "0" that have no important information of the case. The sentences labeled "1", by comparison, contain significant information, which belong to the important components above.

On analyzing sentences labeled "1", we find that they usually contain some special key words or phrases, such as plaintiff's claimant, court's opinion and court's decision. Sentences containing similar keywords or synonyms are more likely to be identified as key sentences. Self-Attention [12] is a special form of Attention to search the connection of words within a sentence. In this paper, Self-Attention mechanism is used to make the model distinguish the categories of sentences by local word information.

3.3   Summary Abstraction Model

The key sentences extraction model extracts most important information from judgment documents and keeps the overall logical consistency. However, the initial summarization are inconsistent and difficult to understand since these sentences are selected directly from the original text. The summary abstraction model is aimed to rewrite and refine the initial summarization.

In this paper, the generation of the final summary is transformed into a Seq2Seq problem. The input sequence is the initial summarization, and the target sequence is the final summary. Seq2Seq is an encoder-decoder framework, in which the encoder compresses input sequence into embeddings with specified length, and the decoder generates specified sequences through these embeddings. According to [14], we adopt RoBERTa-wwm as the framework, and summarization can be regarded as sentence completion [15].

Initial summarization is represented as a sequence$\{A, B, C, D, E\}$, and the final summarization is represented as a sequence$\{F, G, H\}$. Sequence generation based on unidirectional language model can be represented by Eq. (1). Attention map of unidirectional language model is shown in the left of Fig. 3. The shaded part represents the MASK flag, which indicates that these information is invisible. When MASKs of the input sequence are removed, Attention of input sequence becomes bidirectional and Attention of target sequence becomes unidirectional, Attention map of this unified language model is shown in the right of Fig. 3.

$$P(A, B, C, D, E, F, G, H) = P(A)P(B|A)P(C|A, B) \dots$$
$$P(H|A, B, C, D, E, F, G) \qquad (1)$$

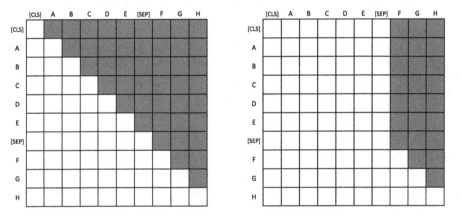

Fig. 3. Attention matrix of unidirectional language model (left) and unified language model (right)

Due to the length limit of RoBERTa-wwm, the sum length of input sequence and target sequence can not exceed 512 words. We segment the initial summarization into sub-paragraphs to retain complete legal information. Each sub-paragraph is sent into the abstraction model to obtain a corresponding summary. All the summaries of sub-paragraphs are merged into a final summary of the whole judgment document.

4 Data and Experiment

4.1 Dataset and Evaluation Metric

The experimental data in this paper is available from CAIL2020[3]. It contains 13.5K Chinese judgment documents, labels of sentences and manual summaries.

ROUGE (Recall-Oriented Understudy for Gisting Evaluation) [16] is a commonly used evaluation index of automatic abstracting, which calculates the overlap rate of the reference summary and the model-generated summary. In this paper, the final summary is evaluated by ROUGE-1, ROUGE-2, ROUGE-L.

ROUGE-N measures the N-gram overlap rate between reference summary and generated summary. ROUGE-1 measures the matching of unigram. ROUGE-2 measures the matching of bigram. ROUGE-L measures the proportion of longest common subsequence between the reference summary and generated summary.

We take the F1 value of ROUGE to balance precision and recall. The calculation of F1 is computed as Eq. (2), where P denotes precision, R denotes recall. Weights $[0.2, 0.4, 0.4]$ are set for the three indicators to get an overall ROUGE score, as shown in (3), to evaluate in a more objective way.

$$F1 = \frac{2 * P(ROUGE) * R(ROUGE)}{P(ROUGE) + R(ROUGE)} \tag{2}$$

$$ROUGE = 0.2 * F1(ROUGE - 1) + 0.4 * $$
$$F1(ROUGE - 2) + 0.4 * F1(ROUGE - L) \tag{3}$$

4.2 Result

In this section, the proposed model is compared internally to reflect the effect of each part. We compare the results of the extraction model, the abstraction model, extraction + abstraction without segmentation (E+A) and the complete model, as shown in Table 1. We can see that the extraction model achieves the highest recall but a poor precision, which leads to a low F1. The abstraction model and Extraction & abstraction (without segmentation) get better precisions but much lower recalls than the extraction model. This is because of the length limit of the abstraction model, summaries of judgment documents suffer

---

[3] http://cail.cipsc.org.cn/.

from a serious legal information loss, such as the fact and reasons, judgment basis and judgment result. The complete model reaches the highest F1. It retains most of the important legal information, segments and sends them into the abstraction model, so it gets an high F1 and is closer to a manual summary of judgment document.

Table 1. The ROUGE scores of each part in our model in test set

Part	ROUGE-1(%)			ROUGE-2(%)			ROUGE-L(%)			ROUGE(%)		
	P	R	F1	P	R	F1	P	R	F1	P	R	F1
Extract	33.65	**83.14**	46.56	24.70	**60.47**	34.08	30.49	**75.13**	42.16	28.80	**70.87**	39.81
Abstract	47.01	30.79	36.95	19.30	12.89	15.34	36.23	23.84	28.54	31.61	20.85	24.94
E+A	**60.01**	43.23	49.86	37.92	27.66	31.70	**50.08**	36.36	41.78	47.20	34.25	39.36
Our Model	57.95	65.84	**60.09**	**41.29**	46.59	**42.61**	49.55	56.05	**51.20**	**47.93**	54.22	**49.54**

The proposed model is also compared to other summary models as shown in Table 2, our Extractive-Abstractive summary model reaches the highest precision and F1, keeping the recall staying a good level. LEAD[4], the baseline of CAIL2020, reflects the level in which the most basic summary method—snippet selection can achieve for judgment documents. TextCNN has the best recall of ROUGE, which indicates that it extracts more complete legal information. However, TextCNN and other summary models have a common problem that the precision of ROUGE is unsatisfactory. This indicates that the generated summaries contain a lot of useless information, and are not satisfactorily refining. TextRank, as a sorting model, is comparable to other neural network models, because we give higher scores to the legal information in this model to make it more suitable for judgment documents.

Table 2. The ROUGE scores of summary models in test set

Model	ROUGE-1(%)			ROUGE-2(%)			ROUGE-L(%)			ROUGE(%)		
	P	R	F1	P	R	F1	P	R	F1	P	R	F1
LEAD	40.02	20.62	26.01	20.69	10.15	13.02	31.54	15.83	20.16	28.90	14.51	18.47
TextRank [17]	38.93	63.34	47.28	25.56	41.62	31.05	33.17	53.94	40.28	31.28	50.89	37.99
FastText [18]	36.32	74.16	47.16	25.07	50.92	32.49	31.49	64.29	40.90	29.89	60.92	38.79
TextCNN [19]	35.47	**79.33**	47.55	25.39	**56.32**	33.96	31.49	**70.41**	42.23	29.84	**66.56**	39.99
TextRNN [20]	35.79	71.72	45.90	24.23	48.37	31.03	30.44	61.07	39.06	29.02	58.12	37.22
Our Model	**57.95**	65.84	**60.09**	**41.29**	46.59	**42.61**	**49.55**	56.05	**51.20**	**47.93**	54.22	**49.54**

The statistical results of the model are shown in Fig. 4. It can be seen that the summarization of judgment documents has a high compression ratio.

---

[4] https://github.com/china-ai-law-challenge/CAIL2020/tree/master/sfzy/baseline.

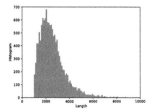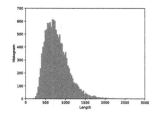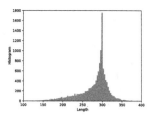

Fig. 4. The length distribution histogram of judgment documents (left), initial summaries (middle) and final summaries (right).

5 Conclusion and Future Work

In this paper, an Extractive-Abstractive summary model for the Chinese judgment documents is proposed. Compared with the existing summary algorithm, the proposed model contains a key sentence extraction model based on the Self-Attention mechanism and a summary abstraction model based on the attention mask mechanism. Such a model could improve the efficiency in case handling and make judgment documents more accessible to the general readers. The experimental results show that the summary generated by our model is more similar to manual summary than other models.

In the future research, we plan to build a knowledge graph based on public judgment documents and integrate more external legal knowledge into our model. To utilize more advanced models, we intend to pre-train a judicial language model with publicly available data and apply it to more legal language processing tasks.

Acknowledgements. This work is supported by The National Social Science Foundation Project of China (No.20BFX077) and National Natural Science Foundation of China (No.61502537).

References

1. Rissland, E.L., Ashley, K.D., Loui, R.P.: Ai and law: a fruitful synergy. Artif. Intell. **150**(1–2), 1–15 (2003)
2. Bench-Capon, T., et al.: A history of AI and law in 50 papers: 25 years of the international conference on AI and law. Artif. Intell. Law **20**(3), 215–319 (2012)
3. Surden, H.: Artificial intelligence and law: an overview. Ga. St. UL Rev. **35**, 1305 (2018)
4. Kågebäck, M., Mogren, O., Tahmasebi, N., Dubhashi, D.: Extractive summarization using continuous vector space models. In: Proceedings of the 2nd Workshop on Continuous Vector Space Models and their Compositionality (CVSC), pp. 31–39 (2014)
5. Cao, Z., Wei, F., Li, S., Li, W., Zhou, M., Wang, H.: Learning summary prior representation for extractive summarization. In: Proceedings of the 53rd Annual Meeting of the Association for Computational Linguistics and the 7th International Joint Conference on Natural Language Processing (Volume 2: Short Papers), pp. 829–833 (2015)

6. Cheng, J., Lapata, M.: Neural summarization by extracting sentences and words. In: Proceedings of the 54th Annual Meeting of the Association for Computational Linguistics (Volume 1: Long Papers), pp. 484–494 (2016)

7. Hochreiter, S., Schmidhuber, J.: Long short-term memory. Neural Comput. **9**(8), 1735–1780 (1997)

8. Rush, A.M., Chopra, S., Weston, J.: A neural attention model for abstractive sentence summarization. In: EMNLP (2015)

9. Chopra, S., Auli, M., Rush, A.M.: Abstractive sentence summarization with attentive recurrent neural networks. In: Proceedings of the 2016 Conference of the North American Chapter of the Association for Computational Linguistics: Human Language Technologies, pp. 93–98 (2016)

10. Vaswani, A., et al.: Attention is all you need. In: NIPS (2017)

11. Sutskever, I., Vinyals, O., Le, Q.V.: Sequence to sequence learning with neural networks. In: Advances in Neural Information Processing Systems (2014)

12. Devlin, J., Chang, M.W., Lee, K., Toutanova, K.: BERT: pre-training of deep bidirectional transformers for language understanding. In: Proceedings of the 2019 Conference of the North American Chapter of the Association for Computational Linguistics: Human Language Technologies, Volume 1 (Long and Short Papers), pp. 4171–4186 (2019)

13. Song, K., Tan, X., Qin, T., Lu, J., Liu, T.Y.: Mass: masked sequence to sequence pre-training for language generation. In: International Conference on Machine Learning, pp. 5926–5936. PMLR (2019)

14. Dong, L., et al.: Unified language model pre-training for natural language understanding and generation. In: Proceedings of the 33rd International Conference on Neural Information Processing Systems, pp. 13063–13075 (2019)

15. Su, J.: From language models to seq2seq: Transformer and mask (2019). https://kexue.fm/archives/6933

16. Lin, C.Y.: Rouge: a package for automatic evaluation of summaries. In: Text summarization branches out, pp. 74–81 (2004)

17. Mihalcea, R., Tarau, P.: Textrank: bringing order into text. In: Proceedings of the 2004 Conference on Empirical Methods in Natural Language Processing, pp. 404–411 (2004)

18. Joulin, A., Grave, É., Bojanowski, P., Mikolov, T.: Bag of tricks for efficient text classification. In: Proceedings of the 15th Conference of the European Chapter of the Association for Computational Linguistics: Volume 2, Short Papers, pp. 427–431 (2017)

19. Kim, Y.: Convolutional neural networks for sentence classification. arXiv preprint arXiv:1408.5882 (2014)

20. Liu, P., Qiu, X., Huang, X.: Recurrent neural network for text classification with multi-task learning. In: Proceedings of the Twenty-Fifth International Joint Conference on Artificial Intelligence, pp. 2873–2879 (2016)

A Framework for Intuitionistic Grammar Logics

Tim S. Lyon$^{(\boxtimes)}$

Computational Logic Group, Institute of Artificial Intelligence,
Technische Universität Dresden, Dresden, Germany
timothy_stephen.lyon@tu-dresden.de

Abstract. We generalize intuitionistic tense logics to the multi-modal case by placing grammar logics on an intuitionistic footing. We provide axiomatizations for a class of base intuitionistic grammar logics as well as provide axiomatizations for extensions with combinations of seriality axioms and what we call *intuitionistic path axioms*. We show that each axiomatization is sound and complete with completeness being shown via a typical canonical model construction.

Keywords: Bi-relational model · Completeness · Context-free · Converse · Grammar logic · Intuitionistic logic · Modal logic · Path axiom

1 Introduction

Having been introduced in 1988 by Fariñas del Cerro and Penttonen [5], *grammar logics* form a prominent class of normal, multi-modal logics that extend classical propositional logic with a set of modalities indexed by characters from an alphabet. Such logics obtain their name due to the incorporation of axioms which can be viewed as production rules in a context-free grammar, and which generate sequences of edges (which can be viewed as words) in a relational model. More significantly however, the class of grammar logics includes many well-known logics that have practical value in computer science; e.g. description logics [17], epistemic logics [11], information logics [27], temporal logics [4], and standard modal logics (e.g. K, S4, and S5) [8].

Another logical paradigm that is useful within computer science is that of *constructive reasoning* (e.g. [18,22]), that is, reasoning where the claimed existence of an object implies its constructibility [3]. One of the most renowned logics for formalizing constructive reasoning is *intuitionistic logic*, which employs a version of implication that is stronger than its classical counterpart. Resting on the philosophical work of L.E.J. Brouwer, propositional intuitionistic logic was provided axiomatizations in the early 20th century by Kolmogorov [19], Orlov [21], and Glivenko [15], with a first-order axiomatization given by Heyting [16].

Work supported by the European Research Council (ERC) Consolidator Grant 771779 (DeciGUT).

P. Baroni et al. (Eds.): CLAR 2021, LNAI 13040, pp. 495–503, 2021.
https://doi.org/10.1007/978-3-030-89391-0_29

The interest in modal and intuitionistic logics naturally gave rise to combinations of the two, thus giving birth to the paradigm of *intuitionistic modal logics*. A diverse set of intuitionistic modal logics have been proposed in the literature [1,2,9,13,14,24,25], though the class of logics introduced by Plotkin and Stirling [24] has become (most notably through the work of Simpson [25]) one of the most popular formulations. In the same year that Plotkin and Stirling [24] introduced their intuitionistic modal logics, Ewald introduced *intuitionistic tense logic* [10], which not only includes modalities that make reference to the future in a relational model ($\Diamond$ and $\Box$), but also includes modalities that make reference to the past ($\blacklozenge$ and $\blacksquare$). As with (multi-)modal and intuitionistic logics, intuitionistic modal logics have proven useful in computer science; e.g. such logics have been used to design verification techniques [12], in reasoning about functional programs [23], and in the definition of programming languages [7].

Due to the practical import of the aforementioned logics, it seems both natural and worthwhile to formulate intuitionistic versions of grammar logics. Hence, the main goal of this paper will be to axiomatize intuitionistic context-free grammar logics with converses, thus generalizing the work of [5,10,24]. In the following section (Sect. 2), we axiomatize and provide a semantics for intuitionistic grammar logics. Afterward (in Sect. 3), we prove the soundness and completeness of our logics, with completeness being shown on the basis of a standard canonical model construction (adapting techniques provided in [10]). In the final section (Sect. 4), we briefly conclude and discuss future work.

2   Intuitionistic Grammar Logics

We define our languages for intuitionistic grammar logics relative to an *alphabet* Σ consisting of a non-empty countable set of characters, which will be used to index modalities. Following [8], we stipulate that each alphabet Σ can be partitioned into a *forward part* $\Sigma^+ := \{a, b, c, \ldots\}$ and a *backward part* $\Sigma^- := \{\overline{a}, \overline{b}, \overline{c}, \ldots\}$ such that each part has the same cardinality and the following is satisfied:

$$\Sigma := \Sigma^+ \cup \Sigma^- \text{ where } \Sigma^+ \cap \Sigma^- = \emptyset \text{ and } a \in \Sigma^+ \textit{ iff } \overline{a} \in \Sigma^-$$

We use a, b, c, ... (possibly annotated) to denote the *forward characters* contained in the forward part Σ^+, and $\overline{a}$, $\overline{b}$, $\overline{c}$, ... (possibly annotated) to denote the *backward characters* contained in the backward part Σ^-. Both forward and backward characters are referred to as *characters* more generally, and we use x, y, z, ... (possibly annotated) to denote them. Intuitively, modalities indexed with forward characters make reference to future states within a relational model, and modalities indexed with backward characters make reference to past states. The *converse operation* $\bar{\cdot}$ is defined to be a function mapping each forward character $a \in \Sigma^+$ to its *converse* $\overline{a} \in \Sigma^-$ and vice versa; hence, the converse operation is its own inverse, i.e. for any $x \in \Sigma$, $x = \overline{\overline{x}}$.

Each of our languages includes *propositional atoms* from the denumerable set $\Phi := \{p, q, r, \ldots\}$. Each language $\mathcal{L}(\Sigma)$ is defined via the following grammar in BNF:

$$A ::= p \mid \bot \mid A \vee A \mid A \wedge A \mid A \supset A \mid \langle x \rangle A \mid [x]A$$

where p ranges over the set of propositional atoms Φ and x ranges over the alphabet Σ. We use $A, B, C, \ldots$ to range over formulae in $\mathcal{L}(\Sigma)$, define $\sim A := A \supset \bot$, and define $A \supset\subset B := (A \supset B) \wedge (B \supset A)$. We interpret formulae on *bi-relational* Σ-*models*, which are inspired by the models for intuitionistic modal and tense logics presented in [2,9,10,24]:

Definition 1 (Bi-relational Σ-Model). *We define a* bi-relational Σ-model *to be a tuple* $M = (W, \leq, \{R_x \mid x \in \Sigma\}, V)$ *such that:*

- W *is a non-empty set of* worlds $\{w, u, v, \ldots\}$;
- *The* intuitionistic relation $\leq \subseteq W \times W$ *is a preorder, i.e. it is reflexive and transitive;*
- *The* accessibility relation $R_x \subseteq W \times W$ *satisfies:*
  - *(F1) For all* $w, v, v' \in W$, *if* wR_xv *and* $v \leq v'$, *then there exists a* $w' \in W$ *such that* $w \leq w'$ *and* $w'R_xv'$;
  - *(F2) For all* $w, w', v \in W$, *if* $w \leq w'$ *and* wR_xv, *then there exists a* $v' \in W$ *such that* $w'R_xv'$ *and* $v \leq v'$;
  - *(F3)* wR_xu *iff* $uR_{\overline{x}}w$;
- $V : W \rightarrow 2^{\Phi}$ *is a* valuation function *satisfying the* monotonicity condition: *for each* $w, u \in W$, *if* $w \leq u$, *then* $V(w) \subseteq V(u)$.

The (F1) and (F2) conditions ensure the monotonicity of complex formulae (see Lemma 1) in our models, which is a property characteristic of intuitionistic logics.[1] We note that we interpret accessibility relations indexed with forward characters as relating worlds to *future* worlds, and accessibility relations indexed with backward characters as relating worlds to *past* worlds. Such an interpretation shows that our models have a tense character, and additionally, shows that our logics generalize the intuitionistic tense logics of [10].

We interpret formulae from $\mathcal{L}(\Sigma)$ over bi-relational models via the following clauses.

Definition 2 (Semantic Clauses). *Let M be a bi-relational Σ-model with* $w \in W$. *The* satisfaction relation $M, w \Vdash^{\Sigma} A$ *between* $w \in W$ *of M and a formula* $A \in \mathcal{L}(\Sigma)$ *is inductively defined as follows:*

- $M, w \Vdash^{\Sigma} p$ *iff* $p \in V(w)$, *for* $p \in \Phi$;
- $M, w \not\Vdash^{\Sigma} \bot$;
- $M, w \Vdash^{\Sigma} A \vee B$ *iff* $M, w \Vdash^{\Sigma} A$ *or* $M, w \Vdash^{\Sigma} B$;
- $M, w \Vdash^{\Sigma} A \wedge B$ *iff* $M, w \Vdash^{\Sigma} A$ *and* $M, w \Vdash^{\Sigma} B$;
- $M, w \Vdash^{\Sigma} A \supset B$ *iff for all* $w' \in W$, *if* $w \leq w'$ *and* $M, w' \Vdash^{\Sigma} A$, *then* $M, w' \Vdash^{\Sigma} B$;
- $M, w \Vdash^{\Sigma} \langle x \rangle A$ *iff there exists a* $v \in W$ *such that* wR_xv *and* $M, v \Vdash^{\Sigma} A$;
- $M, w \Vdash^{\Sigma} [x]A$ *iff for all* $w', v' \in W$, *if* $w \leq w'$ *and* $w'R_xv'$, *then* $M, v' \Vdash^{\Sigma} A$.

---

[1] For a discussion of these conditions and their encompassing literature, see [25, Ch. 3].

Lemma 1. *Let M be a bi-relational Σ-model with $w, u \in W$ of M. If $w \leq u$ and $M, w \Vdash^{\Sigma} A$, then $M, u \Vdash^{\Sigma} A$.*

Proof. By induction on the complexity of A.   □

As will be shown in the subsequent section, given an alphabet Σ, the set of formulae valid with respect to the class of bi-relational Σ-models is axiomatizable. We refer to the axiomatization as $\mathsf{HIK_m}(\Sigma)$ (with H denoting the fact that the axiomatization is a *Hilbert calculus*), and call the corresponding logic that it generates $\mathsf{IK_m}(\Sigma)$. We note that $\mathsf{IK_m}(\Sigma)$ is taken to be the base intuitionistic grammar logic relative to Σ; below, we will also consider extensions of $\mathsf{IK_m}(\Sigma)$ by extending its axiomatization with common modal axioms.

Definition 3 (Axiomatization). *We define our axiomatization $\mathsf{HIK_m}(\Sigma)$ below, where we have an axiom and inference rule for each $x \in \Sigma$.*

A0 Any axiomatization for intuitionistic propositional logic

A1 $[x](A \supset B) \supset ([x]A \supset [x]B)$

A2 $[x](A \wedge B) \supset\subset ([x]A \wedge [x]B)$

A3 $\langle x \rangle(A \vee B) \supset\subset (\langle x \rangle A \vee \langle x \rangle B)$

A4 $[x](A \supset B) \supset (\langle x \rangle A \supset \langle x \rangle B)$

A5 $[x]A \wedge \langle x \rangle B \supset \langle x \rangle(A \wedge B)$

A6 $\sim\langle x \rangle \bot$

A7 $(A \supset [x]\langle \overline{x} \rangle A) \wedge (\langle x \rangle[\overline{x}]A \supset A)$

A8 $(\langle x \rangle A \supset [x]B) \supset [x](A \supset B)$

A9 $\langle x \rangle(A \supset B) \supset ([x]A \supset \langle x \rangle B)$

R1 $\frac{A}{[x]A}(nec)$

We define the logic $\mathsf{IK_m}(\Sigma)$ to be the smallest set of formulae from $\mathcal{L}(\Sigma)$ closed under substitutions of the axioms and applications of the inference rules. A formula A is defined to be a theorem *of $\mathsf{IK_m}(\Sigma)$ iff $A \in \mathsf{IK_m}(\Sigma)$.*

We also consider logics that are extensions of $\mathsf{IK_m}(\Sigma)$ with sets $\mathcal{A}$ of the following axioms.

$$\mathrm{D}_x : [x]A \supset \langle x \rangle A \quad \mathrm{IPA} : (\langle x_1 \rangle \cdots \langle x_n \rangle A \supset \langle x \rangle A) \wedge ([x]A \supset [x_1] \cdots [x_n]A)$$

We refer to axioms of the form shown above left as *seriality axioms*, and axioms of the form shown above right as *intuitionistic path axioms* (IPAs). We use $\mathcal{A}$ to denote any arbitrary collection of axioms of the above forms. Moreover, we note that the collection of IPAs includes multi-modal variants of standard axioms such as T_x, B_x, 4_x, and 5_x, which are shown below.

$$\mathrm{T}_x : (A \supset \langle x \rangle A) \wedge ([x]A \supset A) \quad 4_x : (\langle x \rangle \langle x \rangle A \supset \langle x \rangle A) \wedge ([x]A \supset [x][x]A)$$

$$\mathrm{B}_x : (\langle \overline{x} \rangle A \supset \langle x \rangle A) \wedge ([x]A \supset [\overline{x}]A) \quad 5_x : (\langle \overline{x} \rangle \langle x \rangle A \supset \langle x \rangle A) \wedge ([x]A \supset [\overline{x}][x]A)$$

In the next section, we show that any extension of $\mathsf{HIK_m}(\Sigma)$ with a set $\mathcal{A}$ of axioms is sound and complete relative to a specified sub-class of the bi-relational Σ-models. For each axiom we extend $\mathsf{HIK_m}(\Sigma)$ with, we impose a frame condition on our class of bi-relational Σ-models. Axioms and related frame conditions are displayed in Fig. 1, and extensions of $\mathsf{HIK_m}(\Sigma)$ with seriality and IPA axioms, along with their corresponding models, are defined below.

Axiom	$[x]A \supset \langle x \rangle A$	$(\langle x_1 \rangle \cdots \langle x_n \rangle A \supset \langle x \rangle A) \wedge ([x]A \supset [x_1] \cdots [x_n]A)$
Condition	$\forall w \exists u (wR_x u)$	$\forall w_0, \ldots, w_n (w_0 R_{x_1} w_1 \wedge \cdots \wedge w_{n-1} R_{x_n} w_n \supset w_0 R_x w_n)$

Fig. 1. Axioms and their related frame conditions. We note that when $n = 0$, the related frame condition is taken to be $wR_x w$.

Definition 4 (Terminology for Extensions). *We define the axiomatization* $\mathsf{HIK_m}(\Sigma, \mathcal{A})$ *to be* $\mathsf{HIK_m}(\Sigma) \cup \mathcal{A}$, *and define the logic* $\mathsf{IK_m}(\Sigma, \mathcal{A})$ *to be the smallest set of formulae from* $\mathcal{L}(\Sigma)$ *closed under substitutions of the axioms and applications of the inference rules. A formula A is defined to be an* $\mathsf{IK_m}(\Sigma, \mathcal{A})$-*theorem, written* $\vdash_{\mathcal{A}}^{\Sigma} A$, *iff* $A \in \mathsf{IK_m}(\Sigma, \mathcal{A})$, *and a formula A is said to be* derivable *from a set of formulae* $\mathscr{A} \subseteq \mathcal{L}(\Sigma)$, *written* $\mathscr{A} \vdash_{\mathcal{A}}^{\Sigma} A$, *iff for some* $B_1, \ldots, B_n \in \mathscr{A}$, $\vdash_{\mathcal{A}}^{\Sigma} B_1 \wedge \cdots \wedge B_n \supset A$.

Moreover, we define a bi-relational $(\Sigma, \mathcal{A})$-*model to be a bi-relational Σ-model satisfying each frame condition related to an axiom $A \in \mathcal{A}$. A formula A is defined to be* globally true *on a bi-relational $(\Sigma, \mathcal{A})$-model M, written* $M \Vdash_{\mathcal{A}}^{\Sigma} A$, *iff* $M, u \Vdash^{\Sigma} A$ *for all worlds* $u \in W$ *of M. A formula A is defined to be* $(\Sigma, \mathcal{A})$-*valid, written* $\Vdash_{\mathcal{A}}^{\Sigma} A$, *iff A is globally true on every bi-relational $(\Sigma, \mathcal{A})$-model. Last, we say that a set $\mathscr{A}$ of formulae* semantically implies *a formula A, written* $\mathscr{A} \Vdash_{\mathcal{A}}^{\Sigma} A$, *iff for all bi-relational $(\Sigma, \mathcal{A})$-models M and each $w \in W$ of M, if $M, w \Vdash^{\Sigma} B$ for each $B \in \mathscr{A}$, then $M, w \Vdash^{\Sigma} A$.*

Remark 1. Note that the axiomatization $\mathsf{HIK_m}(\Sigma) = \mathsf{HIK_m}(\Sigma, \emptyset)$ and that a bi-relational $(\Sigma, \emptyset)$-model is a bi-relational Σ-model.

Let us now move on to the next section and prove the soundness and completeness results for our logics.

3 Soundness and Completeness

In this section, we show that the $\vdash_{\mathcal{A}}^{\Sigma}$ and $\Vdash_{\mathcal{A}}^{\Sigma}$ relations coincide, that is to say, we show that each intuitionistic grammar logic $\mathsf{IK_m}(\Sigma, \mathcal{A})$ is sound and complete. As usual, soundness is straightforward to prove:

Theorem 1 (Soundness). *If* $\mathscr{A} \vdash_{\mathcal{A}}^{\Sigma} A$, *then* $\mathscr{A} \Vdash_{\mathcal{A}}^{\Sigma} A$.

Proof. One can prove that if $\vdash_{\mathcal{A}}^{\Sigma} A$, then $\Vdash_{\mathcal{A}}^{\Sigma} A$ by showing that each axiom is valid and each inference rule preserves validity. Then, if we assume that $\mathscr{A} \vdash_{\mathcal{A}}^{\Sigma} A$, it follows that for some $B_1, \ldots, B_n \in \mathscr{A}$, $\vdash_{\mathcal{A}}^{\Sigma} B_1 \wedge \cdots \wedge B_n \supset A$, which further implies that $\Vdash_{\mathcal{A}}^{\Sigma} B_1 \wedge \cdots \wedge B_n \supset A$. The last fact permits us to conclude that $\mathscr{A} \Vdash_{\mathcal{A}}^{\Sigma} A$. □

To establish completeness we combine techniques used for establishing the completeness of intuitionistic logic [6] and intuitionisitc tense logic [10]. Our strategy is rather standard and consists of constructing a canonical model where worlds are pairs of the form $(\mathscr{A}^\omega, \mathscr{B}^\omega)$ with $\mathscr{A}^\omega$ and $\mathscr{B}^\omega$ sets of formulae. If one assumes that $\mathscr{A} \not\vdash^\Sigma_\mathcal{A} A$, then one can show that a pair exists in the canonical model satisfying $\mathscr{A}$, but not A, thus establishing completeness (see Theorem 2 below). We begin by defining two useful notions, viz. the notion of an $\mathsf{IK_m}(\Sigma, \mathcal{A})$-consistent set and the notion of an $\mathsf{IK_m}(\Sigma, \mathcal{A})$-saturated pair.

Definition 5 ($\mathsf{IK_m}(\Sigma, \mathcal{A})$-**Consistent**). *We define a pair of sets of formulae* $(\mathscr{A}, \mathscr{B})$ *to be* $\mathsf{IK_m}(\Sigma, \mathcal{A})$-*consistent iff for no finite subsets* $\mathscr{A}_0 \subseteq \mathscr{A}$ *and* $\mathscr{B}_0 \subseteq \mathscr{B}$ *we have* $\vdash^\Sigma_\mathcal{A} \bigwedge \mathscr{A}_0 \supset \bigvee \mathscr{B}_0$.

Definition 6 ($\mathsf{IK_m}(\Sigma, \mathcal{A})$-**Saturated**). *We define a pair* $(\mathscr{A}, \mathscr{B})$ *to be* $\mathsf{IK_m}(\Sigma, \mathcal{A})$-*saturated iff*

1. $(\mathscr{A}, \mathscr{B})$ *is* $\mathsf{IK_m}(\Sigma, \mathcal{A})$-*consistent;*
2. *if* $\mathscr{A} \vdash^\Sigma_\mathcal{A} A$, *then* $A \in \mathscr{A}$;
3. *if* $\mathscr{A} \vdash^\Sigma_\mathcal{A} A \vee B$, *then* $A \in \mathscr{A}$ *or* $B \in \mathscr{A}$;
4. $\mathscr{A} \cap \mathscr{B} = \emptyset$;
5. $\mathscr{A} \cup \mathscr{B} = \mathcal{L}(\Sigma)$.

Lemma 2. *Suppose that* $(\mathscr{A}, \mathscr{B})$ *is* $\mathsf{IK_m}(\Sigma, \mathcal{A})$-*consistent. Then, there exists a saturated pair* $(\mathscr{A}^\omega, \mathscr{B}^\omega)$ *such that* $\mathscr{A} \subseteq \mathscr{A}^\omega$ *and* $\mathscr{B} \subseteq \mathscr{B}^\omega$.

Proof. Let us enumerate all disjunctions from $\mathcal{L}(\Sigma)$ where each disjunction occurs infinitely often: $\langle B_{0,i} \vee B_{1,i} \rangle_{i \in \mathbb{N}}$. We set $(\mathscr{A}_0, \mathscr{B}_0) := (\mathscr{A}, \mathscr{B})$ and define an infinite sequence of pairs as follows: $\mathscr{A}_{n+1} := \mathscr{A}_n \cup \{B_{j,n}\}$ and $\mathscr{B}_{n+1} := \mathscr{B}_n$, if $(\mathscr{A}_n \cup \{B_{j,n}\}, \mathscr{B}_n)$ is $\mathsf{IK_m}(\Sigma, \mathcal{A})$-consistent (and if $(\mathscr{A}_n \cup \{B_{j,n}\}, \mathscr{B}_n)$ is $\mathsf{IK_m}(\Sigma, \mathcal{A})$-consistent for both $j = 0$ and $j = 1$, then we set $\mathscr{A}_{n+1} := \mathscr{A}_n \cup \{B_{0,n}\}$), and $\mathscr{A}_{n+1} := \mathscr{A}_n$ and $\mathscr{B}_{n+1} := \mathscr{B}_n \cup \{B_{0,i}, B_{1,i}\}$ otherwise.

Let $\mathscr{A}^\omega := \bigcup_{i \in \mathbb{N}} \mathscr{A}_i$ and $\mathscr{B}^\omega := \bigcup_{i \in \mathbb{N}} \mathscr{B}_i$. We now argue that $(\mathscr{A}^\omega, \mathscr{B}^\omega)$ is saturated. It is straightforward to show that for each n, $(\mathscr{A}_n, \mathscr{B}_n)$ is $\mathsf{IK_m}(\Sigma, \mathcal{A})$-consistent and that $\mathscr{A}_n \cap \mathscr{B}_n = \emptyset$ from which the saturation properties 1 and 4 can be deduced (see Definition 6 above). We note that saturation properties 3 and 5 follow from the above construction procedure, and 2 follows from 3 since if $\mathscr{A} \vdash^\Sigma_\mathcal{A} A$, then $\mathscr{A} \vdash^\Sigma_\mathcal{A} A \vee A$ (cf. [6, Lemma 5.3.8]). □

Definition 7. (Canonical Model). *We define the* canonical model $M^C(\Sigma, \mathcal{A})$ $:= (W^C, \leq^C, \{R^C_x \mid x \in \Sigma\}, V^C)$ *as shown below, and let* $w, u \in W^C$ *with* $w := (\mathscr{A}, \mathscr{B})$ *and* $u := (\mathscr{A}', \mathscr{B}')$.

- $W^C := \{(\mathscr{C}, \mathscr{D}) \mid (\mathscr{C}, \mathscr{D}) \text{ is saturated.}\}$;
- $w \leq^C u$ iff $\mathscr{A} \subseteq \mathscr{A}'$;
- $w R^C_x u$ iff (i) for all $A \in \mathcal{L}(\Sigma)$, if $[x]A \in \mathscr{A}$, then $A \in \mathscr{A}'$, and (ii) for all $A \in \mathcal{L}(\Sigma)$, if $A \in \mathscr{A}'$, then $\langle x \rangle A \in \mathscr{A}$;
- $w \in V^C(p)$ iff $p \in \mathscr{A}$.

The following two lemmas are proven in an almost identical fashion to Lemma 3 and 5 of [10].

Lemma 3. *Let $w:=(\mathcal{A}_0,\mathcal{B}_0) \in W^C$. Then, $\langle x \rangle A \in \mathcal{A}_0$ iff there exists a $u:=(\mathcal{A}_1,\mathcal{B}_1) \in W^C$ such that $wR_x^C u$ and $A \in \mathcal{A}_1$.*

Lemma 4. *Let $w:=(\mathcal{A}_0,\mathcal{B}_0) \in W^C$. Then, $[x]A \in \mathcal{A}_0$ iff for each $u:=(\mathcal{A}_1,\mathcal{B}_1)$ and $v:=(\mathcal{A}_2,\mathcal{B}_2)$ in W^C, if $w \leq^C u$ and $uR_x^C v$, then $A \in \mathcal{A}_2$.*

Lemma 5. *The canonical model $M^C(\Sigma,\mathcal{A})$ is a bi-relational $(\Sigma,\mathcal{A})$-model.*

Proof. It is straightforward to show that M^C is a bi-relational $(\Sigma,\mathcal{A})$-model. The proof that M^C satisfies properties (F1)–(F3) uses axioms A8, A9, and A7, respectively (cf. [10]), and the fact that the valuation function V^C is monotonic follows from its definition and the definition of $\leq^C$. Below, we show that M^C satisfies each frame property associated with an axiom from $\mathcal{A}$.

D_x We show that if the seriality axiom $[x]A \supset \langle x \rangle A$ is included in our axiomatization, then R_x is serial. Let $w:=(\mathcal{A},\mathcal{B}) \in W^C$ and observe that the formula $[x](p \supset p) \in \mathcal{A}$ since if it were in $\mathcal{B}$, w would not be $\mathsf{IK_m}(\Sigma,\mathcal{A})$-consistent (and hence, not saturated). Therefore, by applying the seriality axiom D_x, we may conclude that $\langle x \rangle(p \supset p) \in \mathcal{A}$, from which it follows that there exists a $u:=(\mathcal{C},\mathcal{D}) \in W^C$ such that $wR_x^C u$ by Lemma 3.

IPA We show that if $(\langle x_1 \rangle \cdots \langle x_n \rangle A \supset \langle x \rangle A) \wedge ([x]A \supset [x_1] \cdots [x_n]A)$ is included in our axiomatization, then for any $w_0,\dots,w_n \in W^C$, if $w_i R_{x_{i+1}}^C w_{i+1}$ for each $i \in \{0,\dots,n-1\}$, then $w_0 R_x^C w_n$. Let $w_0,\dots,w_n$ be arbitrary worlds in W^C and suppose that $w_i R_{x_{i+1}}^C w_{i+1}$ for each $i \in \{0,\dots,n-1\}$. We aim to show that $w_0 R_x^C w_n$, where $w_0:=(\mathcal{A}_0,\mathcal{B}_0)$ and $w_n:=(\mathcal{A}_n,\mathcal{B}_n)$. First, assume that $[x]A \in \mathcal{A}_0$. Then, by the above axiom, $[x_1] \cdots [x_n]A \in \mathcal{A}_0$, and by our assumption and the definition of the R_x^C relation, $A \in \mathcal{A}_n$. Second, assume that $A \in \mathcal{A}_n$. Then, by our assumption and the definition of the R_x^C relation, $\langle x_1 \rangle \cdots \langle x_n \rangle A \in \mathcal{A}_0$, so by the above axiom, $\langle x \rangle A \in \mathcal{A}_0$. Therefore, $w_0 R_x^C w_n$. □

Lemma 6 (Truth Lemma). *Let $w:=(\mathcal{A},\mathcal{B})$ be saturated. Then, we have $M^C(\Sigma,\mathcal{A}), w \Vdash^\Sigma A$ iff $A \in \mathcal{A}$.*

Proof. We prove the result by induction on the complexity of A and argue the $\vee$, $\supset$, $\langle x \rangle$, and $[x]$ cases since the other cases are simple.

$B \vee C$. $M^C(\Sigma,\mathcal{A}), w \Vdash^\Sigma B \vee C$ iff $M^C(\Sigma,\mathcal{A}), w \Vdash^\Sigma B$ or $M^C(\Sigma,\mathcal{A}), w \Vdash^\Sigma C$ iff $B \in \mathcal{A}$ or $C \in \mathcal{A}$ iff $B \vee C \in \mathcal{A}$. We note that the second '*iff*' follows from IH an the third follows from the fact that w is saturated (see Definition 6).

$B \supset C$. The right-to-left direction is straightforward, so we show the left-to-right direction by contraposition. Suppose that $B \supset C \notin \mathcal{A}$. It follows that $\mathcal{A} \cup \{B\} \nvdash_\mathcal{A}^\Sigma C$, implying that the pair $(\mathcal{A} \cup \{B\}; \{C\})$ is $\mathsf{IK_m}(\Sigma,\mathcal{A})$-consistent, and so, we may extend it to a saturated pair $u:=(\mathcal{C},\mathcal{D})$. Observe that $\mathcal{A} \subseteq \mathcal{C}$, $B \in \mathcal{C}$, and $C \notin \mathcal{C}$. By the definition of $\leq^C$ and IH, it follows that $u \in W^C$ with $w \leq^C u$, $M^C(\Sigma,\mathcal{A}), u \Vdash^\Sigma B$, and $M^C(\Sigma,\mathcal{A}), u \nVdash^\Sigma C$, entailing that $M^C(\Sigma,\mathcal{A}), w \nVdash^\Sigma B \supset C$.

$\langle x \rangle B$. The left-to-right direction is straightforward, so we show the right-to-left direction. Suppose that $\langle x \rangle B \in \mathcal{A}$. Then, by Lemma 3 we know that there exists a $u := (\mathscr{C}, \mathscr{D}) \in W^C$ such that $w R_x^C u$ and $B \in \mathscr{C}$. Therefore, $M^C(\Sigma, \mathcal{A}), u \Vdash^\Sigma B$ by IH, implying that $M^C(\Sigma, \mathcal{A}), w \Vdash^\Sigma \langle x \rangle B$.

$[x]B$. Follows from Lemma 4 and IH.   □

Theorem 2 (Completeness). *If $\mathscr{A} \Vdash_{\mathcal{A}}^\Sigma A$, then $\mathscr{A} \vdash_{\mathcal{A}}^\Sigma A$.*

Proof. Suppose $\mathscr{A} \nvdash_{\mathcal{A}}^\Sigma A$. Then, $(\mathscr{A}, \{A\})$ is $\mathsf{IK_m}(\Sigma, \mathcal{A})$-consistent and can be extended to a saturated pair $w := (\mathscr{A}^\omega, \mathscr{B}^\omega)$. By Lemma 6, $M^C, w \Vdash^\Sigma B$ for each $B \in \mathscr{A}^\omega$, but $M^C, w \nVdash^\Sigma C$ for each $C \in \mathscr{B}^\omega$. Hence, $\mathscr{A} \nVdash_{\mathcal{A}}^\Sigma A$.   □

4   Conclusion

This paper provided sound and complete axiomatizations for intuitionistic grammar logics. We defined a base intuitionistic grammar logic $\mathsf{IK_m}(\Sigma)$, for each alphabet Σ, and provided axiomatizations for extensions of $\mathsf{IK_m}(\Sigma)$ with combinations of seriality axioms and intuitionistic path axioms. In future work, we aim to provide nested sequent systems in the style of [26] for the logics discussed here by making use of the structural refinement methodology of [20]. The goal will be to identify decidable fragments of intuitionistic grammar logics via proof-search. Moreover, due to the connection between modal logics and description logics, it could be worthwhile to investigate the use of intuitionistic grammar logics (or close variants thereof) in knowledge representation.

References

1. Bierman, G.M., de Paiva, V.C.V.: On an intuitionistic modal logic. Stud. Log.: Int. J. Symb. Log. **65**(3), 383–416 (2000). http://www.jstor.org/stable/20016199
2. Božić, M., Došen, K.: Models for normal intuitionistic modal logics. Stud. Log. **43**(3), 217–245 (1984)
3. Brouwer, L.E.J., Heyting, A.: L.E.J. Brouwer: Collected Works, Volume 1: Philosophy and Foundations of Mathematics. North-Holland Publishing Company, American Elsevier Publishing Company, New York (1975)
4. del Cerro, L.F.n., Herzig, A.: Modal deduction with applications in epistemic and temporal logics. In: Gabbay, D.M., Hogger, C.J., Robinson, J.A. (eds.) Handbook of Logic in Artificial Intelligence and Logic Programming (Vol. 4): Epistemic and Temporal Reasoning, pp. 499–594. Oxford University Press Inc., USA (1995)
5. del Cerro, L.F., Penttonen, M.: Grammar logics. Log. Anal. **31**(121/122), 123–134 (1988)
6. van Dalen, D.: Logic and Structure. Springer, Heidelberg (2004). https://doi.org/10.1007/978-3-540-85108-0
7. Davies, R., Pfenning, F.: A modal analysis of staged computation. J. ACM **48**(3), 555–604 (2001). https://doi.org/10.1145/382780.382785
8. Demri, S., de Nivelle, H.: Deciding regular grammar logics with converse through first-order logic. J. Log. Lang. Inf. **14**(3), 289–329 (2005). https://doi.org/10.1007/s10849-005-5788-9
9. Došen, K.: Models for stronger normal intuitionistic modal logics. Stud. Log. **44**(1), 39–70 (1985)

10. Ewald, W.B.: Intuitionistic tense and modal logic. J. Symb. Log. **51**(1), 166–179 (1986). http://www.jstor.org/stable/2273953
11. Fagin, R., Moses, Y., Halpern, J.Y., Vardi, M.Y.: Reasoning About Knowledge. MIT Press, Cambridge (1995)
12. Fairtlough, M., Mendler, M.: An intuitionistic modal logic with applications to the formal verification of hardware. In: Pacholski, L., Tiuryn, J. (eds.) CSL 1994. LNCS, vol. 933, pp. 354–368. Springer, Heidelberg (1995). https://doi.org/10.1007/BFb0022268
13. Fischer Servi, G.: Axiomatizations for some intuitionistic modal logics. Rend. Sem. Mat. Univers. Politecn. Torino **42**(3), 179–194 (1984)
14. Fitch, F.B.: Intuitionistic modal logic with quantifiers. Portugaliae Math. **7**(2), 113–118 (1948). http://eudml.org/doc/114664
15. Glivenko, V.: Sur quelques points de la logique de m. brouwer. Bull. Classe Sci. **15**(5), 183–188 (1929)
16. Heyting, A.: Die formalen regeln der intuitionistischen logik. Sitzungsbericht PreuBische Akad. Wissenschaften Berlin Phys.-Math. Klasse **II**, 42–56 (1930)
17. Horrocks, I., Sattler, U.: Decidability of $\mathcal{SHIQ}$ with complex role inclusion axioms. Artif. Intell. **160**(1–2), 79–104 (2004)
18. Howard, W.A.: The formulae-as-types notion of construction. To HB Curry: Essays Combin. Log. Lambda Calculus Formalism **44**, 479–490 (1980)
19. Kolmogorov, A.: On the principle of tertium non datur. Math. ussr sbornik **32**, 646–667 (1925). In: Van Heijenoort, J. (ed.) From Frege to Gödel: a source book in mathematical logic, 1879–1931, vol. 9. Harvard University Press (1967)
20. Lyon, T.: Refining labelled systems for modal and constructive logics with applications. Ph.D. thesis, Technische Universität Wien (2021)
21. Orlov, I.E.: The calculus of compatibility of propositions. Mathe. USSR Sbornik **35**, 263–286 (1928)
22. Osorio, M., Navarro, J.A., Arrazola, J.: Applications of intuitionistic logic in answer set programming. Theory Pract. Log. Program. **4**(3), 325–354 (2004). https://doi.org/10.1017/S1471068403001881
23. Pitts, A.M.: Evaluation logic. In: Birtwistle, G. (ed.) IV Higher Order Workshop, Banff 1990, pp. 162–189. Springer, London (1991). https://doi.org/10.1007/978-1-4471-3182-3_11
24. Plotkin, G., Stirling, C.: A framework for intuitionistic modal logics: extended abstract. In: Proceedings of the 1986 Conference on Theoretical Aspects of Reasoning about Knowledge, TARK 1986, pp. 399–406. Morgan Kaufmann Publishers Inc., San Francisco (1986)
25. Simpson, A.K.: The proof theory and semantics of intuitionistic modal logic. Ph.D. thesis, University of Edinburgh. College of Science and Engineering. School of Informatics (1994)
26. Straßburger, L.: Cut elimination in nested sequents for intuitionistic modal logics. In: Pfenning, F. (ed.) FoSSaCS 2013. LNCS, vol. 7794, pp. 209–224. Springer, Heidelberg (2013). https://doi.org/10.1007/978-3-642-37075-5_14
27. Vakarelov, D.: Abstract characterization of some knowledge representation systems and the logic nil of nondeterministic information. In: Jorrand, P., Sgurev, V. (eds.) Artificial Intelligence II, pp. 255–260. North-Holland, Amsterdam (1987)

Choosing a Logic to Represent the Semantics of Natural Language

Adam Pease[✉]

Articulate Software, San Jose, CA, USA
apease@articulatesoftware.com

Abstract. We attempt to answer the question of which kind of logical language should be chosen to represent the semantics of a broad selection of natural language sentences, and how prevalent different kinds of sentences are that require different levels of logical expressiveness. We examine these requirements for representing the semantics of text in logic by studying a sample of several balanced corpora. Our method is to create lists of words and sentential constructs that can easily be assessed in text, which are then mapped to requirements for logics of different expressiveness. We then run an automated analysis on thousands of sentences from two English corpora and manually validate a sample.

1 Introduction

Work in linguistic semantics has often employed logics that are quite expressive, exceeding that of first order logic, typically employing various modal operators [4,8,10]. Work in computer science, particularly in industrial applications, often employs languages of lesser expressiveness, informal approaches such as knowledge graphs [15], or the description logic [1] used in semantic web languages and tools. Implicit in these uses is that the logic employed is sufficient for the task at hand. Tools are often chosen based on some combination of an assessment of prevalence and ease of use. When logics are used to represent a wide domain of knowledge, or used to capture knowledge from a variety of textual sources, it would be beneficial to have quantitative metrics that would indicate the proportion of statements that are expressible in a variety of logics.

There is no system that can automatically convert arbitrary text into an expressive logic, and even human coders will have different interpretations of text, which may, at times, result in statements that require a different logic. However, we can attempt a first exploration in this area, with the hope that this will lead to further studies.

Our approach is to start with looking at particular words that typically require particular logics to capture the semantics of sentences in which they appear. We then collect statistics on those words in different corpora. Lastly, we take a small sample of expressive sentences from a corpus and encode them manually, in order to validate whether the word lists are in fact indicative of the logical constructs we believe are required.

© Springer Nature Switzerland AG 2021
P. Baroni et al. (Eds.): CLAR 2021, LNAI 13040, pp. 504–512, 2021.
https://doi.org/10.1007/978-3-030-89391-0_30

While many researchers such as [9] have shown examples where linguistic semantics requires expressive logics, to date there has not been an automated quantitative experiment to determine how prevalent such sentences are in large and balanced linguistic corpora. That is what that paper attempts to address.

2   Different Logics

We will only consider a few broad categories or kinds of logics rather than exhaustively considering many specialized logics or variants within these categories. We attempt to show that those categories can be determined from particular words and simple syntactic constructs. We will also assume that we must go beyond a propositional representation. Propositional logic does not allow for use of variables. While it is often possible to create an abstraction of a single sentence that is propositional, once we have a text with multiple sentences, we assume that it will rarely be possible to avoid some need for variables. This will hopefully be clear once we provide example formalizations of some sample sentences.

Logics less expressive than first order logic have only restricted forms of negation and quantification, such as the atomic negation in standard (AL) description logic, so words that lead to these logical features will be the first test for expressiveness.

Beyond standard first-order (barring a special purpose encoding of a first-order modal logic, which we will consider equivalent) are constructs that require a notion of necessity or possibility, as in the S1-S5 families of modal logics [6]. We will attempt to verify this assertion by showing that in our sample, few examples avoid quantification over formulas.

A next level of expressiveness is that of epistemics and authorship expressions, which attribute a text to a particular person.

Note that for each of these logical features, we need not have 100% accuracy in our analysis. It is acceptable to have words missing for each feature, as we aim simply to have a conservative estimate of expressiveness required. If we fail to identify logically expressive sentences that will simply lead to a more conservative assessment. We do however need to be careful about false positives and a manual coding of the identified expressive sentences should help to provide confidence in that regard.

3   Computation and Lexical Semantics

We employ the Suggested Upper Merged Ontology (SUMO) [11][1] and its associated SUO-KIF [12] language due to its large size (roughly 20,000 terms and 80,000 human-authored logical axioms) and expressive representation in a higher order logic. Its use in modern theorem provers allows the theory and extensions to be tested and employed in practical reasoning [2,13,14]. By choosing a more expressive logic we can use a single language and less expressive formulas will

---

[1] http://www.ontologyportal.org.

simply not take advantage of the full expressiveness of the language. We can also anchor our terms to an existing defined set of terms in the ontology, and not have to use symbols that have an imagined or intended meaning as opposed to a formal and logically specified one. We can also avoid the impractical alternative of having to define all the symbols used from scratch.

Briefly, in order to interpret the formulas below, SUO-KIF is a prefix notation in a standard Lisp S-expression syntax, where only the seven logical operators ("forall", "exists", "=>", "and", "or", "not", "<=>") plus equality ("=") are reseved words in the language, and all other symbols must be defined in SUMO in terms of those operators. Universal quantification is implicit for unquantified variables. Variables are denoted by a leading '?' sign. In this paper we will highlight terms from SUMO given in the text in `typewriter font`.

4   Word Lists

We rely on the Stanford CoreNLP system [7] to identify *negation*. It is a machine learning based system that was trained on a large set of manually-labeled sentences. To indicate *quantifiers* we select the words "some", "many", "few", "all". We will assess sentences with negation or quantifiers as requiring first order logic.

For *modal* expressions we chose a list of "can", "could", "may", "might", "must", "shall", "should" and "would". Some *other modals*, which appear to be less reliable indicators are "ought", "dare", and "need".

Finally, we have words that indicate statements of knowledge or belief, which we can broadly call *epistemic* operators. These include "know", "think", "learn", "understand", "perceive", "feel", "guess", "recognize", "notice", "want", "wish", "hope", "decide", "expect", "prefer", "remember", "forget", "imagine", and "believe". Statements of *authorship* would require a different operator that takes a formula as an argument, but have the same requirement for logical expressiveness as epistemics. They are "say", and "write".

5   Experiment

We wrote a simple open source program in Java[2] that calls the Stanford CoreNLP system to do sentence segmentation, tokenization, lemmatization and dependency parsing as steps to enable this analysis. Those functions enable Stanford's negation detection component as well as checking for the presence of words in our various word lists. We only count a sentence as being in one particular category even if it has multiple kinds of operators. Execution time is dominated by negation detection because of its upstream reliance on dependency parsing, but is still relatively fast, completing analysis of the Brown corpus [5] in just a few minutes on a modern laptop computer. Our results for the Brown Corpus are shown in Table 1.

---

[2] https://github.com/ontologyportal/sigmanlp/blob/master/src/main/java/com/arti culate/nlp/corpora/LogicLevel.java.

In addition, since we are not primarily concerned with works of fiction in commercial applications, we chose a comparably sized portion of the newspaper collection from the Corpus of Contemporary American English [3]. Running on just the year 2012 we get comparable results to the Brown corpus tests, which seem to indicate that these logical features are broadly no more or less prevalent in news than in a balanced corpus that includes works of fiction, poetry and spoken text transcripts. These results are shown in Table 2. Note that percentages are rounded and so do not add up to 100%. Note also that the spacing in the examples reflects tokenizing, where tokens such as in "ca n't" are separated by a space.

Table 1. Brown Corpus statistics

Type of operator	Count	%
Negation	419	10.00%
Epistemic	243	6.00%
Modal	666	16.00%
Other modal	27	0.66%
Quantifier	177	4.30%
Authorship	196	4.80%
Simple	2304	57.00%
Total	4032	

Table 2. COCA 2012 News statistics

Type of operator	Count	%
Negation	513	13.00%
Epistemic	328	8.60%
Modal	369	9.70%
Other modal	27	0.71%
Quantifier	223	5.90%
Authorship	416	11.00%
Simple	1897	50.00%
Total	3773	

6   Experiment Validation

We next selected a random sample of 100 sentences, using Java's `Random` class, that were marked by our automated analysis as not "simple" and attempted to formalize them manually in an expressive logic. Note that we are simply interested in a "upper bound" of how many sentences do not require expressive logics, so we do not need to perform a manual formalization of any of the sentences in the category of "simple", since if a simple sentence required an expressive formalization that would only decrease the upper bound.

Even in the case of a balanced corpus like the Brown Corpus that includes fiction and poetry, only 57% of sentences are "simple" and without negation, modals, authorship or epistemics. This is also likely to be conservative since we do not consider constructs such as metaphors, some of which can require complex logical representations without the explicit keywords that we have measured.

The first randomly selected sentence (from corpus line 45437) marked as being a statement of "authorship" was

"It's just a waste of resources, if you ask me," she said.

We coded the statement in the SUO-KIF logical language, using terms from SUMO. No new terms were needed for this encoding. The interested reader can look at the definitions of these terms by entering them in the online browser[3]. The formalization can be paraphrased as "There is a speaking event, where the agent of the event says that there's an different event that uses a resource, which does not benefit anyone."

There are many possible encodings of this statement, and no doubt many that could be considered "deeper" by explicitly modeling a notion of waste rather than just an absence of benefit, or the implications of politeness or modesty of the phrase "...if you ask me..." But the essential feature relevant to this experiment, which would still be present in other options for formalization, is that the speech has some logical content and stating that content as an explicit logical formula, as opposed to a logically opaque term or proposition, requires logical expressiveness beyond first order logic. The relation in this case is `containsFormula`, which relates a `Physical` thing (which is a class that includes any thing positioned in space and time, and therefore includes `Process`es) and a `Formula`.

```
(exists (?S ?SAY)
  (and
    (instance ?SAY Speaking)
    (agent ?SAY ?SHE)
    (containsFormula ?SAY
      (exists (?IT ?R)
        (and
          (resource ?IT ?R)
          (not
            (exists (?P)
              (benefits ?IT ?P)))))))))
```

---

[3] https://sigma.ontologyportal.org:8443/sigma/Browse.jsp?kb=SUMO&lang=Englis hLanguage&flang=SUO-KIF&term=Speaking.

Statements about propositions are so common that even when one is found there are usually more in the same sentence that aren't signalled by simple keywords, as in

> *Ministers were exploring several options to close that gap, but as talks dragged on Monday, no final solution appeared imminent .*

which was marked as a negation ("...**no** final solution...") but where *appeared* and *imminent* also state relationships (epistemic and temporal, respectively) to a proposition (that a final agreement will be achieved in the negotiation) that require a higher-order logic.

We now present some of a set of randomly chosen sentences from the COCA 2012 news corpus (file `wlp_news_2012.txt`) the first few along with their formalization in SUO-KIF/SUMO. The line number of the corpus is given and then a keyword for how it was classified on the basis of the different word lists given in the body of the paper. There were two sentences out of our random sample of 100 with critical elisions and two that do not require an expressive logic. The two sentences in our sample of 100 that one could argue have been misclassified are

> (corpus line 6504) epistemic: *The testing, to be carried out over the next several weeks, marks a significant expansion of the agency 's probe in Dimock, a tiny crossroads at the center of a national debate over gas drilling and the extraction technique known as hydraulic fracturing, or fracking.*

"...known..." in this case is not an epistemic but just an expression of synonymy. If we create a class of Fracking one could have a simple relation of "`communicationAbout`" that would relate a communication event "...debate..." and a class representing a topic, so it's possible this could be done in a description logic.

> (corpus line 6431) neg: *I ca n't even tell you, again, what a relief this is.*

Read literally, "...can't tell..." is a negation but it isn't since later in the sentence the speaker does tell the listener what he or she wants to say, that [it] is a "relief". It's just a politeness construct. If the referent of "it" is a complex statement that would have to be modeled as a formula, then this is HOL. But if it's just an event, then it could be represented in FOL or even DL

Five sentences of the 100 were fully formalized in SUO-KIF/SUMO - corpus line numbers 65640, 9632, 77220, 70553 and 53967.

Note that one additional sentence (corpus line 45437) is formalized in the text above.

(corpus line 65640) neg: *Ministers were exploring several options to close that gap, but as talks dragged on Monday, no final solution appeared imminent.*

```
(exists (?M1 ?M2 ?N ?M)
  (and
    (attribute ?M1 GovernmentPerson)
    (attribute ?M2 GovernmentPerson)
    (not
      (equal ?M1 ?M2))
    (instance ?M Monday)
    (instance ?N Negotiating)
    (during ?N ?M)
    (agent ?N ?M1)
    (agent ?N ?M2)
    (not
      (expects ?M1
        (holdsDuring
          (ImmediateFutureFn
            (WhenFn ?N)
            (exists (?A)
              (and
                (instance ?A Agreement)
                (result ?N ?A)))))))
    (not
      (expects ?M2
        (holdsDuring
          (ImmediateFutureFn
            (WhenFn ?N)
            (exists (?A)
              (and
                (instance ?A Agreement)
                (result ?N ?A)))))))))
```

Note this sentence is already given in the text above but the formalization is given here. Also to note is that we know from the plural 'Ministers' that there is more than one minister involved in the event. But we do not know that there are more than two involved. The logical form created with two different GovernmentPersons in an agent relation requires two ministers, but does not entail that there are only two.

7 Conclusion

We reviewed all 98 of the randomly chosen sentences. Two sentences were rejected because the news corpus has some elided phrases, replaced with "@ @ @..." that makes it impossible to provide a complete formalization. For two sentences of the 98, it should be possible for formalize them using only a description logic. We did a "complete" formalization of the first 6 sentences. Of the 90 remaining sentences we reviewed that have required the logic determined by the keyword lists, they usually also require several more advanced logical operators. We have posted these validations on line as an appendix to this paper[4]. We believe that we can reasonably conclude that the statistics given in Sect. 5 are conservative. The results show that roughly half of a the sentences in the test corpus require a logical expressiveness of full first order logic or greater. We hope that this may lead researchers and practitioners to reconsider the choice of less-expressive logics for knowledge representation, or at least be more aware about the limitations they impose on the percentage of human communication that requires greater expressiveness.

References

1. Baader, F., Horrocks, I., Sattler, U.: Description logics (chap. 3). In: van Harmelen, F., Lifschitz, V., Porter, B. (eds.) Handbook of Knowledge Representation, pp. 135–180. Elsevier (2008). download/2007/BaHS07a.pdf
2. Benzmüller, C., Pease, A.: Progress in automating higher-order ontology reasoning. In: Konev, B., Schmidt, R., Schulz, S. (eds.) Workshop on Practical Aspects of Automated Reasoning (PAAR-2010). CEUR Workshop Proceedings, Edinburgh (2010)
3. Davies, M.: The corpus of contemporary American English as the first reliable monitor corpus of English. Lit. Linguistic Comput. **25**(4), 447–464 (2010)
4. Gochet, P., Gribomont, E.P.: Epistemic logic. In: Gabbay, D.M., Woods, J. (eds.) Logic and the Modalities in the Twentieth Century, Handbook of the History of Logic, vol. 7, pp. 99–195. Elsevier (2006)
5. Kucera, H., Francis, W.N.: Computational Analysis of Present-Day American English. Brown University Press, Providence (1967)
6. Lewis, C.I., Langford, C.H.: Symbolic logic. The Century Co. (1932)
7. Manning, C.D., Surdeanu, M., Bauer, J., Finkel, J., Bethard, S.J., McClosky, D.: The Stanford CoreNLP natural language processing toolkit. In: Association for Computational Linguistics (ACL) System Demonstrations, pp. 55–60 (2014). http://www.aclweb.org/anthology/P/P14/P14-5010
8. Mineshima, K., Martínez-Gómez, P., Miyao, Y., Bekki, D.: Higher-order logical inference with compositional semantics. In: Proceedings of the 2015 Conference on Empirical Methods in Natural Language Processing, pp. 2055–2061. Association for Computational Linguistics, Lisbon, September 2015. https://doi.org/10.18653/v1/D15-1244, https://www.aclweb.org/anthology/D15-1244
9. Montague, R.: The proper treatment of quantification in ordinary English. In: Hintikka, K.J.J., Moravcsic, J., Suppes, P. (eds.) Approaches to Natural Language, pp. 221–242. Reidel, Dordrecht (1973)
10. Moss, L.S., Tiede, H.J.: Applications of modal logic in linguistics. In: Handbook of Modal Logic (2007)
11. Niles, I., Pease, A.: Toward a standard upper ontology. In: Welty, C., Smith, B. (eds.) Proceedings of the 2nd International Conference on Formal Ontology in Information Systems (FOIS-2001), pp. 2–9 (2001)

---

[4] https://adampease.org/CLAR20201-appendix.pdf.

12. Pease, A.: SUO-KIF Reference Manual. web document (2009). https://github.com/ontologyportal/sigmakee/blob/master/suo-kif.pdf. Accessed 20 June 2020
13. Pease, A.: Arithmetic and inference in a large theory. In: AI in Theorem Proving (2019)
14. Pease, A., Sutcliffe, G., Siegel, N., Trac, S.: Large theory reasoning with SUMO at CASC. AI Commun. **23**(2–3), 137–144 (2010). Special issue on Practical Aspects of Automated Reasoning
15. Singhal, A.: Introducing the knowledge graph: things, not strings (2012). https://blog.google/products/search/introducing-knowledge-graph-things-not/

The Placeholder View of Assumptions and the Curry–Howard Correspondence (Extended Abstract)

Ivo Pezlar$^{(\boxtimes)}$ (iD)

Institute of Philosophy, Czech Academy of Sciences, Jilska 1, 110 00 Praha, Czechia
pezlar@flu.cas.cz

Abstract. Proofs from assumptions are amongst the most fundamental reasoning techniques. Yet the precise nature of assumptions is still an open topic. One of the most prominent conceptions is the placeholder view of assumptions generally associated with natural deduction for intuitionistic propositional logic. It views assumptions essentially as holes in proofs (either to be filled with closed proofs of the corresponding propositions via substitution or withdrawn as a side effect of some rule), thus in effect making them an auxiliary notion subservient to proper propositions. The Curry-Howard correspondence is typically viewed as a formal counterpart of this conception. In this talk, based on my paper of the same name (*Synthese*, 198(11), 10109–10125, 2021), I will argue against this position and show that even though the Curry-Howard correspondence typically accommodates the placeholder view of assumptions, it is rather a matter of choice, not a necessity, and that another more assumption-friendly view can be adopted.

Keywords: Placeholder view of assumptions · Assumption withdrawing · Curry–Howard correspondence · Natural deduction · Intuitionistic propositional logic

1 Introduction

Proofs from assumptions are amongst the most fundamental reasoning techniques. Yet the precise nature of assumptions is still an open topic. One of the most prominent conceptions is the placeholder view of assumptions generally associated with natural deduction for intuitionistic propositional logic. It views assumptions essentially as holes in proofs (either to be filled with closed proofs of the corresponding propositions via substitution or withdrawn as a side effect

---

This is an extended abstract of a paper [8] with the same title published at *Synthese* 2021. Adapted by permission from Springer Nature Customer Service Centre GmbH: Springer Nature, *Synthese* 198(11), 10109–10125, 2021, The placeholder view of assumptions and the Curry–Howard correspondence. Pezlar, Ivo, ©2020. Work on this paper was supported by Grant Nr. 19-12420S from the Czech Science Foundation, GA ČR.

P. Baroni et al. (Eds.): CLAR 2021, LNAI 13040, pp. 513–520, 2021.
https://doi.org/10.1007/978-3-030-89391-0_31

of some rule), thus in effect making them an auxiliary notion subservient to proper propositions (see, e.g., [15], p. 5). The Curry-Howard correspondence is typically viewed as a formal counterpart of this conception (recently, see, e.g., [13]). I this talk, based on my paper [8], I will argue against this position and show that even though the Curry-Howard correspondence typically accommodates the placeholder view of assumptions, it is rather a matter of choice, not a necessity, and that another more assumption-friendly view can be adopted.

Assumption Withdrawing. The rule for implication introduction from natural deduction for intuitionistic propositional logic is arguably the best-known example of the assumption withdrawing rule:

$$\frac{\begin{array}{c}[A]\\\vdots\\B\end{array}}{A \supset B}$$

It prescribes the following inference step: if we can derive B from assumption A, then we can derive $A \supset B$ and withdraw the initial assumption A (it is worth noting that other assumptions than A may be used in deriving B and those remain open after discharging A). Note that this rule effectively embodies the deduction theorem from standard axiomatic systems. In other words, the implication introduction rule is internalizing structural information from the proof level ("B is derivable from A") to the propositional level ("A implies B").[1]

The problematic aspect of this and other assumption withdrawing rules stems from the fact that it behaves differently from the non-assumption withdrawing rules. More specifically, with the implication introduction rule we are deriving the proposition $A \supset B$ not from other propositions as with other standard rules (e.g., conjunction introduction), but from a hypothetical proof. To put it differently, the inference step validated by the implication introduction takes us from a *derivation* starting with a hypothesis to a proposition, not just from propositions to another proposition as do rules without assumptions.[2]

For example, consider the following simple proof of the theorem $A \supset ((A \supset B) \supset B)$ of propositional logic:

$$\cfrac{\cfrac{\cfrac{[A \supset B]^1 \qquad [A]^2}{B}\ \supset\!E}{(A \supset B) \supset B}\ \supset\!I_1}{A \supset ((A \supset B) \supset B)}\ \supset\!I_2$$

---

[1] [13] describes this as a two-layer system. Note that, strictly speaking, the assumptions are not really withdrawn, they are rather incorporated into the propositional level in the form of an antecedent.

[2] This non-standard behaviour is also the reason why [10] describes assumption withdrawing rules as improper rules and introduces the distinction between inference rules and deductions rules. For more, see [7,10].

We start by making two assumptions $A \supset B$ and A. Applying the implication elimination rule (modus ponens) we derive B. What follows are two consecutive applications of implication introduction rule, first withdrawing the assumption $A \supset B$, the second withdrawing the assumption A. Note that it is the fact that B is derivable from $A \supset B$ together with A that warrants the application of the implication introduction rule and the derivation of the corresponding proposition $(A \supset B) \supset B$, at that moment still depending on the assumption A. Analogously with the second application of the implication introduction rule that withdraws this remaining assumption.

A proof that relies on no assumptions is called a closed proof. If a proof depends on some assumptions that are yet to be withdrawn (i.e., open/active assumptions) it is called an open proof. For example, our derivation of $A \supset ((A \supset B) \supset B)$ constitutes a closed proof, since both assumption were withdrawn in the course of the derivation. Assuming we would not have carried out the last inference step, we would get an open proof:

$$\frac{\dfrac{[A \supset B]^1 \quad A}{B} \supset E}{(A \supset B) \supset B} \supset I_1$$

since the assumption A, upon which the derivation of $((A \supset B) \supset B)$ depends, is still active.

Closed proofs are usually preferred to open ones for the simple reason that closed proofs are generally viewed as the fundamental notion in standard proof-theoretic systems. From this perspective, assumptions are just temporary holes in the proof that are preventing us from reaching a closed proof. These open holes can be are either completely discarded via assumption withdrawing rules or filled in with other already closed proofs via substitution. This is the reason why [13] and others[3] call this the placeholder view of assumptions: active assumptions are just auxiliary artefacts of the employed proof system that behave differently than proper propositions, i.e., propositions that do not appear as assumptions.

The Curry-Howard Correspondence. The placeholder view of assumptions is also supported to a large extent by the Curry-Howard correspondence in its basic form which links typed lambda calculus and implicational fragment of intuitionistic propositional logic.[4] Under this correspondence, natural deduction assumptions correspond to free variables of lambda calculus, which fits well with the interpretation of assumptions as open holes in the proof.

For example, assuming only the implicational fragment of intuitionistic propositional natural deduction, we get the following correspondences between the propositional and functional dimensions of the Curry-Howard correspondence:

---

[3] See, e.g., [1].

[4] See, e.g., [14].

Natural Deduction	Lambda Calculus
Assumption	Free variable
Implication introduction	Function abstraction
Implication elimination	Function application

Under this correspondence, the implication introduction rule will then look as follows:

$$[x : A]$$
$$\vdots$$
$$\frac{b(x) : B}{\lambda x.b(x) : A \supset B}$$

Note that the act of withdrawing the assumption A corresponds to λ-binding of the free variable x. The whole proof of the theorem $A \supset ((A \supset B) \supset B)$ would then proceed in the following way:

$$\frac{\dfrac{[x : A \supset B]^1 \qquad [y : A]^2}{xy : B} \supset \text{E}}{\dfrac{\lambda x.xy : (A \supset B) \supset B}{\lambda y.\lambda x.xy : A \supset ((A \supset B) \supset B)} \supset \text{I}_2} \supset \text{I}_1$$

with the concluding proof object (closed term) $\lambda y.\lambda x.xy$ with no free variables representing the final closed proof with no active assumptions. In contrast, the open proof discussed earlier:

$$\frac{\dfrac{[x : A \supset B]^1 \qquad y : A}{xy : B} \supset \text{E}}{\lambda x.xy : (A \supset B) \supset B} \supset \text{I}_1$$

concludes with the proof object $\lambda x.xy$ that still contains the free variable y corresponding to the yet to be withdrawn assumption A.

The Placeholder View of Assumptions and Consequence Statements. The Curry-Howard correspondence is generally viewed as incorporating the placeholder view of assumptions. Probably most recently, this point was explicitly made in [13]. Furthermore, in the same paper Schroeder-Heister advocates for a more general concept of inference that takes us not from propositions to other propositions, but from (inferential) consequence statements $A \models B$ to other consequence statements in order to, amongst other things, equalize the status of assumptions and assertions.[5] The general form of inference rules he discusses is the following:

---

[5] Strictly speaking, we should be writing $A \models_\mathbb{D} B$, i.e., that $A \models B$ can be derived with respect to a set of definitional clauses $\mathbb{D}$ (see [12]), but for simplicity we omit these considerations.

$$\frac{A_1 \models B_1 \quad \ldots \quad A_n \models B_n}{C \models D}$$

where the antecedents can be empty and its correctness means that whenever $A_1 \models B_1, \ldots, A_n \models B_n$, then $C \models D$. As Schroeder-Heister explains:

> This corresponds to the idea that in natural deduction, derivations can depend on assumptions. Here this dependency is expressed by non-empty antecedents, as is the procedure of the sequent calculus. Our model of inference is the sequent-calculus model... ([12], p. 938)

To show that this rule is correct, we have demonstrated that given the grounds for the premises (denoted as $g : A \models B$) we can construct grounds for the conclusion. In other words, the grounds of the conclusion have to contain some operation f transforming the grounds for the premises to the grounds for the conclusion. Schematically:

$$\frac{g_1 : A_1 \models B_1 \quad \ldots \quad g_n : A_n \models B_n}{f(g_1, \ldots g_n) : C \models D}$$

Schroeder-Heister comments on this rule as follows:

> ... [H]andling of grounds in the sense described is different from that of terms in the typed lambda calculus. When generating grounds from grounds according to [the rule immediately above], we consider grounds for whole sequents, whereas in the typed lambda calculus terms representing such grounds are handled within sequents. So the notation $g : A \models B$ we used above, which is understood as $g : (A \models B)$, differs from the lambda calculus notation $x : A \vdash t : B$, where t represents a proof of B from A and the declaration $x : A$ on the left side represents the assumption A. ([12], p. 939)

However, it should be mentioned that he left it "open how to formalize grounds and their handling." (ibid., p. 938) I will argue that even though lambda calculus with the Curry-Howard interpretation can be seen as embodying the placeholder view of assumptions in the intuitionistic propositional logic, within the family of Curry-Howard correspondence based systems we can consider a generalized approach that is free of this view. This generalized approach will treat consequence statements $A \models B$ as higher-order functions $A \Rightarrow B$ that can be naturally captured in Martin-Löf's constructive type theory ([4]), specifically in its higher-order presentation (see [5,6]).

Function-Based Approach to Assumptions. Let us return to the implication introduction rule. Adopting the sequent-style notation for natural deduction,[6] we can rewrite this rule as follows:

$$\frac{x : A \vdash b(x) : B}{\vdash \lambda x.b(x) : A \supset B}$$

---

[6] See, e.g., Gentzen's system NLK, discussed in [9].

where the symbol ⊢ is used to separate assumptions from (derived) propositions.
Notice that the derivation of B from A is coded with an abstraction term from lambda calculus, which means it captures some sort of a function. Reasoning backwards, this should mean that between the assumption (context) and the conclusion (asserted proposition) has to be a relationship that can be understood functionally, otherwise, we would have nothing to code via lambda terms. To put it differently, there has to be some more fundamental notion of a function at play that we are coding through the concrete abstraction term.

We can try to capture this observation via the following rule:

$$\frac{x : A \vdash b(x) : B}{f : A \Rightarrow B}$$

where f is to be understood as exemplifying the more fundamental notion of a function that takes us from A to B.

Note that this rule can be roughly understood as the opposite of the implication introduction rule that goes in the other direction: while the implication introduction rule makes the hypothetical derivation "from A is derivable B" in its premise more concrete in the form of implication proposition $A \supset B$ and the corresponding lambda term $\lambda x.b(x)$, this rule makes the derivation more general in the sense that it is now considered as a function f (not specifically a lambda term) from A to B. Also notice that assumptions are no longer placeholders or contexts, but types of arguments for the function f capturing the corresponding derivation. In other words, assumptions now stand equal to proper propositions, they are not just an auxiliary notion captured via free variables.

Furthermore, capturing derivations in this way allows us to consider grounds for the whole consequence statements as Schroeder-Heister required, not just grounds for the conclusions under some assumptions. More specifically, treating consequence statement $A \models B$ as a function type $A \Rightarrow B$ (in accord with the Curry-Howard correspondence) and a ground g as an object f of this type, we can reformulate the general rule as follows (see [12], p. 938):

$$\frac{g_1 : A_1 \Rightarrow B_1 \quad \dots \quad g_n : A_n \Rightarrow B_n}{f(g_1, \dots g_n) : C \Rightarrow D}$$

Formalization. So far, I have treated $f : A \Rightarrow B$ informally to mean "f is a function from A to B". Utilizing Martin-Löf's constructive type theory ([4]), specifically its higher-order presentation ([5,6]), we can capture it more rigorously as a higher-order judgment of the form $(x)b : (A)B$. To explain why, let us return to the hypothetical judgment $x : A \vdash b(x) : B$ that appears as the sole premise of the implication introduction rule. It tells us that we know $b(a)$ to be a proof of the proposition B assuming we know a to be a proof of the proposition A. In other words, the hypothetical judgment $x : A \vdash b(x) : B$ can be seen as stating that $b(x)$ is a function with domain A and range B.[7] This fact, however, cannot be stated directly in the lower-order presentation of constructive

---

[7] See [4].

type theory. Thus we move towards the higher-order presentation, which is as a generalization of the lower-order presentation using a more primitive notion of a type. The higher-order variant of constructive type theory allows us to form a higher-order notion of a function which can be used to capture the function hidden behind the hypothetical judgment $x : A \vdash b(x) : B$ as an object $(x)b$ of type $(A)B$. Consequently, $(x)b : (A)B$ can then be used to interpret our statement $f : A \Rightarrow B$, as was required. In other words, $(x)b : (A)B$ can be understood as a higher-order judgment declaring that we have (potentially open) derivation of B from A captured by the function $(x)b$.

It is important to emphasize that the higher-order function type $(A)B$ cannot be conflated with the lower-order function type $A \supset B$. The most basic reason is that they are inhabited by different objects: the former by functions, the latter by elements specified by $\supset$-introduction rule, i.e., objects of the form $\lambda x.b(x)$ that are used to code functions. More generally, the notion of a function behind the type $A \supset B$ is parasitic on a more fundamental notion of a function behind the type $(A)B$.[8] From the logical point of view, the main reason we should avoid merging $(A)B$ and $A \supset B$ is that A in $(A)B$ is an assumption of derivation, while A in $A \supset B$ is an antecedent of implication, hence they are objects of different inferential roles. This is perhaps best illustrated by the fact that assuming some function f of type $(A)B$ essentially corresponds to assuming a rule $\dfrac{A}{B}$ in Schroeder-Heister's natural deduction with higher-level rules ([11]).

Conclusion. In this talk, I have argued that the Curry-Howard correspondence is not necessarily connected with the placeholder view of assumptions generally associated with natural deduction systems for intuitionistic propositional logic. Although in the basic form of this correspondence, assumptions, which correspond to free variables, can indeed be thought of as just holes to be filled, we can consider also a functional approach where derivations from assumptions are regarded as functions (see [8]). On this account, assumptions are no longer just placeholders but domains of the corresponding functions. From the logical point of view, this move corresponds to the shift from reasoning with propositions to reasoning with consequence statements.

References

1. Francez, N.: Proof-theoretic Semantics. College Publications (2015)
2. Klev, A.: A comparison of type theory with set theory. In: Centrone, S., Kant, D., Sarikaya, D. (eds.) Reflections on the Foundations of Mathematics. SL, vol. 407, pp. 271–292. Springer, Cham (2019). https://doi.org/10.1007/978-3-030-15655-8_12
3. Klev, A.: Name of the Sinus Function. In: Sedlár, I., Blicha, M. (eds.) The Logica Yearbook 2018. College Publications, London (2019)
4. Martin-Löf, P.: Intuitionistic type theory: Notes by Giovanni Sambin of a series of lectures given in Padua, June 1980. Bibliopolis, Napoli (1984)

---

[8] See [2,3].

5. Nordström, B., Petersson, K., Smith, J.M.: Programming in Martin-Löf's Type Theory: An Introduction. International Series of Monographs on Computer Science, Clarendon Press, Oxford (1990)

6. Nordström, B., Petersson, K., Smith, J.M.: Martin-Löf's type theory. In: Handbook of Logic in Computer Science: Volume 5: Logic and Algebraic Methods. Oxford University Press, Oxford (2001)

7. Pezlar, I.: Towards a more general concept of inference. Log. Univers. **8**(1), 61–81 (2014). https://doi.org/10.1007/s11787-014-0095-3

8. Pezlar, I.: The placeholder view of assumptions and the Curry–Howard correspondence. Synthese **198**(11), 10109–10125 (2021). https://doi.org/10.1007/s11229-020-02706-z

9. von Plato, J.: Gentzen's proof systems: byproducts in a work of genius. Bull. Symb. Log. **18**(3), 313–367 (2012). https://doi.org/10.2178/bsl/1344861886

10. Prawitz, D.: Natural Deduction: A Proof-Theoretical Study. Almqvist & Wiksell, Stockholm (1965)

11. Schroeder-Heister, P.: A natural extension of natural deduction. J. Symb. Log. **49**(4), 1284–1300 (1984). https://doi.org/10.2307/2274279

12. Schroeder-Heister, P.: The categorical and the hypothetical: a critique of some fundamental assumptions of standard semantics. Synthese **187**(3), 925–942 (2012). https://doi.org/10.1007/s11229-011-9910-z

13. Schroeder-Heister, P.: Open problems in proof-theoretic semantics. In: Piecha, T., Schroeder-Heister, P. (eds.) Advances in Proof-Theoretic Semantics. TL, vol. 43, pp. 253–283. Springer, Cham (2016). https://doi.org/10.1007/978-3-319-22686-6_16

14. Sørensen, M.H., Urzyczyn, P.: Lectures on the Curry-Howard Isomorphism, Volume 149 (Studies in Logic and the Foundations of Mathematics). Elsevier Science Inc., New York (2006)

15. Troelstra, A.S., Schwichtenberg, H.: Basic Proof Theory. Cambridge University Press, Cambridge (2000). https://doi.org/10.1017/cbo9781139168717

Paranegations and the Square
of Oppositions

Mariusz Urbański$^{(\boxtimes)}$ ⓘ and Zofia Żmójdzin

Faculty of Psychology and Cognitive Science, Adam Mickiewicz University,
Poznań, Poland
murbansk@amu.edu.pl

Abstract. In this paper, a description of semantics for non-classical
negations of paralogics **CLuN** and **CLaN** is presented in terms of the
theory of oppositions. An outline of a synthetic tableaux method for
these and some other paralogics is given as well.

Keywords: Paralogics · Theory of oppositions · Synthetic tableau
method

1 Introduction

In this paper we describe semantics for non-classical negations of paralogics
CLuN and **CLaN** ([2,4]; see also [7,12]), in terms of relations represented in
the square of oppositions, the relations of contrariness and subcontrariness in
particular (in Sect. 2). Although semantic conditions imposed on these so-called
paranegations are not complicated by themselves, their diagrammatic representations are more vivid and allow for a clear and transparent account of their
interconnections (which we will present in the form of an octahedron of oppositions at the end of Sect. 2). We shall also give a brief description of a certain direct
proof method for these logics, that is, the synthetic tableaux method (STM, in
Sect. 3). In the case of STM semantic justification for the rules for the introduction of paranegated formulas stems directly from the relations represented in the
square of oppositions.

2 The Basic Paralogics and the Square of Oppositions

The basic paralogics are obtained by dropping some requirements imposed on
negation in classical logic. The paraconsistent logic **CLuN**, which allows for gluts
with respect to negation, is obtained by dropping the consistency requirement (if
$v(A) = 1$, then $v(\neg A) = 0$). The paracomplete logic **CLaN**, which allows for gaps

Research reported in this paper were supported by the National Science Centre, Poland
(DEC-2013/10/E/HS1/00172). We would like to thank the anonymous reviewers for
their suggestions and comments.

© Springer Nature Switzerland AG 2021
P. Baroni et al. (Eds.): CLAR 2021, LNAI 13040, pp. 521–532, 2021.
https://doi.org/10.1007/978-3-030-89391-0_32

with respect to negation, is obtained by dropping the completeness requirement (if $v(A) = 0$, then $v(\neg A) = 1$). The logic **CLoN**, which allows for both gluts and gaps concerning negation, is obtained by dropping both requirements. Batens *et al.* [4, p. 30] indicate two reasons why these weak logics are important. The first is, that many paralogics are extensions of them (see [10]). The second is, that these three logics themselves have some interesting applications in research on adaptive logics (see [3]). We focus our attention on **CLuN** and **CLaN**, because semantics for negations in these paralogics may be adequately described within the framework of the square of oppositions, with its four relations of contrariety, subcontrariety, contradictoriness and subalternation (see [5,8]). The case of the third paralogic is more complicated, as the truth values of a formula and its **CLoN**-negation are unrelated to each other. We shall comment on this issue at the end of Sect. 3.3.

We shall start with semantic characteristics of propositional parts of the basic paralogics (see [4]). Their languages are extensions of the language of Classical Propositional Calculus (CPC); we shall consider the version with $\neg$ (classical negation), $\wedge$ (classical conjunction), $\vee$ (classical disjunction) and $\rightarrow$ (classical implication) as the primitive connectives. We shall use the symbols $+$, $\sim$ and $\multimap$ for **CLoN**-, **CLuN**- and **CLaN**-negation, respectively. The notion of well-formed formula (wff for short) is defined as usual. Let Var stands for the set of all the propositional variables of a considered language and $Form_o$, $Form_u$, $Form_a$ for the sets of all the wffs of the logic **CLoN**, **CLuN**, **CLaN**, respectively. Finally, let $Form_o^+$, $Form_o^\sim$, $Form_o^{-\circ}$ stand for the sets of all the wffs of the form $+A$, $\sim A$, $\multimap A$, respectively. We assume also that the notions of truth under a valuation, semantic consequence and validity are defined as usual, relatively to a logic considered.

We shall start with the logic **CLoN**. Its language extends CPC language with a unary connective $+$ (**CLoN**-negation). The semantics is defined in terms of two separate functions, which assign truth values, Truth (**1**) or Falsehood (**0**), to wffs. The assignment functions fulfil the following conditions:

S.1 $\mathbf{v}^{M} : Var \mapsto \{\mathbf{1}, \mathbf{0}\}$

S.2 $\mathbf{v}^{N} : Form_o^+ \mapsto \{\mathbf{1}, \mathbf{0}\}$

A function $\mathbf{v}: Form_o \mapsto \{\mathbf{1}, \mathbf{0}\}$ is a **CLoN**-valuation iff:[1]

V.1 $\mathbf{v}(A) = \mathbf{v}^{M}(A)$ iff $A \in Var$

V.2 $\mathbf{v}(\neg A) = \mathbf{1}$ iff $\mathbf{v}(A) = \mathbf{0}$

V.3 $\mathbf{v}(+A) = \mathbf{v}^{N}(A)$

V.4 $\mathbf{v}(A \wedge B) = \mathbf{1}$ iff $\mathbf{v}(A) = \mathbf{1}$ and $\mathbf{v}(B) = \mathbf{1}$

V.5 $\mathbf{v}(A \vee B) = \mathbf{1}$ iff $\mathbf{v}(A) = \mathbf{1}$ or $\mathbf{v}(B) = \mathbf{1}$

V.6 $\mathbf{v}(A \rightarrow B) = \mathbf{1}$ iff $\mathbf{v}(A) = \mathbf{0}$ or $\mathbf{v}(B) = \mathbf{1}$

---

[1] The conditions V.1, V.2 and V.4 – V.6 define CPC-valuations. Classical negation, $\neg$, may be introduced in **CLoN** (and in other basic paralogics as well) by means of the constant $\bot$, defined as usual: $\mathbf{v}(\bot) = \mathbf{0}$. However, we shall consider $\neg$ as a primitive connective.

The idea underlying **CLoN**-negation is this: the truth value of a formula $+A$ is unrelated to the truth value of A, and thus the assignment of truth value to $+A$ is independent of the truth value of A.[2]

The language of **CLuN** extends the CPC language with a unary connective $\sim$ (**CLuN**-negation). A **CLuN**-valuation is a function $Form_u \mapsto \{1, 0\}$ obtained by replacing the conditions S.2 and V.3 with the following:

S.2$^\sim$ $\mathbf{v^N} : Form_u^\sim \mapsto \{\mathbf{1, 0}\}$
V.3$^\sim$ $\mathbf{v}(\sim A) = 1$ iff $\mathbf{v}(A) = 0$ or $\mathbf{v^N}(\sim A) = 1$

Thus a formula $\sim A$ is true under a valuation $\mathbf{v}$ iff either A is false under $\mathbf{v}$ or $\sim A$ is assigned the value 1 by the assignment function $\mathbf{v^N}$, independently of the valuation $\mathbf{v}$. As a result, both A and $\sim A$ may be true under $\mathbf{v}$, but they cannot both be false: they are *subcontrariae* formulas.

As we claimed above, semantic relations between the formulas A and $\sim A$ may be adequately described within the framework of the theory of oppositions and depicted in the **CLuN**-version of the square of oppositions (see Fig. 1). The relations that hold between pairs of connected formulas are the same as in the classical square of oppositions:

contrariae: $\mathsf{F}\sim A$ and $\mathsf{F}A$;
subcontrariae: $\mathsf{T}A$ and $\mathsf{T}\sim A$;
contradictoriae: $\mathsf{F}A$ and $\mathsf{T}A$, $\mathsf{F}\sim A$ and $\mathsf{T}\sim A$;
subalternae: $\mathsf{T}A$ to $\mathsf{F}\sim A$, $\mathsf{T}\sim A$ to $\mathsf{F}A$.[3]

In Fig. 1 the relation of contrariness is indicated by a dotted line, the relation of subcontrariness – by a dashed line, the relation of contradictoriness – by loosely dotted lines. Arrows indicate the direction of subalternation.

From the **CLuN**-version of the square of oppositions, we may read off in particular, that $\mathsf{T}A$ is semantic consequence of $\mathsf{F} \sim A$, as well as $\mathsf{T} \sim A$ is a semantic consequence of $\mathsf{F}A$. Also, $\mathsf{F} \sim A$ and $\mathsf{F}A$ are *contrariae* formulas, and

---

[2] In what follows we will be using the concept of signed formulas: if A is a formula of a given language, then $\mathsf{T}A$ and $\mathsf{F}A$ are signed formulas (T and F will be referred to as truth-signs). We will refer to them as 'formulas' in cases where no ambiguity can arise. We will use $\#$, $\&$ as variables for truth-signs if needed. Truth-signs do not belong to the vocabularies of languages we will be considering, so the truth values of signed formulas are not determined by valuations. Nevertheless, the truth value of a signed formula $\#A$ (where $\#$ is any of T, F) is dependent upon the truth value of formula A under a certain valuation, so we will speak of the truth value of formula $\#A$ *with respect* to that valuation. Thus a signed formula $\mathsf{T}A$ takes the value $\mathbf{1}$ with respect to a valuation $\mathbf{v}$ iff $\mathbf{v}(A) = 1$ whereas a signed formula $\mathsf{F}A$ takes the value $\mathbf{1}$ with respect to a valuation $\mathbf{v}$ iff $\mathbf{v}(A) = \mathbf{0}$.

[3] The relation of subalternation of A to B amounts to A being a semantic consequence of B.

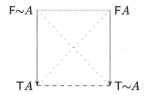

Fig. 1. **CLuN**-version of the square of oppositions

thus they may both be false but cannot both be true (under a certain valuation **v**). The relation of contradictoriness is self-explanatory.

Finally, consider the case of **CLaN**. The language of **CLaN** extends the CPC language with a unary connective $-\circ$ (**CLaN**-negation). A **CLaN**-valuation is a function $Form_a \mapsto \{1,0\}$ obtained by replacing in the definition of **CLoN**-valuation the conditions S.2 and V.3 with the following:

S.2$^{-\circ}$ $\mathbf{v}^N : Form_a^{-\circ} \mapsto \{1,0\}$
V.3$^{-\circ}$ $\mathbf{v}(-\circ A) = 1$ iff $\mathbf{v}(A) = 0$ and $\mathbf{v}^N(-\circ A) = 1$

Thus a formula $-\circ A$ is true under a valuation **v** iff two conditions are met: A is false under **v** and $-\circ A$ is assigned the value **1** by the assignment function $\mathbf{v}^N$. As a result, both A and $-\circ A$ may be false under **v**, but they cannot both be true: they are *contrariae* formulas.

Semantic relations between the formulas A and $-\circ A$ may be depicted in the **CLaN**-version of the square of oppositions (see Fig. 2). Again, the relations that hold between pairs of connected formulas are exactly the same as in the classical square of oppositions (and are indicated by different lines as in Fig. 1):

contrariae: TA and T$-\circ A$
subcontrariae: F$-\circ A$ and FA
contradictoriae: TA and FA, T$-\circ A$ and F$-\circ A$
subalternae: F$-\circ A$ to TA, FA to T$-\circ A$

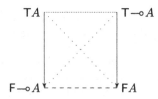

Fig. 2. **CLaN**-version of the square of oppositions

This means, in particular, that F$-\circ A$ is semantic consequence of TA and FA is semantic consequence of T$-\circ A$. The formulas F$-\circ A$ and FA, as *subcontrariae*, may both be true but cannot both be false (again, under a certain valuation **v**).

Although **CLuN**-valuations and **CLaN**-valuations are distinct functions, nevertheless the truth values of the formulas $\sim A$ and $\multimap A$ are related to the truth value of A and, as a result, are related to each other as well. These relations may be represented in an octahedron of oppositions (see Fig. 3; the relations are indicated by different lines as in Fig. 1). To find out what are the relations between **CLuN**-negation, **CLaN**-negation and classical negation just remove all the T's and replace all the F's with $\neg$.

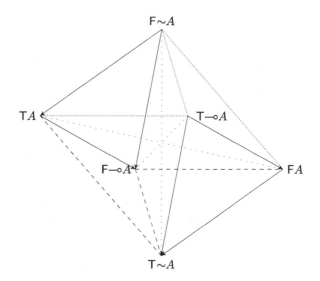

Fig. 3. An octahedron of oppositions for **CLuN**- and **CLaN**-negation

Let us note two further points.[4] First, this octahedron, as it should be expected, is just a fragment of a much more complex structure of oppositional geometry: the "oppositional tetrahexahedron" [9, 11, 13]. Second, there is another square of oppositions identifiable within the octahedron, with the vertices $\mathsf{T}\multimap A$, $\mathsf{F}\sim A$, $\mathsf{F}\multimap A$ and $\mathsf{T}\sim A$. Thus our analysis of the paralogical oppositional space by no means is exhaustive. However, these issues go beyond the scope of the present paper.

3   Synthetic Tableaux Method

Now we shall use our geometric consideration in order to introduce and justify the rules for **CLuN** and **CLaN** negations within the framework of synthetic tableaux method (STM) – a model-seeking and proof method [14–17]. It was developed as a decision procedure for Classical Propositional Calculus (CPC)

---

[4] We owe these remarks to Alessio Moretti.

and some non-classical logics. Roughly speaking, a synthetic tableau for a formula A is defined as a family of interconnected derivations (so-called synthetic inferences) of either A or non-A, based on all the relevant suitably defined sets of basic constituents of A (in the case of propositional logics these basic constituents are signed propositional variables of A). The formulas occurring in a synthetic inference of A can only be (signed) subformulas of A.[5] Recently, STM has been developed also for first-order logic and propositional intuitionistic logic [6]. There, the authors defined a synthetic tableau as a finite labelled tree with an empty root.

The fundamental ideas underlying STM can be traced back to L. Kalmár's proof of the completeness of CPC [15, p. 69]. As the reader will recall, in this proof one makes use of the fact that every valid formula is entailed by every consistent set made up of all of its propositional variables or their negations. However, Kalmár's original proof is system-dependent: it can be applied to every logic which validates certain theorems. STM generalizes its idea. The result is a tableau-style decision procedure which, in contradistinction to Beth-like tableaux, is based on direct reasoning. An STM-proof of a formula A is a synthetic tableau Ω for A such that every element of Ω is a synthetic inference of A. Intuitively it can be said that a formula A is proved if and only if all the possible attempts at 'synthesize' A or non-A lead to A. Thus, "one way or another" is the shortest description of the ideas underlying STM as a proof method.

The set $\mathbf{R}$ of inference rules for CPC consists of the following rules:

$\mathbf{r_{n1}}$ $TA\backslash\backslash F\neg A$ $\mathbf{r_{n2}}$ $FA\backslash\backslash T\neg A$

$\mathbf{r_{d1}}$ $TA\backslash\backslash TA \vee B$ $\mathbf{r_{d2}}$ $TB\backslash\backslash TA \vee B$ $\mathbf{r_{d3}}$ $FA, FB\backslash\backslash FA \vee B$

$\mathbf{r_{c3}}$ $FA\backslash\backslash FA \wedge B$ $\mathbf{r_{c2}}$ $FB\backslash\backslash FA \wedge B$ $\mathbf{r_{c3}}$ $TA, TB\backslash\backslash TA \wedge B$

$\mathbf{r_{i1}}$ $FA\backslash\backslash TA \to B$ $\mathbf{r_{i2}}$ $TB\backslash\backslash TA \to B$ $\mathbf{r_{i3}}$ $TA, FB\backslash\backslash FA \to B$

3.1   The Case of CLaN

In the case of **CLaN** the notion of synthetic inference is defined as follows:

Definition 31. *A finite sequence* $\mathsf{s} = s_1, \ldots, s_n$ *of signed formulas is* a synthetic inference of $\#A$ *iff:*

1. every term of s *is a signed subformula of A;*

---

[5] We will make use of the following notion of an immediate subformula and of a subformula of a given wff [17, p. 322]. If A is a propositional variable, then it has no proper subformulas at all. If A is a formula of the form '$\$B$' (where '$\$$' stands for a negation sign), then B is a proper subformula of A and the only immediate subformula of A as well. If A is of the form '$B * C$' (where '$*$' stands for any of the binary connectives), then both B, C are proper subformulas of A and the only immediate subformulas of A. If C is a proper subformula of B and B is a proper subformula of A, then C is a proper subformula of A. A formula B is a subformula of a formula A iff B is a proper subformula of A or $A = B$.

2. s_1 is a signed propositional variable;
3. s_n is $\#A$;
4. for every s_g $(g = 1, \ldots, n)$ either s_g is a signed propositional variable, or s_g is derivable on the basis of a certain set of formulas such that each element of this set precedes s_g in s;
5. for every s_g $(g = 1, \ldots, n)$ the following hold:
   (a) if s_g is a signed propositional variable $\#\varphi$, then none of $\mathsf{T}\varphi$, $\mathsf{F}\varphi$ occurs at any other place in s;
   (b) if s_g is of the form $\#{-\!\circ}B$, then none of $\mathsf{T}{-\!\circ}B$, $\mathsf{F}{-\!\circ}B$ occurs at any other place in s.

Thus a synthetic inference of a signed formula $\#A$ is a finite sequence of its signed subformulas, which begins with some signed propositional variable and ends with $\#A$ itself. Moreover, every (signed) propositional variable occurs as a term in s only once, no matter of truth-signs (the same pertains to the (signed) paranegated wffs in s), and every formula which is not a (signed) propositional variable is derivable from some earlier formula(s) of s. Derivability relation is defined based on the set $\mathbf{R}$ of classical inference rules extended with the following specific **CLaN** rules:

$$\mathbf{r_{a1}} \quad \mathsf{F}A\backslash\backslash\mathsf{T}{-\!\circ}A \qquad \mathbf{r_{a2}} \quad \mathsf{F}A\backslash\backslash\mathsf{F}{-\!\circ}A \qquad \mathbf{r_{a3}} \quad \mathsf{T}A\backslash\backslash\mathsf{F}{-\!\circ}A$$

The rules $\mathbf{r_{a1}}$ and $\mathbf{r_{a2}}$ are based on subcontrariness relation and are obviously unsound. The rule $\mathbf{r_{a3}}$ is based on subalternation and it is sound.

The notion of synthetic tableau in **CLaN** is given by the following definition:

Definition 32. *Let A be an unsigned formula and let $\#$, $\&$ be distinct truth-signs. A family Ω of finite sequences of signed formulas is a synthetic tableau for A iff every element of Ω is a synthetic inference of $\mathsf{T}A$ or $\mathsf{F}A$, there exists a propositional variable φ such that the first element of every sequence in Ω is $\mathsf{T}\varphi$ or $\mathsf{F}\varphi$ and for every sequence $s = s_1, \ldots, s_n$ in Ω the following hold:*

1. *if s_i $(i = 1, \ldots, n)$ is a signed propositional variable $\#\psi$, then:*
   (a) *there exists in Ω a sequence s^* such that s_i^* is $\& \, \psi$ and, if $i > 1$, then s and s^* do not differ up to the level of their $i - 1$th terms;*
   (b) *if $i > 1$, then for every sequence s^* such that s and s^* do not differ up to the level of their $i - 1$th terms, s_i^* is $\mathsf{T}\psi$ or $\mathsf{F}\psi$;*
2. *if s_i $(i = 2, \ldots, n)$ is of the form $\# \, {-\!\circ}B$ and there exists s_h $(h < i)$ such that s_h is of the form $\mathsf{F}B$, then:*
   (a) *Ω contains a sequence s^* such that s and s^* do not differ up to the level of their $i - 1$th terms and s_i^* is $\& \, {-\!\circ}B$;*
   (b) *for every sequence s^* such that s and s^* do not differ up to the level of their $i - 1$th terms, s_i^* is $\# \, {-\!\circ}B$ or $\& \, {-\!\circ}B$.*

A synthetic tableau Ω for a formula A is a family of interconnected synthetic inferences of $\mathsf{F}A$ or $\mathsf{T}A$. The clause 1a of Definition 32 warrants that introduction of a (signed) propositional variable into a tableau forces branching, which is semantically 'fair': if $\#\psi$ is to be introduced as an ith term of a path s of a tableau, then another branch s* should be created, which is exactly as s up to the level of their $i - 1$th terms and such that its ith term is $\&\psi$ (where $\#, \&$ stand for distinct truth-signs). On the other hand, clause 1b warrants, that this branching is always binary.

Clause 2, in turn, warrants fair branching and binary branching with respect to (signed) **CLaN**-negated formulas (that is, formulas of the form $\mathsf{F} \multimap B$, $\mathsf{T} \multimap B$), provided that they are introduced into a tableau as a result of the application of one of the rules $\mathsf{r_{a1}}$ or $\mathsf{r_{a2}}$.

These two clauses form a kind of cut rule. However, it is a tree-construction rule rather than an inferential rule. Moreover, this cut is very restricted: it can be applied only to propositional variables or to the paranegated formulas (provided that they are subformulas of the initial formula). Therefore, the restrictions here are even stronger than in the case of Smullyan's analytic cut.

Another point is, that if a formula A is of a 'branching-forcing' type (that is, it is a propositional variable or a formula $\& \multimap B$ resulting from the application of one of the unsound rules), then branching a tableau on $\mathsf{F}A$ and $\mathsf{T}A$ can be done only once (because of the clause 5 of Definition 31). Thus, no branch of a tableau can contain the very same wff preceded with T at one place and with F at another (see [17, p. 325–326]).

In order to prove soundness and completeness of the method with respect to the semantics of **CLaN**, we need the following lemmas and a theorem (we shall only outline their proofs; the details can be found in [18] and are analogous to the ones for CPC and **CLuN**, which are given in [14] and [17]).

Lemma 33. *Let s be a synthetic inference of a formula $\#A$. Let X be the set made up of all the terms of s. Let Θ be a subset of X made up of all the signed propositional variables in X. Then every formula in X is derivable via CLaN-rules based on the set Θ.*

The proof of Lemma 33 is based on induction on the degree of complexity of the elements of X (degree of complexity of a formula B is defined as the number of arguments of connectives in B). The synthesizing character of rules of inference guarantees that a formula introduced into a synthetic inference as a result of an application of a rule is of a greater degree of complexity than the premise (or premises) of the rule.

Theorem 34. *Let s be a synthetic inference of a (signed) formula A. Let X be the set made up of all the terms of s. Then there exists a valuation $\mathbf{v}$ such that all the elements of X are true with respect to $\mathbf{v}$.*

Notice that due to the definition of a synthetic inference the following hold ($p_i \in Var$):

1. $\mathsf{T}p_i \in X$ iff $\mathsf{F}p_i \notin X$
2. if $\mathsf{T} \multimap A \in X$, then $\mathsf{F}A \in X$ and $\mathsf{T}A \notin X$

The proof starts with defining the appropriate valuation. Let $\mathbf{v}$ be a **CLaN**-valuation determined by assignment functions $\mathbf{v}^{\mathbf{M}}$ and $\mathbf{v}^{\mathbf{N}}$ such that:

1. for every p_i:
   (a) if $\mathsf{T}p_i \in X$, then $\mathbf{v}^{\mathrm{M}}(p_i) = \mathbf{1}$;
   (b) if $\mathsf{F}p_i \in X$, then $\mathbf{v}^{\mathrm{M}}(p_i) = \mathbf{0}$;
   (c) if neither $\mathsf{T}p_i$ nor $\mathsf{F}p_i$ are in X, then $\mathbf{v}^{\mathrm{M}}(p_i) = \mathbf{0}$;
2. for every formula of the form $-\!\!\circ A$:
   (a) if $\mathsf{T} -\!\!\circ A \in X$, then $\mathbf{v}^{\mathrm{N}}(-\!\!\circ A) = \mathbf{1}$;
   (b) if $\mathsf{F} -\!\!\circ A \in X$, then $\mathbf{v}^{\mathrm{N}}(-\!\!\circ A) = \mathbf{0}$;
   (c) if neither $\mathsf{T} -\!\!\circ A$ nor $\mathsf{F} -\!\!\circ A$ are in X, then $\mathbf{v}^{\mathrm{N}}(-\!\!\circ A) = \mathbf{0}$.

Then we prove that $\mathbf{v}$ has the desired property, by induction on the degree of complexity of the formulas in X and by Lemma 33.

Lemma 35. *For every formula A of the considered language, there exists a synthetic tableau for A.*

The proof of Lemma 35 consists in defining a method of construction of a synthetic tableau for any given formula of the considered language. We start with characterizing a family of all the possible classes of **CLaN**-valuations, determined by truth values assigned to all the propositional variables and paranegated formulas occurring in the elements of X. Then we show that each such class determines a unique synthetic inference of $\#A$ and that all these inferences form a tableau for A, which is in a sense maximal – that is, which contains all the possible branchings (these are so-called canonical synthetic tableaux, see [14]).

All this warrants soundness and completeness of the method:

Theorem 36. *A formula A is **CLaN**-valid iff there exists a synthetic tableau for A such that every path of it leads to $\mathsf{T}A$.*

The detailed proof of this theorem, based on the notion of a minimal error point of a synthetic inference, is given in [18, p. 24–25].

Let us now consider some examples.

Example 1. The formulas p and $-\!\!\circ p$ are *contrariae*, thus $\neg(p \wedge -\!\!\circ p)$ is **CLaN**-valid:

$$\begin{array}{cc}
\mathsf{T}p & \mathsf{F}p \\
\mathsf{F} -\!\!\circ p & \mathsf{F}(p \wedge -\!\!\circ p) \\
\mathsf{F}(p \wedge -\!\!\circ p) & \mathsf{T}\neg(p \wedge -\!\!\circ p) \\
\mathsf{T}\neg(p \wedge -\!\!\circ p) &
\end{array}$$

Example 2. The formulas $\neg -\!\!\circ p$ and $\neg p$ are *subcontrariae* and cannot both be false; thus $\neg(\neg -\!\!\circ p \wedge \neg p)$ is not **CLaN**-valid:

$$\begin{array}{cc}
\mathsf{T}p & \mathsf{F}p \\
\mathsf{F}\neg p & \mathsf{T}\neg p \\
\mathsf{F}(\neg -\!\!\circ p \wedge \neg p) & \\
\mathsf{T}\neg(\neg -\!\!\circ p \wedge \neg p) &
\end{array}$$

$$\begin{array}{cc}
\mathsf{T} -\!\!\circ p & \mathsf{F} -\!\!\circ p \\
\mathsf{F}\neg -\!\!\circ p & \mathsf{T}\neg -\!\!\circ p \\
\mathsf{F}(\neg -\!\!\circ p \wedge \neg p) & \mathsf{T}(\neg -\!\!\circ p \wedge \neg p) \\
\mathsf{T}\neg(\neg -\!\!\circ p \wedge \neg p) & \mathsf{F}\neg(\neg -\!\!\circ p \wedge \neg p)
\end{array}$$

3.2   The Case of CLuN

In the case of the logic **CLuN** the definition of synthetic inference of a formula
$\#A$ is the same as in the case of **CLaN** (with one obvious difference that the
CLaN negation $\multimap$ should be changed to **CLuN** negation $\sim$). Derivability relation is defined based on the set **R** of classical inference rules and the following
specific **CLuN** rules:

$$\mathbf{r_{u1}} \quad \mathsf{T}A\backslash\backslash\mathsf{T}{\sim}A \qquad \mathbf{r_{u2}} \quad \mathsf{T}A\backslash\backslash\mathsf{F}{\sim}A \qquad \mathbf{r_{u3}} \quad \mathsf{F}A\backslash\backslash\mathsf{T}{\sim}A$$

Again, the rules $\mathbf{r_{u1}}$ and $\mathbf{r_{u2}}$ are based on subcontrariness and are unsound.
The rule $\mathbf{r_{u3}}$ is based on subalternation and it is sound.

The definition of a synthetic tableau for a given formula in the case of **CLuN**
differs from the **CLaN** version with respect to clause 2, which this time should
look like this:

2. if s_i $(i = 2, \dots, n)$ is of the form $\#{\sim}B$ and there exists s_h $(h < i)$ such that
   s_h is of the form $\mathsf{T}B$, then:
   (a) Ω contains a sequence s^* such that s and s^* do not differ up to the level
       of their $i - 1$th terms and s_i^* is $\&{\sim}B$;
   (b) for every sequence s^* such that s and s^* do not differ up to the level of
       their $i - 1$th terms, s_i^* is $\#{\sim}B$ or $\&{\sim}B$.

This is because in the case of **CLuN** the formulas $\mathsf{T}B$ and $\mathsf{T}{\sim}B$ are *subcontrariae*. As a result, an attempt to synthesize a **CLuN**-negated formula on the
basis of $\mathsf{T}B$ may lead to $\mathsf{T}{\sim}B$ as well as to $\mathsf{F}{\sim}B$. Thus, every application of
the rule $\mathbf{r_{u1}}$ (resp. $\mathbf{r_{u2}}$) should be accompanied by an application of the rule $\mathbf{r_{u2}}$
(resp. $\mathbf{r_{u1}}$), resulting in splitting current branch of a tableau. Again, soundness
and completeness of the method with respect to the semantics of **CLuN** can be
proved (see [17, p. 325–329]).

Let us consider some examples (taken from [17]).

Example 3. The formulas p and $\sim p$ are *subcontrariae*, thus $\neg(p \wedge \sim p)$ is not
CLuN-valid:

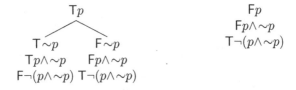

Example 4. The formulas $\neg \sim p$ and $\neg p$ are *contrariae*, thus $\neg(\neg \sim p \wedge \neg p)$ is
CLuN-valid:

$$
\begin{array}{ll}
\mathsf{T}p & \mathsf{F}p \\
\mathsf{F}\neg p & \mathsf{T}{\sim}p \\
\mathsf{F}\neg{\sim}p \wedge \neg p & \mathsf{F}\neg{\sim}p \\
\mathsf{T}\neg(\neg{\sim}p \wedge \neg p) & \mathsf{F}\neg{\sim}p \wedge \neg p \\
 & \mathsf{T}\neg(\neg{\sim}p \wedge \neg p)
\end{array}
$$

3.3   The Case of CLoN

On the one hand, the case of **CLoN** is somewhat more complicated than the cases of **CLaN** and **CLuN**. This is because the truth values of a **CLoN**-negated formula, $+A$, and of an argument of the negation, A, are unrelated to each other: they are assigned to these formulas independently of each other. Thus the square of oppositions in its usual form is not helpful here. All we can say is that none of the classical relations holds neither between $+A$ and A nor their signed versions.

On the other hand, this simplifies the matter of defining appropriate synthetic rules for $+$-introduction. The only prerequisite for introducing a formula $\# + A$ into a tableau is the presence of $\& A$ on a given branch (and in the case of **CLoN** $\#$ and $\&$ need not be distinct!). However, to warrant soundness of the method we still need to take care of the fair-branching condition.

The definition of synthetic inference of formula $\# A$ is the same as in the case of **CLaN** and **CLuN** (only the paranegation should be changed to **CLoN** negation $+$). Derivability relation is defined based on the set **R** of classical inference rules and the following specific **CLoN** rules:

$$r_{o1} \quad \mathsf{F}A\backslash\backslash\mathsf{T}+A \quad r_{o2} \quad \mathsf{F}A\backslash\backslash\mathsf{F}+A \quad r_{o3} \quad \mathsf{T}A\backslash\backslash\mathsf{T}+A \quad r_{o4} \quad \mathsf{T}A\backslash\backslash\mathsf{F}+A$$

None of the rules $r_{o1} - r_{o4}$ is sound. Clause 2 of the definition of a synthetic tableau for a given formula in the case of **CLoN** (which is the only difference between this version and **CLaN** and **CLuN** versions) should look like this:

2. if s_i $(i = 2, \ldots, n)$ is of the form $\#+B$, then:
   (a) Ω contains a sequence s^* such that s and s^* do not differ up to the level of their $i - 1$th terms and s_i^* is $\&+B$;
   (b) for every sequence s^* such that s and s^* do not differ up to the level of their $i - 1$th terms, s_i^* is $\#+B$ or $\&+B$.

Thus, in the case of **CLoN**, (signed) paranegated formulas are introduced into a tableau in the same way as (signed) propositional variables. We may even get rid of the inference rules $r_{o1} - r_{o4}$ and put the clauses for introducing formulas of the form $\&+B$ into tree-construction rules only. In order to do this we would have to change clause 4 of the definition of a synthetic inference (see definition 31) to the following:

4. for every s_g $(g = 1, \ldots, n)$ either s_g is a signed propositional variable, or s_g is of the form $\&+A$, or s_g is derivable on the basis of a certain set of fomulas such that each element of this set precedes s_g in s;

This makes it even more clear that in the case of **CLoN** both (signed) propositional variables and (signed) paranegated formulas are introduced into a tableau as a kind of assumptions and not as derived formulas. Thus a problem arises: does the '$+$' operator represent a negation at all? No information is reversed, no information is cancelled, no failure is present. This is an interesting issue; however, it goes well beyond the scope of the paper.

4 Conclusion

The square of oppositions (or, more generally: oppositional geometry) allows for a clear and transparent representation of the semantics of paranegations in logics **CLaN** and **CLuN**. In the STM setting, the properties of subcontrariness relation offer an intuitive justification for both unsound inference rules and tree-construction rules, which force branching of a tableau if one of the unsound rules is applied. It may be worth investigating if such a diagrammatic representation of semantic interconnections of formulas could also be successfully applied to other logics, and not only with respect to negation. Another possible direction of research are possible connections to non-deterministic semantics [1].

References

1. Avron, A., Konikowska, B.: Multi-valued calculi for logics based on non-determinism. Log. J. IGPL **13**(4), 365–387 (2005)
2. Batens, D.: Paraconsistent extensional propositional logics. Logique et Analyse **90–91**, 195–234 (1980)
3. Batens, D.: A survey of inconsistency-adaptive logics. In: Batens, D., Mortenson, C., Priest, G., Van Bendegem, J.P. (eds.) Frontiers of Paraconsistent Logic, pp. 49–73. Research Studies Press, King's College Publications, Baldock (2000)
4. Batens, D., De Clercq, K., Kurtonina, N.: Embedding and interpolation for some paralogics. The propositional case. Rep. Math. Log. **33**, 29–44 (1999)
5. Bocheński, I.M.: Ancient Formal Logic. North-Holland Publication, Amsterdam (1951)
6. Leszczynska-Jasion, D., Chlebowski, S.: Synthetic tableaux with unrestricted cut for first-order theories. Axioms **8**(4), 133 (2019)
7. Loparić, A., da Costa, C.A.: Paraconsistency, paracompleteness and induction. Logique et Analyse **113**, 73–80 (1986)
8. Łukasiewicz, J.: Aristotle's Syllogistic from the Standpoint of Modern Formal Logic. Oxford UP (1951)
9. Pellissier, R.: "Setting" n-opposition. Logica Universalis **2**, 235–263 (2008). https://doi.org/10.1007/s11787-008-0038-y
10. Popov, V.M.: Sequential axiomatizations for simple paralogics. Log. Investig. **16**, 205–221 (2010)
11. Sauriol, P.: Remarques sur la Théorie de l'hexagone logique de Blanché. Dialogue **7**(3), 374–390 (1968)
12. Sette, A.M., Alves, E.H.: On the equivalence between some systems of nonclassical logic. Bull. Sect. Log. **25**, 68–72 (1996)
13. Smessaert, H.: On the 3D visualisation of logical relations. Log. Univers. **3**(2), 303–332 (2009). https://doi.org/10.1007/s11787-009-0010-5
14. Urbański, M.: Remarks on synthetic tableaux for classical propositional calculus. Bull. Sect. Log. **30**, 194–204 (2001)
15. Urbański, M.: Synthetic tableaux and erotetic search scenarios: extension and extraction. Logique et Analyse **173–174–175**, 69–91 (2001)
16. Urbański, M.: Synthetic Tableaux for Łukasiewicz's Calculus L3. Logique et Analyse **177–178**, 155–173 (2002)
17. Urbański, M.: How to synthesize a paraconsistent negation. The case of CLuN. Logique et Analyse **185–188**, 319–333 (2004)
18. Żmójdzin, Z.: Synthetic tableaux for paralogic CLaN. M.A. thesis (unpublished), Institute of Psychology, Adam Mickiewicz University, Poznań (2011)

Validity Under Assumptions and Modus Ponens

Xuefeng Wen$^{(\boxtimes)}$

Institute of Logic and Cognition, Department of Philosophy, Sun Yat-sen University,
Guangzhou 510275, China

Abstract. Slightly altering and extending McGee's semantics for conditionals, we define a ternary notion of validity for natural language arguments, which can be regarded as a unification of two kinds of validity in the literature. By the new notion of validity, an inference is not just valid or invalid, but valid or invalid under a set of assumptions. Based on this notion, we formulate the validity and invalidity of modus ponens.

Keywords: Validity · Modus ponens · Epistemic modality · Ternary notion of truth

1 Introduction

This paper aims to unify two notions of validity in the literature, and apply it to formulating the validity and invalidity of modus ponens for natural language arguments.

The basic idea is to take McGee's ternary notion of truth given in [10] more formally and define a ternary notion of validity. By the ternary validity, an inference is not just valid or invalid, but valid or invalid under a set of assumptions. So a complete inference is tripart: a set of premises, a conclusion, and a set of assumptions. Assumptions provide contexts for evaluating formulas. Like McGee's semantics, conditional antecedents are treated as making assumptions. To formalize both indicatives and counterfactuals, we build the semantics in the framework of possible worlds semantics, using selection functions initiated by Stalnaker [14] in his conditional logic. To avoid some undesirable consequences of McGee's semantics, we tweak it and allow formulas with undetermined truth values. The new semantics with the new notion of validity shed light on different senses of validity concerning modus ponens.

The rest of the paper is organized as follows. Section 2 provides a new semantics for a formal language containing both conditionals and epistemic modals, together with the new notion of validity based on the semantics. Some semantic propertied are prepared. Section 3 applies the semantically defined logic to analyzing modus ponens, showing how empirical data from natural language arguments are predicted by the logic. Section 4 concludes the paper and suggests some future work.

© Springer Nature Switzerland AG 2021
P. Baroni et al. (Eds.): CLAR 2021, LNAI 13040, pp. 533–542, 2021.
https://doi.org/10.1007/978-3-030-89391-0_33

2   Semantics and Validity

2.1   Semantics

Definition 1 (Formal language). *Given a set At of atoms, the formal language $\mathcal{L}_{CM}$ for the logic of conditionals and epistemic modals is inductively defined by the following BNF:*

$$\mathcal{L}_{CM} \ni \varphi, \psi ::= p \mid \neg\varphi \mid (\varphi \wedge \psi) \mid (\varphi \vee \psi) \mid (\varphi > \psi) \mid \Box\varphi \mid \Diamond\varphi,$$

where $p \in At$.

We omit the outermost parentheses of formulas and stipulate that $\wedge$ and $\vee$ have priority to $>$. For instance, $(((p \wedge q) \vee r) > s)$ can be shortened as $(p \wedge q) \vee r > s$. As usual, we often abbreviate $\Delta \cup \{\varphi, \ldots, \varphi_n\}$ as $\Delta, \varphi, \ldots, \varphi_n$, and $\{\varphi, \ldots, \varphi_n\}$ as $\varphi, \ldots, \varphi_n$.

Among the compound formulas, $\neg\varphi$, $\varphi \wedge \psi$, $\varphi \vee \psi$, and $\varphi > \psi$ are standard Boolean formulas, $\varphi > \psi$ represents conditionals in natural language, and $\Box\varphi$ and $\Diamond\varphi$ are epistemic modal formulas, which read 'it must be the case that φ' and 'it might be the case that φ', respectively. Formulas without $>$, $\Box$, and $\Diamond$ are called *Boolean*. Formulas without $\Box$ and $\Diamond$ are called *modal free*. Atoms and negated atoms are called *literals*. Conditionals whose consequents are literals are called *conditional literals*.

The following definition follows Chellas' selection models [3], which were inspired by Stalnaker's selection models [14].

Definition 2 (Models). *A selection model is a triple $\mathfrak{M} = (W, f, V)$, where $W \neq \emptyset$ consists of worlds, $V : At \to \wp(W)$ is the valuation function, and $f : W \times \wp(W) \to \wp(W)$ the selection function satisfying the following conditions. For all $w \in W$ and $X, Y \subseteq W$,*

(id) $f(w, X) \subseteq X$
(cent) $w \in X$ implies $f(w, X) = \{w\}$
(lim) $f(w, X) = \emptyset$ implies $X = \emptyset$
(arr) $X \subseteq Y$ and $f(w, Y) \cap X \neq \emptyset$ imply $f(w, X) = f(w, Y) \cap X$

A pair $(\mathfrak{M}, w)$ with w in $\mathfrak{M}$ is called a pointed model.

A selection function f chooses for each world w and each proposition X (set of worlds) the closest (or most similar) worlds to w in X. It is not difficult to verify that the conditions above entail the following two conditions, which are less intuitive but more familiar in conditional logics. Together with (id) and (cent), they give rise to Lewis' conditional logic **VC** (a.k.a. **C1**, cf. [7,8]).

(cso) $f(w, X) \subseteq Y$ and $f(w, Y) \subseteq X$ imply $f(w, X) = f(w, Y)$
(pie) $f(w, X \cup Y) \subseteq X$ or $f(w, X \cup Y) \subseteq Y$ or $f(w, X \cup Y) = f(w, X) \cup f(w, Y)$

It follows from (cso) and (pie) that $f(w, X \cup Y) = f(w, X)$ or $f(w, X \cup Y) = f(w, Y)$ or $f(w, X \cup Y) = f(w, X) \cup f(w, Y)$, which will be used in the proofs.

To invalidate modus ponens and validate Import-Export, McGee [10] proposed a semantics based on selection models such that a new parameter other than the pointed model is supplemented to evaluate the truth value of formulas. The new parameter is a set of hypotheses (we call assumptions), used to keep track of the antecedents of conditionals. A conditional is true at a pointed model under a set of assumptions, iff the consequent of the conditional is true at the pointed model under the set of hypotheses supplemented by the antecedent of the conditional. This idea is also adopted in our semantics given below.

Definition 3 (Truth conditions). *Given a model* $\mathfrak{M} = (W, f, V)$, *the ternary satisfaction relation* $\Vdash$ *is defined as follows, in which* $[\![\varphi]\!]^{\mathfrak{M},\Delta} = \{w \in W \mid \mathfrak{M}, w \Vdash^{\Delta} \varphi\}$, $[\![\Delta]\!]^{\mathfrak{M},\emptyset} = \bigcap_{\delta \in \Delta} [\![\delta]\!]^{\mathfrak{M},\emptyset}$, *and* $\mathfrak{M}, w \Vdash \varphi$ *means* $\mathfrak{M}, w \Vdash^{\emptyset} \varphi$.

- $\mathfrak{M}, w \Vdash p$ *iff* $w \in V(p)$;
- $\mathfrak{M}, w \Vdash \neg p$ *iff* $w \notin V(p)$;
- $\mathfrak{M}, w \Vdash^{\Delta} p$ *iff* $f(w, [\![\Delta]\!]^{\mathfrak{M},\emptyset}) \subseteq V(p)$, *where* $\Delta \neq \emptyset$;
- $\mathfrak{M}, w \Vdash^{\Delta} \neg p$ *iff* $f(w, [\![\Delta]\!]^{\mathfrak{M},\emptyset}) \subseteq W - V(p)$, *where* $\Delta \neq \emptyset$;
- $\mathfrak{M}, w \Vdash^{\Delta} \varphi \wedge \psi$ *iff* $\mathfrak{M}, w \Vdash^{\Delta} \varphi$ *and* $\mathfrak{M}, w \Vdash^{\Delta} \psi$;
- $\mathfrak{M}, w \Vdash^{\Delta} \varphi \vee \psi$ *iff* $\mathfrak{M}, w \Vdash^{\Delta} \varphi$ *or* $\mathfrak{M}, w \Vdash^{\Delta} \psi$;
- $\mathfrak{M}, w \Vdash^{\Delta} \varphi > \psi$ *iff* $\mathfrak{M}, w \Vdash^{\Delta,\varphi} \psi$;
- $\mathfrak{M}, w \Vdash^{\Delta} \Box\varphi$ *iff for all* $u \in W$, $\mathfrak{M}, u \Vdash^{\Delta}\varphi$;
- $\mathfrak{M}, w \Vdash^{\Delta} \Diamond\varphi$ *iff for some* $u \in W$, $\mathfrak{M}, u \Vdash^{\Delta} \varphi$.

If $\mathfrak{M}$ is clear from the context, we will simply write $[\![\varphi]\!]^{\Delta}$ for $[\![\varphi]\!]^{\mathfrak{M},\Delta}$, $[\![\varphi]\!]$ for $[\![\varphi]\!]^{\mathfrak{M},\emptyset}$, and $[\![\Delta]\!]$ for $[\![\Delta]\!]^{\mathfrak{M},\emptyset}$ respectively. We write $\mathfrak{M}, w \Vdash^{\Delta} \Gamma$ if for all $\varphi \in \Gamma$, $\mathfrak{M}, w \Vdash^{\Delta} \Gamma$. Note that the above definition does not give truth conditions for *all* formulas. Specifically, negation is not defined yet, though negated atoms are defined. We postpone the truth condition for general negated formulas to Definition 4.

The following lemma is just a reformulation of the truth conditions for $\wedge, \vee, >$, $\Box$, and $\Diamond$.

Lemma 1. *For all models* $\mathfrak{M}$ *and* $\Delta \cup \{\varphi, \psi, \chi\} \subseteq \mathcal{L}_{CM}$,

1. $[\![\varphi \wedge \psi]\!]^{\Delta} = [\![\varphi]\!]^{\Delta} \cap [\![\psi]\!]^{\Delta}$ 2. $[\![\varphi \vee \psi]\!]^{\Delta} = [\![\varphi]\!]^{\Delta} \cup [\![\psi]\!]^{\Delta}$

3. $[\![\varphi > \psi]\!]^{\Delta} = [\![\psi]\!]^{\Delta,\varphi}$

4. $[\![\Box\varphi]\!]^{\Delta} = \begin{cases} W & \text{if } [\![\varphi]\!]^{\Delta} = W \\ \emptyset & \text{otherwise} \end{cases}$ 5. $[\![\Diamond\varphi]\!]^{\Delta} = \begin{cases} W & \text{if } [\![\varphi]\!]^{\Delta} \neq \emptyset \\ \emptyset & \text{otherwise} \end{cases}$

Though the basic idea of the semantics is the same as McGee's, we highlight three differences between McGee's semantics and ours.

First, following Lewis and pace Stalnaker, we do not assume that the closest φ-worlds to w are unique. Consider a world w in which a circuit has two closed switches A and B in series. Then there are at least two closest worlds to w such that A or B is open: one is with A open and B closed, the other B open and A closed. There is no reason to decide that one is closer than the other.

Second, because of the non-uniqueness assumption, we treat negation differently. We cannot just define $\mathfrak{M}, w \Vdash^\Delta \neg\varphi$ by $\mathfrak{M}, w \not\Vdash^\Delta \varphi$, as in McGee's semantics. For if negation is defined like this, then p and $\neg p$ will have asymmetric truth conditions at w under Δ: one with $f(w, [\![\Delta]\!]) \subseteq [\![p]\!]$ and the other $f(w, [\![\Delta]\!]) \not\subseteq [\![p]\!]$, which is equivalent to $f(w, [\![\Delta]\!]) \cap [\![\neg p]\!] \neq \emptyset$. Now the truth condition for p has a universal structure (*all* closest Δ-worlds are p-worlds), whereas for $\neg p$ it has an existential structure (*some* closest Δ-worlds are $\neg p$-worlds), which is unjustified. To treat negation properly, we define the truth conditions of p and $\neg p$ both by the universal structure, and define compound negated formulas by reduction as follows.

Definition 4 (Negation). *The truth set of compound negated formulas are defined inductively as follows. For all models $\mathfrak{M}$ and $\Delta \cup \{\varphi, \psi\} \subseteq \mathcal{L}_{CM}$,*

1. $[\![\neg\neg\varphi]\!]^\Delta = [\![\varphi]\!]^\Delta$ *2.* $[\![\neg(\varphi \wedge \psi)]\!]^\Delta = [\![\neg\varphi \vee \neg\psi]\!]^\Delta$

3. $[\![\neg(\varphi \vee \psi)]\!]^\Delta = [\![\neg\varphi \wedge \neg\psi]\!]^\Delta$ *4.* $[\![\neg(\varphi > \psi)]\!]^\Delta = [\![\varphi > \neg\psi]\!]^\Delta$

5. $[\![\neg\Box\varphi]\!]^\Delta = [\![\Diamond\neg\varphi]\!]^\Delta$ *6.* $[\![\neg\Diamond\varphi]\!]^\Delta = [\![\Box\neg\varphi]\!]^\Delta$

Remark 1. The above definition implies that all formulas can be equivalently transformed into negation normal forms, in which negations are only applied to atoms. Hence, in the proofs by induction on formulas, we need only consider negated atoms, without considering arbitrary negated formulas.

The third difference is that, we allow $f(w, X)$ to be empty, without assuming some absurd world, and since the empty set is a subset of any set, we do not need an additional clause to stipulate that $\varphi > \psi$ is true for any ψ if φ is impossible. Its truth is derivable from other clauses in our semantics, as shown by the following lemma.

Lemma 2. *For all model $\mathfrak{M} = (W, f, V)$ and $\Delta \subseteq \mathcal{L}_{CM}$, if $[\![\Delta]\!] = \emptyset$ then for all $\varphi \in \mathcal{L}_{CM}$, $[\![\varphi]\!]^\Delta = W$.*

Proof. By induction on φ. It is straightforward when φ is Boolean. When $\varphi = \alpha > \beta$, suppose $[\![\Delta]\!] = \emptyset$. Then $[\![\Delta, \alpha]\!] \subseteq [\![\Delta]\!] = \emptyset$, by the inductive hypothesis, we have $[\![\alpha > \beta]\!]^\Delta = [\![\beta]\!]^{\Delta, \alpha} = W$. When $\varphi = \Box\psi$, by the inductive hypothesis, $[\![\psi]\!]^\Delta = W$ and hence $[\![\Box\psi]\!]^\Delta = W$ by Lemma 1. When $\varphi = \Diamond\psi$, by the inductive hypothesis $[\![\psi]\!]^\Delta = W \neq \emptyset$ and hence $[\![\Diamond\psi]\!]^\Delta = W$ by Lemma 1.   □

Moreover, we extend McGee's formal language and incorporate modal operators, whose semantics is defined independently, rather than defined by conditionals as in Stalnaker-Lewisian conditional logics (cf. [14] and [8, p. 22]).

The following lemmas about the semantic properties will be used in the sequel. The proofs of Lemmas 3–5 are easy and left to the reader.

Lemma 3. *For all models $\mathfrak{M}$ and $\Delta \cup \{\varphi, \psi, \chi\} \subseteq \mathcal{L}_{CM}$,*

1. $[\![\varphi > \psi \wedge \chi]\!]^{\Delta} = [\![\varphi > \psi]\!]^{\Delta} \cap [\![\varphi > \chi]\!]^{\Delta}$
2. $[\![\varphi > \psi \vee \chi]\!]^{\Delta} = [\![\varphi > \psi]\!]^{\Delta} \cup [\![\varphi > \chi]\!]^{\Delta}$
3. $[\![\varphi > (\psi > \chi)]\!]^{\Delta} = [\![\varphi \wedge \psi > \chi]\!]^{\Delta}$

Remark 2. Together with Remark 1, Lemma 3 implies that all modal free conditionals can be equivalently transformed into formulas building from conditional literals, using the operators of conjunction and disjunction.

Lemma 4. *For all models $\mathfrak{M} = (W, f, V)$ and $\Delta \cup \{\varphi, \psi\} \subseteq \mathcal{L}_{CM}$, if ψ is Boolean then for all $w \in W$, $\mathfrak{M}, w \Vdash^{\Delta} \psi$ implies $f(w, [\![\Delta]\!]) \subseteq [\![\psi]\!]$.*

Lemma 5. *For all models $\mathfrak{M}$ and $\Delta \cup \Delta' \cup \{\varphi\} \subseteq \mathcal{L}_{CM}$, if $[\![\Delta]\!] = [\![\Delta']\!]$, then $[\![\varphi]\!]^{\Delta} = [\![\varphi]\!]^{\Delta'}$.*

Lemma 6. *For all models $\mathfrak{M}$ and all $\Delta \cup \{\varphi, \psi, \chi\} \subseteq \mathcal{L}_{CM}$, if χ is modal free, then $[\![\chi]\!]^{\Delta, \varphi} \cap [\![\chi]\!]^{\Delta, \psi} \subseteq [\![\chi]\!]^{\Delta, \varphi \vee \psi}$.*

Proof. By induction on χ, noting that we have either $f(w, [\![\alpha \vee \beta]\!]) = f(w, [\![\alpha]\!])$ or $f(w, [\![\alpha \vee \beta]\!]) = f(w, [\![\beta]\!])$ or $f(w, [\![\alpha \vee \beta]\!]) = f(w, [\![\alpha]\!]) \cup f(w, [\![\beta]\!])$. $\qquad\square$

2.2 Validity

Definition 5 (Validity). *Let $\Gamma \cup \Delta \cup \{\varphi\} \subseteq \mathcal{L}_{CM}$.*

1. *The inference from Γ to φ is valid under Δ (denote $\Gamma \vDash^{\Delta} \varphi$), if for all pointed models $(\mathfrak{M}, w)$, $\mathfrak{M}, w \Vdash^{\Delta} \Gamma$ implies $\mathfrak{M}, w \Vdash^{\Delta} \varphi$, i.e., $[\![\Gamma]\!]^{\mathfrak{M}, \Delta} \subseteq [\![\varphi]\!]^{\mathfrak{M}, \Delta}$, where $[\![\Gamma]\!]^{\mathfrak{M}, \Delta} = \bigcap_{\gamma \in \Gamma} [\![\gamma]\!]^{\mathfrak{M}, \Delta}$.*
2. *The inference from Γ to φ is valid (denoted $\Gamma \vDash \varphi$), if it is valid under $\emptyset$; it is fully valid, if it is valid under any Δ.*
3. *φ is valid under Δ (denoted $\vDash^{\Delta} \varphi$), valid (denoted $\vDash \varphi$), or fully valid, if the inference from $\emptyset$ to φ is valid under Δ, valid, or fully valid, respectively.*

With the ternary notion of validity, we can distinguish four forms of the inference from $\{\varphi, \psi\}$ to χ.

Standard Form $\varphi, \psi \vDash \chi$, which reads: φ and ψ imply χ.
Assumptive Form $\vDash^{\varphi, \psi} \chi$, which reads: χ is valid, assuming φ and ψ.
Hybrid Form 1 $\varphi \vDash^{\psi} \chi$, which reads: φ implies χ, assuming ψ.
Hybrid Form 2 $\psi \vDash^{\varphi} \chi$, which reads: ψ implies χ, assuming φ.

The four forms are not always equivalent to each other. An inference can be valid in one form but not in another. We will see in Sect. 3 that the puzzle concerning modus ponens can be resolved by distinguishing the four forms of inferences.

3   Modus Ponens

Modus ponens for material implication is a fundamental rule in classical logic. Presumably, it should also be valid for conditionals. Indeed, in conditional logics proposed by Stalnaker [14] and Lewis [8], the rule $\varphi, \varphi > \psi \,/\, \psi$ is always valid. But McGee [10] gave a famous counterexample to modus ponens for indicative conditionals, which was about the 1980 US presidential election. Opinion polls showed that the republican Ronald Reagan was decisively ahead of the democrat Jimmy Carter, who was in turn decisively ahead of the other republican John Anderson. Then the premises (1a) and (1b) below sound true, while the conclusion (1c) does not, for if Reagan does not win, Carter will.

(1) (a) If a republican wins the election, then if it's not Reagan who wins it will be Anderson.
   (b) A republican will win the election.
   (c) Therefore, if it's not Reagan who wins, it will be Anderson.

Based on such examples, McGee argued that when ψ contains embedded conditionals as above, $\varphi, \varphi > \psi/\psi$ is not valid. Another motivation for McGee to invalidate modus ponens is that, together with some innocuous assumptions, validating both modus ponens and Import-Export leads to collapse of conditionals, i.e. conditionals are logically indistinguishable from material implication (see [4] for a proof). Since Import-Export has not been found any convincing counterexample (cf. [6]) and collapse is generally unacceptable, invalidating modus ponens seems the unique solution to the problem.

Despite the differences given in Sect. 2.1, our semantics inherits most features of McGee's. Modus ponens is still invalid in our semantics, except that with epistemic modals augmented, we can formulate more counterexamples. The following is one based on the same scenario.

(2) (a) If a republican wins the election, then the winner must be Reagan.
   (b) A republican will win the election.
   (c) Therefore, the winner must be Reagan.

We have good reason to believe that (2a) and (2b) are true. But since we cannot completely rule out the possibility of Reagan's lose, (2c) is not true. Thus we obtain another counterexample to modus ponens. Both counterexamples are predicted by our semantics, as the following proposition demonstrates.

Proposition 1. *Modus ponens is invalid in the following forms, where $p, q, r \in At$,*

1. $p, p > (q > r) \nvDash q > r$
2. $p, p > \Box q \nvDash \Box q$

Proof. For 1, consider $\mathfrak{M} = (W, f, V)$, where $W = \{w, u, v\}$, $V(p) = \{w, u\}$, $V(q) = \{u, v\}$, $V(r) = \{u\}$, $f(w, \{u\}) = \{u\}$, $f(w, \{u, v\}) = \{v\}$. Then $\mathfrak{M}, w \Vdash p$ and $\mathfrak{M}, w \Vdash p > (q > r)$, but $\mathfrak{M}, w \nVdash q > r$.

For 2, consider $\mathfrak{M} = (W, f, V)$, where $W = \{w, u\}$, $V(p) = V(q) = \{w\}$, $f(w, \{w\}) = f(u, \{w\}) = \{w\}$. Then $\mathfrak{M}, w \Vdash p$ and $\mathfrak{M}, w \Vdash p > \Box q$, but $\mathfrak{M}, w \nVdash \Box q$. □

Nonetheless, giving up modus ponens completely is too hasty. Indeed, we can keep some forms of modus ponens, as formulated below.

Proposition 2. *Modus ponens is valid in the following forms.*

1. **Standard Form** $\varphi, \varphi > \psi \vDash \psi$, *where ψ is Boolean*
2. **Assumptive Form** $\vDash^{\varphi, \varphi > \psi} \psi$, *where ψ is modal free*
3. **Hybrid Form** $\varphi > \psi \vDash^{\varphi} \psi$

Proof. For 1, given any model $\mathfrak{M} = (W, f, V)$ and $w \in W$, suppose $\mathfrak{M}, w \Vdash \varphi$ and $\mathfrak{M}, w \Vdash \varphi > \psi$. By Lemma 4, we have $f(w, \llbracket \varphi \rrbracket) \subseteq \llbracket \psi \rrbracket$. By (cent), we have $f(w, \llbracket \varphi \rrbracket) = \{w\}$. Then $\mathfrak{M}, w \Vdash \psi$.

For 2, we prove by induction on ψ. We will prove a stronger claim: if ψ is modal free, then for any $\Delta \subseteq \mathcal{L}_{CM}$, $\vDash^{\Delta, \varphi, \varphi > \psi} \psi$. First, it can be verified that for any model $\mathfrak{M}$, $\llbracket \varphi \rrbracket \cap \llbracket \varphi > p \rrbracket \subseteq \llbracket p \rrbracket$ and $\llbracket \varphi \rrbracket \cap \llbracket \varphi > \neg p \rrbracket \subseteq \llbracket \neg p \rrbracket$. When $\psi = p \in At$, for any model $\mathfrak{M} = (W, f, V)$ and $w \in W$, $f(w, \llbracket \Delta, \varphi, \varphi > p \rrbracket) \subseteq \llbracket \varphi \rrbracket \cap \llbracket \varphi > p \rrbracket \subseteq \llbracket p \rrbracket = V(p)$. Hence, $\llbracket p \rrbracket^{\Delta, \varphi, \varphi > p} = W$. It follows that $\vDash^{\Delta, \varphi, \varphi > p} p$. Analogously, we have $\vDash^{\Delta, \varphi, \varphi > \neg p} \neg p$.

When $\psi = \alpha \wedge \beta$, for any model $\mathfrak{M} = (W, f, V)$, $\llbracket \alpha \wedge \beta \rrbracket^{\Delta, \varphi, \varphi > \alpha \wedge \beta} = \llbracket \alpha \rrbracket^{\Delta, \varphi > \beta, \varphi, \varphi > \alpha}, \cap \llbracket \beta \rrbracket^{\Delta, \varphi > \alpha, \varphi, \varphi > \beta} = W \cap W = W$, where the first $=$ is by Lemma 3 and Lemma 5, and the second $=$ is by the inductive hypothesis.

When $\psi = \alpha \vee \beta$, for any model $\mathfrak{M} = (W, f, V)$, $\llbracket \alpha \vee \beta \rrbracket^{\Delta, \varphi, \varphi > \alpha \vee \beta} = \llbracket \alpha \vee \beta \rrbracket^{\Delta, \varphi, (\varphi > \alpha) \vee (\varphi > \beta)} \supseteq \llbracket \alpha \vee \beta \rrbracket^{\Delta, \varphi, \varphi > \alpha} \cap \llbracket \alpha \vee \beta \rrbracket^{\Delta, \varphi, \varphi > \beta} \supseteq \llbracket \alpha \rrbracket^{\Delta, \varphi, \varphi > \alpha} \cap \llbracket \beta \rrbracket^{\Delta, \varphi, \varphi > \beta} = W \cap W = W$, where the first $=$ is by Lemma 3 and Lemma 5, the first $\supseteq$ is by Lemma 6, and the penultimate $=$ is by the inductive hypothesis.

When $\psi = \alpha > \beta$, for any model $\mathfrak{M} = (W, f, V)$, $\llbracket \alpha > \beta \rrbracket^{\varphi, \varphi > (\alpha > \beta)} = \llbracket \beta \rrbracket^{\varphi, \varphi > (\alpha > \beta), \alpha} = \llbracket \beta \rrbracket^{\varphi \wedge \alpha, \varphi \wedge \alpha > \beta} = W$, where the second $=$ is by Lemma 3 and Lemma 5, and the last $=$ is by the inductive hypothesis.

For 3, given any model $\mathfrak{M} = (W, f, V)$ and $w \in W$, suppose $\mathfrak{M}, w \Vdash^{\varphi} \varphi > \psi$. Then $\mathfrak{M}, w \Vdash^{\varphi, \varphi} \psi$, i.e. $\mathfrak{M}, w \Vdash^{\varphi} \psi$. Hence, $\varphi > \psi \Vdash^{\varphi} \psi$. □

The standard form restricted to Boolean formulas is inherited from McGee's semantics, while the other two forms can only be formulated in our framework. Before moving on, let us give two remarks.

Remark 3. The assumptive form does not hold if ψ contains modal operators. This is because modal formulas may be self-refuting. One can easily verify that $\nvDash^{\Diamond p, \Diamond p > p \wedge \Diamond \neg p} p \wedge \Diamond \neg p$, since the assumption $\Diamond p > p \wedge \Diamond \neg p$ can only be true at p-worlds. So under this assumption, $\Diamond \neg p$ cannot be true.

Remark 4. The other hybrid form of modus ponens is not valid. More precisely, $\varphi \nvDash^{\varphi > \psi} \psi$, even if ψ is modal free. One can verify $p \nvDash^{p > (q > r)} q > r$ using the same counter-model for the proof of Clause 1 of Proposition 1.

Both counterexamples like (1) and (2) had been objected by Over [11], among others. Over argued that if the premises of modus ponens have been certainly assumed, the conclusion cannot be false. This intuition is formulated by the assumptive form of modus ponens in our semantics. Though it is not generally valid, its restricted form for the two examples above are valid, as shown by the following proposition.

Proposition 3. *For any $p, q, r \in At$,*

1. $\models^{p,p>(q>r)} q > r$
2. $\models^{p,p>\Box q} \Box q$

Proof. Clause 1 is already contained in Clause 3 of Proposition 2.

For 2, note that $[\![p > \Box q]\!] \subseteq [\![p > q]\!]$. Thus, for any model $\mathfrak{M} = (W, V, f)$ and $w \in W$, $f(w, [\![p, p > \Box q]\!]) \subseteq [\![p]\!] \cap [\![p > \Box q]\!] \subseteq [\![p]\!] \cap [\![p > q]\!] \subseteq [\![q]\!]$, where the last $\subseteq$ is by Clause 1 of Proposition 2. Hence, $\mathfrak{M}, w \Vdash^{p,p>\Box q} q$ for all $w \in W$, which means $\mathfrak{M}, w \Vdash^{p,p>\Box q} \Box q$.   □

Now in the literature concerning the validity of modus ponens, often two notions of validity are distinguished. Mandelkern [9] categorized them as truth-preserving validity, which is the standard one, and informational validity, which was defended in [1], based on the semantics initiated by Veltman [15] and developed by Gillies [5] and Yalcin [16], among others. The two notions of validity yield two forms of modus ponens. The truth-preserving form reads: if φ and $\varphi > \psi$ are true, then ψ is true. The informational form reads: if φ and $\varphi > \psi$ are fully accepted, then rationality requires ψ to be fully accepted. To better understand the three forms of modus ponens formulated in our framework, we can roughly equate the standard form with the truth-preserving form, the assumptive form with the informational form, and the hybrid form with the combination of the truth-preserving form and the informational one.

Bledin [2] argues that, though truth-preserving modus ponens may not be valid, informational modus ponens is still valid. Consider McGee's example again. If we fully accept that a republican will win, and that if a republican wins then if it is not Reagan who wins it will be Anderson, then we must accept that if Reagan does not win, then Anderson will win. The intuition is similar to Over's, which could also be formulated by assumptive modus ponens.

But to dispel the counterexample does not require us to fully accept both premises. Fully accepting that a republican will win is enough for us to infer from 'if a republican wins then if it is not Reagan who wins it will be Anderson' to its consequent, which is predicted by the validity of the hybrid form of modus ponens. Note that fully accepting (1a) only does not make the conclusion true from the other premise, which has been predicted in Remark 4.

We leave the full comparison for future research, but just point out one merit of our framework. Note that the truth-preserving form and the informational form of modus ponens in the literature cannot actually be combined directly, since they rely on different notions of validity. One appeals to truth and the other to acceptance. In our framework, however, we have a ternary notion of validity, which relies on a ternary notion of truth, so that the two notions of validity and the two forms of modus ponens can be unified. Since both truth-preserving validity and informational validity are inadequate for natural language arguments (see e.g. [13] and [12] for criticism of informational validity), a combination or unification of them is desirable.

4 Conclusion and Future Work

We define a logic for conditionals and epistemic modals, based on McGee's ternary notion of truth. The crucial contribution is a ternary notion of validity, by which an inference is not (in)valid per se, but (in)valid under a set of assumptions. Thus, an inference has three different forms: standard form (no premises are assumed), assumptive form (all premises are assumed), and hybrid form (some premises are assumed), which are not equivalent to each other. Armed with this differentiation, we give an analysis of the puzzle concerning the (in)validity of modus ponens. This is a preliminary attempt to unify two kinds of validity proposed in the literature. Future work includes a full comparison to existing works, and applications of the new notion of validity to other puzzles.

Acknowledgements. I thank two referees for their helpful comments. The work was supported by National Social Science Foundation of China for key projects (No. 18ZDA033).

References

1. Bledin, J.: Logic informed. Mind **123**(490), 277–316 (2014)
2. Bledin, J.: Modus ponens defended. J. Philos. **112**(2), 57–83 (2015)
3. Chellas, B.F.: Basic conditional logic. J. Philos. Log. **4**(2), 133–153 (1975)
4. Gibbard, A.: Two recent theories of conditionals. In: Harper, W.L., Stalnaker, R., Pearce, G. (eds.) Ifs: Conditionals, Belief, Decision, Chance, and Time, pp. 211–248. Reidel, Dordrecht (1981)
5. Gillies, A.: Epistemic conditionals and conditional epistemics. Noûs **4**, 585–616 (2004)
6. Khoo, J., Mandelkern, M.: Triviality results and the relationship between logical and natural languages. Mind **128**(510), 485–526 (2019)
7. Lewis, D.: Completeness and decidability of three logics of counterfactual conditionals. Theoria **37**(1), 74–85 (1971)
8. Lewis, D.: Counterfactuals. Harvard University Press (1973)
9. Mandelkern, M.: A counterexample to modus ponenses. J. Philos. **117**(6), 315–331 (2020)
10. McGee, V.: A counterexample to modus ponens. J. Philos. **82**(9), 462–471 (1985)
11. Over, D.: Assumptions and the supposed counterexamples to modus ponens. Analysis **47**(3), 142–146 (1987)
12. Santorio, P.: Trivializing informational consequence. Philos. Phenomenol. Res. (forthcoming)

13. Schulz, M.: Epistemic modals and informational consequence. Synthese **174**(3), 385–395 (2010)
14. Stalnaker, R.: A Theory of conditionals. In: Rescher, N. (ed.) Studies in Logical Theory, pp. 98–112. Basil Blackwell Publishers (1968)
15. Veltman, F.: Defaults in update semantics. J. Philos. Log. **25**(3), 221–261 (1996)
16. Yalcin, S.: Epistemic modals. Mind **116**(464), 983–1026 (2007)

Entailments with Sentential Predicates

Richard Zuber[(✉)]

Rayé des cadres du CNRS, Paris, France
Richard.Zuber@linguist.univ-paris-diderot.fr

Abstract. A simple model accounting for entailments between sentential predicates with propositional attitude verbs is proposed. In this model no reference to propositions is made. Sentential predicates denote specific sets of sentences (of a given natural language). This approach avoids the problem of intensionality of propositional attitude operators and permits to use many tools from the generalised quantifier theory.

1 Introduction

In this paper I discuss, in a preliminary way, properties which give rise to specific entailment relations holding between sentences formed from propositional attitude verbs and operators. I discuss in particular the relation of presupposition of factive verbs and the entailment associated with the so-called *neg-raising verbs*. The propositional operators are of the form *A V that/whether* where *A* is a proper name and V a verb of propositional attitudes. I will also ignore the fact that such verbs can take quantificational noun phrases as grammatical subjects.

They are denoted by O, with additional information concerning the complementizer they take. The class of all propositional operators, which are of category S/S is denoted by PO. The set PA (propositional attitude operator). is a subset of PO. A linguistic object expressing a PO in a given language and taken without the complementizer is called a *sentential predicate* (SP)

Factive predicates, when completed by the grammatical subject referring to a human, form sentential operators which presuppose the truth of their sentential argument: positive forms of sentences formed from factive predicates and their (natural) negations both entail the complement sentence: (1a) and (1b) both entail that sentence P is true:

(1) a. Leo knows/remembers that P.
    b. Leo does not know/remember that P.

Consequently we will consider that *Leo knows that* and *Leo remembers that* are factive PA operators, that is operators presupposing their sentential argument. The verbs *remember* and *forget* are considered as factives.

Another case of intensional sentence-embedding predicates with specific entailments concerns *neg-raising predicates*: when negated sentences with such predicates imply a corresponding sentence in which the negation takes scope in the embedded clause: (2a) entails (2b):

Thanks to at least one referee for useful comments.

P. Baroni et al. (Eds.): CLAR 2021, LNAI 13040, pp. 543–550, 2021.
https://doi.org/10.1007/978-3-030-89391-0_34

(2) a. Leo does not think that life is sad.

    b. Leo thinks that life is not sad.

In the above example we have an intensional operator, formed from the verb of propositional attitude *to think*. This is not the case in general: some neg-transportable operators are not formed from verbs of propositional attitude: the operator *It is true (false) that* is neg-transportable but is not a propositional attitude operator. Observe that (3) entails neither (2a) nor (2b):

(3) It is not true that Leo thinks that life is sad

Given the role of the negation we have to take into account precisely the fact that it has to apply to intensional sentential operators and to make clear what the notion of intensionality of such sentential operators is.

Semantic relations between PA operators are related to principles expressing knowledge of the attitude by agents. They echo various "iteration principles" used in epistemic logics. For instance the so-called KK principle says that for any proposition P if one knows that P then one knows that one knows that P. Thus I will assume the following attitudinal self-awareness principle (ASAP):

ASAP: If any agent has a specific propositional attitude then he/she knows that he/she has this attitude.

The following examples illustrate what I mean by the ASAP: we suppose that (4) entails (5), when taken in *de dicto* readings:

(4) Bo believes/knows/regrets/understands that life is sad.

(5) Bo knows that she believes/knows/regrets/understands that life is sad.

Propositional operators are noted O, O_1, O_2, Q. Propositional operators formed from verbs whose subject NP denotes a are noted O_a. The set of true sentences is noted T and any subset of T is called a *veridical operator* and the set of such operators is noted VER. The set of sentences that the agent a knows to be true is noted K_a and the set of sentences of which a knows whether they are true or not is noted KW_a. If O is a propositional operator then $S \in O$ means that sentence formed from O and having S as propositional argument is true. Thus $S \in T$ means *It is true that S* and $S \in K_a$ means that *a knows that S is true*. Moreover $S \in O$ and $S \notin O$ will be considered as sentences. The distinction between variables in the object language and metalanguage will be ignored.

In D1 we have a semantic definition of propositional attitude operators:

Definition 1. *A propositional operator O_a is a propositional attitude operator, $O_a \in PA$, iff $S \in O_a$ entails a knows whether $S \in O_a$, for any sentence S*

Thus the agent has to be aware that he has the attitude expressed by the main verb of the operator. Since the operators such as *a wrote that* and *a proved that* do not have this property they are not *PA* operators.

In what follows we will consider the entailment between *PO* and not the entailment between sentences.

2   Propositional Attitude Operators

The universe from which we construct the denotational algebra of PA operators consists of the set of (declarative) sentences of a given, fixed, natural language. To be more precise we exclude from the universe sentences whose interpretation is context dependent. In particular we exclude sentences with free variables, indexicals and pronouns externally bound. Thus denotations of propositional operators will be constructed from elements of the power set algebra of the set of sentences whose interpretation does not depend on the context. If Σ is the set of sentences of, say, English, the $\wp(\Sigma)$ can be considered as a Boolean algebra whose elements are sets of sentences and Boolean operations correspond to operations on sets of sentences. The unit of this algebra is the set Σ itself and the zero element is the empty set. The entailment corresponds to the (generalised) cross-categorial entailment (Keenan and Faltz 1985) which is just the partial order of the corresponding Boolean algebra, the denotational algebra of PO.

The POs are interpreted as sets of sentences. Informally, one can consider that PO *It is true that* denotes the set T and PO *It is false that* denotes the set of false sentences. The reason is that linguistic objects of category S/S can be lifted and become of category $S/(S/S)$. Consequently this interpretation is not context dependent and POs denote a set of sentences, taken independently of their truth value.

Thus to construct sets of sentences constituting denotations propositional operators we use the set of (declarative) sentences of a given natural language. We distinguish negated and non-negated sentences. Negated sentences are sentences of the form *It is not true that S*, where S is a sentence. They are noted nS and the set of negated sentences is noted NS. There is obvious semantic dependence between S and nS: S is true iff nS is false. We also need a function corresponding to the deletion of the negation of a negated sentence. Thus:

Definition 2. *Let $S \in NS$. Then $(n)S = S_0$ if $S = nS_0$ and nS otherwise.*

Thus $(n)S$ is the sentence obtained from a negated sentence by deleting its negation: $(n)(nS) = S$. We will also use other Booleanly complex sentences. Thus if S_1 and S_2 are sentences then S_1 *or* S_2 is a sentence. The semantics of such complex sentences is induced by the semantics of the corresponding Boolean connector.

The negation nS of S in D2 corresponds to a syntactic negation. We need also to define semantic negations. Since propositional operators are sets of Boolean objects they have two negations, the Boolean complement and the set of their negated elements:

Definition 3. *Let O be a propositional operator. Then $\neg O$, the Boolean complement of O is defined as $\neg O = \{S : S \notin O\}$. The post-negation of O, noted $O\neg$, is defined as $O\neg = \{nS : S \in O \land S \notin NS\} \cup \{(n)S : nS \in O\}$.*

Informally, we get the post-negation of an element by replacing all sentence which belong to it by their negations. For instance the relationship between the operators K_a and KW_a can be expressed as $KW_a = K_a \cup K_a\neg$.

For Booleanly complex propositional operators the following holds:

Fact 1. *Let O_1 and O_2 be propositional operators. Then: (i) $(O_1 \cap O_2)\neg = O_1\neg \cap O_2\neg$, (ii) $(O_1 \cup O_2)\neg = O_1\neg \cup O_2\neg$, (iii) $(O\neg)\neg = O$.*

The ASAP concerns the positive, non-negated form PA operators. I will consider, in addition that there is a negation of PA operators which preserves the attitudinal property of PA operators: PA operators negated by this negation are also PA operators. Syntactically such attitude preserving negation is not a propositional negation but a negation of the category $(S/S)/(S/S)$ and negated PA operators also satisfy ASAP. It follows from this that $\sim O$, the attitude preserving negation of O, satisfies the following necessary condition:

NASAP: For any sentence S and any propositional operator O_a, if $S \in \sim O_a$ then $S \in \neg O_a$ and a *knows that* $S \notin O_a$.

The positive and the negative versions of the ASAP taken jointly allow us to specify what PA operators presuppose. The conditions expressed by ASAP and NASAP belong to logical, and more generally linguistic, competence of the agent having a specific propositional attitude. For us they are characteristic properties of (positive and negative) PA operators. They can be considered as generalisations of the KK principle.

Recall that propositional operators (PO) denote sets of sentences and thus the set of PA operators is a sub-set of PO. Given ASAP and NASAP principles a PA operator is defined as follows:

Definition 4. *A propositional operator O_a is a propositional attitude operator, or $O_a \in PA$, iff $\forall S((S \in O_a) \rightarrow KW_a(S \in O_a) \wedge (S \notin O_a) \rightarrow (KW_a(S \notin O_a))$*

The attitudinal character of PA operators is preserved by the post-negation:

Fact 2. *If $O_a \in PA$ iff $O_a\neg \in PA$.*

The reason is that a knows whether S iff a knows whether nS. The Boolean complement does not need to preserve the attitudinal character of PA operators.

Thus a propositional operator based on the agent a is a set of sentences such that a knows which sentences belong to it. A non-trivial propositional operator is a set of sentences which is neither empty nor equal to the set of all sentences.

Negative PA operators are obtained from the positive ones by applying to them a specific "attitude inverting" negation. Syntactically this negation takes a propositional operator as argument and gives a propositional operator as result; it is of category $(S/S)/S/S$. Semantically, such a negation preserves the attitudinal force of the operator to which it applies. For this purpose we can use the ASAP principle and definition D4. We have the following definition of the negation $\sim$ of a PA operator O_a:

Definition 5. *Let $O_a \in PA$. Then $\sim O_a = \{S : S \notin O_a \wedge (S \notin O_a) \in KW_a\}$.*

The negation defined in D5 will be called PA preserving negation. It is stronger than "ordinary" negation corresponding to the Boolean complement.

We can now make precise the sense in which PA operators are intensional:

Definition 6. O_a *is normally intensional,* $O_a \in NI$, *iff* $\forall S(S \in O_a \rightarrow \exists S_0(S \equiv S_0) \land S_0 \notin O_a)$

A typical (and basic) NI operator is the operator K_a. The reason is that a human agent is "strongly non-omniscient": if an agent knows the truth of a given sentence then there is always another sentence with the same logical value as a given sentence and such that the agent is not aware of its truth value.

Given that PA operators are defined with the help of K, we have:

Proposition 1. *Any PA operator is normally intensional.*

Proof. : Suppose, *a contrario* that $O_a \notin NI$. Then, by definition D6, there exists a sentence S such that $S \in O_a$ and for all sentences S_0 with the same truth value as S we would have $S_0 \in O_a$. But this is impossible because $O_a \in PA$. □

Thus PA negation preserves normal intensionality.

We define now various semantic relations discussed above. For simplicity all PA operators are based an a fixed agent a and thus O_a, Q_a, O_1, O_2, etc. denote PA operators all based on the agent a. First we define a presupposition:

Definition 7. *Let O_1 be a PA operator and O_2 be a propositional operator. Then O_1 presupposes O_2 iff $O_1 \subseteq O_2$ and $\sim O_1 \subseteq O_2$*

The following facts are obvious:

Fact 3. *(i) Any PA operator O_a presupposes $O_a \cup \sim O_a$, (ii) Any PA operator O_a presupposes $\{S : (S \in O_a) \in KW_a\}$, (iii) If O_1 presupposes O_2 and $O_2 \subseteq O_3$ then O_1 presupposes O_3.*

It follows from fact 3 that any PA operator O_a has a *presupposed part*, the subset $\{S : (S \in O_a) \in KW_a\}$. This set will be called $PP(O_a)$ - presupposed part of O_a. The important point is that $O_a \cup \sim O_a \neq T$ and thus the presupposition indicated in Fact 3 (i) is not trivial.

Factives are specific presupposing PA operators:

Definition 8. *PA operator O_a is factive, $O_a \in FACT$, iff O_a presupposes T.*

The attitude preserving negation also preserves factivity:

Fact 4. *O_a is factive iff $\sim O_a$ is factive.*

A more interesting property of presupposing operators is indicated in

Proposition 2. *Any veridical PA operator is factive.*

Proof. : (after Zuber (2011). We have to show that $\sim O_a \subseteq T$. Suppose *a contrario* that this is not the case. Then there exist S such that $S \in \sim O_a$ and $S \notin T$. Since $\sim O_a$ is a PA operator, given Proposition 1, it is also normally intensional. This means that there exist a sentence S_0 which is false (because S is false) and such that $S_0 \notin \sim O_a$. But then, given the definition of attitudinal negation and the fact that $O_a \in NI$, we have $S_0 \in O_a$. Contradiction, since O_a is veridical. □

The relation between knowledge and factivity is indicated in:

Proposition 3. *If $O_a \in PA$ and $O_a \subseteq K_a$ or $O_a \subseteq\sim K_a$ then O_a is factive.*

Proof. : Observe that if $O_a \subseteq K_a$ then O_a is veridical and thus, given Proposition 2, O_a is factive. Similarly, if $O_a \subseteq\sim K_a$ then O_a is veridical and thus factive. $\square$

To illustrate Proposition 3 observe that: *know that, realise that, reveal that* and *remember that* entail *know that*. Similarly *forget, not remember* and *not know* entail *not know*.

Factivity relates propositional operators to the truth of their arguments since factive operators are veridical ones. Another class of propositional operators related to the truth of their arguments is the class of operators that I will call, following Westerståhl (2012), *midpoint* operators (*MP* operators):

Definition 9. *O is a midpoint operator, $O \in MP$, iff $O = O\neg$.*

MP operators can be defined as in Fact 5:

Fact 5. *$O \in MP$ iff $\forall_S(S \in O) \equiv (nS \in O)$.*

Given the properties of post-negation and definition D9, the set of MP operators is closed with respect to Boolean operations and the post-negation:

Fact 6. *If $O_1, O_2 \in MP$ then $\neg O_1 \in MP$, $O_1\neg \in MP$, $(O_1 \cup O_2) \in MP$ and $(O_1 \cap O_2) \in MP$.*

Facts 5 and 6 allow us to show that MP operators are specific unions and intersections of sets of sentences as indicated in:

Proposition 4. *A propositional operator O is a MP operator iff there exists a propositional operator Q such that $O = Q \cup Q\neg$ (or $O = Q \cap Q\neg$).*

Proof. The implication from right to left is obvious since it follows from the definition of MP that $Q \cup Q\neg$ and $Q \cap Q\neg$ are MP operators.

To prove the implication from left to right we use Fact 5. We decompose the set O into two sets, the set of non-negated sentences which are its elements and the set of the corresponding negated sentences. The first set of sentences constitutes a propositional operator, say Q and the second set constitutes the operator $Q\neg$. The second disjunct of the necessary condition of the proposition is a consequence of Fact 6. $\square$

Thus a MP operator O is decomposable into $Q \cup Q\neg$ or into $Q \cap Q\neg$ or that it is decomposable into a disjunctive or into a conjunctive form.

The set MP has an empirically important subset of propositional operators that I will call *indirectly truth telling* operators:

Definition 10. *O is indirectly truth telling operator, $O \in ITT$ for short, iff $O \in MP$ and O is decomposable into $Q \cup Q\neg$ and $Q \in VER$.*

Thus ITT operators are MP operators that are composed of two parts one containing only true sentences and one containing only false ones.

Definition of MP operators suggests that there may be some propositional operators in NLs which can be decomposed into their disjunctive form. This is indeed the case and it is related, in English, to the distinction between *whether*-clauses and *that*-clauses. One observes that many operators taking *whether* complementizer can be decomposed into disjunctive form:

(6) a. Bo told/informed Dan whether Lea left (or not).
   b. Bo informed Dan that Lea left or Bo told Dan that Lea did not leave.

(7) a. Bo remembers whether Lea left (or not).
   b. Bo remembers that Lea left or Bo remembers that Lea did not leave.

In the above examples the disjunction indicated in parenthesis is not a disjunction between sentences but an exclusive disjunction between propositional operators, The above examples show that operators based on *tell whether, inform whether* and *remember whether* are all MP operators. However, there is a difference between *tell* and *inform whether* on the one hand, and *know* and *remember whether* on the other: only the second group belongs to the ITT class.

We have now enough tools to study the class of neg-transportable operators:

Definition 11. *Let O_a be a PA operator. Then O_a is neg-transportable, $O_a \in NTR$ for short, iff $\sim O_a \subseteq O_a\neg$.*

For neg-transportable operators we have the following propositions:

Proposition 5. *No factive operator is neg-transportable.*

Proof. : Suppose $O_a \in FACT \cap NTR$. Then $\sim O_a \subseteq T$ since $O_a \in FACT$ and $\sim O_a \subseteq O_a\neg$, since $O_a \in NTR$. Contradiction, because $O_a\neg \cap T = \emptyset$. □

Proposition 6. *No neg-transportable operator is a midpoint operator.*

Proof. Suppose *a contrario* that some $O_a \in NTR \cap MP$. Then $\sim O_a \subseteq O_a\neg$. Since $O_a \in MP$ we have $O_a\neg = O_a$. Hence $\sim O_a \subseteq O_a$. Contradiction. □

The class of NTR operators can be equivalently defined as in:

Proposition 7. *O_a is neg-transportable iff O_a presupposes $O_a \cup O_a\neg$.*

Proof. (a) Suppose $O_a \in NTR$. Since $O_a \in PA$ given fact 3, O_a presupposes $O_a \cup \sim O_a$. But then, since $O_a \in NTR$, O_a presupposes $O_a \cup O_a\neg$.

(b) Suppose now that O_a presupposes $O_a \cup O_a\neg$. We have to show that $O_a \in NTR$. Given the supposition we have $\sim O_a \subseteq O_a \cup O_a\neg$. Given that $O_a \cap \sim O_a = \emptyset$, we have $\sim O_a \subseteq O_a\neg$ and thus $O_a \in NTR$. □

The following fact is an obvious consequence of Proposition 7:

Fact 7. *$O_a \in NTR$ iff $O_a\neg \in NTR$.*

The presupposition indicated in P 8 corresponds to the *excluded middle* presupposition (EMP). Thus EMP is equivalent to neg-transportability, and, given Fact 3, is a particular case of the presupposition proper to PA operators in general.

The EMP corresponds to the truth expressed by the *completeness*:

Definition 12. *The propositional operator O is complete, $O \in CMPL$, iff for any sentence S, either $S \in O$ or $nS \in O$.*

A relation between completeness and neg-transportability is indicated in:

Proposition 8. *Any complete PA operator is neg-transportable.*

Proof. Let $O_a \in CMPL$ and, *a contrario* $O_a \notin NTR$. Then for some S we have $S \in\sim O_a$ and $S \notin O_a\neg$. Hence $nS \notin O_a$. But then, since O_a is complete, $S \in O_a$. Contradiction. $\square$

Thus no (non trivial) factive operator is complete.

3   Conclusion

Constructions with verbs expressing propositional attitude play an important role in reasoning. The leading approach in the semantics of such constructions is *propositionalism*: denotations of clausal complements in such constructions are defined with the help of propositions or sets of propositions. This means that propositional operators based on proper nouns denote relations between individuals and sets of propositions. In this note I propose a *sententialist* approach to the semantics of propositional attitude operators. In this approach the universe of the model for propositional attitude operators and predicates they form is constructed from the set of sentences of a given natural language. This approach avoids the basic difficulty meet by of the propositionalists approach, which is the intensionality of PA operators (cf. Partee 1982) and, at the same time allows us to use various formal tools from the generalised quantifier theory. It has also an additional explanatory power since it leads to a simple explanation of various constraints on the semantic relations between PA operators.

References

Keenan, E.L., Faltz, L.M.: Boolean Semantics for Natural Language. D. Reidel Publishing Company, Dordrecht (1985)

Partee, B.H.: Belief-sentences and the limits of semantics. In: Peters, S., Saarinen, E. (eds.) Processes, Beliefs, and Questions, pp. 87–106. D. Reidel Publishing Company (1982)

Westerståhl, D.: Midpoints. In: Graf, T., et al. (eds.) Theories of Everything, pp. 427–439. UCLA (2012)

Zuber, R.: Factives and intensionality. In: Onada, T., Bekki, D., McCready, E. (eds.) JSAI-isAI 2010. LNCS (LNAI), vol. 6797, pp. 104–114. Springer, Heidelberg (2011). https://doi.org/10.1007/978-3-642-25655-4_9

Author Index

Printed in the United States
by Baker & Taylor Publisher Services